A Value & Identification Guide

4TH EDITION

Edited by Ellen T. Schroy

Published by

700 E. State Street • Iola, WI 54990-0001
Telephone: 715/445-2214
Web: www.krause.com

Please call or write for our free catalog of publications.
Our toll-free number to place an order or obtain a free catalog is 800-258-0929
or please use our regular business telephone 715-445-2214.

Library of Congress Catalog Number: 2002105099
ISBN: 0-87349-394-X

Printed in the United States of America

Photos on the front cover are, top left: Amberina cruet, gold shading to red base, red top edge and pouring spout, gold handle and stopper, 6" h, **$275**; center: Swan, Pairpoint, deep amethyst, bulbous base, original label attached, **$115**; top right: compote, Pressed Diamond pattern, yellow, **$65**; bottom left: candy dish, covered, Coin pattern, Fostoria, red, **$70**; bottom right: bride's basket, cased basket, deep maroon shading to pink to white, undulating scalloped rim, slightly ribbed body, ornate silver-plated stand, **$325**.

Photos on the back cover are, clockwise from top left: Cranberry swirl pitcher, quatrafoil top, applied handle, 8-1/4" h, **$165**; tumbler, carnival glass, Peacock at the Fountain, marigold, **$45**; and epergne, single scalloped lily, ruby red, 16" h, 15" d, **$125**. Pictured on the spine is a Cameo glass vase, Daum Nancy, trees in landscape cutting, 9-3/4" h, **$1,500**.

ACKNOWLEDGMENTS

As I finish this edition of *Warman's Glass*, the antiques and collectibles world seems to be rebounding from a slight down turn last fall. I can sense a real enthusiasm for the hobby as dealers gather at shows, information is exchanged between collectors, and research continues.

Part of the fun and excitement of writing *Warman's*, whether this edition or the general price guides, is using the antiques and collectibles I've grown to treasure. But, there are more important things to treasure, those being family and friends who encourage and offer support while a new edition is being credited. To Jeffrey, Mark, Michelle, Linda, Brian, Mom and Dad, Janet, neighbors Jocelyn and her husband Harry, and Mary. I've got to add a whole new list of cyber friends. This new support team includes Larry Baker, Michael Krumme, Woody Keeney, Sam Kissee, Judy Smith, Kathy Bucher, Anne Shatrau, Kathryn Smith, and Lynn Tice, plus others. From tangible offerings, such as baby bottle prices to expert advice on pricing and the weekly bouts of humor we share, this group of friends means a lot. From the cookies offered over the fence, to the words of "you can do this" and hugs, real and cyber, the energy is found to keep researching, writing, and exploring.

This edition probably represents more cyber exploration than any other I've done. Daily readings of postings from WWW.CGA and DGShopper Online have taught me many things, from how to discern colors of carnival glass to what types of patterns to watch for in Depression-era glassware. I greatly enjoy visiting Angela Bowey's Glass Museum On-Line, (http://www.glass.co.nz). My list of bookmarks reads like a "who's who" of the cyber glassworld. E-mail has connected me to pattern-glass experts and leads me to other experts and manufacturers, such as Blenko. You will see many more Internet references in the individual category introductions, leading along these exciting paths.

Real life support also includes the friendly faces at many auction houses, antiques shows, flea markets, and malls. I can't begin to list all of you, those who offer smiles, hand shakes, assistance of all kinds. Through our discussions, I find I am constantly learning and being challenged to discover more. I have always loved the research and information gathering aspects of my career, and through the help of many, I continue to enjoy this fascinating marketplace. I've had great cooperation from auction houses, both large and small, in the form of catalogs, prices realized, press releases, newsletters, and photographs, all of which are appreciated.

Associates at Krause Publications in Iola, Wisconsin, are the best! To Pat Klug, Kris Manty, Patsy Howell, and the other employees, a heart felt thank you for your fine efforts. The professional attitude each brings to this book is appreciated. As I write this section in March 2002, I have no idea to whom I owe these thanks, since many hands will help create the edition you are holding. However, I am confident that this edition will be one *we are all* proud of. From the editors to the production staff to the sales staff and all the others, *thank you.*

Some new categories have been added, like powder jars. Other categories have been rearranged to make the listings easier to read or understand. Some categories have been lengthened to reflect their strong presence in the marketplace. Others are diminished to show the fact that they are not quite as popular in the new century. All are now given to you, the reader, the collector, the dealer, the appraiser, and the student. Enjoy! I'm off to find more glassware to research, to read about, to ponder over, as I continue to learn about glassware, as well as all kinds of antiques and collectibles.

Ellen Louise Tischbein Schroy
135 S. Main St.
Quakertown, PA 18951-1119
e-mail: Schroy@voicenet.com

Contents

Introduction

Warman's Glass offers antiques and collectibles collectors and dealers information about all the major glass collecting categories in one book. As part of Warman's Encyclopedia of Antiques and Collectibles series, *Warman's Glass* gives readers a wealth of information, as well as hundreds of listings, photographs, marks, and illustrations, all relating to the colorful world of glass collecting. It also serves as a companion to *Warman's Antiques and Collectibles Price Guide.*

Warman's Glass includes listings from the antiques marketplace, collectibles marketplace, and studio art of contemporary craftsmen. Because this is a "Warman's" book, you will find detailed information relating to the history to glass type and/or company, reference books, collectors' clubs, and tips to spotting reproductions. Of course, the listings are as detailed as possible. Careful attention has been given to listing correct pattern names, colors, sizes, and other pertinent details.

Warman's Glass covers individual companies, such as Fostoria and Morgantown, as well as the general glass categories such as Depression glass and pattern glass. Since *Warman's Glass* is a price guide, it cannot list every pattern or piece made. Warman's is continually increasing the glass coverage in the Warman's price guides as more knowledge and references are found. For more than 40 years, Warman's guides have been the leaders in the antiques and collectibles field, a tradition this and subsequent editions will continue.

History

Historians date early examples of glassware back as far as the third century B.C. These early combinations of sand and ash were probably the results of accidental mixing at the edges of a fire.

The first real attempts at glassmaking are not well documented, but examples of early utilitarian pieces, such as bottles and bowls, have survived. The Egyptians used glass objects and were very fond of small beads and pieces, which they used as decorations. Because of the great pyramids, historians have carefully documented glassware pieces.

As human civilization developed and spread throughout the world, it became more necessary to preserve and transport foods. Glass bottles and jars, made from local raw materials, were the answer. The color variations found allow modern science to evaluate the type of sand and other minerals that were available to the glassblowers.

As the technologies for glassblowing and later mass production evolved, so did its uses. Utilitarian objects were followed by the production of windowpanes and soon decorative objects. The scientific use of glass led to advances in many fields. We really don't think when taking a Corningware container out of the freezer and putting it directly into the microwave that it is really made of glass and that the ability to use glass in this fashion developed only recently. Glass was first used for storage and only later for cooking. Modern kitchens now include glass as stovetops, in addition to the utilitarian and decorative glassware we have come to take almost for granted. Who knows what kind of developments will occur as glass manufacturers look to the next century!

Glassblowers and manufacturers are credited with many patents for glass techniques, as well as manufacturing advances. However, the real credit for attracting collectors to glass must be given to those who continually strived to develop new colors and shapes. By adding certain minerals and chemicals, glass changes colors and can becomes stronger or weaker. Certain combinations, such as those Findlay used for his beautiful onyx ware, created stunning pieces, but the glass was very brittle, so few examples survive.

Antiques and collectibles glassware is like precious jewels. Glassware is available in every color and hue of the rainbow. Like precious stones, glassware can be engraved, carved, etched, and made into wonderful creations. European glassmakers created masterpieces by engraving crystal objects with detailed portraits and other types of decoration. Cameo glass examples of Gallé and Daum Nancy factories were blown and feature carved layers of different colors, much the same way cameo jewelry brooches are created by carving shells. Etched intaglio designs grace cut glass, as well as later mass-produced pieces made by such companies as Imperial and Fostoria.

Crystal clear glassware was the objective of early blowers as they tried to experiment with different combinations. Cut glass decorators demanded high quality clear-leaded glass for their creations.

Gemlike colors of rich deep blues, amethyst, emerald greens, and blood reds can be found throughout the ages of glass collecting. Experimental color combinations tried by artists such as Louis Tiffany and Frederick Carder at Steuben resulted in the iridescent hues of Favrile and Aurene glass. Cambridge and Heisey produced vivid translucent colors, like Heatherbloom and Alexandrite.

Glassware has always been manufactured to appeal to a woman's eye. Brides choose their trousseau and table settings today just as they did in past generations. Specialized serving pieces, such as berry bowls, cheese domes, and pickle castors were the glories of the past. Today's brides are able to choose from hundreds of crystal patterns, but do not have access to the wide variety of forms of their grandmothers' and great grandmothers' eras. Today's bride may serve berries from a standard round bowl, while her great grandmother served berries from a peachblow basket, in a silver-plated holder, into delicate, matching sauce dishes.

Care and Storing Tips

Glass is easy to care for and store. Most glass was produced for utilitarian purposes. Those lovely sauce bowls were really made for everyday use. Manufacturers designed their glass for heavy use, while appealing to the eye, and many objects were mass-produced. The survival rate is high.

Today's collectors can often purchase mint or fine condition examples of most glass, provided they are willing to pay the price. Pieces that show aging, e.g., some gilding removed by washing, are also desirable, since it may be proof of authenticity.

Glassware can be repaired using modern techniques that produce amazing results. Edges with chips can be ground. The price is lower, but not significantly. Most importantly, the glass is available for re-use. Its beauty can continue to be appreciated.

Take care when purchasing glassware. Examine each piece carefully. Look and feel for wear and imperfections. After purchase, make certain to wrap each piece separately in several layers. Glass can shatter when dropped, but also when exposed to changes in temperature. If you purchase a wonderful piece, carry it around for several hours, and suddenly go out into the cold air, beware. Don't unwrap the glass! Allow it to adjust gradually to the colder temperatures. Likewise, when you take it back indoors, gently unwrap the piece and allow it to come to room temperature before adding it to your collection. Never wash it until its temperature matches that of the environment.

During the summer, care should be taken to gradually cool glass. Storing a newly acquired treasure in a car trunk for hours is fine. Just do not take it into the house and wash it immediately in cold water. Milk glass of the post-World War II era is especially vulnerable to changes in temperatures.

Today, we know that exposing colorless flint glassware to strong sunlight may cause it to chemically react and develop a purple hue. The popular decorating idea of the 1920s through the 1950s of placing shelves of glass in window frames has proven disastrous for many pieces of glass. What our modern home environment will do to glassware is still not clearly established. Colored glassware hues do not appear to fade, but owners are well advised to use caution if they have strong lighting in their display cabinets.

Most antique and collectible glassware should never see the inside of a dishwasher. The temperatures are too severe and the water pressures too great. Gently hand-washing glassware protects the pieces and gives collectors an opportunity to study their collections. Learn the feel of your glassware, remember how heavy it feels, and how sharp the cuttings or patterns feel. This knowledge will help you spot reproductions and copycats.

When storing antique and collectible glassware, make sure the storage area is sturdy. Shelves should be well secured. Periodically check that glass objects are not moving slightly because of normal vibrations. Objects should not touch one another; place pieces of packing materials between stacked objects. Even more precautions should be taken in earthquake-prone areas. It is a good idea to gently remove stoppers from cruets, decanters, etc. periodically to make sure they haven't become stuck. There are many commercial cleaners available to remove interior stains. When trying one of these products, start with the minimum suggested by the manufacturer, and proceed with caution and gentle pressure. Never use harsh chemicals on hand-painted pieces, gold trim, iridized finishes, or things that appear very delicate. Once enamel, gilt, or paint is removed, the price of the piece is diminished.

Glass collectors should maintain an inventory of their collections. This will allow them to have a better idea of what their collection contains, its value, etc. When preparing an inventory, write a detailed description of each piece, what history you might know, the purchase price, dealers' name and address, date, any reference books, etc. Some collectors also photograph their items, giving them an instant identification guide to their collections.

Organization of the Book

Listings: Objects are listed alphabetically by category, beginning with Advertising and ending with Whimsies. If you have trouble identifying the category to which your glassware belongs, use the extensive index in the back of the book. It will guide you to the proper category.

We have made the listings descriptive enough so that specific objects can be identified. We also emphasize items that are actively being sold in the marketplace. Some harder-to-find objects are included to demonstrate market spread—useful information worth considering when you have not traded actively in a category recently. A few categories in this book also appear in *Warman's Antiques and Collectibles Price Guide*, *Warman's Americana and Collectibles*, and *Warman's Depression Glass*. The listings in *Warman's Glass* expand on these two volumes, creating a new companion volume for the general dealer or specialized collector.

History: Collectors and dealers enhance their appreciation of objects by knowing something about their history. We present a capsule history for each category. In many cases, this history contains collecting hints or other useful information. Collectors are encouraged to continue to learn and share their knowledge about their specific interests. Research of the past decades by such people as Ruth Webb Lee, George and Helen McKearin, Alice Metz, and E. McCamley Belknap has been treasured and enhanced by modern researchers such as Regis and Mary Ferson and Jerry Gallagher, as well as the late William Heacock and Hazel Weatherman.

References: Books are listed in most categories to help you learn more about the objects. Included are author, title, publisher, and date of publication or most recent edition. If a small firm or individual has published a book, we have indicated (published by author).

Many of the books included in the lists are hard to find. The antiques and collectibles field is blessed with a dedicated core of book dealers who stock these specialized publications. You will find them at flea markets and antiques shows and through their advertisements in trade publications. Books go out of print quickly, yet many books printed more than 25 years ago remain the standard work in a category. Used book dealers often can locate many of these valuable reference sources. Many dealers publish annual or semi-annual catalogs. Ask to be put on their mailing lists. The Internet now also offers a wonderful source for finding out-of-print glass books.

Periodicals: The newsletter or bulletin of a collectors' club usually provides the concentrated focus sought by specialty collectors and dealers. Some collectors' club newsletters, like the *News Journal* of the Early American Pattern Glass Society, are well worth the cost of the yearly dues. However, there are publications not associated with collectors' clubs that collectors and dealers should be aware of. These are listed in their appropriate category introductions.

In the antiques and collectibles glass field, there are several general periodicals, as well as specialized periodicals to which the glass collector should subscribe:

- *Antique Bottle & Glass Collector*, P.O. Box 187, East Greenville, PA 18041
- *Antique Trader Weekly*, P.O. Box 1050, Dubuque, IA 52001; http://www.csmonline.com
- *AntiqueWeek*, P.O. Box 90, Knightstown, IN 46148; http://www.antiqueweek.com
- *Antiques & Collecting*, 1006 South Michigan Avenue, Chicago, IL 60605
- *Maine Antique Digest*, P.O. Box 358, Waldoboro, ME 04572; http://www.maineantiquedigest.com

Space does not permit listing all the national and regional publications in the antiques and collectibles field. The above is a sampling. A check with your local library will bring many other publications to your attention.

Collectors' Clubs: Collectors' clubs add vitality to the antiques and collectibles field. Their publications and conventions produce knowledge that often cannot be found elsewhere. Many of these clubs are short-lived; others are so strong that they have regional and local chapters.

Museums: The best way to study a specific field is to see as many documented examples as possible. For this reason, we have listed museums where significant collections in that category are on display. Special attention must be directed to the complex of museums which make up the Smithsonian Institution in Washington, D.C. Premiere collections of glassware are available for study at several major museums, including the Chrysler Museum in Norfolk, VA; the Corning Museum of Glass, Corning, NY; and the Toledo Art Museum, Toledo, OH.

Reproductions: Reproductions are a major concern to all collectors and dealers. Throughout this edition, notes and information will alert you to known reproductions and keys to recognizing them. Most reproductions are unmarked; the newness of their appearance is often the best clue to uncovering them. The information is designed to serve as a reminder of past reproductions and prevent you from buying them, believing them to be period.

We strongly recommend subscribing to *Antique & Collectors Reproduction News* (P.O. Box 71174, Des Moines, IA 50325) a monthly newsletter that reports on past and present reproductions, copycats, fantasies, and fakes.

Reproductions are only one aspect of the problem; outright fakes are another. Unscrupulous manufacturers make fantasy items that never existed, e.g., the Eyewinker pattern never included a goblet. Reproduction Eyewinker goblets can easily be found.

Paper labels are now being reproduced and placed on period glassware, as well as reproductions. This statement is made to make you aware of and to question each piece you purchase. Is the piece the proper color, shape, and density? Does the label appear to be original, does it show signs of age that are consistent with a piece of glassware from this time period? Questions, questions, and more questions, are often collectors' constant companion, but can lead to a sense of satisfaction.

Marks: Antique and collectible glass may have manufacturers' marks. Unfortunately, most types of glass are unmarked. It was very difficult to include a mark in a mold. Certain marks, like Heisey's "H" in a diamond, are very small and can be difficult to find. Some of the acid-etched glass marks are also difficult to identify. Careful study of pieces is necessary. Don't be afraid to ask dealers to show you where a piece is marked. Paper labels may have become lost over the years. The dates given on the marks included in this volume are often approximate. Several manufacturers, like Imperial Glass, used several different marks. Therefore, marks should be considered as clues, just as style, color, and other characteristics can lead to the discovery of the maker and date of manufacture.

Price Notes

In assigning prices, we assume the object is in very good condition; if otherwise, we note this in our description. It would be ideal to suggest that mint, or unused, examples of all objects exist. The reality is that objects from the past were used. Because of this, some normal wear must be expected.

Whenever possible, we have tried to provide a broad listing of prices within a category so you have a "feel" for the market. We emphasize the middle range of prices within a category, while also listing some objects of high and low value to show market spread.

We do not use ranges because they tend to confuse, rather than help, the collector and dealer. How do you determine if your object is at the high or low end of the range? There is a high degree of flexibility in pricing in the antiques field. If you want to set ranges, add or subtract 10 percent from our prices.

One of the hardest variants with which to deal is the regional fluctuation of prices, as well as the type of market, be it an auction or flea market. We have tried to strike a balance. Know your region and subject before investing heavily. As traditional auction houses participate in the Internet, more and more collectors are able to purchase treasures outside their geographic region. Buyers should exercise caution, ask questions, and be diligent before bidding. Research and patience are key factors to building a collection of merit. Another pricing segment of glassware is the traditional reference books. Referred to as "book price," collectors should consider this like the prices found as "list prices" on new cars. It's a place to start negotiating.

Another factor that affects prices is a sale by a leading dealer or private collector. We temper both dealer and auction house figures.

Price Research

Everyone asks, "Where do you get your prices?"

They come from many sources.

First, we rely on auctions. Auction houses and auctioneers do not always command the highest prices. If they did, why do so many dealers buy from them? The key to understanding auction prices is to know when a price is high or low in the range. We think we do this and do it well. This fourth edition of *Warman's Glass* represents a concentrated effort to contact more regional auction houses, both large and small. The cooperation has been outstanding and has resulted in an ever-growing pool of auction prices and trends to help us determine the most up-to-date auction prices.

Second, we work closely with dealers. We screen our contacts to make certain they have full knowledge of the market. Dealers make their living from selling antiques; they cannot afford to have a price guide that is not in touch with the market.

Collectors work closely with us. They are specialists whose devotion to research and accurate information is inspiring. Generally, they are not dealers. Whenever we have asked them for help, they have responded willingly and admirably.

Warman's Glass is designed to be a buyer's guide suggesting what you would have to pay to purchase an object on the open market from a dealer or collector. It is not a seller's guide to prices. People frequently make this mistake. In doing so, they deceive themselves. If you have an object listed in this book and wish to sell it to a dealer, you should expect to receive approximately 50 percent of the listed value. If the object will not resell quickly, expect to receive even less.

STATE OF THE MARKET

Glassware collecting in the new millennium is off to a terrific start. Collectors are continuing to add to their treasures. And since glassware is such a durable material, many pieces can be enjoyed by several generations. Today's antiques marketplace is showing a revival in glass collecting in several areas, including carnival glass, which is enjoying a growing number of collectors coming into the hobby. Many times a person becomes a dedicated collector after receiving a piece or two and then discovering that more glittering examples await them. As these examples are added to the cupboard, shelf, or kitchen windowsill, a collection is born and hopefully it will continue to flourish.

Current glass-collecting opportunities reflect new areas of interest, as well as strongly established older categories. Collectors are continually offered a new rainbow of colors and objects. Original boxes are treasured; documentation and advertisements are saved and studied; labels are never removed. Collectors of 18th, 19th, and early 20th century glass face similar challenges: who made the piece, how was it used, when was it made? Solving their quest for information and additional examples may take them down different paths, but the pot of gold at the end of that rainbow is usually a glittering example to add to their treasures.

Specialized antiques and collectibles shows concentrating primarily on glass are doing well in the late 1990s. Dealers continue to offer high quality glassware. More specialized shows, such as cut glass shows and Depression glass shows, are drawing more and more collectors. These specialized shows feature a larger variety of patterns and pieces than found at a general show. These shows expand a collector's horizons. For example, a Depression glass show includes not only the patterns defined as Depression glass, like Cherry Blossom pattern, but also fine glassware produced by Heisey, Cambridge, Fostoria, and others. Specialized shows are a wonderful place to experience the myriad of colors available, learn about the shapes, and see the wealth of sizes produced.

General antiques shows try to present a balanced approach. Promoters actively try to include dealers representing the broad market. You will find dealers offering art glass, cut glass, Depression glass, and pattern glass. General line dealers also offer some glassware items.

Flea markets and antiques malls are like general antiques shows in that they try to appeal to the broad marketplace. Both of these venues can be great places to spend hours searching for examples to add to collections.

Collecting glassware through cyber space is also now possible. By using your favorite search engine, information about specific companies is at your fingertips. Some Web sites include fascinating company histories as well as beautiful photographs. Frequent searching through on-line auctions can yield treasures to add to collections. Some caution needs to be exercised when buying on-line, though: make sure of the seller's return policy and shipping capabilities.

Buying glassware at auction is also a wonderful way to add to a collection. Nothing beats the thrill of finding that perfect piece and waiting for the auctioneer to start the bidding on it. Auction buyers need to be sure to carefully examine the piece before the auction begins and also after winning the bid. Wrap it up carefully and it will bring years of enjoyment to you.

Overall, prices for glassware are remaining stable. Some of the high-end art glasses, like Tiffany and Steuben, have suffered slightly due to reproductions and examples of lesser quality that have been signed later by unscrupulous characters. However, even with this identification problem, the major auction houses continue to be able to do well with stunning examples. Some of the handmade glassware produced in America, such as Cambridge, Fostoria, and Tiffin, are showing steady increases in their prices. Many collectors are choosing to invest in these types of glasswares, enjoying their aesthetic designs, clarity, or color. Another area that is showing an increased interest by collectors is studio art glass. Unique pieces are now entering the secondary market and establishing some exciting prices.

The one aspect of the glassware market that has fallen on hard times is the area of damaged pieces. Little tolerance is now made for broken, chipped, or damaged pieces. Purple sun-tinted glassware has fallen from grace and few collectors seek it out. A mere decade ago found glassware sellers leaving their flint glass out in the sun to turn purple, proving its high flint content. Today this practice is considered dangerous to the glassware and no longer acceptable. Collectors should strive for the best example they can find, whether it's a contemporary drinking glass or a fine piece of Lalique.

Glassware dealers continue to maintain large inventories. It is not unusual for a dealer to work closely with collectors and other dealers to supply patterns or items currently in demand. It always pays to ask dealers if they have any other examples in their inventories. It is this type of customer service that makes glass dealers a special group in the field of antiques.

The Internet and World Wide Web of antiques and collectibles dealers are making an impact of the world of collecting. By connecting to this fascinating world, collectors can now purchase almost any type of glassware. Whether it's from a cyber mall, shop, Web site, or auction, purchases can be made easily. The ability to shop at any hour of the day or night, in the comfort of one's home, will let collectors increase their spending. Dealers are learning the importance of this message and many are going on-line to service this expanding market. This is an area where accurate descriptions are highly desirable, digital images may offer exciting views. However, just like the real world, it's up to the buyer to decide how many dollars to spend. It is also still ultimately up to the purchaser to determine if the description of a newly acquired piece is accurate and perhaps may require more research.

For people interested in carnival glass, there is an on-line collectors' club, WWW.CGA at http://www.woodsland.com. Collectors who specialize in Depression glass can subscribe to an on-line magazine, DG Shopper, http://www.dgshopper.com. Both of these sites offer articles, chat rooms, vendors, and auctions, as well as reference areas filled with images and interesting information. What is hard to describe is the amount of knowledge you can gleam from participating in these kinds of Web sites. It certainly offers collectors a way to connect with more experienced collectors and ask questions about color, manufacturers, care, etc. One of the most fascinating aspects of the Internet is that it is always expanding, giving collectors new areas to explore.

Many glassware collectors enjoy devoting hours to reading about their favorite manufacturers or historical time period. Many of these collectors maintain large personal libraries and eagerly search out materials that pertain to their collections, such as original catalogs and other memorabilia. Museums such as Corning Museum of Glass, Corning, NY, and West Virginia Glass Museum, WV, offer collectors places to research and examine objects. Several collector clubs also maintain excellent museums and offer valuable identification information.

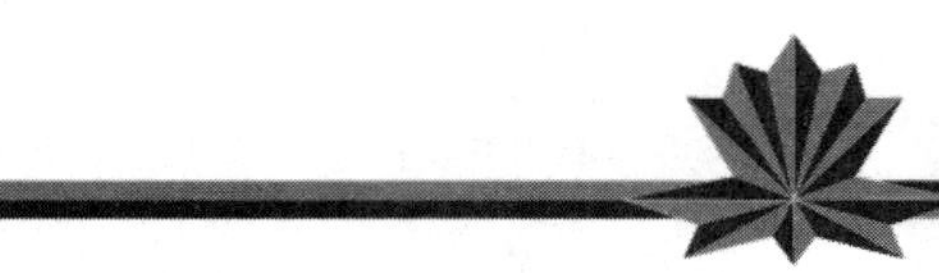

Abbreviations

The following are standard abbreviations which we have used throughout this edition of *Warman's*.

ABP=American Brilliant Period
adv = advertising
ah = applied handle
C = century
c = circa
circ = circular
cov = cover
d = diameter or depth
dec = decorated
DQ = Diamond Quilted
ed = edition
emb = embossed
ext. = exterior
ftd = footed
gal = gallon
ground = background
h = height
hp = hand painted
hs = high standard
illus = illustrated, illustration
imp = impressed
int. = interior
irid = iridescent
IVT = inverted thumbprint
j = jewels
K = karat
l = length
lb = pound
ll = lower left
lr = lower right
ls = low standard
mfg = manufactured
MIB = mint in box
MOP = mother-of-pearl
NE = New England
No. = number
opal = opalescent
orig = original
os = orig stopper
oz = ounce
pat = patent
pcs = pieces
pgs = pages
PUG = printed under the glaze
pr = pair
pt = pint
qt = quart
rect = rectangular
sgd = signed
sngl = single
SP = silver plated
SS = Sterling silver
sq = square
w = width
yg = yellow gold
# = numbered

Glass Comparisons

The quote, "Imitation is the sincerest flattery" from C. C. Colton (1780-1832), comes to mind when thinking about the differences between cut, pattern, carnival, and Depression glassware. Mr. Colton was living during a time when early American glassmakers were struggling to imitate the fine cut glass they used to import from English, Irish, and European glasshouses. As the young America struggled to create her own industries and goods, craftsmen sought to also improve on what they created, making their wares prettier, more practical, and more economical than the imports that were available.

Glassware plays an important part in this struggle, as it was one of the first industries brought to America. The main ingredients for glass production readily existed and the need for containers of every sort and shape helped spur the industry on. Until 1828, when Deming Jarves created the first practical glass pressing machinery, glasswares were hand blown, then hand cut, if decorated at all. Jarves's machinery allowed the Boston & Sandwich Glass Works to begin designing pressed glass in patterns it would design, cut into wooden molds, and then use the molds over and over again making different forms and patterns; this was the beginning of the first mass production of glassware designed to be used on the table.

In 1864, William Leighton, working at Hobbs, Brockunier & Co., developed a new soda lime formula that again revolutionized the glassware industry. Lehighton's non-flint formula allowed glassware to be made more economically, while preserving the clarity and strength of the glass. Improvements to glassmaking formulas and equipment continued as advancements were made, allowing companies to create beautiful patterns of glassware. The styles created followed the fashions of the day, from elegant cut glass to imitations of cut glass, which became known as pattern glass (or pressed glass). When an iridized coloring technique was added to these patterns, carnival glass was born. When more inexpensive colorful tableware was created in the 1930s, Depression-era glass was born.

As communications and competition between the glass manufacturers grew, so did their inventories of patterns and designs. Close examination of patterns of all these types of glassware will show how designers took elements that were popular in one type of glassware and applied it to the succeeding generations: "Imitation is the sincerest flattery."

The question most asked by those trying to identify a piece of glass is, "What is it?" Learning how to discern cut glass, pattern glass, carnival glass, and Depression-era glass is the best place to start. By going to museums, visiting with other collectors, viewing displays of glassware at antiques shows and shops, reading tags on glassware, and reading the stacks of books written on the subject, you can learn how to tell the difference. Listed below are some quick tips to tell the differences; use them as starting points in the journey of discovery.

Cut Glass

1. Object feels sharp to the touch—cutting techniques leave sharp edges.
2. Object will be heavy, since the glass contains lead.
3. Object will be crystal clear and sparkly—the high lead content adds brilliance.
4. Walls of cut glass are thick, allowing for deep cutting.
5. Designs range from simple to elaborate as cutting techniques and equipment evolved. American Brilliant Period cut glass is probably the most desirable in today's antiques market; the intricate designs continue to captivate the user.
6. Some designs were executed in small numbers, as the cutters worked by hand on each piece. Some designs were translated to different forms, i.e. creamers and sugars, or matching goblets. In these cases, the master cutter might make one piece and an apprentice would copy the design to other forms, making slight changes to accommodate the form.
7. Cut glass is rarely marked. Some firms, like Hawkes, developed an acid-etched stamp mark, but never marked all its wares. Some glasscutters "signed" their works by etching, but these, too, are limited.

Cut glass, American Brilliant Period examples, left: dish, 10" d; front: oblong dish 12-1/4" l; right: water pitcher, 10-1/2" h. Photo courtesy of Joy Luke Auctions.

8. Careful examination of the surfaces may show lines and ridges left from the cutting tools. It may also show slight discrepancies in the designs.
9. Some flaws and/or modern damage can be removed with grinding, polishing, etc.
10. Good examples are expensive, usually more than $100.

Cut glass, lamp, mushroom shade, hobstars, prism, strawberry diamond, feathered fan. Photo courtesy of Woody Auction.

Pattern Glass

1. Most pieces are made in clear; some patterns also made in color.
2. Some patterns are found in both flint, which contains lead, and a non-flint formula, which contains soda lime. The flint examples usually will be clearer and slightly heavier.
3. Patterns are table settings, compotes, butter dishes, goblets, platters, etc.
4. Made in large in the number of forms.
5. Medium weight thickness.
6. Patterns range from simple, to elegant, to naturalistic, to geometric.
7. Pattern glass is rarely marked.
8. Mold lines are often clearly evident.

Dakota, pitchers, water, tankard, left: Bird and Fern etching, 4-1/2" d, 12" h, Pattern glass, right: Fern and Berry etching, 4-7/8" w, 9" h.

Banded Portland water set, maiden's blush, pitcher and six tumblers pattern glass. Photo courtesy of Joy Luke Fine Art Brokers and Auctioneers.

9. Some edge flakes can be removed with grinding, polishing, etc.
10. Prices range from $20 to multi-thousands of dollars, depending on the pattern and form.

Depression Glass

1. Most patterns are made in colored glass, but some include clear.
2. Formula used is soda lime, using no flint.
3. Patterns are dinnerware settings, plates, cups and saucers, plus serving pieces.
4. Many patterns are made in extensive number of forms, while some are limited to just dinnerware.
5. Has a light-weight thickness.
6. Patterns range from simple, to elegant, to florals, to geometric, and abstract.

Depression glass examples: Bowknot green tumbler and footed berry bowl.

Depression glass, Diamond Quilted, pink sugar and creamer.

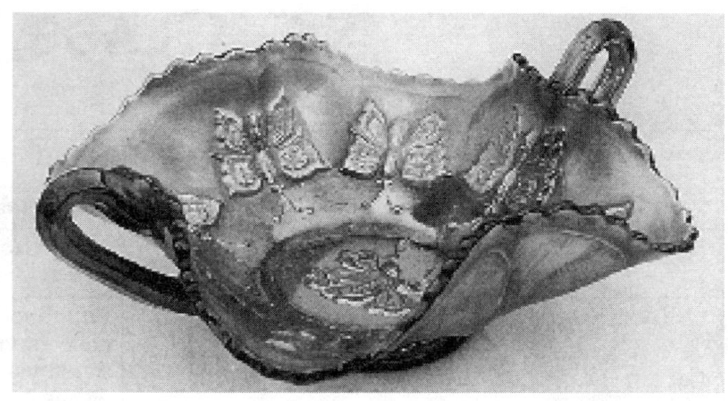

Carnival glass, bonbon dish, Butterflies pattern, two handles, purple, 7-1/4" w, 3-1/8" h.

7. Depression glass is rarely marked.
8. Mold lines are often clearly evident.
9. Removal of edge flakes is often difficult, as glass is thin-bodied.
10. Prices range from $5 to multi-thousands of dollars, depending on pattern, form, and color.

Carnival glass, water pitcher, Heavy Iris pattern, marigold.

Carnival Glass

1. Glass is made in a solid color, clear, blue, red, green, and purple, then sprayed with an iridized coating to give a unique appearance.
2. Base color is determined by looking at an unsprayed area, usually the base.
3. Patterns include accessory pieces, i.e. vases, some serving pieces; very few patterns are made in table sets.
4. Made by many companies, so few pieces are ever marked.
5. Patterns range from florals to geometrics to animals; patterns can be ornate as well as simple.
6. Glass is pressed in medium to heavy thickness.
7. Patterns can feel embossed when touched.
8. Mold seams are often apparent.
9. Removal of chips is difficult if on iridized surface.
10. Prices range from $20 to multi-thousands of dollars, depending on form, pattern, and mostly color.

Carnival glass, bowl, blue, Stag and Holly pattern, 11" d.

 Glass Timeline 

Year	Who	What	Where
1729	Waterford Crystal	Establishes glass house.	Waterford, England
1742	Anders Koskull and George Bogislas Staël von Holstein	Found Ko-Sta glass works.	Sweden
1760s	Baron Henry Stiegel	Founded first flint glass factory. Produced clear (some with enameled decoration), amethyst, cobalt blue, and fiery opalescent wares.	Manheim, PA
1764	Sainte-Anne Glassworks	Founded.	Baccarat, Voges, France
1765-1829	Cut-glass manufacturers	Period known as "*Early Period*." Design motifs reflect English and Irish influence, include prisms, flutes, single star, and diamonds.	
1788-1873	Nailsea area glassmakers	Nailsea glass, with white swirls and loopings or clear or colored ground, later imitated by American glass houses.	Nailsea, England
1817	Baccarat	Royal Warrant issued for opening of Verrerie de Vonâoche éa Baccarat.	Baccarat, Voges, France
1820s	Bohemian	Exported Bohemian glass starts to appear in America.	Bohemia
1820s-1850s	Pattern-glass manufacturers	Period known as "*Lacy Period*." Pressed glass with intricate all-over designs, imitating cut-glass designs.	
1824	Baccarat	Producing quality lead-crystal glass.	Baccarat, Voges, France
1824	Joseph Silvers and Joseph Stevens	Leased Moor Lane Glass House; joined in 1847 by Williams Stevens and Samuel Cox Williams, creating Stevens & Williams.	Briar Lea Hill, England
1828	Deming Jarves	Invents pressing machine used to create pattern glass.	Boston & Sandwich Glass Co., Sandwich, MA
1828	Boston & Sandwich Glass Co.	Incorporates and produces free-blown, blown three mold, and pressed patterns.	Sandwich, MA
1829	Thomas W. Dyott	Promoting glass-canning jars.	Philadelphia, PA
1830-1870	Cut-glass manufacturers	Period known as "*Middle Period*." Design motifs influenced by European designs, include flutes, fine engraved lines, etchings, engraved historical scenes, and some color overlays.	
1837	Deming Jarvis	Establishes Mount Washington Glass Co. for his son, George D. Jarvis.	Boston, MA
1837	Thomas Webb & Sons	Establish glasshouse to produce cameo, satin, cased, iridescent, and ornamental glass.	Stourbridge, England
1845-1891	Hobbs Glass Co.	Company founded by John L. Hobbs and James B. Barnes. First principal product was brilliant cut glass.	Wheeling, WV
1843	McKee Glass Co.	Established as glass manufacturer.	Pittsburgh, PA
1846	Baccarat	Begins production of paperweights.	Baccarat, Voges, France
1849	F. Hale Thomas	Patents mercury glass technique, not copied until 1855 by New England Glass Co.	London, England
1851	Amory and Frances Houghton	Establish Union Glass Company to make pressed-glass and cut-glass blanks.	Somerville, MA

Year	Who	What	Where
1852	McKee Glass Co.	Opens new factory to produce pattern (pressed) glass.	Pittsburgh, PA
1852	Waterford Crystal	Company closes.	Waterford, England
1857	Ludwig Moser	Founded polishing and engraving workshop.	Karlsbad, Czechoslovakia
1858	John Landis Mason	Patents screw-type closure for glass canning jars.	
1858	Deming Jarves	Founds Cape Cod Glass Co. and tries to duplicate wares of Boston & Sandwich Glass Co.	Cape Cod, MA
1860s	Mount Washington Glass Co.	Owned and operated by Timothy Howe and William L. Libbey.	Boston, MA
1863	Central Glass Works	Established as cooperative by workers from J. H. Hobbs, Brockunier.	Wheeling, WV
1863	Hobbs, Brockunier & Co.	Charles Brockunier joins Hobbs Glass Co.	Wheeling, WV
1864	Boda	Established by three glassmakers from Kosta.	Sweden
1864	William Leighton	Develops soda lime formula while at Hobbs, Brockunier & Co. This new (non-flint) formula allows clear glass to be made more economically and revolutionizes industry.	Wheeling, WV
1865	Deming Jarvis	Develops formula for *black glass,* using manganese and powdered charcoal.	Boston and Sandwich Glass Co., Sandwich, MA
1865	George Duncan, Harry B. Duncan, James B. Duncan, Augustus Heisey	George Duncan & Sons forms.	Pittsburgh, PA
1867	Emile Gallé	Opens glasshouse.	Nancy, France
1867-1939	Central Glass Works	Reorganized, new company made bottles, lamps, and barware. Tablewares were added 1900.	Wheeling, WV
1869	William L. Libbey	Builds new factory for Mount Washington Glass Co.	New Bedford, MA
1869-1888	Nicholas Lutz	Employed by Boston and Sandwich Glass Co. Credited with creating techniques for striped and threaded glassware.	Sandwich, MA
1870	Stevens & Williams	Moves factory, employs Frederick Carder, John Northwood, James Hill, and Joshua Hodgetts. Products include art glass, cameo, and peachblow.	Stourbridge, England
1870s-1880s	Challinor, Taylor & Co.	Produced opaque slag glass, including purple, blue, green, and orange.	Tarentum, PA
1872-1898	Vallerystahl and Portieux	Companies merge to produce art glass and later pressed glass.	Vallerystahl, Lorraine, France
1874	Emile Gallé	Begins production of art glass.	Nancy, France
1874	Mount Washington Glass Co.	Factory closed and reorganized. Reopens under A. H. Seabury and Frederick S. Shirley.	New Bedford, MA
1875	Cristalleries de Nancy, aka Daum Nancy	Begins operation, including cameo, colored glassware with enamel decoration, etched, cased, and other techniques. Marks usually are engraved signatures of artist.	Nancy, France
1875	Alfred and Harry Smith	Create Smith Bros. Glass after leaving Mt. Washington Glass. Many pieces marked with red shield trademark.	New Bedford, MA
1876	Äfors	Founded by four master glassblowers.	Sweden

Year	Who	What	Where
1876	Libbey and others	Cut glass made at the exposition.	Centennial Exposition, Philadelphia, PA
1878	Louis Comfort Tiffany	Founds glass house to make stained glass windows. Starts to supply glass materials to others in 1890.	Corona, Long Island, NY
1879	Val St. Lambert	Begins independent glass house, making tablewares for export.	France, Netherlands, and Belgium
1880	Wilhelm Kralik	Patents "*Peloton*" glass process, later patented by others in America and England. Technique incorporates filaments on clear or colored background.	Bohemia
1880	Phoenix Glass Co.	Company established for production of commercial glassware.	Beaver, PA
1880-1917	Numerous cut-glass manufacturers	Period known as "*American Brilliant Period.*" Designs of this period were more complex, cut deeply. Motifs include prisms, notched prisms, hobstars, curved miter splits, fans, pinwheels, stars, blocks, and other earlier period elements.	
1880s	Hobbs, Brockunier & Co.	Producing fine art glass, including amberina, spangled, and opalescent glass.	Wheeling, WV
1883	Joseph Locke	Develops *amberina*. Patent issued July 24, 1883. Transparent glass shading from deep ruby to amber	New England Glass Co., Cambridge, MA
1884	Emile Gallé	Establishes factory and begins production of cameo glass.	Nancy, France
1884	Edward D. Libbey	Given use of name "Amberina."	New England Glass Co., Cambridge, MA
1884-1886	Joseph Locke	Patents and creates first ground *Pomona glass.*	New England Glass Co., Cambridge, MA
1885	Joseph Webb	Perfects *mother-of-pearl satin glass.*	Phoenix Glass Co., Beaver, PA
1885-1891	Frederick Shirley	Develops *Burmese glass*. Translucent glass that shades from soft lemon to salmon pink.	Mt. Washington Glass Co., New Bedford, MA
1886	New England Glass Co.	Develop "*plated amberina*" process, uses paper labels "N.E. Glass Co. 1886 Aurora."	New England Glass Co., Cambridge, MA
1886	Frederick Shirley and Albert Steffin	Develop "*crown milano*" patent, opaque white satin finished with light-beige or ivory-colored ground, further embellished with fancy florals, etc., raised gold accents.	Mt. Washington Glass Co., New Bedford, MA
1887	Joseph Locke	Develop "*agata glass*" formula, by taking piece of peachblow glass and coating it with metallic stain, spattering it with alcohol, and firing.	New England Glass Co., Cambridge, MA
1887	Fostoria Glass Co.	Begins pressed-glass dinnerware production.	Fostoria, OH
1887	Northwood Glass Company	Incorporated by Henry Helling, Henry Floto, William Mann, Thomas Mears, and Harry Northwood.	Martins Ferry, WV
1888	Boston & Sandwich Glass Co.	Closes factory.	Sandwich, MA
1888	A. J. Beatty & Sons	Opens glass-manufacturing plant, produces pattern glass.	Tiffin, OH
1888	McKee Glass Co.	Relocates factory, begins to produce glass kitchenwares, later expands to Depression-era patterns.	Jeanette, PA

Year	Who	What	Where
1888-1900s	Joseph Locke	Second ground "*Pomona glass*" made, process moves to Libbey's Toledo, OH, plant in 1900s.	New England Glass Co, Cambridge, MA
1889	Edward D. Libbey	Patents "*plated amberina*" process, by taking gather of chartreuse or opalescent glass and dipping it into amberina.	New England Glass Co., Cambridge, MA
1889	Edward D. Libbey	Established Libbey Glass Co. First production includes brilliant-period cut glass.	Toledo, OH
1889	George W. Leighton	Patents Findlay Onyx Glass for Dalzell, Gilmore & Leighton Co. This layered opalescent glass was made for a short time due to high production costs.	Findlay, OH
1889	Arthur John Nash	Arrives in America and begins to work for Tiffany Furnaces.	Corona, Long Island, NY
1890	Hawkes, etc.	First acid-etched signatures added to cut glass, but not all pieces were signed.	
1890s	J. Loetz Witwe	Begins production of iridescent and other art glass. Some pieces signed, but not all.	Austria
1891	Fostoria Glass Co.	Moves pressed-glass production to new factory, expands to five factories by 1925.	Moundsville, WV
1891	Seneca Glass Co.	Company founded, chartered in 1896, to produce fine blown and cut crystal. Later produces tablewares.	Morgantown, WV
1891	U. S. Glass Co.	Combines 18 smaller glass houses, develops new patterns, including States series.	Pittsburgh, PA
1892	A. J. Beatty & Sons	Joins U. S. Glass Co, as factory "R."	Tiffin, OH
1892	George Duncan & Sons	Factory burns to the ground, new site found for factory in Washington, PA. Produces many patterns in clear glass. Name changes to Duncan and Miller after John E. Miller joins company.	Washington, PA
1893	Consolidated Lamp and Glass Co.	Founded after merger of Wallace & McAfee Co. and Fostoria Shade & Lamp Co.	Fostoria, OH
1893	Phillip Handel	Founds Handel & Co., known for lamps and decorated glassware.	Meriden, CT
1893	William S. Blake and Julian de Cordova	Establish art glass production, including iridescent Kew Blas wares.	Union Glass Company, Somerville, MA
1894	Indiana Tumbler & Goblet Co.	Produces clear pressed tablewares and bar wares.	Greentown, IN
1894	Mount Washington Glass Co.	Glassworks become part of Pairpoint Manufacturing Co. Also patents *Royal Flemish* technique.	New Bedford, MA
1895	Consolidated Lamp and Glass Co.	After fire in Fostoria, moves to new factory.	Corapolis, PA
1895	Swarovski Family	Perfects glassmaking art.	Wattens, Austria
1896	Bryce Brothers Co.	Founded to manufacture hand-blown stemware for hotel use.	Mt Pleasant, PA
1896	A. H. Heisey	Begins production of clear pressed glassware, known for its clarity and brilliance, and later for vibrant colors.	Newark, OH
1896	Louis Comfort Tiffany	Starts commercial production of art glasswares. Wares often marked.	Corona, Long Island, NY
1897	Indiana Tumbler & Goblet Co.	Adds colors to pressed-glass production lines, also produces first opalescent patterns.	Greentown, IN

Year	Who	What	Where
1897	Victor Durand	Victor and his father lease Vineland Glass Manufacturing Co. Production begins with inexpensive bottles, jars, and glass for scientific and medical purposes.	Vineland, NJ
1898	Harry Northwood	Northwood Glass Co. closes, Northwood moves to Indiana Glass Co.	Indiana, PA
1898	Orrefors Glasbruck	Begins production with glass windows and ink bottles.	Sweden
1898-WWI	C. F. Monroe Co.	Company founded, produces "*Wave Crest Ware*," decorating opal blanks purchased from Pairpoint and European glassmakers. Some wares marked.	Meriden, CT
1898-1915	Northwood, Dugan, Fenton, Heisey, Jefferson, Tarentum, and U.S. Glass Co.	Produce *custard glass*, first introduced in England, brought to U.S. by Harry Northwood. Adding uranium salts produces creamy (ivory) colored glass.	
1899	Macbeth-Evans	Macbeth merges with Evans.	Charleroi, PA
1899	Morgantown Glass Works	Founded, production begins in 1901.	Morgantown, WV
1899	National Glass Co.	Forms as combine of 19 glass companies.	PA, OH, IN, WV, MD
1899	Westmoreland Glass Co.	Founded to produce hand-crafted wares, candy containers, and novelties.	Grapeville, PA
1900	Federal Glass	Opens plant, first wares crystal with needle etching, various decorations and crackle. Later become major Depression-era manufacturer.	Columbus, OH
1900	René Lalique	Begins experimenting with molded glass jewelry.	France
1900	Ludwig Moser	Incorporates as Ludwig Moser & Sons when his two sons join firm. Production expands from clear glass to cut colored glass, cameo, and intaglio cut wares. Inexpensive enameled wares also made.	Karlsbad, Czechoslovakia
1900	Jacob Rosenthal	Develops brown opaque glass, aka "*chocolate glass*."	Greentown, IN
1901	Cambridge Glass Co.	Incorporates, starts production of tableware in clear, later expands to colored wares.	Cambridge, OH
1901	A. H. Heisey Co.	Starts to use paper labels, molded mark introduced later, not every piece marked.	Newark, OH
1901	Imperial Glass Co.	Company organized to produce pressed (pattern) glass.	Bellaire, OH
1901	New Martinsville Glass Manufacturing Co.	Founded, early production included opal glass decorative and utilitarian wares. Later pressed wares included flashed on ruby or gold dec.	New Martinsville, WV
1901	Martin Bach and Thomas Johnson	Organize Quezal Art Glass Decoration Co. Produced art glass that imitated Tiffany. Marked wares starting in 1902 with acid-etched or engraved trademark.	Brooklyn, NY
1901-1933	H. C. Fry Glass Co.	Years of operation, first products were brilliant-period cut glass, introduced pressed tablewares during Depression.	Rochester, PA
1902	Hazel Atlas Glass Co.	Established after merger with Hazel Glass Co. and Atlas Glass & Metal Co.	Washington, PA
1902	H. C. Fry Glass Co.	Produced the first pressed blanks used for cut glass.	Rochester, NY

Year	Who	What	Where
1902	National Glass Co.	Buys Rosenthal's chocolate glass formula to make at its other factories, such as McKee.	
1902	Northwood & Co.	Founded by Harry Northwood and Thomas Dugan. Production includes ornate table patterns, expanding to novelties and pressed patterns by 1907.	Wheeling, WV
1902-1903	Jacob Rosenthal	Develops "*Golden Agate,*" which was used for a pattern designed by Frank Jackson, known as Holly Amber. Production continues until fire destroys factory.	Greentown, IN
1903-1929	Economy Tumbler Glass Co.	Morgantown reorganizes and operates under this name, dropping "Tumbler" in 1923.	Morgantown, WV
1904	Frederick Carder and Thomas G. Hawkes	Establish Steuben Glass Works. Production includes clear, colored, and lustered lines. Wares often marked.	Corning, NY
1904	Phillip Handel	Patents "*chipping*" process for lampshades to create frosted texture.	Meriden, CT
1904	Emile Gallé	Dies, assistants now add star before his name when signing cameo glass.	Nancy, France
1905	Isaac J. Collins	Begins pressed-glass dinnerware production as Hocking Glass Co.	Lancaster, OH
1905	Fenton Art Glass Co.	Began as a cutting shop.	Martins Ferry, OH
1905	René Lalique	Starts to exclusively produce glasswares.	France
1905-1930s	Carnival Glass	Production by Dugan, Fenton, Imperial, Millersburg, Northwood.	
1906	Frank Fenton	Starts construction of new factory, opens in 1907, early production included carnival, chocolate, custard, pressed, opalescent.	Williamstown, WV
1907	Indiana Glass Co.	Founded, early production hand pressed, assembly line production evolves during 1920s, becomes part of Lancaster Colony.	Dunkirk, IN
1907	Lewis E. Smith	Founds L. E. Smith Glass Company. Production includes table and gift wares in clear and color.	Mount Pleasant, PA
1908	René Lalique	Designs packaging for French cosmetic houses.	France
1908	Lancaster Glass Co.	Founded, produces tablewares.	Lancaster, OH
1908-1915	H. Northwood & Co.	Production of intricate carnival glass patterns.	Wheeling, WV
1910	Cambridge Glass Co.	Expands under new leadership, opens factory.	Byesville, OH
1911-1914	Akro Agate	Founded to produce marbles, moves to larger factory in Clarksville, WV by 1914.	Akron, OH, area.
1912	Lotus Glass Co.	Company incorporates, known for the decorating techniques, using blanks from Bryce, Cambridge, Central, Duncan & Miller, Fostoria, Heisey, and Paden City, etc.	Barnesville, OH
1913	Ernest Schneider and Charles Schneider	Founded Schneider Glass. Production includes art glass, tablewares, stained glass, and lighting fixtures. Wares signed with several different marks.	Epiney-sur-Seine, France
1915	Westmoreland Specialty Co.	Introduces line of black glass, quickly copied by contemporaries.	Grapeville, PA
1915-1939	Cambridge Glass Co.	Produces black glass, known as "ebony."	Cambridge, OH

Year	Who	What	Where
1915-1986	Fostoria Glass Co.	American pattern production dates. Made in clear, some blue, green, and pink shading to purple, white, and yellow, but clear most prevalent and popular.	Moundsville, WV
1916	Imperial Glass Co.	Introduces Free-Hand lines, consisting of lustered art glass wares, and Imperial Jewels, an iridized stretch glass, usually found with cross trademark.	Bellaire, OH
1916	David Fisher	Founds Paden City Glass Manufacturing Co. Production concentrates on handmade glass, in clear and colors, often decorated with etching, cut, hand painted, or silver overlay.	Paden City, WV
1916	Tiffin Glass	Starts to use paper labels to mark wares.	Tiffin, OH
1917	Cambridge Glass Co.	Closes Byesville, OH, factory, transferring all workers back to original factory site.	Cambridge, OH
1918	Czechoslovakia	Started to mark objects "Made in Czechoslovakia." Not all glassware was marked.	
1918	Corning Glass Co.	Purchases Steuben. Carder remains and continues to produce art glass.	Corning, NY
1919	Harry Northwood	Dies, company reorganizes, but closes permanently in 1925.	Wheeling, WV
1920	Paul Frank and T. Conrad Vahlsing	Form Lustre Art Glass Company, after leaving Quezal. Production imitates Quezal wares.	
1920	Simon Gate and Advard Hald	Develop cased glassware for Orrefors.	Sweden
1920s	Bryce Brothers Co.	Expands production to colored wares. Also expands type of production.	Mt. Pleasant, PA
1920s	Edward D. Libbey	Renews amberina production; uses script mark on pontil	Toledo, OH
1920s	Fenton Art Glass Co.	Starts production of stretch glass, dolphins, jade green, ruby, and art glass.	Williamstown, WV
1920s	New Martinsville Glass Manufacturing Co.	Starts production of dinnerware patterns, also produces new colors, cuttings, and etchings.	New Martinsville, WV
1920s	Ernest Marius Sabino	Founds Sabino Glass, produces art glass in clear, frosted, and opalescent. Pieces marked with name in mold or etched signature.	France
1920s	Westmoreland Glass Co.	Milk glass production begins, as well as reproduction glassware and decorated items.	Grapeville, PA
1920s-1926	U.S. Glass Co.	Leading exponent of black glass.	
1921-1930	William J. Blenko	Returns to glass manufacturing, opens Eureka Art Glass Co.	Milton, WV
1922	H. C. Fry Glass Co.	Patented heat-resisting ovenware, called *Pearl Oven Ware.*	Rochester, PA
1922	Ludwig Moser & Sons	Buys Meyr's Neffe, its largest Bohemian rival, and continues art glass.	Bohemia
1923	Ysart Family	Develops technique where colored enamels are suspended in clear glass bodies.	Spain
1924	Victor Durand, Martin Bach Jr., Emil J. Larsen, William Wiedebine	Art glass shop opened and produced Quezal-style iridescent art glass. Added cameo and intaglio designs, Art Deco shapes, and Oriental-inspired pieces. Some pieces marked, some use paper sticker, name sometimes scratched on pontil and/or numbered.	Vineland, NJ

Year	Who	What	Where
1924	Fostoria	Introduces colored tablewares. Also creates *black glass* formula.	Moundsville, WV
1924	Lancaster Glass Co.	Becomes subsidiary of Hocking Glass Co., also makes blanks for Standard Cut Glass Co.	Lancaster, OH
1924	John Moncrief	"Discovers" Ysart glass and begins production. Names glassware "Monart," combining their two surnames. Most wares marked with a paper label.	Perth, Scotland
1924	Union Glass Co.	Company closes.	Somerville, MA
1925	Quezal Art Glass Co.	Company closes.	Brooklyn, NY
1925	Consolidated Lamp & Glass Co.	Introduces two new Art Deco-inspired lines, Catalonia and Martele.	Corapolis, PA
1925	Paolo Venini	Opened Venini Glassworks, his descendents still running studio.	Murano, Italy
1926	René Lalique	Adds "France" to his "R. Lalique" marks.	France
1926-1927	H. C. Fry Glass Co.	Produces Foval glass. Art glass in pearly opalescent with jade green or delft blue trim.	Rochester, PA
1927	Jeannette Glass Co.	Ceases all hand operations.	Jeannette, PA
1928	Durand Glass Co.	Perfects *crackle glass* technique, naming it "*Moorish Crackle*" and "*Egyptian Crackle*."	
1928	Hazel-Atlas Factory	Proclaimed "Largest Tumbler Factory" by trade papers.	Clarksburg, WV
1928-1931	A. Douglas Nash	Purchases facilities at Tiffany Furnaces, creating the A. Douglas Nash Corporation, and operates until 1931.	Corona, Long Island, NY
1929-1937	Morgantown Glass	Returns to Morgantown name.	Morgantown, WV
1930	Eureka Art Glass	Changes name to Blenko Glass Co.	Milton, WV
1930	Edward Libbey	Renews interest in art glass, develops new lines for Libbey Glass.	Toledo, OH
1930s	Fenton Art Glass Co.	Production now includes lamps and slag glass forms.	Williamstown, WV
1930s	Imperial Glass Corp.	Imperial Glass Co. reorganizes and continues production, later acquiring molds of other glassmakers as they go out of business.	Bellaire, OH
1930s	Kraft Foods	Introduces *Swankyswigs*, colorful decorated juice tumblers.	
1931	Victor Durand	Dies, Vineland Flint Glass Works merges with Kimble Glass Company a year later, art glass line discontinued.	Vineland, NJ
1931	A. Douglas Nash	Joins Libbey Glass as a designer.	Toledo, OH
1931	Gallé Factory	Production ends.	Nancy, France
1932	Consolidated Lamp and Glass Co.	Closes factory, moving 40 molds to Phoenix.	Corapolis, PA
1932	Keith Murray	Joins Stevens & Williams, designs become more naturalistic.	Stourbridge, England
1932-1960s	Phoenix Glass Co.	Production includes molded, sculptured cameo-type wares.	Beaver, PA
1933-1957	A. H. Heisey Glass Co.	Glass figurines produced during this period. After factory closed, Imperial buys some molds.	Newark, OH
1935	Akro Agate Co.	Begins production of children's wares.	Clarksburg, WV

Year	Who	What	Where
1935-1954	Cambridge Glass Co.	Uses paper labels, as well as five different marks, but not all marked.	Cambridge, OH
1936	Consolidated Lamp and Glass Co.	Reopens factory, 40 molds returned by Phoenix.	Corapolis, PA
1936	Handel & Co.	Company closes.	Meriden, CT
1936-1982	Imperial Glass Co.	Produces No. 400 pattern, better known as Candlewick. Produced mostly in clear, some colors made 1937-41.	Bellaire, OH
1937	Corning Glass Co.	Purchases Macbeth-Evans.	Corning, NY
1937	Libbey Glass Co.	Produces first collector glasses for premier of Walt Disney's Snow White.	Toledo, OH
1937	Hocking Glass	Merges with Anchor Cap Company, creating Anchor-Hocking. Production of ovenware glassware begins.	Lancaster, OH
1938	Robert Gunderson	Buys the Pairpoint Corp and renames it Gunderson Glass Works.	New Bedford, MA
1938	U. S. Glass Co.	Moves corporate offices as pressed glass production decreases.	Tiffin, OH
1939	Morgantown Glassware Guild	Group of former Morgantown employees reopens old factory.	Morgantown, WV
1940s	Fenton Art Glass Co.	Introduces line of "crests"—white trimmed solid color wares, Aqua Crest, Rose Crest, Silver Crest, etc.	Williamstown, WV
1942	Rainbow At Glass Co.	Founded by Henry Manus, primary production was small hand-blown animals and decorative opal, spatter, cased, and crackle wares.	Huntington, WV
1942-1976	Anchor Hocking	*Fire-King* produced in dinnerware, ovenware, and utilitarian wares.	Lancaster, OH
1944	Viking Glass Co.	Forms out of reorganized New Martinsville Glass Co.	New Martinsville, WV
1945	René Lalique	Mark changed to "Lalique France" with out the "R."	France
1948	Akro Agate Co.	Goes out of business.	Clarksburg, WV
1949	Paden City Glass Manufacturing Co.	Expands production to include bottles, ashtrays, and novelties by acquiring American Glass Co.	Paden City, WV
1949	Westmoreland Glass Co.	Re-introduces black glass into production of variety pieces. Also starts to use imprinted mark.	Grapeville, PA
1950s	Barovier, Toso, Emmanno Nason Murano	Studios creating vividly colored glassware.	Murano, Italy
1951	McKee Glass Co.	Closes factory.	Jeannette, PA
1951	Paden City Glass Manufacturing Co.	Closes factory.	Paden City, WV
1952	Waterford Crystal	Company reopens, again making fine crystal tablewares.	Waterford, England
1952-1956	Gunderson Glass Co.	Business reorganized under name of Gunderson-Pairpoint.	Somerville, MA
1953	Welch's	Introduces collector glasses as jelly containers.	
1954	Cambridge Glass Co.	Company closes, some molds purchased by Imperial Glass Co.	Cambridge, OH

Year	Who	What	Where
1955	Duncan and Miller Glass Co.	Plant closes, ending its slogan, "The Loveliest Glassware in America." U.S. Glass purchased molds and machinery in 1956.	Washington, PA
1956	Continental Can	Purchases Hazel-Atlas, continues production.	
1958	A. H. Heisey Glass Co.	Closes factory, some molds sold to Tiffin and T. G. Hawkes Co.	Newark, OH
1958	Federal Glass	Becomes division of Federal Paper Board Co.	
1960	Sabino Glass	Introduces fiery opalescent wares in Art Deco style.	France
1961	Jeannette	Buys old McKee factory.	Jeannette, PA
1962	Consolidated Lamp and Glass Co.	Sold to Dietz Brothers, permanently closes in 1964.	Corapolis, PA
1964	Brockway Glass Co.	Buys out Continental Can's interest in Hazel-Atlas.	
1965	Bryce Brothers Co.	Bought by Lenox Corp.	Mt. Pleasant, PA
1965	Morgantown Glassware Guild	Purchased by Fostoria, which operated original factory until 1971.	Morgantown, WV
1970	Fenton Art Glass Co.	First begins to use oval raised trademark, some paper labels existed prior to this date.	Williamstown, WV
1970	Robert Bryden	Reorganizes Gunderson-Pairpoint.	New Bedford, MA
1970s	Jan Johansson	Develops internally decorated wares for Orrefors.	Sweden
1970s	Viking Glass	Acquires Rainbow Glass Co., continues animal production.	Huntington, WV
1973	Imperial Glass Co.	Sold to Lenox, Inc.	
1975	Kosta Boda	Acquires Äfors.	Sweden
1980	Tiffin Glass Co.	Closes factory.	Tiffin, OH
1982	Westmoreland Glass Co.	Closes factory, tries to reorganize, but fails again in 1984.	Grapeville, PA
1983	Fostoria Glass Co.	Purchased by Lancaster Colony Glass Co., continues some production.	Moundsville, WV
1990	Orrefors Kosta Boda	Orrefors and Kosta Boda merge.	Sweden
1999	L. G. Wright	Closes factory, sells molds.	

ADVERTISING

History: Advertising on glass began with early bottles. Other types of containers, from pickle jars to whiskey bottles, can be found engraved, etched, painted, and labeled. Early manufacturers often used illustrations of the product so that even illiterate buyers could identify a product. The country store of years past was filled with glass jars which contained advertising and slogans.

Another popular way of advertising was a giveaway or premium. Many types of glassware articles were given away by merchants, manufacturers, and salesmen. Carnival glass was popular with the advertiser because it was durable and equally popular with the housewife because it was pretty. Today, carnival glass advertising plates and other forms command a high price.

Usually a collector does not think of glass as a medium when considering advertising collectibles. However, the variety of colors, shapes, and sizes, makes an interesting collection. Many bottles and other types of glass containers have been replaced by plastic containers and the former brown, green, and cobalt blue containers have become collectible.

References: Art Anderson, *Casinos and Their Ashtrays,* 1994, printed by author; Pamela E. Apkarian-Russell, *Washday Collectibles,* Schiffer Publishing, 2000; Donna S. Baker, *Chocolate Memorabilia,* Schiffer Publishing, 2000; Barbara Edmonson, *Old Advertising Spirits Glasses,* Maverick Publications, 1988; Richard Holiner, Stuart Kammermann, *Advertising Paperweights,* Collector Books, 2001; Don and Elizabeth Johnson, *Warman's Advertising,* Krause Publications, 2000; Ray Klug, *Antique Advertising Encyclopedia,* Vol. 1 (1978, 1993 value update) and Vol. 2 (1985), L-W Promotions.

Periodicals: *Advertising Collectors Express,* P.O. Box 221, Mayview, MO 64071; www.tradecardcollectors.com; *Past Times,* P.O. Box 1121, Morton Grove, IL 60053, www.pastimes.org; *The Magazine, Ephemera News,* P.O. Box 95, Cazenovia, NY 13055-0095, www.ephemerasociety.org.

Collectors' Clubs: Antique Advertising Association of America, P.O. Box 1121, Morton Grove, IL 60053, www.pastimes.org; National Association of Paper and Advertising Collectibles, P.O. Box 500, Mount Joy, PA 17552.

Ashtray

Baker's Cocoa 90.00
Barber Supplies, William Marvy, clear, red, white, and blue adv, 5" d 15.00
B. F. Goodrich Vogue Heels, heel shaped, red, white, and blue adv, 3-1/2" x 2-1/4", 1940s 35.00
Chesterfield, MIB 20.00
Coon Chicken Inn, clear, black bell hop, c1930, 4" d 45.00
Dobbs Hats, dark amethyst, hat shape 30.00
Firestone Tire, yellow tire, colorless glass insert, 3-13/16" d. 50.00
G.E.C., blue-green, 3-3/4" sq . 15.00
Goodrich Tire, green, tire shape 40.00
Goodyear, amber, tire shape . . 35.00
Grant's Scotch Whiskey, cobalt blue 15.00
Grapette Soda, milk glass 35.00
Hodges Candy Co., Liberal, KA, blue, pyroglaze dec, 4-1/2" x 3" 9.50
J. S. Hoskins Lumber Co., Baltimore, MD, blue lettering, white ground 25.00
Levy's Jewish Rye Bread, milk glass, Art-Deco shape, illus of black boy eating bread 75.00
Loews L'enfant Plaza, 4" d, colorless, bright blue lettering 5.00
Macbeth Evans, pink 15.00
Reno Cal-Neva, capri blue, red and white design, 3-1/2" d 6.50
Royal Caribbean Cruise Lines, colorless, octagonal, blue crown and anchor logo, 4" d 15.00

Bank

Charles Chaplin, 3-3/4" h, Geo Borgfeldt & Co., painted figure standing next to barrel slotted on lid, name emb on base 220.00
Donald Duck Peanut Butter, Nash Co., 4-1/2" h, lid missing 35.00
Elsie the Cow, colorless cased to white int., milk bottle shape, Save for a Rainy Day, 4-1/2" h 25.00
Esso, clear, emb "Watch Savings Grow". 15.00
Laurel Federal, colorless 12.00
Lincoln Bank, colorless, bottle shape, orig top hat, paper label, 9" h 50.00
Lucky Joe, Nash's Prepared Mustard, Chicago, IL, orig lid, 4-1/2" h 55.00
Pittsburgh Paints, colorless, log cabin shape, paper label 45.00
See Your Savings Daily Shop Peoples Drug Stores, 4-3/4" x 4-3/4" x 3-1/4" 55.00

Basket, marigold carnival glass, John H. Brand Furniture Co., Wilmington, DE 90.00

Beer glass, ftd, Moerlein's Brewery, etched band, National Lager Beer, Good Luck molded in glass, 6-1/4" h . . . 65.00

Biscuit jar, 10-1/2" h, glass lid, "Sunshine Biscuits" emb on front "Loose-Wiles Biscuit Company" on back 350.00

Bottle, Old Tub Whiskey, moon shining black boy, 1930s. 120.00

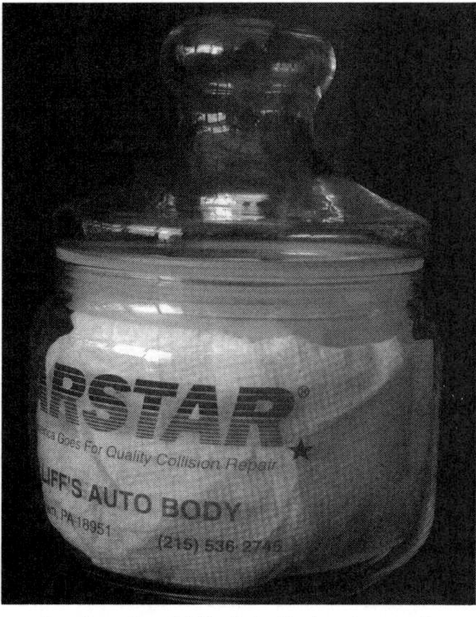

Jar, Car star, Cliff's Auto Body, clear, red and blue lettering, 6-1/4" h, 4" d, **$5.**

Bowl

Citizens Mutual Trust, Wheeling, 1924, Chinese red, Northwood 95.00
Horlacher, Peacock tail pattern, purple carnival glass 85.00
Issac Benesch, amethyst carnival glass, Millersburg mark, 6-1/4" d 400.00
Sterling Furniture Co., purple carnival glass 245.00

Bread plate, Pioneer Flower Mill, San Antonio, clear 50.00

Calling card tray, carnival glass

Fern Brand Chocolates

Amethyst, two turned up sides, 6-1/2" d 700.00
Purple, two turned up sides, 6-1/4" d 175.00

Issac Benesch, Holly Whirl pattern, marigold 125.00

Candy jar, cov, Schrafft's Chocolates, 6" sq, Massachusetts pattern . . . 35.00

Champagne glass, cranberry, Compliments of Frederick Bary Co., trumpet shape, 22" h 175.00

Clock, McCord Motor Gaskets, metal and glass. 95.00

Counter jar

Chicos Spanish Peanuts, glass, tin litho lid and base, minor losses, 12" h. 230.00
Planters Peanuts, 7" dia glass jar with lid, yellow and blue Mr. Peanut image, orig 8" x 8" x 9-1/2" corrugated cardboard shipping carton 90.00

Snickers, Official Snack Food Sponsor of the 1992 U. S. Olympic Team, USA Olympic logo, Barcelona '92 on one side with etched Summer Games logo, Albertville '92 etched on other side, 9-1/4" h **35.00**

Counter plate, El Producto **25.00**

Decanter, Belle of Kentucky, colorless crystal, ribbed, gold letters, orig stopper **100.00**

Dish, marigold carnival glass, Compliments of Pacific Coast Mail Order House, Los Angeles, CA" **700.00**

Dispenser

Hunter's Root Beer, milk glass **50.00**

Radium Vitalizer, vaseline body, emb letters, cylindrical, metal spigot and lid, 10" x 16". **425.00**

Display case, counter top, colorless

Dr. West's Toothbrush **375.00**

Tootsie Rolls, Pure Delicious Chocolate Candy. **350.00**

Eye cup, Optrex Safe Guards Sight, 5" h Optrex bottle with eye cup, cobalt blue, bottom of bottle emb "Optrex" **48.00**

Factices, large perfume display bottle

Ellen Tracey, 11" h **225.00**

Lisson, 13-1/2" h **225.00**

Pavlova, 12" h **200.00**

Romeo Gigli, 17" h. **250.00**

Sharper Image, 12" h, cobalt blue **200.00**

Hat, carnival glass

Horlacher, Peacock Tail pattern, green **90.00**

Miller's Furniture, Harrisburg, basketweave, marigold **95.00**

Humidor, DuraGlass, Dun Rite Wood Novelties, Inc., Brooklyn, NY, Aztec insert under wooden lid, 5-3/4" h, 3-1/2" d **85.00**

Ice cream dish, Borden's, illus of Elsie the Cow **20.00**

Jar, emb

Adam's Pure Chewing Gum, colorless, sq, thumbprint design on stopper, etched label, 11" h . **145.00**

Beich's Candy, colorless, emb lettering, 10" h **60.00**

Bob's Big Boy Restaurant, colorless, Bob's 1985 Collector Series . **30.00**

Buffalo Peanuts, colorless, orig top **125.00**

Candy Bros. Manufacturing Co., St. Louis, colorless, 4-lb size . . . **75.00**

Cavalier Boot Cream, colorless **10.00**

Compressed Lozenges, H. K. Mulford Co., Phila and Chicago, brown, sq, metal screw top, c1880, 11-1/2" h. **85.00**

Dr. Stevens Cough Drops, colorless, paper label **65.00**

Faultless Wonder Nipples, amber, round, frosted glass nipple-shaped cov, emb label, 13" h **800.00**

Kis-Me Chewing Gum, American Chicle Co., colorless, sq, chamfered corners, glass stopper, flanged lip, emb "Kiss-Me," paper label **450.00**

La Palina Cigars, round, knob finial on cov, emb and paper labels, 7" h, 6" d. **75.00**

Lutted's S. P. Cough Drops, colorless, chimney finial on roof cov, emb shingle, log, and window designs, emb label and "Genuine Has J.L. Stamped On Each Drop," ftd, 7" h. **425.00**

Peerless Hardware Soap, colorless, spherical, metal threaded lid, canted, red stencil-style label on raised band. **145.00**

Rexall Drug, colorless, spherical, emb script label, no cov, 4-1/2" h, 5" d. **150.00**

Swift's Toilet Soap, semi ovoid, glass cov, emb label **175.00**

Lamp shade

Eat L. V. Orsinger's Ice Cream, red, two white opaque glass panels, metal frame, six colored jewels, 6" h. **750.00**

Pittsburgh Ice Cream, red and black lettering, "We Serve The Cream of Pittsburgh," milk glass base, 1917 patent **325.00**

Magazine tear sheet, Carder Steuben, from *The House Beautiful,* color illus and text, 1927, one matted, price for pr **40.00**

Marbles, Drakes Cakes, Play The Game, Be Fair, Don't Cheat, Don't Play on the Street, mesh bag full of 15 machine-made glass marbles, late 1940s. **20.00**

Measuring cup

Bryan's Cleaners & Dyers, Pasadene, maroon, 4-5/8" h **18.00**

Crescent Mapleine, white, 3-1/2" h **12.00**

King Midas Enriched Flour, blue and white, 5-1/8" h **20.00**

Lenkerbrok Farms, Inc., colorless, red letters, Pyrex, 8 oz **10.00**

Monarch Inc. Food Service, blue, 4-3/4" h. **14.00**

Mug

Compliments for ...Elling... Harrisburg, PA, Fisherman's pattern, Dugan carnival glass, multicolored, letters partially readable **200.00**

Golden Knight Saving Soap, colorless, emb letters **25.00**

Lease Savers, Customer Quencher, Thermo-Serv **5.00**

Paperweight

American Card Clothing Co., Worcester, MA, 1882, colorless **25.00**

American Glass & Construction Co., Rochester, NY, glass reinforced with wire, rect, 3" x 4-1/2" . . . **20.00**

Bell Telephone, bell shape, cobalt blue **50.00**

Canton, OH, Centennial, 1909, ruby stained, 4-1/4" x 2-3/4" x 3/4" h **45.00**

Columbia National Bank **20.00**

Elgin Watches **35.00**

Golden Pheasant Gunpowder, multicolored. **40.00**

Imperial Glass Co., illus of plant, engraved 1973 . . . . **30.00**

Independent Press Room, Los Angeles, colorless, rect. **20.00**

Leeson & Co., Boston, Linen Thread Importers, colorless, black and white illus, 4-1/8" l **60.00**

Paperweight, J. R. Lesson & Co., Boston, Linen Thread Importers, spinning wheel motif, black lettering, white ground, 2-5/8" x 4-1/8", **$60.**

Lehigh Sewer Pipe & Tile Co., Ft. Dodge, IA, colorless, 4" l . . . **20.00**
Macbeth-Evans Glass Co., Pittsburgh, PA, rect. **25.00**
New York Telephone Bell System, bell shape, cobalt blue **95.00**
Old Bridgeport Double Copper Distilled Pure Rye Whiskey, Brownsville, PA, colorless, 3" d **35.00**
Radekar Lumber Co., men working logs, multicolored scene, milk glass **50.00**
Warfield Grocers Co., Wholesale Grocers, Quincy, IL, 1920, 2-1/2" w, 4" l **35.00**
Wurtz Auto Garage, Degenhart **40.00**

Perfume bottle
California Perfume Bottle, NY, violet scent, orig label **45.00**
Le Golliwogg, de Vigney, Paris, colorless frosted body, painted label, black puff wig, stopper with figural Golliwogg head, 3-1/2" h **95.00**
Lightners Jockey Club, label under glass, glass stopper **315.00**
Lucky Lindy Perfume, Nipoli Co., colorless, 1927 . . . . **30.00**
Owl Drug Co., Oil of Sweet Almond, orig label, 1 oz, cork top **5.00**

Plate, carnival glass
Brazier Candies, purple, hand grip, 6" d **250.00**
Campbell & Beesley Co. , purple **450.00**
Davidson Chocolate Society, purple, 6-1/4" d **245.00**
Eagle Furniture, purple **245.00**
Eat Paradise Soda Candies, Season's Greetings, purple, 6" d **200.00**
Fern Brand Chocolates
Amethyst, 6" d **1,100.00**
Purple, 6" d **225.00**
Greengard Furniture Co., purple **600.00**
Old Rose Distillery, Grape and Cable pattern, green, stippled, 9" d **265.00**
Roods Chocolate, Pueblo, purple **750.00**
Spector's Department Store, Heart and Vine pattern, marigold, 9" d **325.00**
Utah Liquor Co., hand grip, 6" d **300.00**
We Use Brocker's, purple, 7" d **500.00**

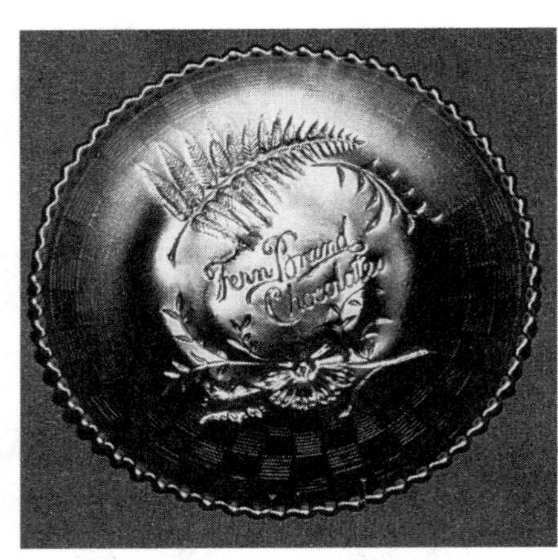

Plate, carnival glass, 6" d, Fern Brand Chocolates, amethyst, **$1,100.** *Photo courtesy of Mickey Reichel Auction Center.*

Plate, pressed glass, Massachusetts, Schrafft's Chocolate adv. **75.00**
Pomade jar, F. B. Strouse, NY, clam-broth, figural bear, 3-3/4" h **375.00**
Salt and pepper shakers, pr
Chef Boy Ar Dee, white, Hazel Atlas **60.00**
Drink Pepsi Cola, colorless, bottle shape, 4-1/4" h **9.00**
General Electric, milk glass, refrigerator shape **35.00**

Seltzer bottle
Barrett & Co. Mineral Water Ashton U Lyne, 6-1/2" h, dark forest green, emb name **35.00**
J & B Jewsbury & Brown Manchester, light cobalt blue, acid etched name on front set in star, chrome top **100.00**

Shoe
Cobalt blue, gold lettering "St. Paul Furnishing Company, Widows and Orphans Protected" **75.00**
Orange, Albert E. Lee Jeweler & Optometrist, Enterprise, Alabama, 1920s, 4-1/2" l **35.00**

Sign
Imperial Glass, 6" x 3-1/4" . . . **300.00**
La Senorite, La Camille, reverse painted on glass, red letters with white outlines, black ground, back light assembly **250.00**

Slide, used in movie theater, black background
Heinz Ketchup, child standing next to giant ketchup bottle **35.00**
"It Might Happen To You! Fire Might Turn A Garage Into A Grave Yard, Is Your Car Insured," see this agency of the Hartford Fire Insurance Co., colored fire disaster scene, Manhattan Slide & Film Co. **25.00**
"Money Gets Away Easily, The Only Safe Plan Is To Carry a Check Book & Keep Your Money in the Bushton State Bank," U.S. Slide Co. . **20.00**
"The New Way Buy From The Sunshine Display Rack The Quality Biscuits of the World Kept Clean and Fresh Under Glass Covers," Advertising Slide Co. **22.00**
"Use Snow Belt Flour," winter scene with church on hill top, U.S. Slide Co. **20.00**

Tray
Houze Glass Co., Point Marion, PA, Season's Greetings, smoke ground, red reindeer, white snowflakes and lettering, 4-3/4" x 3-3/4" **15.00**
Teaberry Gum, amber. **110.00**

Tumbler
Clark's Teaberry Gum, vaseline **45.00**
Columbia Steamship, red and yellow logo, 1957, 5" h **30.00**
Drink Ferro-Phos, colorless, etched, 4-1/4" h. **35.00**
Elsie, Borden's, Bicentennial, 1976, set of 6 . . . . **90.00**
Olsen's Big New Store, etched "Christmas Greetings, 1901" **45.00**
York, First Capital of the U. S. Colonial Courthouse, Courtesy of Rutter Bros. Dairy. **8.50**
Uneeda Milk Biscuit, chocolate slag, Indiana Tumbler and Goblet Co., small base chip **90.00**
Westinghouse Dishwashers, 1950s features, white, 6-3/4" h **6.00**

Wash board, child size, Caroline Washboard, 2 in 1 Junior, colorless . . . **45.00**
Whiskey dispenser, Ask for Sanderson's Whiskey, colorless, etched, 15-1/2" h **475.00**
Whiskey shot glass, colorless
Always Good, Dan's Rye, Brown & Daniel, Chicago, IL. **25.00**
Big Horn Whiskey, Taylor & Williams Distillery, Louisville, KY, c1900 . . . . **20.00**
Blue Rye, John Barth Co., Milwaukee, IL, c1898 . . . . . . **30.00**
John Spengler, Wholesale Liquors, Kansas City, MO **12.00**
Lititz Springs, Straight Rye Whiskey, John C. Horting, Lititz, PA . . **30.00**
The Blochdale, Pennsylvania Pure White Whiskey, 1912 . . . . . . **20.00**

Top Knot Whiskey, partridge, cut and polished **40.00**
White Swan Distilling Co., Indianapolis, IN, c1915 . . . . . **15.00**
Wishing You Luck, Sterling Tavern, Mike and Florence, 2nd & G St., Eureka, CA **35.00**

Agata Glass

History: Agata glass was invented in 1887 by Joseph Locke of the New England Glass Company, Cambridge, Massachusetts.

Agata glass was produced by coating a piece of peachblow glass with metallic stain, spattering the surface with alcohol, and firing. The resulting high-gloss, mottled finish looked like oil droplets floating on a watery surface. Shading usually ranged from opaque pink to dark rose, although pieces in a pastel opaque green also exist. A few pieces have been found in a satin finish.

Reference: Kenneth Wilson, *American Glass 1760-1930: The Toledo Museum of Art*, Volume I, Volume II, Hudson Hills Press and The Toledo Museum of Art, 1994.

Tumbler, glossy peachblow ground, gold tracery, muted black splotches, 3-7/8", **$650.** *Photo courtesy of Joy Luke Fine Art Brokers and Auctioneers.*

Bowl

4" d, green opaque body, mottled border with scalloped gold tracery **650.00**
5-1/4" d, 2-1/2" h, 10-ruffled rim, shaded rose pink, allover blue and gold oil spots **550.00**
5-1/4" d, 3" h, ruffled, peachblow opaque body, allover bright blue staining spots **750.00**
5-3/8" d, deep rose, crimped rim **700.00**
8" d, 3-1/2" h, green opaque body, black mottling, gold border. **995.00**
8" d, 4" h, green opaque body, staining and gold trim **1,150.00**

Celery vase

6-1/4" h, sq mouth, glossy peachblow, ground pontil, some staining remaining **750.00**
6-1/2" h, scalloped sq top, opaque pink shading to deep rose body, glossy finish **750.00**
7" h, sq, fluted top **625.00**

Creamer, opaque pink shading to rose body, applied handle **1,200.00**

Cruet, 6" h, pale green opaque bulbous body, random oil spot dec, applied handle, acid finish, orig faceted dark green stopper **600.00**

Finger bowl

4-1/2" d, ruffled rim, opaque pink shading to rose body, pronounced mottling, deep pink lining . . **800.00**
5-1/4" d, 2-1/2" h, shiny peachblow, black mottling, lacey gold tracery, deep crimps **685.00**
5-1/4" d, 2-5/8" h, crushed raspberry shading to creamy pink, allover gold mottling, blue accents **995.00**
5-1/4" d, 3" h, ruffled, peachblow opaque body, allover bright blue staining spots **750.00**

Juice tumbler, 3-3/4", opaque pink shading to rose body, mottling, deep pink lining **825.00**

Lady's cuspidor, 5" d, 2-1/2" h, New England peachblow coloration, purple mottling **1,800.00**

Lemonade tumbler, 1-5/8" d base, 2-1/2" d top, 5-1/8" h, New England peachblow shading, pronounced mottling, gold tracery **1,250.00**

Pitcher, 6-3/8" h, crimped rim, opaque pink shading to rose body, pronounced mottling, deep pink lining **1,750.00**

Plate, 6-5/8" d, opaque pink shading to rose body, ribbon candy fluted rim **875.00**

Punch cup, 3" d, 2-3/4" h, deep color, oily spots with blue highlights, applied handle with mottling **625.00**

Salt shaker, delicate shading of pink to rose **625.00**

Snuff bottle, 2-3/4" h, opaque pink shading to rose body, carnelian stopper **250.00**

Spittoon, 5-3/8" d, 2-3/4" h, squatty round body, ruffled and scalloped rim **600.00**

Spooner

3-3/4" h, green opaque body, mottled upper band and narrow gold band **950.00**
4-1/2" h, 2-1/2" w, sq top, wild rose peachblow ground, small areas of wear **400.00**

Toothpick holder, 2-1/4" h, flared, green opaque, orig blue oil spots, green trim **795.00**

Juice tumbler, 3-3/4", **$825.**

Tumbler

Green opaque ground, gold border, profuse intense mottling . . . **750.00**
Peachblow ground
- 3-3/4" h, deep metallic stain obscures most of ground, satin finish **950.00**
- 3-7/8" h, gold tracery, bold black splotches **785.00**

Vase

4-1/4" h, quatraform, opaque pink shading to rose body, pinched sides, ruffled scalloped rim **725.00**
4-1/2" h, cylindrical, crimson New England peachblow, gold tracery all over shiny body **685.00**
4-1/2" h, quatraform, flared rim, opaque pink shading to deep rose body, random oil spot dec **900.00**

4-5/8" h, ruffled, four deep dimples, rose-pink, consistent overall gold veining 1,380.00
4-5/8" h, ruffled, pouch shape, four deep dimples, rose-pink shading to creamy yellow, allover mottling 1,875.00
5" h, 6" w, round, acid cut peachblow, four-way scalloped top, good mineral staining 2,900.00
6" h, lily, crimson peachblow, delicate staining 885.00
7-1/4" h, baluster, opaque pink shading to deep rose body, random oil spot dec, satin finish . . 1,650.00
8" h, lily, shiny surface, crimson peachblow ground, large black splotches 1,085.00
8" h, bulbous stick form, deep wild rose shaded color, gold and blue spotting 1,955.00

Whiskey taster, 2-5/8" h, opaque pink shading to rose body, acid finish 750.00

Akro Agate Glass

1932–48

History: The Akro Agate Co. was formed in 1911, primarily to produce marbles. In 1914, the owners moved from near Akron, Ohio, to Clarksburg, West Virginia, where they opened a large factory. They continued to profitably produce marbles until after the Depression. In 1930, the competition in the marble business became too intense, and Akro Agate Co. decided to diversify.

Two of its most successful products were the floral ware lines and children's dishes, first made in 1935. The children's dishes were very popular until after World War II, when metal dishes captured the market.

The Akro Agate Co. also made special containers for cosmetics firms, such the Jean Vivaudou Co. and Pick Wick bath salts (packaged in the Mexicali cigarette jar). Operations continued successfully until 1948. The factory, a victim of imports and the increased use of metal and plastic, was sold to Clarksburg Glass Co. in 1951.

Akro Agate glass is a thick-walled type of glass. Many patterns were made in fired-on, opaque, solid, transparent, and marbleized colors. Colors include black, blue, cobalt blue, cream, green, pumpkin, white, and yellow. Marbleized combinations are limitless, and unusual combinations command the highest prices. An example of an unusual color combination is called "lemonade and oxblood" and usually found in children's dishes. The yellow background has blood red streaks, and while it is striking in appearance, the name might not be popular with today's mothers.

The Akro Agate Company bought Westite molds after the Westite factory burned in 1936. Westite was known for production of household-type fixtures, as well as flower pots, creamers, etc. Westite was made in several colors, but a brown and white marbleized combination was most prevalent, followed by a marbleized green and white combination. The Akro Agate Company began production using these molds and it's own striking color combinations.

Many Akro Agate pieces are marked "Made in USA" and often include a mold number. Some pieces also have a small crow in the mark. Westite pieces are marked with a "W" inside a diamond shape.

References: Gene Florence, *Collectors Encyclopedia of Akro Agate Glassware*, revised ed., Collector Books, 1975, 1992 value update; Roger and Claudia Hardy, *Complete Line of the Akro Agate*, published by author, 1992.

Collectors' Clubs: Akro Agate Art Assoc., P.O. Box 758, Salem, NH 03079; Akro Agate Collector's Club, 10 Bailey St., Clarksburg, WV 26301.

Reproduction Alert: Pieces currently reproduced are not marked "Made In USA" and are missing the mold number and crow.

Apple, cov, pumpkin. 175.00

Ashtray

2-1/4" x 3-1/2", rect, green slag, club shaped cut-out. 150.00
2-7/8" sq, blue and red marble 12.00
2-7/8" sq, blue marble 8.00
2-7/8" sq, red marble 8.00
4" x 2-7/8" sq, red marble 8.00
4", blue, Hotel Lincoln 75.00
4-1/2" w, hexagon, blue and white 35.00
Basket, two handles, orange and white 35.00

Bell

Light blue 60.00
Pumpkin, 5-1/4" h 50.00

Powder jar, Apple, opaque pumpkin color, **$195.**

Flower pot, 5-1/4" d, 5-1/4" h, brown swirls, white ground, Westite, **$17.50.**

Bowl

5" d, emb leaves, white opaque, orange marbleized swirls . . . 35.00
5-7/8" d, 2-7/8" h, dark red marbleized swirls, three toes, marked "#340, Made in USA" 90.00
6" d, cream opaque, brown marbleized swirls, Westite . . 25.00

Cigarette holder, gray and white 15.00

Cigarette lighter top, lemonade and oxblood, square, canted corners, four ball feet 45.00

Cornucopia, orange and white, #765, 3" h 15.00

Demitasse cup

Blue and white marble 12.00
Green and white marble 12.00

Demitasse cup and saucer

Dark green, marble. 20.00
Orange and white marble 20.00

Flower pot

1-1/2" h, opaque green. 7.50
2-1/4" h, ribbed, green and white 9.00
2-1/2" h, Banded Dark, aqua . . 6.00
2-1/2" h, Stack Disk, green and white 11.00
2-1/2" h, Stack Disk, orange and white. 15.00
2-3/4" h, Banded, yellow, marked "300F, Made in USA" with triangle mark 20.00
3-1/4" h, Banded, dark green and white. 18.00
3-1/2" h, Ribs and Flutes, cream 5.00
4" h, Stacked Disk, green and white 22.00
5-1/4" h, white opaque, brown marbleized swirls, Westite . . 17.50
5-1/2" h, scalloped top, blue . . 30.00

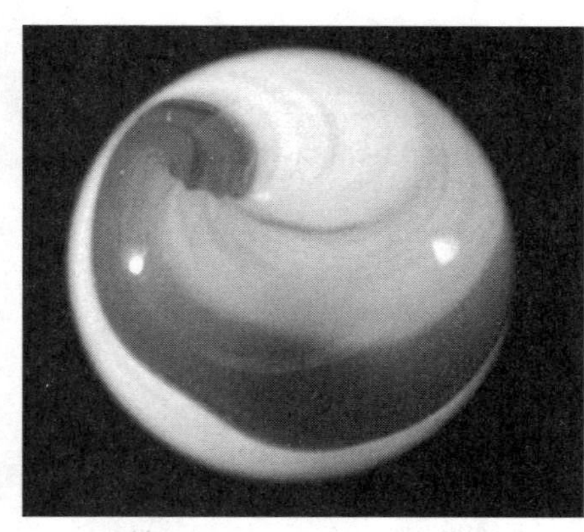

Marble, 5/8" d, Popeye Corkscrew, 1930-35, **$60.**

Lamp

12" h, brown and blue marble, 4" d black octagonal top, Globe Spec Co. **75.00**

13" h, green and brown marble, round 5-1/4" d ribbed base, Houzex **95.00**

Marbles, Chinese Checkers, orig box of 60 . . . . . **125.00**

Match holder, gun shape, white opaque, green marbleized swirls **15.00**

Mexicalli hat, blue and white **20.00**

Mexicalli jar, orange and white, 4-5/8" h **125.00**

Morter and pestle, white, hand-painted flowers **12.00**

Pipe rest, translucent green and white **35.00**

Planter

Chiquita, green, oval, 6" h **5.00**

Graduated Dark, black, scalloped, emb company name and address, 3" h **35.00**

Rect, wire cart holder, orange and white **35.00**

Powder jar

Colonial Lady, white **60.00**

Scottie Dog

Blue opaque **75.00**

White opaque **85.00**

Vase

2-3/8" h, red, white, green streaks **5.00**

3-1/4" h, cornucopia, multicolored **15.00**

3-1/4" h, urn shape, opaque white, orange marbleized swirls, ftd. . **9.00**

3-3/4" h, green marble, smooth top **18.00**

4-1/4" h, lily, marble **15.00**

4-5/8" h, Jean Vivaudou Co., white opaque, blue marbleized swirls, emb handles **12.00**

6-1/4" h, tab handle, marbled . **35.00**

8" h, Ribs and Flutes, cobalt blue **35.00**

8-3/4" h, Seven Darts, pumpkin **35.00**

Children's play dishes, small unless otherwise noted

Bowl

Octagonal, white **10.00**

Stacked Disk and Panel, large, green **18.00**

Cereal bowl

Concentric Ring, blue, large . . **25.00**

Interior Panel, transparent green, large **15.00**

Octagonal, opaque white, large **20.00**

Stacked Disk & Interior Panel, transparent blue, large **45.00**

Creamer

Chiquita

Baked-on cobalt-blue **9.00**

Green **11.00**

Interior Panel, opaque blue, large **42.50**

Octagonal

Blue, large **15.00**

Opaque blue, large **20.00**

Sky blue, large, open handle **22.50**

Yellow, large **23.00**

Stacked Disk

Opaque green **8.00**

Pink **22.50**

Stippled Band, transparent green, 1-1/4" h **25.00**

Creamer and sugar

Chiquita, cobalt blue **20.00**

Interior Panel, turquoise **50.00**

J Pressman, baked-on cobalt blue **12.00**

Octagonal, closed handle, medium blue, white lid, large **38.00**

Stacked Disk

Medium blue **12.00**

Pink **45.00**

Stacked Disk & Interior Panel, turquoise **50.00**

Cup

Chiquita

Opaque green **8.50**

Transparent cobalt blue . . . **13.00**

Concentric Rib, opaque green . **4.50**

Concentric Ring

Opaque green **8.00**

Periwinkle **30.00**

Rose, large **35.00**

Turquoise **32.00**

Interior Panel

Medium blue **6.00**

Pumpkin **35.00**

J Pressman, lavender **30.00**

Octagonal

Green, open handle, large **14.00**

Opaque green, large **15.00**

Plain Jane **14.00**

Stacked Disk

Opaque dark blue **12.00**

Opaque green **5.00**

Oaque light blue **12.00**

Stacked Disk & Interior Panel

Pumpkin **35.00**

Transparent blue, large **40.00**

Stippled Band

Green, large **20.00**

Topaz, 1-1/4" h **20.00**

Cup and saucer

Chiquita

Opaque green **7.00**

Transparent cobalt blue . . . **18.00**

Concentric Ring

Azure trans-optic, 1-1/4" h . **30.00**

Green cup, white saucer . . . **27.00**

Interior Panel

Green and white marble . . . **35.00**

Opaque pumpkin **30.00**

Stacked Disk, green cup, white saucer **10.00**

Stacked Disk & Interior Panel

Green and white marble . . . **35.00**

Transparent cobalt blue . . . **80.00**

Stippled Band

Amber, large **20.00**

Azure **42.00**

Cobalt blue, large **35.00**

Topaz **28.00**

Demitasse cup

J Pressman

Green **9.75**

Pink **30.00**

Demitasse saucer, J Pressman, green **8.00**

Pitcher

Interior Panel, transparent green **30.00**

Octagonal, light blue, 2-7/8" h . **25.00**

Stacked Disk

Opaque blue **35.00**

Opaque green **10.00**

Stacked Disk & Interior Panel

Transparent blue **55.00**

Transparent green **50.00**

Stippled Band, transparent green **15.00**

Stippled Interior Panel

Transparent green **45.00**

Transparent topaz **45.00**

Plate
Concentric Rib
Opaque green **2.50**
Opaque yellow **3.00**
Concentric Ring
Apple green **23.00**
Dark blue **5.00**
Green **3.75**
Light blue **5.00**
J Pressman, 3-3/4" d, baked-on green **4.00**
Interior Panel
Azure blue, large **20.00**
Blue, small **33.00**
Medium blue, large. **15.00**
Transparent green **14.00**
Yellow. **23.00**
Octagonal
Blue, large **10.00**
Lime **5.00**
Opaque blue, large **20.00**
Opaque blue, small **15.00**
Opaque green, large **15.00**
Opaque light green, large. . . **8.00**
Oxblood, marbleized, 4-1/4" d **13.00**
Stacked Disk, opaque green, 3-1/4" d. **4.00**
Stacked Disk & Interior Panel
Cobalt blue small **35.00**
Transparent blue, large . . . **18.00**
Stippled Band
Topaz, large **9.00**
Transparent amber. **12.00**
Transparent green, 4-1/4" d . **6.00**

Saucer
Chiquita, opaque green **2.00**
Concentric Rib
Opaque white. **4.00**
Yellow. **2.50**
Concentric Ring
Ivory **3.00**
Opaque green **3.00**
Pink **4.00**
White **3.75**
Yellow. **3.00**
Interior Panel
Azure blue, large **14.00**
Blue, small **38.00**
Green. **23.00**
Medium blue, large. **16.00**
Transparent green **3.00**
Octagonal
Blue, large **17.00**
Dark pink **6.00**
Opaque blue, large **18.00**
Opaque tan, large **9.00**
Octagonal, pink, large **9.00**
White, large **10.00**
Stacked Disk & Interior Panel, transparent cobalt blue. **30.00**

Stippled Band
Transparent amber **6.50**
Transparent green, 2-3/4" d . **3.00**

Set
Chiquita, green opaque green, six pcs. **70.00**
Concentric Ring, four apple green plates, three orange cups, four yellow saucers, blue teapot, white lid, 13 pcs **250.00**
Interior Panel
Jadeite, 21 pcs **335.00**
Opaque yellow, white teapot lid, large, 21-pc set. **350.00**
Little American Maid, Octagonal, large size, four light green 4-1/4" plates, four yellow 3-1/2" plates, four ivory 3-3/8" bowls, four pumpkin cups, four white saucers, light blue teapot and cov, light blue creamer, ivory cover for sugar, (sugar bowl missing), orig box, 21 pcs **275.00**
Octagonal
Large, four blue plates, four green cups, yellow creamer, yellow sugar with ivory lid, 11 pcs **190.00**
Large, four blue plates, yellow creamer, yellow sugar, yellow teapot, blue sugar lid, blue teapot lid, nine pcs **230.00**
Small, opaque green and white, 23 pcs. **145.00**
Small, open handles, four green plates, four orange cups, four yellow saucers, blue teapot, 13 pcs. **305.00**
Stacked Disk, marbled blue, creamer, sugar, teapot, ivory lid, four pcs **345.00**
Stippled Band
Topaz, 14 pcs **330.00**
Transparent amber, 17 pcs **215.00**
Transparent azure blue, large size, 17 pcs. **470.00**
Transparent green, 14 pcs **355.00**

Sugar
Chiquita
Cobalt blue, transparent **9.00**
Green **11.00**
Interior Panel, lemonade and oxblood **40.00**
Octagonal, white opaque, orange marbleized. **10.00**
Stacked Disk, white **6.00**
Stacked Disk & Interior Panel
Cobalt blue **30.00**
Medium blue **15.00**

Teapot, cov
Chiquita
Opaque green **23.00**
Transparent cobalt blue . . . **32.00**
Concentric Rib
Opaque cobalt blue, white lid **42.00**
Opaque white. **25.00**
Interior Panel
Green, white lid, large **42.00**
Maroon teapot, white lid. . **120.00**
Medium blue, blue lid, large **50.00**
Octagonal
Bright blue, white lid, open handle **24.00**
Medium blue, green lid, large, open handle. **20.00**
Raised Daisy, blue **60.00**
Stacked Disk
Blue teapot, pink lid **38.00**
Green. **21.00**
Medium blue **14.00**
Opaque white. **25.00**
Pink **17.00**
Pumpkin, beige lid **25.00**
Stacked Disk & Interior Panel
Green, white lid **45.00**
Transparent blue, large . . . **85.00**
Stippled Band
Amber, large **50.00**
Azure **90.00**
Topaz **26.00**
Transparent amber **30.00**

Teapot, open
Chiquita, green, opaque **8.00**
Concentric Rib, light blue, opaque **8.00**
Interior Panel
Green luster. **10.00**
Opaque pink **9.75**
Oxblood marble **28.00**
Transparent green, large . . **15.00**
J Pressman, baked-on cobalt blue **8.75**
Octagonal, turquoise, large . . **15.00**
Oxblood, marble **28.00**
Stacked Disk
Medium blue **7.00**
Opaque green **24.00**
Stacked Disk & Interior Panel, transparent cobalt blue. **75.00**
Tumbler
Interior Panel, transparent green **20.00**
Octagonal
Opaque green, large **20.00**
Opaque yellow, large **20.00**
Raised Daisy, yellow, 2" h. . . . **40.00**

Stacked Disk
- Opaque tan. **13.00**
- White. **6.00**

Stacked Disk & Interior Panel
- Transparent blue. **25.00**
- Transparent green. **20.00**

Stippled Band, topaz **14.00**

Stippled Interior Panel
- Transparent green. **20.00**
- Transparent topaz. **20.00**

Water set

Octagonal, open handle, blue pitcher, dark green tumbler . . **65.00**

Playtime, 3" h blue pitcher, three 2" h jadeite tumblers, three 2" h white tumblers, orig box, wear to box **160.00**

Stippled Band, green, pitcher and six tumblers. **105.00**

Amberina Glass

1883

History: Joseph Locke developed Amberina glass in 1883 for the New England Glass Works. "Amberina," a trade name, describes a transparent glass which shades from deep ruby to amber. It was made by adding powdered gold to the ingredients for an amber-glass batch. A portion of the glass was reheated later to produce the shading effect. Usually it was the bottom which was reheated to form the deep red; however, reverse examples have been found. Locke's July 24, 1883 patent described the base as an amber glass containing gold and further claimed that ruby, violet, a greenish, or bluish tint may be developed during the process.

Most early Amberina is flint-quality glass, blown or pattern molded. Patterns include Diamond Quilted, Daisy and Button, Venetian Diamond, Diamond and Star, and Thumbprint.

In addition to the New England Glass Works, the Mount Washington Glass Company of New Bedford, Massachusetts, copied the glass in the 1880s and first sold it under the Amberina trade name and later as "Rose Amber." It is difficult to distinguish pieces from these two New England factories. Boston and Sandwich Glass Works never produced the glass.

Amberina glass also was made in the 1890s by several Midwest factories, among which was Hobbs, Brockunier & Co. Trade names included "Ruby Amber Ware" and "Watermelon." The Midwest glass shaded from cranberry to amber, and the color resulted from the application of a thin flashing of cranberry to the reheated portion. This created a sharp demarcation between the two colors. This less-expensive version was the death knell for the New England variety.

In 1884, Edward D. Libbey was given the use of the trade name "Amberina" by the New England Glass Works. Production took place during 1900, but ceased shortly thereafter. In the 1920s, Edward Libbey renewed production at his Toledo, Ohio, plant for a short period. The glass was of high quality. Amberina from this era is marked "Libbey" in script on the pontil. A round paper label with the company logo may also be found.

References: Gary Baker et al., *Wheeling Glass 1829-1939*, Oglebay Institute, 1994; Neila and Tom Bredehoft, *Hobbs, Brockunier & Co. Glass*, Collector Books, 1997; George P. and Helen McKearin, *American Glass*, reprint, Crown Publishers, 1941, 1948; John A. Shuman III, *The Collector's Encyclopedia of American Art Glass*, Collector Books, 1988, 1994 value update; Kenneth Wilson, *American Glass 1760-1930*, 2 vols., Hudson Hill Press and The Toledo Museum of Art, 1994.

Reproduction Alert: Reproductions abound. Flashed pieces of amberina have invaded the market. Care should be taken when examining a piece to detect scratches and other defects. True amberina glass may shade in color, but will be consistent. Modern reproductions lack the deep coloration and subtle shading of the originals.

Additional Listings: Libbey, Hobbs, Brockunier, Mount Washington.

Bar decanter, 9-3/4" h, 3-3/8" d, blown, bar lip, polished base, attributed to New England, c1840-60, stopper missing, minor wear. **635.00**

Basket

6" h, 5" w, enameled white daisies, int. ribbed design, applied amber handle. **225.00**

7" h, applied amber wishbone dec, loop handle, attributed to New England Glass Works. . . . **1,300.00**

8" h, 5" w, rose bowl shape, enameled white, blue, and gold floral dec, deep amberina coloration, applied amber-green handle. **200.00**

8-1/2" h, 8" w, swirled ribbed design, irid finish to base and handle, applied clear loop handle . . **150.00**

12-1/2" h, 5" w, Swirl pattern, egg-shaped, applied amber glass prunts, tall amber feet, inverted wishbone handle **275.00**

15" h, 10" w, Swirl pattern, gold rose dec, fence design, elaborate gold floral design, applied feet, applied amber rigaree handle **350.00**

Berry bowl, 6" l, 4" w, 1-7/8" h flared oval bowl, lead glass, Gillinder & Sons, small chips, set of four. **85.00**

Berry set, 9" sq master bowl, 10 4-7/8" sq individual bowls, Daisy and Button pattern, minor edge roughness, small flakes, some color variation, assembled 11-pc set **110.00**

Beverage set, Optic Diamond Quilted pattern, 7" h pitcher, three punch cups, two tumblers, New England Glass Works **825.00**

Bonbon, 7" d, 1-1/2" h, wavy six pointed 1-1/2" w rim, fuchsia shading to pale amber, sgd "Libbey" **625.00**

Bowl

4-1/4" h, 8-3/4" d, Optic Diamond Quilted pattern, stand-up color **585.00**

4-1/2" d, 2-1/4" h, tricorn, fuchsia shading to amber, Venetian Diamond design **325.00**

7" d, applied vaseline ribbon edge, pinched feet, attributed to New England. **225.00**

7-1/2" d, Diamond Quilted pattern, rolled over scalloped edge . **195.00**

9" d, six pinched corners, alternating panels of rib and diamond points, ground pontil **200.00**

9" w, square, Daisy and Button pattern. **250.00**

Bride's basket, 8-3/4" l, 6-1/2" w, 13-1/2" h, Reverse Amberina, oval Diamond Quilted bowl, Pairpoint frame, some re-soldering to frame **275.00**

Butter dish, Cov, 7" d, 5" h, Inverted Thumbprint pattern top, amber knob, amber Daisy and Button type pattern base **300.00**

Butter pat, 2-3/4 d, Daisy and Button pattern, sq, notched corners, pr . **250.00**

Carafe, 7-1/8" h, Inverted Thumbprint pattern, reversed color, swirled neck **175.00**

Celery boat, 14" l, 5" w, 2-1/2" h, Daisy and Button pattern, Hobbs, Brockunier & Co., minute roughness on bow **750.00**

Celery vase

Diamond Optic pattern, 6-1/2" h **375.00**

Diamond Quilted pattern, reverse coloration, ruffled rim, 5" d, 6-3/4" h **110.00**

Inverted Thumbprint pattern . **145.00**

Optic Expanded Diamond pattern, New England Glass Works, 6-1/2" h **345.00**

Centerpiece, 14" l, canoe, Daisy and Button pattern, Hobbs, Brockunier & Co. **950.00**

Cologne bottle, 7-7/8" h, blown molded, hexagonal paneled neck and body, oval printies, faceted stopper, attributed to New England, c1840-70, minor imperfections and flaws . . **635.00**

Compote, 8-3/4" d, Inverted Thumbprint pattern **350.00**

Console set, 9-1/4" d bowl, pr 10" h candlesticks **295.00**
Cordial, 4-1/2" h, trumpet shape **225.00**
Cracker jar
- 5" h, 5-1/2" w, Joseph Locke, New England Glass Works, cov missing **550.00**
- 8" h, 5-3/4" d, Inverted Thumbprint pattern, barrel shape, rare glass cov, applied amber knob finial, attributed to Hobbs, Brockunier & Co., c1885 . . . . **785.00**

Creamer, 4-1/2" h, lightly molded ribs, amber applied handle, handle curl missing **40.00**
Creamer and sugar
- 4-1/2" h, Diamond Quilted pattern, crimped top, amber reeded handles **650.00**
- 5-1/4" w, 5" h creamer, 4" w, 7" h sugar, Maple Leaf pattern, Northwood **195.00**

Cruet
- 4-1/2" h, Diamond Quilted, amber applied squared handle, orig amber cut faceted stopper, polished pontil **475.00**
- 5-1/2" h, Inverted Thumbprint pattern, fuchsia trefoil spout, neck, and shoulder, orig stopper, Mt. Washington. **435.00**
- 5-3/4" h, 4" d, Inverted Thumbprint pattern, deep amber shading to cranberry red, replaced stopper **145.00**

Cruet, blown, applied gold handle, original gold ball stopper, **$275.**

- 6" h, gold shading to red base, red top edge and pouring spout, gold handle and stopper **275.00**
- 6-3/4" h, 3" d, applied amber handle, orig amber cut faceted stopper, attributed to New England Glass Works **275.00**

Decanter
- Optic Diamond Quilted pattern, solid amber faceted stopper, 12" h **485.00**
- Reverse Inverted Thumbprint pattern, ground and polished pontil **125.00**

Dish, leaf shape, ftd, pressed, Gillander **1,200.00**
Finger bowl, fluted, fuchsia to amber **375.00**
Finger bowl and underplate, 5" x 2-1/2" h bowl, 6-3/4" d underplate, reverse amberina, Inverted Thumbprint pattern, applied and fire-on enamel blossoms, thistles, Queen Anne's lace, cattails, and ferns, gold rim. **575.00**
Hair receiver, 4-1/2" d, 2" h, two pcs, deep fuchsia shading to amber, partial Libbey label **1,750.00**
Ice cream plate, 5-1/2" sq, Daisy and Button pattern, Hobbs, Brockunier & Co. **95.00**
Juice tumbler, 3-3/4" h, 2-1/2" d, applied reeded amber handle, slight ribbing, tapered body, New England Glass Works **395.00**
Lamp
- Banquet, shaded red to amber glass font, hand-painted flowers and leaves, crystal stem, 5-3/4" sq cranberry glass base with frosted etched flowers, electric, orig pull chain fixture. **125.00**
- Fluid, Lincoln Drape, Aladdin **800.00**

Finger bowl, Inverted Thumbprint pattern, **$375.**

Punch cup, Baby Thumbprint pattern, applied ribbed handle, 3-1/2" h, **$165.**

Lemonade tumbler, 5-1/4" h, Swirl pattern, gold dec, applied handle . . **250.00**
Marmalade, cov, 5-1/4" h, Inverted Thumbprint pattern, white metal cov, Mt. Washington **250.00**
Parfait, 6-1/2" h, Swirl pattern, gold leaf and bud dec. **295.00**
Pickle castor insert, 4-1/4" h, 4" d, Inverted Thumbprint pattern, Mt. Washington. **425.00**
Pitcher
- 4-1/2" h, sq top, Inverted Thumbprint pattern, applied amber reeded handle **325.00**
- 5" h, Daisy and Button pattern, Hobbs, Brockunier & Co. . . **425.00**
- 6" h, Reverse Amberina, Thumbprint pattern, sq lip, names "Meyer" and "Willie" engraved among leaves and flowers dec, applied amber reeded handle, ground pontil **525.00**
- 6-3/4" h, 4" w, Inverted Thumbprint pattern, ruffled rim, applied amber loop handle. **195.00**
- 7" h, Inverted Thumbprint pattern, bright cranberry shading to amber, applied amber handle. **365.00**

Punch cup, Inverted Thumbprint pattern, colorless reeded handle, **$195.**

8" h, Inverted Thumbprint pattern, clear applied reeded handle 210.00
8" h, 5" d, amberina-opalescent, clear reeded handle, ruffled top, wide flange petticoat shape 650.00
8-1/4" h, 6" w, ruffled, melon ribbed form, Inverted Thumbprint pattern, applied amber glass loop handle 325.00
8-3/4" h, deep cranberry shading to amber base, large moondrops dec, applied amber reeded claw handle, New England Glass Co., some wear to base 550.00
10" h, 4-3/4" d, Optic Diamond Quilted pattern, applied amber handle, ground pontil. 235.00

Posy pot, 3" d, applied wishbone feet, berry pontil 300.00

Punch cup
2-1/2" h, applied reeded amber handle, slight ribbing, tapered body, attributed to Mt. Washington 245.00
2-1/2" h, 3-1/2" w, Diamond Quilted pattern, applied reeded amber handle, good coloration to two-thirds of rounded body, set of five. 325.00

Ramekin and underplate, 4-1/4" d, 2-1/4" h, slightly ribbed 250.00

Rose bowl, 5-1/2" d, 5-1/2" h, Diamond Quilted pattern, deep color, pinched tricorn rim, applied amber reeded shell feet, attributed to New England Glass Works 550.00

Salt shaker, elongated Baby Thumbprint pattern, orig top 150.00

Sauce, Daisy and Button pattern . 40.00

Spooner
4-1/2" h, Inverted Thumbprint pattern, New England Glass Works 100.00
5" h, Diamond Quilted pattern, pinched scalloped top 150.00

Sugar bowl, cov, 4-1/4" h, Inverted Thumbprint pattern, New England Glass Works 375.00

Sugar shaker, 4" h, globular, Inverted Thumbprint pattern, emb floral and butterfly lid 425.00

Syrup pitcher
Hobnail pattern, orig pewter top std "Pat. Jan 29 84," Hobbs, Brockunier & Co., three hobs chipped. . 300.00
Inverted Thumbprint pattern, 5-5/8" h, New England Glass Works, fuchsia to amber with rosy tint, silver plate fitting, slight in the making internal air-trap in glass collar 750.00

Toothpick holder
Baby Inverted Thumbprint pattern
Sq top, 2-1/4" h, 1-1/2" w. 295.00
Tricorn 275.00
Inverted Thumbprint
Fluted, polished pontil, 2-3/4" h 175.00
Pedestal base, NTHCS #82 . . . . 235.00
Optic Diamond Quilted pattern, sq
2-3/8" h 295.00
2-1/2" h, shape #28, Mt. Washington 285.00
Venetian Diamond, Libbey . . 200.00

Tumbler, Optic, reverse amberina 140.00

Vase
4-5/8" h, 6" d, deep fuchsia color, shape #3013, flowerform, six petal-like scallops, sgd "Amberina" above "Libbey" in circle . . 1,250.00
5-3/4" h, lily, elongated blossom, brilliant fuchsia shading to Alexandrite blue to amber foot, New England, int. stain. 500.00
5-7/8" h, lily, deep red at rim shading to amber base, polished pontil, Mt. Washington 600.00
6" h, ribbed lily, polished pontil, silverplated base with twigs and leaves. 475.00
6-3/4" h, roll down lip, optic diamond body 300.00
7" h, cylindrical, Inverted Thumbprint pattern, Midwestern type coloration, ruffled rim 165.00

Tumbler, expanded Diamond-Quilted pattern, **$135.** *Photo courtesy of Joy Luke Fine Art Brokers and Auctioneers.*

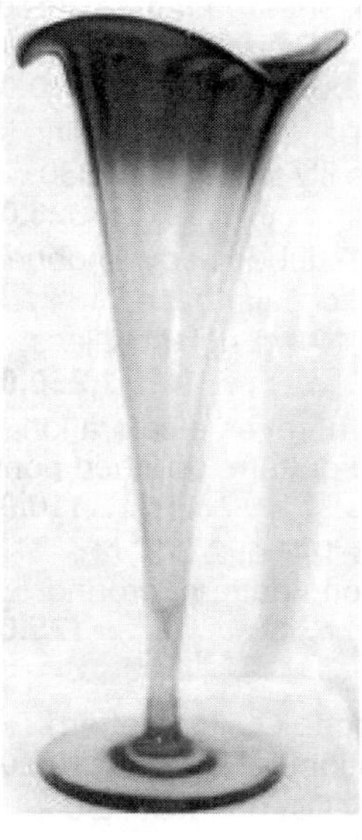

Vase, lily, Mt. Washington, tri-fold rim, deep fuchsia shading to honey amber, wafer base, 10-1/4" h, **$565.** *Photo courtesy of Clarence and Betty Maier.*

7" h, lily, ribbed body, applied amber feet, attributed to New England Glass Works 395.00
7-1/2" h, 11-1/4" l, fan shape, swirled and ribbed, applied amber rigaree edge and wishbone feet, pastoral landscape scene dec highlighted with gold edge, minor loss to painting 195.00
8" h, dark ruby top shades to deep amber base, paneled optic swirls, applied rigaree, indented pontil 185.00
9-1/2" h, corseted, swirled design, tooled amber rigaree trim . . 130.00
10" h, lily, fuchsia highlights. . 675.00
10" h, 5-1/8" d, cylindrical, Swirl pattern, enameled pink and white flowers, green leaves, gold trim, attributed to New England Glass Works 350.00
10-1/2" h, swagged and ruffled lip, snake form entwined around neck, heavy enameled goldfinches perched on thistle blossoms, attributed to Le Gras, c1890 . . . . 595.00
12" h, trumpet, ribbed body, attributed to New England Glass Works 350.00
12-1/4" h, 3-1/4" d, swirled calla lily shape, cranberry shading to golden amber foot, amber applied spiral trim 165.00
11" h, shape #3006, lily, Libbey signature in pontil 875.00
11-1/4" h, shape #3004, sgd "Libbey" 1,200.00

14" h, conical, sheared rim, textured amber serpent spirals lower body, ball knob, mound foot **120.00**

15" h, lily shape, deep red shading to amber, large lily top, flint, c1880 . . . . . **825.00**

23" h, trumpet, ribbed body, knobbed stem, raised circular base, attributed to New England Glass Works **1,250.00**

Water bottle, 7" h, reverse coloration, Diamond Quilted pattern, polished pontil **110.00**

Whimsey, hat, 3-1/4" d, 2-3/8" h, Expanded Diamond pattern, ground pontil **175.00**

Whiskey taster

2-1/2 h, Diamond Quilted pattern, deep coloration **125.00**

2-3/4" h, Baby Diamond Quilted pattern, deep fuchsia to deep amber, minor surface scratches **50.00**

Amberina Glass, Plated

History: The New England Glass Company, Cambridge, Massachusetts, first made plated Amberina in 1886; Edward Libbey patented the process for the company in 1889.

Plated Amberina was made by taking a gather of chartreuse or cream opalescent glass, dipping it in Amberina, and working the two, often utilizing a mold. The finished product had a deep amber to deep ruby red shading, a fiery opalescent lining, and often vertical ribbing for enhancement. Bases are usually yellow gold. Handles are generally applied plain amber pieces. Designs range from simple forms to complex pieces with collars, feet, gilding, and etching.

Edward Libbey's patent used an opalescent glass which was plated with a gold ruby. The pieces also have a vertical ribbed effect, and a wide range of items were made, including creamers, finger bowls, lemonade tumblers, punch cups, toothpick holders, and vases.

A cased Wheeling glass of similar appearance had an opaque white lining, but is not opalescent and does not have a ribbed body.

The New England Glass Company used paper labels which read "N. E. Glass Co. 1886 Aurora." However, these labels were used infrequently and are rarely found.

References: Gary Baker et al., *Wheeling Glass 1829-939*, Oglebay Institute, 1994 (distributed by Antique Publications); George P. and Helen McKearin, *American Glass*, reprint, Crown Publishers, 1941, 1948; John A. Shuman III, *The Collector's Encyclopedia of American Art Glass*, Collector Books, 1988, 1994 value update; Kenneth Wilson, *American Glass 1760-1930*, 2 vols., Hudson Hill Press and The Toledo Museum of Art, 1994.

Reproduction Alert: Examples with rough pontils, inferior linings, and even runny, blurry colors, are appearing on the market.

Bowl

8" d, border of deep dark mahogany, 12 vertical stripes alternating with 12 vertical opalescent fuchsia stripes, off-white casing . . **7,500.00**

8" d, 3-1/2" h, raised ruffled rim, 12-ribbed body, fuchsia-red shaded to amber, cased to opal white interior **4,315.00**

Celery vase, vertical ribbing . **2,750.00**

Cream pitcher, 2-3/4" h, 3-1/2" w, bulbous, vertical ribbing, raspberry shading two-thirds down to golden amber base, elaborate strap handle, deep oil spots dec **1,950.00**

Cruet, 6-3/4" h, faceted amber stopper **3,200.00**

Lamp shade, 14" d, hanging, swirled, ribbed **4,750.00**

Milk pitcher, applied amber handle, orig "Aurora" label **7,500.00**

Parfait, vertical ribbing, applied amber handle, c1886 . . . . . **1,500.00**

Pitcher, 6-1/2" h, vertical ribbing, applied amber handle **4,500.00**

Punch cup, vertical ribs, applied handle **1,500.00**

Salt shaker, vertical ribs, orig top **1,200.00**

Spooner, 4" h, vertical ribbing, ground pontil **2,000.00**

Tumbler, 3-3/4" h, **$1,750.**

Syrup pitcher, vertical ribbing, orig top, applied amber handle **5,600.00**

Tumbler

2-1/2" d, 3-3/4" h, vertical ribbed cylinder, deep fuchsia-red at top shading to golden yellow base, creamy opal lining **1,750.00**

Nine optic ribs, fuchsia top shading to butter cream **1,750.00**

Vase

3-1/4" h, bulbous, vertical ribbing, bluish-white lining **2,500.00**

6-1/4" h, flared cylinder, 12 ribs, deep fuchsia shading to amber, cased in opal white, thin walls **4,025.00**

7-1/4" h, lily shape, raspberry red shading to bright amber, opal white casing **2,750.00**

Animal Collectibles

History: The representation of animals in fine arts, decorative arts, and on utilitarian products dates back to antiquity. Some religions endowed certain animals with mystical properties. Authors throughout written history used human characteristics when portraying animals. It did not take glass manufacturers long to realize that there was a ready market for glass novelties. In the early nineteenth century, walking sticks and witch balls were two dominate forms. As the century ended, glass-covered dishes with an animal theme were very popular.

In the years between World Wars I and II, glass manufacturers such as Fostoria Glass Company and A. H. Heisey & Company created a number of glass animal figures for the novelty and decorative-accessory markets. In the 1950s and early 1960s, a second glass-animal craze swept America led by companies such as Duncan & Miller and New Martinsville-Viking Glass Company. A third craze struck in the early 1980s when companies such as Boyd Crystal Art Glass, Guernsey Glass, Pisello Art Glass, and Summit Art Glass began offering the same animal figure in a wide variety of collectible glass colors, with some colors in limited production.

There are two major approaches to glass animal collecting: (a) animal type; and (b) manufacturer. Most collectors concentrate on one or more manufacturers, grouping their collections accordingly.

References: Elaine Butler, *Poodle Collectibles of the '50s & '60s*, L-W Book Sales, 1995; Candace Sten Davis and Patricia Baugh, *A Treasury of Scottie Dog Collectibles*, Collector Books, Volume I (1998), Volume II (2000); Marbena Jean Fyke, *Collectible Cats*, Book I (1993, 1995 value update), Book II (1996), Collector Books; Lee Garmon and Dick Spencer, *Glass Animals of the Depression Era*, Collector Books, 1993; Everett Grist, *Covered Animal Dishes*, Collector Books, 1988, 1993 value update; Frank L. Hahn and Paul Kikeli, *Collector's Guide to Heisey and Heisey By Imperial Glass Animals*, Golden Era Publications, 1991; Todd Holmes, *Boyd Glass*

Workbook, published by author, 1992; Patricia Robak, *Dog Antiques and Collectibles*, Schiffer Publishing, 1999; Evelyn Zemel, *American Glass Animals A to Z*, A to Z Productions, 1978.

Periodicals: *Boyd Crystal Art Glass Newsletter*, P.O. Box 127, 1203 Morton Ave., Cambridge, OH 43725; *Jody & Darrell's Glass Collectibles Newsletter*, P.O. Box 180833, Arlington, TX 76096; *Jumbo Jargon*, 1002 West 25th St., Erie, PA 16502; *Scottie Sampler*, P.O. Box 450, Danielson, CT 06239-0450; *The Glass Animal Bulletin*, P.O. Box 143, North Liberty, IA 52317-0143.

Collectors' Clubs: Boyd Art Glass Collectors Guild, P.O. Box 52, Hatboro, PA 19040; Cat Collectors, P.O. Box 150784, Nashville, TN 37215-0784, www.catcollectors.com; Folk Art Society of America, P.O. Box 17041, Richmond, VA 23226; Frog Pond, P.O. Box 193, Beech Grove, IN 46107; International Owl Collectors Club, 54 Triverton Road, Edgware, Middlesex HA8 6BE UK; National Elephant Collector's Society, 380 Medford St, Somerville, MA 02145; The Happy Pig Collectors Club, 4542 N. Western Ave., Chicago, IL 60625-2117; Wee Scots, Inc., P.O. Box 450, Danielson, CT 06239-0450, www.campbellscotties.com.

Additional Listings: See specific animal collectible categories in *Warman's Americana & Collectibles*.

Note: Prices for glass animal figures are for the colorless variety unless otherwise noted.

Angelfish, Heisey **125.00**
Bear
- Mirror Images
  - Baby, ruby **60.00**
  - Mama, ruby **80.00**
- Mosser Glass Co., solid, sitting
  - Autumn Amber **45.00**
  - Tawny **12.00**
- New Martinsville
  - Baby **50.00**
  - Mama **150.00**
  - Papa, crystal **200.00**
  - Papa, satinized **225.00**

Bird
- Lalique, frosted colorless, pr, 4" h **125.00**
- Murano, purple, lavender, gold, 21-1/2" l **850.00**

Boar, Baccarat, silver label, round seal, etched mark, 4-1/2" w, 3-1/2" h. . **150.00**
Bridge hound
- Cambridge
  - Amber **45.00**
  - Crown Tuscan **55.00**
  - Emerald **50.00**

Bull, Heisey by Imperial
- Amber **900.00**
- Black **750.00**

Bulldog, Co-Operative Flint **125.00**
Bunny, New Martinsville, head up **60.00**
Butterfly, Westmoreland
- Crystal, 4-1/2" **45.00**
- Green mist, small **25.00**
- Light blue, small **22.50**
- Pink, small **22.50**
- Smoke, small **20.00**

Camel, L. E. Smith
- Amber **70.00**
- Cobalt blue **95.00**
- Colorless **50.00**

Cat, Chat Assis, clear and frosted, Lalique, c1970, engraved "Lalique France," 8-1/4" h, **$920.** *Photo courtesy of David Rago Auctions.*

Cat
- Baccarat, Egyptian, 6-1/4" h. **225.00**
- Bimini, Germany, c1920, multicolored, paper label "Made in Germany" **100.00**
- Mosser Glass Co., sitting, 3" h
  - Chocolate **7.50**
  - Heirloom Pink **7.50**
  - Violet D'Orr **10.00**
- Tiffin
  - Alley Cat, small, black satin **115.00**
  - Sassie Suzie, black satin . **175.00**
  - Sassie Suzie, white milk glass **300.00**

Chanticleer, Fostoria **215.00**
Chick, New Martinsville, orange/red, 1" **65.00**
Colt
- Fostoria
  - Lying down, 2-7/8" **30.00**
  - Standing **50.00**
- Heisey by Imperial, standing. . **85.00**

Deer, Fostoria
- Reclining
  - Silver mist **37.50**
  - White milk glass **37.50**
- Standing
  - Silver mist **37.50**
  - White milk glass **37.50**

Dog
- Baccarat
  - Pointer, silver label, round seal, etched mark, 7" l. **150.00**
  - Sitting, silver label, round seal, etched mark, 4" w, 4-1/4" h **150.00**
- Boyd Crystal Art Glass, Skippy, sitting
  - Crown Tuscan **12.00**
  - Pippin Green **10.00**
- Cambridge, bridge pencil, amber, 1-7/8" **22.00**
- Coop Flint, crystal **65.00**
- L. E. Smith, Scottie, 5" h
  - Black **60.00**
  - White milk glass **85.00**
- Viking, amber, 8" l **60.00**

Dolphin, Baccarat, blue, silver label, round etched seal, 6-1/4" l **185.00**
Donkey, Duncan Miller. **120.00**
Dove, Duncan Miller. **120.00**
Duck
- Baccarat, amethyst, 2-1/2" w, 2-1/2" h **65.00**
- Boyd Crystal Art Glass, Debbie, introduced July 1981
  - English Yew **6.00**
  - Snow **7.00**
- Fostoria, Mama, frosted amber, 4" h **35.00**
- Viking, amber, orig label **45.00**

Ducklings
- Baccarat, pr, frosted **125.00**
- Boyd's Crystal Art Glass, introduced September 1981
  - Furr Green **5.00**
  - Golden Delight **4.00**

Duckling, Fostoria, frosted amber, head back, 2-1/2" h **35.00**
Eagle, New Martinsville **80.00**
Elephant
- Bimini, Germany, c1920, silvered, paper label "Made in Germany" **100.00**
- Co-Operative Flint
  - Amber **85.00**
  - Crystal, 13" h, minor damage **300.00**
  - Green, 7" h, flower frog back **250.00**
  - Pink, 7" h, flower frog back **200.00**
  - Pink, 13" h, tusks repaired **400.00**

Fostoria
- Black **95.00**
- Colorless **65.00**

New Martinsville **85.00**

Fawn

Tiffin, flower floater
- Citron green **325.00**
- Cobalt blue. **500.00**

Flying mare, cobalt blue. **750.00**

Frog

Baccarat, acid stamped mark
- Crystal and green. **95.00**
- Solid green. **100.00**

Co-Operative Flint, pink **200.00**

Gazelle, New Martinsville **60.00**

Giraffe, Heisey **300.00**

Goldfish, Fostoria, vertical **95.00**

Goose

Duncan Miller, bluish cast. . . **210.00**

Heisey
- Wings down **450.00**
- Wings up **85.00**

Paden City, blue **125.00**

Hen

Boyd's Crystal Art Glass, vaseline, 5" **45.00**

Kanawa, blue slag, covered dish **95.00**

New Martinsville **70.00**

Hen in basket, Westmoreland, basketweave base, milk glass, red accents
- 5-1/2" l. **30.00**
- 7-1/2" l. **50.00**

Heron, Duncan **150.00**

Horse

Baccarat, stylized Art Deco, rearing, one black, other colorless, 9" h, marked, one with orig paper label, price for pr **320.00**

Fostoria, #2564, rearing **45.00**

Heisey, plug, crystal **95.00**

L. E. Smith, bookends, pr **48.00**

New Martinsville, rearing. . . . **115.00**

Paden City, sun turned color. **150.00**

Koala Bear in Tree, Baccarat, artist sgd "R Riget," silver label, round seal, etched mark, 5" w, 5" h **200.00**

Mermaid, Fostoria. **200.00**

Monkey, Baccarat, silver label, round seal, etched mark, 2" w, 3" h . . . **150.00**

Mouse, Pee Gee Glass Co., boy and girl mouth, 3" h
- White Delight **14.00**
- Wild Cherry. **16.00**

Ox, Baccarat, red label, round seal, etched mark, 4" w, 2-1/2" h **150.00**

Owl
- Imperial, milk glass **50.00**
- Viking, amber, 3" h **60.00**

Penguins by Archimede Seguso, amber shading to clear glass, original foil labels, 6" h, price for pair, **$145.**

Panther, Indiana
- Amber **225.00**
- Blue **200.00**

Pelican

Baccarat, solid, acid stamped mark **75.00**

Fostoria **65.00**

New Martinsville. **95.00**

Penguin

Archimede Seguso, amber shading to clear glass, orig foil labels, 6" h, price for pr **145.00**

Fostoria **75.00**

Pheasant

Bimini, Germany, c1920, silvered and multicolored, paper label "Made in Germany" **95.00**

Heisey, ringneck **115.00**

Paden City, blue
- Chinese. **150.00**
- Head turned **150.00**

Tiffin
- Copen blue, male and female pr, paperweight bases **800.00**
- Tiffin, crystal, controlled bubbles, single **325.00**

Pig, New Martinsville, mama . . . **325.00**

Piglet, New Martinsville **60.00**

Piranha **125.00**

Polar Bear
- Fostoria **75.00**
- Paden City. **65.00**

Police dog

Mirror Image, ruby **75.00**

German Shepard, New Martinsville **80.00**

Pony

Boyd Crystal Art Glass, Joey, introduced March 1980
- Candy Swirl **18.00**
- Chocolate. **30.00**
- Persimmon. **27.50**

Imperial, Heisey mold
- Caramel slag **40.00**
- Crystal, c1964 . . . . **48.00**

Paden City, 11-1/2"
- Blue **125.00**
- Crystal **75.00**

Porpoise, New Martinsville, wave base **550.00**

Rabbit
- Baccarat, black, 4" w, 2" h . . . **90.00**
- New Martinsville, mama **325.00**

Robin, Westmoreland, 5-1/8"
- Crystal **24.00**
- Pink. **24.00**
- Red. **30.00**
- Smoke **24.00**

Rocking Horse, Guernsey Glass Co., Rocky, reproduction of 1915 Cambridge candy container, 4-1/4" l, 13" h
- Carousel slag **15.00**
- Holly Berry **12.00**

September, 1931 Page 7

Really Something New

A one piece acquarium (green glass) with large sales possibilities

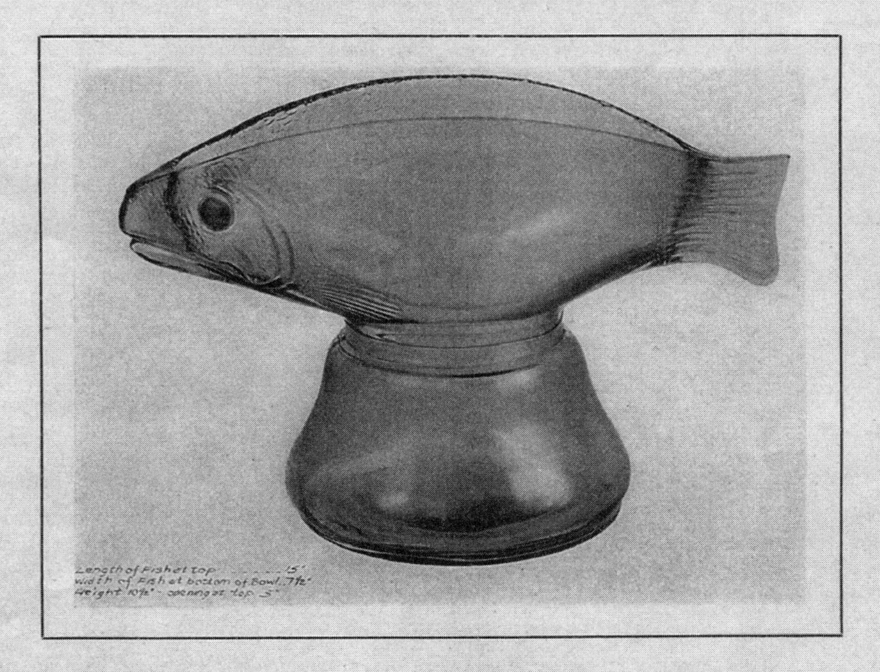

**Fish may use both upper and lower sections.
Packed in individual cartons to
retail at $1.95 each**

GEO. BORGFELDT & CO.

44-60 East 23rd St., cor. Fourth Ave., New York

Tell our advertisers you saw it in The Crockery and Glass Journal

Ad showing the ultimate in aquariums, Crockery and Glass Journal, *September 1931.*

Rooster
- Baccarat, silver label, round seal, etched mark, 3-1/4" w, 4-1/4" h **150.00**
- Bimini, Germany, c1920, silvered, paper label "Made in Germany," 7-1/4" h **100.00**
- Heisey, fighting stance, 8-1/2" h **165.00**
- Lalique, frosted and colorless, pr, 8" h, some damage **275.00**
- L. E. Smith, 8-1/2" h, amber **50.00**
- New Martinsville **80.00**
- Paden City
  - Barn Yard, blue **200.00**
  - Chanticleer, blue **175.00**
  - Elegant, blue **200.00**
  - Head down, blue **200.00**

Seahorse
- Fostoria **175.00**
- New Martinsville **65.00**

Seal
- Mirror Images, baby, ruby **75.00**
- New Martinsville
  - Black, tall handle holder **650.00**
  - Crystal, large, with ball **60.00**
  - Crystal, small, satin finish, clear crystal ball **50.00**

Shark, Baccarat **115.00**

Stag, Bimini, Germany, c1920, silvered, paper label "Made in Germany" **95.00**

Star fish, New Martinsville, 6-1/5" l **40.00**

Stork, Bimini, Germany, c1920, silvered, paper label "Made in Germany," 7-1/4" h **100.00**

Swallow, Baccarat, silver label, round seal, etched mark, 6-1/2" w, 2" h **150.00**

Swan
- Cambridge, 7" x 5" **30.00**
- Duncan Miller
  - 3", orig paper label **85.00**
  - 4-3/4" **85.00**
  - 7-1/2", ruby **42.00**
- L. E. Smith, 8-1/2" h, cobalt blue **65.00**

Swordfish, Duncan Miller
- Blue opalescent **425.00**
- Colorless **275.00**

Thrush, Haley **25.00**

Tiger
- Heisey Club
  - Blue Ice **50.00**
  - Cobalt Blue **95.00**
  - Yellow Mist **50.00**
- Heisey by Imperial
  - Black **65.00**
  - Caramel Slag **100.00**
  - Jade **95.00**
  - Nut Brown **325.00**
  - Yellow **325.00**
- New Martinsville
  - Head down **195.00**
  - Head up **85.00**

Turtle
- L. G. Wright, amber **85.00**
- Viking, green, orig label **30.00**
- Westmoreland, cigarette box **45.00**

Walrus, 10-1/2" l, 5-3/4" h, Murano, attributed to Salviati, solid lattimo white in topaz, shaded to colorless overall surround, applied tusks, eyes, and ears **175.00**

Whale
- Pilgrim, orig labels, purchased at New York World's Fair, 1964, MIB **45.00**
- Vetreria Cendeses Corroso, humpback, aquamarine glass, turquoise blue lips and eyes, etched overall and splotched with metallic oxides to produce corroded effect, base incised "Cenedeses Murano 97V" and "Talberto" **1,380.00**

Wolfhound
- Mirror Image, ruby carnival **150.00**
- New Martinsville **95.00**

Wren, Westmoreland, 2-1/2"
- Crystal mist **17.50**
- Light blue **22.50**
- Pink **20.00**
- Pink mist **24.50**

ARCHITECTURAL ELEMENTS

History: Architectural elements, many of which are hand-crafted, are those items which have been removed or salvaged from buildings, ships, or gardens. Windows, ornaments, and newel post finials are examples of architectural elements found in glass. Part of their desirability is due to the fact that it would be extremely costly to duplicate the items today.

The current trends of preservation and recycling of architectural elements has led to the establishment and growth of organized salvage operations that specialize in removal and resale of elements. Special auctions are now held to sell architectural elements from churches, mansions, office buildings, etc. Today's decorators often design an entire room around one architectural element, such as a Victorian marble bar or mural, or use several as key accent pieces.

References: Ronald S. Barlow (comp.), *Victorian Houseware, Hardware and Kitchenware*, Windmill Publishing, 1991; Len Blumin, *Victorian Decorative Art*, available from ADCA, n.d.; Ernest Rettelbusch, *Handbook of Historic Ornament From Ancient Times to Biedermeier*, Dover Publications, 1996; Stanley Shuler, *Architectural Details From Old New England Homes*, Schiffer Publishing, 1997; Margaret and Kenn Whitmeyer, *Bedroom & Bathroom Glassware of the Depression Years*, Collector Books, 1990, 1992 value update; Kenneth Wilson, *American Glass 1760-1930*, 2 vols., Hudson Hill Press and The Toledo Museum of Art, 1994; Web Wilson, *Great Glass in American Architecture*, E. P. Dutton, New York, 1986.

Periodicals: *Glass Art Magazine*, P.O. Box 260377, Highlands Ranch, CO 80126-0377; *Glass Patterns Quarterly*, P.O. Box 131, Westport, KY 40077; *Stained Glass*, P.O. Box 22642, Kansas City, MO 64113; *The Old House Journal*, Dovetale Publishers, 2 Main St., Gloucester, MA 01930-5726; *Traditional Building*, 69A 7th Ave., Brooklyn, NY 11217-3618; *Victorian Homes Sourcebook*, Victorian Homes, P.O. Box 61, Millers Falls, MA 01349.

Collectors' Club: Antique Doorknob Collectors of America, Inc., P.O. Box 126, Eola, IL 60519.

Museums: Chrysler Museum, Norfolk, VA; Corning Museum of Glass, Corning, NY; National Center for the Study of Frank Lloyd Wright, P.O. Box 444, Ann Arbor, MI, 48106; University of Connecticut, William Benton Museum of Art, Storrs, CT.

Aquarium, 41-1/2" h, 18" h stepped and paneled molded translucent yellow glass bowl, dec with six panels of stylized flowers, set in Art Deco bronzed metal tripod stand, three enameled green handles, legs terminating in stylized dolphins, central light fixture, tri-part base, dark patina, c1925, chips, wear **2,415.00**

Cabinet knob
- Floral emb, center hole to accommodate screw **5.00**
- Hexagonal, geometric, metal screw, large
  - Amber **5.00**
  - Black **8.00**
  - Crystal **4.50**
  - Green **5.00**
  - Pink **5.00**
  - White milk glass **8.00**
- Hexagonal, geometric, metal screw, medium
  - Amber **5.00**
  - Black **8.00**
  - Crystal **4.50**
  - Green **5.00**
  - Lavender **9.00**
  - Pink **5.00**
  - White milk glass **8.00**
- Hexagonal, geometric, metal screw, small
  - Amber **5.00**
  - Black **8.00**
  - Blue **6.00**
  - Crystal **4.50**
  - Green **5.00**
  - Pink **5.00**
  - White milk glass **7.50**

Onion shape, flush mounted, jade-ite 10.00
Round, flush mounted or center metal screw, medium
Amber 8.00
Black 10.00
Crystal 4.00
Green 5.00
Pink 6.00

White milk glass 8.00

Clothes hook, short hook, pink, c1930 . . . . 10.00

Coffee table, 38" d, round glass top, flat circular wrought iron frame, scrolled cross-stretchers and feet, center floral medallion, speckled gilt finish . . . 250.00

Curtain tiebacks, pr
Amberina, orig pewter shanks, New England Glass Works 165.00
Depression glass
Crystal, feather, 7" l. 5.00
Green, flat, floral, 3-1/2" d . . 20.00
Mercury glass, grape dec, 2-1/2" d 50.00
Opalescent glass, large petaled flowers, orig pewter shanks, attributed to Sandwich 125.00

Doorbell pull, cut glass, tapered shank, 1-3/4" d 55.00

Door knobs, pr, glass knob, metal mountings and shaft
Amber, deep color, octagonal . 80.00
Crystal, oval, cut design 45.00
Jadite, hexagonal 125.00
Topaz, center design, hexagonal 85.00

Doors, pr, 89" h, 21" w, stained and painted glass, finches and flowers, Renaissance-style fretwork border, French, 20th C 2,750.00

Drawer pull
Anchor, center flush mounted
Amber 9.00
Crystal 6.50
Green 9.00
Pink 9.00
White milk glass 10.00
Bar, double, crystal, Depression-era 10.00
Round or faceted ends, metal screws
Amber 15.00
Blue 18.00
Crystal 12.00
Green 15.00
Lavender 20.00
Pink 18.50
White milk glass 18.00

Fish bowl, 10-3/4" d vaseline bowl, 39-1/2" h cast iron stand with three feet, center column with spear tip, three supports with hanging tassel on each end, orig green paint, black and gold highlights, marked "#53" under base 850.00

Hand towel holder, double clear glass rods, metal mounting bracket
Blue 40.00
Jade-ite 35.00
Blue milk glass 24.00
Green milk glass 20.00
White milk glass 18.00
Pink 35.00

Lightning rod ball, America, 1870-1920
4" d, chestnut form, deep ruby red, sheared mouths, no metal collars 190.00
4-3/8" d, emb moon and star design, ball form, ruby red, sheared mouths, acceptable collar ship, no metal collars 210.00

Lightning rod ball, ball shape, emb moon and star design, ruby red, sheared mouth, 4-3/8" d, collar chip, America, 1870-1920, **$210.** *Photo courtesy of Norman C. Heckler and Co.*

Panels, Lalique, Juene Faune, clear and frosted, c1929, 12" h, 4" w, price for pr, **$6,900.** *Photo courtesy of David Rago Auctions.*

4-1/2" d, Electra, round ball, emb lettering

Cobalt blue, ground mouths, no metal collars. **160.00**

Ruby red, ground mouths, no metal collars, acceptable collar chip **180.00**

4-1/2" d, plain ball

Gold mercury, ground mouth, metal "Kretzer Brand/ Trademark" collars. **110.00**

Orange milk glass, sheared collared mouths, no metal collars, 4-5/8" d, Electra, emb lettering, cone form, ruby red, sheared collared mouth, no metal collars. **230.00**

5" d, quilt flattened diamond glass ball, grayish green, ground threaded mouth, some mouth chips, 1/2" crack **90.00**

5" d, quilt raised diamond glass ball

Gold mercury, sheared mouth, metal "Kretzer Brand/ Trademark" collars. **275.00**

Ruby red, sheared collared mouth with molded threads, no metal collars **230.00**

Silver mercury, sheared mouth, metal "Kretzer Brand/ Trademark" collars. **275.00**

Newel post knob

6-1/2" h, double cut overlay, white cut to cranberry, stars and circle dec, several small nicks **625.00**

8-1/4" h, pressed glass, electric blue, hobbed pineapple form, brass base, c1840-60. . . . . **200.00**

Panel

4" sq, American Luxfer Prism Co., Chicago, designed by Frank Lloyd Wright, designed based on flower composed of circles and squares, 12-pc set. **1,220.00**

19" x 23", leaded, arched, stylistic design of twin peacocks hovering over urn of fruit and colorful foliage, wings and feathers in swirls and tumults of rich colored art glass, deep royal blue dominant color, sprays of rose pinks, purple, light blue, and white, plated round chunk of amber glass in cupper center, row of blue, green, and yellow chunks surrounded by pink and blue sections form bottom edge, all leadwork finished with black patina, attributed to Tiffany Studios **15,240.00**

Soap dish, wall mounted, transparent blue, c1940 . . . . **12.00**

Toilet paper holder, colorless glass arms, glass rod. **18.00**

Toothbrush holder, wall mounted, opaque blue glass, slots for five toothbrushes, central well for toothpaste tube **20.00**

Towel bar

Opaque glass, one piece, curved ends, mounting brackets, Jade-ite **45.00**

Transparent glass, one piece, curved ends, mounting brackets, white milk glass **20.00**

Transparent glass, one piece, curved ends, mounting brackets

Blue. **35.00**

Pink. **25.00**

Wall sconces, pr, 12" h, 5-1/2" w, Art Deco etched colorless glass fanned shades on "V"-shaped silvered metal wall mounts, France, 1928 . . . **1,150.00**

Window, leaded

13-1/4" h, 30-1/2" h, Gothic interlocking arch motif, etched design inside arched sections, beveled orig frame. **300.00**

15-3/4" x 19-1/8", attributed to John La Farge, early 20th C, four cascading flower blossoms and buds in striated pink, amber, opal and purple glass, amber centers amidst group of striated green and amber leaves, some with rippled and nugget textures, blue-green background segments with red, amber, and frosted geometric border segments, some cracked segments. **1,850.00**

18" d, 29-1/2" h, attributed to Belcher Mosaic Glass Co., passion flower, pink ribbon, and rose bud against variegated amber ground, opalescent roundels, sea green and reddish umber frame of mosaic glass, unsigned **2,875.00**

19" x 15", blue, amber, and colorless segments arranged symmetrically in broad leaf canes, centrally hand painted with bird and floral motif, conserved in wood frames, frame labeled "Frederick Crowninshield/ 43W 18th St, New York, NY," removed from Barnes Building, Beacon Hill, Boston, built 1891, one panel cracked, pr. **865.00**

22-1/4" w x 40-3/4" h, and 18-1/4" w x 22-1/4" h, attributed to Donald McDonald, large floral blooms and leaves, deep green olive green, yellow, and brown, amber and apple green border, unsigned, matched pr **2,875.00**

25-1/2" x 29", La Farge, early 20th C, window centered with round stylized floral and foliage conglomeration of multicolored faceted round, oval, and opalescent nugget glass jewels interspersed with blue-green glass leaf forms, white opal glass ground, surrounded by several geometric tile borders of blue, red, white, opal, opalescent yellow, and green glass mounted in black painted wooden frame, metal rod reinforcements, few cracked segments . . . **9,200.00**

27-1/2" w, 29" h, Tiffany, central tiny white blossoms radiating towards large mottled brown and white pebbled blossoms, pink and green stamens, amber glass surround, geometric green glass border **20,000.00**

30-1/4" x 21-5/8", Tiffany Studios, NY, early 20th C, rect, depicting path through forest, blue sky, mountains, and water in the distance, composed of mottled, double-layered, striated, and textured translucent glass segments, metal tag imp "Tiffany Studios New York," mounted in wooden frame, some cracked segments **20,700.00**

33" w, 31-1/2" h, large massive stag elk, full set of horns, standing in landscape of shrubs and hills, deep cobalt blue over crystal, overlay, acid cut, 19th C **3,000.00**

34" w, 39" h, arched, jeweled navy border framing abstract amber and white mosaic, faceted circles, arched wooden frame, 1900 . . . . **500.00**

36" w, 36" h, blue grapes, green leaves, blue scrolls, opal red ribbon, amber ground, blue pane border, orig wood frame . . . **600.00**

49" h, 27" w, central fleur-de-lis medallion below gothic arches, drapery type dec, arrow and diamond pattern border, price for pr **1,100.00**

66-1/4" h, 24-1/2" w, America, 20th C, rect, geometric colorless glass segments arranged in three dimensional format, pattern of open triangular segments, dark stained wooden frame, losses and a few loose segments, price for three matching windows **1,100.00**

Window, stained, 94" h, 45" h, velvet-like red-orange background of textured art glass with repeating pattern of fleur-de-lis cut from yellowish-red glass, painting of young woman draped in garland of flowers, holding lattice basket of similar blossoms, figure in oval translucent purple glass medallion, border of clear yellow textured glass, faceted jewels, and dark amber glass, frills at top, bottom, and sides composed of yellow and white, background edge of borders with red faceted jewels, lime green rippled glass, greenish-brown glass, textured amber and chocolate brown, low profile rippled glass, lead work with naturally oxidized patina, mounted in wood frame 5,040.00

Avon Glassware Collectibles

History: David H. McConnell founded the California Perfume Co. in 1886. He hired saleswomen, a radical concept for that time. They used a door-to-door technique to sell their first product, "Little Dot," a set of five perfumes; thus was born the "Avon Lady," although by 1979, they numbered more than one million.

In 1929, California Perfume Co. became the Avon Company. The tiny perfume company grew into a giant corporation. Avon bottles began attracting collector interest in the 1960s.

The Avon Company found a new niche in the collectibles market when it coupled its quality cosmetics with glassware made by several different American manufacturers. Several of the company's patterns are now sought by collectors. Many of these collectors are purchasing the glassware to use and are not interested in paying a premium for items in the original boxes.

References: Bud Hastin, *Hastin's Avon Collector's Encyclopedia*, 16th ed., Collector Books, 2000.

Periodical: *Avon Times*, P.O. Box 9868, Kansas City, MO 64134.

Additional Listings: For other Avon collectibles, see *Warman's Americana & Collectibles.*

1876 Cape Cod

This pattern was made in deep ruby red. Most pieces were made by Anchor Hocking, some were made by Wheaton Glass.

Bell 10.00
Bread and butter set, orig box . . 25.00
Butter dish, cov, 3-1/2" x 7", orig box, 1983 . . . . 65.00
Cake knife, 10" l. 17.50
Candleholders, 8-1/2" h, full of Bird of Paradise Cologne, MIB, 1983. . . . 27.50
Candy dish, ftd, 3-1/2" h, orig box 40.00
Champagne 8.00
Cordial, ftd 20.00
Creamer and sugar, set 24.00
Cruet, 5-3/4" h. 14.00
Cup and saucer 14.00
Decanter, MIB 45.00
Dessert bowl, MIB 8.50
Dessert plate 8.00
Dinner plate, 11" d, orig box, 1982 . . . . 37.50
Hurricane lamp 20.00
Goblet 8.00
Luncheon plate 10.00
Mug, ftd, Anchor Hocking, pair in orig box. 30.00
Napkin rings, set of four, 1-3/4" d 55.00
Platter, oval, 10-3/4" x 13-5/8" . . 30.00
Relish, 9-1/2" x 5-1/2" 30.00
Salad plate 7.00
Salt and pepper shakers, pr, 4-1/4" h, orig box, 1978 . . . . 27.50
Sauce boat, 8" l, 3-1/2" h 55.00
Soup/cereal bowl, 7-1/4" d 18.00
Tray, two tiers, MIB 85.00
Trinket box, cov, heart shape . . . 10.00
Tumbler 22.00
Vase, 8" h, orig box, 1984 . . . . . . 65.00
Water pitcher, 48 oz, 7-1/2" h. . . 40.00
Wine goblet 8.00
Wine set, 10" decanter, four matching wine tumblers 35.00

Coin pattern

Made by Fostoria, pieces are dated and often found with orig Fostoria paper labels.

Bowl
Oval, amber 58.00
Round, 8" d, olive green 40.00
Round, 8-1/2" d, olive green . . 95.00
Candlestick, 4" h, amber 33.00
Candlesticks, pr, 4-1/2" h, ruby . . 57.00
Candy jar, cov, amber 62.00
Comport, ftd, crystal, 1977 . . . . . 10.00
Creamer
Amber 32.00
Olive green 32.00
Jelly comport, ftd
Amber 32.00
Olive green 34.00
Shaker, crystal 34.00
Urn cover, amber. 25.00

Hummingbird pattern

Made in crystal with a frosted hummingbird in flight.

Bell 35.00
Cake stand 40.00
Candlesticks, pr 13.50
Champagne, 7" h, sold two in MIB 24.00
Dessert dish, 5" d, 2-1/2" h, orig box, sold two in MIB. 19.00
Dessert plate, 8" d. 8.50
Dinner plate 40.00
Goblet 9.00
Salad bowl, 8-3/4" d 20.00
Salad plate 10.00
Salt and pepper shakers, pr. . . . 15.50
Wine 7.50

Mount Vernon pattern

Made by Fostoria. Made in cobalt blue.

Creamer, orig candle, MIB. 15.00
Dresser tray, orig soaps, MIB . . . 15.00
Goblet
George Washington medallion 10.00
Martha Washington medallion 12.00

Mount Vernon, dresser tray, orig soaps, MIB, 9-1/4" l, **$15.**

Baccarat Glass

History: The Sainte-Anne glassworks at Baccarat in Voges, France, was founded in 1764 and produced utilitarian soda glass. In 1816, Aime-Gabriel d'Artiques purchased the glassworks, and a Royal Warrant was issued in 1817 for the opening of Verrerie de Vonâoche éa Baccarat. The firm concentrated on lead-crystal glass products. In 1824, a limited company was created.

From 1823 to 1857, Baccarat and Saint-Louis glassworks had a commercial agreement and used the same outlets. No merger occurred. Baccarat began the production of paperweights in 1846. In the late nineteenth century, the firm achieved an international reputation for cut glass table services, chandeliers, display vases, centerpieces, and sculptures. Products eventually included all forms of glassware. The firm still is active today.

References: Jean-Louis Curtis, *Baccarat,* Harry N. Abrams, 1992; Paul Jokelson and Dena Tarshis, *Baccarat Paperweights and Related Glass,* Paperweight Press, 1990 (distributed by Charles E. Tuttle Co.).

Additional Listings: Paperweights.

Manufacturer/Distributor: Baccarat Inc., 36 Mayfield Ave., Edison, NY 08837-3821.

Animal, 4" h, parrot

- Blue, sgd in script on side, acid stamped on base, orig paper label 245.00
- Green, sgd in script on side, acid stamped on base 235.00
- Lavender, stamped on base. 225.00

Ashtray, 4-1/2" d, Pinwheel, sgd. 85.00

Atomizer, 5" h, 3-1/2" l, oval, etched crystal body, metal chrome top, marked 90.00

Biscuit jar, cov, 6" h, crystal, etched ground, cranberry flowers, leaves, and vines, marked inside lid. 600.00

Bobeche, 3-3/4" d

- Circular, Rose Tiente Swirl, unmarked 20.00
- Corseted square, Rose Tiente Swirl, marked "Baccarat," pr 45.00

Bookends, pr, 12" h, crystal, serpentine tube on molded rocky form base, etched "Baccarat, France" 150.00

Bowl

- 5-1/2" d, cameo, colorless etched leaf ground, carved chartreuse floral dec 100.00
- 5-1/2" d, cov, teardrop finial . 225.00
- 8" d, Rose Tiente, scalloped, ftd, sgd 115.00
- 8-1/2" d, Rose Tiente Swirl, faintly marked, small chip and bruise 70.00
- 14" d, 3-1/2" h, wide flattened rim, narrow knopped foot, etched "Baccarat, France" 500.00

Box, cov

- 2-3/4" d, amberina, panel and relief diamond pattern, chips on base 60.00
- 2-3/4" d, 2-1/4" h, white airplane design on sides, etched mark 125.00
- 8-3/4" d, 4-1/4" h, Rose Tiente Swirl, rect, raised "Baccarat Depose" mark, few chips on cover . . 280.00

Brandy snifter, crystal, gilded foliate cartouche, monogrammed "N," set of 12 . . . . . . 275.00

Calling card holder, 5-1/2" h, opaline, fan shape, pedestal base, relief butterflies, trees, and flowers, sgd 195.00

Rose bowl, cranberry, lacy enamel decoration, 3" d, **$155.**

Candelabra, pr, crystal, 32" h, four light, diamond-cut baluster standard, four scrolling candle arms terminating I urn form sockets, etched glass globes hung with prisms 2,000.00

Candlesticks, pr

- 7" h, Rose Tiente Swirl, mold marked "Baccarat Depose," chips on table ring 100.00
- 9" h, Swirled. 225.00
- 10-3/4" h, Eiffel Tower shape, Rose Tiente. 225.00
- 14-1/2" h, baluster form, crystal, spiral, dome base, 19th C. . 245.00

Carafe and undertray, 7" h carafe, 7" d undertray, Rosette pattern, amberina, cut fluted rim on unmarked carafe, some cloudiness 100.00

Celery tray, 9-1/2" l, 3-1/2" w, Rose Tiente 45.00

Champagne bucket, 9-1/4" h, tapering cylinder, rect stop fluted molded sides, stamped "Baccarat, France". . . 400.00

Chandelier, 42" h, 29" w, 12 scrolling candle arms, foliate crown surmounting figures, prisms. 12,365.00

Cigar lighter, Rose Tiente, SP top 150.00

Cologne bottle

- 5-1/2" h, Rose Tiente, Diamond Point Swirl, orig stopper 125.00
- 5-3/4" h, amberina, panel and relief diamond pattern, matching stopper 90.00
- 6" h, Rose Tiente Swirl, clear glass stopper numbered to match bottle, silvered mushroom caps fit over brass collar 125.00
- 7" h, Rose Tiente Swirl, clear glass stopper numbered to match bottle, silvered mushroom caps fit over brass collar 125.00
- 7" h, crystal, frosted rosette ground, gold floral swags and bows, cut faceted stopper, pr. 335.00

Cologne bottle set, three bottles ranging from 4-1/2" to 5-1/2" h, Rose Tiente Swirl, orig stoppers, all with chips 150.00

Creamer, 4-1/2" h, lacy, colorless, minor chips 90.00

Crystal ball, 6-1/2" h, solid glass sphere, conforming separate sq holder, labeled and stamped, modern . 290.00

Dealer's sign, crystal 110.00

Decanter

- Conforming stopper, 8-1/2" h, crystal, cut, marked "Baccarat France". 110.00
- Conforming orig stopper, 9-3/4" h, Rose Tiente 125.00
- Conforming stopper, 11" h, Cognas Camus, amber, two silver overlays, one etched "Cognas Camus by Baccarat" with logo, metal top etched "Baccarat France," orig box and paperwork. 185.00
- Conforming stopper, 11-5/8" h, flattened ovoid, scalloped edge, etched flat sides with hunter on horseback, forest animals, scrolling vine, neck with vine etching, similarly shaped and etched stopper, 20th C, price for pr 550.00
- Conforming orig stopper, 14" h, crystal, amphora style, lightly ribbed, collared stem, domed foot, acid stamped mark 260.00

Decanter set, decanter and six cordials, Rose Tiente Swirl 500.00

Desk obelisk, 10" h, cut crystal, sgd with acid "decanter" stamp **250.00**
Dish, 8-3/4" l, oval, lacy, colorless, minor chips.................. **80.00**
Dresser jar, cov, 2-1/2" h, 4-1/2" w, cranberry cut to green base, finely textured bark-like ground, finely cut tiny flowers and leaves, irregular border bands, gold checkerboard type pattern, marked in pontil, monogrammed lid marked "Sterling" **2,350.00**
Dresser set, 2-1/2" d, 4-3/8" h, perfume bottle, 3" h ring holder, two 5-3/16" l pin trays, large tray with signature .. **365.00**
Epergne, 10-3/4" h, four cranberry overlay cut to clear vases, gilt metal holder **550.00**

Fairy lamp

- 3-7/8" h, shaded white to clear **275.00**
- 4" h, Rose Tiente Rosette, dome shade, circular base, marked "Baccarat Depose" **250.00**

Figure

- 3" h, 3-1/4" h, bear's head, crystal, silver label, etched mark... **220.00**
- 3-1/2" h, 4-3/4" l, Sphinx, silver label, round etched mark **150.00**
- 6" h, angel playing horn, colorless **50.00**

Finger bowl

- 4-3/4" d, 6-3/4" d underplate, ruby ground, gold medallions and flowers dec **350.00**
- 5" d, panel cut, set of eight .. **700.00**

Floral centerpiece, pr 11-1/2" h crescent forms, pr of arched 12" l, 4-3/4" h bridges with five sections, pr 12" l, 1-3/4" h rect handles, Rose Tiente, all marked "Baccarat Depose" .. **500.00**

Goblet

- Perfection pattern **40.00**
- Vintage pattern, cone shaped amber bowl, etched grape design, cut stem and base, six-pc set . **125.00**

Paperweight, red strawberries, white flower, green leaves, **$200.**

Hurricane lamp, 6" d, 23" h, 13-1/2" h candlestick base, bobeches, prisms, molded signature with Depose on base and bobeches, price for pr ... **1,995.00**
Ice bucket, 5-1/2" h, Rose Tiente Swirl, married silver plate frame with swivel bail, four ball feet, imp "Baccarat Depose," rubbed frosty rim and base, usage scratches **150.00**

Jar, cov

- 6" h, 3-3/4" d, sapphire blue, Swirl, marked................. **95.00**
- 7" d, cameo cut, gilt metal mounts, imp "Baccarat".......... **350.00**

Jewelry box, cov, 4" d, 2-3/4" h, hinged lid, Button and Bow pattern, sapphire blue, brass fittings........... **145.00**

Lamp, oil

- 6-3/4" h, global, Rosette pattern, amberina, surface wear, couple of chips on base, colorless chimney **130.00**
- 7-3/4" plus chimney, Rosette pattern, amberina, wick adjuster marked "W & W Kosmos," glass chimney stamped "Belgica DE," scratches **150.00**
- 14" h, banquet style, Rosette pattern, amberina, ruby shading to colorless, reeded brass column on pierced base, acanthus leaf feet, glass chimney **200.00**

Lamp, table, 19-1/2" l, 24-1/2" h, central cut glass urn on short brass stem, two horizontal reeded candle arms, fan cut drip pans suspending cut prisms, ovoid glass knop stem, paneled trumpet foot cut with roundels, brass flat leaf base, one with collar at urn for further prisms, other with collars for two etched glass shades, electrified, early 20th C, price for pr **2,875.00**
Mustard jar, cov, 3" d, 5" h, Rose Tiente, Swirl................. **85.00**

Paperweight, sulfide

- Bonapart, 1974, limited edition, spiraled single overlay, orig box **80.00**
- Eisenhower, Dwight D., limited edition, grid-cut base, 1963, 2-3/4" d............... **325.00**
- Henry, Patrick, 1977, limited edition, spiraled single overlay, orig box **95.00**
- Hoover, 1971, limited edition, spiraled single overlay, orig box **90.00**

Paperweight, sulphide of Pope Pius XII, ruby ground, signed, **$165.**

- Jackson, 1972, limited edition, spiraled single overlay, orig box **80.00**
- Pope Pius XII, limited edition, translucent garnet ground, star-cut base, acid etched signature, 2-3/4" d **150.00**
- Truman, 1973, limited edition, spiraled single overlay, orig box **90.00**
- Zodiac, Pisces, c1955...... **165.00**

Perfume bottle, black

- Art-Deco style, D'Orsay..... **225.00**
- 4-3/8" h, 2-1/2" d, orig plastic seal on top of cut glass stopper, bottom etched "63HS," orig packaging for Caron, Paris, France, orig tassel **135.00**

Pitcher, 9-1/4" h, Rose Tiente, Helical Twist pattern............... **295.00**
Plate, 7" d, amberina, panel and relief diamond pattern, cloudy surface, chips **45.00**
Relish tray, 11-3/4" l, 3-1/2" w, oval, amberina, marked "Baccarat Depose" **45.00**
Ring tree, 4" h, blue cut to clear, diamond and fan motif........ **225.00**

Rose bowl

- 3" d, cranberry, lace enamel dec **155.00**
- 5-1/2" h, 2-1/4" d opening, Cuir, round seal mark **400.00**

Stemware

- 16-pc set, set of eight 8" h red wine goblets, and eight 7" h white wine goblets, all signed with acid "decanter" stamp **825.00**
- 47-pc set, rounded cuts on bowl, baluster stem, hexagonal foot, six

water goblets, 10 saucer champagnes, three large wines, seven smaller wines, 10 sherries, 11 cordials **650.00**

49-pc set, rounded cuts on bowl, inverted baluster stem, circular foot, 10 water goblets, 13 saucer champagnes with open stem, 12 sherries, 14 wines. **700.00**

Sugar bowl, cov, 7-1/4" h, lacy, colorless, rim chips **95.00**

Sweetmeat jar, cov, cranberry colored strawberries, blossoms, and leaves, cut back to clear ground of ferns, silver plated cover and handle, sgd . . **350.00**

Toasting goblet, 7" h, #340103, pr **150.00**

Toilette set

Six pcs, Rose Tiente Swirl, gentleman's, 5-1/2" h shaving brush holder, three 7" h tonic bottles (one with pewter top, one with paper label), two 7" h jars with metal covers, cloudy int. on one bottle, bruise on one jar . . . **250.00**

Seven pcs, Rose Tiente Swirl, 6-1/2" h toothbrush holder, 8-1/2" h atomizer without bulb, 5-1/2" h bottle with dome cap, 6-1/2" bottle with metal cap, Paris paper label, cloudy int., 3" h ring tree, 4-1/2" oval tray, 4-1/2" l rect tray, some pieces marked "Baccarat France" **275.00**

Toothpick holder, 2-1/2" h, Rose Tiente **225.00**

Tumbler, 3-1/2" h, Rose Tiente . . **25.00**

Tumble-up, matching tray, Rose Tiente Swirl, 6-1/2" h carafe with cut panel neck, 4" h tumbler, 7" undertray mid "Baccarat Depose" **250.00**

Tumble-up, matching tray, Rose Tiente Swirl, 6-1/2" h carafe with cut panel neck, 4" h tumbler, 7" undertray, marked "Baccarat Depose," **$250.** *Photo courtesy of Cincinnati Art Galleries.*

Vase

6-1/8" h, cobalt blue, white lace dec **250.00**

9-1/4" h, ovoid, crystal, large thumbprint design, acid stamped mark **200.00**

9-3/4" h, colorless, tapered cylindrical, slightly everted rim, vertical tapered flutes on body, press-cut, 20th C. **165.00**

10-1/4" h, inverted-bell form, five etched urns with tall scrolling branches, printed factory mark, 20th C **800.00**

12" h, expanding circular section on short foot, opaline, pale yellow enameled hummingbird, butterfly, and summer blossoms, border of pink thistle blossoms and gilt leaves, marked "Baccarat le 26 Septembre 1860" **1,000.00**

Wash bowl and pitcher, Rose Tiente Swirl **800.00**

Wine, 7" h, green cut to colorless, 11-pc set **850.00**

BARBER BOTTLES

History: Barber bottles, colorful glass bottles found on shelves and counters in barber shops, held the liquids barbers used daily. A specific liquid was kept in a specific bottle, which the barber knew by color, design, or lettering. Some barber bottles indicated the name of the product, like "Bay Rum," while others were more decorative. The bulk liquids were kept in utilitarian containers under the counter or in a storage room.

Barber bottles are found in many types of glass—art glass with various decorations, pattern glass, and commercially prepared and labeled bottles.

References: Ronald S. Barlow, *The Vanishing American Barber Shop*, Windmill Publishing, 1992; *Barbershop Collectibles*, L-W Book Sales, 1996; Keith E. Estep, *Shaving Mug & Barber Bottle Book*, Schiffer Publishing, 1995; Richard Holiner, *Collecting Barber Bottles*, Collector Books, 1986; Ralph & Terry Kovel, *Kovels' Bottles Price List*, 11th ed., Three Rivers Press, 1999; Philip L. Krumholz, *Value Guide for Barberiana & Shaving Collectibles*, Ad Libs Publishing Co., 1989; John Odell, *Digger Odell's Official Antique Bottle and Glass Collector Magazine Price Guide Series*, Vol. 1, published by author (1910 Shawhan Rd, Morrow, OH 45152), 1995.

Note: Prices are for bottles without original stoppers unless otherwise noted.

Advertising

California Perfume Co., Superior Bay Rum, 126 Chambers St., New York, USA, large leaf in background of beige, gray, and black orig label, crown stopper **195.00**

Ed Pinaud Paris Registeres, colorless, orig label, slight sickness to bottle **25.00**

Empire Quinine Hair Tonic, Empire Barber and Beauty Supply Co., Minneapolis, Minn, gallon, orig screw top, ring handle, 3/4 orig contents **25.00**

Klorofil Dandruff Cure, glass label, 2-1/2" d, 7-1/2" h. **170.00**

Koken's Quinine Tonic for the Hair, 7-1/2" h, clear, label under glass **195.00**

Lucky Tiger, red, green, yellow, black, and gilt label under glass, emb on reverse **85.00**

Vegederma, cylindrical, bulbous, long neck, amethyst, white enamel dec of bust of woman with long flower hair, tooled mouth, pontil scar, 8" h. **130.00**

Amber

Hobb's Hobnail. **250.00**

6-3/4" h, Hobnail, three-ring neck, curled lip, bulbous base, polished pontil, one hob broken **200.00**

Amethyst

6-3/4" h, 3-3/4" d, deep amethyst, polished band with matte finish, orange enamel design on band, white and gold floral dec on body, concave base with rough pontil, wear to enameling **200.00**

6-3/4" h, white enameled flowers, orange dot pattern, pontil . . **95.00**

7" h, 3-1/2" d, deep amethyst, white enameled daisies, polished pontil, wear to enameling **110.00**

8" h, cylindrical, bulbous body, long neck, white and orange floral dec, sheared mouth, pontil scar . **90.00**

8" h, Mary Gregory-type dec, white enameled child and flowers **250.00**

8" h, white enameled daisies, round pontil **165.00**

8-1/2" h, enameled flowers, wear to enameling **135.00**

Art glass, 7-1/4" h, cylindrical, bulbous body, long bulbous neck, amethyst and light yellow amber mottled design, all over pink irid, ground mouth, smooth base **325.00**

Blue, 8" h, horizontal brown band design, applied white enamel floral pattern, sheared lip, exposed pontil **115.00**

Canary, 7-1/4" h, Hobnail pattern, three pouring rings, round lip, smooth base **85.00**

Emerald green, cylindrical, corset waisted form, long neck, white enamel and gilt decoration, sheared mouth, pontil scar, white porcelain stopper, American, 1870-1920, 7-1/2" h, some interior residue, **$400.** *Photo courtesy of Norman C. Heckler and Co.*

Cased, 7" h, colorless glass over copper, gold, and blue design, solid brass foot **110.00**

Clambroth

7" h, pyramid shape, scalloped panels **45.00**

8" h, emb "Water" in red letters across front, porcelain stopper **50.00**

Cobalt blue

7-1/4" h, cylindrical, bulbous body, long neck, white enamel, traces of gold dec, tooled mouth, pontil scar **100.00**

8-1/4" h, bulge in straight neck **185.00**

8-1/2" h, bell shape, raised white and orange enameled flowers, sheared lip, exposed pontil **125.00**

Colorless, 6-1/2" h, ribbed, dec band around center, gold trim, raised enamel dot pattern, pontil **75.00**

Crackle, cranberry, swirl **220.00**

Cranberry, 6-3/4" h, rings of hobnails on neck **175.00**

Custard glass, 7" h, marked "MA Co." on bottom **110.00**

Cut glass

5" h, hobstar base, pewter top **90.00**

7" h, 4-1/4" d, zipper cutting on straight neck, floral cutting on bulbous base, unpolished pontil **225.00**

Electric blue, 7-1/2" h, cylindrical corset waisted form, long neck, opalescent wandering vine dec, tooled mouth, smooth base **210.00**

Emerald green

7-1/2" h, cylindrical corset waisted form, long neck, white enamel and gilt dec, sheared mouth, pontil scar, some int. residue **400.00**

7-1/2" h, cylindrical modified corset waisted form, long neck, lighter green enamel and floral gilt dec, tooled mouth, pontil scar . . **275.00**

8-1/2" h, cylindrical bell form, long neck, orange and white enameled floral dec, sheared mouth, pontil scar, some int. haze, 8-1/2" h **210.00**

9" h, white enameled flowers with orange centers, white ceramic stopper **250.00**

Iridescent, 7-1/2" h, Loetz type, crackled green over cobalt blue, blown, ground pontil, c1900 . . . . **250.00**

Latticinio, 8-1/4" h, cylindrical, bulbous, long neck, clear frosted glass, white, red, and pale green vertical stripes, tooled mouth, pontil scar **200.00**

Lime green and amethyst, 8" h, cylindrical, bulbous bodies, long necks, profuse floral gilt dec, tooled mouth, pontil scar, matched pr **350.00**

Lime green

7" h, satin glass, classical bird claw grasping ball, ground mouth, smooth base, pr **100.00**

7-1/8" h, 3" d, white enamel flowers, small dots form band, rough pontil, wear to enameling **200.00**

Milk glass

9" h, Bay Rum, hand painted pink and white flowers, green leaves, pastel ground, rolled lip, pontil **150.00**

9" h, Witch Hazel, painted letters and flowers **115.00**

Opalescent

7-1/4" h, Stars and Stripes pattern, cranberry, pale blue, tooled mouth, smooth base, pr **600.00**

7-1/4" h, Stripes pattern, cranberry, cylindrical segmented melon form, long neck, tooled mouth, smooth base **180.00**

7-1/2" h, Coin Spot pattern, blue **300.00**

Milk glass, painted clover blossom, 10-1/4" h, **$95.**

7-1/2" h, Coin Spot pattern, cranberry. **180.00**

7-1/2" h, Daisy and Fern pattern, blue, bulbous **270.00**

7-1/2" h, Seaweed, pattern cranberry, bulbous **465.00**

7-5/8" h, Daisy and Fern pattern, cranberry, cylindrical segmented melon body, long neck, tooled mouth, smooth base, some minor int. residue **120.00**

7-7/8" h, Spanish Lace pattern, electric blue ground, sq, long neck, tooled mouth, smooth base, pr **250.00**

8-1/4" h, Fern pattern, cranberry, sq, long neck, tooled mouth, smooth base **325.00**

9-1/4" h, Waffle pattern, light blue, rolled lip **125.00**

Sapphire blue

8" h, Mary Gregory-type dec, white enamel dec of girl playing tennis, cylindrical bulbous form, long neck, tooled mouth, pontil scar **150.00**

8-5/8" h, enameled white and yellow daisies, green leaves **125.00**

Spatter glass

8-1/4" h, light blue and white, polished mouth and base . . **200.00**

8-1/2" h, cranberry ground, opalescent white mottling, sq, long neck, tooled mouth, smooth base **160.00**

Opalescent, Coin Spot, cranberry, original pewter top, 7-1/2" h, **$180.**

Tiffany, 7-1/2" h, 4-1/4" d, Favrile, irid gold, purple highlights, unsigned **395.00**

Turquoise, 7-1/4" h, 3-1/4" d, Hobnail pattern, polished pontil **225.00**

Baskets

History: Glass baskets have been made by glassblowers for centuries. Their popularity led to wonderful creations of art glass with thorny handles, as well as plain baskets with simple designs. Cut-glass baskets have often enjoyed a special place because of their beauty. Pressed-glass patterns often also included a basket form to match the compotes and stemware lines.

Unlike their popular natural material counterpart, glass baskets were not made for gathering eggs or going to market, but for holding delicate candies, potpourri, or flowers. Special baskets were made to hold sugar or jelly, while others were made to hold spoons. Small baskets were often included on an elegantly decorated table to hold salt of almonds at each place setting. Larger, usually more ornate baskets were used as centerpieces to hold fruit and/or flowers. Truly elegant table decorations were treasured and often special pieces were used only for specific functions. One served pickles from pickle castors, almonds from baskets, and so on.

Manufacturers of glass baskets include Heisey, Cambridge, Tiffany, and other well-known names. Examples are found in almost every color and generally have applied fixed handles.

Reference: John Mebane, *Collecting Bride Baskets and Other Glass Fancies*, Wallace-Homestead, 1976.

4-1/2" h, Massachusetts pattern, U.S. Glass Co., colorless, applied colorless handle **65.00**

4-1/2" h, 3-3/4" w, satin, mother of pearl, Herringbone pattern, deep pink ruffled edge, pink shaded ground, white int., applied colorless thorn handle. . **450.00**

4-3/4" h, frosted white opaque body, gold accents on handle and rim, "Souvenir of Crosby, Minn" on side in red lettering **30.00**

5" d, Tiffany, pink shading to white stretch glass basket, gold plated metal basket frame. **2,395.00**

5" h, Octagon, Heisey, flamingo . . **90.00**

5" h, 3" d, satin, shaded blue to white, cased, hobnail body, applied frosted colorless handle, pontil **130.00**

5" h, 5-1/2" w, Czechoslovakia, pink, applied black handle **75.00**

5-1/2" h, Czechoslovakia, blue hobnail, black and clear trim and handle . **75.00**

5-1/2" h, 5" w, pressed, colorless, star type design in base, applied smooth colorless handle.............. **25.00**

5-1/2" h, 6" d, squared bowl, white with blue cased int., applied blue thorn handle, polished pontil........ **190.00**

5-1/2" d, 8" h, cut glass, Berlyn pattern, Quaker City Glass Co., applied twisted handle, three-step pedestal base, American Brilliant period **375.00**

6" h, 4-3/4" d, spatter, pink, brown, and white spatter, white int., ruffled edge, applied colorless thorny handle. **175.00**

6" h, 6" w, star shape, sapphire blue, white pattern, applied blue thorn handle, c1890. .... **225.00**

6" h, 7" w, pale blue int. shading to white, opaque white ext., 10 rows of hobnails, applied amber edge, applied amber thorn handle, Victorian . . **110.00**

6-1/2" d, cut glass, intaglio floral cutting, applied twisted handle American Brilliant period **150.00**

6-1/2" h, 5" w, Czechoslovakia, opaque blue, black trim, enameled daisies, roses, and butterfly, applied clear handle...................... **80.00**

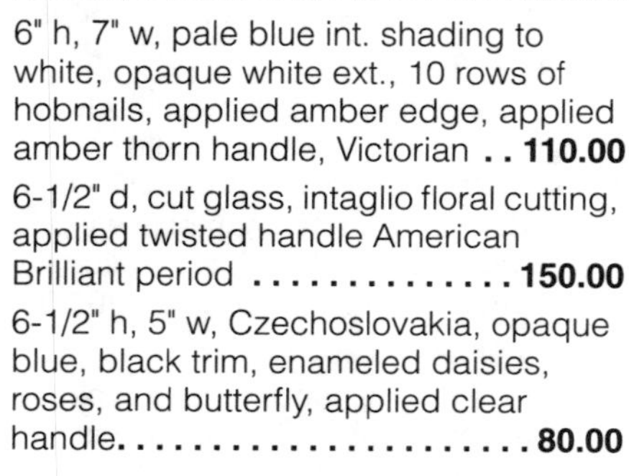

Carnival glass, Basketweave pattern, open edge, ice blue, **$300.** *Photo courtesy of Seeck Antique Auction Center.*

Candy basket, colorless, applied colorless handle, 3" h, **$15.**

6-1/2" h, 5" w, Czechoslovakia, opaque green, white casing, applied black rim and handle **70.00**

6-1/2" h, 5" w, Czechoslovakia, red, blue, and yellow spatter cased with orange, applied clear handle . . . **85.00**

6-1/2" h, 5" w, Czechoslovakia, tomato red, black trim, clear handle **70.00**

6-1/2" h, 5-1/2" w, Czechoslovakia, brilliant orange, black trim, crystal thorn handle **100.00**

6-1/2" h, 7" l, deep brown and green, yellow and white ground, white ext., ruffled edge, applied crystal edge, rope twisted handle, c1890........ **195.00**

6-1/2" h, 7" l, blown hobnail, 12 rows of hobnails, sky-blue int., white ext., applied amber edge and thorn handle **265.00**

6-1/2" h, 9-1/2" l, 8" w, pink opalescent body, overshot vaseline twisted handle, blown-out hobnails on ruffled edges, c1890 .... **324.00**

6-3/4" h, creamy opaque body, applied pink flowers, applied vaseline twist handle.................... **200.00**

6-3/4" h, 5" d, Hobnail pattern, yellow opaque body, crimped edge, applied colorless thorn handle........ **195.00**

7" h, Fenton, Rose Overlay, ruffled **75.00**

7" h, Hobnail pattern, white body, rose int. **95.00**

7" h, Portland pattern, Portland Glass Co., colorless, applied colorless pressed leafy handle.......... **90.00**

7" h, Reverse 44 pattern, U.S. Glass Co., colorless, gold trim applied reeded handle.................... **125.00**

7" h, 6" w, Czechoslovakia, green spangle with mice flecks, cased in white, applied black trim and handle **95.00**

7" h, 6-3/4" l, 5-3/4" w, vaseline opalescent, Diamond Quilted pattern, applied pink flowers and colorless leaves, applied colorless twisted thorn handle.................... **200.00**

7" h, 7-1/2" w, Czechoslovakia, blue, red and white spatter on green spatter ground, black trim and handle... **95.00**

7" h, 9" w, brilliant chartreuse ext., lined in shocking pink, pulled and pinched in middle, applied clear fan center handle, applied clear ruffled feet **100.00**

7-1/4" h, 5-1/4" d, orange, colorless rigaree, applied crystal leaves, applied colorless handle............. **175.00**

7-1/2" h, Cabbage Leaf, pink overlay, yellow int., applied colorless thorn handle.................... **190.00**

7-1/2" h, 4-3/4" d, pink candy stripe swirl overlay, white lining, ruffled edge, applied colorless twisted thorn handle **175.00**

7-1/2" h, 5" w, brilliant pink-purple int., deep brown spatter, applied crystal casing, unusual gather in thorn handle **70.00**

Heisey, vertical grooved base, colorless, **$115.**

7-1/2" h, 5-1/4" w, oxblood red and opaline swirled body, gold aventurine splotches, gold enamel dec, thick crystal casing, crystal handle .. **285.00**

7-1/2" h, 5-1/2" w, shaded green, textured diamond quilted pattern body, swirl top, U-shaped square thorn handle **125.00**

7-1/2" h, 8" l, deep mahogany red to cherry red to pale yellow, white lining, tightly crimped edge, twisted clear rope handle, c1890 .... **265.00**

7-3/4" h, 7" w, satin, mother of pearl, diamond quilted pattern body, deep gold, melon ribbed body, sq crimped top, sq spatter handle, Mt. Washington, c1880.................... **795.00**

8" d, creamy opaque body, rose lining, amber edged ruffled rim, twist handle **185.00**

8" h, 6" d, Diamond Quilted pattern, opalescent vaseline shading to pink, applied pink handle.......... **165.00**

8" h, 6-1/2" w, brilliant yellow and white spatter, pulled down tightly crimped edge, applied sapphire blue handle in V-shape, applied blue leaf feet, slight amount of roughage to one foot, one thorn on handle chipped...... **100.00**

8" h, 6-1/4" w, yellow body, heavy twisted ribs, tightly crimped rim with colorless border, colorless thorn handle **210.00**

8" h, 8-1/2" w, deep mahogany shading to red to pale green, solid opaque white casing, applied crystal edge, applied crystal rope handle, Victorian .. **125.00**

8" h, 11" d, cut glass, Harvard pattern, hobstars and prisms, American Brilliant period **475.00**

8-1/4" h, 6" d, blue, cased white int., spangle in vertical rows, colorless looped thorn handle **190.00**

8-1/2" h, caramel shading to apricot, colorless edge, applied colorless thorn handle **275.00**

8-1/2" h, New Martinsville, Janice, crystal, red handle............ **90.00**

8-1/2" h, Stevens and Williams, opaque white, pink scallops, applied colorless handle **250.00**

8-1/2" h, Tiffin, paneled transparent sky blue **85.00**

8-1/2" h, 10" x 9" body, cased red to white spangled int., white ext., crimped rim with colorless border, applied colorless twisted handle **190.00**

8-3/4" h, 5" d, opalescent light vaseline, green edge, thorny nubs, applied colorless handle **195.00**

8-3/4" h, 7-1/2" w, pot-shaped crystal body, deep pink handle with white latticinio stripes, three matching feet **850.00**

9" h, peachblow, amber ruffle, petal feet, applied amber thorn handle **195.00**

9" h, 5" w, bright yellow ext., tomato red int., three swirled blown out balls, pulled down basket shape, twisted thorn handle, Victorian **175.00**

9" h, 5-1/2" w, apricot to pink opalescent, pedestal rose bowl shape, vertical ribbed int., applied colorless leaves, stems, and vines, applied twisted thorn handle, c1880.... **275.00**

9" h, 6" w, pale pink shading to white ext., brilliant yellow int., cabbage rose design, applied twisted thorn handle, Victorian **125.00**

9" h, 6-1/2" w, Czechoslovakia, pink satin, green satin twisted handle **100.00**

9" h, 7" w, deep pink int., clear casing, mottled pink, purple, and brown swirl effect, wide border of enameled and painted dec done in Turkish manner, applied pale custard handle ... **225.00**

9-1/2" h, 5-1/2" l, green, delicate etched flowers and stems, ruffled rim, applied handle **60.00**

10" h, Czechoslovakia, brilliant orange, blue and white enameled daisy, gold trim, black edge, black handle . **115.00**

10" h, green body, orange flaring scalloped rim, green and orange spatter handle **95.00**

Amethyst glass liner, silver-plated holder, 9" h, **$85.**

10" h, Imperial, Twisted Optic, vaseline **110.00**

10" h, Snail pattern, George Duncan & Sons, clear, pewter handle, cake type **115.00**

10" h, 7-1/2" w, Czechoslovakia, pink, applied black rim and handle . . . **95.00**

10" h, 7-1/2" w, Czechoslovakia, pink, pink spatter, applied vaseline flowers and leaves, clear applied handle **115.00**

10" h, 8" w, opaque white, yellow casing, applied amber thorn handle, four applied feather type feet, ends of two feet chipped **130.00**

10-1/4" h, Czechoslovakia, vaseline and yellow stripes, overlaid red, white, blue, yellow, orange millefiori type pattern, clear twist handle **115.00**

10-1/2" h, 6" d, Czechoslovakia, acid finished clear body, ruffled, applied green leaves, two red cherries, green acid twist handle **125.00**

10-1/2" h, 7" w, pink over opaque creamy white ground, applied amber edge, applied amber feet, melon ribbed body, tall loop amber handle, Victorian **90.00**

10-1/2" h, 11" w, melon-ribbed base, blue cased opalescent, robin's egg blue shading to crystal, crossed crystal handle, two rows of blown hobnails, c1890. . . . . **375.00**

11" h, Cleo pattern, Cambridge, amber, two side handles **45.00**

11" h, pressed, frosted green, applied braided frosted green handle . . . **20.00**

11" h, 10" w, pressed, colorless, circles motif, applied colorless smooth handle **50.00**

11-1/4" h, 8-1/2" w, colorless, jeweled rose cut, engraved, sgd "Heisey," shape #458 . . . . **250.00**

11-1/2" h, Illinois pattern, colorless, applied colorless handle. **110.00**

11-1/2" h, 7-1/2" d, green satin, applied crystal and yellow rose flower, crystal thorn handle **110.00**

11-1/2" h, 8-1/4" w, colorless, floral enamel dec, gold trim, sgd "Heisey" **95.00**

11-3/4" h, 8-1/4" l, colorless, engraved bird on branch with leaves, sgd "Heisey". **300.00**

12" h, Cabbage Rose pattern, colorless, applied colorless handle. **115.00**

12" h, 6-1/2" h, emerald green, engraved floral and bow, sterling silver base, sgd "Hawkes," slight dent to weighted base. **150.00**

Duncan Miller, vaseline, 6" h, **$95.**

12" h, 8-1/4" l, plain sides, painted green ground, white enamel beads along top and bottom, white enameled monogram, sgd "Heisey" **50.00**

12" h, 15" l, Broken Column pattern, colorless, applied colorless handle **125.00**

12-1/2" h, 7-3/8" w, colorless, pair of finely enamel painted Rococo figures on either side, intricate engraved and gilt dec, cut panels below, J. & L. Lobmeyr Co., some loss to gilt. . **110.00**

13" h, 11" w, deep pink int. over pale cream white ext., three rows of hobnails on edge, applied amber edge, four applied amber feet, applied amber thorn cross-form handle, Victorian **200.00**

15" h, 11" d, white ext., deep pink int., melon rib shape, heavily crimped and ruffled, four applied frosted thorn feet, applied frosted crossed V-shaped handle, Victorian **300.00**

15-1/2" h, 8" w, colorless, wide panel pattern, enameled deep blue and red flowers, green leaves, sgd "Heisey" **135.00**

19" h, 12" w, blue aurene, purple highlights, ruffled, applied loop handle, inscribed "Aurene, 455" **5,250.00**

Biscuit Jars

History: The biscuit or cracker jar was the forerunner of the cookie jar. Biscuit jars were made of various materials by leading glass manufacturers of the late nineteenth and early twentieth centuries.

Blue, 5-1/2" h, 4-1/4" d, multicolored enamel and gilt dec, metal lid, wear to dec **70.00**

Bristol glass

- 6" h, 4-5/8" d, light gray body, enameled white, pink, and blue flowers, green leaves, gold stems, SP rim, cov, and handle. . . **145.00**
- 6-1/2" h, allover enameled pink, blue, white and yellow floral dec, green leaves, SP top, rim, and handle **125.00**
- 6-1/2" h, 5-1/4" d, satin finish, opaque beige ground, pink roses, gold leaves, gray foliage, SP top, rim, and handle **195.00**

Three biscuit jars: left: satin glass, ferns decoration, **$110***; center: Wave Crest style, pink floral decoration,* **$120***; right: Wave Crest, decorated with blue and pink flowers and leaves,* **$220.** *Photo courtesy of Joy Luke Fine Art Brokers and Auctioneeers.*

Carnival glass, 7-1/2" h, 4-1/2" w, Harvest pattern, grapes and foliage, blue, Indiana Glass Co. **50.00**

Cased glass, 6-1/4" h, blue, enameled pink roses and green leaves, SP top, rim and handle **145.00**

Cranberry glass

5-1/2" h, 4-1/4" d, white and blue enamel dec, gilt bands, metal lid **90.00**

9" h, 6-1/4" d, two applied clear ring handles, applied clear feet and flower prunt pontil, ribbed finial knob **195.00**

Crown Milano

6" h, 5-1/2" d, barrel shape, pale yellow ground shades to creamy white, deep pink apple blossoms, green leaves, gray-green branches, SP Pairpoint lid and collar, "P" in diamond logo emb in floral motif **695.00**

6-1/2" h, pseudo Burmese coloration, painted acorns and oak leaves, quadruple plate marked "M.W." **445.00**

Cut glass

6-1/2" h, Brilliant period cutting, star cut base, silver plated lid and finial, lid marked "HC & Co. S," 19th C **295.00**

6-1/2" h, Polish, 20th C **65.00**

9-1/2" h, heavy blank, Turkish cutting, 20th C. **100.00**

Fenton glass, 7-1/2" h, 6" d, marigold carnival glass, Grapes pattern, marked "Presnick's Carnival Glass Museum, Lodi, Ohio, 1969" **200.00**

Loetz type, 7-1/4" d, 5" h, dark ext., unmarked **350.00**

Mt. Washington

5-3/4" h, 6" d, silvered metal cover and handle, commemorative inscriptions, melon form jar of acid finish opal glass, enamel dec of gold water lilies, blue-green leaves on shaded sepia ground, red enamel numbers, wear to silvered finish **900.00**

8-1/2" h, colorless ground, tapering body, molded in scrolls, gold highlights, gold single petal blossoms each framed by elaborate gold feather scrolls, small side cartouches of colorless glass framed by fancy gold scrolls, lid sgd "MM 4425," collar, flame finial, and bail with worn gilt finish **1,500.00**

New England Glass Works, melon ribbed, pink floral dec, lid and bail missing **60.00**

Opalescent, 7-3/4" h, William and Mary pattern, English **875.00**

Opalware

9" h, pink shaded, polychrome scene of castle, hand painted stylized florals, quadruple plate lid and frame. **275.00**

10" h, 8" d, pale purple ground, red and purple lilacs, resilvered fittings **320.00**

Opaque

7" h, 4-1/2" d white, satin finish, multicolored floral and leaves dec, Challinor's #313, Challinor, Taylor & Co. **90.00**

9" h, glossy pink, quilted diamond pattern, small hairline in outer layer, quadruple plate lid and frame **110.00**

Pairpoint, 9-1/2" h, burnt orange, floral dec, blown-out floral base, sgd. **350.00**

Pigeon blood, 7" h, melon rib shape, resilvered frame and lid. **425.00**

Pomona, 10-1/2" h, 5-1/2" w, first ground, acanthus leaf design, excellent staining, applied wishbone base, crack in base. **200.00**

Satin glass, 7-1/4" h, pink, molded shell base, enameled floral dec, SP lid and handle **315.00**

Wave Crest, white satin glass, decorated with landscape, figures, and boat, 7" h, **$220.** *Photo courtesy of Joy Luke Fine Art Brokers and Auctioneers*

Smith Brothers, 7" h, 7" d, melon rib shape, enameled pansies, c1875 . . . . **795.00**

Turquoise glass, 71/4" h, 6-1/2" d, enameled bird and flowers, SP base with three ball and claw feet, SP lid, English **495.00**

Vaseline glass, 7" h, threaded, SP rim, lid, and handle **160.00**

Wave Crest

9" h, cream shaded to pale blue ground, hp lavender and pink lilac sprays, green and light brown leaves, rim, bale, and lid marked "Vanbergh Silver Plate Co., Rochester, NY Quadruple Plate" **395.00**

9" h, cream shaded to pale lavender, hp floral spray on each side, marked "Sterling" on lid and rim **295.00**

9" h, yellow roses, molded multicolored swirl ground, incised floral and leaf dec on lid, marked "Quadruple Plate" **400.00**

9-1/2" h, Burmese coloring, "Crackers" in lavender on front, pale blue floral dec, marked "Nakara" **3,500.00**

Black Glass

History: Black glass was one of the colors made during early glass productions as far back as 1600. These early bottles had a thick body and were primarily used for fermenting liquids, where the glass walls had to withstand the pressures of the fermenting ale or wine. The Bohemians developed an opaque black glass which they used as a base for gold matte decorations, often of an Oriental style. Other European glassware manufacturers, as well as the English, produced black glass items; however, its popularity was always limited.

American production of black glass dates back to Deming Jarvis when he was at the Boston and Sandwich Glass Company about 1865. His ingredients included manganese and powdered charcoal. While developing glass with greater strengths and other desirable properties, glass-blowers noticed that the more manganese they added, the darker the purple glass became. Some early "black" glass pieces may actually be very dark purple or even very dark green. Other nineteenth century glass houses, like Atterbury, Dalzell, and Gilmore, produced lamps, bottles, and other items of black glass.

In 1915, Westmoreland Specialty Company introduced a black-glass line and this "new" color was quickly copied by Duncan and Miller, as well as Northwood, Fenton, and Cambridge. Fostoria was one of the last of the major manufacturers to get involved when it began production in 1924, and by that time, demand was beginning to wane. The United States Glass Company became the leading exponent of black glass during the 1920s and continued to hold this lead until around 1926.

Popularity of black glass rose again in 1928 with the introduction of black stemmed wares. Morgantown Glass Works led the way, quickly followed by Fostoria and Central Glass Works. Black tableware sets were introduced during this period. Shapes reflected the design attitudes of the times, and square plates and square footed stemware created a bold statement.

By 1932, demand began to drop off again, as it did for most handmade glass. Cambridge continued its ebony line until 1939. Raw ingredient shortages caused by World War II seriously affected the colored glassware industry, and almost no black glass was produced again until 1949 when Westmoreland issued black variety items. Again, some of the major glass makers, Fostoria Glass Co., Cambridge Glass Co., and Viking, entered the field. Smaller manufacturers like Boyd and Degenhart also joined the marketplace. A large percentage of the black glass offered in today's marketplace comes from the last surge, which lasted into the mid-1950s.

References: Margaret James, *Black Glass, An Illustrated Price Guide*, Collector Books, 1981; Marlena Toohey, *A Collector's Guide to Black Glass*, Antique Publications, 1988.

Animal, cat, Tiffin Glass Co.
- Alley cat, small, black satin . **115.00**
- Sassie Suzie, black satin . . . **175.00**

Ashtray, 4" d, Hazel Atlas, 1930-36
- Cloverleaf pattern, match holder center **65.00**
- 1930-36, square **10.00**

Basket
- 5" h, emb, basketweave bands, two handles. **50.00**
- 7" h, crystal handle, Cambridge **130.00**

Batter set, batter jug and syrup, Paden City Glass Co., colorless body, black cover and tray, 1936 . . . . **75.00**

Berry bowl, Hazel Atlas, Ribbon pattern, c1930 . . . . **25.00**

Bookends, pr
- Horses, L. E. Smith Glass Co., 1950s **60.00**
- Scotties, frosted, made by Imperial for National Cambridge Collectors, Inc. **50.00**

Bowl
- 6-1/2" d, Diamond Glass Ware Co., Victory pattern **30.00**
- 7-1/2" d, Imperial Glass Co., Alternating Flute and Panel, c1930 . . . . **42.00**
- 10" d, United States Glass Co., Deerwood pattern, ftd **100.00**
- 12" d, Cambridge Glass Co., #933, #739 etching **45.00**

Candleholder, Fostoria, 4" h, **$35.**

Bud vase, Cambridge Glass Co.
- Blossom Time, 10" h, gold encrusted dec **325.00**
- #274, partial sticker on foot . . . **35.00**

Butter dish, cov, Heisey Glass Co., rect **110.00**

Cake plate
- Fostoria Glass Co., Fern, two handles, gold trim, 10" d **85.00**
- Mt. Pleasant, L. E. Smith Glass Co., 10" d, low, ftd. **30.00**
- Paden City Glass Co., Black Forest pattern, 2" h pedestal **85.00**

Candelabra, Cambridge Glass Co., Decagon, #638, three-lite. **72.50**

Candleholder
- 2-1/2" h, United States Glass Co., Deerwood **110.00**
- 3" h, Fostoria Glass Co., Oak Leaf **90.00**
- 3" h, Diamond Glass Ware Co., Victory **95.00**
- 4" h, Cambridge Glass Co., Decagon, price for pr **55.00**
- 4" h, Venini, opaque, wafer foot, three knobs on stem, etched "Italia," Venini paper label . . **125.00**
- 5" h, Fostoria Glass Co., Ebony **35.00**
- 6" h, Tiffin Glass Co., frog, bright finish **185.00**
- 9-1/2" h, Cambridge Glass Co., Doric, pr **160.00**

Candy dish, cov, Hazel Atlas, Ovide pattern, 1930-35. . . . . **40.00**

Candy dish, Cambridge Glass Co., #103, 7" d **65.00**

Celery tray
- Heisey Glass Co., Lodestar pattern **50.00**
- Viking, clear swan handle, oval **60.00**

Cereal bowl
- 4-7/8" h, Paden City Glass Co., Orchid, early 1930s **35.00**
- 5" d, Imperial Glass Co., Diamond Quilted, early 1930s. **15.00**

Cigarette box, cov, 4-3/8" l, United States Glass Co., Flower Garden with Butterflies, late 1920s **125.00**

Compote
- Cambridge Glass Co., Blossom Time, gold encrusted dec . **225.00**
- Co-Operative Glass Co., 6-1/2" d, c1924 . . . . **35.00**
- L. E. Smith Glass Co., Veined Onyx, 5" h, ftd. **35.00**
- United States Glass Co., Flower Garden with Butterflies, 7" h, late 1920s **175.00**

Console bowl
- McKee, Autumn pattern, 8-1/2" d **40.00**
- Unknown maker, enameled dec **50.00**

Console set, Fostoria Glass Co., #2402, Deco bowl, pr candleholders **70.00**

Cookie jar, cov, L. E. Smith Glass Co., Amy **95.00**

Cordial decanter, 12 oz, ball shape, applied colorless handle, orig colorless stopper, Cambridge Glass Co., Farber Bros. metal holder, c1933 . . . . . . **95.00**

Creamer
- Diamond Glass Ware Co., Victory pattern **45.00**
- Hazel Atlas, Cloverleaf, 1930-36 . . . . **20.00**
- Imperial Glass Co., Diamond Quilted, early 1930s. **15.00**
- L. E. Smith Glass Co., Mt. Pleasant **20.00**
- United States Glass Co., Deerwood **60.00**

Creamer and sugar tray, Cambridge Glass Co., Decagon **45.00**

Cream soup bowl, 4-3/4" d, Imperial Glass Co., Diamond Quilted, early 1930s. **15.00**

Cup and saucer
- Diamond Glass Ware Co., Victory **45.00**
- Hazel Atlas, Cloverleaf, 1930-36 . . . . **20.00**
- Imperial Glass Co., Diamond Quilted, early 1930s. **20.00**
- L. E. Smith Glass Co., Mt. Pleasant **20.00**

Fern bowl, L. E. Smith Glass Co., Greek Key, 4-1/4" h **25.00**

Fruit bowl, Mt. Pleasant, scalloped, **$40.**

Floor vase, 28-1/2" h, raised bulbous oval body, polished rim, flared at base, American **500.00**
Flower frog, Fenton, September Morn Nymph, flower frog, base, bowl, and stand. **275.00**
Grill plate, 10-1/2" d, Hazel Atlas, Cloverleaf, 1930-36 . . . . **25.00**
Ice bucket
- Cambridge Glass Co., Tally Ho pattern, Farber Bros. chromium plated frame and handle, c1935 . . . . **95.00**
- Imperial Glass Co., Diamond Quilted, early 1930s **85.00**

Mayonnaise, silver dec, L. E. Smith **15.00**
Nappy
- 4-1/2" d, Heisey Glass Co., Dawn **35.00**
- 5-1/2" d, Imperial Glass Co., Diamond Quilted, early 1930s **25.00**

Nut bowl, 5-3/4" d, handle, L. E. Smith Glass Co., Mt. Pleasant **25.00**
Pitcher, Cambridge Glass Co., Gloria, oval, some wear to silver **950.00**
Place card holder, 2-1/2" h, Fostoria **30.00**
Plate
- 6" d, Hazel Atlas, Cloverleaf, 1930-36 . . . . **15.00**
- 6" d, Cambridge Glass Co., Decagon **18.00**
- 6-1/4" d, Fry Glass **10.00**
- 7" d, "V"-shaped open handles **12.00**
- 8" d, Cambridge Glass Co., hp pink flowers **24.00**
- 8" d, Diamond Glass Ware Co., Victory **28.50**
- 8" d, Imperial Glass Co., Diamond Quilted, early 1930s **18.00**
- 8" d, Imperial Glass Co., Molly . **7.00**
- 8-1/4" d, Cambridge Glass Co., #3400 . . . . **10.00**
- 8-1/4" d, Cambridge Glass Co., Decagon. **18.00**
- 8-1/4" d, Fry Glass **15.00**
- 8-1/2" d, gold edge. **10.00**
- 9" d, #30, Westmoreland, wicket border. **18.50**

Relish, two-part, Heisey Glass Co., Lodestar **65.00**
Salt shaker, sterling silver floral dec **15.00**
Sandwich server, center handle
- Co-Operative Flint. **35.00**
- Imperial Glass Co., Diamond Quilted, early 1930s **45.00**
- L. E. Smith Glass Co., Mt. Pleasant, 12" d **40.00**
- United States Glass Co., Flower Garden with Butterflies, late 1920s **115.00**

Saucer
- Cambridge Glass Co., #3400. . **4.50**
- Cambridge Glass Co., Decagon **9.00**
- Fry Glass Co. **5.00**
- Imperial Glass Co., Molly **3.00**

Sherbet
- Diamond Glass Ware Co., Victory **25.00**
- Hazel Atlas, Cloverleaf, 1930-36 . . . . **20.00**
- Imperial Glass Co., Diamond Quilted, early 1930s. **20.00**
- L. E. Smith Glass Co., Mt. Pleasant **20.00**

Snack plate, 8-1/4" sq plate with cup indent, cup, L. E. Smith Glass Co., Mt. Pleasant. **20.00**
Soap dish, Westite **45.00**
Sugar bowl, cov
- Diamond Glass Ware Co., Victory **45.00**
- Hazel Atlas, Cloverleaf, 1930-36 . . . . **25.00**
- Imperial Glass Co., Diamond Quilted, early 1930s. **20.00**
- L. E. Smith Glass Co., Mt. Pleasant **22.00**
- United States Glass Co., Deerwood **60.00**

Sugar shaker, Beaumont Glass Co., Acorn, gilt transfer floral dec, white enamel highlights, 5" h **170.00**
Sweet pea vase, 7" h, 8-1/2" d, Cambridge Glass Co., c1922 . . . **55.00**
Tumbler
- Fostoria Glass Co., Fern, 12 oz, ftd **35.00**
- Heisey Glass Co., Town and Country **40.00**

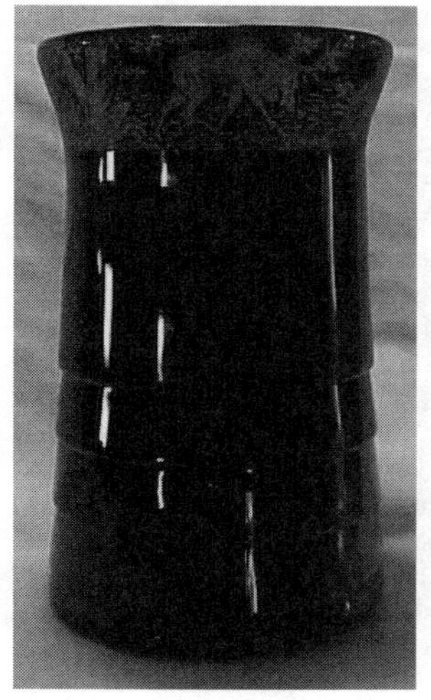
Vase, #210 Regina, Black Forest etch, Paden City, glass chalk used to highlight pattern in photo, 8-1/2" h, **$285.** *Photo courtesy of Michael Krumme.*

Urn, 7" h, 2 handles, L. E. Smith Glass Co., Dancing Girls **40.00**
Vase
- 6" h, Cambridge Glass Co., #1250, Everglades **225.00**
- 6-1/2" h, squatty, Paden City Glass Co., Black Forest pattern . . **175.00**
- 7" h, Eagle Glass Co., Diagonal Star Band, c1898 . . . . **35.00**
- 7-1/2" h, Fostoria Glass Co., Art Deco style **65.00**
- 7-1/2" h, pyramid, ftd **24.00**
- 7-3/4" h, Diamond Glass Ware Co., flared top, silver deposit dec, c1939 . . . . **50.00**
- 8" h, Fostoria Glass Co., fish-bowl shape, designed by George Sakier **125.00**
- 8" h, Fostoria Glass Co., Tut . . **65.00**
- 10" h, Paden City Glass Co., Black Forest pattern **195.00**
- 10" h, Paden City Glass Co., Utopia **195.00**
- 10-1/2" h, Tiffin Glass Co., floral dec, satin. **115.00**
- 12" h, United States Glass Co., Deerwood pattern **120.00**

BLENKO

History: Blenko Glass Company, located in Milton, West Virginia, was founded by British glassmaker William John Blenko. He originally made stained glass for church windows using a method known as the "Norman-slab" method. He arrived in America early in 1893 and created a factory in Kokomo, Indiana, to produce mouth-blown sheet glass. Unfortunately, his efforts were deterred by the poor economics of the time, tariff problems, and even a fire. American glass companies snubbed his efforts and he returned to England in 1905.

He returned to America in 1909, this time locating in Marion, Pennsylvania. By this time, the economic climate had improved, and he also brought a team of English glassworkers. This factory only lasted two years. In 1911, he relocated to Clarksburg, West Virginia, where he employed local skilled workers. The primary emphasis of the factory was on producing window glass. Again, in 1913, the high tariff on window glass shut down Blenko and his factory. After this setback, he returned to his roots and worked as a chemist. In 1919, he accepted a job with the prestigious New York firm of Tiffany, where he worked until 1921. At age 67, he returned to Milton, West Virginia, and created the Eureka Art Glass Company. From rather crude beginnings, the little firm started to grow.

By 1923, Blenko's younger son, William H. Blenko (Sr.) joined the firm and learned the art of glass blowing from his father. Two Swedish glassblowers, Louis Miller and Axel Mueller, joined the firm, bringing their stemware skills to the company. They also began to train local workers as glass blowers. In 1930, Eureka Art Glass changed its name to Blenko Glass Company. Macy's Department Store in New York City began to carry Blenko glasswares in 1932. Another boost to the fledging company came in 1933 when the decorative glassware was featured at the Chicago's World Fair and William H. successfully negotiated a contract with Colonial Williamsburg, assuring its future as a tableware manufacturer. Grandson William H. Blenko Jr. has now been joined by his son Richard Blenko. Today, Richard proudly carries on the business, encouraging company craftsmen to continue the colorful tradition started by William John Blenko. He founded the Blenko Glass Museum, which honors the accomplishments of this American glass maker.

Blenko glassware is handmade and only marked with paper labels. Tall pieces, ranging from 18 inches to 28 inches, are specialties of this manufacturer. Another specialty is crackle glass. Vibrant colors and heavy walls are predominate with the clean modern lines of most pieces.

Visitors to the Milton, West Virginia, factory can enjoy tours and visit the factory outlet. A visit to its Web site, http://www.blenkoglass.com, will also give collectors a good feel for what's currently being offered by this contemporary American glassmaker.

References: Leslie Piña, *Blenko Glass, Cool '50s & '60s Glass,* Schiffer Publishing, 2000; —, *Blenko Glass, 1962-1971 Catalogs,* Schiffer Publishing, 2000; —, *Blenko Glass, 1972-1983 Catalogs,* Schiffer Publishing, 2001.

Periodical: *Antique Notes Newsletter,* P.O. Box 67, Milton, WV 22541-0067.

Videotapes: *Blenko Retro,* Witek & Novak, Inc.; *Hearts of Glass,* Witek & Novak, Inc.

Manufacturer: Blenko Glass Visitor Center Museum and Wholesale Outlet, P.O. Box 67, Milton, WV 22541-0067.

Web sites: http://www.blenkoglass.com, http://www.barnesandwagner.com.

Additional Listings: Crackle Glass.

Ashtray

Freeform, amethyst, 8" l **15.00**

Green, 1951 . . . . **9.00**

Beaker, 9-1/2" h, 6" d top, crackle, 4" l turquoise blue leaves, pontil scar **135.00**

Bottle, stopper, 16" h, crackled, crystal, sgd, price for pr **385.00**

Bowl

3" d, 4" h, amber, scalloped edge **10.00**

6-1/4" d, tangerine, turned in edge **12.00**

6-1/2" d, amber, scalloped edge, heavy base **17.50**

Brandy snifter, crackle, 8" h, crystal, turquoise foot **35.00**

Compote

5-3/4" d, 6" h, red bowl shades to gold, gold stem and foot **20.00**

6-1/2" d, 11" h, bright blue, solid finial **35.00**

10" d, 5-1/2" h, amber, scalloped edge **25.00**

Creamer, red, applied colorless handle **20.00**

Decanter

9" h, amber, sgd **115.00**

10" h, amethyst, orig amethyst stopper **35.00**

13" h, hand blown, tear drop stopper **85.00**

15-1/2" h, 6" h pointed stopper, colorless, hand blown **30.00**

19-1/4" h, 7" d base, 12" l stopper, amberina crackle body, bell shape, hand blown, pontil mark . . . **160.00**

Hour glass, 19" h, colorless body, wood case **45.00**

Muddler, crackled, amethyst **8.00**

Paperweight, snowman, red top hat **25.00**

Pitcher

4-1/4" h, electric blue crackle body, frilled top, applied colorless handle **25.00**

6" h, crackle, blue, applied colorless handle, c1950 . . . . **40.00**

6" h, crackle, green, dimpled, applied colorless handle. . . . **45.00**

6" h, crackle, red, applied yellow handle **55.00**

6-1/2" h, colorless bulbous body, applied colorless handle. . . . **20.00**

10" h, crackle, amberina, applied amber handle **150.00**

11" h, crackle, turquoise, applied turquoise handle, pontil scar**110.00**

Rose bowl, 7" h, 7" d, crackle, bright blue. **35.00**

Tankard, 9" h, gold body, applied colorless handle **25.00**

Vase

4" h, 4" w, emerald green crackle body, double pinched top, hand blown. **35.00**

6-1/2" h, corset shape, bright blue, c1960 . . . . **70.00**

7-3/4" h, 6-1/2" w at top, Rosette, colorless crackle body, four applied rosettes, hand blown, pontil scar **90.00**

8" h, 9" d, crimped, ftd, colorless body, c1950 . . . . **150.00**

8-1/2" h, Florette pattern, flared, colorless. **35.00**

9" h, crackled, blue. **55.00**

9-1/4" h, 6-1/2" w, fluted, hand blown, emerald green crackle body, pontil scar **95.00**

9-1/2" h, 7-1/2" d top, crackle, four 2" d blue rosettes, pontil scar **135.00**

9-3/4" h, crackle, dark green . **50.00**

11" h, 6" w, rose colorless crackle body, waisted cylinder, hand blown, c1950 . . . . **125.00**

11-1/4" h, shaded blue to colorless base, reverse baluster **115.00**

11-1/2" h, blue ground, applied green twist rigaree round neck, c1950 . . . . **125.00**

11-1/2" h, ruby, crystal foot, fan shape **65.00**

12" h, crackle, brilliant orange **135.00**

25" h, avocado crackle body, tapered neck, scalloped edge **40.00**

Water jug, cov, 8-1/2" h, 6" w, blue, double pouring spouts, hand hold indents on both sides **45.00**

Water set, 10" h dark amber pitcher, random small indentations on body, six 6" h tumblers **72.00**

Water bottle, cobalt blue, form introduced in 1938, 8" h, **$21.** *Photo courtesy of Blenko.*

BLOWN THREE MOLD

History: The Jamestown colony in Virginia introduced glassmaking into America. The artisans used a "free-blown" method.

Blowing molten glass into molds was not introduced into America until the early 1800s. Blown three-mold glass used a predesigned mold that consisted of two, three, or more hinged parts. The glassmaker placed a quantity of molten glass on the tip of a rod or tube, inserted it into the mold, blew air into the tube, waited until the glass cooled, and removed the finished product. The three-part mold is the most common and lends its name to this entire category.

The impressed decorations on blown-mold glass usually are reversed, i.e., what is raised or convex on the outside will be concave on the inside. This is useful in identifying the blown form.

By 1850, American-made glassware was relatively common. Increased demand led to large factories and the creation of a technology which eliminated the smaller companies.

Collectors should be aware that reproductions of blown mold glass are offered widely in the marketplace. Some reproductions are specially produced for museums and gift shops. While many are marked, most are not. Modern artists have kept the craft of blown molded glassware alive, and collectors should learn to recognize the characteristics of new glass.

References: George S. and Helen McKearin, *American Glass*, reprint, Crown Publishers, 1941, 1948; Kenneth Wilson, *American Glass 1760-1930: The Toledo Museum of Art, Volume I, Volume II*, Hudson Hills Press and The Toledo Museum of Art, 1994.

Collectors' Club: The National American Glass Club, Ltd., 7417 Allison St., Hyattsville, MD 10784.

Museum: Corning Museum of Glass, Corning, NY; Sandwich Glass Museum, Sandwich, MA.

Additional Listings: Early American Glass and Stiegel-Type.

Basket

3-1/2" h, 3-1/8" d, cobalt blue, plain base, traces of gold dec on ribs, solid applied handle, pontil **125.00**

4-1/2" h, 4" d, colorless, rayed base, solid applied handle, pontil scar **300.00**

Bird cage fountain, 5-1/4" h, colorless, ground mouth, pontil scar, McKearin GI-12. . . . . **50.00**

Bottle, 7-1/4" h, olive green, McKearin GIII-16. . . . . **330.00**

Bowl

4-1/4" d, 1-3/4" h, colorless, outward folded rim, straight sided, 16-diamond base, pontil . . . **215.00**

5" d, colorless, rounded sides, outward folded rim, rayed base, pontil scar. **200.00**

5-3/8" d, colorless, folded rim, 12-diamond base, pontil scar, McKearin GII-6. . . . . **125.00**

6" d, 1-3/4" h, colorless, outward folded rim, straight slanting sides, 16-diamond base, pontil . . **140.00**

6-1/4" d, colorless, folded rim, 12-diamond base, pontil scar **200.00**

6-3/8" d, 5-3/4" h, colorless, folded rim, 16-diamond base, ftd, pontil, tilts to one side, McKearin GII-18 . . . . **4,800.00**

Carafe, 9-1/4" h, dark yellow amber, rayed base, deep pontil scar . **2,400.00**

Celery vase, colorless, Pittsburgh, McKearin GV-21 . . . . **650.00**

Cordial, 2-7/8" h, colorless, ringed base, pontil, heavy circular foot, formed by free-hand, McKearinGII-18. . **550.00**

Creamer

3-1/4" h, colorless, formed mouth and spout, ringed base, applied solid handle with curled end **375.00**

3-1/2" h, colorless, applied handle **125.00**

4-3/8" h, brilliant sapphire blue, ftd, applied round base, applied solid handle, fine curled ending, flared mouth, tooled rim, ringed base with pontil, Boston & Sandwich, c1820, McKearin GI-29 . . . . **2,400.00**

4-1/2" h, 2-3/4" d, cobalt blue, paneled and reeded body, applied handle, attributed to Boston & Sandwich Glass Co., Sandwich, MA, c1825-40, minor wear **3,150.00**

7-1/2" h, colorless, applied handle, small rim chip, check at base of handle **120.00**

Cruet

5-3/8" h, colorless, plain base, formed pouring lip, pontil, McKearin GII-28. . . . . **150.00**

7-3/4" h, cobalt blue, scroll scale pattern, ribbed base, pontil, applied handle, French . . . **265.00**

Cup plate, 3-7/8" d, folded rim, rayed base, pontil scar, three McKearin labels, ex-collection George McKearin and TMR Culbertson, McKearin GII-1 . . . . **600.00**

Decanter, no stopper

Colorless, arch and fern design, snake medallion, 10" h, McKearin GIV-7, minor chips, mold imperfections **165.00**

Colorless, flared mouth, pontil scar, pint, attributed to Keene Marlboro Street Glassworks, Keene, NH, 1820-40, McKearin GIII-20 . **110.00**

Olive amber, sunburst and diamond pattern, 6-3/4" h, attributed to Stoddard Glass Works, NH, early 19th C, mouth repair **520.00**

Yellowish olive, sheared mouth, pontil scar, pint, Keene Marlboro Street Glassworks, Keene, NH, 1820-40, McKearin GIII-16, some light abrasions. **350.00**

Decanter, orig stopper, light sea green, Kent-Ohio pattern, 8-1/2" h, McKearin GII-6 . . . . **2,415.00**

Decanter, period stopper, colorless, flared mouth, pontil scar

Pint, attributed to Keene Marlboro Street Glassworks, Keene, NH, 1820-40, McKearin GIII-16 . **230.00**

Quart, attributed to Keene Marlboro Street Glassworks, Keene, NH, 1820-40, McKearin GIII-15 . **120.00**

Quart, applied crimped snake trailing, attributed to Keene Marlboro Street Glassworks, Keene, NH, 1820-40, McKearin GIII-19 . . . . **550.00**

Sunburst and ray pattern, 10-1/4" h, McKearin GIII-5, attributed to Boston & Sandwich Glass Co., Sandwich, MA, 1840 . . . . . . **225.00**

Sunburst, diamond and zigzag rings and panels, 9-1/4" h, attributed to Boston & Sandwich Glass Co., Sandwich, MA, 1840 . . . . . . **225.00**

Three applied rigaree rings over body, rib and diamond pattern, 8-1/2" h, attributed to New England, c1840 . . . . **200.00**

Three applied rigaree rings over body, rib and diamond pattern, 10-1/4" h, attributed to New England, c1840. . . . . **200.00**

Emerald green, flat cut stopper, gilt enamel dec, 9-1/4" h, third quarter 19th C, minor imperfections **165.00**

Decanter, replaced stopper

Colorless, three applied rings, replaced wheel stopper, 8" h, McKearin GII-18 . . . . **110.00**

Colorless, replaced wheel stopper, 8-1/4" h, McKearin GII-19 . . **115.00**

Unlisted Baroque-type pattern, sapphire blue, flared mouth, pontil scar, quart, French, 19th C, similar to McKearin Plate 5, #2. . . . **350.00**

Creamer, applied handle and pontil, Sandwich, McKearin GII-18, **$1,650.** *Photo courtesy of Pacific Glass Auctions.*

Dish
- 5" d, colorless, outward rolled rim, pontil scar, McKearin GIII-21 .... **130.00**
- 5-1/4" d, colorless, McKearin GII-16 .... **65.00**
- 5-1/2" d, colorless, McKearin GII-18 .... **50.00**
- 6-3/8" d, colorless, folded rim, rayed base, iron pontil **90.00**

Finger bowl, 3-1/2" d, deep teal green, third quarter 19th C, minor imperfections.......... **195.00**

Flask, 5-1/4" h, colorless, arch and diamond pattern, sheared mouth, pontil, Continental **300.00**

Flip glass
- 5-1/2" h, colorless, McKearin GII-18 .... **165.00**
- 5-5/8" h, 4-5/8" h, colorless, eighteen diamond base **135.00**
- 6" h, colorless, McKearin GII-18 .... **125.00**

Hat
- 2-1/8" h, colorless, 15-diamond base, pontil, folded rim.... **275.00**
- 2-1/4" h, colorless, swirled rayed base, pontil, folded rim.... **125.00**
- 2-5/8" h, 2-1/4" d, sapphire blue, folded rim, ringed and pontil base **850.00**

Ink bottle, 2-1/4" d, deep olive green, McKearin GII-2 .... **195.00**

Inkwell
- 1-7/8" h, 2-3/4" d, amber, drum shape, faint ringed base, pontil scar **125.00**
- 2" h, 2-5/8" d, olive green, McKearin GII-18 .... **125.00**

Lamp
- 4" h, 3" d, peg, colorless, heavy applied solid pegs, period tin matching double burners, short factory ground neck, McKearin GII-18, pr.......... **1,450.00**
- 6-1/2" h, colorless, double paw pressed base, orig brass collar, marked "BTM font/Mt Vernon Works," McKearin GI-30 ... **800.00**

Miniature decanter
- 2-5/8" h, colorless, McKearin GIII-12 .... **165.00**
- 3-1/2" h, colorless, ground upper rim, McKearin GIII-12 ..... **125.00**

Mustard
- 3-7/8" h, colorless, flanged lip, iron pontil **50.00**
- 4-1/4" h, colorless, pontil, cork stopper, orig paper label, McKearin GI-15 .... **85.00**
- 5" h, colorless, clear sheared ball finial, flanged, folded lip, pontil, orig matching cov **125.00**
- 5-1/4" h, colorless, plain base, pontil, orig pressed finial finish, hollow blown cov, McKearin GI-24.. **90.00**

Pan, 1-1/2" h, 5" d, colorless, McKearin GI-6.......... **185.00**

Pitcher
- 7" h, colorless, base of handle reglued, McKearin GIII-5... **145.00**
- 8-1/2" h, colorless, tool mark at lower part of applied handle..... **250.00**
- 10-3/4" h, colorless, McKearin GV-17 .... **420.00**

Plate
- 5-3/8" d, colorless, folded rim, plain base, pontil **150.00**
- 9-1/4" d, colorless, sunburst and diamond pattern, attributed to Boston & Sandwich Glass Co., Sandwich, MA, 1840...... **115.00**

Salt, master
- Basket shape, colorless **120.00**
- Galleried rim, rayed base, sapphire blue, 2-1/2" h.......... **1,600.00**
- Hollow stem and base, colorless, pontil **575.00**
- Rayed and ringed base, purple blue, pontil, 2-1/4" h **750.00**

Salt shaker
- 4-5/8" h, colorless, pontil base, orig metal cap **75.00**
- 5" h, colorless, sheared lip, orig metal cap and pontil **75.00**

Sugar, 2-1/2" h, 5" d, brilliant sapphire blue, rolled flanged lip, solid applied base with pontil attributed to Boston & Sandwich, c1820, McKearin GI-29 .... **3,250.00**

Toddy plate, 4-1/4" d, colorless, folded rim, rayed base, pontil **265.00**

Toilet water bottle
- 5-3/4" h, cobalt blue, tam-o-shanter cap.......... **300.00**
- 6-5/8" h, yellow green, tapering ovoid, plain base, pontil, orig matching stopper, Toilet Water Bottle, McKearin GI-3, type II **2,650.00**
- 6-3/4" h, deep sapphire blue, tooled flared mouth, period tam-o-shanter stopper, pontil scar, some light int. residue near base **180.00**
- 6-3/4" h, violet, flared lip, smooth base, period tam-o-shanter stopper.......... **650.00**

Tumbler
- 3-3/8" h, colorless, barrel form, tooled rim, pontil scar, attributed to Keene Marlboro Glassworks, Keene, NH, 1820-40, McKearin GIII-14 .... **190.00**
- 4-5/8" h, colorless, sheared rim, pontil scar, unlisted, similar to McKearin GV-5.......... **110.00**
- 5-5/8" h, colorless, sheared rim, pontil scar, attributed to Boston and Sandwich, McKearin GII-18 .... **130.00**
- 6-1/4" h, colorless, McKearin GII-19 .... **155.00**

Vase, 9" h, colorless, engraved flowers, leaves, and berries, McKearin GV-21 .... **7,500.00**

Vinegar bottle, 6-3/4" h, cobalt blue, ribbed, orig stopper, McKearin GI-7 .... **285.00**

Whiskey taster
- 1-5/8" h, colorless, ringed base, pontil **200.00**
- 2-3/8" h, colorless, applied handle, McKearin GII-18.......... **285.00**

Bohemian Glass

History: The once independent country of Bohemia, now a part of the Czech Republic, produced a variety of fine glassware: etched, cut, overlay, and colored. Glass production has been recorded there as early as the fourteenth and fifteenth centuries. Wheel-cutting techniques were practiced in the sixteenth century. By the mid-nineteenth century, coal replaced wood as fuel and many new factories sprang up. Beautiful examples of exquisite cutting and engraved portraits were skillfully crafted. Bohemian glassware first appeared in America in the early 1820s and continues to be exported to the U.S. today.

Bohemia is known for its "flashed" glass that was produced in the familiar ruby color, as well as in amber, green, blue, and black. Common patterns include Deer and Castle, Deer and Pine Tree, and Vintage.

Most of the Bohemian glass encountered in today's market is from 1875 to 1900. Bohemian glassware was carried around the world by travelers and salesmen. Engravers often decorated pieces to fill the demand of this ground of eager buyers and tailored their decorations to fit the tastes and desires of the buyers. Bohemian-type glass also was made in England, Switzerland, and Germany.

References: Brigitte Klesse and Hans Mayr, *European Glass from 1500-1800, The Ernesto Wolf Collection*, Kremayr & Scheriau, 1987; Sylvia Petrova and Jean-Luc Olivie (eds.), *Bohemian Glass*, Abrams, 1990; Robert and Deborah Truitt, *Collectible Bohemian Glass*, R & D Glass, 1995; —, *Mary Gregory Glassware, 1880-1990*, R & D Glass, 1992, 1998 value update; Kenneth Wilson, *American Glass 1760-1930: The Toledo Museum of Art, Volume I, Volume II*, Hudson Hills Press and The Toledo Museum of Art, 1994.

Reproduction Alert.

Atomizer, 5-3/4" h, broad-shouldered blue glass vessel, facet cut at shoulder to reveal int. silvered glass, enamel dec with white sprays of flowers, gilt highlights, wear to gilt **200.00**

Beaker

4-1/2" h, blue and white overlay, arched panels with gilt ivy and stylized foliage on oval white overlay, flaring base, mid-19th C **225.00**

4-1/2" h, blue and white overlay, multicolored spring floral bouquet on oval white overlay, gilt foliate, arched panels, mid to late 19th C **250.00**

4-1/2" h, colorless, continuous scene of hunters in landscape, band of flowering branches **350.00**

4-5/8" h, waisted cylindrical, multicolored enameled morning glories between cut roundels, pink overlay, white ground **600.00**

4-3/4" h, green flashed, circular and oval cut windows, multicolored enameled flowers, gilt lines **220.00**

4-3/4" h, white overlay, multicolored enameled peasant girl, oval cartouche edged with gilt ivy, loose bouquet of flowers on reverse **450.00**

5" h, cobalt blue, white enameled floral and leaf design, gold accents, cobalt rigaree base trim, J. and L. Lobmeyr, monogram logo enameled on polished pontil, minor rubs to gold **250.00**

5" h, pink flashed opaque, cut stylized leaves and drapery, enamel and gilt flowering branches, flaring base, late 19th C **475.00**

5-18" h, blue and white overlay, rect panel engraved with stag landscape, oval roundels, named scenes, gilt highlights, late 19th C **300.00**

5-1/4" h, white on amethyst overlay, quatrefoil and circular cut windows, painted trailing roses **250.00**

5-1/2" h, amber and ruby flashed, alternating panels engraved with cornucopia, flowers, beehive, and urn, cut panels, scalloped foot **225.00**

5-1/2" h, amber flashed, engraved, animals and building, C scroll panels, flared foot, c1860 . **125.00**

5-3/4" h, flared, colorless, allover pattern of cut circles each containing finely painted ornately blue, and yellow flowers, flashed amber yellow around each circle with black tracery, amber flashed pedestal, black flashed circular base, c1880 . . . . **950.00**

Bonboniere and undertray, cov, 10-1/2" h, allover painted floral garland dec, pear form finial **1,400.00**

Bottle

9-1/4" h, emerald green, gold leaf dec, pr **225.00**

12-1/4" h, blue cut to clear, frosted leaf dec **450.00**

Bowl

3" d, 1-3/4" h, Lityalin, three rows of honeycomb cutting, mottled brown, designed to simulate polished agate, Frederich Eggerman, c1935 . . . . **395.00**

6-1/2" d, 5-1/2" h, cov, translucent crystal ground, studio enameled gold, red, blue, and green foliate elements, delicate black outline, dec repeated on cov and base, in the manner of Steinschonau **635.00**

9-1/2" d, 3" h, amethyst cut to clear, copper wheel engraved forest scene with deer **150.00**

12-1/2" d, double cut overlay, cobalt blue cut to clear **265.00**

Bowl, footed, 10 panels, shaped top, leaf and grape design, 3-1/8" d, 2" h, **$35.**

Bowl, cov, 7-3/8" d, double domed cov, ruby flashed, etched continuous band of rose vines, late 19th/early 20th C **125.00**

Box, cov

3-1/2" d, domed lid, ruby flashed, Vintage pattern, engraved clear and frosted grape clusters and vines, gilt brass fittings **165.00**

3-3/4" d, domed lid, ruby flashed, engraved clear and frosted buildings, scrolling foliate bands, brass fittings **185.00**

Bud vase

6" h, small rim on elongated neck, bulbous body, colorless glass with overall gold irid, polished pontil **115.00**

7-1/2" h, shaded green to pink stem, applied petal ribbon, three blown-out spherical bulbs. . **135.00**

Butter dish, cov, enameled white cut to red, floral and figural cartouches on gilt foliate dec ground **700.00**

Castor set, 18" h, three ruby cut to colorless bottles, matching steeple-shaped stoppers, silver plated metal holder **350.00**

Celery tray, ruby flashed, Deer and Castle pattern, clear and frosted **110.00**

Center bowl

9" d, 11-1/2" h, ribbed and ruffled green irid bowl, elaborate metal base with three cherubs playing flutes **525.00**

9-1/2" d, 3-3/4" h, transparent citron-green encasing seven dark red centered purple-aubergine pad blossoms with trailing stems, attributed to Harbach **325.00**

Cologne bottle, 5" h, cobalt blue, tiered body dec, white and gold flowers and scrolls **175.00**

Compote

6-1/2" d, 3-1/2" h, cranberry, irid int. **290.00**

7" d, amber flashed, cut leaf and floral dec, green band at top, pedestal base **125.00**

7-3/4" h, enameled white cut to red, floral and figural cartouches on gilt foliate dec ground **800.00**

9-1/2" d, 6-1/2" h, amber flashed, Deer and Castle pattern, engraved, clear and frosted animals, castle, and trees **195.00**

Condiment set, Deer and Tree, amber flashed.................... **285.00**

Console set, 10" d bowl, ruby flashed, cut back jumping stag and cartouche, matching candlesticks **275.00**

Cordial glasses, 4-3/8" h, quatrefoil-shaped bowl, gilt rim, pale pink band, slender stem enameled with overlapping leaf pattern, extending to base of bowl, spreading foot, gilt accents, Lobmeyr, 20th C, price for set of six **1,265.00**

Cordial set

8" h cordial decanter with faceted colorless glass stopper, faceted amethyst cased to colorless glass exterior, six 2" h octagonal faceted cordials, c1925, minor nicks and flakes **375.00**

Cruet, ruby stained, etched stag decoration, original stained bulbous stopper, applied clear handle, **$115.**

9" h cordial decanter with faceted colorless glass stopper, topaz, six 2" h rect faceted cordials, c1925, minor nicks and flakes **230.00**

Cream pitcher and sugar, 3-1/4" h x 3-1/4" d cream pitcher, 2-1/4" h x 3-1/2" sugar, Schwarzlot, three hollow bun feet on each, pitcher dec by country scene of well-dressed couple, nobleman with walking stick, wandering troubadour playing mandolin, sugar dec with panoramic rustic scene, including three peasants, villages, and castles, both sigh Lobmeyer signature **1,500.00**

Cruet

Amber cut to clear, floral arrangement intaglio carved on ruby flashed ground of three oval panels with carved frames of floral swags, five cut-to-clear panels at neck, three embellished with gold scrolls, all edged in brilliant gold, 16 decorative panels edged in gold, base and stopper both sgd "4" **750.00**

Iridescent purple over amber, applied threading, polished pontil **110.00**

Decanter

8-1/4" h, octagonal, triple ringed neck, windows engraved with names scenes of Prague on alternating pink and blue flashed areas, yellow flashed ground, enameled black foliage.... **950.00**

11" h, cobalt blue, enameled magnolia branch and garden flowers, stopper serves as shot glass, gold on stopper worn **200.00**

14-3/4" h, octagonal, clear with greenish tint, engraved forest and deer scene, orig stopper... **100.00**

15-1/2" h, ruby cut to clear, geese dec, cut stopper **150.00**

Decanter set

14" h x 4-1/4" w decanter, six 5" h x 2" goblets, ruby cut to clear, ovoid body, cut indentations on slender neck, pinwheel and other cuttings **225.00**

16-1/4" h decanter, four 6-3/4" h goblets, cased ruby red, long neck with elongated cut panels with gilt edge, gilt tracery on ruby panels, border of 12 semi-circles at top and bottom, six multicolored painted circular cartouches with flowers, gilt tracery, pointed stopper with six cut elongated petal shapes with gilt dec, long stemmed goblets with found bowl with ruby red border, cut border of semi-circles, gilt tracery, cut six-sided stem, c1880 ... **1,850.00**

Decanter, cobalt blue, enameled magnolia branch and garden flowers, stopper serves as shot glass, gold on stopper worn, 11" h, **$200.** *Photo courtesy of Cincinnati Art Galleries.*

Dish, cov, 5-3/4" d, 3-3/4" h, cylindrical, green glass overlaid in opaque white, engraved oval facets in zig-zag band, enamel dec with red and blue florets, gilded highlights, polished pontil in center of facet-cut base, conforming lid with circular knob, c1920, minor wear **375.00**

Dresser jar, cov, 4-1/2" d, ovoid, ruby flashed, etched running deer and rococo cartouches, late 19th/early 20th C, price for pr **200.00**

Flask, 6" l, 3-1/2" w, turquoise crackle glass body, enameled blue and white floral dec, orig cork and fittings, c1890 ....**1,500.00**

Flip glass, 6" h, 6" d, colorless, cut, engraved forest scene with fox and birds **125.00**

Goblet

5" h, amber overlay, cut and frosted forest scenes, early 20th C . **95.00**

5-1/2" h, ruby flashed, engraved stag, rocky landscape, enameled stylized foliage and flowers, flaring base **220.00**

6-1/4" h, Annagel, hexagonal bowl, raised enameled bosses, gilt

named scenes, conforming knop and petal base 425.00
6-3/4" h, white and cranberry overlay, thistle form bowl, six teardrop panels alternately enameled with floral bouquets and cut with blocks of diamonds, faceted knob and spreading scalloped foot, gilt trim 600.00
7" h, ruby cut to clear, stag and foliate dec, 12-pc set 750.00
7" h, white ground, fruit and floral dec, 12-pc set 950.00
8-1/2" h, amethyst cut to clear, early 20th C 40.00

Jar, cov
5" h, colorless crystal body overlaid in bright orange, cut facets in geometric motif, applied faceted finials, pr 230.00
6" h, quatraform, green, maroon-red threading, metal rim, swing bail handle and cover 250.00
7" h, barrel shape, bands of clear engraving, red satin discs, barrel finial 165.00

Jug, 8-1/4" h, dark olive green spherical body, irid pulled feather silvery luster, applied offset twisted basket handle, raised pedestal foot, berry prunt at pontil 1,265.00

Lamp, 25" h, candlestick type, amber overlay, cut and frosted foliate panels, pr 500.00

Mantel lusters, pr, 14-1/4" h, slender trumpet form, everted rim hung with prisms, single knopped trumpet foot, white cased cut to clear, acanthus leaves at foot, roundels at rim, enamel dec busts of children and floral bouquets, gilt accents, price for pr 1,840.00

Mug, 6" h, ruby flashed, engraved castle and trees, applied clear handle, sgd "Volmer, 1893" 95.00

Nappy, 5" d, colorless shading to amber, enameled daisy dec, applied ring handle 50.00

Perfume bottle, 7" h, ruby flashed, Deer and Castle, clear and frosted, gold dec 120.00

Pitcher, 4-3/4" h, colorless body, engraved, gilded, and silvered foliate dec, translucent enamel ground, polished pontil, loop handle, early 20th C 450.00

Pokal, cov, 21-1/2" h, amber cut to colorless, 19th C. 500.00

Powder box, 4-1/4" d, round, straight sides, flat top, ruby flashed, etched cov with leaping stag, forest setting,

Finger bowls, Vintage pattern, ruby stained, **$75.**

landscape and birds on sides, clear base. 120.00

Punch set, 11" h, 11-1/2" d tray, curved oval bow, undertray, frosted clear glass, red glass jewels as centers of gold enameled swags and medallions, bowl elaborately engraved, dated 1875 and relating to Carl Buschbeck 345.00

Rose bowl, 7" d, 4" h, green irid, molded swirled organic elements, trifid pewter base rim. 245.00

Scent bottle, 10" h, 5" d, cased cobalt blue, finely cut, gilt and beige floral and foliage dec on top two tiers, gilt and beige baskets and roses on base tier, gilt and beige floral and foliage dec on matching stopper, star cut bottom, pointed stopper, c1840 . . . . . . 1,800.00

Spill vase, 6-3/8" h, overlay, cut white to cranberry, 19th C, very minor chips, pr 420.00

Stein
4-1/2" h, 2-3/4" d, ruby flashed, engraved dog and deer in forest, "Souvenir de Luchon" on front, pewter mounts 250.00
6-1/2" h, 3" d, ruby flashed, engraved cathedral panels, leaves, and scrolls, pewter mounts, ruby inset lid. 320.00

Sugar shaker, ruby flashed, Bird and Castle pattern, clear and forted . 90.00

Teapot, 11" w, cranberry cut to clear, panels of flowers, gilt spout and handle 220.00

Tray, 8-1/2" l, 2" h, oblong colorless body, pedestal foot, gold and turquoise dec, J & L Lobmeyer mark at center 575.00

Tumbler
4" h, colorless, each dec with costumed boy and girl in different outdoor setting, J & L Lobmeyer mark on base, eight-pc set 1,100.00
4" h, ruby flashed, cut design, gold dec, four-pc set 150.00
4-1/4" h, colorless, leaded, enameled German inscription, florals, heart, two hands shaking, dated 1727, pontil scar . . . 550.00

Urn, 7" h, 3-1/8" w at top, colorless glass over layer of vaseline and black flash, engraved border at top, three engraved oval panels with wheat design between them, one panel with girl with watering can in garden, other with house and trees, third with church and trees, black pedestal base with engraved diamond design, oval petal design on foot, c1880 . . . . . . 1,475.00

Vase
3-1/4" h, amethyst, oil-spot dec, polished rim 100.00
5" h, green irid double bulbed body, vertical stripes interspersed with round spots, allover irid, molded base, top rim smoothed . . . 345.00
5-1/4" h, brilliant cobalt blue irid oval body, copper overlay cut in Secessionist motif, smooth base 425.00
5-1/4" h, colorless ground, seven tooled scallops at rim, yellow and maroon swirls, irid dec, attributed to Kralik 375.00
5-1/4" h, mold blown pinched fishbowl sphere, faintly opal persuasion crackled as water, enamel painted fish, water lilies, aquatic plants, attributed to Moser 345.00
5-3/4" h, lemon yellow oval body, green irid pulled feather motif, polished pontil. 1,035.00

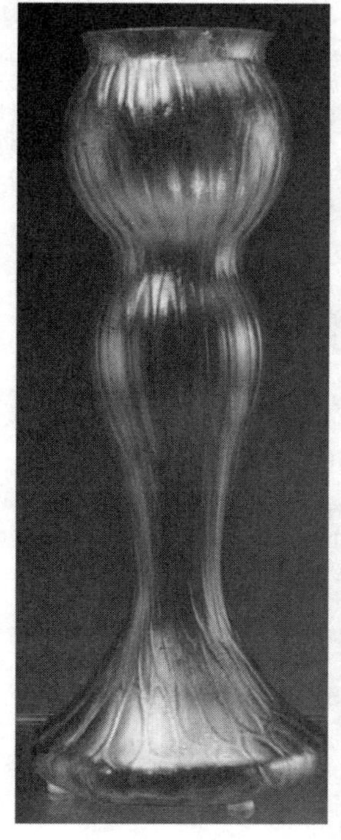

Vase, gold iridescent, elongated teardrop pattern, polished rim, 12" h, **$215.** *Photo courtesy of David Rago Auctions.*

6" h, colorless pinched oval, flared and folded rim, brick red, white, and burgundy spots, foliate etching on int. surface **500.00**

6" h, six ruffle rim, conical body, applied pedestal foot, gold irid int., amber spotted surface, polished base **290.00**

6-3/4" h, amber etched to clear, deer and forest dec **135.00**

7" h, Neptune, green irid, polished rim **100.00**

7" h, green, oil-spot dec, polished rim, blown from top....... **100.00**

7" h, raised trefoil rim over shoulder flaring to circular base, amethyst body dec with broad winding bands of gold oil spot irid, polished pontil.................. **230.00**

7-1/2" h, flattened rim, ovoid form, transparent ruby overlay on colorless glass, freeform lineal gilt dec, eight round facets around shoulder, cut fluted sides, star-cut base, price for pr **250.00**

8-1/2" h, tricorn rim, black basalt surface, intaglio carved lilies and buds, greenish irid cast, incised "C" inside "G" within square for Carl Goldberg........... **325.00**

8-3/4" h, striated blue, green, burgundy-red oval cased to opal body lined in turquoise blue, gilt enamel medallions centered by red glass jewels **320.00**

Beaker, ruby flashed, engraved floral and scrolls decoration, flared foot, c. 1860, **$125.**

9" h, opaque base with gold oil-spot dec coming up from base, polished rim............. **150.00**

9-1/4" h, trumpet form, ruby cut to clear, allover rose and foliate dec **75.00**

9-1/4" h, 3-1/2" d, ovoid body, slender neck, widening at top, white overlay cut to ruby, gold dec on center panels, painted floral sprays on white ground, painted florals circling near top and bottom **150.00**

9-1/2" h, burgundy red oval body cased with opal white, gilded scroll and swag dec, opal, green, and turquoise glass beaded highlights **435.00**

9-1/2" h, satin finish, enameled medallion of roses........ **115.00**

9-1/2" h, Silverina.......... **175.00**

9-3/4" h, 4-3/4" w at top, trumpet shape, cased cranberry, scalloped eight-section cut top edge, ivory and gold enameled intertwined scroll design around top and base in each section, eight cut to clear elongated arches extend from top to base, notched and scalloped base, c1840 .... **1,275.00**

10" h, brilliant cobalt blue body, irid blue oil-spot motif, applied ribbed bright blue handles, polished pontil **865.00**

10" h, green, oil-spot, lightly scalloped rim, broken pontil **175.00**

10" h, transparent gray glass, zig-zag rim dec with gilt trim, ovoid vessel dec with painted floral and geometric design, applied gilt raspberry pulled prunts at shoulder, tapering to ftd base, base marked "2," early 20th C, wear to base and gilt **115.00**

10-1/4" h, emerald green textured ground, gold iris and bud dec, detailed wheel cuttings.... **200.00**

10-1/2" h, irid smooth rose red surface, tapered vessel with four integrated solid supports, polished pontil **490.00**

10-1/2" h, Neptune, polished rim, rubena verde............ **230.00**

10-1/2" h, ocean wave design, variegated red paperweight ground................. **195.00**

11" h, amethyst, oilspot dec, polished rim............. **195.00**

11" h, overlay, gold enameled white cut to cranberry, elongated windows **275.00**

11-1/2" h, Neptune, irid cranberry, finished rim............. **175.00**

12" h, irid gold, elongated teardrop pattern, polished rim **210.00**

13" h, flared quatraform tooled rim, bulbous pinched base, irid dark red body, pulled green and white dec, polished pontil **450.00**

Whiskey glass, 3-1/4" h, clear, engraved, early 19th C, pr **250.00**

Bottles

History: Bottle collecting has been an important segment of the antiques and collectibles hobby for generations. Many bottle collectors specialize in one type of bottle, one manufacturer, or a specific color. Some bottle collectors still practice the age-old tradition of digging to find their treasures. Many collectors prefer pristine examples and haunt antiques shops, malls, and shows, to find additions to their collections. Bottle shows, often sponsored by local clubs, are a treat for bottle collectors, as they can browse tables full of bottles plus the ancillary collectibles, such as trade cards, advertisements, and other associated collectibles.

Cosmetic bottles held special creams, oils, and cosmetics designed to enhance the beauty of the user. Some also claimed, especially on their colorful labels, to cure or provide relief from common ailments.

A number of household items, e.g., cleaning fluids and polishes, required glass storage containers. Many are collected for their fine lithographed labels. Others are collected because of the rainbow of colors in which they were manufactured.

Baby and nursing bottles, used to feed the young and sickly, were a great help to the housewife because of their graduated measure markings, replaceable nipples, and the ease with which they could be cleaned, sterilized, and reused.

Bitters, a "remedy" made from natural herbs and other mixtures with an alcohol base, often was viewed as the universal cure-all. The names given to various bitters mixtures were imaginative, though the bitters seldom cured what their makers claimed. The manufacturers of bitters needed a way to sell and advertise their products. They designed bottles in many shapes, sizes, and colors to attract the buyer. During the Civil War, a tax was levied on alcoholic beverages. Since bitters were identified as medicines, they were exempt from this tax. The alcoholic content was never mentioned. In 1907, when the Pure Foods Regulations went into effect, "an honest statement of content on every label" put most of the manufacturers out of business.

Medicine bottles contained "medicines" of all kinds, from bitters and elixirs to snakebite remedies to serious medicines. These small bottles make very interesting collectibles as their claims rival the best of today's Madison Avenue advertising executives.

Milk bottles have been a favorite with collectors for many years. Some specialize in a particular type of milk bottle, i.e., cream top, while others devote their collection to bottles from a specific geographic area. Milk bottles are being reproduced; most, by use of blank bottles, then being processed with color

slogans, designs, and fictitious farms. Reproduction Elsie the Borden's popular cow, Hopalong Cassidy, and Disney characters have crept into the market. The process has improved and some are virtually undetectable, except to the serious collector. A low price for a very unusual bottle may be a tip off.

Mineral water bottles contained water from a natural spring. Spring water was favored by health-conscious people between the 1850s and 1900s.

Soda bottles, beer bottles, and other popular drink bottles carried our favorite beverages from the manufacturers to the stores' or the distributors' shelves. Painted labels and a myriad of colors attract today's collectors.

References: Joseph K. Baldwin, *Collector's Guide To Patent and Proprietary Medicine Bottles of the Nineteenth Century,* Thomas Nelson, 1973; William E. Covill, *Ink Bottles and Ink Wells,* William S. Sullwold Publishing, 1971; Jeffrey L. Giarde, *Glass Milk Bottles: Their Makers and Marks,* printed by author; Donald E. Lord, *California Milks,* published by author; Peck and Audie Markota, *Western Blob Top Soda and Mineral Bottles,* 2nd ed., published by authors, 1994; George S. and Helen McKearin, *American Glass,* reprint, Crown Publishers, 1941, 1948; Diane Ostrander, *Guide to American Nursing Bottles,* 1984, revised ed. by American Collectors of Infant Feeders, 1992; Carlyn Ring and W. C. Ham, *Bitters Bottles,* published by authors, 1998; Dick Roller (comp.), *Indiana Glass Factories Notes,* Acorn Press, 1994; John Tutton, *Udderly Delightful, Udderly Fantastic, and Udderly Beautiful,* published by author; Jeff Wichmann, *Antique Western Bitter Bottles,* Pacific Glass Books, 1999; —, *The Best of the West Antique Western Bitters Bottles,* Pacific Glass Books, 1999; Kenneth Wilson, *American Glass 1760-1930: The Toledo Museum of Art, Volume I, Volume II,* Hudson Hills Press and The Toledo Museum of Art, 1994.

Periodicals: *Antique Bottle and Glass Collector,* P.O. Box 180, East Greenville, PA 18041, http://www.glswrk-auction.com; *Bottles & Bygones,* 30 Brabant Rd, Cheadle Hulme, Cheadle, Cheshire Sk8 7AU, U.K., *British Bottle Review,* B. B. R. Publishing, Elsecar Heritage Center, Nr Barnsley, South Yorks, S74 8HJ U.K., *Glen Poch's Bottle Collecting Newsletter,* 1537 Silver Strand, Palatine, IL 60074, http://www.antiquebottles.com; *Hawaii Bottle Museum News,* P.O. Box 25152, Honolulu, Hawaii 96825; *Miniature Bottle Collector,* P.O. Box 2161, Pals Verdes Peninsula, CA 90274-8161, http://www.bottlecollecting.com; *The Bitters Report,* P.O. Box 1253, Bunnell, FL 32110.

Collectors' Clubs: American Collectors of Infant Feeders, 5161 W. 59th St., Indianapolis, IN 46254-1107; Antique Bottle & Collectibles Club, P.O. Box 1061, Verdi, NV 89439; Antique Bottle Club of Northern Illinois, 1537 Silver Strand, Palatine, IL 60074; Antique Poison Bottle Collectors Assoc., 312 Summer Lane, Huddleston, VA 24104; Apple Valley Bottle Collectors Club, 3015 Northwestern Pike, Winchester, VA 22603-3825; Baltimore Antique Bottle Club, P.O. Box 36061, Towson, MD 21286-6061; Capital Region Antique Bottle & Insulator Club, 3363 Guilderland Ave., Apt 3, Schenectady, NY 12306-1820; Delmarva Antique Bottle Club, 57 Lakewood Dr., Lewes, DE 19958; Early Tennessee Bottle & Collectibles Society, 220 N. Carter School Rd, Straw Plains, TN 37871-1237; Empire State Bottle Collectors Assoc., 115 Marshia Ave., North Syracuse, NY 13212; Federation of Historical Bottle Collectors, Inc., 2230 Toub St., Ramona, CA 92065; First Chicago Bottle Club, P.O. Box A3382, Chicago, IL 60690; 49'er Historical Bottle Club, P.O. Box 561, Penryn, CA 95663; Forks of the Delaware Bottle Collectors Assoc., 20 Cambridge Place, Catasauqua, PA 18032; Genessee Valley Bottle Collectors Assoc., 17 Fifth Ave., Fairport, NY 14450-1311; Historical Bottle Diggers of Virginia, 242 E. Grattan St., Harrisburg, VA 22801; Hudson Valley Antique Bottle Club, 6 Columbus Ave., Cornwall on Hudson, NY, 12520; Huron Valley Antique Bottle & Insulator Club, 2475 W. Walton Blvd., Waterford, MI 48329-4435; Jersey Shore Bottle Club, P.O. Box 995, Toms River, NY 08754; Las Vegas Antique Bottle & Collectibles Club, 5895 Duneville St., Las Vegas, NV 89118; Little Rhody Bottle Club, http://www.littlerhodybottleclub.com; Middle Tennessee Bottle & Collector's Club, 1750 Keyes Rd, Greenbrier, TN 37073; Midwest Antique Fruit Jar & Bottle Club, P.O. Box 38, Flat Rock, IN 47234-5660; National Assoc. of Milk Bottle Collectors, 4 Ox Bow Rd, Westport, CT 06880-2602; New England Antique Bottle Club, 120 Commonwealth Rd, Lynn, MA 01904; New Mexico Historical Bottle Society, 3256 c/s, Socorro, NM 87801; North Jersey Antique Bottle Collectors Assoc., 117 Lincoln Place, Waldwick, NJ 07463-2114; North Star Historical Bottle Assoc., 3308 32nd Ave. S, Minneapolis, MN 55406-2015; Ohio Bottle Club, 7126 12th St., Minerva, OH 44657; Pennsylvania Bottle Collector's Assoc., 251 Eastland Ave., York, PA 17402-1105; Pittsburgh Antique Bottle Club, 650 Hood School Road, Indiana, PA 15701; Potomac Bottle Club, 4028 Williamsburg Court, Fairfax, VA 22032-1139; Raleigh Bottle Club, P.O. Box 13726, Durham, NC 27709; Richmond Area Bottle Collectors, 4718 Kyloe Lane, Moseley, VA 23120; San Bernardino County Historical Bottle and Collectible Club, 22853 DeBerry, Grand Terrace, CA 92313; San Jose Antique Bottle Collectors Assoc., P.O. Box 5432, San Jose, CA 95159; Sarasota-Manatee Antique Bottle Collectors Assoc., P.O. Box 3105; Sarasota, FL 34230-3105; Southeastern Antique Bottle Club, 143 Scatterfoot Drive, Peachtree City, GA 30269-1853; Yankee Bottle Club, 382 Court St., Keene, NH 03431.

Museums: Billings Farm Museum, Woodstock, VT; Hawaii Bottle Museum, Honolulu, HI; National Bottle Museum, Ballston Spa, NY; National Bottle Museum, Richmond, Surrey, England; Old Bottle Museum, Salem, NJ; Southwest Dairy Museum, Arlington, TX.

Baby and nursing

Acme, clear, lay-down, emb 65.00
Baby's Delight 45.00
Brockway Glass #862 . . . . 10.00
Bunny, Anchor Hocking 16.00
Bunny, Hazel Atlas 15.50
Cala Nurser, oval, clear, emb, ring on neck, 7-1/8" h. 8.00
Cat, Anchor Hocking. 25.00
Cats and kittens, enamel dec with oz measurements. 21.50
Comfy, bottle with orig nipple . . . 15.00
Dominion Glass Co., Canada, 8 oz, narrow mouth, orig filled with Vanilla Extract from Pure Standard Products, orig label, nursery rhyme, "I had a little hobby horse," imp image of little boy riding rocking horse, 1940s 15.00
Dr. Pepper 12.00
Embossed baby, late 1940s 10.00
Empire Nursing Bottle, bent neck, 6-1/2" h 50.00
Evenflo, 3-1/8" h 20.00
Fire King, sapphire blue
- 4 oz 20.00
- 8 oz 60.00
- Binky's nip cap 210.00
- Steri-Seal nipple cover, colorless, emb on cover 25.00

Griptight, banana shape, hole at both ends, colorless, emb name 25.00
Hailwoods Graduated Feeding Bottle, aqua, applied top, flattened bladder shape, 2" neck, markings up to 8 oz on back, front emb with name, 7" h. . 75.00
Happy Baby 12.00
Hygeia, adv on panels. 15.00
Hygienic Feeder, emb, open on both ends 30.00
Little Folk 36.00
Manx Feeding Bottle, bulbous, clear, tooled sq collar, emb "Patent July 4, 1876," 3" h 200.00
Marguerite Feeding Bottle, inside screw, daisy on top 35.00
Mother's Comfort, clear, turtle type 25.00
Nonpareil Nurser, aqua, 5-1/2" h 20.00
Nursery Rhyme, enameled Jack and Jill 15.00
Ovale Nurser, Non-Rolling, Whitall Tatum & Co., 6 oz, applied lip, narrow mouth 10.00
Pepsi, adv. 1994 limited edition. . . 4.00
Plain, 4 oz, "K" inside shield mark 16.00
Pottstown, PA, dairy giveaway, set of five bottles, each enameled with nursery rhyme, one with bank top, other with plastic closure, nipple, yellow and blue congratulations box, never used 25.00
Pyrex, 4 oz, narrow mouth, orig cardboard sleeve 12.00
Pyrex, 8 oz, air vent feature, six-sided, narrow top, pink and blue graphics, orig box 20.00
Sure Feed Ltd. Carfidd, flat turtle shape, long neck, colorless, emb on top 40.00
Sweet Babee Nurser, colorless, emb "Easy Clean, Pat'd May 3, 1910" . 15.00

Teddy's Pet, Peaceful Nights, colorless, emb, turtle shape, 4 oz **70.00**

The Hygienic Feeder, banana shape, hole at both ends, colorless, emb name **25.00**

Tuffy Kap, nipple cov, colorless, emb "Tuffy KAP U.S.A." around cap, "B" in circle on flat top **10.00**

Vitaflo, OH **4.50**

Jones Brewery, Smithton, Pa., "Esquire," 7 oz. **$15.**

Beer

Augusta Brewing Co., Augusta, CA, aqua, painted label, 7" h **15.00**

Buffalo Brewing Co., Sacramento, Cal, dark amber, pint, emb pattern. . . **45.00**

Cal Bottling Co., Export Beer, SF, amber, half pint, tooled top **12.00**

Callie & Co. Limited, emb dog's head, St. Helen's below center, dark green, ring-type blob top, 8-1/4" h **20.00**

Celery Beer, Keller Candy Company Distributors, Oakland, Cal, amber, quart, tooled top **110.00**

Central Brand Extra Lager Beer, aqua, paper label, 9-1/2" h **8.00**

Chattachoochee Brewing Co., Brownsville, AL, aqua, emb, 9-1/2" h **10.00**

Cumberland Brew Co., Cumberland, MD, amber. **10.00**

Etna Brewery, Etna Mills, amber, half pint. **25.00**

Excelsior, aqua, 9-1/4" h. **18.00**

Fredericksburg Bottling Co., green, pint, applied top **55.00**

Germania Brewing Co., aqua, emb, 7-1/2" h **15.00**

Gold Edge Bottling Works, J. F. Deininger Vallejo, amber, emb pattern, generic porcelain stopper. **45.00**

Gold Edge Bottling Works, J. F. Deininger Vallejo, aqua, few scratches **35.00**

Grand Prize Beer, Gulf Brewing Co., Houston, colorless, crown top, paper label, 9" h **10.00**

Hand Brew Co., Pawtucket, RI, aqua **15.00**

H. A. Peterson, Watsonville, Cal, medium amber, quart, scratch or two **70.00**

Honolulu B & M Co., Ltd., Honolulu, H.T., light aqua, pint, crown top . . **45.00**

Honolulu Brewing Co., Honolulu, H.T., light aqua, quart, c1890, few light scratches **80.00**

Iroquois, Buffalo, emb Indian's head, amber **12.00**

John Tons, Stockton, Cal, brilliant yellow-amber, quart, JT monogram **110.00**

John Wieland's Export Beer, SF, red-amber, half pint **35.00**

Los Angeles Brew Co., amber, emb eagle and shield, quart, some interior stain **35.00**

National Brewing Co., Baltimore, amber, emb eagle, blob top. **20.00**

P. B. Milwaukee, brilliant golden amber, pint, tooled top **25.00**

Piel Bros., East New York Brewery, fancy emb logo, aqua **20.00**

Primo Beer, light aqua. **45.00**

Proll Bottling Works, U.S. Lager, SF Cal, medium amber, quart, orig porcelain stopper **330.00**

Property of Frey & Co., San Rafael, medium amber, quart, generic porcelain stopper **55.00**

Richmond Bottling Works, amber, half pint, North Star porcelain stopper **25.00**

Schlitz Brewing Co., amber, painted label, 9-1/2" h **10.00**

Scorborough and Whitby Breweries Crystalis Waters, amber, decorative fountain, pint, bulbous applied top **35.00**

Sebastapol Bottling Works, Cal, amber, pint, tooled top **35.00**

Southern Brewing Co., green, paper label, 9-1/2" h **5.00**

Standard Bottling Co., SF, red-amber, pint, tooled top, very light staining **35.00**

St. Louis Bottling Co., M.C.G. & B. Vallejo, Cal, medium amber, pint, tooled top **35.00**

Sunset Bottling Co., San Francisco, CA, light to medium golden amber, quart, monogram, few scratches . **45.00**

Grolsch Lager Beer, Holland, 15.9 fluid oz, **$20.**

Unmarked, made for Adolphus Busch Company-Bellville, IL, cobalt blue, pint, applied top, recently cleaned, few scratches remaining **100.00**

U.S. Bottling Co., John Fauser & Co., San Francisco, red amber, pint, tooled top **35.00**

Wieland's Little Pop, Cal Bottling, colorless, etched monogram, slight stain. **25.00**

Wm Schmiel, San Jose, California, medium amber, quart, orig porcelain stopper **55.00**

Wonder Bottling Co., W. Noething, Sacramento, Cal, amber, pint, tooled top **45.00**

Beverage

A. M. Binninger & Co., No. 19 Broad St., NY, Old London Jockey Gin, red-amber, quart, sq, large applied top, smooth base **415.00**

A Merry Christmas/Corking Good Stuff/Happy New Year, bald headed man sealing bottle marked "1891 Rye," colorless with brown, yellow, blue and flesh tone colored label under glass, ground mouth, screw threads, metal cap, smooth base, half pint. . . . **700.00**

Arny & Shinn, Georgetown, D. C., "This Bottle Is Never Sold," soda water, squat cylindrical, yellow ground, applied heavy collared mouth, smooth base, half pint, professionally cleaned **150.00**

Bay Rum, 11-1/4" h, amethyst, blown molded, paneled body, partial label, burst bubble, mold imperfections **375.00**

Binninger's Regulator, 19 Broad St., New York, brilliant golden-amber, clock face, emb pattern, applied top, open pontil, 1-1/2 moon shaped slug of glass, numerous bubbles and other irregularities **70.00**

Cole & Southey Washington DC, soda water, squat cylindrical, aquamarine, applied sloping collared mouth with ring, smooth base, half pint, professionally cleaned **110.00**

Drink Howel's Original Orange-Julep, 12" h, cylindrical, colorless, white, gold, red, and yellow orange label under glass, sheared mouth, metal cap, smooth base, America, 1880-90 **125.00**

Grapette, 1946 . . . . **10.00**

J. M. Roseberry & Co., Alexandria, VA, eagle wreath and shield, soda water, attributed to Baltimore Glass Works, Baltimore, MD, 1845-60, squat cylindrical form, yellowish green, applied sloping collared mouth, iron pontil mark, half pint, overall ext. wear, 3/8" flat chip **800.00**

Lange & Bernecker, St. Louis, MO, golden amber, applied top, 1864, 9-1/2" h **415.00**

London Jockey Club House Gin

Golden amber, emb horse and rider, applied top, smooth base, polished, 3/4" l open bubble on one shoulder **310.00**

Light green, emb horse and rider, applied top, smooth base, slight dull haze **770.00**

Olive amber, emb horse and rider, applied top, smooth base, 4" crack **165.00**

M. Flanagan Petersburg Va, Philadelphia XXX Porter & Ale, squat cylindrical, green with olive tone, heavy applied collared mouth, iron pontil mark, half pint, overall ext. wear. **230.00**

Old Tom Long Champ's London Cordiagin, brilliant yellow-olive, massive applied top, smooth base, 9-3/4" h **330.00**

Steinke & Kornahrens/Soda Water/ Return This Bottle/Charleston SC, America, 1845-60, octagonal, cobalt blue, applied sloping collared mouth, iron pontil mark, oversize half pint, 7-3/4" h, professionally cleaned to orig luster, some remaining scratches **650.00**

Udolpho Wolfe's Aromatic Schnapps Schiedam

Amber with olive, applied top, graphite pontil **210.00**

Brilliant green, double rolled collar, smooth base **55.00**

Brilliant yellow, applied top, smooth base, many bubbles **100.00**

Golden amber with streaks of green and puce, applied top, smooth base, some scratching near name **90.00**

Olive-amber, applied top, graphite pontil. **60.00**

Voldner's Aromatic Schnapps Schiedam, amber with some olive, applied top, smooth base, 9-3/4" h **80.00**

W. H. Buck Norfolk VA, soda water, squat cylindrical, deep green, applied heavy collard mouth, iron pontil mark, half pint, some ext. wear and scratches **240.00**

Bitters

A. S. Hopkins Union Stomach Bitters, greenish-yellow, applied tapered collar lip, smooth base, 9-1/4" h **265.00**

Alpine Herb Bitters, amber, sq, smooth base, tooled lip, 9-5/8" h **175.00**

Baker's Orange Grove Bitters, yellowish-amber, smooth base, applied mouth, 90-1/2" h **185.00**

Begg's Dandelion Bitters, medium amber, smooth base, hinge mold mark, 85 percent orig label, 7-1/8" h. . .**110.00**

Bell's Cocktail Bitters, Jas. M. Bell & Co., New York, amber, applied ring, smooth base, 10-1/2" h **450.00**

Ben Franklin, America, 1840-60, tapered barrel form, light blue green, applied collared mouth with ring, pontil scar, 10" h **3,280.00**

Bourbon Whiskey Bitters, barrel shape, plum-puce **495.00**

Brown's Iron Bitters, Brown Chemical Co., medium amber, sq, crude applied sloping collar lip, smooth base, orig front and back labels, 8-1/2" h, some loss to labels, neck with heavy twist lines, orig contents **120.00**

Caldwell's Herb Bitters/The Great Tonic, triangular, beveled and lattice work panels, yellowish-amber, applied tapered lip, iron pontil **400.00**

Cannon's Dyspeptic Bitters, America, 1860-90, sq, beveled corners, emb with cannon balls and ramrods, three full panels with emb cannon barrels, golden amber, applied sloping collared mouth, smooth base, 10" h, 3/4" bruise and repair to top of mouth, some int. residue. **3,250.00**

Cherry Cordial Bitters, America, 1870-90, sq, beveled corners and indented panels, light yellow amber, tooled sloping collared mouth with ring, smooth base, 8-7/8" h roughness to do manufacturer's tool. **140.00**

Clarke's Vegetable Sherry Wine Bitters, aqua, smooth base, applied mouth, 14" h **575.00**

Cunderango, name on two sides, medium blue-green, inset panel, applied lip, 1872-80, 3/4" in-manufacture crevice of glass, couple of onion skin open bubbles . . **1,220.00**

Curtis Cordial Calisaya, The Great Stomach Bitters, medium to light tobacco amber, applied band, smooth base, 1" long crack **330.00**

Drake's Plantation Bitters, puce, Arabesque design, tapered lip, smooth base, 9-3/4" h **295.00**

Dr. A. S. Hopkins Union Stomach Bitters, F. S. Amodon, Sole Prop., Hartford, Conn., USA, sq amber bottle, orig neck seal 98 percent orig graphic front label, 95 percent rear label, orig contents, 9-1/2" h **240.00**

Dr. Bell's Blood Purifying Bitters The Great English Remedy, America, 1860-90, rect, indented panels, bright golden yellow, applied sq collared mouth, smooth base, 9-1/2" h . . **140.00**

Dr. C. W. Roback's Stomach Bitters, Cincinnati, O, medium golden-amber, applied top, smooth base **360.00**

Dr. Harter's Wild Cherry Bitters, St. Louis, amber, single collar lip, smooth base emb "Design 24 Patented," 7-3/4" h **30.00**

Dr. Henley's Wild Grape Root IXL Bitters

Deep bluish-green aqua, applied band top, smooth base. . **2,420.00**

Medium yellow-green, applied band top, smooth base, two minor flat flakes at top. **600.00**

Dr. Hoofland's German Bitters Liver Complaint Dyspepsia, aqua, open pontil, 7" h. **165.00**

Dr J Hostetter's Stomach Bitters

L & W on base, citron, applied top **180.00**

Plain base, medium olive-amber, applied top **250.00**

Dr. Langley's Root & Herb Bitters, 99 Union St. Boston, light green, applied sq collar, smooth base, 8-1/2" h. **155.00**

Dr. Loew's Celebrated Stomach Bitters & Nerve Tonic, green, smooth base, tooled lip, 9-1/4" h **150.00**

Dr. Petzold's Genuine German Bitters Inc. 1862, medium amber, colorful graphic front label, oval, 10-1/2" h **950.00**

Dr. Porter's Medicated Stomach Bitters 75.00

Dr. Walkinshaw's Curative Bitters, Batavia, NY, sq amber bottle, 90 percent orig label, orig contents, 10" h. 315.00

E. G. Lyons & Co. Manufacturers San Francisco, backwards "N," light pastel green, 1868-72, applied square collar, little stain, few minor scratches 5,060.00

Geo. C. Hubble & Co., blue, semi cabin shape, some wear on sides 200.00

Godfrey's Celebrated Cordial Bitters, NY, aqua, pontil, applied mouth, 10" h 1,225.00

Goff's Bitters, H on bottom, amber and colorless, 5-3/4" h 25.00

Greeley's Bourbon Bitters

Apricot puce, barrel shape, applied sq collared mouth, smooth base, America, 1860-80, 9-1/8" h, shallow 3/8" burst bubble on top barrel ring 180.00

Burnt chocolate-puce, barrel shape, applied sq collared mouth, smooth base, America, 1860-80 . . . 360.00

Copper puce, barrel shape, applied sq collared mouth, smooth base, America, 1860-80, 9-1/4" h, shallow 1/4" flake on side of flanged mouth 120.00

Gray topaz, barrel shape, applied sq collared mouth, smooth base, America, 1860-80, 9-1/8" h, one slightly ground spot 190.00

Medium grape puce, barrel shape, applied sq collared mouth, smooth base, America, 1860-80 . . . 600.00

Hall's Bitters, E. Fhall's, New Haven, Ext. 1842

Brilliant canary yellow, applied sq collar, smooth base 600.00

Medium to deep amber, applied sq collar, smooth base 275.00

Hasterlik's Celebrated Stomach Bitters, sq amber, 98 percent front label with eagle, shield, and flags, 9-1/4" h 55.00

Herkules Bitter, America, 1870-90, globular, two flattened label panels, emerald green, tooled mouth with ring, smooth base, 7-1/4" h 2,000.00

H. H. Warner & Co./Tippecanoe, American, 1860-80, cylindrical, yellow amber with olive tone, tooled mushroom mouth, smooth base, 8-3/4" h . . 170.00

Hibernia Bitters

Amber, sq, smooth base, tooled lip, 9-1/4" h 125.00

Golden-amber, applied top, fifth, 1886-90 . . . . 110.00

Holtzermann's Patent Stomach Bitters, amber, complete label, 9-1/2" h 425.00

Hops & Malt Bitters, golden amber, tapered collar lip, smooth base, 9-1/8" h 250.00

I. Newton's Jaundice Bitters, Norwich VT, 1940-60, rect, wide beveled corners, deep aquamarine, tooled flared mouth, pontil scar, 6-7/8" h 700.00

J. C.& Co., molded pineapple form, deep golden amber, blown molded, 19th C, 8-1/2" h. 460.00

John Moffit, Phoenix Bitters, NY, olive amber, eight sided, round collar pontil, 6-3/8" h 2,500.00

John Root's Bitters/1834/Buffalo, N.Y., rect, beveled corners, recessed panels, cabin-type roof, bluish green, applied sloping collared mouth with ring, smooth base, 10" h, 3" crack in one shoulder. 190.00

Johnson's Calisaya Bitters, Burlington VT, 1870-90

Golden yellow, sq, beveled corners, indented panels, 10" h 120.00

Yellow amber, applied sloping collared mouth with ring, smooth base, 10" h, two shallow partial burst bubbles on shoulder . 210.00

Kelly's Old Cabin Bitters, cabin shape, amber, sloping collar lip, smooth base, 9" h 725.00

Keystone Bitters, barrel shape, golden amber, applied tapered collar, sq lip, smooth base, 9-3/4" h. 175.00

Lippman's Great German Bitters, Savannah, Georgia, golden amber, applied top, 1/16" bruise on right corner base 310.00

Louis Taussig & Co., San Francisco, Cal, golden amber, applied top, sq, late 1880s 190.00

Mack's Sarsaparilla Bitters, Mack & Co. Prop'rs, San Francisco, golden amber, applied top 319,99

McKeever's Army Bitters, amber, sloping collared lip, smooth base, 10-5/8" h 1,700.00

Mishler's Herb Bitters, Mishler's Herb Bitter Co., yellow with olive tone, table spoon graduation, smooth base emb "Stoeckels Grad Pat Feb 6 '66," 9-1/8" h, shallow lip flake 350.00

Mist of the Morning Sole Agents Barnett & Lumley, golden amber, sloping collar lip, smooth base, 9-3/4" h 300.00

National Bitters, corn-cob shape

Apricot amber. 715.00

Golden yellow, some roughness at top 770.00

Medium amber 525.00

OK Bitters, medium blue-aqua 6,160.00

Old Homestead Wild Cherry Bitters, America, 1860-90, tall house form, yellow amber, applied sloping collared mouth, smooth base, 9-1/2" h, crudely applied lip has air under some of natural folds, sand grain above door 150.00

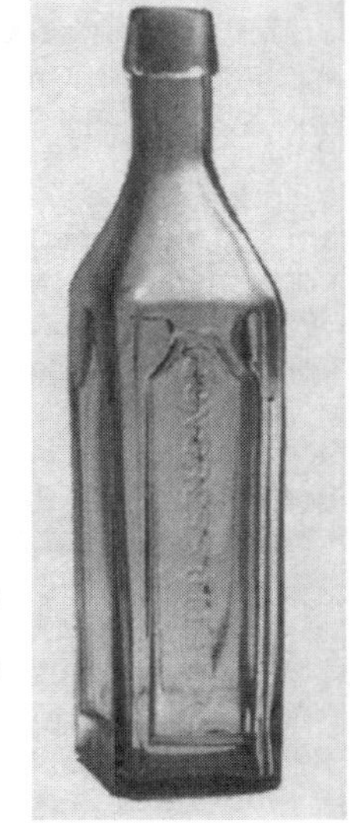

William Allen's Congress Bitters, America, 1860-80, rectangular, indented panels, yellow amber with olive tone, applied sloping collared mouth, smooth base, 10-1/8" h, ***$1,700.*** *Photo courtesy of Norman C. Heckler and Co.*

Old Sachem Bitters and Wigwam Tonic

Aquamarine, barrel form, applied sq collared mouth, pontil scar, America, 1840-60, yellow striation above and to right of word Sachem, 10" h, pinhead size flake on top of mouth 4,750.00

Brilliant apricot, barrel form, applied sq collared mouth, pontil scar, America, 1840-60. . . . . 880.00

Deep plum amethyst, barrel form, applied sq collared mouth, pontil scar, America, 1840-60, 9" h, minor ext. scratches. 550.00

Golden amber, barrel form, applied sq collared mouth, pontil scar, America, 1840-60, 9-1/4" h 600.00

Olive-yellow, barrel form, applied sq collared mouth, pontil scar, America, 1840-60, 9-1/4" h. . . . 1,700.00

Puce copper, barrel form, applied sq collared mouth, pontil scar, America, 1840-60, 9-1/4" h, three pinhead-sized flakes at top corner of mouth 375.00

Pepsin Calisaya Bitters, Dr. Russell Med Co., lime green, smooth base, 8-1/8" h **100.00**
Pineapple Bitters, amber, applied top, smooth base **155.00**
Red Jacket Bitters, Monheimer & Co., sq, amber, tooled lip, smooth base, 9-1/2" h **100.00**
Reed's Bitters, yellow-amber, lady's leg neck, smooth base, 12-3/4" h **425.00**
Sazerac Aromatic Bitters
Milk glass, elaborate P.H.D. monogram on shoulder, applied band top, 10-1/4" h **385.00**
Yellow-olive, elaborate P.H.D. monogram on shoulder, applied band top **1,540.00**
Schroeder's Bitters, Louisville, KY, amber, tooled lip, smooth base, 11-3/4" h **350.00**
Simon's Centennial Bitters, George Washington bust shape, aqua, applied mouth, smooth base, 9-1/8" h. . . **650.00**
Sir Robert, Edgar's English Life Bitters-G E Graves Proprietor Rutland Vt USA, American, 1860-80, sq, beveled corners, yellow amber, applied sloping collared mouth, smooth base, 8-1/2" h, 1/4" shallow burst bubble **170.00**
S. O. Richardson's Bitters, South Reading, Mass, aqua, flared lip, open pontil, pebbly surface **165.00**
S. T. Drake's Plantation Bitters, sq tall log cabin form
Apricot puce, five-logs style, applied sloping collared mouth, smooth base, America, 1860-80, 9-3/4" h **275.00**
Brilliant light yellow, hint of olive, four-logs style, applied sloping collared mouth, smooth base, America, 1860-80 . . . . **770.00**
Cherry amber, six-logs style, applied sloping collared mouth, smooth base, America, 1860-80 . . . **110.00**
Cherry puce, six-logs style, applied sloping collared mouth, smooth base, America, 1860-80 . . . **495.00**
Golden amber, four-logs style, applied sloping collared mouth, smooth base, America, 1860-80 . . . . **110.00**
Light brilliant yellow, four-logs style, applied sloping collared mouth, smooth base, America, 1860-80 . . . . **1,430.00**
Medium deep amber, four-logs style, applied sloping collared mouth, smooth base, America, 1860-80 . . . . **100.00**
Orange-amber, six-logs style, applied sloping collared mouth, smooth base, America, 1860-80, large bubbles **80.00**
Strawberry puce, five-logs style, applied sloping collared mouth, smooth base, America, 1860-80, 9-3/4" h **220.00**
Yellow with olive tone, four-logs style, applied sloping collared mouth, smooth base, America, 1860-80, 10-1/4" h **350.00**
Suffolk Bitters, Philbrook & Tucker, Boston, pig shape, amber, applied mouth, smooth base, 10-1/8" l. . **950.00**
Sunny Castle Stomach Bitters, Jos. Dudenhoefer, Milwaukee, sq, amber, tooled lip, smooth base, 9" h. . . **125.00**
Tippecanoe, Warner & Co., amber, applied mushroom lip, 9" h **95.00**
Traveller's Bitters, America, 1834-70, man standing with cane, oval, amber, 10-1/2" h **265.00**
Warner's Safe Tonic Bitters, America, 1870-90, oval, golden yellow, tooled double collared mouth, smooth base, 7-3/8" h, some minor ext. high point wear **650.00**
Wheeler's Berlin Bitters, Baltimore, 1860s, brilliant emerald, six-sided, applied lip, graphic pontil . . . **15,400.00**
William Allen's Congress Bitters
Aquamarine, rect, indented panels, applied sloping collared mouth, smooth base, America, 1860-80, 10-1/8" h **200.00**
Emerald-blue, rect, indented panels, applied sloping collared mouth, smooth base, America, 1860-80, 10-1/8" h **2,860.00**
Medium golden amber, rect, indented panels, applied sloping collared mouth, smooth base, America, 1860-80, 10-1/8" h **2,640.00**
Yellow amber with olive tone, rect, indented panels, applied sloping collared mouth, smooth base, America, 1860-80, 10-1/8" h **1,700.00**
Zingan Bitters, amber, applied mouth, smooth base, 11-7/8" h **150.00**

Chestnut, freeblown, New England, 1780-30

3-1/4" h, pale green, globular, applied rim **525.00**
3-5/8" h, dark amber, applied rim **500.00**
3-7/8" h, light olive amber, applied rim **575.00**
4-7/8" h, light yellow with olive tone, sheared mouth, applied collar, pontil scar **300.00**
5-1/8" h, yellow olive, sheared mouth, applied round collar, pontil scar. **210.00**
5-1/4" h, light olive amber, applied rim, slightly pinched side, domed kick-up **645.00**
5-3/4" h, light yellow, sheared mouth, applied rim, pontil scar **140.00**
6-1/4" h, light olive yellow, sheared mouth, narrow applied round collar, pontil scar **220.00**
6-3/8" h, olive green, applied rim, high kick-up **635.00**
7-1/8" h, medium yellow olive, short applied sloping collared mouth, pontil scar **170.00**
8" h, yellow olive, applied sloping collared mouth with ring, pontil scar **190.00**
8-1/2" h, light to medium olive yellow, sheared mouth applied ring, pontil scar **250.00**
10-1/4" h, yellow green, olive tone, sheared mouth, applied rim, pontil scar, some minor ext. wear **325.00**

Cosmetic

Boswell & Warner's Colorific, rect, cobalt blue, indented panels, tooled sq lip, c1880, 5-1/2" h **85.00**
De Vry's Dandero-Off Hair Tonic, colorless, paper label, 6-1/2" h . . **15.00**
Edwards Harlene Astol Hair Colour Restorer, three sunken panels, cobalt blue, 7" h **55.00**
Ferd. Muhlens Inc., New York No. 4711 Bath Salts, orig label **20.00**
Florida Water, Reddington & Co., San Francisco, aqua, tooled top **25.00**
Fountain of Youth Hair Restorer, cobalt blue, tooled applied top, 1870s, 7-5/8" h **525.00**
Harrisons Hair Colour Restorer, Amber, Reading, sunken panel, emb on front, 6" h **18.00**
Hind's Honey and Almond Cream, 5-1/2" h **7.50**
Hyacinthia Toilet Hair Dressing, rect, aqua, crude applied lip, open pontil, 6" h **25.00**
Kickapoo Sage Hair Tonic, cylindrical, cobalt blue, tooled mouth, matching stopper, smooth base, 5" h. **160.00**
Kranks Cold Cream, milk glass, 2-3/4" h **6.50**
Mrs. S. A. Allens World's Hair Restorer, amber, rect, three sunken panels, emb name and "London" on base, 7" h **30.00**

Nelson's Extract of Roses and Rosemary, H. P. Wakelee Sole Agent, light cobalt blue, applied top, orig stopper, 7" h, rim flake, some interior haze. **70.00**
Pompeian Massage Cream, amethyst, 2-3/4" h **9.00**
Prichard & Constance, London & New York, Tonic Bath Crystals, orig label **20.00**
The Mexican Hair Renewer, rounded shoulder, rect emb on edges, cobalt blue, 7" h **35.00**
Violet Dulce Vanishing Cream, eight panels, 2-1/2" h **7.50**

Demijohn

10-7/8" h, New England, freeblown, cylindrical, yellowish amber, applied sloping collared mouth, pontil scar **50.00**
12" h, America, blown, late 18th/early 19th C, green, many bubbles, crudely applied top **100.00**
12" h, America, blown, late 18th/early 19th C, olive amber **45.00**
12" h, America, blown, late 18th/early 19th C, red-amber, applied top, smooth base, slight interior stain **45.00**
13" h, America, blown, late 18th/early 19th C, emerald green, crudely applied top, tubular pontil **490.00**
14-1/4" h, America, 1860-80, emb monogram on shoulder and "Trademark" and logo of carboy on base, cylindrical, apple green, applied sloping collared mouth, smooth base, 1/8" irid bruise on base **120.00**
15" h, America, blown, late 18th/early 19th C, sapphire blue, tooled top **310.00**
17-3/8" h, America, 1860-80, cylindrical, four-piece mold, light sapphire blue, applied sloping collared mouth, smooth base, 1/2" flat chip under applied mouth, shallow 1/4" open bubble near base. **220.00**
18-1/4" h, 13-1/2" d, America, blown, late 18th/early 19th C, amber, emb "V K 1859" on side, domed kick-up, imperfections. **175.00**
19" h, 14-1/4" d, America, blown, late 18th/early 19th C, olive green, front shoulder imp with "17" on oval, piece mold construction, sloping collar, domed kick-up and pontil scar, mold imperfections. **145.00**

Figural

Ballet dancer, 12" h, milk glass, pink and brown paint dec highlights, sheared mouth, removable head as closure, pontil scar, attributed to America, 1860-90 . . . . **525.00**
Barrel form, 4-7/8" h, yellow olive green, fancy rigaree trailing around body, two sleigh runner feet serve as base, each emb with repeating sunburst motif, tooled mouth, pontil scar, Europe, 18th C. **450.00**
Bear, 10-5/8" h, dense yellow amber, sheared mouth, applied face, Russia, 1860-80, flat chip on back **400.00**
Big stick, Teddy Roosevelt's, 7-1/2" h, golden amber, sheared mouth, smooth base, flat flake at mouth **170.00**

John Bull, English, 1870-1900, bright orange amber, tooled mouth, smooth base, 11-3/4" h, **$160.** *Photo courtesy of Norman C. Heckler and Co.*

Bull, John, 11-3/4" h, bright orange amber, tooled mouth, smooth base, attributed to England, 1870-1900 . . . . **160.00**
Cherub holding medallion, 11-1/8" h, blue opaque milk glass, sq collared mouth, ground pontil scar, attributed to America, 1860-90. . . . . **120.00**
Chinaman, 5-3/4" h, seated form, milk glass, ground mouth, orig painted metal atomizer head, smooth base, America, 1860-90 . . . . **120.00**
Coachman, 8-3/4" h, back emb "Van Dunck's Genever Trademark Ware & Schmit," applied mouth, smooth base, America, late 19th C. **100.00**

Dog

- 5-1/4" l, colorless, eastern U.S., late 19th/early 20th C, imperfections **2,800.00**
- 7-1/2" l, amber, rigaree detail, eastern U.S., late 19th/early 20th C **3,200.00**

Fish, 11-1/2" h, "Doctor Fisch's Bitters," golden amber, applied small round collared mouth, smooth base, America, 1860-80, some ext. highpoint wear, burst bubble on base **160.00**
Garfield, James, president, 8" h, colorless glass bust set in turned wood base, ground mouth, smooth base, America, 1880-1900 . . . . **80.00**
Indian maiden, Brown's Celebrated Indian Herb Bitters, patented 1867, medium light amber, rolled lip. . **770.00**
Pig, Suffolk Bitters, America, 1860-90, shaded yellow amber, applied double collared mouth, smooth base, 10-1/8" l, minor ext. high point wear. **750.00**
Pineapple, 8-3/4" h, "W & Co./N.Y.," America, 1845-60, brilliant yellow green with strong olive tone, applied double collard mouth, iron pontil mark, 8" meandering crack through body **425.00**
Shoe, dark amethyst, ground mouth, smooth base **125.00**
Washington, George, 10" h, "Simon's Centennial Bitters," aquamarine, applied double collared mouth, smooth base, America, 1860-80 . . . . . . **650.00**

Food

Baking powder, Eddy's, tin top . **12.00**
Banana flavoring, Herberlings, paper label, 8" h. **10.00**
Blueberry, 11" h, 10 lobed flutes, medium green, tooled rolled collared mouth **160.00**
Candy, Prices Patent Candie Company, England, 1840-60, rect wedge form, cobalt blue, applied sloping collared mouth with ring, pontil scar, 7" h **350.00**

Catsup

- Curtis Brothers, colorless, blue label **12.00**
- Cuyuga County Tomato Catsup, aqua, swirl design, 10" h . . . **65.00**

Celery salt, 8" h, Crown Celery Salt, Horton Cato & Co., Detroit, yellow amber, smooth base, ground lip, orig shaker type cap **175.00**
Club sauce, Parker Bros., London, aqua, applied top, open pontil . . **55.00**

Extract

- Baker's Flavoring Extracts, 4-3/4" h, aqua, sq ring lip. **15.00**
- L. C. Extract, label, orig box. **180.00**

Ginger, Crane & Brigham, San Francisco, ginger, blue, slug plate, applied top **55.00**
Honey, Land of Lakes, honeycomb, metal cap **8.00**
Horseradish, Heinz Nobel & Co., emb, two anchors, horse head on lid, 1873, 5" h **275.00**

Ketchup, Shriver's Oyster Ketchup, Baltimore, emerald green, applied top, smooth base, 7-1/2" h. **770.00**

Lemonade, G. Foster Clark & Co., Eiffel Tower, 2-3/4" h **10.00**

Lemon extract, Louis & Company **10.00**

Lime juice

- 10-1/4" h, arrow motif, olive amber, smooth base, applied mouth **85.00**
- 13" h, tapered cylinder, blob top, overall emb lime foliage, emb "L. Rose & Co." **35.00**

Malted milk, Horlick's Malted Milk, Racine, half pint **20.00**

Olive, Chef, 5" h **5.00**

Peanut butter, 5" h, Bennett Hubba **20.00**

Pepper sauce, 8" h, S & P Pat. Appl. For, teal blue, smooth base, tooled lip **50.00**

Pickle

- Applied top, smooth base, green, light interior stain **35.00**
- Cathedral, America, 1845-80
  - Six-sided, light aqua-green, applied top, open pontil, slightly out of shape **80.00**
  - 10-5/8" h, four fancy cathedral arch designs, medium green, sq, beveled corners, tooled rolled mouth, smooth base **650.00**
  - 11-1/2" h, three fancy cathedral designs, greenish-aqua, sq, beveled corners, tooled rolled mouth, smooth base. . . . **150.00**
  - 11-3/4" h, four different fancy cathedral arch designs, protruding irregular panels, aquamarine, tooled sq mouth, iron pontil mark. **170.00**

Olive oil, Preston & Merill, Boston, golden amber, applied top, smooth base, 10-1/2" h **70.00**

Spice

- D. Bernard, San Francisco, light aqua, applied top, smooth base **45.00**
- H. C. Hudson & Co., rich blue-aqua, applied top, smooth base . . . **45.00**
- Unembossed, cornflower blue, applied top, smooth base . . . **75.00**
- Unembossed, greenish-lime, applied top, smooth base . . . **75.00**

Vinegar, jug shape

- Weso Biko Co. Cider Vinegar . **45.00**
- Whitehouse, 10" h **20.00**

Globular

Midwest, 8-1/2" h, pattern molded, globular, 24 ribs swirled to the left, medium reddish amber, outward rolled mouth, pontil scar, 1820-40. . . . **650.00**

Zanesville, OH

- 7-5/8" h, blown, amber, 24 swirled ribs, applied lip, appears to have terminal ring, minor wear and scratches, tiny broken blister, small stones, trace of stain **330.00**
- 7-7/8" h, blown, deep amber, 24 swirled ribs, minor int. stain **470.00**
- Brilliant yellow, 24 swirled ribs, tapering cylindrical neck, folded over rim and pontil, 1820-30 . . . . **3,100.00**

Household

Ammonia

- Golden Key, paper label, 8" h . **5.00**
- Parson's, aqua, 1882 . . . . **20.00**

Blueing, Jennings, aqua, blob top, 7" h **8.00**

Cleaning

- 5" h, jug, yellow amber, Lysol on front, Boots All British on back **24.00**
- 6" h, amber, Lysol London on base **20.00**

Dead Stuck for Bugs, Gottlib Marshall & Co., blue-aqua, emb bug with pin sticking through it, tooled top . . . **45.00**

Glue, Bull Dog Brand Liquid Glue, aqua, ring collar, 3-1/2" **6.50**

Oil, Standard Oil Co., colorless, orig label, 6" h. **7.50**

Polish

- Alma Polish, aqua, name emb on shoulder, marked "M & Go" on base, 5" h **10.00**
- Osborn's Liquid Polish, cylindrical, yellow olive, inward rolled mouth, tubular pontil scar, American, 1840-60, 3-5/8" h **475.00**

Sewing Machine Oil, Sperm Brand, clear, 5-1/2" h. **5.00**

Shoe Polish, Everett & Barron Co., oval, clear, 4-3/4". **5.00**

The Ripley Company, New York, citron, tooled top **25.00**

Gin

8-3/4" h, tapered, yellow olive, applied mushroom mouth, tubular pontil scar, Netherlands, 1780-1830 . . . . **50.00**

9-1/4" h, tapered, yellow olive, applied mushroom mouth, pontil scar, Netherlands, 1780-1830 . . . . **50.00**

9-7/8" h, tapered, yellow olive, flared wide mouth opening to 2-1/8" d, pontil scar, Netherlands, 1780-1830, transformed into wide mouth preserve jar **275.00**

10" h, London Jockey/Clubhouse/Gin, America, 1860-80, sq, beveled corners, brilliant deep yellow green, applied sloping collared mouth with ring, smooth base. **700.00**

Carter Master, hexagonal, cathedral panels, colorless with pale yellowish cast, machined mouth, smooth base, America, 1900-20, 9-7/8" h, **$700.** *Photo courtesy of Norman C. Heckler and Co.*

Ink

Bell

- 2-1/2" h, aqua **10.00**
- 3-1/2" h, "M" emb on body, colorless **35.00**

Boat

- Cobalt blue, shear top. **28.00**
- Dark green, emb "M" on both sides, 2" h **20.00**
- Moss green, sear top, two pen rests, 2-1/2" h **30.00**

Cone, 2-1/2" h

- Carter's 1897, Made in USA
  - Golden amber, few scratches **35.00**
  - Green citron, wide mouth . **145.00**
  - Light to medium brilliant green **90.00**
- Light amethyst, minor interior stain **70.00**
- Medium to deep olive amber, blurred embossing on base **35.00**
- Medium olive with lime, blurred embossing on base **35.00**
- Stanford's, red-amber **35.00**
- Turquoise. **145.00**

Cylindrical

- 2" h, cobalt blue, ringed neck . **28.00**
- 4-1/4" h, Waterman's, colorless, paper label with bottle of ink, wooden bullet shaped case, orig paper label **10.00**

5-1/2" h, ice blue, two rings at bottom, two at top, 1-1/2" neck with pour lip **30.00**

5-5/8" h, America, 1840-60, "Harrison's Columbia Ink," cobalt blue, applied flared mouth, pontil scar, 3" crack, mouth roughness, C #764 . . . . **140.00**

6" h, Hyde London, cobalt blue, emb, 1-1/2" neck with pour lip **60.00**

Figural

2" h, house, domed offset neck for, emb architectural features of front door and four windows, colorless, sheared mouth, smooth base, Carter's Ink, America, 1860-90, some remaining int. ink residue, C #614 . . . . **650.00**

2" h, locomotive, aquamarine, ground mouth, smooth base, C #715 . . . . **800.00**

2-3/8" h, log cabin, rect, colorless, tooled sq collared mouth, smooth base, pinhead sized hole in one base corner, some int. haze, C #680 . . . . **190.00**

2-5/8" h, house, 1-1/2 story cottage form, full label on reverse "Bank of Writing Fluid, Manuf by the Senate Ink Co. Philadelphia," aquamarine, tooled sq collared mouth, smooth base, small area of label slightly faded, C # 682 . . . . **300.00**

3-1/8" h, rect log cabin, colorless, ground mouth, smooth base, 1/8" bruise on int. of mouth, possibly done at manufacture **375.00**

Hexagonal, 9-7/8" h, America, 1900-20, "Carter," cathedral panels, colorless with pale yellow cast, machined mouth, smooth base, similar to C #820. **700.00**

Igloo, J & I.E. M., sheared lip, aqua, recently cleaned **35.00**

Inverted conical

2-3/8" h, Stoddard, NH, 1846-1860, deep yellow-olive, sheared mouth, pontil scar, pinhead flake on mouth edge, C #15 . . . . **170.00**

2-1/2" h, America, 1840-60, medium cobalt blue, tooled mouth, tubular pontil scar, C #23 . . . . **800.00**

2-1/2" h, America, 1840-60, "Woods/Black Ink/Portland," aquamarine, inward rolled mouth, pontil scar, C #12, unearthed with some remaining stain **170.00**

Master

5-1/2" h, cobalt blue, sq, pour lip, emb on side "Hyde London," cleared **60.00**

6" h, cobalt blue, round, pour spout, emb "Hyde London" **85.00**

6-1/2" h, R. L. Higgins, Virginia City, golden amber, applied top, strong embossing. **18,700.00**

7-1/2" h, green, three piece mold, applied top, smooth base, pour spout missing **35.00**

8-1/2" h, aqua, 2" neck, crude applied pour lip, some bubbles **40.00**

10-1/2" h, 18 sides, cobalt blue **95.00**

Octagonal

Aqua, cut away base to lay on side **20.00**

Deep amber, sheared and rolled lip, pontil, 2-1/4" h, 2-1/2" d base **1,100.00**

G. H. Gilbert Co., West Brookfield, MA, orig label **150.00**

Harrison's Columbian Ink, light green **60.00**

Laughlin's And Bushfield Wheeling Va, 2-7/8" h, aquamarine, inward rolled mouth, pontil scar . . . **300.00**

Light forest green with slight amber swirls, burst top, 3-1/2" h. . . . **18.00**

Pitkin, 2" h, pontil, yellow-olive, flakes **480.00**

Square

Caw's Ink, New York, tooled top **25.00**

Temple London, emb top, one pen rest, aqua **24.00**

Teakettle, sapphire blue, long curved spout, orig metal cap, 2" h, C #1257 . . . . **500.00**

Tent

Aqua, ribbing goes from neck to base, single pen rest on side, 2-1/2" h **55.00**

Light cornflower blue, ribbing from bottom of neck to base, single pen rest **85.00**

Triangular, Derby's All British, emb, aqua, sheared lip **30.00**

Umbrella

2-1/8" h, 12-sided, sapphire blue, inward rolled mouth, pontil, scar, America, 1840-60, C #182, professionally cleaned **950.00**

2-1/4" h, New England, 1840-60, octagonal, golden amber, sheared mouth, America, 1840-60, C #145 . . . . **160.00**

2-3/8" h, octagonal, sapphire blue, inward rolled mouth, pontil, scar, America, 1840-60, C #141 . **700.00**

2-5/8" h, octagonal, lime green, labeled "Williams/Black/Empire/ Ink/New York," tooled mouth, smooth base, label 95 percent intact, C #173. . . . . **160.00**

2-5/8" h, octagonal, sapphire blue, inward rolled mouth, pontil, scar, America, 1840-60, C #129. **950.00**

2-5/8" h, octagonal, yellow, inward rolled mouth, pontil, scar, America, 1840-60, C #129 . . . . **1,200.00**

Medicine

A. B. Stewart Druggist, Bodie, Cal., colorless, monogram. **550.00**

Alexander's Silameau, America, 1840-60, violin form, bulbous neck, sapphire blue, applied sq collared mouth, pontil scar, 6-1/8" h, professionally cleaned, some remaining residue **425.00**

A. M. Cole

Druggist, Virginia, pale amethyst, tooled top, 8" h, recently cleaned, 3/8" flake on side of mouth. **415.00**

Virginia City, solid blue western aqua, applied top, inset side panels, cleaned **1,870.00**

American Expectorant, America, 1840-60, octagonal, greenish aquamarine, outward rolled mouth, pontil scar, 5-7/8" h **425.00**

Arnica Liniment, J. R. Burdsall's New York, aqua, applied top, open pontil, 5-1/2" h **35.00**

Arthurs Renovating Syrup, A. A., American, 1845-60, sq, narrow beveled corners, medium blue green, applied sloping collared mouth, iron pontil mark, 9" h **950.00**

Bennetts Hyssop Cure Stockport, rect, aqua, sunken panel, 5-1/2" h **30.00**

Black Swamp Syrup, colorless, light staining on orig label, orig contents, 7" h **50.00**

Boericke & Tafel's Striturations, golden amber, applied top, 7-1/2" h **110.00**

Booth & Sedgwick's London Cordial Gin, American, 1845-60, sq, beveled corners, deep blue green, applied sloping collared mouth with ring, iron pontil mark, 9-3/4" h **375.00**

Brant's Indian Pulmonary Balsam, medium aqua, applied top, smooth base, eight-sided **25.00**

C. Hemistreet & Co., Troy, N.Y., America, 1840-60, octagonal, medium to deep sapphire blue, applied double collared mouth, pontil scar, 6-3/4" h, minor ext. haze **180.00**

C. W. Roback, MD, Dr. Roback Swedish Remedy, America, 1840-60, octagonal, bright aquamarine, applied

sq collared mouth, pontil scar, 6" h 160.00

Dan Patch White Liniment, colorless, complete wrap around label, orig contents, box, 7" h 280.00

Davis & Miller Druggist, Baltimore, attributed to Baltimore Glass Works, Baltimore, MD, 1845-60, cylindrical, brilliant sapphire blue, applied sq collared mouth, iron pontil, mark, 3" d, 7-1/2" h 1,800.00

D. B. White & Co., South Easton, Mass, aqua, applied top, open pontil, 7" h 55.00

Doctor D. Jayne's Alternative, 242 Chestnut St., Phila, medium aqua, applied top, smooth base, inset front panel, 7" h, exterior scratches . . . 25.00

Dr. A. Rogers Liverwort Tar and Canchalagua, A. L. Scovill, Cincinnati, aqua, applied top, smooth base, 7-3/4" h, open bubble at "g" 35.00

Dr. Bowman's Indian Ointment, America, 1840-60, octagonal, aquamarine, applied sloping collared mouth, pontil scar, 6" h 275.00

Dr. Davis' Compound Syrup of Wild Cherry And Tar, America, 1840-60, octagonal, indented panels, greenish aquamarine, applied sloping collared mouth, pontil scar, 6-5/8" h, 1/4" chip under mouth 40.00

Dr. Henley's Celery, Beef and Iron, C B & I Extract Co., America, 1884-94, amber, tooled top, smooth base, 9-1/4" h 120.00

Dr. J. A. Sherman's Rupture Curative Compound, America, 1870-80, rect, indented panels, cobalt blue, blue triations, tooled, applied sq collar, smooth base, 8-1/4" h. 1,000.00

Dr. J. Webster's Cerevisa Angelica Duplex (coat of arms), America, 1840-60, rect, beveled corners, brilliant medium yellowish green, applied sloping collared mouth with ring, pontil scar, 7-1/8" l, some light int. stain on shoulders 1,300.00

Dr. McMunn's Elixir of Opium, round aqua, orig inside paper wrapper, bottle emb "Opium," 4-1/2" h 140.00

Dr. Roback Swedish Remedy, C. W. Roback, MD, America, 1840-60, octagonal, bright aquamarine, applied sq collared mouth, pontil scar, 4-1/2" h 140.00

Dr. Rookes Rheumatic Lixile, dense cobalt blue, slope shouldered rect, double collar, three sunken panels, 5" h 50.00

Dr. Seymour's Balsam of Wild Cherry & Comfrey, America, 1840-60, octagonal, aquamarine, applied sloping collared mouth, pontil scar, 6-1/2" h 475.00

Dr. S. F. Stowe's Ambrosial Nectar, light greenish-aqua, elaborate goblet and floral design, applied band top 35.00

E. A. Buckhout's Dutch Liniment, Prepared At Mechanicsville, Saratoga Co. NY, rect, beveled corners, figure of standing Dutch man, tooled mouth, pontil scar, 4-5/8" h 400.00

E. Anthony, New York, cobalt blue, flared lip, pontil, c1850, 6" h, 3/8" flake on lip, some scratching on side 415.00

Elipizone A Safe Cure For Fits & Epilepsy H. C. Root London, aqua, rect, emb front panel, 6-1/2" h. . . 55.00

From The Laboratory of G. W. Merchant, Chemist, Lockport, N. Y., attributed to Lockport Glass Works, Lockport, NY, 1840-60, rect, chamfered corners, deep yellowish green, applied sloping collard mouth, tubular pontil scar, 5-1/2" h 500.00

G. C. Thaxter Druggist, Carson City, mortar and pestle, aqua, tooled top, 8-1/4" h, recently cleaned 1,320.00

Granular Citrate of Magnesia, kite with letter inside, ring top, cobalt blue, 8" h. 35.00

G. W. House Clemens Indian Tonic, ring top, aqua, 5" h 100.00

Hayman's Balsam of Horehound, ice blue, emb on front panel, 5" h . . . 20.00

Henshaw & Edmands Druggists, Boston, light green, flared lip, tubular pontil, c1850, 10-1/2" h 1,540.00

Hunt's Liniment Prepared By G. E. Stanton, Sing Sing, N.Y., rect, wide beveled corners, bright yellow green, inward rolled mouth, pontil scar, 4-1/2" h 2,000.00

Iceland Balsam For Pulmonary Consumption, Iceland Balsam, America, 1830-50, rect, beveled corners, emb on three sides, yellow olive, short applied sloping collared mouth, pontil scar, 6-1/2" h, professionally cleaned, light emb lettering 5,500.00

I. L. St. John's Cough Syrup, America, 1840-60, octagonal, brilliant aquamarine, applied sloping collared mouth, pontil scar, 6-1/4" h 140.00

I. Newport's Panacea Purifier of the Blood Nerwich, VT, attributed to Stoddard Glasshouse, Stoddard, NH, 1846-60, cylindrical, indented emb panels, yellow olive, applied sloping collared mouth with ring, iron pontil ring, 7-3/8" h, shall chip on sloping collar 1,900.00

J. L. Leavitt, Boston, attributed to Stoddard Glasshouse, Stoddard, NH, 1846-60, cylindrical, yellow olive, applied sloping collard mouth with ring, iron pontil mark, 8-1/8" h 275.00

Jones & Elmes Veterinary Surgeons London, 9" l, 3" neck, oval, dark cornflower blue, c1896. . . . . 50.00

J. R. Nichols & Co., Chemists, Boston, brilliant cobalt blue, tooled top, 9" h, recently cleaned. 80.00

J. W. Doran Pharmacist, Juneau, Alaska, colorless

3" h, hint of haze 360.00
5-1/2" h, light stain. 310.00

Kimball's Anodyne Toothache Drops, Troy, NH, olive green, three pc mold, cylinder, pontil scarred base, 9" h 425.00

K. Konishi & Co. Apothecary Doshiumachi, O.C., last "C" backwards, blue, tooled top, smooth base, 8" h 40.00

L. P. Dodge Rheumatic Liniment Newburg, America, 1840-60, rect, beveled corners, light golden amber, applied sloping collared mouth, pontil scar, 6" h, appears to have been cleaned 750.00

Manchester Wilds Gout & Rheumatic Mixture, aqua, two sunken panels, 6" h 18.00

Monk's Old Bourbon Whiskey For Medicinal Purposes, America, 1845-60, sq, beveled corners, brilliant yellow olive, applied sloping collared mouth, iron pontil mark, 8-1/4" h 1,100.00

N. L. Clark & Co. Peruvian Syrup, aqua, applied top, 8-3/4" h, small lip flake 35.00

O. K. Plantation, triangular, amber, 11" h 200.00

Osgood's India Cholagogua, New York, aqua, applied top, open pontil 80.00

Pinkstones Curechiline Cures Cattle Diseases, shoulder with Curechiline, emb front panel, aqua, 7-1/2" h . . 30.00

Professor Woods Hair Restorative Depots St. Louis & New York, aqua, applied top, open pontil, 7" h, recently cleaned 35.00

Radium Radia, colorless, colorful graphic label wraps around three sides, orig contents, 5-1/4" h 210.00

Rushton & Aspiunwall, No. 86, William S-T & 110 Broadway, New York, medium to light lime-green, applied, tapered collar, open pontil, 6" h **6,050.00**

Sanderson's Blood Renovator Milton VT, America, 1840-60, oval, aquamarine, applied sq collared mouth, pontil scar, 8-1/8" h, very minor ext. high point wear **650.00**

Sand's Sarsaparilla, New York, aqua, applied top, open pontil, 6" h . . . **80.00**

Shaker Anodyne, NTH, Enfield, NH, aqua, front and rear labels, orig contents, 4" h. **250.00**

Shaker Digestive Cordial, AJ White New York, aqua, orig front and rear labels, orig contents, 5-1/2" h . . **110.00**

Smith's Anodyne Cough Drops Montpelier, America, 1840-60, rect, beveled corners, aquamarine, applied sloping collared mouth, pontil scar, 5-7/8" l **140.00**

Smith's Green Mountain Renovator, attributed to Stoddard Glasshouse, Stoddard, NH, 1846-1850, rect, wide beveled corners, yellow olive amber, applied double collared mouth, iron pontil mark, 6-3/4" h. **1,300.00**

Stockton Drug Co., Stockton, CA, citrate, emerald green, crown top, 8" h. **55.00**

Sun Drug Co., Citrate of Magnesia, Los Angeles, Cal, dark emerald green, logo with mortar and pestle with wings design, pinhead size ding on back **125.00**

Swaim's Panacea Philada, America, 1840-60, cylindrical, with indented panels, bright grayish green, applied sloping collared mouth with ring, pontil scar, 7-1/2" h, some minor exterior wear, **$400.** *Photo courtesy of Norman C. Heckler and Co.*

Swaim's Panacea, Philada, golden yellow olive to deeper shade of olive-amber, applied top, sticky ball-type pontil, bent neck, many imperfections and bubbles, orig contents and cork intact. **990.00**

True Daff's Elixir, England, 1830-50, rect, beveled edges, yellow green, applied ring lip, bail pontil base, 4-7/8" h **360.00**

Turner's Balsam, eight sided, aqua, 4-7/8" h **65.00**

Twichell, Philada, large "T," applied top, smooth base, cleaned, scratches, light pitting **35.00**

Unembossed, 27" h, cut and blown, colorless, ball knop on bulbed stopper, bulbous bottle-form stopper with applied ring, ovoid bottle with cut shield, star, thistle, and oval designs, applied round base, attributed to eastern U.S., 19th C **1,955.00**

Use Pritchard's Teething Powders, aqua, rect, emb front panel, 3-1/2" l. **12.00**

Vaughn's Vegetable Lithontriptic Mixture, aqua, 8" h. **125.00**

Warner's Diabetes Cure, brilliant yellow-green, tooled top, "16 oz" above name, 9-1/2" h **550.00**

Warner's Safe Cure

- London, olive green, pint. **90.00**
- Red amber, strong embossing, half pint **50.00**
- Yellow amber, heavy embossing, half pint **45.00**

Web's Cathartic A No. 1 Tonic, amber, 9-1/2" h **60.00**

Whitwell's Liquid Improved Opodeloc, cylindrical, colorless, emb, sloping flanged lip, pontil, two-part mold, 4-5/8" h **110.00**

Winans Bros (Indian) Indian Cure for the Blood, orig contents **525.00**

Wm Radam's Microbe Killer, Germ, Bacteria or Fungus Destroyer, aqua, sheared lip, smooth base, 10-1/2" h **715.00**

Wyeth's Sage Sulphur Compound, orig label. **20.00**

Yerba Santa San Francisco, CA, deep blue-aqua, applied op, 8-1/2" h, open bubble on shoulder **125.00**

Yougatts Gargling Oil, Comstock & Brother New York, aqua, applied top, smooth base, 9" h. **50.00**

Milk

Abbots, pint, emb cottage cheese jar **8.00**

Alta Crest Farm, Spencer, MA, quart, round, green glass, emb cow's head **1,000.00**

Blue Bell Farms, Irvington, NJ, quart, round, orange pyro, Cop-the Cream **140.00**

Borden, in script above Elsie, quart, squat, red pyro **18.00**

Borden's Condensed Milk, quart, Borden Eagle trademark, clear, emb, tin top **100.00**

Borden's, half pint, emb "$.03 deposit," cottage cheese jar **8.00**

Brookfield Dairy, Hellertown, PA, half pint, round, emb baby top **55.00**

Capital Dairy, North Dartmouth, MA, quart, round, clear, emb capital dome emb on front slug plate **15.00**

Cream Top, generic, quart, sq, dish of ice cream, green and orange . . . **15.00**

Crowley's, As good as any better'n some try fresh churned buttermilk, quart, picture of lady, cow, and churn, red pyro. **25.00**

Dairylea, quart, square, red, Miss Dairylea, picture of fruit and vegetables **18.00**

Dykes' Dairy, Youngsville, PA, our milk for your health, man, woman, two children, quart, round, red pyro . **18.00**

Emmadine Farms, quart, toothache square, orange/black pyro **85.00**

Empire State Dairy Co., Brooklyn, half pint, round, emb, state seal in frame **10.00**

Firestone Farms, Columbiana, OH, one half pint, round, clear, emb, Firestone emblem emb in slug plate **25.00**

Fiske, Rumford, RI, qt, round, emb, cream top **15.00**

Florida Store Bottle, $.03, quart, picture of state of Florida, round, emb **22.00**

Gettysburg Ice and Storage Co., Gettysburg, PA, quart, round, clear, emb name. **12.00**

Hankin Dairy, 515 3rd Avenue, Brooklyn, quart, clear, emb, tin top **55.00**

Hoods, quart, round, cow in framed log, red pyro **12.00**

Ingles Dairy, Manchester, NH, Every man's family should have the very best, quart, woman holding child, orange/green pyro. **30.00**

Jon Alm Dairy, Norwich, NY, quart, sq, tall, picture of girl holding glass, red, blue/orange, and brown pyro . . . **30.00**

Maple Farms, Brattleboro, VT, quart, sq, amber **8.00**

Model Farms, Milford, PA, half pint, round, emb in slug plate, Raw Milk **12.00**
Mohawk Farms, Staten Island, NY, quart, large Indian in headdress, round, emb **40.00**
Newport Dairy, quart, squat, round, emb **10.00**
Old Homestead Products, quart, stippled glass, picture of log cabin **40.00**
One Quart Liquid Brighton Place Dairy Rochester, NY, quart, cylindrical, yellow green, machined mouth, smooth base **550.00**
Orange County Milk Association, quart, clear emb, keystone in slug plate, tin top **125.00**
Palmerton Sanitary Dairy, Palmerton, PA, quart, sq, emb, cream top ... **12.00**
Palm Mead, The City of Palms, quart, palm tree, green pyro **25.00**
Saranac Inn Dairy, quart, clear, emb **30.00**
Sheffield Farms, Slawson Decker, NY, quart, logo, round, emb **8.00**
State University of New York, Cobleskill, college seal, quart, sq, tall **25.00**
Universal Store Bottle, 5¢ deposit, quart, round, emb.......... **8.00**
University of Connecticut, Storrs, CT, one half pint, round, clear, emb name **8.00**
White Springs Farm Dairy, Geneva, quart, orange pyro **12.00**
Winona Dairy, Lebanon, NH, for Safety Milk For Health Milk in a Bottle, quart, red pyro **20.00**
WW Schultz Sunnyside Farm, Port Jervis in slug plate, round, emb . . **12.00**
Yasgar Farms, Bethel, NY, 25th Anniversary 1994 (Woodstock), quart, sq, brown/yellow pyro.......... **45.00**

Mineral or spring water

Albergh A. Spring, VT, cylindrical, apricot amber, applied sloping collared mouth with ring, smooth base, quart, rare with misspelling........ **1,000.00**
Alburgh A. Spring, VT, cylindrical, golden yellow, applied sloping collared mouth with ring, smooth base, quart **800.00**
Artesian Water, round, golden chocolate amber, 12-paneled base, iron pontil, 1850-60, pint **450.00**
B. R. Lippincott & Co., Stockton Superior, Mineral Water, Union Glass Works, 1852-58, cobalt blue, applied top, iron pontil, 7-3/8" h........ **450.00**
Buffalo Mineral Water Springs Natures, Materia Medica Trade Mark, yellow, lady sitting on stool, 10-1/2" h **125.00**
Caladonia Spring Wheelock VT, cylindrical, golden amber, applied sloping collared mouth with ring, smooth base, quart.......... **130.00**
Chalybeate Water Of The American Spa Spring Co., N. J., cylindrical, light to medium blue green, olive green slag striation I neck, applied heavy collared mouth, smooth base, pint **400.00**
Champlain Spring, Alkaline Chalybeate, Highgate, VT, cylindrical, emerald green, applied sloping collared mouth with ring, smooth base, quart **200.00**
Chase & Co. Mineral Water, San Francisco, CA, green, applied top, iron pontil, 7-3/8" h **60.00**
Clarke & Co., New York, medium to deep olive green, quart, smooth base **70.00**
Clarke & White, New York, deep to medium moss green **55.00**
Congress & Empire Springs, Saratoga, NY, emerald green, smooth base, many bubbles **125.00**
Congress & Empire Spring Co., Hotchkiss's Sons, New York, Saratoga, NY, brilliant yellow-green, pint, applied top, smooth base, many bubbles **165.00**
D. A. Knowlton, Saratoga, NY, high shouldered cylinder, olive green, applied sloping collared mouth with ring, smooth base, quart...... **100.00**
Eureka Spring Co., Saratoga, NY, aqua, applied top, torpedo style, bottom emb "G. M. Co." and anchor, orig silver plated stand reads "Saratoga Club House" **550.00**
Gettysburg Katalysine Water, yellowish-green, smooth base... **90.00**
Guilford Mineral Sprig Water, Guilford VT, cylindrical, yellow-olive, applied sloping collard mouth with ring, smooth base, quart **475.00**
G. W. Weston & Co., Saratoga, NY, America, 1840-60, cylindrical, yellow olive, applied sloping collared mouth with ring, pontil scar, pint, 1" vertical body crack on reverse **375.00**
Hawthorne Spring Saratoga, NY, brilliant emerald green, slight lip flake **35.00**
Hopkins Chalybeate Baltimore, attributed to Baltimore Glass Works, Baltimore, MD, 1845-60, dense amber, cylindrical, applied double collared mouth, iron pontil mark, pint.... **135.00**
Jackson's Napa Soda Springs, blue, applied top, cleaned **110.00**
John Clarke, New York, America, 1860-80, cylindrical, dark olive amber, applied sloping collared mouth with ring, smooth base, quart, some ext. high point wear, 1/8" potstone bruise **50.00**
Lancaster Glass Works, round, sapphire blue, applied blob top, iron pontil, 1850-60, 7" h **120.00**
Lynch & Clarke, New York, America, 1840-60, cylindrical, yellowish olive, applied sloping collared mouth with ring, pontil scar, pint.......... **275.00**
Lynde & Putnam, Mineral Waters, San Francisco Cala, Union Glass Works, Philada, teal blue, applied top, iron pontil, 7-1/2" h **100.00**
Middletown Healing Springs, Grays & Clark, Middletown, VT, cylindrical, yellow apricot amber, applied sloping collared mouth with ring, smooth base, quart.......... **1,200.00**
Mill's Seltzer Springs, aqua, applied top, smooth base, 7-1/2" h...... **85.00**
Missiquoi, A. Springs, cylindrical, apricot amber, applied sloping collared mouth with ring, smooth base, quart **150.00**
M. T. Crawford/Springfield-Superior Mineral Water, Union Glass Works, Philadelphia, PA, 1845-60, squat cylindrical form, mug base, cobalt blue, heavy applied collared mouth, iron pontil mark, half pint, some int. stain, 1/2" bruise on top of mouth **160.00**
Poland Water, H. Ricker & Sons Proprietors, colorless, tooled top, circular label "Poland Mineral Spring Water," minor interior stain **55.00**
Poland Water, H. Ricker & Sons Proprietors, colorless, tooled top, open pontil, minor roughness on lip edge **310.00**
Round Lake Mineral Water, red amber, 9-1/4" h **750.00**
Rutherford's Premium Mineral Water, ground pontil, dark olive, 7-1/2" h **60.00**
San Francisco Glass Works, tapered neck, blob top, sea green, 6-7/8" h **15.00**
Saratoga Highrock Spring (fancy rock) Saratoga, NY, America, 1860-80, cylindrical, bright medium green, applied sloping collared mouth with ring, smooth base, pint, 1/2" shallow chip on mouth **850.00**

Saratoga Red Spring, America, 1860-80, cylindrical, emerald green, applied sloping collared mouth with ring, smooth base, pint, orig mineral water contents **90.00**

Saratoga Seltzer Water, cylindrical, teal blue-green, applied ring lip, c1890, 7-1/2" h **85.00**

Saratoga (star) Springs, dark olive green, cylindrical, applied sloping collared mouth with ring, smooth base, quart **300.00**

Star Spring, amber, 7-3/4" h . . . **500.00**

Vermont Spring, Saxe & Co., Sheldon, VT, cylindrical, citron, applied sloping collared mouth with ring, smooth base, quart **600.00**

Veronica Mineral Water, amber, sq **10.00**

Vichy Water/Hanbury Smith/N.Y., America, 1860-90, cylindrical, brilliant medium blue green, applied sloping collared mouth, smooth base, pint **100.00**

Wm Goldstein's Ixiflorida Water, aqua, applied top, smooth base, minor stain **45.00**

Poison

Ammonia around shoulder, three sets of ribbing, Poisonous then ribbing and Not To Be Taken, 6-1/2" h, cylinder **4.00**

Bottled By Jeyes, 7" l, dark straw-amber, oval, ribbing down front with name **12.00**

Bowker's Pyrox Poison, colorless **30.00**

British Household Ammonia, Poisonous Not To Be Taken, 6-1/2" h, aqua, name around neck, panel with emb lettering **20.00**

Burdalls Manufacturing Chemists Sheffield Not To Be Taken Internally, 6" l oval, aqua, row of ribbing each side of lettering **22.00**

Carbolic acid, 3 oz, cobalt blue, hexagonal, flat back **48.00**

Chloroform, 5-3/4" h, green, ribbed, label, 1900 . . . . **80.00**

Clark's Ammonia, aqua, offset neck, 8" h **55.00**

Coffin

- 3" h, irregular hexagonal, emerald green, glass stopper, ribbed **30.00**
- 3-1/2" h, cobalt blue, emb, 1890 . . . . **100.00**

Cylindrical, crosshatch dec, cobalt blue, flared mouth with stopper, smooth base, 6-1/4" h **250.00**

Diamond Antiseptics, 10-3/4" h, triangular shape, golden amber, emb **385.00**

Figural, skull, America, 1880-1900, cobalt blue, tooled mouth, smooth base

- 2-7/8" h, small hole in nose area **475.00**
- 4-1/8" h. **1,800.00**

Foultsons Crescent, 5" h, cobalt blue, sunken ribbed front panel, Not To Be Taken and ribbing on side **65.00**

Hobnail, 3-1/2" h, cobalt blue . . . **40.00**

Ikey Einstein Poison, rect, ring top, colorless, 3-3/4" h. **25.00**

Killgerm Disinfectant, oval, aqua, front panel with "Poisonous Not To Be Taken" 6-1/2" l. **25.00**

Kill Pest Non Poisonous Disinfectant, 5" h, aqua, hexagonal, emb lettering on three panels **20.00**

Imperial Fluid Co. Poison, one gallon, colorless **95.00**

J Wilson Bonsetter, light cobalt blue, rect **65.00**

Lysol, 3-1/4" h, cylindrical, amber, emb "Not To Be Taken" **12.00**

McDonalds Steam System, 5-1/2" h, aqua, Poisonous across shoulder **20.00**

Melvin & Badger Apothecaries, Boston, Mass, irregular form, cobalt blue, tooled sq mouth, smooth base, 6-1/4" h **140.00**

Mercury Bichloride, 2-11/16" h, rect, amber **18.00**

Norwich Coffin, 3-3/8" h, amber, emb, tooled lip. **95.00**

Not To Be Taken, cobalt blue, hexagon, 3" h **12.00**

Not To Be Taken Gordon Grand Lysol, 5" h, amber jug shape, emb around neck, cross hatching on two sides. **32.00**

Owl Drug Co., 3-3/8" h, cobalt blue, owl sitting on mortar **70.00**

Plumber Drug Co., 7-1/2" h, cobalt blue, lattice and diamond pattern **90.00**

Poison

- 3" h, hexagonal, cobalt blue **16.00**
- 3-1/2" h, hexagonal, ribbed, cobalt blue **20.00**

Poisonous

- 2-1/2" h, cobalt blue, emb lettering around neck, ribbing down front, cleaned **30.00**
- 4" h, colorless, cylinder, emb lettering on front, ribbing on two sides, sheared lip **15.00**
- 6-1/2" h, formed lip, colorless . **22.00**
- 6-1/2" h, aqua, row of bumps, two lines on each side **40.00**

Skull, America, 1880-1900, cobalt blue, tooled mouth, smooth base, 4-1/8" h, **$1,800.** *Photo courtesy of Norman C. Heckler and Co.*

Poisonous Not To Be Taken

- 3" h, dark cobalt blue, hexagon **15.00**
- 3-1/2" h, cobalt blue, cylinder, Poison on back base, ribbing down front **48.00**
- 5" h, cobalt blue, hexagon . . . **20.00**
- 6-1/2" h, oval, aqua, emb on front panel **20.00**
- 6-1/2" h, oval, aqua, emb on front panel with ribbing, lip chip. . **10.00**
- 7" h, hexagon, aqua, formed lip, Poison on one panel, emb down front **35.00**
- 8" h, oval, cobalt blue, emb on front panel, cleaned **40.00**
- 11-1/2" h, whiskey shaped, green, long neck **50.00**

Poisonous Not To Be Taken J. Salmon & Co., oval, aqua **32.00**

Sano Bolic Disinfectant, 6" h, aqua, cylinder, sheared top. **20.00**

Six-sided, brilliant green, tooled top, 5" h **55.00**

Skull and crossbones, amber, rect, tooled top, 2-1/2" h **55.00**

Sulpholine, 4" h, rect, colorless . **10.00**

Thretipene Disinfectant, 9" h, amber, emb Poison around cylinder shaped shoulder, central ribbing of nine panels, tapers to base, professionally cleaned **225.00**

Tinct Gelsem Poison and Hydrag Subchlor Poison, 5-1/2" h, green ribbed cylinder, orig label in rect panel, pr. **150.00**

Tinct Iodine, 3" h, amber, skull and crossbones **45.00**

Towle's Chlorodyne, 4-1/2" h, colorless **40.00**

Trioloids Poison, triangular, blue, c1900, 3-5/16" h **25.00**

USA Hospital Dept., Acetate Potassa, 6-1/2" h, cylindrical, aqua **65.00**

Vapo Cresolene Co., 4" h, sq, bumps on two panels, cobalt blue **48.00**

Victory Chemical Co., Quick Deal Insecticide, 148 Fairmount Ave., Phila, PA, 8 oz, colorless, 7" h **15.00**

Sarsaparilla

Brown's Sarsaparilla, aqua **12.00**

Bull's Extract of Sarsaparilla, beveled corners, 7" l. **400.00**

Compound Extract of Sarsaparilla, amber, gallon **140.00**

Dalton's Sarsaparilla and Nerve Tonic, blue label. **40.00**

Dr. Beldings Wild Cherry Sarsaparilla, Dr. Belding Medicine Co., Minneapolis, MN, aqua, complete label, orig contents, orig fancy box (top missing), 9-1/4" h **180.00**

Dr. Guysott's Compound Extract of Yellow Dock and Sarsaparilla, peacock green, sloping lip, iron pontil, 9" h **1,350.00**

Dr. Ira Belding's, Honduras Sarsaparilla, colorless, 10-1/2" h . **30.00**

Dr. Townsend's Sarsaparilla

- Brilliant bluish-green, applied top, graphite pontil, orig graphite intact, few scratches **480.00**
- Brilliant green, applied top, graphite pontil, orig graphite intact, few scratches. **480.00**

Foley's Sarsaparilla **20.00**

Guysott's Yellow Dock & Sarsaparilla **40.00**

Lancaster Glassworks, barrel, golden amber **125.00**

Sand's Genuine, rect, aqua **95.00**

Sawyers Eclipse, aqua **35.00**

Skoda's Sarsaparilla, amber . . . **25.00**

Wetherell's, aqua **45.00**

Soda

Alter & Wilson Manuf, light green applied top, 7" h **20.00**

Arny & Shinn/Georgetown, D.C.-A. & S./This Bottle Is/Never Sold, squat cylindrical, blue green, applied sloping collared mouth with ring, smooth base, half pint. **140.00**

Artic Soda Water Works, Honolulu, HI, greenish-aqua, "N. R. Desa Prop" in slug plate, tooled blob top **55.00**

Bacon's Soda Works, light green, blob top, 7" h **9.00**

Bryant's Root Beer, This Bottle Makes Five Gallons, amber, applied top, 4-1/2" h **5.00**

C. A. Cole/Bottler No. 118/N. Howard St. Balt., squat cylindrical form, yellow olive applied sloping collared mouth with ring, iron pontil mark, oversized half pint, 7-1/2" h, some ext. wear and scratches. **850.00**

Cape Arco Soda Works, Marshfield, OR, round, light green, applied top, 7" h. **10.00**

C. Cleminson/Soda & Mineral Water/Troy, NY, squat cylindrical, teal blue, heavy applied sloping collared mouth, iron pontil mark, half pint, 3/8" narrow flat flake on mouth **140.00**

Claussen & Co., Sparkling, San Francisco, aqua, crossed anchors, two stars, applied lip, some interior haze, slight flake off lip **45.00**

Deadwood, SD, blob top **125.00**

Dearborn/83/ed Ave. NY, Cream Soda, squat cylindrical form, deep aquamarine, heavy applied sloping collared mouth, smooth base, quarter pint or less, 5-3/4" h, professionally cleaned **130.00**

Deamer Grass Valley, aqua, blob top, 7-1/4" h **7.50**

Dr. Pepper, Colorado **18.00**

English Soda, light green, applied top, 8" h. **18.00**

Fizz, Southern State Siphon Bottling Co., golden amber, 11" h. **17.50**

G. Norris & Co., City Bottling Works, Detroit, Mich., brilliant blue, tooled blob top, professionally cleaned, some scratching small bruise around lip **70.00**

Guilbert Yreka, aqua, tooled blob top, c1890-98, factory located on Miner St., Yreka, CA, "G" in circle on base **265.00**

Hawaiian Soda Works, Honolulu T.H., Pacific Coast Glassworks, aqua, crown top, few minor scratches. **45.00**

Hippo Size Soda Water, clear, crown top, 10" h **6.50**

Honolulu Soda Water Co., Ltd., T.H., light greenish-aqua, tooled blob top **55.00**

Jackson's Napa Soda, crown cap, 7-1/4" h **7.50**

James Ray/Savannah/ Geo.-Gingerale, Hutchinson Soda Water, tall cylinder, cobalt blue, heavy tooled collared mouth, smooth base, 7-3/4" h, professionally cleaned **170.00**

Los Angeles Soda Works, aqua, 8" h. **5.00**

Mendocin Bottling Works, A L Reynolds, light green, 7" h **8.00**

Mission Dry Sparkling, black 9-3/4" h **4.00**

Nevada City Soda Works, ETR Powell, aqua, applied top, 7" h **9.00**

Oahu Soda Works Aiea, Oahu Bottle Not Sold, light greenish-aqua, tooled blob top, slight stain **55.00**

Orange Crush Co., Pat'd July 20, 1926, light green, 9" h **4.00**

Pacific Soda Works Co., Ltd., Honolulu T. H., light green-aqua, crown top, turn of century. **55.00**

Payne & Co. Soda Water, New Road, London, green, applied top, torpedo style, tiny flake off lip **50.00**

Pioneer Soda Works, Smith & Bryan Co., Reno, Nevada, light lime-aqua **310.00**

Rapid City Bottling Works, light green, crown cap, 8" h **5.00**

Ross' Royal Belfast Ginger Gale, green, diamond shape, paper label, 10" h **7.50**

Sandahl Beverages, clear, 8" h. . . **5.00**

Scott & Gilbert Co., San Francisco, brown, crown top, 10" h **6.00**

Solano Soda Works, aqua, 8" h . . **6.00**

Spring Soda Water Works Co., Waialua Oahu, light green aqua, crown top, emb orchid, turn of century. . **45.00**

Standard Works Soda, "Camm" in cross, S.F., aqua, Hutchinson-style **25.00**

Star Soda Water Works Honolulu T.H., blue aqua, crown top with emb star **125.00**

Sun Rise Soda Water Work, Honolulu, medium blue-aqua, emb **90.00**

Tahoe Soda Springs Natural Mineral Water, light green, 7-1/2" h. **10.00**

Tonopah Soda Works, Nev, 1902-05, light lime-aqua **825.00**

Unembossed, round bottom, cobalt blue, applied top, 8-3/4" h **165.00**

Union Glass Works, dark blue, blob top **20.00**

Steinke & Kornahrens Soda Water Return This Bottle Charleston, SC, 1845-60, octagonal, cobalt blue, applied sloping collared mouth, iron pontil mark, oversized half pint, 7-3/4" h, professionally cleaned, **$650.** *Photo courtesy of Norman C. Heckler and Co.*

W. H. Burt, San Francisco, green, applied top, iron pontil, mineralized **220.00**

Williamstown, NJ Soda, squat cylindrical form, light bluish green, heavy applied sloping collared mouth, iron pontil mark, half pint, ext. wear and scratches, int. stain **75.00**

W. Lant & Co., Coventry, green, applied top, torpedo style, pretty rough, light chipping around top **25.00**

Utility

3-5/8" h, freeblown, flattened chestnut form, short neck, bright green, sheared mouth, pontil scar, American, 1800-30 . . . . **300.00**

5" h, opaque white, polychrome enameled floral dec, some opalescent, pewter fittings and cap **360.00**

7-7/8" h, freeblown, rect, chamfered corners, dark olive amber, applied sloping collared mouth with ring, pontil scar, America, 1800-30, ext. wear **275.00**

9-1/4" h, freeblown, globular, golden amber, heavy applied mouth, pontil scar, attributed to Midwest America, 1800-30, some int. stain **230.00**

Whiskey

Ambrosial B.M. + E.A.W. + Co. on seal, amber, jug shape, applied scroll handle, 19th C, imperfections, 8-7/8" h **265.00**

B AIR No. 1, olive, seal, domed kick-up, 19th C, imperfections, 10-1/4" h **195.00**

Bininger Old Kentucky Reserve Bourbon, 1848, blown two-mold, amber, America, 19th C, 9-1/4" h **395.00**

C. A. Richards & Co., 99 Washington St. Boston Mass, 1860-1880, square with beveled corners, yellow amber with olive tone, applied sloping collared mouth, smooth base, 9-5/8" h, **$120.** *Photo courtesy of Norman C. Heckler and Co.*

Biningers Bourbon Barrel, amber, 8-1/4" h **500.00**

Bottled by Samuel Brothers & Co., Louisville, KY, San Francisco, Cal, "OK" brilliant golden-orange, monogram, applied top **495.00**

C. A. Richards & Co., 18 & 20 Kilby St., Boston, Mass, 1860-90, sq, beveled corners, applied sloping collared mouth m, smooth base, yellow amber, slug plate address, 9-1/2" h **90.00**

C. A. Richards & Co., 99 Washington St., Boston, Mass, 1860-80, dark olive green shading to dense black near base, sq, beveled corners, applied sloping collared mouth, smooth base, partial orig label "Golden Sheaf Whiskey," 9-1/2" h. **150.00**

Caspers Whiskey, Made by Honest North Carolina People, 1870-90, cylindrical, paneled shoulder, cobalt blue, tooled sloping collared mouth with ring, smooth base, 11-3/4" h . . . **325.00**

Chestnut Grove Whiskey, C. W., golden amber, applied band and handle, open pontil, orig labels, dated 1858, 9" h **255.00**

C. Tynan J. H. Cutter Whiskey Salinas Cal, clear, tooled screw top, half pint, small amount of int. stain **80.00**

From the Wine House Liquors and Cigars, Reno, Nev., clear, pint, pumpkin seed shape, 1890s. **1,430.00**

E. G. Booz's Old Cabin Whiskey, 1840, 120 Walnut St., Philadelphia, Whitney Glass Works, golden amber, applied top, chamfered corners **3,740.00**

G. H. Clark's Bourbon Co. KY Whiskey, Moore Reynolds & Co. Sole Agent for Pacific Coast, emb from bottom to shoulder, brilliant golden-amber, c1875-80 . . . . **2,100.00**

Griffith Hyatt & Co., Baltimore, medium to deep pure olive green, applied top, pontil base, applied handle, 7" h. **1,320.00**

G. W. Chesley, Sacramento, Cal., clear, pint, pumpkin seed shape, 1890s, small open bubble, hint of interior stain **110.00**

H. Pharazyn/Phila/Right Secured, 1860-80, Indian Warrior form, brilliant light yellow amber, inward rolled mouth, smooth base, 12-1/2" h, incomplete mouth with roughness, some minor int. residue **800.00**

J & B Jewsbury & Brown, emb star, torpedo shape, applied top, 7" h . **50.00**

J & C McG 1820 on seal, dark olive amber, rounded decanter shape, sheared mouth, vertically applied rigaree, eastern U.S., 10-5/8" h **3,750.00**

J. H. Cutter Old Bourbon, A. P. Hotaling & Co. Sole Agents, medium to deep amber, applied top. **315.00**

Kapp & Streak, 1200 Market St., SF, clear, pint, seed shape, monogram, flake on lower base **210.00**

Lancaster Glassworks, Lancaster, NY, 1860-80, barrel, puce amber, applied double collared mouth, smooth base, 9-5/8" h **180.00**

Lilenthal & Co. Distillers, golden amber, emb crown in monogram, tooled top, flash shape, light scratch, some interior haze. **825.00**

Livingson's Pure Blackberry Brandy Distilled From The Berry, brilliant golden amber, applied top, star on base **1,100.00**

M. Gruenberg & Co., Old Judge, KY Bourbon, San Francisco, yellow-amber, crudely applied top, air vented at shoulder, fifth. **495.00**

Miller's Extract, Martin & Co. Old Bourbon, amber, single roll applied collar, c1871-79. . . . . **1,760.00**

N. Van Bergen & Co., Gold Dust Bourbon, blue-aqua, emb horse, fifth, bubbles, few scratches. **825.00**

Old Bourbon Castle Whiskey F. Chavalier & Co. Sole Agents, medium golden amber, tooled top **145.00**

Old Continental Whiskey, yellow amber, 9-1/4" h **650.00**

Old Gilt Edge Bourbon Wichmann & Lutgen Sole Agents, San Francisco, amber, emb crown, crooked top **660.00**

11-1/4" h, J.H. Henkes, green blown, pressed pontil, **$75.**

Phoenix Bourbon Naber, Alfs & Brune SF, clear, pint, emb bird, slight haze **125.00**
Phoenix Old Bourbon, Naber, Alfs & Brune, SF, Sole Agents, amber, large bird, full face embossing, applied top **1,220.00**
Pride of Kentucky Old Bourbon, Livingston & Co. Sole Agents, dark amber, c1874-79 . . . . **2,860.00**
Ridgeway Straight Corn Whiskey, miniature, stoneware **50.00**
Roth & Co., 214 & 216 Pine St., San Francisco, amber, double roll collar, tooled top, number 3 on base, c1880-85 . . . . **210.00**
Roth & Co., San Francisco, red-amber, monogram, tiny ding on back, scratch on right front **220.00**
Siebe Bros. & Plagmann, SF, Rosedale, OK, Whiskey, Sole Agents, pale aqua, applied top, some scratches, cleaned **25.00**
Simmond's Nabob, amber, scratch on back **65.00**
Spruance Stanley & Co., amber, emb horseshoe and star on base, tooled top **55.00**
Teakettle Old Bourbon, medium amber **1,650.00**
The Arcade, Kerrigan & Leslie, Cheyenne, Wyo, clear, rect, pocket, tooled screw top, few minor scratches **155.00**
The Arcade, W. A. Gaines & Co., Old Crow Whiskey, Cheyene, Wyo, light amethyst, half pint, ground screw top, rect, small open bubble, few light scratches **125.00**
Udolpho Wolfe's Schnapps, Schiedam, olive amber, emb name, 19th C, imperfections, 9-7/8" h . . **385.00**
Unmarked seal, amber, jug shape, applied scroll handle, 19th C, imperfections, 8-1/4" h **195.00**
Wm. H. Spears Old Pioneer Whiskey, walking bear, A. Fenkhausen & Co. Sole Agents, SF, medium amber, slug plate on front and back, 1/8" bleeding pot stone on back **715.00**

Wine

Alloa Glass Works, Scotland, 1830-60, cylindrical, three-piece mold, deep yellow olive, applied sloping collared mouth, pontil scar, 8-1/2" h, 3-3/4" d **325.00**
All Souls College, black, three-piece mold, pontil base, seal reads "A.S.C.R.," for All Souls Common Room, 11-1/2" h **130.00**
CP, 1697, England, c1697, sealed, squat onion form, dark olive green, sheared mouth, string rim, pontil scar, 5" h, 4-1/2" d, some minor ext. wear, shallow chips **9,000.00**
French, olive amber, cylinder, huge tube pontil, deep kick-up, c1780, 13" h **100.00**
London, dark olive, seal reads "Inner Temple," c1845, 9-1/2" h **60.00**

Bride's Baskets

History: Bride's baskets are one of the wonderful types of antiques that have evolved into an exciting collecting area from rather plain beginnings. The term "bride's basket" was first used around 1920. Until that time, the bowls were described by their makers for their intended use, e.g., berry or fruit bowls. The practice of serving berries and cream was popular from the end of the eighteenth century into the beginning of the nineteenth century. Berry sets consisting of a master bowl and matching serving bowls were necessities of a household. Berry bowls were made in most glass types of the period, including vividly colored glass, cut glass, and even pressed glass. By adding a metal frame, or standard, usually with a bail handle, a simple berry bowl became a basket. Ornate silver-plated holders enhanced the beauty of the glassware and were added by companies such as Pairpoint and Wilcox. These bowls were a popular wedding gift in the 1880-1920 era, hence, the name "bride's basket."

The name "bride's basket" is now well-known, and although not as popular now as in the post World War I period, bride's baskets are still collected. Art glass bowls with original silver-plated holders can command high prices.

Over the years, bowls and bases became separated and married pieces resulted. If the base has been lost, the bowl should be sold separately.

Reference: John Mebane, *Collecting Bride's Baskets and Other Glass Fancies*, Wallace-Homestead, 1976.

Reproduction Alert: The glass bowls have been reproduced.

Note: Items listed below have a silver-plated holder, unless otherwise noted.

5-1/4" l, 3-1/4" w, 5-1/2" h, miniature, Double Dahlia with Lens, green, gilt dec, unmarked frame, attributed to Unites States Glass Co., wear to gilt **80.00**

7-1/2" d, orange and white MOP satin with gold tracery, Aurora silver plate holder, figural butterflies and daisies **680.00**

7-1/2" d, 3-3/4" h, rich pink ext. with opalescent stripes, gold lustered int., sq ruffled edge, Monet Stumpf, Patin **125.00**

7-3/4" d, 3-1/4" h, bowl only, cased, light blue int., multicolored enamel leaf dec **50.00**

8" d, blue cased glass shading to white bowl, enameled dec, Victorian. . **100.00**

8" d, 2-1/8" h, bowl only, satin overlay, shaded pink, clear edging on base, gold and silver sanded flowers and leaves dec, ruffled, off-white lining, ground pontil **155.00**

8" d, 10-1/2" h, Loetz-type glass, irid blue, and purple, recessed indentations, ruffled, ground pontil, ftd metal stand. **345.00**

8" d, 10-1/2" h, sq crimped edge bowl, white cased to rose-red, cameo cut winged griffins, floral bouquets and swags, fitted silver-plated metal frame with leaf and berry embellished handle, Mt. Washington Glass Co. bowl, frame marked "Pairpoint" **825.00**

8" d, 11" h, Guttate, satin pink cased, cross type frame, marked "B. Bro's Triple Plate" and "Pat Jan 22, 1884," chips on bowl **225.00**

8-1/4" w, sq, cased, deep rose and white ext., whit int., dragon, floral, and leaf dec, ruffled edge, Mt. Washington **675.00**

8-1/2" d, 8" h, cased, red, yellow, and white marbleized ext., heavy gilt leaf type dec, peach int., mounted into gilded brass frame with four lion's head feet **750.00**

8-1/2" d, 14-1/2" h, heavenly blue satin glass shading to pale white, diamond quilted design, pie crust crimped edge, orig fancy silver-plated holder, Mt. Washington. **400.00**

9" d, Peachblow, shiny finish bowl, applied amber rim, silver-plated Wilcox holder **215.00**

9" d, 12" h, Mt. Washington, Rose Amber, Coin Spot pattern, deep color, fancy silver-plated Pairpoint stand **875.00**

Cased, pink interior with spattered rose decoration, purple rim, silver plated pedestal rim, **$150.**

Pink glass bride's basket decorated with green flowers, silver plated stand, **$375.** *Photo courtesy of Joy Luke Fine Art Brokers and Auctioneers.*

9-1/4" d, blue opalescent, crimped rim, reticulated silver-plated holder marked "Wallingford, Biggins & Rodgers Co." **225.00**

9-1/4" d, Peachblow, yellow flowers dec, orig silver-plated holder... **225.00**

9-1/4" d, 9-1/2" h, cased, light butterscotch and pink, rose and butterfly dec, sand finish on ext., Rogers silver-plated frame with applied cherries, bands and chain on handle **400.00**

9-3/8" d, cased, shaded pink int. with gold floral dec, clear ruffled rim, whit ext........................ **110.00**

9-1/2" d, MOP satin, Diamond Quilted pattern, deep blue shading to pale blue int., blue shading to white ext., applied frosted crimped edge, Mt. Washington **600.00**

9-3/4" d, 2-3/4" h, 3" d, base, bowl only, shaded pink overlay, ruffled edge, white underside, colored enameled flowers and foliage dec, clear and opaque ribbon applied edge **220.00**

9-3/4" d, 11" h, off-white ext., shaded rose int., crystal ruffled edge, Rogers & Bros. silver-plated basket with two small hands, chains, fruit design on holder **300.00**

9-7/8" d, 7-1/2" w, 10-1/2" h, cased, pink int., white ext., crimped rim with clear border, Pairpoint frame **275.00**

10" d, 2-1/2" h, deep rose shading to pink satin bowl, ruffled, enameled floral dec **225.00**

10" d, 11" h, Vasa Murrhina, outer amber layer, center layer with hundreds of cream-colored spots, random toffee-colored spots, dark veins, gold mica flakes, mulberry pink lining, crossed rod thorn handles..... **635.00**

10" w, sq, custard, melon ribbed, enameled daisies, applied rubena crystal rim, twisted and beaded handle, ftd, emb silver-plated frame, marked "Wilcox" **450.00**

10-1/2" d, Hobnail, pink, enameled flowers, ruffled rim, reticulated silver-plated frame **250.00**

10-1/2" h, colorless frosted bowl, overlaid in pink crystal, etched acorn and oak leaf dec, gilt metal frame with basket handles, Victorian...... **250.00**

10-1/2" d, 9" h, Ribbon pattern, clear and frosted shallow colorless bowl, Reed and Barton pedestal stand with Indians hunting buffalo around base, int. scratches in bowl **150.00**

10-1/2" d, 12-1/2" h, oval satin bow, blue int., white ext., pleated rim, applied frosted ribbon edge, ornate ftd Forbes frame **250.00**

10-1/2" d, 14" h, cased, yellow shaded to coral int., white ext., clear ruffled rim, Webster frame, 1" section off applied rim...................... **325.00**

10-1/2" d, 14" h, Dugan Venetian, green, ruffled rim, enameled dainty floral dec on ext., Silverware Mfg Co. frame, National Glass Co., Dugan Factory **140.00**

10-1/2" d, 16-1/2" h, double cased, dark shading to light pink int. and ext. with white core, scalloped ruffled rim, Reed and Barton frame **300.00**

10-3/4" d, 3-1/2" h, bowl only, overlay, heavenly blue, enameled white flowers, green leaves, white underside, ruffled **215.00**

10-3/4" d, 3-1/2" h, bowl only, satin, shaded purple, white underside, dainty purple and white flowers, lacy foliage dec **225.00**

11" d, cased, pink ext., peachblow int., gold stylized flowers, ornate silver-plated holder with aquatic marine life motif, marked "Pairpoint Mfg. Co." **825.00**

11" d, 10-1/2" h, white and vaseline bowl, all-over floral enamel dec, fancy silver-plated frame, sgd "Meriden," minor handle restoration....... **300.00**

11" d, 11-1/2" h, tricorn Crown Milano bowl, six large pansies, pale purple and orange tracery medallions, pale yellow int., orig tricorn ftd Pairpoint stand **3,000.00**

11" d, 15-1/2" h, satin, deep rose, enamel swan and floral dec, heavy bronze holder with birds perched on top....................... **425.00**

11-1/8" d, 3-3/4" h, bowl only, satin, brown shaded to cream overlay, raised dots, dainty gold and silver flowers and leaves dec, ruffled........... **250.00**

11-3/8" d, 3-1/4" h, 2-7/8" d base, bowl only, maroon shaded to cream overlay, fancy leaf edges with circle and slot emb designs, dainty enameled pink flowers, gold leaves, white underside **215.00**

11-1/2" h, sapphire blue bowl, applied ruffled rim, gold tracery and courting scene dec, ornate ftd Meriden stand **325.00**

11-1/2" d, 3-1/4" h, bowl only, cased, dark purple shading to white, yellow enamel dec, sq ruffled rim **180.00**

11-1/2" d, 3-5/8" h, bowl only, shaded green overlay satin, ruffled emb lattice edge, white underside **210.00**

11-1/2" d, 12" h, dark red satin glass shaded to cream, ruffled and crimped rim, silver plated stand **275.00**

11-1/2" d, 13" h, cased, free-form bowl, white int., dark shading to light pink ext., dainty floral enamel and gilt dec on int. and ext., Standard Silver Co. Ltd. pedestal with cherub stem, wear to int. dec **600.00**

11-1/2" d, 13-1/2" h, ruffled white shading to pink to raspberry bowl, cased in white, plum dec, gold ranches, hanging ferns, gold dotted florals, ornate double handled silver frame, figural flowers on handle and base **400.00**

Cased basket, deep maroon shading to pink to white, undulating scalloped rim, slightly ribbed body, delicate silver plated stand, **$325.**

Pink cased, H/P floral, ornate silver plated holder, 11" d bowl, 12" h, **$395**

13" d, 12" h, brilliant yellow cased jack-in-the-pulpit type bowl, heavily ruffled edge, blown out with enameled orange and green dec, metal holder with bronze finish, featuring leaves, berries, vines, and large bird sitting on branch, Victorian **500.00**

13" l, 12-1/2" h, oval satin bowl, shaded raspberry ext., brilliant turquoise int., tightly ruffed pleated and fold-in edge, rect shape, white and gold enameled floral leaf and berry dec on ornate ftd rope handled silver plated orig frame **650.00**

13-1/2" h, robin's egg blue shaded to white, scalloped rim, applied frosted ribbon, frosted Optic Petal pattern, silver-plated base with engraved griffins, butterflies, and bees on sides, full figural swan inside, figural lilies and berries on handle, marked "Reed & Barton" **300.00**

14" d, satin, rose pink, scalloped, rippled, ribbed, and swirled, lacy all-over enamel and gold flower pattern, figural silver-plated base with hummingbird, sgd "Eagle & Co." **1,200.00**

14" l, oval yellow-green bowl, cased in pink, encrusted gold flowers, brass flower-form stand, minor wear from stand. **385.00**

BRISTOL GLASS

History: Bristol glass is a designation given to a semi-opaque glass, usually decorated with enamel and cased with another color.

Initially, the term referred only to glass made in Bristol, England, in the seventeenth and eighteenth centuries. By the Victorian era, firms on the Continent and in America were copying the glass and its forms.

Glass forms commonly found in Bristol glass include cologne bottles, perfume bottles, scent bottles, decanters, finger bowls, and all types of small covered boxes.

Barber bottle, 7-1/2" h, multicolored design, ground pontil **110.00**

Biscuit jar, cov

- 5" d, 7-1/2" h, apple green body, enameled green and yellow flowers and plants, silver-plated rim, cov, handle, and base, figural strawberry finial **195.00**
- 6-1/2" h, white, brown leaves and white flowers. **165.00**

Bowl

- Colorless, cinched, ruffled, crimped, hp **65.00**
- Light blue, Cupid playing mandolin, gold trim **40.00**

Box, cov

- 1-5/8" l, 1" h, turquoise body, gold dec **110.00**
- 2-1/2" d, round, hinged, Cupid on lid, purple floral dec. **150.00**
- 4-1/8" l, 2-3/4" d, 3-1/2" h, oblong, blue, gilt-metal mounts and escutcheon. **550.00**
- 5-3/4" l, 3-5/8" h, egg shape, white body, pink, cream, blue, and yellow flowers **225.00**

Cake stand, celadon green, enameled herons in flight, gold trim. **135.00**

Candlesticks, pr, 7" h, soft green, gold band **75.00**

Compote, fluted, white body, hand painted cat scene, metal base . . **95.00**

Condiment set, cov mustard pot, pepper shaker with orig lid, open salt, milk white, pink and blue flowers and green leaves dec, 4-1/4" x 5-3/4" silver-plated holder **175.00**

Creamer and sugar, cov, white body, multicolored floral dec. **65.00**

Cruet, 6-3/4" h, enameled floral dec **50.00**

Decanter

- 8-3/8" h, gray, encrusted floral engraving, butterflies, gilt trim, vase-like stopper **75.00**
- 9-1/4" h, 3-1/2" d, apple green body, reeded gold trimmed green handles, matching stopper **120.00**
- 11-1/4" h, 3-1/2" d, white body, green and brown leaves and ferns, blue flowers with gold trim, matching stopper. **125.00**
- 11-1/2" h, ruffled stopper, enameled flowers and butterfly. **75.00**

Dresser set, two cologne bottles, cov powder jar, white, gilt butterflies dec, clear stoppers **75.00**

Egg cup, white body, gold bands **25.00**

Ewer

- 4-1/2" h, 2-3/4" d, turquoise, enameled pink flowers, white and green leaves, yellow scrolls, gold trim, applied turquoise handles, pr **190.00**
- 6-3/8" h, 2-5/8" d, pink ground, fancy gold designs, bands, and leaves, applied handle with gold trim **135.00**

Finger bowl, 4-3/8" d, blue, faceted sides, early 20th C, eight-pc set **500.00**

Goblet, 10-3/4" h, pedestal base, opaque blue ground, polychrome enamel floral dec, gilt trim **95.00**

Hatpin holder, 6-1/8" h, ftd, blue, enameled jewels, gold dec **100.00**

Lamp

- 13-1/4" h, blue body, enameled white egret, multicolored flowers and foliage, brass oil fittings, black base **300.00**
- 27" h, glass globe and body, molded in high relief foliate and cherub's head dec, polychrome enameled floral reserves, brass mounts, Victorian, electrified **475.00**

Mantel luster, 3-1/4" d, 7" h, mint green Bristol glass, hp mauve and pink flowers, blue forget-me-nots, green leaves, ruffled edge, remnants of gold trim, polished pontil, c1890, 2" l crystal prisms. **275.00**

Mantle vase, 11" h, painted transfer scene of boy with poodle, large hand painted florals, 19th C, pr. **150.00**

Vase, light pink, handpainted medium pink flowers, green leaves, gold accents, crimped undulating rim, 12" h, **$115.**

Miniature lamp, 10" h, 4-3/4" d, white shaded to soft blue, dainty enameled orange flowers, green leaves, sq ruffled shade, base with matching flowers, brown flying bird, applied opalescent shell feet, orig burner and chimney **885.00**

Mug, 5" h, white, eagle and "Liberty" **375.00**

Patch box, cov, 1" h, 1-1/4" d, hinged, soft pink ground, enameled brown and white bird **100.00**

Perfume bottle

- 3-1/4" h, squatty, blue, gold band, white enameled flowers and leaves, matching stopper.. **100.00**
- 3-7/8" h, hourglass shape, opaque blue, silver-mounted cap .. **175.00**

Pitcher

- 2-1/4" h, 3-1/4" d, turquoise body, gold band, enameled yellow flowers and leaves, applied turquoise handle.......... **65.00**
- 8-1/4" h, light green body, enameled bird and flowers, applied clear handle **95.00**

Plate, 14-1/2" d, white body, hand painted, lavender and ochre French lilacs, green leaves **80.00**

Puff box, cov, round, blue, gold dec **35.00**

Ring box, cov, 1-3/4" h, 1-3/4" d, turquoise body, gold flowers and leaves **50.00**

Rose bowl, 3-1/2" d, shaded blue, crimped edge **65.00**

Salt, 2-3/4" d, light gray body, enameled herons and foliage, silver-plated rim and handle **48.00**

Sugar shaker, 4-3/4" h, white, hp flowers **60.00**

Sweetmeat jar, cov

- 3" d, 5-1/2" h, deep pink, enameled flying duck, leaves, blue flower dec, white lining, silver-plated rim, lid, and bail handle....... **110.00**
- 4-1/2" d, 5-1/2" h, floral garlands and butterflies dec, silver-plated top and bail handle **125.00**

Tumbler, 6-3/4" h, 2-3/4" d, turquoise body, gold and white rope garlands, gold foot **72.00**

Urn, 18" h, pink, boy and girl with lamp **550.00**

Vase

- 4" h, caramel acid finish, hand painted scenic and floral dec, remnants of French retailer's label **50.00**
- 8" h, 2-3/4" w, Fireglow, beige ground, white flowers, green and gold leaves, worn gold accents, matched pr **100.00**
- 8-1/2" h, light pink shading to dark pink, hp enameled design .. **65.00**
- 8-1/2" h, white body, enameled floral and leaf dec, ruffled top, ram's head handles **75.00**
- 9" h, white body, portrait of young boy and girl, facing pr..... **165.00**
- 9-3/8" h, white body, hand painted, flowers, gold trim, raised enameling, pr **150.00**
- 10" h, blue body, cut-out base, enameled floral dec, pr.... **120.00**
- 10-1/8" h, 4-1/4" d base, powder blue, white enamel dec of girl holding bird.......... **70.00**
- 13" h, 6" d, shaded pastel yellow ground, red and purple poppies and white daisies, tapered cylindrical shape.......... **100.00**
- 14" h, coach and horses, scrolls dec **100.00**
- 17" h, 7" w, white body, American cattle scene, artist sgd, pr . **250.00**

Vase, blue ground, hand painted floral decoration, ruffled rim, 7-1/2" h, **$75.**

Burmese Glass

History: Burmese glass is a translucent art glass originated by Frederick Shirley and manufactured by the Mt. Washington Glass Co., New Bedford, Massachusetts, from 1885 to c1891.

Burmese glass colors shade from a soft lemon to a salmon pink. Uranium was used to attain the yellow color, and gold was added to the batch so that on reheating, one end turned pink. Upon reheating again, the edges would revert to the yellow coloring. A yellow top edge is a common indicator that the glassworker reheated the piece at least twice. The blending of the colors was so gradual that it is difficult to determine where one color ends and the other begins.

Although some of the glass has a glossy surface, most pieces were acid finished, resulting in a velvet-type finish. The majority of the items were free blown, but some were blown molded in a ribbed, hobnail, or diamond-quilted design. Glass finishing techniques resulted in ruffled edges, turned down rims, and even included the application of stems, leaves, and flowers. Hand-painted enameled decorations include insects, fish, birds, Egyptian motifs, flowers, leaves, and poetic verses. Artists such as Albert Steffin, Frank Guba, Adolf Frederick, and Timothy Canty often signed their works. Paper labels were also used to mark Burmese objects.

American-made Burmese is quite thin and, therefore, fragile and brittle. English Burmese was made by Thos. Webb & Sons. Out of deference to Queen Victoria, they called their wares "Queen's Burmese."

References: John A. Shuman, III, *The Collector's Encyclopedia of American Art Glass*, Collector Books, 1988, 1994 value update; Kenneth Wilson, *American Glass 1760-1930: The Toledo Museum of Art, Volume I, Volume II,* Hudson Hills Press and the Toledo Museum of Art, 1994.

Collectors Club: Mount Washington Art Glass Society, P.O. Box 24094, Fort Worth, TX 76124-1094.

Reproduction Alert: Reproductions abound in almost every form. Since uranium can no longer be used, some of the reproductions are easy to spot. In the 1950s, Gundersen produced many pieces in imitation of Burmese.

Museums: New Bedford Glass Museum, New Bedford, MA; The Chrysler Museum, Norfolk, VA; The Corning Museum of Glass, Corning, NY; Sandwich Glass Museum, Sandwich, MA; The Toledo Museum of Art, Toledo, OH.

Gundersen

Basket, 8" h, 5" w, matte finish, applied twisted Burmese rope handle .. **300.00**

Charger, 10" d, shallow, disk shape **285.00**

Hat, 3" h, 4" w brim, Diamond Quilted pattern.......... **375.00**

Nut dish, 4" d, coral and gray fronds laden with tiny bittersweet colored blossoms, slightly upward draped sides **345.00**

Plate, 9" d, acid finish........ **650.00**

Toothpick holder **135.00**

Vase, 9-1/2" h, Tappan, acid finish **375.00**

Mount Washington

Basket, 5-1/2" h, 6" w, very pale yellow shading to deep pink, applied frosted loop handle **300.00**

Bonbon

- 5-1/4" l, 1-1/2" h, satin finish, rect, bulged out optic ribbed sides, turned-in edges **345.00**

Tumbler, matte finish, **$175.**

5-1/4" l, 4-1/2" w, 2" h, smooth satin finish, rectangular bowl, bulged-out optic ribbed sides with turned-in edges **285.00**

6-1/2" l, 4-3/4" w, 2-3/8" to top of handle, shiny, lemon-yellow, three applied prunts, applied handle, re-fired heart shaped rim. . . **950.00**

Bowl

5" l, 4-1/2" w, 2" h, rect, thin walls, c1880 . . . . **425.00**

7-1/4" d, 6" h, six ruffled top, three pulled edge, three applied shell feet, large applied berry over pontil **1,100.00**

12" d, glossy, fluted rim, 10 pinched corners **300.00**

Chalice, 8-3/4" h, matte finish, 1890s **1,800.00**

Cider pitcher, 6-3/4" h, minor heat check in handle **385.00**

Compote, 7"d, 4" h, glossy, ruffled top, baluster stem **330.00**

Cream pitcher

2-5/8" h, enameled vintage dec, ruffled rim **295.00**

5-1/2" h, Shape #154, crimped edge with re-fired yellow border. . **485.00**

Cream pitcher and sugar, 4-1/8" h pitcher, 2-5/8" h sugar, Shape #99, diamond quilt design, heat check on creamer **465.00**

Cruet

6" h, salmon shading to white, blue flowers, green leaves and vines **2,950.00**

6-1/8" h, 3-3/4" w, bulbous base, vertical ribbing, acid finish, delicate pink shading two-thirds way down, dainty handle, orig stopper **500.00**

6-1/2" h, satin finish, delicate blush on shoulders, melon ribbed body, soft lemon-yellow handle and faceted stopper. **1,0855.00**

6-1/2" h, three striking chrysanthemum blossoms, two white and one yellow, coral colored detail stripes mushroom stopper, signed "88" in enamel . . . **2,950.00**

7" h, shiny finish, 30 ribs with light pink, blush intensifies on neck and stopper, mushroom stopper, applied handle **1,250.00**

Demitasse cup and saucer, 2-3/8" h, 3-1/8" d cup, 4-5/8" d saucer, undecorated, orig paper label on saucer **585.00**

Dish, 5" d, 3/4" h, shiny finish, deep color. **185.00**

Ewer, 6" h, 2-1/2" d base, long spout, loop handle, applied base, deep color, acid finish, c1880 . . . . **950.00**

Finger bowl, 2-3/4" d, shiny finish, refired crimped rim **435.00**

Ice cream bowl, 9" d 2-3/4" h, deep salmon pink shading to bright yellow, satin finish **950.00**

Jack-in-the-pulpit vase

6-1/2" h, 3" w top, ruffled, matte finish **425.00**

9" h, refired yellow margin of pie-crimped edge, subtle blush of color at mouth and throat, soft yellow standard and base . **750.00**

Jack-in-the-pulpit, 12-1/2" h, elongated prunus blossom dec, gold detail stripes, row of white dots on wafer base. **1,750.00**

Lamp, 19-1/2" h, 10" d shade, fine pink to yellow shaded ground, Frank Guba hand-painted ducks in bright natural colors, three ducks on shade, two on font, fitted with orig Burmese chimney, gilt metal fluid mounts, electrified **11,500.00**

Lamp shade, 5" l, gas light type

Acid finish. **250.00**

Satin finish **300.00**

Jack-in-the-pulpit vase, wide flaring top with deep coloration shading to short body, flared foot, **$750.**

Lemonade set, 7" h x 9" w Egyptian style pitcher, six 4" tumblers, c1880 . . . . **2,250.00**

Milk pitcher

5" w handle to spout, 4" h, satin **850.00**

7-1/4" h, 4" w, tankard, applied loop handle, matte finish. **950.00**

Mustard pot, 4-1/2" h, shiny finish, barrel shape, vertical ribs, bail, metal collar, hinged lid. **425.00**

Pin jar, cov, 2-3/4" h, 4" d, unfired finish, tomato shape, melon ribbed, shaded green ground, large purple and white chrysanthemums, green leaves, fancy SP cov **275.00**

Pitcher

5-1/4" h, 3-1/4" w, acid finish, petticoat shape, deep color, applied loop handle **875.00**

6-3/4" h, 8-1/2" w, satin finish, unadorned. **950.00**

9-1/4" h, 5-1/2" d, ruffled top, rosy salmon shading to canary yellow, applied yellow handle. **485.00**

Rose bowl, 2-1/2" h, 2-1/2" d. . . **285.00**

Rose jar, cov

5" h, 2-1/2" d, petticoat shape, wild rose dec, deep salmon pink shading to yellow, period gold dec cov and metal insert **1,610.00**

5-1/4" h, floral dec **400.00**

Salt shaker

4" h, pillar ribbed, pansies dec, orig top. **325.00**

4-1/4" h, blushed upper half, lemon-yellow lower half, two-part metal top **265.00**

Sugar bowl, cov, 4-1/2" w, 3-1/2" h, wishbone feet, matte finish, berry prunt over pontil. **750.00**

Sugar shaker, 4-1/2" h, 4" w, painted shaded salmon colored ground, enameled blue and white small flowers done in the manner of Timothy Canty, unfired, orig cover **400.00**

Syrup pitcher

6" h, pansy dec, silver plated collar and lid, emb florals and winged insects. **3,750.00**

6-1/2" h, 3" w, bulbous egg form, enameled purple and yellow spider mums, green and brown leaves, applied sq handle, period fancy SP cov **4,025.00**

Tankard pitcher

8-3/4" h, meadow daisies, enameled petals on front, obverse with single flower, colorful butterfly, verse by James Montgomery, applied

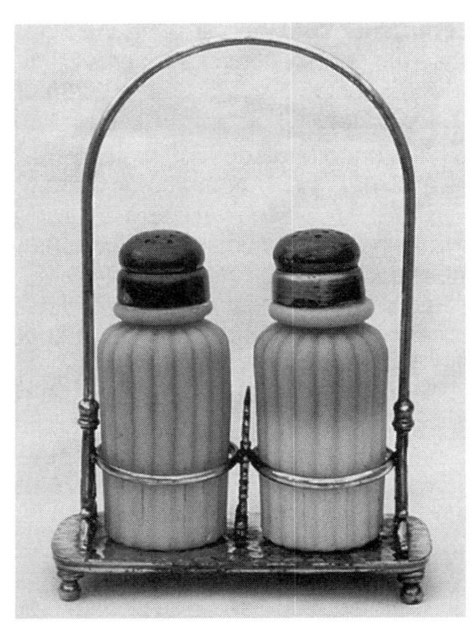

Salt and pepper shakers, pair, silver plated Tufts holder, 7-1/2" h, 4-3/4" w, **$600.**

glossy yellow handle, tight, stable line **1,400.00**
9" h, glossy, applied glossy yellow handle, scratch **650.00**
9" h, rural scene and florals, Longfellow verse **3,500.00**

Toothpick holder
2-1/2" h, shiny finish, pinched tricorn top, Optic Diamond Quilt pattern **535.00**
2-1/2" h, tricorn folded in top, light blue blossoms with bright yellow centers, color blush on lower half of body, shape #4. . . . . **585.00**
2-3/4" h, 3" w, matte finish, sq mouth, bulbous base **325.00**
3" h, 3" w, sq mouth, bulbous base, seven pine cones, needles, and branches **675.00**

Tumbler, 3-3/4" h, 2-3/4" d
Acid finish, painted and enameled English ivy dec. **395.00**
Acid finish, painted field daisies, enameled petals. **900.00**
Pastel salmon shading to a creamy-yellow **285.00**
Matte finish **175.00**
Shiny finish, eggshell thin satin body **375.00**

Vase
3" h, 3-1/2" d, bulbous base, yellow enameled daisy and leaves dec **850.00**
4-1/2" h, shiny finish, scalloped rim, unadorned, Shape 52-1/2" C **585.00**
5-1/2" h, gourd, flared rim, acid finish **550.00**
5-3/4" h, very pale pink to yellow body, white flowers with yellow centers **600.00**
6" h, bulbous, c1880 . . . . **350.00**
6" h, floriform shape, hp fern leaf dec, fitted into gold sgd "Dunham Mfg Co. Triple Plate" holder with Egyptian motif **545.00**
6-1/4" h, acid finish, delicate scalloped rim, int. open blister **250.00**
6-1/2" h, shiny finish, scalloped rim, unadorned, Shape 52-1/2" S **565.00**
7" h, lily, delicate blush to the mouth of the "lily," refired yellow rim **650.00**
7" h, 4" w, double gourd, matte finish, deep salmon pink shading to yellow **500.00**
8" h, gourd shape, roses and forget-me-nots, three lovely peach-colored rose blossoms cling to leafed branch which swirl down rim, around body and down to the base, entwining strands of turquoise-colored forget-me-not blossoms, double gourd shaped **1,050.00**
8" h, Queen's Design, #145 gourd shape, stylized floral dec, multicolored enamel blossoms and buds **2,950.00**
8-1/2" h, 3-1/2" w base, gourd, matte finish **425.00**
8-1/2" h, 3-1/2" w base, gourd, multicolored prunous dec, shades of pale blue and brown, leaves, and stems, 35 white enameled beads on rim, slightly worn . **850.00**
8-1/2" h, 4-1/2" w, double gourd, deep colors **425.00**
8-3/4" h, 5" w, double gourd, matte finish **435.00**
9-3/4" h, lily, unpolished pontil **750.00**
10" h, lily, flesh tone blush, well defined re-fired yellow border **455.00**
10" h, lily, tricorn trumpet, pink rim shading to yellow base **400.00**
10" h, stick, acid finish, scattered sprays of pansies in natural colors **440.00**
10-1/4" h, 5-1/2" w at shoulder, 5-1/4" neck, gourd shape, acid finish **750.00**
11" h, 6" d, white daisies, lemon-yellow ground, No. 146 . . . . **1,750.00**
11-1/2" h, acid finished, ovoid, hp Egyptian desert scene, pyramids and ibis in flight, gilt highlights **4,500.00**
11-1/2" h, 6-1/2" w, gourd, deep salmon pink to yellow, gold, brown, green, tan, and rust bamboo dec **1,875.00**
12" h, ibis in flight, pyramids, palm tree, and sand dunes, rosy-pink blush, drilled 3/8" hole in base **2,750.00**
12" h, lily, satin finish, yellow border as blush to lily **665.00**
12" h, 6-3/4" w, bulbous stick, Queen's pattern, three large open blossoms, seven buds, enameled white, yellow, blue, green, and gold, c1880 . . . . **3,950.00**
12-1/4" h, lily, gross finish . . . **875.00**
12-1/4" h, lily, matte finish . . . **750.00**
12-3/4" h, glossy finish **875.00**
14" h, lily, deep salmon pink shading to brilliant yellow, matte finish, irregular-shaped base **875.00**
15" h, lily, brilliant yellow to deep salmon pink, matte finish . . **950.00**
23-1/2" h, trumpet shape, c1890 . . . . **1,400.00**

Whiskey taster, 2-3/4" tall, molded-in elongated diamond quilted design **285.00**

Pairpoint

Hat, 1-1/4" h, shiny finish, c1930 **450.00**
Jack-in-the-pulpit vase, 5-1/4" h, 6-3/4" w at crown, deep salmon to brilliant yellow, glossy finish, c1920 . . . . **575.00**
Vase, 10" h, 5" d, trumpet, scalloped top, deep color, shiny finish, c1920 . . . . **650.00**

Webb

Bowl
4" d, 2-1/2" h, shiny finish, ruffled, intense salmon shading to yellow **400.00**
6-1/4" d, 3-3/4" h, floral dec, applied colorless rim, marked "Thos Webb" **1,200.00**

Candle cup holder, 1-3/4" h, 4-1/4" d, clear glass candle cup, orig unused candle, holder sgd "S. Clarke Patent Trade Mark Fairy," clear glass cup sgd "S. Clarke Trade Mark Fairy," candle imp "Sam Clarke's New Patent Trade Fairy Mark" **850.00**
Creamer and sugar, 4-1/2" h creamer, 2-1/2" h open sugar, acid finish, wishbone feet, berry pontil, professional repair to one foot on creamer . . **935.00**

Cruet, orig stopper

6-1/2" h, three striking chrysanthemum blossoms, two white and one yellow, coral colored detail stripes mushroom stopper, signed "88" in enamel . . . **2,950.00**

7" h, shiny finish, mushroom stopper, each rib has hint of pink, refired buttery yellow tip of spout **1,250.00**

Epergne

11" h, Queen's Burmese, gilt metal center arrangement supports two crimped bowls, central shat, delicate matching floral motif, sgd bowls and metalwork, fairy lamp candle shades and holders missing **2,300.00**

14" h, 8" center floriform vase, satin finish, pastel yellow stripes, unique pink blush borders, undecorated, shallow bowl-shaped base with muted Burmese color, cone-shaped center rising to support brass fittings that hold three petite Burmese bud vases **1,950.00**

Fairy lamp

3-3/4" h, pyramid, Burmese shade, clear glass base sgd "S. Clarke's Pyramid Fairy" **335.00**

3-3/4" h, pyramid, Burmese shade, unsigned clear glass base . **145.00**

4" h, oval pink to yellow top, ruffled and crimped bowl, colorless Clarkes holder, orig candle . **815.00**

4" h, pyramid, pressed glass base has molded-in "S. Clarke Fairy Pyramid" and dancing fairy logo signature **335.00**

4-3/4" h, pyramid, Burmese shade, clear base sgd "S. Clarke's Pyramid Fairy" **335.00**

5-1/2" h, Cricklite, satin, dome shade, 6" sq base with folded in sides, impressed signature "Thos. Webb & Sons Queens Burmeseware Patented," clear glass candle cup signed, "S Clarke Fairy Trade Mark Patent" . . . **985.00**

5-1/2" h, 5-3/4" w, Cricklite, short crimped skirt flares out from the top of the bowl-shaped base, impressed signature "Thos. Webb & Sons Queens Burmeseware Patented," clear glass candle cup is signed, "S Clarke Fairy Trade Mark Patent," unused wax candle **950.00**

5-1/2" h, 7-1/2" d base, dome shade, frilly pleated skirt, clear glass candle cup sgd "Clarke's Criklite Trade Mark" **1,350.00**

6" h, 7-1/2" d spreading skirt-like pleated base, two acid-etched signatures, "Thos Webb & Sons Queen's Burmeseware Patented" and "S. Clarke's Fairy Patent Trade Mark," clear glass candle cup signed, "Clarke's Criklite Trade Mark" **950.00**

18-1/2" h overall, 3-1/2" h acid finished Burmese shades, colorless pressed Clarke inserts, mounted on silver double arm reeded column with stem base, pr **470.00**

Jar, cov, 3" h, 2-5/8" d, acid finish, rich coloring, brown leaves, blue and white enameled flowers, star-shaped top **300.00**

Perfume bottle, 5" l, flattened elongated oval teardrop, blossom laden branch, blue butterfly, silver screw rim and cap stamped "CM" with hallmarks, cap dented **865.00**

Relish dish, 3" h, 5-3/4" d, 6-1/2" h, 8" w, two hat-shaped bowls, pastel yellow crown, shading to blushed rolled rim, three butterflies and dragonfly dec on each, flattened brim with brilliant golden laden bittersweet blossoms, SP tray, figural calla lily on handle of SP handle **1,500.00**

Rose bowl, 3-1/4" h, prunus blossom dec, sq top **585.00**

Salt, 2-3/4" d, acid finish, bittersweet colored blossoms, gold branches **450.00**

Scent bottle, 4-7/8 l, 1-1/4" w at shoulder, lay down type, shading from blush at shoulder to soft yellow point, mistletoe leaves, white berries dec, sterling screw on top hallmarked "CM," rampant lion, "N" and anchor . **1,400.00**

Sweetmeat jar, cov, 7" h, acid finish, cylindrical, bittersweet and gold foliage, SP collar, lid, and bail handle, sgd **300.00**

Toothpick holder, shiny, soft peach blush fading to buttery-yellow, eggshell-thin body. **435.00**

Vase

3-1/2" h, petal top, deep salmon to yellow, matte finish **250.00**

3-1/2" h, petal top, deep color, large green leaves, red berries, matte finish **475.00**

4" h, Webb, shiny finish, ruffled top **485.00**

4-1/4" h, ruffled, Jules Barbe prunus dec, slight fading to dec . . . **350.00**

6" h, white, front has line-drawn, sepia-colored decoration in Chinoiserie motif depicting oriental man after releasing arrow from bow striking goose in mid air, reverse side is continuation of scene, elaborate border encircling shoulder **950.00**

8" h, gourd shape, roses and forget-me-nots, three lovely peach-colored rose blossoms cling to leafed branch which swirl down rim, around body and down to the base, entwining strands of turquoise-colored forget-me-not blossoms, double gourd shaped **1,250.00**

8-1/2" h, 4" d, acid finish, red buds, green and brown leaves, yellow wafer foot **750.00**

11" h, 6" d base, white daisies with distinctive yellow-dot centers **1,750.00**

14" h, 7" d, bulbous, deep color dec with two monkeys frolicking among bamboo stalks, gold highlighting and trim **13,225.00**

23-1/2" h, circa 1890 . . . . . **1,250.00**

Whiskey taster, 2-3/4" tall, molded-in elongated diamond quilted design **285.00**

Vase, trumpet shaped, 8" h, **$350.** *Photo courtesy of Joy Luke Fine Art Brokers and Auctioneers.*

Cambridge Glass

History: Cambridge Glass Company, Cambridge, Ohio, was incorporated in 1901. Initially, the company made clear tableware, later expanding into colored, etched, and engraved glass. More than 40 different hues were produced in blown and pressed glass.

The Cambridge, Ohio, area was a successful location because a good supply of natural gas and silicon sand were available. The area was also rich in talent because of the National Glass Company, which had brought Arthur J. Bennett to manage its new factory. Under his supervision, National Glass produced the first piece of crystal glassware, a water pitcher, in May 1902. When the company developed financial difficulties in 1907, Bennett recognized its potential and refinanced the company. By 1910, the company had expanded and opened another plant in Byesville, Ohio. It continued operations until 1917, when it closed and all employees were transferred to the plant at Cambridge. With the addition of these talented employees and new capital investments, the Cambridge Glass Company grew. All products were handmade. More than 5,000 molds were used to create the complete line of patterns offered.

One of the distinctive characteristics of Cambridge glassware is the jewel-like colors. Transparent colors include: amber, amethyst, apple green, Carmen (brilliant ruby red), Cinnamon, Crystal, Dianthus (light transparent pink), Eleanor Krystol (gold tint), Heatherbloom (delicate orchid), LaRosa (light pastel pink), Mandarin Gold (very light gold yellow), Mocha, Moonlight (pastel blue), Peach-blue (light pink), pistachio (pastel green), Ritz Blue (bright blue), Royal Blue, Smoke, and Willow Blue. Opaque colors include: Azure Blue (dark blue), Blue Milk (light blue), Coral (flesh-like orange-pink), Crown Tucson (flesh-like pink), Ebony (satin finish black), Ebony (black), Heliotrope (purple), Ivory (light cream), Jade (blue-green), Milk (white), Opal (pearly), Pearl Green (glossy green), Pomona Turquoise, and Violet (light purple). Shaded transparent colors include: Amberina, Mardi Gras, (crystal body with assorted color flecks), Rubina, (later called Sunset), Tomato (yellow-green at top, blending to red and yellow-green at base), and Varitone (Moonlight, LaRosa, Mocha, and Pistachio).

Five different marks were used during the production years, but not every piece was marked. A paper sticker was used from 1935-1954.

The National Cambridge Collectors, Inc. deserves a great deal of credit for the work it does. Incorporated in 1973, it is a nonprofit educational organization devoted to the preservation and collection of Cambridge Glass Company wares. It established a permanent museum in 1982. This group also published excellent reference books, which contain patterns, etchings, and even color comparisons.

The plant closed in 1954. Some of the molds were later sold to the Imperial Glass Company, Bellaire, Ohio.

References: Tom and Neila Bredehoft, *Fifty Years of Collectible Glass, 1920-1970*, Volume 1, Volume II, Antique Trader Books, 2000; Gene Florence, *Elegant Glassware of the Depression Era*, 9th ed., Collector Books, 2000; —, *Glass Candlesticks of the Depression Era*, Collector Books, 1999; —, *Very Rare Glassware of the Depression Years*, 5th Series, Collector Books, 1999; *National Cambridge Collectors, Inc.*, Cambridge Glass Co., Cambridge, Ohio (reprint of 1930 catalog and supplements through 1934), Collector Books, 1976, 1997 value update; —, *Cambridge Glass Co., Cambridge, Ohio, 1949 through 1953* (catalog reprint), Collector Books, 1976, 1996 value update; —, *Colors in Cambridge Glass*, Collector Books, 1984, 1993 value update; —, *Miami Valley Ohio Study Group, Etchings by Cambridge*, Volume I, 1997; Naomi L. Over, *Ruby Glass of the 20th Century*, Antique Publications, 1990, 1993-94 value update; Bill and Phyllis Smith, *Cambridge Glass 1927-1929* (1986) and *Identification Guide to Cambridge Glass 1927-1929* (updated prices 1996), published by authors.

Periodical: *Cambridge Crystal Ball* Newsletter, P.O. Box 416, Cambridge, OH.

Collectors' Club: National Cambridge Collectors, Inc., P.O. Box 416, Cambridge, OH 43725, www.cambridgeglass.org.

Museums: Cambridge Glass Museum, Cambridge, OH; Museum of the National Cambridge Collectors, Inc., Cambridge, OH.

Note: Prices listed are for crystal (colorless) unless otherwise noted.

Miscellaneous patterns and etchings

Aquarium, Madeira, bird and flower etching, floral pattern band etched at top, c1930, 10-1/4" h, 10-1/2" w, 4-3/4" d 1,500.00

Ashtray

Canoe, Ebony, stars dec 125.00

Crown Tuscan

4" d, 3 ftd. 37.50

4" l, shell, no dec. 30.00

Shell, #34, three-toed, orig label

Amber 12.50

Light green 12.50

Mandarin Gold 15.00

Mocha. 12.50

Moonlight blue 15.00

Yellow 12.50

Stack Away, four ashtrays, blue, green, pink, and yellow, wood base 55.00

#3797/150, Ebony, birds dec, 6-1/2" d 195.00

Basket

Crown Tuscan, #55, 6". 75.00

Hunt's Scene, pink, 11" h. . . . 215.00

#119, amber, crystal handle . . 75.00

Beer mug

#55, Martha, frosted green and crystal, 10 oz. 40.00

#56, Martha, frosted green and crystal, 12 oz. 45.00

Bookends, pr

Eagles. 135.00

Lion, amber, NCC 1978 . . . . 195.00

Scotties. 150.00

Bouillon soup, #703, Florentine Green 19.50

Bowl

#933, #739 etching, ebony, 12" d 45.00

#3400 Line, Gold Krystol, Cambridge mark on bottom. 12.00

#3900/49, Valencia, handle, 5" d 40.00

10" d, Flying Nude, Crown Tuscan 250.00

10" d, Windsor Blue, seashell, three toes 250.00

14-1/2" d, Everglades, yellow, swans 225.00

Bridge Hound, #1371, figural dog bridge pencil holder, amber, 1-7/8" h, **$65.** *Photo courtesy of Michael Krumme.*

Bridge hound

#1371, amethyst. 75.00

#1371, ebony 85.00

#1371, peachblow 60.00

#1371, pistachio. 75.00

Bud vase

Crown Tuscan, 10" h. 65.00

Ebony, #274, 10" h, partial orig sticker. 35.00

Butter dish, cov

Gadroon 45.00

#3400, amber. 65.00

Candlesticks, pr

Block, #3797/493, ebony, stars dec, 1-3/4" h. 295.00

Calla Lily, Pristine, Forest Green 125.00

Calla Lily, Pristine, Mandarin Gold **120.00**
Cascade, #400, 1-lite **47.50**
Cherub, #1191, ebony **2,950.00**
Dolphin, double, Crown Tuscan **250.00**
Doric, Helio, 9-1/2" h **225.00**
Everglades **45.00**
Everglades, two-lite, moonlight #3 . . . . . **325.00**
Gadroon, ram's head, 4-1/2" h, cobalt opalescent **150.00**
Statuesque, 8-1/4" h, Crown Tuscan **250.00**
Swan, #1040, 3-1/2" h, Gold Krystol **55.00**
Talisman Rose, #3900/72, two-lite, gold trim **70.00**

Candy box, cov, #107, Crown Tuscan, Charlton dec, 6", ftd **155.00**

Candy dish, cov

#88, Plainware, cobalt blue, 1 lb size **75.00**
#103, Ebony, 7" **65.00**
#110, Windsor Blue, Seashell, 6" h, ftd **300.00**

Cereal bowl

#704 etch, green, 6-3/8" d **37.50**
#3500, Valencia, slight use . . . **50.00**

Champagne

#701 etch, pink, set of four . . **130.00**
#3085, Hunts Scene, pink **48.00**

Cheese and cracker, Lorna **35.00**

Cheese dish, cov, Cordelia, 5" d . **85.00**

Cigarette box, cov

Crown Tuscan **55.00**
#616, small **25.00**

Cigarette holder with ashtray, Two Tone, #1337, amber and crystal . . **45.00**

Cigarette holder with place-card holder, #3400/114, amethyst **50.00**

Cocktail

#3077, Hunts Scene, green . . . **60.00**
#3077, Hunts Scene, pink **60.00**
#3085, Hunts Scene, green . . . **60.00**
#3100/9, Statuesque, 3 oz, forest green, crystal stem **80.00**
#3100/9, Statuesque, 3 oz, Gold Krystol, Crown Tuscan stem **125.00**
#3126, Royal Blue bowl, 3 oz, 6" h **48.00**

Comport

Crown Tuscan, seashell, 7" w, 4" h **48.00**
Honeycomb, 9" d, 4-3/4" h, ftd, rubena **150.00**
Krome Kraft, 71/2" h, cutout grape motif, amethyst **55.00**
Mandarin Gold, #3900, 5-1/2" . **45.00**
Rosalie, #981, green, liner, 5" **125.00**
Statuesque, holding shell with Charleton design, gold trim, Crown Tuscan **275.00**

Condiment set, Pristine, five pcs **98.50**

Cordial

Magnolia **75.00**
Regency, Stradivari, 1 oz **68.00**
#1327, forest green **30.00**
#1341, amethyst, 1 oz **15.00**
#1341, cobalt blue, 1 oz **20.00**
#1341, forest green, 1 oz **15.00**
#1344, amethyst, 1 oz **15.00**
#1344, forest green, 1 oz **15.00**

Cornucopia

#47, Crown Tuscan, shell, 9" l **125.00**
#570, Crown Tuscan, 9", patent number **145.00**
#702, Crown Tuscan **55.00**

Creamer, Martha Washington, amber, clear stick handle **15.00**

Creamer and sugar, Cascade, #400, emerald green **35.00**

Cream soup

Etch 732, amber **18.50**
Willow Blue, #3400/55, orig liner **25.00**

Cup and saucer

Martha Washington, amber . . **12.00**
#703, Florentine Green **35.00**
#3400, crystal cup, cobalt blue saucer **16.50**
#3400, yellow **12.50**

Decanter, orig stopper

#1321, cobalt blue, 28 oz . . . **230.00**
#3121, amethyst **95.00**
#3121, Carmen **150.00**
#84482, Nautilus, crystal **45.00**
#84482, Nautilus, red, 14 oz. **195.00**

Dresser compact, dark amber, gold encrusted etch **195.00**

Finger bowl

Adam, yellow **25.00**
#703, Florentine Green, scratches **12.50**

Flower center

Seashell, #110, #42, 8" **250.00**
Seashell, #110, #44 . . . . . **200.00**

Flower frog

Bashful Charlotte, 6" h

Crystal **95.00**
Green **225.00**
Mandarin Gold **250.00**
Moonlight blue **650.00**
Pink **225.00**

Bashful Charlotte, 11" h

Crystal satin **360.00**
Moonlight blue **600.00**
Moonlight blue satin **775.00**

Blue Jay, 5-1/2" h

Crystal **120.00**
Green **365.00**
Moonlight blue **200.00**

Draped Lady, 8-1/2" h

Amber **190.00**
Blue **260.00**
Crown Tuscan **1,850.00**
Crystal, frosted, ribbed base **75.00**
Dark pink **150.00**
Emerald, light **300.00**
Frosted green **150.00**
Gold Krystol **275.00**
Green **160.00**
Honey, oval base **495.00**
Light pink **160.00**
Midnight blue **325.00**
Moonlight blue, satin **450.00**
Yellow **180.00**

Draped Lady, 13-1/2" h

Moonlight blue **850.00**
Peachblow **550.00**
Pink **180.00**

Eagle, 5-5/8" h

Crystal **350.00**
Pink **365.00**

Frog, #2889, 3-1/2" h, Dianthus Pink **55.00**

Heron

9" h, crystal, fluted base . . **160.00**
12" h, crystal, smooth base **20.00**

Mandolin Lady, 9" h, bend back, green **310.00**

Nude, 6-1/2" h, 3-1/4" d, clear . **95.00**

Rose Lady, 9" h

Amber **260.00**
Custard, #1 base **1,600.00**
Crystal **300.00**
Green **250.00**
Mocha, tall base **275.00**
Peachblow **275.00**
Pink **250.00**

Seagull, crystal **68.50**

Turtle, 3-1/2" x 5-1/2", #1042, crystal **175.00**

Two Kids, 9" h

Crystal **155.00**
Light emerald green **250.00**
Moonlight blue **1,200.00**
Pink, frosted **550.00**

French dressing bottle, Martha Washington, crystal **75.00**

Goblet

Aurora, #1066, Carmen red, 6-1/4" h, 11 oz **30.00**
Cascade, #400 . . . . . **15.00**
Heirloom, 9 oz **17.50**
Heatherbloom, #3111, 10 oz . . **45.00**
Imperial Hunt, #3085, pink . . . **55.00**
King Edward **35.00**
Magnolia **25.00**
Regency, Stradivari, 10 oz. . . . **28.00**

Grapefruit, Marjorie, #7605 .... **50.00**
Ice bucket, Chrysanthemum, pink, silver handle **85.00**
Iced tea tumbler
Candlelight, #3114 .... **35.00**
Cathedral, #1953 .... **20.00**
Lexington, #7966, trumpet, 12 oz, ftd **17.50**
Rosalie, #3035, Heatherbloom, 12 oz, ftd **195.00**
Icer and insert, Adonis........ **68.00**
Ivy ball
#1066, Aurora, amber and crystal **45.00**
#1066, Aurora, amethyst and crystal **75.00**
#1236, Crown Tuscan....... **95.00**
#1236, Crown Tuscan, Charleton roses dec **250.00**
#1236, Royal blue.......... **85.00**
#3100/9, Statuesque....... **275.00**
Jug
Hunts Scene, 64 oz, pink, gold edge, wear to top edge .. **1,495.00**
Minerva................. **300.00**
Nautilus, amethyst, crystal handle **215.00**
#3400, Optic, ball shape, Heatherbloom........... **450.00**
#3400/141, 80 oz, amethyst . **250.00**
Lamp, Geisha Girl
Amber.................. **350.00**
Light emerald **400.00**
Lamp, Martha Washington, 9", electric, portable.................. **95.00**
Muddler, rooster **25.00**
Mustard, cov, Two Tone, amber, #1329 .... **50.00**
Old fashioned tumbler, #704 etch, green, ftd, 10 oz, gold trim worn . **45.00**
Olive dish, #704 etch, green, 6-1/2" l **45.00**
Oyster cocktail, #1066 Aurora, 3-7/8" h, 5 oz, royal blue **28.00**
Parfait, #3085, Hunts Scene, pink **85.00**
Pitcher
#119, Etch 695, amber, ice lip, 63 oz **250.00**
#3400/141, Doulton, dark green **115.00**
#3900/114, Lexington, cut ... **65.00**
Plate
Crown Tuscan, 7" d......... **45.00**
Martha Washington, amber, lunch **12.00**
#704 etch, green, 7" d **14.50**
#704 etch, green, 8" d **18.50**
#704 etch, green, 10-1/2" d .. **80.00**
#3400, Heatherbloom, 10-1/4" d **125.00**
#3400, light green, 10-1/2" d, slight use.................... **37.50**
#3400, Moonlight blue, 9-1/4" d **30.00**
#3400, yellow, 10-1/2" d...... **35.00**
#3900, Adonis, 8" d **22.00**
Punch bowl set
#3200, bowl, 10 cups **190.00**
Swan, bowl and 12 cups.. **2,200.00**
Punch cup
Swan handle **24.00**
Wild Rose................ **22.00**
Relish, #3400
Amber, two parts, two handles, 8-3/4" l **35.00**
Amethyst, three parts, 6-1/2" l . **35.00**
Salad dressing bowl, divided, Pristine, one orig ladle **28.00**
Salad plate, Cascade, #400, 6-1/2" d **10.00**
Salt and pepper shakers, pr, Daffodil, #360, chrome lid.............. **80.00**
Seafood cocktail, Seashell, #110
Crown Tuscan, 4-1/2" oz **95.00**
Dolphins................. **70.00**
Sherbet
Aurora, #1066, 4-1/2" h, 7 oz, forest green.................. **18.00**
Carmine................. **17.00**
Colonial Dame, green and crystal, 6-1/2 oz **12.00**
Daffodil, #3779, 6 oz, low **24.00**
Imperial Hunt, #3085, tall, pink **40.00**
Nearcut Star.............. **12.50**
Regency, Stradivari, low **12.00**
Sherry, Amethyst, trumpet, 2-1/2 oz **20.00**
Shot glass, Aero Optic, Gold Krystol, pinched form **22.50**
Smoker set, Square, #3797/152, three-pc set in orig display box . **125.00**
Soup, flat, #703, Florentine Green **75.00**
Sugar, Martha Washington...... **17.50**
Swan
3", Style #1
Amber................ **85.00**
Carmen, sgd........... **125.00**
Cobalt blue, sgd........ **145.00**
Crown Tuscan........... **75.00**
Crystal................ **30.00**
Ebony, sgd **95.00**
Forest Green........... **200.00**
Gold Crystal **40.00**
Light emerald, sgd **45.00**
Royal blue............ **125.00**
3", Style #3, red **110.00**
4-1/2", Style #1
Crystal frost, red and black enamel **350.00**
Pink.................. **85.00**

Swan, Crown Tuscan, 8-1/2" l, **$150.** *Photo courtesy of Michael Krumme.*

4-1/2", Style #3, milk glass ... **95.00**
6-1/2", Style #3
Forest Green **95.00**
Milk glass............. **250.00**
Red **325.00**
7", crystal, sgd **33.00**
8-1/2", Style #1, gold crystal. **450.00**
8-1/2", Style #2, crystal...... **95.00**
8-1/2", Style #3
Forest Green **125.00**
Milk glass............. **300.00**
Red **325.00**
Torchiere
#3500/88, Gadroon, forest green top, crystal stem and foot .. **65.00**
#3500/90, crystal, ashtray foot **48.00**
#3500/90, Royal Blue, ashtray foot **85.00**
Torte plate, #704 etch, green, 13" d, wear to gold trim **75.00**
Tray
Daffodil, handles **60.00**
#3500/112, three-part, 15" ... **38.50**
Tumbler
Adam, yellow, ftd **25.00**
Carmine, crystal, 12 oz **25.00**
Daffodil, #3779, 9 oz, low.... **28.00**
Gyro Optic, #3143, amber, 3-1/4" h, flat **10.00**
Heatherbloom, #3111, 12 oz, ftd, Optic **55.00**
Martha Washington, #1203, amber, 5" h.................. **15.00**
Nautilus, amethyst, 12 oz, 4-3/4" h................ **25.00**
Urn
8" h, Crown Tuscan........ **140.00**
10" h, Minerva, #3500/41 ... **295.00**
Vase
Amber
Diamond Optic, #3400, 8" h **65.00**
Wide Panel Optic, keyhole, 10" h **85.00**
Wide Panel Optic, keyhole, 12" h **110.00**

CAMBRIDGE Introduces

—The 3011 Figured Stem Line

as above. This comes in various color combinations with foot in crystal.

Patent has been applied for on this outstanding and beautiful line.

Ad, Crockery and Glass Journal, *September 1931, showing the #3011 Figure Line.*

Amethyst
#309, 4-1/2" h. **45.00**
#1299, 11" h. **275.00**
Keyhole, 10" h **115.00**
Azurite, gold bands, 10" h . . **125.00**
Carmen, keyhole, 10" h. **125.00**
Crown Tuscan
#42, shell, 7-1/2" h **145.00**
#1238, keyhole, 12" d **95.00**
#1309, 5", orig sticker **45.00**
Emerald green, #1299, 11" h **115.00**
Everglades, 10-1/2" h, Moonlight blue **350.00**
Flying Nude, Crown Tuscan, hp roses and violets dec, creamy pink molded shell bowl held by nude woman, 9" h, 12" l. **175.00**
Forest Green, #1309, 5" h, orig sticker. **35.00**
Hunt's Scene, #797, 8" h, flip, amber, gold edge. **400.00**
Nautilus, 7" h, Crown Tuscan, ftd **67.50**
Roses, 9" h **325.00**
Songbird and Butterfly, #402, 12" h
Blue **375.00**
Pink **275.00**
Tall Flat Panel, swung, 19-1/4" h, sgd **105.00**

Water set, Gyro Optic, Moonlight blue, pitcher, six tumblers **250.00**
Wine
#1066 Aurora, 4-11/16" h, 3 oz, optic, Moonlight blue **35.00**
#3400, Amy, 2-1/2 oz **16.50**
Lily of the Valley **28.00**
Statuesque **195.00**

Patterns and etchings

Apple Blossom

Line #3400, 1930s. Made in amber, blue, crystal, dark green, light green, pink, and yellow.

Basket, crystal, 7" **475.00**
Berry bowl, #3400, yellow **47.50**
Bonbon, #3400/1180, 5-1/4" d, blue **60.00**
Bowl
#3400/2, low, ftd, yellow **65.00**
#3400/4, 12" d, four toes, crystal **90.00**
#3400/4, 12" d, four toes, green, gold edge. **130.00**
#3400/4, 12" d, four toes, pink, gold edge worn **125.00**
#3400/118, amber, handle, 10" d **65.00**
#3400/1185, green, 10" d . . . **145.00**
#3400/1240, oval, yellow **75.00**
Butter, cov, #3400/52, pink. . . . **500.00**

Apple Blossom etch, goblet, original labels, **$35.**

Candlesticks, pr, #3400/646
Pink **110.00**
Yellow. **85.00**
Celery/relish
4-part, #3500/142, crystal **65.00**
5-part, yellow **90.00**
Champagne, yellow **25.00**
Cheese and cracker, #3400/6, yellow **65.00**
Cheese comport, amber **50.00**
Cocktail
Crystal **14.00**
Yellow. **48.00**
Cocktail shaker, #3400/78, crystal, no stopper **95.00**
Comport
4-toes, #3400, yellow. **60.00**
7", #14, yellow **85.00**
Console bowl
#3400/4, yellow **45.00**
#3400/5, rolled edge, yellow . . **45.00**
Creamer and sugar, #3400/68
Crystal **35.00**
Yellow. **60.00**
Cream soup and liner, #3400, yellow **110.00**
Cup and saucer, #3400
Crystal **25.00**
Pink **80.00**
Yellow. **22.00**
Finger bowl, #3130, yellow **95.00**
Goblet, #3130, crystal **25.00**
Gravy liner, #1091, yellow **95.00**
Ice bucket, green. **100.00**
Jug, #3400/100 76 oz, crystal . . **390.00**
Juice tumbler, #3130, ftd, green. **30.00**

Martini pitcher, #1408, 60 oz, crystal **1,200.00**
Mayonnaise, #3400/11, green, three toes **95.00**
Mayonnaise ladle, green **35.00**
Pickle tray, 9" l, #3400/59, yellow **70.00**
Pitcher, #1205, yellow. **395.00**
Plate
6" d, #3400, crystal. **8.50**
6" d, #3400, yellow **8.00**
6" d, #3400/1181, handle, green **42.50**
7-1/2" d, #3400, tea, crystal . . **14.00**
8" sq, #3400, yellow **40.00**
8-1/2" d, #3400, pink **20.00**
8-1/2" d, #3400, yellow **20.00**
9-1/2" d, #3400, yellow **65.00**
Relish
#1083, two parts, blue **145.00**
#3400/67, yellow, 12" l **95.00**
#3400/91, 8" d, three handles **60.00**
#3400/120, five parts, yellow **125.00**
Sandwich plate, #3400/8, yellow, 11-1/2" d, handle. **60.00**
Sherbet, #3130, crystal **20.00**
Table center, 12", #3400/5, crystal **130.00**
Tumbler
5 oz, ftd, yellow. **25.00**
9 oz, ftd, crystal **14.00**
9 oz, yellow. **28.00**
10 oz, #3025, ftd, crystal, black foot **45.00**
12 oz, #3130, ftd, yellow. **40.00**
12 oz, mushroom shape, crystal **25.00**
Whiskey, ftd, 2 oz
Crystal **30.00**
Green **85.00**
Yellow **65.00**
Wine, #3130, green. **85.00**

Blossom Time

Etching. Made on crystal and some colors.

Bell, crystal **90.00**
Bonbon, 6" d, two handles, crystal **25.00**
Bud vase, #274, 10" h, black, gold encrusted **325.00**
Cake plate, two handles, crystal **40.00**
Candy, cov, Martha blank, crystal **95.00**
Cheese and cracker set, Martha blank, crystal **85.00**
Compote, black and gold. **225.00**
Cornucopia, crystal **125.00**
Hat, crystal **300.00**
Hurricane base, #1617, gold encrusted, price for pr **125.00**
Ice bucket, crystal **125.00**

Salt and pepper shakers, pr, crystal **50.00**

Candlelight

Etching 1940s-50s. Made on crystal and Crown Tuscan with gold decoration. Prices listed below for crystal.

Bowl, 12" d, ftd, #3400/4 . . . . . . **130.00**
Cheese, ftd, #3400. . . . . **70.00**
Cordial, cut **225.00**
Juice tumbler, ftd, 5 oz, #3114 . . **38.50**
Mayonnaise, two-pc set, gold edge, #3400/11. . . . . **130.00**

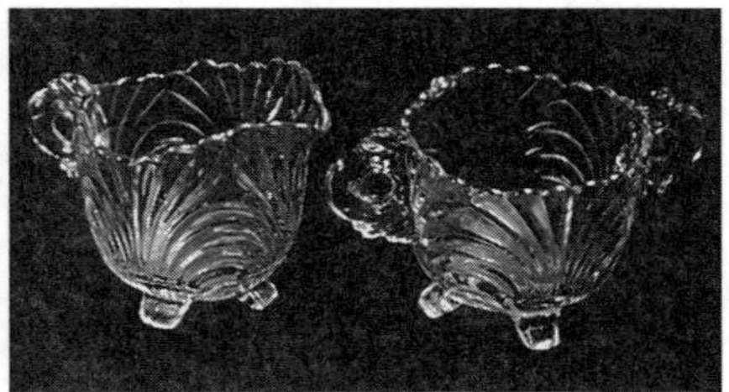

Caprice pattern, small creamer and open sugar, blue, **$50.**

Caprice

Extensive pattern from 1940s-1957. Made in amber, amethyst, cobalt blue, crystal, emerald green, Mandarian gold, Moonlight blue, (blue), pink, pistachio, and white milk glass. Some pieces have satinized panels and are referred to as Alpine. Reproductions have been made by Summit Art Glass, which now owns several molds, and are shown with an asterisk.

Ashtray, #34
- Alpine. **27.50**
- #34, Pistachio **12.50**

Banana bowl, blue **400.00**

Basket
- #146, crystal, 4", two handles, sq **24.00**
- #153, blue **60.00**

Bonbon
- #147, blue **50.00**
- #148, Alpine, oval, two handles, 4-1/2". **80.00**
- #154, sq, two handles, 6" **48.00**

Bowl
- #51, blue **300.00**
- #52, blue, 9" d **300.00**
- #58, blue **360.00**
- #60, blue, silver overlay, ruffled, 11" d, deep **350.00**
- #61, Alpine, 4 ftd, 12-1/2" . . . **125.00**
- #66, Alpine, crimped, ftd, 13" d **175.00**
- #66, blue, ruffled, ftd **200.00**

Bridge set
- #169, heart, crystal*. **45.00**
- #170, club, Alpine* **125.00**
- #171, diamond, crystal. **40.00**
- #172, spade, blue*. **110.00**
- #172, spade, crystal* **40.00**
- #173, cloverleaf, blue* **95.00**

Bubble, #256, 4" d, enamel flowers, blue **400.00**
Butter dish, #52, quarter pound, crystal* **225.00**
Cake stand, #36, crystal. **155.00**

Candlestick
- #67, crystal, 2-1/2" h, pr **35.00**
- #69, two-lite, crystal, pr **300.00**
- #70, Alpine, pr **200.00**
- #70, blue, pr **160.00**
- #638, three-lite, keyhole, blue, pr **230.00**
- #647, two-lite, keyhole, blue, pr **190.00**
- #1338, three-lite, blue, pr . . . **250.00**
- #1356, two-lite, blue, base only **495.00**
- #1577, five-lite, crystal **260.00**

Candy dish, cov, three ftd
- Alpine **130.00**
- Pink. **230.00**

Celery
- #103, blue. **330.00**
- #126, four-part, blue. **460.00**

Champagne
- #300, blue, tall **40.00**
- #301, crystal. **14.00**

Cheese stand, blue **600.00**
Cigarette box, cov, crystal **50.00**

Cigarette holder
- #204, blue. **60.00**
- #205, blue, 2-1/4" **75.00**

Claret, blue **200.00**

Coaster, #20
- Blue, 5-1/2" d **30.00**
- Crystal, 5-1/2" d **15.00**
- Pink, 5-1/2" d. **40.00**

Cocktail, #300, blown
- Blue. **85.00**
- Crystal **30.00**

Comport, #136
- Crystal, tall, 6" d **48.00**
- Pink, tall, 6" d **170.00**

Condiment set, #109, five-pc, blue **550.00**

Cordial
- #300, blown, blue. **120.00**
- #300, crystal. **50.00**
- #301, crystal. **38.00**

Creamer and sugar, tray, blue
- Individual size* **60.00**
- Medium size* **70.00**
- Large size* **90.00**

Creamer and sugar, tray, crystal, individual size* **40.00**

Cruet, orig stopper
- #100, blue, 5 oz. **350.00**
- #101, Alpine*. **175.00**

Cup and saucer
- Blue **48.00**
- Crystal **20.00**
- Mandarin Gold. **36.00**

Decanter set, #187 35-oz ball-shaped decanter, five #188 2-oz tumblers, amethyst. **560.00**

Finger bowl
- Liner, pressed, #16, blue. **60.00**
- #18, blue, flat, 5" d. **90.00**
- #19, blue, ruffled, 5" d **95.00**

Fruit saucer, crimped, blue, 5" d. **90.00**

Goblet
- #1, amber, thick, blown **500.00**
- #1, amethyst, thick, blown. . . **350.00**
- #300, blue **40.00**
- #300, crystal, 7-3/4" h, 9 oz . . . **30.00**

Ice bucket
- Alpine **300.00**
- Crystal, orig tongs **60.00**

Iced tea tumbler
- #301, blown, crystal **30.00**
- #310, flat, 12 oz, blue **140.00**
- #310, flat, 12 oz, crystal **35.00**

Ivy ball, #232
- Blue, 5" d **350.00**
- Crystal, 5" d **130.00**

Jelly
- #135, blue, crimped, 7" **75.00**
- #144, blue, 2 handles, 4". **32.50**

Jug
- Alpine, ball, 80 oz **500.00**
- Blue, ball, 80 oz. **350.00**
- Crystal, ball, 80 oz. **150.00**

Juice tumbler
- #300, blue, ftd, 5 oz. **45.00**
- #300, crystal, ftd, 5 oz. **14.00**
- #300/2, crystal, 5 oz **18.00**
- #310, blue flat, 5 oz. **125.00**

Lemon plate, #152
- Blue, 6" d **35.00**
- Pink, 6" d **50.00**

Mayonnaise
- #106, blue, two pcs* **160.00**
- #111, blue, three pcs **330.00**

Mustard, #87, blue, base only. . **125.00**

Nut bowl
- #93, blue, 2-1/2" **60.00**
- Crystal, 2-1/2. . . . . **38.00**

Oil and vinegar set, #99
- Blue, three pcs **260.00**
- Crystal, three pcs **130.00**

Oil bottle, #117, crystal. **50.00**

Old Fashioned tumbler, #310, blue 125.00
Oyster cocktail, #300, crystal .. 20.00
Parfait, #300
- Blue, 5 oz 300.00
- Pink, 5 oz 170.00

Pitcher, Doulton, amber 2,200.00
Plate
- Alpine, 14" d, #28 .... 120.00
- Blue
  - 6-1/2" d, blue 42.50
  - 7-1/2" d, blue 40.00
  - 8" d, handle, #131 .... 40.00
  - 8-1/2" d................ 45.00
- Crystal
  - 6" d.................... 10.00
  - 7" d.................... 45.00
  - 7-1/2" d, crystal 20.00
  - 8-1/2" d, crystal 14.00
  - 9-1/2" d, #24* 50.00
- Mandarin Gold, 8-1/2" d 30.00

Platter, crystal, 14" l, ftd 30.00
Relish
- #122, three parts, crystal 30.00
- #124, three parts, crystal, Alpine dec, 8-1/2" l*............. 55.00
- #126, four parts, blue* 430.00
- #199, two parts, crystal 30.00

Rose bowl, #235, Alpine, ftd, 6" 295.00
Salad bowl
- #49, blue, 8" d............ 270.00
- #57, blue, 10" d........... 290.00
- #80, pink, cupped, 13" d ... 500.00

Salad dressing set, #112, blue, two bottles, handle.............. 495.00
Salt and pepper shakers, pr, #96, blue, flat*.................. 125.00
Sandwich set, amber, four cups, saucers, 8-1/2" plates, creamer and sugar, 12" d four-ftd plate 350.00
Saucer, Mandarin Gold......... 5.00
Sherbet
- #300, blue, 6 oz 32.00
- #300, crystal, 6 oz 13.00
- #301, crystal.............. 10.00

Sugar, #133, blue 110.00
Tumbler
- #11, blue, ftd, 5 oz 60.00
- #11, crystal, ftd, 5 oz 14.00
- #12, blue, 3 oz 100.00
- #180, blue, barrel, 5 oz...... 40.00
- #184, blue, 12 oz 58.00
- #188, Alpine, 2 oz.......... 75.00
- #188, blue, 2 oz * 55.00
- #188, Mandarin Gold, 2 oz... 35.00
- #300, blue, ftd, 2-1/2 oz, rare 300.00
- #300, crystal, ftd, 10 oz 20.00
- #300/2, blue, ftd, 12 oz...... 40.00
- #300/2, crystal, ftd, 12 oz.... 22.00

Vase
- #237, blue, 4-1/2" h 275.00
- #239, amber, 8-1/8" h 190.00
- #239, cobalt blue, 8-5/8" h...290.00
- #242, amber, 6" h..........125.00
- #243, cobalt blue, 8" h......400.00
- #245, crystal, plain top, 5-1/2" h 130.00
- #249, blue, ruffled, 3-1/2" h ..430.00
- #340, blue, ruffled, 9-1/2" h ..800.00
- #344, blue, straight top, 4-1/2" h 225.00
- #345, blue, ruffled, 5-1/2" h ..240.00

Whiskey
- #300, blue, 2-1/2 oz........225.00
- #300, emerald green, 2-1/2 oz 50.00

Wine
- #6, blue, thick*............195.00
- #6, crystal, thick*...........35.00
- #300, blue, 2-1/2 oz.........80.00
- #300, crystal, 2-1/2 oz.......27.50

Chantilly

Late 1940s-1950s etching. Made only in crystal.

Bowl
- 5-1/2" d, sterling base 70.00
- 8" d, three parts, sterling base 195.00
- 10" d, divided, sterling base ..90.00
- 10-1/2" d, Martha blank 100.00
- 11-1/2" d, #3900/28 ....65.00
- 11-1/2" d, two handles, #3900/45 ....120.00
- 12-1/2" d, #430 ....65.00
- 13" d, four toes, 3400/160 ...100.00

Butter, cov, #3400/52.........200.00
Candlesticks, pr 200.00
Candy, cov, #313, sterling knob.225.00
Celery, Martha blank 65.00
Champagne, #3600, 6" h, 7 oz ..35.00
Cheese and cracker, 13-1/2" d, #3900/34..................240.00
Cocktail
- #3600....................35.00
- #3625, crystal 20.00

Cocktail icer, crystal 58.00
Cocktail shaker, glass lid 150.00
Comport, #3900/136, 5-1/2" h...65.00
Cordial
- #1327, 1 oz, crystal.........95.00
- #3625, 4-3/4" h, 1 oz, crystal..65.00

Cordial decanter, #3400/156, sterling base 260.00
Creamer and sugar
- #138, sterling base 85.00
- #252 Martha blank..........55.00

Cruet, straight top, handle, matching tray 150.00
Cup and saucer, #3900/17 .....36.00
Decanter, #1321 .... 600.00
Dressing bottle, silver base... 150.00
Goblet
- #3600 .... 40.00
- #3625 .... 45.00

Iced tea tumbler, ftd, #3625.... 30.00
Jug, 20 oz, #3900/117 .... 250.00
Juice tumbler, #3600 .... 35.00
Marmalade, glass cov 75.00
Mayonnaise, #3900/111, three pcs 80.00
Oil cruet, 4 oz............... 95.00
Pitcher
- 20 oz, sterling base 300.00
- 76 oz, #3900/115, ice lip ... 275.00
- 86 oz, #1561, ice lip, gold rim 245.00

Plate, #3900/24, dinner........ 75.00
Relish
- #324, Martha blank, two parts, two handles 38.00
- #324, Martha blank, three parts 68.00
- #3400/90, two parts, 6" d, handle 35.00
- #3500, three parts, handle... 70.00

Salad dressing and underplate, divided, crystal 75.00
Salad plate, 7" d, blown, #131 . 150.00
Salt and pepper shakers, pr
- #3400, handle, sterling top.. 125.00
- #3900/1177, crystal 55.00

Sherbet, #3625, tall 22.00
Sherry, #7966 .... 85.00
Sherry decanter, #1321...... 400.00
Tumbler, #3625, ftd, 6-1/2" h, 10 oz 36.00
Vase, 11" h 195.00
Wine
- #3600 .... 42.00
- #3625 .... 48.00

Cleo

Introduced in 1930. Made in amber, Moonlight blue, crystal, green, Dianthus pink, and yellow.

Basket, two handles, 7", Moonlight blue 40.00
Berry bowl, crystal........... 55.00
Bonbon, two handles, crystal... 60.00
Bowl
- 10" d, w handles, Dianthus pink 110.00
- 12" d, Decagon, green 50.00

Bread and butter plate, Moonlight blue, 6" d.................. 30.00
Candlesticks, pr, #627, 4" h
- Dianthus pink 95.00
- Green 85.00
- Moonlight blue 65.00
- Moonlight blue, gold trim ... 125.00

Celery, crystal 95.00
Centerpiece, #7, Dianthus pink, 8-1/8" 165.00
Cereal bowl, crystal...........85.00
Champagne, #3126, amethyst and crystal.....................32.50
Cocktail, #3077, Dianthus pink . . 75.00
Console bowl, 12" d, Decagon, Dianthus pink 95.00
Creamer, Moonlight blue 45.00
Cream soup and liner, Moonlight blue 195.00
Cup, Dianthus pink............30.00
Cup and saucer, crystal 42.00
Dessert plate, Moonlight blue, 7" d 30.00

Dinner plate

- Moonlight blue, Decagon . . . 100.00
- Dianthus pink, 10-1/2" d 195.00

Fruit bowl, ftd, large, crystal . . . 100.00

Goblet, #3077

- Dianthus pink..............65.00
- Moonlight blue.............65.00

Gravy and liner, double, #917, Dianthus pink 350.00
Iced tea tumbler, flat, Dianthus pink 95.00

Ice pail, #851

- Dianthus pink.............135.00
- Ice Pail, #851, yellow.......170.00

Mayonnaise Liner, #873, Dianthus pink 25.00
Pitcher, crystal, no lid 500.00
Powder box, cov 500.00
Seafood icer, liner, underplate, green, gold trim 125.00
Sherbet, #3077, Dianthus pink, low 38.00
Tumbler, #3400/38, cobalt blue, 12 oz 24.00

Vegetable bowl

- 9-1/2" l, crystal............195.00
- 9-1/2" l, Dianthus Pink 130.00

Wine, #3077, Moonlight blue....95.00

Cigarette box, covered, Crown Tuscan, dolphin feet, **$55.**

Decagon

Made the 1930s-1940s in amber, black, Moonlight blue, green, pink, red, and Ritz blue (cobalt blue).

Bell, pink................... 18.00

Bonbon

- #749, pink, two handle, 6-1/2" 24.00
- #749, Ritz blue, two handles, 6-1/4" 42.50
- #758, pink, handle, 5-1/2" d . . 27.50
- #1169, green, handle 50.00

Bouillon, ftd, Moonlight blue . . . 20.00

Bouillon and saucer

- Pink..................... 19.50
- Ritz blue 45.00

Bowl

- 5-1/2" d, cupped, deep, green 55.00
- 6" d, ftd, green 24.00
- 6-3/4" d, flat rim, green...... 24.00
- 8-1/2" d, #971, handle, amber 37.50
- 8-1/2" d, #971, handle, pink . . 45.00
- 12" d, flat, Moonlight blue.... 75.00
- 13" d, #754, green 110.00

Café parfait, #3077

- Amber.................... 24.00
- Green 32.50

Candelabra, #638, three-lite, black 72.50

Candlesticks, pr

- #627, 4" h, black........... 55.00
- #646, 5" h, Moonlight blue . . . 45.00

Candy, cov, #864, Moonlight blue 120.00
Celery, green................ 37.50

Champagne, #3077, 5-1/2"

- Moonlight blue 24.00
- Ritz blue 20.00

Cheese and cracker, Moonlight blue 65.00
Club plate, 10" d, pink 45.00

Cocktail, #3077

- 4-1/2" h, Moonlight blue 25.00
- 4-1/2" h, Ritz blue 15.00

Creamer, #867

- Green 25.00
- Moonlight blue 32.50
- Ritz blue 25.00

Creamer and sugar

- Moonlight blue 35.00
- Pink..................... 30.00
- Ritz blue 18.00

Cream soup, orig liner

- Green 35.00
- Moonlight blue 30.00
- Pink..................... 32.50

Cruet

- #193, 6 oz, Moonlight blue . . 195.00
- #619, pink................ 75.00

Cup and saucer

- Amber 12.00
- Crystal cup, black saucer....20.00
- Moonlight blue.............15.00
- Pink 14.50
- Ritz blue..................30.00

Fruit bowl, 5-1/2" d, pink........5.50

Goblet, #3077, 9 oz

- Amber 20.00
- Amethyst 35.00
- Moonlight blue.............32.50
- Ritz blue..................35.00

Gravy boat and liner, #1091, green or pink.......................125.00
Guest set, #488, 22-oz jug, lid, tray, and tumbler, pink 160.00

Ice bucket

- Amber 45.00
- Pink 85.00

Jug, #937, 68 oz, ice lip

- Moonlight blue............165.00
- Pink 95.00

Juice Tumbler, 5 oz, ftd, Moonlight blue 25.00

Mayonnaise, #873, ftd, handle

- Amber 30.00
- Pink, with liner 60.00

Mayonnaise, ftd, handle, ladle, Moonlight blue 75.00
Muffin tray, 11-1/2", Moonlight blue 35.00

Nut

- Individual, green, ftd, 2-1/2" d. 30.00
- Master, pink, 6" d...........72.50

Oil bottle, stopper, #197, 6 oz, pink 75.00
Oil and vinegar tray, #619, handle, pink........................45.00

Pickle tray, #1082, 9"

- Amber 22.50
- Green....................35.00

Plate

- 6" d
  - Amber.................5.00
  - Amethyst, marked, polished base 18.00
  - Black..................18.00
  - Moonlight blue 12.50
  - Pink...................12.50
  - Ritz blue 12.50
- 8" d
  - Amethyst, marked........25.00
  - Moonlight blue 15.00
  - Pink...................15.00
- 8-1/4" d
  - Amber..................8.00
  - Black..................18.00
  - Moonlight blue 15.00
  - Ritz blue 19.50

8-1/2" d
Amber **8.00**
Amethyst, polished base . . **22.00**
8-3/4" d
Amber **11.50**
Green **18.50**
9" d, Moonlight blue **60.00**
Platter, 12-1/2" l, oval, Moonlight blue **75.00**
Relish, #1067, two parts, 9"
Amber **22.50**
Green **35.00**
Moonlight blue **37.50**
Salad dressing bottle
#1261, ftd, amber **120.00**
#1263, amber **110.00**
Salt and pepper shakers, pr
Amber, ftd **45.00**
Moonlight blue **85.00**
Ritz blue **125.00**
Salt shaker, #396
Amber **22.50**
Ritz blue **40.00**
Sandwich tray, amber **30.00**
Saucer
Amber **4.00**
Black **9.00**
Pink **4.50**
Server, center handle
Green **27.50**
Moonlight blue **45.00**
Pink **40.00**
Sherbet, #3077
Amber, low **12.00**
Moonlight blue, low **20.00**
Pink, low **18.00**
Sherbet, #3120, Moonlight blue, tall **16.00**
Shrimp cocktail, liner, #968, amber **25.00**
Soup bowl, flat, bell rim, light blue **80.00**
Soup bowl, #808, flat rim
Amber **25.00**
Green **75.00**
Moonlight blue **80.00**
Sugar and creamer tray
#1095, black **45.00**
#1096, amber **24.00**
#1099, pink **45.00**
Sugar bowl, #867, Moonlight blue **32.50**
Sugar pail, #1169, pink **65.00**
Sugar shaker, #813, pink **165.00**
Syrup, cov, #175, pink **125.00**
Tray, #489, green **35.00**
Tumbler, ftd
3-1/2" h, amber **10.00**
3 oz, ftd, Ritz blue **30.00**
4-1/2 oz, #3055, green **20.00**
5 oz, #3077, Moonlight blue . . **22.50**
5 oz, #3077, ftd, pink **19.50**
8 oz, ftd, Moonlight blue **12.00**
12 oz, #3065, green **35.00**
12 oz, #3065, pink, optic **35.00**
12 oz, #3077, ftd, green **42.50**
12 oz, #3077, ftd, Moonlight blue **20.00**
Tumbler tray, #973, green, blue . **35.00**
Vase, #84, green, ftd, 8" h **95.00**
Vegetable bowl, pink, 9-1/2" l, oval **50.00**
Wine, #3077
Amethyst **30.00**
Moonlight blue **35.00**
Pink **18.00**
Ritz blue **40.00**

Diane

1934-1950s etching. Made in amber, blue, Crown Tuscan, crystal, crystal with gold encrusted dec, emerald green, Heatherbloom, some pink, some red, and yellow.

Bobeches, pr, crystal **100.00**
Bonbon, crystal, 8-1/2" **25.00**
Bonbon plate, #3900/131, 8" d, two handles, crystal **48.00**
Bowl, 12" d
#3400, crystal, gold encrusted **110.00**
#3400/4, red, wear to gold . . **350.00**
#3900/62, three ftd, crystal . . . **60.00**
Candlesticks, pr
#627, crystal **85.00**
#637, crystal, keyhole **75.00**
Candy dish, cov, #3500/57, three parts, crystal **85.00**
Champagne, #3122 . . . . **32.00**
Cheese comport, #3400/7, crystal **50.00**
Cigarette box, cov, crystal, gold encrusted, 3-5/8" x 4-1/2" **150.00**
Cigar holder, ashtray foot, #1337, crystal, gold encrusted **350.00**
Claret, #3122, amber **50.00**
Cocktail, #3122, crystal, 3 oz . . . **35.00**
Cocktail shaker, glass lid, crystal **150.00**
Console bowl, #3400 line, center ftd, pink **800.00**
Cordial, #1066, crystal **95.00**
Cordial pitcher, #3400/119, 12 oz, tilt, crystal **250.00**
Corn dish, crystal **40.00**
Demitasse cup and saucer, crystal **145.00**
Goblet, crystal **30.00**
Iced tea tumbler, 15 oz, 5-1/2", flat, crystal **60.00**
Jug, #3900/117, 20 oz **395.00**
Juice tumbler
Amber, #3122 . . . . **45.00**
Crystal, ftd **15.00**
Marmalade, cov, #147, crystal . **165.00**
Mayonnaise, #1491, crystal, sterling silver base **85.00**
Mustard, metal lid and orig spoon **45.00**
Oyster cocktail, #3122, crystal . **35.00**
Pitcher, Doulton, crystal **500.00**
Plate
#3400, crystal, 6" d, two handles **32.50**
#3400, crystal, 8" d **22.50**
#3400, crystal, 10-1/2" d **135.00**
#3900, 8" d, crystal **16.50**
Relish
#393, five parts, crystal **60.00**
#394, five parts, crystal, 10" l . **85.00**
#862, four-part center handle, crystal **110.00**
#3400/91, three parts, 8" d, ftd, pink **90.00**
#3500/652, three parts, crystal, 12" l **125.00**
Salad dressing bowl, #1491, crystal, divided, 5-1/2" d **65.00**
Salt and pepper shakers, pr, crystal **95.00**
Sandwich server, #3400/10, center handle, crystal **135.00**
Sherbet, #3122, low
Amber **32.00**
Crystal **24.00**
Sherry, #7966, 2 oz, crystal **75.00**
Tumbler
#498, 12 oz, crystal, 5-1/4" h . **65.00**
#1066, 5 oz, crystal **80.00**
#3109, 14 oz, 4-1/8" h, crystal, gold encrusted **85.00**
#3122, 10 oz, flat, crystal **65.00**
#3900/117, 5 oz, crystal **75.00**
#3900/118, 5 oz, crystal **75.00**
Urn, #3500/44, crystal, ftd, 8" h **350.00**
Vase, 12" h, keyhole, crystal **110.00**
Wine, #3122, 2-1/2 oz, crystal . . **45.00**

Elaine

Line #1402. Made 1934-1950s. Made only in crystal.

Ball jug, #3400 . . . . **275.00**
Bitters bottle, loose tube **275.00**
Bowl
#1402/122, three parts, 10-1/2" d, deep **395.00**
#3400/4, 12" d, ftd **60.00**
Bud vase
6" h **55.00**
10" h **55.00**

Cake plate, #3900/35, 13-1/2" d, two handles **75.00**

Candlesticks, pr

#1338, three-lite **165.00**
#3400/647, two-lite **110.00**
#3500/94, two-lite, ram's head **350.00**
#3500/154, three-lite **350.00**

Candy, cov **150.00**

Champagne

#3035 . . . . **30.00**
#3500 . . . . **35.00**
#3121 . . . . **45.00**

Claret, #3121 . . . . **40.00**

Cocktail

#3035 . . . . **30.00**
#3500 . . . . **42.50**

Compote

#3500/36, 6" **60.00**
#300/37, tall, two handle **175.00**

Cordial, #3035, 1-1/2 oz **45.00**

Corn dish **75.00**

Creamer and sugar, #1402/33 . . **65.00**

Crescent salad **195.00**

Fruit basket, #3500/18, 12" **350.00**

Goblet

#3121 . . . . **40.00**
#3500, short bowl **45.00**

Iced tea tumbler, ftd, #3500 . . . . **40.00**

Ice pail, #1402/52, Tally-Ho, chrome handle, tons **145.00**

Icer and liner **80.00**

Jug

#3400/38, 80 oz **245.00**
#3400/141, 80 oz **395.00**

Juice tumbler, ftd

#3035 . . . . **32.50**
#3121 . . . . **35.00**
#3500 . . . . **35.00**

Mayonnaise bowl, 6" d, ftd, handle, #3500/59 . . . . **80.00**

Nappy, 5" d, handle **50.00**

Nut, #3400/71, four ftd **60.00**

Oil bottle, #3400/69, 6 oz **110.00**

Pitcher, #3400/141 . . . . **275.00**

Plate

6" d, #3400/1181, two handles **32.50**
6" d, #3900 . . . . **16.50**
6-1/2" d **7.50**
8" d, #3500 . . . . **22.00**
10-1/2" d **75.00**
14" d, #3900/166 . . . . **100.00**

Relish

#1402/91, three parts, 8" l **70.00**
#3400/67, five parts, 12" l **75.00**
#3500/60, two parts, handle, 5-1/2" l **32.50**
#3500/61, three parts **45.00**
#3500/67, six-pc inserts **185.00**
#3500/71, three parts, center handle **125.00**
#3500/97, 14" l **125.00**
#3900/125, three parts, 9" l. . . **65.00**

Salad dressing bowl, #1402/95, divided, orig liner **120.00**

Salt and pepper shakers, pr, #3900/17, ftd **70.00**

Shaker, glass top **55.00**

Sherbet

#3121, tall **24.00**
#3500, low **30.00**

Tumbler

#498, 12 oz, 5-1/2" h. **110.00**
#3121, 10 oz **25.00**
#3400/115, 14 oz, flat **65.00**

Wine, #3500 . . . . **60.00**

Wine bottle, stopper **1,600.00**

Farber Brothers

Basket, #5563

Cobalt blue liner **75.00**
Green liner **35.00**

Bitters bottle, amber **75.00**

Bonbon, #5567, duo center handle, amber **125.00**

Candlesticks, pr, flat top, red, 8-1/2" h **295.00**

Claret, #3167, cobalt blue **125.00**

Coaster

Black **35.00**
Light blue **37.50**

Cocktail

#5461, tulip, 3 oz, mocha **20.00**
#6018, 3 oz, amethyst **27.50**
#6095, 3 oz, cobalt blue **145.00**
#6095, 3 oz, mocha **24.00**

Cocktail set, two amber, two green, two smoke, six-pc set **60.00**

Cocktail shaker, #3400, crystal, cobalt blue handle, ball, tilt **48.00**

Compote, 5-1/2" h, 5-1/4" d, royal blue insert **75.00**

Compote, 7-1/2" h, Krome Kraft base

Amethyst **45.00**
Cobalt blue **50.00**
Green **45.00**
Frosted crystal **45.00**

Cordial, chrome base

Amber **20.00**
Amethyst **24.00**
Cobalt blue **37.50**
Light blue **37.50**

Cordial decanter, #3400/119, forest green **75.00**

Cordial set, seven pcs, chrome plate **55.00**

Decanter

#113-3, amethyst **85.00**
#3400, amethyst, 24 oz **75.00**
#3400/119, black, straight sided **125.00**

Jug, ball, amber, 4 oz **25.00**

Marmalade, cov, Krome Kraft lid and base

Amber **35.00**
Amethyst **35.00**
Cobalt blue **85.00**

Mustard, cov, cobalt blue **50.00**

Oil and vinegar set, 3 oz, amethyst, #5453 . . . . **40.00**

Oil bottle

#3400, 3 oz, amber **30.00**
#3400, tilted, 3 oz, amethyst . . **40.00**

Pickle dish, oval, cobalt blue . . . **70.00**

Pitcher

#6130, 22 oz, amethyst **125.00**
#6131, 76 oz, mocha **145.00**
#6131/3400, 76 oz, ice lip, amethyst **250.00**

Preserve dish, amber **45.00**

Relish, #3500

Two-part, Gadroon, chrome base, amber **20.00**
Two-part, Gadroon, chrome base, crystal **30.00**
Two-part, Gadroon, chrome base, green **45.00**
Three-part, amethyst **45.00**
Three-part, green, chrome base **50.00**
Four-part, 7-1/4" d, chrome base, amethyst **60.00**
Four-part, 7-1/4" d, chrome base, crystal **40.00**
Four-part, 7-1/4" d, chrome base, green **50.00**

Salt and pepper shakers, pr, ball shaped, Krome Kraft base

Amber **35.00**
Amethyst **40.00**

Sugar bowl, cov, cobalt blue, Krome Kraft lid and base **55.00**

Tumbler

#3400, cobalt blue, 6 oz, 3-1/2" h **7.50**
#5633, 12 oz, amethyst **35.00**
#5633, 12 oz, mocha **27.50**

Wine

Amethyst, Duchess Filigree chrome base **20.00**
Amethyst, #3400/92, 2-1/2 oz . **16.50**
Cobalt blue, 3-1/2" h **30.00**

Gloria

Tableware line.

Bonbon, #3400/1179, yellow, 5-1/2" **50.00**

Bowl, #3400/1185, amber, handle, 10" d **95.00**

Bud vase, ebony, silver encrusted, 10" h. 695.00
Champagne, amber 48.00
Cup, #3400/50, crystal, square, four-toed 95.00
Goblet, #3130, yellow 50.00
Mayonnaise, ftd, green. 125.00
Plate, #3400, yellow, 8-1/2" d . . . 22.50
Salt and pepper shakers, pr, #3400/76, crystal, glass stops, etched bases. 165.00

Plainware, console set, crystal, **$95.**

Mt. Vernon

Tableware line. Made late 1920s-1940s. Made in amber, Carmen, crystal, emerald green, Heatherbloom, light green, Royal blue, and violet.

Candlesticks, pr
- Dolphin, green 225.00
- Milk glass 350.00

Cocktail, crystal 9.00
Comport, 6-1/2", Heatherbloom . 85.00
Cup, crystal. 6.00
Decanter, 40 oz
- Crystal. 55.00
- Milk glass 150.00

Juice tumbler, red, 5 oz, ftd 45.00
Mug, cobalt blue, handle 60.00
Pitcher, forest green 300.00
Plate, 13" d, cobalt blue, some use 95.00
Relish, crystal, five parts 35.00
Sherbet, low, crystal 7.00
Tumbler, 9 oz, barrel, crystal . . . 15.00

Nude

3011 Line.

Ashtray, Moonlight blue 800.00
Brandy
- Crystal. 200.00
- Brandy, pistachio 145.00

Champagne
- Carmen. 175.00
- Pink. 650.00

Cigarette holder
- Carmen 595.00
- Crystal, ashtray foot. 700.00
- Crystal, frosted 850.00

Claret, Carmen 175.00
Cocktail, crystal. 200.00
Compote
- Shell. 295.00
- Short, Carmen 660.00
- Tall, Carmen. 730.00
- Tall, Crown Tuscan, shell 295.00
- Tall, Moonstone 430.00
- Tall, Pistachio. 1,250.00

Cordial, crystal 680.00
Goblet
- Banquet, Carmen 700.00
- Banquet, Ritz Blue. 650.00
- Table, Carmen 250.00
- Table, Smoke, crackle 760.00

Ivy ball
- Amethyst 295.00
- Carmen 385.00
- Crystal 500.00

Mint dish, crystal. 760.00
Sauterne, topaz. 375.00
Seashell, tall, emerald green. . . 600.00
Wine
- Amber 325.00
- Amethyst 300.00

Portia

Etching made from 1932 to early 1950s. Made in amber, crystal, crystal with gold encrusted dec, green, Heatherbloom, and yellow. Prices shown are for crystal, (except where noted), colors would be somewhat higher.

Ashtray
- #3500/97, sq, 14" d 45.00
- #3500/129, sq 45.00

Bowl, #3400/1240, oval, ftd 110.00
Candle bobeches, pr 125.00
Celery tray
- #1402/94, 12" l. 70.00
- #3900/120 . . . . . 75.00

Claret, #3126, 4-1/2 oz 35.00
Cocktail
- #3121. . . . . 32.50
- #3130. . . . . 24.00

Cocktail icer, two pcs 75.00
Cocktail shaker, #3400/175 . . . 165.00
Cordial
- #3144. . . . . 125.00
- #1355. . . . . 125.00
- #3121. . . . . 65.00

Corn dish, crystal 50.00
Cornucopia, double candlesticks, pr 230.00
Cranberry dish, #3400/49, 3-1/2" d 48.00
Cream soup liner, #3400 . . . . . 30.00
Cup, #3400 . . . . . 35.00
Cup and saucer
- #3400 . . . . . 42.50
- #3900/17. . . . . 38.00

Decanter
- #1321, 28 oz. 350.00
- #3400/113. . . . . 300.00

Decanter set, #3400, 12-oz flask with stopper, eight #1344 shot glasses 950.00
Finger bowl, 5" d 55.00
Goblet, #1066. . . . . 35.00
Ice bucket. 225.00
Jug, #3900/116, ball, gold trim. 395.00
Marmalade, #3400/140. . . . . 75.00
Martini pitcher, orig plunger, #1408, 60 oz 1,500.00
Oil and vinegar bottle 375.00
Oyster cocktail, #3109. . . . . 40.00
Parfait, #3121 . . . . . 95.00
Pitcher, ball, yellow, gold etched 180.00
Plate
- #3400, 8" d 17.50
- #3500, 6". 14.50

Relish
- #1402/91, three parts, 8" d round, Tally Ho. 58.00
- #3400/67, three parts, 12" l . . 55.00
- #3400/200, three parts 55.00
- #3500/65, four parts, 12" d. . . 55.00
- #3500/97, handle, 14" l. 95.00
- #3900/124, two parts, 7". 48.00

Salt and pepper shakers, pr, #3900/1177, glass tops. 65.00
Seafood, icer and liner 80.00
Sherbet, #3121. . . . . 25.00
Sherry, #796, 2 oz
- Crystal 50.00
- Crystal, gold encrusted 60.00

Tankard pitcher 500.00
Tumbler, #3400/38, 12 oz. 45.00
Vase, small, gold etched 40.00
Wine, #3121 . . . . . 50.00

Rose Point

Etching made from 1936 to 1953. Made on crystal, some pieces have gold trim, some have sterling silver trim, and others are gold encrusted. A few examples are known on a Crown Tuscan base. Prices listed are for crystal, unless otherwise noted.

Ashtray, five-pc set. 385.00
Basket
- #3500/51, 5" 296.00
- #3500/55, square 65.00
- #3500/55, square, set in sterling silver sgd base. 295.00

Berry bowl 125.00
Bobeches. 75.00

Bonbon
#3400/201 . . . . **195.00**
#3400/202, ftd **195.00**
#3400/204 . . . . **195.00**
#3400/205 . . . . **195.00**
Bowl
#993, 12-1/2" d **155.00**
#1359, 10" d, ruffled. **165.00**
#1359, 10-1/2" d **135.00**
#1398, 13" d. **275.00**
#1402/122, 10-1/2" d, three parts **495.00**
#3400/4, 12" d, ftd, crystal. . . **130.00**
#3400/48, 11" d, four ftd, fancy edge **350.00**
#3400/1185, 10" d, two handles **140.00**
#3500/21, 12-1/2" d, ftd, handle, oval **400.00**
#3900, 11" d, ftd, handle **125.00**
Brandy, #3121, low, repaired. . . . **75.00**
Bud vase
#274, 10" h, gold encrusted . **165.00**
#6004, 6" h. **95.00**
#6004,6" h, gold encrusted . . **155.00**
Butter dish, cov, #3900/52, quarter pound **750.00**
Cabaret plate, #3900/1397, 14-1/2" d **95.00**
Café parfait, #3121, 5 oz. **125.00**
Cake stand, 3400/35 . . . . **48.00**
Canapé set, #693/3000, two pcs, sterling rim **500.00**
Candelabra, pr
#496, two-lite, with hurricane globes **800.00**
#1268, with bobeches **425.00**
Candlestick
#647, keyhole, pr. **160.00**
#1338, pr **230.00**
#3121. . . . . **295.00**
#3400/646, 1-lite, 5", pr **130.00**
#3400/647, two-lite, pr. **190.00**
#3500, ram's head, pr **300.00**
#3500/74, ram's head, pr. . . . **280.00**
#3900, two-lite, pr **190.00**
#3900/67, 6", pr **185.00**
#3900/72, two-lite, pr. **165.00**
Candy dish, cov
#3500. . . . . **230.00**
#3500/57, Crown Tuscan, gold trim **165.00**
#3500/57, three parts, gold trim **135.00**
Celery tray, #3900/120 . . . . **65.00**
Champagne
#3121, tall **32.50**
#3500. **40.00**
Cheese comport, #3400, gold trim **50.00**

Mustard, covered, Rose Point, #151, 3 oz, original foil label, **$295.** *Photo courtesy of Michael Krumme.*

Cigarette holder
#1066, oval, ashtray foot . . . **500.00**
#1337 . . . . **295.00**
Claret, #3121 . . . .**110.00**
Cocktail, #3121, 6" h, 3 oz **35.00**
Cocktail icer, #968, 4-1/2" h, two pcs **80.00**
Cocktail shaker, #3400/175 . . . **295.00**
Comport
#3500, 6". **60.00**
#3500/148, 6" **135.00**
#3900/136, 5-1/2" **125.00**
Console bowl
#3400/4, flared, gold encrusted **165.00**
#3400/97, oval **225.00**
Console set, 12" d #3400/12 bowl, pr of #3400/647 candlesticks, Crown Tuscan, gold dec **700.00**
Cordial
#3121 . . . . **75.00**
#7966 . . . . **175.00**
Cordial decanter, #1320, 40 oz **950.00**
Corn relish, #447 . . . . **95.00**
Cracker plate, #3400/6, 11-1/2" d, two handle **75.00**
Creamer and sugar
#3500/14. . . . . **70.00**
#3900 . . . . **50.00**
Cruet, orig stopper, 6 oz. **125.00**
Cup and saucer
#3400 . . . . **50.00**
#3900 . . . . **70.00**
French salad dressing bottle, #1263 . . . . **700.00**

Goblet
#3121, 10 oz **48.00**
#3500, luncheon **65.00**
Hurricane lamp, Martha base, gold encrusted, pr **900.00**
Ice bucket, #3400/851, gold encrusted **300.00**
Iced tea tumbler
#3121. **55.00**
#3500. **60.00**
Lamp, Crown Tuscan **1,275.00**
Jug, ball
#3400. . . . . **400.00**
#3900/115, 76 oz. **450.00**
#3900/118, 32 oz. **600.00**
Juice tumbler, #3121, 5 oz **42.50**
Lazy Susan **400.00**
Marmalade, #157. . . . . **225.00**
Martini pitcher, small. **700.00**
Mayonnaise
#3400/11, four toes **60.00**
#3900/19, ftd, spoon **100.00**
Mustard, #151, 3 oz, sterling lid **265.00**
Oil bottle, #3900/100, 6 oz **195.00**
Oyster cocktail, #3121, 4-1/2" h, 4 oz **45.00**
Parfait
#3121. . . . . **120.00**
#3500. . . . . **125.00**
Pickle, #3900/123, ftd, 7". **65.00**
Pitcher
#3400/100 . . . . **450.00**
#3400/141, Doulton **525.00**
Plate
#3400, 5" d, handle **50.00**
#3400, 6" d **20.00**
#3400, 7" d **22.50**
#3400, 8-1/2" d **25.00**
#3400, 10-1/2" d **170.00**
#3500, 7-1/2" d **22.50**
#3500, 8-1/2" d **25.00**
#3500/39, 12" d, ftd. **190.00**
#3900, 8" d **25.00**
#3900/131, 8" d, two handles, ftd **95.00**
Relish
#394, two parts, 10" l. **95.00**
#394, five parts **170.00**
#3400/90, two parts, 6" d, handle **55.00**
#3500/60, two parts, 5-1/2" l . . **50.00**
#3500/62, four parts, two handles **125.00**
#3500/64, 10" l. **130.00**
#3500/67, six parts, 12" l, gold encrusted **600.00**
#3500/68, two parts, 5-1/2" . . . **60.00**
#3500/71, three parts, center handle, gold encrusted. . . . **245.00**

#3500/87, four parts, 10" d, handle . . . 100.00
#3500/97, 14" l, oval . . . 1250.00
#3500/152, four parts, 11" l, two handles. . . 200.00
#3900/125, three parts, 9" l. . . 70.00
#14032, three parts, 8" d, handle . . . 190.00

Salad dressing bowl, #1402/133, twin . . . 95.00

Salt and pepper shakers, pr
#1177, worn chrome tops, #837 center handle tray . . . 150.00
#1468, egg shape . . . 195.00
#1470, ball shake, small . . . 195.00
#3400/77, plastic tops . . . 70.00

Server, #3400/10, center handle 155.00
Sherbet, #3121, low . . . 32.50
Sherry decanter, #1321, 28 oz. 650.00
Shrimp cocktail, liner, #3900 . . . 90.00
Shot glass, #3400/92, 2 oz. . . . 140.00
Sugar bowl, #3900, gold encrusted dec . . . 55.00

Torte plate
13" d, three ftd . . . 95.00
14" d, ftd, gold encrusted . . . 145.00
14-1/2" d, #3900/167 . . . 160.00

Tray, #3400/59, 9" . . . 110.00

Tumbler
#3121, 2-1/2 oz, ftd. . . . 85.00
#3121, 9 oz. . . . 40.00
#3121, 10 oz, ftd. . . . 50.00
#3121, 12 oz, ftd. . . . 35.00
#3400/38, 5 oz . . . 135.00
#3400/38, 12 oz, mushroom . . 95.00
#3400/92, 2-1/2 oz . . . 165.00
#3500 . . . 55.00

Urn, cov, small. . . . 850.00

Vase
#278, Crown Tuscan, gold encrusted, 11" h . . . 475.00
#278, crystal, sterling silver base, 11" h, ftd . . . 375.00
#279, 13" h . . . 500.00
#797, flip, 8" h. . . . 300.00
#1237, key, 10" h. . . . 135.00
#1238, key, 12" h. . . . 185.00
#1309, 5" h, crystal . . . 200.00
#1309, 5" h, crystal, gold encrusted . . . 295.00
#1430, 8" h . . . 450.00
#1528, 10 oz. . . . 375.00
#3400/103, Crown Tuscan, gold encrusted, 6-1/2" h. . . . 350.00
#6004, 12" h . . . 150.00
Black amethyst, etched gold dec, 5-1/4" d top, 3-1/2" d base 1,500.00

Wine
#3121 . . . 65.00
#3500, 2-1/2 oz, short. . . . 125.00

Tally Ho

Tableware pattern made in amber, amethyst, cobalt blue, crystal, crystal with gold trim, forest green, and Carmen.

Bowl, 12-1/8", flat rim, Carmen . . 75.00
Champagne, 6-1/2", #1402, amethyst . . . 30.00
Cheese and cracker, gold trim . . 60.00
Claret, 4-1/2 oz, red. . . . 45.00
Cocktail, cobalt blue . . . 35.00
Cocktail shaker, cobalt blue . . . 40.00
Comport, #1402/100, 5" h, forest green, crystal stem and foot . . . 60.00
Cordial, Carmen, thick. . . . 65.00
Cup and saucer, cobalt blue. . . . 55.00
Decanter set, decanter, stopper, six-handled 2-1/2 oz tumblers, amethyst. . . . 185.00

Goblet
Luncheon, Carmen . . . 30.00
Water, 10 oz, Carmen . . . 35.00

Ice bucket, cobalt blue . . . 175.00

Pitcher
Amethyst, 88 oz. . . . 200.00
Crystal, metal spout and lid. . 105.00

Plate, 9", Carmen. . . . 20.00
Platter, 14" l, handle, cobalt blue. 75.00
Punch bowl set, bowl and eight mugs, Carmen. . . . 800.00
Punch cup, crystal, Carmen handle . . . 12.00
Relish, three parts, 8-1/4" l, handle, cobalt blue . . . 25.00
Salad dressing bowl, divided, four satin horizontal bands . . . 48.00
Sugar, cobalt blue . . . 55.00
Tankard, amber . . . 95.00

Tumbler
9 oz, flat, cobalt blue . . . 18.00
10 oz, flat, Carmen . . . 20.00

Bushel basket, figural basketweave exterior, two molded handles, slightly flared foot, canary, **$115.**

Wildflower

Etching made from the 1940s to 1950s. Made mainly on crystal, some with gold trim, some gold encrusted, some other color pieces made. Prices listed below crystal, unless noted otherwise.

Ball jug, #3400 . . . 300.00
Basket, 6" h, two handles, sq, #3500/55 . . . 55.00

Bonbon
#3400/1179, crystal, 5-1/2" d, two handles . . . 40.00
#3500/54, gold encrusted, 6" d, two handles . . . 65.00

Bowl
10" d, two handles, #3400/1185 . . . 95.00
10" d, crystal, Gold Krystol, matching 12-1/2" d plate, sgd . . . 375.00
11" d . . . 85.00

Bud vase, 10" h, pink . . . 200.00
Butter, cov, #3400/52 . . . 200.00

Candlestick
#638, three-lite . . . 80.00
#646, one-lite, pr . . . 75.00
#3900/72, two-lite, pr . . . 145.00
#3900/72, two-lite, pr, gold encrusted. . . . 165.00

Candy dish, cov
#3400, three-part, 8" d . . . 95.00
#3400/9, four ftd . . . 180.00
#3500/57, three-part, 8" d. . . 150.00

Celery/relish
#3400/67, five parts, 12" l. . . . 55.00
#3500/64, three parts, 10" l, two handles, gold trim . . . 75.00

Celery service, #397 . . . 60.00

Champagne, #3121, 6-1/2" h, 6 oz
Crystal . . . 40.00
Crystal, gold trim . . . 50.00

Cheese and cracker set, #3400/6, gold encrusted . . . 110.00
Cheese comport, #3400/7 . . . 50.00
Claret, 4-1/2 oz . . . 42.00
Cocktail, #3121, 6" h . . . 32.00

Compote
#3400/6. . . . 37.50
#3500/148, 6" . . . 60.00

Console set, 12" d ruffled bowl, pr of keyhole candlesticks, crystal . . 195.00
Cordial, #3121, 5-1/4" h, 1 oz. . . 75.00
Creamer and sugar, #3500/15, individual size, crystal. . . . 48.00
Dresser compact, pink . . . 250.00
Finger bowl . . . 85.00
Goblet, #3121, 8-1/4" h. . . . 48.00
Hurricane lamps, #1604 . . . 500.00
Iced tea tumbler, #3121, ftd, 12 oz . . . 45.00
Juice tumbler, #3121, ftd . . . 35.00

Mayonnaise
#3900/129, three pcs, crystal **140.00**
#3900/129, three pcs, crystal, gold encrusted, wear to gold **80.00**
#3900/129, three pcs, pink . . **165.00**
Pickle, 9" **48.00**
Pitcher, #3900/117, 20 oz **450.00**
Plate
#3400/6, 6" d **20.00**
#3400/35, 11" d, two handles, gold trim **120.00**
#3400/1181, 6" d, two handles **35.00**
#3400/1186, 12-1/2" d, two handles, gold trim **100.00**
#3900/166, 14-1/4" d, gold trim **130.00**
Oyster cocktail **38.00**
Relish
Two parts, 7" l, handles **55.00**
Three parts, 6-1/2" d, gold rim. **60.00**
Five parts, 10" l **95.00**
Salt shaker, #3400, ftd. **30.00**
Seafood cocktail, insert, orig plate **50.00**
Sherbet, #3121, gold trim **30.00**
Sugar bowl, #3400 . . . . **45.00**
Sweet pea vase, 3-3/4" h, green **300.00**
Torte plate, #3900/65, 14" d . . . **115.00**
Tray, #3400/1181, 6" w, gold encrusted crystal **65.00**
Tumbler, #3121, 10 oz **45.00**
Vase
4" h, blown **195.00**
7" h. **195.00**
8-1/2" h, crystal **95.00**
8-1/2" h, crystal, gold encrusted **195.00**
10" h, ftd. **135.00**
10" h, keyhole **65.00**
11" h, ftd. **165.00**
12" h, flip **800.00**
Wine, #3121, 3-1/2" h. **60.00**

Cameo Glass

De Latte Nancy

1921

History: Cameo glass is a form of cased glass. A shell of glass was prepared; then one or more layers of glass of a different color(s) was faced to the first. A design was then cut through the outer layer(s), leaving the inner layer(s) exposed.

This type of art glass originated in Alexandria, Egypt, between 100 and 200 A.D. The oldest and most famous example of cameo glass is the Barberini or Portland vase found near Rome in 1582. It contained the ashes of Emperor Alexander Serverus, who was assassinated in 235 A.D.

Emile Gallé is probably one of the best-known cameo glass artists. He established a factory at Nancy, France, in 1884. Although much of the glass bears his signature, he was primarily the designer. Assistants did the actual work on many pieces, even signing Gallé's name. Glass made after his death in 1904 has a star before the name Gallé. Other makers of French cameo glass include D'Argental, Daum Nancy, LeGras, and Delatte. The French cameo glassmakers produced some of the most beautiful examples found in today's antique glass marketplace.

English cameo pieces do not have as many layers of glass (colors) and cuttings as do French pieces. The outer layer is usually white, and cuttings are very fine and delicate. Most pieces are not signed. The best-known makers are Thomas Webb & Sons and Stevens and Williams.

Marks: A star before the name Gallé on a piece by that company indicates that it was made after Gallé's death in 1904.

References: Victor Arwas, *Glass Art Nouveau to Art Deco*, Rizzoli International Publications, 1977; Alastair Duncan and George DeBartha, *Glass by Gallé*, Harry N. Abrams, 1984; Ray and Lee Grover, *English Cameo Glass*, Crown Publishers, 1980; Kyle Husfloen, *Antique Trader's American & European Decorative and Art Glass Price Guide*, 2nd ed., Krause Publications, 2000; Tim Newark, *Emile Galle*, The Apple Press, 1989; Albert C. Revi, *Nineteenth Century Glass*, reprint, Schiffer Publishing, 1981; John A. Shuman, III, *Collector's Encyclopedia of American Art Glass*, Collector Books, 1988, 1999 value update; Wolf Ueker, *Art Nouveau and Art Deco Lamps and Candlesticks*, Abbeville Press, 1986; Kenneth Wilson, *American Glass 1760-1930: The Toledo Museum of Art, Volume I, Volume II*, Hudson Hills Press and The Toledo Museum of Art, 1994.

Additional Listings: See Daum Nancy, and Galle, as well as other makers.

American

Gillander American Glass Co., attributed to
Lamp shade, 4-1/2" h, 3-7/8" fitter ring, crimped rim, flared cased body
Blue, cameo-etched white blackberry design, minor rim chips **250.00**
Pink, cameo-etched three birds among blossoms, minor rim chips **250.00**
Vase, 4" h, overlaid in white, cameo-etched morning glory blossoms, buds, and leafy vines, shaded blue cased to white oval body **825.00**
Harrach, vase, 8" h, 4" d, cameo-etched bright white carved daffodils, leaves, and stems, frosted and green ground **950.00**
Honesdale Glass, vase, 12" h, green cameo-etched to clear, gold dec trim **1,295.00**
Mount Washington
Bowl, 8" d, 4" h, sq, ruffled edge, two winged Griffins holding up scroll and spray of flowers design, blue over white ground **1,475.00**
Lamp
17" h, 10" d shade, fluid font and shade composed of opal white opaque glass overlaid in bright rose pink, acid-etched butterflies, ribbons, and bouquets centering cameo portrait medallions in classical manner, mounted on silverplated metal fittings, imp "Pairpoint Mfg. Co 3013," electrified **3,105.00**
21" h, 10" d shade, brilliant deep yellow over white, base figural woman with basket of flowers, matching floral design on shade, fancy brass base and font, orig chimney. . . . **8,500.00**
24" h, deep rose over white, portrait of woman dec on shade and base, silver-plated fittings **7,500.00**

Unknown English Maker, bowl, ruby red ground, cameo-etched white honeysuckle flowers, vine, and butterfly, 3" d, 1-3/4" h, ***$1,175.*** *Photo courtesy of Clarence and Betty Maier.*

English

Florentine Art, cruet, 6-1/2" h, ruby-red body, textured white enamel meadowland scene, Meadowlark on tall plant stalk, smaller scene on reverse, white rim, trefoil spout, clear frosted handle, teardrop shaped stopper, pontil mark sgd "59" **750.00**
Stevens and Williams
Bowl, 6-1/4" d, 4" h, ftd, cased yellow ground, cameo-etched seaweed, applied glass prunt **250.00**
Decanter, 15-1/2" h, citron yellow and colorless ground, sapphire blue overlay, wheel cut and engraved cactus rose blossoms on

spiked leaf-forms, matching teardrop stopper **1,265.00**

Lamp, 8" h, yellow ground, cameo-etched red fuchsias and leaves, sgd **2,750.00**

Vase

4-1/4" h, flared du Barry rose oval, overlaid in white, cameo-etched wild geranium plant and grasses, linear borders . **850.00**

4-1/4" h, 3-1/4" w, pale blue ground, cameo-etched dainty carved leaves, single large butterfly, band of white beaded cutting at throat, base fully sgd "Stevens & Williams Art Glass, Sturbridge" **1,250.00**

4-1/2" h, broad bright blue oval, overlaid in opaque white glass, cameo-etched and cut clusters of cherries on leafy boughs, circular mark on base "Stevens & Williams Art Glass Stourbridge" **1,265.00**

6-1/4" h, Rose du Barry, lush pink rose oval body, cameo-etched with white six-petaled blossoms and buds, intricate leaves, butterfly at reverse, linear border **1,610.00**

9" h, double bulbed gourd shape, reverse colored, du Barry rose over white cased to colorless, cameo-etched exotic pink blossoms, circular mark on base "Stevens & Williams Stourbridge" **2,185.00**

9" h, flared elongated neck, bulbed body, dusky rose overlaid in white, cameo-etched overall in passion flowers motif, elaborate top and medial borders, tiny chip under base edge **2,000.00**

Unknown maker

Cologne bottle, 6" h, 4-1/4" w, ball shaped, matte yellow, highly detailed white cameo-etched flowers, leaves, and fern font, monogrammed silver screw-on cap, some denting to top **900.00**

Marmalade jar, cov, 5-1/4" h, carved white flowers and leaves, medium blue ground, notch in lid for spoon . **1,650.00**

Perfume bottle, 5-1/2" h, 4-3/4" h, citron yellow ground, cameo-etched white flowers, leaves, vines, and buds, carved butterfly, three applied frosted feet, sterling repoussé cover . . **1,550.00**

Plaque, 5-1/2" l, 3-1/2" w, citron yellow, five cameo-etched white carved carnation flowers, leaf **1,275.00**

Scent bottle, 2" h, 1-3/4" d, ball shaped, white cameo-etched morning glories, clear frosted ground, chartreuse lining, orig collar and screw-on cap with English hallmarks **950.00**

Sweetmeat jar, cov, 3" h, 4-3/4" d, frosted deep cranberry ground, cameo-etched opaque white apple blossoms and leaves, silver plated top, rim, and handle **1,100.00**

Vase

3-1/8" h, frosted yellow oval body cased to white, crimson red overlay, cameo-etched and cut various plants and grasses below double border design ... **1,725.00**

3-3/4" h, 3" h, carved fuchsia flowers and leaves, lime green triple cameo-etched band **650.00**

4-1/8" h, bright sapphire blue ground, white layer, cameo-etched single blossoming branch, notched border **850.00**

5-1/4" h, cornflower blue oval body, cameo-etched white overlay in blossom motif, goldenrod on reverse, spiked border **850.00**

7" h, 5" w, corset shape, cranberry, white overlay, cameo-etched sprays of sweet peas, leaves, branches, butterfly in flight **1,750.00**

7-1/4" h, flared rim, bulbous base, white to frosted colorless glass body, overlaid in green and pink, cameo-etched grapes on leafy vines, other flowers **815.00**

Thomas Webb & Sons

Bowl, 3-1/2" d, 1-5/8" h, red glass overlaid in white, cameo-etched and engraved honeysuckle and butterfly on reverse, polished pontil, late 19th C **865.00**

Bowl and undertray, 5-1/8" d bowl, 6" d underplate, brilliant red layered in sapphire blue, overlaid in white, cameo-etched floral design and butterflies, plate with central medallion, each pc stamped "Thomas Webb & Sons/Cameo" **1,380.00**

Cologne bottle

4-3/4" h, white over yellow sphere, intricately cameo-etched decumbent fuchsia with elaborate borders above and below, butterfly at center, mounted with silver rim, hinged ball cover, English hallmarks, tiny glass chip on butterfly **980.00**

Webb, vase, blue ground, white decoration, etched "Thomas Webb & Sons" in banner, 6" h, **$3,200.**

5" h, square blue body, four panels of white overlaid cameo-etched and etched blossoms, silver ball cover, damage at two corners, small chips, some cover dents **490.00**

5" h, square yellow body, four panels of white overlaid cameo-etched and etched blossoms, screw-on silver cover, several chips to white dec, cov dents **520.00**

5-1/2" h, brilliant red oval body, layered in white, cameo-etched and etched blossoming leafy vines, stylized border, repeated on conical silver hallmarked screw top, base with semicircular mark "Thomas Webb & Sons". . **1,500.00**

Cup and saucer, handleless, 2-3/4" h, 5" d, cranberry over crystal, cameo-etched prunous blossoms, leaves, and branches, 10 blossoms on cup with large butterfly and 25 buds **550.00**

Decanter, 9-1/2" h, bulbous, yellow bottle cased with white over bright red layer, cameo-etched blossoming leafy vines, applied glass handle attached metal chain to decanter, silver rim, hinged floral motif cap, imp "sterling" and English hallmarks....... **3,000.00**

Perfume bottle

3-3/4" l, flattened teardrop shape, bright blue, cameo-etched forget-me-nots all around, two butterflies on shoulder, one chip on surface flower, wear to gilt metal screw cap **435.00**

4" l, teardrop shape, blue glass overlaid in white, cameo-etched sweet pea blossoms, silver hinged top, glass stopper, hallmarks, c1883, stopper stuck . . . **1,265.00**

5-1/2" l, 2-3/4" w, sq, citron yellow, white overlay, allover cameo-etched wild roses, leaves, and buds, orig silver spring-hinge cov. **2,750.00**

5-3/4" l, swan's head, yellow glass layered in opaque white, intricately carved details, registered mark "Rd 11109" on underside, chased silver hinged cap, London hallmarks, monogrammed, c1884, minor nick to cameo on bill. **3,450.00**

Posey pot, 2" h, squatty bulbous form, crimson red ground, cameo-etched white morning glory vines, butterfly in flight **865.00**

Scent bottle, 4" l, flattened teardrop shape, sapphire blue, cameo-etched white ferns and grasses dec, butterfly at side, gilt metal hinged cover . **920.00**

Vase

3-1/4" h, double bulbed shape, bright crimson red body, white overlay, cameo-etched passion flower motif, pendant leafy vine above and on reverse, late "Webb" on base **700.00**

3-1/4" h, red oval body, layered in white, cameo-etched wild geraniums, spike-leafed stems on reverse, dec borders. **980.00**

4-1/8" h, flared oval, crimson layered in white, cameo-etched all around in stylized Asian influence foliate dec **1,050.00**

4-1/2" h, bulbous pastel yellow body, white layer cameo-etched as dahlia plant on front, maidenhair fern on back, linear borders **490.00**

4-1/2" h, pale raisin color oval body, layered in white cameo, leafy bough and delicate blossom clusters cameo-etched around shoulder, linear border above **575.00**

4-3/4" h, small flared rim, green amber ovoid body, overlaid in opaque white, cameo-etched gentian blossoms, butterfly on reverse, rim nicks **1,150.00**

5" h, flared oval, bright yellow-green overlaid in white, cameo-etched rosa rigosa blossom and bud, flying butterfly on back. . . . **500.00**

5" h, tricolor, bright citron yellow-green oval body, layered in white over red, cameo-etched intricate rose blossom, thorny branch, single butterfly on reverse, linear border. **1,100.00**

5-1/2" h, flared bulbous red oval body, layered white and cameo-etched five detailed seashells, various seaweed clusters, base marked "Thomas Webb & Sons/Cameo" . . . **2,645.00**

5-5/8" h, tricolor, baluster, frosted colorless cased to white int., layered in white over Webb red, cameo-etched trumpet blossom and buds pendant from linear border. **700.00**

5-3/4" h, raised rim, bright red oval body, layered in white, six cameo-etched trumpet blossoms on decumbent leafy vine, repeating feather border **1,500.00**

7" h, flared red oval body, white layer cameo-etched rose blossoms, buds, leaves, and thorned branches, reverse with delicate blossoming bough, linear borders **1,840.00**

7" h, simulated ivory bulbous body, cameo-etched ivy above berries on leafy vines, motif enhanced by sepia coloration, semicircular mark on base "Thos. Webb & Sons" **815.00**

7-1/4" h, gourd form, transparent green body, solid applied top stem as handle, three oval aperture openings cut into body, white layered and cameo-etched fruit and leaf laden branches, unsgd, chipped, small annealing crack at stem end **3,250.00**

7-1/2" h, 6-1/2" w, pillow, brilliant blue, white cameo-etched wild roses, two large roses, 12 leaves, large butterfly in flight, full signature **2,750.00**

8-3/4" h, lily, flared colorless ground, transparent red overlay, acid-etched four stylized repeating blossoms, Webb cartouche at lower edge **1,100.00**

9" h, Old Ivory, double gourd body, scenes with warriors on horseback, half-man half-animal figures, bird-serpents, kings and queen, all in elaborate frames, floral backgrounds, orig circular mark on base "Thomas Webb & Sons Cameo," George Woodall design **23,000.00**

9-3/4" h, flared rim, elongated neck, chartreuse oval body, overlaid in opaque white, cameo-etched clematis blossom on budding vine, butterfly on reverse, small chips to upper rim. **1,265.00**

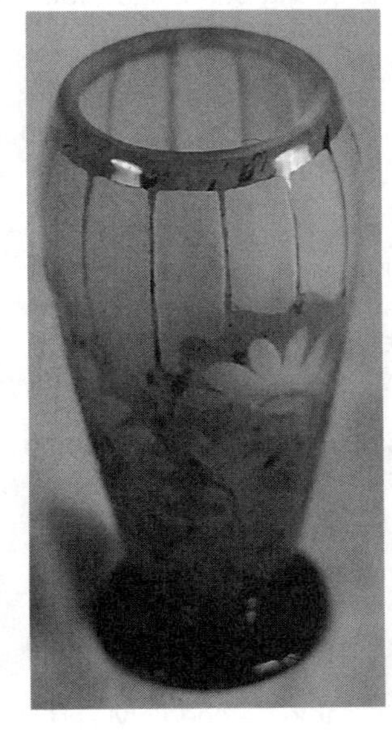

Charder Le Verre Francais, vase, 11" h, **$650.**

French

Arsall

Vase

4" h, densely foliaged royal purple islands on calm waterway, frosty gray sky, cameo sgd "Arsall" **325.00**

5" h, flared, pink mottled yellow overlaid ground, green layer cameo-etched decumbent blossoms, buds, and leafy stems, sgd "Arsall" in design **325.00**

7-3/4" h, entwining morning glory vines in pumpkin and olive green, circling gray ground with pink tint around rim, cameo sgd "Arsall" among leaves at base **500.00**

16-1/4" h, flared rim, large frosted pink-white oval body, layered in orange and sienna, cameo-etched realistic iris blossoms, spiked leaves, side sgd "Arsall" **1,575.00**

Burgun and Schverer

Vase

7-1/4" h, urn form, three handled, translucent fiery amber

cameo-etched and painted body, medallion cartouches of regional ethnic costumed people, elaborate B & S mark on base. **6,900.00**

7-3/4" h, frosted gray oval shaded to purple-amethyst, overlaid in purple-amethyst, cameo-etched blossoming leafy plants, some martele background, fitted with dec silvered metal foot, glass base inscribed with BS & Co. thistle and cross mark, two side chips at lower side. **345.00**

9-1/4" h, translucent yellow-green oval body, internally swirled in burgundy and green, overlaid in amethyst and green, cameo-etched iris blossoms and leaves, stars, and martele in background, base marked with BS & Co. elaborate thistle and cross mark. **7,760.00**

Charder

Vase

8-1/4" h, ftd bulbous shape, blue cameo-etched foliate design, cameo sgd "Charder" . . **500.00**

15" h, gourd shape, white ground, orange cameo-etched stylized flowers, cameo sgd "Charder" **800.00**

Chouvenin, vase, satin ground, brown overlay cameo-etched as wind blown trees, enameled details, yellow highlights, cameo sgd "Chevenin" **550.00**

Christian, vase, 11-1/2" h, pink leaves and thistles accented with small amounts of light brown tint, clear ground completely cameo-etched geometric florals, sgd "Vallerystahl" on base. **1,850.00**

Crystallerie D'Art, vase, 13" h, creamy opal white oval, bright forest green over pastel green layers, cameo- etched stylized Art Deco blossoms and leaves, sgd and marked on base "o. 31 of 100 exemplaries" **880.00**

D'Argental

Atomizer

4" h, cylindrical amber perfume bottle, green and brown overlay, cameo-etched landscape of leafy trees, wild geese in flight, sgd "D'Argental" on side, gilt metal fittings marked "Le Parisien Made in France," "BTE, S.G.D.G.". **825.00**

D'Argental, atomizer, cameo-etched green and forest green landscape scene of geese in flight, amber ground, signed "d'Argental" in cameo, hardware signed "LE Parisien, Made in France," 4-1/2" h, **$490.** *Photo courtesy of David Rago Auctions.*

4-1/2" h, cameo-etched green and forest green landscape, geese in flight, amber ground, sgd "d'Argental" in cameo, hardware sgd "L. E. Parisien/Made in France" **490.00**

Box, cov, 6-7/8" d, compressed spherical form, yellow ground, mauve overlay, cameo-etched roses, lid, with central knob, sgd in cameo **1,200.00**

Cabinet vase, 4-1/2" h, 2-1/2" d body, deep blue cameo-etched to dull gold, floral dec, sgd "D'Argental". **400.00**

Center bowl, 8-3/4" d, double conical contour, wide everted mouth, frosted ground, cameo-etched orchid blossoms and leaves, sgd in cameo "D'Argental" with cross de Lorraine, c1900 . . . . **2,400.00**

Perfume bottle, 5-1/4" h, lime green ground, light and dark burgundy overlay, cameo-etched flowers, buds, and leaves, carved signature, gold washed metal top sgd "Le Parisien". **1,200.00**

Vase

5" h, frosted oval, mauve and purple-black overlay, cameo-etched spring snowdrops, blossoms, and buds, silver rim wrap, side sgd "D'Argental (cross)" **520.00**

6-3/4" h, frosted pastel green oval body, overlaid in gray-black, cameo-etched blossoms, pods, and leafy poppy plants, side sgd "D'Argental (cross)" **435.00**

D'Argental, vase, lake and village scene, 18" h, **$1,400.**

9-3/4" h, fiery amber oval body, layered in maroon and brown, cameo-etched pendant blossoming trumpet vine, lower side sgd "D'Argental," some int. bubbles in glass **1,035.00**

10" h, swollen neck over elongated ovoid body, amber yellow glass layered in orange and brown, cameo-etched maple leaves and seeds, cameo signature with cross near base, c1920 . . . . **1,035.00**

11-1/2" h, opal white oval body, overlaid in green and gray, cameo- etched shaded levels of riverside scene, tall leafy foreground trees, sgd "D'Argental" in cameo in lower scene. **1,725.00**

13-3/4" h, opalescent yellow and maroon ground, lake and village showing through birch lined marsh, slight iridescence, cameo sgd "D. Argental" **1,600.00**

Daum Nancy

Basket, 6" h, 6-1/2" d, green shaded to clear textured ground, sprays of enamel leaf, branch, and berry design, handle with matching cameo-etched pattern, sgd "Daum Nancy" with cross of Lorraine, possible internal fracture in bowl **350.00**

Bowl

2-1/2" h, mottled brilliant purple and yellow ground, ext. cameo-etched deep blue and bright red grape leaves and vines, int. with bunch of purple grapes, sgd **1,600.00**

4-3/4" d, cameo-etched deep blue grape pods, autumn color leaves and vines, mottled yellow, pink, and amethyst ground, quad fold trim, cameo sgd **900.00**

Box, cov

3-1/2" d, 2-3/4" h, brilliant yellow and clear mottled ground, cameo-etched green, yellow, and red floral and leaf dec, sgd **1,550.00**

4-3/4" d, 2-3/4" h, cameo-etched green grapes and leaves, tan ground **500.00**

Bud vase

9" h, bulbed and elongated neck, flattened oval form, dome base, colorless glass layered in amethyst, cameo-etched and engraved with lilies on stalks, textured ground of stylized floral medallions, gilt highlights, inscribed "Daum (cross) Nancy '93" on base, c1893 .. **1,350.00**

10" h, flared elongated neck, bulbed yellow body layered in green, mottled bright pink, cameo-etched stylized leafy design, pedestal foot sgd "Daum (cross) Nancy" **1,150.00**

Cabinet vase

1" h, 2" w, pillow shape, pale yellow and clear frosted ground, cameo-etched naturalistic landscape in browns, blue, and green, sgd "Daum"... **1,100.00**

1-1/8" h, 2" l, pillow shape, brilliant orange yellow ground, cameo-etched trees and snow winter landscape, sgd **1,200.00**

1-3/4" h, cameo-etched landscape with birch trees, leaves, branches, and green grass, pale opalescent white ground, sgd **1,200.00**

1-3/4" h, 1-1/4" w, cameo-etched tropical island scene, shades of gray, purple, and soft peach, palm trees and oasis, sgd "Daum" **900.00**

2" h, pale yellow and pink ground, cameo-etched yellow flowers, green leaves and stems, sgd "Daum Nancy" **1,100.00**

2" h, cameo-etched winter scene, various trees, snowy landscape, sgd **1,000.00**

2" h, 1-1/2" w, cameo-etched landscape of trees and leaves in green and yellow, sgd. **1,200.00**

2-1/2" h, cameo-etched rain scene, frosted clear ground, trees and foliage, sgd "Daum Nancy"............. **1,600.00**

3" h, scenic, cameo-etched green trees, blue and purple landscape sgd "Daum Nancy" **1,100.00**

4" h, deeply carved red poppies and green leaves, pink ground, vertical lines, gold rim and stopper with dragonflies, sgd, cross mark.......... **5,000.00**

7-1/2" h, amethyst ground, cameo-etched iris floral cutting, "Parfum de Vertus," gilt highlights, base sgd "Daum Nancy"............. **1,450.00**

Cream pitcher, 3" h, 2-1/2" d, enamel and cameo-etched, flattened shape, brilliant orange poppy dec, green leaves, stems, and buds, textured opalescent apricot ground, gold trim, sgd "Daum Nancy" **2,150.00**

Dish, 6-1/4" d, 3-1/4" h, tricorn, mottled green, amber, and colorless, padded white trumpet blossoms, green leafy vines, rim sgd "Daum Nancy (cross) 1875" **750.00**

Ewer, 12" h, colorless frosted oval body, overlaid in bright rose-red, deeply etched as convolvulus blossoms, matching flowers and dec on silver foot, handle, rim, and hinged cov, imp hallmarks and "sterling," glass base sgd in gold "Daum (cross) Nancy" ... **4,900.00**

Flask, 5-3/4" h, 1-1/2" w, turquoise blue shading to clear, textured ground, cameo-etched and enameled mistletoe dec, gold washed metal, orig stopper, orig leather bound carrying case, sgd **2,100.00**

Ice bucket, 5-1/2" h, 5-1/4" w, shaded green to clear, elaborate scroll and floral cameo dec, gold paint, fancy bronze rim and handle, sgd "Daum Nancy" **1,350.00**

Jar, cov, 3" h, 2-3/4" w, deep amethyst colored glass, cased in crystal, cameo-etched flowers, leaves, and vines, enameled and gilded, sgd "Daum Nancy" **600.00**

Perfume bottle, 5" h, tapered form, translucent green shaded to colorless glass, cameo-etched asters on textured ground, gold enamel highlights, mounted with chased silver cap and base, worn enamel signature under base, c1895, metal mount re-attached **815.00**

Perfume flacon, 6" l, elongated bottle, colorless glass layered in red, cameo-etched branches of bleeding heart, gilt highlights, enamel signature on base int., hammered silver screw top mount and base, French hallmarks, c1900, minor nick to cameo **920.00**

Salt, open

1-1/8" h, 2" w, enameled and cameo-etched, summer landscape, trees and plants, clear frosted ground, enameled green, brown, purple, and yellow, sgd **900.00**

1-1/8" x 2-1/8" w, enameled and cameo-etched, pale vaseline opalescent ground, single layer cutting of flowers, leaves, and stems, gold dec, sgd "Daum Nancy" **1,200.00**

1-3/4" h, 2" w, double handles, enameled and cameo-etched, landscape dec with branches, boughs, and cones .. **1,250.00**

2" l, 1" h, rose ground, lightly gilted morning glory vine dec, script sgd "Daum Nancy" with cross................ **425.00**

2-1/2" h, 3-1/2" l, ftd, enameled and cameo-etched, green ground, cut leaves and vines, gold dec, sgd "Daum Nancy" **650.00**

2-1/2" h, 3-1/2" l, pale opalescent vaseline ground, cameo-etched leaves and vines, gold enameled dec, sgd "Daum Nancy" **850.00**

Tumbler, 3-1/2" h, colorless textured ground, acid-etched and enameled mistletoe, gilt highlights, side engraved "1 May 1910," bottom engraved "Daum Nancy" **275.00**

Vase

3-1/2" h, 3" w, olive green ground, rough textured finish, gold leaf and vine dec, "Je mours ou je n attache" carved below neck, sgd in gold under base . **350.00**

4-1/2" h, frosted opalescent red, yellow, and green rainbow ground, enameled cameo-etched thistle florals, cameo sgd "Daum Nancy" **800.00**

4-1/2" h, oval bud, fiery opalescent amber with red striations, cameo-etched thistle pods and thorny stems, enameled burgundy-red, sgd "Daum Nancy (cross)" at side **815.00**

4-1/2" h, 2" d, slightly opalescent frosted ground, textured background, cameo-etched wild roses, irregular gold rim, sgd **450.00**

5" h, 3-1/2" w, pale pink and yellow opalescent ground, cameo-etched leaves and strawberry dec, applied silver repoussé base........ **450.00**

6" h, peaceful river scene seen through mocha brown trees, foliaged islands silhouetted in background against mottled orange sunset, cameo sgd "Daum Nancy (cross)". **1,000.00**

6-1/4" h, 6-1/2" d, colorless spherical body, deep red pedestal foot, emerald green transparent body, cameo-etched all over with six repeating thistles in arched foliate frame, sgd in motif "Daum Nancy (cross)".. **980.00**

6-3/4" h, 3-1/2" w at shoulder, enamel and cameo-etched, textured acid finish clear ground, mottled pale yellow and pink, heavily carved Shasta daisy flowers, enameled with yellow, gold, tan, and brown, dark green leaves veined in yellow, green and yellow textured base, sgd, dripped as lamp base **700.00**

7-1/2" d, deep purple cameo overlay, rose colored ground, sgd in cameo........ **1,725.00**

8-3/4" h, marquetry-applied orange florals, fine wheel carved detail, sgd "Daum Nancy"............. **4,025.00**

9-3/4" h, cameo-etched and enameled dragonflies, gold gilt dec **1,725.00**

9-3/4" h, 5-1/2" d, highly textured ground, cameo-etched large pink parrot tulips and leaves, sgd **1,200.00**

10-1/4" h, ftd baluster, frosted apricot ground, overlaid in pine green, cameo-etched trees and lake scene, sgd in cameo "Daum Nancy" **1,600.00**

11-1/2" h, mold blown, woodland scene, dark green foliage, peering village, mottled orange and yellow sky, sgd on bottom **10,200.00**

13-1/4" h, 4-1/2" w, deep emerald green, cameo-etched fleur-de-lis dec with gold, textured and sculptured ground, sgd **250.00**

13-1/2"h, 2-1/2" w, cameo-etched floral design of pale yellow marsh flower, multicolored leaves, spatter of pale pink and yellow shading to brilliant green and brown ground, sgd **4,100.00**

15-1/4" h, carved and enameled daffodils among foliage, dark matte green mottled shades into raised base, gray opal background has cobalt, iron red, and coral mottling, engraved "Daum Nancy" with croix de Lorraine at top of foot, some peppering in design **6,750.00**

17-1/2" h, flared rim, elongated bulbed colorless cylinder, overlaid in vitrified autumn orange and yellow colors, cameo-etched leaves and seed pods above and below, base incised "Daum Nancy (cross)" **2,100.00**

Vase, 9-3/4" h, signed "Daum Nancy," **$1,500.**

Degue

Vase

6" h, 5" w, pink mottled on clear ground, heavily textured surface, cameo-etched Art Deco cutting, sgd **650.00**

14" h, frosted ground, red shading to blue cameo tulips, cameo-etched "Degue Made in France" **700.00**

14-1/2" h, glossy finish Art Deco stylized tortoise shell teasels, mottled minty ground acid finished ground, script engraved "Degue" on foot, inscribed "Made in France" on base **1,100.00**

17-1/2" h, ftd oviform, pink to purple cameo-etched foliate design, hand etched "Degue" **800.00**

Delatte

Vase

9" h, cameo-etched amethyst leaves and vine, orange ground, sgd "A. Delatte/Nancy" . **750.00**

10" h, mottled white and colorless satin ground, cameo-etched amethyst iris dec, cameo sgd "Delatte Nancy"....... **600.00**

De Vez

Cabinet vase, 2-1/2" h, cameo-etched mountains, lake, trees, and bands on mottled amber and pink ground, light dark blue overly, sgd "deVez" **2,070.00**

Rose bowl, 3-1/2" d, cobalt blue foliated trees and mountains, pink to yellow sky and water, scalloped rim, sgd **500.00**

Vase

3-3/4" h, light green to forest green cameo-etched trees, hills, and stream, mottled pink and light blue ground, sgd "deVez" **920.00**

5-3/4" h, cameo-etched landscape with mountains, waterfront, trees, and vines, shades of pink and green **750.00**

6" h, flared hyacinth form, pink opal layered in pastel yellow and blue, cameo-etched genre river scene with three cows wading before a watching cloaked figure, trees, blossoms above, cameo sgd "de Vez" **1,035.00**

6" h, maroon and fiery amber oval body, cameo-etched cottages,

mother and child under tall trees, sgd "De Vez" at side, polished rim **980.00**

6-1/4" h, fiery amber and maroon oval, cameo-etched riverfront vista, sgd "De Vez" in cameo **990.00**

6-1/4" h, opaque cream-colored oval, layered in rose-red and maroon, cameo-etched poppy blossoms, seed pods, leafy stems, sgd "De Vez" at lower edge.............. **1,380.00**

8" h, tubular, three color scenic brown castle and trees, blue mountains, frosted ground, sgd **1,400.00**

9" h, pink and maroon, rose blossom border and riverside mountain, sgd "De Vez" in cameo............... **850.00**

9-1/4" h, 3" w, cameo-etched landscape with three sailboats, mountains, and buildings, sgd **1,200.00**

12" h, 7" w, pale pink and blue ground, bright green cameo-etched five large birds, scenic landscape, sgd **1,650.00**

Galle

Atomizer, 7-3/4" h, cameo-etched purple bleeding hearts, frosted ground, orig hardware, sgd "Galle" in cameo **925.00**

Bowl, 5" l, 2-1/2" h, oval, flared mottled green gray oval, cased to pink, layered with mauve, acid-etched stylized leafy plants, sgd "Galle" at side **635.00**

De Vez, cabinet vase, cameo-etched mountains, lake, trees, and birds, mottled amber and pink ground, light and dark blue overlay, signed "de Vez," 2-1/2" h, **$690.** *Photo courtesy of David Rago Auctions.*

Bud vase, 3-5/8" h, elongated cylindrical neck over bulbous body of pale amber yellow overlaid in purple, cameo-etched flower and bud, cameo signature **375.00**

Cabinet vase

2-1/2" h, cameo-etched orange flowers, leaf, and vine, frosted ground, sgd "Galle" in cameo **520.00**

3-1/2" h, 3-1/4" d, glossy cranberry red, shaded yellow and crystal frosted ground, cameo-etched currants, leaves, and branches dec, sgd. **650.00**

3-3/4" h, cameo-etched amethyst floral design, amber ground, fire polished, sgd "Galle" in cameo **535.00**

4-1/2" h, 2-1/2" h, purple to frosted peach shading to colorless base, cameo-etched florals, sgd "Galle," slightly irregular rim, possibly polished **275.00**

Ceiling shade, Plaffonier, 11-1/2" d, 6-1/2" d, conical flared shale, frosted shades of green and gray layered in burgundy red-maroon over green, cameo-etched and etched buds and blossoms, leafy stems around rim, sgd "Galle" at side in motif, three gilt metal chains and ceiling mount....... **3,220.00**

Lamp base, 9" h, yellow ground, cameo-etched amethyst florals and buds, cameo sgd "Galle".. **450.00**

Lamp, 10-1/2" h, 10" d conical flared shade, oval base, colorless glass cased to fiery yellow, layered in dark maroon under burnt umber, cameo-etched and cut as exotic blossoms and leafy stems, sgd "Galle" on shade and base, two circular "Galle/Nancy/Paris" paper labels on base **8,625.00**

Night light, 2-1/4" d, 4-1/2" h, cameo-etched glass shade dec with three blue and purple butterflies, amber ground, iron base, sgd "Galle" in cameo **750.00**

Perfume lamp, 7-1/4" h, 4" d, yellow frosted ground, cameo-etched deep rose cyclamens, six large open blossoms, five buds, numerous leaves and stems, sgd **1,350.00**

Toothpick holder, 2-1/2" h, cameo-etched chartreuse and medium green seed pods and leafy branches, frosted and orange ground, sgd **500.00**

Vase

4-1/4" h, bright frosted red oval body layered in aubergine-black, cameo-etched as wild geranium blossoms and leafy stems, sgd "Galle" on motif, collar ridge for atomizer. **435.00**

4-5/8" h, slightly flattened colorless oval, overlaid in amethyst shaded to purple, cameo-etched clematis blossom and leafy vine, glossy fire polished surface, base incised "Galle/depose" **1,265.00**

5" h, 3-1/2" w, pale pink and peach ground, cameo-etched lavender and green floral dec, star signature **700.00**

5-5/8" h, flared rim and pedestal foot, fiery yellow oval ground, overlaid in rose red, cameo-etched delicate leafy stems and berries, sgd "Galle" in motif **1,500.00**

5-3/4" h, flattened oval, elliptical rim, amethyst and green layers, cameo-etched with raised center blossoms, leafy vines, sgd "Galle" at side, two small chips to stems **490.00**

6-1/2" h, elongated neck on flattened banjo shaped oval, fiery yellow layered in rose red, cameo-etched berry laden leafy branches, sgd "Galle" at side **1,380.00**

7-1/2" h, colorless satin ground, yellow-orange base, overlaid with cranberry, cameo-etched berries, cameo sgd "Galle," rim ground **770.00**

8" h, bulbed frosted colorless oval, pinched quatraform, burnt sienna amber cameo-etched spider mums, petals, and "Galle" at reverse.... **1,265.00**

8" h, olive green over colorless glass cased to bright orange, acid-etched water lilies and water grasses, sgd "Galle" on side............... **1,380.00**

8-1/4" h, flattened bulbous body, elongated neck, cased pink layered in amethyst and green, cameo-etched wisteria clusters and leafy stems, sgd "Galle" on side................ **920.00**

8-3/4" h, bud, trumpet form, fiery amber layered in blue and purple, cameo-etched and cut wild rose blossoms and buds, leaf border below, sgd "Galle" in design **1,380.00**

9-3/4" h, flared rim, cream colored ovoid body, overlaid in orange and deep red, cameo-etched landscape of Rio de Janeiro, sgd "Galle," and "Rio de Janeiro" **4,140.00**

10-1/2" h, 5-1/2" w, blue mountains, frosted pale pink and clear ground, deep brown landscape design, sgd **3,900.00**

11" h, bud, tall flattened bottle-form, amethyst overlay, cameo-etched blossoms, bud, and vines, sgd "Galle" on back **1,150.00**

12" h, ruffled rim, elongated colorless cylinder, overlaid in orange-amber, cameo-etched poppy blossoms, fire polished shiny surface, side sgd in vertical Oriental-style, applied tooled camphor foot . . **1,150.00**

12" h, trumpet, elongated neck with flared rim, bulbous frosted gray body overlaid in burnt sienna orange, cameo-etched poppy pods, blossoms, and leafy stems, reverse sgd "(star) Galle". **1,265.00**

12-1/2" h, frosted colorless translucent oval body, overlaid in amethyst purple, cameo-etched iris blossoms, buds, and spiked leaves, fire polished all over, partial martele background, sgd "Galle" at lower side **2,300.00**

13" h, flattened oval, colorless shaded to blue body, layered in bright pink and olive green, cameo-etched and cut decumbent bleeding heart blossoms and leafy stems, sgd "Galle" in design on side **5,175.00**

13-1/4" h, large conical frosted colorless body, layered in pale green and dark green, cameo-etched and carved as tall iris blossoms and spike leaves, Oriental-style, "Galle" vertically on one spike, four tiny leaf edge chips **1,380.00**

14" h, raised rim, ovoid amber glass body, overlaid in orange and green, cameo-etched flower clusters, sgd "Galle" **8,625.00**

Vase, 11-3/4" h, signed Galle, **$1,200.**

16" h, flared rim, elongated ovoid amber body, overlaid in orange and deep red, cameo-etched phlox, sgd "Galle" . . . **8,100.00**

17" h, baluster form, pedestal base, pale amber body, overlaid in salmon and maroon, cameo-etched hollyhocks, sgd "Galle" **5,750.00**

17-3/4" h, swollen cylindrical form, amber yellow body, overlaid in orange and red, cameo-etched trailing hibiscus buds and blossoms, sgd "Galle" **8,100.00**

21" h, elongated salmon shading to pale yellow ovoid body, overlaid in brown, cameo-etched trumpet blossoms, sgd "Galle" **3,450.00**

Lamatrine

Vase

3-1/2" h, cameo-etched, striking enamel landscape with stubby trees along waterway, mottled opal sky, script imp signature and number, short factory stress lines at rim and internal nicks **500.00**

6-1/2" h, tranquil forest landscape, pastel rainbow streaked interior gives sky soft glow, enamel highlights **1,200.00**

Legras

Bowl

2-3/4" h, cameo-etched colorless body, quatraform rim, enameled sunset snow scene, side sgd "Legras" **375.00**

3" h, cameo-etched colorless body, enameled stylized grape arbor border, side sgd "Legras" **350.00**

4-3/4" l, 1-3/4" h, frosted colorless shaped oval, scenic dec of shepherd and flock of sheep among mountainous landscape, enameled natural colors, sgd "Legras" at end, rim roughness **175.00**

Vase

4-1/2" h, panoramic view of lake reflecting distant orchid color trees, amber tinted sky, darker trees with olive foliage shad bare path in foreground, enamel highlights. **350.00**

7-1/2" h, satin ground with yellow opalescent highlights, light green, dark green, and amethyst cameo-etched leaves and florals, cameo sgd "Legras" **2,100.00**

8" h, tall enameled conifer trees overlooking lake reflecting mountain range, cameo sgd "Legras," narrow ring stain on int. **300.00**

8-1/2" h, frosted colorless oval body, cameo-etched and dec in pink and maroon enameled flowering branches, rim marked "Legras," stamped by retailed "Ovington New York/France" **575.00**

8-3/4" h, scalloped oval shape, cameo-etched landscape scene, green, brown, peach, and frosty white, chips . . **50.00**

9-1/2" h, slender, shepherd and flock sheltered by tall silhouetted trees, coral, frost, and citron sky, sgd "Legras" in foreground, chips, slightly polished rim. **150.00**

12" h, burgundy flowering branches on pale apricot textured ground, enamel highlights, cameo sgd "Legras" **350.00**

12-1/4" h, flared rim, frosted colorless oval, cameo-etched maroon enameled stylized Art Deco swags, geometric dec, side sgd in cameo "Legras" **575.00**

12-1/2" h, elongated bulbous fiery opalescent amber body,

overlaid in white and green, cameo-etched deep leaf and seed pod motif, lower edge sgd in cameo "Legras" **825.00**

14-1/4" h, elongated white flecked pink oval body, cameo-etched with three maroon enameled Art Deco stylized fountains with arching water sprays, side sgd in cameo "Legras" **635.00**

15" h, panoramic summer morning, three swans swimming in tranquil lake, tall foliaged trees in background, cameo sgd "Legras" **900.00**

15-1/2" h, angular oval yellow and brown on white within colorless glass body, three repeating cameo-etched Art Deco foliate elements, mahogany brown enameling, side inscribed "Legras" **1,150.00**

22" h, raised rim, bulbed cornelian beige-pink oval body, cameo-etched seaweeds, aquatic plants, and creatures, enameled dark red and green highlights, side sgd in cameo "Legras" **1,725.00**

Le Verre Francais

Bowl, 9" d, 7" h, bulbous, bright orange frosted ground, overlaid in tortoiseshell brown, cameo-etched and polished stylized repeating geometric elements, sgd "Charder" at side, "LeVerre Francais" below **920.00**

Lamp shade, 5-1/2" h, 3" d fitter ring, double bulbed red on mottled yellow and turquoise blue ground, cameo-etched butterfly, rim inscribed "Le Verre Francais, France" **1,100.00**

Perfume lamp night light base, 3-1/4" h, cased red to yellow, overlaid in tortoiseshell brown, cameo-etched stylized blossoms, rim inscribed "Le Verre Francais," fitted with metal light cap ..**375.00**

Punch bowl, 12" h, 14-1/2" w, large pedestal bowl, textured ground, acid finish, gray, pink, and green, cameo-etched pattern of horse chestnut burrs in mottled browns and rust tortoise shell colors, pedestal base of mottled dark purple, sgd on base **1,600.00**

Vase

3-3/4" h, mottled yellow amber body, overlaid in red shaded to olive green, cameo-etched foliate design, platform base sgd "Le Verre Francais" **550.00**

5-3/4" h, 4-1/4" w, acid finish, shading from clear at shoulder to dark purple, purple wafer base, cameo-etched daisy design, sgd **850.00**

7-1/2" h, raised rim on ovoid frosted body, tortoiseshell brown overlay, three cameo-etched foliate repeating elements, sgd "Le Verre Francais" on foot **690.00**

10" h, 14" w, bulbous, mottled brilliant yellow, orange, brown and green ground, large cut border of three Art Deco style flowers, three additional cut cameo bands, sgd "La Verre Francais" **450.00**

11-1/2" h, trumpet, flared mottled amethyst cone, green cameo-etched leaf dec, applied colorless foot with pink, blue, white cane twist within.. **980.00**

11-3/4" h, ftd oval, yellow speckled orange layered in tango red shaded to aubergine foot, cameo-etched stylized Art Deco blossoms and dots, disk sgd "Le Verre Francais," base sgd "France" **1,380.00**

13" h, elongated oviform, bun foot, yellow ground, orange cameo-etched flowers shading to blue, etched "Le Verre Francais" **1,200.00**

14" h, tapered bulbous body, cylindrical neck, mottled yellow ground, overlaid with green shading to red, cameo-etched geometric bands, engraved "Le Verre Francais" **1,200.00**

15-3/4" h, swelled oval, mottled pink, white, and orange layered in lavender and aubergine, cameo- etched and polished stylized rose blossoms on thorny stems, marked "Charder" at side, "Le Verre Francais" on foot, "France/Ovington" on base **1,100.00**

16" h, elongated ftd oval, bright mottled orange ground, overlaid in spotted tortoiseshell brown, cameo-etched and polished with three tall beetles below and between Art Deco border, striped candy cane mark at one side, other side marked "Le Verre Francais" **1,150.00**

16-1/2" h, elongated ftd oval, bright mottled orange, overlaid in spotted tortoiseshell brown, cameo-etched and polished with three tall beetles below and between Art Deco border, striped candy cane mark, sgd "Le Verre Francais" on foot **1,500.00**

17-1/2 h, mottled yellow and colorless ground, shaded red toned cameo-etched iris dec, flattened bulbous foot, script engraved "Le Verre Francais" **1,430.00**

19" h, mottled yellow vasiform overlaid in orange, cameo-etched in five repeats of pendent berries above and below Art Deco borders, 1/2" inch signature cane twist embedded at lower edge **1,725.00**

21-1/2" h, mottled orange-amber bulbed oval body, purple-lavender blue overlay, cameo-etched as grapes on whirling grapevines, foot inscribed "Le Verre Francais," colored cane embedded below **2,100.00**

21-3/4" h, elongated flared orange and yellow oval body, overlaid in mottled tortoiseshell brown to aubergine foot, cameo-etched stylized Moroccan Poppy blossoms and seed pods, leafy border, foot sgd "Le Verre Francais" **1,500.00**

22" h, floral oval, transparent orange layered in mottled aubergine, blue-white spots, cameo-etched and polished convoluted leaf and vine elements, striped candy cane at edge, "Le Verre Francais" on foot **1,380.00**

Mabut, vase, 9" h, oval cylindrical form tapering to dome base, gray and deep blue cased to chartreuse, cameo-etched and engraved lily blossoms, base inscribed "Verrerie de la Paix J. Mabut," c1900 .... **2,185.00**

Michel

Lamp, 17" h, 8" d domed shade, frosted yellow ground overlaid in red, cameo-etched mountainous landscape as seen through arcade of columns, baluster base, cameo sgd "Michel" **5,000.00**

Vase

3" h, rainbow ground, chocolate leaves, sgd "Michel" with cross de Lorraine, two nicks in design **150.00**

10-1/4" h, 5-1/4" d, orange and yellow, deep blue overlay, cameo-etched sailing ship on one side, lighthouse on obverse, flower border **1,400.00**

12-1/4" h, yellow ground, overlaid in burgundy and reddish brown rain scene with trees, cameo sgd "Michel" **1,100.00**

Mueller Freres

Cabinet vase

2" h, single mulberry violet with foliage, raspberry tinted frosty ground, cameo sgd "Mueller" **200.00**

3-1/2" h, 5" d, red cameo-etched leaf design, yellow ground **575.00**

4" h, 3-3/4" d, navy blue cameo-etched to orange, classical female figures in landscape, sgd "Muller Luneville," polished spot on edge of rim **300.00**

Lamp, 14-3/4" h, domed cameo shade, mottled orange body, brown overlay, cameo-etched leaves and berries on vines with tendrils, sgd in cameo, openwork wrought iron four arm base, curling vine motif **4,000.00**

Vase

4-7/8" h, frosted yellow-gray oval, red and maroon overlay, cameo-etched cyclamen blossoms, buds, and turning leaves, side sgd in cameo "Muller Fres Luneville".. **750.00**

5" h, 4" w, squatty, cameo-etched bleeding hearts and leaves, orange and yellow acid spatter ground, sgd "Mueller fre Luneville"........... **1,200.00**

5-1/4" h, fiery amber oval body, overlaid in orange, olive green, and black, cameo-etched trumpet-shaped blossoms, buds, and spiked leaves, sgd "Muller Fres Luneville," small chip to one leaf **575.00**

5-1/4" h, 5" w, brilliant orange and black, cameo-etched landscape design, sgd . **600.00**

5-1/4" h, 5-1/2" w, deep maroon, cranberry finely cameo-etched peony, pale yellow opalescent ground **1,800.00**

6" h, 3" w, mottled pale green, blue, brown, and orange ground, cameo-etched five sailboats, green and brown painted landscape, sgd "Mueller Fres Luneville" **1,800.00**

6-1/4" h, 6-1/4" w, scenic, cameo-etched blue mountains and trees, mottled white and pale pink ground, sgd **1,100.00**

8-3/4" h, oviform, rounded neck, frosted yellow ground, overlaid in burgundy, cameo-etched sheep, shepherd, and trees, lake scene, cameo sgd "Muller Freres Luneville"..... **1,200.00**

9-1/2" h, burnt orange ground, tree lined lake in silhouette, cameo-etched three figures picking fruit, another playing a musical instrument, sgd in cameo "Muller Fres Luneville" **990.00**

10" h, oval trumpet opal white body, green overlay etched and martele wheel-cut poppy pods and blossoms, base inscribed "Muller Croismare pres Nancy" **2,300.00**

Muller Freres, atomizer, cobalt, 9" h, **$550.**

Muller Freres, cabinet vase, cameo-etched red leaf design, yellow ground, 5" d, 3-1/2" h, **$500.** *Photo courtesy of David Rago Auctions.*

11-1/2" h, 3-1/2" w, glossy surface, cameo-etched green iris, white and green shaded ground, sgd......... **1,500.00**

13-1/2" h, red ground, overlaid in black, cut forest with deer at lake's edge, marked "Muller Fres Luneville"....... **2,200.00**

21" h, tapered, bun feet, mottled cream, deep yellow and blue ground, overlaid in blue, cameo-etched Oriental poppies and foliage, cameo sgd "Muller Freres Luneville" **5,600.00**

Pantin, vase, 9" h, elongated vasiform, slightly irid colorless glass, overlaid in translucent aqua, cameo-etched with wild flowers, textured int., base with etched circular signature "Cristallerie de Pantin, STV & C," c1900 .. **1,265.00**

Richard

Bowl, 6" l, 2-3/4" h, brilliant cased poppy red, brown overlay, acid-etched stylized foliate motif, sgd "Richard" at side..... **460.00**

Vase

4" h, powder blue ground, overlaid in amethyst, cameo-etched floral cuttings, cameo sgd "Richard" .. **550.00**

4-1/4" h, orange ground, overlaid in cobalt blue, cameo-etched florals, cameo sgd "Richard" **275.00**

7-1/4" h, yellow cased oval, layered in brown, cameo-etched mountainous village waterfront scene, applied brown-black handles at each side, sgd "Richard" at side...... **825.00**

13-1/4" h, striking orange ground, overlaid in deep cobalt blue, mountain lake, fir tree, and

castle silhouette, cameo sgd "Richard" **2,325.00**

13-1/2" h, 8" w, landscape with mountain and lake, trees, castle and bridge, brilliant bright orange, deep cobalt blue cameo overlay, sgd .. **3,000.00**

Wine, 7-3/4" h, cobalt blue scenic water and sailboats, frosted ground, notched stem..... **400.00**

Saint Louis, vase, 11" h, Rubina Verde, cameo-etched life size orchids, gold highlights, metal base, unmarked **600.00**

Unknown French maker, vase, 11" h, pinched trefoil mouth over cylindrical form, pale translucent green, layered in opaque white, etched with snow laden trees, enamel dec of pine cones and boughs in shades of green and brown, spurious signature **4,600.00**

Germany

Heckert, Fritz

3-1/4" h, frosted ground, pale cranberry cameo-etched floral and leaf dec, sgd **350.00**

3-1/4" h, 2-1/2" w, frosted clear and yellow ground, amethyst cameo-etched floral leaf and branch pattern, sgd **800.00**

Raspiller, G., Strasbourg, c1910, vase, 14" h, flared rim, elongated frosted orange oval body, overlaid in dark brown, cameo-etched iris blossoms and buds with dragonfly alighting, sgd "G. Raspiller" in cameo lower side, minor nicks **865.00**

Weis, cabinet vase, 1-1/2" h, pumpkin ground, mocha vintage design, cameo sgd "Weis" **250.00**

CAMPHOR GLASS

History: Camphor glass derives its name from its color. Most pieces have a cloudy white appearance, similar to gum camphor; others have a pale tint. Camphor glass is made by treating the glass with hydrofluoric acid vapors.

Other similar types of opaque glassware exist and there is confusion between camphor, clambroth, Bristol, and opaline. All are made using similar manufacturing techniques and have similar characteristics. Today, terms such as camphor and clambroth are giving way to opaline or opaque. Perhaps these names are not quite as descriptive, but they are more meaningful to modern collectors.

Biscuit jar, cov, white body, blue floral dec, brass-plated fittings **70.00**

Bookends, pr, 7" h, horse heads, white body **85.00**

Powder jar, covered, pink, embossed flowers, lovebirds finial, **$65.**

Bottle, 6-1/2" h, orig stopper.... **40.00**

Bowl

7-1/2" d, 3-1/2" h, white body, flared, scalloped rim, ftd **85.00**

10" d, fluted rim, polished pontil **125.00**

Box, cov, 5" d, hinged, enameled holly spray **75.00**

Candlesticks, pr, 7" h, hp roses . **75.00**

Creamer, Wild Rose and Bowknot pattern, white body, rose trim ... **40.00**

Cruet, hp enameled roses, orig stopper **45.00**

Goblet, 7" h, butterscotch bowl, gold dec, blue ring, red jewels **90.00**

Hair receiver, white body, gold scroll dec **50.00**

Lemonade set, pitcher, eight tumblers, white body, applied white handle **165.00**

Mustard, cov, Wild Rose and Bowknot pattern, white body, rose trim ... **45.00**

Powder jar, green, dog finial, 4-1/2" h, 4-1/2" w, **$75.**

Perfume bottle, 8-1/2" h, pinch type, mushroom cap **50.00**

Place card holder, 3-3/4" h, ftd .. **35.00**

Plate

6-1/2" d, Easter Greeting..... **30.00**

7-1/4" d, hp owl **40.00**

Powder jar, cov, sq, blue body, bird finial, c1920 .... **65.00**

Ring tree, 4-1/2" h, white body .. **20.00**

Rose bowl, hp violets, green leaves **50.00**

Salt and pepper shakers, pr, Swirl pattern, blue, orig tops......... **45.00**

Scent bottle, 8" h, white body, gold scrolling dec................ **50.00**

Sugar shaker, 3-1/2" h, tinted yellow ground, pressed leaf dec, silver plated top **55.00**

Toothpick holder, bucket shape. **30.00**

Vase

8" h, fan shape, clear leaf design and trim................. **85.00**

10-1/2" h, Grecian shape, double handles, clear base **120.00**

CANDLEWICK

History: Candlewick, Imperial Glass Corporation's No. 400 pattern, introduced in 1936, was made continuously until October 1982 when Imperial declared bankruptcy. In 1984, Imperial was sold to Lancaster-Colony Corporation and Consolidated Stores International, Inc. Imperial's assets, including inventory, molds, buildings, and equipment, were liquidated in 1985. Imperial's Candlewick molds were bought by various groups, companies, and individuals.

At the liquidation sale, the buildings and site were purchased by Anna Maroon of Maroon Enterprises, Bridgeport, Ohio, with the intent of developing the site into a tourist attraction, Imperial Plaza. The Imperial glass outlet, The Hay Shed, the Bellaire Museum, and a few small businesses moved into the building, but the project failed, and the Imperial building deteriorated and was demolished in July 1995.

The Hay Shed outlet relocated to a building near the Imperial site and operates as a consignment shop for Imperial and other glass. At its 1996 convention, the National Imperial Glass Collector's Society started a drive to establish an Imperial museum and preserve the heritage of glassmaking that took place at Imperial for more than 80 years.

Candlewick is characterized by the crystal-drop beading used around the edges of many pieces; around the bases of tumblers, shakers, and other items; in the stems of glasses, compotes, and cake and cheese stands; on the handles of cups, pitchers, bowls, and serving pieces; on stoppers and finials; and on the handles of ladles, forks, and spoons. The beading is small on some pieces, and larger and heavier on others.

A large variety of pieces was produced in the Candlewick pattern. More than 650 items and sets are known. Shapes include round, oval, oblong, heart, and square. Imperial added or discontinued items as popularity and demand warranted. The largest assortment of pieces and sets were made during the late 1940s and early 1950s.

Candlewick was produced mostly in crystal. Viennese blue (pale blue, 1937-1938), Ritz blue (cobalt, 1938-1941), and ruby red (red, 1937-1941) were made. Amber, black, emerald green, lavender, pink, and light yellow pieces also have been found. From 1977 to 1980, four items of 3400 Candlewick stemware were made in solid-color Ultra blue, Nut Brown, Verde Green, and Sunshine yellow. Solid-black stemware was made on an experimental basis at the same time.

Other decorations on Candlewick include silver overlay, gold encrustations, cuttings, etchings, and hand-painted designs. Pieces have been found with fired-on gold, red, blue, and green beading. Blanks, i.e., plain pieces, were sold to many companies which decorated them with cuttings, hand paintings, and silver overlay, or fitted them with silver, chrome, or brass bases, pedestals, or lids. Shakers sold to DeVilbiss were made into atomizers. Irving W. Rice & Co. purchased Candlewick tray handles and trays, assembled boudoir sets, and sold Candlewick clocks.

References: Myrna and Bob Garrision, *Imperial's Boudoir, Etcetera,* 1996; National Imperial Glass Collector's Society, *Imperial Glass Encyclopedia, Vol. I: A–Cane,* The Glass Press, 1995; —, *Imperial Glass Catalog Reprint,* Antique Publications, 1991; Virginia R. Scott, *Collector's Guide to Imperial Candlewick,* 4th edition, available from author; Mary M. Wetzel-Tomalka, *Candlewick: The Jewel of Imperial,* Books I and II, available from author; —, *Candlewick, The Jewel of Imperial, Personal Inventory & Record Book,* available from author, 1998; —, *Candlewick, The Jewel of Imperial, Price Guide '99 and More,* available from author, 1998.

Periodicals: *Glasszette,* National Imperial Glass Collector's Society, P.O. Box 534, Bellaire, OH 43528; *Spyglass Newsletter,* Michiana Association of Candlewick Collectors, 17370 Battles Rd, South Bend, IN 46614; *The Candlewick Collector Newsletter,* National Candlewick Collector's Club, 6534 South Ave., Holland, OH 43528; *TRIGC Quarterly Newsletter,* Texas Regional Imperial Glass Collectors, 2113 F. M. 367 East, Iowa Park, TX 76367.

Collectors' Clubs: Candlewick Crystals of Arizona, 1122 W. Palo Verde Drive, Phoenix, AZ 85013; Fox Valley Northern Illinois Imperial Enthusiasts, 38 W. 406 Gingerwood, Elgin, IL 60123; Maryland Imperial Candlewick Club, 23 Ashcroft Court, Arnold, MD 21012; Michiana Association of Candlewick Collectors, 17370 Battles Rd, South Bend, IN 46614; National Candlewick Collector's Club, 6534 South Ave., Holland, OH 43528; National Imperial Glass Collector's Society, P.O. Box 534, Bellaire, OH 43528; Ohio Candlewick Collector's Club, 613 S. Patterson, Gibsonburg, OH 43431; Texas Regional Imperial Glass Collectors, 2113 F. M. 367 East, Iowa Park, TX 76367.

Museum: Bellaire Museum, Bellaire, OH 43906.

Reproduction Alert

When Imperial Glass Corp. was liquidated in 1985, all the molds were sold but no accurate records were kept of all the buyers. It is known that Mirror Images, Lansing, Michigan, purchased more than 200 of the molds, and Boyd Crystal Art Glass, Cambridge, Ohio, purchased 18 small ones. Other molds went to private individuals and groups.

Since the late 1980s, Boyd Crystal Art Glass has used Candlewick molds to make items in various slag and clear colors. Boyd has marked its reproductions with its trademark, a "B" inside a diamond, which is pressed on the bottom of each article.

In 1985, Mirror Images had Viking Glass Co., New Martinsville, West Virginia, make the six-inch Candlewick basket, 400/40/0, in Alexandrite, and a four-piece child's set (consisting of a demitasse cup and saucer, six-inch plate, and five-inch nappy) in pink. In 1987, Viking produced clear plates, bowls, saucers, flat-based sugars and creamers (400/30 and 400/122), and the 400/29 tray for Mirror Images in crystal. These pieces have ground bottoms, are somewhat heavier than original Candlewick pieces, and are not marked. Shapes of items may differ from original Candlewick.

In late 1990, Dalzell-Viking Corporation, successor to Viking, began making Candlewick in Mirror Image's molds. It made five-piece place settings in crystal, black, cobalt, evergreen, and red. Most of these are marked, either "DALZELL" for the first-quality pieces, or "DX" for seconds. In January 1991, Dalzell added handled plates, bowls, and a five-section 400/112 center-well relish in crystal. A new pastel shade, Cranberry Mist, was added in 1992.

Since late 1995, Dalzell Viking has offered Candlewick Gold, clear with gold beads; Candlewick Pastels, also called Satins, in azure, crystal, green, yellow, and cranberry; 8-inch, 10-inch, and 12-inch plates, cups, and saucers, and 6-inch bowls were made, all marked only with a paper label.

In 1996, Dalzell added a punch bowl set with gold beads and also began to make Candlewick with silver beads. The Pastel Satin production has been extended to include the following: 400/231 three-piece square bowl set; 400/161 butter dish; 400/154 deviled-egg tray; 400/68D pastry tray with a heart center handle; 400/87C and /87F vases; a six-inch bowl on an eight-inch oval tray; and a four-ounce sherbet, similar to 400/63B compote. Dalzell also added Candlewick Frosts, dark amber, plum, blue, and sage green with frosted finish. All of the above are marked only with a Dalzell Viking paper label.

Ashtray

400/18 bridge, crystal **6.00**
400/134/1, crystal **6.00**
400/150, 6" d, round, large beads, caramel slag **14.00**
400/150, 6" d, round, large beads, cobalt blue **30.00**
400/150, 6" d, round, large beads, crystal. **8.00**
400/150, 6" d, round, large beads, pink **14.00**
400/450, nested set, 4", 5", and 6", crystal. **20.00**
400/450, nested set, 4", 5", and 6", pink **32.00**
400/450, nested set, 4", 5", and 6", patriotic dec, pink **72.00**
400/450, nested set, 4", 5", and 6", patriotic dec, red, white, and blue **175.00**

Atomizer

400/96 shaker, atomizer top, made by DeVilbiss **125.00**
400/167 shaker, atomizer top, amethyst. **75.00**
400/167 shaker, atomizer top, aqua **75.00**
400/247 shaker, atomizer top, amethyst. **75.00**
400/247 shaker, atomizer top, aqua **65.00**

Banana stand, 11" d, two turned-up sides, four-bead stem, crystal. . **800.00**

Basket, crystal

400/37/0, 11", applied handle **130.00**
400/40/0, 6-1/2", turned-up sides, applied handle. **30.00**
400/273, 6", rolled-in edge . . **350.00**

Bell, crystal400/108, 5". **85.00**
400/179, 4", four-bead handle **50.00**

Bonbon

400/51T, 6", heart shape, curved-over center handle, beaded edge, crystal. **25.00**
400/51T, 6", heart shape, curved-over center handle, beaded edge, light blue . . . **75.00**
400/51T, 6", heart shape, curved-over center handle, beaded edge, ruby red, crystal handle **200.00**

Bowl

400/1F, 5" d, crystal **12.00**
400/3F, 6", nappy, crystal **10.00**
400/13B, 11" d, center, light blue **25.00**
400/13F, 10" d, slight use marks **39.50**
400/42B, 4-3/4" d, crystal **12.00**
400/52, 6" d, divided, crystal . **15.00**
400/62B, 7" d, two handles, red **250.00**
400/63B, 10-1/2" d, belled, crystal **60.00**
400/69B, 8-1/2". **35.00**
400/73H, 9" w, heart-shape, handle **125.00**

400/74B, 8-1/2" d, four ball toes, black 275.00
400/74B, 8-1/2", four ball toes, crystal 125.00
400/74SC, 9" d, four ball toes, crimped, black 200.00
400/74SC, 9" d, four ball toes, crimped, crystal 85.00
400/74SC, 9" d, four ball toes, crimped, light blue 100.00
400/74SC, 9" d, four ball toes, crimped, red 200.00
400/75B, 10-1/2" d, crystal . . . 35.00
400/92B, 11" d, float bowl, cupped edge, crystal 35.00
400/104B, 14" d, belled, large beads on sides 75.00
400/106B, 12" d, belled, crystal 70.00
400/131B, 14" l, oval, crystal . 350.00
400/427B, 4-3/4" d, 6" d, 7" d, and 8-1/2" d, crystal, price for nested set 65.00

Bridge set, 400/118, four pcs, crystal 34.00

Bud vase, crystal

400/25, 3-3/4" h, beaded foot, ball shape, crimped top 35.00
400/28C, 8-1/2", trumpet shaped top, crimped, beaded ball bottom 50.00
400/107, 5-1/4" h, beaded foot, large beads, crimped top 45.00
400/227, 8-1/2" h, beaded ball bottom, narrowed top slants, applied handle 100.00

Butter dish, covered, #400/144, **$40.**

Butter, cov, crystal

400/144, 5-1/2" d, round, two-bead finial 40.00
400/161, quarter pound, graduated beads on cov 30.00
400/276, 6-3/4" x 4", California, beaded top, c1960 . . . . 95.00
400/276, 6-3/4" x 4", California, plain top, c1951 . . . . 115.00

Cake stand, crystal

400/67D, 10" d, dome ftd, wedge marks on plate, one-bead stem, c1939 . . . . 80.00
400/103D, 11" h, tall, three-bead stem 75.00
400/160, 14" d, 72 candle holes 300.00

Canapé plate, 400/19, 6" d, off-center indent, crystal 15.00

Candleholders, pr, crystal

400/CV, 5" h, round bowl, beaded, vase insert, two pcs 175.00
400/CV, 5" h, round bowl, fluted, vase insert, two pcs 175.00
400/79R, 3-1/2" h, rolled saucer, small beads 30.00
400/81, 3-1/2" h, dome ftd, small beads, round handle 100.00
400/86, mushroom, pr 90.00
400/100, two-lite 50.00
400/115, 9" h, oval, beaded base, three candle cups 200.00
400/115/1-2, 9" h, oval, beaded base, three candle cups, two eagles. 500.00
400/175, 6-1/2" h, three-bead stem 150.00
400/190, 5" h, handle 100.00
400/207, 4-1/2" h, three toed 160.00
400/224, 5-1/2" h, ftd, three sections of arched beads on stem . . 450.00
400/280, 3-1/2" h, flat 30.00
400/1752, 6-1/2" h, three-bead stem, adapter, prisms 250.00

Candy dish, cov, crystal

400/59, 5-1/2" d, two-bead finial 35.00
400/110, 7" d, three-part, two-bead finial, cut and mirror finish . 400.00
400/140, 8" d, one-bead stem, flat, c1944 . . . . 150.00
400/140, 8" d, one-bead stem, ftd, beaded foot dome, c1943 . 225.00
400/245, 6-1/2" d, round bowl, sq cov, two-bead finial 125.00
400/260. . . . . 85.00

Celery tray, crystal

400/46, 11" l, oval, scalloped edge 50.00
400/58, 8-1/2" l, oval 37.50
400/105, 13" l, oval, two curved beaded handles. 40.00

Champagne, saucer, crystal

3400, flared belled top, 5 oz, four graduated beads in stem. . . 18.50
3400, Wild Rose etch 35.00

Cheese and cracker set, 400/88, 5-1/2" ftd 400/88 cheese compote, 10-1/2" d 400/72D handled plate, crystal . . 45.00

Cheese, toast or butter dish, 400/123, 7-3/4" d plate with cupped edge, domed cov with bubble knob, crystal 200.00

Cigarette holder, eagle 95.00

Cigarette set, crystal

400/29/6, six-pc set 60.00
400/29/64/44, dome ftd 3" 400/44 cigarette holder, small beads, four nested 400/64 ashtrays, c1941 . . . . 60.00

Claret, 3400/5, flared belled top, four graduated beads in stem, crystal 55.00

Clock, 4", large beads, New Haven works, crystal 400.00

Coaster, crystal

400/78, 4" d, 10 rays 7.00
400/226, 3-1/2" d, spoon rest . 12.00

Cocktail

3400, flower cut 20.00
4000/190, bell-shaped bowl, beads around foot, 4 oz, three bead stem, crystal 20.00

Compote, crystal

400/48F, 8" d, beaded edge, four-bead stem 65.00
400/48F, 8" d, beaded edge, five-bead. 350.00
400/67B, 9" d, flat, large bead stem, c1943 . . . . 65.00
400/67B, 9" d, ribbed bowl, dome ftd, large bead stem 75.00
400/220, 5" d, three-part, beaded edge, arched 90.00

Console set, crystal

400/100, 12" 400/92F flat bowl, cupped edge, pr two-lite candleholders, center circle of large beads. 95.00
400/8692L, 13" 400/92L mushroom bowl on 400/127B 7-1/2" d base, pr 400/86 mushroom candleholders 200.00

Condiment set, crystal

400/1589, jam set, two cov 400/89 marmalade jars, three-bead ladles, oval 400/159 tray. 95.00
400/2946, oil and vinegar, pr 400/164 and 400/166 beaded foot cruets, kidney-shaped 400/29 tray 90.00

Cordial, 3400, flared belled top, four graduated beads in stem, crystal 20.00

Cordial bottle, 15 oz, beaded foot, three-bead stopper

400//82, crystal, handle, c1938 . . . . 195.00
400/82, crystal, handle, red stopper and base, c1938. . . . . 275.00
400/82/2, crystal, no handle, c1941 . . . . 175.00

Cruet, #400/70, **$55.**

Creamer and sugar set

400/29/30, flat base, beaded question-mark handles, 400/30, 7" l 400/29 tray, crystal **30.00**
400/30, flat base, beaded question-mark handles, sterling silver floral dec **100.00**
400/31, beaded foot, plain handles, c1937, crystal. **40.00**
400/31, beaded foot, plain handles, c1937, blue **60.00**
400/31, plain foot, question-mark handles, c1941, crystal **30.00**

Cup and saucer, beaded question-mark handles

400/35, tea, round 400/35 cup, 400/35 saucer **15.00**
400/37, coffee, slender 40/37 cup, 400/35 saucer **15.00**
400/77, after dinner, small, slender 5-1/2" d beaded saucer **20.00**

Decanter

400/18, crystal **365.00**
400/163, beaded foot, round stopper, crystal. **195.00**
400/163, beaded foot, round stopper, crystal with red foot and stopper, c1938 . . . . **250.00**

Deviled egg tray, 400/154, 11-1/2" d, 12 indents for eggs, heart-shaped center handle, crystal **115.00**

Epergne set, 400/196, 9" ftd 400/196FC flower candle holder, one-bead stem, 7-3/4" h two-bead peg vase, beaded top, peg to fit into candle cut, crystal **175.00**

Fruit tray, 400/68F, center handle, crystal **350.00**

Goblet, water, crystal

400/190 Line, bell-shaped bowl, hollow trumpet-shaped stem with beads around foot, 10 oz . . . **22.50**
3400 Line, flared bell bowl, four graduated beads in stem, 9 oz **16.00**

Iced tea tumbler, crystal, 12 oz, ftd

400/18, domed beaded foot, rounded top. **40.00**
400/19, beaded base, straight sides **22.00**

Icer, no inserts, 400/533, crystal . **75.00**

Ice tub, 400/63, 8", crystal **110.00**

Jelly server, crystal

400/52, 6" d, divided dish, beaded edge, handles **18.00**
400/157, 4-3/4" d, ftd, one-bead stem, two-bead cov. **50.00**

Juice tumbler, 400/19, beaded base, straight sides, 5 oz, ftd, crystal . . **12.50**

Ladle, three beads, crystal

Large **12.00**
Medium **12.00**
Small **12.00**

Lamp, hurricane

400/79R, 3-1/2" saucer candle-holder, 9" chimney, two-pc set, Bohemian, cranberry flashed chimney, gold bird and leaves dec **125.00**
400/79R, 3-1/2" saucer candleholder, 9" chimney, two-pc set, crystal. **75.00**
400/152R, candleholder, chimney, and 100/152 adapter, crystal, three pcs **95.00**

Lemon tray, #400/221, 5-1/2" l, handle, crystal. **55.00**

Manhattan pitcher, 400/18, 40 oz, crystal. **245.00**

Marmalade, 400/89, four-pc, crystal **45.00**

Mayonnaise set, bowl, plate with indent, and ladle, crystal

400/23, 5-1/4" d 400/32D bowl, 7-1/2" d 400/23B plate, 400/135 three-bead ladle **30.00**
400/52/2, 6-1/2" d 400/52/B bowl with two handles, 400/52D handled pate, 400/135 three-bead ladle **40.00**

Mint dish, 400/51F, 5" d, round, applied handle. **20.00**

Mint tray, 400/149, 9" d, heart-shaped center handle **30.00**

Mirror, domed beaded base, crystal, brass holder and frame, two-sided mirror flips on hinges, made for I. Rice Co., 1940s **85.00**

Mustard jar, 400/156, beaded foot, notched beaded cov with two-bead finial, 3-1/2" glass spoon, fleur-de-lis handle, crystal. **40.00**

Nappy, 400/3F, 6" d, beaded edge, crystal **10.00**

Pastry tray

400/49D, handle, 400/19, crystal **28.00**
400/68D, 11-1/2" d beaded plate, center heart-shaped handle, crystal. **35.00**
400/68D, 11-1/2" d beaded plate, center heart-shaped handle, crystal, floral cutting. **80.00**

Pitcher, crystal

400/16, 16 oz, beaded question-mark handle, plain base **125.00**
400/18, 16 oz, plain handle, beaded base **200.00**
400/18, 80 oz, plain handle, beaded base **300.00**
400/24, 80 oz, beaded question-mark handle, plain base **150.00**

Plate, crystal

400/1D, 6" d, bread and butter. **8.00**
400/3D, 7" d, salad. **7.00**
400/5D, 8-1/2" d, salad/dessert **10.00**
400/7D, 9" d, luncheon **15.00**
400/10D, 10-1/4" d, dinner . . . **30.00**
400/13D, 12" d, scratch mark. **24.50**
400/72C, 10" d, w handles, crimped **25.00**
400/72D, 10" d, handles **30.00**
400/75V, 13" d, cupped, floral cut **50.00**
400/92D, 14" d **40.00**
400/98, 9" l, oval, indent **20.00**
400/145D, 12" d, two open handles **30.00**

Platter, crystal

400/124D, 13" l **90.00**
400/131D, 16" l **190.00**

Dessert bowl, #400/19, ***$15****; plate, 6" d, #400/1D,* **$8.**

Punch bowl set, crystal

400/20, 13" d six-quart 400/20 bowl, 10" belled 400/128 base, 12 400/37 punch cups, 400/91 ladle, 15-pc set **250.00**

400/20, 13" d six-quart 400/20 bowl, 17" d 400/20V plate, 12 400/37 punch cups, 400/91 ladle, 15-pc set **225.00**

400/210, 14-1/2" d 10-quart 400/210 bowl, 9" belled 400/210 base, 12 400/37 punch cups, 400/91 ladle, 15-pc set **450.00**

Relish, beaded edge, crystal

400/54, two parts, 6-1/2" l, two-tab handles **15.00**

400/55, four parts **30.00**

400/57, 8-1/2" l, oval **20.00**

400/84, two parts, 6-1/2" l **25.00**

400/102, 13" l. **85.00**

400/208, three parts, three toes, 10" d **175.00**

400/215, three-part on one side, one section on other, 5-1/2" l, two tab handles **100.00**

400/256, two parts, 10-1/2" l, oval, two tab handles. **25.00**

400/262, three parts, 10-1/2" l, two tab handles **100.00**

Relish and dressing set, 400/1112, 10-1/2" five-part 400/112 relish, 400/89 jar fits center well, long three-bead ladle, crystal, c1942 . . . . **115.00**

Rose bowl, 400/132, crystal . . . **425.00**

Salad fork and spoon, 400/75, five-bead handles, crystal **32.00**

Salad set, crystal

400/735, 9" d handled heart-shaped 400/73H bowl, 700/75 fork and spoon set. **110.00**

400/75B, 10-1/2" d beaded 400/75B bowl, 13" d cupped 400/75V plate, five-bead handles 400/75 fork and spoon set. **85.00**

400/75B, 10-1/2" d bowl, 14" d plate, Lily of the Valley center **125.00**

Salt and pepper shakers, pr, beaded foot, crystal

400/96, bulbous, eight beads, chrome tops **25.00**

400/116, one ball stem **225.00**

400/190, trumpet foot, chrome tops **90.00**

Salt dip, crystal

400/61, 2". **10.00**

400/19, 2-1/4". **10.00**

400/61, 2", star cut. **15.00**

Salt spoon, 400/616, crystal, 3". . **10.00**

Sauce boat set, 400/169, oval gravy boat with handle, 9" oval plate with indent. **135.00**

Sauce bowl, 400/243, 5-1/2" d, crystal **110.00**

Saucer, 400/56 . . . . **6.00**

Sherbet, 400/190, belled bowl, 5 oz, tall, crystal **18.00**

Marmalade, covered, spoon, #400/1989, **$30.**

Sugar, 400/18, domed foot **115.00**

Tidbit server, 400/2701, two tiers, 7-1/2" d and 10-1/2" d plates joined by metal rod, round handle at top

Crystal **60.00**

Emerald green **350.00**

Toast plate, 400/123, crystal . . . **75.00**

Torte plate

400/20D, 17" d, flat, crystal . . **50.00**

400/20V, 17" d, cupped, crystal **50.00**

Tray

400/29, 7", crystal. **15.00**

400/42E, 5-1/2" l, upturned handles, crystal. **20.00**

400/51T, 6" l, handle bent to center of dish, crystal **25.00**

400/62E, 8-1/2" l, black, hand painted gold flowers, handle **250.00**

400/159, 9" l, oval, crystal. . . . **40.00**

Tumbler, water, ftd, crystal

400/18, domed beaded foot, rounded top, 9 oz. **32.00**

400/19, beaded base, straight sides, 10 oz, 4-3/4" h **18.00**

400/19, 12 oz **22.50**

3400, 12 oz. **19.50**

Vase, crystal

400/87C, 8" h, crimped beaded top, graduated beads down sides **50.00**

400/87F, 8-1/2" h **45.00**

400/87R, 7" h, rolled beaded flange top, solid glass arched handles with small bead edging, flat foot **40.00**

400/143C, 8" h, crimped, flip, cut leaves **195.00**

Vegetable bowl, cov, 65/1, 8" l . **350.00**

Wine

400/190 Line, belled bowl, hollow trumpet stem with beads, 5 oz, crystal **28.00**

3400 Line, flared belled bowl, four graduated stems in base, 9 oz, crystal **27.50**

3400 Line, flared belled bowl, four graduated stems in base, 9 oz, ruby bowl **100.00**

3400 Line, flared belled bowl, four graduated stems in base, 9 oz, yellow, c1977 . . . . **30.00**

Carnival Glass

History: Carnival glass, an American invention, is colored pressed glass with a fired-on iridescent finish. It was first manufactured about 1905 and was immensely popular both in America and abroad. More than 1,000 different patterns have been identified. Production of old carnival glass patterns ended in 1930.

Most of the popular patterns of carnival glass were produced by five companies—Dugan, Fenton, Imperial, Millersburg, and Northwood. Northwood patterns frequently are found with the "N" trademark. Dugan used a diamond trademark on several patterns.

Color is the most important factor in pricing carnival glass. The color of a piece is determined by holding it to the light and looking through it.

References: Gary E. Baker et al., *Wheeling Glass*, Oglebay Institute, 1994 (distributed by Antique Publications); Elaine and Fred Blair, *Carnival Hunter's Companion: A Guide to Pattern Recognition*, published by authors (P.O. Box 116335, Carrolton, TX 75011), 1995; Carl O. Burns, *Collector's Guide to Northwood Carnival Glass*, L-W Book Sales, 1994; —, *Imperial Carnival Glass 1909-1930 Identification and Values*, Collector Books, 1996; Bill Edwards, *Standard Encyclopedia of Carnival Glass*, 6th ed., Collector Books, 1998; Ruth Grizel, *A Notebook of Imperial's Modern Carnival Glass*, WGCN (P.O. Box 143, North Liberty, Iowa, 52317-0143); Marion T. Hartung, *First Book of Carnival Glass to Tenth Book* of Carnival Glass (series of 10 books), published by author, 1968 to 1982; William Heacock, James Measell, and Berry Wiggins, *Dugan/Diamond*, Antique Publications, 1993; —, *Harry Northwood, The Wheeling Years, 1901-1925*, Antique Publications, 1991; Heart of America Carnival Glass Assoc., Educational Series 1 (1990); Educational Series 2, (1992), Educational Series 3 (1996) (3048 Tamarak Dr., Manhattan, KS

66502); James Measell, *Imperial Glass Encyclopedia, Volume II, Cape Cod-L,* National Imperial Glass Collectors' Society, 1997; Marie McGee, *Millersburg Glass,* Antique Publications, 1995; Tom and Sharon Mordini, *Carnival Glass Auction Price Reports, 1989-1996,* published by authors (36 N. Mernitz, Freeport, IL 61032); Lloyd Reichel, *Carnival Glass Collectors Book I (1971) and II (1971),* published by author, (P.O. Box 236, Jamestown, MO 65046); Jerry Reynolds, *Iridescent Hatpins & Holders of the Carnival Glass Era,* published by author (1305 N. Highland Pkwy, Tacoma, WA 98406); The Australian Carnival Enthusiasts Associated, Inc., *Carnival Glass of Australia,* Australian Carnival Enthusiasts Associated, Inc.; *The Sanctified Cross-Eyed Bear's Price Trend Guide for Carnival Glass and Individual Sales Supplemental Guide for 1996,* 3rd edition, The Sanctified Cross-Eyed Bear (P.O. Box 1296, Huntsville, AL 35807), 1996; Cecil Whitney, *The World of Enameled Carnival Glass Tumblers,* published by author (1041 Cheshire Lane, Houston, TX 77018), 1985.

Periodical: *Network,* PageWorks, P.O. Box 2385, Mt. Pleasant, SC 29465.

Collectors' Clubs: Air Capital Carnival Glass Club, 15201 E. 47th St., Derby, KS 67037; American Carnival Glass Assoc., 9621 Springwater Lane, Miamisburg, OH 45342; Australian Carnival Enthusiasts Assoc. (SA) Inc., P.O. Box 1028, New Haven, SA, 5018; Australian Carnival Enthusiasts Assoc. (Victoria) Inc., RSD Fryerstown, Victoria, 3451; Canadian Carnival Glass Assoc., 107 Montcalm Dr., Kitchner, Ontario N2B 2R4 Canada; Carnival Club of Western Australia, 179 Edgewater Drive, Edgewater, Western Australia 6027; Carnival Glass Collectors Assoc. of Australia, Inc., 24 Kerstin St., Quakers Hill, NSW 2763; Collectible Carnival Glass Assoc., 2360 N. Old S. R. 9, Columbus, IN 47203-9430; Gateway Carnival Glass Club, 108 Riverwoods Cove, East Alton, IL 62024; Great Lakes Carnival Glass Club, 612 White Pine Blvd., Lansing, MI 48917; Heart of America Carnival Glass Assoc., 43-5 W. 78th St., Prairie Village, KS 66208; Hoosier Carnival Glass Club, 944 W. Pine St., Griffith, IN 46319; International Carnival Glass Assoc., P.O. Box 306, Mentone, IN 46539; Keystone Carnival Glass Club, 719 W. Brubaker Valley Rd, Lititz, PA 17543; L'Association du Verra Carnaval du Quebec, 3250 Rue Leon Brisbois, Ile Bizard, QC, H9C IT6 Canada; Lincoln-Land Carnival Glass Club, N951, Hwy 27, Conrath, WI 54731; National Duncan Glass Society, P.O. Box 965, Washington, PA 15301; National Imperial Glass Collectors, P.O. Box 534, Bellaire, OH 43906; New England Carnival Glass Club, 10 Seminole Rd, Canton, MA 02021-1212; Northern California Carnival Glass Club, 4325 Raiders Way, Modesto, CA 95355; Pacific Northwest Carnival Glass Club, 5340 Market Rd, Bellingham, WA 98226; San Diego County Carnival Glass Club, 5395 Middleton Rd, San Diego, CA 92019; San Joaquin Carnival Glass Club, 3906 E. Acacia Ave., Fresno, CA 93726; Southern California Carnival Glass Club, 31091 Bedford Dr., Redlands, CA 92373; Tampa Bay Carnival Glass Club, 101st Ave. N, Pinellas Park, FL 34666; Texas Carnival Glass Club, 4736 CR 310, Cleburne, TX 76031; The Carnival Glass Society (UK), 162 Green Lane, Edgeware, Middsix HA8 8EJ, England; WWW.CGA at http://www.woodsland.com.

Videos: "Hooked on Carnival," Volumes I and II, Glen and Steve Thistlewood, P.O. Box 83, Alton, Hampshire Gu34 4YN England.

Museums: National Duncan Glass Society, Washington, PA; Fenton Art Glass Co., Williamstown, WV.

Acanthus, Imperial, bowl
- 7-1/2" d, smoke **50.00**
- 8" d, ruffled, purple **45.00**

Acorn, Fenton, bowl, 8" d, marigold **100.00**

Acorn Burrs, Northwood
- Punch cup, pastel **85.00**
- Punch set
  - Ice blue. **6,000.00**
  - Ice green. **17,000.00**
  - Marigold **2,200.00**
  - Purple **1,750.00**
  - White. **6,000.00**
- Water set, pastel **525.00**

Advertising and Souvenir
- Elks, Detroit, 1910, Fenton, bowl, purple **975.00**
- John Brand, open basket, marigold **90.00**

Amaryllis, Northwood, compote, purple **150.00**

Apple Blossom Twigs, Dugan, bowl, low, ruffled
- Basketweave ext., purple . . . **175.00**
- Marigold. **70.00**

April Showers, Fenton, vase
- 6" h, squatty, amethyst. **125.00**
- 13" h, blue **50.00**

Asters, ice cream bowl, marigold, 9" d **125.00**

Basketweave, Dugan, flower basket, miniature, marigold. **15.00**

Beaded, Dugan, basket, amethyst **80.00**

Beaded Bulls Eye, Imperial, vase, 9" h, purple **170.00**

Beaded Cable, Northwood, rose bowl
- Marigold. **75.00**
- White **425.00**

Beaded Shell, Dugan, mug, blue **115.00**

Beauty Twig, Dugan, bud vase, marigold, 9" h **100.00**

Blackberry, Fenton
- Basket, open edge, ruffled, blue **90.00**
- Bowl, 3" h, 6-1/2" d, open edge, basketweave ext., amber/horehound **255.00**
- Vase, swung, open edge, dark marigold **2,250.00**

Blackberry Bramble, Fenton, compote, ruffled, green **35.00**

Blackberry Spray, Fenton
- Hat, red. **300.00**
- Hat, reverse amberina opal, ruffled **1,000.00**
- Jack in the pulpit, crimped edge, red **800.00**

Blackberry Wreath, Millersburg
- Compote, green **75.00**
- Ice cream bowl
  - 5/12" d, amethyst **50.00**
  - 6-3/4" d, marigold **45.00**
  - 10" d, green **200.00**
- Sauce, three-in-one, green. . . **85.00**

Blaze, ice cream bowl, 9" d, marigold **60.00**

Border Plants, Dugan
- Bowl, ruffled, domed, purple **185.00**
- Plate, hand grip, peach opalescent **175.00**

Brocaded Acorns, **Fostoria**, plate, 7-1/2" d, lavender **225.00**

Boutonniere, Millersburg, compote, amethyst, satin **110.00**

Bull's Eye and Beads, vase, 12" h, amber **260.00**

Bushel Basket, Northwood
- Amethyst. **250.00**
- Aqua opalescent **300.00**
- Blue **145.00**
- Ice green **250.00**
- Green **275.00**
- Marigold, dark **65.00**
- Marigold, pastel **250.00**
- Sapphire blue. **2,000.00**
- White. **200.00**

Butterfly, Fenton, calling card tray, blue **55.00**

Butterfly, Northwood, bonbon, handle, plain ext.
- Green **65.00**
- Horehound **145.00**
- Purple **40.00**

Butterfly and Berry, Fenton
- Bowl, 9" d, scalloped, three claw and ball feet, bronze, green, and blue irid, cobalt blue ground . . . **450.00**
- Vase, 7" h, tightly crimped edge, blue **80.00**

Butterfly and Fern, Fenton, tumbler, amethyst **50.00**

Butterfly and Plume, Fenton, water pitcher, bulbous, green. **900.00**

Butterfly and Tulip, Dugan
- Bowl, sq, ftd, purple **1,200.00**
- Ice cream bowl, 10" d, ftd, marigold **285.00**

Captive Rose, Fenton, plate
- 9-1/2" d, amethyst. **400.00**
- 9" d, blue **500.00**

Carolina Dogwood, Westmoreland, bowl, 7-3/4" d, six ruffled, blue opalescent 425.00

Caroline, Dugan
- Bowl, 9" d, peach opalescent . 95.00
- Plate, hand grip, peach opalescent 100.00

Cherry, Dugan, bowl
- 9" d, collar base, pastel opalescent 135.00
- Ftd, pastel opalescent 95.00

Cherry, Millersburg
- Milk pitcher, marigold 750.00
- Spooner, green 125.00

Coin Spot, Dugan, compote, peach opalescent 80.00

Colonial, Imperial, lemonade mug, marigold, clear handle and base . 22.50

Concave Flute, Westmoreland, bowl, flat, marigold, 9" d 55.00

Concord, Fenton, ice cream bowl, ruffled
- Amethyst 300.00
- Green, gold, red, and blue irid 350.00
- Pumpkin marigold 250.00

Corinth, Dugan
- Banana boat, 8-1/2" l, two sides up, teal 25.00
- Jack in the pulpit vase, 8-1/2" h, yellow 80.00

Corn Vase, Northwood, vase, flower base, ice green 270.00

Cosmos, Millersburg, ice cream bowl, 6" d, green 65.00

Cosmos and Cane, berry bowl, white 40.00

Country Kitchen, Millersburg, butter, cov, amethyst 445.00

Courthouse, Millersburg, bowl
- 7-1/2" d, low, ruffled, amethyst 725.00
- Ruffled, amethyst, light base, radium 650.00

Cut Flowers, Jenkins, vase, 10" h, green 110.00

Dahlia, Dugan
- Berry bowl, amethyst 65.00
- Water pitcher, ftd, purple 550.00

Dandelion, Northwood
- Tumbler
  - Marigold 55.00
  - Purple 24.00
- Water set, tankard pitcher, six tumblers
  - Green 1,300.00
  - Ice blue 5,000.00
  - Purple 1,300.00

Diamond Lace, Imperial, water set, five pcs, purple 525.00

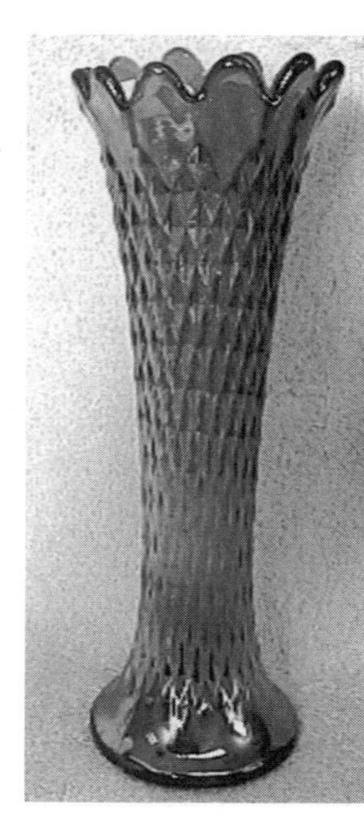

Diamond Point, vase, sapphire blue, 10" h, **$500.** *Photo courtesy of Seeck Antique Auction Center.*

Diamond Point, Imperial, flower basket, handle, miniature, ice blue 80.00

Diamond Point, Northwood, vase, 10" h, ice blue 300.00

Diamond Ring, Imperial, bowl, ruffled, 8" d
- Marigold 50.00
- Smoke 50.00

Diamonds, Millersburg
- Pitcher, marigold, chip base filled 35.00
- Tumbler, marigold 40.00

Dogwood Sprays, Dugan, bowl
- Domed, ruffled, purple 50.00
- Tricorn, dome ftd, peach opalescent 50.00

Dolphins, Millersburg, compote, amethyst, rosalind int. 1,500.00

Double Loop, Northwood, chalice
- Blue 35.00
- Purple 35.00

Double Star, Cambridge
- Tumbler, green 35.00
- Water pitcher, green 100.00

Double Stem Rose, Dugan
- Bowl, domed foot, peach opalescent 160.00
- Plate, dome foot, white 175.00

Dragon and Lotus, Fenton
- Bowl
  - Ruffled, plain back, amber 120.00
  - Three-in-one, light amethyst, irid pink and blue highlights 225.00
- Ice cream bowl
  - Cobalt blue 185.00
  - Marigold, chip 40.00

Dragon and Strawberry, Fenton, bowl, ftd, large, green 1,500.00

Dragonfly, hatpin, marigold. 95.00

Drapery, Northwood
- Candy dish
  - Ice blue. 175.00
  - N mark, marigold 135.00
- Rose bowl
  - Aqua opalescent 450.00
  - Electric blue 500.00
  - White. 425.00
- Vase
  - 8" h, marigold, small chip . . 35.00
  - 8" h, white 175.00
  - 8-3/4" h, ice lime green. . . 125.00

Dutch Mill, ashtray, marigold . . . 30.00

Egyptian Scarab, hatpin, pastel . 60.00

Embossed Scroll, Imperial
- Berry set, File pattern ext., six pcs, pastel 175.00
- Compote, large, deep amethyst 80.00
- Plate
  - Green 60.00
  - Purple 500.00
- Sauce, ruffled, File ext., purple 75.00

Embroidered Mums, Northwood, bowl, 9" d, ruffled
- Blue 400.00
- Marigold 400.00

Fanciful, Dugan
- Bowl, ruffled, peach opalescent 160.00
- Ice cream bowl, peach opalescent 160.00

Fans, English, pitcher, marigold. 90.00

Fashion, Imperial, rose bowl, green 300.00

Feather Stitch, Fenton, plate, marigold 600.00

Fine Cut, Jenkins, vase, 10" h, marigold 80.00

Fine Cut and Roses, Northwood
- Candy dish, ftd, amethyst 75.00
- Rose bowl
  - Dark marigold, chips 60.00
  - Ice blue. 195.00
  - White. 225.00

Fine Rib, Dugan, Fenton, or Northwood, vase, 9" h, fiery amethyst 375.00

Fish Net, Dugan, epergne, crimped edge, center lily vase, pastel opalescent 275.00

Fish Scale and Beads, Dugan
- Bowl, low, candy ribbon crimping, pastel, 7" d 155.00
- Plate, 7" d, white 125.00

Fleur De Lis, Millersburg, bowl, ruffled, large, amethyst **525.00**
Floral and Grape, Fenton, water set, pitcher, two tumblers, blue **150.00**
Flowering Dill, Fenton, hat, amethyst **40.00**
Flowers and Frames, Dugan, bowl
- Dome foot, peach opalescent **155.00**
- 9" d, peach opalescent..... **175.00**

Fluffy Peacock, tumbler, cobalt blue **95.00**
Flute, Millersburg, berry bowl, aqua **20.00**
Flute and Cane, Imperial, bowl, 8-1/2" d, deep ruffle, marigold... **25.00**
Frosted Block, Imperial, bowl, 8-1/2" oblong, marigold **30.00**
Fruits and Flowers, Northwood
- Bonbon, handled, stemmed
  - Electric blue, 4" h, 8-1/2" d. **250.00**
  - Green **275.00**
  - Sapphire blue.........**2,500.00**
- Bowl, 7" d, green.......... **110.00**

Garden Mums, Northwood, bowl, 5-1/4" d, amethyst **375.00**
Garden Path Variant, Dugan, bowl, 10" d, white **300.00**
Gay Nineties, Millersburg, water set, amethyst **15,500.00**
Good Luck, Northwood
- Bowl
  - Pie crust edge, basketweave ext., green **225.00**
  - Pie crust edge, pastel ... **250.00**
  - Ribbed, dark marigold... **175.00**
  - Ribbed back, blue...... **450.00**
- Plate, dark ice blue.......**3,400.00**

Grape, Imperial
- Berry bowl, master, ruffled, purple **95.00**
- Bowl, ruffled, green......... **90.00**
- Cup and saucer, marigold ... **40.00**
- Decanter, stopper, marigold.. **75.00**
- Tumbler
  - Marigold............... **40.00**
  - Pastel................. **30.00**
  - Smoke **60.00**
- Water pitcher
  - Marigold............... **85.00**
  - Smoke **200.00**

Grape and Cable, Northwood
- Banana boat, amethyst..... **210.00**
- Berry bowl, 6" d, ruffled, basketweave ext., pastel **40.00**
- Bonbon, stippled, handle, basketweave ext.
  - Green................. **65.00**
  - Purple................. **80.00**
- Bowl
  - 7-1/4" d, basketweave ext., green **80.00**
  - Ruffled, basketweave ext., marigold **35.00**
  - Ruffled, plain ext., purple . **250.00**
  - Stippled, pie crust edge, ice blue **750.00**
- Breakfast creamer
  - Pastel **100.00**
  - Purple **165.00**
- Candle lamp, marigold **600.00**
- Centerpiece bowl, ftd, turned-in
  - Ice green........... **1,500.00**
  - White.................**600.00**
- Compote, cov, marigold .. **1,300.00**
- Cracker jar, cov
  - Marigold **450.00**
  - Purple **600.00**
- Dresser tray
  - Ice blue............ **1,100.00**
  - Marigold **140.00**
- Hatpin holder
  - Green **400.00**
  - Pastel **45.00**
- Ice cream bowl, 10-1/2" l, white, sgd **175.00**
- Nappy, pastel **75.00**
- Orange bowl, banded, blue . **800.00**
- Pin tray, ice blue **875.00**
- Plate
  - 7-3/4" d, hand grip, basketweave ext., green, sgd **135.00**
  - 8" d, two sides up, basketweave ext., green **120.00**
  - 9" d, plain back, marigold..**80.00**
- Powder jar, cov, amethyst... **200.00**
- Punch bowl set
  - Blue, 14 pcs **15,000.00**
  - Marigold, 14 pcs **1,700.00**
  - Purple, 14 pcs **2,100.00**
  - White, 14 pcs.........**3,000.00**
- Punch cup
  - Green................. **35.00**
  - Marigold............... **22.50**
- Sherbet, amethyst **40.00**
- Spooner, marigold, chip..... **25.00**
- Sugar bowl, cov, green..... **175.00**
- Sweetmeat, cov
  - Amethyst **95.00**
  - Blue **3,200.00**
  - Purple **300.00**
- Tumbler
  - Amethyst **35.00**
  - Marigold............... **35.00**
- Water set
  - Marigold, seven pcs **225.00**
  - Purple, seven pcs **400.00**
- Whiskey decanter and stopper, handle, purple **500.00**
- Whiskey glass, purple **35.00**

Grape and Gothic Arches, Northwood, creamer, pastel, sgd "N" **75.00**

Grape Delight, Dugan
- Nut bowl, white............ **90.00**
- Rose bowl
  - Amethyst **145.00**
  - Marigold.............. **125.00**
  - White **100.00**

Grape and Cable, Northwood, two tumblers and water pitcher shown, amethyst, auctioneer's label on front, **$350 for pitcher and six tumblers.** *Photo courtesy of Joy Luke Fine Art Brokers and Auctioneers.*

Grape Leaves, Millersburg or Northwood, bowl, dark ice blue 2,450.00

Grapevine Lattice, Dugan
- Bowl, low, ruffled, white 85.00
- Plate, 7" d, white 75.00

Greek Key, Northwood
- Bowl, ruffled, basketweave ext.
  - Amethyst 55.00
  - Green 65.00
- Plate, 9" d, basketweave ext., green 825.00

Hanging Cherries, Millersburg
- Bowl, 8-1/2" d, ftd, peach opalescent 145.00
- Tumbler, green 105.00
- Water pitcher
  - Amethyst 700.00
  - Green 1,400.00

Hattie, Imperial, bowl, ruffled, 9-1/2" d, purple 245.00

Heart and Vine, Fenton, bowl, ruffled, amethyst 60.00

Hearts and Flowers, Northwood
- Bowl, ruffled
  - Pie crust edge, marigold . 500.00
  - Ribbed back, ice blue ... 500.00
- Compote
  - Blue 625.00
  - Renninger's Blue 1,100.00
  - Sapphire opalescent ... 2,000.00
  - White 200.00
- Plate, marigold 1,850.00

Heavy Grape, chop plate, marigold 135.00

Heavy Iris, tankard, marigold .. 375.00

Hobstar Flower, Imperial, compote, ruffled, stemmed, purple 65.00

Holly, Fenton
- Bowl
  - Crimped, ruffled edge, 9" d, marigold 135.00
  - Low, ruffled, blue 100.00
  - Ruffled, aqua 85.00
- Compote
  - Goblet shape, blue 50.00
  - Ribbed, blue 40.00
  - Ruffled, green 135.00
- Goblet, red 875.00
- Hat
  - Crimped, ruffled edge, red 450.00
  - Four sides up, aqua 60.00
  - Ruffled, blue 55.00
  - Ruffled, red, amber, yellow 150.00
- Ice cream bowl, scalloped, 9" d
  - Blue 130.00
  - Marigold 25.00
- Plate
  - 9-1/4" d, white 300.00
  - 9-1/2" d, white 210.00

Holly and Berry, Dugan, bowl, ruffled, peach opalescent 110.00

Holly Sprig (Whirl), Millersburg
- Bonbon, two handles, green . 80.00
- Bowl
  - 6" d, deep, crimped, ruffled edge, green 70.00
  - 8-1/2" d, crimped, ruffled, amethyst 550.00
  - 9-3/4" d, ruffled, amethyst . 115.00
  - 9-3/4" d, ruffled, green ... 120.00
- Calling card tray, green 80.00

Horse Head Medallion
- Bowl, ruffled, blue 150.00
- Nut bowl, ftd, vaseline 550.00

Inverted Strawberry, Cambridge, lady's spittoon, marigold, sgd "Near Cut," 3" h, 5-1/2" w 750.00

Kittens, Fenton
- Banana boat, two sided, marigold 75.00
- Bowl, four sided, marigold .. 150.00
- Cereal bowl, marigold 290.00
- Cup, marigold 55.00

Lattice and Grape, Fenton, tumbler, marigold 30.00

Lattice and Points, Dugan, vase, 9-1/2" h, marigold 40.00

Leaf and Beads, Northwood, rose bowl, ftd
- Blue 65.00
- Electric blue 85.00
- Floral int., green 325.00
- Marigold 60.00
- Purple 85.00

Leaf Chain, Fenton
- Bowl, blue, 9" d 100.00
- Plate, 7" d, marigold, 7" d ... 100.00
- Plate, white, 7" d 300.00

Leaf Column, Northwood, vase, 10" h, white 125.00

Lined Lattice, Dugan, vase
- 9-1/2" h, white 75.00
- 11" h, light lavender/smoke . 220.00

Lion, Fenton, bowl, ruffled, 7" d, marigold 110.00

Little Fishes, Fenton, sauce, ftd, dark marigold 200.00

Little Stars, Millersburg, bowl, 8" d, low, ruffled, pastel marigold ... 105.00

Long Thumbprint, Dugan, vase, 7" h, aqua 35.00

Lotus and Grape, Fenton
- Bowl, low, ruffled, marigold .. 65.00
- Bowl, 7" d, ftd, marigold 25.00

Louisa, Westmoreland
- Plate, ftd, marigold 70.00
- Rose bowl, amethyst 105.00

Lustre Rose, Imperial, ice cream bowl
- Collared base, flared edge, smoke 150.00
- Ice cream bowl, ftd, pastel, 10" d 220.00
- Plate, 9" d, amber 120.00

Many Fruits, Dugan, punch bowl and base, ruffled, purple 850.00

Many Stars, Millersburg, ice cream bowl, five points, marigold ... 1,400.00

Maple Leaf, Dugan, water wet, purple, six pcs 210.00

Mayan, Millersburg, bowl, 7-3/4" d, green 85.00

Memphis, Northwood, punch cup, marigold 7.50

Mikado, Fenton, compote, ruffled, blue 650.00

Milady, Fenton, tumbler, blue ... 75.00

Morning Glory, funeral vase, marigold, 11" h, **$200.** *Photo courtesy of Seeck Antique Auction Center.*

Morning Glory, Millersburg, vase, 7" h, pastel, radium 200.00

Nippon, Northwood, bowl, pie crust edge
- Ice blue 375.00
- White 285.00

Northern Star, Fenton, plate, 6" d, two sides turned up, very light marigold 20.00

Octagon, Imperial, wine, marigold 25.00

Ohio Star, Millersburg, vase, green 2,800.00

Omnibus, U.S. Glass, tumbler, marigold 225.00

Orange Tree, Fenton
- Bowl, ruffled, 9" d, white **110.00**
- Hatpin holder, blue **275.00**
- Ice cream bowl
  - 7-3/4" d, trunk center, electric blue **250.00**
  - 8-1/2", green........... **350.00**
- Loving cup
  - Blue **250.00**
  - Dark marigold **150.00**
- Mug
  - Aqua and marigold **85.00**
  - Blue, 3-1/2" h **185.00**
  - Marigold............... **25.00**
  - Persian Blue............ **60.00**
- Orange bowl, blue **150.00**
- Plate
  - 9" d, white **175.00**
  - 9-1/4" d, marigold....... **425.00**
  - 9-1/4" d, white **250.00**
- Punch bowl, matching base, blue **360.00**
- Shaving mug, electric blue.. **150.00**
- Tumbler, marigold.......... **70.00**
- Water pitcher, ice green, damage at spout **2,100.00**
- Water set, blue, six pcs, chips to tumblers **400.00**

Paneled Dandelion, Fenton, water set, tankard pitcher, six tumblers
- Amethyst............... **550.00**
- Blue.................... **525.00**
- Dark marigold........... **360.00**
- Green **750.00**

Pansy, Imperial
- Bowl, ruffled, 8-1/2" d, purple **225.00**
- Dresser tray, stippled, amber **135.00**

Panther, Fenton, bowl, ruffled, claw feet, blue, 10" d **900.00**

Peacock and Dahlia, Fenton
- Bowl, spatula ftd, amethyst.. **100.00**
- Plate, 7" d, ruffled, blue..... **450.00**

Peacock and Grape, Fenton
- Bowl
  - Ftd, lime opalescent..... **585.00**
  - Ruffled, pumpkin marigold **325.00**
- Ice cream bowl, spatula foot
  - Amethyst **120.00**
  - Green................. **60.00**
- Plate, collar base, marigold **1,100.00**

Peacock and Urn, Fenton
- Bowl, 8" d, ruffled, marigold . **150.00**
- Compote, blue **45.00**
- Ice cream bowl, dark marigold **600.00**
- Plate, 9" d
  - Blue **550.00**
  - Deep marigold......... **375.00**
  - White **400.00**
- Sauce bowl, pastel......... **95.00**

Peacock at the Fountain, Northwood
- Bowl, marigold............**235.00**
- Compote, ice blue....... **1,100.00**
- Fruit bowl, ruffled
  - Blue..................**850.00**
  - Marigold **300.00**
- Pitcher, light blue........ **2,000.00**
- Punch set, dark marigold, eight pcs **850.00**
- Table set, blue **1,200.00**
- Tumbler
  - Light blue **175.00**
  - Dark marigold...........**25.00**

Peacock at the Urn, Millersburg, compote, stemmed, ruffled, green **1,300.00**

Peacock at the Urn, Northwood
- Ice cream bowl, individual size
  - Blue...................**75.00**
  - Marigold **65.00**
- Ice cream set, purple **550.00**

Peacock, Millersburg, berry bowl, 6" d, amethyst...................**120.00**

Peacocks, Northwood
- Berry bowl, 5-1/4" d, amethyst. **90.00**
- Bowl
  - Pie crust edge, ribbed ext., dark marigold **170.00**
  - Ruffled, electric blue.....**650.00**
  - Ruffled, ribbed ext., marigold **325.00**
  - Ruffled, ribbed ext., purple **225.00**
- Plate
  - Ribbed ext., cobalt blue . . **850.00**
  - Ribbed ext., ice blue... **2,400.00**
  - Ribbed ext., lime green . . **700.00**
  - Ribbed ext., white.......**425.00**
  - Stippled, ribbed back, blue **800.00**

Peacocks, Northwood, plate, stippled, ribbed back, blue, **$800.** *Photo courtesy of Mickey Reichel Auction Center.*

Peacocks on the Fence, Northwood
- Bowl
  - Ruffled, 9" d, ice green . **1,100.00**
  - Ruffled, ribbed back, blue **600.00**
  - Ribbed back, whimsy type, ice blue **2,000.00**
- Plate, 9" d
  - Ice green **300.00**
  - Lavender **550.00**
  - Ribbed back, white **475.00**

Peacock Tail, Fenton, dish, triangular, sides pulled up to 2" peach, 7" d, marigold **85.00**

Peacock Tail Variant, Millersburg, compote, green............. **125.00**

Persian Garden, Dugan
- Bowl, 11" d, ruffled, peach opalescent **185.00**
- Plate
  - 6" d, white **65.00**
  - 6-1/2" d, blue **135.00**
  - 6-3/4" d, dark marigold ... **80.00**
  - 7-12" d, white.......... **125.00**

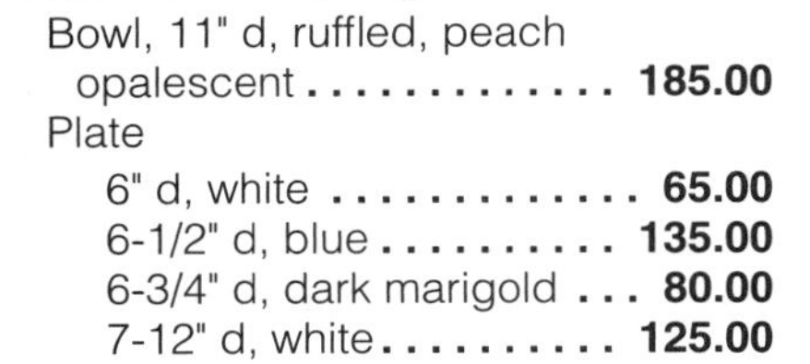

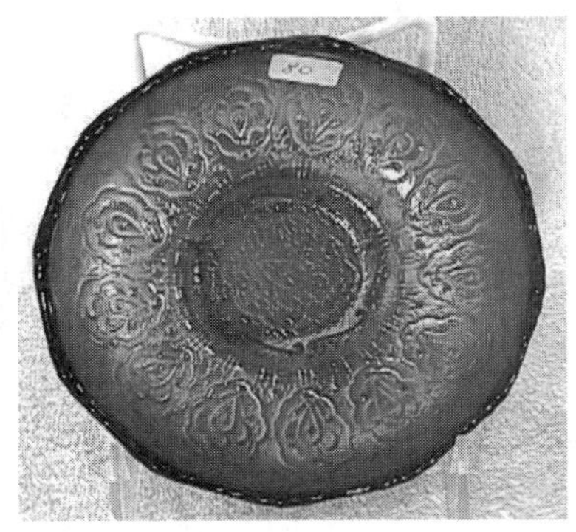

Persian Medallion, ice cream-shaped sauce, red, **$675.** *Photo courtesy of Seeck Antique Auction Center.*

Persian Medallion, Fenton
- Bonbon
  - Aqua, four sided **200.00**
  - Reverse amberina **850.00**
- Bowl, 8-1/2" d, three-in-one edge, amethyst.............. **140.00**
- Compote, amethyst **125.00**
- Hair receiver, sq top, marigold **50.00**
- Ice cream bowl, crimped edge, amethyst.............. **165.00**
- Plate, 6" d
  - Blue **135.00**
  - Marigold.............. **50.00**

Petal & Fan, Dugan, bowl
- 5" d, peach opalescent, ruffled **75.00**
- 10" d, peach opalescent ... **200.00**

Pine Cone, Fenton
- Ice cream bowl, 6-3/4" d, blue **110.00**

Poppy Show, Northwood, bowl, ruffled, blue, **$1,400.** *Photo courtesy of Mickey Reichel Auction Center.*

Plate, 6" d
- Amethyst............**225.00**
- Blue, silvery iridescent **95.00**
- Marigold **70.00**

Plume Panels, Fenton
- Compote, green...........**40.00**
- Vase
  - 10-1/2" h, red...........**650.00**
  - 12" h, green...........**100.00**

Poinsettia, Imperial, milk pitcher, smoke....................**375.00**

Pony, Dugan, bowl, amethyst ..**435.00**

Poppy, Millersburg, ice cream-shaped salver compote, amethyst ... **2,500.00**

Poppy Show, Northwood
- Bowl, ruffled, blue, marked **1,400.00**
- Plate
  - Amethyst............ **1,150.00**
  - 9"d, green **3,000.00**

Question Marks, Dugan
- Bonbon, two handled, stemmed, amethyst **75.00**
- Compote, crimped ruffled edge, peach opalescent........**140.00**

Rainbow, Northwood
- Bowl, basketweave back, green **105.00**
- Compote, amethyst **95.00**

Rambler Rose, Dugan, tumbler, blue **35.00**

Raspberry, Northwood, milk pitcher, green, gold bronze color, 7-1/2" h **165.00**

Rays and Ribbons, Millersburg, bowl, fluted, amethyst **200.00**

Ribbed Pillar, Northwood, vase, swung
- 8" h, ice green opalescent, damage to feet **450.00**
- 11" h, celeste blue, orig gold trim **525.00**

Ribbon Tie, Fenton, bowl, three-in-one, amethyst **130.00**

Rings, Jeanette, vase, gold irid, 8" h **45.00**

Ripple, Imperial, vase
- 10-1/2" h, green **50.00**
- 10-1/2" h, pastel **150.00**
- 10-3/4" h, swung, amber.... **100.00**
- 11-1/2" h, pastel **165.00**
- 12" h, swung, purple....... **135.00**

Robin, Imperial
- Mug
  - Marigold.............. **45.00**
  - Red **24.00**
- Water pitcher and four tumblers, marigold.............. **750.00**

Rococo, Imperial
- Bowl, ruffled, marigold **20.00**
- Vase
  - Marigold.............. **120.00**
  - Ruffled, 3-1/2" h, smoke... **65.00**

Rose Columns, Millersburg, vase, green...................**5,500.00**

Rose Show, Northwood, bowl, ruffled, sapphire blue, **$2,250.** *Photo courtesy of Mickey Reichel Auction Center.*

Rose Show, Northwood
- Bowl, dark marigold **1,500.00**
- Plate, electric blue **2,100.00**

Round-Up, Dugan
- Bowl, 8-1/2" d, low
  - Pastel opalescent **195.00**
  - Ruffled, marigold **85.00**
- Plate, 8-3/4" d, white....... **175.00**

Rustic, Fenton, vase
- 6-1/2" h, white............ **70.00**
- 19-1/2" h, 5-1/4" d, marigold. **700.00**
- 20" h, 5" d base, green....**1,500.00**

Sailboats, Fenton, bowl, 6" d, ruffled, marigold **75.00**

Scales, Westmoreland, bowl, amethyst **40.00**

Shell and Sand, bowl, 8" d, ruffled, teal green.................... **125.00**

Singing Birds, Northwood
- Berry bowl, master, green .**2,500.00**
- Mug
  - Amethyst...............**75.00**
  - Aqua opalescent **1,350.00**
  - Green, straight sides **165.00**
  - Light blue **550.00**
  - Marigold, dark **70.00**
- Tumbler, green, sgd "N" **135.00**
- Water set, seven pcs, purple. **550.00**

Single Flower, Dugan
- Bowl, three-in-one, peach opalescent **35.00**
- Plate, 7" d, peach opalescent . **40.00**

Ski Star, Dugan
- Banana boat, peach opalescent **50.00**
- Bowl
  - 8" d, ruffled, peach opalescent **50.00**
  - 10" d, tri-corner, dome ftd, peach opalescent **125.00**
  - 11" d, ruffled, peach opalescent **400.00**

Smooth Ray, Westmoreland, bowl
- 8" deep, teal **25.00**
- 9-1/2" d, deep ruffled, vaseline **35.00**

Soldiers and Sailors, Fenton, plate, marigold................ **2,250.00**

Spearhead and Rib, Fenton, vase, dark marigold, ruffled top, 14" h.. **50.00**

Spiralex, English, vase, 11" h, peach opalescent.................**45.00**

Springtime, Northwood
- Tumbler, green **65.00**
- Water pitcher
  - Green **900.00**
  - Marigold **600.00**

S-Repeat, Dugan
- Punch cup, amethyst........**12.50**
- Punch set, 14 pcs, purple . **5,000.00**

Stag and Holly, Fenton
- Ice cream bowl, 8" d, spatula foot
  - Cobalt blue............**350.00**
  - Marigold **90.00**
- Plate, spatula ftd, marigold, bruise on one foot **100.00**

Starfish, Dugan, compote, peach opalescent.................**85.00**

Star of David and Bows, Northwood, bowl, amethyst..............**70.00**

Stippled Flower, Dugan, bowl, tri-corner, peach opalescent **65.00**

Stippled Rays, Fenton, bowl
- 6" d, amberina...........**300.00**
- 6-1/2" d, six ruffles, Scale Band ext., red...................**300.00**

Stippled Rays, Northwood, bowl, amethyst...................**60.00**

Stippled Strawberries, Jenkins
- Bowl, pie crust edge, blue ..**300.00**
- Plate, 9" d, ribbed back, green **1,250.00**

Stork and Rushes, Dugan
Mug, banded top, amethyst . . 70.00
Tumbler
Beaded edge, blue 55.00
Lattice banded, marigold. . 20.00
Stork and Rushes, Dugan, water set, deep blue, 8" h pitcher, four 4" h tumblers. 400.00
Strawberry, Millersburg and Northwood
Bowl
8" d, crimped ruffled edge, green, radium, Millersburg 275.00
8-1/2" d, pie crust edge, stippled, blue 450.00
9" d, plain back, pastel marigold 200.00
9"d, stippled, pastel. 250.00
Compote
Amethyst 400.00
Marigold, Millersburg. . . . 450.00
Ice cream bowl, amethyst. . . 150.00
Plate
Basketweave ext., marigold 76.00
7-1/2" d, hand grip, green, "N" mark. 300.00
9" d, amethyst, marked . . 170.00
9" d, green, "N" mark 265.00
9" d, marigold, "N" mark . 150.00
Strawberry Scroll, Fenton, tumbler, blue 140.00
Sunflower, Millersburg, pin tray
Green 90.00
Pastel 75.00
Swan, Dugan, master salt
Celeste blue 20.00
Florentine ice green 50.00
Swirl, Northwood, compote, tricorn, 3-1/2" d, marigold 100.00
Swirl Hobnail, Millersburg, spittoon, dark marigold 800.00
Ten Mums, Fenton, bowl, 9-1/2" d, three-in-one edge, amethyst . . . 300.00
Thin Rib, Dugan, vase
5" h, squatty, peach opalescent 80.00
15" h, pastel 25.00
Thin Rib, Northwood, vase, 10" h, blue, electric highlights 115.00
Thistle, Fenton
Banana boat
Blue 500.00
Deep marigold. 140.00
Green. 600.00
Bowl
Crimped ruffled edge, blue 175.00
9" d, three-in-one, green . . 70.00

Three Fruits, Northwood
Bowl
Ruffled, basketweave ext., marigold, sgd 200.00
Ruffled, collar base, stippled, pastel opal sapphire blue 950.00
Ruffled, meander ext., stippled, ftd, butterscotch aqua opal 450.00
Stippled, pumpkin marigold 400.00
Stippled, ribbed back, collar base, white 250.00
Plate
Basketweave ext., green . 200.00
9" d, stippled, marigold. . . 185.00
9" d, stippled, ribbed back, dark marigold 375.00
9" d, stippled, ribbed back, amethyst. 450.00
9-1/2" d, pale amethyst horehound 800.00
Tiger Lily, Imperial, tumbler, pastel 125.00
Top of the Morning variant, hatpin, pastel 75.00
Tree Trunk, Northwood, vase, 12" h, 4-3/4" d base, amethyst, sgd . . . 245.00
Trout and Fly, Millersburg, ice cream bowl, low
Amethyst 750.00
Green. 350.00
Tulip, Millersburg, plate, 9" d, marigold 90.00
Tulip and Cane, Imperial, goblet, marigold 40.00
Triplets, (Daisy Dear), Dugan, bowl, 7" d, ruffled, vaseline 20.00
Twins, Imperial, berry bowl, 6" d, marigold 40.00
Two Flowers, Fenton
Bowl, ruffled, ftd, large, blue . 150.00
Rose bowl, ftd, blue. 100.00
Victorian, Dugan, bowl, 11" d, ruffled
Amethyst 400.00
Pastel. 475.00
Purple 250.00
Vineyard, Dugan, water pitcher, marigold 90.00
Vintage, Fenton, Millersburg, Northwood
Bowl
8" d, candy ribbon edge, green 175.00
8" d, cherry red 1,600.00
9" d, ruffled, green 60.00
Compote, marigold 65.00

Plate
7" d, blue 200.00
7-1/2" d, amethyst 450.00
Vintage Leaf, Fenton
Ice cream bowl, tightly crimped, lavender 150.00
Plate, marigold 1,400.00
Waffle Block, Imperial, punch bowl, teal. 100.00
Water Lily and Cattails, Northwood
Butter, cov, marigold 325.00
Tumbler, pastel 850.00
Whirling Leaves, Millersburg, bowl, 8-1/2" d, ruffled
Amethyst. 150.00
Green, cut leaves 400.00
Wide Panel, Imperial, vase, 10" h, red 300.00
Wide Rib, Dugan, vase, 11" h, cobalt blue 50.00
Wild Blackberry, Fenton, bowl, crimped ruffled edge, green . . . 225.00
Wild Strawberry, Northwood
Bowl
10" d, basketweave back, amethyst 250.00
10" d, basketweave back, marigold 135.00
10" d, pastel. 225.00
Plate, 701/4" d, hand grip, green 175.00
Windflower, Dugan, nappy, handle, marigold 80.00
Windmill, Imperial, milk pitcher, green, Helios finish. 75.00
Wishbone, Northwood
Bowl
Ruffled, three ftd, amethyst 110.00
Ruffled, three ftd, white . . 300.00
Three ftd, marigold 135.00
Wishbone, Northwood, epergne, single lily, green. 550.00
Wishbone and Flowers, bowl, three ftd, green. 140.00
Zig Zag, Millersburg, bowl, amethyst, three-in-one, amethyst 450.00
Zippered Heart, Imperial, berry set, seven pcs, pastel 250.00
Zipper Loop, Imperial, lamp
8" h, 4-3/4" base, marigold . . 325.00
9" h, 5-1/8" base, marigold . . 285.00

CENTRAL GLASS WORKS

History: Central Glass Works, Wheeling, West Virginia, was established as a cooperative in 1863 by workmen from J. H. Hobbs, Brockunier and Company. It

failed shortly thereafter and was reorganized as a stock company in 1867. Production continued until 1939.

Early goods were bottles, lamps, and barware. Around 1900, production began of crystal and decorated tablewares, as well as barware and tumblers for homes and famous hotels. In 1919, Central Glass acquired the molds for Benjamin W. Jacob's very successful Chippendale pattern. The trademark, Krys-Tol (and sometimes the pattern date) is marked in the mold. Chippendale was made in more than 300 forms and widely distributed. It achieved such great popularity in England that molds were sent to an English firm in 1933.

Central Glass produced a large line of optic glassware, as well as selling blanks to decorating companies. Several etched patterns were also popular.

Reference: Hazel Marie Weatherman, *Colored Glassware of the Depression Era, Book 2,* Glassbooks, Inc., 1982.

Bonbon, Balda, Morgan etch, two handles, black **95.00**

Bowl

9-1/2" d, Frances, green **35.00**

11" d, Frances, green, crimped **40.00**

11" d, Frances, green, rolled, three toes **40.00**

11-1/2" d, Balda, lavender, rolled edge **50.00**

Butter dish, cov, Chippendale pattern, colorless **20.00**

Candlestick

Butterfly, 6" h, black, gold encrusted, pr **195.00**

Frances, 3-1/2" h, green, pr . . . **40.00**

Ribbed, 9" d, deep blue, silver trim, single **42.00**

Candy dish, cov, green, 8-1/2" d . **65.00**

Champagne, Balda, light amethyst, 5-3/4" h **30.00**

Cocktail, Balda, lavender **30.00**

Console set, bowl and pr candlesticks

Memphis, colorless **50.00**

Zoricor, colorless **55.00**

Creamer

Balda, lavender **30.00**

Chippendale, colorless **25.00**

Frances, green. **15.00**

Cream soup and liner, Balda, lavender **40.00**

Decanter set, decanter, six cordial glasses, Balda, lavender **660.00**

Fruit bowl, Frances, 10" d, three toes, green **35.00**

Goblet

Acorn, colorless. **15.00**

Balda, lavender **30.00**

Frances, colorless **18.00**

Hester, colorless **15.00**

Morgan, blue and crystal. **95.00**

Sheila, colorless. **15.00**

Veninga, colorless **15.00**

Hair receiver, cov, Chippendale, colorless **15.00**

Mayonnaise, Morgan, ftd, two handles, matching ladle, rose **165.00**

Pitcher, water, Acorn, colorless . **35.00**

Pitcher, Balda, lavender **300.00**

Ring holder, Chippendale, colorless **15.00**

Server, Morgan, 10" d, center handle, green **135.00**

Sherbet, 4-7/8" h, Balda, lavender, 4-7/8" h **18.00**

Sugar bowl, cov

Balda, lavender **30.00**

Chippendale, colorless. **25.00**

Frances, green **15.00**

Tumbler

Balda, lavender, 5-1/8" d, ftd . **25.00**

Balda, light amethyst, 3" d, ftd **37.50**

Hester, colorless. **15.00**

Lotus Etch, crystal and pink, 2-3/4 oz, ftd **37.50**

Lotus Etch, crystal and pink, 7 oz, ftd **27.50**

Morgan, cone shape, 4-1/2" h, 6 oz, cone shape **40.00**

Tumble-up, Thistle etching **25.00**

Water set, Greek, pink and crystal, pitcher and six 7-oz tumblers . . **495.00**

Wine

Balda, lavender, 5-1/2" h, 2-1/2 oz **40.00**

Chippendale, colorless. **20.00**

CHILDREN'S DISHES

History: Dishes made for children often served a dual purpose—play things and a means of learning social graces. Dish sets came in two sizes. The first was for actual use by the child when entertaining her friends. The second, a smaller size than the first, was for use with dolls.

Children's dish sets often were made as a sideline to a major manufacturing line either as a complement to the family service or as a way to use up the last of the day's batch of materials.

Children's toy dishes were made by many of the major manufacturers, such as Cambridge, Akro Agate, Jeannette Glass Co., and Hazel Atlas. Collectors prefer complete sets and mint pieces; sometimes this is difficult to achieve because the pieces were toys and enjoyed by children of years ago.

Children's toy dishes are commonly sold in combinations such as berry sets, table sets, and water sets. Due to the small size of the items, the display desirability of a grouping of pieces has increased their value.

Unlike toy dishes meant for play, children's feeding dishes are the items actually used in the feeding of a child. Their colorful designs of animals, nursery rhymes, and children's activities are meant to appeal to the child and make mealtimes fun. A special type of plate, known as an "ABC plate," helped teach children their alphabet and sometimes numbers before their formal education began.

References: Maureen Batkin, *Gifts for Good Children, Part II, 1890-1990,* Antique Collectors' Club, 1996; Mildred L. and Joseph P. Chalala, *A Collector's Guide to ABC Plates, Mugs and Things,* Pridemark Press, 1980; Gene Florence, *The Collectors Encyclopedia of Akro Agate Glassware, Revised Edition,* Collector Books, 1975, 1992 value update; Roger and Claudia Hardy, *The Complete Line of Akro Agate: Marbles, General Line and Children's Dishes With Prices,* published by authors, 1992; Doris Lechler, *Children's Glass Dishes, China and Furniture, Volume I,* Collector Books, 1982, 1991 value update; Doris Lechler, *Volume II,* Collector Books, 1986, 1993 value update; Doris Lechler, *French and German Dolls, Dishes, and Accessories,* Antique Publications, 1991; Doris Lechler, *Toy Glass,* Antique Publications, 1989; Irene and Ralph Lindsey, *ABC Plates & Mugs,* Collector Books, 1997; Lorraine May Punchard, *Child's Play,* published by author, 1982; —, *Playtime Kitchen Items, and Table Accessories,* published by author, 1993; Noel Riley, *Gifts for Good Children,* Richard Dennis Publications, 1991; Margaret & Kenn Whitmyer, *Children's Dishes,* Collector Books, 1984, 1995 value update.

Collectors' Clubs: ABC Plate/Mug Collectors, 67 Stevens Ave., Old Bridge, NJ 08857; Toy Dish Collectors, P.O. Box 351, Camilus, NY 13031.

Additional Listings: Also see Akro Agate.

Reproduction Alert: Reproductions exist in several types of children's glass and are indicated with an asterisk (*).

Child-sized dishes

ABC plate

6" d, Barley pattern, colorless . **45.00**

6" d, Cane pattern, alphabet on stippled rim, colorless. **48.00**

6" d, Christmas Eve, Santa on chimney, colorless. **75.00**

6" d, Deer and Tree pattern, colorless **50.00**

6" d, Ding Dong Bell, colorless **75.00**

6" d, dog, standing on grass, tree in center, colorless **70.00**

6" d, dog's head center, colorless **45.00**

6" d, duck, amber **45.00**

6" d, elephant with howdah, three waving Brownies, Ripley & Co., colorless **135.00**

6" d, floral bouquet with bow, colorless **50.00**

6" d, hen and chicks, colorless **45.00**

6" d, Jumbo, emb alphabet border **95.00**

6" d, Little Bo Peep, center scene, raised alphabet border..... **50.00**
6" d, plain center, colorless, white scalloped edge **65.00**
6" d, President Garfield, profile bust center, colorless, frosted alphabet border.................. **60.00**
6" d, Starburst pattern, alphabet border, scalloped rim, New Martinsville, colorless...... **40.00**
6" d, Star Medallion pattern, colorless................ **40.00**
6" d, Thousand Eye pattern, blue **70.00**
6" d, Thousand Eye pattern, vaseline **65.00**
6" d, young Girl, portrait, colorless **65.00**
6" d, Westward Ho pattern ... **90.00**
6-1/4" d, colorless and frosted, Christmas Morning, frosted center, stippled alphabet border .. **175.00**
6-1/4" d, colorless and frosted, rabbit in cabbage patch, frosted center, stippled alphabet border ... **65.00**
6-1/2" d, dog in center, colorless **110.00**
6-3/4" d, Independence Hall, 1776-1876, colorless and frosted **145.00**
7" d, Centennial Exhibition, 1776-1876, American eagle center, colorless............... **110.00**
7" d, clock face center, Arabic and Roman numerals, alphabet center, frosted and colorless **75.00**
7" d, Easter Greetings, alphabet border with gilt letters, floral center, beaded edge, milk glass ... **45.00**
7" d, Emma, girl's head in center, beaded rim, Higbee bee mark, colorless................ **90.00**
7" d, plain center, emb alphabet border, beaded rim, milk glass **55.00**
7" d, stork, marigold carnival glass **65.00**
7-3/4" d, Arabic and Roman numerals, colorless **50.00**
8" d, Frosted Stork, flake.... **125.00**

Bowl

Breakfast of Champions **55.00**
Children, red dec **12.00**
Davy Crockett, brown and white **20.00**
Dutch Girl **10.00**
Little Bo Peep, divided, white, fired-on red dec **75.00**
Wheaties, red and white..... **25.00**

Cereal bowl, Circus, red, Pyrex . **15.00**

Mug, Ranger Joe, white ground, blue lettering, Hazel Atlas, **$15.**

Mug

A is for Alligator, color lettering on white, Hazel Atlas **15.00**
Batman, Fireking blue print ... **20.00**
B is for Bunny, color lettering on white, Hazel Atlas **15.00**
Bo Peep, red and white...... **10.00**
Circus, red and white **6.00**
Circus Clowns, red and white . **12.00**
C is for Cow, color lettering on white, Hazel Atlas **15.00**
Cowboy and Indian, red on white, Hazel Atlas **15.00**
Crockett, brown and white.... **10.00**
Davy Crockett, red on white, Hazel Atlas **25.00**
D is for Donkey, color lettering on white, Hazel Atlas **15.00**
Esso Tiger **5.00**
G is for Goose, color lettering on white, Hazel Atlas **15.00**
H is for Horse, color lettering on white, Hazel Atlas **15.00**
Hopalong Cassidy, green on white **35.00**
Indians, red **12.50**
Ranger Joe, blue dec on white, Hazel Atlas **15.00**
Ranger Joe, red on white, Hazel Atlas **15.00**
Robin Hood, red and white ... **15.00**
Smokey the Bear, Glasbake .. **15.00**
Space Scene, black dec on white, Hazel Atlas **25.00**
Space Scene, blue dec on white, Hazel Atlas **25.00**
Space Scene, red dec on white, Hazel Atlas **25.00**
Superman, Federal **25.00**

Tumbler

D is for Duck, color lettering on white, Hazel Atlas, 3-1/8" h .. **9.50**
Nursery Rhymes, Jack and Jill, red, Hazel Atlas, 4-5/8" h........ **6.00**
Nursery Rhymes, Mary Had Little Lamb, light blue, Hazel Atlas, 4-5/8" h.................. **6.00**
N is for Night Crawler, pink and red, 5" h.................... **18.00**
Nursery Rhymes, Little Miss Muffet, green, Hazel Atlas, ribbed, 4" h **6.00**
P is for Penguin, black lettering on white, 5" h............... **18.00**
V is for Vulture, light blue and dark blue, 5" h **30.00**
X is for Xema, blue and green, 5" h **18.00**

Akro Agate, tumblers, Interior Panel and Stacked Disk, cobalt blue, **$50.**

Play dishes

Akro Agate

Dinner set, Interior Panel, small, amber, orig box, 21 pcs... **200.00**

Tea set

Concentric Ring, two green plates, two green cups, two white saucers, green teapot, eight pcs **85.00**
Octagonal, large, green and white, Little American Maid, orig box, 17 pcs **225.00**
Octagonal, large, two blue plates, two blue cups, two pink saucers, pink teapot and lid, eight pcs **180.00**
Stippled Band, transparent green, small size, orig box, 14 pcs, box lid missing **355.00**

Water set, Play Time, pink and blue, orig box, seven pcs **125.00**

Bohemian, decanter set, ruby flashed, Vintage dec, five pcs **135.00**

Contemporary glass, Mosser glass. The Jennifer pattern was made to resemble Depression glass Cameo pattern. It was made in pink, green, or yellow, all values the same. The Lindsey pattern is its modern version of

Cambridge's Caprice pattern. It was made in cobalt blue or moonlight blue, both colors valued the same.

Berry set, master bowl, four rimmed bowls, Jennifer 20.00
Console set
Jennifer 20.00
Lindsey 25.00
Cup and saucer
Eight-pc set, Jennifer 22.00
Lindsey 20.00
Dessert set, cake plate, four plates, Jennifer 25.00
Dinner plate
Four-pc set, Jennifer 20.00
Four-pc set, Lindsey 20.00
Goblet, four-pc set, Jennifer . . 20.00
Grill plate, four-pc set, Jennifer 25.00
Ice tub, Jennifer 12.00
Juice set, juice pitcher, four tumblers, Jennifer 25.00
Punch set, punch bowl and six cups, Lindsey 35.00
Relish set, elongated three-part dish, salt dips, Lindsey 25.00
Salad set, divided relish, four sq plates, Jennifer 22.00
Table set, cov butter, creamer, sugar, Jennifer 18.00
Tumbler, cone shape, Jennifer 10.00
Vase, Jennifer 10.00
Water set, pitcher, four tumblers, Lindsey 30.00

Depression-era glass
Bowl, Little Deb, ribbed 15.00
Creamer
Blossom, Delphite 60.00
Cherry Blossom, pink 55.00
Doric and Pansy, pink 55.00
Doric and Pansy, ultramarine 75.00
Laurel, green 35.00
Laurel, green, Scottie dec. 115.00
Laurel, ivory, Scottie dec. . . 85.00
Laurel, plain 20.00
Moderntone, bright pink . . . 20.00
Moderntone, pastel pink . . . 18.00
Moderntone, rust 26.50
Twentieth Century, fired-on pastel pink 18.00
Cup
Cherry Blossom, Delphite* . 50.00
Cherry Blossom, pink 45.00
Doric and Pansy, pink 32.50
Doric and Pansy, ultramarine 60.00
Homespun, crystal 22.00
Homespun, pink 32.00
Laurel, green 30.00
Laurel, green, Scottie dec . 60.00
Laurel, ivory, Scottie dec . . 40.00
Laurel, plain 18.00
Moderntone, blue 15.25
Moderntone, bright pink . . 22.50
Moderntone, burgundy . . . 14.50
Moderntone, gold 18.00
Moderntone, gray 20.00
Moderntone, pastel blue . . 16.00
Moderntone, pastel yellow. 16.00
Twentieth Century, fired-on pastel blue 12.50
Twentieth Century, fired-on pastel green 12.50
Mixer, Glassbake, three ftd . . 40.00
Plate
Cherry Blossom, 6" d, Delphite 28.00
Cherry Blossom, 6" d, pink 22.50
Doric and Pansy, pink 15.00
Doric and Pansy, ultramarine 20.00
Homespun, crystal 10.00
Homespun, pink 15.00
Laurel, green 17.50
Laurel, green, Scottie dec . 55.00
Laurel, ivory, Scottie dec . . 35.00
Laurel, plain 10.00
Laurel, red trim 15.00
Little Hostess, blue, 5-1/4" d 10.00
Little Hostess, yellow, 5-1/4" d 10.00
Moderntone, aqua 15.00
Moderntone, blue 12.00
Moderntone, bright pink . . 15.00
Moderntone, chartreuse . . . 9.00
Moderntone, dark green . . 15.00
Moderntone, gold 12.50
Moderntone, gray 15.50
Moderntone, green 12.00
Moderntone, lemon yellow. 15.00
Moderntone, pastel blue . . 12.00
Moderntone, pastel green . 12.00
Moderntone, pastel pink . . 12.00
Moderntone, pastel yellow. 12.50
Moderntone, rust 12.50
Moderntone, tan 15.00
Moderntone, turquoise 12.50
Twentieth Century, fired-on pastel blue 12.00
Twentieth Century, fired-on pastel green 12.00
Twentieth Century, fired-on pastel pink 12.00
Saucer
Cherry Blossom, Delphite . 15.50
Cherry Blossom, pink 10.50
Doric and Pansy, pink 12.00
Doric and Pansy, ultramarine 18.50
Homespun, crystal 9.00
Homespun, pink 12.00
Laurel, green 10.00
Laurel, green, Scottie dec . 55.00
Laurel, ivory, Scottie dec . . 25.00
Laurel, plain 8.00
Moderntone, blue 9.75
Moderntone, green 9.75
Moderntone, pink 9.75
Twentieth Century, fired-on pastel yellow 5.00
Set
Cherry Blossom, Delphite, 14-pc set 435.00
Cherry Blossom, pink, 14-pc set 525.00
Diana, crystal, gold trim, rack, 12-pc set 125.00
Doric and Pansy, pink, 14-pc set 425.00
Doric and Pansy, ultramarine, 14-pc set 525.00
Homespun, pink, 14 pcs, orig box 600.00
Laurel, McKee, red trim, 14-pc set 355.00
Little Hostess, green, gray, chartreuse, and maroon, 16-pc set 250.00
Moderntone, burgundy, 14-pc set, orig box 350.00
Sugar
Cherry Blossom, Delphite . . 50.00
Cherry Blossom, pink 47.50
Doric and Pansy, pink 35.00
Doric and Pansy, ultramarine 45.00
Laurel, green 40.00
Laurel, green, Scottie dec 115.00
Laurel, ivory, Scottie dec . . 85.00
Laurel, plain 20.00
Moderntone, beige 20.00
Moderntone, bright pink . . . 22.00
Moderntone, chartreuse . . . 15.00
Moderntone, gray 15.00
Moderntone, pastel pink . . . 18.00
Moderntone, rust 24.50
Twentieth Century, fired-on pastel pink 18.00
Teapot
Homespun, crystal 75.00
Homespun, pink 190.00
Little Hostess, turquoise . . . 85.00
Moderntone, burgundy . . . 150.00
Moderntone, gray 115.00
Moderntone, green 95.00
Moderntone, lemon 75.00
Moderntone, pink 75.00
Moderntone, white 75.00

Goofus glass, banana stand, folded, two cupids 35.00

Milk glass

Butter, cov

Versailles, emb roses, raised scalloped draping, blue trim, Ditheridge, c1900 . . . . . **165.00**
Wild Rose. **65.00**

Creamer, Wild Rose **65.00**
Cup, Nursery Rhyme **24.00**
Ice cream platter, Wild Rose . **60.00**

Mug

Gooseberry **35.00**
Little Bo Peep. **85.00**

Punch bowl, Wild Rose **45.00**
Punch bowl set, Wild Rose, lemon stain dec. **225.00**
Stein, Monk, rings on top **25.00**
Table set, cov butter, creamer, cov sugar, spooner

Thumbelina **95.00**
Wild Rose, four pcs **275.00**

Pattern glass (colorless unless otherwise noted)

Banana stand, Beautiful Lady, stemmed **45.00**

Berry bowl

Fine Cut X **20.00**
Flute **8.00**
Lacy Daisy **8.00**
Pattee Cross. **10.00**
Wheat Sheaf. **9.00**

Berry set, Wheat Sheaf, seven pcs **85.00**

Butter, cov

Alabama. **215.00**
Amazon **75.00**
Austrian, canary. **250.00**
Button Arches, ruby stained, enamel flowers, souvenir **175.00**
Doyle's 500, amber **100.00**
Drum **145.00**
Hawaiian Lei. **60.00**
Hobnail with Thumbprint base, blue **95.00**
Lion Head **175.00**
Mardi Gras **125.00**
Michigan, rose stain. **185.00**
Pennsylvania, dark green **115.00**
Stippled Forget-Me-Not . . **100.00**
Tulip and Honeycomb . . . **105.00**
Wee Branches, alphabet base **110.00**

Cake stand

Beautiful Lady, 4" h, 5" d, c1905 . . . . **25.00**
Fine Cut and Fan **40.00**
Hawaiian Lei. **35.00**
Palm Leaf Fan **35.00**
Rexford. **35.00**
Ribbon Candy, green. **48.00**

Candlesticks, pr, Star, Cambridge, light blue **35.00**
Castor set, glass bottles, SP metal base

American Shield, four bottles **125.00**
Gothic Arches **165.00**

Condiment set

English Hobnail. **45.00**
Hickman, open salt, pepper shaker, cruet, and leaf-shaped tray **75.00**

Creamer

Alabama **60.00**
Amazon, pedestal. **35.00**
Austrian, canary **75.00**
Buzz Saw **15.00**
Colonial, blue **22.00**
Dewdrop **30.00**
Drum **70.00**
Fernland **18.00**
Grapevine with Ovals **40.00**
Hawaiian Lei **15.00**
Hobnail with Thumbprint base, amber **40.00**
Hobnail with Thumbprint base, blue. **40.00**
Lamb. **75.00**
Lacy Medallion, green, gold trim, souvenir **25.00**
Liberty Bell **65.00**
Lion Head **65.00**
Mardi Gras, ruby stain **75.00**
Nursery Rhyme **30.00**
Pennsylvania. **35.00**
Pert **30.00**
Sawtooth Band, Heisey. . . . **55.00**
Stippled Forget-Me-Not . . . **80.00**
Tappan, amethyst **35.00**
Tulip and Honeycomb. **20.00**
Twin Snowshoes **20.00**
Twist, opalescent, blue **80.00**
Wee Branches **80.00**
Whirligig **230.00**

Cruet, English Hobnail, green. **25.00**
Cup and saucer, Lion **50.00**
Goblet, Vine, cobalt blue **60.00**
Honey jug, Mardi Gras, ruby stain, 2-1/2" h **85.00**
Horseradish dish, Menagerie, bear **120.00**
Ice cream platter, ABC **125.00**

Lemonade pitcher

Lily of the Valley **125.00**
Oval Star **65.00**

Mug, handle

Austrian. **45.00**
Fighting Cats. **35.00**
Grape and Festoon with Shield, cobalt blue **90.00**
Grapevines **20.00**

Mug, Degenhart, stork, cobalt blue carnival, 2-5/8" h, **$50.**

Grapevine with Ovals **21.00**
Heron **20.00**
Liberty Bell. **125.00**
Michigan **45.00**
Old Butterfly. **30.00**
Ribbed Forget-Me-Not. . . . **25.00**
Robin, amber **25.00**
Robin, translucent blue, Atterbury, 2-1/2" h **35.00**
Robin in Tree, amber **45.00**
Stippled Forget-Me-Not . . . **60.00**
Wee Branches **25.00**

Nappy, Michigan **50.00**
Pepper shaker, English Hobnail **10.00**

Pitcher

Brick Work **45.00**
Colonial **20.00**
Hobb's Hobnail **45.00**
Michigan, rose stain **50.00**
Nursery Rhyme **100.00**
Oval Star **30.00**
Pattee Cross, gold trim . . . **48.00**
Waffle and Button **35.00**

Plate

Dog's Face. **140.00**
Sitting Dog, numerals border **125.00**
Wee Branches **48.00**

Punch bowl

Inverted Strawberry **75.00**
Oval Star, gold trim **55.00**
Rex. **110.00**
Thumbelina **30.00**
Whirligig. **20.00**

Punch bowl set, punch bowl and six cups

Flattened Diamond and Sunburst **75.00**
Star Arches **75.00**
Tulip and Honeycomb **90.00**
Wheat Sheaf **75.00**

Punch cup, clear, embossed birds at fountain, 2" h, **$5.**

Punch cup
- Inverted Strawberry, Cambridge **17.50**
- Thumbelina **35.00**
- Wheat Sheaf **8.00**

Spooner
- Amazon, pedestal, sawtooth rim **30.00**
- Austrian, canary **90.00**
- Colonial, green **20.00**
- Diamond and Panels **20.00**
- Doyle's 500, amber **35.00**
- Duncan & Miller #42, some gold trim **30.00**
- Hawaiian Lei **35.00**
- Lion Head **90.00**
- Mardi Gras **45.00**
- Menagerie Fish, amber ... **150.00**
- Michigan, rose stain **120.00**
- Mitered Sawtooth **26.00**
- Pennsylvania **20.00**
- Stippled Forget-Me-Not ... **80.00**
- Tulip and Honeycomb **20.00**
- Twist, opalescent, vaseline . **75.00**
- Whirligig **40.00**

Sugar, cov
- Alabama **90.00**
- Amazon, pedestal **45.00**
- Austrian, canary **150.00**
- Beaded Swirl **40.00**
- Colonial, blue **30.00**
- Drum **65.00**
- Fernland **20.00**
- Hawaiian Lei, with bee **40.00**
- Liberty Bell **135.00**
- Lion Head **125.00**
- Mardi Gras **65.00**
- Michigan **55.00**
- Nursery Rhyme **48.00**
- Oval Star **30.00**
- Stippled Forget-Me-Not .. **115.00**
- Tappan, amethyst **45.00**
- Tulip with Honeycomb **25.00**

Table set, four pcs, cov butter dish, creamer, cov sugar, spooner
- Arrowhead in Oval **100.00**
- Beaded Swirl **125.00**
- Clear and Diamond Panels, blue **185.00**
- Hobnail Thumbprint Base, four-pc set on matching tray **75.00**
- Oval Star, four pcs **75.00**
- Sweetheart **90.00**
- Thumbelina, three pcs **85.00**

Tray, Doyle's 500, amber **50.00**

Tumbler
- Michigan **15.00**
- Nursery Rhyme **20.00**
- Oval Star **15.00**
- Pattee Cross **15.00**
- Sandwich Ten Panel, sapphire blue **145.00**

Water set, Nursery Rhyme, pitcher, six tumblers **225.00**

CONSOLIDATED GLASS COMPANY

History: The Consolidated Lamp and Glass Company was formed as a result of the 1893 merger of the Wallace and McAfee Company, glass and lamp jobbers of Pittsburgh, Pennsylvania, and the Fostoria Shade & Lamp Company of Fostoria, Ohio. When the Fostoria, Ohio, plant burned down in 1895, Corapolis, Pennsylvania, donated a seven-acre tract of land near the center of town for a new factory. In 1911, the company was the largest lamp, globe, and shade works in the United States, employing more than 400 workers.

In 1925, Reuben Haley, owner of an independent design firm, convinced John Lewis, president of Consolidated, to enter the giftware field utilizing a series of designs inspired by the 1925 Paris Exposition (l'Exposition Internationale des Arts Décorative et Industriels Modernes) and the work of René Lalique. Initially, the glass was marketed by Howard Selden through his showroom at 225 Fifth Avenue in New York City. The first two lines were Catalonian and Martele.

Additional patterns were added in the late 1920s: Florentine (January 1927), Chintz (January 1927), Ruba Rombic (January 1928), and Line 700 (January 1929). On April 2, 1932, Consolidated closed it doors. Kenneth Harley moved about 40 molds to Phoenix. In March 1936, Consolidated reopened under new management, and the "Harley" molds were returned. During this period, the famous Dancing Nymph line, based on an eight-inch salad plate in the 1926 Martele series, was introduced.

In August 1962, Consolidated was sold to Dietz Brothers. A major fire damaged the plant during a 1963 labor dispute and in 1964 the company permanently closed its doors.

References: Ann Gilbert McDonald, *Evolution of the Night Lamp*, Wallace-Homestead, 1979; Jack D. Wilson, *Phoenix & Consolidated Art Glass, 1926-1980*, Antique Publications, 1989.

Collectors' Club: Phoenix and Consolidated Glass Collectors, P.O. Box 3847, Edmond, OK 73083-3847.

Almond dish, Ruba Rombic, smoky topaz, 3" l **235.00**

Animal
- Dragonfly, brown and green stained milk glass **80.00**
- Screech owl, brown stained milk glass **90.00**

Ashtray, Santa Maria, green wash **200.00**

Banana boat, Lovebirds
- Frosted and clear, 13" l **350.00**
- Green wash, 13" l **675.00**
- Pink, brown, blue-green, white milk glass ground, 15" l, 6" h ... **730.00**

Basket, Catalonian, green **48.00**

Berry bowl
- Criss-Cross, cranberry opalescent, 8" d **175.00**
- Master, Cone, pink, glossy, silverplated rim **110.00**

Bonbon, Ruba Rombic, 6" d, smoky topaz **125.00**

Bowl, Ruba Rombic pattern, jungle green, light rim chips, 8-1/2" d, **$750.** *Photo courtesy of David Rago Auctions.*

Bowl
- Catalonian, yellow, 9-1/2" d ... **45.00**
- Coronation, Martelé, flared, blue, 5-1/2" d **75.00**
- Dancing Nymph, dark blue wash, 8" d **365.00**
- Leaf, green, 10" l, 4" w **35.00**
- Ruba Rombic, Jungle Green, light rim chips, 8-1/2" d **750.00**
- Ruba Rombic, Smokey Topaz, oval, 12" l, 6" w, 4-1/4" h, small rim flakes **1,295.00**
- Waterlilies, green, 14-1/4" d, 3-5/8" h, some roughness at rim **630.00**

Box, cov
Five Fruits, frosted, emb fruits, 7" l, 5" w, 2-1/4" h **75.00**
Martelé line, Fruit and Leaf pattern, scalloped edge, 7" l, 5" w. . . **85.00**
Butter dish, cov
Cosmos
Pink band. **200.00**
Yellow, pink, and blue dec, 8" d, 6" h. **160.00**
Florette, pink satin. **385.00**
Guttate, white, gold trim **150.00**
Candlesticks, pr
Five Fruits, Martelé line, green **60.00**
Hummingbird, Martelé line, oval body, jade green, 6-3/4" h . **245.00**
Ruba Rombic, smoky topaz . **215.00**
Tropical Fish, blue wash **500.00**
Celery tray, Florette, pink **35.00**
Cigarette box, cov
Phlox, slate blue **150.00**
Santa Maria, white, 5-1/4" l, 4" w, 2-1/4" h. **175.00**
Cocktail, Dancing Nymph, French Crystal **90.00**
Cologne bottle, orig stopper, 4-1/2" h, Cosmos **120.00**
Compote, Fish, green. **90.00**
Console bowl, Cockatoo, blue, frosted highlights. **250.00**
Cookie jar
Con-Cora, white milk glass, hp pink and green roses dec, gilt trim, 6-1/4" h, 6-1/2" d. **185.00**
Regent Line, #3758, Florette, rose pink over white opal casing, 6-1/2" h, 6-1/2" d. **370.00**
Creamer and sugar
Catalonia, light green **95.00**
Cosmos, white milk glass with fired-on colors **185.00**
Ruba Rombic, Sunshine Yellow **265.00**
Shell & Seaweed, pink, floral dec, emb shells **995.00**
Cruet, orig stopper
Bulging Loops, pink satin . . . **300.00**
Cone, yellow satin. **300.00**
Florette, pink satin. **225.00**
Cruet, replaced stopper, Cone, pink satin, 5" h. **110.00**
Cup and saucer
Catalonian, green **30.00**
Dancing Nymph, ruby wash. **265.00**
Fish tray, amber, 9-1/4" l, 6" w . **350.00**
Goblet, Dancing Nymph, French Crystal **90.00**
Humidor, Florette, pink satin. . . **225.00**
Jar, cov, Con-Cora, #3758-9, pine cone dec, irid **165.00**

Jug
Five Fruits, half gallon, French Crystal **250.00**
Spanish Knobs, 5-1/2" h, handle, pink **125.00**
Juice tumbler, Catalonian, green, 3-7/8" h **15.00**
Lamp
Cockatoo, figural, orange and blue, black beak, brown stump, black base, 13" h **450.00**
Criss-Cross, spherical base, cream ground, gold dots dec, later silk shade **110.00**
Dogwood, brown and white. . **135.00**
Elk, chocolate brown, blue clock mounted between horns, black glass base, 13" h, shallow annealing mark **1,000.00**
Flower Basket, bouquet of roses and poppies, yellows, pinks, green leaves, brown basketweave, black glass base, 8" h. **300.00**
Foxglove, white, lavender blue flowers, mint green leaves, c1943, orig fittings, 10-1/4" h **150.00**
Lovebirds, two green lovebirds, orange crest, brown and yellow stump, black base, 10-1/2" h **350.00**
Owl, brown, black eyes, black glass base, 8-1/2" h **400.00**
Mayonnaise comport, Martelé Iris, green wash. **55.00**
Miniature lamp
7" h, Cosmos, fish net ground **350.00**
9" h, Cosmos, pink, yellow and blue dec, electrified **90.00**
10" h, blue satin glass, spherical shade, sq base **395.00**
10-1/4" h, white milk glass, sq base with emb floral dec **295.00**
Night light, Santa Maria, block base **450.00**
Old fashioned tumbler, Catalonian
Lavender, 3-7/8" h **24.00**
Yellow, 3-7/8" h. **20.00**
Pickle castor, Cosmos **525.00**
Pitcher, water
Catalonian, yellow **135.00**
Florette, pink satin **200.00**
Plate
Bird of Paradise, amber wash, 8-1/4" d **40.00**
Catalonian
Green, 7" d **25.00**
Purple wash, 7-1/2" d **20.00**
Yellow, 7" d **15.00**
Yellow, 10-1/4" d **40.00**

Dancing Nymph
French Crystal, 8-1/4" d . . . **115.00**
Pink, 8-1/4" d **145.00**
Five Fruits
Green, 8-1/2" d **40.00**
White, 12" d **65.00**
Martelé
Orchid, pink, birds and flowers, 12" d **115.00**
Martelé, Vine, smokey topaz, 6" d **65.00**
Martelé, Vine, smokey topaz, 8-1/4" d **85.00**
Platter, Dancing Nymph, Palace
Dark blue wash. **1,000.00**
Palace, French Crystal **500.00**
Puff box, cov
Hummingbirds, milk glass . . . **75.00**
Lovebirds, blue. **95.00**
Rose bowl, Shell & Seaweed
Blue shaded to white, enameled bell shaped flowers, molded shells around base, 5" h. **295.00**
Blue shaded to white, molded shells around base, 5" h. **210.00**
Pink shaded to white, enameled bell shaped flowers, molded shells around base, 5" h. **275.00**
Yellow shaded to white, enameled daisies, molded shells around base, 5" h. **225.00**

Salt shaker, Bulging Loops pattern, pigeon blood, 3-1/4" h, **$100.**

Salt shaker
Apple Blossom, milk white opaque **35.00**
Beaded Dahlia
Cased, clear with pink casing, 2-1/2" h **30.00**
Light blue, 2-1/2" h. **30.00**
Medium blue opaque, 2-1/2" h **30.00**
Bulging Petal, flat
Cased, clear with pink casing, 2-1/8" h **20.00**

Dark blue opaque, 2-1/8" h. **30.00**
Flat, light blue opaque, 2-1/8" h **30.00**
Cone, pink opaque, 3" h **45.00**
Cord and Tassel
Blue opaque, glossy, 2" h, damage to lid **35.00**
Green opaque, satin finish, 2" h, damage to lid **20.00**
Pink opaque, satin finish, 2" h, damage to lid **30.00**
Cosmos, tall, blue opaque, 3-1/2" h **30.00**
Cotton Bale
Pink opaque, satin finish, 2-1/2" h, split in lid **30.00**
Pink, semi-transparent, variegated, glossy, 2-1/2" h, split in lid **30.00**
Flaming, clear, pink casing, satin, 3" h **45.00**
Florette, clear, pink casing, satin, 2-1/4" h **30.00**
Guttate
Green opaque, 3" h. **48.00**
Pink opaque, 3" h, damage to lid **15.00**
Narrow Base Scroll, clear, pink casing, 3-7/8" h, lid split **30.00**
Overlapping Leaf, pink, blue, or green opaque, 1-7/8" h **40.00**
Palm Leaf, green or blue opaque, 2-1/2" h **30.00**
Pineapple
Blue opaque, 3-1/8" h, damage to lid **15.00**
Green opaque, glossy, 3-1/4" h **35.00**
Pink opaque, satin finish, 3-1/4" h **35.00**
Pink and purple opaque variegated, satin finish, 3-1/4" h **35.00**
Scroll and Net
Blue or green opaque, 3" h. **25.00**
Clear, pink casing, 3" h **25.00**

Sauce, Criss-Cross, cranberry opalescent **55.00**
Scent bottle, orig stopper, Cosmos, pink and blue floral. **140.00**
Sherbet
Catalonian, green, ftd **20.00**
Dancing Nymph
Blue, ftd. **85.00**
French Crystal, ftd **80.00**
Pink satin, ftd **140.00**

Snack set, Martelé Fruits, pink . . **45.00**
Spooner
Cosmos **140.00**
Criss-Cross, cranberry opalescent **75.00**
Shell & Seaweed, pink satin, enameled florals, emb shells, wear to plated handles and collar **165.00**

Sugar bowl, cov
Argus Swirl, shaded opaque pink, satin finish, applied pressed leaf form finial, 3-1/4" d, 5" h, small rim chip **80.00**
Catalonian
Green. **30.00**
Yellow. **40.00**
Guttate, cased pink **120.00**

Sugar shaker, orig top
Cone, green **95.00**
Guttate
Cased pink, pewter top **200.00**
Cranberry, pewter top . . . **450.00**

Sundae, Martelé Russet Yellow Fruits **35.00**
Sweet pea vase, Catalonian, ruby wash **75.00**

Syrup pitcher, Cosmos pattern, white netted background, pink and blue flowers, yellow centers, green leaves, 6-1/2" h, **$275.**

Syrup pitcher
Cone, squatty
Pale blue, cased, 6-1/4" h **100.00**
Pink **295.00**
Cosmos, SP top **275.00**
Guttate, pink, satin, cased, 6-1/2" h, check at top of handle **230.00**

Toilet bottle, Ruba Rombic, cased jade green. **650.00**
Toothpick holder
Florette, cased pink **75.00**
Guttate, cranberry **185.00**

Tumbler
Catalonian, ftd, green, 5-1/4" h **30.00**
Cosmos **85.00**
Dancing Nymph, frosted pink, 6" h **175.00**
Guttate, pink satin **60.00**
Katydid, clambroth **165.00**
Martelé Russet Yellow Fruits, ftd, 5-3/4" h **5.00**
Ruba Rombic, jade, 5-1/2" h . **325.00**

Umbrella vase, Blackberry **550.00**
Vase
Bird of Paradise, crystal, fan . . **90.00**
Catalonian
Honey Amber, 7-3/4" h, 5-1/2" d **90.00**
Lavender, fan, 6-5/8" h **45.00**
Spanish Knob, green, flared, 4" h **45.00**
#1101, triangle, rubena, 10" h **90.00**
#1183, three tiers, honey, 6" h **165.00**
Chickadee, four colors
Custard body **175.00**
Milk glass body. **195.00**
Cocktaoo, satin milk glass and blue **450.00**
Con-Cora
Milk glass, hp flowers, 12" h, 8-1/2" d. **95.00**
#8c, pine cone dec, irid . . . **65.00**
#6x13, tall, pine cone dec . **65.00**
#4916C, pine cone dec, irid **75.00**
Criss-Cross Variant, sq rim, satin finish, cranberry body, stripes have central oval, but edges not serrated, stripes close together, possibly from sugar shaker mold, 5" h, 2-3/8" d **250.00**
Dancing Nymph, crimped
Ruby stain, reverse French Crystal highlights, 5" h . . **135.00**
Crimped, rust stain, reverse highlights, 5" h **140.00**
Dogwood
Green and white, 10-3/4" h **595.00**
Peach flowers, brown stems, white ground, 10-1/2" h . **200.00**
Florentine, collared, flat, green, 12" h **275.00**
Freesia, white ceramic wash, fan **225.00**
French, blue milk glass, silver irid to rams heads on sides, 7-3/4" h **55.00**
Hummingbird, #2588, turquoise on satin custard, 5-1/2" h **90.00**

Katydid
- Blue wash, fan shaped top, 8-1/2" h **300.00**
- White frost, 8-1/4" h **115.00**
- White frost, fan shaped top, 8-1/2" h **165.00**

Lovebirds, custard yellow ground, pale green birds, coral colored flowers, 11-1/4" h, 10" w ... **600.00**
Martelé, frosted, 10-1/2" h... **475.00**
Narcissus, gold satin, 6-1/2" h **200.00**
Nut Hatch, French Crystal .. **225.00**
Peonies, pink, green and brown, 6-1/4" h................. **80.00**
Pine Cones, Con-Cora blank, #3916C, irid, 7" h **75.00**
Poppy, green cased **550.00**
Purple leaf and berry design, opalescent, 9-3/4" h **225.00**
Regent Line, #3758
- Cased blue stretch over white opal, pinched, 6" h..... **175.00**
- Milk glass, French Daisy dec **75.00**

Ruba Rombic
- French Silver, 9-1/2" h ..**4,000.00**
- Jungle Green, c1931, 6-3/8" h **815.00**

Spanish Knobs, red, fan, 6" h **125.00**
Starflower, blue, 6-3/4" h, 6-3/4" d **190.00**

Water set, Guttate, 9" h pitcher, seven 3-5/8" h tumblers, white opaque, gilt handle and rims, wear to gilt, small flakes **160.00**

Contemporary Drinking Glasses

History: Contemporary collector glasses date back to the premiere of Snow White and the Seven Dwarfs in December 1937. Libbey Glass and Walt Disney designed tumblers with a safety edge and sold them through variety stores and local dairies. The glasses were popular with the public, and today, collector glasses can be found with almost every Disney character and movie theme. In 1953, Welch's began to use decorated tumblers as jelly containers and featured Howdy Doody and his characters. These glasses were eagerly received, and Welch's soon added other cartoon characters, like Mr. Magoo, to the designs. By the late 1960s, fast food restaurants began to use tumblers as advertising premiums. Soft drink manufacturers like the Coca-Cola Co. and Pepsi-Cola Co. saw the advertising potential and helped develop marketing plans for the characters and soft drink products.

Contemporary collector glasses are usually produced in series, and it is important to collectors to assemble all the different color variations and items in a series.

Care should be taken when using these tumblers as several early examples were decorated with a lead-based paint. Collectors should try to purchase examples with brightly colored decorations, and avoid faded examples. Because these bright tumblers were mass produced, collectors may be able to find very good to excellent examples.

References: Mark E. Chase and Michael Kelly, *Collectible Drinking Glasses,* 2nd ed., Collector Books, 1999; Collector Glass News, *Collector Glass News 2001 Prices Realized Book,* Collector Glass News, 2001; Carol Markowski Huffman and Tom Hoder, *Tomart's Price Guide to Character & Promotional Glasses,* 3rd ed., Tomart Publications, 2000.

Periodicals: *Collector Glass News*, 108 Poplar Forest Dr., P.O. Box 308, Slippery Rock, PA 16057; *Root Beer Float*, P.O. Box 571, Lake Geneva, WI 53147.

Collectors' Club: Promotional Glass Collectors Association, 97 Bigham Drive, Central Point, OR 97502, www.pgcaglassclub.com.

Al Capp
- Daisy Mae, pink, 1949, 4-3/4" h **14.00**
- Lil Abner, red, 1949, 4-3/4" h... **6.00**
- Lonesome Polecat, maroon, 1949, 4-3/4" h **9.00**
- Mammy Yokum, light green, 1949, 4-3/4" h **6.00**
- Marryin Sam, light blue, 1949, 4-3/4" h **6.00**
- Pappy Yokum, dark green, 1949, 4-3/4" h **15.00**
- Sadie Hawkins, 1975, 6" h.... **46.00**
- Shmoos, orange, 1949, 4-3/4" h **6.00**

American Greeting Corp.
- Christmas is a Gift of Love..... **5.00**
- Holly Hobbie, Coke, Happiness Is **4.00**

Amtrak, mug, red and blue logo, 5-1/4" h set of four **10.00**

Arby's
- Actors
  - Laurel and Hardy **10.00**
  - W. C. Fields, 1979......... **8.00**
- Arkansas Razorbacks, 1977 ... **4.00**
- BC Ice Age
  - Anteater, 1981............ **8.00**
  - Thor on wheels, 1981 ...... **8.00**
- Bicentennial Stars and Stripes, 1976 .... **9.00**
- Dudley takes tea at sea, 12 oz, 1976 .... **23.00**
- Memphis State Univ. Tigers, mug **5.00**
- Monopoly, Collect $200 as You Pass Go, 1985 .... **28.00**
- Wizard of Id, Wizard, 1983 ... **14.00**
- Zodiac, Libra, 1976.......... **3.00**

Braum's Mug, Frost Before Using, black lettering and cow image, **$3.**

Archie Comic Publications
- Archie Gets a Helping Hand, ©1971, 4 oz **6.00**
- Jughead Wins the Pie Eating Contest, ©1971, 4 oz....... **4.00**
- Reggie Makes the Scene, Veronica etched in bottom, ©1971, 4 oz **6.00**

Armour, Transportation Series, The Pony Express, 5" h **4.00**
Betty Boop, King Features Syndicate, 1988 .... **9.00**
Big Boy, Christmas, fountain type, Big Boy making snow angels **3.00**
Borden's, Elsie and Friends, Bicentennial theme **4.00**
Bozo the Clown, 1950s **9.00**

Burger Chef
- Endangered Species Collection, Bald Eagle, 1978 .... **5.00**
- Presidents & Patriots, John F. Kennedy................ **3.00**

Burger King
- Burger Thing, 1979.......... **5.00**
- Coca-Cola, Star Wars, R2D2, C3PO, 1977.................... **5.00**
- Dr. Pepper, D. D. Lewis, Dallas Cowboys, 5-1/2" h **10.00**
- Duke of Doubt, 1979 .... **5.00**
- King Series, 1978........... **6.00**

Chili's, Big Chili's Reunion, 1985, 6" h **5.50**

Chuck E. Cheese
- All The Characters & Lots of Activity, 5-1/2" h................. **20.00**
- Milk glass mug, pedestal, 1981 **3.00**

Cinderella, 1950, Cinderella attending stepsisters **8.00**

Coca-Cola

Atlanta, mug **7.00**

Caltex/Coca-Cola, 1996 Worldwide Olympic Partner, 1928-1996 Coca-Cola logo, back reads "South African Olympic Team Proud Sponsor of the South African Team to the 1996 Olympic Games in Atlanta," red star on white circle Texaco logo **15.00**

Classic Golf, red and green plaid background, white lettering . . **10.00**

Coca-Cola Around The World, eight-pc set, orig box, 1960s **120.00**

Coke/Eat'N Park, Pittsburgh Steelers Hall of Fame, 1996, set of four **16.00**

Enjoy Coca-Cola, Dallas Cowboys, bell shaped, 6" h **6.50**

Heritage Collector Series, Monticello **26.00**

King Kong, New York Subway . . **3.50**

Kollect-A-Set, Swee' Pea **4.00**

Magnificent Ladies, flared, #5 . . **4.00**

Mickey's Christmas Carol, Goofy as Marley's Ghost, 1982 . . . . **3.50**

NFF, California Flag **6.00**

Olympics, Enjoy Coca-Cola, 1976, slogan in English, Japanese, Hebrew, Arabic, and Chinese, set of four, MIB **40.00**

Dairy Queen

Beatles, Canada, 16 oz **12.00**

Boy and girl with cone and sundae, 1976 . . . . **6.00**

Davy Crockett

American Pioneer, grew up in the forests, shooting deer, red . . . **32.00**

Canadian, Walt Disney #4 . . . . **12.00**

Davy the Scout, orange, brown, green, and yellow, 4-3/4" l . . . **10.00**

Fighting bear, on horse, Indian pal, brown, frosted, 5" h **35.00**

Frontier Hero, green scene, yellow hide, canoes, 4-5/8" h **10.00**

Hero of the Alamo, white scene, yellow hide, 5-5/8" h **3.00**

Indian Fighter, green scene, yellow hide, 5" h **3.00**

D. C. Comics

Batman, Super Series, 1976 . . **12.00**

Superman, Super Powers, 1993 . . . . **10.00**

Disney

Alice in Wonderland, #6 . . . . . . **50.00**

America on Parade, 5-5/8" h . . . **6.00**

Lady & The Tramp

Jock, 6-1/4" h **70.00**

Peg, 6-1/4" h **65.00**

Pedro, 6-1/4" h **90.00**

Toughy, 6-1/4" h **75.00**

Trusty, 6-1/4" h **60.00**

Mickey Mouse Club

Donald building brick wall . **14.00**

Mouse Club, Mickey waving **8.00**

Mickey Mouse dreaming of Minnie, Fanta, 1986 . . . . **20.00**

Mickey Mouse, Goofy, and Pluto, yellow **9.00**

Nice Shot, Mickey shooting basketball, 6-1/4" h. **6.00**

101 Dalmatians, French, 3-7/8" **15.00**

Pinocchio, Jiminy Cricket, green, 4-3/4" h **25.00**

Sleeping Beauty, touching the spindle, 1958 . . . . **18.00**

Snow White and Seven Dwarfs, Happy, 4-5/8" h. **12.00**

Domino's Pizza, Dick Tracy . . . **175.00**

Dr. Pepper

Happy Days

Ralph, 1977 . . . . **10.00**

The Fonz, 1977 . . . . **11.00**

Star Trek, Kirk, Spock, McCoy and The Enterprise, 1978, set of four **140.00**

Duo Penotti

Flintstones, Barney with Bamm-Bamm, Fred holding Pebbles, Fred and Wilma with cradle, orig lid **4.00**

Flintstones, Betty and Wilma shopping, Barney making pizza, Fred cracking egg, orig lid **4.00**

Wacky Racers **4.00**

Esso Tiger, slogan in eight languages, 5-1/2" h **15.00**

Famous Americans

Battle of Bunker Hill, brown and white, 5-1/2" h. **11.00**

Betsy Ross, red and white, 5-1/2" h **14.00**

Daniel Webster, blue and white, 5-1/2" h **11.00**

Francis Scott Key, red and white, 5-1/2" h **11.00**

Nathan Hale, red and white, 5-1/2" h **11.00**

Sam Houston, brown and white, 5-1/2" h **11.00**

Hanna-Barbera

Barney, Pizza Hut, 1986 . . . . . **10.00**

Flintstone children, gold lettering, 3-1/4" h **55.00**

Fred, Wilma, and Dino, "Wilma," mug, 1991 . . . . **3.00**

Going to the Drive-In, Hardee's, 1991 . . . . **10.00**

Here's Your Lunch Fred, Wilma and Fred, European, gold rim, 4-3/4" h **35.00**

Huckleberry Hound, 24K and blue design, Huckleberry on front, Snaglepuss, Yogi Bear, and Kellog's "K" on back, 401/2" h **110.00**

Yogi Bear, 24K gold and blue design, Yogi in front in TV screen, film stock circling back, allover gold stars, 4-1/2" h **250.00**

You Really like Football, don't you Fred, Football is it, mug, 1994 **5.00**

Hardee's, Ziggy, Try to Have a Nice Day **3.00**

Hess Gas Station, classic truck series, 1996, set of four **20.00**

Indy 500

1978 Airport Hilton **12.00**

1979 Airport Hilton **10.00**

1980 Airport Hilton **3.00**

1981 Airport Hilton **3.00**

1982 Airport Hilton **3.00**

1983 Airport Hilton **3.00**

1984 Airport Hilton **3.00**

1985 Airport Hilton **3.00**

Kellogg's, 1977 Collectors Series

Tony the Tiger **6.00**

Toucan Sam **6.00**

Kentucky Derby

1945 . . . . **300.00**

1948, frosted bottom **120.00**

1950 . . . . **330.00**

1952 . . . . **135.00**

1953 . . . . **75.00**

1954 . . . . **175.00**

1955 . . . . **135.00**

1956, one star, two tails **135.00**

1956, two stars, two tails **118.00**

1957 . . . . **65.00**

1958, gold bar **85.00**

1958, Iron Leige **100.00**

1959 . . . . **45.00**

1960 . . . . **50.00**

1964 . . . . **24.00**

1974, Cannero II **5.00**

1982, Preakness **20.00**

1986 . . . . **3.00**

1986, Preakness **12.00**

1987, Festival **4.00**

1991, Breeder's Cup **5.00**

1996 . . . . **3.00**

Marathon Oil, Apollo, carafe, 1970s **7.50**

McDonald's

Adventure Series

Big Mac nets the Hamburglar, 1980 . . . . **3.00**

Captain Crook sails the bounding main, 1980 . . . . **5.00**
Mayor McCheese rides a runaway train, 1980 . . . . . . **3.00**
Baltimore Orioles Greatest Moments, 1998, set of six **21.00**
Big Mac, slogan in several languages, late 1970s **5.00**
Camp Snoopy
#2, Civilization is overrated! **26.00**
There's No Excuse For Not Being Properly Prepared **16.00**
Capt. Cook, 12 oz, thick base **11.00**
Great Muppet Caper
Hot Air Balloon, 5-1/2" h, ©Henson Assoc., Inc., 1981 . . . . **6.00**
Kermit, 5-1/2" h, ©Henson Assoc., Inc., 1981 . . . . **7.00**
Miss Piggy, 5-1/2" h, ©Henson Assoc., Inc., 1981 . . . . **7.50**
Monopoly, black and white . . . **15.00**
Nascar Bill Elliot, 1998, stock cars, set of four **15.00**
Topps Baseball, Cal Ripken . . . **7.00**

Mountain Dew, Do the Dew, bulbous, 6" h. **8.00**

Pepsi
Batgirl and Robin, subduing Catwoman, sample glass, 16 oz, Brockway, wraparound action, mint. **1,595.00**
Beaky Buzzard, white letter, Federal, ©Warner Bros., 1973 . . . . **6.00**
Bugs Bunny
Broadway, ©Warner Bros., 1973, 16 oz **12.00**
Brockway, ©Warner Bros., 1973, 16 oz, black letters **18.00**
Christmas Collection, 1982. . . . **3.00**
Cool Cat and Beaky Buzzard, ©Warner Bros., 1976, 16 oz. **15.00**
Daffy Duck, ©Warner Bros., 1973, 12 oz **12.00**
DC Comics
Aquaman **4.00**
Superman, More Powerful than an Locomotive, sample glass, 16-oz Brockway, sample sticker on bottom, 1977 . . . . . **1,465.00**
Disney, Happy Birthday Mickey, 1978 . . . . **3.00**
Elmer Fudd, Brockway, ©Warner Bros., 1973, 16 oz, black letters **3.00**
Foghorn Leghorn, Brockway, ©Warner Bros., 1973, 16 oz, black letters **3.00**
Harvey Cartoons
Big Baby Huey, 5" h **5.00**

Dalmatians, white dogs with black spots, green grass, "Dalmatians" in white lettering, **$5.**

Richie Rich, 6" h, white letters **10.00**
Wendy, 5" h **10.00**
Henry Hawk, Brockway, ©Warner Bros., 1973, 16 oz **12.00**
Hoss' Family Steak & Sea House, 4-1/8" h, white **4.00**
Pepsi & Pete, Libbey logo on bottom, 1940s **205.00**
Pepsi Fest East 94, Charlotte, NC **3.00**
Porky Pig, Brockway, ©Warner Bros., 1973, 16 oz **15.00**
Ringling Bros. and Barnum & Bailey Circus, 100th Anniversary **3.00**
Slow Poke Rodriguez, Brockway, ©Warner Bros., 1973, 12 oz, black letters. **15.00**
Tasmanian Devil, Brockway, ©Warner Bros., 1973, 16 oz, white letters. **18.00**
Tweety, Sylvester, and Spike, ©Warner Bros., 1976, 16 oz, some color registration off **8.00**
Wisconsin Badgers, Brockway, wrestling, 16 oz **6.00**
Yosemite Sam
Brockway, ©Warner Bros., 1973, 16 oz, white letters **3.00**
©Warner Bros., 1978, Tim Horton Donuts **5.00**

Pike's Peak, Streamline Cog Train at Summit House, Auto Highway, Pikes Peak Cog Railroad, 5" h **9.00**

Pizza Hut, Boris and Bullwinkle, faded, registration off on most colors . . . **45.00**

Popeye, Popeye's Fried Chicken, Popeye through the years, 1982 . . **7.00**

Red Lobster, Tropical Explosion, 7" h **5.00**

Red Steer Restaurant, Bicentennial Collection, 1976
Cataldo Mission **5.00**
Oregon Trail **5.00**
Silver City **5.00**

7-Eleven
Indiana Jones & the Temple of Doom, spiked room **4.00**
Marvel Comics, The Incredible Hulk, 1977 . . . . **16.00**
Quickshop, Thor, 16 oz. **30.00**

Space
Harolds Moonshot, space capsule shape **14.00**
Milestones in Space, Apollo 11, 6-3/4" h **15.00**

Spot the Dog
#1 . . . . **30.00**
#3 . . . . **7.00**
#4 . . . . **10.00**
#5 . . . . **10.00**
#7 . . . . **7.00**

Sunday Funnies
Gasoline Alley. **10.00**
Little Orphan Annie. **10.00**

Superman, Superman in Action, 1964, orange and aqua, 5-3/4" h **20.00**

Taco Bell, Star Trek series
Fal-Tor-Pan, 1984, ©Paramount Pictures Corp., 16 oz **12.00**
Lord Kruge, 1984, ©Paramount Pictures Corp., 16 oz **12.00**
Spock Lives 1984, ©Paramount Pictures Corp., 5-3/4" h **14.00**

Ultramar Petroleum
Batman, ©DC Comics, 1989, 4-1/4" h. **15.00**
Fill It Up Pup **3.00**

Universal Studios, Battlestar Galactica, Apollo, 1979, 16 oz . . **15.00**

Warner Bros.
Marriott's Great America
Bugs Bunny, 1975, 4-3/4" h **17.50**
Tweety, 1975, 4-3/4" h **27.50**
Ultamar, Daffy Duck, 1989, 4" h **3.00**
2000 IXL Collectibles Extreme Sports
Bugs & Elmer on mountain bike, #1 of six. **7.00**
Wile E. & Road Runner snowboarding, #2 of six . . **8.00**
Dally rollerblading, #3 of six **7.00**

Sylvester and Tweety skydiving, with orig lid, #4 of six **9.00**
Taz skateboarding, with orig lid, #5 of six **9.00**
Pepe water skiing, #6 of six . **7.00**

Welch's Looney Tunes

Bugs Bunny, Daffy Duck, and Elmer Fudd, jelly jar, ©Warner Bros., 1994, 10-oz round bottom, orig lid, #11 of 12 .... **7.00**
Daffy Duck and Porky Pig, jelly jar, ©Warner Bros., 1994, 10-oz round bottom, orig lid, #4 of 12..... **6.50**
Roadrunner and Wile E. Coyote, jelly jar, ©Warner Bros., 1994, 10-oz round bottom, orig lid, #8 of 12 .... **8.00**
Sylvester and Tweety, jelly jar, ©Warner Bros., 1994, 10-oz round bottom, orig lid, #6 of 12..... **5.50**
Tasmanian Devil, jelly jar, ©Warner Bros., 1995, 10-oz round bottom, orig lid, #5 of six **6.00**

Wizard of Oz, Swift

Cowardly Lion, Baum, fluted, yellow **12.00**
Scarecrow **6.00**
Wizard, Baum, fluted red..... **10.00**
Woodsman, S & Co., wavy, green **8.00**

CORALENE

History: Coralene refers to glass objects which have the design painted on the surface of the piece, along with tiny colorless glass beads which were applied with a fixative. The piece was placed in a muffle to fix the enamel and set the beads. The design and technique were named "coralene" by Mt. Washington Glass, believed to be the originator of American coralene decoration.

Several American and English companies made glass coralene in the 1880s. Seaweed or coral were the most common design. Other motifs were Wheat Sheaf and Fleur-de-Lis. Most of the base glass was satin finished.

Reproduction Alert: Reproductions are on the market, some using an old glass base. The beaded decoration on new coralene has been glued and can be scraped off.

Bowl

4-1/2" d, blue ground, flowers and leaves, SP holder **165.00**
5-1/2" d, blue MOP satin herringbone pattern, pink seaweed coralene, deeply crimped top, applied rim **625.00**
5-1/2" d, peachblow, ruffled, yellow coralene seaweed dec.... **190.00**

Cruet, pink satin, yellow coralene, orig stopper **410.00**

Fairy lamp, 7" h, six rows of yellow coralene, white opaque shade with yellow tinting, brass-colored metal holder **375.00**

Mug, 3-5/8" h, light blue shading to white satin body, DQ, MOP, yellow coralline, gold rim, applied frosted reeded handle.............. **525.00**

Pickle castor, 7" h, rubena inverted thumbprint insert, coralene butterflies, floral wreath, bird finial cov, cucumbers and leaves on vine, ring handle, low silverplated frame, marked "Derby Silver Co. #147"............. **825.00**

Pitcher

5-1/4" h, cased white ground, bright pink lining, gold seaweed coralene, applied amber reeded handle **225.00**
6-1/4" h, shaded yellow ground, white lining, coralene seaweed dec **350.00**
6-1/2" h, pink and white satin stripes, yellow branch coralene, rose int., bulbous shape, tricorner mouth, amber applied handle, polished pontil.................. **500.00**

Sweetmeat, blue ground, flowers and leaves, SP holder............ **400.00**

Toothpick holder, 2-1/2" h, glossy peachblow, sq raised rim, bulbous body, opaque lining, yellow seaweed coralene dec **275.00**

Tumbler, 3-3/4" h, satin glass, medium to light pink, white int., gold seaweed coralene, gold rim **225.00**

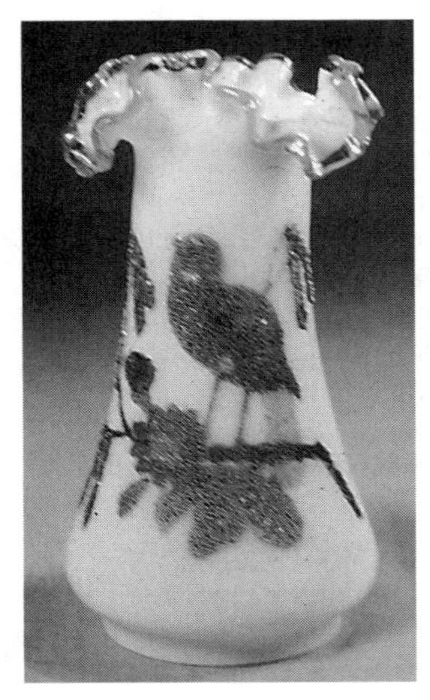

Vase, decorated with bird design, **$145.**

Vase

4-1/2" h, 3-3/8" d, Diamond Quilted pattern, shaded pink, yellow beaded coralene starts in centers of diamonds, white enameled beading around top edge.. **500.00**
5" h, yellow satin ground, blue coralene overlay, sgd "Webb," some beading missing **150.00**
5-3/8" h, golden yellow snowflake MOP satin ground, white lining, yellow wheat coralene dec . **520.00**
5-1/2" h, 4" d, butterscotch MOP, Coinspot pattern, heavy coralene beading, pink and white flowers, yellow centers, green leaves **525.00**
5-1/2" h, 4-5/8" d, fan-shaped top, opaque pink satin ground blends to frosted base, allover dec of yellow three leaf sprays with coralene beads.......... **235.00**
6" h, white cased to yellow, yellow coralene beading, ruffled rim **250.00**
7" h, pink shaded and cased to white, diamond pattern, gold beading within design, price for pr **440.00**
7" h, ruffled pink top shading to white mother of pearl, coralene flowers and butterfly **90.00**
7-1/2" h, blue ground, bulbous, yellow coralene seaweed dec **265.00**
7-1/2" h, peachblow satin, deep rose shading to pale pink, yellow coralene seaweed dec, gold trim top, white casing, polished pontil, c1870, marked "PATENT" .. **850.00**
7-3/4" h, 4-3/4" d, pink and green striped satin ground, off-white lining, heavy yellow beaded coralene **475.00**
8" h, blue ground, large pink, green, and white center coralene rose, Japanese **400.00**
8" h, 5" d, alternating pink, white, and green striped satin ground, shades to white base, yellow coralene beading............... **520.00**
8-1/2" h, green shaded ground, green beading, gold tracery **350.00**
8-1/2" h, yellow shaded to pale pink cased to opal white, diamond and cross pattern, yellow beading, gold trim, slight bead loss...... **175.00**

Vase, orange shading to yellow cased satin glass, allover coralene decoration, 5" h, **$395.** *Photo courtesy of Joy Luke Fine Art Brokers and Auctioneers.*

8-1/2" h, 7" w, sapphire blue, two pastel colored coralene lilies, stems, and foliage, reverse with cream colored foliage, four clear scrolled feet, gold enamel trim, Moser, some loss of glass beads **950.00**

10" h, blue satin ground, seaweed coralene, applied camphor root handles, annealing line, some areas of missing coralene . **325.00**

10-1/2" h, Diamond Quilted pattern, MOP pink satin shaded ground, yellow wheat coralene . . . **1,200.00**

Water set, 9" h satin glass MOP pitcher, DQ, glossy finish, yellow coralene seaweed dec, bulbous, three-spout top, applied reeded shell handle, three matching 4" h tumblers, two small blisters on pitcher, Mt. Washington **750.00**

CRACKLE GLASS

History: The history of crackle glass has not definitely been established. It is known that the Venetians made some examples as early as the 16th century. The Bohemians are also credited with early examples. Their method of creating this sparkly finish was to plunge red hot glass into cold water and then reheat it as the piece was re-blown. Martin Bach claimed his Egyptian and Moorish Art Nouveau influenced designs were reproductions of these ancient civilizations glass when he created his form of crackle for the Durand Glass Company in 1928. By the late 1930s to the early 1970s, crackle was quite popular in the West Virginia glass houses, including Pilgrim, Blenko, Kanawha, and Viking, and many others.

One popular theory for the development of this technique was to hide imperfections in the glass. By creating a crackling effect, defects could be disguised. Other companies used this technique to create more reflective surfaces on a plain body, adding sparkle and interest without the costly process of cutting or hand decorating.

There are several ways to create the crackle effect: (1) The glassblower takes a hot glob of glass and while still attached to the blow pipe, he dips it into cold water. The glass blob is then returned to the hot oven and reheated, sealing the cracks. The glass is then shaped, producing a large crackle design. (2) A desired style is created, then submerged in cold water and after the crackle effect is achieved, it is then reheated to seal the large cracks. (3) The hot glass is rolled in moist sawdust or covered with sand in order to give the surface a coarse finish, then it is submerged in water, causing the surface to crack, without destroying the glass; a second layer of glass is then added and reheated until the cracks fuse together slightly, adding stability. Kanawha uses a hot mold process, where the molds are preheated to accept the molten glass. Harmon Glass blew its glass into metal paste molds that had been lined with paste and cork.

Like many other types of glassware, crackle glass can be found from colorless to a rainbow of intense colors. Collectors may use colors to date some examples of Blenko and Pilgrim glass, as their color production has been carefully documented.

References: Judy Alford, *Collecting Crackle Glass with Values*, Schiffer, 1997; Leslie Pina, *Crackle Glass Too, 1950s-2000*, Schiffer, 2001; Stan and Arlene Weiman, *Crackle Glass Identification and Value Guide*, Book I (1996), Book II (1998), Collector Books.

Collectors' Club: Collectors of Crackle Glass Club, P.O. Box 1186, Massapequa, NY 11758.

Museum: Pilgrim Glass Corp., P.O. Box 395, Ceredo, WV 22507.

Basket, 7-1/2" h, 6" w, white crackle ext., brilliant blue int., crystal V-shaped thorn handle, Victorian **125.00**

Beaker, 7" h, 5-1/2" d top, Leaf pattern, crystal, green applied leaves, hand blown, Blenko, c1940-50 . . . . **90.00**

Bottle, stopper, 16" h, crystal, sgd "Blenko," pr **395.00**

Brandy snifter, 8" h, crystal, turquoise foot, Blenko. **35.00**

Candleholders, amberina, squatty form, pr. **30.00**

Cigarette lighter, 7" h, amberina, metal top **35.00**

Cocktail shaker, Macbeth Evans, crystal. **18.00**

Ad, Pilgrim Glass Pitcher Collection, available in 18 shapes and 5 colors, China Glass & Tablewares, *February 1962.*

Cruet, 6" h, amber, hand blown, Rainbow Glass Co, c1940-60 . . . **35.00**

Decanter, orig stopper

7-1/2" d, 5-1/4" d, blue, straight neck, bulbous base, air bubbles in colorless ball stopper. **75.00**

8-1/2" d, amber, hand blown, pontil mark **70.00**

8-1/2" h, orange, hand blown, Rainbow Glass Co, c1940-60 . . . . **65.00**

10-1/2" h, amberina, hand blown, pontil mark **85.00**

Dish, 8-3/4" w, 6" l, 3-1/2" h, smoke gray, crimped folded up sides, hand blown, pontil mark, Blenko **85.00**

Drink mixer, 8-1/4" h, blue, applied crystal open-end handle, hand blown, Pilgrim Glass Co., orig label **75.00**

Lamp, 18" h, 12" d dome shade, gold Aurene, spherical ball above metal base, attributed to Steuben. . . **4,025.00**

Muddler, amethyst, Blenko **8.00**

Finger bowl, cranberry color, **$65.**

Pitcher
- 4" h, blue, applied reeded handle 20.00
- 5-1/4" h, blue, applied clear handle, mold blown, Kanawha 30.00
- 5-1/4" h, green, applied green handle, mold blown, Kanawha 25.00
- 5-1/2" h, 5" d, amberina, applied glass handle, hand blown, pontil mark 65.00
- 6" h, dark green, dimpled, Blenko 45.00
- 10-1/2" h, amberina, red top shades to orange to amber to orange, slender body, wide flaring top, applied orange handle, hand blown, pontil scar 115.00
- 12-1/2" h, amberina, mold blown, Kanawha 55.00
- 13" h, lemon-lime, applied handle, hand blown, pontil mark, Pilgrim Glass Co. 115.00

Plate, green, U.S. Glass 5.00

Punch cup, clear, cobalt blue ring handle, Fry 45.00

Rose bowl, 5-1/4" h, 4-1/4" w, reddish-orange, pinched top, hand blown, pontil mark, Pilgrim Glass Co. 60.00

Tankard
- 7" h, bright yellow, applied crystal handle, Pilgrim Glass Co. . . . 65.00
- 7-1/2" h, peach crackle body, enamel and gold overlay, applied handle, polished pontil, Moser, c1920 . . . . 125.00
- 12" h, clear, applied clear handle 35.00

Tumbler, 5-1/4" h, clear body, Delft green handle, Fry 70.00

Vase
- 4-3/4" h, deep blue, two pulled up sides 15.00
- 5" h, flashed cranberry, hand blown 35.00
- 5" h, 3" d, two shades of orange, flared at top, hand blown, pontil scar, Blenko 35.00
- 7" h, amber, flared crimped top, straight body, bulbous foot, hand blown, pontil mark, Bischoff Glass Co. 45.00
- 7-1/4" h, 7-1/2" w, Jonquil, crimped, ftd, Blenko 125.00
- 7-3/4" h, dark orange-red, slender, flared top, mold blown, Kanawha 40.00
- 9" h, blue, Blenko 55.00
- 9-3/4" h, dark green, Blenko . . 50.00

Vase, double gourd shape, gold iridescent, polished rim, Bohemian, 10-1/2" h, **$210.** *Photo courtesy of David Rago Auctions.*

- 10" h, baluster, flared neck, clear, free blown 35.00
- 10-1/2" h, double gourd shape, gold irid, polished rim, Bohemian 210.00
- 10-1/2" h, 8-1/2" d, reddish-orange, crimped top, hand blown, pontil mark, Blenko 135.00
- 10-3/4" h, crystal, crackled on bottom half only, sgd "R. Strong 7/76," ground pontil 125.00

CRANBERRY GLASS

History: Cranberry glass is transparent and named for its color, achieved by adding powdered gold to a molten batch of amber glass and reheating at a low temperature to develop the cranberry or ruby color. The glass color first appeared in the last half of the 17th century, but was not made in American glass factories until the last half of the 19th century.

Cranberry glass was blown, mold blown, or pressed. Examples often are decorated with gold or enamel. Less-expensive cranberry glass, made by substituting copper for gold, can be identified by its bluish purple tint.

References: William Heacock and William Gamble, *Encyclopedia of Victorian Colored Pattern Glass: Book 9, Cranberry Opalescent from A to Z,* Antique Publications, 1987; Kenneth Wilson, *American Glass 1760-1930,* 2 vols., Hudson Hills Press and The Toledo Museum of Art, 1994.

Collectors' Club: Pilgrim Glass Cranberry Collector's Club, P.O. Box 395, Ceredo, WV 25307.

Additional Listings: See specific categories, such as Bride's Baskets, Cruets, Jack-in-the-Pulpit Vases, etc.

Reproduction Alert: Reproductions abound. These pieces are heavier, off-color, and lack the quality of older examples.

Barber bottle, Inverted Thumbprint pattern 270.00

Basket
- 5-1/2" h, 6" w, star-shaped top, ruffled edge, colorless thorn loop handle, c1890 . . . . 195.00
- 7" h, 5" w, ruffled edge, petticoat shape, colorless loop handle, c1890 . . . . 250.00
- 7-1/2" h, 6-3/4" w, boat-shaped basket, dark cranberry, allover gold dec, white florals, wide gold band, brass ftd vase with flower form handle 200.00
- 8" h, 5" w, deep color, ruffled edge, applied colorless handle, Victorian 90.00
- 8-1/2" h, 5" w, rose bowl form, Diamond Quilted pattern, ruffled edge, applied wishbone feet, V-shaped loop handle 150.00
- 9" h, 5" w, deep cranberry int., amber casing on ext., white and gold aventurine flecks, applied amber feet, amber U-shaped handle 90.00

Barber bottle, Hobnail pattern, cork stopper, silver top, 8-1/4" h, **$275.**

9" h, 5" w, very deep cranberry int., slight ribbed int., applied colorless wishbone rigaree around top, 12 applied feet, applied colorless twisted loop handle, Victorian, flake on one foot **100.00**

Biscuit jar, 4" h, 6-1/2" d, Inverted Thumbprint pattern, SP lid and rim **595.00**

Bottle

7-3/4" h, 4" d, flattened bulbous, frosted, gold church scene, small boats on back, gold around top **135.00**

8" h, 3" d, gold mid-band, white enameled trim, colorless faceted stopper. **145.00**

8-1/2" h, 3-1/4" d, Inverted Thumbprint pattern, white enameled dot flowers and bands, gold trim, colorless cut faceted stopper. **155.00**

9-3/4" h, 3-1/2" d, dainty white enameled flowers around middle, white enameled dots dec, colorless teardrop stopper **175.00**

Bowl

5-1/2" d, 6-1/2" d underplate, swirl pattern **65.00**

7-3/4" d, paneled, flower dec, brass standard, mirrored base. . . **120.00**

Brandy jug, 8" h, Inverted Thumbprint pattern, applied colorless handle, colorless hollow stopper, pontil . . **90.00**

Bride's bowl, 9" sq, 3-1/2" h, finely executed enameled apple blossom dec, fancy ornate SP orig holder marked "Middletown Silver Co.," Mt. Washington **950.00**

Butter dish, cov, round, Hobnail pattern **125.00**

Candlestick

10-1/2" h, applied yellow eel dec **120.00**

10-5/8" h, heavily encrusted gold and polychrome dec, pr. . . **190.00**

Celery vase, 10" h, Thumbprint pattern, enameled flowers and birds, ornate handles, ftd mount, orig silverplated Jas. Tufts Co. frame. **550.00**

Claret jug, 10-3/4" h, 4-5/8" d, French emb pewter hinged top, foot, and handle **320.00**

Cologne bottle

7" h, dainty blue, white, and yellow enameled flowers, green leaves, gold outlines and trim, orig colorless ball stopper. **195.00**

8-5/8" h, 2-3/8" d, gold scrolls, small gold flowers, matching sq cranberry bubble stopper . . **185.00**

Creamer, 5" h, 2-3/4" d, Optic pattern, fluted top, applied colorless handle **95.00**

Cruet, orig stopper

6-1/2" h, 2-3/4" d, applied colorless wafer foot, applied colorless twisted rope handle with flower prunt at base, colorless ribbed bubble stopper **135.00**

10-1/2" h, 3-7/8" d, acid cut herringbone double band around middle, applied colorless foot, applied colorless handle, colorless cut faceted stopper. **190.00**

13" h, 4" d, heavy gold roses dec, colorless cut faceted stopper **195.00**

Cup and saucer, gold bands, enameled purple and white violets, gold handle. **135.00**

Decanter

10" h, cut to colorless, flattened colorless oval, obverse medallion engraved "Mollies Pony 1869" centering scene with horse, cut star on reverse, conforming teardrop stopper, some internal bubbles **990.00**

10-1/2" h, 3-1/4" d, cut to colorless, matching mushroom bubble stopper **250.00**

11-1/2" h, 3-7/8" d, bulbous base, pinched-in sides, lacy gold enamel dec, dark red flowers, gold enameled centers, applied colorless handle, colorless cut faceted stopper. **250.00**

Compote, iridescent interior, Bohemian, 6-1/2" d, 3-1/2" h, **$225.** *Photo courtesy of David Rago Auctions.*

Epergne

14" h, 12" d, three cranberry vases with applied vaseline rigaree, deep cranberry base. **1,495.00**

19" h, 11" d, five pcs, large ruffled bowl, tall center lily, three jack-in-the-pulpit vases . . **1,150.00**

Fairy lamp, 4-1/2" h, applied colorless hand tooled petals, colorless insert marked "Clarke" **350.00**

Finger bowl, Inverted Thumbprint pattern, **$85.**

Finger bowl, scalloped, matching underplate. **145.00**

Jack-in-the-pulpit vase, 6" h, tulip form, orig Pilgrim Glass label . . . **35.00**

Mantel lusters, pr, orig prisms . **550.00**

Muffineer (sugar shaker)

Inverted Thumbprint pattern, nine panels **150.00**

Parian Swirl pattern **125.00**

Optic pattern, orig top **225.00**

Mug, 4" h, 2-3/4" d, Baby Inverted Thumbprint pattern, applied colorless handle and pedestal foot **65.00**

Music box, 12-1/4" h, 5-1/4" d decanter, emb ribs with etched leaves and stars, orig colorless cut bubble stopper, not working **310.00**

Night light, 6-1/4" h, 3-1/4" d, cranberry shade with white sanded scallops, grapes, and leaves, openwork brass top rim, gold-washed ormolu ftd frame **275.00**

Perfume bottle

3-1/2" h, ball form body, white enamel floral dec, orig clear ball stopper. **80.00**

7-1/4" d, 2-3/4" d, gold stars dec, star cut under base, colorless bubble stopper **150.00**

Pitcher

6-1/4" h, 4-3/8" d, Ripple pattern, bulbous, round mouth, applied colorless handle. **110.00**

Pitcher, applied handle, quadrafoil top, 8-1/4" h, **$195.**

6-1/2" h, 4-1/8" d, Ripple and Thumbprint pattern, bulbous, round moth, applied colorless handle **110.00**
7-1/2" h, 4-1/2" d, Optic pattern, bulbous, round mouth, applied colorless reeded handle . . . **145.00**
8-1/4" h, Inverted Thumbprint, crimped rim, applied colorless handle **160.00**
9-3/4" h, white and gilt enamel dec, polished pontil, wear to gilt . . **90.00**
10" h, 5" d, bulbous, ice bladder int., applied colorless handle. . . **220.00**
11-3/8" h, 9" w, bulbous shape, colorless loop handle, white and blue floral leaf dec, int. vertical ribs, c1895 .... **275.00**
Venetian pattern, large **120.00**

Rose bowl
3-3/4" h, 3-3/4" d, worn gold rim, six-crimp top **95.00**
4" h, optic ribs, scalloped turned in rim, colorless ruffled applied pedestal base **125.00**

Salt, master
Crystal rigaree around middle **150.00**
Enameled floral dec, ftd **200.00**

Sauce, Hobbs Hobnail pattern . . **45.00**
Smoke bell (for lamp), 6-1/2" d, swirled, ruffled edge.......... **600.00**
Spooner, Paneled Sprig pattern **125.00**
Sugar bowl, cov, 6-1/8" h, 4" d, applied wafer foot, colorless ribbed bubble finial **115.00**
Tankard, 11" h, 5-1/4" d, hinged silver plated top and collar, applied colorless handle.................... **285.00**
Tray, 13-1/4" l, 7-1/4" w, 1-3/4" h, two fan handles, blue and white enameled marsh scene with egret in center, attributed to Moser **2,500.00**
Tumble-up, Inverted Thumbprint pattern.................... **195.00**
Tumbler, Inverted Thumbprint pattern **65.00**
Urn, 11-1/2" h, two applied colorless handles, enameled flowers and leaves **400.00**

Vase
6-3/8" h, 4-3/8" d, frosted, white daisies, blue forget-me-nots, green leaves, price for pr....... **210.00**
7-1/2" h, emb ribs, applied colorless feet, three swirled applied colorless leaves around base **110.00**
8" h, vertical bands below diamond points, deep cut to colorless **315.00**
8" h, vertical bands of ribbed thumbprints cut to colorless, ground pontil **110.00**
8-7/8" h, bulbous, white enameled lilies of the valley dec, cylinder neck **115.00**

Water set, Frazier pattern, enameled flowers, pitcher, six matching tumblers **265.00**
Whiskey jug, 8-1/2" h, ribbed optic type pattern, applied colorless handle, colorless hollow stopper, pontil mark **180.00**

Wine decanter
8-1/2" h, 4-1/2" d, small gold stars dec, orig gold trim cranberry bubble stopper.......... **165.00**
10-3/4" h, 4-3/4" d, flattened bulbous shape, colorless wafer foot, applied colorless spun rope handle, orig bubble stopper **185.00**
12" h, opaque white cased over cranberry, enameled flowers and gilt scrollwork dec, pr **500.00**
13" h, 4" d, gold roses and foliage dec, applied colorless handle, colorless cut faceted stopper **200.00**
13-1/2"h, blown swirl, colorless applied ruffled top, three colorless applied feet, gilt and enamel surface dec of leaves and flowers, some paint wear **350.00**

Sugar shaker, tin top, 5", **$115.**

CROWN MILANO

History: Crown Milano is an American art glass produced by the Mt. Washington Glass Works, New Bedford, Massachusetts. The original patent was issued in 1886 to Frederick Shirley and Albert Steffin.

Usually, it is an opaque-white satin glass finished with light-beige or ivory-colored ground embellished with fancy florals, decorations, and elaborate and thick raised gold.

Through continuing research into the Mount Washington Glass Company, experts have now determined that shiny Crown Milano was originally named "Colonial Ware." Documentation of this includes the name used in an 1894 issue of the *Jewelers Circular and Horological Review*, which featured both Colonial Ware glass and Crown Milano.

When marked, pieces carry an entwined CM with crown in purple enamel on the base. Sometimes paper labels were used. The silver plated mounts often have "MW" impressed or a Pairpoint mark as both Mount Washington and Pairpoint supplied mountings.

References: John A. Shuman III, *The Collector's Encyclopedia of American Art Glass*, Collector Books, 1988, 1994 value update; Kenneth Wilson, *American Glass 1760-1930*, 2 vols., Hudson Hills Press and The Toledo Museum of Art, 1994.

Collectors Club: Mount Washington Art Glass Society, P.O. Box 24094, Fort Worth, TX 76124.-1094

Museum: New Bedford Glass Museum, New Bedford, MA.

Atomizer, 6-1/2" h, trumpet vine dec, swirled body................ **600.00**

Biscuit jar
5-1/2" h, squatty, round, opal ground, all-over hand painted rose blossoms, buds, leaves, and

thorny stems, gold outlines, SP rim, bail, and cover, imp "MW," purple "CM" and crown mark **400.00**

5-1/2" d, 4" h, muted shades of gold, sepia and brown single-petaled rose blossoms with jewel centers, buds, and leaves, raised gold branches, alternating melon and cream colored jagged swirls, turtle plodding across floral emb lid, bail handle, sgd "M.W.4416/a" **1,385.00**

6" h, painted Burmese ground, all-over bamboo design, green, gold and brown enamel, ornate silver hardware......... **1,150.00**

7" h, enameled floral dec, SP collar, lid, and bail handle, base sgd, lid marked "Pairpoint"....... **750.00**

7" d, 6" h, blown blank, hobnail dec, underwater scene, jeweled starfish and enameled sea creature, sea plants, period fancy SP hardware and cover, marked "MW" . **1,610.00**

7-1/2" d, 9" h, colorful painting of couple in Colonial garb covers entire front, reverse side is a small white reserve, outlined in raised gold, gold line-drawn florals, cream colored body, base is signed "3912/80", lid is signed, "M.W.4419/c" **975.00**

Bowl

4" h, cov, delicate multicolored flowers, applied gold scrolling, handles, finial, base marked "CM" under crown in blue **700.00**

6" h, cov, shiny finish, Colonial opalware, applied reeded prunt handles, multicolored blossoms and elaborate gold enameling, red wreath and crown mark and number "1013," some wear **800.00**

9" d, 3" h, tricorn, rolled edge, roses, asters, cornflowers, pansies and bachelor buttons, shaded yellow ground, gold trim, gold scrolls on ext., sgd "C. M. Monogram 74" **1,740.00**

10" d, 4-1/4" h, heavy walls, square and crimped top rim, coppery and gilt enamel oak leaf and acorn dec, ivory satin ground, marked "300," work gold rim **175.00**

Bride's basket

4" h, 8" d, multicolored roses, asters, and pansies, lusterless white ground, tricorn, colored and cut rim bowl, SP mounting, black crown mark, worn **500.00**

11-1/2" h, 11" d, six large pansies, purple and orange tracery medallions, pale yellow int., tricorn, tightly ruffled, orig tricorn ftd stand, sgd "Pairpoint" **2,950.00**

12" h, 9" w, triangular, gold edged fluted bowl, white ground, pink roses, yellow and purple pansies dec, gold dec, soft beige int. with gold scrolls, ornate SP Pairpoint stand **3,165.00**

Candlesticks, pr, 8-1/4" h, 3-3/4" d base, silver-plated base and socket, opal glass cylinder, deep maroon background, gold leaf and bow encircle central portrait of young woman in low-cut pink dress, sgd on metal "Pairpoint Mfg. 6139"....... **1,750.00**

Cracker jar, 8-1/2" h, 5-1/2" d, yellow and purple mums, pink and yellow roses, gold dec, stationary handle, Aldoph Frederick dec, c1895-1900 .... **985.00**

Creamer and sugar

4" h, reeded handle on creamer, two reeded handles on cov sugar, opal white glass dec with raised gilt and brown floral vines, red and white highlights, sepia foliate scrollwork, cream-colored ground, polished pontils, paper label inside sugar lid **1,725.00**

4-1/2" h creamer, 4-3/4" h cov sugar with two applied leaf handles, petticoat shape, blue cornflowers, purple asters, pink, and yellow roses, red wild roses, soft beige ground, heavy gold embellishments, faint hairline in sugar, sgd "Crown Milano" **1,250.00**

Melon ribbed bodies which shades from pale pink to natural white to pale green at base, blue cornflowers and green foliage, silverplated fittings, sgd "3905/201"........... **1,500.00**

Demitasse cup and saucer, raised golden vine laden with single-petaled blossoms, buds, and tiny leaves meander around satin white ext., raised gold borders, coral colored ring of dots centers in four blossoms, black rings in other three blossoms, sepia colored rococo scrolls entwine floral dec, pale pink tint, sgd with logo, 2" h cup, 5" d saucer.................. **1,750.00**

Ewer

7-1/2" d, 6-1/2" h, Colonial Ware, shiny white body, two reserves of colorful blossoms framed by rococo borders of raised gold scrolls, gold cross-hatching across cream colored shoulder, some loss to wash of color around rope handle, sgd "0100" **1,250.00**

8" h, 8" d, bulbous, gold lotus blossoms, green and gold pods outlined in raised gold, light green ground, aqua serpentine handle with gold scales, spout dec with aqua and scrolled leaves, c1894 .... **1,650.00**

10" h, beige, tan, rust, jeweled shadow flowers outlined in heavy gold, seven green jewels on each flower, rope handle, c1893 .... **1,375.00**

10" h, 8" w, pillow, handled, landscape dec, central front cartouche with idyllic English countryside, shepherd, sheep, and thatched roof house, plants and trees in bloom, heavily raised gold floral and scroll design around perimeter of design, soft green ground, numerous gold floral traceries of pansies, roses, and asters, gold scrolling on neck and handle, sgd and numbered **4,315.00**

11-1/2" h, yellow shaded body, all-over white enameled blossom clusters, connected by delicate raised gold leaves and vines, applied twisted handle, sgd **1,450.00**

12" h, opaque white ground, freeform pastel enamel clusters, raised gold swirled stripes **1,350.00**

12" h, white neck and body, background shadow dec of sepia colored scrolls and florals, spout with raised gold dec, abstract dec, twisted handle with brushed gold highlights, hundreds of individual dots in dark blue, light blue, rust, coral, pink, yellow, green, black and gold form stylized florals and geometric designs...... **1,750.00**

Fern vase, 9-1/2" h, elongated and flared neck bulbed over globular body, acid finished opal white glass, enamel dec with scrolled border on neck, gold ferns over ochre form silhouettes on body, polished pontil, minor wear to gilt **865.00**

Jar, cov

4" h, squatty, star molded, custard colored ground, apricot chrysanthemums and jeweled starfish, SP rim, bail handle, and floral cov, imp "M. W. 4417" **675.00**

5-1/4" h, melon ribbed bowl, enamel dec, applied gold bead dec, SP rim, bail and crab motif cov, one bead missing, worn SP **600.00**

5-1/2" h, deeply ribbed melon form, applied yellow-amber surface, gold enameled roses and thorny branches, silver plated rim, bail handle, crab dec cov, marked "MN4415," base stamped "CM" under crown in blue..... **1,400.00**

6-3/4" h, melon ribbed bowl, blue body, gold enhanced floral dec, SP rim and raised cov, unsgd.. **350.00**

10-1/2" h, molded floral ground, pink, green, and white blossoms and broad leaves, elaborate SP Rogers Bros. handled frame, some corrosion to stand **1,350.00**

Jardiniere, 6" h, 8" d, blue, yellow, and pink chrysanthemum blossoms, shiny pink ground, scrolling gilt borders, blue crown mark, numbered **400.00**

Lamp, banquet, 23" h, 9" d, Colonial Ware, shiny ground, base and globe-shaped shade dec with sprays of golden roes an blossoms, touches of gold accent molded-in dec of florals, swags, and geometric designs, opaque white chimney, brass burner sgd "Made in United States of America" . **2,950.00**

Pickle castor, 9" h, shaded pink to white ground, pink and white enameled flowers, allover raised hobnail pattern, period fancy SP Pairpoint frame **1,725.00**

Pin tray, 5-3/4" d, glossy, folded rim, pansy dec, red wreath mark with crown **275.00**

Plate, white finish, colorful spring flowers, center pink cabbage rose, five elaborate raised gold rococo embellishments, signed, 7" d, **$550.** *Photo courtesy of Clarence and Betty Maier.*

Pitcher, 12" h, hand painted, portrait of costumed couple in center, attributed to Frank Guba, scrolled gilt borders, applied rope twist handle, red crown and wreath mark **675.00**

Rose bowl

4-1/4" h, swirled gold enamel stylized sq floral, yellow shaded opal ground, unsgd **250.00**

4-1/2" h, 5" d, shaded Burmese yellow to soft brown ground, purple, pink, and yellow orchids, green and brown foliage, sgd and numbered in purple **500.00**

Rose jar, 8-1/2" h, raised bulbed rim, molded stylized borders, oval body with eight ribs, hand painted roses, gold dec, unsgd **500.00**

Salt shaker

2-1/2" h, hen, hand painted dec **350.00**

4" h, ribbed, dainty blue and white daisy blossoms, Burmese-colored background **185.00**

Sugar shaker

3" h, 4" d, melon-ribbed shape, chalk-white body, sprays of violet-colored Johnny-Jump-Up blossoms, silvery-bright metal collar and lid, embossed with butterfly, dragonfly, and blossoms **585.00**

3" h, 4" d, melon ribbed, tomato shape, white ground, tendrils with multicolored ivy leaves, two part metal collar and lid emb with butterfly, dragonfly, and blossoms **585.00**

Syrup pitcher

4" h, white body with six panels, each dec with sprays of pink single petaled summer roses, framed by gold tinted molded-in ribbed columns, dark patina on shaped silver plated spout and lid, numbered "744 230" on base **485.00**

6" h, 4" w, melon ribbed body, alternating pale pink with gold netting and brilliantly colored Dresden type floral dec, handle, sgd and numbered **2,875.00**

Sweetmeat jar, cov, 5" h, ivory ground, deeper colored ribs, worn enameled floral design, SP fittings and lid, sgd "M.W." **550.00**

Tumbler

3-3/4" h, shiny finish, gold bow and swag enameling, red wreath mark, pr **525.00**

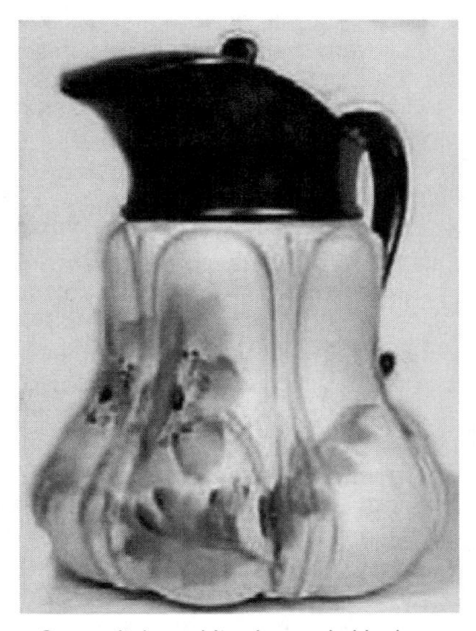

Syrup pitcher, white six-paneled body, sprays of pink single petaled summer roses, gold-tinted molded-in ribbed columns, dark patina on silver plated spout and lid, marked "744 230" on base, 4" h, **$485.** *Photo courtesy of Clarence and Betty Maier.*

Colonial Ware, shiny body, shades of raised gold, swags of finely detailed roses and daisies descend from free-flowing ribbon, numbered "1026" **585.00**

Vase

4" h, amber and umber organic swirls, beaded pinwheel dec, ribbed and swirled lusterless ground, black crown and CM mark **550.00**

4-1/2" h, bulbous, eight pulled-up ribs, soft beige ground, deep beige traceries, heavily raised gold enameled petit point dec of stylized iris, leaves, and scrolls **875.00**

4-1/2" h, white satin body with tint of lilac at neck, three fully opened chrysanthemum blossoms, two partially opened buds, raised gold borders, rich gold rim, raised DQ design, sgd............. **685.00**

4-1/2" h, 4-1/4" d, jeweled, gilt enameled apple blossoms, gold beaded dec, two applied handles, orig paper label on base, three beads missing........... **675.00**

4-1/2" h, 5" w, squatty bulbous form, painted gingko dec, green and brown leaves, shaded pale pink ground................. **550.00**

5" h, onion-shape, narrow neck with four turned-down folds, shadow dec, buff colored fern leaves, gold dec of four large fern leaves in two shades of gold, 24 molded-in swirls, white int. **885.00**

5" h, 6" d, bulbous, ribs, pulled edges, gingko dec, green and brown leaves, pink ground, Albertine **785.00**

5" h, 7" w, bulbous, peach and yellow mottled ground, gold wild rose dec, leaves, buds, and stems, glass jewels, two applied leaf handles **1,200.00**

5-1/2" h, squatty, pastel yellow body, gold outlined pink and lavender orchid blossoms, applied ribbed handles, sgd **990.00**

6" h, flared eight-lobed rim on ribbed sphere, peach colored ground, polychrome spring blossoms, overlaid with gold medallions, purple crown "CM" mark with "583" below **1,725.00**

6" h, onion shape, 24 molded swirls, narrow neck, four turned down folds, flower like mouth, four large fern leaves and shadow of buff colored fern leaves, white int., attached SP stand **400.00**

6" h, 5-3/4" d, butter yellow neck and mouth, four fold-down sides, 24 swirling molded-in ribs, cream-colored body, blue and white forget-me-nots, leaves, and foliage. **1,485.00**

6" h, 5-3/4" d, cream-colored body, 24 swirling molded-in ribs, white peony blossoms **1,250.00**

6" h, 6" d, springtime blossoms, glorious pastel hues, opposite side of flowering white dogwood, four raised gold circular embellishment, large circle with cherub riding mystical sea creature, one with a sun face surrounded by stylized dolphins, two smaller circles with geometric designs, Crown Milano logo and "583" **1,950.00**

6-1/4" h, deeply ruffled quatraform rim, swirled opal oval, blue medallions under gold outlined white peony blossom and buds, unsigned **1,035.00**

7" h, raised quatreform neck, two twisted handles over pinched globular vessel of glossy finished opal glass, gilt dec with sprays of flowers, polished pontil, red enamel crown and laurel wreath mark, wear to gold enamel **865.00**

8" h, mauve, creamy white, and peach-yellow peony blossoms, soft lemon ground, green and sepia foliage, gold dec around neck **765.00**

8-1/2" h, melon ribbed, cream ground, three long-stemmed thistles, each crowned with blossom of individual raised gold petals, pastel pink, aqua, and green leaves with off-white highlights, raised leaves and veins **1,450.00**

8-1/2" h, melon ribbed oval, bulbed molded border motif, hand painted pink rose blossoms, unsgd **1,200.00**

8-3/4" h, 6-1/2" w, ball shaped, 2-1/2" neck, allover gold fern dec, beige and white ground, gold and beige scrolls around neck **1,200.00**

9" h, Colonial Ware, sprays of colorful enamel blossoms, shadow foliate branches of single petaled roses and buds, neck with gold embellishments, sgd logo and "0615" **1,000.00**

9" h, white, pearlescent pink-white Lotus Blossoms, purple and green pads, trailing stems, background gray shadow dec **1,500.00**

Vase, egg-shaped body, cylindrical neck, flattened bulbous top, two applied handles, gold floral decoration, blue highlights, beige flower bud, star mark, 10" h, **$950.**

9-1/4" h, opaque white body, cup-shaped top, exquisite floral decoration, two applied handles, orig paper label **1,750.00**

9-1/2" d, h, encrusted gold, thorny rose branches laden with single-petaled blossoms, buds and leaves, orig paper label . . **1,450.00**

9-3/4" h, extended thick neck, bulbous base, pink tinted body, raised gold and blue enameled pansy dec, one sgd, matching pr **1,900.00**

10-1/2" h, creamy yellow ground, green, brown, and gilt enamel blossoms, leaves, and blackberries, unsgd **450.00**

10-1/2" h, petticoat shape, white body, pastel pansies, free-form gold accents **850.00**

10-1/2" d, shaded yellow lusterless ground, gilt enameled green and brown scrolling designs, winged dragons **2,550.00**

12" h, Colonial Ware, shiny finish, dainty pastel pink roses, festoons of leafy vines, two rows of applied rigaree, brushed gold on rigaree, rim, and base, sgd with Colonial Ware crown in wreath logo and "1041" **1,750.00**

12" h, cone shape, flared, fluted top, Albertine, gold dec, gilded prunts, marked, c1893 . . . . **770.00**

12-1/4" h, creamy lusterless ground, gilt enameled pink, green, and blue thistle dec, unsgd **1,500.00**

12-1/2" h, 5-1/2" w, soft beige ground, green and pink thistles, light green/blue leaves, gold trim **1,100.00**

13-3/4" h, double bulbed elongated shape, pink seed thistle blossoms, green, brown, and white leaf dec, unsgd **1,250.00**

14-1/2" h, Burmese colored ground, white, yellow, amber, and brown cymbidium orchids, unsgd **2,500.00**

18" h, Colonial Ware, shiny, scene of youthful couple dancing, lady in formal yellow and pink gown, elegant hat, pink bows on shoes, male partner with baby blue satin waistcoat, fancy pantaloons, tricorner hat, walking stick, ruby colored garter, elaborate rococo scrollwork of raised gold, some loss to gold embellishments on applied wafer base, crown in wreath mark and "1029" . **1,750.00**

Vase, cov, 5" h, 8-1/2" d, Colonial Ware, shiny finish, bowl form, applied reeded prunt handles, conforming cov, multicolored blossoms, elaborate gold enameling, red wreath, crown mark, and "1013" on base, some gold wear **825.00**

CRUETS

History: Cruets are small glass bottles used on the table and hold condiments such as oil, vinegar, and wine. The pinnacle of cruet use occurred during the Victorian era when a myriad of glass manufacturers made cruets in a wide assortment of patterns, colors, and sizes. All cruets had stoppers; most had handles. Cruets also have pouring lips or spouts. Perfume bottles are often the same size, but do not have a pouring lip.

Pattern glass manufacturers included cruets as part of their patterns. Later, Depression-era manufacturers included cruets in many of their patterns, Some cruets were sold in sets, with a different bottle each for oil and vinegar, often with a matching tray to hold the bottles.

References: Elaine Ezell and George Newhouse, *Cruets, Cruets, Cruets*, Vol. I, Antique Publications, 1991; William Heacock, *Encyclopedia of Victorian Colored Pattern Glass: Book 6, Oil Cruets from A to Z*, Antique Publications, 1981.

Amber, four indents on body, sapphire blue handle, matching hollow stopper, ground pontil, 7-3/4" h, **$165.** *Photo courtesy of Clarence and Betty Maier.*

Amber

Baby Inverted Thumbprint, tall narrow form, orig stopper, 8" h **130.00**

Blown, ftd ovoid body, short neck, tricorn rim, blue daisies and gold leaves, applied handle, amber ball stopper, 8" h **125.00**

Amberina

4-1/2" h, Diamond Quilted, amber applied squared handle, orig amber cut faceted stopper, polished pontil **475.00**

5-1/2" h, Inverted Thumbprint pattern, trefoil spout, attributed to Mt. Washington Glass **385.00**

Blue

5" h, Diamond Quilted, enamel floral dec, os **110.00**

7" h, sq, multicolored floral dec, amber applied rope handle, orig amber faceted stopper . . . **220.00**

Bluerina, 7-1/4" h, deep royal blue neck fades to clear at shoulder, Optic Inverted Thumbprint design in body, applied clear glass handle, teardrop shaped airtrap stopper, in-the-making thin elongated bubble in neck. . **500.00**

Bohemian, amber cut to clear, floral arrangement intaglio carved on ruby flashed ground of three oval panels with carved frames of floral swags, five cut-to-clear panels at neck, three embellished with gold scrolls, all edged in brilliant gold, 16 decorative panels edged in gold, base and stopper both sgd "4". **750.00**

Burmese, 6-1/2" h, three striking chrysanthemum blossoms, two white and one yellow, coral colored detail stripes mushroom stopper, signed "88" in enamel. **2,950.00**

Cambridge glass, Caprice pattern, blue, 5 oz, os. **350.00**

Custard glass

Chrysanthemum pattern, 7" h **250.00**

Wild Bouquet pattern, fired-on dec **500.00**

Cut glass

Alhambra pattern, Meriden, os, 9" h **550.00**

Chrysanthemum pattern, Hawkes, 5-1/2" h, os **150.00**

Greek Key engraved border, pedestal, ns, 10" h **50.00**

Vintage pattern, three pour spout, 7" h, sgd "Tuthill" **200.00**

Fostoria, June Night pattern, oil and vinegar type bottle, crystal **300.00**

Frosted blue, 12" h, 3" d, enameled large pink and white flower, green leaves, applied blue handle, matching blue frosted bubble stopper, gold trim **165.00**

Green, 9-1/4" h, 3-1/8" d, white enameled dec, applied green handle, green bubble stopper **165.00**

Opalescent, Hobail pattern, cranberry, applied clear handle, replaced clear stopper, **$485.**

Greentown

Cactus pattern, chocolate, ns **125.00**

Leaf Bracket pattern, chocolate, os **265.00**

Imperial glass, Candlewick pattern, 400/2946, oil and vinegar, pr 400/164 and 400/166 beaded foot cruets, kidney-shaped 400/29 tray **90.00**

Lavender, blown, ftd spherical body, slender cylindrical neck, gold flowers and bows, applied colorless handle and foot, colorless facet cut stopper, 7-1/4" h **225.00**

Opalescent glass

Daisy Fern pattern, blue, Parian mold, orig stopper. **225.00**

Hobnail pattern, cranberry, Hobbs, Brockunier & Co., Wheeling, WV, 7-1/2" h **485.00**

Stripes pattern, pale blue ground, orig hollow stopper, solid amber handle, polished pontil mark **485.00**

Swirl pattern, green, applied clear handle, os, 6-1/2" h **170.00**

Swirl pattern, white, applied sapphire blue handle, sapphire blue stopper **285.00**

Tokyo pattern, green, no stopper, 4-1/2" h **70.00**

Wild Bouquet pattern, blue, orig stopper **495.00**

Opaque, white opaque, applied white handle, orig white stopper, 6" h, attributed to New England Glass Works **850.00**

Pattern glass

Amazon, orig bar-in-hand stopper, 8-1/2" h 185.00
Beveled Star, green, os 225.00
Big Button, ruby stained, os . 250.00
Croesus, large, green, gold trim, os 395.00
Cut Log, os 60.00
Daisy and Button with Crossbars, os 5.00
Dakota, etched, ns 55.00
Delaware, cranberry, gold trim, os 295.00
Diamond, light amber opalescent, tall clear stopper, 8-1/2" h. . . 50.00
Esther, green, gold trim, os. . 465.00
Fandago, ns 85.00
Fluted Scrolls, blue dec, os . 265.00
Inverted Honeycomb, blue, amber applied handle, orig blue stopper, 8-1/4" h 80.00
Inverted Thumbprint, blue, enamel floral dec, reeded handle, OS, 5-3/4" h 110.00
Louise, os 70.00
Mardi Gras, ns 35.00
Millard, amber stain, os 345.00
Pressed Diamond, amber, paneled stopper, 6-1/2" h 90.00
Riverside's Ransom, vaseline, os 225.00
Tiny Optic, green, dec, os . . 150.00

Peachblow

Petticoat form, three lip top, acid finish, New England, 6-3/4" h, 4" d base 1,950.00
Petticoat shape, orig cut amber stopper, Wheeling, 6-1/2" h 1,750.00

Blown, amethyst, applied handle, green stopper, 9-1/4" h, **$115.**

Sapphire blue

7-1/4" h, Hobnail pattern, faceted stopper, applied blue handle, damage to three hobs. 385.00
7-1/2" h, hp bridal white leafed branches, orig stopper with teardrop shaped airtrap . . . 185.00
7-1/2" h, 3-1/4" d, enameled pink, yellow, and blue flowers, green leaves, applied clear handle and foot, cut clear stopper. 165.00

Satin

5" h, Diamond Quilted, MOP, pink, thorn handle and stopper . . 595.00
8-1/4" h, Diamond Quilted, white shaded to gold, clear frosted handle, orig frosted clear knobby stopper 595.00

Spatter, 7-1/2" h, deep mottled burgundy, ftd, flattened pillow form, cased opal int., clear applied reeded handle, os. 190.00

Threaded glass, vaseline body and threads, 6-1/2" h 115.00

Tiffin glass, English Hobnail, white milk glass, 3-1/2" h, os. 20.00

Vaseline, Hobnail pattern, os, 7-1/2" h 400.00

Cup Plates

History: Many early cups were handleless and came with deep saucers. The hot liquid was poured into the saucer and sipped from it. This necessitated another plate for the cup, hence the "cup plate."

The first cup plates made of pottery were of the Staffordshire variety. From the mid-1830s to 1840s, glass cup plates were favored. The Boston and Sandwich Glass Company was one of the main manufacturers of the lacy glass type.

It is extremely difficult to find glass cup plates in outstanding (mint) condition. Collectors expect some marks of usage, such as slight rim roughness, minor chipping (best if under the rim), and in rarer patterns, a portion of a scallop missing. Some allowances are made for the techniques used to create this little plates. As such, overfills or underfills of the molds may detract slightly from the value. Condition can detract from the value, but color may drastically increase it. Most cup plates were made of clear glass, but many deeply colored green, blue, and purple cup plates are known, as well as some opaque white and fiery opalescent cup plates.

References: Ruth Webb Lee and James H. Rose, *American Glass Cup Plates*, published by author, 1948, Charles E. Tuttle Co. reprint, 1985; Kenneth Wilson, *American Glass 1760-1930*, 2 vols., Hudson Hills Press and The Toledo Museum of Art, 1994.

Notes: The numbers used are from the Lee-Rose book in which all plates are illustrated. Prices are based on plates in average condition.

LR 1, clear, flint, polished pontil . 35.00

LR 2, 3-5/8" d, amber, blown, 18 ribs, Midwest origin. 1,200.00

LR 4-A, 4-1/8" d, clear, swirled red and white latticino, gold flecks in rim, attributed to Nicholas Lutz, Sandwich 185.00

LR 10, 3-5/8" d, clear, plain rim, New England origin. 75.00

LR 11, 2-13/16", clear, New England origin, small shallow rim chips and roughage. 85.00

LR 13, 3-3/4" d, deep blue, A-type mold, plain rim, New England origin 75.00

LR 21, 3-7/16" d, clear, 15 scallops with shelves rim, stars between shoulder fans, strawberry diamond center, New England origin. 115.00

LR 22-A, 3-7/16" d, clear, 15 scallops with shelves, circles between shoulder fans, six pointed star center, New England or Sandwich origin . . . 100.00

LR 22-B, 3-7/16" d, clear pontil, New England origin, slight roughage . 95.00

LR 26, 3-7/17" d, clear, 15 even scallops, 11 lance points center, attributed to New England Glass Co. or Sandwich. 165.00

LR 28, 3-1/4" d, clear, 17 even scallops, 12 lance points, attributed to New England Glass Co. or Sandwich origin 35.00

LR 36, 3-1/4" d, opal opaque, 17 even scallops, seven stalk sheaves with round points, rosettes in spandrels between eight central leaves, New England origin. 475.00

LR 37, 3-1/4" d, opalescent, 17 even scallops, seven stalk sheaves with round points, rosettes in spandrels between eight central leaves, attributed to New England Glass Co. or Sandwich 475.00

LR 45, 3-9/16" d, pale opalescent, 19 even scallops, rope top and bottom, wide cap ring, attributed to New England Glass Co. or Sandwich, mold overfill, slag deposit near center 120.00

LR 46, 3-1/2" d, lavender, 15 even scallops, geometric shoulder design, strawberry diamond pattern, Eastern origin 125.00

LR 51, 3-3/4" d, clear, pontil, 15 scallops with points between, stippled center background, New England origin, moderate rim roughage, few shallow flakes 185.00

LR 52, 3-3/4" d, opalescent, 15 scallops with points between, stippled, Eastern origin....................**200.00**

LR 58, 3-3/8" d, cloudy, unlisted color, plain rope, band of radial lines on inner and outer edge of underside of shoulder, bull's eyes on plain band, waffle center, Eastern origin....**285.00**

LR 70, 3-7/16" d, colorless, plain rope, Midwest origin **125.00**

LR 75-A, 3-13/16" d, clear, rope rim top and bottom, strawberry diamond between border sheaves, attributed to New England Glass Co., one tiny rim flake **90.00**

LR 79, 3-3/8" d, pink tint, rope top and bottom, rope table ring with tiny feet, New England origin **60.00**

LR 80, 3-3//4" d, opalescent, rope top and bottom, plain table ring, New England origin **250.00**

LR 81, 3-3/4" d, fiery red opalescent, rope top and bottom, rope table ring with tiny feet, New England origin **360.00**

LR 82, 3-5/8" d, clear, plain rim, five-pointed star center, attributed to New England Glass Co........**125.00**

LR 82, 3-5/8" d, opalescent, plain rim, five-pointed star center, attributed to New England Glass Co., minor rim roughness..................**375.00**

LR 88, 3-11/16" d, deep opalescent opaque, rope top, shoulder baskets, pinwheel with stars center, attributed to New England Glass Co. or Sandwich **250.00**

LR 95, 3-5/8" d, opalescent opaque, 10 sided, rope top and bottom, New England origin **180.00**

LR 100, 3-1/4" d, clear, plain rim, stippled background, attributed to Philadelphia area, normal mold roughness..................**110.00**

LR 121, 3-16" d, clear, lacy, portholes shoulder pattern, stippled, Midwest origin, slight rim roughage **115.00**

LR 135, 3-7/16" d, clear, 24 bull's eyes, points between, peacock feather pattern, Midwest origin.........**85.00**

LR 150,-B, 2-15/16" d, clear, plain rim, rope on bottom, Midwest origin ..**60.00**

LR 163, 3-1/4" d, light green, 24 scallops, radial lines beneath, irregular stippling, Midwest origin **75.00**

LR 179, 3-7/16" d, lavender, 10 scallops, rope top and bottom, attributed to Philadelphia, PA, area **145.00**

Hearts and star motif, colorless, Pairpoint, **$15.**

LR 197-E, 3-1/8" d, clear, Midwest origin **75.00**

LR 200, 96 sawtooth scallops, Midwest origin **45.00**

LR 215-C, 3-5/8" d, clear, Scotch Plaid, 60 even scallops, Curling, Ft. Pitt Glass Works..................... **35.00**

LR 242-A, 3-1/2" d, black amethyst, lacy, 60 even scallops, Eastern origin, mold overfill and underfill **675.00**

LR 247, 3-7-16" d, emerald green, lacy, 12-sided, 60 scallops, attributed to New England Glass Co. or Sandwich, small chip on one scallop.......... **750.00**

LR 257, 3-3/8" d, clear, attributed to New England Glass Co. or Sandwich **40.00**

LR 259, 3-7/16" d, clear, 12 large stippled scallops, points between, Eastern origin **200.00**

LR 271, clear, attributed to New England Glass Co. or Sandwich. **65.00**

LR 272, clear, 43 scallops, Eastern origin **70.00**

LR 276, 3-7/16" d, blue, lacy, 55 even scallops, arcs of central quadrants outlined in heavy dots, dots in centers of central diamond-shaped figures, coarse rope table ring, Boston and Sandwich Glass Co. **395.00**

LR 284, 3-3/16" d, clear, 24 large bull's eyes divided by points, attributed to Philadelphia, PA, area, minute rim roughness **260.00**

LR 323, 3-1/2" d, opalescent, attributed to New England Glass Co. or Sandwich **80.00**

LR 332-B, 2-1/2" d, clear, attributed to New England Glass Co. or Sandwich **55.00**

LR 343-B, 3-7/16" d, plain, dotted below, fire polished, attributed to Philadelphia, PA, area **35.00**

LR 391, 3-7/16" d, clear, Eastern origin **20.00**

LR 395, 3-3/4" d, clear, 44 points, unknown origin...............**20.00**

LR 396, 3-1/4" d, clear, Sandwich origin **15.00**

LR 399, 3-5/16" d, clear, Eastern origin, normal mold roughness.......**110.00**

LR 412, 3-3/16" d, clear, 10 sided, star center, Sandwich origin **120.00**

LR 416, 3-1/16" d, clear, unknown origin, minor roughness........**25.00**

LR 433, 4-1/8" d, clear, two chips, mold roughness **80.00**

LR 456, 3-3/8" d, clear, 41 even scallops, Sandwich origin **40.00**

LR 458-A, 3-1/2" d, clear, unknown origin **20.00**

LR 459-M, 3-3/4" d, jade opaque, 43 even scallops, 12 hearts on shoulder, Sandwich origin **475.00**

LR 500, 3-1/4" d, clear, 48 even scallops, unknown origin **65.00**

LR 503, 3-1/4" d, clear, 56 even scallops, Eastern, possibly Sandwich, origin **20.00**

LR 522, 3-5/16" d, amber, flint, 66 even scallops, Sandwich origin **375.00**

LR 538, 3-1/4" d, clear, 66 even scallops, Sandwich origin **20.00**

LR 561-A, octagonal, colorless, gray striations, Washington, tilted head, Midwest orig.............. **4,500.00**

LR 565-A, 3-9/16" d, clear, 25 flat scallops, points between, Sandwich origin **35.00**

LR 575, 3-1/2" d, clear, 25 large scallops with two smaller ones between, Sandwich origin **75.00**

Glass, historical

LR 568, 3-7/16" d, clear, Harrison, 67 even scallops, swags and black lozenges on shoulder, attributed to Sandwich, mold roughness **85.00**

LR 576, 3-9/16" d, medium blue, Victoria, 25 large scallops, two small scallops between, Sandwich origin **100.00**

LR 586-B, 3-7/16" d, clear, Ringgold, Palo Alto, stippled ground, small letters, Philadelphia area, 1847-48 ....**650.00**

LR 605-A, 3-1/2" d, clear, octagonal, seven scallops between corners, ship, stippled and plain rope rigging . **100.00**

LR 615-A, 3-7/8" d, clear, Constitution, 25 scallops, points between, unknown origin **650.00**

LR 653, 3" d, clear, plain rim, acorns on shoulder, central eagle in laurel wreath, Midwest origin **175.00**
LR 670, 3-7/16" d, 36 bull's eyes, Midwest or Pittsburgh origin **75.00**
LR 676, 3-11/16" d, clear, 60 even scallops, "Fort Pitt" in banner held by central eagle, Curling's Ft Pitt Glass works **95.00**
LR 677-A, 3-3/16" d, clear, 44 even scallops, Midwest origin **45.00**
LR 695, 3" d, clear, Midwestern origin, normal mold roughness. **150.00**
LR 836, 4-3/4" d, Geo. Peabody, Heart & Crown. **90.00**

Custard Glass

History: Custard glass was developed in England in the early 1880s. Harry Northwood made the first American custard glass at his Indiana, Pennsylvania, factory in 1898.

From 1898 until 1915, many manufacturers produced custard glass patterns, e.g., Dugan Glass, Fenton, A. H. Heisey Glass Co., Jefferson Glass, Northwood, Tarentum Glass, and U.S. Glass. Cambridge and McKee continued the production of custard glass into the Depression.

The ivory or creamy yellow custard color is achieved by adding uranium salts to the molten hot glass. The chemical content makes the glass glow when held under a black light. The more uranium, the more luminous the color. Northwood's custard glass has the smallest amount of uranium, creating an ivory color; Heisey used more, creating a deep yellow color.

Custard glass was made in patterned tableware pieces. One of the most desirable forms is a table set, consisting of a covered butter, creamer, covered sugar, and spooner, all pieces must match as far as coloration and decoration. It also was made as souvenir items and novelty pieces. Souvenir pieces often include a place name or hand-painted decorations, e.g., flowers. Patterns of custard glass often were highlighted in gold, enameled colors, and stains.

Reproduction Alert: L. G. Wright Glass Co. has reproduced pieces in the Argonaut Shell and Grape & Cable patterns. It also introduced new patterns, such as Floral and Grape and Vintage Band. Mosser reproduced toothpicks in Argonaut Shell, Chrysanthemum Sprig, and Inverted Fan & Feather. Look for signs of wear on vintage pieces of custard glass, and loss to any decoration. Also pay close attention to the details of the piece, remembering that the period piece of custard glass will have

References: Gary E. Baker et al., *Wheeling Glass 1829-1939*, Oglebay Institute, 1994, distributed by Antique Publications; William Heacock, *Encyclopedia of Victorian Colored Pattern Glass, Book IV: Custard Glass from A to Z*, Peacock Publications, 1980; William Heacock, James Measell and Berry Wiggins, *Harry Northwood: The Early Years 1881-1900*, Antique Publications, 1990; —, *Harry Northwood, The Wheeling Years, 1901-1925,* Antique Publications, 1991.

Collectors' Club: Custard Glass Collectors Society, 591 S. W. Duxbury Ave., Port Saint Lucie, FL 34983.

Banana boat
- Grape & Gothic Arches, Northwood **200.00**
- Grape and Thumbprint, Northwood **375.00**

Berry bowl, master
- Argonaut Shell, Northwood . . **150.00**
- Beaded Circle, Northwood . . **185.00**
- Cherry and Scale, Fenton . . . **120.00**
- Intaglio, ftd. **125.00**
- Louis XV, Northwood, gilt dec, 11" l, 5" w **125.00**
- Ring Band, Heisey. **125.00**
- Victoria, Tarentum **175.00**

Bowl
- Delaware, U.S. Glass. **65.00**
- Wild Bouquet, slight loss to gold edge **235.00**

Butter dish, cov
- Argonaut Shell, Northwood . . **250.00**
- Beaded Circle, Northwood . . **275.00**
- Cherry and Scale, Fenton . . . **240.00**
- Chrysanthemum Sprig, Northwood, blue **750.00**
- Fan, Dugan **225.00**
- Geneva, Northwood, red and green dec **165.00**
- Intaglio, gold and green enamel dec **250.00**
- Inverted Fan and Feather, Northwood. **250.00**
- Jefferson Optic, Jefferson . . . **200.00**
- Maple Leaf, Northwood **200.00**
- Wild Bouquet, Northwood . . . **275.00**
- Winged Scroll, Heisey, dec . . **185.00**

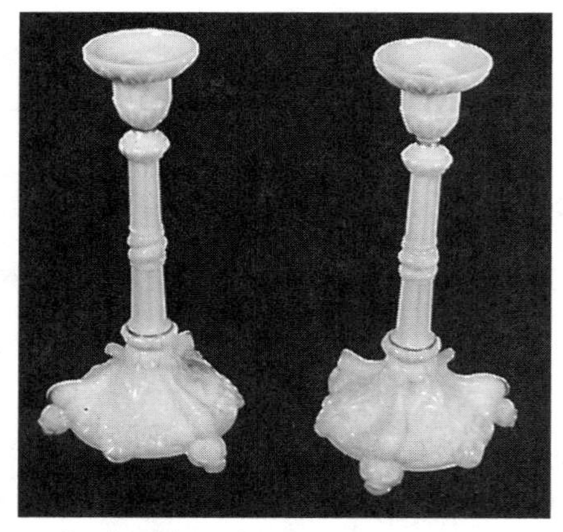

Candlesticks, pair, architectural-style columns, spreading foot with scrolls, **$200.**

Celery
- Ivorina Verde, Heisey **250.00**
- Victoria, Tarentum, gold trim. **190.00**

Cigarette box, Ivorina Verde, Heisey **250.00**

Cologne bottle, orig stopper
- Ivorina Verde, Heisey **250.00**
- Northwood Grape, Northwood, nutmeg stain **425.00**

Compote, Intaglio, Northwood . **385.00**

Condiment set
- Chrysanthemum Sprig, Northwood, four pcs **2,000.00**
- Ring Band, Heisey, five pcs . **800.00**

Cracker jar, cov, Grape & Cable, Northwood, two handles **700.00**

Creamer, Jackson, worn gold rim, **$90.**

Creamer
- Argonaut Shell, Northwood . **150.00**
- Beaded Circle, Northwood, slight gold loss. **350.00**
- Cherry and Scale, Fenton. . . **145.00**
- Delaware, U.S. Glass, rose dec **85.00**
- Diamond with Peg, Jefferson . **90.00**
- Fan, Dugan. **100.00**
- Fluted Scrolls, Heisey. **85.00**
- Intaglio, gold and green enamel dec, slight loss of gold at rim . . . **225.00**
- Inverted Fan and Feather, Northwood **150.00**
- Jackson, Northwood. **100.00**
- Jefferson Optic, Jefferson . . . **95.00**
- Louis XV, Northwood **85.00**
- Maple Leaf, Northwood **125.00**
- Northwood Grape, Northwood, nutmeg stain **115.00**
- Ribbed Drape, Jefferson . . . **120.00**
- Ring and Beads, Heisey. **50.00**
- Vermont, U.S. Glass Co. **100.00**
- Victoria, Tarentum. **125.00**
- Wild Bouquet, Northwood . . **145.00**
- Winged Scroll, Heisey, dec . . **110.00**

Cruet

Argonaut Shell, Northwood, gold trim 885.00
Beaded Circle, Northwood, slight gold loss 1,250.00
Georgia Gem, Tarentum, green, orig stopper 300.00
Louis XV, Northwood, clear faceted stopper 185.00
Maple Leaf, Northwood 950.00
Ribbed Drape, Jefferson 400.00
Ring Band, Heisey 400.00
Wild Bouquet, Northwood . . . 525.00

Custard cup

Empress, Riverside, green, gold trim 45.00
Winged Scroll, Heisey 65.00

Goblet

Beaded Swag, Heisey 75.00
Grape & Cable, Northwood . . . 70.00

Humidor, Winged Scroll, Heisey 225.00

Jelly compote, green, late period, **$75.**

Jelly compote

Argonaut Shell, Northwood . . 110.00
Beaded Circle, Northwood . . 365.00
Chrysanthemum Sprig, Northwood 200.00
Geneva, Northwood. 100.00
Intaglio, Northwood, gold trim 150.00
Maple Leaf, Northwood, green and gilt dec, 4-1/2" d, 4-3/8" h, wear to gilt 140.00
Ribbed Drape, Jefferson 190.00
Ring Band, Heisey. 200.00

Lamp, Heart with Thumbprint, Tarentum, kerosene 400.00

Mug

Dandelion, Northwood, nutmeg stain 150.00
Diamond with Peg, Jefferson . 60.00
Punty Band, Heisey 70.00
Ring Band, Heisey 60.00

Nappy, Winged Scroll, Heisey . . 65.00

Pickle dish

Beaded Swag, Heisey 265.00
Vermont, U.S. Glass 60.00

Pin dish, Delaware, U.S. Glass, dec 80.00

Pitcher

Cherry and Scale, Fenton. . . 350.00
Chrysanthemum Sprig, Northwood 375.00
Intaglio, gold and green enamel dec 425.00
Inverted Fan and Feather, Northwood 400.00
Maple Leaf, Northwood 385.00
Ring Band, Heisey, floral dec 450.00
Vermont, U.S. Glass 250.00
Winged Scroll, Heisey, dec. . 290.00

Plate

Grape & Cable, Northwood, nutmeg stain 60.00
Prayer Rug, Imperial. 45.00
Three Fruits, Northwood 35.00

Punch bowl, matching base, Grape & Cable, Northwood 900.00

Punch cup

Grape & Cable, Northwood . . 50.00
Inverted Fan and Feather, Northwood 200.00
Ring Band, Heisey 60.00

Ring tray, Delaware, green dec, U.S. Glass, 3-1/2" x 6-1/2" 70.00

Salt and pepper shakers, pr

Argonaut Shell, Northwood . . 350.00
Beaded Circle, Northwood . . 275.00
Carnelian, Northwood 450.00
Fluted Scrolls with Flower Band, Northwood. 150.00
Geneva, Northwood 185.00
Georgia Gem, Tarentum, orig top 100.00
Heart, Northwood 175.00
Intaglio, gold and green enamel dec 175.00
Louis XV, Northwood 350.00
Maple Leaf, Northwood. 475.00
Trailing Vine, Couderspot Glass 165.00

Sauce/berry bowl, individual size

Argonaut Shell, Northwood, dec 90.00
Beaded Circle, Northwood . . . 65.00
Chrysanthemum Sprig, Northwood 85.00
Delaware, US Glass, rose stain 65.00
Fan, Dugan 70.00
Geneva, Northwood, oval 45.00
Georgia Gem, Tarentum 40.00
Intaglio, gold and green enamel dec, wear to gold at rim 100.00
Inverted Fan and Feather, Northwood. 55.00
Louis XV, Northwood, gold trim 45.00
Maple Leaf, Northwood. 80.00
Peacock and Urn, Northwood. 45.00
Ribbed Drape, Jefferson. 45.00
Victoria, Tarentum 50.00

Left: Chrysanthemums Sprig, covered sugar, ***$200****; right: Louis XV water pitcher,* **$400.**
Photo courtesy of Joy Luke Fine Art Brokers and Auctioneers.

Spooner

Beaded Circle, Northwood, slight gold loss **350.00**
Chrysanthemum Sprig, Northwood **125.00**
Everglades, Northwood **145.00**
Fan, Dugan **85.00**
Intaglio, gold and green enamel dec, some loss to gold trim **225.00**
Louis XV, Northwood **75.00**
Ribbed Drape, Jefferson **65.00**
Trailing Vine, Couderspot Glass, blue **70.00**
Victoria, Tarentum **65.00**
Wild Bouquet, Northwood **70.00**
Winged Scroll, Heisey **100.00**

Sugar, cov

Argonaut Shell, Northwood . . **150.00**
Beaded Circle, Northwood, 6-3/4" h, slight gold loss **485.00**
Cherry and Scale, Fenton . . . **145.00**
Chrysanthemum Sprig, Northwood, blue, gold dec **395.00**
Delaware, U.S. Glass, rose dec **85.00**
Diamond with Peg, Jefferson **110.00**
Everglades, Northwood **125.00**
Fan, Dugan **100.00**
Fluted Scrolls, Heisey **85.00**
Intaglio, gold and green enamel dec, some loss to gold trim at rim **225.00**
Jackson, Northwood **100.00**
Northwood Grape, Northwood, nutmeg stain **115.00**
Ribbed Drape, Jefferson . . . **120.00**
Ring and Beads, Heisey **50.00**
Vermont, U.S. Glass Co. **100.00**
Winged Scroll, Heisey **175.00**

Syrup pitcher, orig top

Geneva, Northwood **250.00**
Ring Band, Heisey **315.00**

Table set, covered butter, creamer, cov sugar, and spooner

Carnelian **850.00**
Geneva, Northwood **550.00**
Georgia Gem, Tarentum, gold trim **300.00**
Louis XV, Northwood, gold trim **500.00**
Ring Band, Heisey **550.00**

Toothpick holder

Argonaut Shell, Northwood, dec **465.00**
Chrysanthemum Sprig, Northwood, blue, gold trim **315.00**
Diamond with Peg, Jefferson . **85.00**
Ivorina Verde, Heisey **85.00**
Maple Leaf, Northwood **475.00**
Ribbed Drape, Jefferson . . . **150.00**

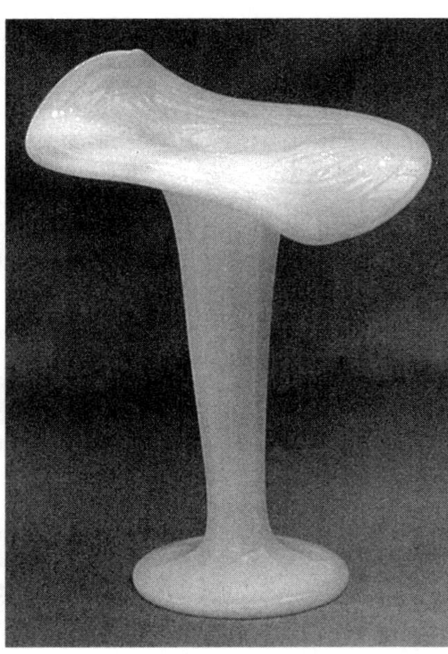
Jack-in-the-pulpit vase, bamboo-type decoration on flared top, **$75.**

Vermont, U.S. Glass, green dec **145.00**

Tumbler

Argonaut Shell, Northwood . . . **90.00**
Chrysanthemum Sprig, blue, gold trim **185.00**
Delaware, U.S. Glass, green dec **65.00**
Fan, Dugan **60.00**
Fluted Scrolls, Heisey **45.00**
Grape & Cable, Northwood, nutmeg stain **50.00**
Grape & Gothic Arches, Northwood **65.00**
Maple Leaf, Northwood, 3" d, 4" h, wear to dec **35.00**
Prayer Rug, Imperial **80.00**
Punty Band, Heisey, souvenir . **40.00**
Ribbed Drape, Jefferson, floral dec **100.00**
Winged Scroll, Heisey **70.00**

Vase

Grape Arbor, Northwood, nutmeg stain, 5" d, 3-7/8" h **85.00**
Prayer Rug, Imperial **65.00**
Victorian, baluster, crown-style top, gold dec, intertwining foliage around center, 15" h, 4-1/2" h, matched pr **2,500.00**

Whiskey, Diamond with Peg, Jefferson souvenir **45.00**

Wine

Beaded Swag, Heisey **70.00**
Diamond with Peg, Jefferson . . **50.00**
Punty Band, Heisey **50.00**
Tiny Thumbprint **50.00**

Cut Glass, American

History: Glass is cut by grinding decorations into the glass by means of abrasive-carrying metal or stone wheels. A very ancient craft, it was revived in 1600 by Bohemians and spread through Europe to Great Britain and America.

American cut glass came of age at the Centennial Exposition in 1876 and the World Colombian Exposition in 1893. The American public recognized American cut glass to be exceptional in quality and workmanship. America's most significant output of this high-quality glass occurred from 1880 to 1917, a period now known as the American Brilliant Period.

The Early Period was from 1765 to 1829, and glass from this period is rare. Early Period designs reflect the influence of English and Irish cut glass. Motifs include prisms, flutes, single star, diamonds, and a simple form of the strawberry diamond. The Middle Period from 1830 to 1870 produced simple, typically American designs in reaction to European patterns. Flute cuttings, engraved fine lines, etching, engraving historical scenes, and cut colored glass were predominate. Brilliant Period patterns are much more complex and usually cut deeper into the blank. Motifs include prisms, notched prisms, hobstars, curved miter splits, fans, and pinwheels, as well as stars and blocks and many design components of the earlier periods.

All cut glass blanks were hand blown until 1902. The H. C. Fry Glass Company of Rochester, Pennsylvania, produced the first pressed blanks in 1902.

About 1890, some companies began adding an acid-etched "signature" to their glass. This signature may be the actual company name, its logo, or a chosen symbol. Signatures are often rather pale and may be difficult to find. Today, signed pieces command a premium over unsigned pieces since the signature clearly establishes the origin. However, signatures should be carefully verified for authenticity since objects with forged signatures have been in existence for some time. One way to check is to run a finger tip or fingernail lightly over the signature area. As a general rule, a genuine signature cannot be felt; a forged signature has a raised surface.

Many companies never used the acid-etched signature on their glass and may have affixed paper labels to the items originally. Dorflinger Glass and the Meriden Glass Co. made cut glass of the highest quality, yet never used an acid-etched signature. Furthermore, cut glass made before the 1890s was not signed. Many of these wood-polished items, cut on

blown blanks, were of excellent quality and often won awards at exhibitions.

Consequently, if collectors restrict themselves only to signed pieces, many beautiful pieces of the highest quality glass and workmanship may be missed.

References: Bill and Louis Boggess, *Collecting American Brilliant Cut Glass 1876-1916*, Schiffer Publishing, 1992; —, *Identifying American Brilliant Cut Glass*, 3rd ed., Schiffer Publishing, 1996; —, *Reflections on American Brilliant Cut Glass*, Schiffer Publishing, 1995; City of Corning, New York, Centennial, *Corning, N. Y., 1891, Illustrated*, Corning-Painted Post Historical Society, 1990; Jo Evers, *Evers' Standard Cut Glass Value Guide*, Collector Books, 1975, 2000 value update; Kyle *Husfloen*, Antique Trader's American & European Decorative and Art Glass Price Guide, 2nd ed., Krause Publications, 2000; Bob Page and Dale Fredericksen, *A Collection of American Crystal*, Page-Fredericksen Publishing, 1995; —, *Seneca Glass Company 1891-1983*, Page-Fredericksen Publishing, 1995; J. Michael Pearson, *Encyclopedia of American Cut & Engraved Glass*, Vols. I to III, published by author, 1975; Albert C. Revi, *American Cut & Engraved Glass*, Schiffer Publishing, 2000; Estelle F. Sinclaire & Jane Shadel Spillman, *The Complete Cut & Engraved Glass of Corning*, 2nd ed., Syracuse University Press, 1997; Jane Shadel Spillman, *American Cut Glass, T. G. Hawkes and His Competitors*, Antique Collectors' Club, 1999; Martha Louise Swan, *American Cut and Engraved Glass*, Wallace-Homestead, 1986, 1994 value update; Kenneth Wilson, *American Glass 1760-1930*, 2 vols., Hudson Hills Press and The Toledo Museum of Art, 1994.

Collectors' Club: American Cut Glass Assoc., P.O. Box 482, Ramona, CA 92065.

Museums: Chrysler Museum, Norfolk, VA; Corning Museum of Glass, Corning, NY; High Museum of Art, Atlanta, GA; Huntington Galleries, Huntington, WV; Lightner Museum, St. Augustine, FL; Toledo Museum of Art, Toledo, OH.

Note: A common abbreviation associated with Cut Glass is ABP—American Brilliant Period

Ambrosia bowl, 12" d, 10-1/4" h, panel and cut fruit design **150.00**

Ashtray, 4" x 3", billiard table shape, engraved Kingfisher, sgd "Hawkes" **100.00**

Atomizer

4" h, 2-1/2" sq, Harvard pattern, gold washed atomizer, ABP **145.00**

6-1/2" h, all-over cutting, marked "DeVilbiss," ABP **145.00**

8" h, 2-1/2" h sq, Harvard pattern, gold washed atomizer, ABP **125.00**

Banana bowl, 11" d, 6-1/2" d, Harvard pattern, hobstar bottom, ABP... **210.00**

Basket

5-1/2" h, 6" d, brilliant and gravic style cutting, Wild Rose pattern, applied crystal handle, sgd "Tuthill," ABP **1,125.00**

6" h, 6" d, step cut base with large hobstar, band of four hobstars with diamond point, fan and cane cutting, triple notched handle, ABP **950.00**

6" h, 7" d, four cut hobstars, strawberry, diamond, and fan cutting, triple notched square cut handle, brilliant blank, ABP **350.00**

6" h, 8" d, low form, eight-sided, allover brilliant cut design of hobstars and numerous brilliant cuttings, applied twisted rope handle, ABP **225.00**

6-1/2" h, 8" d, low, floral and leaf design, applied crystal twisted rope handle, ABP........ **150.00**

6-1/2" h, 5" d, pattern of two large pinwheels, star cut base, notched handle, sgd "Frye," ABP .. **160.00**

7" h x 7" d, two large Florentine stars, hobstar, crosshatch, rope twist handle, attributed to Meriden **350.00**

7-1/2" h, 8-1/2" d, allover heavy brilliant pattern, and of Harvard with hobstars, viscera cutting, applied crystal twisted rope handle, low form, ABP **325.00**

7-1/2" h, 8-1/2" d, four large hobstars, two fans applied crystal rope twisted handle, ABP.. **350.00**

7-1/2" h, 8-1/2" d, hobstars and Harvard pattern cutting, low bowl, twisted crystal handle, ABP **200.00**

8" h, 7" d, Cactus pattern, Pairpoint **275.00**

8" h, 7" d, hobstars, fans, tiny buttons, cut scalloped rim, three applied feet, cut notched applied handle **300.00**

8" h, 8-1/2" d, Angelica pattern, applied loop crystal rope handle, deep cut pattern, sgd "Fyre" **550.00**

8" h, 9" d, six cut flowers and leaves, bands of cane, notch and cut etch, twisted rope handle, ABP.. **125.00**

8-1/2" h, 6-1/2" w, square-shaped, three large cut hobstars with panels of floral cut leaf design, double notched handle, ABP **500.00**

9" h, 10-1/2" d, low flaring basket, bands of 12 hobstars around side with fan cutting and panels of cross hatching, cut with huge hobstar in base, flat arched handle with notched edges and leaf cutting in center, clearly sgd "Hoare" on int. **3,500.00**

9-1/2" h, 11-1/2" d, five large hobstars, fancy emb floral silver handle and rim, ABP...... **225.00**

10-1/2" h, 10-3/4" d, brilliant and heavy glass blank, four hobstars with fan and strawberry point cutting, double notched handle, ABP.................. **425.00**

12-1/2" h, 8" d, allover scrolls and leaf design, quadruple notched handle resembles snake with tongue coming out, sgd "Hawkes Gravic" **900.00**

13" h, 9" d, notched cut step pedestal, open flaring shaped basket, band of hobstars, brilliant cutting, applied crystal rope twisted handle, large hobstar cut base, ABP............ **1,850.00**

14" h, 9" w, engraved thistles and leaves, triple notched handle **200.00**

14-1/2" h, 10" d, cut cosmos and Harvard type band, double notched handle, ABP **175.00**

14-1/2" h, 10" d, cut plums, leaf, and floral design, double notched handle, ABP **750.00**

16" h, 10" d, ruffled shaped form, dahlia-like flower cut with leaves, elaborate swirls, cut and notched applied loop handle, base sgd "Hawkes Gravic Glass".. **1,800.00**

17" h, 11-1/2" d, numerous cut hobstars, step cutting, heavy serrated edge, large star cut base, triple notched handle, ABP **2,900.00**

17-1/2" h, 12" w, floral and leaf design, large double notch handle, ABP.................. **500.00**

18" h, 10" d, Harvard design, pattern of four cut carnations and leaves, double notched handle, ABP **850.00**

18" h, 12" d, alternating hobstars and pinwheels, double notched handle, extremely heavy and brilliant blank, ABP................ **1,200.00**

18" h, 12" d, floral and brilliant pattern, poppy-like design, bands of triple diamond cut pattern, ABP **2,900.00**

21" h, 13-3/4" h, heavy blank, hobstars and pinwheels, double notched handle, ABP ... **1,500.00**

21" h, 16" d, floral and leaf design, double notched handle, American Brilliant and Floral Period .. **600.00**

Beaker, 8-1/2" h, 6-1/2" w, crystal blank with gravic cutting, finely engraved all over with wild rose buds, blooms, and leaves **100.00**

Bell

4-1/2" h, Monarch pattern, J. Hoare **225.00**

4-1/2" h, starred top, beaded flutes on handle, large feathered band with vesicas of hobstars and crosshatching. **225.00**

4-1/2" h, three large hobstars with pillar of crosshatching, fan in between, notched handle . **150.00**

4-3/4" h, Delft pattern, J. Hoare **175.00**

5-1/2" h, strawberry diamond bands, crosshatching in fan, handle cut to pattern **325.00**

5-3/4" h, hobstars, fans, strawberry diamond, ABP **275.00**

6-3/4" h, sharply cut strawberry diamond and fans, pattern also cut on stem end knob **550.00**

7" h, Colonial pattern, Dorflinger **600.00**

8" h, hobstars, fans, crosshatching, cut handle, cut by Thomas Hazelbauer for Hawkes . . . **850.00**

Bonbon

7-1/2" l, 6" w, loop handle, Hobstar and Gothic Arch dec, c1900 **75.00**

8" d, 2" h, Broadway pattern, Huntly, minor flakes **135.00**

9" l, Arcadia pattern, scoop shape, by Sterling **175.00**

Bone dish, 7" l, 5" w, Russian pattern, crescent shape, set of four **360.00**

Bowl, hobstar, strawberry, diamond, and other cuttings, notched scalloped rim, signed Hawkes, **$300.**

Bowl

7" d, low, Pontiac pattern, sgd "Clark" **60.00**

7-3/4" d, 3-1/2" h, China Aster pattern, highly cut pattern, sgd "Hawkes Gravic" **450.00**

8" d, Checker Board pattern . **250.00**

8" d, clusters of hobstars and cross hatched diamonds, ABP **90.00**

8" d, feathered buzz saws, nail head filled diamonds, ABP, minor flakes **90.00**

8" d, Heart pattern **250.00**

8" d, hobstars, arches, and cane, ABP, chips **50.00**

8" d, hobstars, fans, and pointed diamonds, sgd "Hawkes," ABP, minor chips **100.00**

8" d, large feathered buzz saws and hobstar medallions, ABP. . . **100.00**

8" d, low, circle motifs of hobstar and cane **150.00**

8" d, low, "Y" in center, three large hobstars **80.00**

8" d, Napoleon pattern, sgd "Hawkes". **550.00**

8" d, sunbursts and feathered arches, ABP **90.00**

8" sq, four large hobstars in corners, double-mitre vesicas with cane and Russian motifs. **115.00**

8" d, 2" h, eight lobes, hobstars and triangular panels cut on base, cross hatching and small star cutting **90.00**

8" d, 3-1/2" h, slanted sides cut in pattern of eight hobstars, hobstar base, vertical panels of notches, ABP **50.00**

8" d, 3-3/4" h, large hobstar with band of eight hobstars, ABP, large chip on rim **110.00**

8-3/4" d, low, cranberry cut to clear, Venetian pattern **2,100.00**

9" d, deep cut, medallions, large pointed ovals, arches, and base, ABP **110.00**

9" d, demonstration type, cutting process shown through four divided sections, sgd "J. Hoare" **2,500.00**

9" d, divided, Garland pattern, hobstars, feathered fan, and crosshatching, sterling rim, Gorham **250.00**

9" d, low, large feathered hobstars, hobstar, cane, and fan motif **500.00**

9" d, Manitou pattern, clear uncut tusk surrounded by brilliant overall cutting, Hoare **400.00**

9" d, six large deep cut hobstars and Gothic arches, ABP, minor flakes **250.00**

9" w, sq, #98 pattern, sgd "Sinclaire" **850.00**

9" d, 4" h, hobstar, fan. **125.00**

9" d, 4-1/4" deep, Russian pattern, ABP **275.00**

9" d, 5-1/2" h, hobstar, checkerboard, ABP **135.00**

9-1/4" d, 5" h, golden amber blank attributed to Union Glass Co, Somerville, MA, upper bowl cut in cane pattern above faceted edge, eight scallop rim, star-cut base, unsigned **3,450.00**

9-1/2" d, Bermuda pattern, blown out and crimped, Bergen. **325.00**

9-1/2" d, 2" h, low, engraved fish swimming in swirling water, sgd "Sinclaire, Fish #1" **400.00**

10" d, deep cut buttons, stars, and fans, ABP **220.00**

10" d, Lotus pattern, Eggingston **275.00**

10" d at top, 5" h, 10" d underplate, daisy and button cutting, hobstars, and other devices, ABP, chips **115.00**

10" d, 4" h, rolled rim, Harvard pattern, Mt. Washington. . . **350.00**

11" d, 5" h, engraving of glass basket with large bouquet of flowers within scroll, large pattern of diamonds, Hawkes-type **150.00**

12" d, Holland pattern, rolled rim, sgd "Hawkes" **700.00**

12" d, 4-1/2" h, rolled down edge, cut and engraved flowers, leaves, and center thistle, notched serrated edge. **275.00**

Box, cov

5" d, 2-3/4" h, cut paneled base, cover cut with large eight-pointed star with hobstar center surrounded by fans, C. F. Monroe **275.00**

6-1/2" d, hinged, hobstars, cross hatching, fan, Hawkes, ABP **400.00**

6-1/2" d, 4-1/4" h, Bishop's hat shape, large center hobstar, cross hatching and fans on lid, silver plated fittings **850.00**

Bread tray

11-1/2" x 8", Blazed Star **90.00**

12" x 7-1/2", Wedgemere pattern, Libbey, tooth chip. **250.00**

13-3/4" x 6-1/4", hobstars and cane, rim flake **250.00**

Bud vase, 3" h, green cut to clear, split miters and punties, floral engraving, silver rim, pattern "Stone Engraving #2" by Dorflinger **900.00**

Butter dish, covered, late period floral cutting, pressed leaves, cut cane pattern motif, **$200.**

Butter dish, cov
Hobstar, ABP **250.00**
Russian and florals, 7" d **385.00**

Butter pat
Cypress, Laurel **35.00**
Flat stars and crosshatching, 2-1/2" d, price for set of four **150.00**
Hobstar, elongated thumb hold, ABP, set of four **200.00**
Ray center, split vesica and star border, sgd "Unger Bros," 2-1/2" d, price for pr. **200.00**

Cake stand
Alhambra pattern, tear drop stem, pattern cut base, Meriden, 9-1/2" x 7-1/2" **1,100.00**
Vintage pattern, scalloped rim, sgd "Tuthill," 8" d, 3-1/2" h **800.00**

Candelabra
15" h, Prism pattern, five sterling holders, Meriden **1,250.00**
16" h, Clarke cricket lights, hollow stems with diamond cuts, brass fittings, sgd with Clarkes patent, price for pr. **1,000.00**

Candlesticks, pr
8" h, hobstars, hobnail, and diamonds, hollow teardrop stems, rayed bases **975.00**
9-1/2" h, hobstars, teardrop stem, hobstar base **250.00**
10" h, faceted cut knobs, large teardrop stems, ray base . . **425.00**
12" h, Adelaide pattern, amber, Pairpoint **250.00**

Candy basket
3-3/4" h, engraved florals, sterling rim and handle, Hawkes . . . **175.00**
4" h, egg shaped, two large pinwheels, hobstar, crosshatch and fan motif, twist handle **150.00**
4" d, 6" h, Beaver pattern, Fry, hobstars, whirling stars, cross hatching, cut notched rim and handle, ABP **225.00**

Candy dish, 7-3/4" l, oval, deeply cut Elfin pattern, Hoare **90.00**

Canoe
2" l, Harvard pattern, ABP. . . . **75.00**
10" l, ends in shape of "Woodbark & String" boat ends, crosscut diamond, Hawkes **1,200.00**
11-1/4" l, Harvard pattern sides, hobstar base, ABP **185.00**
13-1/2" l, 4-1/2" w, floral and leaves **85.00**

Caviar dish, cov
6" x 8-1/2", stars, hobstars, crosshatching, blind miters **1,150.00**
8" h, hobstar, strawberry diamond, and fan **650.00**

Celery boat, 11-1/2" w, 4-1/2" d, 2" h, elliptical, Hobstar and Fan dec, c1895-1905 . . . . **175.00**

Celery tray
10" l, 4-1/2" w, hobstar center, buzzstars, ABP. **85.00**
11" l, nailhead filled diamonds and sunbursts, ABP. **90.00**
11" x 6", Pattern #70450, Marshall Field catalog, Boggess, pg 156, #568 . . . . **140.00**
12" l, Bakers Gothic pattern, folded, sgd "Libbey" **85.00**

Celery vase
7-3/4" h, blown, scalloped rim, bowl cut with panels, strawberry diamonds, and fans, knop stem, star cut foot, Pittsburgh . . . **275.00**
8-1/4" h, waisted with band of alternating cross hatched diamonds and ovals, foliate band at rim, Bakewell, Pittsburgh, c1825 . . . . **375.00**
10" h, notched prisms with band of hobstars, faceted knob, skirt base, attributed to J. Hoare **675.00**

Center bowl
9-1/2" d, 4-1/2" h, Kohinoor & St. Louis motif, sgd "Hawkes". **250.00**
14-3/4" d, 3-1/2" h, broad flat rim, topaz yellow, large polished pontil, Sinclair, Corning, NY, c1925 . . . . **275.00**

Centerpiece, 10-3/4" d, wheel cut and etched, molded, fruiting foliage, chips **490.00**

Chalice
10" h, hobstar, vesica, hobnail, crosshatch, prism, and fan motif, faceted cut knob, hobstar base **750.00**
14" h, hobstar and fan motif, one fan left out for monogram, tear drop stem **650.00**

Chamberstick
2" x 4", star of crosshatching and hobstars with notched border, notched handle, sgd "Hawkes" **800.00**
2-1/2" x 4-1/2", base cut in notched prisms, four ball feet, swirled cut handle, sterling silver holder **750.00**

Champagne
Double teardrop stems, strawberry diamonds and fans, set of six **360.00**
Flared bowls, delicate stems, hobstar chain, set of nine . . **450.00**
Kalana Lily, pattern, Dorflinger **75.00**
Monarch pattern, saucer style, set of 12 . . . . **1,200.00**
Rayed Button Russian pattern, Russian bases, tumbler type, set of six, ABP. **500.00**
Stone engraved rock crystal, Dorflinger, c1890. . . . . **85.00**

Champagne bucket, 7" h, 7" d, sgd "Hoare," ABP **400.00**

Champagne pitcher
10" h, hobstars and cane, double thumbprint handle. **210.00**
11" h, Prism pattern, triple notch handle, monogram sterling silver top. **425.00**
12-1/2" h, Cane pattern, other cuttings, sterling silver rim, ABP **400.00**
12-3/4" h, large 36 point hobstars, cane, prism, strawberry diamond, star, and fan motif, pattern cut handle **1,300.00**
13-1/4" h, all-over cut hobstars, cane bars, stars, and fan, 24-point hobstar base, triple notch handle, fluted spout **600.00**

Cheese and cracker
9" d, Aberdeen pattern, Jewel **850.00**
10" d, center spire, Dorlinger's #18 . . . . **260.00**

Cheese dish, cov
6" h, 7" d, dome, matching underplate, allover copper wheel engraving of farmhouse, trees, cows, lambs, and deer . . **3,700.00**
6" h, 9" d, plate, cobalt blue cut to clear, Bull's Eye and Panel, large miter splints on bottom of plate, ABP **250.00**
8" h, 10-1/2" d plate, swirling pattern serving plate, matching high dome

cov, faceted knob top, ABP, flat edge chip, minor wear **550.00**

Cider pitcher

Hobstar, cross-cut diamond, jewels and fan, zipper cut and tear drop handle **325.00**

Hobstars, zippers, fine diamonds, honeycomb cut handle, 7" h, ABP **175.00**

Pinwheel and chain of hobstar cut, triple notch handle **220.00**

Split vesica motifs, hobstar, star, and tan, triple notch handle ... **150.00**

Cigarette set, 4-1/4" x 3-1/2" cov box, two ashtrays, Millicent pattern, Hawkes, sgd **145.00**

Cigar holder, 3-1/2" l, notched miters and stem in swirl miter........ **350.00**

Claret decanter

9-1/2" h, whiskey jug form, shoulder step-cut, loop handle lapidary cut, Lancet Hobstar dec, discoloration on int. base, c1890-95 .... **165.00**

10" h, Buzz and Hobstars dec, cut spherical stopper, notch-cut handle, c1905-15........ **110.00**

Cocktail glass, 4-1/4" h, Greek Key, three engraved flowers and leaves, Pairpoint **70.00**

Cocktail shaker

10-1/2" h, 4-1/2" w, steeple case with rider, horse, and fox, band of heavy-cut diamonds, notched thumbprint on base, glass sgd "Hawkes," cover and rim marked "Sterling" **450.00**

12-1/2" h, 5-1/2" w, mallard duck in flight over marsh, fancy sterling silver rim and cover, both glass and sterling rim sgd "Hawkes" . **210.00**

Cologne bottle

4" d, 6" h, sterling silver cap with fitted secondary glass stopper, c1895-1900 .... **490.00**

5-1/4" h, alternating bull's eye and cross-cut squares, faceted cup stopper, sgd "Libbey" **325.00**

6" h, Hob and Lace pattern, green cased to clear, pattern cut stopper, Dorflinger **625.00**

6-1/4" h, sq, red cut to clear, Octagon Diamond pattern, horizontal stepped shoulder, matching starred stopper, ABP, chips at inner stopper edge **575.00**

7-1/2" h, Holland pattern, faceted cut stopper............... **275.00**

7-1/2" h, 2-3/4" d, Parisian pattern, sq shape, Dorflinger, ABP, pr **700.00**

8-3/4" l, lay-down, diamond of hobnail with clusters of punties **110.00**

Compote

6" h, flared rim, deep bowl with hobstars and pointed triangles, similar cut base, minor flakes, ABP **95.00**

6" h, hobstar and arches, flared pedestal, ABP **150.00**

6" d, 8" h, Tuthill, wild rose pattern, large teardrop stem, cut designs all over, sgd **250.00**

7" d, 5-7/8" h, colorless, shallow round bowl, floral and foliate cut dec, ball connector, stepped round silver base with engraved "LL O'D" initials, engraved "Hawkes/Sterling/ 49 PWTS" on base, price for pr **500.00**

7-1/2" d, 8" h, hobstar, cane, strawberry diamond motif, scalloped rim, 32-point hobstar scalloped foot base....... **400.00**

8" d, 5-5/8" h, bowl cut with floral sprays offset by cross cup lappets joined by beaded garlands, Hawkes sterling trumpet foot **230.00**

9" h, Hawkes, blank #1224 .. **200.00**

9" h, Pairpoint, intaglio cut fruit **445.00**

9" h, deep cut buzz saws and pointed arches below, thumbprint stem, ABP **110.00**

9" h, deep cut sunburst, arches and buttons, zippered stem, starcut petal base, ABP **150.00**

9" h, sunburst and fan cuttings, zipper stem, star cut base, minor flakes, ABP **190.00**

9" d, 6" h, Hobstars, fans, buttons, miters, octagonal notched standard, ABP........... **150.00**

9-1/4" d, 7" h, Pittsburgh, blown, cut panels, strawberry diamonds and fans, foliage band at rim, finely scalloped lip, knob stem, star cut foot, minor wear and scratches **385.00**

9-1/2" h, deep star and arch cutting, star cut base, ABP **180.00**

Condiment dish, 11" d, 6-1/2" h, notched center handle, tripartite condiment servers **2,100.00**

Console set

12" d #1074 bowl, pr 3-1/2" h #12928 candleholders, Elfin Green, engraved Como pattern, Sinclaire **350.00**

12" d ftd bowl with wide flat rim, pr 9-1/8" h baluster form candlesticks, cross-hatched diamond and flute cutting, ABP............ **750.00**

15" d bowl, 14" h candlesticks, bright floral and webbed motif on bowl, matching candlesticks with horizontal stepped cutting on upper shafts, trefoil T. G. Hawkes mark on each base, "1925" engraved at center of rayed base **3,125.00**

Cookie tray, 7" x 8-1/2", hobstar, Harvard, and silver diamond, sidebands of hobstar and crosshatching, fully cut....... **275.00**

Cordial

3-3/4" h, feathered star with curved miters, hobstar and fan, apple core stem with double teardrop, star base................. **375.00**

6" h, Uncatena, Pairpoint, straight stem, price for pr **175.00**

6-1/2" h, engraved floral and ribbon, elongated punties **40.00**

Cracker jar, cov, 7" d, floral cut, silver plate and bail handle, Pairpoint **275.00**

Creamer and sugar

3" h, hobstar, ABP.......... **50.00**

6" d, 4" h, large center hobstar with triangular panels of cross hatching, handles with large notches and end in three-leaf clover at base, unsigned brilliant heavy blank **350.00**

6-1/2" h, hobstar and arches, stepped hexagonal pedestal, ABP **415.00**

8-1/2" d, hobstars and sunburst, plantation size, ABP...... **385.00**

Zenda, sgd "Libbey" **90.00**

Cruet, orig stopper

6" h, Chrysanthemum patter, tri-pour spout, cut handle and stopper, sgd "Hawkes," ABP.......... **350.00**

6" h, hobstars, crosshatching and double miter cuts, triple pour spout **150.00**

7" h, buzz saws, ABP **70.00**

9-1/2" h, Alhambra pattern, honeycomb handle, tall pyramidal shape, ABP **675.00**

9-1/2" h, sunburst, arches, and horizontal cut ovals, St. Louis handle, ABP............ **250.00**

Cup and saucer, Star pattern, triple notched handle, Dorlinger **300.00**

Decanter, orig stopper

6-1/2" h, blown, colorless, cut panels, fans, and diamond point roundels, applied foot and two rings, Pittsburgh, small chips **220.00**

7-1/4" h, blown, colorless, cut flutes, diamond point, strawberry diamonds and panels, three applied rings, Pittsburgh, small flakes, lip ground. **110.00**

7-3/8" h, blown, colorless, cut panels, strawberry diamonds and fans, three applied rings, Pittsburgh, pinpoint flakes, mismatched stopper **55.00**

8" h, blown, colorless, cut panels, strawberry diamonds and fans, applied foot, three applied rings, Pittsburgh, slight stain in bottom, very small chips **250.00**

8-1/2" h, blown, colorless, cut panels and fans, three applied rings, Pittsburgh, small flakes **140.00**

11-1/2" h, stars, arches, fans, cut neck, star cut mushroom stopper **95.00**

12-3/4" h, hobstar and fan pattern, large notched handle, sgd "Hoare," firing check at handle **75.00**

13" h, cranberry cut to clear, bulbous body, fan and diamond cutting, notched panel neck, applied cut handle, faceted stopper, star-cut base, ABP **3,450.00**

13" h, paneled neck above sunburst, fine diamond and pineapple cuttings, ABP, minor flake at bottom of stopper **100.00**

13-3/4" h, Buzz dec, period cut glass snake stopper, c1905-15. . . **175.00**

14" d, eight panels, hollow pointed stopper, sgd "Hawkes" **220.00**

15" h, Mercedes pattern, lapidary cut ring, pattern stopper, Clarke **950.00**

Dish

5" d, heart shape, handle, ABP **45.00**

5" d, hobstar, pineapple, palm leaf, ABP **45.00**

8" d, scalloped edge, allover hobstar medallions and hobs, ABP . **175.00**

Dresser box, cov, mirror lid, ABP

4" h, 8" w, heavy brilliant blank, panel side cuttings, star cut bottom, lid cut with center hobstar surrounded by chain of hobstars with notched fan cuttings, orig hinged beveled mirror, marked "C. F. M. Co. Sterling" trim, fully sgd at hinge, slight dent at hinge. **750.00**

7" h, 7" w, Harvard pattern variation, three-ftd, silver plated fittings, orig beveled mirror on swivel hinge under lid, cut by Bergen Glass Co, couple of minute flakes . . . **750.00**

Epergne

11" h, one piece, bowl cut in intaglio thistle, lily cut in honeycomb and cross hatch, rolled rim **850.00**

14", four lilies, copper wheel engraved floral and fern, John Illig **900.00**

14-1/2" x 11", engraving #8, heavy blank, pedestal bowl, two piece, sgd "Sinclaire" **650.00**

Fern dish

3-3/4" h, 8" w, round, silver-plate rim, C. F. Monroe, minor roughness to cut pattern, normal wear on base, no liner **200.00**

5" h, 9-1/2" d, brass rim, C. F. Monroe **400.00**

Finger bowl, 4-1/2" d, engraving #4 pattern, sgd "Sinclaire" **250.00**

Flask, 11" l, lay-down, strawberry diamond, clear sides, sterling top, attributed to Dorflinger **200.00**

Flower center

4-1/4" h, 5-1/2" d, hobstars with strawberry diamond points and fans, 16-point rayed base, blue and notch cut neck **315.00**

4-1/2" h, Bengal pattern, sgd "Sinclaire". **700.00**

5" h, 6" d, hobstars, flashed fans, hobstar chain and base, ABP **325.00**

5-1/2" h, Kings pattern, wafer base, sgd "Hawkes". **900.00**

6-1/2" h, 8" d, Queens pattern, sgd "Hawkes" **1,100.00**

6-1/2" h, 10" d, Grecian pattern, sgd "Hawkes" **4,900.00**

7-1/2" h, paneled zipper and pointed stem above bulbous bowl, star cut sunburst arches and medallions **200.00**

7-1/2" h, zippered neck, bulbous bowl with sunburst, arrows, and four pointed ovals, ABP **110.00**

7-3/4" h, 12" d, etched and wheel cut motif, honeycomb flared neck, some wear **500.00**

8" h, 12" d, large hobstars, strawberry diamond, crosscut bar motif, sgd "J. Hoare" **800.00**

Ginger jar, cov, 5" h, Russian pattern **325.00**

Goblet, strawberry diamond and fans, teardrop stem, **$65.**

Goblet

Buzzstar, pineapple, 7" h, marked "B & B," ABP **40.00**

Clear Button Russian pattern, facet cut teardrop stem, ABP. . . . **140.00**

Intaglio vintage cut, 8-1/2" h, sgd "Sinclaire" **80.00**

Rayed Button Russian, 6" h, teardrop stems, sgd "Hawkes," set of nine **1,200.00**

Strawberry diamond and fans, double teardrop stems, wood polished, set of 12. . . . . **800.00**

Strawberry diamond, pinwheel, and fan, notched stem, seven-pc set **350.00**

Grain cart, 11-1/2" x 4" x 4", Harvard pattern, very rare **2,000.00**

Gravy boat

6" l, blowout panels, scalloped standard, stepcut neck and spout **550.00**

8" l, matching underplate, hobstar and fan, stepcut lip **450.00**

Hair receiver

4-1/4" d, deep cut arches, diamonds, engraved florals **. 60.00**

5-1/2" d, Harvard pattern, two pcs **140.00**

Honey jar, **cov,** 6" h, Boston pattern, sterling silver rim and lid, Mt. Washington. **400.00**

Horseradish jar, cov

4-1/2" h, Brunswick pattern, triple notched handle, sterling finial, Higgins & Seiter **525.00**

5" h, Boston pattern, Gorham sterling silver lid, Mt. Washington . . **225.00**

Humidor, cov

6-3/4" h, 6" d, deep cranberry cut to clear, Prism and Punty pattern, elaborate sterling silver cover, Mt. Washington, ABP, several chips on base rim, cover dented, two jewels missing **650.00**

7-1/2" d, Middlesex, hollow stopper, sponge holder in lid, Dorflinger, ABP **490.00**

9" h, hobstars, beaded split vesicas, hobstar base, matching cut glass lid with hollow for sponge, ABP **575.00**

9" h, Monarch pattern, hobstar base, matching cut-glass lid with hollow for sponge, Hoare, ABP ... **625.00**

Ice bucket

6" d, Jewel pattern, hobstar bases, two handles, 8-1/2" d underplate, Clark, ABP **550.00**

6" d, 7-1/2" h, Crescent pattern, two handles, Higgins and Seiter **375.00**

6-1/2" d, 5-1/2" h, Hobstar and Fan dec, c1895-1910 .... **150.00**

7" d, 6-1/2" h, Harvard pattern, floral cutting, eight sided form, ABP, minor edge flaking on handles **100.00**

7" h, hobstars and notched prisms, 8" d underplate, double handles, ABP **940.00**

Ice cream bowl, 10" d, 4" h, Interlaced Hobstars dec, c1895-1900 .... **200.00**

Ice cream server, floral engraved **175.00**

Ice cream set

Cluster pattern, 15" x 9" tray, six 7" d matching plates, Eggington **3,100.00**

Russian pattern, eight 7" d dishes, 8-1/2" d serving bowl, 11" d cake plate, some chips to edges, ABP, price for 10-pc set **500.00**

Ice cream tray

10" x 10-1/4", Carolyn pattern, sgd "J. Hoare" and "F. W. Hoffman" **2,750.00**

14" x 7-1/2", 24-point hobstar center surrounded by cane, pinwheel border................. **100.00**

15" x 11", hobstars, arches, and gravic cut florals, ABP, minor flakes **150.00**

Ice tub, two handles, hobstars, ABP **395.00**

Jar, 6" h, 6" d, deep cranberry cut to clear, star and leaf design, star cut bottom, Sinclaire, no lid....... **875.00**

Jelly compote

4-1/2" d, 9" h, hobstar, band of flat star, attributed to Clark **350.00**

8" d, hobstar, vesica, strawberry diamond and cane, tear drop stem **250.00**

Jug, 7" h, spherical body, offset stoppered spout, applied notched handle, Sinclaire, ABP **520.00**

Knife rest, pinwheel cutting, **$90.**

Knife rest, 4-1/2" l, ABP....... **145.00**

Lamp, ABP

13" h, 6-1/2" d mushroom shade with engraved and clear cut large flowers and leaves, vining tendrils, notch cup stepped base with matching pattern cut on bottom **350.00**

13-1/2" h, domed shade with strawberry diamond and horizontal ribbed cutting, Hawkes-Sinclair manner, silvered metal two-socket electrical fittings **690.00**

14" h, teardrop shade with engraved tulip blossoms, star-cut closed top, columnar shaft with sq silver plated platform base, dec with cherubs in vineyard scene, attributed to Pairpoint **550.00**

15" h, 5" h x 10" d mushroom shade done cut with gravic cut style daisies and leaves, matching base, orig prisms, Pairpoint style . **500.00**

18" h, mushroom shade, Pattern #69359, orig pendants, T. B. Clark **2,450.00**

21" h overall, 14" h vasiform cut and engraved standard, double stepped reticulated silver plated bases, matching faceted finial, pr **490.00**

21-1/2" h, 12" d mushroom shade, hobstar pinwheel motif .. **2,000.00**

21-3/4" h, standard with egg-shaped knop over flattened knop, two further egg knops, round knop, each cut with diagonal floral bands, bronzed metal leaf endcaps, round spreading foot, bronzed metal base **490.00**

22" h, daisy and button floral design **850.00**

23" h, large mushroom shade, pedestal base, shade cut with 10 large hobstars with panels of cross-hatching base cut in Queen pattern with step cutting below fixture, orig ring and prisms **2,750.00**

23-3/4" h, 10" d shade, large expanding cut star in heavy brilliant period pattern of band of daisy-like flowers and leaves, matching conforming base, inverted trumpet form, with matching band of flowers, notched prism band, band of strawberry, diamond, and fan circling base, orig prisms **2,000.00**

26" h, 10-1/2" d Turkish domed shade with pagoda top, Harvard pattern shade and base, 40-step notched prism cut base, silver plated fittings, orig cut prisms **3,750.00**

32" h, 7" d font, 9-1/2" w base, banquet type, solid medium green, strawberry, diamond, and fan pattern, three-section, large flaring hollow blown base, cut knob and large matching cut font, orig double wick hardware, attributed to Dorflinger factory **5,250.00**

Letter opener, 11-1/2" l, engraved hollow handle with seaweed motif, ivory blade, sterling silver fitting **600.00**

Liquor decanter, 14-1/2" h, Creswick pattern, long narrow neck, triple notched handle, pattern cut stopper, sgd "Eggington" **900.00**

Liquor goblet, stemmed, buzzstar, pineapple, marked, "B & B," ABP **25.00**

Loving cup

5" h, bow time of crosshatch and fan, star base, three handles .. **175.00**

6-1/2" h, sterling rim, prism cut, three triple notched handles, ABP **575.00**

Luncheon set, mirror black crystal, opaque white rim wraps, 12-1/2" d centerpiece bowl, six 8-1/2" d luncheon plates, 6-1/2" dessert plates, 12 4-3/4" bowls, Sinclaire, 26-pc set **750.00**

Mayonnaise bowl, 5" d, deep cut, hobstar, medallions, and arches, ABP **50.00**

Mayonnaise set, bowl, underplate, ladle, Tiger Lily pattern, sgd "Sinclaire" **475.00**

Miniature

Banana bowl, 4" d, hobstar, miter, nailhead diamonds, attributed to Hawkes **200.00**

Dish, 2-1/2" d, double handles, cut hobstars, zippered miters, and fans **100.00**

Flower center, 2-1/2" x 3", hobstar, bow tie of crosshatching and fans **200.00**

Loving cup, 3" h, Pattern #20, sterling silver rim, Dorflinger **300.00**

Paperweight, 1-1/2" x 2", miniature, cut in double miter, Harvard **300.00**

Pitcher, 2-1/2" h, large fans, alternating diamonds of strawberry diamond and crosshatching, star base, triple notched handle **225.00**

Punch bowl, 3" w, 3" h, two-pc bowl and stand, strawberry diamond **600.00**

Vase, 5" h, Brunswick pattern, sgd "Hawkes" **500.00**

Milk pitcher, pinwheel, strawberry diamond and notched fan **190.00**

Mint set, Star of David center, sterling rims, sterling handle on master, master dish and four individuals, price for five-pc set **250.00**

Mustard pot, cov

3" d, 5" h, ftd, bands of punties, notched oblong flutes, sterling top **200.00**

3-1/2" h, panel and notched prism, underplate, sgd "Maple City Glass" **225.00**

Napkin ring, hobstars and bow-tie fans **90.00**

Nappy, two handles

6" d, hobstar center, intaglio floral, strawberry diamond button border, 6" d **45.00**

6" x 7", step-cut pulled handle, checker board bottom, diamond cut sides **70.00**

7" d, four part, hobstar in each section, double thumbprint handles, 7" **160.00**

9" d, deep cut arches, pointed sunbursts and medallions, ABP **135.00**

Nut dish, 7" d, swirl effect, hobstar, beading, crosshatch and fan motif **110.00**

Orange bowl

9-3/4" x 6-3/4" x 3-3/4" h, hobstars and strawberry diamond, ABP **200.00**

10" d, pinwheel, notched prism and hobstar in vesicas, ABP ... **185.00**

Paperweight

2-1/2" w, 4" h, book shape, Russian pattern **400.00**

3" d, eight sided, zipper cut, ray base, Gorham sterling silver top **175.00**

3" d, hobstar shape, cut hobstar and prisms, sterling silver top .. **250.00**

Parfait

Renaissance, faceted and teardrop stems, Dorflinger, six-pc set **240.00**

7" h, two hobstars alternating with two large fans around top, bottom notched with fans and hobnails **110.00**

Perfume bottle

3-1/4" l, canary yellow, cut facets, silver mounted cap **300.00**

3-1/2" l, cranberry overlay, shaped sides, notched cuts, S. Mordan & Co., silver mounted cap ... **325.00**

3-1/2" l, pistol shape, sterling silver fittings **225.00**

5-1/2" h, 3" d, six-sided, alternating panels of Harvard pattern and engraved florals, rayed base, matching faceted stopper, ABP **175.00**

6-1/2" h, bulbous, allover cutting, orig stopper, ABP **220.00**

7" l, oval cut column, hinged sterling silver cov with polychrome portrait center **225.00**

Perfume flask, 5-1/2" l, diamond cut cylindrical bottle, screw mount on one end, hinged spring cap on other, hallmark "EG," well worn orig velvet lined leather case **230.00**

Pickle tray, 7" x 3", checkerboard, hobstar **45.00**

Picture frame, 5" x 6-1/2", strawberry diamond border, sgd "Hawkes" **275.00**

Pitcher, floral cutting, basketweave-type base cutting, applied notched handle, **$375.**

Pitcher

6-3/8" h, blown, cut panels, strawberry diamonds, fans, roundels, and rays with foliage rim, fluted lip, Pittsburgh, recut rim with chip **95.00**

7-1/2" h, tusk shape, Russian pattern, button strap handle, J. Hoare **800.00**

9" h, cranberry cut to clear with detailed woodland scene, tapered straight sided form, elaborate star and fan-cut base, applied colorless handle, American **635.00**

9-1/2" h, button and daisy cut wide borders, floral center, ABP . **125.00**

11" h, pedestal, rock crystal, engraved iris, carnation, tulip, daisy, and lily panels, pattern cut handle, sgd "Hawkes Gravic" **1,600.00**

12-1/2" h, Wild Rose pattern, pedestal, sgd "Tuthill" ... **5,200.00**

14-1/8" h, baluster, vertical flutes with bead and lozenge cuts, crosshatched and diamond-cut diamonds at base, mounted with sterling bead-edged spout, monogrammed **250.00**

Place card holder, 2-1/2" x 2", faceted ball on faceted base, attributed to Dorflinger **150.00**

Plate

7" d, Aberdeen pattern, Jewel Cut glass **1,100.00**

7" d, Acme pattern, J. Hoare. **800.00**

7" d, Albion pattern, sgd "Hawkes" **800.00**

7" d, Alexandria pattern, sgd "Hawkes" **1,150.00**

7" d, bands of cane and fans in center, hobstars and crosshatching border, attributed to J. Hoare **200.00**

7" d, bands of hobstars with notched miters, alternating with flat stars and feathered fans, large center hobstar with hobnail and fan **400.00**

7" d, Carolyn pattern, sgd "J. Hoare" **800.00**

7" d, Genoa pattern, sgd "Clark" **300.00**

7" d, Glenda pattern, sgd "Libbey" **500.00**

7" d, Hindu pattern, J. Hoare. **400.00**

7" d, Hobstar, intersecting miters, crosshatching **125.00**

7" d, Hobstars surrounded by tusks, hob-diamonds, crossbands of hobstars **550.00**

7" d, Mars pattern, Pitkins and Brooks 550.00
7" d, Paul Revere pattern, sgd "Hawkes" 275.00
7" d, Russian pattern 125.00
7" d, Russian pattern, hobstar center 275.00
7" d, Salem, heart shaped, Pairpoint 125.00
7" d, Zella pattern, Irving . . . 175.00
10" d, Carolyn pattern, J. Hoare 525.00
12" d, alternating hobstar and pinwheel 100.00

Pokal, cov, 16" h, 6-1/2" w, Harvard pattern, tall cut knob, ABP 850.00

Powder box, cov
3" h, star and zipper cut, emb silvered lid, ABP 75.00
3" d, 3" h, emb florals on sterling silver lid, c1890-1900 . . . . . 100.00
4-1/2" d, flashed hobstar on top, alternating pinwheel and vesica motif 120.00
5" d, 4" h, Wild Rose pattern, engraved roses on lid, hobnail band on bowl, on standard, sgd "Tuthill" 700.00
5-1/2" d, buzz saw base and large buzz saw lid 125.00
5-1/2" d, Venetian, Hawkes . . 350.00

Punch bowl
11" h, 10" w, two-pc, Elgin pattern, Quaker City 600.00
11" h, 10" w, two-pc, pinwheel and hobstar pattern, heavy blank with unusual lapidary cut domed base, ABP 500.00
12" d, 10" h, interlaced hobstars dec, stand base, c1895-1900 . . 385.00
12-1/4" d, 5" h, four star-cut devices spaced by notched vertical ribbing, star-cut base, silver rim mounted with ornate grape clusters and vines, silver marked "sterling" with mark for Wilcox 1,035.00
14" d, two pcs, large stars with fields of cane and crosshatching 2,300.00
14" d, 7" h, five large hobstars, central large hobstar, ABP . 550.00
17" h, 11-1/2" d, chalice shape, pedestal base, engraved all over with pattern of stars among leaves and hanging blossoms, band of leaf etching around top and base 500.00

Punch cup
Cranberry cut to clear, cross-cut diamond, clear handle, 2-1/2" h 95.00

Punch bowl, two-piece, heavy blank, interlaced hobstars, mitered arches, **$550.**

Hobstars, pedestal, handle 85.00
Monarch pattern, pedestal, sterling silver base marked "Shreve & Co., San Francisco," J. Hoare, 4-1/2", price for four-pc set 525.00

Punch ladle
11-1/2" l, silver plated emb shell bowl, cut and notched prism handle 165.00
14" l, 5-1/4" w, Harvard pattern, ornate Pairpoint silver plate stem and double spout bowl 325.00

Ramekin, underplate, 3" x 1-3/4", Hobnail pattern, Dorflinger 125.00

Relish
6" l, pinwheel, hobstars, fans, and prisms, ABP 90.00
8" l, two handles, divided, Jupiter pattern, Meriden 120.00
8" l, 3" w, double handles, hobstars, fans, and crosshatching . . . 120.00
13" l, leaf shape, Clear Button Russian pattern, ABP 375.00

Ring tree, 4" x 3", green cut to clear, hobstar and strawberry diamond motif 900.00

Rose bowl
6-1/2" h, ABP 175.00
8" d, 7-1/2" h, ftd, allover strawberry diamond, ray base, Mt. Washington 575.00
10" d, 9-1/2" h, sphere shape, integrated disk foot, overall Russian pattern variant cutting without buttons, top rim polished, base also cut, ABP 575.00

Rum jug
7-1/2" h, allover notched prisms 325.00
7-1/2" h, strawberry diamond pattern, faceted stopper . . 275.00

Salad bowl and underplate
10" d, 6" h bowl, 11-1/2" d underplate, Spilane (Trefoil & Rosette) pattern, cross-cut vesicas, notched prism, hobstars and fans, sgd "Libbey" 2,200.00
10" d, 7" h, strawberry diamonds, minute nicks 325.00

Salad serving fork and spoon, silver plated, cross-cut diamond glass handles 300.00

Salad set, 9" salad bowl, 11" d matching underplate, fan, crosshatching, stars and miter cuts, large 24-point hobstar center . . 700.00

Salt, open, individual
Feather 20.00
Sawtooth, ftd. 30.00

Salt, open, master, 3" d, pedestal, scalloped base, serrated rim, crosshatch diamond motif. 75.00

Salt shaker
Alhambra pattern, 3-1/4" h, sterling top marked "Meridan" 175.00
Garland pattern, green, 4" h, sterling silver lid 60.00
Notched prism columns, replaced top 30.00

Sandwich tray, 10" d, gravic floral cut, center handle, ABP 90.00

Scent bottle, 6-1/4" l, cane pattern, tapered bottle, hinged cover and rim, imp "Tiffany & Co Sterling," ABP, cover misaligned, glass stopper missing 175.00

Sherry
Russian pattern, Dorflinger, 4-1/2" h 80.00
Russian pattern with star buttons, 4-1/2" h. 45.00

Spooner
4-1/2" h, Crescent pattern, two handles, Higgins & Seiter . 250.00
5" h, hobstar and arches, ABP 90.00

Sweet pea vase
3-1/2" h, 6" w, Kalana Pansy, Dorflinger 110.00
5-1/2" x 8-1/2", hobstar, cane, crosshatching and fan motif 200.00

Swizzle stick, 6" l, pinwheel and diamond cut body. 200.00

Syrup pitcher, 4" x 3-1/2", hobstar, miter and cane cutting, sterling flip top lid **300.00**

Tankard pitcher

10-1/4" h, Harvard cut sides, pinwheel top, mini hobnails, thumbprint notched handle, ABP **200.00**

11" h, hobstar, strawberry diamond, notched prism and fan, flared base with bull's eye, double thumbprint handle **275.00**

11" h, vertical rows of hobstars and stars, crosscut diamond and fan motif. **240.00**

12" h, diamond band and leaf design, large applied notched handle, ABP **200.00**

13" h, bowling pin shape, alternating vertical bands of hobnail and engraved wild florals, attributed to Tuthill **3,000.00**

17-1/4" h, 7" w base, three rows of hobstars, diamond point cutting, fancy silver rim, applied loop cut handle, ABP **700.00**

Tantalus set, three matching 6" h Dorflinger cut glass bottles in patent #210 with orig matching stoppers, elaborate metal holder sgd "The Tantalus Betjemann's Patented London 6588," some minor flaking to bottles **1,100.00**

Tazza

6-1/2" d, 8" h, Pattern #100, Elmira **375.00**

8" d, shallow bowl, buzz star and arches, paneled zippered stem, starcut base, ABP **125.00**

Teapot, 7" h, Old Irish pattern, long elegant spout, Hawkes. **900.00**

Tobacco jar, 9" h, 6" d, straight sided canister, panels of fine cut cane pattern alternating with faceted thumbprints, matching cut glass top with star cutting repeated on base, ABP **1,150.00**

Tonic bottle, 6-1/2" h, Victoria pattern, sterling top, sgd "Hawkes". **500.00**

Toothpick holder

3" h, on standard, notched top, feather intersecting miters with crosshatching, sgd "Hawkes" **200.00**

3" h, Queens pattern, sgd "Hawkes" **800.00**

Tooth powder bottle, 4" h, flat, stars, hobnail, and notched prisms, sterling dispenser and lid **750.00**

Tray

4-1/2" w, 1-3/4" h, cutting of diamond notches, star cut base, floral emb silver plated rim, C. F. Monroe **75.00**

10" l, allover hobstars, ABP . **495.00**

10" l, deep cut hobstar medallions and cross hatched arches, ABP **225.00**

12" d, engraved cherries, plus strawberries, and gooseberries, sgd "Hawkes Gravic". . . . **2,700.00**

12" l, similar to Hawkes Nelson pattern, sgd "Straus" **700.00**

12" l, 8" w, cane pattern, ABP **400.00**

14" x 7-1/2", Sillsbee pattern, Pairpoint **335.00**

Tumble-up, pitcher and matching tumbler, 6-1/2" h, alternating panels of cut large diamond and engraved grapes, attributed to Pairpoint. . **450.00**

Tumbler

Bristol Rose pattern, Mt. Washington **75.00**

Clear Button Russian pattern . **95.00**

Cut panels, fans, sheaves, roundels, strawberry diamonds, 3-1/8" h, flint, Pittsburgh **40.00**

Harvard, rayed base. **45.00**

Hobstars **40.00**

Hobstars, strawberry diamonds, fans, hobstar cluster and base, set of six. **360.00**

Panel, sgd "Hawkes," rare . . **400.00**

Russian Button pattern, set of nine **350.00**

Star of David pattern, 4" h, set of four **300.00**

Vase

5" h, 2" w, Kalana, lily dec, Dorflinger **150.00**

8" h, monogrammed and inscribed silver flared neck, body cut with thumb notching and elongated panels, ABP, c1901, minor chips **230.00**

8" h, trumpet set, hobstar and diamond arches, ABP **90.00**

9" h, cylindrical, star, strawberry diamond, cross-cut diamond and fan, attributed to Dorflinger **130.00**

9" h, deep cut zippered ribs with panels of sunburst and fine cut, ABP, minor flake **150.00**

9-1/2 h, deep cut arched stars, windows, and zippered ribs, ABP **100.00**

10" h, arches, pointed triangles and buzz stars, ABP **100.00**

Vase, ruby stained decoration cut to clear, T.B. Clark, 8" h, **$150.**

10" h, corset shape, hobstar, crosshatching, prism and punty motifs. **275.00**

10" h, fan shape, hobstar base with panels of flutes on side. . . . **300.00**

10" h, ovoid shape bowl, cut with buzz saw, button and daisy, deep arches, zipper cut paneled stem, faceted paperweight and fine cut foot, ABP **275.00**

10" h, trumpet, zipper and thumbprint cut, star cut paperweight base. **100.00**

10" h, 8" d, bulbous, Roosevelt pattern, Quaker City **700.00**

10-1/4" h, engraved dragon, clear ground, deep amber flashing, applied sterling rim, both glass and silver rim sgd "Hawkes" . . . **250.00**

10-1/2" h, flared cylindrical form, raised on standard, disk foot, deeply engraved with scalloped rim, rose and bud on body, Hawkes trefoil acid stamp, minor wear **350.00**

11" h, bulbous top, fluted rim, tapering cylindrical stem, wide base, bulbous top cut with double row of thumbprints and diamond patterns and cross hatching, step cutting underneath, stem cut with hobstars, cross hatching, and flat flutes, heavy brilliant blank, clearly sgd "Hawkes" **550.00**

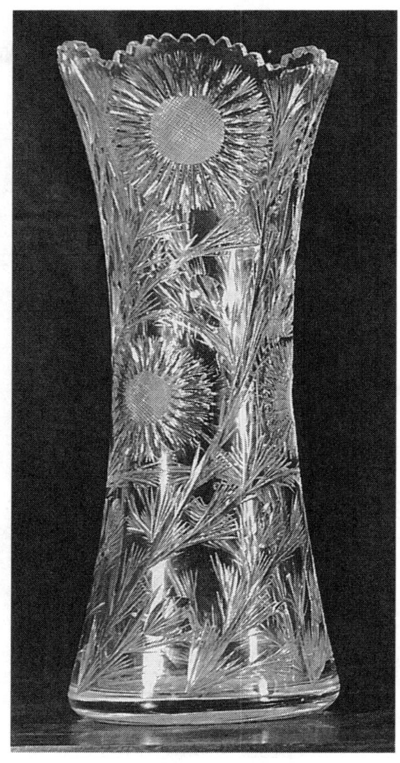

Vase, sunflower motif, 12" h, **$450.**

11" h, sunburst and finecut pattern, zippered panel stem, star cut base **175.00**
11-1/2" h, 6" w, medium green, floral engraving, gold band, sgd "Hawkes," int. crazed **150.00**
12" h, corset shape, vertical rows of punties, prism and crosshatching, attributed to Clark **250.00**
12" h, hobstars, florals, and zippered ribs **85.00**
12" h, pedestal, Stratford pattern, Herbeck **600.00**
12" h, pedestal, tulip, hobstar and geometric cane motif **1,150.00**
12" h, strawberry diamond, buzzstars. ABP **150.00**
12" h, 5-1/2" w, triangular, three large and three small hobstars, double notched pedestal and flaring base, ABP **150.00**
12-1/4" h, corset shape, cone and file band, deep cut leaves and flowers **85.00**
12-1/2" h, 6-1/2" d, floral and diamond point engraving, sgd "Hawkes" **250.00**
14" h, bowling-pin shape, Comet pattern, sgd "J. Hoare," professionally repaired **200.00**
14" h, bowling-pin shape, three 24-point hobstars on sides surrounded by notched prisms, strawberry diamond, hobstars, star, and checkered diamond fields **700.00**
14" h, corset shape, Harvard pattern, deep floral engraving **925.00**
14" h, trumpet shape, 8" w at top, Venetian pattern, Hawkes, ABP **750.00**
15" h, corset shape, Primrose pattern, Dorlinger **1,250.00**
16" h, corset shape, well-cut hobstar, strawberry diamond, prism, flashed star and fan **300.00**
16" h, tapered cylinder, bulbed scalloped top, intricately carved in a variety of motifs, ABP, some small int. rim chips **1,840.00**
16" h, 5-1/2" d, trumpet form, circular foot with sunburst, Vertical Graduated Hobstars dec, c1895-1900 . . . . **110.00**
17" h, 7" w at widest point, tulip shape, hobstar, strawberry diamond and fan, 24-point hobstar base **425.00**
19" h, corset shape, alternating vertical Russian and Buzz and Snowflake panels **220.00**
19-1/2" h, funeral, hobstars, strawberry diamond, and fan motifs **500.00**
22-1/2" h, 11" d, baluster shape, alternating Buzz and Harvard Spear dec **220.00**

Water carafe

Brunswick pattern, thin neck, sgd "Hawkes" **240.00**
Harvard pattern, ABP **185.00**
Hobstars and notched prisms, ABP **125.00**
Pinwheel and Fan cutting, notched neck, 8" h, 4" w **125.00**
Russian pattern, 7-1/2" h, 6" w, all-over brilliant design, minor flaking to pattern, ABP **225.00**
Thumbprint and chain of hobstar, honeycomb neck, sgd "Hawkes" **180.00**
Wedgemere pattern, Libbey, 9" h, ABP **1,200.00**

Water pitcher

9-1/2" h, Harvard pattern panels and intaglio cut sprays of flowers and foliage, ABP **300.00**
10" h, Keystone Rose pattern **190.00**
11" h, Harvard pattern, rayed base, double punty handle, sgd "Hawkes," ABP **400.00**

Water set, pitcher and tumblers, two bands of hobstars, flat pillar cut, three panels of intaglio wild florals, sgd "Sinclaire," six pcs **575.00**

Whiskey jug

6-1/4" h, bulbous, thistle and grape cutting, orig stopper, sgd "Sinclaire" **295.00**
8" h, Laurette pattern, pinwheel, crosshatch and hobstar buttons, corncob stopper, strap handle, Lucerne **400.00**

Wine

4" h, flint, cut panels, strawberry diamonds, and fans, Pittsburgh **60.00**
4-1/8" h, flint, Gothic Arch, sheaf like ferns, Pittsburgh **75.00**
4-1/4" h, flint, strawberry diamonds, fans, leaves, and panels, Pittsburgh **65.00**
4-1/2" h, Vintage, sgd "Egginton" **250.00**
4-3/4" h, Hobdiamond pattern, vaseline, Dorlinger **325.00**
4-3/4" h, Hoblace pattern, yellow cut to clear, Dorlinger **500.00**
6" h, buzz saws and cross hatched diamonds, ABP, one chipped, set of four **100.00**

Wine hock

7-1/2" d, vesica, crosshatch, cane and fan, tear-drop stem **70.00**
8-1/2" h, rock crystal, lotus flowers with clear fingers, diamond cut round base of bowl, sgd "Brierly" **200.00**

CUT VELVET

History: Several glass manufacturers made cut velvet glass during the late Victorian era, c1870-1900. An outer layer of pastel color was applied over a casing. The layers were fused and blown into a mold. Then the piece was molded or cut in a high-relief ribbed of diamond-quilted shape, exposing portions of the casing. The pieces are usually acid finished, which gives them a satin velvety feel, hence the name "cut velvet." Some glossy pieces have been found.

This exquisite glassware was made in many forms. Bowls, ewers, pitchers, and vases are the most common. Ruffled edges, rigaree, and applied clear handles are sometimes added to enhance the beauty or usefulness of a piece. Although two-toned bodies have been found, most are single colors, shaded by the shape and technique. Colors include amethyst, apple green, apricot, dark blue, butterscotch, gold, light blue, pink, rose, tan, turquoise, and yellow. Casings generally are white, but yellow, pink, and blue were also used.

Basket, 11-1/2" h, 9" w, brilliant yellow ext., Diamond Quilted pattern, bright pink shaded int., tightly crimped and ruffled edge, applied crystal loop handle **300.00**

Biscuit jar, cov, pink, SP mountings and lid **275.00**

Celery vase, 6-1/2" h, deep blue over white, Diamond Quilted pattern, box-pleated top **725.00**

Creamer, 5-1/4" h, raised ribbed pattern, butterscotch body, white lining **200.00**

Cruet, 6" h, shiny pink, Diamond Quilted pattern, clear faceted stopper, clear handle **750.00**

Finger bowl, 4-1/2" d, Diamond Quilted pattern, blue **185.00**

Rose bowl, 3-1/4" d, 3-3/4" h, egg shape, raised Diamond Quilted pattern, rose body, white lining, six crimp top **195.00**

Tumbler, blue exterior, white cased interior, 3-5/8" h, **$90.**

Vase

4-1/4" h, 3" d, bulbous, deep pink shading to pale pink, DQ pattern, ruffled top, Mt. Washington . **225.00**

5-1/4" h, blue body, quatrefoil top **145.00**

6-1/2" d, stick type, raised Diamond Quilted pattern, rose body, white lining **250.00**

6-3/4" h, bulbous, raised Diamond Quilted pattern, pink body, ruffled rim **220.00**

7-1/2" h, 3-1/2" w, bulbous shape, ruffled top, Herringbone pattern, Alice Blue, white lining, c1880 . . . . **450.00**

9" h, cylindrical, raised Diamond Quilted pattern, blue body, ruffled rim **250.00**

Vase, conical-shaped neck over bulbous body, raised Diamond Quilted pattern, pink body, white interior, **$225.**

9" h, deeply ruffled top, deep orange body, DQ pattern **675.00**

9" h, slight flare to end of elongated neck, robin's egg blue, diamond quilt body, daisy blossom-like design at base **385.00**

10" h, ruffled and crimped top, purple cased to opal white body, Diamond Quilted pattern, Victorian **575.00**

11-1/2" h, 6" w, glossy satin, Herringbone pattern, deep blue shading to pale blue, bright opaque white lining, applied crystal edge **250.00**

13-1/2" h, 6" w, double gourd, long pumpkin stem neck, pale gold Diamond Quilted body **650.00**

Czechoslovakian Items

History: Objects marked "Made in Czechoslovakia" were produced after 1918 when the country claimed its independence from the Austro-Hungarian Empire. The people became more cosmopolitan and liberated and expanded the scope of their lives. Their porcelains, pottery, and glassware reflect many influences.

A specific manufacturer's mark may be identified as being much earlier than 1918, but this only indicates the factory existed in the Bohemian or Austro-Hungarian Empire period.

Czechoslovakian glassware can range from exquisite cut glass to Art-Deco designs executed in bright colors. Vivid color combinations of orange, blue, and black with white are common. Spatter-type wares and bright streaks of color also are readily found. Modern Czech craftsmen are producing some lovely pieces and should be included in any collection of Czechoslovakian glassware. The mass-produced bowls, perfume bottles, vases, and other types of items are starting to command high prices as collectors seek these colorful pieces of glassware.

References: Dale and Diane Barta and Helen M. Rose, *Czechoslovakian Glass & Collectibles* (1992, 1995 values), Book II (1996) Collector Books; *Bohemian Glass*, n.d., distributed by Antique Publications; Ruth A. Forsythe, *Made in Czechoslovakia*, Antique Publications, 1993; Jacquelyne Y. Jones-North, *Czechoslovakian Perfume Bottles and Boudoir Accessories*, Antique Publications, 1990; Leslie Piña, *Pottery, Modern Wares 1920-1960*, Schiffer Publishing, 1994.

Periodical: *New Glass Review*, Bardounova 2140 149 00 Praha 4, Prague, Czech Republic.

Collectors' Club: Czechoslovakian Collectors Guild International, P.O. Box 901395, Kansas City, MO 64190; Friends of the Glass Museum of Novy Bor, Kensington, MD 20895.

Atomizer, 7-1/2" h, brilliant period cut glass **115.00**

BasketAmber, six-prong cobalt blue handle **45.00**

Bright yellow, six-prong cobalt blue handle **60.00**

Lemon yellow, black trim, clear handle, emb floral design, 7-1/2" h, 6-1/2" w, matched pr **100.00**

Multicolored spatter cased in cobalt blue, cobalt blue handle, 7" h **100.00**

Pink, six-prong cobalt blue handle **50.00**

Powder blue, glossy, floral design, black trim, clear frosted handle, 7-1/2" h, 6-1/2" w **90.00**

Red, colorless handle **95.00**

Yellow and orange spatter, clear twisted thorn handle **110.00**

Bowl

Cased, yellow int., black ext., polished pontil **60.00**

Clear and smoke with oxblood and orange drippings, 9" d, 4" h **100.00**

Flared opal-green oval, three black applied ball feet, black rim wrap, design attributed to Michael Powolny, 10-1/2" d, 5" h **290.00**

Low, glossy finish yellow and orange spatter, deep purple base, 7-1/2" w **75.00**

Multicolored spatter cased in cobalt blue, cov **85.00**

Orange ground, large randomly spaced multicolored murrines, 10" d, ftd **375.00**

Box, cov

6" d, amber ground, white enameled boy and bird, orig paper label "Bohemian glass, made in Czechoslovakia". **75.00**

7" d, 3-1/2" h, lemon yellow, enamel dec of black tree with brilliant orange fruit, black leaves, sgd "Delafine Ltd" **150.00**

Candlesticks, pr, 15" h, Papillon, raised candle cup over segmented standard, double-tiered dome base, cobalt blue glass with strong blue and gold spotted irid, minor nicks, c1930 . . . . **980.00**

Chandelier, 28-1/2" d, 23" l drop, yellow-green glass standard, alabaster bulbed segments, supporting 12 yellow-green curved arms, each fitted with shallow bobeche, painted metal ceiling mount, c1930. . . . . **750.00**

Console bowl, 11" d, orange and purple cased in clear, polished pontil, acid Czechoslovakia mark **75.00**

Console set

7" h, 7-1/2" bowl, pr candlesticks, threaded, acid stamped "Czechoslovakia". **135.00**

10" x 6" x 2-1/2" bowl, Art-Deco design, turquoise raised drapery, knotted corners, bowl and pr candlesticks **85.00**

Art-Deco covered crystal container has cut panels with linear-cut trim and sports a stained faux-leopard wrap against an amber ground, unsigned, 4-1/2", 5" l, **$35.**

Decanter set, figural owl decanter, four matching cups, blue ground, painted eyes. **200.00**

Dresser set, 6" h colorless bottle, covered powder with enameled florals **50.00**

Fairy lamp, 5" h, two pcs, ruby flashed, cut back design of jumping stag, orig paper label "Egermann, Czechoslovakia". **90.00**

Fernery, 4-1/2" d, amber cased with cream mottling, orig frog **95.00**

Flask, 12-1/2" h, Burmese-type ground, birds perched on stems, foliage, moon, sgd "Tischler #426" **500.00**

Inkwell, 3-1/4" h, colorless, figural, sitting Scottie dog, SP collar, marked **85.00**

Jack-in-the-pulpit vase, 12" h, white and yellow irid, deep red interior, green-red criss-cross looping, marked "Czechoslovakia" **325.00**

Jam jar, cov, 4" h, 3-1/2" d, pear shape, glossy finish, multicolored spatter, applied black trailing **75.00**

Jar, cov

4" h, mottled red and yellow, applied florals. **50.00**

4" h, swirled cased orange and yellow, colorless finial **35.00**

5" h, 4-1/2" d, crystal, Art-Deco style cut panels with linear cut trim, stained faux leopard wrap against amber ground **170.00**

Lamp

9" h, vanity, cased red mushroom shade, coralene floral dec on matching base **250.00**

9" h, vanity, mushroom shade hand dec with windmill scene, matching base, orig bulb **250.00**

22" h, figural, bronzed metal figure of kneeling woman supporting diamond hobbed art glass mottled art glass shade, minor damage to shade **250.00**

25" h overall, pale pink and deep blue cased to clear honeycomb pattern glass, orig cast iron and metal fittings **95.00**

Lamp shade, beaded **50.00**

Luncheon set, partial, flowing irid magenta, orange, brown and lavender, mother of pearl ground, sgd, 40 pcs **280.00**

Perfume bottle

3" h, colorless, integrated engraved stopper **125.00**

4" h, mottled blue and turquoise, art glass stopper under brass hinged cap **90.00**

5" h, colorless, etched and engraved stopper **125.00**

5" h, red, black stopper, ground pontil on dauber, paper label marked "Made in Czechoslovakia" **100.00**

6" h, amethyst, faceted, integrated engraved stopper **145.00**

6-3/4" h, amber, large intaglio floral stopper. **175.00**

Pitcher, 9-1/2" h, cranberry, white enameled boy with bird, orig paper label "Bohemian glass, made in Czechoslovakia" **110.00**

Plate, 9-1/2" d, gilt foliate designs, wide burgundy border, Epiag, early 20th C, light wear, 11-pc set **290.00**

Powder box, cov, round, yellow, black knop **60.00**

Rose bowl, 5-1/2" h, enameled florals and orange lattice dec **80.00**

Scent bottle, 6-1/4" h, molded green malachite glass, elaborate cherub and foliate design, conforming stopper with floral bouquet, polished base, pr **260.00**

Vase

4-3/4" h, blue, ftd, applied black rim, cased **70.00**

5" h, irid opalescent, red threading, red int., ground pontil, marked "Czechoslovakia". **165.00**

5" h, 5" w, bright red, applied cobalt blue rim, applied cobalt blue leaf dec around center **75.00**

5-1/8" h, tripod, ovoid, mottled red internally striped in black, red glass legs supporting struts applied and tooled all in one piece, polished at top rim **270.00**

5-1/2" h, spatter, satin finish, polished rim, silver mark . . **150.00**

6" h, cased red over white, irid finish **110.00**

6-1/2" h, ftd urn form, rose pink irid bowl, blue oil-spot motif, partial acid stamp "CZECHO/SLOVAKIA" **1,000.00**

6-1/2" h, bright yellow, mottled base **75.00**

7" h, raised rim, ovoid form, circular foot, lightly irid opaque yellow dec at bottom half with blue oil spot irid, dark blue ground, oval acid stamp "Czechoslovakia" in polished pontil, c1930, minor wear. **1,035.00**

7" h, ribbed orange, bright cobalt blue leaf trim, matched pr . **100.00**

7" h, 3" w, glossy finish, ivory, bulbous tortoise shell spatter base, pr **145.00**

7-1/2" h, raised rim, bright yellow cased oval body, hand-painted blue clown above spiked design elements, painted black rim, sgd

Vase, spatter, satin finish, finished rim, signed with silver mark, 5-1/2" h, **$115.** *Photo courtesy of David Rago Auctions.*

"Czech/Slovakia" on base, pr **290.00**

8" h, green, fine orange threading at fan-shaped rim, ground pontil **220.00**

8" h, mottled red over yellow, blown out mold of ribs and snails . **100.00**

8" h, yellow and orange spatter, four clear feet **90.00**

8" h, wave design of charcoal and white with bubbles, colorless cased ground, applied black serpent **90.00**

8-1/2" h, red and white mottled ground, black snake dec, ruffled **125.00**

8-1/2" h, yellow, orange, red, blue spatter, cobalt applied trim, clear feet **95.00**

8-1/2" h, 5" w, glossy finish, bulbous, red and gray spatter, applied reeded black handles, pr.. **155.00**

9" h, orange, black center spiral and rim **95.00**

9" h, wrought iron reticulated frame, blown-in glass body with splotched blue, orange and green cased to white, base stamped "Czechoslovakia"........ **460.00**

9" h, 3" w, red, cobalt blue spiral and trim **95.00**

9" h, 4" w, bright red, bulbous base, flaring rim, applied cobalt blue leaf dec around center **100.00**

10" h, 5" w, acid finish, orange and yellow spatter, clear ground, dark purple base **100.00**

10-1/4" h, cadmium yellow, applied and stretched cobalt blue Papillion shell handles, cobalt blue rim, acid stamped "Czechoslovakia" in oval, gaffer's sliver chip at polished pontil, minor short scratches **700.00**

10-1/2" h, applied black rim, three horizontal ribs, wide ftd flange, marked "Czechoslovakia".. **150.00**

10-1/2" h, trumpet form, deep rose bowl with blue oil-spot motif, acid stamped "CZECHO/SLOVAKIA" **1,800.00**

10-1/2" h, 8" w, matte finish, bright orange, yellow, white, and green spatter, pr **150.00**

11" h, 5" w, pale blue ground, white and pink spatter **90.00**

11-3/4" h, swollen cylindrical form, cobalt blue mold blown glass, irid luster, two arched full-length handles on Secessionist-style bronze mounts **2,300.00**

12" h, ribbed bright orange, brown, yellow, and orange spatter base **110.00**

14-3/4" h, raised rim, irid colorless oval body cased to opal glass, internal layer of bright red, green, orange, and olive green splotched dec, base stamped "Czechoslovakia" **520.00**

15" h, 9-1/4" h, acid finish, brilliant yellow and orange swirls, dark lavender spatters, flaring acid finish pedestal base with lavender flames up the side........ **200.00**

Wine

5" h, orange bowl, black stem, enameled jester design **50.00**

5" h, red bowl, black stem.... **35.00**

Daum Nancy

History: Daum Nancy glassware originates in the Nancy, France, region and most pieces are attributed to members of the Daum family. Also known as Cristalleries de Nancy, the glassworks has been in operation since 1875.

Daum family members include the founder, Jean Daum (1825-1885), Jean-Louis Auguste Daum (1853-1909), Jean-Antonin Daum (1864-1930), Paul Daum (1890-1944), Henri Daum, (1894-1930), Michel Daum (1900-), and Jacques Daum (1919-). Both Jean-Louis Auguste and Jean-Antonin were greatly influenced by Emile Gallé.

Cameo glasswares were carefully crafted in addition to colored glassware with enameled decoration, etch glass, cased glass, and several other techniques. Crystal glassware and pate-de-verre were reintroduced into the firm's lines during the late 1960s.

All items made are marked with an engraved signature, which varies from artist to artist.

References: Victor Arwas, *Glass Art Nouveau To Art Deco*, Rizzoli International Publications, Inc., 1977; Harold Newman, *An Illustrated Dictionary of Glass*, Thames and Hudson, 1977; Wolf Ueker, *Art Nouveau and Art Deco Lamps and Candlesticks*, Abbeville Press, 1987.

Reproduction Alert: Examples of period Daum Nancy items have been copied and reproduced. Most lack the details and exquisite cutting of the originals.

Animal

15" h, catalog #02039, stork, head overlooking back, modern, crystal, inscribed "Daum France" .. **230.00**

18-1/2" h, catalog #02038, stork, head extended upward, modern, crystal, inscribed "Daum France" **235.00**

Beverage set, 9" h ribbed oviform pitcher, applied handle, carved circular stopper, six matching footed goblets, clear glass, finely carved with thistle blossoms, gilt highlights, enameled "Daum Nancy" **2,250.00**

Bottle, 4-1/2" h, cameo, rhomboid shape, short, narrow cylindrical neck, everted rim, mottled and streaked green and white, dark red splashes on base, green and gray overlay, cut pendant leafy branches and stems of deep orange berries, sgd in cameo, c1900 .... **2,000.00**

Bowl

6" d, 2" h, trefoil rim, colorless and brick-orange body, frosted int., dec as branches of mistletoe with white berries, gold enhancement, base sgd "Daum (cross) Nancy" . **920.00**

6-1/2" d, 4-3/4" h, colorless glass cased to red, gold foil inclusions, blown into wrought iron three-ftd stand, base of bowl inscribed "Daum (cross) Nancy France, L. Marjorelle," c1920 .... **815.00**

6-3/4" d, 3-1/8" h, mottled yellow-pink dish, metal foil inclusions blown into simple wrought iron framework, base sgd "Daum Nancy/L. Majorelle" **1,100.00**

7-3/4" h, circular, pinched quatrefoil rim, burgundy mottled yellow ground, etched berried branches, black enamel highlights, enameled "Daum Nancy/France" .. **1,800.00**

8-1/2" h, 5-1/4" h, flared, ftd, inverted rim, mottled burgundy ground, overlaid in puce, etched wooded lake scene, cameo sgd "Daum Nancy" **1,600.00**

Box, cov

2-3/4" h, sq, frosted colorless, white, and amber ground, amethyst-purple blossoms and buds, delicate green leafy stems, conforming cov, sgd in green "Daum Nancy (cross)" .. **2,100.00**

6" w, 5-1/4" h, brilliant blue mottled ground, shades of turquoise blue and cobalt blue, gold foil dec, sgd "Daum Nancy" **275.00**

Candlesticks, pr, 6-3/4" h, 9" l, three-lite, molded colorless form, engraved "Daum (cross) Nancy," c1960 .... **175.00**

Centerbowl, 23" l, 8" h, modern, crystal, heavy walled elliptical colorless, inscribed "Daum France" **175.00**

Chandelier, 41" l, flared trumpet hanger, wide domed shade, rich yellow glass etched with vertical geometric devices, etched "Daum Nancy" **25,000.00**

Cologne bottle, 6" h, mold blown Art Deco sq colorless bottle, cased to opaque amethyst, capped with conforming orange stopper, lower edge engraved "Daum (cross) Nancy," pr **920.00**

Coupe, 16" d, flared circular form, etched geometric pattern, faceted base, smoky topaz, incised "Daum Nancy France" **1,100.00**

Creamer, 3-1/8" h, 3" d, cameo, squared bulbous, round mouth, mottled gold shading to mottled brown frosted ground, enameled green leaves and brown berries, single acid cutting, cameo sgd **1,750.00**

Cruet, 7-1/4" h, green ground, stylized foliate branch with white enamel berries, gold enamel accents, applied brushed gold highlights, sterling silver edged matching flag sided stopper, orig silver holder with cut out edge, gold enamel sgd "Daum Nancy," cross of Lorraine **1,850.00**

Cup and saucer, 3-1/4" d cup, 5-1/4" d saucer, etched and enameled black on white to colorless, handled cup with Dutch lowlands scene, woman walking on tree lined roadway, passing sailboats, saucer with scene of windmill, farm, each pc marked in gold "Daum (cross) Nancy" **1,150.00**

Dealer's sign, crystal, France .. **60.00**

Decanter, 9" h, bulbous Art-Deco style, bubbly orange, applied aubergine handle and stopper, sgd "Daum (cross) Nancy/France" at lower edge .. **690.00**

Egg, 5" h, fiery opalescent egg-shaped oval, acid etched eggshell texture, shallow cameo, cut ducks in groups of three, sgd on glass base, mounted to gilt metal beaded pedestal foot **1,600.00**

Flower pot, 5-3/4" h, heavy walled colorless molded body, internally dec by tiny bubbles, lower edge engraved "Daum (cross) Nancy-France" . **345.00**

Goblet

5-1/2" h, colorless glass, black and gold enameled floral and painted dec, sgd............. **1,250.00**

Dali, sgd, orig presentation box **400.00**

Hops pitcher, 3" h, flattened miniature, fiery yellow amber, scrolling stylized etched and enameled black and gold dec, base marked "Daum (cross) Nancy" **1,850.00**

Jar, cov

2-1/4" h, 4" w, light and dark blue textured crystal ground, cameo carved pale gray and black poppies, leaves, and buds, gold accents, sterling lid with "E" monogram and emb poppies, minute wear to edge rim of jar **200.00**

3-3/4" h, apple shape, green bowl, matching cove, bright orange finial, side inscribed "Daum (cross) Nancy" **260.00**

Jar, open, 1-3/4" h, polished rim, colorless, white and purple bowl, wheat shaft and grasses dec, base sgd "Daum (cross) Nancy" in gold . **850.00**

Lamp base

10-1/2" h, oviform, yellow ground overlaid in burgundy, etched and polished with stylized flowering vines, carved "Daum Nancy France," drilled and mounted in gilt-metal base. **1,500.00**

15-3/4" h, elliptical mottled amber and brown vase, deeply etched and wheel-cut mushrooms growing wild under branches, pine cones and needles, all over naturalized enameling, drilled and mounted with gilt metal lamp fittings top and base **4,600.00**

Lamp, table

19-1/2" h, trumpet form standard, domed shade with open top, tangerine ground shading to yellow, etched and enameled sailboats, enameled "Daum Nancy". **8,500.00**

20" h, 11-1/4" d domed gray glass shade, etched vertical lines, etched "Daum Nancy France," wrought iron standard dec with pine cone clusters, circular foot with conforming dec, stamped "Katona" **2,500.00**

20-1/4" h, gray-white glass elongated slender dome shade acid etched in furrows, zig-zag border, wrought iron mount, base, and shade inscribed "Daum Nancy France" with cross de Lorraine **135,000.00**

21" h, domed reverse painted shade, blackberries and foliate design, bronze Art Nouveau Edgar Brandt base, France, early 20th C **14,950.00**

21-1/2" h, 12" d orange domed glass shade with scalloped rim, etched stylized chrysanthemums, etched "Daum Nancy France," reticulated scrolled wrought iron base **2,200.00**

Miniature

Pitcher, 2-1/2" h, 3" w, clear glass, int. ribbing, black enameled landscape, gold trim, applied loop handle, sgd "Daum Nancy" **2,000.00**

Vase

1-1/2" h, shaped cylindrical, mottled tangerine ground, etched and enameled snow scene with trees, enameled "Daum Nancy" **800.00**

1-3/4" h, bright yellow ground, enameled brown landscape design. **850.00**

Perfume bottle, cameo, gold iridescent and foliage, purple ground, replaced stopper, 7-1/2" h, **$1,430.** *Photo courtesy of Jackson's Auctioneers & Appraisers*

Paperweight, cactus **125.00**

Perfume flacon, 5-3/4" h, colorless bottle, shaded emerald green at top, etched poppy blossoms and pod, starry background, mounted with silver taster foot, screw rim, and swirled cov, base marked "Daum (cross) Nancy" **1,380.00**

Platter, 17-3/4" d, round, topaz ground, ext. etched with concentric textured Art-Deco style rings, base edge inscribed "Daum (cross) Nancy France," minor scratches **650.00**

Salt, open

1-1/4" h, 1-1/4" w, bucket shape, two tab handles, snowy landscape scene **900.00**

1-1/2" d, 1-1/4" h, bucket shape, winter scene of windmill and boats, opaque ground, sgd **690.00**

2" d, 1-1/8" h, small oval form, colorless glass, etched with border band of florets, grisaille enamel, band of raised florets, gold enamel highlights, c1900 . . . . **375.00**

Sculpture, 8-1/4" h, clear and frosted, designed by Folon, #81 of limited edition of 300, etched "Folon Daum France 81/300" **175.00**

Toothpick holder, 2" h, orange and yellow mottled ground, winter trees in snowy landscape dec, base sgd "Daum (cross) Nancy". **1,150.00**

Vase

3" h, flattened form, gray and tan ground, enameled floral dec, molded "Daum Nancy/France" **1,300.00**

3-1/2" h, oviform, mottled frosted white ground shading to violet base, etched and enameled violets, cameo sgd "Daum Nancy" **2,000.00**

3-1/2" h, 7-1/4" d, quatraform rim, mottled burgundy red bowl-form, three encased gold foil elements, lower edge inscribed "Daum (cross) Nancy," some int. scratches **460.00**

3-3/4" h, enameled winter scene of sailing chips, windmills, and trees, sgd "Daum Nancy" on base **860.00**

3-7/8" h, squared rim, goblet form, yellow-orange mottled ground, winter trees above snowy ground, minimal chip on pedestal foot, base inscribed "Daum (cross) Nancy" **2,185.00**

4" h, bulbed oval, sunset red and orange, overlaid in dark burgundy-black, cameo-etched leafy waterfront trees with boats, lower side sgd "Daum (cross) Nancy" **865.00**

4-1/2" h, diamond form, cased yellow and mottled orange body, etched and enameled orange poppy blossoms and buds, delicate green stems, gold enhanced leaves, side sgd "Daum Nancy (cross)" **1,785.00**

4-1/2" h, ftd trumpet form, rich opalescent ground, etched and enameled thistle branch, engraved "Daum Nancy" **700.00**

4-1/2" h, squared form, acid textured body enameled dec with glossy purple violets among emerald green foliage, gilt highlights, int. mottled gray-white and purple, cameo sgd "Daum Nancy" with croix de Lorraine, small rim nicks **1,000.00**

4-1/2" h, waisted lozenge form, opalescent ground, delicate enamel and gilt foliate dec, painted "Daum Nancy" **1,500.00**

4-1/2" h, 2" w, single layer of pale opalescent yellow, cutting of thistles and leaves, sgd . . . **350.00**

4-3/4" h, square etched colorless body, cased to yellow and deep purple, overall painted naturalized cornflowers, side sgd in cameo "Daum Nancy (cross)" . . . **3,550.00**

4-7/8" h, barrel, mottled red, orange, and green body, overlaid in olive green, etched riverside landscape, lower side sgd "Daum (cross) Nancy" **1,380.00**

4-7/8" h, square cylinder of colorless and sky-blue glass, etched and painted as leafy birch trees at riverside, "Daum (cross) Nancy" inscribed in base **2,415.00**

4-7/8" h, square cylinder of green over colorless, cameo-etched iris blossom, border scene above and gold enamel highlights, "Daum (cross) Nancy" in gold on base **690.00**

5" h, oval body, gold highlighted iris blossoms, raised on hallmarked silver pedestal foot, side sgd "Daum (cross) Nancy" **375.00**

5-1/4" h, blue-green bowl-form, amber splotches raised on aubergine-black pedestal foot, smooth flougravure finish, inscribed "Daum (cross) Nancy" on lower side **600.00**

5-1/2" h, enameled, conical vessel, four pinched sides, enamel painted yellow and amethyst frosted surface, orange blossoms, tall spike leaves, "Daum Nancy (cross)" painted on side . . **1,610.00**

5-1/2" h, etched and enameled, pinched trumpet form, mottled yellow shading to apricot, etched and enameled white flowering branches, cameo sgd "Daum Nancy" **2,200.00**

5-1/2" h, etched, Art Deco, monochromatic translucent yellow sphere, alternating glossy and etched panels, base rim inscribed "Daum (cross) Nancy France" **345.00**

6" h, bulbous, fluted panels, smoky gray, wheel carved "Daum Nancy France" **500.00**

6" h, elongated oval, intercalaire etched, seagreen glass internally dec with burgundy trailings, etched aquatic foliage, gilt highlights, seagreen finely enameled with seaweed, fish, and squid, enameled "Daum Nancy" . **6,000.00**

6" h, wheel-carved, fire-polished, squatty bulbous form, everted rim, opalescent ground, overlaid with cranberry and spruce, etched and carved wild roses on thorny branches, martele surface, engraved "Daum Nancy" **4,500.00**

6-1/4" h, elliptical opalescent body, free-form decorative rim, etched tall leafy trees in foreground, red landscape in distance enhanced by enamel dec, base sgd in black "Daum (cross) Nancy" . . **4,100.00**

6-1/4" h, tooled double pointed rim, yellow amber tapered cylinder, brown and black sailboats in harbor scene, base inscribed "Daum (cross) Nancy" . . **2,300.00**

6-3/4" h, two handled oval, opaque green shaded into orange-amber, delicate cameo-etched spring flowers painted in natural palette, enhanced by gold repeating on applied handles, base inscribed in gold "Daum (cross) Nancy" **2,875.00**

6-7/8" h, raised rim, urn-form, frosted amber, orange, and mottled green body, etched and realistically colored orchid blossoms, delicate stems, above wild grasses, side sgd "Daum Nancy (cross)" **1,265.00**

7" h, broad oval bowl form, pedestal foot, colorless glass, rose red mottled powders below bright royal blue border, internally decorated, base inscribed "Daum (cross) Nancy" **435.00**

7" h, offset rect, gilt highlighted poppies, apricot textured ground, gold sgd "Daum Nancy" with croix de Lorraine, gilt rim has small nick in corner **750.00**

7-3/4" h, bulbous, polished rim, monochromatic topaz body, repeating etched panels of Art Deco geometric devices, lower edge engraved "Daum (cross) Nancy France" **375.00**

7-3/4" h, oviform, everted rim, overlaid in red and blue, etched and wheel-carved iris blossoms and foliage against martele ground, engraved "Daum Nancy" **3,250.00**

8-3/4" h, compressed cylindrical, mottled sky-blue ground, etched mountainous landscape with trees and lake in foreground, enameled "Daum Nancy" **4,000.00**

8-7/8" h, colorless, blown, applied blue and brown glass medallion, diagonal cut lines, engraved "Daum France," orig paper label **225.00**

9-1/4" h, baluster, overlaid in orange and green, etched and carved poppy blossoms and foliage, frosted martele ground, engraved "Daum Nancy" **2,000.00**

9-1/4" h, slender bud, creamy amber, blue foot, smooth flougravure finish, inscribed "Daum (cross) Nancy" on lower side **650.00**

9-1/2" h, ftd trumpet form, opalescent ground, etched and enameled thistle blossoms, gilt highlights, gilded "Daum Nancy" **2,000.00**

10-3/4" h, elongated oval, mottled white, colorless, and deep purple-blue body, etched overall and cameo enamel painted as naturalized stalks of wheat and grasses, gold accents and embellishments, base marked in gold "Daum (cross) Nancy" **5,750.00**

11-3/4" h, waisted cylinder, mottled autumnal colors, etched thorny branches and leaves, cameo sgd "Daum Nancy" **1,400.00**

12-1/4" h, flattened flask form, mottled burgundy and lemon ground, overlaid in puce, etched wooded lace scene, sailboats, cameo sgd "Daum Nancy" **2,500.00**

13-1/4" h, modern, crystal, heavy walled colorless trapezoidal body, inscribed "Daum" near base, tiny top chips **175.00**

Vase, cameo-etched, pink and white flowers on gray, blue, and green ground, signed "Daum Nancy," 4-1/4" h, 2-1/4" w, **$2,000.** *Photo courtesy of David Rago Auctions.*

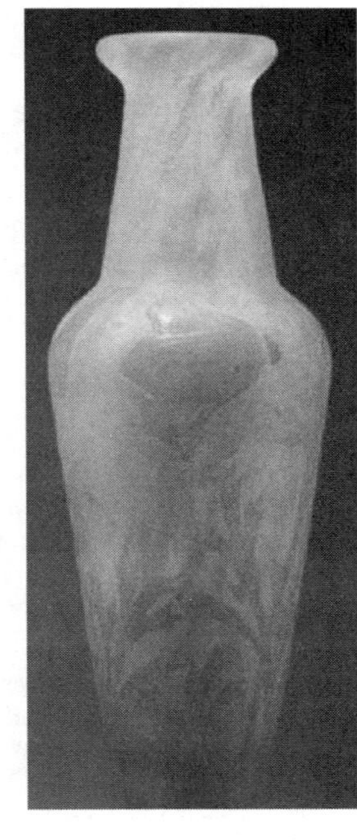

Vase, cameo-etched, marquetry applied orange florals, wheel carved details, signed, 8-3/4" h, **$4,025.** *Photo courtesy of David Rago Auctions.*

14" h, small mouth over shouldered vessel tapering to pedestal base, mottled gray, colorless, and chartreuse glass layered in vitrified colors of striated purple, green, and orange, cameo-etched clusters of berries on thorny branches, sgd in cameo "Daum Nancy (cross)," c1900. . . **1,725.00**

14-1/2" h, flared oviform, flattened sq foot, deep smoky topaz, etched vertical skyscraper motif bands, wheel carved "Daum Nancy France" **7,000.00**

15-1/2" h, raised rim, oval shaded gray to sky-yellow to gray, vitrified autumn colors on falling leaves above and below landscape scene, medial cameo mark "Daum Nancy (cross)". **6,900.00**

19-3/4" h, cylindrical, bulbous base, frosted ground shading to emerald green, etched and enameled storks in flight, lotus blossom lake below en-griasille, gilt highlights, gilt sgd "Daum Nancy" . . **5,750.00**

20" h, trumpet form, bulbous foot, lavender ground, deep violet overlay, etched and wheel-carved flowering clematis blossoms and foliage, fine martele ground, cameo sgd "Daum Nancy" **6,000.00**

27" h, elongated extended neck, bulbous body, mottled pastel blue-green, multicolored yellow-red acid finished surface, etched repeating geometric and foliate dec, marked "Daum Nancy (cross)" in cameo at side . **2,100.00**

Veilleuse lamp shade, 6" h, mottled frosted yellow, amber, and orange, side inscribed "Daum (cross) Nancy" **460.00**

Water pitcher, 9-1/2" h, smoke, etched Art-Deco design, acid sgd "Daum Nancy" **150.00**

Wine, 3-1/2" h, entire surface of glass cut and polished with gold dec, sgd, set of nine **325.00**

DEGENHART GLASS

History: John (1884-1964) and Elizabeth (1889-1978) Degenhart operated the Crystal Art Glass factory of Cambridge, Ohio, from 1947 to 1978. The factory specialized in reproduction pressed-glass novelties and paperweights. More than 50 molds were worked by this factory including 10 toothpick holders, five salts, and six animal-covered dishes of various sizes.

When the factory ceased operation, many of the molds were purchased by Boyd Crystal Art Glass, Cambridge, Ohio. Boyd has issued pieces in many new colors and has marked them all with a "B" in a diamond.

Degenhart pressed-glass novelties are collected by mold (Forget-Me-Not toothpick holders or all Degenhart toothpick holders), by individual colors (Rubina or Bloody Mary), or by group colors (opaque, iridescent, crystal, or slag).

Correct color identification is a key factor when collecting Degenhart glass. Because of the slight variations in the hundreds of colors produced at the Degenhart Crystal Art Glass factory from 1947 to 1978, it is important for beginning collectors to learn to distinguish Degenhart colors, particularly the green and blue variations. Seek guidance from knowledgeable collectors or dealers. Side-by-side color comparison is extremely helpful.

Later glass produced by the factory can be distinguished by the "D" in a heart trademark or a "D" by itself on molds where there was insufficient space for the full mark. Use of the "D" mark began around 1972, and by late 1977, most of the molds had been marked. From 1947 to 1972, pieces were not marked except for owls and the occasional piece hand stamped with a block letter "D" as it came out of the mold. This hand stamping was used from 1967 to 1972.

Collecting unmarked Degenhart glass made from 1947 to 1970 poses no problem once a collector becomes familiar with the molds and colors which were used during that period. Some of the most desirable colors, such as Amethyst & White Slag, Amethyst Carnival, and Custard Slag, are unmarked. Keep in mind that some colors, e.g., Custard (opaque yellow), Heliotrope (opaque purple), and Tomato (opaque orange red), were used repeatedly, and both marked and unmarked pieces can be found, depending on production date.

References: Gene Florence, *Degenhart Glass and Paperweights*, Degenhart Paperweight and Glass Museum, 1982.

Collectors' Club: Friends of Degenhart, Degenhart Paperweight and Glass Museum, Inc., 65323 Highland Hills Rd, P.O. Box 186, Cambridge, OH 43725.

Museum: The Degenhart Paperweight and Glass Museum, Inc., Cambridge, OH. The museum displays all types of Ohio valley glass.

Reproduction Alert: Although most of the Degenhart molds were reproductions themselves, there are contemporary pieces that can be confusing such as Kanawha's bird salt and bow slipper; L. G. Wright's mini-slipper, Daisy & Button salt, and five-inch robin-covered dish; and many other contemporary American pieces. The three-inch-bird salt and mini-pitcher also are made by an unknown glassmaker in Taiwan.

Bell, 2" h, 1976
- Lavender **12.00**
- Vaseline **15.00**

Bernard and Eldena, 7/8" w, 2-3/4" h, price for pr
- Amethyst Carnival **15.00**
- Cobalt Carnival **15.00**
- Cranberry Ice Carnival **18.00**
- Crystal Carnival **15.00**
- Green Carnival **15.00**
- Ice Blue Carnival **15.00**

Boot, 2-1/2" h, black slag, "D" in heart mark **25.00**

Candy jar, cov, amberina. **24.00**

Child's mug, Stork and Peacock. **25.00**

Coaster, introduced 1974, marked 1975, crystal. **9.00**

Creamer and sugar, Daisy and Button, carnival. **45.00**

Cup plate
- Heart and Lyre, mulberry **18.00**
- Seal of Ohio, sunset **15.00**

Hand, marked, Crown Tuscan . . . **22.00**

Hat, Daisy and Button
- Amber **12.00**
- Amberina. **20.00**
- Blue **18.00**

Hen, covered dish, ebony, 3-1/2". **24.00**

Jewel box, heart shape, blue . . . **38.00**

Owl, 1-3/4" w, 3-1/2" h, introduced 1967, large "D" mark
- Antique Blue **45.00**
- Bloody Mary **75.00**
- Chad's Blue **45.00**
- Cobalt Blue **35.00**
- Cobalt Blue Carnival **125.00**
- Crystal **10.00**
- Dark Rose Marie **45.00**

Emerald Green 45.00
Light Blue 10.00
Light Bluefire. 45.00
Midnight Sun. 45.00
Pink. 45.00
Purple Slag 35.00
Red Carnival. 110.00
Tiger 45.00

Paperweight, early 1950s, John Degenhart
2-1/2" d, 2-1/2" h, five multicolored flowers, each with controlled bubble center. 175.00
3" d, 3" h, dark blue flower, green ground 250.00
3-1/4" d, multicolored floral bouquet 250.00
3-1/2" d, multicolored floral bouquet, five teardrop controlled bubbles 250.00

Pooch
Amethyst. 40.00
Baby Green. 22.00
Bittersweet 15.50
Brown 15.00
Canary 17.50
Charcoal 20.25
Cobalt Blue. 28.00
Fawn 17.50
Henri Blue. 15.50
Heather Bloom 27.50
Milk Glass, blue 15.50
Periwinkle 31.00
Rosemary Pink 18.00
Royal Violet. 24.00
Willow Blue 20.00

Portrait dish, portrait of Elizabeth Degenhart, 5-1/2" d, emb name and "First Lady of Glass"
Amethyst. 50.00
Clear 30.00

Priscilla, Rose Marie, June, 1976 65.00

Robin, covered dish
Blue, 5-1/2" w 40.00
Taffeta, marked. 55.00

Salt and pepper shakers, pair, birds, blue opaque, **$18.**

Salt and pepper shakers, pr, bird, sapphire 18.00

Tomahawk, 2" w, 3-3/4" l, "D" in heart mark
Amethyst Carnival 18.00
Chocolate Slag 15.00
Cobalt Blue 15.00
Cobalt Blue Carnival 15.00
Crystal Carnival 15.00
Pink Carnival 15.00

Toothpick holder
Basket, milk glass, white 18.00
Beaded Heart, lemon custard . 20.00
Colonial Drape and Heart, custard 20.00
Degenhart Bird, vaseline, 2-3/4" h 24.00
Elephant's Head, jade 24.00
Forget-Me-Not, Bloody Mary . . 24.00

Wine glass, Buzz Saw
Cobalt Blue 20.00
Milk Glass, blue 22.00
Vaseline 20.00

DEPRESSION GLASS

History: Depression glass was made from 1920 to 1940. It was an inexpensive machine-made glass and was produced by several companies in various patterns and colors. The number of forms made in different patterns also varied.

Depression glass was sold through variety stores, given away as premiums, or packaged with certain products. Movie houses gave it away from 1935 until well into the 1940s.

Like pattern glass, knowing the proper name of a pattern is the key to collecting. Collectors should be prepared to do research.

References: Tom and Neila Bredehoft, *Fifty Years of Collectible Glass, 1920-1970, Volume 1, Volume II,* Antique Trader Books, 2000; Debbie and Randy Coe, *Elegant Glass: Early, Depression & Beyond,* Schiffer Publishing, 2001; Shirley Dunbar, *Heisey Glass, The Early Years, 1896-1924,* Krause Publications, 2000; Gene Florence, *Anchor Hocking's Fire-King & More,* 2nd ed., Collector Books, 2000; —, *Collectible Glassware from the '40s, '50s, '60s,* 6th ed., Collector Books, 2001; —, *Collector's Encyclopedia of Depression Glass,* 15th ed., Collector Books, 2001; —, *Elegant Glassware of the Depression Era,* 9th ed., Collector Books, 2000; —, *Florence's Glassware Pattern Identification Guide,* Collector Books, Vol. I, 1998, Vol. II, 1999; —, *Glass Candlesticks of the Depression Era,* Collector Books, 2000; —, *Pocket Guide to Depression Glass & More, 1920-1960s,* 12th ed., Collector Books, 2000; —, *Stemware Identification Featuring Cordials with Values,* 1920s-1960s, Collector Books, 1997; —, *Very Rare Glassware of the Depression Era,* 1st Series (1988, 1991 value update), 2nd Series (1991), 3rd Series (1993, 1995 value update), 4th Series (1996, 1997 value update), 5th Series (1996, 1999 value update), Collector Books; Philip Hopper, *Forest Green Glass,* Schiffer Publishing, 2000; Ralph and Terry Kovel, *Kovels' Depression Glass & American Dinnerware Price List,* 5th ed., Crown, 1995; Carl F. Luckey and Debbie Coe, *Identification & Value Guide to Depression Era Glassware,* 4th ed., Krause Publications, 2002; Jim and Barbara Mauzy, *Mauzy's Depression Glass,* 3rd ed., Schiffer, 2001; James Measell and Berry Wiggins, *Great American Glass of the Roaring '20s & Depression Era,* Book 2, Antique Publications, 2000; Leslie Piña and Paula Ockner, *Depression Era Art Deco Glass,* Schiffer Publishing, 1999; Leslie Piña, *Fifties Glass,* 2nd ed., Schiffer Publishing, 2000; Sherry Riggs and Paula Pendergrass, *Glass Candle Holders of the Depression Era and Beyond,* Schiffer Publishing, 2001; Ellen T. Schroy, *Warman's Depression Glass,* 2nd ed., Krause Publications, 2000; Kent G. Washburn, *Price Survey,* 4th ed., published by author, 1994; Hazel Marie Weatherman, *Colored Glassware of the Depression Era,* Book 2, published by author 1974, available in reprint; —, *1984 Supplement & Price Trends for Colored Glassware of the Depression Era, Book 1,* published by author, 1984.

Collectors' Clubs: Big "D" Pression Glass Club, 10 Windling Creek Trail, Garland, TX 75043; Buckeye Dee Geer's, 2501 Campbell St., Sandusky, OH 44870; Canadian Depression Glass Assoc., 119 Wexford Rd, Brampton, Ontario L6Z 2T5, Canada; Clearwater Depression Glass Club, 10038 62nd Terrace North, St. Petersburg, FL 33708; Crescent City Depression Glass Club, 140 Commerce St., Gretna, LA 70056; Depression Era Glass Society of Wisconsin, 1534 S. Wisconsin Ave., Racine, WI 53403; Depression Glass Club of Greater Rochester, 657 East Ave., Rochester, NY 14609; Depression Glass Club of North East Florida, 2604 Jolly Rd, Jacksonville, FL 33207; Fostoria Glass Collectors, Inc., P.O. Box 1625, Orange, CA 92668; Gateway Depressioners Glass Club of Greater St. Louis, 2040 Flight Drive, Florissant, MO 63031-2216; Greater Tulsa Depression Era Glass Club, P.O. Box 470763, Tulsa, OK 74147-0763; Heart of America Glass Collectors, 14404 E. 36th Terrace, Independence, MO, 64055; Illinois Valley Depression Glass Club, RR 1, Box 52, Rushville, IL 62681; Iowa Depression Glass Assoc., 5871 Vista Dr., Apt 725, West Des Moines, IA 50266; Land of Sunshine Depression Glass Club, P.O. Box 560275, Orlando, FL 32856-0275; Lincoln Land Depression Glass Club, 1625 Dial Court, Springfield, IL 62704; Long Island Depression Glass Club, P.O. Box 148, West Sayville, NY 11796; National Depression Glass Assoc., Inc., P.O. Box 8264, Wichita, KS 67209; Northeast Florida Depression Glass Club, P.O. Box 338, Whitehouse, FL 32220; North Jersey Dee Geer's, P.O. Box 741, Oradell, NJ 07649; Peach State Depression Glass Club, 4174 Reef Rd., Marietta, GA 30066; Permian Basin Depression Glass Club, 1412 Alamosa St., Odessa, TX 79763; Phoenix and Consolidated Glass Collectors' Club, P.O. Box 182082, Arlington, TX 76096-2082; Southern Illinois Diamond H Seekers, 1203 N. Yale, O'Fallon, IL 62269; 20-30-40 Society, Inc., P.O. Box 856, LaGrange, IL 60525; Western Reserve Depression Glass Club, 8669 Courtland Drive, Strongsville, OH 44136.

Web Site: *DG Shopper Online,* the WWW Depression-era glass magazine, http://www.dgshopper.com; Mega Show, http://www.glassshow.com; Facets Antiques & Collectibles Mall, http://www.Facets.net

Videotape: "Living Glass: Popular Patterns of the Depression Era," 2 vols., Ro Cliff Communications, 1993.

Reproduction Alert: Reproductions of Depression glass patterns can be a real problem. Some are easy to detect, but others are very good. Now that there are reproductions of the reproductions, the only hope for collectors is to know what they are buying and to buy from reputable dealers and/or other collectors. Most of the current Depression glass reference books have excellent sections on reproductions. The following items with an asterisk (*) have been reproduced, but beware that there are more reproductions being brought into the marketplace.

Note: The examples listed here are only a small sampling of the patterns and variety of objects found in this large collecting area. Please refer to one of the reference books mentioned for more detailed listings of a particular pattern or manufacturer.

Ashtray

Adam, Jeannette Glass Co., 4-1/2" d
- Green **25.00**
- Pink **32.00**

Cloverleaf, Hazel Atlas, 5-3/4" d, green **20.00**

Diana, Federal Glass Co., pink . **4.00**

Early American Prescut (Anchor Hocking), crystal
- 4" d **3.00**
- 7-3/4 d **12.00**

Floragold, Jeannette Glass Co., irid **10.00**

Forest Green, Anchor Hocking Glass Co., 4-5/8" sq, green **5.50**

Harp, Jeannette Glass Co., crystal **4.50**

Homespun (Fine Rib), Jeannette Glass Co., crystal or pink **6.00**

Manhattan (Horizontal Ribbed), Anchor Hocking Glass Co., crystal **11.00**

Moroccan Amethyst, Hazel Ware, amethyst
- 6-7/8" triangular **12.50**
- 8" sq **17.50**

Pineapple & Floral, 4-1/2" d, amber **20.00**

Sandwich, Indiana Glass Co., crystal, club **3.50**

Soreno, Anchor Hocking, aquamarine, 8" **14.50**

Sunflower, Jeannette Glass Co., green **14.00**

Windsor (Windsor Diamond), Jeannette Glass Co., 5-3/4" d, pink **35.00**

Berry bowl, individual

Adam, Jeannette Glass Co., pink **16.50**

Anniversary, Jeannette Glass Co., 4-7/8" d, irid **4.50**

Bowknot, green **16.00**

Cherry Blossom, Jeannette Glass Co., delphite* **15.00**

Colonial Fluted (Rope), Federal Glass Co., green **11.00**

Coronation (Banded Fine Rib, Saxon), Hocking Glass Co., ruby, 4-1/2" d, two handles **9.50**

Doric & Pansy, Jeannette Glass Co., ultramarine **20.00**

Fruits, Hazel Atlas, green **28.00**

Heritage, Federal Glass Co.
- Blue **55.00**
- Crystal **9.50**

Madrid, Federal Glass Co., amber **6.00**

Normandie (Bouquet and Lattice), Federal Glass Co., 5" d, irid . . **5.00**

Old Café, Hocking Glass Co., ruby **6.00**

Patrician (Spoke), Federal Glass Co., amber **12.00**

Pyramid (No. 610), Indiana Glass Co., green **25.00**

Rose Cameo, Belmont Tumbler Co., green **12.00**

Sharon (Cabbage Rose), Federal Glass Co., pink **10.00**

Windsor (Windsor Diamond), Jeannette Glass Co., 4-3/4" d, crystal **4.00**

Berry bowl, master

Aunt Polly, U.S. Glass Co., blue **45.00**

Cameo (Ballerina, Dancing Girl), Hocking Glass Co., pink . . **150.00**

Colonial Fluted (Rope), Federal Glass Co., crystal **16.00**

Coronation (Banded Fine Rib, Saxon), Hocking Glass Co., ruby, 8" d, two handles **27.50**

Doric, Jeannette Glass Co. delphite **135.00**

Floral and Diamond Band, pink **13.00**

Florentine No. 2 (Poppy No. 2), Hazel Atlas, 9" d, yellow **30.00**

Heritage, Federal Glass Co.
- Crystal **40.00**
- Pink **45.00**

Indiana Custard, (Flower and Leaf Band), Indiana Glass Co., French Ivory **32.00**

Lorain, Indiana Glass Co., green **85.00**

Newport (Hairpin), Hazel Atlas, amethyst **35.00**

Raindrops (Optic Design), Federal Glass Co., green **45.00**

Strawberry, U.S. Glass Co., green or pink **20.00**

Windsor (Windsor Diamond), Jeannette Glass Co., 8-1/2" d, green **17.50**

Berry set, Capri, Seashells, 8-3/4" d bowl, six 4-3/4" bowls **50.00**

Bonbon

Flower Garden with Butterflies (Butterflies and Roses), U.S. Glass Co., black **265.00**

Moonstone, Anchor Hocking Glass Co., opal, heart shape **14.00**

Royal Ruby, Anchor Hocking, ruby **18.00**

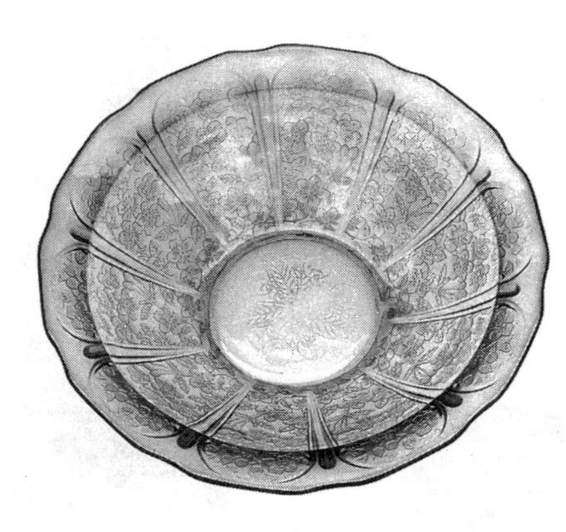

Bowl, Cherry Blossom, 8-1/2" d, green, **$22.**

Bowl

Adam, Jeannette Glass Co., green, 9" d **45.00**

American Pioneer, Liberty Works, crystal, 9" d **24.00**

Bamboo Optic, Liberty, 4-1/4" d, green **6.00**

Carolyn, Lancaster, 11" d, topaz **36.00**

Cube (Cubist), Jeannette Glass Co., 4-1/2" d, green **7.00**

Diamond Quilted (Flat Diamond), Imperial Glass Co., 7" d, green or pink **10.00**

Early American Prescut, (Anchor Hocking), crystal, ruffled, 5-1/4" d **6.50**

Floragold, Jeannette Glass Co., 5-1/4" d, ruffled, irid **16.00**

Georgian (Lovebirds), Federal Glass Co., 6-1/2" d, green **65.00**

Iris (Iris and Herringbone), Jeannette Glass Co., 9-1/2" d, irid **10.00**

Jody, Lancaster, 12" l, oval, topaz **35.00**

Jubilee, Lancaster Glass Co., 8" d, pink **265.00**
Manhattan (Horizontal Ribbed), Anchor Hocking Glass Co., crystal, 7" d, two handles **16.00**
Moonstone, Anchor Hocking Glass Co., cloverleaf, opal **13.00**
Moroccan Amethyst, Hazel Ware, amethyst, 5-3/4" sq. **12.50**
Oyster and Pearls, Anchor Hocking Glass Co., 5-1/4" w, heart shape, ruby **15.00**
Primo (Paneled Aster), U.S. Glass Co., 7-3/4" d, green **25.00**
Queen Mary, pink, 6" d **20.00**
Roxana, Hazel Atlas, golden topaz **12.00**
Sandwich, Anchor Hocking, crystal, scalloped, 8" d **12.50**
Sharon (Cabbage Rose), Federal Glass Co., 8" d, amber **5.00**
Sphinx, Lancaster, 12" d, green **135.00**
Tulip, Dell Glass Co., 13-1/4" l, amber, crystal, or green **40.00**
Windsor (Windsor Diamond), Jeannette Glass Co., pointed edge, pink, 10-1/2" l **35.00**

Butter dish, covered, Columbia, clear, **$16.**

Butter dish, cov

Adam, Jeannette Glass Co., pink* **95.00**
Anniversary, Jeannette Glass Co., pink. **60.00**
Block Optic (Block), Hocking Glass Co., green. **50.00**
Cameo (Ballerina, Dancing Girl), Hocking Glass Co., yellow **1,400.00**
Colonial (Knife and Fork), Hocking Glass Co., green **60.00**
Colonial Block, Hazel Atlas, Hazel Atlas, green or pink **45.00**
Doric, Jeannette Glass Co. green **90.00**
Floral (Poinsettia), Jeannette Glass Co., green **90.00**
Georgian (Lovebirds), Federal Glass Co., green **80.00**
Hex Optic (Honeycomb), Jeannette Glass Co., green **75.00**
Holiday (Buttons and Bows), Jeannette Glass Co., pink . . . **45.00**
Miss America, (Diamond Pattern), Hocking Glass Co., crystal* **200.00**
Moderntone, Hazel Atlas, cobalt blue, metal cov **100.00**
Royal Lace, Hazel Atlas, pink **150.00**
Sandwich, Anchor Hocking, low, crystal **45.00**
Sandwich, Indiana Glass Co., amber dome, crystal base **55.00**
Sierra Pinwheel, Jeannette Glass Co., green **75.00**
U.S. Swirl, U.S. Glass Co., green or pink **115.00**
Windsor (Windsor Diamond), Jeannette Glass Co., pink . . . **60.00**

Cake plate

Adam, Jeannette Glass Co., green **32.00**
Anniversary, Jeannette Glass Co., crystal, round **7.50**
Block Optic (Block), Hocking Glass Co., crystal **18.00**
Cameo (Ballerina, Dancing Girl), Hocking Glass Co., 10" d, green **22.00**
Cherry Blossom, Jeannette Glass Co., pink*. **25.00**
Doric, Jeannette Glass Co. pink **30.00**
Harp, Jeannette Glass Co., crystal, gold trim, ruffled, 9" d **30.00**
Holiday (Buttons and Bows), Jeannette Glass Co., 10-1/2" d, pink **100.00**
Miss America, (Diamond Pattern), Hocking Glass Co. **25.00**
Primo (Paneled Aster), U.S. Glass Co., green or yellow **23.50**
Sunflower, Jeannette Glass Co., green or pink. **16.00**
Thistle, Macbeth-Evans, green **150.00**

Candlesticks, pr

Adam, Jeannette Glass Co., 4" h, pink **100.00**
Bamboo Optic, Liberty, hexagon base, pink **25.00**
Holiday (Buttons and Bows), Jeannette Glass Co., 3" h, pink **110.00**
Laced Edge (Katy Blue), Imperial Glass Co., Imperial, two-lite, green **180.00**
Madrid, Federal Glass Co., 2-1/4" h, pink* **28.00**
Moonstone, Anchor Hocking Glass Co., opal. **18.00**
Old Colony (Lace Edge, Open Lace), Hocking Glass Co., pink **250.00**
Patrick, Lancaster Glass Co., pink **150.00**
Tea Room, Indiana Glass Co., green **48.00**

Candy dish, cov

Cloverleaf, Hazel Atlas, green **45.00**
Floragold, Jeannette Glass Co., irid **15.00**
Flower Garden with Butterflies (Butterflies and Roses), U.S. Glass Co., heart shape, pink **195.00**
Fortune, Hocking Glass Co., pink **25.00**
Iris (Iris and Herringbone), Jeannette Glass Co., crystal* **150.00**
Moroccan Amethyst, Hazel Ware, amethyst, tall **32.00**
Ovide, Hazel Atlas, Platonite . **12.00**
Princess, Hocking Glass Co., green* **65.00**
Queen Mary (Prismatic Line, Vertical Ribbed), Hocking Glass Co., crystal. **22.00**
Ribbon, Hazel Atlas, black . . . **38.00**

Candy jar, cov

Aunt Polly, U.S. Glass Co., green **26.00**
Cube (Cubist), Jeannette Glass Co., pink **28.00**
Diana, Federal Glass Co., amber **36.00**
Moonstone, Anchor Hocking Glass Co., opal. **30.00**

Casserole, cov

Adam, Jeannette Glass Co., green **90.00**
Dewdrop, Jeannette Glass Co., crystal. **24.00**
Floral (Poinsettia), Jeannette Glass Co., pink. **28.00**
New Century, Hazel Atlas, crystal or green **60.00**

Cereal bowl

Adam, Jeannette Glass Co., 5-3/4" d, green **46.00**
Aurora, Hazel Atlas, pink **14.00**
Bubble, Anchor Hocking Glass Co., sapphire blue, 5-1/4" d. **19.50**
Cherry Blossom, Jeannette Glass Co., green*. **35.00**
Daisy (No. 620), Indiana Glass Co., fired-on red. **25.00**
Floragold, Jeannette Glass Co., irid **35.00**

Forest Green, Anchor Hocking Glass Co., green **16.50**
Hobnail, Hocking Glass Co., crystal, red trim **4.25**
Horseshoe (No. 612), Indiana Glass Co., green or yellow **25.00**
Old Café, Hocking Glass Co., crystal or pink **8.00**
Ring (Banded Rings), Hocking Glass Co., decorated **5.00**
Royal Ruby, Anchor Hocking, ruby, 4-3/4" d, ftd **24.50**
Thistle, Macbeth-Evans, green **27.50**

Cheese and cracker set

Jubilee, Lancaster Glass Co., yellow **255.00**
Patrick, Lancaster Glass Co., pink **150.00**

Chip and dip set, Soreno, Anchor Hocking, avocado, 8-1/2" d bowl, 5" bowl, brass frame, orig box **45.00**

Chop plate

Columbia, Federal Glass Co., flashed. **12.00**
Windsor (Windsor Diamond), Jeannette Glass Co., 13-5/8" d, green **18.00**

Coaster

Adam, Jeannette Glass Co., pink **32.00**
Cherry Blossom, Jeannette Glass Co., green or pink **15.00**
Floragold, Jeannette Glass Co., irid **10.00**
Harp, Jeannette Glass Co., crystal **4.50**
Miss America, (Diamond Pattern), Hocking Glass Co., crystal . . **20.00**
Primo (Paneled Aster), U.S. Glass Co., green or yellow **8.75**

Cocktail

American Pioneer, Liberty Works, amber **45.00**
Block Optic (Block), Hocking Glass Co., green **35.00**
Bubble, Anchor Hocking, crystal, 4-1/2 oz **4.00**
Iris (Iris and Herringbone), Jeannette Glass Co. **24.00**
Patrick, Lancaster Glass Co., pink or yellow **85.00**
Ring (Banded Rings), Hocking Glass Co., decorated or green **18.00**

Comport

Anniversary, Jeannette Glass Co., crystal, ruffled **6.50**
Floragold, Jeannette Glass Co., irid, 5-1/4" d, ruffled **695.00**
Floral and Diamond Band, U.S. Glass Co., green **16.50**

Manhattan (Horizontal Ribbed), Anchor Hocking Glass Co., crystal, 5-3/4" h **32.00**
Miss America, (Diamond Pattern), Hocking Glass Co., crystal . **14.00**
Pineapple & Floral (No. 618), Indiana Glass Co., diamond shape, crystal **3.00**
Windsor (Windsor Diamond), Jeannette Glass Co., crystal . **6.00**

Console set

Block Optic (Block), Hocking Glass Co., 11-3/4" d bowl, pr 1-3/4" h candlesticks, amber. **160.00**
Diamond Quilted (Flat Diamond), Imperial Glass Co., 10-1/2" d bowl, pr candlesticks, green **55.00**

Cookie jar, cov

Manhattan (Horizontal Ribbed), Anchor Hocking Glass Co., crystal **35.00**
Mayfair (Open Rose), Hocking Glass Co., green* **575.00**
Princess, Hocking Glass Co., blue **875.00**
Royal Lace, Hazel Atlas, cobalt blue **500.00**
Sandwich, Anchor Hocking, crystal **45.00**

Cordial

Diamond Quilted (Flat Diamond), Imperial Glass Co., pink. . . . **15.00**
Hobnail, Hocking Glass Co., crystal **6.00**
Jubilee, Lancaster Glass Co., yellow **245.00**

Creamer

Adam, Jeannette Glass Co., green **22.00**
Bamboo Optic, Liberty, ftd, green **10.00**
Block Optic (Block), Hocking Glass Co., yellow **15.00**
Cameo (Ballerina, Dancing Girl), Hocking Glass Co., 4-1/4" h, pink **85.00**
Christmas Candy (No. 624), Indiana Glass Co., crystal. **12.00**
Cube (Cubist), Jeannette Glass Co., green **10.00**
Floragold, Jeannette Glass Co., irid **10.00**
Georgian (Lovebirds), Federal Glass Co., green, 3" **15.00**
Holiday (Buttons and Bows), Jeannette Glass Co., pink . . **12.50**
Newport (Hairpin), Hazel Atlas, cobalt blue **20.00**
Ovide, Hazel Atlas, black **7.00**
Raindrops (Optic Design), Federal Glass Co. **8.00**

Sandwich, Anchor Hocking, crystal **7.50**
Sandwich, Indiana Glass Co., crystal, diamond shape **9.50**
Strawberry, U.S. Glass Co., small, crystal irid **12.00**
Sunflower, Jeannette Glass Co., green or pink. **20.00**
Tulip, Dell Glass Co., amethyst or blue **20.00**
Vernon (No. 616), Indiana Glass Co., green or yellow **25.00**

Creamer and sugar, cov

Colonial Block, Hazel Atlas, Hazel Atlas, pink **40.00**
Florentine No. 1 (Old Florentine, Poppy No. 1), Hazel Atlas, ruffled, green. **45.00**
Forest Green, Anchor Hocking Glass Co., green **14.00**
Iris (Iris and Herringbone), Jeannette Glass Co., crystal **30.00**
Lake Como, Hocking Glass Co., opaque white, blue scene. . . **65.00**
Madrid, Federal Glass Co., amber **15.00**
Moderntone, Hazel Atlas, cobalt blue **22.00**
Moonstone, Anchor Hocking Glass Co., opal **18.00**
Normandie (Bouquet and Lattice), Federal Glass Co., irid **14.00**
Patrician (Spoke), Federal Glass Co., amber **20.00**
Pretzel (No. 622), Indiana Glass Co. **9.00**
Sandwich, Anchor Hocking, no lid **30.00**
Tea Room, Indiana Glass Co., with tray, pink **75.00**
Windsor (Windsor Diamond), Jeannette Glass Co., crystal. **10.00**

Cream soup

American Sweetheart, Macbeth-Evans , monax . . . **120.00**
Floral (Poinsettia), Jeannette Glass Co., green or pink **735.00**
Madrid, Federal Glass Co., amber **15.00**
Mayfair, Federal Glass Co., amber **18.00**
Moderntone, Hazel Atlas, 5" d, ruffled, amethyst **30.00**
Patrician (Spoke), Federal Glass Co., amber **16.00**
Petalware, Macbeth-Evans, Cremax **12.50**
Windsor (Windsor Diamond), Jeannette Glass Co., green . **30.00**

Cruet, Sandwich, Indiana Glass Co., crystal, 6-1/2 oz **45.00**

Cup

Adam, Jeannette Glass Co.
Green **22.00**
Pink **24.00**
Anniversary, Jeannette Glass Co.
Irid **4.00**
Pink **9.00**
Aurora, Hazel Atlas
Cobalt blue **18.00**
Green **9.00**
Bamboo Optic, Liberty
Green **7.00**
Pink **10.00**
Bowknot, unknown maker, green **15.00**
Cherry Blossom, Jeannette Glass Co., crystal or pink* **20.00**
Cloverleaf, Hazel Atlas, green . **8.00**
Egg Harbor, Liberty
Green **6.00**
Pink **8.00**
Harp, Jeannette Glass Co., crystal **26.00**
Heritage, Federal Glass Co., crystal **7.00**
Mayfair (Open Rose), Hocking Glass Co., pink **18.00**
Miss America, (Diamond Pattern), Hocking Glass Co., crystal.. **10.00**
Moroccan Amethyst, Hazel Ware, amethyst **5.00**
Peanut Butter, unknown maker, crystal **4.00**
Pretzel (No. 622), Indiana Glass Co., crystal **6.00**
Pineapple & Floral (No. 618), Indiana Glass Co., amber or red **10.00**
Queen Mark, pink **7.00**
Round Robin, green **7.00**
Sunflower, Jeannette Glass Co., pink **16.00**
Victory, Diamond Glass-Ware Co., pink **8.00**

Cup and saucer, Circle, green, **$8.50.**

Cup and saucer

Cameo (Ballerina, Dancing Girl), Hocking Glass Co., crystal.. **14.00**
Capri, Hobnails **9.50**
Colonial Fluted (Rope), Federal Glass Co., crystal **7.00**
Diamond Quilted (Flat Diamond), Imperial Glass Co., blue **24.00**
Dogwood, Macbeth-Evans, green **40.00**
Doric & Pansy, Jeannette Glass Co., ultramarine **21.00**
Forest Green, Anchor Hocking Glass Co., green **8.00**
Fortune, Hocking Glass Co., crystal **12.50**
Lake Como, Hocking Glass Co., opaque white, blue scene... **42.00**
Lorain, Indiana Glass Co., crystal or green **15.00**
Madrid, Federal Glass Co., amber **9.00**
Parrot (Sylvan), Federal Glass Co., green **55.00**
Patrician (Spoke), Federal Glass Co., amber **20.00**
Royal Lace, Hazel Atlas, green **25.00**
Royal Ruby, Anchor Hocking, ruby, round **12.00**
Sandwich, Anchor Hocking, Forest Green **49.50**

Cup and saucer, Cloverleaf, pink, **$16.50.**

Custard cup, Sandwich, Anchor Hocking, crystal, 5 oz **7.50**

Demitasse cup and saucer

Diana, Federal Glass Co., crystal **12.00**
Iris (Iris and Herringbone), Jeannette Glass Co., irid **350.00**

Dessert bowl

Fortune, Hocking Glass Co., crystal or pink **4.50**
Moonstone, Anchor Hocking Glass Co., crystal **8.00**
Royal Ruby, Anchor Hocking, ruby, sq **5.25**
Star, Federal Glass Co., amber . **4.00**

Domino tray

Cameo (Ballerina, Dancing Girl), Hocking Glass Co., 7" l, pink **250.00**
Round Robin, unknown maker, green **40.00**

Dresser tray, Floral (Poinsettia), Jeannette Glass Co., green ... **700.00**

Egg cup

Egg Harbor, Liberty, green ... **12.00**
Egg Harbor, Liberty, pink **14.00**
Old English (Threading), Indiana Glass Co., crystal **10.00**
Ovide, Hazel Atlas, green **4.50**

Flower frog, Floral (Poinsettia), Jeannette Glass Co., green ... **850.00**

Fruit bowl

Bubble (Bullseye Provincial), Hocking Glass Co., crystal, 4-1/2" d **5.00**
Cherry Blossom, Jeannette Glass Co., crystal **32.00**
Dogwood, Macbeth-Evans, green **250.00**
Floragold, Jeannette Glass Co., irid **8.50**
Heritage, Federal Glass Co., crystal **18.50**
Iris (Iris and Herringbone), Jeannette Glass Co., 11-1/2" d, ruffled. **15.00**
Oyster and Pearls, Anchor Hocking Glass Co., pink **10.00**
Raindrops (Optic Design), Federal Glass Co., green **11.00**
Royal Ruby, Anchor Hocking, ruby **6.00**
Thistle, Macbeth-Evans, pink **200.00**

Goblet

Block Optic (Block), Hocking Glass Co., green **24.00**
Bubble (Bullseye Provincial), Hocking Glass Co., forest green **15.00**
Colonial Block, Hazel Atlas, crystal **9.00**
Diamond Point, ruby stained, 7-1/2" h **35.00**
Hobnail, Hocking Glass Co., crystal **7.50**
Iris (Iris and Herringbone), Jeannette Glass Co., 5-1/2" h, irid, clear foot **25.00**
Jubilee, Lancaster Glass Co., 7-1/2" h, yellow **75.00**
Moonstone, Anchor Hocking Glass Co., 10 oz **18.50**
Moroccan Amethyst, Hazel Ware, amethyst **10.00**
Old English (Threading), Indiana Glass Co., amber, green, or pink **30.00**
Ring (Banded Rings), Hocking Glass Co., crystal **7.00**
Royal Ruby, Anchor Hocking, ruby, ball stem **13.50**
Wexford, Anchor Hocking, crystal, 9-1/2" oz **9.50**

Grill plate, Miss America, clear, **$15.**

Grill plate, divided
- Adam, Jeannette Glass Co., 9" d, green or pink **20.00**
- Block Optic, 9" d, yellow **42.00**
- Bubble (Bullseye Provincial), Hocking Glass Co., 9-3/8" d, sapphire blue **22.00**
- Cherry Blossom, Jeannette Glass Co., 9" d, green or pink **22.00**
- Dogwood, Macbeth-Evans, 10-1/2" d, green or pink. **20.00**
- Doric, 9" d, pink **25.00**
- Floral (Poinsettia), Jeannette Glass Co., 9"d, green **185.00**
- Florentine No. 1 (Old Florentine, Poppy No. 1), Hazel Atlas, 10" d, yellow **22.00**
- Horseshoe (No. 612), Indiana Glass Co., 10-3/8" d, green or yellow **85.00**
- Madrid, Federal Glass Co., amber **9.00**
- Normandie (Bouquet and Lattice), Federal Glass Co., irid **9.00**
- Parrot (Sylvan), Federal Glass Co., 10-1/2" d, amber **32.00**
- Princess, Hocking Glass Co., 9-1/2" d, green or pink. **15.00**
- Rosemary (Dutch Rose), Federal Glass Co., 9-1/2" d, amber . . . **8.50**
- Royal Lace, Hazel Atlas, 9-7/8" d, cobalt blue **35.00**
- Thistle, Macbeth-Evans, 10-1/2" d, pink **28.00**

Hot plate
- Georgian (Lovebirds), Federal Glass Co., green **48.00**
- Parrot (Sylvan), Federal Glass Co., 5" d, amber **875.00**

Iced tea tumbler
- Adam, Jeannette Glass Co., green, ftd, 12 oz **60.00**
- Circle, Hocking Glass Co., green or pink, ftd, 12 oz. **17.50**
- Dewdrop, Jeannette Glass Co., crystal, ftd, 12 oz **17.50**
- Diamond Quilted (Flat Diamond), Imperial Glass Co., green or pink, ftd, 12 oz **10.00**
- Early American Prescut, (Anchor Hocking), crystal, 6" h, 15 oz **25.00**
- Florentine No. 1 (Old Florentine, Poppy No. 1), Hazel Atlas, yellow, ftd, 12 oz **24.00**
- Hobnail, Hocking Glass Co., crystal, ftd, 12 oz **8.50**
- Homespun (Fine Rib), Jeannette Glass Co., crystal or pink, ftd, 12 oz **32.00**
- Miss America, (Diamond Pattern), Hocking Glass Co., pink, ftd, 12 oz **85.00**
- Moroccan Amethyst, Hazel Ware, amethyst, 6-1/4" h, 16 oz . . . **17.50**
- Princess, Hocking Glass Co., pink, ftd, 12 oz **50.00**
- Roulette (Many Windows), Hocking Glass Co., green, ftd, 12 oz . **25.00**
- Royal Ruby, Anchor Hocking, ruby, 13 oz, flat **15.00**
- Ships (Sailboat, Sportsman Series), Hazel Atlas, cobalt blue **18.00**

Juice pitcher, Royal Ruby, Anchor Hocking, ruby, 42 oz, tilt ball type **60.00**

Juice tumbler, ftd
- Bubble, Anchor Hocking
  - Crystal, 5-1/2 oz. **5.00**
  - Forest green bowl, crystal base, 5-1/2 oz **14.50**
- Fortune, Hocking Glass Co., crystal **8.00**
- Holiday (Buttons and Bows), Jeannette Glass Co., pink . . **55.00**
- Moroccan Amethyst, Hazel Ware, amethyst, 2-1/2" h, 4 oz **12.50**
- Old Café, Hocking Glass Co., crystal or pink **10.00**
- Peanut Butter, unknown maker, crystal. **9.00**
- Royal Ruby, Anchor Hocking, ruby, 5 oz, flat. **12.50**
- S-pattern, Macbeth Evans, pink **14.00**
- Star, Federal Glass, crystal, 3-3/8" h, 4-1/2 oz **5.00**
- Thumbprint, Federal Glass Co., green **6.00**
- Wexford, Anchor Hocking, crystal, 5-1/2 oz **9.50**

Lemonade tumbler, Floral (Poinsettia), Jeannette Glass Co., green. **60.00**

Mayonnaise set, underplate, orig ladle
- Christmas Candy (No. 624), Indiana Glass Co., crystal. **24.00**
- Diamond Quilted (Flat Diamond), Imperial Glass Co., blue **65.00**
- Flower Garden with Butterflies (Butterflies and Roses), U.S. Glass Co., amber **70.00**
- Jubilee, Lancaster Glass Co., pink **315.00**
- Landrum, Lancaster, topaz . . **150.00**
- Patrick, Lancaster Glass Co., yellow **80.00**

Mint tray, Old Café, Hocking Glass Co., ruby **15.00**

Mug
- Block Optic (Block), Hocking Glass Co., green. **35.00**
- Cherry Blossom, Jeannette Glass Co., pink **250.00**
- Moderntone, Hazel Atlas, white. **8.50**

Nappy
- Coronation (Banded Fine Rib, Saxon), Hocking Glass Co., crystal or ruby. **15.00**
- Floragold, Jeannette Glass Co., irid **8.00**
- Floral and Diamond Band, (Poinsettia), Jeannette Glass Co., pink **11.00**

Old fashioned, Moroccan Amethyst, Hazel Ware, amethyst, 3-1/4" h, 8 oz **15.00**

Pickle
- Aunt Polly, U.S. Glass Co., green or irid **17.50**
- Cherryberry, U.S. Glass Co., crystal **10.00**
- Pyramid (No. 610), Indiana Glass Co., green or pink **35.00**

Pitcher
- Adam, Jeannette Glass Co., 32 oz, pink **125.00**
- Aunt Polly, U.S. Glass Co., crystal **175.00**
- Bamboo Optic, Liberty, 8-1/2" h, green. **50.00**
- Coronation (Banded Fine Rib, Saxon), Hocking Glass Co., pink **500.00**
- Crystal Leaf, Macbeth Evans, pink **45.00**
- Floragold, Jeannette Glass Co., irid **40.00**
- Florentine No. 1 (Old Florentine, Poppy No. 1), Hazel Atlas, ice lip, pink **115.00**
- Forest Green, Anchor Hocking Glass Co., 22 oz, green **22.50**
- Fruits, Hazel Atlas, green **85.00**
- Hex Optic (Honeycomb), Jeannette Glass Co., 32 oz, 5" h, green or pink **24.00**

Horseshoe (No. 612), Indiana Glass Co., 64 oz, green **250.00**
Jubilee, Lancaster Glass Co., pink **950.00**
Mac Hob, Macbeth Evans, 72 oz, crystal. **40.00**
Miss America, (Diamond Pattern), Hocking Glass Co., crystal, 8" h* **45.00**
New Century, Hazel Atlas, ice lip, 80 oz, cobalt blue **45.00**
Ring (Banded Rings), Hocking Glass Co., 60 oz, decorated or green **25.00**
Sandwich, Anchor Hocking, crystal, ice lip **85.00**
Star, Federal Glass Co., crystal, 60 oz. **14.00**
U.S. Swirl, U.S. Glass Co. green **55.00**
Windsor (Windsor Diamond), Jeannette Glass Co., 4-1/2" h, pink. **115.00**

Plate, Adam, pink, 9", **$38.50.**

Plate

Adam, Jeannette Glass Co.
- 6" d, sherbet, green **9.50**
- 7-3/4" d, salad, green. **17.00**
- 9" d, dinner, pink **38.50**

American Pioneer, Liberty Works, 6" d, crystal. **12.50**
American Sweetheart, Macbeth-Evans , 9" d, monax **10.00**
Anniversary, Jeannette Glass Co., 9" d **5.00**
Aunt Polly, U.S. Glass Co.
- 6" d, blue **12.00**
- 8" d, crystal **20.00**

Aurora, Hazel Atlas, 6-1/2" d, cobalt blue **12.00**
Bamboo Optic, Liberty, octagonal
- 5-3/4" d, bread and butter, green **4.00**
- 7" d, salad, green. **7.50**
- 8" d, luncheon, pink **10.00**
- 10" d, dinner, green. **24.00**

Block Optic
- 6" d, crystal. **1.50**
- 8" d, green **5.50**
- 9" d, dinner, green. **27.50**

Bowknot, 7" d, green **12.50**
Bubble (Bullseye Provincial), Hocking Glass Co.
- 6-3/4" d, crystal. **3.50**
- 9-3/8" d, dinner, forest green **20.00**
- 9-3/8" d, dinner, ruby **22.00**

Cameo (Ballerina, Dancing Girl), Hocking Glass Co.
- 8" d, crystal. **14.00**
- 8" d, green **12.00**
- 8" d, pink. **36.00**

Capri, Hobnails, 9-7/8" d **10.50**
Cherry Blossom, Jeannette Glass Co.
- 6" d, green*. **6.00**
- 7" d, pink. **17.00**
- 9" d, crystal* **18.00**

Christmas Candy (No. 624), Indiana Glass Co.
- 6" d, teal **16.00**
- 9-5/8" d, crystal. **12.00**

Circle, Hocking Glass Co., 8-1/4" d, green or pink. **12.00**
Colonial Fluted (Rope), Federal Glass Co., 8" d, green. **10.00**
Columbia, Federal Glass Co., 9-1/2" d, pink. **32.00**
Daisy (No. 620), Indiana Glass Co.
- 6" d, amber **3.00**
- 6" d, 8-3/8" d, crystal. **5.00**
- 6" d, 9-3/8" d, dark green . . . **7.50**

Diana, Federal Glass Co.
- 6" d, amber **3.00**
- 9-1/2" d, crystal. **6.00**

Dogwood, Macbeth-Evans
- 6" d, pink. **9.50**
- 8" d, green **9.00**

Doric
- 6" d, green or pink **6.50**
- 7" d, green **20.00**
- 9" d, pink. **18.00**

Doric & Pansy, Jeannette Glass Co., ultramarine, dinner **35.00**
Early American Prescut, (Anchor Hocking), crystal
- 11" d **10.00**
- 13-1/2" d **12.00**

Egg Harbor, Liberty, luncheon, green or pink **10.00**
Floragold, Jeannette Glass Co., 8-1/2" d, dinner, irid **35.00**
Floral (Poinsettia), Jeannette Glass Co.
- 6" d, sherbet, green **7.50**
- 8" d, salad, pink. **15.00**
- 9" d, dinner, delphite **145.00**

Floral and Diamond Band, (Poinsettia), Jeannette Glass Co., 8" d, luncheon, green or pink **40.00**
Florentine No. 1 (Old Florentine, Poppy No. 1), Hazel Atlas
- 6" d, sherbet, crystal **6.50**
- 8-1/2" d, salad, green **9.00**
- 10" d, dinner, green **16.00**

Florentine No. 2 (Poppy No. 2), Hazel Atlas, 10" d, yellow, dinner **15.00**
Fortune, Hocking Glass Co., 8" d, luncheon, crystal or pink . . . **17.50**
Georgian (Lovebirds), Federal Glass Co., green
- 6" d, sherbet **6.50**
- 8" d, luncheon **10.00**
- 9-1/4" d, dinner **30.00**

Harp, Jeannette Glass Co., crystal, gold trim, 7" d. **15.00**
Heritage, Federal Glass Co., crystal, 9-1/4" d. **14.50**
Hobnail, Hocking Glass Co., 8-1/2" d, luncheon, crystal . . . **5.50**
Holiday (Buttons and Bows), Jeannette Glass Co., pink
- 6" d, sherbet **6.00**
- 9" d, dinner **17.50**

Homespun (Fine Rib), Jeannette Glass Co., 9-/2" d, dinner, crystal or pink **17.00**
Horseshoe (No. 612), Indiana Glass Co.
- 6" d, sherbet, green or yellow **9.00**
- 8-3/8" d, salad, green or yellow **10.00**
- 9-3/8" d, luncheon, green . **13.00**

Iris (Iris and Herringbone), Jeannette Glass Co.
- 8" d, luncheon, crystal . . . **125.00**
- 9" d, dinner, irid **45.00**

Jubilee, Lancaster Glass Co.
- 7" d, salad, pink. **25.00**
- 9-3/4" d, luncheon **16.50**

Laced Edge (Katy Blue), Imperial Glass Co., 10" d, blue **90.00**
Madrid, Federal Glass Co.
- 6" d, amber **4.00**
- 8-7/8" d, amber **8.00**

Manhattan (Horizontal Ribbed), Anchor Hocking Glass Co., 7" d, crystal. **6.00**
Mayfair (Open Rose), Hocking Glass Co., 8-1/2" d, pink **25.00**

Miss America, (Diamond Pattern), Hocking Glass Co., dinner, crystal **15.00**
Moderntone, Hazel Atlas, 7-3/4" d, cobalt blue **12.50**
Moroccan Amethyst, Hazel Ware, amethyst
  5-3/4" d, sherbet **12.50**
  9-3/4" d, dinner **12.50**
Newport (Hairpin), Hazel Atlas
  6" d, sherbet, amethyst **7.50**
  6" d, 8-1/2" d, luncheon, cobalt blue.................. **16.50**
  6" d, 8-1/2" d, dinner, fired on color **15.00**
Normandie (Bouquet and Lattice), Federal Glass Co., 6" d, irid . . **3.00**
Old Café, Hocking Glass Co., crystal or pink
  6" d, sherbet **4.00**
  10" d, dinner **10.00**
Old Colony (Lace Edge, Open Lace), Hocking Glass Co., crystal
  Dinner **33.00**
  Luncheon **23.00**
  Salad.................. **25.00**
Parrot (Sylvan), Federal Glass Co.
  5-3/4" d, sherbet, amber . . . **24.00**
  7-1/2" d, green **40.00**
  9" d, dinner, green........ **38.00**
Patrician (Spoke), Federal Glass Co.
  7-1/2" d, amber **15.00**
  9" d, amber **12.00**
  11" d, amber **6.00**
Patrick, Lancaster Glass Co.
  7" d, sherbet, pink........ **20.00**
  7-1/2" d, salad, yellow..... **20.00**
  8" d, luncheon, pink **45.00**
Peanut Butter, unknown maker, crystal, 8" d, luncheon....... **5.00**
Petalware, Macbeth-Evans
  6" d, sherbet, cremax, gold trim **50.00**
  8" d, salad, fired-on color . . . **8.00**
  9" d, dinner, monax....... **10.00**
Pineapple & Floral (No. 618), Indiana Glass Co.
  6" d, sherbet, amber **6.00**
  8-3/8" d, salad, amber or crystal **8.00**
Pretzel (No. 622), Indiana Glass Co., 9-3/4" d, dinner, crystal **10.00**
Primo (Paneled Aster), U.S. Glass Co., 10" d, dinner, green **22.50**
Princess, Hocking Glass Co.
  5-1/2" d, sherbet, apricot . . **10.00**
  8" d, salad, green **15.00**
  9-1/2" d, dinner, pink...... **35.00**
Queen Mary (Prismatic Line, Vertical Ribbed), Hocking Glass Co., 6" d, crystal **4.00**

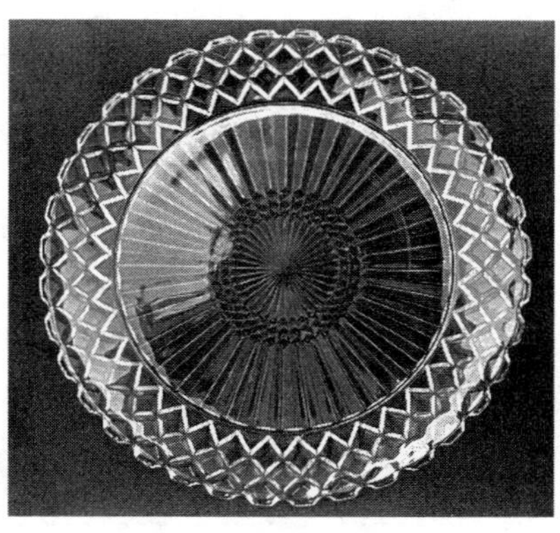

Plate, Waterford, crystal, 9-1/2" d, **$12.50.**

Romansque, 8" d, octagonal
  Gold.................. **8.00**
  Green................. **9.00**
Rose Cameo, Belmont Tumbler Co., 7" d, salad, green......... **16.00**
Rosemary (Dutch Rose), Federal Glass Co.6-3/4" d, salad, green **11.00**
  9-1/2" d, dinner, green **15.00**
Roulette (Many Windows), Hocking Glass Co., 8-1/2" d, luncheon, crystal.................. **7.00**
Round Robin
  6" d, sherbet, irid or green . . **7.00**
  8" d, luncheon, green..... **12.50**
Roxana, Hazel Atlas, 6" d, sherbet, crystal.................. **4.00**
Royal Lace, Hazel Atlas
  6" d, sherbet, green...... **15.00**
  8-1/2" d, luncheon, cobalt . **30.00**
  9-7/8" d, dinner, pink **20.00**
Royal Ruby, Anchor Hocking, ruby
  6-1/4" d, sherbet **4.00**
  7" d, salad **3.00**
  7-3/4" w, salad, sq **2.00**
  8-3/8" w, luncheon, sq **11.00**
  9-1/8" d, dinner **14.00**
Sandwich, Anchor Hocking, 9" d, crystal................. **20.00**
Ships (Sailboat, Sportsman Series), Hazel Atlas, 9" d, dinner, cobalt blue **32.00**
Sierra Pinwheel, Jeannette Glass Co., 9" d, dinner, green **18.00**
Starlight, Hazel Atlas, 9-1/2" d, dinner, crystal............ **7.00**
Tea Room, Indiana Glass Co.
  6-1/2" d, sherbet, pink **32.00**
  8-1/4" d, luncheon, green . **37.50**
Thistle, Macbeth-Evans, 8" d, luncheon, green.......... **22.00**
Vernon (No. 616), Indiana Glass Co., 8" d, luncheon, green or yellow **10.00**

Waterford (Waffle), Hocking Glass Co., dinner, crystal **12.50**
Windsor (Windsor Diamond), Jeannette Glass Co.
  6" d, sherbet, crystal....... **3.75**
  9" d, dinner, green or pink . **25.00**

Platter

Bubble, Anchor Hocking Glass Co., sapphire blue, 12" l........ **19.50**
Cherry Blossom, Jeannette Glass Co., green **48.00**
Daisy (No. 620), Indiana Glass Co., crystal or dark green....... **11.00**
Dogwood, Macbeth-Evans, Macbeth Evans, 12" l, oval, pink **650.00**
Georgian (Lovebirds), Federal Glass Co., green **70.00**
Indiana Custard, (Flower and Leaf Band), Indiana Glass Co., French Ivory **30.00**
Laced Edge (Katy Blue), Imperial Glass Co., 13" l, blue...... **165.00**
Madrid, Federal Glass Co., amber **14.00**
Petalware, Macbeth-Evans, Monax **20.00**
Royal Lace, Hazel Atlas, pink . **40.00**
Windsor (Windsor Diamond), Jeannette Glass Co., 11-1/2" l, oval, green.................. **25.00**

Popcorn bowl, Forest Green, Anchor Hocking Glass Co., green **16.50**

Puff box, cov, Moonstone, Anchor Hocking Glass Co., opal **25.00**

Punch bowl

Forest Green, Anchor Hocking Glass Co., green **25.00**
Moroccan Amethyst, Hazel Ware, amethyst **85.00**
Sandwich, Anchor Hocking, crystal or white milk glass......... **30.00**

Punch bowl set

Dewdrop, Jeannette Glass Co., bowl, 12 cups, crystal...... **95.00**
Royal Ruby, Anchor Hocking, bowl, 12 cups, ruby **110.00**

Punch cup

Forest Green, Anchor Hocking Glass Co., green **4.50**
Royal Ruby, Anchor Hocking, ruby **5.00**
Sandwich, Anchor Hocking, crystal or white milk glass.......... **3.50**

Relish

Doric, Jeannette Glass Co. green **32.00**
Early American Prescut, (Anchor Hocking), crystal, four-part, 11 d.................... **10.00**

Lorain, Indiana Glass Co., four-part, 8" d, crystal or green **17.50**
Miss America, (Diamond Pattern), Hocking Glass Co., four-part, crystal **11.00**
Pretzel (No. 622), Indiana Glass Co., three-part, crystal **9.00**
Princess, Hocking Glass Co., four-part, apricot **100.00**
Tea Room, Indiana Glass Co., divided, green **30.00**

Salad bowl

Cherryberry, U.S. Glass Co., green **22.00**
Cloverleaf, Hazel Atlas, yellow **48.00**
Cube (Cubist), Jeannette Glass Co. **15.00**
Early American Prescut, (Anchor Hocking), crystal, 10-1/2" d . **10.00**
Forest Green, Anchor Hocking Glass Co., green **6.50**
Fortune, Hocking Glass Co., crystal **15.00**
Hobnail, Hocking Glass Co., crystal **5.00**
Horseshoe (No. 612), Indiana Glass Co., green or yellow **24.00**
Landrum, Lancaster, pink . . . **110.00**
Pineapple & Floral (No. 618), Indiana Glass Co., amber* **10.00**
Royal Ruby, Anchor Hocking, ruby
- 6-5/8" d **24.50**
- 11-1/2" d **45.00**

Tea Room, Indiana Glass Co., pink **135.00**
Twisted Optic, Imperial, blue . **15.00**

Salt and pepper shakers, pr

Adam, Jeannette Glass Co., green **100.00**
American Sweetheart, Macbeth-Evans , monax . . . **325.00**
Cameo (Ballerina, Dancing Girl), Hocking Glass Co., green* . . **70.00**
Cube (Cubist), Jeannette Glass Co., green or pink **36.00**
Diana, Federal Glass Co., amber **100.00**
Floral (Poinsettia), Jeannette Glass Co., green* **45.00**
Florentine No. 2 (Poppy No. 2), Hazel Atlas, yellow **48.00**
Hex Optic (Honeycomb), Jeannette Glass Co., green or pink . . . **30.00**
Manhattan (Horizontal Ribbed), Anchor Hocking Glass Co., crystal **50.00**
Moderntone, Hazel Atlas, white **18.00**
New Century, Hazel Atlas, crystal **25.00**
Ovide, Hazel Atlas, black or green **28.00**
Patrician (Spoke), Federal Glass Co., amber **50.00**
Princess, Hocking Glass Co., green **50.00**
Ribbon, Hazel Atlas, green . . . **25.00**
Waterford (Waffle), Hocking Glass Co., crystal, tall **7.00**

Sandwich server, center handle

Bamboo Optic, Liberty, octagonal
- Green **20.00**
- Pink **25.00**

Daisy (No. 620), Indiana Glass Co., amber **14.50**
Flower Garden with Butterflies (Butterflies and Roses), US Glass Co., green **75.00**
Landrum, Lancaster, topaz . . . **55.00**
Old English (Threading), Indiana Glass Co., amber **60.00**
Ring (Banded Rings), Hocking Glass Co., decorated or green **15.00**
Sandwich, Anchor Hocking, crystal **45.00**
Sandwich, Indiana Glass Co., crystal, 13" **24.50**
Spiral, Hocking Glass Co., green **30.00**
Twisted Optic, Imperial, canary **35.00**

Saucer

Adam, Jeannette Glass Co., green or pink **7.00**
Aurora, Hazel Atlas
- Cobalt blue **6.00**
- Green **2.00**

Bamboo Optic, Liberty, green or pink **3.00**
Block Optic (Block), Hocking Glass Co., crystal **2.00**
Bubble (Bullseye Provincial), Hocking Glass Co., crystal . . . **1.50**
Cloverleaf, Hazel Atlas, green or pink **4.00**
Harp, Jeannette Glass Co., crystal **10.00**
Heritage, Federal Glass Co., crystal **4.00**
Madrid, Federal Glass Co., amber **4.00**
Miss America, (Diamond Pattern), Hocking Glass Co., crystal . . . **4.00**
Peanut Butter, unknown maker, crystal **3.00**
Star, Federal Glass, amber **4.00**
Twitch, No. 92, Bartlett-Collins, green **3.00**

Sherbet

Adam, Jeannette Glass Co., green **40.00**
April, Macbeth Evans, 4" h, ftd, pink **15.00**
Bowknot, unknown maker, green **24.00**
Cherry Blossom, Jeannette Glass Co., pink **17.00**
Cloverleaf, Hazel Atlas, green **12.00**
Coronation (Banded Fine Rib, Saxon), Hocking Glass Co., green **70.00**
Doric, Jeannette Glass Co. delphite **10.00**
Florentine No. 1 (Old Florentine, Poppy No. 1), Hazel Atlas, yellow **16.00**
Florentine No. 2 (Poppy No. 2), Hazel Atlas, yellow **8.00**
Forest Green, Anchor Hocking Glass Co., Boopie, green **7.00**
Fruits, Hazel Atlas, pink **7.50**
Hex Optic (Honeycomb), Jeannette Glass Co., green or pink **5.00**
Iris (Iris and Herringbone), Jeannette Glass Co., 2-1/2" h, irid **15.50**
Lorain, Indiana Glass Co., yellow* **35.00**
Madrid, Federal Glass Co., amber **7.00**
Moderntone, Hazel Atlas, cobalt blue **13.00**
Moonstone, Anchor Hocking Glass Co., opal **7.00**
Normandie (Bouquet and Lattice), Federal Glass Co., irid **8.00**
Old Café, Hocking Glass Co., ruby **12.00**
Old English (Threading), Indiana Glass Co., green **20.00**
Parrot (Sylvan), Federal Glass Co., cone shape, green **24.00**
Peanut Butter, unknown maker, crystal **4.00**
Raindrops (Optic Design), Federal Glass Co., crystal **4.50**
Rose Cameo, Belmont Tumbler Co., green **16.00**
Royal Ruby, Anchor Hocking, ruby, ftd **10.50**
Sandwich, Anchor Hocking, crystal **9.50**
Sunflower, Jeannette Glass Co., green **13.50**
Thumbprint, Federal Glass Co., green **7.00**
Wexford, Anchor Hocking, crystal, 7 oz **6.50**
Windsor (Windsor Diamond), Jeannette Glass Co., pink . . **13.00**

Snack set, plate with indent, matching cup
- Columbia, Federal Glass Co., crystal **35.00**
- Dewdrop, Jeannette Glass Co., crystal **9.00**
- Harp, Jeannette Glass Co., crystal **47.00**
- Moroccan Amethyst, Hazel Ware, amethyst **15.00**
- Sandwich, Anchor Hocking, 9" d, crystal **7.00**
- Sandwich, Indiana Glass Co., crystal **9.50**

Soup bowl
- Holiday (Buttons and Bows), Jeannette Glass Co., 7-3/4" d, pink **50.00**
- Indiana Custard, (Flower and Leaf Band), Indiana Glass Co., French Ivory........ **32.00**
- Laced Edge (Katy Blue), Imperial Glass Co., blue **18.00**
- Royal Ruby, Anchor Hocking, ruby, 7-1/2" d, orig label........ **24.50**

Sugar, cov
- Bamboo Optic, Liberty, ftd, green **10.00**
- Bubble, Anchor Hocking Glass Co., sapphire blue, ftd **30.00**
- Cameo (Ballerina, Dancing Girl), Hocking Glass Co., 3-1/4" h, pink **100.00**
- Cube (Cubist), Jeannette Glass Co., 3", green or pink **25.00**
- Diana, Federal Glass Co., amber or crystal **10.00**
- Egg Harbor, Liberty, green or pink **3.50**
- Floragold, Jeannette Glass Co., irid **15.00**
- Georgian (Lovebirds), Federal Glass Co., 3" d, green **15.00**
- Heritage, Federal Glass Co., crystal **27.50**

Sugar bowl, Georgian, green, **$15.**

- Holiday (Buttons and Bows), Jeannette Glass Co., pink .. **25.00**
- Madrid, Federal Glass Co., amber **7.00**
- Ring (Banded Rings), Hocking Glass Co., decorated........ **10.00**
- Royal Ruby, Anchor Hocking, ruby, ftd........ **26.50**
- Sandwich, Anchor Hocking, crystal **27.50**
- Sandwich, Indiana Glass Co., crystal, diamond shape **8.50**
- Sierra Pinwheel, Jeannette Glass Co., pink........ **20.00**
- Tulip, Dell Glass Co., blue ... **20.00**
- Vernon (No. 616), Indiana Glass Co., crystal........ **12.00**

Syrup pitcher, Cameo (Ballerina, Dancing Girl), Hocking Glass Co., green........ **225.00**

Table set, Early American Prescut, (Anchor Hocking), crystal, 1/4 lb cov butter, pr cruets with stoppers, creamer, cov sugar, salt and pepper shaker with plastic tops **55.00**

Tid-bit server
- Anniversary, Jeannette Glass Co., crystal........ **14.00**
- Bubble (Bullseye Provincial), Hocking Glass Co., ruby ... **35.00**
- Christmas Candy (No. 624), Indiana Glass Co., crystal........ **12.00**
- Dogwood, Macbeth-Evans, pink **90.00**
- Laced Edge (Katy Blue), Imperial Glass Co., two tiers, blue...**110.00**

Tray
- Cube (Cubist), Jeannette Glass Co., pink........ **5.00**
- Floral (Poinsettia), Jeannette Glass Co., 6" sq, green **195.00**
- Harp, Jeannette Glass Co., rect, crystal........ **35.00**
- Manhattan (Horizontal Ribbed), Anchor Hocking Glass Co., 14" d, crystal inserts........ **50.00**
- Patrick, Lancaster Glass Co., 11" d, pink........ **145.00**
- Windsor (Windsor Diamond), Jeannette Glass Co., 4" sq, green **12.00**

Tumbler
- Bamboo Optic, Liberty, 5-1/2" h, 8 oz, ftd, pink........ **15.00**
- Block Optic (Block), Hocking Glass Co., 3-1/4" h, green **27.50**
- Bubble, Anchor Hocking, Forest Green bowl, crystal base. **PRICE?**
- Cherryberry, U.S. Glass Co., 3-5/8" h, irid **20.00**

Tumbler, Adam, cone shape, pink, **$35.**

- Columbia, Federal Glass Co., 4 oz, crystal **30.00**
- Crystal Leaf, Macbeth Evans
  - 3-1/2" h, green **5.00**
  - 4-1/2" h, 9 oz, pink **10.00**
  - 4-3/4" h, 12 oz, pink **12.00**
- Dogwood, Macbeth-Evans, 4-3/4" h, pink **45.00**
- Doric, Jeannette Glass Co. 5-1/2" h, pink **60.00**
- Early American Prescut, (Anchor Hocking), crystal, 4-1/2" h, 10 oz, orig label........ **12.50**
- Floragold, Jeannette Glass Co., irid, 5" h, 10 oz **20.00**
- Forest Green, Anchor Hocking Glass Co., 9 oz, green **7.00**
- Hex Optic (Honeycomb), Jeannette Glass Co., 7 oz, 4-3/4" h, green or pink **8.00**
- Horseshoe (No. 612), Indiana Glass Co., 9 oz, ftd, green **22.00**
- Madrid, Federal Glass Co., 5-1/2" h, amber **18.00**
- Mayfair (Open Rose), Hocking Glass Co., 6-1/2" h, ftd, pink **40.00**
- Moderntone, Hazel Atlas, cone, white **5.00**
- Moroccan Amethyst, Hazel Ware, amethyst, 4-1/2" h, 10 oz.... **12.50**
- Patrician (Spoke), Federal Glass Co.
  - 4" h, amber **25.00**
  - 5-1/2" h, amber........ **40.00**
- Peanut Butter, unknown maker, crystal or milk glass **7.00**
- Princess, Hocking Glass Co., 9 oz, green........ **28.00**

Tumbler, Dogwood, 5", pink, **$45.**

Pyramid (No. 610), Indiana Glass Co., 8 oz, ftd, crystal or pink **50.00**
Rose Cameo, Belmont Tumbler Co., green **22.50**
Ships (Sailboat, Sportsman Series), Hazel Atlas, 9 oz, cobalt blue **14.00**
Star, Federal Glass, amber, 3-7/8" h, 9 oz.................... **9.50**
Vernon (No. 616), Indiana Glass Co., yellow **35.00**

Vase

Moonstone, Anchor Hocking Glass Co., 6-1/2" h, crystal, ruffled.. **8.00**
Moroccan Amethyst, Hazel Ware, 8-1/2" h, amethyst, ruffled... **40.00**
Old Café, Hocking Glass Co., 7-1/4" h, ruby **24.00**
Old English (Threading), Indiana Glass Co., 12" h, amber, green, or pink.................... **60.00**
Pineapple & Floral (Poinsettia), Jeannette Glass Co., cone, red **45.00**
Tea Room, Indiana Glass Co., 11" h, green **200.00**

Vegetable, open

Cameo (Ballerina, Dancing Girl), Hocking Glass Co., green .. **30.00**
Christmas Candy (No. 624), Indiana Glass Co., teal **235.00**
Colonial (Knife and Fork), Hocking Glass Co., green **25.00**
Daisy (No. 620), Indiana Glass Co., dark green **10.00**
Doric, Jeannette Glass Co. pink **30.00**
Florentine No. 2 (Poppy No. 2), Hazel Atlas, yellow, cov **55.00**
Horseshoe (No. 612), Indiana Glass Co., 8-1/2" d, green or yellow **30.00**
Lake Como, Hocking Glass Co., opaque white, blue scene, 9-3/4" l.................. **60.00**
Madrid, Federal Glass Co., 10" l, oval, amber* **18.00**
Normandie (Bouquet and Lattice), Federal Glass Co., irid **18.00**
Parrot (Sylvan), Federal Glass Co., amber **65.00**
Pineapple & Floral (No. 618), Indiana Glass Co., amber or crystal . **30.00**
Rosemary (Dutch Rose), Federal Glass Co., green.......... **37.00**
Royal Ruby, Anchor Hocking, ruby, 8" l, oval................. **25.00**
Sharon (Cabbage Rose), Federal Glass Co., amber, oval **20.00**
Star, Federal Glass Co., amber **10.00**
Tea Room, Indiana Glass Co., green **75.00**

Wall pocket, Anniversary, Jeannette Glass Co., pink............... **30.00**

Whiskey

Diamond Quilted (Flat Diamond), Imperial Glass Co., pink **12.00**
Hex Optic (Honeycomb), Jeannette Glass Co., green or pink..... **8.50**
Hobnail, Hocking Glass Co., crystal **5.00**
Miss America, (Diamond Pattern), Hocking Glass Co., crystal .. **22.00**
Raindrops (Optic Design), Federal Glass Co., green........... **9.00**
Roulette (Many Windows), Hocking Glass Co., green or pink.... **15.00**
Ships (Sailboat, Sportsman Series), Hazel Atlas, cobalt blue **30.00**
Thumbprint, Federal Glass Co., green.................... **6.50**
Tulip, Dell Glass Co., amethyst **20.00**

Wine

Anniversary, Jeannette Glass Co., crystal **8.00**
Cameo (Ballerina, Dancing Girl), Hocking Glass Co., green... **65.00**
Iris (Iris and Herringbone), Jeannette Glass Co., 4" h, irid **25.00**
Circle, Hocking Glass Co., green or pink **15.00**
Hobnail, Hocking Glass Co., crystal **6.50**
Mayfair (Open Rose), Hocking Glass Co., pink **75.00**
Moroccan Amethyst, Hazel Ware, amethyst **10.00**
Royal Ruby, Anchor Hocking, ruby, 2-1/2 oz, ftd............. **14.00**
Wexford, Anchor Hocking, crystal, 5-1/2 oz.................. **9.50**

Duncan and Miller

History: George Duncan, his sons Harry B. and James B., and Augustus Heisey, his son-in-law, formed George Duncan & Sons in Pittsburgh, Pennsylvania, in 1865. The factory was located just two blocks from the Monongahela River, providing easy and inexpensive access by barge for materials needed to produce glass. The men, from Pittsburgh's south side, were descendants of generations of skilled glassmakers.

The plant burned to the ground in 1892. James E. Duncan Sr., selected a site for a new factory in Washington, Pennsylvania, where operations began on Feb. 9, 1893. The plant prospered, producing fine glassware and table services for many years.

John E. Miller, one of the stockholders, was responsible for designing many fine patterns, the most famous being Three Face. The firm incorporated and used the name The Duncan and Miller Glass Company until the plant closed in 1955. The company's slogan was, "The Loveliest Glassware in America." The U.S. Glass Co. purchased the molds, equipment, and machinery in 1956.

References: Tom and Neila Bredehoft, *Fifty Years of Collectible Glass, 1920-1970*, Volume 1, Volume II, Antique Trader Books, 2000; Gene Florence, *Elegant Glassware of the Depression Era*, 9th ed., Collector Books, 2000; Gail Krause, *The Encyclopedia of Duncan Glass*, published by author, 1984; —, *A Pictorial History of Duncan & Miller Glass*, published by author, 1976; —, *The Years of Duncan*, published by author, 1980; Naomi L. Over, *Ruby Glass of the 20th Century*, Antique Publications, 1990, 1993-94 value update, Book II, 1999.

Collectors' Club: National Duncan Glass Society, P.O. Box 965, Washington, PA 15301, http://www.duncan-glass.com.

Museum: Duncan Miller Glass Museum, Washington, PA.

Miscellaneous patterns and etchings

Animal

Donkey and pheasant, crystal **425.00**
Goose, fat, crystal **275.00**
Heron, crystal............ **150.00**

Ashtray, tropical fish, Blue Opalescent **50.00**

Bowl

Candlelight Garden, Teakwood **50.00**
Chrysanthemum, blue, 13-1/2" d **145.00**
Laguna, Biscayne Green, divided, orig spoon, 8" d **60.00**
Murano, 10" d, crimped
Milk glass.............. **55.00**
Twilight............... **145.00**

Candlesticks, pr, American Way
Crystal **25.00**

Pink Opalescent **65.00**
Ruby **65.00**

Candlesticks, pr, Sculptured Fish, crystal, one with small crack . . . **500.00**

Candy dish, Murano, 7" d, crimped, crystal **38.00**

Celery vase, Homestead, 5" h, milk glass **28.00**

Champagne
Cascade, crystal **35.00**
Lily of the Valley, crystal **35.00**
Willow, crystal **30.00**

Cigarette holder, #538, ruby **55.00**

Claret, Dover, red and crystal, 5 oz, 5-1/4" h **22.50**

Cocktail
Cascade, crystal **35.00**
Willow, crystal **30.00**

Console bowl, #16, winged shape, cobalt blue **250.00**

Console set
American Way, star plate and pr candlesticks, citron **35.00**
Candlelight Garden, Biscayne Green, bowl and pr candle blocks **175.00**

Cornucopia vase
Swirl#121, Blue Opalescent, shape #1, 11" **135.00**
#121, Blue Opalescent, shape #2, upswept tail **75.00**
#121, Pink Opalescent, shape #2, 11" **195.00**
Deep ruby, shape #3, 14" h **125.00**
Three Feathers
Blue Opalescent, 8" h **125.00**
Pink Opalescent, 8" h **125.00**

Creamer, Zipper Slash, amber stain, etched dec **45.00**

Cruet, Starred Loop, orig stopper, crystal **36.00**

Goblet
Cascade, crystal **40.00**
Croecus, crystal **35.00**

Cigarette jar base, Nautical, opalescent, **$60.** *Photo courtesy of Michael Krumme.*

The New "Puritan"

The new "Puritan" pattern stands out conspicuously for its utterly unaffected design, and its elemental comeliness of shape. The raised thread-like lines of self-color, which make up the entire scheme of ornamentation upon the surface of the ware, seem to flow naturally about the topmost and outermost edges of the variously shaped units. When one looks at the entire group as a whole, there is seen a striking similarity to the slightly rippled depths of a woodland pool when it is disturbed by a pebble cast into its depths. A complete range of pieces from demi-tasse through various sized plates and miscellaneous items, to huge flower and fruit bowls, and all the other needed equipment for dining and decorative purposes, is obtainable in crystal, green and rose, and whether the particular bit is flared, crimped, rolled or cupped, the plain curving lines of the "Puritan" decoration are in complete harmony.

The
Duncan & Miller Glass Co.
Washington, Pa.

REPRESENTATIVES:
Paul Joseph, 200 Fifth Avenue, New York.
Murt Wallace, 157 Summer St., Boston, Mass.
F. T. Renshaw, 58 E. Washington St., Chicago, Ill.
Wm. C. Byrnes, Burd Bldg., 9th and Chestnut Sts., Philadelphia
Pacific Coast Representative:
Percy Pownall—Home Address, 105 S. Oak St., Inglewood, Cal.
E. B. Hill, A. A. Graesser, Factory Representatives.
Washington, Pa.

An advertisement, introducting No. 21, Crockery and Glass Journal, *1931.*

Eternally Yours, crystal **15.00**
Festival of Flowers, crystal . . . **28.50**
Plaza, cobalt blue **37.50**
Starlight, crystal **38.00**
Touraine, crystal, 6-7/8" h, orig paper label **18.00**
Willow, crystal **32.00**

Iced tea tumbler
Cascade, ftd, crystal **35.00**
Croecus, ftd, crystal **35.00**
Starlight, ftd, crystal **38.00**
Willow, ftd, crystal **32.00**

Juice tumbler, Eternally Yours, crystal **18.00**

Old fashioned tumbler, Barware, #502, cobalt blue and crystal, 8 oz, ftd. **18.50**

Oyster cocktail, Lily of the Valley, crystal **35.00**

Plate
Cascade, crystal, 7-1/4" d . . . **22.00**
Chantilly cutting, #115, 7-1/2" d, two handles, crystal **22.00**

Relish, Sanibel, three-part, Blue Opalescent, 13" l **75.00**

Salad plate, Chantilly cutting, #115, 7-1/2" d, crystal **18.00**

Serving tray, Sanibel, Blue Opalescent, sides turned up, 11" d **75.00**

Sugar shaker, Duncan Block, crystal **40.00**

Swan
3-1/2", crystal, #30 . . . . **20.00**
4", crystal, #30, solid **28.00**
5-1/2", crystal, #122 Sylvan . . **38.00**
6-1/2", opal pink **95.00**
7", medium green, pall mall . . **55.00**
7-1/2", crystal bowl **12.00**
7-1/2", red bowl **40.00**
10", green **65.00**
10", ruby, partial sticker **285.00**
10-1/2", crystal bowl **24.00**
10-1/2", dark green bowl **55.00**
10-1/2", red bowl **75.00**
13", chartreuse **115.00**

Tumbler, Touraine, 5-1/2" h, ftd, orig paper label **18.00**

Umbrella
6-3/4" h, 3" d, Daisy & Button, vaseline, round foot with pattern, orig metal handle and tip, flake on one rim point **450.00**
7" h, 6-1/2" w, Daisy & Button, amber, ftd, orig metal handle and tip **350.00**
7" h, 6-1/2" w, Daisy & Button, colorless, orig metal handle and tip, rim flake **250.00**

Urn
Crystal, round applied handles, 5-1/2" sq base **25.00**
Light chartreuse
No handles, 5-1/2" sq base **36.00**
Round applied handles, 3" sq base **45.00**
Milk glass, green handles, 5-1/2" sq base **395.00**
Ruby
No handles, 3" sq base . . . **35.00**
Round applied handles, 3" sq base **45.00**

Vase, Chanticleer, #128, Blue Opalescent, 3-1/2" h **125.00**

Water set, Button Panels, crystal, gold trim, seven-pc set **160.00**

The
DUNCAN and MILLER GLASS CO
Manufacturers of Fine Table Glassware
WASHINGTON PA.

Tell our advertisers you saw it in THE CROCKERY AND GLASS JOURNAL

An ad introducing "The New Puritan," Pottery, Glass & Brass Salesman, *May 1930.*

Whiskey
- Ducks and Cattails etching, crystal, 2 oz, orig label 28.00
- Seahorse, etch #502, red and crystal, ftd, 2 oz 45.00

Wine
- Alden, cobalt blue and crystal, 3 oz 45.00
- Festival of Flowers, crystal 26.50
- Willow, crystal 35.00

Patterns and etchings

Astaire—Cordial, ruby 45.00
Finger bowl, ruby 35.00
Plate, ruby, 7-1/2" d 12.50
Tumbler, ruby, 10 oz 18.00

Canterbury, #115—Extensive dinnerware pattern made in Cape Cod blue (opalescent), chartreuse, cranberry pink, crystal, jasmine yellow, ruby, and sapphire blue. Made 1937.

Ashtray, rect, crystal 10.00
Basket
- 5-1/2" d, cranberry pink 70.00
- 10" l, oval, crystal 85.00

Bowl
- 6-1/2" d, crystal, handle 12.00
- 6-1/2", sapphire blue 30.00
- 8" d, 2 part, crystal 16.00
- 12" d, flared, crystal 25.00

Cake plate, 14" d, chartreuse . . . 30.00
Candlesticks, pr, 3-1/2" h, crystal 25.00
Candy box, cov
- Chartreuse, three-part 55.00
- Crystal, three-part, 6" d, 3-1/2" h 65.00
- Crystal, three-part, 8" d, gold overlay flowers on lid 35.00

Celery tray, 11" l, crystal 25.00
Champagne, sapphire blue 20.00
Cheese comport, crystal 25.00
Cigarette box, ruby, small 125.00
Claret, sapphire blue 25.00
Cocktail, crystal 10.00
Comport
- Crystal, 5-1/2" h 45.00
- Emerald green, crystal foot, 5-1/2" h 72.00
- Ruby, crystal foot, orig label, 5-1/2" h 140.00

Condiment tray, four-part, crystal 20.00
Console bowl, small 45.00
Cordial, blown, cut, crystal 20.00
Creamer and sugar, tray, crystal
- 2-3/4" h, 3 oz 35.00
- 3-3/4" h, 7 oz 25.00

Cruets, pr, orig stoppers, on tray, crystal 75.00
Cup and saucer, crystal 17.50
Decanter, stopper, crystal 100.00
Flower arranger
- Jasmine yellow 65.00
- Dark green, 5-1/2" h 55.00

Goblet
- Chartreuse 20.00
- Crystal, 9 oz, ftd 12.00

Ice cream, crystal 6.00
Mayonnaise, plate, orig ladle . . . 40.00
Oyster cocktail, jasmine yellow . 15.00
Plate
- 8" d, chartreuse 15.00
- 8-1/2" d, sapphire blue 15.00
- 9" d, chartreuse 18.00
- 11-1/4" d, crystal 25.00

Relish, three parts
- 11" d, crystal 25.00
- Three handles, crystal, silver overlay 27.50

Salt and pepper shakers, pr, crystal 24.00
Sherbet, crimped, sapphire blue 15.00
Sugar, large, crystal 12.00
Tumbler
- Crystal, 6-1/4" h 15.00
- Pink opalescent 45.00

Vase
- Biscane green, #115, crimped top, partial gold label, 7" h 145.00
- Crystal
  - 3" h 12.00
  - 5-1/2" h 24.00
  - Inverted candle type, 7-1/4" h 115.00
- Sapphire blue, 4-1/2" h 20.00

Violet vase, cranberry pink opalescent 40.00
Wine, crystal 25.00

Caribbean—Extensive dinnerware pattern made in amber, blue, crystal, and ruby. Made 1936-55.

Ashtray, 6" d, blue 35.00
Bowl
- 5" d, blue 35.00
- 8-1/2" d, blue 70.00

Candy, cov, 7" d, flared, blue . . . 95.00
Champagne, blue 45.00
Cheese dish, cov, blue 35.00
Cocktail, 3-3/4" oz, 4-1/8" h, blue 45.00
Console bowl, 12" d, flared edge, crystal 40.00
Creamer, blue 25.00
Cruet, orig stopper, crystal 75.00
Cup and saucer, crystal 22.00
Epergne, 9-1/2" h, blue 95.00
Fruit plate, 6" d, handle, blue . . . 20.00
Goblet, blue 40.00
Mayonnaise, 5-3/4" d, handle, orig liner, spoon, blue 85.00
Milk pitcher, blue 295.00
Plate
- 6-1/4" d, crystal 6.00
- 7-1/2" d, blue 20.00
- 8-1/2" d, blue 35.00
- 8-1/2" d, crystal 18.00
- 10-1/2" d, crystal 45.00

Punch bowl, crystal 90.00
Punch cup, crystal, red handle . . 15.00
Relish, two parts, round, 6" d, blue 30.00

Master salt, blue swan, **$65.**

Salt and pepper shakers, pr, metal tops, crystal 35.00
Server, 6-1/2" d, center handle, blue 48.00
Torte plate, 16" d, crystal 35.00
Tumbler, 5-1/2" h, ftd, crystal 22.00
Vase
- 5-3/4" h, ftd, ruffled edge, blue 60.00
- 7-1/2" h, ftd, flared, bulbous, crystal 48.00
- 9" h, flared, blue 125.00

Water pitcher, blue 965.00
Wine, blue, 3 oz, 4-3/4" h 45.00

First Love—Extensive dinnerware etched pattern made only on crystal. Made in 1937.

Ashtray, 5" l, rect 35.00
Bowl
- 5-1/2" d, handle 40.00
- 10" d, flared 50.00

Bread and butter plate, #111, 6" d 15.00
Bud vase, 9" h 75.00
Butter dish, 7" sq, Terrace blank 120.00
Cake plate, 14-1/2" d, small base 60.00
Candelabra, pr, two-lite, #30 . . . . 85.00
Candlesticks, pr, 4" h 60.00
Candy, open, three-part 40.00
Celery tray, #30, two handles, 12" l 65.00
Champagne 26.00
Cheese and cracker 95.00

Cocktail, #65111-1/2 . . . . 20.00
Comport, 5-1/2" 50.00
Cornucopia vase
Three Feathers blank
4" h 75.00
8" h 145.00
#117 . . . . 60.00
Creamer and sugar, matching tray, individual size 35.00
Cup and saucer 20.00
Decanter, 32 oz 295.00
Deviled egg plate, 12" d 115.00
Dinner plate, #111, 11" d 45.00
Goblet
Low 25.00
Tall 28.00
Honey dish, 5" x 3" 30.00
Ice bucket, orig handle 75.00
Iced tea tumbler, ftd, #5111-1/2, 6-1/2" h, 12 oz 15.00
Luncheon plate, #30, 8-1/2" d . . 22.00
Martini pitcher 165.00
Mayonnaise, 5-1/4" x 3", divided, 7-1/2" underplate 40.00
Nappy, 5-1/2" x 2", handle, heart shape 30.00
Oyster cocktail, 3-3/4" 22.00
Perfume bottle, 5" h, #5200 . . . . 65.00
Relish
Two parts, two handles, Terrace blank 30.00
Three parts, feather 50.00
Four parts, 9" 45.00
Five parts, 10" d 65.00
Salad dressing bottle 200.00
Salad plate, #115, 7-1/2" d 20.00
Salt and pepper shakers, pr . . . 32.00
Tray, tab handles, 10" w 55.00
Urn, 7" h 50.00
Tumbler, 8 oz, flat 30.00
Vase, 10" h, cylinder 72.00

Hobnail

Bowl, 12" d, crimped rim, blue . . 65.00
Candlesticks, pr
Amethyst 75.00
Blue opalescent, 4" h 60.00
Champagne, pink 20.00
Cologne bottle, 8 oz
Blue opalescent 115.00
Pink opalescent 85.00
Cruet, orig stopper, amber 60.00
Cup and saucer, blue opalescent 22.00
Goblet, ftd, 9 oz, blue opalescent 40.00
Hat, 6", blue opalescent 195.00
Ivy ball, #118
Amber, 5", small opening 25.00
Light green, 5", small opening 36.00
Milk glass, 5", small opening . 40.00

Plate
8" d, blue opalescent 15.00
8-1/2" d, pink 30.00
Violet vase, green, ftd, ruffled . . . 30.00

Indian Tree—Made in crystal.

Candy, cov, #115, three compartments 75.00
Champagne 25.00
Creamer and sugar, #115 . . . . . 55.00
Iced tea tumbler, ftd 22.00
Juice tumbler, ftd, 4-3/4" h 22.50
Pickle/olive, 8-1/2" 40.00
Plate, 8-1/2" d 18.00
Sherbet/champagne, tall 12.00

Language of Flowers —Made in crystal.

Bowl, 12" d, flared 37.50
Candlesticks, pr 45.00
Compote, 6" h 35.00
Oyster cocktail, crystal 15.00
Sherbet, crystal 15.00
Sugar, large 20.00

Mardi Gras, #42—Extensive dinnerware pattern made in crystal; some colors known.

Candlesticks, pr, Pharaoh, crystal, flower cutting 55.00
Cup, cobalt blue, Radiance 12.00
Jelly compote, crystal, 5" h 32.00
Punch bowl and base, crystal, 12-1/2" d 250.00
Punch cup, crystal 15.00
Sherry, flared, crystal 30.00
Sugar, cov, large, crystal 50.00
Tumbler, crystal , 4" h, 8 oz, gold trim, six-pc set 120.00
Vase, 10-1/4" h, yellow 95.00
Water carafe, crystal, 8-1/2" d . . 135.00

Passion Flower—Bowl, 12-1/2" d, crystal 30.00
Cornucopia, 8-1/2" l 65.00
Creamer and sugar, #38, crystal 40.00
Plate, 14-1/2" d, crystal 30.00
Relish, divided, crystal, 10-1/2" l . 25.00

Sandwich #41—Extensive dinnerware pattern made in amber, cobalt blue, crystal, green, and pink. Made by Duncan and Miller from 1924 to 1935. The molds have been sold and some forms of this pattern have been made by other companies, such as Lancaster Colony and Tiffin.

Ashtray, individual, sq 8.00
Basket, 10", oval, loop handle . . 150.00
Bonbon, 5" l, heart shape, ring handle 18.00
Bowl
11-1/2" d 48.00
12" d, shallow 50.00
Bread and butter plate, 6" d 6.00

Cake plate, pedestal, 13" d 85.00
Candelabra, pr
10" h, pr 150.00
16" h, 3-lite, bobeches and prisms 225.00
Candy basket, ftd, loop handle . 50.00
Candy, cov, ftd 55.00
Celery tray, 10" l 22.50
Champagne, 5-1/4" h 10.00
Cheese comport 15.00
Coaster 15.00
Cocktail 15.00
Comport, 7" 25.00
Creamer, 4" 12.00
Creamer and sugar, tray, individual size 37.50
Cruet, stopper 40.00
Cruet set, five pcs 70.00
Cup and saucer 16.00
Dessert plate, 7" d 7.50
Deviled egg plate 80.00
Dinner plate, 9-1/2" d 50.00
Float bowl, 11-1/2" d 50.00
Fruit bowl
5-1/2" d 10.00
12" d, flared 45.00
Goblet, water, 9 oz, ftd 18.00
Grapefruit bowl, rimmed, 7" 18.00
Ice cream bowl, 5 oz 12.00
Jelly compote 10.00
Juice tumbler, ftd 13.00
Mayonnaise, 5" d 20.00
Nappy, 5" d 8.00
Pickle, 7" l, oval 15.00
Relish
Two parts, round, ring handle . 15.00
Two parts, 5-1/2" d, handle . . . 15.00
Three parts, 6" x 10" 27.50
Three parts, 10-1/2", oblong . . 20.00
Four parts, 10" d, round, two handles 45.00
Salad bowl, 10" d 70.00
Salad plate, 8" d 11.00
Salt and pepper shakers, pr
Metal tops 20.00
Orig tops, 3-3/4" h 35.00
Sandwich plate, 16" d 115.00
Sherbet 10.00
Sugar, 2-3/4" 10.00
Syrup jar 65.00
Torte plate, 12" d 50.00
Tray, 7" l, oval 15.00
Tumbler
4-3/4" h, 9 oz, ftd 12.00
5-1/4" h, 13 oz, flat 18.00
5-1/4" h, 13 oz, ftd 15.00
Vase
9-3/4" h, ftd 70.00
10" h, ftd, #41 . . . . 90.00

Water pitcher, ice lip 135.00
Wine 20.00

Sanibel—Bowl

8" d, blue opalescent 80.00
14" d, yellow opalescent 85.00

Celery tray, 13" l, three-part, pink opalescent 45.00
Floating garden bowl, 13-1/2" l, pink opalescent 50.00
Mint tray, 7" l, blue opalescent . . 30.00
Plate, 8" d, pink opalescent 30.00
Relish, two parts, blue opalescent 30.00
Salad plate, 8-1/2" d

Blue opalescent 25.00
Yellow opalescent 25.00

Spiral Flutes—Made in amber, crystal, green, and pink. Introduced in 1924.

Almond bowl

Amber 15.00
Green 15.00

Bowl

4-1/4" d, amber 4.50
6-3/4" d, flange, green 9.00
9" d, amber 30.00

Celery tray, 10-3/4" x 4-3/4", green 20.00
Chocolate box, cov, amber 225.00
Cigarette holder, green, cutting . 70.00
Cocktail, 2-1/2 oz, ftd 10.00
Compote, 6" d, amber 20.00
Console bowl, 12" d, pink 40.00
Creamer, green 10.00
Cup and saucer, amber 10.00
Demitasse cup and saucer, green 20.00
Dessert plate

Green, 6" d 3.50
Pink, 6" d 5.00

Dinner plate, crystal, 10-1/4" d . . 22.00
Finger bowl, 4-1/4" d, green or pink 10.00
Grapefruit, ftd, green 20.00
Juice tumbler, ftd, 4-1/2" h, pink . 20.00
Luncheon plate, amber, 8-1/2" d . . 8.00
Luncheon, green, 8-1/2" d 9.50
Mug, 7" h, amber 40.00
Nut bowl, individual, green 20.00
Parfait, 5-1/2" h, green 20.00
Pickle, 8-1/2" l, green 18.00
Relish, 10" x 7-1/2" d, oval, two inserts, green 75.00
Salad plate, green, 7-1/2" d 6.00
Saucer, green 2.50
Seafood sauce cup, green 24.00
Sherbet, 4-3/4" h, green or pink . . 10.00
Tumbler

3-1/4" h, ftd, green 10.00
5-1/4" h, ftd, green 12.50

Vase, 8-1/2" h, green 20.00

Tear Drop—Extensive dinnerware pattern made only in crystal. Made from 1936 to 1955.

Ashtray, individual 5.00
Basket, ruby handle, large size 125.00
Bonbon, 6" 27.50
Bowl

8" x 12", oval, handle, orig paper label 40.00
12" sq, handle 42.50

Bread and butter plate, 6" d 5.00
Butter dish, cov, quarter pound . 22.00
Cake plate, 13" d, ftd 48.00
Candy dish, 7-1/2" d, heart shape 15.00
Candy dish, cov, three parts . . . 45.00
Celery tray, 11" l, two handles, oval 15.00
Champagne, 5-1/8" h, bead stem 10.00
Cocktail, 3-1/2 oz 12.00
Condiment set, five pcs 75.00
Cordial 25.00
Creamer and sugar 15.00
Cruet, orig stopper, 3 oz 24.50
Cup and saucer

Circle handle 10.00
Open handle, orig label 16.50

Dinner plate, 10-1/2" d 35.00
Goblet, 7" h 15.00
Heart, 7-1/2" d, two parts, orig paper label 22.00
Iced tea tumbler, ftd, 14 oz 18.00
Lemon plate, 7" d, four handles . 15.00
Luncheon plate, 8-1/2" d 8.00
Marmalade, cov, orig spoon 40.00
Mayonnaise, ftd, spoon 21.00
Nut, two parts, handle, 6" d 25.00
Old fashioned tumbler, #5300, 3-1/4" h 15.00
Olive dish, oval, two handles . . . 18.00
Oyster cocktail, 3-1/2 oz, ftd 8.00
Relish

Two parts, two handles 15.00
Five parts, 12" l, orig label . . . 25.00

Salad plate, 7-1/2" d 6.00
Saucer 3.00
Sherbet

Flared, 3-7/8" 12.50
Low, 2-1/2", 5 oz 8.00

Soup plate, 6-1/4" d, orig paper label 10.00
Sweetmeat, center handle, 6-1/2" 30.00
Torte plate, 13" d, rolled edge . . 30.00
Tumbler

5-1/4" h, 14 oz, flat 9.00
6-3/8" d, ftd, flared top 18.00

Wine, 4-3/4" h, #5301 . . . . 14.00

Terrace

Ashtray, red, sq 35.00
Bonbon, rolled up handles, cobalt blue 20.00
Bowl, 5", crystal 12.50
Candy, cov

Cobalt blue, tall 400.00
Crystal, floral sterling overlay, 6" h 135.00

Champagne, red 95.00
Comport, 7", amber 45.00
Creamer, crystal 15.00
Cup, crystal 15.00
Cup and saucer, crystal 20.00
Demitasse set, cup, saucer, and plate 45.00
Ice tub, 5-1/2", tab handles, flower cutting 75.00
Jug, floral sterling overlay 350.00
Mayonnaise bowl, divided, Eternally Yours cutting 40.00
Plate

Cobalt blue, 7-1/2" d 37.50
Crystal

7-1/2" d, use marks 5.00
8-1/2" d 12.50

Relish

Four parts, 9" d, round, floral sterling overlay 45.00
Five parts, gold trim 125.00

Tray, 4" d, round, handle, floral sterling overlay 135.00
Tumbler

Cobalt blue 30.00
Red 37.50

DURAND

History: Victor Durand (1870-1931), born in Baccarat, France, apprenticed at the Baccarat glassworks where several generations of his family had worked. In 1884, Victor came to America to join his father at Whitall-Tatum & Co. in New Jersey. In 1897, father and son leased the Vineland Glass Manufacturing Company in Vineland, New Jersey. Products included inexpensive bottles, jars, and glass for scientific and medical purposes. By 1920, four separate companies existed.

When Quezal Art Glass and Decorating Company failed, Victor Durand recruited Martin Bach Jr., Emil J. Larsen, William Wiedebine, and other Quezal men and opened an art-glass shop at Vineland in December 1924. Quezal-style iridescent pieces were made. New innovations included cameo and intaglio designs, geometric Art-Deco shapes, Venetian Lace, and Oriental-style pieces. In 1928, crackled glass, called Moorish Crackle and Egyptian Crackle, was made.

Durand died in 1931. The Vineland Flint Glass Works was merged with Kimble Glass Company a year later, and the art glass line was discontinued.

Many Durand glass pieces are not marked. Some have a sticker with the words "Durand Art Glass," others have the name "Durand" scratched on the pontil or "Durand" inside a large V. Etched numbers may be part of the marking.

Reference: Kenneth Wilson, *American Glass 1760-1930: The Toledo Museum of Art*, Volume I, Volume II, Hudson Hills Press and The Toledo Museum of Art, 1994.

Ashtray, 5" d, irid blue and green ground, match holder center... **750.00**

Bowl

- 4-1/4" d, 2" h, irid blue body, white heart and vine dec, base marked in silver "V Durand #3"...... **575.00**
- 4-1/2" d, 2" h, irid blue, white heart and vine design, highly irid surface, sgd **500.00**
- 5" d, luster glass, opal and blue floral, sgd and numbered. **3,350.00**
- 8" d, 6-1/2" h, orange cased to opal, irid green leaf and vine dec, sgd "Durand" in "V".........**1,500.00**
- 9-3/4" d, butterscotch, partial silver sgd **325.00**

Box, cov, 3-1/2" d, King Tut, green luster ground, gold luster dec . **1,200.00**

Box, 4-1/2" d, 3-1/4" h, King Tut, Lady Gay Rose, round, gold int., applied ambergris disk foot, cover cut-star at center top pontil mark, unsigned **1,610.00**

Candlesticks, pr

- 2-3/4" h, mushroom, red, opal pulled florals, pale yellow base... **700.00**
- 7" h, irid opal white with random dec, int. gold luster, unsigned .. **375.00**
- 9-1/2" h, amber baluster, pulled blue tip feathers, etched wheat and leaves on flanged rim..... **325.00**
- 10" h, No. 315, transparent ambergris baluster form, simple foliate cutting on top bobeche rim, unsigned **520.00**

Charger

- 14" d, transparent green ground, five center colorless, green, and gray feathers, few small seed bubble **900.00**
- 14-1/4" d, transparent blue ground, five center colorless, lighter blue, and gray feathers, numerous bubbles within glass surround **750.00**

Compote, cov, 10-1/2" h, Spanish yellow cased glass, etched and wheel-cut Bridgeton Rose floral dec cut to clear, conforming matching cover, base marked with "Durand" in "V," possibly added later **375.00**

Compote, open

- 3" h, Luster Ware, irid gold wrapped in infused threads, bluish gold connector and base, some loss to threading...............**200.00**
- 5-1/2" d, 4-1/2" h, irid gold and opal, King Tut, sgd............**325.00**
- 8" d, white feather center design, blue ground, pale green stem and foot **750.00**

Decanter, 12" h, blue cut to clear, mushroom shaped stopper, unsgd **600.00**

Dessert set, 10 white rimmed ruby ftd bowls, seven plates, 15" d center bowl, pr ruby with topaz candlesticks . **950.00**

Dish and undertray, 4-1/2" d dish, 7" d undertray, transparent Spanish Yellow, green rim wraps, unsgd.......**225.00**

Plate, green and white pulled center, unsigned, 8" d, **$200.**

Ginger jar, cov

- 7-1/4" h, Luster Ware, irid gold finish, dome cov with applied amber rosette finial, sgd "Durand," numbered 1964-6 in silver, flat gaffer's chip beside polished pontil **750.00**
- 10-1/2" h, gold and green King Tut dec **1,950.00**

Goblet, 5-1/2" h, irid ruby ground, pale yellow stem and base, sgd **500.00**

Jack-in-the-pulpit vase, 10-3/4" h, gold irid, strong orange and fuchsia highlights **700.00**

Jar, 8-1/2" h, gold ground, blue swirl vine dec **1,200.00**

Lamp base

- 8" h, turquoise green over opal, silver and blue leaves, random irid threading, gilt-metal Egyptian Revival platform base, replaced socket **800.00**
- 8-1/2" h, ruffled rim, oval vasiform lamp shaft, transparent amber, blue pulled feathers, cut Bridgeton Rose design, mounted to gilt-metal lamp fittings, metal work, sockets replaced............... **230.00**
- 9-1/2" h Lustre Ware vase, irid blue gourd form, stretched magenta and golden hues on shoulder, blue swollen neck, mounted on ornamental cast metal base with bronze-like patina **1,900.00**
- 11" h glass shaft, 40" h with finial and riser, King Tut, green irid vasiform shaft, elaborate gilt-metal and giltwood Egyptian Revival lamp fittings............... **1,200.00**
- 12" h vase, blue, green, orange King Tut dec, opal ground, drilled**400.00**
- 12" h vase, flared neck over broad shouldered vessel, irid blue, spider web threading, mounted in gilt-metal lamp fittings, c1925, minor breaks to threading . **635.00**
- 12" h vase, irid blue body, wrapped in fine threading, mounted with ornate metal cap and base, some threads missing, base marked "Lion Electric Mfg. Design Patent" **950.00**
- 13-1/2" h vase, Lustre Ware, cased golden orange, fastened to metal base, few carbon particles **500.00**
- 23-1/2" h, brilliant blue, allover spider web dec, purple, gold, and blue highlights **1,000.00**

Mantel lamp, 6-1/2" h, opal glass oval, applied gold threading and irid, mounted to elaborate gilt-metal single socket lamp base, some thread loss, pr....................... **550.00**

Mint bowl, 6" d, shallow, gold scalloped rim, sgd "V. Durand". **195.00**

Plate

- 7-3/4" d, cobalt blue ground, opal pulled feather, cross hatched pontil, sgd **500.00**
- 8-1/2" d, ruby, paneled, 10-sided, hand blown, sgd **215.00**
- 8-5/8" d, feather pattern, blue, opal, and clear, cross hatched cut center **225.00**

Rose bowl, 4" h, colorless, air traps, sgd and numbered **350.00**

Sherbet and underplate, 2-3/4" h green sherbet, applied white rim, Phantom luster finish, 6" d matching underplate................. **200.00**

Stemware, cobalt blue cut to clear **175.00**

Vase

4" h, colorless sphere, controlled bubble, int. dec, base inscribed "V. Durand 1995-4," gold irid, sgd "V Durand/1995-4" **300.00**

4-1/4" h, oviform, irid blue, white cobweb dec, sgd "Durand" **800.00**

6" h, ambergris oval, flared rim, overall lustrous gold surface, inscribed "V. Durand 1710-6" **375.00**

6" h, oval, fine blue irid, inscribed "Durand 1722 1/2-6" **435.00**

6-1/4" h, King Tut, classic baluster form, irid green swirls and coils, warm orange glass cased to white, lustered orange int., Larson foot **690.00**

6-1/4" h, threaded, gold irid **1,355.00**

6-1/4" h, vasiform, irid gold, gold threading, gold irid on int. of flared mouth, polished pontil, unsigned, c1925, some threading loss at shoulders................ **575.00**

6-1/2" h, gold threaded body, sgd "Durand/1901," some loss to threading................ **290.00**

6-3/4" h, flared oval, opal ground, green gold leaves, silvery gold threading, gold irid int., sgd "V. Durand 1812-6" on base, some thread loss.............. **635.00**

6-3/4" h, ruffled rim, blue and white pulled feathers over irid gold ground, Shape 1706 .... **1,100.00**

7" h, flared trumpet, integrated pulled King Tut dec, inscribed "Durand" in script straight across polished pontil........... **690.00**

Vase, gold iridescent, signed "V Durand/1990-8," 8" h, **$520.** *Photo courtesy of David Rago Auctions.*

7" h, irid amber, intaglio florals, unsgd................. **195.00**

7-1/8" h, baluster, ftd, King Tut, pale green ground, gold swirling dec, sgd "Durand"........... **750.00**

7-1/2" h, blue and gold coil dec **800.00**

8" h, collared oval, ambergris, extended folded rim, blue irid, inscribed "V. Durand 20161-8" **1,265.00**

8" h, gold irid, sgd "V Durand/ 1990-8"................ **520.00**

8" h, tooled beehive, brilliant blue irid ambergris, silver signature **1,000.00**

8-1/4" h, blue and gold hearts, vine dec, gold threading, white ground, gold int., blue foot, unsigned **1,380.00**

8-1/2" h, flared rim, oval ground, red and white crackled surface, bright irid gold luster, rough base **1,610.00**

8-1/2" h, folded over white rim, light green, shiny, sgd and numbered **600.00**

8-3/4" h, Moorish Crackle, red and white crackle on gold ground, shape 1928, unsigned ... **2,200.00**

8-3/4" h, pulled feather and threading, unsigned, some loss to threading **365.00**

8-3/4" h, 8" w, deep orange-gold, purple and blue irid surface, sgd, numbered 1710, minor int. wear **600.00**

9" h, flared, bulbous, irid blue, sgd and numbered **1,600.00**

9" h, gold irid oval cased to white, inscribed "Durand" across pontil, water stained int. **625.00**

9-1/4" h, irid cobalt blue, vertical gold heart and vine motif, purple shading, incised signature **1,250.00**

9-3/4" h, Lady Gay Rose, flared orange lined oval body, cased to white, red-rose surface, King Tut irid swirling gold and silver design **1,495.00**

9-3/4" h, yellow tinted opal, scattered gold and royal blue leaves, wrapped in irid gold threads, unsigned, hairline across base, some threading missing... **200.00**

10-1/4" h, King Tut, shape no. 1819, raised and flared rim, elongated ovoid amber body, pulled opal white dec, strong gold luster, polished pontil inscribed "Durand" **2,530.00**

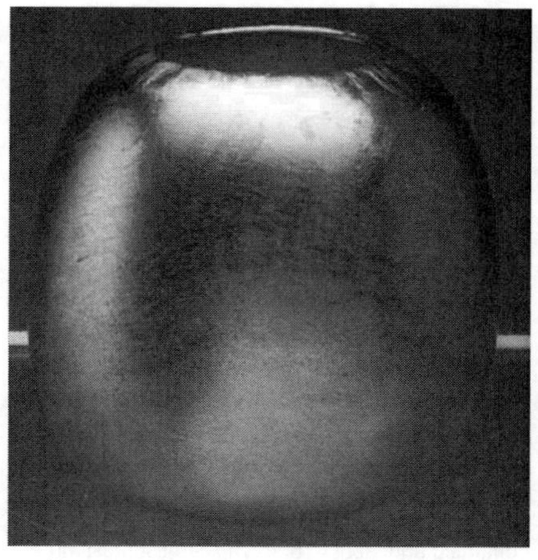

Vase, gold iridescent, signed "V Durand/ 1995-4," 4" h, **$300.** *Photo courtesy of David Rago Auctions.*

10-1/2" h, gold coil dec from top to bottom, white ground ... **1,380.00**

10-12" h, Lustre Ware, irid blue, small drilling hole started in polished pontil, but never completed **1,100.00**

10-1/2" h, 10 prominent vertical ribs, oval amber body, rough deeply crackled surface with over all irid, base inscribed "Durand" **1,840.00**

11" h, platinized gold leaves on tangled vines, irid golden luster over rich irid cobalt blue, marigold int.................. **2,100.00**

12" h, crackle, emerald green over gold, sgd "V Durand" ... **2,530.00**

12" h, flared cylinder, bright transparent green shaded to clear, five pulled green and white striped pulled peacock feathers... **750.00**

12" h, flared 10-ribbed yellow amber body, emerald green crackled surface, base inscribed "V. Durand".............. **1,610.00**

12" h, 4-3/4" w, oyster white exterior, random threading, heart leaf dec, brilliant yellow irid interior, gold irid foot, very minor loss to threading **800.00**

12-1/4" h, flared trumpet, shaded purple-blue luster, applied gold pedestal foot, heart and vine dec, marked "Durand 20120-12" **1,725.00**

15" h, "Genie" form, elongated tapered neck, bulbous amber body, fine gold irid, flattened indentation on bulbed side, base inscribed "V Durand 1974-15" **1,150.00**

Early American Glass

History: The term "Early American glass" covers glass made in America from the colonial period through the mid-19th century. As such, it includes the early pressed glass and lacy glass made between 1827 and 1840.

Major glass-producing centers prior to 1850 were Massachusetts (New England Glass Company and the Boston and Sandwich Glass Company), South Jersey, Pennsylvania (Stiegel's Manheim factory and many Pittsburgh-area firms), and Ohio (several different companies in Kent, Mantua, and Zanesville).

The Lacy Period of American glass began with the advent of pressing machines in the 1820s and continued until about 1850. The earliest pressing machines led to a revolution in the way glassware was made, as well as the detailed patterns now referred to as lacy. Lacy patterns tried to convey the delicate and intricate cut-glass patterns in the new pressing techniques without using the more time-consuming copper wheel grinding and engraving methods.

Intricate lacy patterns often contain florals and scrolls, as well as historical and commemorative elements. Many lacy patterns have such an elaborate pattern that they resemble embroidery or lacy backgrounds, hence their name. Lacy patterns were adapted to create almost every type of glass household item, from decanters and drawer pulls to goblets, plates, salts, and vegetable dishes.

Researchers today often contend that many other lacy patterns were also designed to hide small blemishes in the batches of glass used by early manufacturers. Many lacy patterns do indeed hide some imperfections such as pieces of sand and even small pebbles. Lacy patterns remain a vivid reminder of the pride and craftsmanship of early moldmakers and glasscrafters.

Early American glass was collected heavily between 1920 and 1950. It has now regained some of its earlier popularity. Leading sources for the sale of Early American glass are the auctions of Early Auction Co., Garth's Auction, Inc., Norman C. Heckler & Co., and Robert W. Skinner Auctions.

References: Raymond E. Barlow and Joan E. Kaiser, *The Glass Industry in Sandwich, Vol. 2, Vol. 3, and Vol.4*, distributed by Schiffer Publishing; William E. Covill, *Ink Bottles and Inkwells*, William S. Sullwold Publishing, 1971; Lowell Inness, *Pittsburgh Glass, 1797-1891*, Houghton Mifflin, 1976; Ruth Webb Lee, *Early American Pressed Glass, 36th Edition*, Lee Publications, 1966; Ruth Webb Lee, *Sandwich Glass Handbook*, Charles E. Tuttle, 1977; George and Helen McKearin, American Glass, Crown, 1975; —, *Two Hundred Years of American Blown Glass*, Doubleday and Company, 1950; Helen McKearin and Kenneth Wilson, *American Bottles and Flasks*, Crown, 1978; L.W. and D. B. Neal, *Pressed Glass Dishes of the Lacy Period, 1825-1850*, published by author, 1972; Adeline Pepper, *Glass Gaffers of New Jersey*, Schribners, 1971; Dick Roller (comp.), *Indiana Glass Factories Notes*, Acorn Press, 1994; Jane S. Spillman, *American and European Pressed Glass*, Corning Museum of Glass, 1981; Kenneth Wilson, *American Glass 1760-1930*, 2 vols., Hudson Hills Press and The Toledo Museum of Art, 1994; —, *New England Glass and Glassmaking*, Crowell, 1972.

Periodicals: *Antique Bottle & Glass Collector*, P.O. Box 187, East Greenville, PA 18041.

Collectors' Clubs: Early American Glass Traders, RD 5, Box 638, Milford, DE 19963; Early American Pattern Glass Society, P.O. Box 266, Colesburg, IA 52035; Glass Research Society of New Jersey, Wheaton Village, Glasstown Rd, Millville, NJ 08332; The National American Glass Club, Ltd., P.O. Box 8489, Silver Spring, MD 20907.

Museums: Bennington Museum, Bennington, VT; Chrysler Museum, Norfolk, VA; Corning Museum of Glass, Corning, NY; Glass Museum, Dunkirk, IN; Historical Glass Museum Foundation, Redlands, CA; New Bedford Glass Museum, New Bedford, MA; Sandwich Glass Museum, Sandwich, MA; Toledo Museum of Art, Toledo, OH; Wheaton Historical Village Assoc. Museum of Glass, Millville, NJ.

Additional Listings: Blown Three Mold, Cup Plates, Flasks, Sandwich Glass, and Stiegel-Type Glass.

Blown molded

Basket vase, 8" h, aqua, applied handle, America, mid/late 19th C, imperfections **495.00**

Bottle
- 6-1/4" h, colorless, high kick-up, swirled rib pattern, America, mid/late 19th C, imperfections **115.00**
- 7-1/4" h, aqua, swirled rib pattern, America, mid/late 19th C, imperfections **120.00**
- 7-7/8" h, amethyst, paneled, white loop designs, metal screw cap, England or Eastern U.S., 19th C **950.00**
- 8-1/4" h, cobalt blue, white spiral canes, England or Eastern U.S., 19th C **1,150.00**

Bowl
- 4-3/4" d, 3-1/8" h, cobalt blue, expanded diamond, applied foot **250.00**
- 4-7/8" d, 2-7/8" h, puce, 16 vertical ribs, broken swirl to right, inward folded rim, ftd, pontil **265.00**
- 5" d, 3-5/8" h, cobalt blue, 15 swirled ribs, flared lip, applied foot . **440.00**
- 5-7/8" d, 3" h, amber, folded rim, early 19th C, minor burst bubble **690.00**
- 6-1/2" d, 1-7/8" h, light green, lily pad dec, rolled rim, attributed to NJ **1,495.00**
- 6-1/2" d, 4-5/8" h, amber, folded rim, Midwestern **715.00**

Canister
- 9-5/8" h, colorless, two applied rings and finial, Pittsburgh **110.00**
- 9-7/8" h, colorless, dolphin, minor roughage to base, single . . **200.00**
- 11" h, colorless, two applied rings, pressed lid with chips **140.00**
- 11-1/8" h, colorless, three applied blue rings, colorless applied finial, Pittsburgh **770.00**

Celery vase, gadrooned gather at base, New England or PA, c1830-40 . . . . **200.00**

Cologne bottle
- 4-3/4" l, amethyst, round, pulled neck, inverted diamond pattern, mismatched faceted stopper, ground lip, pontil scar, imperfections, England or America, early 19th C **95.00**
- 5-1/2" l, amethyst, oval, vertical ribs, slight right twist at neck, flared lip, pontil scar, England or America, early 19th C **115.00**

Compote, 10" d, 7-3/4" h, flint, colorless, bowl with cut sheaf of wheat pattern, knop stem, star foot, Pittsburgh, wear and small flakes **385.00**

Creamer
- 3" h, amethyst, 18 ribs swirled to the right, modified pear form, applied handle, inward rolled rim with pour spout, pontil scar, c1820-50 . . . . **600.00**
- 3-1/4" h, sapphire blue, faint darker blue striations, 14 ribs, tooled rim with pour spout, applied handle, attributed to Pittsburgh, 1820-60, small pc of rigaree at tail end of handle missing. **150.00**
- 3-1/2" h, cobalt blue, 20-diamond pattern, ovoid, applied handle, sheared rim with pour spout, pontil scar, 1770-1830 . . . . **450.00**
- 4-5/8" h, deep sapphire blue, 11-diamond pattern, elongated ovoid, applied solid handle, tooled rim, pour spout, applied ribbed base with inward rolled rim, pontil scar, c1820-40 . . . . **650.00**

Decanter
- 5-1/2" h, colorless, ribbed body and stopper, 19th C. **235.00**
- 6" h, colorless, engraved leaf dec, ribbed band around base, 19th C **245.00**
- 6-3/4" h, 3-1/2" d base, dark olive green, flange lip, ribbed neck, swirled ribbed upper body above sunburst motif (McKearin GII-2, Type 1), ribbed lower body, attributed to Mt. Vernon Glass Factory, Vernon, NY, c1820-40,

stopper missing, minor wear **2,875.00**

7-1/2" h, amethyst, conical shape, swirled rib pattern, flared lip, pontil scar, England or America, early 19th C **100.00**

8-5/8" h, 3-7/8" d base, pale green, fluted and hoped, ribbed lower body, attributed to New England, c1820-40, stopper missing, very minor imperfections. **3,500.00**

10-1/2" h, olive, opalescent loops, England or Eastern U.S., 19th C **1,150.00**

11-1/8" h, 3-3/8" d, amethyst, ribs twisted into spiral patterned neck, America, 19th C, minor wear **635.00**

Ewer

Colorless, vertical ribs, applied handle, 19th C. **145.00**

Olive green, applied handle, flaring rim, white speckles and striations, 6-1/8" h, England or America, mid to late 19th C, minor flaking and scratches. **450.00**

Flask, swirled rib pattern, America, mid/late 19th c., **$250.** *Photo courtesy of Pacific Glass Auctions.*

Flask

5-3/4" h, aqua, vertical ribbed half pint, America, mid/late 19th C, imperfections. **120.00**

5-3/4" h, colorless, vertical ribbed half pint, America, mid/late 19th C, imperfections. **110.00**

6-1/2" h, aqua, diamond quilted half pint, America, mid/late 19th C, imperfections. **120.00**

6-1/2" h, cobalt blue, ribbed two-mold, crowned rampant lion with ax within shield panel, pint, England or Eastern U.S., 19th C, imperfections. **290.00**

6-1/2" h, colorless, half pint, flattened side with honeycomb-diaper pattern, America, mid/late 19th C, imperfections **150.00**

7" h, aqua, pink, swirled rib pattern, America, mid/late 19th C, imperfections **130.00**

8-5/8" h, cobalt blue, ovoid, swirled ribs, pint, England or Eastern U.S., 19th C, imperfections. **275.00**

9-3/4" h, cobalt blue, ovoid, applied colorless rigaree and Prince of Wales feathers, quart, England or Eastern U.S., 19th C, imperfections **325.00**

10-3/4" h, cobalt blue, white speckle dec, England or Eastern U.S., 19th C, very minor imperfections **260.00**

Flip glass, colorless, ribbed side, engraved scallop crosshatch and zigzag dec, 19th C **125.00**

Gaffing tool holder, 4-3/4" h, peacock blue, applied base, segmented stem **580.00**

Gemel bottle, 7" h, cobalt blue, England or Eastern U.S., 19th C, imperfections. **250.00**

Goblet

6-1/2" h, deep amethyst, applied pedestal foot, polished pontil, Ohio, c1830 . . . . **165.00**

7" h, colorless, applied foot, hollow hourglass stem and bowl, copper wheel engraved ivy and "B.D.C.," attributed to New England Glass Co. **125.00**

Hat, colorless, polished pontil, applied cockade. **40.00**

Jug, 4" h, bulbous, aqua, ribbed, sloping lip, applied handle, and base, America, mid/late 19th C, imperfections **375.00**

Pan, 7" d, colorless, applied cobalt blue rim, ground pontil **165.00**

Pitkin

7" h, aqua, half post neck, 30 ribs with broken swirl, flake at pontil and bottom edge. **330.00**

7-1/4" h, olive green, half post neck, 36 ribs with broken swirl. . . **275.00**

Pitcher

5-1/2" h, aqua, applied handle and base, America, mid/late 19th C, imperfections **395.00**

8-1/4" h, colorless, pillar ribbed, applied handle, attributed to Pittsburgh, PA, c1870, imperfections **300.00**

9" h, colorless, applied thread and handle, New England, late 19th C **250.00**

9-1/4" h, 5-1/2" d, pale aqua, applied thread at neck, trefoil handle, attributed to Saratoga Mountain Glass Works, Saratoga, NY, c1844-60, slight roughness to spout **2,100.00**

11-1/4" h, olive amber, white speckles, applied scrolling handle, England or America, mid to late 19th C, minor losses to speckling **320.00**

Preserving jar, 7-1/4" h, colorless, tin lid, recessed gallery lip for wax . **220.00**

Salt, master

2-1/4" h, 2-1/8" d, light amethyst, 17 ribs swirled to the right, double ogee bowl with short stem drawn from same gather, applied plain foot, tooled rim, pontil scar, Midwest, 1820-50 . . . . **800.00**

2-1/2" h, light green, diamond pattern on petal foot, late 18th C/early 19th C, minute chips **815.00**

2-1/2" h, 2-3/4" d, cobalt blue, checkered diamond, applied solid foot, Amelung **850.00**

2-7/8" h, cobalt blue, 16 ribs swirled slightly to the right, double ogee bowl, short stem of same gather, applied circular foot, sheared mouth, pontil scar, Midwest, 1820-60. . . . . **90.00**

3" h, colorless, double ogee bowl, short stem, applied petal foot, sheared rim, pontil scar, 1770-1830 . . . . **175.00**

3-5/8" h, colorless with pale gray cast, 15 ribs, outward folded rim, pontil scar, freeblown foot, flat rim chip **170.00**

Spirit bottle, 8" h, olive amber, squatty, domed kick-up, white speckles, England or America, mid to late 19th C **450.00**

Sugar bowl, cov

5-1/8" h, colorless, applied chain dec, attributed to Thomas Cains, Boston, first half 19th C. . . . **920.00**

Colorless, dip molded, eight vertical ribs, Pittsburgh, PA, c1815-40 . . . . **225.00**

Sweetmeat jar, cov, 16-3/4" h, 6-1/4" d, colorless, blown in a dip mold, trumpet form lid, applied knop finial, bowl form container raised on hollow stem, circular foot with polished pontil, slight greenish cast to bowl, early 19th C **690.00**

Tumbler

3-1/8" h, cobalt blue, paneled, pinpoint flakes on foot **125.00**

3-1/8" h, cobalt blue, Ashburton, pinpoint flakes on foot **150.00**

4" h, olive green, old paper label, broken blisters, Midwestern **715.00**

Vase

4" h, lilypad, flaring rim, two applied handles and base, America, mid/late 19th C, imperfections **350.00**

6" h, swirl-ribbed, gauffered rim, pressed pattern glass hexagonal standard, circular base, minor imperfections **125.00**

8" h, emerald green, flared baluster, circular foot, attributed to Pittsburgh, 19th C....... **2,185.00**

Whiskey bottle, 7-1/4" h, amber, pear-shape, applied handle, "Griffith Hyatt & Co. Baltimore" around semicircular panel enclosing paper label, circular panel on reverse enclosing paper label of *U.S.S. Constitution*, wear, losses to labels **750.00**

Wine

5-1/8" h, colorless, Pittsburgh-type engraved foliage, tapered stem and bowl, applied foot **85.00**

6-3/8" h, colorless, folded rim, hollow stem, applied dome foot attributed to Amelung **600.00**

Free blown

Bank, 6-1/2" h, free blown and pattern molded, sea green with mulberry colored spiral striation patterned molded bowl with coin slot, applied rigaree trailing and three applied birds, free blown pedestal base, applied flat circular foot, knob contains U.S. dime1841, tooled rim, pontil scar, 1841-60 .... **17,000.00**

Bowl, 5-1/2" h, aquamarine, tooled rim, pontil scar, attributed to New York State glasshouse, 1840-70......... **475.00**

Cologne bottle, 8-1/8" h, slender conical form, brilliant medium amethyst, inward rolled mouth, pontil scar **325.00**

Compote, 7-1/4" h, colorless, copper wheel engraving of vintage pattern, leaves and fruit, ground rim, pontil scar, attributed to Pittsburgh district, Pittsburgh, PA, 1840-70....... **210.00**

Creamer

3-1/2" h, cobalt blue, ovoid, applied base and handle, sheared rim with pour spout, pontil scar, 1830-60 .... **400.00**

3-1/2" h, sapphire blue, ovoid, applied base and handle, sheared rim with pour spout, pontil scar, 1830-60................ **250.00**

Flask, 5-1/8" h, deep olive amber, sheared mouth, pontil scar, 1800-30, some minor ext. wear......... **160.00**

Jar

4-1/2" x 6-3/8", golden amber, cylindrical, wide flat folded rim, tubular pontil **325.00**

8" h, colorless, two horizontal ribs, domed cov, air trap finial... **200.00**

Lamp, fluid

9-3/4" h, marbrie font, white loops over clear glass, fluted and paneled opalescent white baroque pressed glass base, New England, 19th C **215.00**

13" h, brass font and connector, cylindrical free-blown blue and white latticinio glass standard, sq marble base, attributed to New England, late 19th C **260.00**

Lamp, suspension, 20" h, domed clear glass smoke shade suspending three chains supporting deep oval globe with etched and engraved grape clusters and foliage, foliate emb brass collar with three hooks, America, 19th C, surface scratches............ **980.00**

Pitcher, free blown, attributed to South Jersey glasshouse, 1840-60, bulbous body, type 1 lily pad decoration, applied solid handle, applied circular foot, golden amber, sheared rim with pour spout, pontil scar, McKearin plate 17, **$7,000.** *Photo courtesy of Norman C. Heckler and Co.*

Pitcher

5-1/2" h, lily pad, bulbous body, type-I lily pad dec, applied solid handle, applied circular foot, golden amber, sheared rim, pour spout, pontil scar, attributed to South Jersey glass house, 1840-60, McKearin plate 17 .... **7,000.00**

6" h, lily pad, bulbous body, type-II lily pad dec, applied handle, applied flat circular foot, bluish aquamarine, tooled rim, pour spout, pontil scar, attributed to Ellenville Glassworks, Ellenville, NY, 1830-60 .... **6,000.00**

Sand shaker, opaque blue.... **275.00**

Sock darner, amber, labeled "Dug at Lyndeboro site" **95.00**

Sugar bowl, cov, 7-3/8" h, light green, applied sq base, applied double solid handles, flanged cover with elaborate applied swan finial, sheared rim, pontil scar, attributed to South Jersey **5,500.00**

Vase

7-1/2" h, 3-1/2" d base, amethyst, trumpet shape, folded rim, circular base, attributed to New England, mid-19th C, minor imperfections **1,840.00**

8" h, cobalt blue, applied rings at rim and neck, attributed to New England, 19th C, minor wear **750.00**

12" h, 4-1/4" d base, ruby overlay, trumpet shape, gauffered rim, circular base, attributed to New England, late 19th C, minor imperfections, price for pr **1,360.00**

Wine, 7-1/2" h, panel cut flared bowl, baluster stem, applied foot, pr . **225.00**

Wine funnel, 3-3/8" x 5-3/4", colorless, engraved border of leaves and flowers, eight cut flutes continue down stem **95.00**

Lacy

Compote, 4-1/4" h, 6-1/2" d, 4-1/4" h, Heart and Shield pattern, colorless, New England Glass Co., small rim chip **750.00**

Dish, rect, open chain border and handles **200.00**

Salt, open

Basket of flowers, colorless, BF 1b, New England, second quarter 19th C, minor imperfections.... **165.00**

Basket of fruit, light green, IV 2, attributed to Jersey Glass Co., 19th C, imperfections......... **225.00**

Basket of fruit, opalescent, NE 1, New England, second quarter 19th C, minor imperfections.... **220.00**

Beaded scroll, colorless, MV 1, New England, second quarter 19th C, minor imperfections....... 155.00

Boat, colorless, BT 9, New England, second quarter 19th C, minor imperfections............ 175.00

Eagle, colorless, EE 1a, New England, second quarter 19th C, minor imperfections....... 185.00

Eagle, colorless, EE 7, New England, second quarter 19th C, minor imperfections............ 195.00

Sugar bowl, cov

5-1/4" h, Acanthus Leaf pattern, canary yellow, octagonal, Boston and Sandwich Glass Co., slight roughage.............. 2,900.00

5-3/4" h, Gothic Arch pattern, canary yellow, Boston and Sandwich Glass Co., c1840....... 2,500.00

Tray, Hairpin, 9-1/4" l, 8" w, 1-3/8" h, peacock shape, Boston and Sandwich, c1830-40, rim chip......... 9,750.00

Tumbler, 3-1/4" h, Eye and Scale pattern, colorless, pillar flute motif, Boston and Sandwich Glass Co., 1827 .... 900.00

Honey dish, colorless, lacy type pattern, minor roughness, 5" w, **$20.**

Pillar molded

Candlestick, 11-3/4" h, 5-1/4" d, colorless, flint, large eight pillar socket flares at top, eight pillar ribs, circular plain foot.................. 3,600.00

Celery vase, 9-1/2" h, colorless, copper wheel engraved panels, Pittsburgh, c1820 .... 145.00

Decanter, 10-5/8" h, eight pillar mold, colorless with amethyst highlights on each rib, heavy collar molded mouth, ground pontil scar, attributed to Pittsburgh, 1835-70 .... 1,000.00

Ewer, 11-3/4" h, flint, colorless, applied foot and handle, pewter top, hinged lid with finial, Pittsburgh......... 495.00

Pitcher, 5-3/4" h, flint, colorless, applied handle and tooled lip, Pittsburgh 315.00

Rose bowl, colorless, Pittsburgh 30.00

Pressed

Back bar bottle, 10-1/4" h, fancy pattern mold, cylindrical, pale opalescent yellow green, opalescent stripes swirled to the right, rolled mouth, ground pontil scar, 1870-1900 . 200.00

Bar bottle, Horn of Plenty, pewter slid stoppers, attributed to New England, second quarter 19th C, marbles missing, price for pr 500.00

Celery vase, 10" h, flint, colorless, round foot, hexagonal foot and bowl with oval and round thumbprint and Gothic Arches, chips on foot... 145.00

Chamber stick, 1-7/8" h, miniature or toy, deep amethyst, American, 1840-70 .... 140.00

Cologne bottle, 5-1/2" h, hexagonal, canary yellow, Star and Punty, cut stopper with ground edges.... 330.00

Compote, cov, Petal and Loop, 8-5/8" h, 6-3/4" d, minor imperfections 285.00

Compote, open, Colonial, 5-3/4" d, 5-7/8" h, fiery opalescent, rim chip 535.00

Decanter, matching stopper

10-7/8" h, Strawberry Diamond and Fan pattern, three neck rings, cut panels at shoulder and base, Pittsburgh, second quarter 19th C 310.00

13-3/8" h, Diamond Point, Pittsburgh, second quarter 19th C.... 300.00

Spooner

4-1/8" h, cobalt blue, Bigler variant 415.00

4-3/8" h, fiery opalescent, Excelsior, chips on base........... 330.00

Sugar bowl, cov

5-3/8" h, Gothic Arch, flint, vaseline, octagonal, acanthus leaf lid, small flakes on base, lid with rim chips 550.00

9-7/8" h, 5-1/4" d, Diamond Thumbprint pattern, colorless, minor imperfections 300.00

Syrup pitcher, 8-1/4" h, colorless, hexagonal, Star and Punty, applied hollow handle, tin top with hinged lid, pewter finial................ 220.00

English Glass

History: The English have been manufacturing fine glassware for centuries. This category is a catchall for some examples of the many fine glasswares produced by the English. English glassmakers, just like their contemporaries around the world, often did not mark their wares. Research and a familiarity with techniques and colors often allow collectors and dealers to correctly attribute a lovely piece of glass as English.

References: Victor Arwas, *Glass Art Nouveau to Art Deco*, Rizzoli International Publications, Inc., 1977; Ray and Lee Grover, *English Cameo Glass*, Crown Publishers, Inc., 1980; Charles A. Hajdamach, British Glass, 1800-1914, Antique Collectors' Club, 1991; Albert C. Revi, *Nineteenth Century Glass*, reprint, Schiffer Publishing, 1981.

Barber's bowl, 7-1/2" h, 5-1/2" d, cylindrical, spring green ground, white enameled dec of stylized leaves, gold band of diamonds and half diamonds 750.00

Basket

6" h, 6-1/2" w, deep cranberry, rolled over rim, applied crystal ruffled edge, shell ftd base, applied crystal looped handle, Victorian 175.00

7" h, 8" w, vaseline opalescent shading to pink, diamond quilted design, petal shaped edge, pale pink handle............. 100.00

12" h, 10" w, heavy threaded body, applied rigaree shell base with double row of rigaree, three large rows of applied rigaree including two done in shell pattern, double crossed crystal handle with matching applied rigaree .. 450.00

Beverage set, 8-3/4" h x 5-3/4" w pitcher, two 4" tumblers, deep emerald green shading to purple, allover enameled floral dec of Queen Anne's lace, leaves, and wild roses, applied transparent green handle...... 850.00

Bowl

5" d, 3" h, opalescent yellow shading to vaseline, applied blue edge, yellow rigaree, Victorian 50.00

8" w, 3-3/4" h, triangular shape, Tartan, blue, white, and pale pink, clockwise swirl on ext., reversed on int., applied feet, sgd "Tartan Rd. No. 46498," registered by Henry Gething Richardson, Wordsley Flint Glass Works, near Stourbridge, Feb. 24, 1886 .... 1,250.00

Candlesticks, 10" h, cut glass, Anglo/Irish, 19th C, set of four .. 850.00

Celery vase, 7-1/4" h, 4-7/8" d, emb ribs, blue opalescent, marked "RD. #217752" **95.00**

Centerpiece, 20-1/2" h, 15-1/2" d, three parts, center vase, compote dish, and base, cut glass, Anglo/Irish, 19th C **1,500.00**

Compote

6" h, 8" w, deep rose shading to pink satin int., white ext., silver plated stand, Victorian. **150.00**

11-3/4"h, baluster form pedestal, fan and diagonal cut bowl, Irish **400.00**

Creamer, 4-1/2" h, 3-3/4" d, daisies and panel type pattern, vaseline opalescent, marked "Rd. #176566" **75.00**

Dish, cov, 9-1/2" d, cut glass, crosshatching and fans, Anglo/Irish, 19th C, chips, pr **400.00**

Hanging basket

8-1/2" h, 3" w basket, pink overlay over white, crystal stand with thorn handle and holder **200.00**

9" h, 5-1/2" h x 3-1/4" w basket, pink and white cut overlay basket, clear applied thorn handle cut with flower and leaf design, clear crystal ribbed thorn base. **600.00**

Humidor, 6-1/4" h, 4-1/4" w, white milk glass, shades from yellow to brown, large pink and burgundy enameled roses, green leaves, brass finish, emb flower finial, Victorian, small chip on rim **50.00**

Jar, cov, 5-1/2" h, spatter, minor roughness **65.00**

Pokal, cov, 17-3/4" h, 8" d, cut glass, wide paneled cut design, tulip like edge, Anglo-Irish, matching pr . **700.00**

Rose bowl, spatter, cased **75.00**

Service, cut glass, cut with alternating vertical bands of diagonal flutes and cross-cut diamonds, each with central cut shield engraved with "H," paneled waisted stems with star-cut bases, 11 6-3/4" h water goblets, 10 5-3/4" h wine goblets, eight 4-3/4" h sherry glasses, seven 4-1/2" d finger bowls, four 3-7/8" h cordial glasses, two 15" h decanters with stoppers, two 12-3/8" h ewers with associated stoppers, two 7-1/2" h ftd vases, one 10-1/2" h ftd vase, one 12-1/2" d decanter, Anglo-Irish, Waterford-type, late 19th C, descended in the family of businessman philanthropist John Hopkins **3,750.00**

Sugar shaker, cut-glass base, star-cut base, star-shaped holes in hall-marked sterling silver top, **$85.**

Spirits bottle, 5" h, 6-1/8" d, free blown, cylindrical squatty shape, dense olive green, sheared mouth, string rim, pontil scar, 1/2" chip on string rim, small chips, some ext. wear, 1680-1730 . . . . **325.00**

Syrup pitcher, 7" h, 3-1/2" w, pear shape, body shades from blue to white, beige flowers, green leaves and ferns, silver plated top and handle, Victorian **100.00**

Sweetmeat

6" h, 6" w, vaseline, applied vaseline rigaree in middle, fancy Sheffield holder **100.00**

8" h, 10" l, two bowls, vaseline, applied ruby red edge, fancy metal holder with center handle . . **125.00**

Urn, cov, 12" h, colorless cut crystal, Anglo Irish, pr. **800.00**

Vase

5" h, marbleized, striated red, yellow, orange, blue, and green, cased, opal white lining, enamel dec at flared neck and rim **215.00**

8" h, floriform, opalescent yellow, internally dec by four stylized flowers, attributed to Powell or Whitefriars **350.00**

10" h, 5-3/4" d, colorless crystal over blue overlay, crystal rigaree around top and near base, blue overlay pedestal foot, multicolored enameled birds and flowers **425.00**

10-1/4" h, Moss Agate, cobalt blue ground, multichromatic swirls of color overlaid with colorless glass, engraved mark "W. & C. England," (Webb Corbett), minor tooling blemish at shoulder. **700.00**

Wine glass

6-5/8" h, double-series opaque twist stem, bell shaped bowl, conical foot, late 18th/early 19th C, price for pr. **265.00**

6-5/8" h, plain stem, bell shaped bowl, conical foot, late 18th/early 19th C. **125.00**

EPERGNES

History: Epergnes were made by early glass craftsmen. Beautiful glassware used for serving food was often an important decorating element in early society, and epergenes of glass and silver adorned many dining rooms. Epergnes usually consist of one or multiple lily-type vases supported on elaborate frames and are often found with large round bases which could be filled with additional fruit or floral displays. Epergnes can be found in almost every glass color and historical period, right up to the present. Their peak popularity was during the Victorian period when they were considered necessary to every well-appointed dining room.

Reference: John Mebane, *Collecting Bride's Baskets and Other Glass Fancies*, Wallace-Homestead, 1976.

4-3/4" h, 4-3/8" d base, single bulbous Burmese ruffled vase, red berries, green and brown leaves dec, enameled highlights, notched mirrored plateau, base cov in red velvet, Webb . . **350.00**

7-1/2" h, 5-5/8" w, amberina, single lily, gold washed Art Deco metal base **100.00**

8" h, 7" w, three Burmese fairy lamps with satin glass shades, prunus blossom dec, colorless pressed glass candle cups, gilt metal ftd stand fitted with four undecorated Burmese satin glass flower holders, ruffled rims **3,200.00**

8-1/2" h, clear glass base with two tree trunk apertures, each has hanging pink cased basket, English. **350.00**

8-1/2" h, trumpet form, blue edge, highly dec figural glass dragon encircling stem, enameled florals and gold highlights, no holder **75.00**

8-1/2" h, 10-1/2" d, Hobnail, white milk glass, three ruffled lily-shaped horns, ruffled base, Fenton **95.00**

10-1/2" h, blue, center trumpet vase, three smaller trumpets, white enameled floral dec, brass frame with applied leaves and chains **275.00**

10-3/4" h, 7" d, single lily, blue satin, hand painted flowers, ruffled top and base **600.00**

12" h, 7-1/2" d, cranberry, center ruffled top single lily, fancy crystal applied

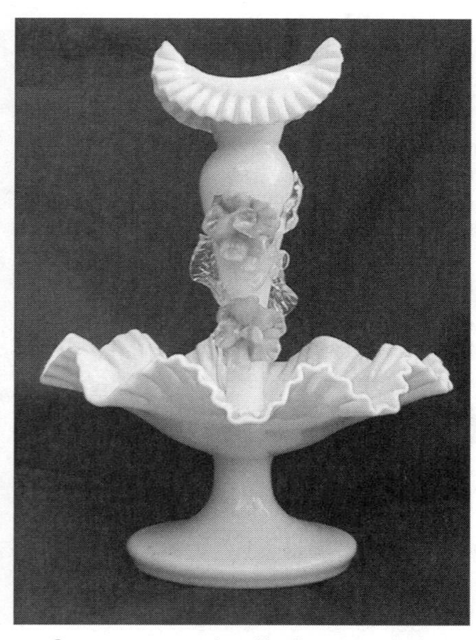

Opaque cream-colored body, two applied pink and white striated flowers, vaseline rigaree, 10-1/2" h, 7-1/2" w, **$195.**

spiral trim, ruffled cranberry bowl, brass connection **250.00**

13-1/2" h, 10" w, colorless ground, eight miniature baskets with handles and berry prunts, all hanging from center vase, Stevens and Williams **475.00**

13-1/2" h, 10-1/2" h, three lily holders, center taller lily, each raspberry with crystal threading, molded gilded leaves, mirror plateau base .. **2,400.00**

14" h, amethyst trumpet shaped single lily, etched grape and vine pattern, marble base with peacock and flower ornament **510.00**

14" h, green trumpet shaped single lily, ruffled top, matching disk base, silver plated pedestal base **400.00**

14-1/2" h, 10-1/2" d, ruffled lift out opalescent vase, nickel plated foot and vase holder................. **275.00**

15" h, Baccarat, three trumpet shaped vases with scalloped edges, Rose Tiente coloration............. **475.00**

16" h, 10-1/2" d, shaded blue int., white ext., green and maroon flowers and lacy foliage on int., lift out center lily **450.00**

16" h, 14" d, fluted center white with blue trim 10-1/2" h horn, three 9-1/2" h blue horns, jack-in-the-pulpit style fluted crest, fluted white base with blue trim, small chip.............. **450.00**

17" h, 12-1/4" d, three ribbed lilies, center 10" h x 5-1/2" d, ruffled edge with pink shading to colorless edge . **900.00**

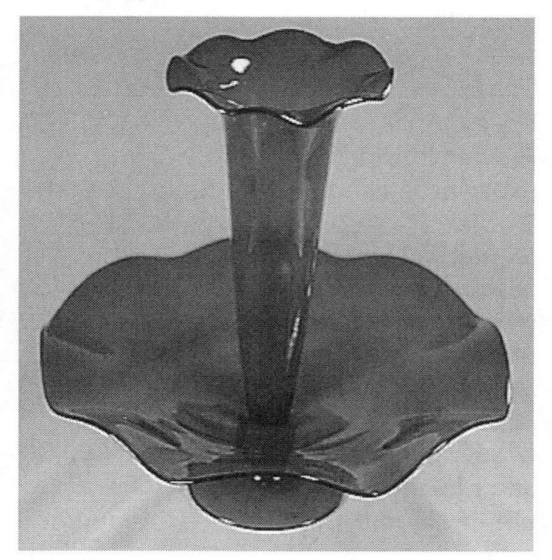

Ruby glass, 15" d, 16" h, **$250.**

19" h, 11" d, three lilies, pale translucent green shading to white opalescent ruffled rim, matching deep base **1,750.00**

19" h, 11" d, three lilies, pink and white cased, ruffled bowl, heavy wire holder with figural strawberries and leaves winding around 10" l lilies **350.00**

20" h, three lilies, cranberry, two clear twisted basket arms, Victorian . **600.00**

20" h, three lilies, turquoise and white cased, scalloped bowl, fancy rigaree around lilies................ **450.00**

21" h, three lilies, light green shading to opalescent body shading to cranberry base, ruffled, matching base .. **950.00**

21" h, 16" d, cranberry, enter flower vase, two candleholders supported with colorless glass branches, cut and etched leaf and berry design, cranberry prism drops, Victorian........ **575.00**

23" h, green opalescent, four lily-shaped vases stemming from flower bowl, Victorian.............. **660.00**

24" h, emerald green, central lily-shaped vase, five diamond cut bowls with fluted edges, silver plated frame marked "WMF EP IX," c1880 .... **2,650.00**

Cut glass, three 9" h trumpets, one 13-1/2" trumpet, three-handled hanging baskets, 10-1/2" d bowl, strawberry, diamond, and fan design, attributed to Dorflinger, American Brilliant Period **5,500.00**

European Glass

History: European glassmakers have been creating utilitarian and decorative glassware items for centuries. The necessity of food and beverage storage vessels created a demand for early pieces. Other items, such as wine goblets, and other types of stemware, exist today as fine examples of the many craftsmen who worked throughout Europe.

Because of the variation in raw materials from one region to another, differences in techniques and colors exist. These differences provide clues to scholars and collectors when determining the origin of a piece. The existing examples also reflect the political and religious views of the periods. It was not unusual for a reigning monarch to shelter and encourage a glassblower. Unfortunately, wars and changes in monarchs caused shortages of money and materials for glassmakers. During some periods, production halted and often years passed before techniques were reinstated or developed by later craftsmen.

Brilliant colors, exquisite detailed cuttings, and engravings are frequently found on European glassware. The addition of enamel and gilt decorations further enhanced the glassware. Utilitarian pieces, such as bowls and bottles, were frequently left plain. Most pieces are unmarked. Glass composition, design, and texture are the most important keys to identifying regions and periods.

Today, European craftsmen are beginning to capture international markets with innovative and colorful glassware. Leading auction houses, such as Skinner's and William Doyle Galleries, Inc., include these examples and are finding that they do quite well with today's collectors.

Basket

6" h, 5-1/2" w, ruby cut glass, red and white candy stripe spiral twist handle.................. **175.00**

7" h, 12" w, amber, wide banner of enameled floral dec in Persian manner, gold, blue, red, and green, two large applied open handles, applied matching ruffled glass base, Austria............ **125.00**

8-1/2" h, 8" w, irid green, applied crystal handle with prunts... **65.00**

10-1/2" h, 6" w, olive green, mottled white, maroon, blue, and gold, applied fancy loop handle with gold dec, crackle finish, base inscribed "Eleveille Harris," French **150.00**

12-1/2" h, 9-1/2" d, cranberry shaded to clear, engraved and cut bouquets of wild roses, triple notched handle.......... **150.00**

14" h, 8" w, deep red border shading to pale green and clear, highly irid surface, applied clear shaped handle.................. **100.00**

Beaker, 4-1/2" h, German, engraved, seven irate women fighting over pair of trousers, verse **825.00**

Bowl

3-3/4" h, heavily walled, conical, translucent amber ground, etched graduated depths with descending, overlapping squares, etched artist's monogram of Jean Luca, c1925, French **800.00**

4-3/4" d, 3" h, colorless glass, pinched quatreform rim, green and aubergine leaves and berries against mustard colored background, sgd "Leg." (Legras) at side, "Made in France" stamped on base **175.00**

7-3/4" d, 3" h, splotched and mottled amber, blue, and turquoise powders within colorless glass round, internal silver foil spangles, foot inscribed "Muller Fres Luneville" **345.00**

8" d, 4-5/8" h, raised rim on squatty bowl, amber glass, top with two applied handles, four decorative prunts or irid colorless glass, irid gold papillon ground, polished pontil, Austria, base nicks . **290.00**

10" d, 5" h, flared, blended and mottled burgundy and moss green, white network design, WMF **120.00**

Box, cov

2-1/4" d, French, early 19th C, colorless glass lid with sulfide profile cameo of Napoleon, signature for "Andrieu".... **230.00**

5" d, 2-3/4" h, transparent green, orange-amber int., etched naturalistic crab on cov, seaweed springs around base, black etched mark "Nancea".......... **435.00**

Bud vase

6" h, pastel green, white stag on black disk base, Bimini, Austria **135.00**

6-1/4" h, clear, white swirl dec, Bimini, Austria............ **95.00**

Center bowl, 10-1/4" h, 9-3/4" d, half round, colorless, frosted pedestal base of figural Atlas, arms extended supporting bowl, labeled and stamped "Sevres Cristal France" **520.00**

Centerpiece set, 14" d x 5-1/2" h heavy walled bowl with folded-in edge, maroon, colorless, white, and olive green dec, matching pr of 4-1/2" h candleholders, WMF Wurttenberg **230.00**

Compote, 3-3/4" h, conical lime green body, circular black glass foot, everted circular rim, black enameled lattice dec, attributed to Wiener Werkstaette, early 20th C................ **225.00**

Cordial service, two 9" h decanters, nine matching 2-1/2" tumblers, stylized Art Deco foliate and orange, amber, green blue, and black enamel motif, bottles sgd "Serves" at side.... **700.00**

Figure, 5-3/4" h, black, white, and red, Bimini, Austria............... **125.00**

Flower holder, 6" h, 7-1/2" w, irid, diamond quilted, oyster design .. **60.00**

Goblet, 7" h, 3" d top of bowl, hand painted magenta, yellow, and green flowers and foliage on ext., flower painted in center of int., long delicate green stem, gilt edge around green base, each numbered "350" and artist initialed "W.R." on bottom, Austrian, c1890, set of eight **3,600.00**

Jack-in-the-pulpit vase, 8-1/4" h, green, deep brown random threading, slight irid finish **125.00**

Jar, 6-7/8" h, 4-3/4" d base, formed from squatty bottle, globular, elongated neck, expanded sheared mouth with string rim, pontil scar, olive amber, painted red, tan, gold, blue, white, and flesh tone dec of George Washington, 16-star flag painted on reverse, Netherlands, c1730-60, some scaling to paint dec **1,700.00**

Jar, cov, 13" h, ftd, colorless, molded and etched, crown, motto, dated "1847" **250.00**

Lamp, floor, eight sections on main shade divided into alternating panels of dark green to white slag glass, orange, red, green, and white chunk glass, center white chunk glass, small shades hang from main shade, base with thick stem, four footed base with matching glass chunk design, Austria.. **3,920.00**

Lamp, table

16" h, 11-1/2" d molded mushroom cap colorless shade, irid raised honeycomb design, adjustable turned brass lamp shaft, weighted base, Austrian........... **575.00**

18" h, 13" w, oval shade covered with various size chunks of colored glass, red, green, yellow-orange, seven pieces of raised white chunk glass radiate from large chunk of red-orange glass, two supporting arms lead to matching base, which also has chunk design, Austria **2,800.00**

Lamp shade

5-1/4" h, 2-1/4" fitter rim, bell form, red striped ruffled edge, four green heart leaves, random green threading, irid amber spotted surface, Austrian, minor chips at top edge **260.00**

13-3/4" d, shallow frosted colorless body, molded fanciful floral design, sgd "Degue" at side, "France" on rim, not drilled, small unseen chip inside rim **230.00**

Marble, 1-5/8" d, end of day, blue, red, white, and yellow streaks, mica flecks, German, 1880-1915 .... **425.00**

Perfume bottle, 4-1/4" l, tapered body, ball form knob, black glass, silver foil dec **150.00**

Pitcher, 9" h, colorless bottle body, etched all over, enameled violet blossoms, gold enhanced, mounted with elaborate silvered metal handle, spouted rim, and hinged cov imp "V (ship) S," (Verre de Serves) mark repeated on glass base **935.00**

Plaque

3-1/4" d, sulfide encrusted cameo, profile bust of Napoleon, press molded colorless plaque with scalloped edge, attributed to France, mid-19th C **230.00**

4-3/4" d, sulfide, encrusted cameo, profile of Shakespeare, colorless glass roundel, black background, attributed to England, mid-19th C, round giltwood frame..... **250.00**

Pokal, amber, decorated with castle and trees, 8-3/4" h, **$35.** *Photo courtesy of Joy Luke Fine Art Brokers and Auctioneers.*

Pokal, cov, 11-3/4" h, colorless lead glass, hollow Sileasian stem on goblet and cov finial, goblet finely engraved with falconers and coat of arms, German inscription translates as "Let your allegiance soar as the falcons fly," small chip on cov finial base, blown and engraved in Germany, late 19th C **2,400.00**

Powder box, 5-1/2" d, 3-1/2" h, hinged top, squatty form, frosted colorless glass, enamel dec with polychrome

medallions, gilt linear highlights, gilt metal mount, attributed to France, c1930 .... **175.00**

Rose bowl

4-1/2" h, tricorn, spotted red rose body, amber-gold irid pulled wavy banded dec, polished pontil, Austrian **575.00**

4-3/4" h, ruffled rim, purple ground, irid coin spot circles, matching vertical lines, polished pontil, Austrian **420.00**

Server, 10-1/2" l, 10-1/2" w, 13" h, Wiener Werkstatte, Austria, second quarter 20th C, Art Deco, scalloped rim on shallow sq light yellow tinted transparent glass bowl, repeating linear and circle cut glass border, raised on base composed of round silver pan on four colorless glass rod legs over sq platform with four oval bezel-mounted green, pink, purple and black stones, imp marks, few rim chips and scratches **2,185.00**

Tea canister

4" h, sq, canary, chamfered corners, emb sunburst motif, crudely sheared mouth, smooth base, applied brass collar and cap, smooth base, Russian, c1860 .... **100.00**

4-3/4" h, sq, canary, chamfered corners, emb waffle pattern on four panels, crudely sheared mouth, smooth base, tin soldered cap, smooth base, Russian, c1860, 5/8" l chip on mouth **60.00**

Trinket box, cov, 3-1/2" l, 2-1/2" d, 3" h, French, early 20th C, black glass box, hinged lid, brass mounts, enameled dec on lid and front, floral sprays on back, gilt edging **225.00**

Tumbler

3-3/4" h, colorless, beaded teardrops, octagonal cartouche with sulfide encrusted profile cameo of man, attributed to England, first half 19th C... **520.00**

3-7/8" h, colorless, pressed with stylized fern and horizontal flute banding, octagonal cartouche with sulfide of posy clasped by hands, attributed to England, first half 19th C **175.00**

Vase

3-3/4" h, oyster white, deep pink and green threading, one side of ruffled rim turned up............ **100.00**

4-1/8" h, 5-1/4" d, flared bowl-form, colorless body layered in black and amber, etched and engraved stylized leaf motif, dec abstractions in Josef Hoffman manner, labeled "Made in Germany" **175.00**

5-1/2" h, ruby, mottled ivory, satiny sheen, Austrian, rim has been polished **50.00**

5-3/4" h, Cyprus, melon ribbed, enameled white dove on blue shield, yellow floral branches, decorative rim and base, enamel monogram "F. H." (Fritz Heckert) and "M. R." (designer Max Rade,) numbered 130/6......... **300.00**

6" h, stick, enameled, grayed pastel colors over colorless ground, sgd "Juenvit H. Paris" **110.00**

6-1/4" h, 9-1/2" w, deep red shading to clear, pale green mottled finish, highly irid, ruffled **850.00**

8" h, clear, Art Deco cut dec of trees, woodsman, Karhula **135.00**

8" h, opalescent, spherical form, concentric molded dot pattern, molded "VERVIL FRANCE" **400.00**

8" h, 11-1/2" d, frosted and selectively polished white bulbous ground, molded medial band of alternating male and female lions in high relief, amethyst patine in recesses, base imp "D'Avesen Made In France"........ **1,840.00**

8-1/8" h, cut glass, waisted baluster form, applied with ribbon-tied husk swag girdle, flute cut neck and trumpet foot with reeded gilt-metal mounts, body cut with diamonds and palmettes, Continental, early 20th C, price for pr....... **750.00**

8-3/4" h, broad flat rim, raised neck, tapered cylindrical body, translucent light amethyst glass internally dec with mottled opaque blue, green, rose, and white rising from base, inscribed "Muller Fres Luneville" near base, France, c1925 .... **865.00**

9" h, cameo-etched, white ground, rainbow colored woodbine vines with berries, cameo initialed "BW" **225.00**

9-1/4" h, colorless flattened body, enameled red and blue stylized basket of flowers painted in Marcel Goupy style, cartouche on base marked "France" **815.00**

9-1/2" h, round colorless flattened form, applied handles, polychrome enameled medallions front and back with parrots and blossoms, in Marcel Goupy manner, cartouche on base marked "France".. **815.00**

9-1/2" h, triple gourd, amethyst ground, confetti designs, irid, attributed to Kralik........ **150.00**

9-3/4" h, slender baluster form, cranberry flashed ground, gilt enamel quatrefoils, panels embellished with pastel and white florals, late 19th C/early 20th C, price for pr **200.00**

9-3/4" h, 4" w, elongated egg-shaped, frosted green ground, enameled winter scene of houses, trees, and woman stacking wood, Legras, base numbered "#4114" **350.00**

10" h, broad bulbous oval, transparent olive green, etched and selectively frosted in repeating curvilinear Art-Deco elements, "Legras" etched in motif, internal blemish at mid section **800.00**

10" h, highly irid, multicolored design pulled and infused across dimpled body, Graf-Harrach, attributed to Austria................. **800.00**

10" h, tapered, variegated greens mingled with coppers on ext., vibrant irid rainbow highlights, attributed to Austria....... **275.00**

10-1/2" h, transparent topaz colored goblet-form, green and yellow repeating Art Deco devices, base inscribed "M. Goupy" ... **1,380.00**

10-3/4" h, enameled lakeside scene with sailboats, polished pontil, attributed to Legras....... **265.00**

11" h, enameled butterflies on tall cattails, intricate band of lilies and more butterflies on frosted ground, enameled "Leg" for Legras. **350.00**

11" h, 3-1/2" d w, cylinder, finely enameled border of pink, magenta, and white poppies, stylized design at top and base, colorless center with stylized yellow, white, and light green buds and foliage, Art Nouveau style, French, c1910 .... **675.00**

11" h, 4-1/2" h, clear ground, painted and frosted in the matter of Daum, blue sailing ships against bright yellow/orange ground **100.00**

11-3/4" h, enameled Golden Pheasant among tall grasses, pale pink satin ground, enamel sgd "Leg for Legras," small open bubble on reverse........ **750.00**

12" h, raised ruffled rim, transparent royal purple body, acid textured

and etched stylized Art-Deco lily blossom and scrolling leaves, blue irid on raise dec, polished pontil, Austrian **920.00**
12-1/4" h, 5-1/2" w, deep cobalt blue over crystal, cut band of floral and leaf design, large square star cut base, slight roughage on base **100.00**
12-3/8" h, cylinder, gold irid surface, combed dec, blue-green luster, polished pontil, Austrian. . . **815.00**
12-1/2" h, emerald green bulbed body, all over irid, mounted in bronzed metal frame with swirling foliate design, Austrian. . . . **635.00**
13" h, caramel reverse swirl designs over pearlized taupe cylindrical body, pinched sides, ruffled rim, irid magenta and gold, Austrian **200.00**
13" h, 6-1/2" w, mottled pink and yellow, white ground, five leaf-like pulled decorations near base, highly irid surface. **225.00**
13" h, 7" w, deep red mottled ground, swirled pattern, highly irid . **200.00**
14-1/2" h, 5" w, cobalt blue, flaring rim, pedestal base, cut all over with raised panels mixed with recessed diamond and heart-shaped panels, heavy gold dec, intricate tiny leaves, slight wear to gold . **400.00**
15" h, gooseneck, cased rose glass overlaid with threading network, polished pontil, Pallme-Konig **290.00**
15-1/2" h, yellow ground, stylized cameo orange scarabs, applied handle **950.00**
16" h, gold and copper aventurine, pigeon-blood ground, ormolu mounts, French, price for pr **750.00**
22-1/2" h, 7" w, deep emerald green shading to clear, realistic cut pattern of large oriental poppy, leaves, and buds, Austrian, attributed to Moser or Harrach **575.00**

Veilleuse, (night light), 5-1/2" h, bulbous mottled green and blue shade, patinated wrought iron mount surrounded by three curling tendrils, inscribed "Robj, Paris," c1920 . . **650.00**

Wall sconces, pr, 12" h, 5-1/2" w, Art Deco etched colorless glass fanned shades on "V"-shaped silvered metal wall mounts, France, 1928 . . . **1,150.00**

Wine, 5-3/4" h, freeblown, engraved, colorless, large bowl with engraved bird and floral motif, lettered "Fn Die Huhe," long stem with wide knop, domed circular foot with inward rolled edge, tooled rim, pontil scar, early 19th C **325.00**

Pair of vases, gold and copper aventurine on pigeon blood ground, ormolu mounts, French, 16" h, **$750.** *Photo courtesy of David Rago Auctions.*

Fairy Lamps

History: Fairy lamps, which originated in England in the 1840s, are candle-burning night lamps. They were used in nurseries, hallways, and dim corners of the home.

Two leading candle manufacturers, the Price Candle Company and the Samuel Clarke Company, promoted fairy lamps as a means to sell candles. Both contracted with glass, porcelain, and metal manufacturers to produce the needed shades and cups. For example, Clarke used Worcester Royal Porcelain Company, Stuart & Sons, and Red House Glass Works in England, plus firms in France and Germany. Clarke's trademark was a small fairy with a wand surrounded by the words "Clarke Fairy Pyramid, Trade Mark."

Fittings were produced in a wide variety of styles. Shades ranged from pressed to cut glass, from Burmese to Nailsea. Cups are found in glass, porcelain, brass, nickel, and silver plate.

American firms selling fairy lamps included Diamond Candle Company of Brooklyn, Blue Cross Safety Candle Company, and Hobbs-Brockunier of Wheeling, West Virginia.

Fairy lamps are found as two pieces (cup and shade) and three-pieces (cup with matching shade and saucer). Married pieces are common.

References: Bob and Pat Ruf Pullin, *Fairy Lamps*, Schiffer Publishing, 1996; John F. Solverson (comp.), *Those Fascinating Little Lamps: Miniature Lamps Value Guide*, Antique Publications, 1988; Kenneth Wilson, *Americana Glass 1760-1930: The Toledo Museum of Art, Volume I, Volume II*, Hudson Hills Press and the Toledo Museum of Art, 1994.

Periodical: *Light Revival*, 35 West Elm Ave., Quincy, MA 02170; *Night Light Newsletter*, 38619 Wakefield Ct., Northville, MI 48167.

Collectors' Club: Night Light Club, 38619 Wakefield Ct., Northville, MI 48167.

Reproduction Alert: Reproductions abound.

Amber, 3-5/8" h, 3" d, pyramid, white opal swirl glass shade, clear marked Clarke candle cup **125.00**

Burmese

3-1/2" h, 5-1/4" d, Webb shade, Tunnecliffe porcelain base with gold rim, clear candle holder marked "S. Clarke Fairy, Patent" **1,200.00**

4" h, acid finished pyramid dome shade, clear marked Clarke base, two slight bruises on base . **175.00**

5-1/2" h, 7-1/2" d, Cricklite, frilly pleated skirted base, clear candle holder marked "Clarke's Cricklite Trade Mark" **1,085.00**

5-3/4" h, undecorated dome shade, Burmese quadrafold base, clear marked Clarke candle cup, bottom edge of shade lightly ground **325.00**

7" h, salmon pink shaded to yellow, acid finish, matching ruffled base marked "Clarke's Patent Fairy Lamp," clear marked Clarke candle cup, brass frame with two scrolling arms........... **825.00**

Cased, 6-1/4" h, glossy aqua blue, ribbed dome shade, non-matching complimentary blue satin base, lined white set in Clarke sgd cup.... **225.00**

Cranberry

4-1/4" h, pyramid shade with three rows of down-turned petals, matching cranberry petaled base, clear marked Clarke candle cup, some of the petals have been ground and polished **150.00**

4-1/2" h, crown shape, overshot shade, clear base, clear marked Clarke candle cup, c1887 . **220.00**

Figural

3-3/4" h, owl, custard, satin finish, Fenton **35.00**

4-1/4" h, dog's head, satinized white glass, matching pyramid-sized base, blue eyes, faint caramel-colored streak runs throughout head......... **450.00**

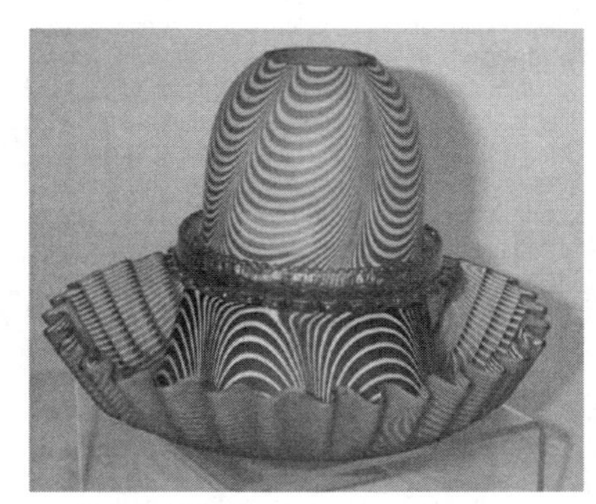

Blue, white Nailsea loopings, clear marked Clarke candle cup, 5" h, **$395.** *Photo courtesy of Joy Luke Fine Art Brokers and Auctioneers.*

Nailsea

4-3/4" h, citron ground, clear marked Clarke Cricklite candle cup and base **190.00**

4-3/4" h, white loops pulled through red, frosted ribbed base, roughness on base of shade **100.00**

5" h, pink and white, clear marked Clarke candle cup and base **200.00**

Opalescent

4-1/8" h, blue pyramid done shade, rose and foliage dec creamware base sgd "Clarke & Tunnicliffe" **450.00**

5-3/8" h, Cleveland Swirl, pink, white, and opaque, upward fluted base, clear marked Clarke candle cup, several small chips on top post of base **600.00**

5-3/4" h, Cleveland Swirl, blue, white, and opaque, dome shade with emb ribs, six-sided ruffled matching under bowl, clear marked Clarke candle cup, slight roughness to base of shade, base lighter than shade........ **350.00**

Opaque

4-3/4" h, white, hand-painted nativity scene, base marked "Fenton," orig Fenton label **70.00**

4-3/4" h, white, two hand-painted bluebirds on front, one on back, sgd "Hand Painted by J. Stevens," base marked "Fenton," orig Fenton label **80.00**

Overshot

3" h, 3-3/4" d, green pyramid shade, clear marked Clarke candle cup **125.00**

3-1/2" h, yellow swirl cased pyramid shade, clear marked Clarke candle cup **175.00**

Peachblow

3-7/8" h, cream lining, acid finished rose shaded pink, black lacy flower and leaf dec, clear marked Clarke candle cup, gold washed metal stand, attributed to Thomas Webb **350.00**

3-7/8" h, 3-3/4" h, green leaves dec, clear marked Clarke candle cup, attributed to Thomas Webb **400.00**

3-7/8" h, 4-1/2" h, 2-7/8" d, colorless, opalescent overshot, crown-shaped pyramid shade, clear marked Clarke candle cup, made for Queen Victoria's 1887 Jubilee **190.00**

3-7/8" h, 5-1/4" h, clear marked Clarke candle cup, Mt. Washington **250.00**

3-7/8" h, 6-3/8" h, blue, white, brown, and green enamel dec, white int., clear marked Clarke Cricklite candle cup **425.00**

Ruby, 3-3/4" h Diamond Quilted dome, 6-3/4" d white crimped petticoat base, clear marked Clarke candle cup, attributed to Fenton, small shade rim chips...................... **80.00**

Sapphire blue, 4-5/8" h, Diamond Quilted, melon ribbed, clear marked Clarke candle cup **175.00**

Satin

3-1/2" h, rose Diamond Quilted, MOP shade, white lining, married to clear marked Clarke candle base, roughness to dome rim **90.00**

3-1/2" h, 2-7/8" d, rose Diamond Quilted, MOP shade, white lining, clear marked Clarke candle cup **185.00**

3-5/8" h, apple green opaque shade, emb Swirl pattern, clear marked Clarke candle cup **150.00**

3-3/4" h, blue Diamond Quilted, mother of pearl pyramid shade, Clarke sgd base **150.00**

3-3/4" h, pink Diamond Quilted, mother of pearl pyramid shade, Clarke sgd base **150.00**

3-3/4" h, pink cased pyramid shade with white lining, Clarke sgd base **125.00**

4" h, pale pink smocked pattern pyramid shade, Clark sgd base **100.00**

4-1/4" h, 5-3/4" w base, blue, lined cream, matching ruffled base, unsigned white satin cup . . **200.00**

5" h, dark pink shading to light pink dome with imp stars, ruffled inverted saucer-shaped base, clear cup **550.00**

6" d, lavender ruffled dome top, three gold inset jeweled medallions, ruffled base . . . **350.00**

6-3/4" h, 5-1/2" w, swirled, white shade and base with pale blue ruffles **380.00**

7-1/2" h, orange pyramid shade, 12 rows of frosted tooled loopings, make-do frosted finger shade cup **225.00**

Spatter, 5-1/2" h, white spatter, chartreuse cased in crystal ground, swirled rib mold, heavy applied crystal feet and base trim, clear marked Clarke candle cup **550.00**

Vaseline, 3-1/2" h, 2-7/8" d, ribbed dome, green marked Clarke candle base. **175.00**

Verre Moiré

4" h, red frosted ground, white loopings, clear Clarke candle cup marked "S. Clarke's Patent Pyramid Trade Mark" and "C.W.S. Night Light" **495.00**

4-3/4" h, blue dome shade, clear marked Clarke candle cup. **325.00**

4-3/4" h, citron dome shade, Clarke sgd base, clear marked Clarke candle cup **225.00**

4-7/8" h, rose dome shade, Clarke sgd base, clear marked Clarke candle cup **430.00**

5-1/4" h, cranberry frosted ground, white loopings, clear base, clear marked Clarke candle cup . **250.00**

6-1/4" h, citron, matching three-cornered ftd base, clear marked Clarke candle cup, very minor roughness to bottom edge of shade **725.00**

6-1/2" h, 8" w, sweeping white loopings blend into delicate blue background, done shaped shade, triangular shaped base with pinch-in folds, clear glass cup holder with ruffled edge, sgd "S. Clarke Patent Trade Mark Fairy" **945.00**

FENTON GLASS

History: The Fenton Art Glass Company began as a cutting shop in Martins Ferry, Ohio, in 1905. In 1906, Frank L. Fenton started to build a plant in Williamstown, West Virginia, and produced the first piece of glass there in 1907. Early production included carnival, chocolate, custard, and pressed glass, plus mold-blown opalescent glass. In the 1920s, stretch glass, Fenton dolphins, jade green, ruby, and art glass were added.

In the 1930s, boudoir lamps, Dancing Ladies, and slag glass in various colors were produced. The 1940s saw crests of different colors being added to each piece by hand. Hobnail, opalescent, and two-color overlay pieces were popular items. Handles were added to different shapes, making the baskets they created as popular today as then.

Through the years, Fenton has beautified its glass by decorating it with hand painting, acid etching, color staining, and copper-wheel cutting. Several different paper labels have been used. In 1970, an oval raised trademark also was adopted.

References: Tom and Neila Bredehoft, *Fifty Years of Collectible Glass, 1920-1970*, Volume 1, Volume II, Antique Trader Books, 2000; Robert E. Eaton Jr. (comp.), *Comprehensive Price Guide to Fenton Glass: The First Twenty-Five Years*, 1995, Antique Publications, 1995, 1997 value update; —, *Comprehensive Price Guide to Fenton Glass: The Second Twenty-Five Years*, 1995, Antique Publications, 1995, 1997 value update; —, *Comprehensive Price Guide to Fenton Glass: The 80s' Decade*, Antique Publications, 1996, 1997 value update; Fenton Art Glass Collectors of America (comp.), *Fenton Glass: The Third Twenty-Five Years Comprehensive Price Guide*, 1995, Antique Publications, 1995; Shirley Griffith, *A Pictorial Review of Fenton White Hobnail Milk Glass*, published by author, 1984; William Heacock, *Fenton Glass: The First Twenty-Five Years (1978), The Second Twenty-Five Years (1980), The Third Twenty-Five Years (1989)*, available from Antique Publications; Alan Linn, *Fenton Story of Glass Making*, Antique Publications, 1996; James Measell (ed.), *Fenton Glass: The 1980s Decade*, Antique Publications, 1996; Naomi L. Over, *Ruby Glass of the 20th Century*, Antique Publications, 1990, 1993-94 value update; Ferill J. Rice (ed.), *Caught in the Butterfly Net*, Fenton Art Glass Collectors of America, Inc., 1991; John Walk, *Fenton Glass Compendium, 1940-1970*, Schiffer, 2001; —, *Fenton Glass Compendium, 1970-1985*, Schiffer, 2001.

Web Site: Fenton Art Glass Company, Inc., http://www.fentonartglass.com.

Collectors' Clubs: Fenton Art Glass Collectors of America, Inc., P.O. Box 384, Williamstown, WV 26187, http://www.collectoronline.com/club-FAGCA.html; National Fenton Glass Society, P.O. Box 4008, Marietta, OH 45750, http://www.axces.com/nfgs; Pacific Northwest Fenton Assoc., P.O. Box 881, Tillamook, OR 97141-0881, http://www.glasscastle.com/pnwfa.html.

Videotape: Michael Dickensen, "Glass Artistry in the Making Fenton," Fenton Art Glass, 1992.

Museum and Factory Tour: Fenton Art Glass Co., 420 Caroline Ave., Williamstown, WV 26187

Ashtray

#848 Mandarin Red **75.00**

#1700 Lincoln Inn, aqua. **25.00**

#1700 Lincoln Inn, ruby **25.00**

#3773 Dogwood Flowered Hobnail, pipe **65.00**

#3810 Hobnail, milk glass, two pcs **18.00**

#3872 Hobnail, Topaz Opalescent, fan shape **15.00**

#7377 Apple Blossom Crest, 6-1/2" **45.00**

Banana bowl

#3720 Hobnail, milk glass . . . **40.00**

#5824 Silver Crest, low, ftd. . . **50.00**

#7324 Silver Crest **75.00**

#9028 Lace Work, white milk glass, 11-1/2" **45.00**

Basket

#187 Ivory Crest, crystal handle, c1940-41, 10-1/2". **75.00**

#192 Mulberry, crystal handle, c1942, 10-1/2" **475.00**

#203 Black Rose, crystal handle, 7" **250.00**

#389 Cranberry Hobnail, crystal handle, 10-1/2". **285.00**

#389 Topaz Hobnail, crystal handle, 10-1/2" **450.00**

#680 Aqua Crest, crystal handle, 5" **120.00**

#711 Silver Crest, crystal handle, 7" **45.00**

#920 Peach Crest, crystal handle, 10" **165.00**

#1353 Coin Dot, French Opalescent, 12" **200.00**

#1435 Coin Dot, Cranberry Opalescent, 4-1/2" **110.00**
#1437 Coin Dot, Cranberry Opalescent, 7" **115.00**
#1522 Cranberry Coin Dot, crystal handle, 10-1/2" **385.00**
#1523 Aqua Crest, crystal handle, 13" **250.00**
#1890 Priscilla, Emerald Green, 12" **195.00**
#1921 Aqua Crest, dark aqua coloring, c1940-43, 5" **95.00**
#1924 Coin Dot, French Opalescent, 5" **35.00**
#1924 Green Overlay, 4-1/2" . . **55.00**
#1936 Daisy & Button, amber crystal handle **55.00**
#3734 Hobnail, white milk glass, double crimped, round, 11-1/4" **47.50**
#3736 Hobnail, Blue Marble, 6-1/2" **50.00**
#3830 Hobnail, Cranberry Opalescent, 10" **95.00**
#3834 Hobnail, French Opalescent, 4-1/2" **60.00**
#3835 Hobnail, Cranberry Opalescent, 5-1/2" h **125.00**
#3837 Hobnail, Cranberry Opalescent, 7" **110.00**
#6437 Aventurine, green with blue, 11" h **125.00**
#6137 Beatty Waffle, Green Opal **47.50**
#6437 Vasa Murrhina, 11" . . . **125.00**
#6458 Vasa Murrhina, blue mist, 11" **95.00**
#7237 Rose Crest, crystal handle, 7" h **45.00**
#7308 Silver Crest, crystal handle, 8" h, sgd **40.00**
#7336 Silver Crest, crystal handle, 6-1/2" **45.00**
#7437 Burmese, hand painted pink peach and light olive green, sgd by artist Alice Farley, c1970, 5-1/2" h, 5" w **115.00**
#7437 Burmese, Maple Leaf decal **75.00**
#7437 DV Violets in the Snow, milk glass **75.00**
#9137 Olde Virginia Thumbprint, 7" h **30.00**
#9138 Poppy, Blue Satin, 7" d, 11" h **65.00**
#9235 Embossed Rose, 9" h . **40.00**

Beverage set

#230 Celeste Blue, pitcher and six tumblers, cut **350.00**
#222 Rib Optic, Blue Opalescent, six tumblers, royal blue coasters **550.00**
#3967 Hobnail, Cranberry Opalescent, 80-oz pitcher, four #3947 barrel tumblers **275.00**
Christmas Snowflake, Cobalt Blue water pitcher, six tumblers (L.G. Wright) **210.00**

Bell

#1966BA Daisy and Button, Blue Satin **17.50**
#3677MI Hobnail, white milk glass **14.50**

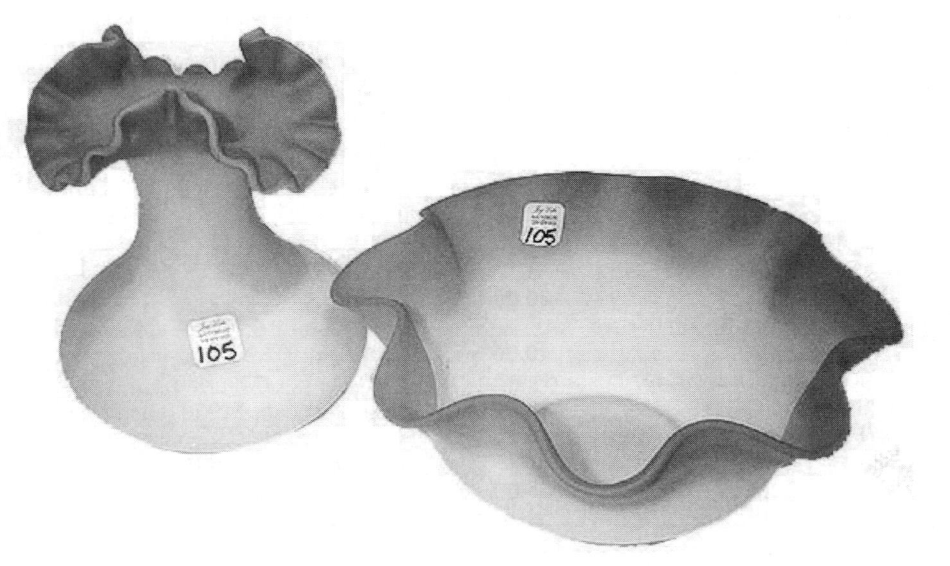

Left: Burmese vase, 7-1/2" h, right: Burmese bowl, 9" d, ruffled rim, sold as lot for **$165.** *Photo courtesy of Joy Luke Fine Art Brokers and Auctioneers.*

#7466 CV hp Christmas Morn . **45.00**
#8267CU Medallion, Custard . **17.50**
#8267CU Medallion, Custard, hp holly dec **27.50**
#8466 OI Faberge, Teal Marigold **55.00**
#8466 RE Faberge, Rosalene . **45.00**
#9064 Velva Rose, Whitton . . . **25.00**

Bicentennial plate, white milk glass, orig box and wrappings

No. 1 . . . . **25.00**
No. 2 . . . . **25.00**
No. 3 . . . . **25.00**
No. 4 . . . . **25.00**

Bonbon

#349 San Toy, tricorner, handle, crystal, 1930s, 5-1/2" d **25.00**
#389 Hobnail, Green Opalescent, sq, 6" **25.00**
#389 Hobnail, Topaz Opalescent, crimped, 6" **27.50**
#1533 Dolphin, tangerine stretch, crimped, sq **85.00**
#1621 Dolphin Handle, Green . **32.50**
#1621 Dolphin Handle, satin finish dec, 6" l oval **50.00**
#1621 Dolphin Handle, satin finish dec, 6" l oval, crimped **50.00**
#3935 Hobnail, blue opalescent, 5", handle **30.00**
#3937 Hobnail, blue opalescent, 4-1/2", handle **24.00**
#7225 Aqua Crest, 5-1/2" **30.00**
#7225 Silver Turquoise Crest, 5-1/2" **20.00**
#7333 Silver Turquoise Crest, 7", heart shape, handle **60.00**
#7377 Apple Blossom Crest, double crimped, 8" **55.00**
#8230 Rosalene Butterfly, two handled **35.00**

Bowl

#100 Jade Green, crimped, three toes, 7" d **35.00**
#230 Peach Crest, 6-1/2" d . . . **45.00**
#249 Ming, Fenton Rose, three toes **110.00**
#349 San Toy, ftd, handle, crystal, 8" d **35.00**
#711 Emerald Crest, Beaded Melon, 7" d **35.00**
#846 Chinese Yellow, cupped . **75.00**
#846 Pekin Blue, cupped **37.50**
#848 Chinese Yellow, eight Petal **45.00**
#848 Cobalt Blue, 9" d **45.00**
#950 Mandarin Red, 11" oval **125.00**
#1010 Silvertone, amethyst, three toes, 7" d **35.00**
#1427 Coin Dot, cranberry Opalescent, 7" d **85.00**

#1427 Snow Crest, Ruby Overlay, Dot Optic, 7" d **60.00**
#1522 Blue Ridge, triangle, 10" d, c1939 . . . . **150.00**
#1562 Satin Etched Silvertone, oblong bowl **55.00**
#1601 Ebony, oval, dolphin handles, ftd **145.00**
#1605 Stag and Holly, green, ftd **130.00**
#1800 Sheffield, halo etching, 11-1/2" d **50.00**
#1800 Sheffield, Silvertone dec, 13" sq, silver iridized around base **65.00**
#1932 Pink, crimped, three toes, 7-1/2" d **18.00**
#1933 San Toy, satin, 5" d, three toes, cupped **45.00**
#1933 San Toy, satin, 6-3/4" d, three toes, crimped **45.00**
#1933 San Toy, satin, 6-3/4" d, three toes, flared **45.00**
#3624 Hobnail, white milk glass, double crimped, 10-1/2" d . . **30.00**
#3731 Hobnail, white milk glass, double crimped, 10" d, ftd . . **40.00**
#3824 Hobnail, Green Opalescent, 11" d **70.00**
#3924 Hobnail, Cranberry Opalescent, 9" d, ruffled **95.00**
#3924 Hobnail, Peach Blow, 9" d **50.00**
#7220 Aqua Crest, 10" d, double crimped **75.00**
#7221 Silver Crest, 10" d, yellow jonquil dec, gold trim **46.00**
#7222 Emerald Crest, low dessert **28.00**
#7223 Silver Crest, double crimped, 13" d **95.00**
#7224 Aqua Crest, 13" d **130.00**
#7224 Silver Crest, 10" d, ruffled **50.00**
#7227 Emerald Crest, double crimped, 7" d **18.00**
#7227 Silver Crest, double crimped, 7" d **15.00**
#7316 Silver Crest, 10" d **50.00**
#7330 Silver Crest, 9" sq, ftd . **70.00**
#7330 Silver Turquoise, ftd, square **55.00**
#7423 Milk Glass bowl, hp Yellow roses **65.00**
#7498 Silver Crest, 8" d, metal center handle **12.50**
#8222 Custard, Basketweave, open edge, 5" d **19.50**
#8222 Rosalene, Basketweave **30.00**
#9020 Peach Crest, 10" d **90.00**
#9020 Peach Crest, Charleton dec **105.00**

Cake plate

#3513 Pink Pastel, ftd, 12-1/2" d **65.00**
#5813 Silver Crest, low, ftd . . . **45.00**
#7213 Ebony Crest, 13" d . . . **135.00**

Candlestick

#249 Stretch, Celeste Blue, 6" h, pr **165.00**
#316 Stretch, green **22.50**
#349 Wisteria, crystal **35.00**
#445 Flame, 8-1/2" h **95.00**
#848 Black, pr **36.00**
#848 Crystal, pr **22.50**
#848 Jade Green, c1921-30 . . **15.00**
#848 Ruby, pr **25.00**
#950 Cornucopia, satin poinsettia, pr **75.00**
#950 Ming, pink, pr **130.00**
#951 Silver Crest Cornucopia, single **37.50**
#1010 Silvertone, amethyst, three toes, pr **65.00**
#1010 Silvertone, crystal, three toes **15.00**
#1524 Coin Dot, Cranberry Opalescent, 5-3/4" h, pr . . . **195.00**
#1800 Silvertone, Sheffield, blue **24.00**
#1800 Silvertone, Sheffield, crystal, Halo Etch, 4" h, pr **55.00**
#3974 Hobnail Topaz Opalescent **60.00**
#7270 Aqua Crest, 4-3/4" h, pr **98.00**
#7271 Silver Crest, low, ruffled, pr **45.00**
#7271 Silver Turquoise, pr **45.00**
#7272 Silver Crest, single **17.50**
#7474 Flame Crest, 6" h, pr . . **125.00**
#8473 Rosalene, Water Lily, pr **65.00**

Candy box, cov

#192 Diamond Optic, Cranberry **125.00**
#835 Stretch, Celeste Blue, half pound, c1917-28 . . . . **75.00**
#7258 Thumbprint, pink, oval . **30.00**
#7280 Silver Crest **70.00**
#7380 Custard hp pink daffodils, Louise Piper, dated March 1975 . . . . **160.00**
#7380 Ebony, hp white daisies, ftd **40.00**
#9088 Wild Strawberry, Custard Satin **35.00**
#9282 Roses, orange **35.00**
#9284 Roses, Colonial Green, ftd **35.00**
#9394 UE three pcs, Ogee, Blue Burmese **110.00**
#9394 RE three pcs, Ogee, Rosalene **100.00**

Ruby Iridized, Butterfly, for FAGCA **100.00**

Candy dish, cov

#835 Aquamarine **70.00**
#835 Cameo Opalescent **45.00**
Hobnail Topaz Opalescent, ftd **130.00**

Champagne

#1620 Plymouth, red **17.50**
#1700 Lincoln Inn, red **24.00**

Christmas plate, #8279

No. 2, Old Brick Church, 1971, Blue Satin **25.00**
No. 9, Church of the Holy Trinity, 1978, Carnival **35.00**

Cologne bottle, white and red, Charlton dec, orig stopper, chip inside bottle **85.00**

Comport

#680 Emerald Crest, low, ftd, 7" w, 3-3/4" h **45.00**
#1533 Stretch, Florentine Green, ftd, crimped, dolphin handle, 6" **125.00**
#3628 Thumbprint, Colonial Green, 6" d **22.00**
#3628 Thumbprint, Colonial Green, 7-1/2" d **27.50**
#3728 PO Plum Opal Hobnail 5-1/2" **75.00**
#7228 Emerald Crest, ftd **30.00**
#7228 Silver Crest, ftd, 8" **20.00**
#7228 Silver Turquoise, ftd, 7" **35.00**
#7329 Apple Blossom Crest, low, ftd **65.00**
#7329GC Gold Crest, low, ftd **35.00**
#8422 Flowered, ftd, Rosalene **30.00**
#8422 Waterlily ftd, Rosalene . **30.00**
#8476 Jefferson, chocolate, cov **225.00**
#9222 Roses, Blue Marble . . . **25.00**
#9222 Roses, Orange **35.00**

Cocktail shaker, #6120 Plymouth, Crystal **55.00**

Condiment set

#3809 Hobnail, seven pcs . . . **40.00**
#6909 Teardrop, white milk glass, three pcs **70.00**

Console bowl, Ming, oval

Green **85.00**
Pink **85.00**

Console set

#950 Ming, bowl and pr candlesticks, c1930, satin etched, green **150.00**
#950 Ming, bowl and pr candlesticks, c1930, satin etched, pink **175.00**
#1522 Aqua Crest, 10-1/2" d bowl in dark aqua, white milk glass swirl base, pr #1523 candles . . . **145.00**

#1900 Daisy and Button, Mermaid Blue, pr two-lite candlesticks, cloverleaf bowl 190.00
#3904 Hobnail, Rose Pastel, 9" decorated bowl, pr of low candlesticks 75.00

Cracker jar, #1681 Big Cookies
Jade. 125.00
Lilac, no lid, handle 250.00

Creamer
#1461 Coin Dot, Cranberry Opalescent, 4". 65.00
#1502 Diamond Optic, Black . 35.00
#1502 Diamond Optic, Ruby . . 30.00
#1924 Coin Dot, cranberry opalescent, 4" h. 75.00
#6464 RG Aventurine Green w/Pink, Vasa Murrhina 45.00

Creamer and sugar, cov
#489 Hobnail, Topaz Opalescent, miniature 25.00
#680 Silver Crest, reeded handles 55.00
#1903 Daisy and Button, Blue Opalescent 35.00
#9103 Fine Cut & Block (OVG) 20.00

Creatures (animals and birds)
#5174 Springtime Green Iridized Blown Rabbit. 45.00
#5178 Springtime Green Iridized Blown Owl 45.00
#5193 RE Rosalene Fish, paperweight 25.00
#5197 Happiness Bird, Blue Satin 20.00
#5197 Happiness Bird, Cardinals in Winter 32.50
#5197 Happiness Bird, Custard 20.00
#5197 Happiness Bird, Custard, hp flowers. 30.00
#5197 Happiness Bird, Rosalene 40.00
Alley Cat
Amethyst Carnival, 11" h. . 125.00
Burmese 75.00
Pink Carnival. 75.00
Stiegel Green Carnival 75.00
Atterbury Duck, blue and white, covered dish type 95.00

Cruet
#208 Coin Dot, Cranberry, 7" h 150.00
#207 Coin Dot, French Opalescent 100.00
#3869 Hobnail, French Opalescent 45.00
#7701 QJ 7" Burmese, Petite Floral 175.00

Cup and saucer
#1700 Lincoln Inn, red. 42.00
#7208 Aqua Crest. 35.00
#7208 Emerald Crest 45.00

Decanter set
#389 Blue Opalescent, decanter and four wines. 250.00
#3761 Hobnail, Cranberry Opalescent. 375.00

Dresser tray
#957 Daisy & Button, amber, 10-3/4" l, fan shape, small chip 15.00
#957 Daisy & Button, cranberry stained and crystal, 10-3/4" l, fan shape 40.00

Epergne
#1948 Diamond Lace, Aqua Crest, French Opalescent, c1948-55, four pcs 195.00
#3701 Hobnail, milk glass, four pcs 60.00
#3801 Hobnail, milk glass, miniature, four pcs 50.00
#3902 Petite Blue, Opal 4" h. 125.00
#3902 Petite French Opal, 4" h 40.00
#4802 Diamond Lace, white milk glass, c1948-55, two pcs. . . 95.00
#7308 Silver Crest, three vases 145.00

Epergne flower (single)
Amber Crest, center flower, 5-1/2" h 20.00
Rose Crest, center flower, 5-3/4" h 20.00

Fairy light
#1167 RV Rose Magnolia Hobnail three-pc Persian Pearl Crest, Signed Shelly Fenton 80.00
#3380 CR Hobnail, three-pc Cranberry Opal 75.00
#3608 Hobnail amber, two-pc 30.00
#3804 CA Hobnail three-pc Colonial Amber. 25.00
#3804 CG Hobnail three-pc Colonial Green 20.00
#5108 Owl, Custard 25.00
#8406 WT Heart, Wisteria. . . . 65.00
#8406 PE Heart, Shell Pink. . . 25.50
#8408 BA Persian Medallion three-pc Blue Satin. 35.00
#8408 VR Persian Medallion, three-pc Velva Rose—75th Anniv. 75.00

Flower pot, #401 Snow Crest, green 35.00

Fruit bowl, #846 Mandarin Red, 9-3/4" d, black glass stand 85.00

Ginger jar
#893 Persian Pearl w/base and top 150.00
#893 Crystal, wisteria satin etching, three pcs 125.00

Goblet
#203 Silver Crest 60.00
#389 Hobnail, French Opalescent 20.00
#1503 Diamond Optic, green, 9 oz 18.50
#1611 Georgian, ruby, 5-1/2" h 15.00
#1620 Plymouth, ruby 22.00
#1700 Lincoln Inn, pink 27.50
#1700 Lincoln Inn, red. 30.00
#1700 Lincoln Inn, red, amberina stem 30.00
#1700 Lincoln Inn, royal blue . 30.00
#1942 Flower Windows Blue . . 55.00
#3845 Hobnail, Green Pastel, 5-1/2" h 24.00

Guest set, two pcs
#200, Florentine Green 375.00
Opal Curtain Optic, topaz, blue handle 1,350.00

Hat
#2 Hobnail, French Opalescent, 2-1/2" h 27.50
#1455 Coin Dot, Cranberry Opalescent, 3-1/4" h 80.00
#1455 Coin Dot, French Opal 5" 45.00
#1492 Coin Dot, Cranberry Opalescent, 3-1/4" h 80.00
#1922 Ivory Crest, 6" h 55.00
#1922 Peach Crest, 10" h . . . 125.00
#1922 Swirl Optic, French Opalescent 110.00
#1933 Daisy & Button, amber, #3 . . . . 25.00

Hurricane lamp
#170 Coin Dot, French Opalescent chimney, white milk glass base 150.00
Custard, hp daisies 85.00
Topaz Opal Daisy and Fern. . 300.00

Hurricane shade
Hobnail, Peach Blow, 7-1/2" h . 95.00
Snow Crest, emerald green. . . 95.00

Ivy ball
#1925 green cased, 6-1/4" h . . 65.00
#1956 Silver Crest, ftd 65.00

Jardiniere, #3996 Hobnail, milk glass, 6" 12.50

Jug
#192 Diamond Optic, 8", handle, mulberry 230.00
#192 Gold Crest, handle, 7" h . 45.00
#192 Silver Crest, handle, 6" h 45.00
#192A Rose Crest, handle, c1946-48, 9" h. 95.00
#711 Black Rose Crest, Beaded Melon, 6" 125.00
#711 Peach Crest, 8" h, handle 75.00
#6068 Cased Lilac, Handled, 6-1/2" 50.00

Of course Shelley is too young to court . . .

. . . but it really doesn't matter, for her Fenton Courting Lamps are actually lamps of many uses.

In the bedroom, in the living room, or wherever these richly colored lamps are used, they add a gentle light.

Adapted to oil or electricity, the attractive price and versatility of these handmade "early American" lamps will lead many of your customers to buy them in pairs.

Suggest Fenton Courting Lamps for the patio – They will make every party an occasion.

May we send you our catalog?

THE FENTON ART GLASS COMPANY • WILLIAMSTOWN, WEST VIRGINIA

FEBRUARY 1962 CHINA GLASS & TABLEWARES

thirty-seven

#7264 Aqua Crest, 9" h, handle, roses dec. **70.00**
Hobnail, blue opalescent, 4-1/2" **70.00**

Juice tumbler
#1700 Lincoln Inn, crystal, 4 oz, ftd **12.50**
#3945 Hobnail, Blue Opalescent **18.00**

Lamp
#670 boudoir, black embossed, satin shade **200.00**
#670 boudoir, Coin Spot, French Opalescent **225.00**
#670 boudoir, Jade **250.00**
#670 boudoir, pink, floral cut . **250.00**
#1790 Colonial, orange, courting, oil **65.00**
#2606 Candy Stripe French Colonial, 20" **650.00**
#2700 Ruby Overlay Mariners **150.00**
#3782 CA Courting, Hobnail, Amber, Kerosene **65.00**
#3792 Courting, Hobnail, Amber, electric. **85.00**
#7312 BD Hurricane Candle Lamp, Five Petal Blue Dogwood . . . **75.00**
#7398 Black Rose, Hurricane, White Base, 9" h **100.00**

Lamp shade, Silver Crest, Grape pattern, 8" d **55.00**

Lavabo
#3867 Hobnail, white milk glass **130.00**
#4467 Thumbprint, white milk glass **125.00**

Liquor set, #1934 Flower Stopper, floral silver overlay, eight-pc set **250.00**

Liquor tray, #1934, light blue satin, 12". **140.00**

Mayonnaise set, #3903 Hobnail, Cranberry Opalescent, three pcs **150.00**

Mother's Day plate
1972, blue satin, no box **20.00**
1979, amethyst carnival, Madonna of the Rose Hedge, orig box, stand, and literature **25.00**

Mustard, cov, spoon, #3889 MI, Hobnail **35.00**

Nut bowl
#3428 Cactus, Topaz Opalescent, Levay. **25.00**
#7229 Silver Crest, 4", ftd **18.00**
Sailboats, Marigold Carnival . . **50.00**

Olive, #1700 Lincoln Inn, olive, handle **24.00**

Paperweight, eagle, chocolate, orig literature **25.00**

Perfume bottle, Peach Crest, DeVilbiss **75.00**

Pitcher
#100 Honeycomb & Clover, Crystal/Gold **45.00**
#821 Cannonball, cobalt dec **150.00**
#1653 Ming Green, black handle **165.00**
#8464 Water Lily, blue satin, 36 oz **65.00**
#9166 Jacqueline, honey amber **75.00**
Burmese, hp log cabin scene **275.00**
Christmas Snowflake, Cranberry Opal, water (L.G. Wright) . . **350.00**
Coin Dot, Cranberry Opalescent, #1353 . . . . **250.00**
Daisy & Fern, Topaz Opal, water (L.G. Wright). **170.00**
Dot Optic, Cranberry Opalescent **250.00**
Plum Opal, Hobnail, water, 80 oz. **190.00**

Plate
#107 Ming Rose 8" **30.00**
#175 Leaf, Blue Opalescent, 7" d **25.00**
#1614 9-1/2" Green Opalescent, New World label. **65.00**
#1621 Dolphin Handled, Fenton Rose, 6" **25.00**
#1720 Emerald Crest, 8" d . . . **35.00**
#1720 Emerald Crest, 10" d . . **50.00**
#5118 Leaf, 11" Rosalene (Sample) **120.00**
Lafayette & Washington, Light Blue Iridized, sample **80.00**
Silver Crest
8-1/2" d. **30.00**
10-1/2" d, dinner **40.00**

Powder box
#192 Diamond Optic, Cranberry **125.00**
#6080 Wave CrestBlue Overlay **120.00**
Coral **230.00**

Punch bowl, #3820 Hobnail, milk glass, octagon, chip on top edge **99.00**

Relish, #7333SR, Silver Rose, heart shape, gold roses outlined in black dec, c1956-58 . . . . **65.00**

Ring tree, #9299 Owl, blue satin **19.50**

Rose bowl
Beaded Melon, Goldenrod, 3-1/2" **50.00**
Beatty Waffle, green opalescent, 4-1/2" **50.00**
Black Rose, 6-1/2" **40.00**
Crystal, Wisteria satin etching, crimped, #894 . . . . **35.00**
French Opalescent, #201. . . . **65.00**
Ivory Crest, #201, crimped, c1940-41, 5" **35.00**
Rose Burmese, #7424, hand-painted roses, sgd by artist, 1971, 3-1/2" h, 2" w **110.00**
Silver Crest, #711
5". **75.00**
6", ftd. **55.00**

Salad bowl, #7220 Aqua Crest, 10" d **75.00**

Salt and pepper shakers, pr
#1605 Rib Optic, Cranberry Opalescent **95.00**
#1605 Rib Optic, Lime Opalescent **85.00**
#3806 Hobnail, Blue Opalescent, flat, chrome top **70.00**
#3806 Hobnail, Cranberry Opalescent, flat. **50.00**
#7206 Silver Crest, ftd **120.00**
Georgian, amber, ftd **55.00**

Sandwich tray, #1502 Emerald Crest, 10" d, handle **160.00**

Sherbet
#1620 Plymouth, Amber **15.00**
#1700 Lincoln Inn, light blue, 4-3/4" h **19.50**
#1700 Lincoln Inn, ruby, 4-3/4" h **25.00**
#1942 Flower Windows, Crystal **35.00**
#4441 Small, Thumbprint, Colonial Blue. **35.00**
#4443 ThumbprintColonial Blue **20.00**
Ruby **12.00**

Slipper, Hobnail
Blue Opalescent **25.00**
Crystal **20.00**
Milk glass, white **15.00**

Temple jar
#7488 Chocolate Roses on Cameo Satin **25.00**
Cranberry Swirl, three pcs, c1939 . . . . **250.00**

Tidbit tray
#7294 Aqua Crest, two tiers . . **70.00**
Silver Crest
Single 8-1/2" d plate **30.00**
Two tiers, 6-1/2" d and 8-1/2" d plates **50.00**
Two tiers, 8-1/2" d and 12-1/2" d plates **65.00**
Three tiers, 6" d, 8-1/2" d, 12" d plates **95.00**
Three tiers, 6" d, 8-1/2" d, 12-1/2" d plates **95.00**

Toothpick holder
Daisy and Button, chocolate, hat shape **45.00**

Hobnail, Topaz Opalescent .. **35.00**
Strawberry, Carnival, orange . **12.00**

Tumbler

#1634 Diamond Optic, Aqua .. **6.00**
#3700, Grecian Gold, grape cut **15.00**
#3947 Hobnail, Cranberry Opalescent, 12 oz, 5" h **35.00**
#9242 Roses.............. **12.00**

Vase, Peacock, #791, Mandarin Red, flared top, 8" h, **$145.** *Photo courtesy of Michael Krumme.*

Vase

#36 Crystal Crest, double crimped, 6" h **85.00**
#36 Gold Crest, double crimped, triangle, 6-1/4" h **35.00**
#36 Gold Crest, triangle, 6" h . **30.00**
#184 Wisteria, crystal, 10" h .. **75.00**
#186 Aqua Crest, 8" sq...... **65.00**
#186 Blue Ridge, tulip, 8" h, c1939 .... **125.00**
#186 Peach Crest, triangle, 8" h **55.00**
#192 Aqua Crest, 5" h....... **75.00**
#194 Coin Dot, Blue Opalescent, 11" h, double crimped **160.00**
#194 Coin Dot, Blue Opalescent, 11" h, two handles **160.00**
#201 Ivory Crest, cupped, flared, 6" h **55.00**
#201 Ivory Crest, double crimped, 6" h **45.00**
#201 Ivory Crest, square, 5" h **55.00**
#203 Peach Crest, double crimped, 5" h **55.00**
#203 Rose Crest, triangle, 5" h **55.00**
#208 Coin Dot, Cranberry Opalescent, 5-1/2" h....... **65.00**
#349 San Toy, flared, crystal, 8" h **55.00**
#389 Hobnail, Blue Opalescent, 8" h, ftd **60.00**
#389 Hobnail, Green Opalescent, fan, ftd **40.00**
#389 Hobnail, Topaz Opalescent, miniature, fan, 3-5/8" h **40.00**
#389 Hobnail, Turquoise Pastel, fan, ftd, 4" h **40.00**
#621 Ming, cupped, satin etched, pink, c1930, 9" h **95.00**
#711 Ivy Green, 5" h **70.00**
#711 Peach Crest, 5" h **55.00**
#711 Silver Crest, double crimped, tulip, 4" h **40.00**
#711 Silver Crest, jack-in-the-pulpit, 6-3/4" h **45.00**
#847 Mandarin red, fan, 5-1/2" h **60.00**
#847 Periwinkle Blue, fan **62.50**
#894 Spiral Optic, Blue Opalescent, flared, 10" h............ **130.00**
#894 Spiral Optic, Blue Opalescent, tulip, 10" h **140.00**
#1441 Coin Dot, Cranberry Opalescent, 7" h **145.00**
#1452 Peach Crest, 13-1/2".. **150.00**
#1453 Coin Dot, Cranberry Opalescent, 6-1/2" h **75.00**
#1457 Coin Dot, Cranberry Opalescent, 7" h **120.00**
#1523 Ivory Crest, cornucopia, c1940-41............... **125.00**
#1523 Ivory Crest, tulip, c1940-41, 7" h **55.00**
#1923 Spiral Blue Opalescent, tulip/violet **80.00**
#1959 Daisy & Button, blue pastel, fan, 8" h **55.00**
#1959 Daisy & Button, green pastel, fan, 8" h **45.00**
#2250 Polka Dot, Cranberry, tulip shape, 8" h **95.00**
#2857 Burmese, Shiny, Wild Rose with Bowknot, made for LeVay, 7-1/2" h **125.00**
#3005 Snow Crest, amber, 7-1/2" h **45.00**
#3653 Hobnail, Colonial Green, 5" h **15.00**
#3652 Hobnail, milk glass, swung, 18" h **24.00**
#3756 Plum Opal, bud, 8" h... **35.00**
#3759 Plum Opal, Hobnail, Swung................. **150.00**
#3850 Hobnail, Blue Opalescent, 5" h **55.00**
#3850 Hobnail, French Opalescent, triangle, 5" h **38.00**
#3850 Hobnail, Topaz Opalescent, triangle, 5" h **75.00**
#3855 Hobnail, Blue Opalescent, miniature, flared, 3-3/4" h ... **30.00**
#3856 Hobnail, French Opalescent, 6" h **30.00**
#3858 Hobnail, Cranberry Opalescent, 8" h, chip...... **35.00**
#3956 Hobnail, Blue Opalescent, crimped, 6" h............ **28.50**
#3957BO Hobnail, Blue Opalescent, fan, 6-1/4" h **45.00**
#3959 Hobnail, Blue Opalescent, fan, 8" h **65.00**
#5155 Peach Crest, 10-1/2" h, hand **360.00**
#5858 Jamestown Blue, 8" h, factory defect inside top **55.00**
#6056 Peach Crest, 6" h..... **60.00**
#6056 Silver Jamestown Crest, 6" h.................... **40.00**
#6454RG Vasa Murrhina, 4" .. **65.00**
#6456AO Vasa Murrhina, 8" .. **55.00**
#7157 Peach Crest, Beaded Melon, tulip, 6" h **50.00**
#7251RB Burmese, roses dec, 11" h.................. **250.00**
#7253 Burmese, 7" h **75.00**
#7253BR Burmese, roses dec, 7" h................... **175.00**
#7258 Silver Crest, 8" h **50.00**
#7262 Silver Crest, 12" h ... **100.00**
#7269 Silver Crest, fan top, 12-3/4" h............... **125.00**
#7345 Emerald Crest, crimped, 4-1/2" h................ **35.00**
#7350 Gold Crest, 5-1/2" h... **50.00**
#7354 Aqua Crest, double crimped, 4-1/2" h................ **45.00**
#7355 Rose Crest, fan, 4-1/2" h................ **35.00**
#7357 Crystal Crest, fan, 6-1/4" h................ **85.00**
#7451 Blue Satin, 6" h **24.50**
#7460 Amberina Overlay crimped, 6-1/2" **80.00**
#7528 Peach Rest, double crimped, 8" h................... **55.00**
#7547 Burmese, hp Pink Dogwood, 5-1/2" h................ **75.00**
#8254 Mermaid Planter/Vase, Dark Carnival **100.00**
#8802 French Blue, Sandcarved, oval, 12" h............. **160.00**
#9254 Blue Marble, Handkerchief, 6-1/2" h................ **20.00**
Aristocrat Bud Vase, #98 Cutting, Fenton Rose............ **45.00**
Art Glass, vaseline with white opalescence, two applied cobalt blue handles and rim, 10" h, 6" w **1,100.00**
Fan vase, Rose Crest, 6-1/2" h **70.00**
Hand vase, Aqua Crest **290.00**
Hanging Heart, opaque jade green ground, cobalt blue rim, irid surface, 11-1/2" h, 6" w .. **1,700.00**
Ivory Crest, 10"............ **65.00**

Wine bottle, #1667 Rib Optic, cranberry.................. **190.00**

Wine, #389 Hobnail, French Opalescent **20.00**

Findlay Onyx Glass

History: Findlay onyx glass, produced by Dalzell, Gilmore & Leighton Company, Findlay, Ohio, was patented for the firm in 1889 by George W. Leighton. Due to high production costs resulting from a complex manufacturing process, the glass was made only for a short time.

Layers of glass were plated to a bulb of opalescent glass through repeated dippings into a glass pot. Each layer was cooled and reheated to develop opalescent qualities. A pattern mold then was used to produce raised decorations of flowers and leaves. A second mold gave the glass bulb its full shape and form.

A platinum luster paint, producing pieces identified as silver or platinum onyx, was applied to the raised decorations. The color was fixed in a muffle kiln. Other colors such as cinnamon, cranberry, cream, raspberry, and rose were achieved by using an outer glass plating which reacted strongly to reheating. For example, a purple or orchid color came from the addition of manganese and cobalt to the glass mixture.

References: Neila and Tom Bredenhoft, *Findlay Toothpick Holders*, Cherry Hill Publications, 1995; James Measell and Don E. Smith, *Findlay Glass: The Glass Tableware Manufacturers, 1886-1902*, Antique Publications, 1986; Kenneth Wilson, *American Glass 1760-1930: The Toledo Museum of Art, Volume I, Volume II*, Hudson Hills Press and The Toledo Museum of Art, 1994.

Collectors' Club: Collectors of Findlay Glass, P.O. Box 256, Findlay, OH 45839.

Creamer, Onyx, platinum-colored blossoms, creamy-white background, opalescent applied handle, **$435.** *Photo courtesy of Clarence and Betty Maier.*

Bowl
- 7" d, 2-3/4" h, silver onyx **320.00**
- 7-1/2" d, cream onyx **390.00**
- 7-1/2" d, raspberry onyx **425.00**

Butter dish, cov, 5-1/2" d, silver onyx **850.00**

Celery, 6-1/4" h, cream........ **450.00**

Creamer, 4-1/2" h, platinum colored dec, opalescent glass handle
- Cream onyx **525.00**
- Raspberry onyx **550.00**

Dresser box, cov, 5" d, cream, round **675.00**

Mustard, cov, 3" h
- Cream onyx, hinged metal cov, orig spoon marked "sterling"... **400.00**
- Raspberry onyx, hinged metal cov, orig spoon marked "sterling" **600.00**

Pitcher
- 7-1/2" h, cream, applied opalescent handle, polished rim chip.. **800.00**
- 8" h, cream onyx, amber florals and handle, minor bubbles in inner liner **700.00**

Salt and pepper shakers, pr, 3" h, platinum onyx **550.00**

Spooner, cinnamon ground, tulip, daisy, and thistle motif, 4-1/4" h, **$650.**

Spooner, 4-1/2" h
- Cream onyx, bright silver dec, few small rim flakes.......... **485.00**
- Platinum blossoms, rough edge **265.00**
- Raspberry onyx **650.00**

Sugar bowl, cov, 5-1/2" h
- Cream onyx **475.00**
- Raspberry onyx **650.00**

Sugar shaker, 6" h
- Raspberry onyx **495.00**
- Silver onyx **475.00**

Syrup, 7" h, 4" w, silver dec, applied opalescent handle.......... **1,150.00**

Toothpick holder, 2-1/2" h
- Cinnamon onyx........... **425.00**
- Cream onyx, metallic silver dec, minimal flaking at rim **475.00**

Tumbler, raspberry onyx, Floradine pattern **785.00**

Water set, water pitcher, four barrel-shaped tumblers, cream **2,500.00**

Fire-King

History: Fire-King dinnerware and kitchenware were products of the Anchor Hocking Glass Corporation. In 1905, Isaac J. Collins founded the Hocking Glass Company along the banks of the Hocking River near Lancaster, Ohio. On March 6, 1924, fire completely destroyed the plant, but it was rebuilt in six months. Hocking produced pressed glass dinnerware, many patterns of which are considered Depression glass.

In 1937, Hocking Glass Company merged with the Anchor Cap Company and became Anchor Hocking Glass Corporation. Shortly thereafter, the new company began to manufacture glass ovenware that could withstand high temperatures in a kitchen oven.

Production of oven-proof glass marked "FIRE-KING" began in 1942 and lasted until 1976. Dinnerware patterns include Alice, Charm, Fleurette, Game Bird, Honeysuckle, Jane Ray, Laurel, Primrose, Turquoise Blue, Swirl, and Wheat. Utilitarian kitchen items and ovenware patterns also were produced.

At the 2002 Housewares Fair, Anchor Hocking released a new line of oven-safe Fire King in Jade-ite.

Housewives eagerly purchased Fire-King sets and could also assemble sets of matching dinnerware and ovenware patterns. Advertising encouraged consumers to purchase prepackaged starter, luncheon, baking, and snack sets, as well as casseroles. Oven glassware items included almost everything needed to completely stock the kitchen.

Fire-King patterns are found in azurite, forest green, gray, ivory, jadeite, peach luster, pink, plain white, ruby red, sapphire blue, opaque turquoise, and white with an assortment of rim colors. To increase sales, decals were applied. Collectors tend to focus on the older patterns and colors, as well as ovenware items. Fire-King was sold in sets. Add an additional 25 percent to 35 percent to the price of the individual pieces for an intact set in its original box.

Anchor Hocking used a molded mark for Fire-King, as well as oval foil paper labels.

References: Gene Florence, *Anchor Hocking's Fire King & More*, 2nd ed., Collector Books, 2000; —, *Collectible Glassware from the '40s, '50s, '60s*, 6th ed., Collector Books, 2001; —, *Kitchen Glassware of the Depression Years*, 6th ed., Collector Books, 2001; Shirley Glyndon, *The Miracle in Grandmother's Kitchen*, published by author, 1983; Gary and Dale Kilgo and Jerry and Gail Wilkins, *Collectors Guide to Anchor Hocking's Fire-King Glassware*, K & W Collectibles Publisher, 1991; —, *Collectors Guide to Anchor Hocking's Fire-King Glassware, Volume II*,, K & W Collectibles Publisher, 1998; April M. Tvorak, *Fire-King*, 5th ed., published by author (P.O. Box 126, Canon City, CO 81215), 1997; —, *Fire-King '95*, published by author, 1995; —, *Fire-King II*, published by author, 1993; —, *History and Price Guide to Fire-King*, VAL Enterprises, 1992

Periodicals: *Fire-King Monthly*, P.O. Box 70594, Tuscaloosa, AL 35407; *Fire-King News*, K & W Collectibles, Inc., P.O. Box 374, Addison, AL 35540.

Collectors' Club: Fire-King Collectors Club, 1406 E. 14th St., Des Moines, IA 50316.

Dinnerware

Alice

Jade-ite, white with blue trim, and white with red trim. Introduced as Quaker Oats premium, 1945.

Cup and saucer

Jade-ite 9.00
White, blue trim 16.50
White, red trim 20.00

Dinner plate, 9-1/2" d

Jade-ite 22.00
White, blue trim 24.00
White, red trim 27.50

Anniversary Rose

Translucent white, rose design, 22K gold trim, heat resistant, 1964-65.

Berry bowl 4.00
Creamer 5.00
Cup and saucer 5.00
Dinner plate, 10" d 4.50
Platter, 9" x 12" 7.00
Salad plate, 7-3/8" d 4.00
Soup bowl 6.00
Sugar, cov 5.00
Vegetable bowl 6.00

Blue Mosaic

Solid white, blue mosaic pattern, 1966-68.

Berry bowl 4.00
Creamer 5.00
Cup 5.00
Dinner plate, 10" d 8.00
Salad bowl 5.00
Salad plate 6.00
Saucer 2.00
Snack plate 8.50
Soup bowl 6.00
Sugar, cov 5.00
Vegetable bowl 6.50

Bubble

Heat resistant, often found with blue and silver paper labels, 1930s-60s.

Berry bowl, individual

Crystal 4.50
Sapphire blue 19.00
White 4.50

Berry bowl, large, crystal 7.00

Bowl

8" d, crystal 6.50
8-3/8" d, Peach Lustre 8.00

Bread and butter plate

Crystal 2.75
Sapphire blue 4.00

Cereal bowl

Crystal 9.50
Sapphire blue 15.00

Creamer and sugar

Sapphire blue 60.00
White 12.50

Cup and saucer

Crystal 4.00
Sapphire blue 6.00

Dinner plate, 9-1/4" d

Crystal 6.50
Sapphire blue 8.00

Fruit bowl

Crystal 4.50
Ruby 10.00
Sapphire blue 15.00
White 5.00

Grill plate, sapphire blue, 9-1/4" d 15.00
Mug, Peach Lustre 3.00
Platter, sapphire blue 16.00
Salad plate, sapphire blue 4.00

Saucer

Crystal 75
Sapphire blue 1.00

Soup bowl

Crystal 9.50
Sapphire blue 16.00

Sugar Bowl

Crystal 6.00
Sapphire blue 25.00

Vegetable bowl 6.00

Candleglow

Cake plate, 9" d, round 9.00
Casserole, 1-1/2" sq, knob cover . 9.00
Custard cup 2.00

Charm

Azur-ite and Jade-ite, square shapes, 1950s.

Bowl, 4-3/4" d

Azur-ite 5.00
Jade-ite 16.00

Cereal bowl, 6" d, Azur-ite 18.00

Creamer

Azur-ite 6.50
Jade-ite 18.00

Cup and saucer

Azur-ite 11.00
Jade-ite 15.00

Dessert plate, Azur-ite, 7-1/4" d . 15.00

Dinner plate, 9-1/2" d

Azur-ite 20.00
Jade-ite 25.00

Luncheon plate, 8-3/8" d

Azur-ite 8.00
Jade-ite 35.00

Platter

11" x 8", Azur-ite 15.00
Jade-ite 30.00

Salad bowl, 7-3/8" d

Azur-ite 15.00
Jade-ite 30.00

Salad plate, 6-5/8" d, Jade-ite . . . 6.00

Sugar

Azur-ite 6.00
Jade-ite 17.00

Children's Ware, alphabet mug 12.00

Colonial Lady, snack set, ruby and crystal 10.00

Country Kitchens, cake plate, 9" d 5.00

Diamond, mug, Peach Lustre . . . 3.00

Fishscale, demitasse cup and saucer, Lustre 35.00

Fleurette

Bowl, 4-1/2" d 5.00
Creamer 8.00
Cup 3.50
Dinner plate, 9-1/8" 6.00
Platter, 9" x 12", oval 15.00
Salad plate, 7-3/8" d 10.00
Saucer 1.50
Soup plate, 6-5/8" d 12.00
Sugar, cov 9.00
Vegetable bowl, 8-1/4" d 12.50

Fruits

Hand painted on white.

Baking dish, 1-1/2 qt, oblong . . 20.00
Casserole, cov, 1-1/2 qt 25.00
Meat loaf dish, 5" x 9", quart . . . 12.50
Mixing bowl, 6" d, Colonial 16.00

Game Bird

White background, four different decals, heat resistant.

Ashtray 5.00
Bread and butter plate 9.00
Chili bowl, 5" d 5.00
Creamer, Pheasant dec 10.00

Dessert bowl

Canada Goose dec 5.00
Mallard Duck dec 5.00
Pheasant dec 5.00

Dinner plate, 10" d

Canada Goose dec 9.00
Mallard Duck dec 9.00
Pheasant dec 9.00
Ruffled Grouse dec 9.00

Mug

Canada Goose dec 18.50
Mallard Duck dec 10.00
Pheasant dec 15.00
Ruffled Grouse dec 12.00

Sugar, Pheasant dec 10.00

Tumbler
- Canada Goose dec **22.00**
- Mallard Duck dec **12.00**
- Pheasant dec. **12.00**
- Ruffled Grouse dec **12.00**

Golden Anniversary

White.

Bowl, 8" d. **6.00**
Creamer. **3.50**
Cup and saucer. **5.00**
Dinner plate. **3.00**
Fruit bowl, 4-7/8" d **4.00**
Plate, 7-1/2" d. **2.00**
Platter, oval **10.00**
Soup bowl **7.50**
Saucer **1.00**
Sugar, open **3.50**

Golden Shell Swirl

Milk white swirl, 22K gold scalloped edges, ovenproof, 1963-76.

Berry bowl, 4-7/8" d. **3.00**
Cereal bowl **6.00**
Creamer. **3.00**
Cup and saucer. **4.25**
Demitasse cup and saucer **12.00**
Dessert bowl, 4-3/4" d. **3.50**
Dinner plate, 10" d. **9.00**
Luncheon set, 16 pcs, orig box . **80.00**
Salad plate, 7-1/4" d **4.00**
Soup plate, flat, 7-5/8" d **12.00**
Souvenir plate, 10" d, World's Fair, 1964 . . . . **45.00**
Saucer . . . . **.75**
Sugar bowl, cov **8.00**
Vegetable bowl **8.00**

Honeysuckle, cup and saucer . . **6.00**

Ivory, snack set, gold trim **5.00**

Jade-ite

Restaurant Ware, heat resistant; 1950-56.

Berry bowl, small. **6.00**
Bowl, 10" d. **15.00**
Bread and butter plate, 5-1/2" d . . **4.00**
Breakfast bowl, 4-7/8" d, 10 oz, ftd **14.00**
Butter dish, cov. **75.00**
Cereal bowl, flared **18.00**
Chili bowl. **12.00**
Coffee mug, 7 oz. **12.00**
Cup and saucer. **10.00**
Demitasse cup and saucer **95.00**
Dinner plate, 9" d. **20.00**
Egg cup, double **20.00**
Hot chocolate mug **20.00**
Grill plate
- Three sections, 9-5/8" d. **15.00**
- Three sections, 9-5/8" d, tab handle **35.00**
- Five sections, 9-5/8" d **18.00**

Luncheon plate, 8" d **12.00**
Milk pitcher. **32.00**
Pie plate, 6-3/4" d **12.00**
Platter
- 8-7/8" d, oval, partitioned **20.00**
- 11-1/2" l, oval **55.00**

Refrigerator dish, 4" x 4", clear top **18.00**
Relish, five parts. **18.00**
Salad plate, 6-3/4" d **6.00**
Sandwich plate, 9-3/4" l, oval. . . **15.00**
Saucer. **3.75**

Jane Ray

Made in Ivory, Jade-ite, Peach Lustre, white, and white with gold trim. First jade-colored heat resistant dinnerware, 1945-63.

Bowl, 5-7/8" d, Jade-ite. **25.00**
Bread and butter plate, 6-1/4" d, Jade-ite, orig label. **195.00**
Cereal bowl
- Ivory **8.00**
- Jade-ite. **15.00**
- White. **8.00**

Chili bowl
- Ivory **8.00**
- Jade-ite. **9.00**
- White. **8.00**

Creamer
- Ivory **19.00**
- Jade-ite. **24.00**
- Peach Lustre. **20.00**
- White. **19.00**

Cup and saucer
- Ivory **7.00**
- Jade-ite. **12.00**
- Peach Lustre. **10.00**
- White. **9.00**

Demitasse cup, Peach Lustre . . **15.00**
Dinner, plate, Jade-ite, 9-1/8" d . **10.00**
Oatmeal bowl, 8" d
- Ivory **8.00**
- Jade-ite. **12.00**
- White. **8.00**

Salad plate, 7-3/4" d
- Ivory **12.00**
- Jade-ite. **20.00**
- White. **12.00**

Soup bowl, 7-5/8" d
- Ivory **8.00**
- Jade-ite. **30.00**

Starter set, Jade-ite, 12 pcs, orig box, orig labels **75.00**
Sugar
- Ivory **19.00**
- Jade-ite. **35.00**
- Peach Lustre. **20.00**
- White. **19.00**

Vegetable bowl, 8-1/4" d
- Ivory **24.00**
- Jade-ite **35.00**
- White **24.00**

Kimberly mug, yellow/maroon, 9 oz **2.50**

Leaf and Blossom

Bowl. **9.00**
Dinner plate, 10" d, green and pink **8.00**

Meadow Green

Bowl, 4-1/2" d **4.00**
Casserole, cov
- 1-1/2 qt **18.50**
- 2 qt **8.00**

Casserole, French **6.00**
Cereal bowl, 4-7/8" d. **5.00**
Custard **3.00**
Dinner plate, 10" d **8.00**
Fruit bowl, 4-5/8" d **4.50**
Loaf dish, 5" x 9" **9.50**
Mug **7.50**
Salad plate, 7-1/4" d **6.00**
Soup bowl. **9.50**

Milano pitcher, aqua, ice lip . . . **35.00**

Peach Lustre

Copper tinted lustre, scratches easily, heat resistant, 1951-65.

Bowl, 4-7/8" d, Peach Lustre **4.50**
Creamer
- Gray Laurel **5.00**
- Peach Lustre **4.50**

Cup and saucer
- Gray Laurel **5.50**
- Peach Lustre **6.00**

Custard cup, ruffled, Peach Lustre **1.00**
Dessert bowl, 4-7/8" d
- Gray Laurel **4.50**
- Peach Lustre **4.00**

Dinner plate, 9" d
- Gray Laurel **8.25**
- Peach Lustre **6.50**

Salad plate, 7-1/2" d, Peach Lustre **3.00**
Serving plate, 11" d
- Gray Laurel **15.00**
- Peach Lustre **14.00**

Soup bowl, 7-5/8" d
- Gray Laurel **6.00**
- Peach Lustre **9.50**

Sugar, cov, Peach Lustre **10.00**
Sugar, open, ftd
- Gray Laurel **6.00**
- Peach Lustre **4.50**

Vegetable bowl, 8-1/4" d
- Gray Laurel **12.00**
- Peach Lustre **9.00**

Philbe

Made in blue, crystal, green, and pink, from 1937-38.

Candy jar, cov, 4" d, low, blue.. **800.00**

Cereal bowl, 5-1/2" d
- Blue **65.00**
- Crystal **20.00**
- Green **42.00**
- Pink **42.00**

Cookie jar, cov, crystal **625.00**

Creamer, 3-1/4" h, ftd
- Blue **135.00**
- Crystal **40.00**
- Green **115.00**
- Pink **115.00**

Cup and saucer
- Blue **225.00**
- Crystal **95.00**
- Green **175.00**
- Pink **175.00**

Grill plate, 10-1/2" d, blue **75.00**

Iced tea tumbler, ftd, blue **165.00**

Iced tea tumbler, crystal **90.00**

Luncheon plate, 8" d
- Blue **50.00**
- Green **40.00**
- Pink **40.00**

Sandwich plate, 10" d
- Blue **110.00**
- Crystal **30.00**
- Green **65.00**
- Pink **65.00**

Sherbet, 4-3/4" h, blue **1,500.00**

Sherbet plate, 6" d, crystal **35.00**

Sugar, 3-1/4" h, ftd
- Blue **135.00**
- Crystal **45.00**
- Green **115.00**
- Pink **115.00**

Tumbler, ftd, blue **175.00**

Primrose

Bowl
- 4-5/8" d **4.50**
- 8-1/4" d **1.00**

Casserole, open, quart **5.00**

Creamer **8.00**

Cup **3.00**

Custard **4.00**

Dinner plate, 9-1/8" d **7.00**

Plate, 7-1/4" d **5.00**

Platter, 12" l, oval **15.00**

Saucer **1.00**

Set
- Luncheon, orig box, 19 pcs **110.00**
- Ovenware, orig box, 11 pcs **50.00**

Snack plate with cup **7.00**

Sugar
- Cov **10.00**
- Open **5.00**

Rainbow jug, ball, orange **48.00**

Red Rose mug **3.00**

Royal Ruby #R4000

Bowl
- 4-1/2" d **7.50**
- 6-1/2" d **15.00**

Creamer **6.00**

Cup and saucer **8.00**

Dessert bowl **6.00**

Dinner plate **10.00**

Salad plate **10.00**

Saucer **2.00**

Sugar **6.00**

Sapphire Blue

Light blue, also made in Ovenware.

Bowl
- 4-3/8" d **24.50**
- 5-3/8" d **24.50**

Cake pan, 8-3/4" l, tab handles **30.00**

Casserole, cov, individual, 10 oz. **13.00**

Cereal bowl, 6" d **22.00**

Coffee dripolator, Silex, two cups, filter insert **50.00**

Custard cup, 5 oz **5.00**

Measuring cup, 8 oz, spout **30.00**

Mug **25.00**

Hot plate, tab handle **30.00**

Loaf pan **28.00**

Nurser bottle, 4 oz **24.00**

Percolator top, 2-1/8" d **12.50**

Pie plate
- 8-3/8" d **9.00**
- 9" d, 1-1/2" deep **12.50**
- 9-5/8" d, 1-1/2" deep **12.50**
- 10-3/8" d, Juice Saver **150.00**

Refrigerator jar, cov, 5-1/8" x 9-1/8" **40.00**

Roaster
- Cov, 8-3/4" l **60.00**
- Open, 10-3/8" l **50.00**

Utility Bowl
- 6-7/8" d **16.00**
- 10-7/8" d **22.00**

Shell

Molded swirl design, scalloped edge, 1963.

Berry bowl, Jade-ite **6.00**

Candy dish, 7" d, Jade-ite **35.00**

Cereal bowl
- Golden White, 6-3/8" d **10.00**
- Jade-ite, 6-3/8" d **28.00**

Creamer
- Golden White **6.00**
- Jade-ite **7.50**

Cup and saucer
- Golden White **4.00**
- Jade-ite **8.00**
- St Denis, breakfast type, Jade-ite **30.00**

Demitasse cup and saucer, Lustre **15.00**

Dinner plate, 10" d, Lustre **10.00**

Fruit bowl, Jade-ite **7.00**

Place setting, 10" d plate, 7-1/4" d plate, cup and saucer, Jade-ite, four pcs **75.00**

Salad plate, 7-1/4" d, Jade-ite **25.00**

Sugar
- Golden White **6.00**
- Peach Lustre, cov **10.00**

Vegetable bowl
- Jade-ite **37.50**
- Lustre **6.00**

Sierra, bowl, avocado/brown **3.00**

Summerfield

Baking pan, 1-1/2 quart **20.00**

Custard cups, set of eight **15.00**

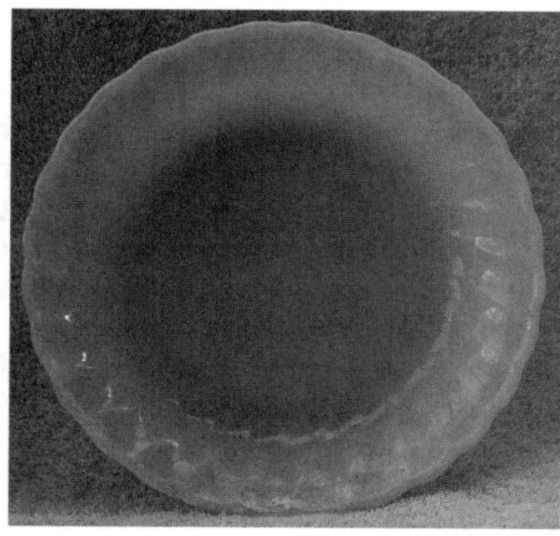

Soup bowl, Swirl, Jade-ite, 7-5/8" d, **$8.50.**

Swirl

Made in Azure-ite, ivory, ivory with gold trim, ivory with red trim, Jade-ite, pink, sunrise, white, and white with gold trim.

Bowl
- Lustre, 8-1/2" d **11.00**
- Sunrise **8.00**

Casserole, open, white, 10 oz **1.50**

Creamer, flat
- Azure-ite **6.00**
- Ivory **4.00**
- Pink **9.00**
- White **4.50**

Creamer, ftd
- Ivory **5.00**
- Jade-ite **6.00**
- White **5.00**
- White with trim **6.00**

Cup and saucer
- Azur-ite **8.50**
- Ivory **4.00**
- Lustre trim **10.00**
- Jade-ite **6.00**
- Pink **4.00**

White 7.00
White with trim 10.00
Dinner plate, 9-1/8" d
Azur-ite.......... 12.50
Ivory.......... 4.50
Jade-ite 11.00
Mixing bowls, nested set, 5-7/8", 7", 8", 9", Jade-ite 180.00
Platter, 12" x 9"
Azur-ite.......... 18.00
Ivory.......... 7.00
Sunrise.......... 20.00
White 7.00
White with trim 20.00
Salad plate, 7-1/8" d
Azur-ite.......... 6.50
Jade-ite 8.50
Sunrise.......... 8.00
Salad plate, 7-3/8" d, Lustre trim . 10.00
Soup bowl, 7-5/8" d
Azur-ite.......... 9.00
Ivory.......... 8.00
Jade-ite 8.50
Pink 12.00
White 4.00
White with trim 5.00
Sugar, flat, tab handles
Azure-ite.......... 6.00
Ivory.......... 4.00
Pink 9.00
White 4.50
Sugar, ftd, open handles
Ivory.......... 5.00
Jade-ite 6.00
White 5.00
White with trim 6.00

Three Band, cup, Peach Lustre . 2.00

Turquoise Blue

Some pieces with 22K gold trim, heat resistant, 1957-58.

Batter bowl 475.00
Bowl
4-1/2" d 8.00
6-1/2" d 25.00
8" d.......... 22.50
Bread and butter plate, 6" d 20.00
Cereal bowl, 5" d 12.00
Chili bowl, 5" d 18.50
Coffee mug 16.50
Creamer.......... 10.00
Cup.......... 5.00
Deviled egg plate, gold edge ... 15.00
Dinner plate
9" d.......... 15.00
10" d.......... 44.00
Mixing bowl, splash proof, nested set of three, one qt, two qt, three qt .. 80.00
Mug 16.50
Relish, three parts, gold trim 15.00
Salad plate, 7" d 12.00
Saucer
Round.......... .75
Square 1.00
Set, starter, orig box, 12 pcs... 100.00
Snack set, 9" d, plate with ring and cup, gold trim 12.50
Soup bowl, 6-5/8" d 16.00
Sugar bowl.......... 10.00
Vegetable bowl, 8" d 30.00

Vienna Lace

Creamer 2.50
Dessert bowl 2.00
Dinner plate, 10" d 3.00
Platter, oval.......... 8.00
Sugar, cov.......... 5.00
Vegetable bowl, 8-1/4".......... 8.00

Wheat

Bowl, 4-5/8" d 3.50
Cake pan
Round, 8" d.......... 11.00
Sq, 8" w.......... 10.00
Casserole, cov, 1-1/2 qt 15.00
Creamer 5.50
Custard.......... 4.50
Plate, 10" d 7.50
Platter, 12" l, oval 12.50
Soup bowl, 6-1/2" d 8.00
Sugar, cov.......... 9.50
Vegetable bowl, 8-1/4" d 12.00

Kitchenware

Batter bowl, 7-1/2" d, one handle
Jade-ite.......... 24.00
White, hand-painted floral ... 20.00
Butter dish, clear lid, 2-3/4" x 6-3/4"
Clear.......... 5.00
Ivory 9.00
Jade-ite.......... 27.50
Casserole, 10 oz, individual size, tab handle, Sapphire Blue.......... 13.00
Coffee maker, Silex, two cups, two pcs 20.00
Hot plate, Sapphire Blue, handle 22.00
Loaf pan, Sapphire Blue, 9" x 5". 20.00
Measuring cup, Sapphire Blue, one spout 18.00
Mixing bowl
Beaded rim, 4-7/8" d, white ... 6.00
Sapphire Blue, turned rim.... 23.00
Swirl, 6" d, jadeite.......... 12.00
Swirl, 9" d, white 10.00
Turquoise Blue, quart, round . 15.00
Turquoise Blue, quart, tear shape 18.00
Mixing bowl set, Tulip pattern, Non-Splash, one-, two-, three-, and four-quart sizes, orig box 200.00
Mug
Jade-ite.......... 8.00
Sapphire Blue, thick 30.00
Nurser, Sapphire Blue, 4 oz...... 8.50
Pie plate, Sapphire Blue, 8" d 7.00
Refrigerator dish
4-1/2" x 5-1/2", open, Jade-ite . 16.00
5" x 9", cov, emb lid, Jade-ite . 40.00
Table server, Sapphire Blue 20.00
Utility bowl, Sapphire Blue
6-7/8" d 15.00
8-1/4" d 18.00

Ovenware, covered individual casserole, light blue, **$8.50.**

Ovenware

Baker, Sapphire Blue, 6 oz, individual 3.25
Cake pan, 8" sq, Primrose, white, decal 9.00
Casserole, cov
Ivory, knob, 1-1/2 qt, knob lid . 15.00
Peach Lustre, copper tint, French-style, tab lids, orig label 5.00
Sapphire Blue, one pint...... 14.00
Custard cup, 6 oz, crystal, orig label 2.00
Mixing bowl set, nested, three bowls 60.00
Mug 27.50
Pie plate
Crystal, 10 oz, deep, orig label. 3.00
Ivory, 15 oz 16.00
Pie plate cover, Sapphire Blue, 9" d.......... 15.00
Popcorn popper, Sapphire Blue. 35.00
Set, Peach Lustre, copper tint, 1-1/2 qt casserole, 5" x 9" deep loaf, 9" d pie plate, 6" x 10" utility pan, 8" round cake plan, 6-oz custard cup, orig box and labels 45.00

FLASKS

History: A flask, which usually has a narrow neck, is a container for liquids. Early American glass companies frequently formed them in molds, which left a relief design on the front and/or back. Historical flasks with a portrait, building, scene, or name are the most desirable.

A chestnut is hand-blown, small, and has a flattened bulbous body. The pitkin has a blown globular body with a spiral rib overlay on vertical ribs. Teardrop flasks are generally fiddle shaped and have a scroll or geometric design. Pocket flasks are generally small enough to fit conveniently in a pocket and can have a variety of designs.

Dimensions may differ for the same flask because of the variations in the molding process. Color is an important pricing factor, with scarcer colors demanding higher prices. Aqua and amber are the most common colors. Flasks found with a "sickness" or opalescent scaling, which obscures the clarity, are worth much less.

Decorators have long favored the shapes and colors of flasks and often included them in decorating schemes. Of course, reproduction flasks were soon made to meet this need.

References: Gary Baker et al., *Wheeling Glass 1829-1939*, Oglebay Institute, 1994, distributed by Antique Publications; George L. and Helen McKearin, *American Glass*, Crown Publishers, 1941 and 1948; Kenneth Wilson, *American Glass 1760-1930*, 2 vols., Hudson Hills Press and The Toledo Museum of Art, 1994.

Periodical: *Antique Bottle & Glass Collector*, P.O. Box 187, East Greenville, PA 18041.

Collectors' Clubs: Federation of Historical Bottle Collectors, Inc., 2230 Toub St., Ramona, CA 92065; The National American Glass Club, Ltd., P.O. Box 8489, Silver Spring, MD 20907.

Chestnut

Blown, Zanesville, OH, 24 vertical ribs, amber, half pint, 4-3/4" h, minor wear **250.00**

Free blown, Germany, 1650-1700, olive yellow, sheared mouth, applied decorated string rim, smooth base, 10" h. **325.00**

Wharton Whisky, 1850, brilliant yellow-amber, quarter pint, pocket, applied top, round bottom. **110.00**

Historical

Baltimore Monument-Sloop, Baltimore Glass Works, Baltimore, MD, 1840-60, light yellow with olive tone, sheared mouth, pontil scar, half pint, some ext. high point wear and scratches **2,100.00**

Clasped Hands-Cannon, Pittsburgh district, Pittsburgh, PA 1860-80

- Aquamarine, applied collared mouth with ring, smooth base, pint, McKearin GXII-41, some minor int. haze **70.00**
- Golden yellow, applied collared mouth with ring, smooth base, pint, McKearin GXII-41, some minor exterior scratches below cannon, 1/8" chip on top of mouth . . **300.00**

Columbia, American Eagle, aqua, pint, sheared lip, open pontil, McKearin GI-121. **450.00**

Double Eagle

- Coventry Glass Works, Coventry, CT, 1830-48, yellow olive, sheared mouth, pontil scar, pint, McKearin GII-70 . . . . **200.00**
- Granite Glass Works, Stoddard, NH, 1846-50, yellow olive, sheared mouth, pontil scar, pint, McKearin GII-81, slight misshapen shoulder **250.00**
- Kentucky Glass Works, Louisville, KY, 1850-55, attributed to, brilliant copper, sheared mouth, pontil scar, pint, McKearin GII-24, 2" vertical crack **325.00**
- Kentucky Glass Works, Louisville, KY 1850-55, pale blue, sheared lip, open pontil, orig cork, McKearin GII-26, open bubble on one side **385.00**
- Louisville Glass Works, Louisville, KY, 1855-60, vertically ribbed, pale blue green, sheared mouth, pontil scar, pint, McKearin GII-32A, manufacturer's mouth roughness, some int. haze. **575.00**
- Pittsburgh district, Pittsburgh, PA, 1860-80, lime green, quart, applied band, smooth base, McKearin GII-101, 2" crack **80.00**
- Pittsburgh district, Pittsburgh, PA, 1860-80, yellow olive, applied collared mouth with ring, smooth base, pint, McKearin GII-105, pinhead flake at base **150.00**
- Stoddard glasshouse, Stoddard, NH, 1846-60, light yellow amber with olive tone, sheared mouth, pontil scar, half pint, McKearin GII-86a **180.00**
- Stoddard glasshouse, Stoddard, NH, 1846-60, olive amber, sheared mouth, pontil scar, quart, McKearin GII-79 . . . . **160.00**
- Stoddard glasshouse, Stoddard, NH, 1846-60, yellow amber with olive tone, sheared mouth, pontil scar, pint, McKearin GII-82. . . . . .**110.00**

Eagle, calabash, applied top and pontil, McKearin GII-143, few minor scratches, hint of int. stain **145.00**

Eagle-Cornucopia, attributed to Keene Marlboro Street Glassworks, Keene, NH, 1830-50

- Bright aquamarine with bluish bone, sheared mouth, pontil scar, pint, McKearin GII-74. . . . . **140.00**
- Brilliant aquamarine, sheared mouth, pontil scar, pint, McKearin GII-74, small int. open bubble on shoulder **90.00**
- Brilliant yellowish green with olive tone, sheared mouth, pontil scar, pint, McKearin GII-63. . . . . **180.00**
- Emerald green, sheared mouth, pontil scar, pint, McKearin GII-74, pinhead sized flake on top of mouth, two 3/8" potstone cracks **210.00**
- Olive amber, pint, New England, 19th C, McKearin GII-72 . . **165.00**
- Olive amber, pint, New England, 19th C, McKearin GII-73 . . **165.00**
- Olive, pint, New England, 19th C, McKearin GII-73. . . . . **165.00**
- Pale aquamarine, sheared mouth, pontil scar, pint, McKearin GII-72,

Left: G.R.J.A. star and seeing eye on reverse, brilliant amber, McKearin GIV-43, ***$525;*** *center: Cornucopia-urn, emerald green, McKearin GIII-17,* ***$660;*** *right: General Taylor, Fell's Point, Balto, pale amethyst, McKearin GI-73,* **$825.** *Photo courtesy of Pacific Glass Auctions.*

some minor int. stain near base **130.00**

Yellow amber with olive tone, sheared mouth, pontil scar, pint, McKearin GII-72 . . . . **120.00**

Yellowish olive amber, sheared mouth, pontil scar, pint, McKearin GII-72 . . . . **150.00**

Eagle-Cornucopia, attributed to early Pittsburgh district, 1820-40, sheared mouth, pontil scar

Colorless, half pint, McKearin GII-11 . . . . **600.00**

Light greenish-aquamarine, pint, McKearin GII-6 . . . . **475.00**

Eagle-Grape, light aqua, quart, America, mid-19th C, McKearin GII-55, imperfections **150.00**

Eagle-Stag, Coffin and Hay Manufacturers, Hammonton, NJ, 1836-47, aquamarine with pale yellowish green tint, sheared mouth, pontil scar, half pint, McKearin GII-50 . . . . **325.00**

Eagle-Westford Glass Co., Westford Glass Co., Westford, CT, 1860-73, bright medium reddish amber, malformed applied double-collared mouth, smooth base, half pint, McKearin GII-65 . . . . **120.00**

Eagle-Willington/Glass Co., Willington Glass Works, West Willington, CT, 1860-72

Bright medium yellowish-olive, applied double collared mouth, smooth base, half pint, McKearin GII-63 . . . . **210.00**

Golden red amber, applied double collared mouth, smooth base, quart, McKearin GII-61, some ext. highpoint wear. **200.00**

Medium yellow olive, double collared mouth, smooth base, pint, McKearin GII-64 . . . . **150.00**

Yellow-olive, sloping collared mouth, smooth base, quart, McKearin GII-61 . . . . **200.00**

For Pike's Peak Prospector-Hunter Shooting Deer, attributed to Ravenna Glass Works, Ravenna, OH, 1860-80, aquamarine, applied mouth with ring, smooth base, quart, McKearin GXI-47, 1/4" shallow flake **325.00**

G.R.J.A., star and arm, seeing eye, attributed to Stoddard, brilliant amber, sheared lip, open pontil, McKearin GIV-43. **525.00**

Horse and Cart-Eagle, Coventry Glass Works, Coventry, CT, 1830-48, bright light yellow amber with olive tone, sheared mouth, pontil scar, pint, McKearin GV-9 . . . . **170.00**

Liberty Eagle, Willington Glass Co., West Willington, CT, medium green, applied top, smooth base, heavily emb, McKearin GII-62 . . . . **310.00**

Lowell/Railroad-Eagle, Coventry Glass Works, Coventry, CT, 1830-48

Olive, half-pint, America, mid-19th C, McKearin GV-10. . . . . **160.00**

Olive amber, half-pint, America, mid-19th C, McKearin GV-10 . . . . **170.00**

Yellow amber with olive tone, sheared mouth, pontil scar, half pint, McKearin GV-10, some minor ext. highlight wear, lettered emb weak. **170.00**

Masonic-Eagle, Keene Marlboro Street Glassworks, Keene, NH, 1815-30

Deep bluish aquamarine, shared mouth, pontil scar, pint, McKearin GIV-27 . . . . **275.00**

Deep greenish aquamarine, wide tooled collared mouth, pontil scar, pint, McKearin GIV-5 . . . . . **850.00**

Light blue green, inward rolled mouth, pontil scar, half pint, McKearin GIV-28 . . . . **300.00**

Light yellow amber with olive tone, sheared mouth, pontil scar, half pint, McKearin GIV-24 . . . . **160.00**

Olive amber, pint, McKearin GIV-17 . . . . **175.00**

Olive amber, sheared mouth, pontil scar, pint, McKearin GIV-71 **150.00**

Pale bluish-green, tooled collared mouth, pontil scar, pint, McKearin GIV-7a **950.00**

Masonic-Eagle, White Glass Works, Zanesville, OH, 1820-30

Brilliant aquamarine, inward rolled mouth, pontil scar, pint, McKearin GIV-16 . . . . **3,000.00**

Light blue green, sheared mouth, pontil scar, pint, McKearin GIV-32 . . . . **325.00**

Light yellow amber, sheared mouth, pontil scar, pint, McKearin GIV-32, shallow bubble burst on left column of Masonic emblem **500.00**

Masonic-NEG Eagle, attributed to New England Glass Bottle Co., Cambridge, MA, 1820-30, deep greenish aquamarine, sheared mouth, ground pontil, half pint, McKearin GIV-26 . . . . **1,200.00**

Pike's Peak, America, mid-19th C, aqua

Half pint, McKearin, GXI-10 . .**110.00**

Half pint, McKearin, GXI-18 . **100.00**

Pint, McKearin GXI-9. . . . . . . **100.00**

Quart, McKearin GXI-22 . . . . **115.00**

Railroad-Eagle, two-toned golden to red amber, McKearin GV-7a, some minor high point wear. **250.00**

Seeing Eye Masonic, attributed to Stoddard glasshouse, Stoddard, NH, 1846-60, olive amber, sheared mouth, pontil scar, pint, McKearin GIV-43, moderate ext. highpoint wear . . **150.00**

Success to the Railroad, Coventry Glass Works, Coventry, CT, 1830-48

Brilliant light yellowish olive, sheared mouth, pontil scar, pint, McKearin GV-8, pinhead sized flake on side of mouth **325.00**

Yellow amber with olive tone, sheared mouth, pontil scar, pint, McKearin GV-8, narrow 1/2" area on top of mouth ground . . . **160.00**

Success to the Railroad, Keene Marlboro Street Glassworks, Keene, NH, 1830-50

Brilliant yellow amber with olive tone, sheared mouth, pontil scar, pint, McKearin GV-3, sandgrain on medial rib **160.00**

Light yellow amber with olive tone, sheared mouth, pontil scar, pint, McKearin GV-3 . . . . **250.00**

Olive amber, pint, McKearin GV-3 . . . . **300.00**

Success to the Railroad, Lancaster Glass Works, Lancaster, NY, 1849-60

Aquamarine, sheared mouth, tubular pontil scar, pint, McKearin GV-1a, 3/8" brush on inside of mouth, other minor mouth roughness . . . **200.00**

Golden amber, pint, sheared mouth-pontil scar, McKearin GV-1 . . . . **4,320.00**

Success to the Railroad, Mount Vernon Glass Works, Vernon, NY, 1830-44

Deep yellow olive, sheared mouth, pontil scar, pint, McKearin GV-5 . . . . **160.00**

Forest green, sheared mouth, pontil scar, pint, McKearin GV-5, pinhead sized flake on medial rib. . . **375.00**

Union, clasp hands

Amber, half pint, Eastern U.S., 19th C, McKearin GXII-17. . . . . . **145.00**

Aqua, pint, Eastern U.S., 19th C, McKearin GXII-29 . . . . **135.00**

Light to medium amber, half pint, emb eagle on reverse, applied top, smooth base, McKearin GXII-33, partial cork inside **200.00**

Pale green, pint, Eastern U.S., 19th C, McKearin GXII-38 ..... **135.00**
Pale green, pint, Eastern U.S., 19th C, McKearin GIV-40 ...... **145.00**

Union, Old Rye, clasped hands, eagle on reverse, light blue, pint, applied band, smooth base, McKearin GXII-25 .... **110.00**

Pattern molded

4-5/8" l, Midwest, 1800-30, 24 ribs swirled to the right, golden amber, sheared mouth, pontil scar **190.00**

7-3/8" l, Emil Larson, NJ, c1930, swirled to the right, amethyst, sheared mouth, pontil scar, some exterior highpoint wear...................... **250.00**

6-1/2" h, Midwestern, Broken Swirl (Diamond), green aqua, sheared lip, pontil, 20 ribs, under-blown, strong pattern.................... **880.00**

Pictorial, Sailor-Banjo Player, Maryland Glass Works, Baltimore, MD, 1840-60, aquamarine, inward rolled mouth, pontil scar, half pint, McKearin GXIII-8, **$180.** *Photo courtesy of Norman C. Heckler and Co.*

Pictorial

Baltimore/Glass Works and anchor-Resurgam Eagle, Baltimore Glass Works, Baltimore, MD, 1860-70, variegated yellow amber, applied collared mouth, smooth base, pint, McKearin GXIII-54, two 1/4" shallow flakes at side of base **475.00**

Bridgetown, NJ, sailboat and star, aqua, half pint, sheared lip, tubular type pontil, McKearin GX-8, some scratches, roughness at top **160.00**

Cornucopia, New England, 19th C
Amber, half-pint, McKearin GIII-II **100.00**
Amber, pint, McKearin GIII-6 **100.00**
Olive, half-pint, McKearin GIII-II **100.00**
Olive, pint, McKearin GIII-6 . **100.00**

Cornucopia-Large Medallion, Midwest America, 1820-40, very pale blue green, sheared mouth, pontil scar, half pint, McKearin GIII-1 .... **3,000.00**

Cornucopia-Urn
Attributed to Coventry Glass Works, Coventry, CT, 1830-48, bright green, sheared mouth, pontil scar, pint, McKearin GIII-4, small flake appears to have been ground **230.00**
Attributed to Lancaster, NY, emerald green, pint, sheared lip, tubular pontil extending to edge of base, McKearin GIII-17......... **660.00**
Attributed to New England, 1830-50, yellow olive, sheared mouth, pontil scar, half pint, McKearin GIII-2, small chip **130.00**
Urn of fruits, attributed to Coventry Glass Works, Coventry, CT, 1830-48, olive amber, pint, McKearin GIII-4, lip chip, 6-3/4" h **85.00**

Cornucopia-Urn, Lancaster Glass Works, NY, 1849-60, blue green, applied sloping collared mouth, pontil scar, pint, McKearin GIII-17, some minor stain **350.00**

Fisherman Hunter, light green aqua, calabash, applied top, pontil, America, mid-19th C, McKearin GXIII-6, few minor scratches **155.00**

Flora Temple/Horse, Whitney Glass Works, Glassboro, NJ, 1860-80, cherry puce, applied collared mouth with ring, smooth base, pint, handle, McKearin GXIII-21 .... **170.00**

Hunter
Amber, quart, calabash, America, mid-19th C, McKearin GXIII-4, imperfections **90.00**
Aqua, quart, calabash, America, mid-19th C, McKearin GXIII-4, imperfections **90.00**

Hunter Fisher, wine color, calabash, iron pontil, graphite still intact, McKearin GXIII-4 .... **880.00**

Isabella/Glass Works and Anchor-Factory, Isabella Glass Works, Brooklyn, NJ, 1850-60, aquamarine, sheared mouth, pontil scar, qt, McKearin GXIII-55, 3/4" open bubble burst to right of factory........ **210.00**

Log Cabin, Spring Garden Glassworks, Baltimore, light aqua, pint, applied band, smooth base, McKearin GXIII-58, slight wear on cabin.......... **150.00**

Monument-Sloop, Baltimore Glass Works, Baltimore, MD, 1840-60, medium variegated yellow green, sheared mouth, pontil scar, half pint, McKearin GVI-2, some exterior highpoint wear, overall dullness **1,100.00**

Sailor-Banjo Player, Maryland Glass Works, Baltimore, MD, 1840-60, aquamarine, inward rolled mouth, pontil scar, half pint, McKearin GXIII-8 **180.00**

Sheaf of Wheat-crossed farm tools, Westford Glass Co., Westford, CT, reddish-amber, applied top, smooth base, McKearin GXIII-35...... **260.00**

Sheaf of Wheat-Star, attributed to Bulltown Glass Works, Bulltown, NJ, 1858-60, bright medium green, applied double collared mouth, pontil scar, pint, McKearin GIII-39............ **750.00**

Sheaf of Wheat-Westford Glass Co., Westford Glass Works, Westford, CT, 1860-73
Golden amber, reddish tone, applied double-collared mouth, smooth base, pint, McKearin GXIII-35 .... **120.00**
Reddish amber, applied double-collared mouth, smooth base, pint, McKearin GXIII-35 .... **140.00**
Yellow olive, applied double-collared mouth, smooth base, pint, McKearin GXIII-36 .... **120.00**
Yellow olive, applied double-collared mouth, smooth base, pint, McKearin GXIII-37 .... **120.00**

Sloop and Star, half pint, flattened staved barrel form, aqua, America, late 19th C **90.00**

Summer Tree, Winter Tree, aqua, quart, America, mid-19th C, McKearin GX-16, imperfections............... **120.00**

Summer-Winter
Attributed to Baltimore Glass works, Baltimore, MD, 1860-70, citron with olive tone, applied double collared mouth, smooth base, pint, McKearin GX-15......... **900.00**
Light blue-aqua, applied top, pontil, calabash, double roll collar, McKearin GXIV-46 .... **155.00**

Pitkin type

Midwest, 1800-30
4" h, ribbed and swirled to the right, 26 ribs, brilliant golden amber, outward rolled mouth, pontil scar, some ext. high point war, some minor int. stain, 1/4" shallow chip near base............. **1,200.00**

Pitkin, ribbed and swirled to the right, 16 ribs, Midwest, 1800-1830, olive green with a yellow tone, sheared mouth, pontil scar, 6-1/4" h, some interior stain, **$350.** *Photo courtesy of Norman C. Heckler and Co.*

6-1/4" l, ribbed and swirled to the right, 16 ribs, olive green with yellow tone, sheared mouth, pontil scar, some int. stain. **300.00**

New England, 1783-1830

5" h, 36 ribs swirled to the right, yellow olive, sheared mouth, pontil scar **400.00**

5-1/4" h, 36 swirled ribs, olive green, sheared mouth, half post neck, pontil scar **255.00**

5-1/4" l, ribbed and swirled to the left, 36 ribs, light olive yellow, sheared mouth, pontil scar . **375.00**

6" l, ribbed and swirled to the right, distinct popcorn pattern, 36 ribs, yellow-olive, sheared mouth, pontil scar, 1/4" fissure **220.00**

6-1/2" h, 31 ribs, broken swirl, olive green, sheared mouth, half post neck, pontil scar **315.00**

6-7/8" h, 36 ribs, ribbed and swirled to left, light yellow amber, sheared mouth, pontil scar **500.00**

Portrait

Adams-Jefferson, New England, 1830-50, yellow amber, sheared mouth, pontil scar, half pint, McKearin GI-114 . . . . **325.00**

Father of His Country, Washington, plain reverse, medium to light emerald green, pint, applied sq collar, shaped base, pontil, McKearin GI-48 . **2,640.00**

General Jackson, Pittsburgh district, 1820-40, bluish-aquamarine, sheared mouth, pontil scar, pint, McKearin GI-68 . . . . **1,500.00**

Gen. Taylor, Baltimore Glass Works, Baltimore, MD, 1830-50, pint, medium amethyst, sheared mouth-pontil scar, McKearin GI-73 . . . . **16,100.00**

Gen. Taylor, portrait and Fell's Point Balto, monument on reverse, pale amethyst, sheared lip, open pontil, McKearin GI-73 . . . . **825.00**

Lafayette-DeWitt Clinton, Coventry Glass Works, Coventry, CT, 1824-25, yellowish-olive, sheared mouth, pontil scar, half pint, 1/2" vertical crack, weakened impression, McKearin GI-82 . . . . **2,100.00**

Lafayette-Masonic, Coventry Glass Works, Coventry, CT, 1824-45, yellowish-olive, sheared mouth, pontil scar, half pint, McKearin Gi-84, some minor exterior highpoint wear . **1,700.00**

Rough and Ready Taylor-Eagle, Midwest, 1830-40, aquamarine, sheared mouth, pontil scar, pint, McKearin GI-77 . . . . **1,200.00**

Washington-Albany Glass Works/NY, Albany Glass Works, Albany, NY, 1847-50, greenish-aquamarine, sheared mouth, pontil scar, half pint, McKearin GI-30 . . . . **2,200.00**

Washington/Captain Bragg, aqua, quart, America, mid-19th C, McKearin GI-42 imperfections. **190.00**

Washington-Eagle, Kensington Glass Works, Philadelphia, PA, 1820-38, bright aquamarine, sheared mouth, pontil scar, pint, McKearin GI-14 . . . . **375.00**

Washington, Lockport Glass Works, Lockport, NY, 1845-60, quart, medium green, double-collared mouth-iron pontil mark, McKearin GI-60 . . **4,025.00**

Washington-Monument, Baltimore Glass Works, Baltimore, MD, 1830-50, jade green, sheared mouth, pontil scar, pint, McKearin GI-20, ext. high point wear. **2,400.00**

Washington-Sheaf of Wheat, Dyottville Glass Works, Philadelphia, PA 1840-60, medium yellow-olive, inward rolled mouth, pontil scar, half pint, McKearin GI-59 . . . . **9,000.00**

Washington-Taylor, Dyottville Glass Works, Philadelphia, PA, 1840-60

Bright bluish-green, applied double collared mouth, pontil scar, quart, McKearin GI-42 . . . . **400.00**

Brilliant olive yellow, sheared mouth, pontil scar, pint, McKearin GI-38 . . . . **900.00**

Washington-Taylor, Dyottville Glass Works, Philadelphia, PA, 1840-80

Medium green, double collared mouth-pontil scar, quart, McKearin GI-39 . . . . **300.00**

Sapphire blue, sheared mouth-pontil scar, pint, McKearin GI-40a, minor edge roughness **4,890.00**

Scroll

America, 1845-60

Brilliant golden amber, applied collared mouth, iron pontil mark, pint, McKearin GIX-10. . . . . **425.00**

Brilliant golden amber, sheared mouth, pontil scar, pint, McKearin GIX-14, 3/8" potstone crack near medial rib **140.00**

Cornflower blue, sheared mouth, pontil scar, pint, McKearin GIX-10 1-4" flake on int. of mouth . . **190.00**

Medium lime green, sheared mouth, iron pontil mark, McKearin GIX-11, 1/4" flat flake on top of mouth **325.00**

Miniature, cobalt blue, inward rolled mouth, pontil scar, 2-5/8" h, approx. 1 oz, McKearin GIX-40, extremely rare, deep color **5,000.00**

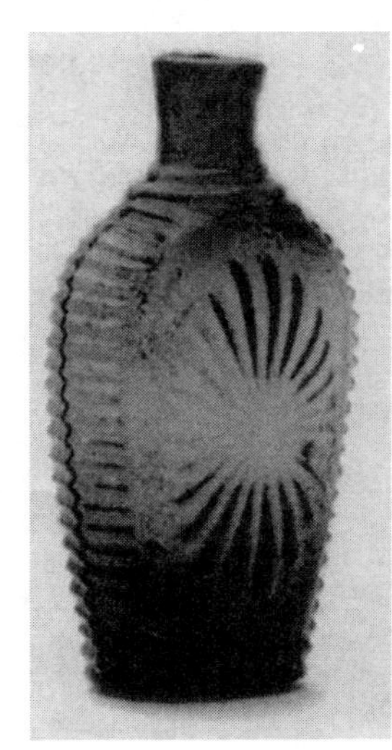

Sunburst, Coventry Glass Works, Coventry, CT, 1814-30, variated brilliant yellowish green with olive tone, sheared mouth, pontil scar, half pint, McKearin GVIII-18, **$850.** *Photo courtesy of Norman C. Heckler and Co.*

Sunburst

Baltimore Glass Works, Baltimore, MD, 1820-30, attributed to

Colorless, light gray hue, sheared and tooled mouth, pontil scar, pint, McKearin GVIII-26, some light overall int. haze. **375.00**

Copper amber, sheared and tooled mouth, pontil scar, pint, McKearin GVIII-20 . . . . **1,900.00**
Deep yellow olive, sheared and tooled mouth, pontil scar, pint, McKearin GVIII-26 . . . . . . **2,750.00**
Olive green, sheared and tooled mouth, pontil scar, half pint, McKearin GVIII-27 . . . . . . **3,000.00**

Coventry Glass Works, Coventry, CT, 1814-30
Brilliant light olive yellow, sheared mouth, pontil scar, pint, McKearin GVIII-3 . . . . **450.00**
Brilliant light yellowish olive, sheared mouth, pontil scar, half pint, McKearin GVIII-16 . . . . **500.00**
Brilliant medium yellowish olive, sheared mouth, pontil scar, McKearin GVIII-3, some highpoint wear **325.00**
Variegated brilliant yellowish amber with olive tone, sheared mouth, pontil scar, half pint, McKearin GVIII-18 . . . . **850.00**

Keene Marlboro Street Glassworks, Keene, NY, 1815-30
Brilliant yellow amber with olive tone, sheared mouth, pontil scar, half pint, McKearin GVIII-8, 3/4" faint fissure in one of rays **200.00**
Pale yellowish amber, sheared mouth, pontil scar, pint, McKearin GVIII-2, some ext. highpoint wear **350.00**
Yellow olive, "P & W," sheared mouth, pontil scar, half pint, McKearin GVIII-10 . . . . **350.00**
Yellow olive, sheared mouth, pontil scar, pint, McKearin GVIII-8, some ext. highpoint wear **325.00**

New England, 1820-30, attributed to, blue green, inward rolled mouth, pontil scar, half pint, McKearin GVIII-29 . . . . **190.00**

Fostoria Glass

History: Fostoria Glass Co. began operations at Fostoria, Ohio, in 1887, and moved to Moundsville, West Virginia, its present location, in 1891. By 1925, Fostoria had five furnaces and a variety of special shops. In 1924, a line of colored tableware was introduced. Fostoria was purchased by Lancaster Colony in 1983 and continues to operate under the Fostoria name.

Fostoria is known for tableware and stemware of high quality. These fine wares included clear, colored, etched, gilded, lustered, and pressed items. Fostoria reacted to the market and the times by actively competing with its contemporaries, such as Cambridge, Heisey, and Westmoreland. Some of the Fostoria patterns and colors were designed to directly compete with these companies. Careful study of its patterns will show the similarities in design and color. Fostoria's Azure blue compare to Cambridge's blue. Etched patterns such as June or Navarre compare to Cambridge's Rose Point and Heisey's Orchid pattern.

Fostoria produced patterns in a wide range of items, allowing a bride to set her table with everything from ashtrays to vases. Plates of every size and use complemented the stemware. She could use a different piece of stemware to serve grapefruit, oysters, parfait, sherbets, as well as water and wine.

One of the most popular patterns ever produced by Fostoria is American. Its production began in 1915 and continued until the merge with Lancaster Glass. Most production was in clear glass, although some color pieces were made. This pattern was very popular with World War II brides and made in many forms. More than 50 different sizes of bowls were made for use as serving pieces.

References: Tom and Neila Bredehoft, *Fifty Years of Collectible Glass, 1920-1970*, Volume 1, Volume II, Antique Trader Books, 2000; Gene Florence, *Elegant Glassware of the Depression Era*, 9th Edition, Collector Books, 2000; Ann Kerr, *Fostoria: An Identification and Value Guide of Pressed, Blown, & Hand Molded Shapes* (1994, 1997 values), *Etched, Carved & Cut Designs* (1996, 1997 values) Collector Books; Milbra Long and Emily Seate, *Fostoria Stemware*, Collector Books, 1995; Leslie Piña, *Fostoria Designer George Sakier*, Schiffer Publishing, 1996; —, *Fostoria*, Schiffer Publishing, 1995; JoAnn Schleismann, *Price Guide to Fostoria*, 3rd ed., Park Avenue Publications, n.d.

Collectors' Clubs: Fostoria Glass Assoc., 109 N. Main St., Fostoria, OH 44830; Fostoria Glass Collectors, P.O. Box 1625, Orange, CA 92668, http://www.fostoriacollectors.org; Fostoria Glass Society of America, P.O. Box 826, Moundsville, WV 26041, http://www.fostoriaglass.org.

Museums: Fostoria Glass Museum, Moundsville, WV; Huntington Galleries, Huntington, WV.

Note: Prices listed are for crystal (colorless), unless otherwise noted.

Animal

Chanticleer, 10-3/4" h **225.00**
Colt, laying **45.00**
Colt, standing, 3-7/8" h **50.00**
Deer, standing **45.00**
Duckling, frosted amber, head back **35.00**
Duck, Mama, frosted amber . . **35.00**
Flying fish, ruby **55.00**
Pelican **65.00**
Polar bear **75.00**
Seal **85.00**

Bookend

Eagle **125.00**
Owl **250.00**
Seahorse **200.00**

Bookends, pr, Lyre **100.00**

Figure

Lotus, Silver Mist **250.00**
Lute, black **350.00**
Lute, Silver Mist **250.00**

Madonna, #2635

Crystal **55.00**
Frosted, thin, 4" **30.00**
Silver Mist **55.00**

Window Box, #2373, with frog
Ebony, small **85.00**
Green, large **75.00**
Rose, small **90.00**

Miscellaneous patterns and etchings

After Dinner cup and saucer

Blank #5098, Fern etching, crystal **45.00**
Queen Anne **45.00**

Almond, Grape Leaf

Regal Blue **55.00**
White milk glass **35.00**

Bottle, stopper, Crown, #2749 Windsor, gold **150.00**

Bowl

#2315, Paradise, ftd, rolled edge, orchid **85.00**
#2324, green, 10" d **60.00**
#2530, Coronet, handle, 11" d **60.00**
#2536, Daisy etch, handle, c1935-43, 9" d **125.00**
#2545, Flame, oval, 12-1/2" l, oval **45.00**
Oriental, blown, 8-1/4" d, 3-1/4" h **295.00**

Brandy, #6012, 2 oz **22.00**

Candleholders, pr

#2297, turquoise, 7" h **42.50**
#2395-1/2, black **50.00**
#2447, topaz **75.00**
#2447, wisteria **200.00**
#2470-1/2, wisteria **300.00**
#2472, Fuchsia, etch #310, duo **100.00**
#2496, Shirley, 5-1/2" h **125.00**
#2545 . . . . **75.00**
#2630, Milkweed **36.00**
#2666, Flora, wheat cutting . . **30.00**

Candlestick, Rebecca at the Well
Crystal satin **125.00**
Marsh Green **225.00**

Candlesticks, pr, duo, designed by George Sakier **65.00**

Candy dish, cov

Crown, #2749 Windsor, royal blue **95.00**
Crown, #2750 Hapsburg
Gold **95.00**
Royal blue **95.00**
Topaz yellow **65.00**

Candy dish, open, green, designed by George Sakier **30.00**

Ad, new goblet designs for 1933, Crockery and Glass Journal, *March 1933.*

Cake plate
Fern, ebony, gold trim, two handles, 10" d **85.00**
Italian Lace, #514 dec **30.00**
Centerpiece bowl, Grape, #2371, oval, two-pc flower holder, orchid . . . **255.00**
Chalice, cov, Crown
#2749 Windsor, gold, 9-1/2" h **125.00**
#2750 Hapsburg, gold **125.00**
#2750 Hapsburg, ruby **135.00**
Champagne
Blank
#890, burgundy **75.00**
#5097, orchid **42.00**
#5098, azure blue **40.00**
#5098, rose **40.00**
#5098, wisteria **95.00**
#5099, wisteria **95.00**
#6003, green **30.00**
#6003, wisteria **85.00**
#6008, crystal, dimple optic **40.00**
Cellini **30.00**
Chapel Bell, #6080 . . . . **10.00**
Christiana, #6030, 5-1/2" h . . . **10.00**
Distinction, red **14.00**
Fern, #5298, pink **55.00**
Fuchsia, #6004, crystal and wisteria **45.00**
Heraldry, #6012 . . . . **10.00**
Laurel, crystal **35.00**
Oriental **20.00**
Precedence, #6108, onyx bowl **38.00**
Shirley **32.00**
Shooting Stars **30.00**
Simplicity, gold band **35.00**
Westchester, empire green . . . **65.00**
Westchester, ruby **65.00**
Whirlpool **25.00**
Champagne set, Spiral Optic, crystal body, green stem **85.00**
Cigarette box, cov, Oriental . . . **225.00**
Claret
Blank #5097, orchid **65.00**
Blank #5098, rose **65.00**
Precedence, black and crystal **50.00**
Sampler, 4" h **25.00**
Simplicity, gold band **50.00**
Splendor, #6131, 7 oz, 5-1/2" h, blue **15.00**
Wilma, blue, blank #6016 . . . . **38.00**
Coaster, #2272 . . . . **6.00**
Cocktail
Cellini **30.00**
Heraldry, #6012 . . . . **9.00**
Laurel **15.00**
Simplicity, gold band **25.00**
Spiral Optic, crystal body, green stem **18.00**
#6008 . . . . **8.00**

Comport
#2327, turquoise, 7-1/2" **40.00**
#2362, Paradise, green, 11" . **175.00**
#2470, rose, 6" low **28.00**
#2470, topaz, 6" low **28.00**
#2496, Shirley **65.00**
#2560, Coronet **35.00**
#2749/386, Windsor Crown, cobalt blue, 9" **95.00**
#2749/386, Windsor Crown, gold, 9" **60.00**
#5099, azure blue, 6" **135.00**
Rebecca at the Well, satin avocado green, marked "HFM" for Henry Ford Museum, c1960, 10-1/2" d, 12-3/4" h, small nick on outer rim **295.00**
Console bowl
#2297, "C" rolled edge, turquoise, 10-1/2" d **55.00**
#2496, Italian Lace **55.00**
Console set, green, bowl, pair #2324 candlesticks, silver overlay design, designed by George Sakier **295.00**
Cordial
Heraldry, #6012 . . . . **28.00**
Loop Optic, #5097, mother of pearl, amber stem, 3-1/2" h **35.00**
Precedence, black and crystal **70.00**
Simplicity, gold band **45.00**
Westchester, #6012, ruby **60.00**
Creamer and sugar
Coronet, table size **25.00**
Shirley, tea size **75.00**
Skyflower, table size **45.00**
Wistar, table size **48.00**
#4020 Line, crystal bowl and handles, wisteria base **75.00**
Cruet, orig stopper, Glacier **45.00**
Cup and saucer
Coronet **19.75**
Florentine **25.00**
Shirley **35.00**
Decanter, #4020, ftd, orig stopper, crystal, green foot **125.00**
Goblet
Announcement, #6103/666, 7-1/4" **12.00**
Arcady etch **42.00**
Betsy Ross, milk glass **18.00**
Cellini **30.00**
Comet, #4020, 11 oz **22.00**
Diadem, #6202
Crystal bowl, green stem . . **35.00**
Topaz bowl, crystal stem . . **35.00**
Eloquence, #6120, white bowl, onyx base **55.00**
Fuchsia, #6004, crystal and wisteria **65.00**
Grand Majesty, etched blue bowl
9 oz **30.00**
13 oz **35.00**
Heraldry, #6012 . . . . **18.00**
Laurel **35.00**
Lotus, 11 oz, crystal, mist base **21.00**
Lovelight, #6107/671, 8-1/4" . . **20.00**
Needlepoint, #64, 12 oz, amber **22.00**
Oriental **27.50**
Pine, 5-7/8" h **20.00**
Precedence, black and crystal **45.00**
Rhapsody, #6055, 6-1/8" h . . . **12.00**
Sampler, 10 oz, 5-1/2" h **25.00**
Simplicity, gold band **45.00**
Spiral Optic, 7-1/2" h, #5093, crystal body, green stem, set of six **150.00**
Trellis, crystal **30.00**
Triumph, #6112, 10 oz, gold . . **15.00**
Westchester
Burgundy **75.00**
Regal blue **75.00**
Ruby **75.00**
Whirlpool **30.00**
#5099, wisteria **65.00**
#6008 . . . . **12.00**
Grapefruit, Royal, amber **45.00**
Grapefruit and liner, Oriental . . . **65.00**
Iced tea tumbler
Blank
#4020, ebony base **42.00**
#5000, green **32.00**
#5099, wisteria **115.00**
#6003, wisteria **95.00**
Fuchsia, #6004, crystal and wisteria **55.00**
Laurel **35.00**
Sceptre, azure blue **38.00**
Simplicity, gold band **45.00**
Tradition, red **22.00**
Trellis **30.00**
Jelly, cov, Garland, crystal **95.00**
Jug
Daisy, #5000 . . . . **350.00**
Milkweed, three pint **125.00**
Oriental, #303 . . . . **595.00**
Shirley, #6011 . . . . **425.00**
Woodland **95.00**
Juice tumbler, ftd
Blank
#5098, wisteria **65.00**
#5099, wisteria **55.00**
#6008, crystal **10.00**
Christiana, #6030 . . . . **11.00**
Comet, #4120, crystal, ebony foot **24.00**
Fern, #4120, crystal, ebony foot **24.00**
Laurel, 4-3/4" h **35.00**
Sceptre, topaz **30.00**

Stardust, 4-5/8" h 15.50
Trellis 25.00
Wistar/Betsy Ross, #2620, 3-3/4" 12.00

Mayonnaise and ladle, Coronet, crystal 38.00

Mayonnaise and underplate
Shirley 125.00
Wistar 55.00

Mint tray, Seascape, Pink Opalescent, 7-1/2" l 30.00

Nappy, handle
Flared, Shirley 45.00
Wistar 22.00

Nut cup, Grape Leaf, milk white, individual size 10.00

Old fashioned, Whirlpool 20.00

Oyster cocktail
Cellini 25.00
Florentine, 3-1/2" 15.00
Fuchsia, #6004, crystal and wisteria 40.00
Sceptre 20.00
Trellis 25.00
Whirlpool 20.00

Pansy vase, Coronet 40.00

Parfait
Blank#5098, Fern etching 45.00
#5099, azure blue 75.00
Oriental 28.00
Spinet 10.00

Pitcher
#2666/807, 10" h, lilac 20.00
#5000, Daisy 295.00
#5000, Minuet Green 350.00

Place card holders, #2538/543, Azure Blue, set of eight 165.00

Plate
Oriental, 8-1/2" d 15.00
Simplicity, 6" d, gold band 25.00
Trellis, 7-1/2" d 20.00
Wistar/Betsy Ross, 7" d, #2620 10.00

Relish
#2419, four parts, Daisy etch . 55.00
#2470, five parts, 12" l, topaz . 45.00
#2496, Shirley, three parts, 10" l 75.00
Silver Spruce, three parts, 10" l 35.00

Salad dressing bottle, Oriental . 165.00

Salad set, Thistle, 12" bowl, 13-1/2" d plate 95.00

Sauce dish, #2496, Italian Lace, oval 28.00

Saucer
Arcady 10.00
Florentine, crystal 3.00
Minuet, green 5.00

Seafood cocktail
Empire Green 35.00
Silver Mist 25.00

Server, center handle, Morning Glory cutting 45.00

Sherbet
Argus, ruby 16.00
Betsy Ross, milk glass, 4" h . . 12.50
Blank#4020, ebony base 38.00
#5098, topaz 30.00
#5098, wisteria 55.00
#5099, wisteria 45.00
Lovelight, #6107/671, 9 oz . . . 10.00
Oriental, crystal 22.50
Pine, 4-3/8" 15.00
Spinet, #6033/821, 4" 15.00
Spray, #6055/841, 4-1/2" 10.00
Westchester, #6012, low, ruby 25.00
Wistar/Betsy Ross, 4-1/8", #2620 . . . . 12.00
Wisteria, 6-1/8" h, c1931-38 . . 55.00
Woodland, #2921
Brown 15.00
Crystal 12.00

Sugar bowl
Flemish 15.00
Fuchsia, etch #310 . . . . 24.00
Glacier 15.00

Tankard, #300, Oriental 375.00

Tidbit tray, Starflower, #2630, three-toed tray 32.00

Toothpick holder
Brazilian 55.00
Frisco 45.00

Torte plate, Coronet, 14" d 45.00

Tray, #2470, 8-3/4" l, pink 30.00

Tumbler
Blank
#5098, rose, 9 oz, ftd 32.00
#5099, topaz, 10 oz, ftd . . . 20.00
#5099, wisteria, 9 oz, ftd . . 65.00
Cellini, ftd 25.00
Congo, 5" h, pink 45.00
Florentine, 5-1/2", ftd 20.00
Laurel, 6" h, ftd 18.50
Oriental, #4911, 8 oz 20.00
Queen Anne Etch, #4020
Amber, 5-5/8" h, ftd 45.00
5" h, ftd 22.00

Vase
#01-713c, Images, lilac 150.00
#03-721c, Interpretations, lilac 150.00
#101, Images, 4" h, white cased 200.00
#2292, Royal Blue, 8" h, flared 175.00
#2292, Spiral Optic, 8" h, flared, amber 65.00
#2385, fan, azure blue 95.00
#2470, Regal blue, 9-1/2" h . 195.00
#2518, Empire Green 150.00
#2560, Coronet, handles 55.00
#4100, flip, loop optic, amber, 8" h 25.00
#4100, flip, loop optic, light green, 8" h 48.00
#4100, flip, seaweed dec, azure blue, 8" h 95.00
#4105, 9-3/4" h, Draped Optic 160.00
Images, rolled edge, lilac, orig pamphlet, 7" h 200.00
Sakier, designed by George Sakier
6" d, spherical, Art Deco, black opaque glass, unmarked 1,450.00
6-1/2" d, spherical, Art Deco, clear yellow, unmarked 1,250.00
8" h, bulbous, fluted, green 700.00
13" h, cylindrical, fluted, purple-blue 725.00

Whiskey
Blank 4020
Ebony base 28.00
Wisteria 55.00
Whirlpool 20.00

Wine
Argus, ruby 25.00
Blank
#877, empire green 65.00
#5097, rose 35.00
#6008 . . . . 12.00
Laurel 35.00
Oriental, 2-1/2 oz 25.00
Precedence, black and crystal, tulip shape 50.00
Simplicity, gold band 45.00
Westchester, ruby 85.00
Woodland, #2921
Brown 15.00
Crystal 12.00

Patterns

Acanthus

Plate Etching #282. Dinnerware pattern. Made 1930-1933. Made in amber, green, or amber with crystal base and green with crystal base.

After Dinner cup and saucer, amber 50.00

Bowl, amber, scroll design 70.00

Candlestick, amber 55.00

Cocktail, amber with crystal base 25.00

Goblet, green with crystal base . . 28.00

Jelly, amber 20.00

Lemon dish, amber 24.00

Plate, 8" d, green 20.00

Server, center handle, amber . . . 25.00

Sugar, cov, handle, green 185.00

Tumbler, ftd, 5-1/4" h 22.50

Alexis

Pattern #1630. Made 1909-1925 in crystal.

- **Celery vase**, tall 35.00
- **Creamer and sugar**, hotel, cutting 95.00
- **Decanter**, Kentucky Tavern, no stopper 75.00
- **Jug**, half gallon 195.00
- **Sweet pea vase** 35.00
- **Toothpick holder** 65.00
- **Vase**
  - 8" h 65.00
  - 9" h 45.00
- **Wine** 9.50

Argus

Pattern #2770. Giftware line. Made for Henry Ford Museum. Made 1960s-1985. Made in cobalt blue, crystal, gray (1972), olive green, and ruby.

- **Bowl**, 4-1/2" d, ruby 18.50
- **Candy**, cov, cobalt blue 125.00
- **Cocktail**, 2-7/8" h, crystal 10.00
- **Compote**, cov, 8", cobalt blue.... 40.00
- **Cream pitcher**, ruby 67.50
- **Creamer and sugar,** cov, cobalt blue 125.00
- **Dessert plate**, 8" d, olive green .. 9.00
- **Fruit bowl**
  - Cobalt blue 24.00
  - Ruby 35.00
- **Goblet**
  - Cobalt blue 25.00
  - Ruby 35.00
- **Iced tea tumbler**, ruby 38.00
- **Juice tumbler**
  - Cobalt blue 25.00
  - Ruby 32.00
- **Old fashioned tumbler**, ruby 30.00
- **Plate**
  - Cobalt blue 25.00
  - Ruby 55.00
- **Sherbet**
  - Cobalt blue 25.00
  - Ruby 28.00
- **Wine**
  - Cobalt blue 25.00
  - Ruby 35.00

American

Line #2056. Made 1915-1986. Made in some amber, blue, crystal, green, some pink shading to purple (late 1902s), red (1980s), white, and yellow. Dalzell Viking continues to make some forms. Prices for colors fluctuate greatly. Some pieces are made under the Whitehall label. Prices listed below are for crystal, unless otherwise noted.

- **Almond**
  - Individual size.... 28.00
  - Large, 4-1/2" l 40.00
- **Appetizer**, insert.... 37.50
- **Ashtray**
  - Large 100.00
  - Oval 25.00
  - Oval, with match stand 30.00
  - Square 6.00
- **Baby bowl**, flared 25.00
- **Basket**, reed handle, 4" x 9".... 125.00
- **Beer mug**.... 75.00
- **Bell**.... 650.00
- **Biscuit jar** 800.00
- **Bitters bottle**.... 50.00
- **Bonbon**, 6" d, ftd 16.00
- **Boudoir set,** oval ash tray with match stand, quart pitcher, 8-oz tumbler, Eiffel Tower candlestick, 10" tray.... 795.00
- **Bowl**
  - 4-1/2" d 14.50
  - 8" d, 5-1/8" h, ftd, deep 250.00
  - 8-1/2" d, two handles.... 60.00
  - 10" d, ground base 55.00
  - 11" d, rolled edge 42.50
  - 11" d, three corners.... 42.50
  - 11-3/4" d, oval, deep 45.00
- **Brick ice cream tray**.... 75.00
- **Bud vase, 6" h**
  - Crystal, cupped.... 32.00
  - Crystal, flared, ftd 32.00
  - Milk glass.... 45.00
  - Ruby 95.00
- **Bud vase, 8" h**
  - Crystal, flared 48.00
  - Milk glass, ftd, flared 75.00
- **Butter dish, cov**
  - Metal holder, label.... 140.00
  - Quarter pound.... 45.00
  - Round 125.00
- **Cake plate**
  - Crystal, 10" d, two handles 32.00
  - Crystal, 12" d, three toes 45.00
  - Ruby, handle 125.00
- **Cake salver/stand**
  - Round 185.00
  - Square.... 295.00
- **Candleholders, pr**
  - Two-lite, bell.... 175.00
  - Two-lite, flat 110.00
  - 3" 25.00
  - 3-1/2" h.... 55.00
  - 6" h, hexagon base 95.00
  - 7" h, columnar, sq 95.00
- **Candle lamp**, chimney and cup 175.00
- **Candy dish, cov**
  - Crystal, footed.... 65.00
  - Crystal, three parts 135.00
- **Candy dish**, ruby, ftd.... 145.00
- **Celery dish**, 10".... 38.00
- **Celery vase**, 6" h 70.00
- **Centerpiece bowl**, 9-1/2" d 42.50

American pattern, relish, three parts, 6" x 9", **$35**

- **Cheese and cracker** 95.00
- **Cheese comport** 25.00
- **Chip and dip**.... 190.00
- **Cigarette box**, cov 40.00
- **Claret** 75.00
- **Coaster**.... 10.00
- **Cocktail**, ftd, cone, 2-7/8" h 12.50
- **Cologne bottle**, stopper.... 145.00
- **Commemorative bowl**, ftd.... 490.00
- **Comport**, cov, 9" d, high standard 65.00
- **Condiment bottle**, stopper 125.00
- **Condiment set**
  - Cloverleaf tray 595.00
  - Oval tray.... 195.00
- **Console bowl**.... 35.00
- **Cookie jar**.... 325.00
- **Cordial decanter**, stopper 225.00
- **Cosmetic box, cov**
  - 1-1/2" 700.00
  - 2-1/2" 700.00
- **Creamer and sugar**
  - Hexagonal 1,800.00
  - Table size 35.00
  - Tea size.... 47.50
- **Creamer and sugar, matching tray**
  - Green 165.00
  - Table size 48.50
  - Tea size.... 50.00
- **Cruet**, orig stopper, 5 oz.... 65.00
- **Cup and saucer**.... 22.50
- **Decanter, stopper**
  - Gin, rye, or scotch 180.00
  - In metal holder 295.00
- **Dinner plate**, 9-1/2" d.... 45.00
- **Finger bowl** 90.00
- **Floating garden bowl**
  - 10" d 80.00
  - 11" d 110.00
- **Fruit Bowl**, 16" h.... 120.00
- **Goblet, water**
  - Hexagon foot, 7" h 22.00
  - Low, 9 oz 12.50
- **Hat**
  - 2-1/2" h, milk glass 75.00

3", crystal 25.00
3", milk glass 75.00
4", crystal 50.00
4", milk glass 95.00
Honey jar, cov, orig spoon. 400.00
Hurricane lamp and chimney . 450.00
Ice bucket, metal handle 70.00
Ice cream bowl 58.00
Ice cream platter 300.00
Iced tea tumbler
Flat, flared 28.00
Footed, 20 oz. 25.00
Icer bowl 75.00
Icer insert 75.00
Ice tub
5-1/2", cov, underplate. 145.00
6-1/2" 60.00
Jam pot set 185.00
Jelly compote, cov 55.00
Jewel box, cov. 500.00
Jug, three pints, ice lip. 60.00
Juice tumbler
Flat 22.00
Footed 20.00
Ketchup bottle, stopper 145.00
Lemon dish, cov 30.00
Luncheon tumbler, ftd 12.00
Marmalade, cov, orig spoon . . . 145.00
Mayonnaise, two pcs, ground base
. . . . 55.00
Muffin tray, handle, ruby 125.00
Mustard, cov 80.00
Napkin ring 35.00
Nappy, handle
Crystal
5" d, tricorn 22.00
8" x 4-3/4", deep 125.00
9-1/2" x 3", flared 125.00
Ruby, three toes. 55.00
Old fashioned tumbler 10.00
Olive dish, 6" l 14.00
Oyster cocktail 3-1/4", ftd 18.00
Pastry stand 500.00
Party set 54.00
Perfume bottle, round, replaced stopper 675.00
Pickle dish, 8" 28.00
Picture frame, oval 35.00
Pin tray
Jenny Lind, milk glass 50.00
Oval 400.00
Rectangular, 5" l. 125.00
Pitcher
Half gallon
Regular, 8" h 95.00
Straight, ice lip 135.00
Pint, 5-3/8" h. 48.00
Three pints, ice lip 95.00

Platter
10-1/2" l, oval 48.00
12" l. 65.00
Pomade set 875.00
Preserve, cov 135.00
Puff box, cov
Amber. 470.00
Crystal 495.00
Punch bowl set, 14" bowl with high foot, 12 cups 850.00
Punch bowl base, low 95.00
Punch cup, flared
Ear handle 18.00
Flared, round handle, 8 oz . . . 18.00
Relish
Three parts, 6" x 9" 35.00
Three parts, 9-1/2" l 40.00
Four parts, 6-1/2" x 9". 85.00
Four parts, 11" l, sq 225.00
Relish boat
8-1/2" l. 24.00
12" l. 35.00
12" l, two parts 60.00
Ring tree. 750.00
Rose bowl
3-1/2" d 40.00
5-1/2" d 40.00
Salad plate
Crescent 110.00
Round, 7" d. 18.00
8-1/2" d 32.00
Salt dip, orig spoon 20.00
Salt and pepper shakers, pr
Chrome tops. 38.00
Glass tops. 75.00
Nickel tops 65.00
Tray, chrome tops 68.00
Tray, glass tops. 145.00
Sandwich plate, 11" d 35.00
Sandwich tray, center handle . . 48.00
Sauce boat 40.00
Saucer. 3.00
Serving plate, center handle . . . 35.00
Sherbet
Flared 15.00
Hexagon foot 15.00
High, 4-1/2" h 15.00
Low, round base, 5 oz, 3-1/2" h
. . . . 15.00
Shrimp and dip 595.00
Soap dish 3,100.00
Straw jar, cov 185.00
Sugar bowl, cov
Table size, handle. 24.00
Tea size. 8.50
Sugar cube holder. 335.00
Sugar shaker 75.00
Sundae, 6 oz, 3-1/8" h. 18.00
Sweet pea vase 85.00

Syrup
Bakelite handle 175.00
Glass lid, underplate, three pcs
. . . . 425.00
Tom and Jerry mug 42.00
Tom and Jerry punch bowl . . . 250.00
Tomato juice tumbler, ftd 10.00
Toothpick holder 35.00
Torte plate
13-1/2" l, oval. 95.00
14" d 65.00
20" d 160.00
Tray
Oval
6-1/2" l. 42.00
10-1/2" l, handles 75.00
Rect
6-3/4" l. 35.00
10-1/2" l. 125.00
14-1/8" l, cobalt blue, five parts
. . . . 200.00
Trifle bowl, 8" d 250.00
Trophy bowl, 8-1/2", handles . . 130.00
Tumbler
3 oz, ftd 17.00
5 oz, 3-5/8" h, flat. 12.00
8 oz, flat. 18.00
Utility tray
Crystal, 9" l. 65.00
Ruby 125.00
Vase
6" h, flared 50.00
6" h, straight sides. 30.00
7-1/2" h, square foot, flared . . . 68.00
8" h, straight. 68.00
9" h, sq, ftd 37.50
9-1/2" h, flared, swung. 295.00
10" h, flared, ftd 90.00
10" h, sq, ftd, crystal 90.00
10" h, sq, ftd, milk glass 150.00
10" h, straight sides. 90.00
11" h, swung 175.00
12"h, straight sided 155.00
16" h, swung 345.00
19" h, swung 375.00
Vegetable bowl
7" d, round 45.00
9" l, oval, divided 38.00
Wash bowl, 19" d, flared 500.00
Watercress set 110.00
Wedding bowl
Crystal, cov 195.00
Milk glass. 225.00
Whiskey, 2-1/2" 22.00
Wine. 25.00
Wine decanter, stopper. 85.00
Youth plate 60.00
Youth set, plate, mug, and bowl 165.00

American Lady

Line #5056. Made 1933-73. Made in crystal, and crystal with amber, burgundy, emerald green or Regal blue bowl.

Bowl, #495, crystal **10.00**
Claret, #27
Amethyst **55.00**
Emerald green and crystal . . . **35.00**
Cocktail, crystal **75.00**
Goblet, 6-1/8" h
Amethyst **42.00**
Burgundy **40.00**
Crystal **35.00**
Regal blue **125.00**
Iced tea tumbler, #63
Amethyst **42.00**
Burgundy and crystal **35.00**
Regal blue **135.00**
Juice tumbler
Amethyst **55.00**
Crystal **30.00**
Oyster cocktail, #33, crystal . . . **30.00**
Plate, amethyst **35.00**
Sherbet, 4-1/8" h
Amethyst **42.00**
Crystal **32.00**
Tumbler, 5-3/9" h, amber and crystal **15.00**
Wine, crystal **42.00**

Baroque

Line #2496. Made 1936-66. Made in azure blue, black amethyst, cobalt blue, crystal, gold tint, green, pink, red, and topaz yellow.

Bonbon, three toes, azure blue . **40.00**
Bowl
7" d, crystal, cupped **95.00**
7" d, topaz yellow, ruffled, three feet **20.00**
10-1/2", handle, crystal **95.00**
11" d, rolled edge, crystal **85.00**
12" d, crystal, flared **30.00**
12" d, topaz yellow, flared **60.00**
Cake plate, handle, crystal **65.00**
Candelabra, pr, crystal
Two-lite, #2484 . . . . **295.00**
Three-lite, #2484 . . . . **450.00**
Candlestick
One-lite, #2496, topaz yellow, pr **65.00**
Two-lite, crystal, pr **45.00**
Two-lite, topaz yellow, pr. . . . **130.00**
Two-lite, 8-1/4" h, 16 prisms, azure blue **90.00**
Curved, 4" h, Azure blue, pr . **135.00**
Single, candle drips, #2484, Silver Mist, pr **250.00**
5-1/2" h, topaz yellow, pr. . . . **130.00**
Candy, cov
Crystal, three parts **125.00**
Gold tint, three parts **175.00**
Celery
Azure blue **85.00**
Crystal **20.00**
Comport
5-1/2" w, topaz yellow **40.00**
6-1/2" w, topaz yellow **45.00**
Flared
Azure blue **85.00**
Gold tint **68.00**
Short,
Azure blue **38.00**
Topaz yellow **40.00**
Condiment set, salt and pepper shakers, mustard with spoon, tray, gold tint **385.00**
Console bowl
#2484, winged, azure blue . . **195.00**
#2496, 10-1/2" d, azure blue . **175.00**
11" d, rolled, gold tint **125.00**
Creamer and sugar
Individual size, topaz yellow . . **55.00**
Table size
Azure blue **95.00**
Crystal **30.00**
Topaz yellow **40.00**
Creamer and sugar, matching tray
Regular size, topaz yellow, 1937-40 . . . . **135.00**
Tea size, crystal **85.00**
Cup and saucer
Azure blue **45.00**
Crystal **28.00**
Gold tint **45.00**
Topaz yellow **30.00**
Dessert, handle, azure blue **90.00**
Goblet, water
Azure blue **45.00**
Crystal **27.00**
Gold tint **45.00**
Ice bucket
Crystal **95.00**
Gold tint **145.00**
Topaz yellow **130.00**
Iced tea tumbler, 6" h, ftd
Azure blue **90.00**
Crystal **50.00**
Topaz yellow **95.00**
Jelly cov
Azure blue **250.00**
Crystal **75.00**
Jug, crystal **225.00**
Mayonnaise, underplate
Azure blue **65.00**
Crystal **85.00**
Gold tint **125.00**
Topaz yellow **50.00**
Mint, 4-1/4" d, tab handle, azure blue **48.00**
Nappy, handle
4" d, round, crystal **12.00**
4" d, square, azure blue **45.00**
4" w, square, crystal **12.00**
4-1/2" d, round, ftd, azure blue **42.50**
5" d, ftd, crystal **55.00**
Nut bowl, three toes
Azure blue, cupped **65.00**
Crystal **60.00**
Gold tint **75.00**
Topaz yellow **35.00**
Oil and vinegar, azure blue . . . **595.00**
Oil, orig stopper, crystal **90.00**
Oyster cocktail, azure blue **22.00**
Pickle dish
Azure blue **55.00**
Gold tint **38.00**
Pitcher, ice lip, azure blue, light use **1,400.00**
Plate
6" d, azure blue **12.50**
6" d, gold tint **16.00**
6" d, topaz yellow **10.00**
7" d, azure blue **22.00**
7" d, gold tint **22.00**
8" d, azure blue **20.00**
Preserve, cov, topaz yellow . . . **270.00**
Punch cup, crystal **22.00**
Relish
Two parts, 6" w, square, topaz yellow **35.00**
Two parts, 6-1/2" l, azure blue **85.00**
Three parts, azure blue **95.00**
Three parts, crystal, Corsage etch **65.00**
Three parts, crystal, silver overlay **55.00**
Three parts, topaz yellow **55.00**
Four parts, azure blue, 10" l . **395.00**
Rose bowl, topaz yellow **95.00**
Salt and pepper shakers, pr
Individual size, azure blue . . **340.00**
Table size
azure blue **170.00**
Topaz yellow **120.00**
Sauce bowl
Azure blue, divided, with underplate **195.00**
Topaz yellow **50.00**
Saucer, crystal **3.50**
Server, center flame-shaped handle, crystal **60.00**
Sherbet
Azure blue **49.00**
Crystal **18.00**
Gold tint **30.00**
Topaz yellow **24.00**
Sweetmeat
6", sq, handle, azure blue. . . . **48.00**
9-1/2", cov, topaz yellow. . . . **300.00**
Tidbit, three toes, azure blue . . . **65.00**

Torte plate, 14" d
- Crystal **40.00**
- Topaz yellow **45.00**

Tumbler
- 5" h, ftd, azure blue **45.00**
- 5-3/4" h, flat, 14 oz, crystal ... **40.00**

Vase
- 6-3/4" h, crystal **95.00**
- 7" h, azure blue **195.00**
- 8" h, azure blue **225.00**

Beacon

Cutting #767. Made 1937-55, in rock crystal.

Champagne **25.00**
Cocktail **9.00**
Goblet, water **28.00**
Iced tea tumbler **28.00**
Plate, 7-1/2" d **9.00**
Sherbet **8.00**
Sweetmeat **25.00**
Tumbler, ftd, 9 oz **12.00**

Beverly

Plate Etching #276. Made 1927-34. Made in azure blue (1928-31); amber, crystal, green (1927-34); orchid (1927-28); and amber and green with crystal bowl (1927-34).

After dinner cup and saucer
- Amber **45.00**
- Green **65.00**

Ashtray, crystal **12.00**
Berry bowl, green **20.00**
Bouillon and liner
- Amber **20.00**
- Green **24.00**

Candy box, cov, 3", crystal **90.00**
Celery, crystal **25.00**
Cereal bowl, green **30.00**
Comport, 8", ftd, #2350, amber .. **85.00**
Cordial, green **75.00**
Cream soup, amber **38.00**
Creamer and sugar, amber **58.00**
Demitasse cup and saucer
- Amber **45.00**
- Green **30.00**

Finger bowl
- Amber **24.00**
- Green **25.00**

Fruit bowl, green **22.00**
Goblet, amber **32.50**
Oyster cocktail, amber **25.00**
Pitcher, water, #5000
- Amber, ftd **250.00**
- Green, ftd **350.00**

Plate
- Amber
  - 6-1/8" d **7.00**
  - 10-1/4" d **35.00**
- Crystal
  - 6" d **4.00**
  - 7-1/2" d **5.00**
  - 8-1/2" d **7.50**
- Green
  - 7-1/2" d **8.00**
  - 10-1/4" d **35.00**

Platter, 15" l, amber **120.00**
Salt and pepper shakers, pr, #5000
- Crystal **135.00**
- Green **60.00**

Saucer
- Amber **4.00**
- Crystal **3.50**

Sherbet, amber **20.00**
Tumbler, ftd, 12 oz, green and crystal **22.00**
Underplate, 6-1/4" d, amber **6.00**
Urn, ftd, green **125.00**
Wine, amber **38.00**

Bouquet

Plate Etching #342. Made 1949-1960 and only in crystal.

Bud vase, #2630, 6" h **45.00**
Candlesticks, pr, #2630, duo ... **75.00**
Champagne, 4-3/4" h **24.00**
Cocktail **18.00**
Creamer and sugar, #2630 .... **38.00**
Dinner plate, 9-1/2" d **30.00**
Goblet, 6-1/4" h **30.00**
Juice tumbler, ftd, 4-1/2" h **20.00**
Oyster cocktail **24.00**
Salad bowl, 10-1/2" d, deep **70.00**
Sherbet **24.00**
Tumbler, ftd, 5-7/8" h **26.00**

Buttercup

Etching #340. Made only in crystal.

Ashtray, #2364, 2-3/8", individual size **20.00**
Candlestick
- #2324, 4" h **30.00**
- #6023, two-lite, pr **95.00**

Champagne **24.00**
Cocktail **24.00**
Fruit bowl, 13" d **75.00**
Goblet
- #6030, luncheon, 7 oz **35.00**
- Water **30.00**

Oyster cocktail **20.00**
Pitcher, ftd **450.00**
Plate
- 7-1/2" d **16.50**
- 9-1/2" d **50.00**

Relish, three parts, 10" **60.00**
Salt and pepper shakers, pr, #2364 .... **48.00**
Server, center handle **50.00**
Sherbet, #6030, 6 oz **22.00**
Vase
- #4143, 7-1/2" d, ftd, blown .. **195.00**
- #6021, 6" h, ftd **65.00**

Wine, #6030 .... **35.00**

Camelia

Plate Etching #344. Made 1952-65 only in crystal.

Butter, cov, quarter pound **55.00**
Candlestick, #2630, 7" l, single .. **65.00**
Candy, cov **65.00**
Champagne **22.50**
Cocktail **24.00**
Iced tea tumbler **25.00**
Juice tumbler, ftd **20.00**
Parfait **25.00**
Pitcher, #2630, 6-1/8" h, pint ... **115.00**
Wine **30.00**

Capri

Pattern #6045. Made 1952-65. Blown lead-glass stemware made in solid crystal and crystal bowls on bitter green or cinnamon base.

Claret-wine, crystal with cinnamon base **22.00**
Cordial, crystal with bitter green foot **35.00**
Finger bowl, crystal **8.00**
Goblet, crystal with cinnamon base **20.00**
Iced tea tumbler, ftd, crystal with cinnamon base **17.00**
Juice tumbler, crystal with bitter green base **10.00**
Plate, 7" d, crystal **8.00**
Sherbet
- Crystal, 4" h **15.00**
- Crystal with cinnamon base, 4" h **18.00**

Century

Made 1949-85 only in crystal.

Bowl
- 4-1/2" d, thin **20.00**
- 5" d **15.00**
- 8" d, two handles, deep, oval . **50.00**
- 11" d, ftd, rolled **45.00**

Butter dish **28.75**
Cake salver, ftd, cutting **50.00**
Candlesticks
- Pr, duo **95.00**
- Triple, pr **125.00**

Cereal bowl **22.50**
Cocktail **18.00**
Comport, 4-3/8" **20.00**
Creamer and sugar
- Large, floral silver overlay **50.00**
- Large, no dec **40.00**
- Matching tray, individual size . **40.00**

Cruet, orig stopper **50.00**
Cup and saucer **22.00**
Dessert bowl, two handles **45.00**
Fruit bowl, 5" d **25.00**
Goblet, water **30.00**

Ice bucket 50.00
Iced tea tumbler, 5-7/8" h, ftd 20.00
Juice tumbler 15.00
Mayonnaise, divided, two ladles 42.50
Pitcher
Ice lip, 7" h 95.00
Pint 70.00
Plate
7" d 12.00
7-1/2" d 18.00
8" d 24.00
9" d 40.00
9-1/2" d 27.00
10" d 60.00
10" d, handle 18.00
Preserve, cov, ftd 40.00
Relish
Two parts, 7-1/2" l 18.50
Three parts, handle 35.00
Salad plate, crescent 35.00
Salt and pepper shakers, pr 40.00
Salt and pepper shakers, pr, matching tray, individual size 65.00
Server, center handle 45.00
Serving bowl, center handle, 9-1/2" oval 20.00
Sherbet 20.00
Sugar, cov, large 15.00
Tray, for creamer and sugar 15.00
Tumbler, 12 oz, ftd 27.50
Vase, 8-1/2" h, oval 65.00
Vegetable, oval 45.00
Wine 28.00

Chintz

Plate Etching #338. Made in the 1950s only in crystal.

Bonbon, 7-5/8" 28.00
Bowl
10" d, handle 75.00
10-1/2" d, handle 65.00
10-1/2" d, four toes 70.00
Cake plate, #2496, handle 28.00
Candlesticks, pr, #2496
One-lite, 4" h 70.00
One-lite, 5-1/2" h 130.00
Two-lite 130.00
Candy dish, cov, three parts 225.00
Champagne, 6 oz, tall 38.00
Cheese and cracker 145.00
Cheese compote, 3-1/2" h 50.00
Cocktail, 5", 4 oz 35.00
Comport, 5-1/2" d, 4-3/4" h 40.00
Console set, bowl and pr double candlesticks 125.00
Cordial 80.00
Creamer and sugar
Matching tray, individual size 120.00
Table size 75.00
Cruet, orig stopper 195.00
Cup 25.00
Dessert bowl, two handles 70.00
Goblet, water
6-1/8" h 45.00
7-3/4" h 48.00
Iced tea tumbler, ftd 45.00
Jelly, cov 65.00
Jug, #5000 725.00
Juice tumbler, ftd, 5 oz 35.00
Mayonnaise and underplate, #2496 65.00
Nappy, triangular, handle 40.00
Pickle 35.00
Plate
7" d 16.50
7-1/2" d 17.50
9-1/2" d 75.00
Relish
Two parts, 6" sq 35.00
Three parts 75.00
Sauce dish, handle 80.00
Server, center handle 95.00
Sherbet, 4-3/8", 6 oz, low 22.50
Sugar, 3-1/2", ftd 15.00
Torte plate, 14" d
Lacy Leaf etch 48.00
No decoration, minor scratches 70.00
Tray, 10-1/2" d, handle 50.00
Tumbler, ftd, 6" h 38.00
Wine, 4-1/2 oz 45.00

Coin

Line #1372. Made 1958-82. Made in amber, blue, crystal, empire green, olive green, and ruby red.

Ashtray
5" d, ruby red 38.00
5-1/2", amber 35.00
3" x 9", oblong, empire green 20.00
7-1/2" d, center raised coin, ruby red 30.00
7-1/2" d, plain center, ruby red 27.50
Bowl
8" d, amber 35.00
8" d, olive green 45.00
8-1/2" d, ftd, amber 95.00
Bud vase, amber 22.50
Cake salver, crystal 145.00
Candlestick, 4" h, amber 38.00
Candlesticks, pr
Amber
4" h 75.00
4-1/2" h 40.00
Crystal, 4-1/2" h 44.00
Olive green
Flat top, 4-1/2" h 65.00
Regular top, 4-1/2" h 65.00
8" h, olive green 95.00
Candy box, cov
Empire green 245.00
Olive green 58.00
Ruby red 95.00
Candy dish, cov
Amber 68.00
Amber, Avon dates 62.00
Blue 75.00
Olive green 48.00
Ruby, frosted 55.00
Candy jar, cov
Amber 40.00
Blue 125.00
Cigarette box, cov
Amber 40.00
Blue 225.00
Crystal 175.00
Cigarette urn, ftd
Amber 52.00
Olive green 64.00
Cigarette urn, rolled edge
Amber 55.00
Ruby red 55.00
Comport, ftd
Empire green 40.00
Olive green 45.00
Ruby red, 8-1/2" 75.00
Condiment set, amber, crystal base 225.00
Creamer
Amber 10.00
Amber, Avon 32.00
Crystal 45.00
Olive green 15.00
Creamer and sugar, crystal 22.00
Cruet, olive green, 7 oz 50.00
Highball, 12 oz, crystal 55.00
Iced tea tumbler, ftd, 14 oz, 5-3/16" h
Crystal 45.00
Ruby red 150.00
Jelly comport, ftd
Amber 35.00
Blue 85.00
Nappy, handle
Empire green 85.00
Olive green 32.00
Ruby red 24.00
Old fashioned tumbler, crystal 45.00
Patio lamp and shade, amber 250.00
Pitcher
Amber 125.00
Olive green 65.00
Plate, 8" d, ruby red 40.00
Punch cup, crystal 45.00
Punch set, bowl, base, 12 cups, crystal 650.00
Salt and pepper shakers, pr, blue 125.00
Salt shaker
Olive green 17.50
Ruby red 32.50

Sugar, cov, olive green **30.00**
Tumbler, crystal **45.00**
Urn, cov, ftd
- Amber **45.00**
- Olive green **95.00**

Vase, 8" h
- Crystal **55.00**
- Olive green **58.00**
- Ruby red, ftd **45.00**

Vase, 10" h, crystal **225.00**
Wedding bowl, 8-1/2" d
- Amber **50.00**
- Blue **195.00**
- Crystal **60.00**
- Empire green **325.00**
- Ruby red **60.00**

Colonial Dame

Pattern #5412. Made 1948-82. Designed to compliment Colony pattern dinnerware. Made in solid crystal and Empire Green with crystal base.

Champagne, Empire Green **28.00**
Claret/wine, Empire Green **30.00**
Cocktail, 3-1/2 oz, 4", Empire Green **12.00**
Cordial, 3-1/4", crystal **20.00**
Goblet, 11 oz, 6-3/8", Empire Green **35.00**
Iced tea tumbler, Empire Green with crystal base **35.00**
Juice tumbler, ftd, Empire Green with crystal base **28.00**
Oyster cocktail, crystal **8.00**
Plate, 7" d, crystal **8.00**
Sherbet/champagne, 6-1/2 oz, 4-5/8", Empire Green **28.00**
Wine, Empire Green **36.00**

Colony

Line #2412. Made 1938-72 only in crystal.

Almond, ftd **28.00**
Bowl
- 7" w, triangular, ftd **20.00**
- 8-1/4" d, flared **65.00**
- 8-1/2" d, handle **35.00**
- 10-1/2" l, low, ftd **75.00**
- 11" d, flared **60.00**
- 11" l, oval, ftd **55.00**
- 14" l, oval, ftd **70.00**

Butter dish, cov, 1/4 lb **65.00**
Candlesticks, pr
- 3" h **70.00**
- 7-1/2" h **95.00**
- Two-lite **120.00**

Celery dish **30.00**
Centerpiece, 13" **90.00**
Cheese and cracker set **50.00**
Cocktail **20.00**
Comport, cov, low **65.00**
Creamer and sugar **35.00**
Creamer and sugar, matching tray
- Individual size **65.00**
- Table size **45.00**

Cruet, stopper **55.00**
Cup and saucer **22.50**
Cup, three toes **22.00**
Goblet, 5-1/4" h **25.00**
Ice bowl, ftd **200.00**
Ice cream, 5-1/2" w, sq **55.00**
Iced tea tumbler **25.00**
Ice jug, ftd, three pints **200.00**
Inkwell, cascade, brass hinged lid **150.00**
Mayonnaise, underplate **25.00**
Muffin tray **40.00**
Nappy, 4-1/2" **22.00**
Nut bowl, 5-1/2" d, three ftd **18.00**
Oil bottle, stopper **55.00**
Oyster cocktail **20.00**
Pitcher, ftd, 48 oz **225.00**
Plate
- 6" d **15.00**
- 7-1/2" d **18.00**
- 8" d **18.00**
- 9" d **35.00**
- 10" d, handle **35.00**

Platter, 12-1/2" l **95.00**
Punch cup **20.00**
Relish
- Two parts, handle **35.00**
- Three parts, 10-1/2" l, handle . **35.00**

Rose bowl, 6" d **130.00**
Salt and pepper shakers, pr
- Matching tray, individual size . **58.00**
- Table size **42.00**

Salver, 12" d, ftd **100.00**
Sandwich server, center handle . **35.00**
Sherbet **19.00**
Sponge cup, 3" d, round **30.00**
Sugar bowl, 2-7/8" h **12.50**
Sugar bowl, large **15.00**
Torte plate, 15" d **50.00**
Tumbler
- 8 oz, flat **28.00**
- 12 oz, flat **32.50**

Urn, cov
- Patterned **85.00**
- Plain **125.00**

Vase
- 7" h, ftd, cupped **95.00**
- 7-1/2" h, flared **45.00**
- 12" h, flared **325.00**

Wine, 4-1/4" h **25.00**

Two Art Deco spherical vases, one black opaque glass, other clear yellow, designed by George Sakier, 6" x 6-1/2", **$2,440 for pair***; two fluted vases, one 13" h purple-blue, other 8-1/4" h green bulbous form, designed by George Sakier,* **$1,320 for pair.** *Photo courtesy of David Rago Auctions.*

Contour

Pattern #2638, #6060, and #2666. Made 1955-77. Made in amber, crystal, and crystal with pink.

Ashtray, amber, two lips **25.00**
Award tray, 7-1/2" w, dated 1953, for sales proficiency **55.00**
Candleholders, pr, 6" h, crystal . **40.00**
Champagne, crystal and pink . . **20.00**
Creamer and sugar on tray, individual size, irid crystal **48.00**
Goblet, water, crystal **30.00**
Iced tea tumbler, crystal and pink **25.00**
Relish
- Two parts, crystal **28.00**
- Three parts, crystal. **35.00**

Sherbet, 4-1/2", crystal **15.00**

Corsage

Plate Etching #325. Made 1935-60 only in crystal.

Bowl
- 9" d, handle, #2536. . . . . **90.00**
- 11-1/2" d **50.00**
- 12" d **95.00**

Candlesticks, pr, two-lite, #2496 . . . . **130.00**
Champagne **32.00**
Cocktail, 5" h. **20.00**
Comport, #2496, 5-1/2" **50.00**
Cordial, 1 oz **55.00**
Creamer and sugar **75.00**
Cup and saucer **28.00**
Iced tea tumbler, ftd **30.00**
Jug, #5000 . . . . **625.00**
Nappy, tricorner, handle **50.00**
Oyster cocktail. **22.00**
Plate, 8-1/2" d **18.00**
Relish
- Two parts, Lafayette blank, #2440 . . . . **60.00**
- Three parts **75.00**
- Five parts, chipped. **70.00**

Sauce dish, 6-1/2" l, oval **70.00**
Sherbet, tall. **20.00**
Tumbler, ftd, 6" **25.00**
Wine, 3 oz, 5-1/4" h, crystal **30.00**

Dolly Madison

Cutting #876. Made 1939-74. Made in rock crystal with hand-cut flutes. Designed and sold as a companion to Raleigh pattern tableware.

Champagne **35.00**
Cocktail. **30.00**
Goblet **35.00**
Iced tea tumbler. **36.00**
Oyster cocktail. **30.00**
Sherbet **35.00**

Fairfax

Pattern #2375, dinnerware line. Made 1927-60. Made in amber and green (1927-41); orchid (1928); azure and rose (1928-41); topaz (1929-36); selected items in ebony (1930-42); and selected items in ruby (1935-39).

After dinner creamer, rose **35.00**
After dinner cup
- Azure blue **35.00**
- Green. **15.00**

After dinner cup and saucer
- Azure blue **65.00**
- Green. **38.00**
- Rose. **38.00**

Almond, ftd, topaz. **32.00**
Baker, oval
- Amber, 9" l **48.00**
- Azure blue, 9" l. **75.00**
- Orchid, 9". **75.00**

Berry bowl
- Amber, 5" d **10.00**
- Rose, 5" d **15.00**
- Topaz, 5" d. **12.50**

Bonbon, cov, two handles
- Rose. **20.00**
- Topaz **22.50**

Bouillon
- Rose. **18.50**
- Topaz. **23.00**

Bouillon with liner
- Amber **15.00**
- Green. **17.50**

Bowl
- Azure blue, 12" d. **60.00**
- Green, 5" d. **6.00**
- Rose
  - 8" d **27.50**
  - Rose, 9-1/2" d **10.00**

Butter dish, cov
- Amber **95.00**
- Green. **125.00**
- Rose. **125.00**

Cake plate, #2375, 10" d, handle
- Amber **35.00**
- Azure blue **50.00**

Canapé plate, 6" d, amber. **12.00**
Candlesticks, pr
- #2324
  - Azure blue, 4" h. **68.00**
  - Green, 4" h **64.00**
- #2375, azure blue, 3" h **60.00**
- #2394
  - Azure blue, three toes. **85.00**
  - Green, three toes **65.00**
  - Rose, three toes **60.00**
  - Topaz, three toes **55.00**
- #2395-1/2", 5" h, scroll, topaz . **25.00**
- #2415, combination bowl and candleholder, green **125.00**

Candy, cov, three parts, green . . **68.00**
Champagne
- #5097, orchid **42.00**
- #5298
  - Azure blue **40.00**
  - Green. **28.00**
  - Rose. **40.00**

Cheese and cracker set, #2375
- Azure blue **75.00**
- Rose **75.00**
- Topaz **80.00**

Claret
- #5097, orchid **65.00**
- #5098, rose. **65.00**
- #5299, topaz. **35.00**

Cocktail, #5098, rose **35.00**
Combination bowl and candlesticks, #2415, azure blue **160.00**
Comport
- 4-1/2", crystal **30.00**
- 5", topaz **135.00**
- 5-1/2" d, #5297, tall, green . . . **60.00**
- 5-3/4" d, rose **75.00**
- 6", #2400, azure blue **45.00**
- 6", #2400, green **35.00**
- 6", #2400, topaz **24.00**
- 7", azure blue **75.00**
- 7", green **48.00**
- #5009, azure blue. **135.00**
- #5297, 5-1/2" h, green **60.00**
- #5298, blown, low, rose **125.00**

Confection, cov
- Orchid. **130.00**
- Rose **90.00**

Cordial, amber, #5298 . . . . **45.00**
Cracker plate, #2375, handle, topaz **30.00**
Creamer, azure blue, individual size **30.00**
Creamer and sugar
- Individual size
  - Amber **70.00**
  - Rose. **70.00**
  - Ruby **60.00**
  - Topaz. **70.00**
- Matching tray, table size, azure blue **350.00**
- Table size
  - Azure blue **45.00**
  - Green, ftd. **50.00**
  - Orchid, flat. **125.00**
  - Rose. **43.00**
  - Ruby **95.00**
  - Topaz, ftd. **45.00**
- Tea size
  - Azure blue **78.00**
  - Ebony. **95.00**
  - Rose. **68.00**
  - Topaz. **50.00**

Cream soup
Azure blue 47.00
Green 48.00
Rose 40.00
Cream soup, liner
Orchid 55.00
Topaz 15.00
Cruet, open, topaz 70.00
Cup and saucer
Amber 15.00
Azure blue, ftd 28.00
Green 25.00
Orchid 26.00
Rose 28.00
Topaz 25.00
Dessert bowl, large, handle, rose 48.00
Finger bowl, blown
Green 15.00
Rose 15.00
Fruit bowl, 5" d, azure blue 42.00
Goblet, water, #5299
Azure blue 65.00
Topaz 28.00
Grape fruit, liner, amber, #945-1/2 . . . . . 25.00
Gravy boat, liner
Green 75.00
Rose 85.00
Topaz 90.00
Grill plate
Amber, 10-1/4" d 20.00
Rose, 10-1/4" d 40.00
Ice bucket, azure blue 45.00
Iced tea tumbler
#5000, green 45.00
#5298, azure blue 45.00
Icer
Black 15.00
Green 10.00
Rose 10.00
Topaz 65.00
Icer insert, topaz 65.00
Mayonnaise and liner, topaz . . . 75.00
Mayonnaise, ftd, green 45.00
Mayonnaise underplate, orchid . 14.00
Nut bowl, individual, three toes
Azure blue 30.00
Green 18.50
Oil bottle and stopper, ftd, rose 135.00
Oyster cocktail
#5000, orchid 32.00
#5098, green 30.00
Parfait
#5298, rose 40.00
#5299, topaz 35.00
Pickle dish
8" l, green 20.00
8-1/2" l, divided, rose 20.00
Pitcher, ftd, #5000, orchid 350.00

Plate
Amber
6" d 5.50
7-1/2" d 12.00
Azure blue
6" d 18.00
7-1/2" d 20.00
8-3/4" d 22.00
9-1/2" d 45.00
Green
6" d 6.00
7" d 7.50
7-1/2" d 16.00
8-3/4" d 18.00
9-1/2" d 20.00
Orchid
6" d 15.00
9-1/2" d 60.00
Rose
6" d 8.00
7-1/2" d 16.00
8-3/4" d 20.00
9-1/2" d 15.00
10-1/2" d 40.00
Topaz
6" d 10.00
7-1/2" d 12.00
8-3/4" d 18.00
Platter
Green
12-1/4" l 45.00
14-1/8" l 45.00
15-1/2" l 50.00
Topaz, 10-1/2" l, oval 30.00
Relish
Two parts, azure blue 38.00
Two parts, green 32.00
Two parts, topaz 17.00
Three parts, green 42.00
Three parts, rose 58.00
Salad bowl, green, 9-1/4" d 25.00
Salt and pepper shakers, pr
Azure blue, metal lid, ftd 80.00
Green 60.00
Rose, glass tops, ftd 125.00
Sandwich server, topaz 38.00
Sauce boat
Azure blue 50.00
Crystal, flower cutting 15.00
Sauce boat and liner
Green 110.00
Orchid 125.00
Saucer
Amber 2.00
Green 3.00
Rose 2.50
Topaz 3.00
Server, center handle
Orchid 75.00
Rose 30.00

Service tray, amber 95.00
Shaker, ftd, azure blue 40.00
Sherbet
Azure blue, #5298, low 32.00
Topaz, 6 oz 11.00
Sugar bowl
Individual size
Amber 10.00
Azure blue 15.00
Green 10.00
Table size
Ftd, green 10.00
Ftd, flat top, rose 15.00
Topaz 12.50
Sugar pail, rose 75.00
Sweetmeat, handle
Azure blue 36.00
Green 34.00
Rose 24.00
Topaz 18.50
Tomato, icer, rose 52.50
Torte plate, orchid, 13" d 70.00
Tray, 8" l, oblong, azure blue 65.00
Tumbler
#5000, ftd, green 25.00
#5098, ftd, rose 32.00
#5296, 9 oz, ftd
Azure blue 20.00
Topaz 13.00
#5298, ftd, azure blue 25.00
Vase
#2369, crystal, 7" h, ftd 150.00
#4100
Amber, flip, loop optic, 8" h 90.00
Crystal, flip, cutting, 10" h. 130.00
#4105, green, loop optic, 10" h 130.00
#22902, green, 8" h, ftd 80.00
Vegetable bowl
Azure blue, cov, oval 70.00
Green, 10" l, oval 45.00
Whipped cream bowl, azure blue 36.00
Whipped cream pail, handle
Azure blue 75.00
Rose 60.00
Topaz 35.00
Whiskey, #5298, ftd, topaz 25.00
Wine
Azure blue 47.50
Topaz 30.00

Glacier

Acid-Etched Design #2510. Made 1935-44 only in crystal.

Candlesticks, pr, two-lite 225.00
Candy, cov, ftd 95.00
Creamer, ftd 9.00

Cruet, orig stopper 45.00
Cup and saucer 20.00
Ice bucket 60.00
Iced tea tumbler 28.00
Jelly, cov 25.00
Mustard, cov 85.00
Nappy, sq 10.00
Old fashioned tumbler 12.00
Onion soup, cov 25.00
Pickle dish, handle 9.00
Plate, 8" d 9.00
Relish, two parts 38.00
Rose bowl, 5" d 25.00
Salad bowl 25.00
Sugar, large 18.00
Sweetmeat, two handles, oblong 25.00
Torte plate, 15" d 35.00
Tray, oval 35.00
Tumbler, 9 oz 18.00

Heather

Etching #343. Made only in crystal.

Bonbon, three-toed 30.00
Bowl
- 5" d 30.00
- 8" d, flared 50.00
- 8-1/4" d, handle 45.00
- 10-3/4" d, flared, ftd 70.00
- 12" d, flared 55.00

Bud vase
- 6" h 65.00
- 8-1/2" h, #5902 .... 120.00

Butter dish, cov, 1/4 lb 95.00
Cake plate, handle 65.00
Candlesticks, pr, #2630, two-lite 125.00
Candy, cov 75.00
Cereal bowl, 6" d 40.00
Champagne 22.00
Cheese and cracker 120.00
Cocktail 35.00
Compote 40.00
Comport, 4-3/8" h 35.00
Creamer and sugar
- Individual size, matching tray. 80.00
- Table size 65.00

Cup and saucer 35.00
Goblet
- Low 40.00
- Tall 40.00

Iced tea tumbler 40.00
Juice tumbler 30.00
Mayonnaise, two pcs 70.00
Muffin tray, handle 75.00
Mustard 42.00
Nappy, three-toed, tricorner 32.50
Party plate set, two pcs 70.00
Pickle, 8" 30.00
Plate
- 6" d 15.00
- 7-1/2" d 20.00
- 8" d 22.50
- 9-1/2" d 60.00
- 13" d 45.00

Platter, 12" l 90.00
Relish
- Two parts, 7-3/8" l, #2360, handle 30.00
- Three parts 58.00

Salad, crescent 55.00
Salt and pepper shakers, pr 85.00
Sherbet 35.00
Sugar
- Individual size 17.50
- Large 25.00

Torte plate 85.00
Tumbler
- 4-7/8" h, ftd 18.50
- 6-1/8" h, 12 oz, ftd 25.00

Vase, 5" h, #6021 .... 130.00
Vegetable, oval 70.00
Wine 45.00

Hermitage

Pattern #2449. Made 1931-45. Made in amber, crystal, and green (1931-42); topaz (1932-38); gold tint (1938-44); wisteria (1932-38); and selected items in ebony (1932-38).

Ashtray set, set of four stacking ashtrays, crystal 25.00
Beer mug, ftd, 12 oz, crystal 35.00
Berry bowl, 5" d, light blue 20.00
Bowl, 8" d, topaz, ftd 45.00
Celery, 11", green 70.00
Coaster, green 15.00
Cocktail, cone, topaz 10.00
Coupe salad, 6-1/2"
- Crystal 8.50
- Light blue 35.00

Crescent salad, wisteria 95.00
Cup and saucer, crystal 18.50
Decanter, topaz 195.00
Goblet, crystal, 5-1/4" h 12.50
Icer, 4-3/4"
- Crystal 12.50
- Green 15.00
- Topaz 12.00

Icer with tomato juice insert, wisteria 125.00
Jug, three pints
- Crystal 125.00
- Topaz 130.00

Mayonnaise, light blue 45.00
Plate
- Amber, 8" d 20.00
- Crystal, 9" d 24.00

Sandwich plate, green, 12" d 20.00
Sherbet, 3", low, wisteria 15.00
Tumbler
- 2-7/8" h, ftd
  - Crystal 10.00
  - Green 12.00
  - Topaz 15.00
- 4-1/4" h, ftd, topaz 15.00

Vase, 6" h, green 70.00
Whiskey, amber, 2-3/8" h 15.00

Holly, goblet, #6030, 10 oz., 7-7/8" h, **$40.**

Holly

Cutting #815. Made 1942-80 only in rock crystal.

Bowl, 12" d, flared 65.00
Candlesticks, pr
- #2324, 4" h 75.00
- #6023, two-lite 95.00

Champagne 30.00
Claret, 6" 35.00
Cocktail
- 3-1/2 oz, 5-1/4" h 30.00
- 5-1/4" 32.50

Cordial, 1 oz, 3-7/8" 65.00
Creamer and sugar 75.00
Goblet, #6030, 10 oz
- 6-1/2" h 35.00
- 7-7/8" h 40.00

Iced tea tumbler, #6030, 12 oz, 6" h 35.00
Juice tumbler, ftd, 4-5/8" h 30.00
Lily pond bowl, 12" d 95.00
Mayonnaise, underplate, spoon 85.00
Oyster cocktail 30.00
Pickle, 8" 24.00

Plate, 7-1/2" d. **20.00**
Salt and pepper shakers, pr, #2364, 2-5/8" **45.00**
Sherbet, 6 oz **30.00**
Tray, center handle **65.00**
Wine **35.00**

Jamestown

Pattern #2719. Made 1958-85. Made in amber, azure blue, azure tint, crystal, green, pink, ruby, and smoke.

Bowl, 4-1/2" d, amber **12.00**
Butter dish, cov
Crystal **75.00**
Pink **50.00**
Creamer and sugar, amber **45.00**
Fruit bowl
Amethyst **30.00**
Crystal **24.00**
Ruby **35.00**
Goblet, luncheon, amber **12.00**
Goblet, water, 5-7/8" h
Amber **15.00**
Amethyst **30.00**
Azure blue **32.00**
Crystal **25.00**
Green **32.50**
Pink **32.00**
Ruby **32.00**
Smoke **18.00**
Iced tea tumbler, ftd, 12 oz, 6" h
Amber **15.00**
Amethyst **32.00**
Azure blue **34.00**
Green **32.00**
Pink **35.00**
Ruby **40.00**
Smoke **17.00**
Jelly cov, crystal **68.00**
Jug, #2719/456, smoke, three pints, 7-5/16" h **75.00**
Juice tumbler, ftd, 4-3/4" h
Amber **15.00**
Amethyst **28.00**
Azure blue **30.00**
Crystal **22.00**
Green **28.00**
Pink **30.00**
Ruby **20.00**
Pitcher
Amber **125.00**
Green **140.00**
Smoke **75.00**
Plate
Amber **15.00**
Amethyst **28.00**
Ruby **35.00**
Salt and pepper shakers, pr
Blue **84.00**
Cinnamon **27.50**
Green **75.00**
Pink **65.00**
Smoke **55.00**
Sherbet, 7 oz, 4-1/2" d
Amber **10.00**
Amethyst **28.00**
Azure blue **30.00**
Crystal **20.00**
Green **25.00**
Pink **30.00**
Ruby **30.00**
Smoke **6.50**
Tumbler
5-1/4" h, flat, ruby **22.00**
6" h, ftd
Amber **10.00**
Azure blue **24.00**
Green **24.00**
9 oz, flat
Crystal **24.00**
Smoke **10.00**
12 oz, flat
Azure blue **20.00**
Crystal **26.00**
Wine
Amber **15.00**
Azure blue **35.00**
Green **32.00**
Pink **35.00**
Ruby **32.00**

June

Made 1928-44. Made in azure blue, crystal, rose pink, and topaz yellow.

After dinner creamer and sugar
Azure blue **215.00**
Rose pink **300.00**
Topaz yellow **125.00**
After dinner cup and saucer
Azure blue **200.00**
Rose pink **200.00**
Topaz yellow **125.00**
Ashtray
Azure blue **75.00**
Rose pink **55.00**
Baker, oval, rose pink **180.00**
Bar tumbler, topaz yellow, 2 oz . **75.00**
Berry bowl, 5" d
Azure blue **65.00**
Crystal **45.00**
Rose pink **60.00**
Topaz yellow **40.00**
Bonbon, azure blue **25.00**
Bouillon
Azure blue **60.00**
Crystal **24.50**
Topaz yellow **40.00**
Bouillon and liner
Crystal **40.00**
Rose pink **85.00**
Bowl
9" d, two handles, topaz yellow **85.00**
11-1/2" d, three-toed, rose pink **85.00**
12" d, #2394, crystal **65.00**
Canapé plate, crystal **35.00**
Candlesticks, pr
#2349
Azure blue, three toes. . . . **135.00**
Topaz yellow, three toes . . **125.00**
#2375
Azure blue **135.00**
Topaz yellow **75.00**
#2375-1/2, mushroom, topaz yellow **150.00**
#2395-1/2
Azure blue, scroll, 5" h . . . **225.00**
Crystal, scroll, 5" h **125.00**
Pink, scroll, 5" h **250.00**
Topaz yellow, scroll, 5" h. . **150.00**
Candy, cov, topaz yellow **495.00**
Celery
Azure blue **145.00**
Crystal **80.00**
Rose pink **115.00**
Topaz yellow **110.00**
Centerpiece bowl
Rose pink, 12" d **125.00**
Topaz yellow, 12" d **80.00**
Cereal bowl, topaz yellow **85.00**
Champagne
Azure blue **60.00**
Crystal **35.00**
Rose pink **68.00**
Topaz yellow **50.00**
Chop plate
Rose pink, 13" d **230.00**
Topaz yellow, 13" d **160.00**
Claret, topaz yellow **125.00**
Club plate, blue **300.00**
Cocktail
Azure blue **70.00**
Rose pink **65.00**
Topaz yellow **40.00**
Comport
Azure blue, 6-1/2" h **110.00**
Crystal, 4" **45.00**
Pink **175.00**
Topaz yellow, #2400, 6" **45.00**
Console bowl, #2394, azure blue, three toes **175.00**
Console set, 12" d ftd bowl, pr 3" h candlesticks, topaz yellow **105.00**
Cordial, crystal **85.00**
Creamer and sugar
Individual size, crystal **125.00**
Table size, topaz yellow **125.00**

Cream soup
- Azure blue . . . 95.00
- Topaz yellow, orig liner . . . 120.00

Cup and saucer
- Crystal . . . 30.00
- Rose pink . . . 44.00
- Topaz yellow . . . 55.00

Dessert bowl, handle, topaz yellow . . . 110.00

Finger bowl
- Azure blue . . . 100.00
- Crystal . . . 45.00
- Rose pink . . . 100.00

Finger bowl, underplate, topaz yellow . . . 125.00

Fruit cocktail insert, topaz yellow . . . 32.50

Goblet, water
- Azure blue . . . 75.00
- Crystal, #5298 . . . 45.00
- Rose pink . . . 75.00

Grapefruit and liner
- Crystal . . . 130.00
- Topaz yellow . . . 250.00

Ice bucket, crystal . . . 95.00

Iced tea tumbler, ftd
- Azure blue . . . 75.00
- Crystal . . . 45.00
- Rose pink . . . 85.00
- Topaz yellow . . . 45.00

Icer bowl
- Crystal . . . 60.00
- Topaz yellow . . . 55.00

Icer and tomato insert
- Azure blue . . . 295.00
- Crystal . . . 80.00
- Topaz yellow . . . 165.00

Jug, #5000, topaz yellow . . . 695.00

Juice tumbler, ftd, azure blue . . 65.00

Lemon dish
- Azure blue . . . 45.00
- Rose pink . . . 45.00

Mayonnaise and liner, azure blue . . . 190.00

Mayonnaise ladle, crystal . . . 19.50

Mayonnaise, underplate, ladle, topaz yellow . . . 165.00

Mint, 4-1/2" d, three-toed, #2394 45.00

Oil and vinegar bottle, crystal . 300.00

Oyster cocktail, 5-1/2 oz
- Azure blue . . . 55.00
- Crystal . . . 30.00
- Rose pink . . . 50.00
- Topaz yellow . . . 35.00

Parfait
- Crystal . . . 95.00
- Rose pink . . . 135.00
- Topaz yellow . . . 65.00

Pickle, 8" l, green . . . 20.00

Pitcher, #5000
- Crystal . . . 500.00
- Rose pink . . . 895.00
- Topaz yellow . . . 425.00

Plate
- Azure blue
  - 6" d . . . 28.00
  - 7-1/2" d . . . 32.00
  - 8-1/4" d . . . 25.00
  - 9-1/2" d . . . 85.00
- Crystal
  - 6" d . . . 10.00
  - 7-1/2" d . . . 15.00
- Rose pink
  - 6" d . . . 25.00
  - 7" d . . . 18.50
  - 7-1/2" d . . . 20.00
  - 8-1/4" d . . . 22.00
  - 10-1/4" d . . . 175.00
- Topaz yellow
  - 6" d . . . 25.00
  - 7-1/2" d . . . 25.00
  - 8-1/2" d . . . 30.00
  - 9-1/2" d . . . 65.00
  - 10-1/4" d . . . 125.00
  - 11" l . . . 175.00

Platter
- Crystal, 12" l . . . 90.00
- Rose pink, 12" l . . . 230.00

Relish, two parts, rose pink . . . 70.00

Salt and pepper shakers, pr
- Azure blue . . . 250.00
- Crystal . . . 60.00
- Topaz yellow . . . 175.00

Sauce boat and underplate, #2375, topaz yellow . . . 200.00

Server, center handle
- Azure blue . . . 195.00
- Topaz yellow . . . 70.00

Sherbet
- Azure blue , 6" . . . 35.00
- Crystal . . . 25.00
- Rose pink . . . 60.00
- Topaz yellow . . . 24.00

Sugar
- Cov, topaz yellow . . . 230.00
- Open, rose pink . . . 32.50

Sweetmeat
- Crystal . . . 50.00
- Rose pink . . . 55.00

Tomato juice insert, topaz yellow . . . 20.00

Tumbler
- 9 oz, ftd
  - Azure blue . . . 44.00
  - Crystal . . . 30.00
  - Rose pink . . . 44.00
- 12 oz, ftd, topaz yellow . . . 40.00

Vase, #2417, topaz yellow, 8" h . 395.00

Vegetable, oval
- Azure blue . . . 165.00
- Topaz yellow . . . 125.00

Whipped cream bowl
- Rose pink . . . 35.00
- Topaz yellow . . . 45.00

Whiskey, ftd
- Azure blue . . . 225.00
- Rose pink . . . 150.00
- Topaz yellow . . . 75.00

Wine
- Azure blue . . . 115.00
- Crystal . . . 55.00
- Topaz yellow . . . 75.00

Kashmir

Plate Etching #281. Made 1930-34. Made in crystal, azure blue, topaz, green, and crystal with azure, topaz, or green base.

After dinner cup and saucer, topaz . . . 55.00

Berry bowl, azure blue . . . 38.00

Celery, azure blue . . . 85.00

Cereal bowl, 6", topaz . . . 35.00

Champagne
- Azure blue . . . 42.50
- Topaz . . . 28.50

Cheese comport, #2375, azure . 45.00

Cocktail, crystal bowl, green base . . . 28.00

Cruet, azure blue . . . 995.00

Jug, ftd, #4020, crystal, green base . . . 300.00

Mayonnaise, ftd, azure blue . . . 40.00

Pickle, azure blue . . . 28.00

Pitcher, #5000, topaz . . . 295.00

Soup, flat, azure blue . . . 195.00

Tumbler, ftd, #4020, 10 oz, crystal, green base . . . 24.00

Lafayette

Pattern #2440. Made 1931-60. Made in amber, green, and rose (1933-38); burgundy, empire green, and regal blue (1935-42); crystal (1931-60); gold tint (1938-44); ruby red (1935-39); topaz (1932-38); and wisteria (1931-38).

Almond, individual, crystal . . . 8.00

Bonbon, 5" d, handle
- Amber . . . 9.50
- Burgundy . . . 40.00

Cake plate, crystal . . . 20.00

Candlesticks, pr, two-lite, #2447, wisteria . . . 200.00

Celery, wisteria . . . 145.00

Champagne, wisteria . . . 60.00

Claret, wisteria . . . 195.00

Comport, #2400, 6", wisteria . . 125.00

Creamer and sugar, wisteria . . 125.00

Cup, regal blue . . . 20.00

Cup and saucer, wisteria . . . 35.00

Finger bowl, #869, wisteria 65.00
Goblet, wisteria 25.00
Iced tea tumbler, ftd, #5299, wisteria 60.00
Pickle, 9" l, wisteria 75.00
Plate
- Crystal, 9" d 15.00
- Burgundy, 8" d, handle 75.00
- Wisteria
  - 6" d 15.00
  - 8" d 20.00
  - 8-1/2" d 25.00
  - 9-1/2" d 65.00

Platter, wisteria, 12" l 165.00
Relish, two parts
- Burgundy, handle 50.00
- Regal blue 85.00

Sauce boat and liner, burgundy 130.00
Sauce bowl, rose 70.00
Sugar, 3-5/8", crystal 15.00
Tidbit tray, topaz, metal handle . . 65.00
Torte plate, 13" d, empire green . 70.00
Vase, 5" h, wisteria 195.00
Whiskey, #5299, ftd, wisteria . . . 165.00
Wine, #5298, wisteria 165.00

Lido

Plate Etching #329. Made 1937-55. Made in azure blue, crystal, and azure blue with crystal base (1937-43).

Bowl, 10-1/2" d, handle, four-toed, azure blue 140.00
Candle, duo flame, single, crystal 40.00
Candlesticks, pr, #2496, crystal . 75.00
Candy, cov, three parts, crystal . . 65.00
Champagne, saucer, #6017
- Azure blue 48.00
- Crystal 32.00

Cheese and cracker, azure blue 170.00
Cocktail, crystal 30.00
Comport, #2496
- Azure blue, 6-1/2" 225.00
- Crystal, 6" 45.00

Console bowl, flame, crystal 75.00
Cordial, crystal 55.00
Creamer and sugar, #2496, crystal 40.00
Dessert, two handles, crystal . . . 70.00
Goblet, #6017
- Azure blue with crystal base . . 38.00
- Crystal 35.00

Ice bucket, crystal 110.00
Iced tea tumbler, crystal 35.00
Jug, #6011, crystal 295.00
Juice tumbler, #6018, crystal . . . 24.00
Nappy, tricorner, handle, crystal . 30.00
Pitcher, 53 oz, ftd, crystal 145.00
Plate, 7-1/2" d, crystal 12.00
Relish
- Azure blue, three parts, handle 100.00
- Crystal 65.00

Salad plate, 7" d, crystal 14.00
Sauce, oval, crystal 58.00
Sherbet, crystal 30.00
Tidbit, three toes, crystal 45.00
Tumbler, 12 oz, ftd, crystal 22.00

Manor

Plate Etching #286. Made 1931-44. Made in crystal (1931-44); green (1931-35); topaz (1931-38); green bowl with crystal base (1931-35); topaz bowl with crystal base (1931-37); and crystal bowl with wisteria base (1931-35).

After dinner cup, green 45.00
Ashtray, #2412, crystal 15.00
Bowl, 12" d, #2433, green 225.00
Candlesticks, pr, #2433, 3" h
- Crystal 125.00
- #2433, 3" h, topaz 75.00

Champagne, #6007
- Crystal 40.00
- Wisteria 110.00

Claret, 4-1/2 oz, crystal bowl, green base 30.00
Cocktail, 3-1/2 oz, crystal bowl, wisteria base 30.00
Comport
- 6", green 35.00
- #2433, tall 195.00

Creamer and sugar, tea size, crystal 65.00
Cup and saucer, green 45.00
Finger bowl, crystal 65.00
Fruit bowl, green 42.00
Goblet
- #6003, 6-1/4" h
  - Crystal 40.00
  - Wisteria 125.00
- #6007, 6-1/2" h, crystal 45.00

Iced tea tumbler, #6007
- Crystal 40.00
- Wisteria 125.00

Icer bowl, orig insert, topaz 50.00
Ice tub, crystal 95.00
Jelly comport, #2419, crystal . . 48.00
Jug, #4020
- Crystal 525.00
- Wisteria 1,500.00

Oyster cocktail, #6007, crystal . 30.00
Plate
- 7-1/2" d, crystal 22.00
- 8-1/2" d, green 45.00

Relish, four parts, crystal 65.00
Sherbet, #6007, crystal 30.00
Syrup pitcher, glass lid, crystal 175.00
Sweetmeat, green 65.00
Tumbler, #6003, 9 oz, crystal bowl, topaz base 20.00
Vegetable bowl, oval, green 75.00
Whiskey, ftd, #6003, crystal 25.00

Stem #6013, cocktail, crystal bowl and foot, **$15.**

Mayfair

Pattern #2419. Made 1930-44. Made in crystal (1930-44); azure blue and green (1930-31); topaz (1930-38); gold tint (1938-44); amber and rose (1930-1942); and selected items in ebony, wisteria, and ruby red (1930-42).

After dinner cup and saucer
- Ebony 12.00
- Green 25.00

Ashtray, Rosette intaglio etch, crystal 20.00
Baker, rose 45.00
Celery, 11", topaz 16.00
Creamer and sugar, tea size, #2419
- Ebony 45.00
- Rose 38.00
- Topaz 38.00

Cup and saucer
- Amber 10.00
- Ebony 12.00

Fruit, 5" d, crystal 7.50
Gravy, attached underplate, topaz 65.00
Plate, 10" d, crystal 20.00
Relish, four parts
- Amber, New Garland etch 55.00
- Topaz, 8-3/4" l, handle 45.00
- Topaz, Daisy etch 55.00

Saucer, amber 1.75

Mayflower

Plate Etching #332. Made 1939-55 only in crystal.

Bonbon, three-toed 65.00

Bowl, 8-1/2" d, handle......... **35.00**
Cake plate, handle........... **25.00**
Candlesticks, pr
One-lite.................. **70.00**
Two-lite.................. **125.00**
Champagne................ **32.50**
Cocktail.................... **22.00**
Compote, #2560 Coronet blank, 6"
.... **35.00**
Cordial................... **75.00**
Creamer................... **36.50**
Cup and saucer............. **24.00**
Goblet, water.............. **38.00**
Iced tea tumbler, 12 oz........ **30.00**
Mayonnaise and ladle........ **45.00**
Muffin tray, handle........... **85.00**
Oyster cocktail.............. **32.00**
Pitcher, #4140.............. **595.00**
Plate
7" d...................... **22.00**
9-1/2" d.................. **65.00**
Relish, three parts........... **85.00**
Salt and pepper shakers, pr... **75.00**
Server, center handle, flame.... **80.00**
Sugar..................... **18.00**
Vase, 7" h, two handles....... **140.00**
Wine...................... **45.00**

Meadow Rose

Plate Etching #328. Made 1936-75. Made in crystal and azure blue with crystal base (1936-44).

Bowl, oval, flame............ **135.00**
Cake plate, handle, crystal..... **22.00**
Candlesticks, pr, #2496
One-lite, azure blue....... **175.00**
Two-lite, flame, crystal..... **425.00**
Three-lite, crystal......... **195.00**
Champagne, saucer, #6016
Azure blue................ **48.00**
Crystal................... **38.00**
Cocktail, 3-1/2 oz, crystal...... **25.00**
Cordial, #6016, crystal........ **60.00**
Creamer and sugar
Individual size, crystal...... **70.00**
Table size, crystal.......... **75.00**
Cup and saucer, crystal....... **35.50**
Goblet, #6016, crystal......... **35.00**
Iced tea tumbler
Azure blue, ftd............ **55.00**
Crystal................... **35.00**
Juice tumbler, 5 oz, crystal.... **25.00**
Mayonnaise, three pcs, crystal. **80.00**
Nappy, #2496, crystal, flared rim, 5" d
.... **28.00**
Oyster cocktail, crystal....... **30.00**
Pitcher, bulbous, 7" h, crystal.. **195.00**
Plate
Azure blue, 7-1/2" d........ **30.00**
Crystal
7-1/2" d................ **22.50**
10" d, handle............ **55.00**
13-1/2" d............... **45.00**
Relish, three parts
Azure blue................ **90.00**
Crystal................... **45.00**
Salt and pepper shakers, pr, azure blue...................... **260.00**
Sandwich tray, #2375, crystal, 11" d
.... **95.00**
Sherbet, 4-1/2", crystal........ **32.50**
Sugar, crystal............... **17.50**
Tray, 11" l, handle, crystal...... **50.00**
Tumbler, 13 oz, ftd, crystal..... **32.00**
Underplate, 7" d, center ring, crystal
.... **15.00**
Wine, crystal................ **45.00**

Midnight Rose

Plate Etching #316. Made 1933-57 only in crystal.

Bowl, 10-3/4" d, ftd........... **65.00**
Candlesticks, pr
#2467, three-lite........... **115.00**
#2470, one-lite............ **145.00**
#2481, 5" h, price for pr..... **125.00**
Celery, 11"................. **60.00**
Champagne................ **35.00**
Cocktail................... **22.00**
Creamer and sugar, matching tray
.... **60.00**
Cup and saucer............. **35.00**
Goblet.................... **42.00**
Iced tea tumbler............ **40.00**
Juice tumbler.............. **30.00**
Mayonnaise, two parts, oval.... **68.00**
Oyster cocktail............. **30.00**
Pickle, 9"................. **30.00**
Plate
7" d...................... **15.00**
7-1/2" d.................. **24.00**
10" d, dinner.............. **110.00**
Platter, 14" d............... **68.00**
Relish
Two parts................ **45.00**
Five parts, round, #2462, 11" d
.... **85.00**
Sauce bowl................ **65.00**
Sherbet, #6009............. **18.50**
Torte plate, 14" d, slight use.... **60.00**
Vase, 7" h................. **165.00**
Wine..................... **45.00**

Navarre

Plate Etching #327. Made 1936-82. Made in crystal (1936-82); azure bowl with crystal base (1973-82); and pink bowl with crystal base (1973-78).

Navarre, iced tea tumbler, crystal, **$45.**

Bell
Azure blue................ **125.00**
Azure blue base, crystal handle
.... **80.00**
Crystal, large claret........ **85.00**
Bonbon, three-toed, crystal.... **65.00**
Bowl, crystal
6" w, sq, two parts......... **40.00**
12" d, flared.............. **95.00**
Brandy snifter, crystal....... **165.00**
Cake plate, crystal, handle..... **75.00**
Candelabra, #2545, crystal... **595.00**
Candlesticks, pr
#2472, crystal............ **195.00**
#2482, three lites, crystal... **325.00**
#2495, two lites, flame, crystal
.... **90.00**
#2496
One-lite, crystal......... **75.00**
Two-lite, crystal......... **90.00**
Three-lite, crystal....... **190.00**
Candy, cov, three parts, crystal **225.00**
Celery, crystal, 11" l.......... **95.00**
Celery/relish, 12" l, five parts, crystal
.... **100.00**
Champagne flute
Azure blue bowl, crystal base
.... **175.00**
Crystal................... **175.00**
Champagne/saucer, 6 oz, 5-5/8"
Azure blue................ **75.00**
Crystal................... **35.00**
Pink..................... **60.00**
Cheese and cracker, crystal.. **165.00**
Claret, 4-1/2 oz
Azure blue bowl, crystal base
.... **125.00**
Crystal................... **50.00**
Pink bowl, crystal base...... **75.00**
Cocktail, #6016, crystal....... **25.00**

Comport

#2400

Crystal, 4-1/2" **45.00**

Crystal, 6-1/2" **81.00**

#2496, crystal, 5", flared **85.00**

Console bowl, 11-1/2" d, flared, crystal **70.00**

Cordial, 3-7/8" h, crystal **50.00**

Cracker plate, crystal **55.00**

Creamer and sugar, crystal

Individual size **45.00**

Table size. **50.00**

Creamer and sugar, matching tray, crystal. **165.00**

Cup and saucer, crystal **45.00**

Goblet, water

Azure blue **125.00**

Crystal **45.00**

High ball, flat, crystal. **65.00**

Ice bucket, Baroque style, crystal **160.00**

Ice tea tumbler, ftd

Azure blue **52.00**

Crystal **45.00**

Pink **55.00**

Jug, #5000, crystal. **625.00**

Juice tumbler, ftd, 5 oz, crystal. . **40.00**

Magnum, 7-1/4", 16 oz, crystal . **175.00**

Mayonnaise, two parts, crystal . . **75.00**

Nappy, round, handle, crystal . . . **40.00**

Old fashioned tumbler, crystal . . **75.00**

Pickle, #2496, crystal. **75.00**

Pitcher, crystal **500.00**

Plate, crystal

7" d. **15.00**

7-1/2" d **18.00**

8" d. **15.50**

8-1/2" d **28.50**

Relish, crystal

Two parts, 6", sq **40.00**

Three parts, 10" l, #2496 . . . . . **75.00**

Five parts, 13" l, #2419 . . . . . **145.00**

Salt and pepper shakers, pr, #2364, 2-1/4", crystal **125.00**

Sauce dish, #2496, crystal **125.00**

Sherbet, 6 oz, 4-3/8", crystal **35.00**

Sugar, crystal **25.00**

Tidbit tray, three-toed, crystal . . . **58.00**

Torte, 14" d. **95.00**

Tray, oblong, 8" l, crystal **70.00**

Tumbler, ftd

Crystal

5 oz **25.00**

10 oz **28.00**

13 oz **35.00**

Pink, 5-7/8" h, orig Lenox label **75.00**

Vase, #2470, crystal

9-1/2" h. **350.00**

10" h, ftd. **150.00**

Wine, 5-1/4", crystal **60.00**

Nectar

Plate Etching #332. Made 1936-43 only in crystal.

Cocktail, #6011. . . . . **9.00**

Cordial, #6011 . . . . **14.00**

Creme de menthe, #6011, 2 oz . **30.00**

Neo Classic

Made 1934-late 1950s. Made in crystal and regal blue, burgundy, empire green, ruby with crystal base, and crystal bowl with amber base.

Champagne, saucer, #6011

Burgundy **20.00**

Crystal **18.50**

Empire green **28.00**

Cocktail, crystal **18.50**

Goblet, #6011, 10 oz

Burgundy **35.00**

Ruby **48.00**

Iced tea tumbler, ftd, 12 oz

Burgundy **25.00**

Empire green **28.00**

Sherry, burgundy **26.00**

Tumbler, #6011, 10 oz, Regal Blue **25.00**

Whiskey, #6011, 2 oz

Regal Blue **35.00**

Ruby **35.00**

Wine, #6011, 5" h, 3 oz, burgundy **18.00**

New Garland

Plate Etching #284. Made in 1929-35. Made in amber, rose, and topaz. Also made in rose with crystal base (1931-34); and crystal bowl with amber base (1930-31).

After dinner cup, green **25.00**

After dinner cup and saucer, topaz **50.00**

Baker, 10", topaz. **60.00**

Bowl, 12" d, topaz. **65.00**

Claret, rose bowl, crystal optic base **20.00**

Fruit, 5-1/2" d, topaz **18.00**

Goblet, #4020, 11 oz, topaz **30.00**

Plate

Amber, 9" d. **15.00**

Topaz

6" d. **8.00**

8" d. **10.00**

Platter, 12" l, amber **30.00**

Salad dressing bottle, topaz . . **260.00**

Sherbet, #4020, high, 7 oz, topaz **24.00**

Vase, #2430, 8" d, topaz. **190.00**

Whiskey, #4020, 10 oz, ftd, topaz **16.00**

Oak Leaf

Brocade Plate Etching #290. Made in 1928-31. Made in crystal, green, and rose (1928-31); selected items in ebony (1929-31).

Bonbon, #2375

Crystal **24.00**

Green. **40.00**

Pink **55.00**

Bowl

Crystal, 12" d. **125.00**

Pink **195.00**

Centerpiece, oval, green. **85.00**

Cigarette box, cov, ebony. **48.00**

Comport, pink, tall. **250.00**

Ice bucket, iridized blue **200.00**

Lemon tray, handle, orchid etching, gold trim **60.00**

Lunch tray, octagon, fleur-de-lis handle, green. **75.00**

Plate, 7" d, crystal **25.00**

Salver, 12" d, rose **60.00**

Soup plate, deep liner, 8-1/2" d, green **20.00**

Sweetmeat, amber **24.00**

Tumbler, 5 oz, crystal **18.00**

Pioneer

Pattern #2350. Made 1926-60. Made in crystal, amber, and green (1926-41); blue (1926-27); and selected items in rose, azure blue (1929-36); ebony (1929-41); and burgundy, empire green, regal blue, and ruby (1934-41).

After dinner cup and saucer, amber **17.50**

Ashtray, amber **8.00**

Bouillon with liner, blue **20.00**

Bowl

5-1/2" d, amber **5.00**

9-1/4" l, oval, amber. **15.00**

Celery, 11" l, amber **22.00**

Cream soup, flat, amber **9.00**

Cup and saucer

Amber **14.00**

Burgundy. **20.00**

Cup

Fat, green **7.50**

Ftd, green **7.50**

Demitasse cup and saucer, amber **17.50**

Lunch tray, handles, amber **44.00**

Mahjong set, 8-3/4" d snack plate with sherbet, amber. **30.00**

Plate

Amber

7" d **6.00**

7-1/2" d **4.00**

9-1/2" d **10.00**

Blue, 9-1/2" d. **25.00**

Green

6" d **4.00**

7-1/2" d **4.50**

9" d 7.00
10-1/2" d. . . . 25.00
Platter, 10-3/4" l, oval, amber . . . 15.00
Sauce boat, amber 22.50
Saucer, green 3.00
Sugar, cov, green 40.00
Vase, 3" h, amber 18.00

Priscilla

Pattern #2321. Made 1925-30. Made in amber, blue, crystal, and green (1925-30), and azure blue and rose (1929-30).

Bouillon, crystal 10.00
Creamer, rose 10.00
Custard cup, handle, green 12.50
Goblet, 9 oz
Amber 24.50
Crystal. . . . 15.00
Mayonnaise, crystal 25.00
Mug, ftd, green 60.00
Pitcher, blue 90.00
Plate, 8" d, blue. . . . 20.00

Raleigh

Pattern #2574. Made 1939-55 only in crystal.

Bonbon. . . . 15.00
Bowl, 13" d 30.00
Cake plate, 10" d 15.00
Creamer and sugar, #681, ftd . . 20.00
Cruet, orig stopper 50.00
Cup and saucer 12.50
Mayonnaise, underplate, and ladle 35.00
Nappy, handle. . . . 15.00
Plate
7-1/2" d 6.00
8-1/2" d 8.50
Relish, three parts, 10" l 40.00
Torte plate, 13" d 30.00
Tray, crystal. . . . 15.00
Whipped cream bowl. . . . 30.00

Rambler

Pattern #1827. Made 1911-15 only in crystal. Some items were reproduced in 1969.

Berry bowl, 4-1/2" d 10.00
Champagne, hollow stem 30.00
Creamer and sugar 30.00
Goblet 28.00
Iced tea tumbler, ftd 25.00
Nappy, 10" d 20.00
Oyster cocktail. . . . 20.00
Plate, 8" d 10.00
Relish, five parts, crystal, plain or gold trim. . . . 70.00
Sherbet 14.00
Tumbler, water 15.00

Randolph

Pattern #2675. Made 1961-65 only in handmade milk glass.

Bowl, 5-3/4" sq 10.00
Candlesticks, pr, 6" h 45.00
Creamer. . . . 17.50
Cup and saucer. . . . 17.50
Egg cup 15.00
Nappy, sq. . . . 14.00
Plate, 9" d, luncheon 14.50
Preserve, cov, ftd. . . . 27.50
Salt and pepper shakers, pr, chrome top 15.00
Sugar, open 10.00

Rogene

Plate Etching #269. Made 1924-1929 only in crystal.

Champagne. . . . 15.00
Goblet, #5082 . . . . 20.00
Jug, ftd, No. 7 . . . . 360.00
Mayonnaise. . . . 60.00
Pitcher, ftd 225.00
Plate, #2283
6" d. . . . 8.00
7" d. . . . 10.00
8" d. . . . 15.00
Tumbler, 13 oz 45.00

Romance

Plate Etching #341. Made 1942-72 only in crystal.

Bowl
10" l, oval, handle, orig paper label 65.00
11" l, oblong, shallow. . . . 70.00
Candlesticks, pr
#2594
5-1/2" h, orig paper label . . 75.00
8" h, three-lite 225.00
#6023, two-lite 115.00
Celery. . . . 50.00
Champagne. . . . 35.00
Cheese and cracker plate 40.00
Claret 60.00
Cocktail 30.00
Compote
7-5/8", tall. . . . 75.00
8", Sonata. . . . 125.00
Console bowl 45.00
Cordial. . . . 75.00
Creamer and sugar, table size . . 75.00
Cup and saucer. . . . 47.50
Fruit bowl, 12" d 65.00
Goblet 35.00
Iced tea tumbler 35.00
Jug, #6011. . . . 550.00
Juice tumbler 32.00
Lily pond, 12" d 75.00
Mayonnaise, plate, spoon. . . . 85.00
Oyster cocktail, 4 oz. . . . 25.00
Pickle. . . . 40.00
Plate
6" d. . . . 20.00
7-1/2" d 24.00
9-1/2" d 65.00
11" d 42.00
Relish, three parts 50.00
Salt and pepper shakers, pr, crystal
Individual size. . . . 65.00
Table size, #2364 . . . . 78.00
Sandwich server, plume center handle 85.00
Sherbet
High 30.00
Low. . . . 25.00
Torte plate, 14" d 65.00
Tumbler, 6" 25.00
Wine, 5-1/2"h. . . . 50.00

Rose

Cutting. Found on crystal.

Champagne 35.00
Cocktail 30.00
Cordial 75.00
Creamer and sugar, matching tray, tea size 95.00
Creamer, table size. . . . 45.00
Cup and saucer 45.00
Finger bowl, blown. . . . 45.00
Goblet. . . . 36.00
Iced tea tumbler. . . . 36.00
Jug
#2666, contour 195.00
#6011 . . . . 395.00
Juice tumbler. . . . 30.00
Oyster cocktail. . . . 30.00
Plate
7-1/2" d 22.00
8-1/2" d 25.00
Relish
Two parts 65.00
Three parts 75.00
Sherbet. . . . 30.00
Wine 35.00

Royal

Plate Etching #273. Made 1925-32. Made in amber, black, blue, and green.

Bouillon cup, 3-1/2" d, green. . . 18.50
Candlesticks, pr
Amber. . . . 55.00
Green, 3". . . . 50.00
Candy box, cov, light green, three parts, fleur-de-lis finial. . . . 125.00
Centerpiece bowl, 12" d, rolled edge, amber 45.00
Champagne, amber 20.00
Console bowl, amber. . . . 32.00
Cordial, crystal 35.00
Cup and saucer, amber 15.00
Finger bowl, amber 25.00
Goblet, amber. . . . 25.00
Grapefruit, blown, ftd
Amber. . . . 48.00
Crystal 40.00

Jelly comport, 5", amber **35.00**
Parfait, amber **35.00**
Pickle, 6-3/8" l, eight-sided oval, worn gold edge **15.00**
Plate
Amber
6" d **6.50**
7-1/2" d **7.00**
8" d **10.00**
Green, 10" d.............. **30.00**
Platter, amber, 12" l, slight scratches **40.00**
Relish, amber, eight-sided oval, worn gold edge
8-3/8" l **18.50**
10-1/4" l **22.00**
Soup, flat, amber **35.00**
Tumbler, water, ftd, 9 oz, amber . **18.00**
Underplate, 6-1/8" d, amber **6.50**
Urn, 10" h, ftd, #2324, amber... **125.00**
Vase, #2292
Amber, flared, 7" h **95.00**
Gold edge, 8" h **95.00**

Seville

Plate Etching #274. Made 1926-34. Made in amber, blue, crystal, and green.

Bowl, amber................. **10.00**
Butter, cov, crystal........... **85.00**
Candy box, cov, #2331, crystal.. **80.00**
Centerpiece, 11" d, blue **95.00**
Cheese and cracker, crystal.... **40.00**
Cream soup, amber **30.00**
Dinner plate, amber **12.00**
Goblet, amber, 7" h **30.00**
Plate, 7-1/2" d, green **6.50**
Saucer, amber **3.00**
Salad plate, amber **6.00**
Sherbet, amber
4" h...................... **18.50**
5-1/4" h.................. **22.00**
Tumbler, ftd, 5", amber **20.00**
Underplate, 6-1/2" d, green...... **5.00**

Sprite

Cutting #823. Made 1950-68. Made in combination gray and polished cutting on crystal only.

Champagne................. **20.00**
Goblet, 6-1/8" h **25.00**
Iced tea tumbler, ftd, 6" h **25.00**
Juice tumbler, ftd, 41/2" h **21.50**
Mayonnaise, #2630/477, three-pc set **36.00**
Sherbet **18.50**
Torte plate, 14" d **42.00**

Sun-Ray

Pattern #2510. Made 1935-44. Made in amber, azure blue, crystal, green, and topaz (1935-38); gold tint (1938-40); and selected items in ruby red (1935-40).

Almond, crystal **24.00**
Ashtray, crystal.............. **18.00**
Bonbon, 7-1/2" d, three-toed, crystal **22.50**
Bowl, 12" d, handle, crystal **45.00**
Celery, 10" l, crystal **32.50**
Coaster.................... **10.00**
Compote, low, crystal......... **35.00**
Console set, bowl and pr candlesticks, crystal **275.00**
Creamer and sugar, individual size, crystal **30.00**
Decanter, #25010-1/2, orig stopper, oblong, crystal, rye, or scotch... **85.00**
Goblet
Amber................... **25.00**
Golden Ray, 9 oz, topaz..... **20.00**
Ice bucket, crystal **95.00**
Jelly, ftd, cov
Crystal **75.00**
Golden Ray.............. **125.00**
Jug, ice lip, crystal **135.00**
Mayonnaise and underplate, crystal **45.00**
Nappy
Round, handle, ruby, 5" d.... **45.00**
Tricorn
One handle, ruby, 5" l **45.00**
Two handles, crystal **17.50**
Nut cup, amber.............. **20.00**
Oil bottle, stopper, crystal **75.00**
Pickle, ruby................. **75.00**
Plate, 6" d, crystal............ **10.00**
Relish, two parts
Crystal **32.50**
Golden Ray............... **85.00**
Salt, individual, crystal **20.00**
Sherbet, crystal **19.50**
Sugar, 2-3/4", crystal.......... **10.00**
Sweetmeat, divided, 6" l, 4" w, ruby **75.00**
Torte plate, 16-1/2" d
Crystal **70.00**
Ruby red................. **75.00**
Tray, oval, 7" l, 5" w, ruby **75.00**
Tumbler, green **18.00**
Vase, 9" h, sq, ftd, crystal **75.00**

Trojan

Made 1929-44. Made in rose pink, some green, and topaz yellow.

Ashtray, topaz yellow **55.00**
Baker, oval, topaz yellow **100.00**
Berry bowl, topaz yellow **30.00**
Bonbon, handle, topaz yellow .. **50.00**
Bowl, 12" d, topaz yellow **125.00**
Cake plate, handle, rose pink... **85.00**
Candlesticks, pr, #2394, topaz yellow **65.00**
Celery, topaz yellow........... **95.00**
Cereal bowl, topaz yellow **75.00**
Champagne
Rose pink................. **40.00**
Topaz yellow **38.00**
Cocktail, topaz yellow **40.00**
Combination bowl, #2415, topaz yellow **250.00**
Comport
Rose pink, 6" **90.00**
Topaz yellow, 4-1/2"......... **40.00**
Cordial
Rose pink................ **150.00**
Topaz yellow **75.00**
Cream soup and liner, topaz yellow **70.00**
Cruet, topaz yellow **600.00**
Cup and saucer
Rose pink................. **60.00**
Topaz yellow **40.00**
Demitasse cup and saucer, topaz yellow **75.00**
Dessert bowl, large, handle, topaz yellow **95.00**
Goblet, topaz yellow **55.00**
Grapefruit and icer, topaz yellow **145.00**
Iced tea tumbler, ftd
Rose pink................. **95.00**
Topaz yellow **50.00**
Jug, #5000, topaz yellow...... **595.00**
Juice tumbler, ftd **35.00**
Lemon plate, handle
Rose pink................. **65.00**
Topaz yellow **24.00**
Mint, 6" d, ftd, master, topaz yellow **75.00**
Plate, topaz yellow
6" d **9.50**
7-1/2" d **8.00**
8-1/2" d **16.00**
Relish, two parts
Rose pink................. **95.00**
Topaz yellow **65.00**
Service tray, insert
Rose pink................ **295.00**
Topaz yellow **300.00**
Soup, 7" d, flat
Rose pink................ **195.00**
Topaz yellow **195.00**
Sugar bowl, topaz yellow **40.00**
Sugar pail, topaz yellow **250.00**
Tomato juice insert, topaz yellow **20.00**
Tumbler, water, ftd, topaz yellow . **32.50**

Vase
Crystal, deep etch, c1913-18, 6" h . . . 95.00
Topaz yellow, bulbous bottom, 8" h . . . 400.00

Vernon

Plate Etching #277. Made 1927-34. Made in amber, crystal, and green (1927-34); azure blue (1928-34); and orchid (1927-28).

Berry bowl, green . . . 30.00
Bouillon and saucer, azure blue 50.00
Candlesticks, pr, mushroom, green . . . 90.00
Candy, cov, three parts
Green . . . 100.00
Orchid . . . 130.00
Centerpiece bowl, 13" l, oval, orchid . . . 195.00
Cereal bowl, orchid . . . 55.00
Cheese and cracker plate, round, orchid . . . 90.00
Chop plate, orchid . . . 140.00
Cup and saucer, orchid . . . 24.00
Finger bowl
Green . . . 20.00
Orchid . . . 35.00
Finger bowl and liner, azure blue . . . 35.00
Goblet, green . . . 42.50
Grapefruit and insert, green . . . 95.00
Gravy boat and liner, green . . . 175.00
Parfait, orchid . . . 55.00
Pitcher, orchid . . . 500.00
Plate, 9-1/2" d, orchid . . . 35.00
Server, center handle, orchid . . . 90.00
Sherbet, orchid . . . 28.00
Tumbler, etched, ftd, crystal . . . 15.00
Vegetable bowl, oval, green . . . 85.00

Versailles

Plate Etching #278. Made 1928-44. Made in azure blue, green, rose, topaz, and gold tint.

After dinner creamer and sugar
Azure blue . . . 250.00
Green . . . 65.00
After dinner cup and saucer
Azure blue . . . 175.00
Rose pink . . . 125.00
Ashtray
Azure blue . . . 65.00
Rose . . . 70.00
Topaz . . . 65.00
Baker, oval, azure blue . . . 165.00
Bar tumbler, 2 oz, azure blue . . . 95.00
Berry Bowl, azure blue . . . 55.00
Bonbon
Azure blue . . . 42.00
Rose pink . . . 65.00
Topaz . . . 35.00
Bowl
Azure blue, #2394, 12" d . . . 125.00
Green
5" d . . . 35.00
12" d . . . 135.00
Topaz
5" d . . . 40.00
9-1/2" d, scroll handles . . . 45.00
Candlesticks, pr
#2375-1/2
Azure blue . . . 175.00
Green, mushroom . . . 150.00
#2395
Azure blue, 3" h . . . 180.00
Green, 3" h . . . 225.00
Celery, green . . . 90.00
Centerpiece, 11" d, round
Azure blue . . . 140.00
Green . . . 135.00
Cereal bowl
Rose, 6-1/2" d . . . 95.00
Topaz, 6-1/2" d . . . 70.00
Champagne
#5099, 6 oz, 6-1/8" h
Azure blue . . . 50.00
Green . . . 35.00
Rose . . . 70.00
Topaz . . . 45.00
#5298, azure blue . . . 45.00
Cheese comport, green . . . 125.00
Claret, #5298, 6" h, 4 oz
Azure blue . . . 165.00
Rose . . . 195.00
Cocktail
Green . . . 45.00
Rose . . . 67.50
Topaz . . . 60.00
Comport
#2375, 7-1/2" w, 6-1/2" h
Azure blue . . . 125.00
Rose . . . 130.00
#2400, 6"
Rose . . . 125.00
Topaz . . . 85.00
#5098, rose, 5" . . . 135.00
Cordial, rose . . . 195.00
Cracker plate, handle, azure blue . . . 95.00
Creamer and sugar
Azure blue . . . 125.00
Green . . . 125.00
Cream soup
Azure blue, liner . . . 55.00
Rose . . . 85.00
Topaz . . . 20.00
Cruet, topaz . . . 350.00
Cup and saucer
Azure blue . . . 45.00
Green . . . 45.00
Rose . . . 45.00
Topaz . . . 30.00
Decanter, stopper missing, topaz . . . 750.00
Dessert bowl, large, handle, azure blue . . . 155.00
Fruit bowl
Azure blue . . . 35.00
Rose . . . 65.00
Topaz, 5" . . . 28.00
Fruit cocktail insert, rose . . . 42.50
Goblet
Azure blue . . . 65.00
Rose . . . 85.00
Topaz . . . 65.00
Grapefruit and liner, green . . . 150.00
Gravy boat, rose . . . 325.00
Ice bucket, azure blue . . . 165.00
Iced tea tumbler, #5099, 12 oz, 6" h, ftd
Azure blue . . . 75.00
Rose . . . 75.00
Topaz . . . 50.00
Icer bowl and tomato juice insert, topaz . . . 175.00
Jug, #5000, ftd
Azure blue . . . 695.00
Green . . . 600.00
Rose . . . 795.00
Juice tumbler, ftd
Azure blue . . . 35.00
Rose . . . 52.50
Topaz . . . 35.00
Lemon plate, handle
Azure blue . . . 48.00
Rose pink . . . 60.00
Mayonnaise ladle, green . . . 35.00
Mayonnaise, underplate
Rose . . . 125.00
Topaz . . . 40.00
Mayonnaise, underplate, and spoon, azure blue . . . 135.00
Mint, #2394, 4-1/2", green . . . 50.00
Nut dish, individual size, azure blue . . . 65.00
Oyster cocktail, 5-1/2" oz
Azure blue . . . 55.00
Green . . . 50.00
Rose . . . 48.00
Topaz . . . 35.00
Parfait
Azure blue . . . 145.00
Green . . . 95.00
Pitcher, #5000
Azure blue . . . 795.00
Green . . . 595.00
Rose . . . 595.00
Topaz . . . 495.00
Plate
Azure blue
6" d . . . 24.50

7" d **26.00**
8-3/4" d **55.00**
9-1/2" d **95.00**
10-1/4" d **65.00**

Green
7-1/2" d **28.00**
8-1/2" d **28.50**
10-1/4" d **90.00**

Rose
6" d **22.50**
10-1/4" d **95.00**

Topaz
4" d **15.00**
6" d **20.00**
7-1/2" d **24.00**
8-1/2" d **32.00**
9-1/2" d **50.00**

Platter
Green, 12" l **100.00**
Rose, 15" l **300.00**
Topaz, 15" l **95.00**

Relish, two parts, 8-1/2" l
Azure blue **70.00**
Green **55.00**
Rose **48.00**
Topaz **38.00**

Salt and pepper shakers, pr
Azure blue **260.00**
Rose **220.00**

Sauce boat and liner, topaz . . . **250.00**
Seafood insert, green **22.50**
Server, center handle, rose **80.00**
Service tray, insert, green **375.00**
Serving bowl, two handles, azure blue **110.00**

Sherbet
Azure blue **35.00**
Green **30.00**
Rose **37.50**
Topaz **14.75**

Soup bowl, green **195.00**

Sugar bowl
Azure blue **40.00**
Green **20.00**

Sugar pail, azure blue **300.00**
Sweetmeat, green **45.00**

Tomato juice insert
Green **22.50**
Rose **25.00**

Tumbler, ftd
Azure blue
5-1/4" h, orig paper label . . **45.00**
6" h, #5298 . . . . **70.00**
Rose, #5298, 6" h. **45.00**

Vase, rose pink, #2385, fan **695.00**

Whipped cream pail
Azure blue **185.00**
Rose **275.00**

Whiskey, ftd, rose **125.00**

Wine
Azure blue **85.00**
Rose, 5-3/8" h **125.00**

Vesper

Plate Etching #275. Made 1926-34. Made in amber and green (1926-34); and selected items made in blue (1926-28).

After dinner cup and saucer
Amber **65.00**
Green **50.00**

Berry bowl, amber **16.00**
Bouillon, green. **14.00**

Bowl
5" d, amber **22.00**
10" d, ftd, #2524, amber **85.00**

Candlesticks, pr
3" h, green **70.00**
4" h
Amber, #2324 . . . . **115.00**
Blue, #2324 . . . . **145.00**

Candy dish, cov, 1/2 lb, green . **120.00**
Centerpiece bowl, 13-1/2" d, amber **125.00**

Cereal bowl
Amber **40.00**
Green **45.00**

Champagne, amber **40.00**
Claret, green, 4-1/2 oz, 5-5/8" h . **65.00**
Cocktail, amber **35.00**

Comport
Regular stem, green **125.00**
Twist stem
Amber **45.00**
Blue **125.00**

Console bowl
Amber, rolled edge, 11" d. . . . **45.00**
Blue, #2297, three toes, 12" d **300.00**
Green, ftd, 13" d **65.00**

Creamer and sugar
Amber **75.00**
Blue **250.00**
Green, ftd **85.00**

Cream soup, green **30.00**
Cup and saucer, amber **45.00**

Fruit bowl, 5-1/2" d
Amber **35.00**
Blue **45.00**

Goblet
Amber **45.00**
Blue **125.00**

Grapefruit, ftd, blown, green . . . **70.00**

Ice bucket
Amber **65.00**
Blue **550.00**

Iced tea tumbler, amber **45.00**
Jug, #5000, green. **650.00**
Oyster cocktail, 3", ftd, amber . . **45.00**
Parfait, blue **95.00**

Plate
Amber
7-1/2" d **14.00**
8" d **14.00**
8-1/2" d **18.00**
9-1/2" d **60.00**
10-1/2" d **65.00**

Blue
8-3/4" d **55.00**
10" d **65.00**

Green
6" d **12.00**
8-1/2" d **25.00**
9-1/2" d **50.00**

Platter, amber, 12" l **95.00**
Soup, flat, 7" d, blue **65.00**

Tumbler, #5000
Amber, 9 oz, ftd **30.00**
Green, 9 oz, ftd **35.00**

Vase, #2292, green, trumpet, 8" h **165.00**
Wine, green **50.00**

Stem #6013, goblet, crystal bowl and foot, **$20.**

Victoria

Pattern #4024. Made 1934-43. Made in crystal, regal blue bowl and crystal base, burgundy bowl and crystal base, empire green, and selected pieces made in ruby.

Celery, #183, crystal with frosting **75.00**
Cocktail, 1-3/4" h, 1 oz, empire green **20.00**
Cordial, 3-1/8" h, regal blue. **50.00**
Goblet, 5-3/4" h, empire green . . **25.00**

Oyster cocktail, crystal 10.00
Relish, canoe shape, satin highlights 85.00
Sherbet, crystal............... 8.00

Wakefield

Cutting #820. Made 1942-72 only in rock crystal.

Candlesticks, #6023 .... 75.00
Claret, #6023 .... 20.00
Finger bowl 10.00
Goblet, luncheon, #6023/63 .... 18.00
Jug, ftd 90.00
Juice tumbler, 4-1/2" h, ftd..... 22.00
Plate
6" d 8.00
7" d 9.00
8" d 12.00
Sherbet, 4-7/8" h............ 22.00
Tumbler, 5-3/4" h, ftd.......... 24.00

Willow

Etching #335. Made 1939-45 only in crystal.

Candlesticks, pr, 4" h 95.00
Celery 48.00
Champagne 25.00
Cocktail.................... 18.00
Cordial 65.00
Creamer and sugar
Individual size............ 85.00
Table size 60.00
Cup and saucer 32.00
Fruit bowl 10.00
Goblet, 9 oz 35.00
Jug, ftd 360.00
Juice tumbler.............. 16.00
Mayonnaise 48.00
Olive 35.00
Pickle 42.00
Plate
7-1/2" d 28.00
9-1/2" d 60.00
Sherbet.................... 35.00
Sugar, 3", crystal............ 20.00
Wine 45.00

Willowmere

Plate Etching #333. Made only in crystal.

Bowl
11" d, handle.............. 65.00
11-1/2" d, crimped 65.00
12" d, flared............... 55.00
Cake tray, 10-1/2" d, handle 75.00
Candlesticks, pr
Coronet blank 75.00
#2560-1/2, 4" h 60.00
Celery, 11"................. 70.00
Champagne 35.00
Cocktail.................... 30.00
Creamer and sugar
Individual size............. 50.00
Table size, ftd 70.00
Cup and saucer.............. 42.00
Demitasse cup and saucer 36.00
Goblet, 7-1/4" h 40.00
Iced tea tumbler, 12 oz 38.00
Mayonnaise and liner......... 48.00
Oyster cocktail 20.00
Pitcher, #5000 .... 395.00
Plate
7" d......................... 14.00
7-1/2" d 22.00
13-3/4" d, light use.......... 45.00
Relish
Two parts................. 48.00
Four parts 70.00
Five parts................ 125.00
Server, center handle, #2560 ... 50.00
Sherbet, tall 30.00
Torte plate, 14" d.............. 65.00
Tumbler, 12 oz, ftd, #6024...... 30.00
Vase, #2568, 9" h 225.00
Wine, 3-1/2 oz 16.00

Fry Glass

History: The H. C. Fry Glass Co. of Rochester, Pennsylvania, began operating in 1901 and continued in business until 1933. Its first products were brilliant-period cut glass. It later produced Depression glass tablewares. In 1922, the company patented heat-resisting ovenware in an opalescent color. This "Pearl Oven Glass," produced in a variety of pieces for oven and table, included casseroles, meat trays, and pie and cake pans. Most pieces of the oven glass are marked "Fry," with model numbers and sizes.

Fry's beautiful art line, Foval, was produced only in 1926 and 1927. It is pearly opalescent, with jade green or delft blue trim. It is always evenly opalescent, never striped like Fenton's opalescent line. Foval examples are rarely signed, except for occasional silver-overlay pieces marked "Rockwell."

Reference: Fry Glass Society, *Collector's Encyclopedia of Fry Glass*, Collector Books, 1989, 1998 value update.

Collectors' Club: H. C. Fry Glass Society, P.O. Box 41, Beaver, PA 15009.

Reproduction Alert: In the 1970s, reproductions of Foval were made in abundance in Murano, Italy. These pieces, including items such as candlesticks and toothpicks, have teal

Art glass

Candleholder, Azure blue 25.00
Compote
6" d, 6-7/8" h, opaque pale green 450.00
7-7/8" d, 3-1/2" h, amethyst flared bowl, crystal stem, 4-1/4" d amethyst disk foot 180.00
Cordial, 5-1/2" h, 2 oz, crystal optic bowl, green twist stem 28.00
Creamer, 4" h, pinched top, yellow body, three blue-green loops, applied deep blue handle 175.00
Goblet, Royal Blue, 6-1/4" h 35.00
Ivy ball
Emerald green, crystal swirl connector................ 60.00
Rose, crystal swirl connector. 65.00
Lamp shade, 6" h, 6-1/4" d at base, 2" fitter ring, opalescent blue 95.00
Lemonade tumbler, applied handle, colorless, fired on yellow and gold trim, 12 oz 45.00
Pitcher
9-1/4" h, Diamond Optic pattern, chrome green, ground pontil 85.00
9-1/4" h, 7" w, Crackle, cov, colorless, green handle and knob 230.00
Plate, 7-1/2" d, jade, sterling silver floral overlay.................... 185.00
Relish, two parts, irid, holder ... 60.00
Sherbet, black, Thistle Petal foot 24.00
Tumbler
10 oz, conical, colorless, sterling silver floral overlay, sgd "Rockland" 110.00
13 oz, 5-1/2" h, thin colorless body, red fired top band, black glass scalloped feet 38.50
Vase
10" h, amber crackle body, applied blue loop handles, ground bottom 85.00
12" h, opalescent body, pink loopings................ 215.00
Wine, Royal Blue, 3-3/4" h 35.00

Cut and etched glass

Bowl
8" d, pineapple design, wheel cutting, sgd 120.00
11" d, 6" h, hobstars and pinwheel cutting, sgd 400.00
Goblet
Rose etch, #7816, 10 oz..... 24.00
Wild Rose etch, #51 .... 30.00
Ice cream tray, 14" l, 7" w, Nelson pattern variation, allover cutting, sgd "Fry"..................... 290.00
Iced tea set, Japanese Maid, deeply etched, ftd pitcher, six handles, ftd tumblers 525.00
Jug, Wild Rose etch, 64 oz, cut fluted neck..................... 165.00

Juice tumbler, Wild Rose etch, 3-5/8" h, 5 oz, cut fluted base **20.00**

Nappy, 6" d, pinwheel and fan with hobstar center, sgd **60.00**

Sherbet, 4" h, Chicago pattern . . **75.00**

Soda tumbler, Wild Rose etch, 5" h, 12 oz, handle, 16-point cut star base **28.00**

Tumbler

Pinwheel, zipper, and fan motifs, sgd, six-pc set **180.00**

Wild Rose etch, #51, 3-1/2" h, 8 oz, cut fluted base **24.00**

Wine, Wild Rose etch, 5-1/4" h, 3 oz, cut fluted stem **28.00**

Bowl, opalescent swirls, cobalt blue rim, 8-1/2" d, **$85**

Foval

Bouillon cup and saucer, pearl white, two cobalt blue handles **85.00**

Bud vase

9-1/2" h, pearl white, Delft blue wafer attachment **125.00**

10" h, pearl white, cobalt blue foot **140.00**

Canapé plate, 6-1/4" d, 4" h, cobalt blue center handle **175.00**

Candlesticks, pr, 12" h, pearl white candlesticks, jade green threading and trim **1,380.00**

Center bowl, 10-1/2" d, pearl white, Delft blue rim **125.00**

Compote

6-3/4" d, alabaster white bowl and foot, jade green stem **120.00**

8-3/4" d, 6-3/4" h, opalescent pearl white bowl, pale blue loopings and blue foot **175.00**

Creamer and sugar

Delft blue handles **325.00**

Green jade handles **425.00**

Cream soup, opalescent **55.00**

Cruet, pearl white body, cobalt blue handle, orig stopper **125.00**

Cup and saucer, pearl white, Delft blue handles **65.00**

Decanter, 9" h, ftd, applied Delft blue handle **195.00**

Eggcup, jade base **145.00**

Fruit bowl, 9-7/8" d, 5-1/4" h, pearl white, ridged, delft blue foot . . . **520.00**

Goblet, fiery opalescent pearl white body, pink loopings **90.00**

Lemonade pitcher

6" h, Pearl Ware, Delft blue handle **145.00**

6-1/4" h, Icicle pattern, green handle **95.00**

Parfait, 6-1/2" h, pearl white body, Delft blue stain **175.00**

Perfume bottle, 7-1/2" h, Foval body, Delft blue stopper, etched flower on pearl glass dauber, pearl bottle with flared rim, slender vessel dec with similar etched blossoms, leafy stems, Delft blue ftd base, c1930 . . . . . **300.00**

Pitcher, alabaster body, jade green base and handle **295.00**

Plate, 9-1/2" d, pearl white, Delft blue rim **75.00**

Sugar bowl, open, 3" h, 5-1/2" w, pearl white body, green opalescent handles **230.00**

Tankard pitcher, 10-1/2" h, 5" w, applied Delft Blue large loop handle and foot, strong pearlescence . **675.00**

Teacup and saucer, Delft blue handles **95.00**

Teapot, 10" w, 6" h, pearl white

Cobalt blue spout, handle and knob **350.00**

Green, spout, handle, and knob, two small chips **330.00**

Toothpick holder, pearl white, Delft blue handle **85.00**

Tumbler, 3-7/8" h, waisted **40.00**

Vase

7-1/2" h, jade green, rolled rim and foot **225.00**

9" h, trumpet, pearl white, jade green foot **395.00**

Wine, pearl white, Delft blue stem **165.00**

Reamer, Ovenware, **$35.**

Ovenware

Bean pot, #1924, 1 quart **45.00**

Bread maker, 9" l **25.00**

Butter dish, cov, Pearl Oven Ware **75.00**

Casserole, cov

#1938, 8-3/8" d, Pearl Oven Ware **50.00**

#1932-9D, Pearl Oven Ware . . **65.00**

Pearl Oven Ware, etched gold dec lid, metal holder, 1938 . . . . . . **75.00**

Child's pie plate, Pearl Oven Ware **50.00**

Custard cup, flared, opaque **12.00**

Hot plate, 3 ftd, 8" d **35.00**

Grill plate, 10-1/2" d, marked "Pearl Oven Ware" **35.00**

Pie plate **35.00**

Platter

14-3/4" l, oval, leaf cutting **75.00**

17" l, Oven Ware **65.00**

Reamer, 7-1/4" d, 3-1/8" h, vaseline **130.00**

Trivet, 8" d, #1959, Oven Ware . . **30.00**

GALLÉ

1867–1904

History: Emile Gallé was one of the most famous glassmakers and designers from Nancy, France. Born in 1846, he learned the art of glassmaking from his father. He furthered his studies in art at Weimar and traveled frequently to Paris and London to study glass and glass techniques.

Gallé opened his own glasshouse in 1867, and began production of art glass in 1874 with his father. This Nancy factory did very well and soon expanded into cameo and cased glasswares. Gallé was a leading exponent of the Art Nouveau movement in glassmaking, furniture, and other decorative arts.

Complicated cameo-cutting techniques allowed intricate glassware to be crafted to Gallé's exacting standards. One of the more common techniques of the factory was the production of cameo ware with detailed floral patterns on an opaque white background. Opaque-colored backgrounds of many other colors were also used. Much like his contemporary, Louis Tiffany, Gallé was a designer and left much of the actual crafting to others. The Art Nouveau movement, as well as the increasing interest in Japanese and other Oriental-style decoration, influenced the lovely glass creations he designed.

Examples of Gallé's wares were exhibited at the Paris Expositions of 1878 and 1884. They were also exhibited there in 1889 and 1900 and received wide acclaim for their beauty. Gallé's influence on other glasshouses, such as De Verre, in the Nancy region, was felt as the "School of Nancy" grew around his factory.

After Gallé's death in 1904, the factory continued production until 1931. Most pieces of Gallé glass were signed. Cameo glasswares have the bold signature cameo carved into the piece. Pieces made after Gallé's death are signed with the classic signature and a star.

References: Victor Arwas, *Glass Art Nouveau to Art Deco*, Rizzoli International Publications, Inc., 1977; Tim Newark, *Emile Gallé*, The Apple Press, 1989; Harold Newman, *An Illustrated Dictionary of Glass*, Thames and Hudson, 1977; Albert C. Revi, *Nineteenth Century Glass*, reprint, Schiffer Publishing, 1981.

Museums: Bergstrom-Mahler Museum, Neenah, WI; The Chrysler Museum, Norfolk, VA; The Corning Museum of Glass, Corning, NY; The Toledo Museum of Art, Toledo, OH.

Cameo

Bonbonniere, cov, 4" h, Verre Parlant, egg shaped, frosted body, violet overlay, cameo-etched rooster and phrase "Le cou de Village," cameo sgd "Galle" **1,750.00**

Bowl

3-1/2" w, 3" h, fire polished, burgundy leaves, berry dec, translucent ground, sgd "Galle" in cameo **1,200.00**

5" d, 4-1/2" h, round, small pedestal base, cameo-etched lime green flowers and leaves over frosted gray and pink ground, top rim pulled to make five points, sgd, two spots repolished, inclusion on int. base **400.00**

11" l, 3-1/4" h, frosted body, blue and violet overlay, cameo-etched water lilies floating on water, cameo sgd "Galle" **1,300.00**

Box, cov

3-1/2" h, frosted fiery amber-yellow base and cover, orange sienna layer cameo-etched all over as blossoming leafy plants, sgd "Galle" on cover and base, some color variation **1,265.00**

4" d, 3" h, chartreuse dec with panoramic crimson florals on leafy burgundy branches, sgd "Galle" in cameo on cov and base. **1,500.00**

4-3/8" d, compressed spherical shape, flat lid, amber ground, purple overlay, cameo-etched stalk of starflowers, lid and base sgd in cameo **800.00**

Brush pot, 5-1/2" h, sq, dark yellow body, overlay small trumpet flowers and leaves, enameled white, green, and maroon, gilt highlights, sgd in cameo, c1900 .... **3,300.00**

Bud vase, 4" h, tricolor, frosty citron ground, raspberry primroses, mahogany foliage, sgd "Galle" in cameo, polishing to ext. rim, few short scratches **700.00**

Cabinet vase

2-3/8" h, conical oval, pink within frosted glass, green and amethyst overlay, cameo-etched as blossoming cluster, sgd "Galle" at lower edge **490.00**

2-1/2" h, 2-1/4" w, squatty, gray acid ground, lavender at throat, cameo-etched green leaves and purple and green floral spray, sgd **350.00**

2-1/2" h, 3-1/2" d, frosted green, yellow, and clear ground, cameo-etched green and yellow maple leaves and seedlings, sgd, two chips in design **450.00**

3-1/2" h, flattened sphere, green, orange, and frosted, cameo-etched acorns and oak leaf branches, sgd "Galle" on reverse **600.00**

Coupe, 4-3/8" d, 2-1/4" h, frosted turquoise body, magenta-red overlay, crisply cameo-etched leafy blossoming plants, side sgd "Galle" **750.00**

Creamer, 3-1/4" h, 2-1/4" d, frosted peach ground, cameo-etched red berries and leaves, two acid cuttings, applied frosted handle, cameo sgd **1,600.00**

Decanter, 9-1/2" h, transparent amber body, flattened and ribbed body engraved with Rampion lion on one side, scrolled fleur-de-lis on obverse, mushroom stopper, applied buttons to sides, engraved "Gallé depose" beside leafy vine **1,400.00**

Ewer, 9-1/4" h, compressed spherical body and spout, applied handle and vines, colorless body, wheel carved lines simulating opening calla lily, sgd "E Gallé" on base, c1900 .... **3,500.00**

Floor vase, 30-1/2" h, 6-1/4" d top, 12" d base, highly carved ferns in shades of brown and burgundy, crystal and pink ground with clear carved shaded green ferns in background, sgd **8,500.00**

Lamp, table

14-1/2" h, 12" d, wrought iron base cast with stylized foliage issuing three down-turned arms, each with flared frosted yellow glass shade, red overlay, cameo-etched trumpet flowers and foliage, each cameo sgd "Galle" **6,500.00**

25" h, 18" d domed shade, frosted yellow ground, red and crimson overlay, cameo-etched peony blossoms and foliage, baluster vase base, both shade and base cameo sgd "Galle" **170,000.00**

30" h, 18" d domed shade, deep yellow ground, periwinkle and indigo overlay, cameo-etched berried branches, cameo sgd on shade and ftd base "Galle" **30,000.00**

Lamp, wall, 9-1/4" h, 9" " w, half-round frosted amber glass wall pocket, cinnamon overlay, cameo-etched various blossoms, mounted to gilt bronze floral frame and metal back housing light socket, sgd "Galle" on side in cameo **5,500.00**

Perfume, 4" h, 4-1/4" w, raised rim, wide flattened quatraform bottle, mottled pink ground, moss green and brown overlay, double cameo-etched in riverscape scene with man in boat, conforming stopper, sgd "Galle" at reverse **2,650.00**

Perfume bottle, 4-1/4" h, 3-3/4" d, cameo-etched deep burgundy berries and leaves, green ground, sgd "Galle" in cameo **1,725.00**

Perfume bottle, cameo-etched deep burgundy berries and leaves, green ground, signed "Galle" in cameo, 4-1/4" h, 3-3/4" d, **$1,725.** *Photo courtesy of David Rago Auctions.*

Plaffonier, domed circular shade, 20" d, frosted yellow ground

Crimson red overlay, mold blown and cameo-etched oranges among foliage, cameo sgd "Galle" **17,000.00**

Red overlay, cameo-etched poppies, cameo sgd "Galle" **6,750.00**

Scent bottle, 4-1/4" h, ebony spider mums and buds silhouetted against tropical sunset background, mushroom stopper with matching floral motif and marked with coordinating number to bottle, sgd "Galle" in cameo . **2,660.00**

Toothpick holder, 2-1/2" h, tapered cylinder, frosted colorless body, orange-amber overlay, cameo-etched broad blossom and bud on leafy stem, sgd "Galle" in cameo **690.00**

Tumbler, 2-3/4" h, frosted colorless and pink opal body, white, blue, and green overlay, four cameo-etched petaled blossoms and leaves, sgd in cameo **800.00**

Vase

3-1/2" h, olive green catkins dangling above leaves, peach and chartreuse ground, sgd "Galle" in cameo, altered height **160.00**

4-1/2" h, trumpet form, citron body, mint auburn orchids and leaves, sgd "Galle" in cameo **850.00**

5-3/4" h, raised rim, flattened fiery amber oval body, olive green overlay, cameo-etched long-leafed branches with figs pendent **1,150.00**

6" h, banjo, dark foliaged trees, reflective waterway, distant blue ridge mountains, frost and citron sky, sgd "Galle" in cameo . **600.00**

6" h, bulbed, orange and colorless body, red overlay, cameo-etched trailing blossoms, buds, and leafy stems, side sgd "Galle," some int. debris flecks. **575.00**

6" h, flared green-gray ftd oval, purple overlay, cameo-etched leafy branches laden with berries, reverse side sgd "Galle," some minor int. stain **750.00**

6" h, oval pink, white, and frosted colorless glass, layered in lavender-purple under green, cameo-etched as pendant wisteria blossom clusters, sgd "Galle" at lower side. **1,265.00**

6" h, tapered, clusters of mulberry colored flowers encircling frosty white body, sgd "Galle" in cameo, internal bubble almost hidden in design **375.00**

6-3/4" h, frosted yellow-amber banjo body, pastel blue-green overlay under mauve, cameo-etched mountain landscape. **1,955.00**

7" h, oviform, everted rim, rich yellow body, sky blue and hunter green overlay, cameo-etched cornflowers and foliage, cameo sgd "Galle" **2,750.00**

7" h, 3-1/2" w, banjo shape, deep purple fuchsia floral dec, frosted clear and yellow ground, sgd **800.00**

7" h, 5" w, bulbous, flaring rim, marbleized shades of orange, small bubbles and dark brown swirls throughout, inscribed "Cristallerie de Galle," small bruise at base **900.00**

7-1/2" h, pink poppies and green lappets and seed pods silhouetted against frosty gray ground shading into teal, sgd "Galle" in cameo after star **1,800.00**

7-3/4" h, colorless body cased and layered with brilliant pink and amethyst, olive green around raised calyx-rim, deeply cameo-etched detailed blossoms, seed pods, berries, and leaves, "Galle" Asian influence mark at side. **5,175.00**

7-3/4" h, fire polished, aqua ribbed body whirling to tricorn rim, dec with periwinkle blue morning glory vines cascading and surrounding glossy surface, sgd "Galle" in cameo, polished 1/8th nick on base **1,200.00**

8" h, flattened oviform, frosted yellow ground, white and violet overlay, cameo-etched mountainous lake scene, cameo sgd "Galle" **2,000.00**

8-1/4" h, pinched quatraform rim, shaded blue to frost to pink tapered body, bright pink and olive green overlay, cameo-etched blossoming leafy plants, sgd "(star) Galle" **1,265.00**

9" h, elongated ovoid pastel yellow and frosted colorless body, burgundy and rose overlay, cameo-etched bleeding hearts blossoms, sgd "Galle" in lower design **1,610.00**

8-3/8" h, 6" d, marquetry wheel carved and cameo-etched, trumpet, ridge raised rim, colorless heavy walled body, cased to opal-pink, amethyst-mauve overlay over creamy pink-beige, etched and martelé carved as highly detailed trumpet blossoms and undulating leaf forms, "Galle" Asian influence mark at lower edge, some internal specks and blemishes within glass . . **5,750.00**

9-3/4" h, plum colored clematis blossoms and leafy vines encircling crimson pink ground, ext. polished at rim, sgd "Galle" in cameo **800.00**

10" h, elongated trumpet form, everted rim, frosted ground shading to peach, lime green, and brown overlay, cameo-etched ferns, cameo sgd "Galle" **1,500.00**

10-1/4" h, mold blown, raised rim, spherical, yellow, amber, dark amethyst overlay, cameo-etched flowering rhododendron branches, sgd "Galle" in cameo on lower body **9,200.00**

11" h, tapered cylindrical form, notched at neck, colorless body, ochre and mauve overlay, cameo-etched and engraved with trumpet flowers, sgd in cameo near base **2,760.00**

11" h, flared rim, pedestal base, ovoid gray and salmon body, light brown overlay, cameo-etched grapes on vine, sgd "Galle" **6,100.00**

11-1/2" h, flared blue-gray oval body, blue, green, lavender, and purple overlay, cameo-etched riverside landscape, mountains, tall fir trees, side sgd "Galle" **2,645.00**

11-1/2" h, three-color scenic, amber to frosty sky, mocha foliage trees lining stream in foreground, chartreuse trees in background, cameo sgd "Galle" in the lower landscape area, some surface scratches **1,000.00**

12" h, flattened oval, frosted yellow body, blue and green overlay, cameo-etched trees against mountainous landscape, cameo sgd "Galle" **3,000.00**

12-1/2" h, bulbous, pink and colorless frosted body, elongated slender neck, white, green, and lavender overlay, cameo-etched blossoming leafy branches, sgd "Galle" in cameo on reverse **1,380.00**

12-1/2" h, 5-1/2" w, 3-1/4" d mouth, elongated oval body, short straight neck, shaded gray frosted ground, cameo-etched pine cones and tassels dec, shading from dark brown to light coffee color, sgd **800.00**

13-3/4" h, ribbed transparent, frosted, and fire-polished aquamarine oval, tricorn rim, applied aubergine cupped pedestal foot, glossy sapphire blue overlay, cameo-etched two bumblebees among blossoms, leafy morning glory vines, center star blossom, sgd "Verre Parlant Lupine et Caitate," and "Galle" at side **5,750.00**

14-3/4" h, 6-1/4" w, round, flat base, tapered stem opens to wide ovoid shoulder, rolled-in top rim with four indentations, large orange nasturtiums and leaves circle around shaded gray, pink, and pale orange ground **1,550.00**

15" h, 6-1/4" w, 2" d mouth, ovoid bulbous base, elongated tapered neck, slightly flaring mouth, green, blue, and white over clear frosted ground, pale peach int., cameo-etched floral cutting, sgd **4,000.00**

15-1/4" h, flared elongated trumpet, green and pink frosted body, dark olive green and lavender overlay, cameo-etched tall spiked blossoms, leafy stems, medial cameo mark "(star) Galle" **1,495.00**

15-1/2" h, 5-1/2" w, 3-1/2" w mouth, colorless shaded to yellow frosted body, lavender overlaid cameo-etched columbine flowers, sgd **2,000.00**

16" h, flared trumpet-form oval, frosted pale blue and colorless body, amethyst and mauve green overlay, cameo-etched hydrangea blossom clusters, leafy stems, sgd "Galle" in design on reverse **2,645.00**

17" h, pilgrim flask form, rich yellow frosted body, periwinkle and indigo overlay, cameo-etched mountainous landscape and chalets, cameo sgd "GALLE," orig paper label **19,500.00**

23" h, elongated flared ovoid body, frosted colorless, pink, and lavender body, purple-amethyst overlay, cameo-etched wisteria blossom cluster, long leafy stems at side, "(star) Galle" in cameo **2,875.00**

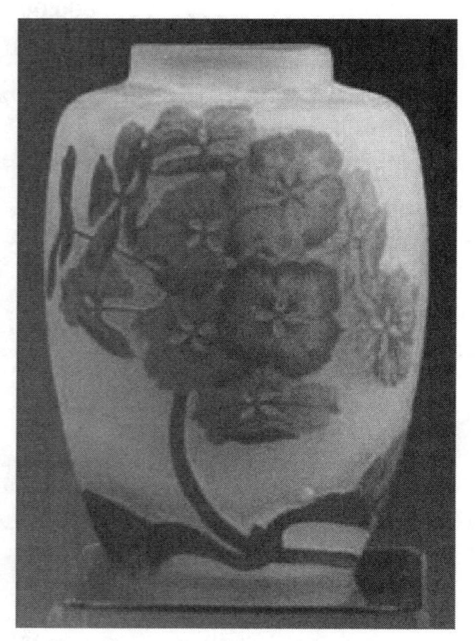

Vase, three colors, blue and green forget-me-nots and vine, mottled pink ground, 8" h, **$2,750.** *Photo courtesy of David Rago Auctions.*

Enameled

Bowl, 9" l, 5" h, ruffled rim, oval form, translucent green glass, enameled nasturtium blossoms on trailing leafy vines, shades of yellow, red, cream, and gold, base with intricate inscribed signature "Cristallerie de Galle a Nancy" among leaves, c1885, wear **920.00**

Cabinet vase

2-5/8" h, wide blue-green oval cased to opal, overlaid olive green, etched with seed pods on leafy branch, rim wrapped with conforming leaf and pod silver collar, sgd "Galle" at side, lightly dented **825.00**

3-1/4" h, frosted pink oval, layered in lime green, etched broad leaf blossoming plant, sgd "Galle" in cameo **435.00**

Candle lantern, 11-1/2" h, hexagonal, Moorish cut-out windows, enameled bees and flowering branches, base marked "Galle Faience E & G Depose," restored **350.00**

Cup, 2" h, 2-3/4" w, pale amber body, seven enameled fleur-de-lis dec, applied rope handle, sgd "E. Galle Nancy," set of four **600.00**

Cup and saucer

2-1/4" h cup, 5" d saucer, pale topaz transparent crystal, matching pastel stylized floral designs, cups inscribed "E. Galle Nancy" on base, price for eight-pc set **1,495.00**

2-5/8" d cup, 4-1/4" d saucer, handleless cup, scalloped edge, blue, green, rose, white, and gold repeating border dec, plate inscribed "Galle" and retailer "Gilman Collamore & Co. New York" **345.00**

Flacon, 5-1/4" h, 5-1/2" l, Verre Parland, figural bird, transparent topaz bird-form vessel, applied disk foot, notched handle, body enameled with multi-colored scrolling devices, golden stylized bird with phrase "Je Suis ill Roi," base engraved "E. Galle - Nancy," topaz stopper above beak rim **3,105.00**

Perfume bottle, 6" h, 3-1/2" w, clear crystal body, blue enameled floral and ribbon design, sgd "E. Galle Nancy" **1,650.00**

Tray, 10-1/4" d, scalloped and folded pale topaz, enameled praying mantis above stylized leaf and blossom branches, black, brown, blue, and red, disk foot, marked "E. Galle a Nancy" **1,265.00**

Tumbler, 4-1/2" h, faceted, slightly tapering cylinder, enameled French peasant woman holding umbrella in the rain, two acanthus leaves, inscription on reverse, blue, yellow, red, and white, enameled "Emile Gallé Depose," c1870 . . . . **1,650.00**

Vase

3-3/4" h, 5" d, aquamarine transparent bowl form, six-sided angular rim, raised star above gold centered pink cameo-etched

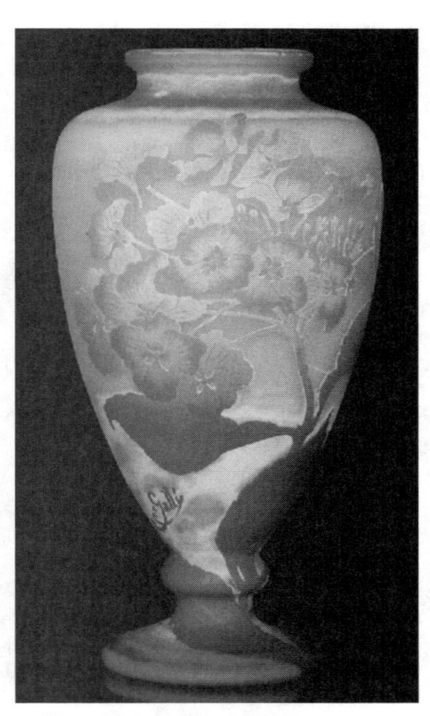

Vase, 14" h, three colors, blue poppies, green foliage, fading peach to opaque ground, signed in cameo, **$2,800.** *Photo courtesy of Freeman\Fine Arts of Philadelphia, Inc.*

blossoms, gold enameled leaves, base inscribed "Galle/Depose/ GesGesch" in flower outline **1,840.00**

4" h, raised rim, squatty body of pale topaz, two applied "C" handles, enameled polychrome butterfly, wild grasses and flowers, enamel signature "E. Galle Nancy" on base, c1890 . . . . **920.00**

4-3/4" h, transparent colorless sphere, applied rope twist collar, enameled Japonesque fish over blue waves, floral elements, gold painted ocean waves, ripples, base inscribed "E. Galle a Nancy," two sliver chips under collar at rim **1,380.00**

5" h, bulbous emerald green transparent oval body, surface etched all over and cameo cut chrysanthemums, enhanced by enamel polychrome coloring, sgd "Galle" at lower side **1,035.00**

6-1/4" h, three-footed ribbed body, enameled pastel Japonesque floral dec, base marked "E. Galle/a Nancy," rim polished **320.00**

6-7/8" h, trefoil rim, cylindrical topaz vessel, etched and enameled polychrome thistles and wildflowers, base with intricate inscribed signature "Galle" with thistle, traced in gold enamel, c1885, loss to enamel **690.00**

9" h, double bulbed form, molded spiral ribbed topaz glass, enameled light blue and mauve trumpet flowers, gilt enamel at rim, base sgd "Crystallerie de Emile Galle a Nancy," wear to enamel **1,840.00**

12" h, double bulbed transparent colorless glass, ribbed, blue enameled fleur-de-lis with gold accents, base inscribed "Emile Galle Nancy" **980.00**

Whimsey, 4-1/4" h, three blue and amethyst butterflies on frosted cap with "Galle" mark, mounted on wrought iron tripod holder **1,265.00**

Wine, 4-3/8" h, colorless rib-molded bowl, amber knop, topaz cupped stem foot, three applied red, amber, green jewels as etched blossom centers, gold enameled outlines, "E. Galle" etched on leaf on foot, some wear to gold **1,380.00**

Goofus Glass

History: Goofus glass, also known as Mexican ware, Hooligan glass, and Pickle glass, is a pressed glass with relief designs that were painted either on the back or front. The designs are usually in red and green with a metallic gold ground. It was popular from 1890 to 1920 and used as a premium at carnivals.

The cold painted, unfired, decoration did not wear well and easily chipped off. This may be why the name goofus was derived—the manufacturers "goofed" with this technique. The goofus decoration was applied to colorless, transparent green, blue, or amber grounds, as well as opalescent and milk glass grounds. Surfaces were sometimes acid etched (giving a satin ground), crackled, or pressed in a basketweave pattern.

Goofus glass was produced by several companies: Crescent Glass Company, Wellsburg, West Virginia; Imperial Glass Corporation, Bellaire, Ohio; LaBelle Glass Works, Bridgeport, Ohio; and Northwood Glass Co., Indiana, Pennsylvania, Wheeling, West Virginia, and Bridgeport, Ohio. Goofus glass made by Northwood includes one of the following marks: "N," "N" in one circle, "N" in two circles, or one or two circles without the "N."

Goofus glass lost its popularity when people found that the paint tarnished or scaled off after repeated washings and wear. No record of its manufacture has been found after 1920.

Reference: Carolyn McKinley, *Goofus Glass*, Collector Books, 1984.

Periodical: *Goofus Glass Gazette*, 9 Lindenwood Ct, Sterling, VA 20165.

Web site: http://home.sundial.sundial.net/gballens/index.html.

Animal covered dish, 6-1/4" l, 5-1/4" w, 7" h, turkey, gold ground, Westmoreland **125.00**

Ashtray, red rose dec, emb adv . **12.00**

Basket, 5" h, strawberry dec **50.00**

Bonbon, 4" d, Strawberry pattern, gold, red, and green dec **40.00**

Bowl

4-1/2" d, red roses dec, gold trim **20.00**

5-1/2" d, La Belle Rose pattern, sq **35.00**

6-1/2" d, Grape and Lattice pattern, red grapes, gold ground, ruffled rim **45.00**

7" d, Iris pattern, gold and red dec **35.00**

7" d, thistle and scrolling leaves, red dec, gold ground, ruffled rim **35.00**

8-3/4" d, fluted, beaded rim, relief molded, teardrops and red hearts **45.00**

9" d, Carnation pattern, red flowers, relief molded **30.00**

9" d, Cherries pattern, red dec, gold ground. **30.00**

9" d, Roses pattern, red roses, ruffled, relief molded **30.00**

10" d, Dahlias pattern, scalloped **50.00**

10" d, pears and apples dec. . **35.00**

10-1/2" d, red roses, molded, gold ground. **45.00**

10-1/2" d, water lilies dec **50.00**

11" d, red cherries, relief molded, ruffled **35.00**

Bread plate, 7" w, 11" l, Last Supper pattern, red and gold, grapes and foliage border. **65.00**

Cake plate

11" d, Dahlia and Fan, red dec, gold ground. **40.00**

12" d, red roses dec, gold ground **20.00**

Candle holder, red and gold. . . . **20.00**

Candy dish, 8-1/2" d, figure eight design, serrated rim, dome foot. . **60.00**

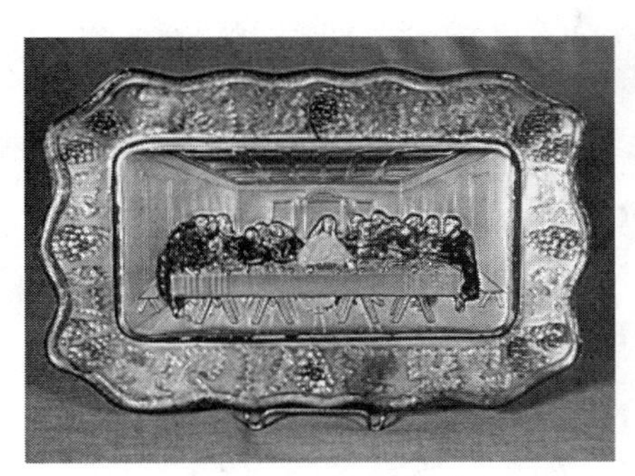

Bread plate, The Last Supper, **$65.**

Child's plate, 6-1/2" d, "This Little Pig Went To Market" in center, circle of children holding hands around perimeter, beaded edge, gold ground **125.00**

Coaster, 3" d, red floral dec, gold ground **12.00**

Compote

- 4" d, Grape and Cable pattern **35.00**
- 6" d, Strawberry pattern, red and green strawberries and foliage, ruffled **40.00**
- 6-1/2" d, Poppy pattern, red flowers, gold foliage, green ground, sgd "Northwood" **40.00**
- 9-1/2" d, red and green floral and foliage dec, green ground, crimped and fluted rim, pedestal foot, sgd "Northwood" **40.00**
- 9-1/2" d, Strawberry pattern, red and green strawberries and foliage, gold ground, ruffled **50.00**
- 10-1/4" d, red fruit, relief molded **65.00**

Decanter

- La Belle Rose, orig stopper . . **50.00**
- Single Rose pattern, basketweave ground, emb rose stopper . . **65.00**

Dish, 11" d, chrysanthemum sprays, red and gold, scalloped rim **75.00**

Dresser tray, 6" l, Cabbage Rose pattern, red roses dec, gold foliage, clear ground **35.00**

Fairy lamp, red roses dec, green trim, clear candle cup **45.00**

Flask, Zigzag pattern, milk glass ground, gold paint, metal screw top **50.00**

Jar, cov, butterflies, red and gold **35.00**

Jewel box, 4" d, 2" h, basketweave, rose dec. **50.00**

Miniature lamp, 12" h, Cabbage Rose pattern **45.00**

Mug, Cabbage Rose pattern, gold ground **35.00**

Nappy, 6-1/2" d

- Cherries pattern, red cherries, gold foliage, clear ground **35.00**
- Strawberry pattern, red strawberries, green leaves, molded applied ring handle **20.00**

Oil lamp, 21" h, "Gone-with-the-Wind" shape, gold ground, red floral dec **480.00**

Perfume bottle, 3-1/2" h, pink tulips dec **20.00**

Pickle jar

- Aqua, molded, gold, blue, and red painted floral design. **50.00**
- Colorless, 12-3/4" h, c1910-20, price for pr **150.00**

Pin dish, 6-1/2" l, oval, red and black florals **20.00**

Pitcher, red rose bud dec, gold leaves **60.00**

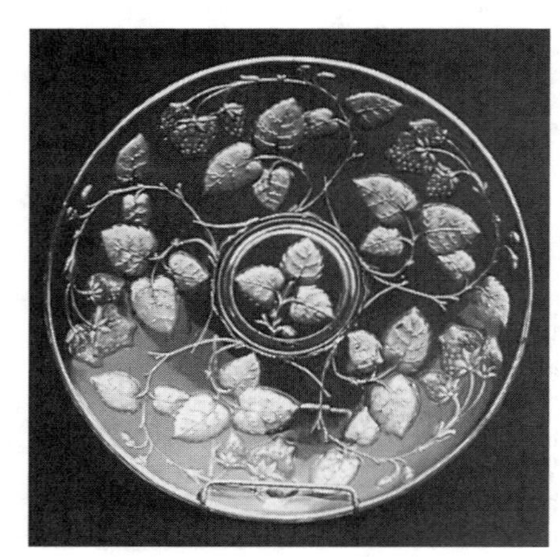

Plate, allover leaf pattern, **$40.**

Plate

- 6"d, Rose and Lattice pattern, relief molded **20.00**
- 6" d, Sunflower pattern, red dec center, relief molded **20.00**
- 7-1/2" d, apples, red dec, gold ground. **24.00**
- 7-3/4" d, Carnations pattern, red carnations, gold ground **20.00**
- 8" d, red applies, relief molded **20.00**
- 8-1/2" d, Gibson Girl cameo, red and gold **45.00**
- 8-1/2" d, red apples, gold ground, relief molded **35.00**
- 10-1/2" d, grapes dec, gold ground, irid pink edge **35.00**
- 11" d, Dahlia pattern, red and gold **40.00**
- 11" d, roses, red and gold, scalloped rim **45.00**
- 12" d, Bird and Strawberry, gold, blue and red dec. **100.00**
- 12" d, Intaglio Grape, gold, scalloped rim, some wear to paint **35.00**

Platter, 18" l, red rose dec, gold ground **65.00**

Powder jar, cov

- 3" d, puffy, rose dec, red and gold **40.00**
- 4-1/2" d, Cabbage Rose pattern, white cabbage rose, relief molded **35.00**

Salt and pepper shakers, pr

- Grape and Leaf pattern. **45.00**
- Poppy pattern **40.00**

Syrup pitcher

- Red roses dec, lattice work ground, orig top. **85.00**
- Strawberry pattern, red strawberries, green foliage, gold ground . **75.00**

Toothpick holder, red rose and foliage dec, gold ground **40.00**

Tray, 8-1/4" d, 11" d, red chrysanthemum dec, gold ground **45.00**

Trinket box, 4" d, 1-1/2" h, round, stylized rose on lid with gold ground, clear base **15.00**

Tumbler, 6" h, red rose dec, gold ground. **35.00**

Vase

- 6" h, Cabbage Rose pattern, red dec, gold ground. **65.00**
- 6-1/2" h, Grape and Rose pattern, red and gold dec, crackle glass ground **45.00**
- 7-1/4" h, Grapes pattern, purple dec **45.00**
- 7-1/2" h, brown, red bird. **40.00**
- 8" h, Grapes pattern, purple dec **45.00**
- 9" h, bird sitting on grapevine, red and gold, satin glass ground **45.00**
- 9" h, Poppies pattern, blue and red dec, gold ground **55.00**
- 10-1/2" h, Peacock pattern. . . **75.00**
- 12" h, Parrot pattern, red and blue bird, molded foliage. **85.00**
- 12" h, red roses, molded, gold ground **90.00**

GREENTOWN GLASS

History: The Indiana Tumbler and Goblet Co., Greentown, Indiana, produced its first clear, pressed glass table and bar wares in late 1894. Initial success led to a doubling of the plant size in 1895 and other subsequent expansions, one in 1897 to allow for the manufacture of colored glass. In 1899, the firm joined the combine known as the National Glass Company.

In 1900, just before arriving in Greentown, Jacob Rosenthal developed an opaque brown glass, called "chocolate," which ranged in color from a dark, rich chocolate to a lighter coffee-with-cream hue. Production of chocolate glass saved the financially pressed Indiana Tumbler and Goblet Works. The Cactus and Leaf Bracket patterns were made almost exclusively in chocolate glass. Other popular chocolate patterns include Austrian, Dewey, Shuttle, and Teardrop and Tassel. In 1902, National Glass Company bought Rosenthal's chocolate glass formula so other plants in the combine could use the color.

In 1902, Rosenthal developed the Golden Agate and Rose Agate colors. Golden Agate was the color used for the Holly Amber pattern, designed by Frank Jackson, in January 1903. More than 30 forms were developed for this pattern, which featured a gold-colored body with a marbleized onyx color on

raised design elements. All work ceased on June 13, 1903, after a fire of suspicious origin destroyed the Indiana Tumbler and Goblet Company Works.

After the fire, other companies, e.g., McKee and Brothers, produced chocolate glass in the same pattern designs used by Greentown. Later reproductions also have been made, with Cactus among the most-heavily copied patterns.

References: James Measell, *Greentown Glass*, Grand Rapids Public Museum, 1979, 1992-93 value update, distributed by Antique Publications; Brenda Measell and James Measell, *A Guide To Reproductions of Greentown Glass*, 2nd ed., The Printing Press, 1974; James Measell, *Greentown Glass, The Indiana Tumbler & Goblet Co.,* Grand Rapids Public Museum, 1979, 1992-93 value update, distributed by Antique Publications; Kenneth Wilson, *American Glass 1760-1930: The Toledo Museum of Art, Volume I, Volume II*, Hudson Hills Press and The Toledo Museum of Art, 1994.

Collectors' Clubs: Collectors of Findlay Glass, P.O. Box 256, Findlay, OH 45839; National Greentown Glass Assoc., 19596 Glendale Ave., South Bend, IN 46637.

Videotapes: "Centennial Exhibit of Greentown Glass" and "Reproductions of Greentown Glass," National Greentown Glass Assoc., P.O. Box 107, Greentown, IN 46936.

Museums: Grand Rapids Public Museum, Ruth Herrick Greentown Glass Collection, Grand Rapids, MI; Greentown Glass Museum, Greentown, IN.

Reproduction Alert

Animal covered dish
- Bird with Berry
  - Blue . . . 475.00
  - Chocolate, minor repair . . 650.00
- Cat, hamper base
  - Amber . . . 465.00
  - Blue . . . 465.00
  - Chocolate . . . 425.00
- Dolphin, chocolate, chip off tail . . . 195.00
- Hen on Nest
  - Blue . . . 265.00
  - Chocolate . . . 725.00
- Rabbit, dome top, amber . . . 250.00
- Robin, nest base, opaque white . . . 225.00

Berry set, Leaf Bracket, chocolate, seven pcs . . . 275.00

Bowl
- Cactus, chocolate
  - 6-1/2" d . . . 100.00
  - 7-1/2" d . . . 120.00
- Herringbone Buttress, green, 7-1/4" d . . . 135.00
- Holly Amber
  - 7-1/2" l, oval . . . 375.00
  - 8-1/2" d . . . 395.00
- Geneva, chocolate
  - 9-3/8" l, 5-7/8" w, oval, flat rim flake . . . 110.00
  - 10-1/4" d . . . 450.00
- No. 11, blue, 6-1/4" d . . . 200.00

Butter, cov
- Cactus, chocolate . . . 300.00
- Cupid, chocolate . . . 575.00
- Daisy, opaque white . . . 100.00
- Herringbone Buttress, green 250.00
- Holly Amber . . . 1,875.00
- Leaf Bracket, chocolate . . . 250.00
- Oval Lattice, colorless . . . 75.00
- Shuttle, chocolate . . . 1,100.00

Cake stand, Holly Amber . . . 2,500.00

Celery vase, Beaded Panel, colorless . . . 100.00

Compote
- Cactus, chocolate . . . 225.00
- Geneva, 4-1/2" d, 3-1/2" h, chocolate . . . 150.00
- Holly Amber, 8-1/2" h, 12" d, cov . . . 2,500.00

Cookie jar, Cactus, chocolate . 300.00

Cordial
- Austrian, canary . . . 125.00
- Overall Lattice, colorless . . . 45.00
- Shuttle, colorless . . . 45.00

Creamer, Austrian pattern, **$40.**

Creamer
- Austrian, colorless . . . 40.00
- Cactus, chocolate . . . 125.00
- Cord Drapery, colorless . . . 65.00
- Cupid, Nile green . . . 400.00
- Holly Amber
  - 4" h, 3-1/2" w, golden agate, professionally polished rim, small burst bubble . . . 75.00
  - 4-1/2" h . . . 650.00
- Indian Head, opaque white . . 450.00
- Indoor Drinking Scene, chocolate, 5-1/2" h . . . 500.00
- Shuttle, chocolate, tankard style, 6-1/8" h . . . 80.00

Cruet, orig stopper
- Cactus, chocolate . . . 325.00
- Chrysanthemum Leaf, chocolate . . . 1,275.00
- Dewey, vaseline . . . 300.00
- Geneva, chocolate . . . 1,000.00
- Holly Amber . . . 1,850.00
- Leaf Bracket, chocolate . . . 275.00
- Wild Rose and Bowknot, chocolate . . . 350.00

Cruet stopper, 2-1/4" l, 9/16" d, chocolate . . . 70.00

Dish, Dolphin, chocolate, sawtooth edge, 7-1/2" l, 3-1/2" w, 4-1/4" h . 200.00

Dresser tray, Wild Rose and Bowknot, chocolate . . . 350.00

Goblet
- Beehive, colorless . . . 65.00
- Diamond Prisms, colorless . . . 70.00
- Overall Lattice, colorless . . . 40.00
- Shuttle, chocolate . . . 500.00

Honey, cov, Holly Amber . . . 850.00

Jelly compote
- Cactus, chocolate . . . 200.00
- Pleat Band, chocolate . . . 130.00

Lemonade tumbler, Cactus, chocolate . . . 100.00

Mug
- Elf, green . . . 115.00
- Herringbone Buttress, chocolate . . . 80.00
- Holly Amber, 4-1/2" h, ring handle . . . 550.00
- Indian drinking scene, chocolate, 8" h . . . 450.00
- Outdoor drinking scene, Nile green . . . 200.00
- Overall Lattice, colorless . . . 45.00
- Serenade, colorless . . . 75.00
- Shuttle, ruby stained . . . 50.00
- Troubadour, 6-1/2" h, opaque white, cov . . . 70.00

Mustard, cov, Daisy, opaque white . . . 75.00

Nappy
- Holly Amber . . . 385.00
- Leaf Bracket, chocolate, triangular . . . 85.00
- Masonic, chocolate . . . 85.00

Paperweight, Buffalo, Nile green . . . 600.00

Parfait, Holly Amber **600.00**
Pitcher, water
Cord Drapery, colorless **95.00**
Fleur De Lis, colorless **265.00**
Racing Deer and Doe, colorless **200.00**
Ruffled Eye, chocolate **550.00**
Shuttle, chocolate. **3,500.00**
Squirrel, colorless. **200.00**
Teardrop and Tassel, cobalt blue **200.00**
Plate, Serenade, 8-1/2" d, chocolate **125.00**
Punch cup
Cord Drapery, colorless **20.00**
Shuttle, colorless **15.00**
Relish
Cord Drapery, amber **110.00**
Holly Amber, oval **300.00**
Leaf Bracket, 8" l, oval, chocolate **75.00**
Rose bowl, Austrian, colorless. . **45.00**
Salt and pepper shakers, pr
Cactus, chocolate. **150.00**
Holly Amber **500.00**
Salt, open, wheelbarrow shape, Nile green **350.00**
Sauce
Cactus, chocolate, ftd **65.00**
Geneva, chocolate **90.00**
Holly amber. **250.00**
Leaf Bracket, chocolate **50.00**
Six Fluted, chocolate **225.00**
Water Lily and Cattails, chocolate **100.00**
Wild Rose and Bowknot, chocolate **95.00**
Spooner
Austrian, colorless **65.00**
Cactus, chocolate. **80.00**

Nappy, Leaf Bracket pattern, chocolate, **$85.**

Cupid, colorless. **145.00**
Holly Amber. **475.00**
Wild Rose and Bowknot, chocolate **150.00**
Sugar, cov
Cupid, opaque white **115.00**
Dewey, cobalt blue **145.00**
Syrup pitcher
Cord Drapery, chocolate, 6-1/2" h **350.00**
Holly Amber, 5-3/4" h, SP hinged lid **2,000.00**
Indian Feather, green. **175.00**
Toothpick holder
Cactus, chocolate, 2-3/4" h . . . **75.00**
Holly Amber, 2-1/4" h **585.00**
No. 11, green. **85.00**
Tumbler
Cactus, chocolate, 4" h, 3" d . **85.00**
Cord Drapery, chocolate . . . **245.00**
Dewey, canary **65.00**
Fleur de Lis, chocolate. **75.00**
Geneva, chocolate **115.00**
Holly Amber **400.00**
Icicle, chocolate **150.00**
Leaf Bracket, chocolate **125.00**
Sawtooth, chocolate. **70.00**
Shuttle, chocolate. **70.00**
Teardrop and Tassel, blue . . . **65.00**
Wildflower, amber. **45.00**
Vase, Holly Amber, 6" h. **500.00**
Wine
Cord Drapery, colorless **85.00**
Shuttle, colorless **20.00**

Handel & Co.

History: Handel & Co. was established in 1893 by Philip Handel. This Meriden, Connecticut, firm is known mainly for lamps, although it also did some decorating on glasswares. Vases and other items were etched, enameled, or painted.

Handel & Co. patented a method of "chipping" glass in 1904. This method required that a piece be sandblasted, covered with glue, and refired, creating a "chipped ice" or frosted finish. This textured finish was applied to many items, including lamp shades.

Well known for its beautiful lamps, the company also produced its own metalwork, including spelter bases with a patinated bronze finish. Styles ranged from plain to sculptured nudes and stylized tree trunks. A patent was issued to Handel for a pond lily lamp in 1902. Several variations of this lamp were made.

The period before World War I saw a rapid expansion in the production of lamps; many new patents were taken out by Philip Handel. The company also made great strides in adapting kerosene lamps to electric. The company's production slowed during the war years and was affected by the death of Philip Handel in 1914. However, the company successfully reorganized and began a second prosperous period directly after World War I. A national sales force helped to market the beautiful lamps to the middle class. The high-quality lamps were loved, but prices soon rose out of the range of the average buyer, resulting in declining sales and hard economic times of the company. It continued to produce some glassware and lamps, and even tried china decorating before closing in 1936.

Most of the decorators signed their works, along with a vertical mark. Decorators included Henry Bedigie, F. Gubisch, Albert Parlow, George Palme, William Runge, and Walter Wilson.

References: Victor Arwas, *Glass Art Nouveau to Art Deco*, Rizzoli, 1977; Robert De Falco, Carole Goldman Hibel, John Hibel, *Handel Lamps, Painted Shades & Glassware*, H & D Press, 1986; John A. Shuman III, *The Collector's Encyclopedia of American Art Glass, Collector Books, 1988, 1994 value update*; Kenneth Wilson, *American Glass 1760-1930: The Toledo Museum of Art, Volume I, Volume II*, Hudson Hills Press and The Toledo Museum of Art, 1994.

Museums: New Bedford Museum, Bedford, NH; The Corning Museum of Glass, Corning, NY; The Toledo Museum of Art, Toledo, OH.

Decorative objects

Ashtray, 3" d, 1" h, glossy brown exterior, Boston Terrier painted on interior, sgd "Handelware" and artist marked, wear to dog's face **100.00**

Fernery, 4" h, 9" d, opalware, ftd, white glass, painted yellow and pink spider mums, green leaves, stems, buds, sgd in gold on base............ **1,800.00**

Humidor

- 5" h, 5" d, opalware, green and brown shaded background, transfer and hand-painted owl dec, silver-plated collar and lid with monogram, sgd "Handel Ware #4038" **550.00**
- 6" h, 4-1/2" w, dark brown and green ground, male and female golfers in appropriate attire, base sgd "Handelware PJ Handel, Meriden, CT #2379/136"......... **1,500.00**
- 7-1/2" h, 5-1/2" w, dark green and brown glossy ground, three running dog heads, sgd "Handelware".......... **1,100.00**
- 7-1/2" h, 6" w, dark brown and green ground, scene of doe and buck, metal cover with full pipe finial, sgd with shield mark and #4060/3 .... **1,000.00**
- 8-1/4" h, hinged top, grizzly bear motif, sgd "Handel Ware/4060/g" **1,050.00**

Humidor, 8-1/4" h, hinged top, grizzly bear motif, signed "Handel Ware/4060/g," **$1,050.** *Photo courtesy of David Rago Auctions.*

Jewelry box, cov, 4-1/2" w, 3-1/2" h, soft beige opal ground, pink carnation dec, sgd "Handelware #71/941" **675.00**

Pattern plate, 14" x 16", engraved steel, rect plates engraved with various patterns to use as a guide for the artists decorating the hand-painted Handel glass lamp shades, patterns include apple blossoms on branches; chrysanthemums, No. 1002; carnations, No. 146; lily of the valley, No. 992; flower baskets, No. 7188, and others, signed "Handel," price for set of five **1,725.00**

Sketch book, 13" x 10-1/2", orig cover inscribed "P. J. Handel August 22nd, 1904," labeled "Pearl E. Lambert, Richmond, Oil Craft Painting," approx. 10 pages showing Handel wares, including lamps, leaded shades, hanging domes, lilies, numerous orig artist sketches, black and white line drawings of designs used on Handel porcelain and opal humidors, orig design numbers and prices for shades, watercolor of two elves advertising Pabst Blue Ribbon done by unknown Handel artist, pages loose, some wrinkling and minor edge tears . **700.00**

Tazza, 5-1/2" w, 9" h, shaded cream, and green opal ground, strawberries, leaves, and blossoms dec, beaded white top, sgd "Handelware" . **1,000.00**

Vase

- 6" h, Teroma, enameled panoramic landscape of tall foliaged trees and shrubs, stamped "Teroma Handel" in oval, numbered...... **1,100.00**
- 6-1/2" h, 4-3/4" d, Teroma Art, landscape scene, naturalistic fall colors, artist sgd "John Bailey" **1,500.00**
- 8" h, Teroma, etched ext. surface hand-painted wood landscape scene, in muted colors, unsigned, tiny chip near base **690.00**
- 9-3/4" h, 4-1/2" w, Teroma Art, landscape and mountain design, purple and blue mountains, green and yellow trees and leaves, Shape #4218 .... **2,500.00**
- 10" h, Teroma, serene scene of snow capped mountains towering over Alpine village, tall cypress trees and growth of yellow shrubs in foreground, ink stamped "Teroma Handel" and numbered, artist sgd "John Bailey" in scenery. **1,200.00**
- 11" h, flared and ftd oval, colorless glass overlaid in golden amber double etched repeating stylized floral motif, etched "Palme" in design, and "Handel 4258" on base, some rim skips, int. etching **1,150.00**

Lamp shades

20" d, sunset overlay, nine shaped slag glass panels in striated tones of rose and yellow, border of green slag glass, patinated metal overlay of tropical trees, joints reinforced **7,495.00**

22" d, 9" h, leaded, hexagonal, fragmented green leaves rise up to one leaning cattail in middle of each panel, four more plants at top of shade, cream to white background, sgd "Handel," one cracked panel **9,000.00**

22" d, overlay, striated deep red, orange, and yellow, overlay of trees, apron with green background with pine needle overlay, one panel cracked **5,600.00**

Boudoir lamp, 8" h, 5" d, decorated with red flowers, yellow centers, signed "Handel/7808," **$1,380.** *Photo courtesy of David Rago Auctions.*

Lamps

Boudoir

7" d, interior painted with poppies and wildflowers, molded shade #7158 DB **3,100.00**

7" d, parrot, zig-zag border, shade painted with two colorful parrots perched on branches, bronzed base with pierced carved foot **8,960.00**

8" d, obverse and reverse painted scenic landscape, tree trunk base **2,520.00**

8" h, 5" d, dec with red flowers, yellow centers, sgd "Handel/7808" **1,380.00**

13" h, one-light lily, naturalistic stem form supporting floriform shade of overlapped green and white slag glass petals, green slag glass bud, bronzed metal lily pad form base, brown patina, raised mark on mark, c1903 . . . . **460.00**

13-1/2" h, 7" d tucked under dome shade, pond lilies and cat-o-nine tails on blue ground, marked "Handel 6554," two rim chips, Handel metal single socket base, corroded finish, finial missing **1,840.00**

14" h, 7" d bell-shaped reverse painted shade, natural palette meadow landscape, rim sgd "Handel 6231," bronzed metal ribbed single socket base imp "Handel" **2,645.00**

14" h, 7-1/2" d, six-sided conical moonlit scenic shade, blue, green, sunset pink on int., landscape hand painted on ext. surface, sgd "Handel 6232," six-sided metal base with gray-green patina, imp "Handel," cap indented. . **2,185.00**

14" h, 7" x 5" scenic dome shade, chipped ice finish, windmill and landscape, orange, green, and brown, bronze finish base **1,750.00**

14" h, 7 x 5" scenic dome shade, sunset landscape and trees in shades of brown, No. 6112 . . . . **1,600.00**

14" h, 8-1/4" w squared domed shade with scalloped border, chipped sand-finish, int. painted with red flowers and foliage, each sgd "Handel 6698," one with "C. M.," metal bases painted white, tag stamped "HANDEL," pr. . **2,750.00**

Ceiling, 25" d bent slag glass paneled shade, octagonal forest scene bronzed frame, green pine cone needle apron, Handel three-socket cluster fixture with hanging hood, two panels cracked **3,750.00**

Chandelier and sconces, 14" x 14" hanger, five 5" x 5" diameter bell-shaped shades in caramel brickwork pattern, four matching scones in cream and caramel slag brickwork, all shades sgd "Handel" **8,960.00**

Desk

8" w shade, Design No. 6975, cylindrical lipped shade, chipped finish, painted on int. with fully rigged sailing ship in tropical bay, palm trees, fool moon, green, brown, blue, and gray, pivoted bronzed metal base, adjustable arm, orig Handel cloth tag, one tiny chip on inner shade rim . **2,350.00**

11-1/2" h, 8" l loaf shade, reverse painted with Treasure Island scene, sgd "Handel," pattern number 6575, bronzed base with adjustable crescent arm on oval leaf molded foot, firm's cloth label attached, rough area on shade, flat chip on edge **1,700.00**

14" h, 8" l, bright yellow ground, band of pink roses against black, orig sgd base **1,100.00**

19" h, 7-1/2" d six-sided paneled amber slag glass shade, six green dec elements at rim, harp type bronzed metal base, adjustable swivel socked **1,500.00**

Floor

24" d leaded glass shade, border of pink tulips, green leaves, bronze base **6,500.00**

67" h torchiere, oval glass shade acid-etched and enamel painted with shield coat of arms, mounted on orig metal weighed lamp base, three significant chips at top rim of shade **425.00**

Hanging globe, 10" h, 10" d, chipped ice finish, Birds in Flight dec, red trees, green leaves, Baltimore Oriole-type birds flying among branches, one perched, brass finish hanging attachments. **3,250.00**

Table

13-1/2" d six-sided shade, blue and white slag bent upper panels, white apron overlaid with metal band with tree clusters, shade sgd on rim, slender vasiform base with spreading round foot **5,600.00**

14" h, 7" d shade, tulip dec, orig green and white slag glass set into five petals, base as formed as long stem with leaves, irregular foot representing leaf, base sgd "Handel" **940.00**

15" d, 21" h, obverse and reverse painted shade, Hawaiian, pale yellow background shading to orange, palm trees, ferns, shade sgd "6310," pr **5,500.00**

16" d, Shade No. 6958, black ground, pink roses, 12 blue and yellow parrots **13,500.00**

18" d, Bird of Paradise, blue green ground, purple, fuchsia, blue, yellow, and orange birds, orig lamp base supported with three columns, sgd "B. D. #7036" **10,500.00**

19" h, 12" d Tam o'Shanter shade, converted fluid type, obverse painted shade with green stylized leaf motif, shaded int., rim sgd "Handel Co. 2642," mounted on three-arm spider with swastika border above cast metal six-band base, corrosion, socket repair **550.00**

19-1/2" h, 15-1/2" d dome shade, leaded mosaic glass segments depicting pink flowers on brown vine, multicolored ground, two-socket shaft over floriform circular bronzed metal base, dark brown patina, base imp "Handel," c1912, few cracked segments **2,300.00**

20" d, 22" h, caramel slag panel with green painted and metal overlay Art Nouveau shade, orig sgd bronze base, some damage to metal overlay **1,450.00**

20" h, 14" domed reverse painted shade, butterscotch yellow ground, stylized Arts and Crafts multicolored border design, two-socket ribbed organic design base, imp "Handel," repaired copper finish, sockets replaced, int. glass bubble on shade **1,380.00**

21" h, 14" d hipped Arts and Crafts-style shade, tan-brown textured shade, light reflective opal white int., molded basketweave border design, four drop-ring buckles, mounted on baluster-form copper-colored Handel base, finish worn................. **2,300.00**

21" h, 14" d textured Teroma-style obverse and reverse painted dome shade, colorless ground, six red roses, thorny leafy green stems, marked in red "Handel 1521," and "A.C." in the design, bronzed sq two-socket base, imp "Handel," rewired, replaced fitter cap **2,300.00**

22" h, 15" d domed glass shade basketweave molded with vertical ribs and horizontal ridges, painted with profusion of pastel rose blossoms in shades of pink, rose, and yellow, interspersed green leaves, imp "Handel" top rim, mounted on ridged quatraform single socket base with "Handel" threaded label, small int. chip on rim **2,185.00**

22" h, 17" d reverse painted shade, clumps of trees in fields, mountains in background in reds and oranges, brilliant yellow skyline, ice chipped shade, sgd "Handel 6957" **5,040.00**

22" h, 18" d textured domed shade, clear cased to opal white reflective int., outside hand painted with repeating foliate Arts and Crafts style motif below yellow amber color, inner rim inscribed "Handel 6778 HG," three-socket Handel tripartite base, bronzed finish **4,600.00**

22-1/2" h, 16" d molded octagonal Teroma shade with dropped apron, hand-painted yellow-pink roses on latticework ground, sgd "Handel," at edge, mounted on three-socket bulbed and sectioned bronzed base stamped "Handel," base refinished **2,645.00**

22-1/2" h, 18" d textured dome reverse painted Meadowlands scenic shade, maroon red and green grass, blue gray and orange clouds, blue sky overhead, rim inscribed "Handel 6937," three-socket ribbed quatraform bronzed platform base... **5,500.00**

22-1/2" h, 18-3/4" d umbrella-shaped metal overlay shade depicting leafy bamboo trees, lower leaf border, mauve, green, white, and caramel striated bent slag glass panels, yellow, green, and white striated border panels, two socket bronze base with bamboo trunk shaft, round base, imp "Handel" on base edge, shade possibly originally a hanging dome **2,760.00**

23" h, 18" d reverse painted and obverse shade, pastoral scene of twilight, three-color sky of frosty gray, pale yellow, and coral, silhouetted by grove of lush dark green foliaged trees, network design on ext., striated bronze base, three-light fixture with acorn pulls, shade boldly signed, "Handel, 5360," also sgd with conjoined artist initials "J.R.," base unsigned **5,250.00**

23" h, 18" d reverse painted dome shade, interior painted with four exotic birds on branches, peonies, and foliage, wings intensely painted in fuchsia and purple, citrine yellow highlights on flowers, and birds' tails and throats, metal tripod base molded with leaves, dec bands, and round foot, large amber glass teardrop prisms hang from glass faceted circles, shade sgd "Handel 7026"..... **13,400.00**

23" h, 18" d reverse painted dome shade, stylized roses, leaves, and butterflies on pastel colored ground, shade sgd "Handel 6688," stamped "Handel Lamps" on rim, three-light scrolled tripod base, relief dec with leaves, stepped circular base, warm brown patina, cloth Handel tag on felt base, c1919 .... **16,100.00**

23" h, 18" d reverse painted dome shade, riverfront landscape with split rail fence, moon through autumn trees, inscribed "Handel 8025," heavy bronzed base with four scrolled legs around central shaft, sq platform, base unsigned, restored.............. **5,175.00**

23-1/2" h, 18" conical obverse painted Daffodil shade, hand painted green and yellow naturalized blossoms, marked "Handel 5648," mounted on three-socket gilt metal tripartite base with Handel label, old repaint on metal base **5,750.00**

23-1/2" h, 18" d textured dome shade, hand-painted realistic pastel rose blossoms, three crystal yellow butterflies in flight, sgd "Handel 7032," mounted on dark gold metal three-socket base with split tripartite columns.. **10,350.00**

23-1/2" h, 18" d textured domed shade, three brilliantly colored macaws among exotic jungle foliage and wisteria blossoms, sgd "Handel 6974," mounted on three-socket bronzed metal base with Japonesque motif, tiny rim chip, one socket replaced **16,100.00**

24" h, 18" d reverse painted domical shade, exotic birds in flight, greens, blues, and turquoise, tail feathers extend downward and fan out, black leaves, lemon yellow vines with leaves, orange-red background, blue, yellow, and white six petaled flowers, bronzed metal base with polygonal form, foot molded as pierced Chinese stand, shade sgd "Handel Lamps, Pat'd No. 979664" on collar, "Handel 9021" directly on shade **77,800.00**

24-1/2" h, 16" d textured domed reverse painted shade, hand-painted delicate wild roses and varicolored leaves on thorny branches, edge sgd "Handel," mounted on three-socket ribbed shaft in orig white paint, Japonesque fretwork stepped platform base, some wear to paint **5,475.00**

24-1/2" h, 17" diagonal paneled glass shade, 10 sunset orange slag glass bent panels above shaped green slag border, framed in bronzed leafy tree overlay motif, raised on bronzed simulated tree trunk base with dark patination, needs rewiring **4,025.00**

24-1/2" h, 18" d textured glass dome shade, two pairs of long-tailed brightly colored birds perched in brilliant yellow-green blossoming

foliage, black background, edge sgd "Handel 7026 Palme," mounted on three-socket Handel gilt metal and gesso base, urn-form tripartite shaft with amber glass beads **11,500.00**

28" h, 18" d shade composed of four tapered curved panels, two etched and enameled with brilliant orange parrots, two with brown-amber jungle leafage, lower edge sgd "Handel 7686 Palne," mounted on Handel lamp base, replacement socket, rewired **4,025.00**

Wall scones, pr, 10" h, one-light, lily form, naturalistic stems supporting floriform shade of overlapped green and white slag glass panels, two green slag glass buds, bronzed metal lily pad form wall mounts, rich red brown patina, raised Handel signature, c1903 . . . . **1,380.00**

HEISEY GLASS

1900–58

History: The A. H. Heisey Glass Co. began producing glasswares in April 1896, in Newark, Ohio. Heisey, the firm's founder, was not a newcomer to the field, having been associated with the craft since his youth.

Many blown and molded patterns were produced in crystal, colored, milk (opalescent), and Ivorina Verde (custard) glass. Decorative techniques of cutting, etching, and silver deposit were employed. Glass figurines were introduced in 1933 and continued in production until 1957 when the factory closed. Imperial Glass Corporation purchased several of the molds after they closed.

Heisey sold blanks to Tiffin Glass and the T. G. Hawkes Company. No glassware was marked until November 1901, when paper labels became popular. The "H" in diamond mark was introduced later. This mark was never used on the foot or bowl, only on the stem; however, not every piece was marked.

All Heisey glass is notable for its clarity. Popular patterns were widely sold through stores, and today's collectors delight in finding Heisey glass advertisements in women's magazines of the era.

Heisey colors include rainbow hues of Alexandrite, amber, black, blue, cobalt blue, dawn, emerald green, flamingo (pink), heliotrope, marigold (deep amber-yellow), Moongleam (green), red, Sahara (yellow), tangerine, vaseline, and zircon.

References: Neila Bredehoft, *Collector's Encyclopedia of Heisey Glass, 1925-1938*, Collector Books, 1986, 1999 value update; —; *Fifty Years of Collectible Glass, 1920-1970*, Volume 1, Volume II, Antique Trader Books, 2000; —; *Heisey Glass, 1896-1957*, Collector Books, 2001; Lyle Conder, *Collector's Guide to Heisey's Glassware for Your Table*, L-W Books, 1984, 1993-94 value update; Shirley Dunbar, *Heisey Glass, The Early Years, 1896-1924*, Krause Publications, 2000; Gene Florence, *Elegant Glassware of the Depression Era*, 9th, Collector Books, 2000; —, *Glass Candlesticks of the Depression Era*, Collector Books, 1999; Frank L. Hahn and Paul Kikeli, *Collector's Guide to Heisey and Heisey by Imperial Glass Animals*, Golden Era Publications, 1991, 1998 value update.

Collectors' Clubs: Bay State Heisey Collectors Club, 354 Washington St., East Walpole, MA 02032; Heisey Collectors of America, 169 W. Church St., Newark, OH, 43055, http://www.heiseymuseum.org; National Capital Heisey Collectors, P.O. Box 23, Clinton, MD 20735.

Museum: National Heisey Glass Museum, Newark, OH.

Reproduction Alert: Some Heisey molds were sold to Imperial Glass of Bellaire, Ohio, and certain items were reissued. These pieces may be mistaken for the original Heisey. Some of the reproductions were produced in colors which were never made by Heisey and have become collectible in their own right. Examples include: the Colt family in Crystal, Caramel Slag, Ultra Blue, and Horizon Blue; the mallard with wings up in Caramel Slag; Whirlpool (Provincial) in crystal and colors; and Waverly, a seven-inch, oval, footed compote in Caramel Slag.

Note: Glassware is colorless (clear, crystal, or etched), unless another color is indicated.

Miscellaneous accessories, etchings, and patterns

After dinner cup, Yeoman, #1184, Moongleam **35.00**

Animal
- Asian Pheasant **280.00**
- Gazelle **1,450.00**
- Giraffe **195.00**
- Goose
  - Wings down **450.00**
  - Wings half up **80.00**
- Mallard, wings up **150.00**
- Plug horse, Oscar **115.00**
- PonyBalking **195.00**
  - Kicking **175.00**
  - Standing **95.00**
- Rabbit **225.00**
- Ringneck pheasant **195.00**
- Sealyham terrier **125.00**
- Scottie **145.00**
- Sparrow **145.00**

Ashtray
- Lodestar, dawn **110.00**
- Victorian, monogrammed **25.00**

Basket
- #417
  - Colorless, sgd, minor base nick **80.00**
  - Medium green, floral and band engraving, sgd, 8-1/4" h, 6-1/2" h **175.00**
  - Pale amethyst, sgd, 8-1/2" h, 6" w **300.00**
  - Pink, sgd, 8-1/2" h, 6" w . . **125.00**
- #459
  - Butterfly and floral engraving, sgd, 13-1/2" h, 7" w **175.00**
  - Daisy and leaf engraving, sgd, 14" h, 7" w **175.00**
- #460, heavy press, cut-glass imitation, patent date 2-22-16, sgd, 12" h, 7-1/2" w **225.00**
- #465, paneled, sgd, 12-3/4" h, 9-1/4" l **100.00**
- #477, leaf and floral engraving, sgd, 10-1/2" h, 10-1/2" l **100.00**
- #480
  - Floral cutting, round shape, sgd, 9-1/2" h, 8" w **175.00**
  - Floral leaf and basketweave engraving, sgd, 10-1/2" h, 8" w **225.00**
- Bow Tie, flamingo **125.00**
- Daisy **140.00**

Beer mug, fisherman etching . . **275.00**

Berry bowl, Beaded Swag, opalescent, metal foot **25.00**

Beverage set, Gallagher, pitcher and six handled lemonades **450.00**

Bitters bottle, #5003, tube **165.00**

Bonbon #1210, 8" d, handle, Moongleam **35.00**

Bookends, pr
- Fish **185.00**
- Horse heads **225.00**

Bowl
- 9-1/2" d, 3" h, cut basket of flowers design, three applied glass feet **70.00**
- 10" d, Priscilla, ftd, marked . . **295.00**
- 11" d, #143, floral, flamingo . . **95.00**
- 12" d, Yeoman, #1184, floral, flamingo **35.00**

Candelabrum
- #300
  - Hemisphere, five-light, 3-1/2" d **150.00**
  - Upper Hemisphere, five-light **150.00**
- #1445, Grape Cluster, one-lite, 4" prisms **325.00**

Candle block, #1469, 3" pr. **85.00**

Candlesticks, pr
- #22, Windsor, 7-1/2" h. **140.00**
- #99, Little Squatter **35.00**
- #112, Mercury
  - Flamingo, 3" h **48.00**
  - Sahara yellow **70.00**
- #114, Pluto, Hawthorne orchid **155.00**
- #118, Miss Muffet, diamond optic base, Moongleam **55.00**
- #121, Pinwheel **90.00**
- #126, Trophy, flamingo pink . **275.00**
- #142, Cascade, three-lite, crystal **75.00**

Loving cup, Colonial, crystal, **$95.** *Photo courtesy of Joy Luke Fine Art Brokers and Auctioneers.*

#1433, Thumbprint and Panel **140.00**
#1504, Regency, two-lite **98.00**
Trident, Alexandrite **995.00**
Tea Rose, two-lite, fern blank. **120.00**

Card box, cov, Windsor, Royal Sensation cutting **125.00**
Celery/pickle, #1184, Yeoman, 9" l, Sahara yellow, diamond optic . . . **20.00**
Center piece, Buttress, low **35.00**
Champagne, Rampo, Moongleam green saucer-shaped bowls, applied flamingo pink base, six-pc set . . **360.00**
Champagne flute, #422 Cumberland, #3336 Lady Leg, 7" h, 4-1/2 oz . . **38.00**
Cigarette box, horse head finial **125.00**
Cocktail
Pompeii, 3 oz **35.00**
Rooster stem **40.00**
Rosealie, 3 oz **10.00**
Cocktail shaker
#4225, Cobel
Quart **55.00**
Pint, rooster stopper, etched "US" **150.00**
Two quart **55.00**
#4225, Sportsman etching, two quart, #455 etching **290.00**
Cologne, #1489, cut stopper, 4 oz **155.00**
Commemorative plaque, 5-1/2" h, cobalt blue, diamond shape, emb "H," manufactured by Heisey Collectors of America **100.00**
Console set, Moongleam, Cattail cutting, bowl, four candlesticks . **295.00**
Cordial
5th Avenue-Mitchell, #829 . . . . **45.00**
Puritan, 1 oz **18.00**
Cornucopia, Warwick, #1426, 9" h **190.00**

Creamer and sugar, cov
#325, Pillows, crystal, gold trim **165.00**
#354, Wide Flat Panel, oval, hotel size, Sahara yellow. **175.00**
#479 Petal, Moongleam **75.00**
#1506, Whirlpool, individual size **65.00**
Crème de Menthe, Puritan, 2-1/2 oz **16.00**
Cruet, orig stopper
Greek Key. **135.00**
Saturn **60.00**
Whirlpool. **60.00**
Yeoman, #1184, Moongleam, diamond optic **85.00**
Cup
#502 Crinoline etching, #1509 Queen Ann blank **38.00**
Stanhole, crystal, black knob . **12.00**
Custard cup, Pinwheel & Fan, Moongleam green **20.00**
Decanter
#305 Punty and Diamond Point, orig stopper. **185.00**
#367 Prism Band, flamingo pink, crystal #48 cut stopper . . . **200.00**
#4027 Tally Ho **365.00**
Floral bowl, Tear Drop, pink. . . . **90.00**
Fruit basket, #480, cutting, 8" . **245.00**
Goblet
#458 Olympiad, #3411 Monte Cristo, 8-3/8" h, 9 oz **60.00**
#3324 Delaware, flamingo, diamond optic **20.00**
#3333 Old Glory, Renaissance cutting **30.00**
#3350 Wabash, flamingo, 7" h **22.50**
#3368 Albemarle, 8-1/2" h, 8 oz, diamond optic **35.00**
#4091 Kimberly, #1015 Dolly Madison, rose cutting, 10 oz **85.00**
#8005, Galaxy. **25.00**
Horseradish jar, #352 . . . . **55.00**
Iced tea tumbler
Fred Harvey, ftd, amber **45.00**
Kimberly, #4091, Dolly Madison, #1015, rose cutting **70.00**
Jar, 11-1/2" h, 5" w, floral cutting, gold banding, sgd. **70.00**
Jug, Charter Oak, #3362, flamingo, diamond optic, half gallon. **200.00**
Juice tumbler, Whirlpool **15.00**
Lamp, Dolphin, candlestick type **180.00**
Madonna, 9" h, frosted **110.00**
Mayonnaise ladle, #6, Alexandrite **245.00**
Mug, Whaley, #4163, 16 oz, etched club drinking scene. **150.00**

Mustard, cov
Coarse Rib, marigold satin, marked in top and base. **65.00**
Flat Panel, #352. . . . . **48.50**
Nappy, Prison Stripe, #357, 4-1/2" d **22.00**
Nut dish, individual, swan shape **22.50**
Perfume, 6-1/4" h, amber and crystal, floral and leaf cutting, long crystal stopper, pr **150.00**
Pickle, #1191, Lobe, flamingo . . . **30.00**
Pickle jar, cov, gold band dec . . **55.00**
Pitcher
Coarse Rib, quart, 7-1/4" h . . **145.00**
Priscilla, quart, 5" h **120.00**
Puritan, quart, 6" h. **135.00**
Plate, Yeoman, #1184
Sahara, 6" d. **8.00**
Yeoman, #1184
Sahara, 7" d **8.50**
#847 streamline cutting, 8" d **55.00**
Punch bowl set, Whirlpool **185.00**
Punch cup
Fancy Loop, #1205, 4-1/2" h, 5 oz **48.00**
Locket on Chain **35.00**
Pillows **35.00**
Punch ladle, #11 . . . . **95.00**
Relish
Crenoline, three parts **65.00**
Normandie, #1466 Relish, star etch **95.00**
Rose bowl
Mermaid, 6" d **500.00**
Plateau, #3369, flamingo. **65.00**
Salad plate
#4004 Impromptu, 7" d **12.00**
#4901 Kimberly, #1015 Dolly Madison, rose cutting, 8" d . . **40.00**
Sherbet
Gascony Line, #3397, Ambassador, #452 etching, 2-3/8" h, 6 oz . **35.00**
Olympia, #3408 . . . . **14.00**
Priscilla, 4 oz, high **15.00**
Puritan, 3 oz, low. **16.00**
Sherry
Puritan, 2 oz. **18.00**
Renaissance, #3333, Old Glory stem, 2 oz **24.00**
Soda tumbler
#170, Cleopatra, diamond optic, 5 oz **20.00**
#235, Newton, Fronetnac etch, 8 oz **20.00**
#3389, Duquesne, #3389, ftd, tangerine, 12 oz **210.00**
#3397, Gascony, #3397 line, Ambassador, #452, etching, 12 oz, 5-1/2" h **35.00**

#3416 Barbara Fritchie, #457 Springtime etching, restored rim, 12 oz, 5-5/8" h **15.00**
#3480, Koors, Flamingo, 5 oz, set of eight **175.00**
#4054, Coronation, #4054, 10 oz **9.50**
#4083, Stanhope, #4083, ftd, zircon bowl and foot, 8 oz....... **155.00**
#4091, Kimberly, Dolly Madison, #1015, rose cutting, 5 oz ... **55.00**

Sugar, cov, #1225 Pineapple and fan, gold trim **48.00**
Sugar cube tray, Narrow Flute, flower and leaf cutting **45.00**
Syrup pitcher
Punty Band **200.00**
Urn **130.00**
Toothpick holder
Fancy Loop, emerald, small base flake, wear to gold trim.... **120.00**
Waldorf Astoria, #333 ...... **110.00**
Tumbler
#1417 Arch, orig red and white factory identification label, 9 oz **55.00**
Tumbler, #3404, Titania etch, ftd, 6-1/4" h **30.00**
Vase
Cathedral, #1413, flared, Sahara yellow **250.00**
Molded, flared rim, oval form, round stepped base, three scrolled handles, colorless, repeating etched scrolled floral bands, raised diamond mark, 7-5/8" h ... **200.00**
Pineapple and Fan, 6" h, green, worn gold trim **40.00**
Prison Stripe, #357, cupped, 5" **55.00**
Rooster, crystal............ **70.00**
Wine
Creole, Alexandrite, crystal stem **175.00**
Gascony, 2 oz, Sportsman etch **60.00**

Patterns

Acorn

Plate, dinner **60.00**
Sherbet, Flamingo pink......... **20.00**
Syrup **80.00**

Arcadia—#1025

Champagne, saucer.......... **18.00**
Goblet, water **20.00**

Banded Flute—#150

Chamberstick............... **45.00**
Claret **25.00**
Cup **100.00**
Flower center............... **60.00**
Horseradish jar **85.00**
Plate, 6" d.................... **50.00**
Punch set, 14" d punch bowl, high base, five cups.............. **295.00**
Salt shaker **50.00**
Water carafe **125.00**
Wine...................... **50.00**

Beaded Panel & Sunburst—#1235

Punch bowl and stand, 7-3/4" h, 14-1/2" w, 5-3/4" h x 9-1/2" w stand, chip under bottom bowl rim, c1896-1905, sgd **625.00**
Water bottle................ **115.00**

Carcassone—#390

Cordial, Sahara yellow........ **115.00**
Sherbet, crystal **20.00**

Chintz—#1401 (Empress Blank) and #3389 (Duquesne Blank). Made in Alexandrite orchid, crystal, flamingo pink, Moongleam green, and Sahara yellow; 1931-38.

Bread and butter plate, crystal, sq, 6" w......................... **8.00**
Celery tray, 10" l, crystal **20.00**
Champagne, crystal **22.00**
Claret, crystal................ **20.00**
Cocktail, Sahara yellow........ **42.00**
Cordial, #3389, Duquesne, crystal **115.00**
Creamer, Sahara yellow........ **40.00**
Cup and saucer, crystal **30.00**
Dinner plate
Crystal, sq, 10-1/2" w........ **45.00**
Sahara yellow, sq, 10-1/2" w .. **90.00**
Finger bowl, Sahara yellow..... **15.00**
Goblet, crystal **25.00**
Grapefruit, crystal **22.00**
Ice bucket, ftd, crystal......... **90.00**
Iced tea tumbler, #3389, 12 oz, ftd, Sahara yellow............... **25.00**
Juice tumbler, #3389, 5 oz, ftd, crystal **15.00**
Luncheon plate, crystal, sq, 8" w **18.00**
Luncheon, Sahara yellow, sq, 8" w **25.00**
Mint dish, Sahara yellow **32.00**
Nasturtium bowl, 7-1/2" d, crystal **20.00**
Oyster cocktail, #3389, Sahara yellow **25.00**
Pickle and olive bowl, two parts, 13" d, crystal..................... **20.00**
Pitcher, three pints, dolphin foot, Sahara yellow............... **185.00**
Platter, 14" l, oval, crystal....... **28.00**
Preserve bowl, handle, crystal .. **18.00**
Salad plate, Sahara yellow, sq, 7" w **20.00**
Sandwich tray, center handle, 12" sq, crystal..................... **40.00**
Sugar, Sahara yellow **42.00**
Tumbler, ftd, 10 oz
Crystal **25.00**
Sahara yellow, ftd, 10 oz **30.00**

Colonial

Candy dish, cov............. **60.00**
Celery, 12".................. **35.00**
Champagne **18.00**
Claret **18.00**
Coaster................... **10.00**
Cordial **15.00**
Cruet, Flamingo pink, octagonal stopper **620.00**
Crushed fruit jar
Large **190.00**
Small.................. **180.00**
Custard cup, flared, handle **10.00**
Goblet.................... **20.00**
Horseradish and mustard, cov, pr **75.00**
Jug, pint **165.00**
Plate
4-3/4" d.................. **4.75**
6" d, scalloped **10.00**
Punch bowl, matching base, 13" d **175.00**
Sherry, 2 oz................ **18.00**
Tumbler, 6 oz, ftd **50.00**
Wine, 2 oz................. **18.00**

Creole—#3381

Soda tumbler, 12 oz, ftd, diamond optic Alexandrite bowl, crystal foot **167.50**
Wine, 2-1/2 oz, Alexandrite.... **165.00**

Crystolite—Blank #1503. Made in amber, crystal, Sahara yellow, and Zircon/Limelight.

Ashtray, zircon **65.00**
Basket, 6" h................ **175.00**
Cake plate **325.00**
Candle block, sq **20.00**
Candlesticks, pr
Block.................. **85.00**
Round.................. **40.00**
Two-lite **55.00**
Three-lite................ **75.00**
Candy dish, cov............. **75.00**
Celery tray, 12" l, rect......... **35.00**
Cheese comport, ftd **25.00**
Cheese plate, 8" d, two handles. **45.00**
Cigarette holder, ftd.......... **55.00**
Coaster
Sahara yellow............ **35.00**
Zircon **45.00**
Creamer **25.00**
Cruet, stopper............... **55.00**
Cup **22.50**
Floater bowl, 12" l, oval **48.00**
Floater candles, 4-1/2" sq, pr .. **38.00**
Gardenia bowl, 12" d **175.00**
Heart, one handle **30.00**
Jelly compote, 4-1/2" h, 5" d ... **28.00**

Mayonnaise set
- Oval, three pcs **65.00**
- Round, three pcs **48.00**

Mint, ftd **18.00**
Nappy **18.50**
Nut, master, swan, 7" **45.00**
Oil bottle, no stopper **30.00**
Plate, 7" d **10.00**
Puff box, cov, filigree holder . . . **125.00**
Punch cup **10.00**

Relish
- Three parts, #1503, 8" **55.00**
- Five parts, #1503, 10" **65.00**
- Five parts, 10" d, aluminum lazy Susan **90.00**

Sherbet **15.00**
Spring salad bowl **70.00**
Sugar, cov **30.00**
Tumbler, 6" h, ftd **30.00**
Urn, 7" h **20.00**

September, 1931 *Page 5*

Expressing Fine Traditions in Early American Glass

Simple lines and delightful sturdiness are carried out with true craftsmanship in recent Early American glass by Heisey. In this glass is expressed the many fine traditions of the period.

An example is the new 1404 line — the Thumb Print pattern. The charm of its design was inspired by the famous Sandwich glass, of which the Heiseys own the original models.

A variety of stemware and other pieces is offered in the 1404 pattern, in clear crystal, Sahara gold, Moon Gleam green, and Flamingo rose.

It is a design with a great deal of appeal—right in the fashion to go with the vogue for Early American dining-rooms.

Other glass in this period offered by Heisey is the Scroll Design—No. 1405—and fine lead-brown stemware with quaint Chintz etchings. You will want to stock one or another of these patterns for the fall.

A. H. HEISEY & COMPANY
Newark, Ohio

Shown here is the goblet of the new 1404 line, the Thumb Print pattern. Available in stemware and other pieces in the following colors: Clear Crystal, Moon Gleam, Flamingo and Sahara.

SALES OFFICES

E. G. Nock, 358 Fifth Avenue Building, New York.
W. S. Redfield, 1560 Merchandise Mart, Chicago.
H. S. Bokee, 122 W. Baltimore Street, Baltimore.
H. M. Bortz, 218 E. Sedgwick Street, Philadelphia.
G. A. Granville, 111 Summer Street, Boston.
R. C. Irwin, 1560 Merchandise Mart, Chicago.
R. E. Phillips, 129 Putnam Avenue, Zanesville, Ohio.
C. S. Whipple, 622 S. Westlake Avenue, Los Angeles.
Davis & Braisted Co., 120 N. 4th Street, Minneapolis.
Hal M. Copeland, 3608 Springdale Avenue, Baltimore.
The Edminster Co., 612 Howard Street, San Francisco.
E. F. Redfield, 6432 Oak Street, Kansas City, Mo.

Tell our advertisers you saw it in THE CROCKERY AND GLASS JOURNAL

Ad, Line #1404, Thumb Print pattern, introduced in Crockery and Glass Journal, *September 1931.*

Empress Blank—#1401. Made in Alexandrite, cobalt blue, flamingo pink, Moongleam green, Sahara yellow, and some tangerine. This pattern was also made later in crystal and the name changed to Queen Ann.

Ashtray
- Alexandrite **150.00**
- Sahara yellow **90.00**

Bowl
- 6" d, dolphin foot, Moongleam green **45.00**
- 7-1/2" d, dolphin foot, Sahara yellow **50.00**
- 11" d, ftd, flower frog, Sahara yellow **75.00**

Candelabra, three-lite, Sahara yellow, crystal bobeches, pr **950.00**
Candlesticks, pr, 6" h, dolphin foot, pink **185.00**
Candy dish, cov, silver overlay, ftd **75.00**
Celery tray, 13" l, Sahara yellow . **25.00**

Creamer and sugar
- Moongleam, individual size . . . **95.00**
- Sahara yellow **60.00**

Cream soup, Sahara yellow **25.00**

Cruet, orig stopper
- Flamingo **140.00**
- Moongleam green foot and stopper **250.00**

Cup and saucer
- Alexandrite, sq **115.00**
- Moongleam green, sq **50.00**
- Sahara yellow, round **45.00**

Dinner plate, crystal, square, 10-1/2" d **90.00**
Goblet, pink, etched **50.00**
Grapefruit, 6" sq, Sahara yellow . **20.00**
Iced tea tumbler, ftd, pink, etched **50.00**
Ice tub, #1401, arctic etch **170.00**
Jelly compote, 6" h, Sahara yellow **35.00**
Lemon server, cov, oval **50.00**

Luncheon plate
- Alexandrite, 7-1/2" d **45.00**
- Sahara yellow, 7-1/2" d **22.00**

Mayonnaise, dolphin feet, Sahara yellow **50.00**
Mint dish, #1185, Moongleam, 6", ftd **45.00**

Nut dish
- Individual, Alexandrite **175.00**
- Sahara yellow **20.00**

Relish, three parts
- Crystal **25.00**
- Minuet etch **90.00**
- Sahara yellow **35.00**

Salad plate
- Alexandrite, round, 8" d **80.00**

Sahara yellow
Round, 8" d **20.00**
Sq, 8" w **22.00**
Salt and pepper shakers, pr, Sahara yellow..................... **75.00**
Sherbet plate, Moongleam, 6" d. **10.00**
Sherbet, Sahara yellow
Round, 6" d.............. **13.00**
Sq, 6" w................. **13.00**
Tray, center handle, 12" sq, Sahara yellow..................... **65.00**
Vegetable bowl, 10" l, Sahara yellow **45.00**

Greek Key—Made in crystal.

Almond dish, individual **35.00**
Banana split dish, 9" l, ftd **25.00**
Butter dish, cov **170.00**
Candy dish, cov, ftd **65.00**
Celery tray, 12" l **45.00**
Creamer and sugar, medium size **100.00**
Cruet, no stopper **35.00**
Egg cup **45.00**
Flower center **75.00**
Horseradish, cov **60.00**
Ice tub, cov **65.00**
Jelly compote, handle **25.00**
Nappy **10.00**
Orange bowl, 14" d, flared rim .. **65.00**
Pitcher, three pints **200.00**
Plate
4-1/2" d **12.00**
6" d **15.00**
7" d **18.00**
8" d **20.00**
9" d **24.00**
Sherbet, low, flared.......... **50.00**
Spooner **90.00**
Straw jar, top missing........ **250.00**
Tankard, three quarts **250.00**
Tray, 13" l, oblong **60.00**
Tumbler, 12 oz, flared rim...... **30.00**
Water bottle **185.00**

Heisey Minuet—#503, etching.

Champagne, #5010 Symphone, 61/8" h, 6 oz................. **55.00**
Cordially **175.00**
Goblet, #5010 Symphone, 8-1/8" h, 9 oz **65.00**
Iced tea tumbler, ftd, #5010 Symphone, 6-15/16" h, 12 oz ... **60.00**
Mayonnaise, ftd, #1511 Toujours **85.00**
Oyster cocktail, #5010 Symphone, 3-3/8" h, 4-1/2 oz **48.00**
Plate
7" d, #1511 Toujours........ **24.00**
8" d, #1511 Toujours........ **24.00**
Sundae, #5010 Symphone, 3-1/2" h, 6 oz....................... **45.00**
Wine...................... **75.00**

Ipswich—Blank #1405. Made in Alexandrite, cobalt blue, crystal, flamingo pink, Moongleam green, and Sahara yellow.

Candlestick centerpiece, ftd, vase, prisms, pr **300.00**
Champagne/sherbet, tall, #150 . **12.00**
Cocktail shaker............. **285.00**
Creamer.................... **20.00**
Finger bowl, underplate, Moongleam green **45.00**
Juice tumbler, ftd, Sahara yellow **42.00**
Mantel lusters, pr, cobalt blue, orig inserts and prisms **900.00**
Plate
7" sq, flamingo pink......... **25.00**
8" sq, Sahara yellow **30.00**
Sherbet, Sahara yellow **35.00**
Sugar, flamingo pink **30.00**
Tumbler, Sahara yellow **52.00**

Lariat—Blank #1540. Made in crystal; limited production in amber and black.

Ashtray, 4" d **15.00**
Bonbon, 7-1/2" d, hand painted dec **100.00**
Bowl, 12" d.................. **40.00**
Bud vase, 15" h, swung....... **185.00**
Buffet plate, 21".............. **70.00**
Camellia bowl, 9-1/2" d........ **40.00**
Candlesticks, pr
One-lite, low............... **40.00**
Two-lite, #1150............. **95.00**
Three-lite **125.00**
Candy basket, Moonglo cutting . **45.00**
Candy, cov.................. **45.00**
Caramel, cov, 7"............. **75.00**
Celery tray, 10" l **30.00**
Champagne................. **15.00**
Cheese dish, cov, ftd.......... **40.00**
Coaster **12.50**
Cocktail, Moonglo cut **12.00**
Coffee cup.................. **15.00**
Creamer and sugar, individual size, floral cutting **30.00**
Deviled egg plate, 13" d **125.00**
Floral bowl, small, 9" d **27.00**
Gardenia bowl, 12" d.......... **32.00**
Goblet
Crystal **20.00**
Moonglo.................. **35.00**
Hurricane lamps, dec, pr **100.00**
Iced tea tumbler, 12 oz
Crystal **27.50**
Moonglo.................. **35.00**
Juice tumbler, ftd, 5 oz **10.00**
Mayonnaise and underplate ... **20.00**
Plate
7" d, dessert **8.00**
8" d, salad................ **12.00**
10-1/2" d, service **24.00**
14" d, floral cutting **48.00**
Punch bowl, set, 14" d punch bowl, 21" d underplate, eight punch cups, orig hooks, and ladle......... **225.00**
Punch cup **12.50**
Relish
Two parts, 11", two handles, oval **40.00**
Three parts, 10-1/2" **24.00**
Three parts, 12" **28.00**
Salad bowl, 10-1/2" d......... **40.00**
Sandwich plate, 13" d **28.00**
Sherbet, Moonglo............ **30.00**
Wine **15.00**

Narrow Flute—#393.

Goblet..................... **28.50**
Jelly, two handles, 5" **45.00**
Jug, three pints.............. **75.00**
Mustard, cov................ **40.00**
Nut dish, Moongleam......... **15.00**
Strawberry dip plate, with rim . **195.00**

New Era—#4044. Made in crystal, frosted crystal, and some cobalt blue with crystal stem and foot. Original pattern made 1934-41. Stemware, candlesticks, and celery added 1944-57. Made pieces of this Art Deco-style tableware were monogrammed. Deduct 20 percent for monogrammed pieces.

Ashtray.................... **30.00**
Candlesticks, pr............. **90.00**
Celery **40.00**
Champagne **22.50**
Cocktail, 3-1/2 oz **22.50**
Console bowl................ **85.00**
Cordial **48.00**
Cup and saucer.............. **50.00**
Floral bowl, 11" d, frosted **40.00**
Luncheon plate **40.00**
Nut cup.................... **50.00**
Pilsner **50.00**
Plate, 6" d **25.00**
Relish, three parts **45.00**
Rye bottle, orig stopper, monogram **115.00**
Sherbet.................... **20.00**
Wine **37.50**

Octagon—Blank #500, #1229, and #1231 (ribbed). Made in crystal, Dawn, flamingo pink, Hawthorne orchid, Marigold, Moongleam green, and Sahara yellow.

After dinner cup and saucer, flamingo pink **25.00**
Basket, 5" h, Hawthorne orchid etching **120.00**
Bonbon, sides up............ **10.00**

Celery dish, Moongleam green . . 35.00
Creamer and sugar, Moongleam green 75.00
Hors d'oeuvre plate, 13" d, flamingo pink 30.00
Ice tub, Hawthorne orchid etching 65.00
Muffin plate, 12" d, Moongleam green 47.50
Nut dish, individual, flamingo pink 15.00
Plate, 8" d, luncheon, Moongleam green 20.00
Salad bowl, 12-1/2" d, Sahara yellow 25.00
Soup plate, 9" d, Sahara yellow . . 20.00
Vegetable bowl, 9" d, flamingo pink 20.00

Old Dominion—Blank #3380, 1930-39.

Bar tumbler, Moongleam green . 30.00
Bouillon cup, two handles, ftd, flamingo pink 20.00
Champagne/saucer, marigold, Empress etch bowl, crystal stem . 30.00
Cigarette holder 20.00
Cocktail, marigold, Empress etch bowl, crystal stem 30.00
Cordial, diamond optic, Sahara yellow 145.00
Creamer and sugar, cov, etched, Sahara yellow 70.00
Cup and saucer, flamingo pink . . 40.00
Goblet, marigold, 8-3/4" 55.00
Grapefruit, 6" d, Moongleam green 40.00
Nappy, 8" d, Sahara yellow 40.00
Plate
- 6" d, Sahara yellow, round 9.00
- 7" w, flamingo pink, square . . . 18.00
- 9" d, colorless, round 20.00
- 10-1/2" w, Moongleam green, square 65.00

Oyster cocktail 65.00
Sandwich plate, 12" d, center handle, flamingo pink 60.00
Sherbet, low, marigold, Empress etch bowl, crystal stem 25.00
Soda tumbler, 12 oz, ftd, diamond optic Alexandrite 90.00
Wine, Sahara yellow 20.00

Old Colony—Etching made on #1401 Empress blank, #3390 Caracassone blank, and #3380 Old Dominion blank. Made on cobalt blue, crystal, flamingo pink, marigold, Moongleam green, and Sahara yellow; c1930-39.

Beverage set, 11 oz pitcher, six goblets, Sahara yellow, Carcassone blank, sq base 525.00
Bouillon cup, Moongleam green 30.00
Cocktail, 3 oz, Sahara yellow, Old Dominion blank, round base 28.00
Finger bowl, #4075
- Crystal 8.00
- Flamingo pink 12.00
- Marigold 28.00
- Moongleam green 18.00
- Sahara yellow 15.00

Creamer, dolphin foot, flamingo . 35.00
Mayonnaise, 5-1/2" d, dolphin foot, flamingo pink 75.00
Plate
- 6" d, crystal, round 8.00
- 7" w, flamingo pink, square . . . 15.00
- 8" d, Sahara yellow, round . . . 30.00
- 9" d, Moongleam green, round 72.00
- 10-1/2" d, crystal, round 32.00
- 10-1/2" d, crystal, square 30.00

Soda tumbler, 9 oz, ftd, Sahara yellow 28.00
Sugar, dolphin foot, Moongleam green 35.00
Vase
- Crystal, 9" h 80.00
- Flamingo pink, 9" h 135.00
- Moongleam green, 9" h 175.00
- Sahara yellow, 9" h 160.00

Wine, 2-1/2 oz
- Crystal 50.00
- Flamingo pink 145.00
- Moongleam green 175.00
- Sahara yellow 135.00

Old Sandwich—Blank #1404. Made in amber, cobalt blue, crystal, flamingo pink, Moongleam green, and Sahara yellow.

Ashtray, Moongleam, individual size 67.50
Beer mug
- Amber 450.00
- Stiegel blue 400.00

Bowl, 11" d, oval, ftd, Moongleam green 120.00
Catsup bottle 35.00
Champagne, yellow 35.00
Creamer and sugar, oval, Flamingo pink 50.00
Decanter, Moongleam green . . 185.00
Finger bowl, crystal 15.00
Goblet, 12 oz 20.00
Iced tea tumbler, ftd, 12 oz 15.00
Jug, Sahara yellow, half gallon . 225.00
Parfait 15.00
Plate, square
- 7" w, flamingo pink, square . . . 20.00
- 8" w, green 35.00

Popcorn bowl, cupped, Moongleam green 70.00
Salt shaker 30.00
Soda tumbler
- 8 oz, Moongleam green 48.50
- 10 oz, flat, tangerine 495.00

Water tumbler, Sahara 35.00

Old Williamsburg—crystal.

Candelabra, three-lite, #301, short base 310.00
Cocktail 10.00
Epergne, 5-1/2" d, marked "Heisey by Imperial" 18.00
Wine 14.00

Orchid Etching—#1507 on #1519 Waverly blank, and #1509 Queen Ann blank. Made only in crystal; 1940-57.

Ashtray, 3" sq 30.00
Bowl
- 10" d, Queen Anne blank 68.00
- 11" d, three dolphin feet 165.00
- 13" d 100.00

Butter dish, cov. 245.00
Cake plate, 13-1/2" d, ftd. 245.00
Candlesticks, pr
- One-lite, mercury 90.00
- Two-lite, Trident blank, #134 . 120.00
- Two-lite, Waverly blank 120.00
- Three-lite 250.00

Celery, 11-3/4" l 65.00
Champagne 55.00
Cheese and cracker set, 12" d . 135.00
Cigarette holder, ftd 165.00
Cocktail, 4 oz. 40.00
Cocktail shaker, sterling foot . . 200.00
Comport
- 6", Waverly blank 50.00
- 7", oval 150.00

Condiment bottle, orig stopper 250.00
Cordial 115.00
Creamer and sugar
- Individual size 110.00
- Table size 95.00

Cup and saucer, ftd. 70.00
Gardenia bowl, #1519 Waverly, 9-1/4" d 85.00
Goblet, #5025
- Luncheon, 10 oz 40.00
- Water 68.00

Iced tea tumbler, 12 oz 65.00
Jelly, underplate, spoon 165.00
Jug, 1/2 gallon, ice lip 525.00
Juice tumbler, ftd 80.00
Mayonnaise, liner, orig spoon, ftd 165.00
Mint, three toes 75.00
Oil bottle, stopper, ftd 225.00
Parfait 80.00
Pitcher, tankard 625.00
Plate, 7-1/2" d 48.00

Relish, three parts
- Queen Anne blank **75.00**
- Waverly blank, 11" l. **65.00**

Serving tray
- 12" d, center handle, Queen Ann blank. **200.00**
- 13" d **150.00**

Sherbet, low **25.00**
Torte plate, 14" d **90.00**
Wine, 3 oz **85.00**

Peerless—Blank #300, crystal.

Champagne, 4 oz, saucer type . **16.00**
Cocktail, 4-3/8" h **15.00**
Cordial, 3-3/8" h **15.00**
Goblet
- 5-1/8" h **18.00**
- 5-1/2" h, Colonial. **18.50**
- 6-3/8" h **18.50**

Pitcher
- 7-1/2" h, quart **165.00**
- 9-1/2" h, half gallon **265.00**

Sherbet, 3", 3 oz **10.00**
Wine, 3-7/8" h **15.00**

Pied Piper—crystal.

Beverage set, pitcher and six goblets **500.00**
Champagne, saucer **30.00**
Oyster cocktail. **15.00**

Plantation—Blank #1567. Made in crystal and some amber.

Cake plate, ftd, 12-1/2" d **85.00**
Candlesticks, pr, two-lite **150.00**
Candy, cov, three parts **250.00**
Cheese comport **75.00**
Coaster, 4" d **60.00**
Comport **40.00**
Creamer and sugar **35.00**
Cruet, orig stopper **155.00**
Epergne candle holder, ftd, 5" h **165.00**
Gardenia bowl, 13" d **45.00**
Honey, ivy etch, 6-1/2" **80.00**
Hurricane lamps, globes, electrified, pr **1,150.00**
Iced tea tumbler, ftd **75.00**
Marmalade jar, pineapple shape, cov, sgd spoon **115.00**
Mayonnaise, liner, matching underplate, etched **115.00**
Plate, 8-1/2" d **25.00**
Punch bowl, some wear. **450.00**
Relish, four parts **70.00**
Salt shaker, slightly cloudy. **30.00**
Sandwich plate, 14" d **65.00**
Sherbet. **25.00**
Sugar shaker **115.00**
Syrup **150.00**
Tumbler, ftd, 12 oz, pressed **80.00**
Vase, 5" h, ftd **35.00**
Wine. **35.00**

Pleat and Panel—Blank #1170. Made in crystal, flamingo pink, and Moongleam green.

Candle dish, cov, flamingo pink . **55.00**
Champagne, 5 oz, flamingo pink. **25.00**
Cheese and cracker set, flamingo pink **45.00**
Compote, cov, 7" h, flamingo pink, gold trim **75.00**
Creamer and sugar, hotel size . . **25.00**
Cruet, orig stopper, Moongleam **175.00**
Goblet, 5-1/4" h, 7-1/2 oz, luncheon, flamingo pink **30.00**
Iced tea tumbler, flamingo pink. . **25.00**
Jelly compote
- Flamingo pink **30.00**
- Moongleam green **25.00**

Lemon dish, cov, 5" l, flamingo pink **45.00**
Marmalade jar, ftd **25.00**
Nappy, 8" d, flamingo pink **58.00**
Plate
- 6" d, flamingo pink. **12.00**
- 7" d, crystal **10.00**
- 7" d, flamingo pink. **15.00**

Sandwich plate, 14" d, Moongleam green **35.00**
Spice tray, 10" d, flamingo pink. . **35.00**

Provincial—Blank #1506. Made in crystal, Moongleam green, and Zircon/Limelight.

Butter dish, cov. **85.00**
Candy dish, zircon **500.00**
Goblet **15.00**
Mustard, cov **50.00**
Nut bowl, 5" d **15.00**
Oil bottle, 4 oz **15.00**
Plate, 18" d. **40.00**
Relish, 12" **35.00**
Snack plate, 7" d, two handles . . **20.00**
Violet vase, 3-1/2" h, Moongleam green **65.00**

Ridgeleigh—Blank #1469. Made in crystal, Sahara yellow, and zircon; 1935-44.

Ashtray
- Club shape **10.00**
- Square, 6" **35.00**

Candlesticks, pr
- 2" sq. **80.00**
- 7" h, bobeches and prisms . . **150.00**

Celery and relish tray, oblong, two parts **40.00**
Centerpiece bowl, 11" d **225.00**
Cigarette holder **20.00**
Claret, 4 oz. **35.00**
Coaster, stacking set of six **36.00**
Creamer **20.00**
Cruet, orig stopper **50.00**
Floral bowl, 11-1/2" w. **55.00**
Goblet, luncheon **18.50**
Jelly, handle, 6". **20.00**
Marmalade, violet vase base, slotted chrome cover **50.00**
Nappy, pink. **8.00**
Old fashioned tumbler, 8 oz . . . **20.00**
Pitcher, half gallon, ice lip **80.00**
Plate, 8" d **10.00**
Platter, small **40.00**
Punch bowl **170.00**
Salt and pepper shakers, pr, double-cone shape **4.00**
Salt dip **15.00**
Sherbet. **20.00**
Tidbit tray, 11" and 13" plates . . **75.00**
Tumbler, 8 oz **45.00**
Vase, Sahara yellow, cylinder, 8" h **245.00**
Wine **25.00**

Rose—Etching #1515 on #1519 Waverly blank. Made only on crystal. 1949-57.

Ashtray. **35.00**
Bowl, 12" d, crimped **75.00**
Butter dish, cov **250.00**
Cake plate, 15" d, pedestal . . . **325.00**
Candlesticks, pr, low, flat **65.00**
Candy dish, cov, seahorse. . . . **250.00**
Celery, 12". **48.00**
Champagne, saucer. **35.00**
Claret, #5072, 4 oz **135.00**
Cocktail **32.50**
Compote, low, ftd, 6-1/2" h **95.00**
Cordial **150.00**
Cracker plate, 12" d **130.00**
Creamer and sugar, individual size **125.00**
Cup and saucer **75.00**
Goblet, crystal, 9 oz **60.00**
Honey, ftd, 6-1/4" d **80.00**
Iced tea tumbler, 12 oz, ftd **65.00**
Juice tumbler, ftd, 5-1/2" h, 5 oz **58.00**
Mayonnaise, underplate, ftd . . . **85.00**
Plate, 8-1/2" d **65.00**
Relish
- Three parts **65.00**
- Four parts, 9" d, round **70.00**

Salad plate, 7" d **20.00**
Salt and pepper shakers, pr, pewter tops **95.00**
Server, center handle **175.00**
Sherbet. **40.00**
Sugar, ftd **35.00**
Tumbler, ftd, 12 oz **50.00**
Underplate, 7-1/2" d **50.00**
Vegetable bowl **95.00**
Wine, 3 oz **115.00**

Depression glass, Beaded Block, vaseline square plate, **$8.50**, and iridescent round plate, **$17.50**.

Depression glass, Royal Ruby, punch set, punch bowl, and six cups, **$200** for the set.

Depression glass, Swirl, ultramarine plate, **$30**, and bowl, **$30**.

Early American, creamer, Banded Lily Pad, Southern New Jersey type, bulbous body, applied handle, crimped foot, c1830-50,
3-3/4" h, slight damage to three lily pads, **$1,760**. Photo courtesy of Pacific Glass Auctions.

Early American, decanter, pillar molded, Pittsburgh, 12 vertical sided ribs swirling at shoulder,
brilliant yellow with touch of olive, c1850-60, 12" h, **$360**. Photo courtesy of Pacific Glass Auctions.

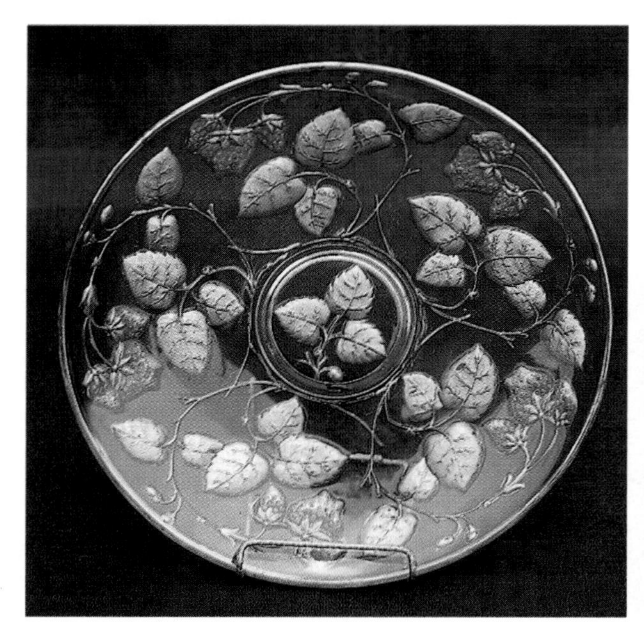

Goofus glass, plate, 11" d, allover leaf pattern, **$40**.

Goofus glass, bread plate, Last Supper, gold exterior with multicolored figures, grapes, and foliage border, **$65**.

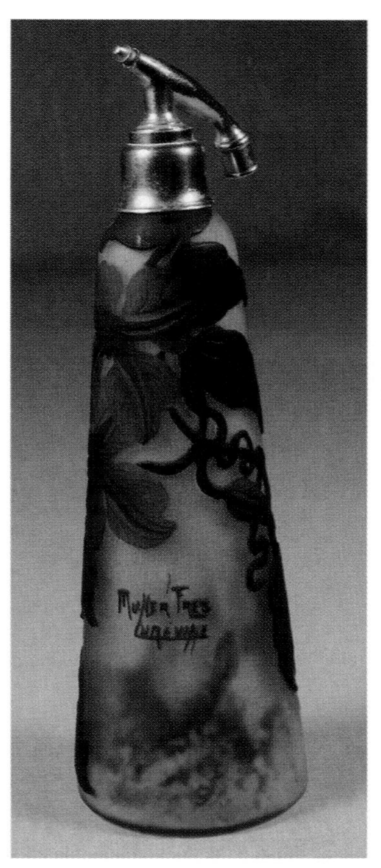

Cameo glass, atomizer, cobalt, "Muller Freres," 9" h, **$550.**

Cameo glass, vase, signed "Galle," 11-3/4" h, **$1,200.**

Cameo glass, vase, "Charder Le Verre Francais," 11" h, **$650.**

Cameo glass, atomizer, 7-1/2" h, signed "G. Raymiller," **$500**.

Cameo glass, vase, "D'Argental," lake and village scene, 18" h, **$1,400.**

Opalescent glass, Coin Spot pattern, cranberry ground, **$115**; pitcher with straight neck, applied clear handle, **$350**.

Bohemian glass, cruet, ruby stained, etched stag decoration, original stained bulbous stopper, applied clear handle, **$115**.

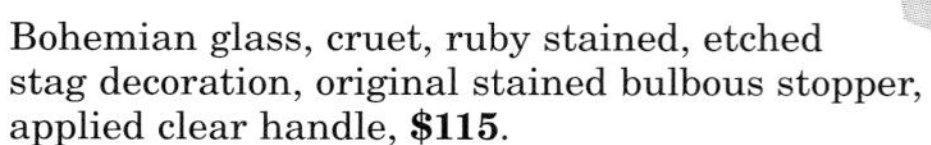

Opalescent glass, cruet, Hobnail pattern, cranberry, applied clear handle, replaced original stopper, **$485.**

Cranberry glass, sugar castor, English, 5-3/4" h, **$145.**

Blown glass, cruet, amethyst, applied handle, green stopper, 9-1/4" h, **$115**.

Quezal, candlestick, white King Tut decoration on blue iridescent ground, fully signed, 7" h, **$1,050**. Photo courtesy of David Rago Auctions.

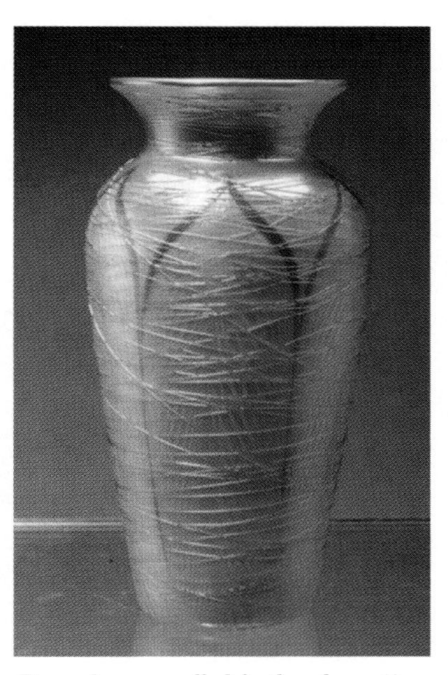

Durand, vase, pulled feather decoration, threading, some loss to threading, unsigned, 8-3/4" h, **$365**. Photo courtesy of David Rago Auctions.

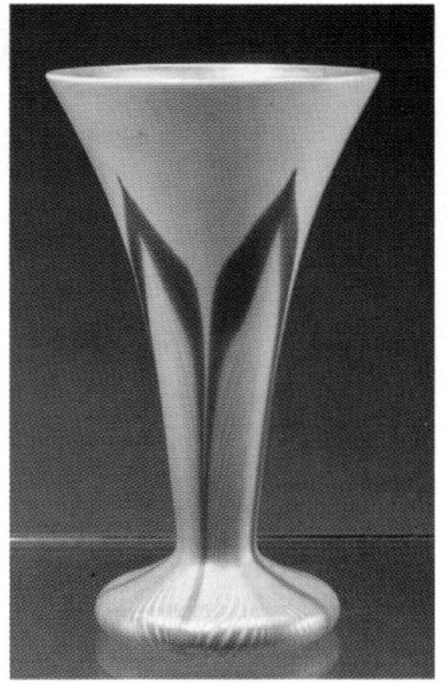

Art glass, possibly Durand or Quezel, vase, green and gold pulled feather, iridescent gold interior, **$250.**

Barber bottle, milk glass, painted clover blossom, 10-1/4" h, **$95.**

Custard glass, creamer, Jackson, worn gold rim, **$90**.

Bohemian, glass decanters, 11-1/4" h, “Castle and Deer” pattern, price for pair, **$650.**

Bride’s basket, cased, white exterior, rose shading to pink interior, gold scrolled decoration on crimped border, silver-plated holder, 11" d bowl, **$450**.

Cambridge glass, plate, “Helio” color, Laurel Wreath-type engraving, 8" d, **$65**.

Cambridge, animal covered dish, turkey, c1906, clear, **$60**.

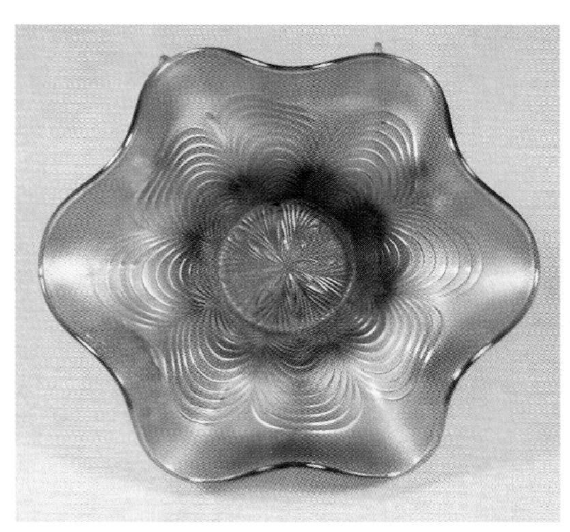

Carnival glass, bowl, Rosalind variant, 6" d, 3" h, **$650**.

Cambridge glass, bushel basket, figural basket weave exterior, two molded handles, slightly flared foot, canary, **$115.**

Carnival glass, vase, Tree Trunk, Northwood, 9-1/2" h, **$300.**

Carnival glass, Orange Tree, loving cup, blue, **$250**. Photo courtesy of Seeck Antique Auction Center.

Carnival glass, Town Pump, Northwood, purple, **$725**. Photo courtesy of Seeck Antique Auction Center.

Burmese glass, jack-in-the-pulpit vase, wide flaring top with deep coloration shading to short body, flared foot, **$750**.

Cut velvet, vase, conical-shaped neck over bulbous body, raised Diamond Quilted pattern, pink body, white interior, **$225**.

Amberina glass, punch cup, Baby Thumbprint pattern, applied ribbed handle, 3-1/2" h, **$165**.

Baccarat glass, paperweight, red strawberries, white flower, green leaves, **$200.**

Cut glass, vase, ruby stained decoration cut to clear, T. B. Clark, 8" h, **$150**.

Spanish—#3404.

Champagne, 5-1/2 oz, crystal
Barcelona, #941, cutting 40.00
Strawberry diamond cutting, 5-7/8" h 50.00
Cocktail, 3-1/2 oz, crystal, Barcelona, #941, cutting 38.00
Goblet
Cobalt blue 155.00
Crystal, Barcelona, #941, cutting 58.00
Strawberry diamond cutting, 7-1/2" h, 10 oz 65.00
Soda tumbler
4-1/4" h, 5 oz, cobalt blue, strawberry diamond cutting . 95.00
6-1/4" h, 12 oz, #457 Springtime etching, restored rim 15.00

Tudor—#411.

Champagne 12.00
Goblet 12.00
Mayonnaise, Hawthorne orchid . 95.00

Twist—Blank #1252. Made in some Alexandrite, crystal, flamingo pink, marigold amber/yellow, Moongleam green, and Sahara yellow.

Baker, Moongleam green. 30.00
Bowl, 9" d, flamingo pink 35.00
Candlesticks, pr, crystal 125.00
Celery tray, 13" l
Flamingo 35.00
Marigold. 45.00
Cheese plate, Kraft, Moongleam green 62.50
Console bowl, 12-1/2" d, Moongleam green, gold bird border 85.00
Creamer and sugar, oval, Sahara yellow 165.00
Cruet, orig stopper, Moongleam green 80.00
Cup and saucer, flamingo 55.00
Floral bowl, 9" d, Moongleam green 70.00
Goblet, 9 oz, flamingo pink 40.00
Ice bucket, Moongleam green. . . 95.00
Juice tumbler
5 oz, 4-3/8" h, ftd, flamingo pink 48.00
6 oz, flamingo pink 30.00
Lemon plate, two handles, Moongleam green 20.00
Nasturtium bowl, Moongleam green 110.00
Pickle tray, 7" l, flamingo pink . . . 20.00
Plate
6" d, flamingo pink. 18.00
7" d, flamingo pink. 22.00
8" d, marigold 15.00

Twist, oil bottle, 2-1/2 oz, #78 stopper, flamingo, original label, **$95.**

Relish, flamingo pink, 13" l 40.00
Salt and pepper shakers, pr, flat, Sahara yellow 85.00

Victorian—#1425. Made in cobalt blue, crystal, Sahara yellow, and some zircon; 1933-53.

Ashtray, monogrammed. 25.00
Champagne/saucer, two-ball stem 17.50
Claret, two-ball stem, 4 oz 20.00
Cologne bottle, orig stopper . . . 50.00
Creamer 25.00
Goblet, 5-1/2" h. 26.00
Juice tumbler, 5 oz. 10.00
Punch bowl set, 15" d bowl, 12 cups 325.00
Sherbet, 3-1/2" 15.00
Soda tumbler, 4" h, 5 oz, straight 20.00
Sugar 27.50
Wine, 2-1/2 oz. 20.00

Waverly—Blank #1519. Made in crystal and some amber. Often found with Orchid or Rose etchings.

Bowl
10" d, crimped, rose etch 95.00
12" d, rose etch, seahorse foot, floral 235.00
Box, cov, 5" l 35.00
Butter dish, cov, rose etching . 175.00
Candle epergnette, two parts . . 25.00
Candlesticks, pr, two-lite, #942 Harvester cutting. 125.00
Candy box, cov, 6" l, bow tie knob 40.00
Champagne 28.00
Compote, 6" d, low foot 20.00
Creamer and sugar
Orchid etch 75.00
Plain. 55.00
Cup and saucer 12.00
Epergne, 5" d, orig blue label . . . 24.00
Honey dish, 6-1/2" d, ftd 15.00
Iced tea tumbler 30.00
Mayonnaise, 5-1/2" d, three ftd, rose etch 55.00
Plate
7" d 8.00
8" d, Narcissus etching 20.00
11 d 20.00
Relish
Two parts, 6-1/2" 25.00
Three parts 35.00
Salt and pepper shakers, pr, plume shape, sterling top 50.00
Sherbet 18.00
Torte plate 55.00
Vegetable bowl, 9" d 35.00

Yeoman—Blank #1184. Made in some cobalt blue, crystal, flamingo pink, Hawthorne orchid, marigold, Moongleam green, and Sahara yellow.

Ashtray, Hawthorne orchid 35.00
Banana split dish, Moongleam green, ftd 35.00
Bonbon, Sahara yellow, 6-1/2" d, handle 45.00
Candle vase, short prisms, inserts, crystal. 95.00
Celery tray, 13" l, Moongleam green 40.00
Coaster, 4-1/2" d
Crystal 4.00
Flamingo pink 7.00
Moongleam green. 15.00
Sahara yellow 12.00
Compote, Moongleam green, 5" w, 3-3/4" h 45.00
Cream soup, Moongleam green . 20.00
Creamer and sugar, Hawthorne orchid 60.00
Cruet, orig stopper
Flamingo pink 80.00
Moongleam green, 4 oz 85.00
Sahara yellow, 2 oz 75.00
Cup and saucer, flamingo pink . . 25.00
Egg cup, Flamingo pink. 25.00
Goblet, Moongleam green. 45.00
Grapefruit, ftd, marigold 48.00
Gravy, underplate, Moongleam green 35.00
Hors d'oeuvre tray, 13" d, center handle, Sahara yellow 65.00
Marmalade jar, cov, Sahara yellow 50.00
Oyster cocktail, crystal. 12.00

Parfait, crystal **15.00**
Plate
6" d
Crystal **4.00**
Flamingo pink. **18.00**
Hawthorne orchid. **20.00**
Marigold. **18.00**
Moongleam green **15.00**
8" d, crystal. **15.00**
10-1/2" d, crystal. **18.00**
Relish, three parts, Moongleam green, handle **60.00**
Salt, open, flamingo pink **10.00**
Sherbet, flamingo pink **12.00**
Soda tumbler, flamingo pink, 4-1/2 oz **10.00**
Sugar shaker, Moongleam green **70.00**
Tray, 11" l, three parts, crystal. . . **20.00**
Tumbler
8 oz, Sahara yellow, ftd. **18.00**
10 oz, flamingo pink, straight sides **20.00**
Whiskey, 2-1/2 oz
Crystal. **5.00**
Flamingo pink **10.00**
Moongleam green. **18.00**
Sahara yellow **15.00**

Hobbs, Bockunier & Co.

History: The Hobbs Glass Company was located in Wheeling, West Virginia, from 1845 until 1891. Its principal production was brilliant cut glass. John L. Hobbs and James B. Barnes founded the firm after leaving the New England Glass Company. Their sons, John H. Hobbs and James F. Barnes, soon joined the business. In 1863, the name was changed to Hobbs, Brockunier & Co. to reflect changes in management by John L. Hobbs, John H. Hobbs, and Charles Brockunier. Brockunier was formerly a superintendent at the New England Glass Company. William Lehighton Sr. was in charge of production.

Lehighton devised a formula for soda lime glass in 1864. His formula was responsible for production of a cheaper, but also clear type, of glassware, which revolutionized the glass industry.

By the 1880s, the firm was producing fine art glass, including amberina, spangled, and several opalescent patterns. It is generally these colored wares that are considered when the name Hobbs, Brockunier is mentioned.

References: Neila and Tom Bredehoff, *Hobbs, Brockunier & Company Glass,* Collector Books, 1997; Kenneth Wilson, *American Glass 1760-1930: The Toledo Museum of Art, Volume I, Volume II,* Hudson Hills Press and The Toledo Museum of Art, 1994.

Barber bottle, Francesware Hobnail pattern, frosted ground, amber stain **125.00**
Basket, Leaf and Flower pattern, ruby stain, scalloped, pressed rope handle **65.00**
Berry bowl, master
Francesware Swirl pattern. . . . **85.00**
Hexagon Block pattern, pointed scalloped rim, 7" d **25.00**
Hobbs' Hobnail, cranberry, white opal edge, ruffled rim, polished pontil, 7-3/4" d, 3" h. **110.00**
Bowl
5-1/4" d, Hobnail pattern, cranberry opalescent, ruffled **75.00**
7" l, Francesware Hobnail pattern, oval **45.00**
8" d, 4" h, satin, soft pink ground, applied yellow edge, thirty crimps **450.00**
10" w, 3-3/4" h six-sided, Daisy and Button, vaseline. **265.00**
Bride's basket, 10-3/4" h, 9" d x 3" h bowl, Daisy and Button, amberina with deep fuchsia, red to bright amber, orig fancy Meriden silver-plated holder, numerous edge flakes and chips **100.00**
Bride's bowl, 13" d, 7" h, white border with hobnails, shading into opalescent canary, crimped ruffles, white edging, unmarked silver plated standard. **125.00**
Butter dish, cov
5-1/2" d, 5-1/2" h, Dewdrop pattern, vaseline opalescent **275.00**
6-1/4" d, 8" h, Daisy & Button pattern, amber, bell cover, orig flat metal clapper attached to cork set in handle, reticulated flange, several flat chips under flange **70.00**
Cake plate, Hand, frosted base. **250.00**
Candy box, cov, Buttons and Bows, vaseline, c1880-90 . . . . **350.00**
Canoe, 9-1/2" l, 4-1/2" h, Daisy & Button, amber, orig silver plated frame marked "Homan Mfg Co." **110.00**
Castor set, Francesware Swirl pattern, salt and pepper shakers, oil and vinegar cruets, orig SP holder . . **650.00**
Celery vase
6-1/4" h, Francesware, Dewdrop pattern, amber dec rim, damage to one hob **50.00**
6-1/2" h, 5" w, cranberry opalescent, opaque white swirls, satin finish, flared ruffled rim, polished pontil **100.00**
Compote, 7" d, Hexagon Block pattern, amber stain, high standard, pointed scalloped rim **65.00**
Creamer
Francesware Hobnail pattern, clear and frosted, applied handle . **45.00**
Hexagon Block pattern, ftd, applied handle **35.00**
Hobbs' Block pattern, clear, applied handle **35.00**
Hobbs' Hobnail pattern, rubena, sq top, polished pontil, 4" h . . **220.00**
Hobbs' Spangled, amber, deep blue plated int., melon ribbed, 3-1/2" h **70.00**
Leaf and Flower pattern, amber stain, applied handle **45.00**
Creamer and sugar, cov, Hobbs' Hobnail, colorless, amber stain, 4" h, 5-1/2" h, open bubble on lid **90.00**
Cruet
6" h, crackle, colorless, bell-shaped base, two-ball stopper, colorless handle **100.00**
7" h, Rubena Verde, tee-pee shape, flashed ruby-red color at trefoil spout and two-thirds way down, intense vaseline lower third, handle, and faceted stopper **550.00**
Custard cup, Hexagon Block pattern, applied handle, ftd **50.00**
Finger bowl, Hobbs' Hobnail pattern, rubena satin **90.00**
Goblet
Hexagon Block pattern, amber stain **50.00**
Hobbs' Block pattern, amber stain **95.00**
Hanging canoe, 8" l, 4" h, Daisy & Button, blue. **70.00**

Tankard pitcher, Coin Spot, canary-vaseline, three strand braided air-twist handle, 8-1/2" h, **$500.** *Photo courtesy of Clarence and Betty Maier.*

Jack-in-the-pulpit vase, 8" h, 4-3/4" d, trumpet shape, fold down in front, back half of top tightly crimped, white opaque body, bead of cranberry glass running down the entire circumference, colorless wafer base **250.00**

Lamp shade, Francesware Swirl pattern, bulbous **90.00**

Lemonade set, Francesware Hobnail pattern, frosted ground, amber stain, pitcher and six lemonade mugs. **425.00**

Match safe, 4-1/4" l, 3" w, 2-1/4" h, Daisy & Button, amber, two compartments, striker on front, small annealing line **30.00**

Miniature lamp, Francesware Swirl pattern **425.00**

Molasses can, 5-3/4" h, Mario, #341, half pint, c1872. . . . . **175.00**

Mustard cov, Francesware Swirl pattern **90.00**

Oil lamp, Snowflake pattern

- Cranberry font, orig pie crimp chimney, #1 burner, patented 1865, replacement Greek Key iron base **1,200.00**
- White font, pearl chimney, 10-1/2" h, flaw in handle **450.00**

Pitcher

- 5" h, 5" w, spangle, light gold ground, diamond quilted body, gold mica flecks, white lining, applied amber shell reeded handle **285.00**
- 7-1/4" h, Hobnail pattern, frosted rubena, applied handle. . . . **350.00**
- 7-3/4" h, sq mouth, shaded pink satin ground, yellow coralene seaweed dec, applied frosted handle **750.00**
- 8" h, 7" w, blue opalescent, colorless applied handle, ground polished pontil **400.00**
- 8-1/2" h, Francesware Hobnail pattern, frosted ground, amber stain. **250.00**

Plate, 7" d, Daisy & Button, vaseline, set of four, rim chips **130.00**

Salt shaker, Stripe, blue opalescent, ring neck **110.00**

Sauce

- Francesware Hobnail pattern, frosted, amber stain, ruffled rim **35.00**
- Francesware Swirl pattern, oval **35.00**
- Hexagon Block pattern, amber stain, pointed scalloped rim **25.00**
- Hobbs' Block pattern, scalloped rim **15.00**

Spooner

- Francesware Hobnail pattern, frosted, amber stain, ruffled rim **55.00**
- Francesware Swirl pattern . . . **65.00**
- Hexagon Block pattern, amber stain, pointed scalloped rim **30.00**
- Hobbs' Block pattern, scalloped rim **35.00**
- Leaf and Flower pattern, scalloped **35.00**

Sugar bowl, cov

- Francesware Hobnail pattern, frosted, amber stain **95.00**
- Francesware Swirl pattern, faceted knop finial. **95.00**
- Hexagon Block pattern, amber stain, ftd **125.00**
- Hobbs' Block pattern, frosted, amber stain **115.00**

Sugar bowl, cov, Leaf and Flower pattern, ruby stain **145.00**

Sugar shaker

- Francesware Swirl, frosted, amber stain, 4-1/2" h **300.00**
- Inverted Thumbprint pattern, frosted, amber top. **120.00**
- Venetian Diamond pattern, cranberry **125.00**

Syrup pitcher

- Cranberry ground, opalescent hobnails, orig pewter top marked "Pat. Mar 20 83" **400.00**
- Hobbs' Hobnail, colorless, amber stain, 6-3/4" h, number of hobs chipped, internal fractor at handle **110.00**
- Hobbs' Optic, light cranberry, front of lid marked "Pat. Apr. 26, 81, Mar 26, 82," 6-1/4" h. **140.00**
- Seaweed, cranberry opalescent, 6" h **1,150.00**

Toothpick holder

- Daisy and Button pattern, amberina **300.00**
- Francesware Hobnail pattern, frosted, amber stain, 2-1/2" h **65.00**

Tumbler

- Francesware Hobnail pattern, frosted, amber stain **45.00**
- Francesware Swirl pattern. . . . **45.00**
- Hexagon Block pattern, amber stain **35.00**
- Hobbs' Block pattern. **20.00**
- Hobbs' Hobnail, 3-7/8" h, rubena **60.00**
- Hobbs' Polka Dot, rubena, engraved fern and berry dec, 3-3/4" h, minor flake. **30.00**

Vase, 6-1/4" h, 4-1/2" d, Polka Dot pattern, cranberry hobnail opalescent, polished pontil **145.00**

Waste bowl, Francesware Hobnail pattern, frosted ground, amber stain, 4" d **55.00**

Water pitcher, cranberry, melon ribbed, ivy mold, ruffled edge **185.00**

Water set, Francesware Hobnail pattern, frosted, amber stain, 8-1/2" h pitcher, six 4" h tumblers, bruise on pitcher, rim flakes on tumblers . . **150.00**

Water tray, Francesware Hobnail pattern, frosted, amber stain, leaf shape, 12" l. **145.00**

Witch ball, 6-1/2" d, Hobnail pattern, vaseline **300.00**

Imperial Glass

History: Imperial Glass Co., Bellaire, Ohio, was organized in 1901. Its primary product was pattern (pressed) glass. Soon other lines were added, including carnival glass, Nuart, Nucut, and Near Cut. In 1916, the company introduced Free-Hand, a lustered art glass line, and Imperial Jewels, an iridescent stretch glass that carried the Imperial cross trademark. In the 1930s, the company was reorganized into the Imperial Glass Corporation, and the firm is still producing a great variety of wares.

Probably the most well-known Imperial glass pattern is Candlewick. Because of the high collectibility of this pattern, it is listed in a separate category. It is one of those patterns known by pattern name first, and the manufacturer second. Imperial produced many other patterns, including Cape Cod and Crystolite, but these never achieved the success of the Candlewick line.

Imperial recently acquired the molds and equipment of several other glass companies—Central, Cambridge, and Heisey. Many of the retired molds of these companies are once again in use.

Marks: The Imperial reissues are marked to distinguish them from the originals.

References: Margaret and Douglas Archer, *Imperial Glass*, Collector Books, 1978, 1998 value update; Sean and Johanna S. Billings, *Peachblow Glass, Collector's Identification & Price Guide*, Krause Publications, 2000; Tom and Neila Bredehoft, *Fifty Years of Collectible Glass, 1920-1970, Volume 1, Volume II*, Antique Trader Books, 2000; Carl O. Burns, *Imperial Carnival Glass*, Collector Books, 1999; Gene Florence, *Elegant Glassware of the Depression Era*, 9th ed., Collector Books, 2000; Myrna and Bob Garrison, *Imperial's Boudoir, Etcetera*, 1996; National Imperial Glass Collectors Society, *Imperial Glass Encyclopedia: Volume I, A-Cane*, Antique Publications, 1995; —, *Vol. II: Cape Cod- L*, Antique Publications, 1998; —, *Imperial Glass 1966 Catalog*, reprint, 1991 price guide, Antique Publications; Virginia R. Scott, *Collector's Guide to Imperial Candlewick*, published by author (275 Milledge Terrace, Athens, GA 30606); Mary M. Wetzel-Tomlka, *Candlewick: The Jewel of Imperial Books I and II*, published by author (P.O. Box 594, Notre Dame, IN 46556-0594); —, *Candlewick The Jewel of Imperial, Personal Inventory & Record Book*, published by author, 1998; —, *Candlewick The Jewel of Imperial, Price Guide 99 and More*, published by author, 1998.

Collectors' Clubs: National Candlewick Collector's Club, 17609 Falling Water Road, Strongsville, OH 44136, plus many regional clubs; National Imperial Glass Collectors Society, P.O. Box 534, Bellaire, OH 43906, http://www.imperialglass.org.

Art glass

Bowl, 11" d, low, inward rim, opal white glass flashed overall with brilliant orange stretched irid, c1920, minor wear to irid **200.00**

Pitcher, 80 oz, ice lip, Spun, teal . **85.00**

Tumbler, 14 oz, straight sided, Spun, teal **20.00**

Vanity jar, 7-5/8" h, Spun, pink, reeded **95.00**

Vase

- 4-3/4" h, 8" d, opaque white body, irid golden-orange ext., impressionistic blue dec of eight heart-shaped blossoms, blue vines, blue rim, brilliant irid golden-orange int., gold paper label. . . . **1,000.00**
- 6-1/2" h, Mosaic, deep cobalt blue body, shaded and swirled with opal, irid orange lining **550.00**
- 6-3/4" h, baluster, flared neck, gold ground, blue pulled loop dec, white int. neck flashed irid orange-gold, polished pontil. . . . **950.00**
- 8-1/8" h, flared mouth over slender waisted body, flared base of cobalt blue and opal swirled glass, golden orange luster int., polished pontil, c1924 . . . . **425.00**
- 8-1/2" h, 4-1/2" w, deep blue Heart and Vine dec, applied cobalt blue glass rim, apricot colored throat **1,495.00**
- 9-1/2" h, bulbous, wide flared neck, white glass cased to cobalt blue ext., int. rim flashed with irid orange, polished pontil **575.00**
- 10-1/2" h, heavy walled body swelling to top, cream colored glass, strong gold irid dec, on ext., three branches of holly leaves rising from base, polished pontil **575.00**

Carnival glass

Basket, 10", Plain Jane, teal **85.00**

Bell

- Hobnails, marigold **25.00**
- Santa, white **45.00**
- Star Medallion, ice green. . . . **27.50**
- Suzanne, cobalt blue. . . . **55.00**

Bottle, 5" h, Corn, smoke. . . . **300.00**

Bowl, Fashion, red **40.00**

Candlesticks, pr

- Hex shape, irid smoke. . . . **75.00**
- Premium pattern, irid smoke . **100.00**
- Rose, ice blue and amber **20.00**

Compote

- Acanthus, red **35.00**
- Hobstar Flower, ruffled, purple **65.00**
- Zodiac, smoke, cov **35.00**

Candy dish, imitation cut glass pattern, embossed mark, c1970, 6" l, **$12.**

Creamer and sugar, Acanthus, red **35.00**

Dish, Pansy, oblong, marigold . . **27.50**

Dresser tray, Pansy, amber **95.00**

Lily bowl, Beaded Block, irid, 5" d **65.00**

Milk pitcher

- Amelia, 5-3/4" h, marigold . . . **45.00**
- Poinsettia, smoke **375.00**
- Windmill, green. . . . **75.00**

Mug

- Robin, marigold **45.00**
- #474, smoke. . . . **15.00**

Nappy, 5" d, handle, Heavy Grape, electric purple **110.00**

Perfume, pink. . . . **40.00**

Pickle dish, Grape, amber. . . . **25.00**

Plate

- Embossed Scroll, flat, 9" d, purple **500.00**
- Nu-Homestead
  - Ribbed back, marigold . . **700.00**
  - Vaseline **75.00**
- Mums, amethyst. . . . **75.00**

Relish, two parts, Arrow, red . . . **45.00**

Rose bowl, purple, iron cross mark **500.00**

Salad set, Optic & Button, light marigold, iron cross mark, two pcs **50.00**

Sauce bow, Embossed Scroll, ruffled, File ext., 6" d, purple **75.00**

Sugar bowl, Flute, electric purple **75.00**

Sugar shaker, ice blue. . . . **35.00**

Tumbler, Grape, smoke **60.00**

Vase

- Daisy, ice blue **25.00**
- Floral with Button, 7" h, 3" d, red **45.00**

Loganberry, 10" h, green 300.00
Morning Glory
Olive green, 6-1/2" h 60.00
Smoke, 6-1/2" h, 4" d flare at top 50.00
Ripple, swung
Amber, 10-3/4" h 100.00
Purple, 12" h 135.00
Swirl, ice pink, tall 35.00
Swirled Interior, fan shape, two handles, smoke and multicolor irid 80.00
Thin Rib & Drape, marigold, 5" h 40.00
Three Swans, 9" h, necks curve to form handle, irid blue, emb "IG" 75.00
Water carafe, Grape, ice green. . 35.00
Water pitcher, Grape
Marigold. 65.00
Smoke 200.00
Water set
Diamond Lace, five pcs, purple 525.00
Grape, amber, seven pcs . . . 150.00
Robin, cobalt blue, seven pcs 175.00

Humidor, Checkerboard pattern, faceted knob finial, **$90.**

Engraved or hand cut

Bowl
6-1/2" d, flower and leaf, molded star base 25.00
7-1/2" d, Amelia 9.00
9-1/2" d, three sprays with flowers, molded star base 45.00
Candlesticks, pr, 7" h, Amelia . . . 35.00
Celery vase, three side stars, cut star base 25.00
Nut dish, Design No. 112, 5-1/2" d 30.00
Pitcher, 6" h, daisies, molded star base 65.00
Plate, 5-1/2" d, Design No. 12. . . 15.00
Sherbet, Design No. 300, engraved stars, ftd. 15.00
Syrup, Design No. 112, SP top. . 45.00
Table set, cov butter, reamer, cov sugar, and spooner, Design No. 4, cut star pattern 215.00
Tankard, Design No. 110, flowers, foliage, and butterfly cutting 60.00
Tumbler, buzz star dec. 20.00

Jewels

Bowl
6-1/2" d, purple Pearl Green luster, marked 75.00
8-1/2" d, 3-1/2" h, round base ending in cornered top, blue and purple jewel finish, stretch type irid, sgd 300.00
Candlesticks, pr
7-3/4" h, dark purple stretch form 500.00
9" h, 3-3/4" d, bright orange, small pulled pontil on one 500.00
Compote, 7-1/2" d, irid teal blue. 65.00
Creamer, Jewel Ware, amethyst, pearl, and green luster 80.00
Plate
8" d, irid pale green 50.00
9" d, white luster 70.00
Rose bowl, amethyst, green irid. 75.00
Vase
5-1/2" h, bulbed gold irid, lightly stretched luster, base molded cross trade mark 325.00
5-1/2" h, 6-1/2" w, round body ending in square dimpled top, dark blue, silver blue irid, sgd "Imperial" on base 250.00
6" h, 4-1/2" d, classic baluster, brilliant blue glossy ext., orange irid lining. 550.00
7-3/4" h, classic baluster, white body, mirror bright tray-blue surface, deep orange irid interior rim 320.00
8" h, Jewel Ware, flared rim, irid silver, mulberry ground . . . 180.00
11" h, bulbous, orange ext. and int., white top rim, some nicks. . 195.00

Lustered (free hand)

Bud vase, 7" h, 3-1/4" d, bulbous base, tall cylindrical neck, orange and heart vine dec, irid purple ground . . . 600.00
Candlesticks, pr
9-1/4" h, Free Hand Ware, orange mirror luster 275.00
10" h, slender baluster, cushion foot, clear, white heart and vine dec, tall cylindrical irid dark blue socket, orig paper label 440.00
10-3/4" h, cobalt blue luster, white vine and leaf dec 325.00
10-3/4" h, 4-1/8" d, crystal, selenium red knobs, threaded dec around stem, polished pontil. . . . 1,550.00
Hat, 9" w, ruffled rim, cobalt blue, embedded irid white vines and leaves 120.00
Ivy ball, 4" h, Spun, red, crystal foot 90.00
Lamp shade, 5" l, Art Nouveau, irid ivory, gold, and green feather pattern, colored threading, sgd. 190.00
Pitcher, 10" h, pale yellow luster, white pulled loops, applied clear handle 240.00
Rose bowl, 6" d, Free Hand Ware, irid orange, white floral cutting. 85.00
Vase
4-7/8" h, Free Hand Ware, raised and flared rim, wide shouldered vessel, pale amber glass, strong gold irid ext., polished pontil, spurious signature 460.00
5-3/4" h, Free Hand Ware, ovoid form, dark blue ground, orange leaves on vines, overall irid surface, white rim wrap to flared neck, gold foil label, polished pontil 1,265.00
6" h, Free Hand Ware, bulbous yellow, orange int. rim 200.00
6" h, Free Hand Ware, classic form, cobalt blue, orange int. 350.00
6-1/4" h, 4-1/2" d, classic shape, bulbous base, flaring neck, glossy yellow ext., orange lining . . 400.00
6-1/2" h, flared orange lined rim, opal oval body, chartreuse green heart and vine dec 750.00
6-1/2" h, 6" d, bulbous, flaring top, blue pulled loop over bright orange exterior, orange and white lining 650.00
6-5/8" h, 4-1/8" d, Free Hand Ware, ovoid tapering body, short neck, flattened flaring rim, oyster white irid body, green hearts and vines dec, deep bronze int. 350.00
7" h, irid metallic finish, green, purple, and blue, white veining 350.00
7" h, opal white irid body, bright blue heart and vine dec, applied cobalt blue wrap, subtle orange lustered int. 800.00
7-1/4" h, brilliant orange irid flared oval body cased to white, lustered green pulled dec, unsigned polished white pontil 345.00

7-1/4" h, Free Hand Ware, lustrous marigold ground, wide brackish net design, opal rim trim, short surface scratches 500.00

7-1/2" h, 4-1/4" d, bulbous, slender neck, flaring top, blue glossy finish, orange interior 450.00

8" h, Free Hand Ware, orange ext. and int., polished white pontil, unsigned 575.00

8-1/2" h, cylindrical, irid green heart and vine design, white ground, marigold lining, some wear 385.00

8-1/2" h, irid green, blue, and purple concentric lines over red ground, polished pontil 330.00

8-1/2" h, 2-1/2"w, slender, white drag loops over yellow, bright orange interior 400.00

8-1/2" h, 3" d, yellow ground, white drag loop dec, orange irid interior, small black spot on interior rim from firing 400.00

8-3/4" h, 2-1/2" w, white opal ground, orange interior casing, green hanging hearts and vines, minor wear to interior lining 350.00

8-3/4" h, 3" d, cylindrical, flaring and rim, brilliant orange, applied blue threading, minute wear to threading in two spots 400.00

9-7/8" h, elongated flared neck, squatty opal glass body, ext. cased to yellow, white dragged loop dec, int. neck flashed irid orange, polished pontil, c1924 . . . . 375.00

10" h, red irid ext., int. with irid alligatored caramel surface over white irid 450.00

10" h, tall slender form, irid orange ext., deep orange throat. . . 195.00

10" h, 5-1/2" d, bulbous, flaring neck and top rim, blue pulled drag loops over orange, brilliant orange interior 900.00

11" h, tricorn rim, extended tooled handles on oval body, brilliant golden bronze, heart and vine dec, orig label on base. 2,300.00

11" h, Free Hand Ware, cobalt blue, opal leaves, entwined vines, rainbow luster, applied opal rim trim 650.00

11-1/4" h, Free Hand Ware, tall slender ovoid body, tapering slightly to flared rim, glossy cobalt blue ext., white hearts and random vine dec, orig irid int. 600.00

11-1/4" h, irid purple, amber, and white pulled ext., purple int. 300.00

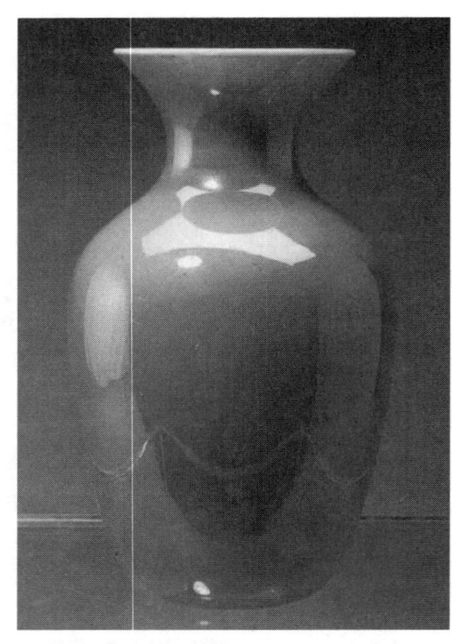

Vase, Free Hand Ware, orange exterior and interior, polished white pontil, 8" h, **$575.** *Photo courtesy of David Rago Auctions.*

11-1/4" h, 4-1/2" w, dark blue matte finish, pale blue drag loops, blue and purple irid interior. 800.00

11-1/4" h, 5" w, oyster white exterior, deep orange neck, hanging heart and vine dec 850.00

11-1/2" h, Free Hand Ware, orange ground, deep blue Drag Loops over white, iridescent surface 875.00

Nuart

Ashtray 22.00

Ashtray, marked "Nuart" 20.00

Lamp shade

Crystal, cluster electric type, frosted int., flower etching, marked "Nuart" 35.00

Marigold. 50.00

Pearl ruby, fan and star etching, marked "Nuart" 45.00

Vase6" h, green, polished pontil, tucked in top 275.00

7" h, bulbous, irid green 125.00

Nucut

Berry bowl

4-1/2" d, handles 15.00

7-1/2" d, marked "Nucut". 22.00

Bowl, 8-1/2" d, Rose Marie, pink, ftd, marked "Nucut" 45.00

Celery tray, 11" l, marked "Nucut" 18.00

Creamer, marked "Nucut" 20.00

Fern dish, 8" l, brass lining, ftd. . 30.00

Nappy, 6" w, heart shape, marked "Nucut" 22.00

Orange bowl, 12" d, Rose Marie 48.00

Punch bowl set, 13" d punch bowl, six cups, Rose Marie, marked "Nucut" 185.00

Salad bowl, 10-3/4" d, marked "Nucut" 35.00

Sauce, 4-1/2" d, handles, marked "Nucut" 18.00

Tumbler, flared rim, molded star, marked "Nucut". 15.00

Pressed

Animal

Cygnet, light blue 35.00

Owl, milk glass 50.00

Ashtray, caramel slag, 6-1/2" sq 25.00

Bar bottle, Cape Cod, crystal . 150.00

Basket

Cape Cod, #160/73/0, crystal 350.00

Slag, caramel basket, milk glass handle, 5-1/2". 50.00

Berry bowl

Katy, blue opalescent, flat rim 30.00

Pansy, red slag. 45.00

Birthday cake plate

Cape Cod, crystal 295.00

Tradition, crystal 125.00

Bowl

Beaded Block

Blue opalescent, 6-1/2" d . 75.00

Green, 7-1/2" d 45.00

Cane, crystal, 7-1/2" d 20.00

Cape Cod, crystal

5", heart shape. 25.00

5-1/2" d 12.00

9" d, ftd 95.00

11" l, oval 90.00

Katy, blue opalescent, 8" d, low 65.00

Mt. Vernon, crystal, 6-1/2" d . . 10.00

Pillar Flutes, blue, 6" d 24.00

Roses pattern, milk glass, 9" d 25.00

Windmill, amethyst, fluted, 8" d, 3" h 45.00

Bowl, cov, purple slag, #680 . . . 65.00

Bud vase, Candlewick, crystal, fan, floral cutting, 8-1/2" h 90.00

Butter dish, cov

Candlewick, crystal, quarter pound 32.00

Cape Cod, 4" d. 30.00

Canapé plate, Fish

Red 20.00

Teal 15.00

Candlesticks, pr
Candlewick, #207, crystal, three toes . . . 260.00
Crocheted Crystal, crystal, two-lite . . . 45.00
Dolphin, reproductions of Boston and Sandwich candlesticks, made for Metropolitan Museum of Art, blue and white . . . 250.00
Katy, blue . . . 75.00
Katy, green opalescent, two-lite . . . 98.00
Pillar Flutes, blue, two-lite . . . 55.00
Candy dish, cov, Candlewick, crystal, three parts . . . 180.00
Candy jar, cov
Cape Cod
Crystal, 1 lb . . . 100.00
Milk glass, 1 lb . . . 145.00
Grapes, ruby . . . 45.00
Celery, Pillar Flutes, blue . . . 25.00
Center bowl, Cape Cod, #160/751, crystal, ruffled edge . . . 65.00
Cereal bowl, Katy, blue opalescent, deep . . . 65.00
Champagne, Cape Cod
Azalea . . . 24.00
Verde green . . . 13.50
Cheese and cracker, Candlewick, crystal . . . 65.00
Cheese stand, Molly, blue opalescent . . . 75.00
Cigarette holder, Candlewick, eagle, crystal . . . 95.00
Claret, Cape Cod, Verde green . . 15.00
Coaster, Cape Cod, No. 160/76, crystal . . . 10.00
Cocktail
Cape Cod, crystal . . . 12.00
Shaeffer, Stiegel Green, 4-3/8" h, set of four . . . 100.00
Cocktail shaker, Shaeffer, Stiegel Green, chrome lid . . . 185.00
Cologne bottle, Hobnail, blue milk glass, ruffled stopper, pr . . . 75.00
Compote, cov, Cape Cod, crystal, ftd . . . 85.00
Compote, open
Antique Buttons, amber, 4-3/4" d . . . 18.50
Crocheted Crystal, crystal
7-1/4" d, leaf cut design . . . 24.00
8-1/2" d . . . 24.00
Hobnail, 5", crimped, green . . . 15.00
Katy, 4-3/4" d, white . . . 45.00
Pillar Flutes, light blue . . . 25.00
Cordial, Cape Code, 1-1/2 oz . . . 12.00
Creamer and sugar
Beaded Block, deep blue . . . 95.00
Cape Cod, crystal . . . 25.00
Diamond Quilted, green . . . 25.00
Grape, white milk glass . . . 24.00
Molly
Blue opalescent . . . 95.00
Ruby . . . 25.00
Pillar Flutes, light blue . . . 50.00
Cruet, orig stopper, Cape Cod, #160/119, amber . . . 28.00
Cup and saucer
Katy, crystal . . . 15.00
Molly
Blue opalescent . . . 40.00
Pink . . . 8.50
Pillar Flutes, light blue . . . 28.00
Decanter, orig stopper, Cape Cod, #160/163, crystal . . . 75.00
Fruit bowl, Cape Code, crystal, 4-1/2" d . . . 15.00
Goblet
Cape Cod, #1602
Antique blue . . . 30.00
Crystal . . . 6.50
Verde green . . . 20.00
Red . . . 135.00
Monticello, crystal . . . 15.00
Tradition, crystal . . . 15.00
Gravy boat, liner, Candlewick, crystal . . . 190.00
Ivy ball, Hobnail, 6-1/2" h, ftd
Blue opalescent . . . 35.00
Green opalescent . . . 45.00
Juice tumbler
Cape Cod
flat, 6 oz . . . 6.50
ftd, amber . . . 22.50
Provincial, purple, 3-5/8" h . . . 9.00
Lily bowl, Diamond Block, green, 5" d . . . 20.00
Macaroon jar, cov, Grapes, ruby, woven handle . . . 85.00
Mayonnaise, Laced Edge, blue opalescent . . . 75.00
Mayonnaise ladle, Katy, white . . 45.00
Mint dish
Cape Cod, 6" d, handle . . . 35.00
Heart, red glossy slag . . . 18.50
Mug
Cape Cod, crystal . . . 58.00
Chesterfield, vaseline . . . 35.00
Oil bottle, Candlewick, crystal . . 55.00
Oyster cocktail, Cape Cod, #1602, crystal . . . 7.00
Parfait, Cape Cod, crystal . . . 12.00
Perfume bottle, milk glass, melon-shaped base, crystal stopper . . . 45.00
Pickle, Cape Cod, 9-1/2" l, oval . 35.00
Pitcher
Cape Cod
#160/19, ice lip, crystal . . . 85.00
#160/24, two quarts, ftd . . . 85.00
Tradition, crystal, ice lip . . . 50.00
Windmill, red slag . . . 60.00
Plate
Cape Cod, crystal
7-1/4" d . . . 8.00
8" d . . . 10.00
11-1/2" d, handle . . . 35.00
14" d . . . 65.00
Cape Cod, Verde green, 8" d . 15.00
Coin, crystal, 9" d, 1964 coins . 25.00
Diamond Quilted, black, 8" d . 15.00
Katy, blue opalescent
8" d . . . 65.00
9-1/2" d . . . 65.00
Plate
Molly
Amber, 7-3/4" d . . . 3.50
Black, 8" d . . . 7.00
Blue opalescent, 8" d . . . 25.00
Pillar Flutes, light blue, 8" d . . . 16.50
Tradition
Crystal, 8" d . . . 6.00
Light blue, 8-1/4" d . . . 15.00
Twisted Optic, amber
6" d . . . 2.50
8" d . . . 5.00
Windmill, glossy, green slag, IG mark . . . 48.00
Punch bowl set, bowl and 10 cups, Monticello, crystal . . . 95.00
Relish
Candlewick, crystal, floral cutting . . . 60.00
Cape Cod, crystal, 9-1/2" l, oval . . . 22.00
Tradition, white milk glass, three parts, 12" l, handle . . . 35.00
Rose bowl, Molly, black, silver deposit floral dec, 5" h . . . 45.00
Salad fork and spoon, Candlewick, crystal . . . 45.00
Salt and pepper shakers, pr, Cape Cod
Crystal, worn tops . . . 12.00
Fern green . . . 75.00
Verde green, orig tops . . . 40.00
Ultra blue . . . 95.00
Saucer, Molly, black . . . 3.00
Sherbet
Cape Cod, #1602, crystal, ftd . . 6.50
Hoffman House, ruby, 4-1/8" h . 12.50
Molly, blue opalescent . . . 30.00
Mt. Vernon, ruby . . . 30.00
Provincial, purple . . . 15.00
Tradition, crystal . . . 6.00
Twisted Optic
Amber . . . 5.00
Green . . . 6.00
Victorian, yellow . . . 12.00

Soup bowl, Katy, blue opalescent **85.00**
Sugar bowl, Diamond Quilted, black **10.00**
Sundae, Cape Cod, 6 oz **4.50**
Tea cup, Candlewick, crystal **8.00**
Tea saucer, Cape Cod, crystal . . . **3.00**
Toothpick, Ivory, orig label **24.00**
Tray
- Cabochon, yellow, 3-part, 15" x 12" **45.00**
- Molly
  - Blue opalescent, 10-1/2" l, handles **40.00**
  - Pink, 10-3/4" l, handles. . . . **45.00**

Tumbler
- Candlewick, crystal, 12 oz . . . **16.00**
- Georgian, red **18.00**
- Katy, blue opalescent, 10 oz . **62.50**
- Molly, blue opalescent, ftd . . . **50.00**
- Shaeffer, Stiegel Green, 2-1/2" h **65.00**

Vase
- Beaded Block, deep blue opal **95.00**
- Candlewick, #400/143C, silver overlay, 8" h **195.00**
- Cape Cod, flip, crystal **85.00**
- Katy
  - Blue opalescent, 5-1/2" h. . **60.00**
  - Cobalt blue. **65.00**
  - Green opalescent, 5-1/2" h **65.00**
- Loganberry, white milk glass, crimped, 10" h **65.00**
- Pillar Flutes, blue, 6" h. **45.00**

Whiskey set, Cape Cod, No. 160/280, crystal, raised letters Bourbon, Rye, and Scotch, metal rack **650.00**
Wine, Cape Cod
- Azalea, 5-1/2" h. **30.00**
- Crystal, 5 oz **9.50**

INKWELLS

History: Most of the commonly found inkwells were produced in the United States or Europe between the early 1800s and the 1930s. The most popular materials were glass and pottery because these substances resisted the corrosive effects of ink.

Inkwells were a sign of the office or wealth of an individual. The common man tended to dip his ink directly from the bottle. The years between 1870 and 1920 represent the golden age of inkwells when elaborate designs were produced. Glass inkwells are well represented in this interesting collecting area.

Inkwells are frequently sold by their Covill number (C#), referring to the excellent reference book by William E. Covill Jr.

References: Veldon Badders, *Collector's Guide to Inkwells: Identification and Values*, Book I (1995, 1998 value update), Book II, 1998, Collector Books; William E. Covill, Jr., *Inkbottles and Inkwells*, William S. Sullwold Publishing, out of print; Jean and Franklin Hunting, *The Collector's World of Inkwells*, Schiffer Publishing, 2000.

Collectors' Clubs: St. Louis Inkwell Collectors Society, P.O. Box 29396, St. Louis, MO 63126; The Society of Inkwell Collectors, 10 Meadow Drive, Spencerport, NY 14559, http://www.soic.com.

Amber, 4-1/2" h, 2-1/2" sq, fine stippling on base, deep plain dimple on each side, polished brass hinged mountings **240.00**
Amethyst, 2-1/4" h, 2-1/4" sq, sq, flat cut faceted shoulder and corners, nickel plated collar and hinged lid **160.00**
Austrian
- 2-3/8" h, 5-1/4" d, green irid, flattened circular form, emb feather design, hinged bronze cov marked "D.G.M.A.K.K. OEST PAT.A.," colorless glass liner. **475.00**
- 2-1/2" h, 4" d, irid emerald green, well defined ridges, urchin form, brass color hinged top stamped "DRGM," attributed to Rindskopf, clear glass insert, slight damage to insert edge **200.00**
- 3-1/2" h, art glass green irid ground, irid threading, bronze floral base, hinged cap, marked "DRGM." **360.00**

Blown three mold
- 1-5/8" h, Keene Marlboro Street Glassworks, Keene, NH, 1820-40, cylindrical, deep olive amber, tooled disc mouth, pontil scar, McKearin GIII-28. . . . . **180.00**
- 1-5/8" h, Mount Vernon Glass Works, Vernon, NY, 1820-40, dense olive amber, tooled disc mouth, pontil scar, McKearin GII-15 . . . . . **150.00**
- 1-3/4" h, Boston and Sandwich Glass Works, Sandwich, MA, 1860-90, cylindrical, vertical flues, fiery opalescent milk glass, crudely sheared mouth, smooth base, small areas of roughness and flaking, C #1173 . . . . **200.00**

Colorless
- 3-1/4" d, 3-3/4" h, pressed panels, flake on base. **70.00**
- 5-1/2" l, 4" w, 3-1/2" h, sq, gilded metal frame with cherub, pen holder in front **130.00**

Figural
- 1-7/8" h, snail, America, 1830-70, colorless glass, ground mouth, smooth base, flat chip on int. **140.00**
- 2-3/4" h, Benjamin Franklin head shape, France, 1830-60, colorless glass with pale gray cast, sheared mouth, smooth base, C#1289 . . . . **230.00**

Free blown glass, 1-3/4" h, attributed to America, 1840-60, sq, opaque electric blue, flared mouth, pontil scar **120.00**
Paperweight
- 3-3/4" h, turquoise and electric blue, pyramid form inkwell, obelisk form paperweight with flat front, building molded into back, chip on inkwell **30.00**
- 4-3/4" h, upright red rose, three striped green aventurine leaves in round stopper, initial cane underneath rose, colorless glass bottle base, Kaziun **350.00**
- 6-1/4" h, 4-1/2" d, multicolored concentric millefiori, base with 1848 date canes, Whitefriars **175.00**

Pattern molded glass, 2" h, America, 1840-60, cylindrical, vertical ribs, cobalt blue, sheared rim, pontil scar, C #1066 . . . . **140.00**
Pitkin type, 1-7/8" h, New England, 1780-1830, 36 ribs swirled to left, cylindrical, deep yellow-olive, tooled mouth, pontil scar, C #1160 . . . **400.00**
Teakettle, attributed to America, 1830-60, cut and polished octagonal form
- 1-5/8" h, orange amber, ground mouth, applied brass collar, smooth base, brass cap missing, C #1268 . . . . **325.00**
- 2" h, opalescent electric blue, ground mouth, smooth base, C #1255 . . . . **400.00**

Blown three mold, Mount Vernon Glass Works, Vernon, NY, 1820-40, dense olive amber, tooled disc mouth, pontil scar, 1-5/8" h, McKearin GII-15, **$150.** *Photo courtesy of Norman C. Heckler and Co.*

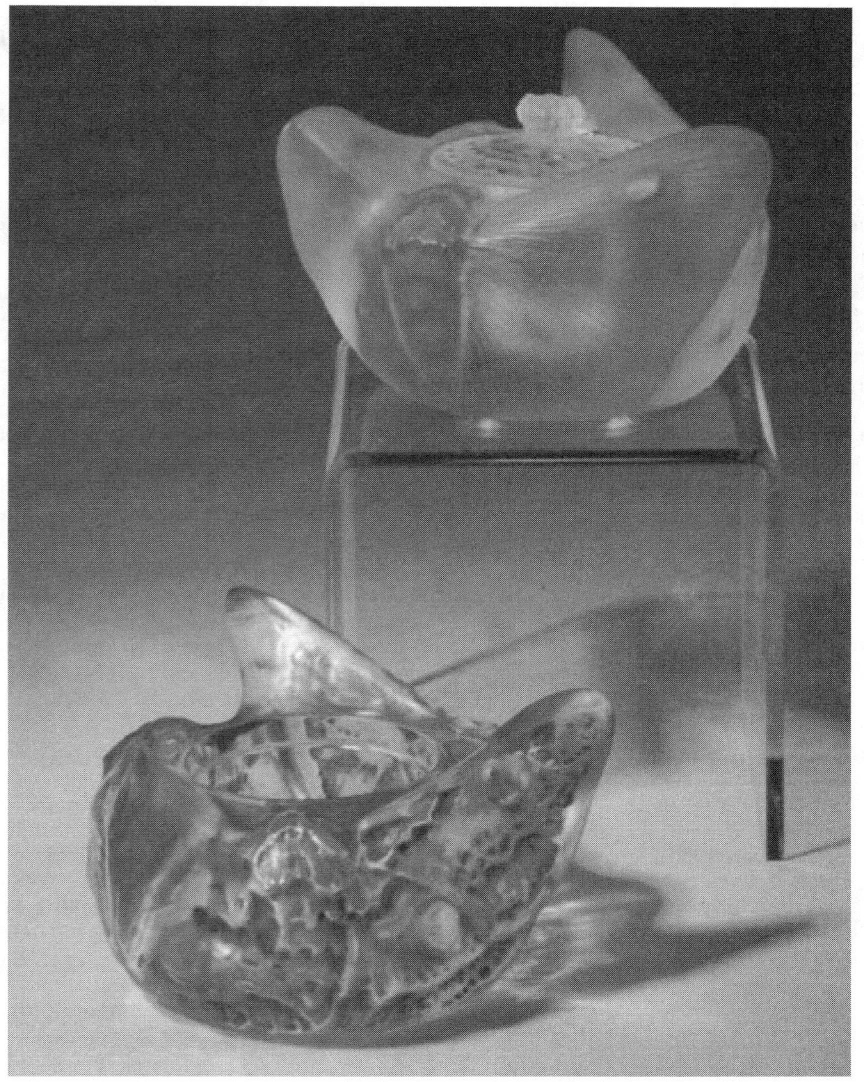

Lalique, Trois Papillons, foreground: clear and frosted earlier version with sepia patina (missing cover), rear: clear and frosted, raised wing version, engraved mark "R. Lalique France," also molded "R. Lalique," each 3-1/2" d, sold as pair, **$1,380.** *Photo courtesy of David Rago Auctions.*

2-1/8" h, canary, ground moth, smooth base, missing closure, C #1268. . . . . **250.00**

2-5/8" h, brick red and burgundy slag glass, ground mouth with brass cap, smooth base, two small chips, C#1261 . . . . **110.00**

3-1/4" h, additional applied ink reservoir on top, opaque blue, gilt highlighted dec, ground mouth, smooth base, no collar and cap, wear to gilt. **350.00**

Teakettle, attributed to America, 1830-60, 2" h, five loped body form, raised floral and leaf dec, fiery opalescent milk glass ground, orange painted and gilt dec highlights, ground mouth with brass collar and cap, smooth base, similar to C#1223 . . . . **275.00**

Tiffany

4-1/2" h, double bulbed transparent green-amber Favrile glass, dark red pulled feather motif dec, base inscribed "X 1353," hinged silver rim and cap both imp "Tiffany & Co. Maker Sterling S3099" **2,990.00**

5-1/2" h, raised neck with median band of depressions, swirled blue and silver irid overall, glass liner, polished pontil, hinged bronze cap with raised scrolled dec, brown patina, circular paper label, minor wear **8,650.00**

Jack-in-the-Pulpit Vases

History: Trumpet-shaped jack-in-the-pulpit glass vases were in vogue during the late 19th and early 20th centuries. The vases were made in a wide variety of patterns, colors, and sizes by many manufacturers.

The form imitates the wildflower known as jack-in-the-pulpit. These vases are generally found with a bulbous base, slender stem, and a flaring throat that develops into a lovely diamond-shaped back. Art glass examples provide collectors with lovely shaded and colorful additions to their glassware collections.

3-1/2" h, 6-1/2" w, red carnival glass, Leaf and Berry pattern **300.00**

4" h, squatty, blossom form, white satin ground, emerald green lining, seven applied and frosted feet **75.00**

4-1/4" h, satin glass, peachblow colored ground, applied camphor glass ruffled pedestal foot **400.00**

4-1/2" h, opaque jade green, ruffled emb ribbed base, enameled small white flowers, gold trim **95.00**

5" h, opaline, ruffled purple top .. **90.00**

5-1/2" h, 3-1/2" w, spangled blue, yellow, and brown, white ground, silver flecks all over, applied crystal edge, swirled, Mt. Washington **250.00**

5-3/4" h, spangle, white ground, pink lining, mica flecks, ruffled rim, clear edging **125.00**

5-3/4" h, 6-1/4" d, Leaf Chalice pattern, opalescent blue............. **85.00**

6" h, cranberry, tulip form, orig Pilgrim Glass label.................. **35.00**

6" h, bright gold Aurene, strong irid, Steuben, sgd "Aurene 2699".. **1,450.00**

6" h, vaseline, clear bulging opalescent body, cranberry flared rim, ftd.. **165.00**

6" h, 5" w, frosted pink and white stripes, large bulbous base, broad flange, Webb.................... **375.00**

6-1/2" h, Loetz type, gold luster, pinched body **200.00**

6-1/2" h, opalescent white, squatty open form top **75.00**

6-1/2" h, 3" w top, Burmese, matte finish, ruffled top, Mt. Washington, c1880.................... **425.00**

6-3/4" h, Burmese, crimped edge, delicate coloration........... **230.00**

6-3/4" h, Silver Crest, #711, Fenton **45.00**

6-3/4" h, Stevens and Williams, rainbow swirl, trefoil crimped top **500.00**

7" h, cased pink over white, enameled bell flowers, Victorian......... **100.00**

7-1/4" h, creamy opaque ext., white and yellow flowers, green leaves gold trim, deep rose pink int., amber edge, ormolu leaf feet **165.00**

7-1/4" h, spatter, green, peach, yellow, and white spatter at top, green diamond quilted pattern body........... **75.00**

7-1/4" h, 3-3/8" d top, 2-3/4" d base, peachblow, deep salmon pink top and throat shades to creamy bulbous base **175.00**

7-1/2" h, Nailsea, frosted chartreuse green ground, white loopings, applied frosted feet **165.00**

7-1/2" h, opalescent, chartreuse, ruffled **90.00**

7-1/2" h, 4-1/2" w, salmon stretch tri-fold top shading to silvery white body and disk base, sharp pontil........ **225.00**

8" h, 4-3/4" d, trumpet shape, fold down in front, back half of top tightly crimped, white opaque body, bead of cranberry glass running down the entire circumference, colorless wafer base, Hobbs Brockunier **250.00**

8" h, 7" w, Burmese, scalloped rim, applied base, Pairpoint **725.00**

8-1/2" h, spatter, white, green, and cranberry **115.00**

8-1/2" h, Squirrel and Acorn pattern, opalescent, blue............. **150.00**

8-1/2" h, Squirrel and Acorn pattern, opalescent, green **145.00**

8-1/2" h, Squirrel and Acorn pattern, opalescent, vaseline.......... **175.00**

8-1/2" h, 4-1/2" h, opalescent, white flared top with ruffled rim, swirled body, colorless base **125.00**

9" h, Burmese, undecorated, pie-crimped edge, deep blushed throat shades to soft yellow base, Mt. Washington................. **785.00**

9" h, pink cased over white, turned up trumpet form top, row of applied blue glass around middle of body, early 1900s **150.00**

9" h, emerald green crooked neck, tree bark surface, snipped rim manipulated to blossom form, gold irid surface, polished pontil, Loetz......... **690.00**

9" h, 5" w, cranberry, white opal edge, applied crystal base, Hobbs, Brockunier **325.00**

9-1/4" h, pale red alternating with white vertically striped body, applied pale green rigaree, pale green and yellow linen fold foot **450.00**

9-1/2" h, 5" w, lusterless white, Mt. Washington, randomly scattered floral dec, flared pie crimped top **300.00**

9-3/4" h, vaseline opalescent ... **180.00**

9-3/4" h, 4-3/4" d top, Crown Milano, painted opalware, Burmese yellow base, Peachblow pink top, white mid section, small flower and leaves floral dec, 36 crimps at top, Mt. Washington **785.00**

10" h, cranberry, applied crystal rigaree and feet.................... **225.00**

10" h, 3-1/2" d, amber color blown glass vase, paperweight base with controlled bubbles.................... **75.00**

10" h, 4" w, Burmese, Mt. Washington, tightly pleated ruffled top, delicate pink with re-fired yellow edge, yellow steam and base **450.00**

11" h, Fine Diamond Optic, green opalescent, Fenton, oval mark, orig label.......................**115.00**

11-3/4" h, cased floriform, gold irid flower, green and gold pulled feather dec opaque opal body, unsigned, attributed to Martin Bach, Quezal, two int. skips in blossom **1,400.00**

12" h, green, silver-blue irid spots, Loetz, c1920 .... **450.00**

12-1/2" h, trumpet, satin, white, lavender and white flowers, green leaves, ruffled rim, Mt. Washington **375.00**

13" h, heavily cased clear over purple-amethyst body, irid flared top with continuous winding green stem from calla lily top to base, overshot dec, etched by artist "C. Funk 87" .. **225.00**

13-1/4" h, amberina, Inverted Thumbprint pattern, New England Glass Works **325.00**

13-1/2" h, blue opalescent, eight-petal top, yellow enameled inside of top and down front **275.00**

13-1/2" h, brilliant yellow baluster form, colorless glass overlay, black rim wrap, Czechoslovakian............ **225.00**

14" h, purple stretch, butterscotch pulled feather design on base . **270.00**

15-3/4" h, cased, blue, white lining, ruffled, applied crystal spiral trim, clear foot with scalloped shell trim... **250.00**

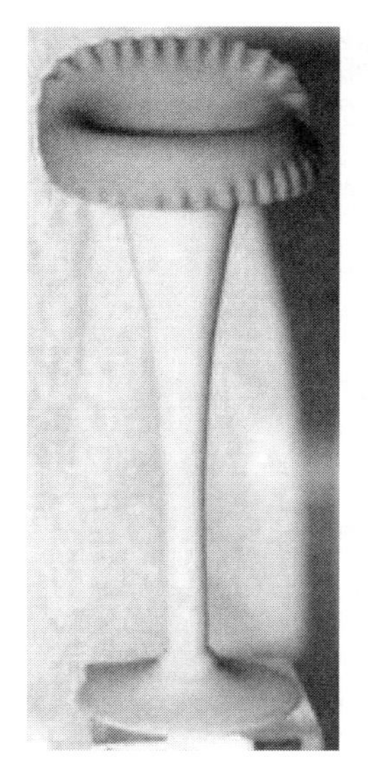

Burmese, pie-crimped edge, blush of color at mouth and throat, Mt. Washington, 9" h, **$785.** *Photo courtesy of Clarence and Betty Maier.*

Kitchen Glassware

History: The Depression era brought inexpensive kitchen and table products to center stage. Anchor Hocking, Hazel Atlas, McKee, U. S. Glass, and Westmoreland led in the production of these items.

Kitchen glassware complimented Depression glass. Many items were produced in the same color and style. Because the glass was molded, added decorative elements included ribs, fluting, arches, and thumbprint patterns. Kitchen glassware was thick to achieve durability. The resulting forms were difficult to handle at times and often awkward aesthetically. After World War II, aluminum products began to replace Kitchen Glassware. Today's microwaves are seeing a resurgence in kitchen glassware forms.

Kitchen glassware was made in large numbers. Although collectors do tolerate signs of use, they will not accept pieces with heavy damage. Many of these products contain applied decals; these should be in good condition. A collection can be built inexpensively by concentrating on one form, such as canister sets, measuring cups, etc.

References: Ronald S. Barlow, *Victorian Houseware*, Windmill Publishing, 1992; Tom and Neila Bredehoft, *Fifty Years of Collectible Glass, 1920-1970, Volume 1, Volume II,* Antique Trader Books, 2000; Gene Florence, *Anchor Hocking's Fire King & More,* 2nd ed., Collector Books, 2000; ——, *Collectible Glassware from the '40s, '50s, '60s*, 6th ed., Collector Books, 2001; ——, *Kitchen Glassware of the Depression Years*, 6th ed., Collector Books, 2001; Linda Campbell Franklin, *300 Years of Housekeeping Collectibles*, Books Americana, 1992; ——, *300 Hundred Years of Kitchen Collectibles*, Krause Publications, 1997; Joe Keller and David Ross, *Jadeite: An Identification and Price Guide,* Schiffer Publishing, 1999; Gary and Dale Kilgo and Jerry and Gail Wilkins, *Collectors Guide to Anchor Hocking's Fire-King Glassware*, K & W Collectibles Publisher, 1991; —, *Collectors Guide to Anchor Hocking's Fire-King Glassware, Volume II,*, K & W Collectibles Publisher, 1998.

Anchor Hocking, Post–1930

Federal Glass Co.

Hazel Atlas

Hocking Pre–1938

Jeannette Glass Co.

Owens Illinois

CLIMAX

MACBETH No PEARL GLASS

Periodicals & Web Sites: *DG Shopper Online,* The WWW Depression Era Glass Magazine, http://www.dgshopper.com/~dgshoppr; *Fire-King News,* P.O. Box 473, Addison, AL 35540.

Collectors' Clubs: Glass Knife Collectors Club, 711 Kelly Dr., Lebanon, TN 37087; National Reamer Collectors Assoc., 47 Midline Court, Gaithersburg, MD 20878.

Museums: Corning Glass Museum, Corning, NY; Kern County Museum, Bakersfield, CA; Landis Valley Farm Museum, Lancaster, PA.

Apothecary set, Chalaine **195.00**

Ashtray

Butterfly, crystal, Jeannette ... **7.00**

Cowboy hat, Delphite, Jeannette **22.75**

Green, fluted, Federal....... **12.00**

Jade-ite.... **60.00**

Banana split dish, Jeannette, oval, crystal **5.00**

Batter bowl

Anchor Hocking, set of 7", 8", 9", and 10" d, rimmed, transparent green **95.00**

Hocking, crystal, spout...... **15.00**

Tufglass, two handles, two spouts **45.00**

Batter pitcher, two cups

Cobalt blue.... **125.00**

Milk glass, Federal **15.00**

Pink, U.S. Glass **55.00**

Beer mug, yellow **40.00**

Berry bowl, Hazel Atlas, crimped

Large

Green.... **21.00**

Pink **25.00**

Small

Cobalt blue **15.00**

Green.... **7.00**

Pink **7.00**

Bowl

5-1/2" d, red, platonite, Criss-Cross **12.50**

6" d, Delphite, Pyrex.... **13.00**

6" d, Jade-ite, Jeannette..... **16.00**

6" d, Jennyware, Jeannette, crystal **8.00**

6-1/2" d, cobalt blue.... **23.00**

7-1/2" d, cobalt blue, Hazel Atlas **45.00**

7-3/4" d, cobalt blue **55.00**

8" d, Delphite, vertical rib **85.00**

8" d, green, Hocking **15.00**

8-1/2" l, oval, Pyrex, beige, two handles, blue dec, 1-1/2 quart **15.00**

9" d, Delphite, Pyrex **17.00**

10" d, emerald glo.... **50.00**

Butter box, cov, Federal, green, two-pound size.... **145.00**

Butter dish, cov, one-pound size

Criss Cross

Cobalt blue.... **120.00**

Crystal.... **20.00**

Green **85.00**

Hazel Atlas

Cobalt blue.... **195.00**

Green **60.00**

Iridescent, round **25.00**

Hocking, crystal.... **25.00**

Jade-ite **95.00**

Cake plate, Snowflake, pink **35.00**

Canister

3" h, Jade-ite, Jeannette

Allspice.... **65.00**

Ginger.... **65.00**

Nutmeg.... **65.00**

Pepper **65.00**

5-1/2" h, coffee, Jade-ite, sq, Jeannette **55.00**

6" h, green, screw-on lid, smooth **38.00**

8 oz, smooth sides, green, Hocking **28.50**

20 oz, tea, Delphite, round .. **275.00**

20 oz, tea, screw-on lid, Vitrock **27.00**

29 oz, cereal, Delphite, sq .. **375.00**

29 oz, sugar, Delphite, sq ... **425.00**

40 oz, coffee, Delphite, round **400.00**

40 oz, sugar, Delphite, round **450.00**

Rice, Ruff N'Ready, green.... **24.00**

Sellers, clambroth, small..... **34.00**

Casserole, cov

Cupid & Arrow.... **140.00**

Pyrex, white.... **25.00**

Cereal bowl, green, Federal **8.00**

Coffee measuring cup, Kitchen Aid advertisement, coffee measurement indicators, red and black, 4-3/8" h **18.00**

Coffeepot, four cups, Pyrex **15.00**

Creamer, Criss Cross, crystal ... **15.00**

Creamer and sugar

Hocking

Crystal, dec **12.00**

Green **24.00**

Jeannette, green **15.00**

Chopper, one-cup clear glass measuring cup base, metal lid and chopper, green wooden knob, some wear, **$20.**

Cruet, stopper
- Crystolite, amber 30.00
- Hocking, transparent green .. 25.00

Cup, handle
- Federal, green 5.00
- Hazel Atlas, diamond quilted, pink 10.00

Curtain tiebacks, pr
- 2-1/2" d, knob-type, pink..... 35.00
- 3-1/2" d, flat, floral, green and pink 20.00
- 4-1/2" d, flat, floral, amber.... 25.00

Custard cup
- Glassbake, crystal 1.00
- Hazel Atlas, ftd, green 5.00
- Tufglas, green.............. 6.00

Drawer pull, crystal
- Double type 10.00
- Knob 3.00

Drippings jar, cov, Jade-ite, Jeannette 32.00

Egg cup, double
- Black.................... 12.00
- Green, Hazel Atlas 7.00
- Yellow, Hocking............. 7.50

Egg nog set, bowl, six cups, white, Hazel Atlas 30.00

Epsom salt container, ribbed, jade 150.00

Fish bowl, 6" d, transparent green 22.00

Fork and spoon, amber handle . 45.00

Funnel, green
- Medium 35.00
- Large 110.00

Furniture caster
- Hazel Atlas, 3" d, transparent green 40.00
- Hocking, green, set of four ... 14.00

Ginger jar, Chalaine blue....... 55.00

Grease jar, Tulips, cov, Hocking . 15.00

Hand beater, 32-oz measuring cup base
- Green.................... 45.00
- Green, stippled texture 45.00

Ice bucket, Hocking, crystal, handle 25.00

Iced tea spoons, colored handles, set of 12 .... 60.00

Icing tray, 10-1/2" d, Chalaine blue 175.00

Ink blotter, Scottie Dog, Jade-ite. 65.00

Juicer, lemon/lime, green, Federal 20.00

Juice tumbler, Hocking, pink, ribbed, 3-3/8" h 6.50

Knife
- Block, 8-1/4" l
  - Crystal, orig box 35.00
  - Green 45.00
- Buffalo, crystal, orig box 39.00
- Dur-x, three leaf
  - Blue, orig box 72.00
  - Crystal, 8-1/2" l 19.00
  - Crystal, 9-1/4" l 21.00
  - Crystal 9-1/4" l, orig box ... 28.00
  - Green, orig box.......... 62.00
  - Light pink, orig box....... 58.00
  - Pink 53.00
- Pinwheel, crystal 22.00
- Plain, 9-1/8" l, green......... 40.00
- Rose Spray, pink, orig box ... 28.00
- Star
  - Blue, orig box 72.00
  - Crystal................. 19.00
  - Pink 54.00
- Stonex
  - Dark amber, MIB........ 375.00
  - Light amber, MIB 300.00
  - Opalescent 40.00
- Three Star
  - Blue................... 38.00
  - Crystal, orig box 68.00
  - Pink 25.00
- Thumbguard, crystal, dec, Westmoreland 52.00

Loaf pan, cov, 5" x 8", Glassbake, clear, knob finial 35.00

Match holder, Jeannette, Delphite, round
- Black lettering "Matches"... 145.00
- No lettering.............. 70.00

Mayonnaise ladle
- Amber, flat 9.75
- Pink, transparent 20.00

Measuring cup
- 2 oz, 1/4 cup, Delphite, Jeannette 72.00
- 2 oz, 1/4 cup, Jade-ite, Jeannette 85.00
- 2.6 oz, 1/3 cup, Delphite, Jeannette 82.00
- 2.6 oz, 1/3 cup, Jade-ite, Jeannette 85.00
- 8 oz, crystal, one spout, Fire-King 18.50
- 8 oz, crystal, one spout, Hocking 16.00
- 8 oz, Delphite, Jeannette 90.00
- 8 oz, green, Hazel Atlas 32.00
- 8 oz, green, transparent..... 18.00
- 8 oz, Jade-ite, Jeannette ... 100.00
- 8 oz, milk white, Hazel Atlas.. 25.00
- 16 oz, cobalt blue, Hazel Atlas 225.00
- 16 oz, crystal, U.S. Glass 20.00
- 16 oz, fired-on green 20.00
- 16 oz, green, Hocking 32.00
- 16 oz, green, stick handle, U.S. Glass 50.00
- 16 oz, milk glass, white 22.00
- 32 oz, green 46.00

Mixing bowl
- 5-3/4" d, yellow banded dot, Pyrex 8.00
- 6" d, crystal, Hazel Atlas..... 12.00
- 6" d, crystal, Jeannette...... 16.00
- 6" d, Delphite Blue, Jeannette, vertical ribs............. 100.00
- 6-1/2" d, Amber, Federal..... 10.00
- 6-1/2" d, cobalt blue, Hazel Atlas 35.00
- 6-1/2" d, green, Restwell 10.00
- 6-5/8" d, cobalt blue, Hazel Atlas 75.00
- 7-1/4" d, yellow banded dot, Pyrex 10.00
- 7-1/2" d, cobalt blue, Hazel Atlas 42.00
- 7-3/4" d, amber, Federal..... 15.00
- 8" d, Delphite Blue, Jeannette, vertical ribs............. 85.00
- 8-1/2" d, cobalt blue, Hazel Atlas 90.00
- 9-1/2" d, amber, Federal..... 18.00
- 11" d, Vitrock, white 15.00
- #90, Pyrex, set of three, crystal, measure, mix, and pour.... 25.00

#120, Pyrex, three quarts, crystal 12.00
Nested set
Amber, Paneled, Hocking, set of six 145.00
Cobalt blue, 6-5/8" d, 7-5/8" d, 8-1/2" d, 9-5/8" d, Hazel Atlas 320.00
Green, Paneled, Hocking, set of five 165.00
White, ivy dec, Hazel Atlas . 50.00

Mug
Ranger Joe, Hazel Atlas, blue or red 9.50
Red Transparent, New Martinsville, polka dot pattern 15.00

Napkin holder
Lady, blue and white 90.00
Nar-O-Fold, white, marked "Napkin Company, Chicago, reg. U.S.A." 50.00

Patio set, Jeannette, orig box ... 55.00
Percolator lid, green, Hocking .. 12.00
Pie lifter, Pine Cone 15.00
Pie plate, individual size, heart shape, Cupid & Arrow 25.00

Pitcher, Hazel Atlas, light blue, **$45.**

Pitcher
Cobalt blue, Louis Glass Co.. 140.00
Crystal, painted, Hocking 18.00
Fired-On, orange, ball shape, tilt 20.00
Green, Criss-Cross, Hocking.. 15.00
Green, tall, Hocking........ 36.00
Jade-ite, sunflower in base ... 40.00
Pheasants dec, green, Hocking 25.00
Pink........ 80.00

Plate, 8" d, green, Federal 6.00

Platter
Glassbake, crystal, large 20.00
Pyrex, 14" l, oval 12.00

Provision jar, cov
8 oz, green, Hocking 40.00
16 oz, green, Hocking 45.00

Range shaker
Black, Arch
Flour........ 35.00
Salt and pepper, pr 45.00
Sugar........ 40.00
Chalaine, salt, pepper, sugar, and flour, set 450.00
Custard
Arch, flour 25.00
Arch, sugar 28.00
Three small lines, spice ... 25.00
Delphite
Arch, sugar 250.00
Rib, salt and pepper, pr... 85.00
Green, emb
Flour........ 75.00
Salt........ 40.00
Sugar........ 90.00
Jade-ite, Jeannette, flour
Round 85.00
Sq........ 40.00
Pink
Emb, salt and pepper, pr.. 110.00
Jenny 28.00
Seville
Arch, sugar 35.00
Three large lines, flower... 25.00
Three large lines, ginger .. 35.00
Three large lines, spice ... 65.00
Ultramarine, Jenny 35.00

Reamer, lemon
Criss Cross, pink 325.00
Hazel Atlas, pink........ 35.00
JeannetteDelphite........ 100.00
Jade-ite 35.00

Reamer, orange
Criss Cross
Blue 375.00
Crystal 10.00
Green........ 60.00
Pink 250.00
Federal
Large, loop handle, crystal 14.00
Small pointed cone, green. 25.00
Hazel Atlas, cobalt blue, tab handle 325.00
Jeannette
Delphite 138.00
Pink........ 175.00
Ultramarine........ 148.00
Lindsay
Green 475.00
Pink........ 425.00
McKee, Chalaine Blue...... 360.00
Sunkist
Black........ 800.00
Caramel 375.00
Chaline 275.00
Crown Tuscan........ 375.00
Opalescent........ 200.00
U.S. Glass, Handy Andy, green 50.00

Refrigerator dish, Hazel Atlas, cobalt blue, 4" x 4", **$25.**

Refrigerator dish, cov
3" x 5-3/4", Criss Cross, cobalt blue 165.00
4" x 4", Criss Cross, cobalt blue 35.00
4" x 4", Delphite blue, Jeannette 45.00
4" x 5", Jade-ite 65.00
4" x 8", Criss Cross, green.... 60.00
4" x 8", Delphite 65.00
4" x 8", floral carved, transparent green, U.S. Glass 30.00
4" x 8", ultramarine........ 62.00
4" x 10", Jade-ite 110.00
4-1/4" x 5", cobalt blue, Hazel Atlas 115.00
4-1/2" x 4-1/2" sq, Jade-ite, Jeannette 15.00
4-1/2" x 4-1/2", sq, pink, Jennyware 35.00
4-1/2" x 4", crystal, vertical ribs, Hocking........ 14.00
6" x 3", transparent green, Tufglass 45.00

6-1/2" sq, Poppy Cocklebur, transparent green, U.S. Glass **55.00**
8" x 8", sq, Amber, Federal . . . **25.00**
8" x 8", sq, Criss Cross, crystal **25.00**
8" x 8", sq, pink, Federal **95.00**
8-1/2 x 4-1/2", Jade-ite, Jeannette **32.00**
32 oz, round, Jade-ite, Jeannette **35.00**
32 oz, round, Ultramarine, Jeannette **90.00**

Relish, 8-1/2 x 13" oval, Delphite, divided, Pyrex. **20.00**

Rolling pin, blown
6-1/4" l, translucent aqua, England, 19th C, imperfections **90.00**
12-3/4" l, amethyst, sailor's token, transfer dec of British flags, ships, sailor's prayers, mottoes, declarations of love, England, 19th C, wear to transfers, chips . **150.00**
13-1/4" l, colorless and white, blue and red speckles, bulbous hand holds, England, 19th C, imperfections. **300.00**
14" l, black, white speckles, small button knop ends, England, 19th C, imperfections. **175.00**
14" l, dark amber, white speckles, small button knop ends, England or eastern U.S., 19th C, imperfections **225.00**
14-1/2" l, pale translucent green, small button knop ends, England, 19th C, imperfections **155.00**
14-3/4" l, colorless, white, and amethyst loop design, bulbous hand holds, England or eastern U.S., 19th C, imperfections . **245.00**
15" l, pale aqua, white marbrie, elongated bulbous hand holds, England, 19th C, imperfections **225.00**
15-1/8" l, amber, white speckles, small button knop ends, England, 19th C, imperfections **190.00**
15-1/4" l, cobalt blue, sailor's token, transfer dec of British flags, ships, sailor's prayers, mottoes, declarations of love, England, 19th C, wear to transfers, chips . **150.00**
16" l, blue, transfer printed dec and verses, small button knop ends, England or eastern U.S., 19th C, imperfections. **210.00**
16" l, white cased to opalescent, sailor's token, transfer dec of British flags, ships, sailor's prayers, mottoes, declarations of love, England, 19th C, wear to transfers, chips. **150.00**
16-1/2" l, amethyst, sailor's token, transfer dec of British flags, ships, sailor's prayers, mottoes, declarations of love, England, 19th C, wear to transfers, chips . **150.00**
17" l, colorless, white loop designs, bulbous hand holds, England or eastern U.S., 19th C, imperfections **190.00**
17" l, white cased to opalescent, sailor's token, transfer dec of British flags, ships, sailor's prayers, mottoes, declarations of love, England, 19th C, wear to transfers, chips. **150.00**

Root beer dispenser, amber . . **350.00**

Salad fork and spoon, blue. . . . **55.00**

Salt and pepper shakers, pr
Cobalt Blue, red lids, Hazel Atlas **30.00**
Delphite, round. **125.00**
Ribbed, Jade-ite, Jeannette . . **22.00**
Roman Arches, black, minor damage to lids **45.00**
Round, Jade-ite, Jeannette . **105.00**
White, Hazel Atlas, red dec, 3-1/2" h **24.00**

Salt box
4" x 5-1/2" d, round, yellow, no writing on lid. **100.00**
Green, wood lid **900.00**
Pink, glass lid **150.00**
Ultramarine. **175.00**

Sherbet
Federal, pink. **5.00**
Hocking, plain yellow **7.50**

Soup bowl, Glassbake. **2.00**

Spice jar, Hazel Atlas, cobalt blue **75.00**

Spice shaker
Delphite
Paprika, black lettering . . **185.00**
Pepper, round, black lettering **90.00**
Pepper, sq, black lettering **150.00**
Ultramarine, Pepper, round, Jeannette **48.00**
White
Cinnamon, red and blue dec, Hocking. **12.00**
Ginger, red and blue dec, Hocking. **12.00**
Nutmeg, red and blue dec, Hocking. **12.00**
Paprika, red and blue dec, Hocking. **12.00**

Spoon, clear, Higbee. **25.00**

Straw holder, crystal, lid missing **100.00**

Sugar bowl, cov
Criss-Cross design, transparent green, Hazel Atlas. **35.00**
Federal, ftd, green. **12.50**

Sugar cube dispenser, crystal . **225.00**

Sugar shaker
Amber, paneled. **225.00**
Delphite, round **185.00**
Green
Hex optic **250.00**
Pinch. **250.00**
Plain **145.00**
Spiral. **250.00**
Jade-ite, Jeannette, round . . . **85.00**

Sundae, ftd, pink, Federal **12.00**

Syrup pitcher
Crystal
Gold catalin handle **12.00**
Flower etch **35.00**
Green, Hazel Atlas **65.00**

Thermos, Cambridge, cobalt blue **450.00**

Tom and Jerry set, Hazel Atlas
Seven pc, Auld Lang Syne . . . **15.00**
Seven pc, eggnog. **15.00**
Seven pc, red and green dec . **15.00**
Nine pc, red and green dec . . **25.00**
Nine pc, red and green dots . . **25.00**

Towel bar, 24" l, crystal, orig hardware **15.00**

Tray, sq, Jeannette, handle, pink. **18.00**

Trivet, 9" d, round, Pyrex, crystal. **12.00**

Tumbler
Federal, Lido, 15 oz, ftd, pink . **15.00**
Hazel Atlas
Crystal, flat **4.50**
Pink, diamond quilted. **12.00**
White, 3-1/2" h, 9 oz **5.00**
White, 4-1/2" h, 16 oz **7.00**
Hocking, cobalt blue, flat **1.50**
Jeannette, Cosmos pattern, irid **4.50**

Vase
Hazel Atlas, 6-3/4" h, milk glass, c1930 . . . . **12.00**
Hocking, bud, dark amethyst . **18.00**
Jeannette, bud, Jade-ite **14.00**

Water bottle, clear, glass lid, Hocking **24.00**

Water cooler, Smith, cobalt blue **400.00**

Water dispenser, 17" h, black base, crystal bowl, silver trim. **95.00**

Water set, Jeannette, pitcher, seven tumblers, irid **32.00**

LALIQUE

LALIQUE

R.LALIQUE

History: René Lalique (1860-1945) first gained prominence as a jewelry designer. Around 1900, he began experimenting with molded-glass brooches and pendants, often embellishing them with semiprecious stones. By 1905, he was devoting himself exclusively to the manufacture of glass articles.

In 1908, Lalique began designing packaging for the French cosmetic houses. He also produced many objects, especially vases, bowls, and figurines, in the Art Nouveau and Art Deco styles. The full scope of Lalique's genius was seen at the 1925 Paris l'Exposition Internationale des Arts Décorative et Industriels Modernes. He later moved toward his well known Art-Deco forms.

The mark "R. LALIQUE FRANCE" in block letters is found on pressed articles, tableware, vases, paperweights, and automobile mascots. The script signature, with or without "France," is found on hand-blown objects. Occasionally, a design number is included. The word "France" in any form indicates a piece made after 1926.

The post-1945 mark is generally "Lalique France" without the "R," but there are exceptions.

References: Patricia Bayer, *The Art of Rene Lalique*, Book Sales, 1996; Nicholas Dawes, *Lalique Glass*, Crown, 1986; Hugh D. Guinn (ed.), *Glass of René Lalique at Auction*, Guindex Publications, 1992; *Lalique Glass From the Collection of Charles and Mary Maguil*, Clark Art Institute; *Lalique Glass the Complete Illustrated Catalogue for 1932*, Dover Publications, 1981; Robert Prescott-Walker, *Collecting Lalique Glass*, Wallace-Homestead, 1996; 1986; Mary Lou Utt, et. al., *Lalique Perfume Bottles*, Crown, 1990.

Periodicals: Lalique Magazine, 400 Veterans Blvd., Carlstadt, NJ 07072; T & B, P.O. Box 15555, Plantation, FL 33318.

Collectors' Club: Lalique Collectors Society, 400 Veterans Blvd., Carlstadt, NJ 07072.

Videotape: Nicholas M. Dawes, "World of Lalique Glass," Award Video and Film Distributors, 1993.

Reproduction Alert: The Lalique signature has often been forged; the most common fake includes an "R" with the post-1945 mark.

Animal

2-3/4" h, fox, frosted, circular, engraved script sgd "R. Lalique France" **550.00**

7" l, fish, sgd "Lalique, France," orig paper label **550.00**

8-1/4" h, Chat Assis, sitting, clear and frosted, c1970, engraved "Lalique France" **920.00**

9-1/4" h, Chat Couche, clear and frosted, c1970, engraved "Lalique France" **575.00**

Architectural panel, 12" h, 4" w, Jeune Faune, clear and frosted, Marcilhac 879, No. 4, price for pr **6,900.00**

Ashtray

3-1/2" h, Soucis, opal figure of vase with flowers at center, base stamped "R. Lalique France" **460.00**

5-1/2" d, Tobago, clear and frosted, c1960, molded "R. LALIQUE," Marcilhac 273, No. 295 ... **230.00**

8" d, frosted cherubs, orig paper label **185.00**

Atomizer, cylindrical

2-1/2" h, Epines, clear, molded thorny bramble design, lavender patina, raised molded signature, gilt metal atomizer fittings, damage to orig bulb and net **300.00**

3-3/4" h, relief molded frieze of six nude maidens, holding floral garland, waisted gilt metal mount, Le Provencal fragrance, molded "R Lalique, Made in France".. **265.00**

4-3/4" h, relief molded frieze of six nude maidens, holding floral garland, waisted gilt metal mount chased with ribbon tied floral festoons, stamped "LE Parisiene Bte S.G.D. G. Made in France/O/F," base low relief molded "R. Lalique Made in France"......... **900.00**

Automobile hood ornament

2-1/2" h, Tete D'Epervier, opalescent, orig chrome collar, c1928, molded "LALIQUE FRANCE," Marcilhac 499, No. 1138 .... **2,615.00**

3-3/4" h, Sirene, clear and frosted, c1920, molded "R. LALIQUE," engraved "R. Lalique France," Marcilhac 497, No. 831.. **2,870.00**

4-1/4" h, Tete D'Aigle, clear and frosted, c1960, molded "R. LALIQUE FRANCE," engraved "Lalique France," Marcilhac 499, No. 1138 .... **575.00**

4-1/2" h, Faucon, clear and frosted, c1925, molded "R. LALIQUE," wheel-cut "FRANCE," Marcilhac 498, no. 1124 .... **2,870.00**

4-1/2" h, St. Christophe, clear and frosted, c1985, molded "LALIQUE FRANCE," Marcilhac 501, No. 1142 .... **690.00**

6" l, Pintade, clear and frosted, orig chrome collar, c1929, molded "R LALIQUE," Marcilhac 504, No. 1164 .... **4,315.00**

7" h, Tete de Coq, clear and frosted, c1950, molded "LALIQUE FRANCE," Marcilhac 499, No. 1137 .... **575.00**

8" h, Coq Houdon, clear and frosted, c1929, wheel-cut "R. LALIQUE FRANCE," Marcilhac 504, No. 1161 .... **4,600.00**

10" l, Victorie, amethyst-tinted, c1938, molded "R. LALIQUE

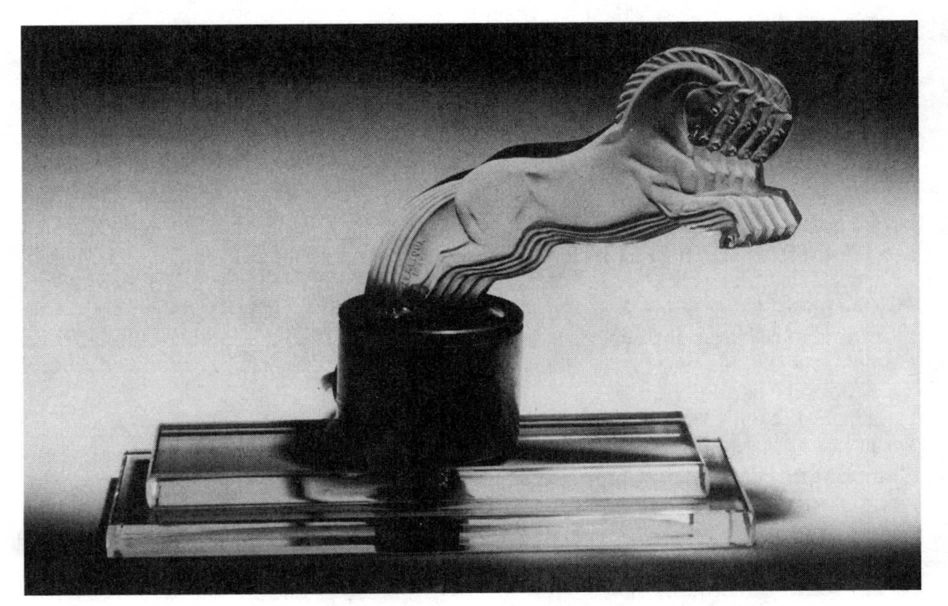

Automobile Mascot, Cinq Cheveaux, clear and frosted, c1925, orig Breves Galleries chromium plated brass mount, modern glass base, molded "R. Lalique," wheel-cut "France," **$8,850.**

FRANCE," Marcilhac 502, No. 1147 .... **20,125.00**

Bonbonier, 8-1/2" d, 1-3/4" h, Georgette, opalescent cover, three dragonflies on brown satin-lined box, molded "R. LALIQUE" **1,250.00**

Bowl

6-1/4" d, Edelweiss, clear, c1937, wheel-cut "R. LALIQUE FRANCE," Marcilhac 437, No. 10-913. **690.00**

6-1/4" d, 2-1/2" h, Graines D'Asperges No. 4, clear, opalescent intertwining twig and berry design in relief on ext. base and sides, inscribed "R. Lalique France No. 3222" **290.00**

8-1/4" d, Couquilles No. 2, opalescent, molded "R. LALIQUE," engraved "France," Marcilhac 748, No. 3201 .... **575.00**

9-3/4" d, Nemours, clear and frosted, black enamel highlights, c1970, Marcilhac 299, No. 404 ... **535.00**

10" d, Nemours, clear and frosted, sepia patina, brown enameled highlights, c1929, molded "R. LALIQUE FRANCE," M 299, No. 404 .... **920.00**

Box, cov

2-3/4" sq, Cerises, black celluloid, c1923, molded "R. LALIQUE," Marcilhac 236, No. 72 .... **850.00**

3-1/2" d, Emiliane, clear and frosted, engraved "R. Lalique France," Marcilhac 235, No. 70 .... **350.00**

5-1/4" d, Roger, topaz, c1926, molded "LALIQUE," Marcilhac 237, No. 75................ **630.00**

Candlesticks, pr, 2-1/8" h, sq, colorless, molded stylized leaves, short cylindrical base, c1943, edge sgd "R. Lalique," M 2127 .... **350.00**

Ceiling light, 14-1/2" d, Lierre, clear and frosted, sepia patina, c1927, orig hooks and hanging cord, molded "R LALIQUE FRANCE," m p 673, No. 2469 .... **3,775.00**

Center bowl, 13" d, Marguerites, dainty blossoms in relief around rim, radiating stems around sides and base, clear, blue-green patina, etched "R. LALIQUE, FRANCE" on base, minor scratches.................. **575.00**

Champagne glass, 8" h, Champagne Ange, engraved "Lalique France," set of six in orig box **1,150.00**

Charger, 15-3/4" d, Argues, opalescent, raised seaweed forms in spiral formation, c1933, block letter etched stamp "R. Lalique France" **815.00**

Cigarette box, 4" sq, Fouad I, clear and frosted, sepia patina, molded "R. LALIQUE," presentation inscription, Marcilhac 222............... **120.00**

Cold drink service, jug and six tumblers

8" h jug, Blidah, amber, c1931, Setubal tray, all stenciled "R. LALIQUE FRANCE," Marcilhac 797, No. 3681, p 799, No. 3684 (tray) **2,185.00**

9" h, jug, Bahia, amber, c1931, matching tray, all stenciled "R. LALIQUE FRANCE," Marcilhac 798, No. 3683 .... **2,870.00**

Coupe

9-1/4" d, Gui, clear, green patina, wheel-cut "R. LALIQUE FRANCE," Marcilhac 751, No. 3224... **490.00**

15-1/2" d, Flora-Bella, clear and opalescent, c1930, stenciled "R. LALIQUE FRANCE," Marcilhac 299, No. 407 .... **2,990.00**

Decanter set, 10" h decanter, six glasses, Nippon, clear, stenciled "R LALIQUE FRANCE," glasses script sgd "R. Lalique France," Marcilhac 443, No. 3173 .... **1,150.00**

Display perfume bottle

11-1/4" h, Je Reviens, dark and light blue, Art Deco, for Worth, c1932, molded "LALIQUE MADE IN FRANCE," Marcilhac 953, B **575.00**

12-1/2" h, L'Air Du Temps, clear and frosted, for Nina Ricci, c1960, sealed, orig contents...... **980.00**

Dresser bottles, graduated from 5" to 7" h, Fleurettes, silver mounted neck, swollen rect colorless form, each edge dec with border of florettes, frosted glass with gray patina to borders, broad dome stopper, c1919, molded signature on base, silver hallmarks, M 575-577, price for set of three **1,380.00**

Dressing table set, Perles, 5-1/4" l pin tray, cov powder box, soap dish, opalescent, c1926, stenciled and engraved marks, Marcilhac 344, No. 604, 605, 606 .... **1,150.00**

Figurine

6-3/4" h, Christ, crucified on cross, radiating linear bands surrounding figure, clear, inscribed "R. Lalique, France" on base, Marcilhac 1223 .... **460.00**

9-1/2" h, Danseuse, clear and frosted, c1980, engraved "Lalique France," Lalique Design No. 119080 .... **865.00**

Hand mirror, 11-3/4" l, Narcisse Couche, clear, dec with bands of stylized leaves, centered by Narcissus in repose, sepia patina, edge inscribed "R. Lalique France, No. 675" in script, mirror loose, shows wear, nicks to glaze **1,100.00**

Hat pin

9-3/4" l, Feuilles, clear foil backed glass, sepia patina, orig silvered metal mount, c1912, Marcilhac 566, No. 1558.......... **1,955.00**

9-3/4" l, Scrabees, clear foil backed glass, sepia patina, orig silvered metal mount, c1912, Marcilhac 566, No. 1559.......... **1,625.00**

Inkwell, cov, 3-1/2" d, Trois Papillons, clear and frosted, c1912, engraved "R. Lalique France" and molded "R. LALIQUE," Marcilhac 315, No. 426 .... **1,150.00**

Jardiniere, 18" l, Acanthes, clear and frosted, sepia patina, 1927, wheel-cut "R. LALIQUE FRANCE," engraved No. 3460, Marcilhac 773, No. 3460. **980.00**

Medallion, 1-1/4" d, Chose Promise, for Fioret Fragrances, clear and frosted, c1920, silk-lined box, molded "R. LALIQUE," M 937, No. 4, unpierced **520.00**

Necklace, 40" l, Fueilles De Lierre, 20 opalescent green elements, orig golden silk cord, c1919, engraved "R. Lalique," M 558, No. 1505 .... **2,990.00**

Paperweight, 3" h, Deux Aigles, deep amber, 1914, wheel-cut "R. Lalique," Marcilhac 380, No. 801....... **690.00**

Pendant

1-3/4" d, Ange et Columbe, clear and frosted, sepia patina, gilt backing, c1920, engraved "R. Lalique," Marcilhac 570, J . **575.00**

2" l, Gui, yellow, modern beaded cord, c1920, molded "LALIQUE," Marcilhac 579, No. 1655 .. **415.00**

2" l, Lys, clear and frosted, c1920, engraved "R. Lalique," Marcilhac 580, No. 1657........... **535.00**

Perfume bottle

2-1/4" h, Chamille, clear and frosted, c1927, molded "R. LALIQUE FRANCE," Marcilhac 335, No. 516 .... **630.00**

3-1/4" h, Epines No. 4, clear and frosted, gray patina, c1920, engraved "R. Lalique France," Marcilhac 343, No. 593 ... **460.00**

3-3/4" h, Amphitrite, clear and frosted, blue patina, c1920, molded "R. LALIQUE," engraved

"France," No. 514, Marcilhac 335, No. 514 .... 2,990.00
- 3-3/4" h, Deux Fleurs, double flower blossom bottle, press molded flower center stopper, acid-etched "R. LALIQUE, FRANCE" on base, minor nicks on stopper, straw marks.................. **175.00**
- 3-3/4" h, Telline, clear and frosted, gray patina, c1920, engraved "R. Lalique France, No. 508" Marcilhac 333, No. 508 .... **800.00**
- 4" h, Roses, clear and frosted, for D'Orsay, c1912, molded "LALIQUE" with extended L, Marcilhac 933, No. 3.... **2,415.00**
- 4-1/4" h, Fleurs Concave, clear and frosted, blue patina, c1912, engraved "R. Lalique France," Marcilhac 327, No 486 .. **1,150.00**
- 4-1/2" h, La Belle Saison, clear and frosted, sepia patina, for Houbigant, c1925, molded "R. LALIQUE MADE IN FRANCE," Marcilhac 941, No. 3.... **1,150.00**
- 4-1/2" h, Palerme, clear, c1926, molded "R. LALIQUE," Marcilhac 336, No. 518 .... **630.00**
- 4-1/2" h, Tzigane, clear and frosted, for Corday, c1938, orig red silk and gilt card presentation box, Marcilhac 920, No. 1...... **520.00**
- 5" h, Pan, clear and frosted, gray patina, c1920, molded "R. LALIQUE," Marcilhac 332, No. 504 .... **1,150.00**
- 5-1/4" h, Ambre, black, for D'Orsay, c1912, molded "LALIQUE," Marcilhac 933, No. 1.... **1,610.00**
- 5-1/4" h, Quatre Flacons, four bottles fitted in opalescent and clear glass and satin box, presentation for Houbigant, c1928, stoppers missing, Marcilhac 969, No. 2 .... **575.00**
- 5-1/2" h, Relief, clear, for Forvil, c1924, molded "R. LALIQUE PARIS FRANCE," Marcilhac 338, No. 7 .... **380.00**
- 6" h, Ambre Antique, clear and frosted, sepia patina, for Coty, c1910, molded "R. LALIQUE," Marcilhac 927, No. 3.... **1,725.00**

Perfume burner, 5-1/4" h, Danseuses Egyptiennes, clear, black enamel highlights, chrome fittings, orig wick, c1926, molded "R. LALIQUE FRANCE," Marcilhac 962, No. 1 .... **535.00**

Plate
- 10-1/2" d, Fleurons No. 2, opalescent, stenciled "R. LALIQUE FRANCE," Marcilhac 751, No. 3224 .... **490.00**

Plate, Fish Ballet, 1967, **$95.**

- 11" d, Ondines, opalescent, c1921, wheel-cut "R. LALIQUE FRANCE," engraved "No. 3003," Marcilhac 699, No. 3003.......... **1,840.00**
- 14" d, Algues, opalescent, c1933, wheel-cut "R. LALIQUE FRANCE," Marcilhac 308, No. 10-390. **750.00**

Pot de crème, 3-3/4" h, Cigalia, clear and frosted, green patina, for Roger et Gallet, c1924, Marcilhac 970, No. 1 .... **800.00**

Powder box, cov
- 3" d, Fleurs d'Amour, for Rogert et Gallett, c1922, aluminum with red patina, molded "R. LALIQUE," Marcilhac 970............ **115.00**
- 4" d, Le Lys, clear and frosted, for D'Orsay, c1920, molded "R. LALIQUE," Marcilhac 968, No. 1 .... **200.00**
- 4" d, Trois Figurines, clear and frosted, for D'Orsay, c1920, molded "R. LALIQUE," Marcilhac 968, No. 3.............. **210.00**
- 4-1/4" d, Enfants, clear and frosted, sepia patina, c1942, engraved "R. Lalique," Marcilhac 345, No. 610 .... **460.00**
- 4-1/2" d, Helene, clear and frosted, sepia patina, c1942, stenciled "R. LALIQUE," Marcilhac 348, No. 635 .... **460.00**

Sculpture
- 13-1/2" h, surtout de table, illuminated, Fauevettes A, clear and frosted glass, birds on branch dec, orig nickel-plated metal illuminating base, wheel-cut "R. LALIQUE," Marcilhac 486, No. 1171 .... **7,475.00**
- 16" h, Coq De Jungle, clear and frosted, stenciled "R LALIQUE FRANCE," Marcilhac 493, No. 1124, signature partially obliterated by polishing........... **1,840.00**

Statuette
- 5-3/8" h, Moyenne Violee, opalescent, blue patina, c1912, engraved "Lalique," Marcilhac 398, No. M29.............. **5,175.00**
- 14" h, Grande Nue Socle Lierre, clear and frosted, sepia patina, c1919, mounted on plinth of Macassar ebony, engraved "R. Lalique," Marcilhac 400, No. 836 .... **17,250.00**
- 27" h, Source De La Fontaine Calypso, clear and frosted, c1924, mounted on ebonized wood plinth, designed by Rene Lalique for use in monumental fountain which welcomed visitors to Paris Exposition of 1925, wheel-cut "R LALIQUE," Marcilhac 400, No. 837 .... **23,000.00**

Stemware, Logelbach pattern, colorless, molded leaf stems, 11 5-7/8" h water goblets, 12 5-3/8" h wines, 11 4-3/4" h champagnes, bases acid stamped "R. Lalique," model created 1925, M 5026, 5027, 5029, price for 34-pc set **920.00**

Table ornament
- 4" l, Anenome Ferme and Anenome Ouverte, clear and frosted, black enamel highlights, stenciled "R. LALIQUE," Marcilhac 488, No. 1179 and No. 1180, price for pr **380.00**
- 6-1/2" h, Pavot, clear and frosted, black enamel highlights, c1928, stenciled "R. LALIQUE," Marcilhac 475, H **230.00**

Tea cup and saucer, 4-3/4" d saucer, Cactus, clear, black enamel highlights, c1933, stenciled "R. LALIQUE," Marcilhac 819, No. 3096 and 3907 .... **575.00**

Tumbler, 4-3/8" h, flared cylindrical, colorless, bottom portion with pinched and woven form, dec with four applied colored glass prunts to side, one to base, green, turquoise, and amethyst, etched "Lalique France" on bases, rim nicks, 11-pc set **525.00**

Vase
- 4-3/4" h, Bouchardon, clear and frosted, sepia patina, c1926, molded "R. LALIQUE," Marcilhac 435, No. 981 .... **2,615.00**
- 4-3/4" h, Grenade, black, c1930, stenciled "R. LALIQUE," engraved

"France," Marcilhac 448, No. 10-45 .... **2,530.00**

4-3/4" h, Grenade, sapphire blue, c1930, stenciled "R. LALIQUE," Marcilhac 448, No. 10-45. **2,530.00**

5" h, Dahlias, clear and frosted, sepia patina, black enameled highlights, engraved "R. Lalique France, No. 928," Marcilhac 425, No. 938............... **2,615.00**

5" h, Malines, clear and frosted, c1924, engraved "R. Lalique France No. 957," M 429, No. 957 .... **750.00**

5" h, Meudon, clear, c1933, stenciled "R. LALIQUE France," Marcilhac 460, No. 10-878 .... **380.00**

5" h, Rampillon, opalescent, blue-gray patina, c1927, wheel-cut "R. LALIQUE FRANCE," Marcilhac 437, No. 991........... **1,100.00**

5-1/4" h, Avalon, opalescent, c1935, stenciled "R. LALIQUE FRANCE," Marcilhac 436, No. 986 .. **1,725.00**

5-1/2" h, Beautrellis, topaz, c1927, wheel-cut "R. LALIQUE FRANCE," Marcilhac 436, No. 989 .. **1,355.00**

5-1/2" h, Honfleur, clear and frosted, c1926, wheel-cut "R. LALIQUE FRANCE," engraved "No. 994," Marcilhac 437, No. 994 ... **980.00**

5-1/2" h, Mossaic, opalescent, post-war ftd version, c1950, stenciled "LALIQUE FRANCE," Marcilhac 437, No. 992 ... **630.00**

6" h, Annecy, clear, black enameled highlights, c1935, stenciled "R. LALIQUE FRANCE," Marcilhac 461, No. 10-884 .... **1,485.00**

6" h, Charmonix, opalescent, c1933, stenciled "R. LALIQUE FRANCE," Marcilhac 458, No. 1090 .. **920.00**

6" h, Coqs et Plumes, clear and frosted, c1928, wheel-cut "R. LALIQUE FRANCE," Marcilhac 445, No. 1033........... **865.00**

6-1/4" h, Gui, cased, opalescent, blue patina, c1943, stenciled "R. LALIQUE FRANCE," Marcilhac 424, No. 948............ **800.00**

6-1/2" h, Biches, clear and frosted, sepia patina, c1932, engraved "R. Lalique France," Marcilhac 456, No. 1082............... **980.00**

6-1/2" h, Formose, cased, opalescent yellow, sepia patina, c1924, molded "R. LALIQUE," Marcilhac 425, No. 934 .. **3,220.00**

6-1/2" h, Formose, emerald green, c1924, engraved "R. Lalique France, No. 934," Marcilhac 425, No. 934 .... **5,250.00**

6-1/2" h, Ormeaux, clear and frosted, c1926, engraved "R. Lalique France," Marcilhac 435, No. 984 .... **630.00**

6-1/2" h, Ormeaux, opalescent, c1926, engraved "R. Lalique France," Marcilhac 435, No. 984 .... **490.00**

6-3/4" h, Albert, deep topaz, c1925, wheel-cut "R. LALIQUE," Marcilhac 430, No. 958 .... **1,955.00**

6-3/4" d, Gui, white opalescent, green patina, c1920, molded "R. LALIQUE," Marcilhac 427, No. 948 .... **800.00**

6-3/4" d, Gui, white opalescent, gray patina, c1920, molded "R. LALIQUE," Marcilhac 427, No. 948 .... **630.00**

7" h, Druides, opalescent, green patina, c1924, molded "R. LALIQUE," Marcilhac 425, No. 937 .... **1,485.00**

7" h, Koudour, clear, black enamel highlights, c1926, engraved "R. Lalique France," molded "R. LALIQUE," Marcilhac 432, No. 968 .... **6,900.00**

7" h, Laurier, opalescent, c1922, wheel-cut "R. LALIQUE FRANCE," engraved "947," Marcilhac 427, No. 427 .... **1,355.00**

7" h, St. Franciois, clear and opalescent, c1930, stenciled "R. LALIQUE FRANCE," Marcilhac 450, No. 1055 .... **2,070.00**

7-1/4" h, Amiens, opalescent, c1929, wheel-cut "R. LALIQUE," Marcilhac 443, No. 1023 .... **1,840.00**

7-1/4" h, Oursin, molded as sea urchin, clear and frosted, c1935, stenciled "R. LALIQUE," Marcilhac 442, No. 10-888........ **1,840.00**

7-1/4" h, Quatre Panneaux, clear and frosted, sepia patina, c1928, stenciled "R. LALIQUE FRANCE," Marcilhac 469, No. 10-920 .... **1,485.00**

7-1/2" h, Myrrhis, topaz, c1926, molded "R. LALIQUE," Marcilhac 435, No. 983 .... **1,485.00**

7-1/2" h, Ornis, clear and frosted, gray patina, c1926, wheel-cut "R. LALIQUE FRANCE," Marcilhac 434, No. 966 .... **1,725.00**

7-1/2" h. St. Tropez, opalescent, c1937, stenciled "R. LALIQUE FRANCE," Marcilhac 467, No. 10-915............... **1,150.00**

8" h, Aras, clear and frosted, c1922, molded "R. LALIQUE," Marcilhac 421, No. 919, neck reduced **380.00**

8" h, Tourbillons, clear, black enameled highlights, c1926, wheel-cut "R. LALIQUE," Marcilhac 433, No. 973.......... **40,250.00**

8-1/4" h, Grimperaux, pale smokey topaz, geometric bands of birds on branches, powdery white patina, slighted flared, six feet, c1926, engraved "R. Lalique," inscribed "No. 987," M 987 .... **1,495.00**

8-1/4" h, Plumes, cased opalescent, c1920, engraved "Lalique," molded "R. LALIQUE," Marcilhac 427, No. 944........... **1,100.00**

8-3/8" h, Plumes, raised rim, sloped shoulder tapering to base, molded plumes in low relief in opalescent glass, raised "R. LALIQUE" on base, Marcilhac 944, rim cut down **980.00**

8-1/2" h, Domremy, opalescent, c1926, engraved "R. Lalique France," Marcilhac 435, No. 979 .... **960.00**

8-1/2" h, Domremy, opalescent with sepia patina, c1926, engraved "R. Lalique France No. 979," Marcilhac 434, No. 979........... **1,840.00**

8-1/2" h, Domremy, topaz, sepia patina, c1926, stenciled "R. LALIQUE," Marcilhac 434, No. 979 .... **2,615.00**

8-3/4" h, Languedoc, clear and frosted, sepia patina, c1932, engraved "R. Lalique France," Marcilhac 443, No. 1041 . **5,750.00**

9" h, Boreno, clear and frosted, blue enameled highlights, c1930, wheel-cut "R. LALIQUE FRANCE," Marcilhac 450, No. 1056 . **2,070.00**

9" h, Borrome, clear and frosted, sepia patina, c1928, engraved "R. Lalique France," Marcilhac 422, No. 1017.............. **2,300.00**

9" h, Epicea, clear and frosted, gray patina, c1923, molded "R. LALIQUE," wheel-cut "FRANCE," Marcilhac 421, No. 921 ... **980.00**

9" h, Poissons, cased red glass, c1921, engraved "Lalique," molded "R. LALIQUE," Marcilhac 422, No. 925.......... **14,850.00**

9-1/4" h, Malesherbes, opalescent, gray patina, c1928, stenciled "R. LALIQUE," Marcilhac 432, No. 10-14 .... **1,485.00**

9-1/2" h, Bands des Roses, clear and frosted, sepia patina, c1919, molded "R. LALIQUE" with extended L, Marcilhac 419, No. 910 . . . . **1,840.00**

9-1/2" h, Ceylan, opalescent, c1924, wheel-cut "R. LALIQUE FRANCE," Marcilhac 418, No. 905 . . **6,000.00**

9-1/2" h, Martinets, clear and frosted, c1970, engraved "Lalique France" **855.00**

9-1/2" h, Perruches, clear and frosted, c1919, molded "R. LALIQUE," Marcilhac 410, No. 876 . . . . **2,870.00**

9-3/4" h, Ecailles, deep topaz, c1932, stenciled "R. LALIQUE FRANCE," M 456, No. 1080 . . . . **3,450.00**

10" h, Perruches, cased opalescent, blue patina, c1919, molded "R. LALIQUE," Marcilhac 410, No. 876 . . . . **6,400.00**

10" h, Royat, flared, colorless, rim tabs, raised ribs of triangular chains frosted and polished, c1936, base inscribed "Lalique" in script, nicks, M 10-921 . . . . **290.00**

10-1/2" h, Sauterelles, grasshoppers perched on waving blades of grass, clear and frosted, blue and green patina, c1912, engraved "R. Lalique," Marcilhac 414, No. 888 . . . . **7,475.00**

11" h, Camargue, clear and frosted, sepia patina, c1943, engraved "Lalique France," Marcilhac 472, No. 10-937 . . . . **4,025.00**

11-1/2" h, Davos, amber, c1932, engraved "R. Lalique," M 455, No. 1079 . . . . **3,775.00**

Wall mirror, 25-1/2" w, 33" h, Entrelacs, clear, gilded highlights, nickel-plated metal frame, 1951, Marcilhac 259, G, with assembly hardware **20,125.00**

Water glass

4-7/8" h, Jaffa, ribbed cylindrical form, frosted cactus motifs, inscrolled "Lalique France" on base, Marchilac 3680, price for set of 12 . . . . **920.00**

5" h, Reims, Art Deco, clear and frosted, base with zig-zag frieze, c1942, stenciled "R. LALIQUE FRANCE," Marcilhac 771, No. 3426, price for set of 10 . **1,045.00**

Wine cooler, 10" h, St. Emilion, clear and frosted, engraved "R. Lalique France," Marcilhac 472, No. 10-939 . . . . **1,150.00**

Wine glass

4-1/8" h, Arbois, clear, c1937, acid stamp "R. LALIQUE," Marcilhac 5363 . . . . **100.00**

5" h, Bourgueil, clear, c1930, acid stamp "R. LALIQUE," Marcilhac 5200 . . . . **100.00**

5" h, Monogramme, clear, black enamel for SH, c1924, Marcilhac 831, No. 5045, made for Rene Lalique's daughter Suzanne's wedding to Paul Haviland, 1924 . . . . **1,610.00**

7-1/2" h, Hagueneau, Art Deco, clear, c1924, stenciled or engraved "R. LALIQUE FRANCE," Marcilhac 829, No. 5022, set of 12 . . **2,300.00**

Lamps and Lighting

History: Lighting devices have evolved from simple stone-age oil lamps to the popular electrified models of today. Aimé Argand patented the first oil lamp in 1784. Around 1850, kerosene became a popular lamp-burning fluid, replacing whale oil and other fluids. In 1879, Thomas A. Edison invented the electric light, causing fluid lamps to lose favor, and creating a new field for lamp manufacturers. Companies like Tiffany and Handel became skillful at manufacturing electric lamps, and their decorators produced beautiful bases and shades.

References: James Edward Black (ed.), *Electric Lighting of the '20s-'30s* (1988, 1993 value update), *Volume 2 with Price Guide* (1990, 1993 value update), L-W Book Sales; John Campbell, *Fire & Light in the Home Pre 1820,* Antique Collectors' Club, 1999; J. W. Courter, *Aladdin Collectors Manual & Price Guide #19,* published by author (3935 Kelley Rd, Kevil, KY 42053), 2000; —, *Aladdin, the Magic Name in Lamps, Revised Edition,* published by author, 1997; *Electric Lighting of the '20s-'30s, Vol. 1* (1994, 1998 value update), *Vol 2, (1994),* L-W Book Sales, Carole Goldman Hibel, John Hibel, John Fontaine, *The Handel Lamps Book,* Fontaine Publishers, 1999; Donald B. Johnson and Leslie Pina, *1930s Lighting: Deco & Traditional by Chase,* Schiffer Publishing, 2000; Richard Miller and John Solverson, *Student Lamps of the Victorian Era,* Antique Publications, 1992, 1992-93 value guide; Herb Millman and John Dwyer, *Art Deco Lighting,* Schiffer Publishing, 2001; Jo Ann and Francis Thomas, *Early Twentieth Century Lighting Fixtures,* Collector Books, 1999; Jo Ann Thomas, *Early Twentieth Century Lighting Fixtures: Selections from the R. Williamson Lamp Catalog,* Collector Books, 1999; —, *Lighting Figures of the Depression Era,* Collector Books, 2000; Catherine M. V. Thuro, *Oil Lamps,* Wallace-Homestead, 1976, 1998 value update; —, *Oil Lamps II,* Collector Books, 1983, 2000 value update; John J. Wolfe, *Brandy, Balloons & Lamps: Ami Argand, 1750-1803,* South Illinois University Press, 1999; *Pairpoint Lamp Catalog: Shade Shapes Ambero through Panel; Pairpoint Lamp Catalog: Shade Shapes Papillon through Windsor & Related Material,* Schiffer Publishing, 2001.

Periodicals and Internet Resources: *International Guild of Lamp Researchers,* http://www.dapllc.com/lampguild; *Light Revival,* 35 West Elm Ave., Quincy, MA 02170; http://www.aladdincollector.com; http://www.lavaworld.com; http://www.oillamp.com.

Collectors' Clubs: Aladdin Knights of the Mystic Light, 3935 Kelley Rd, Kevil, KY 42053, http://www.aladdinknights.org; Historical Lighting Society of Canada, P.O. Box 561, Postal Station R, Toronto, Ontario M4G 4El, Canada; Incandescent Lamp Collectors Association, Museum of Lighting, 717 Washington Place, Baltimore, MD 21201; International Coleman Collectors Club, 2282 W Caley Ave., Littleton, CO 80120, http://www.colemancollectors.com; Night Light, 38619 Wakefield Ct, Northville, MI 48167; Rushlight Club, Inc., 260 Maryland Ave., NE, Washington, DC 20002, http://www.rushlight.org.

Museums: American Sign Museum, Cincinnati, OH; Kerosene Lamp Museum, Winchester Center, CT; Pairpoint Lamp Museum, River Edge, NJ.

Astral

America, 19th C, 22" h, cut and acid-etched shade, 22 star and quatrefoil design cut prisms, brass front, brass fluted standard, stepped brass and marble base, minor dents to font, chips to marble **1,610.00**

America, 19th C

23" h, acid-etched shade, foliate standard ending in stepped marble base, electrified, minor imperfections **460.00**

26-1/2" h, acid-etched globe, gilt brass lotus font hung with prisms above overlay shaft cut ruby to clear, stepped marble base, electrified **865.00**

Cornelius & Co., Philadelphia, 24" h, patent date April 18, 1845, marble base, later blue rimmed wheel cut and acid finish shade, electrified, gilt wear, minor base chips **635.00**

Boudoir

Aladdin

14-1/2" h, 8" d, reverse painted bell shade, pine border, floral molded polychromed metal base . . **225.00**

G-16, Alacite **500.00**

Cut glass, 9" h, mushroom shade, flared base, sunburst design . . . **400.00**

Danse De Lumiere, 11" h, molded glass figure of woman with outstretched arms, bearing stylized feather drapery, oval platform base with internal light fixture, molded title and patent mark, c1930, mold imperfections **400.00**

French, 11" d, 6" d, weighted brass base, crystal glass paneled insert, brass emb leaves and berries, rod curving upward holding night light, brass chains, and mounts, glass night light, holds candle **215.00**

Handel, 14-1/2" h, 8" d ribbed glass domed shade with squared scalloped rim, obverse painted with snowy winter scene, pastel yellow orange sky, sgd "Handel 5637" on rim, raised on bronzed metal tree trunk base, threaded Handel label **3,335.00**

Lady, sitting, with flowers, fired-on pink **95.00**

Lady with Harp, fired-on blue. . **125.00**

Mushroom, attributed to Pairpoint, obverse painted, Moorish-style dec, highlighted with clusters of pink and green roses, textured ground, stamped "Patented April 29th, 1913," brass and metal mount with two handles, chip to base of shade, 14" h, 14" d **690.00**

Pairpoint, 14" h, 7-1/4" linen-fold style shade, reverse painted repeated motifs of colorful parrots on yellow ground, stamped "Pairpoint" in large gold caps, green patina base marked "Pairport, C3064," two frosty chips on shade **1,300.00**

Phoenix, 14" h, 8" reverse painted shade, brilliant yellow and orange, green trees, blue and orange mountains, pr. **850.00**

Southern Belle

- Fired-on blue. **115.00**
- Fired-on pink. **115.00**

Chandelier

Art glass, Italy, 20th C, round brass ceiling mount with link chain suspending shaped center standard conjoining three extending curved arms supporting upright bell-form shades with ring and ruffled ribbed pendants, leaf and flower-form inserts in opalescent quilted glass, transparent glass highlights, 26" h (excluding chain), 21" d **460.00**

Arts & Crafts, early 20th C, 20" d, 22-1/2" total drop, four conical riveted and pierced shade caps, metal strapwork housing four curved butterscotch white striated slag glass panels, round domed ceiling pan with hammered textured copper patina, suspending four chains terminating in four metal shades, one panel cracked, wear to patina **700.00**

Bradley & Hubbard, 25" d, hand beaten curled heavy brass frame, six caramel colored bent slag glass panels, 19" of heavy brass chain and mounting. **980.00**

Leaded glass, 22-1/2" d, 11" h, cone shade with hexagonal segments of striated green and amber slag glass, large drop apron with irregular border, highlighted by bright red and orange striated glass stylized flowers on curvilinear green and caramel ground, three-light fixture, unsigned, few cracked segments **500.00**

Mosaic Company, 13-1/2" h, sq caramel crown over green medallion with extended ribbon scrolling, green leaf apron, caramel background **350.00**

Muller Fres, 23" d, 42" h, one center and three side bell-form shades of mottled orange, yellow, and blue, each marked "Muller Fres Luneville," black wrought iron ceiling mount with elaborate foliage dec framework, minor chip on side rims **1,500.00**

Steuben, Corning, NY

- Five shade mounts, bell-form gold luster glass shades, gold hearts and threading, gold Aurene int., silver fleur-de-lis acid stamp, domed brass ceiling mount, chain drop supporting fixture, raised leaf dec, 19" d, 39-1/2" drop, chips to some top rims **1,265.00**
- Round domed fixture with etched curvilinear and floral motifs, extensions suspending six bell-form glass shades with ruffled rims, creamy white luster and pulled gold Aurene striations on rims, gold Aurene int., circular domed ceiling mount, three chain drops, silver fleur-de-lis acid stamp, 20-1/2" d, 23" drop, dents on shade mounts. **6,325.00**

Unknown maker

- Leaded, closed domed bottom of cream to butterscotch leaded glass, bright gold finish band with row of beading, upper section with additional brickwork segments with applied metal lyre, four layers of dark red glass, top band with leaf dec in bright gold **1,385.00**
- 15" d reverse painted shade, 23" h, eight panels of five-petal blue flowers with red centers, leaves painted with pink veins hang from top of panels, ornate hanger dec with ribbons and leaves . . . **750.00**

Shieldon Swirl, 8-3/4" h, blue opalescent font, clear base, two small chips and roughness under base, **$350.** *Photo courtesy Green Valley Auctions Inc.*

Desk

Austrian, 17" h, closed top teardrop opal green irid shade with Loetz-type papillon surface and spiraled gold threading, single socket base with ribbed foliate cast motif, base marked "Rose Bros. & Co., Lancaster, PA" **1,500.00**

Bradley & Hubbard, 13" h, 8-1/2" d adjustable tilt shade, narrow ribbed panels, reverse painted green, blue, and brown Arts and crafts border motif, single socket metal base **460.00**

Emeralite, NY, c1916, 13" h, 8-7/8" l, flared glass shade with allover textured etched floral motif, high areas painted light mauve, lower int. painted with green, blue, yellow, and red scrolled foliate band on russet ground, raised on adjustable metal frame, standard on weighted sq metal base, raised foliage dec, metal manufacturer's tag, minor patina spotting on base **1,100.00**

Handel

- 14" h, 10" w, orig chipped ice dec opal shade, floral etched pattern, sgd "Handel, No. 6573" . . **1,300.00**
- 15" h, 8" flared glass cylindrical shade, green textured surface cased to reflective opal white,

marked "Mosserine Handel 6010," adjustable bronzed metal weighted base, threaded Handel label on felt liner 1,380.00

Student

21-1/2" h, Harvard style, heavy brass, weighted iron base, modern cased green 6-1/2" d shade, marked "P.E.G. 423" 300.00

22" h, double, brass frame, electrified, cased green shades 605.00

23-1/2" h, brass frame and adjustable arm, white glass shade, early 20th C 260.00

Tiffany Studios

13-1/2" h, 7" d swirl dec irid green ribbed dome Damascene shade cased to white, marked "L.C.T" on rim, swivel-socket bronze harp frame, rubbed cushion platform, five ball feet, imp "Tiffany Studios New York 419" 3,750.00

Tiffany Studios, 17-1/2" h, 7" d swirl dec irid green cased dome Damascene shade, marked "L.C.T. Favrile," swivel-socket dark patina bronze harp frame with baluster shaft, ribbed cushion platform, five ball feet, imp "Tiffany Studios New York 7907" 4,025.00

Tiffany Studios, 18" h, 10-1/2" d gold irid Steuben bell shade, swivel socket dark etched bronze wide harp frame, adjustable shaft above leaf and petal base, imp "Tiffany Studios New York 569" . . 1,100.00

Tiffany Studios, 18-1/4" h, 10-1/4" w, later molded, textured striated butterscotch and white glass domed shade with radiating tile motif, adjustable swivel socket, harp frame, trumpet shaped shaft and base, ribbed and fringe details in relief, dark brown and green patina, imp "Tiffany Studios New York 613" on base, some corrosion spots 2,185.00

Early American

Banquet

20-1/2" h, blue cut to clear overlay punty font, matching standard, double stop marble base, collar missing, font has been drilled 3,550.00

28-1/2" h, 10" d floral etched ruby ball shade, brass, sgd "The Rochester Company," electrified 500.00

28-3/4" h, 10" d reverse frosted gold dec ball shade sgd "Baccarat" on fitter, artist sgd "Beaucaire," brass font shell sgd "Miller," spelter stem and foot, electrified 700.00

37-1/2" h, Monarch, yellow cased font and baluster stem, slightly lighter yellow cased ball shade, brass connector and pieced foot, Consolidated Lamp & Glass Co., electrified through base . . . 700.00

Blown, colorless, 10" h, drop burners, pressed stepped base, chips on base, pr 385.00

Hand, 2-7/8" h, Hobbs Glass Co., Snowflake pattern, cranberry ground, white opalescent pattern, applied clear handle 550.00

Hour glass, 7" h, clear blown glass, pine and oak frame, whittled baluster posts, old brown finish, glued break in bottom plate 275.00

Lace maker's

10" h, free blown, clear, cut circles ring font 325.00

17-1/2" h, cranberry thumbprint shade, electrified brass base, multiple small dents on base 170.00

Parlor

13" h, white opaque, base and shade emb with dec flowers on stippled panels, burner electrified 120.00

16" h, white opaque four panel base and shade, transfer floral dec, hand colored red and blue, electrified through burner. . . 75.00

Peg

6-1/2" h, acid cut-back purple floral and leaf, clear background . 45.00

8" h, blue satin shading dark to light, 10 bulging panels, each with fleur-de-lis, frosted swirled rib ruffle top shade 90.00

15" h, amber irid Loetz type, random applied threading, period brass push-up candlesticks, cream irid shades with random crackled surface, one shade damaged, other with chip, price for pr 300.00

16-1/2" h, cranberry cut to clear, two rows of thumbprints, attached to period brass beehive push-up candlestick, cranberry shade with white threading around rim 200.00

Stem, Optic Opalescent Seaweed, 9" h, cranberry opalescent font, clear stem and base, orig burner 1,300.00

Floor

Bradley and Hubbard, 56" h, 7" d, small domed leaded glass shade, green slag glass, gold key border, open framework adjustable standard, domed circular foot 400.00

Duffner & Kimberly, 28-1/2" d leaded shade, Red Poppy pattern, large red blossoms in striated and wavy glass, variegated green and white foliage, purple background, Duffner & Kimberly bronze senior floor base, shade sgd "Duffner & Kimberly of New York" 72,800.00

Handel, harp base, bronze finish, two parrots on yellow ground shade, sgd "Handel #7073 G A". 8,000.00

Tiffany

55" h, 9-1/2" d linenfold shade, 12-sided etched bronze shade #1936 with panels of gold-amber favrile fabrique glass, swing socket harp base, tripod legs, spade feet, shade and base imp "Tiffany Studios New York," bronze base hammered "423" 1,380.00

Dogwood flowers on irregular shaped border, pale pink and light blue panels, yellow-green background, orig cap, shade sgd vertically "Tiffany Studios New York" 89,500.00

Tiffany/Aladdin, 50" h, 10" d spun bronze shade, reflective white int., marked "Tiffany Studios New York," adjustable bridge lamp base with Arabian Nights motif, orig dark bronze patina, elaborate platform base, stamped "Tiffany Studios New York 576" 2,990.00

Wilkinson, 64" h, 24" d leaded domed shade, opal white segments banded by wide border of multicolored and shaded blossoms with buds rising through brickwork and around top rim, elaborate five-socket ribbed floor base with medial leaves, stepped lappet bordered platform 7,200.00

Fluid, America, 19th C

8" h, pressed, Loop pattern, vaseline, hexagonal standard, tiered hexagonal base, attributed to New England, 19th C, minor imperfections. 415.00

8" h, pressed, three-printie block pattern, vaseline, knop and paneled hexagonal base, attributed to New England, 19th C, minor imperfections 375.00

9-1/4" h, 4-1/4" w, pressed, cobalt blue, arched faceted font, hexagonal tiered standard, hexagonal base, attributed to

New England, 19th C, minor imperfections.............. **3,150.00**

9-5/8" h, cut, amethyst glass font cut with oval and vesica cut designs, brass column standard, sq marble base, New England, 19th C, scratches.... **520.00**

9-5/8" h, pressed, low relief swans and reeds around colorless font, yellow-green swan form standard, stepped hexagonal base, Atterbury, base imp "pat. Sept 29, 1868," base cracked.................. **290.00**

10" h, cut double overlay, cobalt blue cut to white to clear, oval and circle cut designs on font, ring-turned brass standard and marble base, small chips to marble, gilt dec worn....... **460.00**

10-3/4" h, cut double overlay, pink cut to clear cut to white, punty, oval, and slash cut designs on font, standard, and base, attributed to New England, 19th C, crack on standard......... **550.00**

10-3/4" h, molded horizontal ribbed glass, white loop swirl within colorless font, fluted brass standard, sq stepped marble and brass base, New England, 19th C **865.00**

11" h, cut double overlay, cobalt blue cut to clear cut to white, quatrefoil, punty, and oval cut designs on font, standard, and base, attributed to New England, 19th C............ **1,610.00**

11-1/2" h, colorless pressed pattern, prism and flattened sawtooth pattern font, faceted standard, octagonal base, New England, 19th C, minor flaws from mold, price for pr............ **490.00**

Fluid, colorless, wide loop panels, handle with curl, replaced chimney, **$95**

12-1/8" h, cut double overlay, opaque pink cut to white cut to clear, round punty cut designs, leafy gilt bronze molded standard, sq stepped marble base, New England, 19th C, patination worn **490.00**

12-1/4" h, cut overlay, white cut to clear, gilt outlined quatrefoil, oval, star, and vesica cut designs, opaque white fluted pressed glass standard, baroque base, New England, 19th C, gilt wear . **635.00**

12-5/8" h, cut overlay, ruby cut to clear, pinwheel, quatrefoil, and punty cut designs, ribbed clambroth glass baroque standard and base, New England, 19th C **1,380.00**

12-3/4" h, cut overlay, cobalt blue cut to white to clear, oval, circle, and star cut designs, fluted brass standard, stepped brass and marble base, small chips to marble base **520.00**

12-3/4" h, colorless pattern glass with bull's eyes, painted brass standard on stepped marble base, emb brass band, gilt embellishments, minor wear. **460.00**

12-3/4" h, cut overlay, white cut to clear, Washington cut, oval cut designs, fluted opalescent fluted standard, sq stepped base, New England, 1860-87, imperfections **275.00**

13" h, cut overlay, opaque white cut to ruby font, punty vesicas, and oval cut designs, fluted brass standard, stepped marble base, New England, 19th C, minor imperfections.. **1,150.00**

13" h, pressed, Diamond Thumbprint pattern, colorless, ribbed gilt brass standard, marble base, brass collars and burners, New England, mid-19th C, minor imperfections, price for pr **1,035.00**

13" h, pressed, double punty and rib colorless font, wheel-cut dec, blue opal faceted baroque base, New England, 19th C, minor imperfections.... **690.00**

13" h, 6" d, cut double overlay, white overlay cut to ruby font, punty and elongated oval cut designs, clear wafer, clambroth pressed glass reeded standard, baroque base with gilt accents, attributed to Boston & Sandwich Glass Co., Sandwich, MA, second half 19th C, hairline cracks, gilt wear, flaws **460.00**

13-1/4" h, cut overlay, cranberry cut to clear, oval cutting on font, brass fluted standard with stepped brass and marble base, small chips to marble base **550.00**

13-1/4" h, cut overlay, transparent green cut to clear, floral and vine gilt band, punty and oval cut design, octagonal opal fluted standard, sq base with gilt borders attributed to Boston & Sandwich Glass Co., Sandwich, MA, 1860-70, minor gilt wear **1,035.00**

13-1/4" h, cut overlay, white cut to cranberry, oval, star, and quatrefoil cut design, reeded brass standard, stepped brass and marble base, tiny chips to marble base **865.00**

13-1/2" h, blown and pressed, colorless, conical blown font cut with strawberry diamonds, fans, blaze, and vesicas above 13 panels, joined by bladed knop and two wafers to a hollow knop stem with cut printies, joined to cut corner stepped base by bladed knop and two wafers, pewter and base burner, New England, second quarter 19th C, minor imperfections, price for pr **1,150.00**

13-5/8" h, pressed, colorless faceted diamond petal pattern, wheel cut dec, opaque lavender ribbed stand, baroque base, New England, 19th C **920.00**

13-3/4" h, cut double overlay, opaque ruby cut to white cut to clear, quatrefoil punty, and oval cut designs, opaque white ribbed standard, fluted baroque base, New England, 19th C, worn gilt accents **1,150.00**

13-7/8" h, opaque white font, gilt leafy scroll dec, clambroth baroque base with gold accents, New England, 19th C, one shallow chip under base **460.00**

17" h, 7" d, cut overlay, white cut to clear font, petal, leaf, and vine cut designs, foliate brass ring, white cut to clear glass standard with elongated oval and punty designs, mercury flash int. on circular acorn and oak leaf design molded brass base, attributed to Boston & Sandwich Glass Co., Sandwich, MA, 19th C....... **1,265.00**

Hanging

American, 19th C

18" h, patinated metal and cut glass, hall type, candle socket, Gothic arches, diamonds and flowerheads dec.................. **1,380.00**

23" h, clear blown glass, hall type, elaborate wheel cut dec of birds and deer in landscape, foliate devices, pressed brass mounts **2,415.00**

Arts and Crafts, brass washed metal, four lanterns, hammered amber glass **1,000.00**

Candle, 12" w, 6-1/2" h heavy blue opaline shade, fancy gold trim, pearl like jewel highlights, fancy stamped brass chains and canopy, outside of body satinized, glossy bottom protruding disk, some wear to gold trim **400.00**

Cranberry, glossy cranberry shade, white enameled Arabesque dec, mounted in yellow brass frame with satinized vertically ribbed cranberry and white spatter font shell and drop in font, white milk glass smoke bell with cranberry edge. **2,250.00**

Handel, 10" d, hall type, spherical form, acid cut, translucent white, brown, vase and foliate dec, ornate orig hardware **4,200.00**

Satin glass, blue Diamond Quilted mother of pearl shade mounted in jeweled brass frame, cobalt blue edged white milk glass smoke bell . . **3,500.00**

Steuben, 13" w, 6-1/2" d, gold calcite dome, large star cut center, orig rim and chains, unsgd. **1,100.00**

Tiffany, 18" l, 15" d, attributed to Tiffany Glass and Decorating Co., late 19th C, square green and opalescent diamond-shaped glass jewels arranged as central pendant chandelier drop, twisted wire frame. **2,990.00**

Lantern

15-1/4" h, hexagonal, six acid-etched glass panels mounted in black painted tin Gothic frame, supporting single candle socket, clear glass panels at bottom, hanging chain and hook at top, America, 19th C **320.00**

Oil (kerosene)

Acanthus Leaf, 12" h, jade green font, double stepped clambroth colored semi-opaque base, minor roughness, several small base chips **1,900.00**

Acorn and Drapery, 9-1/2" h, cut and frosted free blown font, three ring knob, pewter collar, stepped pressed base, New England Glass Works. **250.00**

Blackberry, 8" h, Boston and Sandwich **225.00**

Chapman, 8-1/4" h, clear, Atterbury & Co. **75.00**

Columbian Coin, 9-1/4" h, milk glass, Central Glass Co. **125.00**

Duncan Ribbed Band, two handles **90.00**

Gem, 7-1/2" h, clear font, amber pressed textured match striker panels on stem, Atterbury & Co. **150.00**

Hobnail, blue font, 4-1/2" h **120.00**

Hobbs' Optic, flat, finger **575.00**

Inverted Thumbprint and Fan, opalescent Coin Spot font, clear base, 8-1/2" h, flakes. **200.00**

Inverted Thumbprint and Prism stem, medium green, 9-1/2" h, normal flaking and roughness **130.00**

King Melon Optic Dot, opal white, finger grip handle, Crimp & Galfurid chimney. **155.00**

Little Beauty, orig label **60.00**

Loop, 9-1/4" h, flint, clear, slight roughness to base. **85.00**

Match holder base, vaseline, 8-1/2" h, 4-3/4" d foot, flake on corners . . **250.00**

Moon and Star, amber font, blue base, brass connector, attributed to Adams & Co., 11-3/4" h, flakes on step between stem and base, chip under base **120.00**

Optic, 8-7/8" h, silver stained band, frosted leaves and flowers, Beaumont Glass Works, Bellaire, OH. **285.00**

Queen of Hearts, 8" h, clear font, medium green base, Dalzell, Gilmore & Leighton, Findlay, OH **275.00**

Ripley, two handles. **70.00**

Riverside Fern, 10" h, green font, clear base, paneled stem, round foot, emb beading underneath, Riverside Glass Works. **125.00**

Riverside Panel, 7-1/2" h, green font, clear base, Riverside Glass Co. **125.00**

Snowflake, cranberry opalescent, large **745.00**

Star, 8" h, clear font, amber base, Atterbury & Co., two flakes, minor mold roughness **65.00**

St. Louis, 10-1/2" h, amber font, clear base, brass connector, United States Glass Co., connector slightly bent **50.00**

Waffle and Thumbprint, 10-5/8" h, flint, clear, several small nicks **100.00**

Wave, 9-1/4" h, clear, panel base, marked "October 7, 1873," Atterbury & Co. **75.00**

Piano

Handel

9" h, 22" l, 7" d conical leaded glass shade with straight apron of green slag and granite glass segments arranged in geometric design, mounted to adjustable socket, curved "dog's leg" shaft above weighed lappet dec base imp "Handel". **1,265.00**

Handel, 15" h, 7" d leaded glass shell-shaped shade, three rows of overlapping green slag glass panels, base sgd "Handel" **1,235.00**

Tiffany, 6-3/4" h, 19" l tripartite gold amber glass turtleback shade, framed in bronze, three center gold irid turtleback tiles, single-socket swiveling "dog leg" shaft, shade and weighted base imp "Tiffany Studios New York" **4,025.00**

Table

Arts & Crafts, America, early 20th C, 24-3/4" h, 16-1/4" d octagonal oak framed shade insert with leaded glass panels of striated amber and pink glass, raised on four oak arms, lighted sq oak base with heart shaped cut-outs, filled with striated pink and amber slag glass inserts **625.00**

Bigelow and Kennard, Boston, early 20th C

19" h, 13-1/4" d domed leaded shade, fiery opal white brickwork above amber, slate blue, and white lappet border motif, converted fluid lamp font with three-arm spider inserted within Japonesque art pottery base with shaded pink, blue, green glaze, imp "600" **1,840.00**

22" h, 18" d domed leaded shade, red cluster gladiola blossoms, green leaf stalks, opal white glass segments, blue and mottled segments, rim tagged "Bigelow Studios Boston," and "Bigelow Kennard," three-socket stem shaft above ftd bronze platform base **3,740.00**

24" h, 18" d, hemispherical shade, upper shade with brown, green, and translucent white segments depicting leaves with amber border segments over graduating translucent white tile segments, above lower shade border of brown, green, and translucent white panels depicting pine cones and leaves, amber border segments, imp metal maker's tags, three-socket bronze base with fluted columnar shaft, sq base with sq feet, metal maker's tag on base, several cracked segments **4,025.00**

26" h, 18" d domed leaded shade, opalescent white segments in geometric progression border, brilliant green leaf forms repeating motif, edge imp "Bigelow Kennard Boston/Bigelow Studios," three socket over Oriental-style bronze base cast with foo dog handles, Japonesque devices. . . . **2,875.00**

Bradley & Hubbard

12" h, six-sided bent panel slag glass shade, brickwork frame, metal base with three owl shaft, "B & H" imp on base, shade labeled, damage to some panels and glass eyes **690.00**

21-1/2" h, 15" sq octagon shade, Prairie School, shade with geometric overlay on green and white slag glass panels with red squares, sgd on base and shade **1,150.00**

22" h, 20" d dome shaped leaded shade, caramel colored pieces in honeycomb pattern, rimmed at base, border of pink and ivory panels, framed with continuous double narrow green strip, base sgd "Bradley & Hubbard Mft. Co. Patent Applied For," brass finished pedestal with design of draped swags and medallions above raised leaves, wide paneled foot, raised rim, two or three panels with cracks. **1,600.00**

23-1/2" h, 18" d bent glass shade, eight emerald green slag panels, octagonal flame motif in green-black metal frame, two-socket black painted metal base with "B&H" triangular patent mark **575.00**

Classique, 22-1/2" h, 18" d, brilliantly colored sunset scene with trees, bell shaped shade, bronze six-sided base **1,350.00**

Duffner & Kimberly

20" h, 16" pyramid leaded shade, butterscotch, white, ink, and red flowers, green and white background with butterscotch highlights, simple stem with band design, circular foot with petal shapes rising from it, base sgd, two acorn pulls **3,360.00**

23" h, 19" d leaded geometric shade, strong green honeycomb sections, elongated caramel glass top border, orig three-socket base, orig patina **2,240.00**

26" h, 20" d Viking shade, shade sectioned into six segments by metal bands and faux rivets, bands join at top under ornate cap and finial with three bird heads, at base, bands end with mythological creature with large ears and extended tongue, leaded glass segments in reds, yellows, greens, two bands of royal purple and orange diamonds, mottled green glass overlapping scales on top, Gothic base with three graduating levels, 15 simulated talons that join together to form stem with faux rivets, three large creatures with tongues extended and teeth barred, three feet, shade sgd "The Duffner & Kimberly Co., New York," base sgd "516" **36,400.00**

26" h, 22" pyramid leaded shade, deep red poppy blossoms of rippled segments, background of blue-green foliage, lime green upper section, orig sgd base **20,720.00**

Gorham

Leaded shade, floral overlay design on shade and base, matching finial, four-socket Handel cluster base **4,480.00**

Leaded shade with bird, 22" h, 12" d red striated glass belly and head, outstretched brown wings, rippled green leaves, tan branch, knot base in orig patina **5,040.00**

Handel, Meriden, CT, early 20th C

15" h, 10" l, 5-1/2" d elongated oval glass shade, glossy irid int., ext. handpainted with colorful woodland scene with center bird in flight on front and back, sgd on rim "Handel 6427," mounted on integrated oval base with "Handel" threaded label. **5,462.00**

20" h, 12" d brilliant yellow shade with sunrise, green trees, reddish-orange accents, sgd "Handel, #4216," chip out of shade rim **1,350.00**

23" h, 17-7/8" d reverse painted dome shade, brilliant blue and red parrots among trees and wisteria blossoms, base cast with blossoming prunus branches, brown patina, shade painted "Handel 6874R". **22,000.00**

23" h, 18" d reverse painted shade, chipped ice finish, orange-yellow ground, panels of red, blue, and green foliate dec and leaves, 1" rim orange and red band, textured bronze finish base, shade sgd "Handel #7918". **2,000.00**

25" h, 18" d, eight panel bent glass shade of striated green and white slag glass with geometric tile metal overlay, dropped apron with grapevine overlay, three socket base with stylized Art Nouveau floral panel, bronze patinated metal base, raised "Handel" mark under base, imperfections **1,955.00**

Jefferson

21" h, 6" d, reverse painted shade, scenic woodland setting with dirt road, tall cypress trees, several grassy areas, pale purple sky, base marked "B2364". **1,800.00**

21-1/2" h, 18" d reverse painted shade with dark conifers lining banks of river, silhouetted against inverted peachblow sky, setting sun, baluster form base marked "Jefferson" on side of foot, replaced double sockets, shade unsigned **1,300.00**

Miller, 21" h, 16" reverse painted shade with setting sun, snowy country landscape on one side, obverse with stone bridge over stream with house, ext. with shadowing texturing on snowy areas, gold washed base marked "M L Co." **950.00**

Moe Bridges, 23" h, 18" d shaped domed reverse painted shade, expansive riverside landscape, sgd on lower rim "Moe Bridges Co. 186," orig gilt metal base, replaced sockets, worn finish **1,650.00**

Pairpoint, 18-3/4" h, Cologne shade, large purple and blue grape pods among fall leaves, base with applied flamed torches and bows on stem, unmarked shade, base attributed to Miller, marked "E. M. & Co." . . **1,300.00**

Pittsburgh

19" h, 14" d, obverse painted shade with jungle scene, sgd base **1,225.00**

21" h, 16" d obverse and reverse painted shade, three groupings of dark trees with rust-colored leaves painted on obverse, frame three pairs of swans on lake surrounded by green foliage, pale purple and blues on pond, eight lily pads on stem, flowers on foot, fine dark patina. **1,950.00**

21-1/2" h, 18" d, obverse and reverse painted shade, night scene of Indian encampment, teepee, and burning campfire, dugout canoe on riverbank, large conifers painted on obverse, darkened purple clouds painted on reverse, full yellow moon reflect on water, base with stylized flower and leaves on large gourd-shaped form with two handles **3,360.00**

Reverse painted, America, early 20th C

20-1/2" h, 16" d domed shade, painted on int. and ext. with fir trees

by lake at sunset, naturalistic colors, white metal two-light lamp fitting, elongated oval standard, stepped domed base, dark brown-gray patina, spotting to metal finish **750.00**

22-5/8" h, 16-3/4" d, domed hammered textured frosted yellow-green glass shade, reverse painted rim border of pink and purple tulip blossoms, filed of green grass, two-socket fixture with scrolled wrought iron shaft with applied painted iron flower dec, bronze and verdigris patina on bracketed square cast-iron base, imp "L 619" on base, minor chips to shade edge, imperfections **1,045.00**

24-3/4" h, 16-3/4" d, attributed to Jefferson Company, scenic, domed frosted shade with hammered metal textured surface, reverse painted with cottages on hillside, trees and footbridge overlooking water, case metal base with two-socket fixture, raised foliage, scroll, and floral motifs, bronze patina, rim nicks, patina wear **1,840.00**

Riviere Studios, attributed to, 26-1/2" h, 27-1/2" d paneled geometric shade, shaped base of striated green and white slag glass, metal overlay of pierced leaves on trailing vines overall, beaded and braid trim, four claw feet, green patina, four-socket fixture with wiring for illuminated base, wear, minor repairs. **2,300.00**

Sale M. Bros., America, early 20th C, 26-1/4" h, 18-1/4" domed shade with six caramel and green bent slag glass panels, embossed floral and foliate metal framework, two-socket fixture on baluster-shaped ribbed and embossed metal base with verdigris on black patina, raised maker's mark under base, patina wear, replaced finial **575.00**

Tiffany and Pittsburgh Lamp Co., 22-1/2" h, 16" d domed leaded shade, horizontal bands of lozenge shapes in pale amber and white among arched segments in mottled soft green and white, circular opalescent white glass jewel highlights, lozenge, "X" and brick border, imp metal tag reads "Tiffany Studios New York 1595," raised on Pittsburgh bronze owl base, few cracked segments, loose sockets **14,950.00**

Tiffany, 16" d Woodbine shade, dichroic segments, yellow, red, and streaks of purple leaves, confetti glass background, library base with orig patina, both shade and base sgd **30,250.00**

Unique Lamp Co.

23" h, 16" d leaded shade, border of yellow five-petal flowers with orange centers, dark green striated odd shaped leaves randomly placed, light green rows of rect glass segments, ftd base, pierced cap and ornate finial are later replacements **1,465.00**

27" h, 24" d leaded wisteria shade, irregular border formed by heavily laden purple-blue wisteria blossoms, striated glass almost white, clumps of partial flowers between full flowers in deeper shades, striated brown vines, tops of leaves streamed with sunlight are paler shades of peach, green, yellow, and cream, base case with knots and gnarls simulating bark, large foot, shade sgd "Handel" on tab, base with cloth "Handel Lamp" tag on felt, lamp sold in Nov of 2001, auctioneer believes shade was made by Unique, base crafted by Chicago Mosaic **13,440.00**

Unknown maker, 20" h, 18" d shade, flared out bottom with row of hexagonal cut glass, next row with large pink to red swirls set apart by deep green pieces of glass, four more rows of green and white striated segments, base foot with stylized swirls and cuts in metal, dark black to deep brown patina **900.00**

Wilkinson Co.

24-1/2" h, 18" d leaded dome, pink and white waterlily blossoms interspersed with green and red ripple glass leaves and buds, amber granite glass ground, three-socket cast bronze base with beaded lappet motif **3,450.00**

27-1/2" h, 20" d scalloped conical leaded glass shade, yellow centered pink and peach colored blossoms, green leaves bordering amber and green slag glass segments arranged in ladderwork progression, locking mechanism with three baluster shaft, bulbed turnings, stepped platform base, imp "Wilkinson Co/Brooklyn, NY" **3,220.00**

28" h, 28" d leaded conical shade, large scrolling apron, white, green, rose, and gold geometric design, highly decorative Wilkinson base **8,960.00**

31" h, 21" d leaded shade, yellow, red, and cream pond lilies, various shades of green lily pads, light blue glass segments as water, cattails interspersed as rough textured

Table, Tiffany, double bronze branches, each branch with three iridescent glass shades, central bronze stem hollowed on one side to accept separate candle snuffer (missing), base imp "Tiffany Studios 10456," each shade signed "LCT," minor roughness on shade bases, 15-1/2" h, 22" w, **$12,500.** *Photo courtesy of Joy Luke Fine Art Brokers and Auctioneers.*

brown-orange glass segments, top of shade ranges from cream, orange, and turquoise, four ftd base cast with water lilies and buds, stems, and cattail leaves rise up from base to three-light socket, acorn pulls, base sgd in two places 7,280.00

Williamson, Richard, & Co., Chicago, 25" h, 20" d peaked leaded glass dome, amber slag bordered by red tulips, pink and lavender-blue spring blossoms, green leaf stems, carved glass, mounted on four-socket integrated shaft with stylized tulip blossoms above leafy platform, imp "R. Williamson & Co./Washington & Jefferson Sts./Chicago, Ill," restored cap at top rim 3,220.00

Wall sconce

Bradley and Hubbard, wall mount bracket, sapphire blue expanded bull's eye shade 400.00

Bronze, 21-1/2" l, 5-3/4" h, curved two-arm wall fixtures with dark brown patina, supporting bell-form shades of irid amber cased with opalescent glass, five green and amber pulled feather designs, few chips on upper shade apertures 1,350.00

Lamp Shades

History: Lamp shades were made to diffuse the harsh light produced by early gas lighting fixtures. These early shades were made by popular Art Nouveau manufacturers including Durand, Quezal, Steuben, and Tiffany. Many shades are not marked.

Lamp shades offer a glass collector exciting shapes and colors. Many of the art glass and decorated shades make lovely cabinet pieces. Preservationists also seek period lamp shades as replacements for antique lighting fixtures.

References: Dr. Larry Freeman, *New Lights on Old Lamps,* American Life Foundation, 1984; Denys Peter Myers, *Gaslighting in America: A Pictorial Survey, 1815-1910,* Dover Publications, Inc., 1978; Jo Ann Thomas, *Early Twentieth Century Lighting Fixtures,* Collector Books, 1980.

Reproduction Alert: Lamp shades have been widely reproduced.

Aladdin, satin, white, dogwood dec 85.00

Art glass

3-5/8" h, 2-1/4" d aperture, Carder Steuben, bulbous, white with green body, gold dragged loop and gold border, fleur-de-lis paint stamp . 175.00

3-3/4" h, 2-1/4" d aperture, amber glass with irid gold, 10 ribbed bulbous shade, tapered and flared 115.00

3-3/4" h, 2-1/4" d aperture, King Tut drapery pattern on irid gold, attributed to Carder Steuben 490.00

4" d, white opal hobnails, blue ground, Fenton. 90.00

4" h, 10 ribbed bell form, flared ruffled rim, irid gold, attributed to Steuben, minor scratches 165.00

4-1/4" h, 10 ribbed bell form, flared ruffled rim, irid gold, attributed to Steuben, minor scratches 165.00

4-1/4" h, 2-1/8" d aperture, slightly paneled hexagonal irid gold body, white dragged loop dec 200.00

4-1/4" h, 2-1/8" d aperture, green dragged loop and gold border on white ground, attributed to Carder Steuben 375.00

4-1/2" h, 2" d aperture, tulip form, ribbed transparent green crown, opal feathering edged in bluish bold extending into greenish-gray opal, rim slightly scalloped, attributed to Tiffany, chip on fitter ring 950.00

4-1/2" h, 2-1/8" d aperture, shouldered form, ruffled rim, gold and white fishnet design on translucent gold ground 230.00

4-1/2" h, 2-1/4" d aperture, white and gold pulled feathers with green borders, irid gold ground, small fitter rim chips 230.00

4-1/2" h, 3-1/4" d, Tiffany Favrile, gold irid, fluted edge, sgd "L.C.T. Favrile," price for pr 2,915.00

4-5/8" h, 2-1/4" d aperture, bell form, green heart-shaped leaves, trailing vines, gold irid ground, price for pr 390.00

4-7/8" h, 2-1/8" d aperture, bulbous, green pulled feathers with gold borders, white ground. 150.00

5" h, 2" d aperture, irid gold, opal pulled feathers tipped in green, wrapped in golden threads, Lustre Art 300.00

5" l, 5" d, gold and black heart dec, ivory ground, random gold trailings, highly irid gold int., Durand, set of four 900.00

5-1/8" h, 2-1/8" d aperture, irid gold pulled feathers with brown borders 375.00

5-1/8" h, 2-1/4" d aperture, trumpet shape, gold dragged loop dec on white ground 175.00

5-1/4" h, 2" d, aperture, ribbed, irid bluish gold luster, one with smeared Steuben silver stamped logo, price for pr 550.00

5-1/4" h, 2-1/8" d outer rim, bell shape, 16 ribs, opal, gold int., rim marked "Luster Art," three-pc set. 250.00

5-1/4" h, 2-1/4" d aperture, Steuben, gold Aurene, unsigned 125.00

5-1/2" h, dark green, platinum feathers, gold lining, sgd "Quezal" 650.00

5-1/2" h, Zipper pattern, green pulled dec, opal ground, gold lining, Fostoria 225.00

5-1/2" h, 8-1/2" w, 4" d fitter ring, gas, frosted glass, ruffled six panel top, emb pattern of 15 vertical rows of banding separated by 15 vertical plain ribs, cranberry top edge, price for three-pc set 250.00

5-1/2" l, 6-1/4" w, 2-1/2" d fitter, green pulled feather, butterscotch loopings, white ruffled edge, gold int., unsigned Quezal, set of four. 600.00

6" h, 2" d outside rim, Bohemian, attributed to Loetz, bell form, gold papillon surface, green and red raised spots and vertical stripes 435.00

6" h, 2-1/8" d aperture, trumpet form, white pulled feather dec, irid gold ground, small minor fitter rim nicks, price for pr. 350.00

6" h, 2-1/4" d aperture, Steuben, gold Aurene, unsigned 145.00

6" h, 3" d fitter, bright yellow and fuchsia, clear frosted ground, cameo-etched floral cutting . . . 250.00

6" h, 3-1/4" fitter ring, gas, bands of white, yellow, and pink, sgd "Tartan Rd. No. 46498," registered by Henry Gething Richardson, Wordsley Flint Glass Works, near Stourbridge, Feb. 24, 1886 . . . . 285.00

7" h, Pairpoint, puffy, flower basket, reverse painted pink and yellow poppies and roses 425.00

8" h, long tapered ruffled bell form, intricate gold and green zipper pattern, gold irid int., Fostoria. 290.00

8-1/2" d, irid green oil spotting, ribbon work, white glass int., attributed to Loetz, c1900 . . . . 250.00

9" d, 4" fitter rim, Handel, round crackle glass gall, transfer printed Art Deco parrots, gilt metal and tassel mountings 635.00

9-1/2" h, gold Egyptian crackle, blue and white overlay, bulbous, ruffed rim, sgd "Durand" 225.00

Large Art Deco frosted lavender glass faceted ceiling fixture in the style of Ruba Rhombic, with jutting angles and incised ribs. Unmarked, 15" x 11", **$1,200.** *Photo courtesy of David Rago Auctions.*

10" d, tam o'shanter, handpainted green silhouette village scene with windmill and harbor, sgd "Handel 2862" **. 325.00**

14" d, Pairpoint, Saville design reverse painted shade, monochrome green, three sets of bird pairs amid scrolling foliate elements **1,840.00**

14-1/4" h, Muller Fres shade mounted in bronze luminere mount, France and America, 20th C, bronze male torso finial on shade mount suspending mottled yellow, orange, and purple glass shade inscribed "Muller Fres Luneville," bronze base, shade mount imp "Riddle Design pat. pend. Made in USA, 713" **1,035.00**

15" h, 6" d, Handel, tulip shape, caramel and green, soldered repair to base **600.00**

Ceiling

Arts & Crafts, early 20th C, shade 10-3/4" d, 19" drop, with metal domed shade cup over riveted conical shade with ruffled rims, four oval cut-outs supporting curved and textured white opalescent glass inserts, round domed cast iron ceiling mount with hammer textured surface, suspending chain supporting shade, cracks **690.00**

Degue, 13-5/8" d, ceiling type, Art Deco style geometric design, etched colorless glass, sgd "Degue," suspended on four cords, orig ceiling plate **575.00**

Macbeth Evans, 10" d drilled bowl, dogwood pattern, pink, frosted int. **150.00**

Leaded

12" d, 5" h, domed, segments of mottled green glass, metal rim tag reads "Tiffany Studios, New York 1411," few cracked segments.......... **5,750.00**

15-1/2" d, 35" drop, attributed to Tiffany Studios, NY, early 20th C, leaded glass shade with graduating quadrangular mottled green glass segments with medial band of stylized acorns in mottled yellow-green glass, beaded domed bronze ceiling mount issuing long cylindrical shaft with three-socket fixture, suspending three beaded chains supporting bronze shade mount with rope twist trim, unsigned, few cracked segments, some scratches to patina.................. **10,350.00**

16" d, 3-1/2" opening, attributed to Bigelow & Kennard, rose pink slag glass segments, green acorn shaped leaf on vine dec belt, areas of restoration **1,150.00**

16" d, 20" h, Pomegranate, three rows of light green mottled glass, wide row of repeating pomegranates, three pieces of yellow glass on bottom of each fruit, sgd with large "Tiffany Studios New York 1457" tag............. **8,960.00**

21" d, 14" h, attributed to Wilkinson, green, amber, and red, border of mottled brown, orange and red, some small fractures in panel **350.00**

22" d, 9-1/2" h, conical leaded dome, white opalescent brickwork segments above and below border of repeating red amber ripple glass pine cones, shaded green needle leaves, yellow border glass, rim tag "Bigelow Kennard Boston Studios," four border glass segments broken out........ **2,760.00**

23" d, 16" h, A. Hart, shade composed of 11 segments, yellow-green glass background, more than 100 purple, blue, and pink flowers with yellow centers, odd-shaped cream pieces of glass form irregular top border, 11 pieces of chunk glass form last row, sgd "A. Hart" **2,300.00**

24-1/2" d, 5-1/4" h, broad parasol shape, 32 tapered panels in Prairie School manner, rim tag "Bigelow Kennard Boston," small split in metal rim **1,610.00**

25" d, 15" h, standard globe, curtain border apron with 48 vertical rows of quadrangular, rippled butterscotch glass, band of repeating design of seven pieces of glass, blue-gray glass used as next interlocking border, rest of shade with rippled butterscotch segments, pierced cap with decorative finial, orig hanging hardware, sgd "Tiffany Studios, New York" . **22,400.00**

25-1/4" d, 11-1/2" h, attributed to John Morgan and Sons, NY, early 20th C, shade composed of striated green, amber, and white slag glass segments and round transparent purple "jewels" against striated caramel and white slag glass ground, verdigris bronze leaves surrounding ceiling hook suspending four chains supporting six-socket domed shade, similar bronze leaf dec, dropped apron, few cracked segments **8,500.00**

26" d, 14" h, attributed to Wilkinson, conical, raised amber slag grown and brickwork shoulder above wide colorful border of grape clusters, puffed bend glass apples, pears, peaches, and figures of birds **690.00**

27" d 14" h, attributed to New York maker, bunches of pale purple grapes and green leaves, irregular shaped border, some vines worked in metal, imp crown of metal grape leaves rises 4" about shade............ **3,920.00**

Smoke bell

3" h, 4" w, white milk glass, aqua blue edge, metal loop **75.00**

4" h, 4-1/4" w, white milk glass, medium blue edge, metal loop **85.00**

6-3/4" h, 5-3/4" w, white milk glass, forest green edge, applied milk glass loop, some smoke staining **50.00**

7-1/4" h, 6-1/2" w, white milk glass, blue edge, applied milk glass loop ... **95.00**

LIBBEY GLASS

1896–1906

History: Edward Libbey established the Libbey Glass Company in Toledo, Ohio, in 1888 after the New England Glass Works of W. L. Libbey and Son closed in East Cambridge, Massachusetts. The new Libbey company produced quality cut glass which today is considered to belong to the American Brilliant Period.

In 1930, Libbey's interest in art-glass production was renewed, and A. Douglas Nash was employed as a designer in 1931.

The factory continues production today as Libbey Glass Co.

References: Carl U. Fauster, *Libbey Glass Since 1818-Pictorial History & Collector's Guide,* Len Beach Press, 1979; Bob Page and Dale Frederickson, *Collection of American Crystal*, Page-Frederickson Publishing, 1995; Kenneth Wilson, *American Glass 1760-1930*, 2 vols., Hudson Hills Press and The Toledo Museum of Art, 1994.

Manufacturer: Libbey Glass, One Sea Gate, Toledo, OH 43666.

Additional Listings: Amberina Glass and Cut Glass.

Art glass

Bell, 5-3/4" h, colorless, acid etched dec "1893 World's Fair," circular logo surrounded by acid-etched florals and banners, shoulder int. molded "1893 World's Columbian Xposition (sic)", twisted frosted handle with star at top, metal clapper **285.00**

Bonbon, 7" d, 1-1/2" h, amberina, shape #3029, six pointed 1-1/2" w fuchsia rim, shallow pale amber bowl, sgd **600.00**

Bowl

7" d, amberina, ruffled, flared rim, sgd.................. **350.00**

8-1/4" d, Wave pattern, scalloped rim, turned over ruby border, amberina body, three applied amber feet, acid stamped "Libbey" in circle, c1900.......... **450.00**

10" d, 4" h, amberina, fold down rim, sgd.................. **850.00**

11" d, 3-3/4" h, Cluthra, pink and crystal, numerous large pink bubbles, sgd **395.00**

12-1/2" d, black cut to colorless, sgd **1,250.00**

Bud vase, 9" h, elongated, ribbed, colorless **615.00**

Cologne bottle, 8-1/2" h, honey amber on nine optic panels, deep fuchsia neck, quatraform opening, color blushed on orig stopper, Libbey, #3041 .... **1,750.00**

Compote

8" d, 4" h, amberina, 1-3/4" wide crimson rim, honey amber bowl, applied standard, wafer base, sgd **985.00**

10-1/2" w, 4" h, colorless, pink Nailsea-type loops, flaring top, sgd "Libbey" **595.00**

Console set, green and white pulled feather, sgd **825.00**

Hair receiver, cov, 4-1/2" w, 2" h, two pcs, amberina, deep fuchsia shading to amber, partial label **1,750.00**

Pickle Castor, amberina, Swirled Rib pattern, ftd Meriden frame..... **475.00**

Pitcher, 5-1/2" h, ribbed opal body, combed peppermint pink striping, applied cased glass handle, colorless foot stamped "Libbey" in circular mark **350.00**

Rose bowl, 3-1/2" w, 2-1/2" h, melon ribbed bowl, beige ground, two pansies and leaves, white beads, sgd "Libbey Cut Glass" **550.00**

Tazza, 7" d, 5-3/4" h, colorless, opalescent feet, white and pink pulled feather bowl, pr **300.00**

Vase

8" h, amberina, flared rim with 12 scallops, 12 optic ribs, knob and wafer base, factory drilled hole at base, sgd slightly off center of pontil **575.00**

8" h, oviform, ribbed, wasted neck, wafer and ball stem....... **720.00**

8" h, 5" d, rose, clear foot with opalescent rim, K-535 of 1933 Libbey-Nash catalog...... **350.00**

8-1/4" h, tapered optic fern and pink threaded design, colorless foot, sgd **325.00**

9" h, cylindrical, slightly flaring, light vertical ribbing, blue threaded dec, opal ground, c1933....... **275.00**

10" h, tapered, paneled, turned down pink opalescent mushroom cap, marked "Libbey" in circle on base **725.00**

10" h, turquoise zipper pattern, colorless ground, sgd..... **425.00**

11-1/4" h, 4" d, deep red ball shaped bowl, 7-1/2" l hollow amber stem, 4" d circular base, sgd .. **1,000.00**

11-1/2" h, 2-1/2" w, amberina, deep fuchsia shading to amber, slight ribbing, flaring edge, orig label **850.00**

12" h, amberina, slender, Shape #3003, deep fuchsia at top shades to honey-amber, half original Libbey paper label remains and encircles signature on pontil **985.00**

15" h, floriform, amberina, c1917 .... **990.00**

Dish, shallow, opaque white, painted Sana Maria, made at 1893 Columbian Exposition, 6-1/2" d, **$635.** *Photo courtesy of Clarence and Betty Maier.*

Cut glass

Banana boat

12-1/2" l, 6-3/4" w, 6-3/4" h, hobstars, cane, and trellis cutting, double saber signature, flake and chip out of edge................ **900.00**

13" x 7" x 7", scalloped pedestal base, 24-point hobstar, hobstar, cane, vesica, and fan motifs, sgd **1,500.00**

Basket

14-1/2" h, 9-3/4" w, cut carnation, graphic style cutting, unusual cut handle, sgd **275.00**

18-1/2" h, 9" w, pedestal base, berry and leaf design, notched edge, fancy cut handle, sgd ... **1,000.00**

19-1/2" h, 8-3/4" w, pedestal base, floral pattern of roses, band of diamond point and leaves, double notched handle, sgd **800.00**

Berry bowl, 5" d, Regis pattern, sgd **50.00**

Bowl

8" d, Colonna pattern, crimped edge **350.00**

8" d, Comet pattern, sgd ... **550.00**

8" d, hobstar, bands of strawberry diamond and fans, sgd **110.00**

9" d, Gloria pattern **325.00**

9" d, 4" h, Snowflake pattern, sgd **950.00**

9" d, Somerset pattern, sgd . **150.00**

Candlestick

6" h, Flute pattern, sgd..... **100.00**

8" h, cut in flutes with multiple woven air controlled swirl stems, sgd **175.00**

8" h, #0493 pattern, twisted stem, sgd...................**110.00**

10" h, Empress pattern, sgd, price for pr................ **2,200.00**

Candy dish, cov, 7" d, divided, clover shape, hobstar and prism, sgd.. **90.00**

Chamberstick, 5" h, Pannel pattern, hollow core, star base, sgd.... **550.00**

Champagne, Rock Sharpe, #1014, Frontenac Cut **35.00**

Charger, 14" d, hobstar, cane, and wreath motifs, sgd........... **300.00**

Cocktail

Rock Sharpe, #1014, Frontenac Cut **28.00**

Vanity Cut, #300, 4-5/8" h, 4 oz, crystal................. **25.00**

Cordial

American Prestige pattern, c1930 .... **50.00**

Hobstar, strawberry diamond and hob diamond, sgd, 5" h ... **150.00**

Rock Sharpe, #1013 variant.. **25.00**

Cordial set, 11-1/4" h decanter, six 3-1/2" h goblets, Knickerbocker pattern, Walter Dorwin Teague/Edwin W. Fuerst manner, each stamped "Libbey," c1939 .... 400.00

Flower center

6" x 8", Kingston pattern, unusual shape 400.00

10-1/2" d, 6-1/2" h, Venetia pattern 600.00

12" d, 7-1/2" h, Gloria pattern, sgd 1,600.00

Goblet, Rock Sharpe, #1014, Frontenac Cut 45.00

Grapefruit stemware, 7" x 5", hobstar and notched mitres, stars, and fans 225.00

Ice cream tray, 10 x 14", Gloria pattern 275.00

Jug, 11" h, Harvard pattern, pattern cut handle, heavy cut deep blank 2,300.00

Nut cup, 1-1/2" h,, faceted pedestal, sgd, six-pc set 220.00

Perfume bottle, 7-1/2" h, cobalt blue cut to clear, engraved floral motif, two handles, sgd.......... 450.00

Pitcher, 10" h, copper wheel cut leaves and butterfly dec, sgd 195.00

Plate

6" d, Sultana pattern, shows four stages of cutting, large engraved "Libbey" in center, sgd "Libbey" 2,300.00

7" d, Azora pattern.......... 375.00

7" d, Diana pattern, sgd... 2,750.00

7" d, Delphos pattern..... 2,300.00

7" d, Gloria pattern.......... 195.00

8" d, Ellsmere pattern, sgd .. 675.00

10" d, Isabella pattern 2,000.00

Strawberry diamond and fans border, sunburst center, sgd. 75.00

Punch ladle, 13" l, hobstar, strawberry diamond and fan motif, Gorham sterling silver shell shaped dipper 1,10.00

Salad bowl, 9" d, 4" h, Savona pattern, hobstar, star center, engraved fruit and wreath, sgd.......... 1,900.00

Toupee stand, 3" x 6", hobstar, cane, and vesica motif, sgd....... 1,300.00

Tray

9" d, Aztec pattern, sgd... 7,000.00

11-1/2" d, Regis pattern, sgd 1,300.00

12" d, large hobstars, strawberry diamond, star, and crosshatch motif, very thick blank..... 900.00

Tumbler, 4", Herringbone pattern, sgd 700.00

Tumble-up

5-3/4" h, medicine jar insert, engraved corn pattern, sgd "Libbey" on all four pcs .. 1,600.00

Star burst, hobstar, fern, and fan motifs, minor handle check 725.00

Vase, amberina, lily shape, tricorn, **$575.**

Vase

7" h, Empress pattern, trumpet shape, sgd.......... 300.00

8-3/4" h, eight faceted panels, deeply cut iris, frosted foliate motif, stamped "Libbey" in circle. 635.00

9" h, 7" w, flared, Comet pattern, sgd 375.00

9" h, 9" w, rippled top, multiple scenes of engraved houses, church, boats, and forest, sgd "Libbey" 2,000.00

10" h, Harvard pattern, trumpet shape 125.00

12" h, floral pattern, flutes and horizontal ladder, precise cutting, colorless blank, 1906-19 trademark 450.00

13-1/2" h, baluster, emerald green cut flower panels, ftd, sgd base 700.00

Water carafe on stand, 9" h, Ellsmere pattern, sgd.......... 700.00

Water set, pitcher and six tumblers, engraved cherries, sgd...... 5,500.00

Wine, Harvard pattern, faceted cut knob stems, sgd, 12-pc set.... 350.00

Pressed patterns

Butter dish, cov, 7-1/4" d, 6" h, Maize, pale green kernels, gold trimmed husks 500.00

Candlesticks, pr, Silhouette pattern, colorless candle cup, opalescent figure of camel in stem 385.00

Celery vase, 6-1/2" h, 5" w, Maize, Pomona dec, amber kernels, blue leaves.......... 395.00

Champagne

Caprice, colorless bowl, lapis stem, 8-1/4" h 115.00

Silhouette pattern, colorless bowl, figural squirrel stem 200.00

Talisman pattern, colorless, ruby threading, 6" h.......... 135.00

Cocktail, Silhouette pattern, colorless bowl, black figure

Of bear in stem 250.00

Of kangaroo in stem 300.00

Goblet

Liberty Bell pattern, 12 oz, 7" h, crystal 25.00

Silhouette pattern, colorless bowl, black figure of cat in stem, sgd 300.00

Pitcher, 8-3/4" h, 5-12" d, Maize, barrel shaped, creamy opaque kernels, green husks, applied strap handle.... 575.00

Plate, Optic Swirl pattern, green . 45.00

Salt and pepper shakers, pr, Maize 75.00

Sherbet

#3006-2, 5-1/2" h, 6 oz, crystal 20.00

Silhouette pattern, black rabbit, sgd 145.00

Sherry, 5" h, Silhouette pattern, colorless bowl, black monkey silhouette in stem 125.00

Spooner, Maize, creamy opaque kernels of corn, blue husks, gold trim 190.00

Sugar bowl, cov, 2-3/4" h, Optic Rib pattern, pale blue opalescent, satin finish, gold enameled "World's Fair 1893" 175.00

Sugar shaker, Maize, creamy opaque kernels of corn, yellow husks, gold trim, orig top.......... 245.00

Toothpick holder, Maize, creamy opaque kernels of corn, blue husks, gold trim.......... 300.00

Tumbler, Maize, creamy opaque kernels of corn, yellow husks, 4" h 125.00

Water carafe, Maize, creamy opaque kernels of corn, yellow husks, gold trim 325.00

Wine, 7" h, Silhouette pattern, colorless bowl, black cat silhouette in stem, sgd 200.00

LOETZ

History: Loetz is a type of iridescent art glass that was made in Austria by J. Loetz Witwe in the late

1890s. The Loetz factory at Klostermule produced items with fine cameos on cased glass, good quality glassware for others to decorate, as well as the iridescent glasswares more commonly associated with the Loetz name.

Marks: Some pieces are signed "Loetz," "Loetz, Austria," or "Austria." Not all pieces of glassware attributed to Loetz are signed.

Reference: Robert and Deborah Truitt, *Collectible Bohemian Glass: 1880-1940*, R & D Glass, 1995.

Basket

6-1/2" h, 5" w, brilliant green mottled on clear ground, highly irid blue and purple finish. **100.00**

10-1/2" h overall, 4-1/2" h x 7" w glass, oyster white glass, mottled medium yellow raindrop patter, four bands of pulled deep ruby brown horizontal stripes, pinched and dimpled, four pulled down edges, fancy ormolu and silver bronzed Art Nouveau holder with Japanese chrysanthemum dec **600.00**

16" h, 10" w, mottled oyster white int., deep gold mottled ground, applied tall crystal loop handle with floral prunts **250.00**

17-1/2" h, 10" w, deep red to clear, green hooked and pulled design, highly irid surface, applied crystal handle **250.00**

18-1/4" h, 11-1/2" w, medium green, purple and blue irid **200.00**

Bottle, 11-3/4" h, bulbous, extended neck, everted rim, four upturned handles, rose gold irid ground, rainbow irid oil spot dec **19,800.00**

Bowl

6-1/2" h, squatty, three applied handles, gold irid on green body, polished pontil, wear **575.00**

8-5/8" d, round, applied blue edge on curved rim, medial ring of applied blue prunts, green transparent glass, polished pontil, light scratches **400.00**

10" d, 3" h, oyster white ground, diamond quilted design, applied deep black-green edge, highly irid surface **120.00**

13" l, 7-1/2" h, large shell form, resting on seaweed base, green ground, blue irid. **1,700.00**

Bride's bowl, 12" h, 9-1/2" d glass basket, clear to green glass, mottled with deep purple spatter, brilliant green and purple irid finish, silver plated Victorian holder **300.00**

Candlesticks, pr

9-1/2" h, slender baluster form, raised circular foot, gold irid **300.00**

15-3/8" h, cobalt blue ground, annulated round tapering stem, stepped cushion foot, bell form nozzle, conical drip pan, rainbow irid oil spot dec **2,400.00**

Centerpiece bowl

10" h, 15" l, deep gold bronze with deep purple dec glass bowl, highly irid surface, fancy bronze Art Nouveau holder with pine cone and leaf dec **1,500.00**

13" d, speckled green irid finish, blown-out scrolls, ormolu ftd frame marked "L. Henry," bowl unmarked **550.00**

Chalice, 5-1/2" h, blue-green irid round, tear drop motif, engraved "Loetz, Austra," c1900 . . . . **2,550.00**

Chandelier, five hanging irid shades with purple and blue highlights, Art Nouveau-style fixture **3,500.00**

Compote

10" d, 9-1/2" h, brilliant irid green, diamond quilted raised pattern, highly irid surface, fancy Art Nouveau reticulated floral design metal holder **300.00**

10-5/8" d, 5-1/4" h, bright orange int., deep black ext., white flaring circular rim, three ball feet, c1920 . . . . **310.00**

Dish, 8-1/2" d, 2-3/4" h, three applied pulled out handles, brilliant gold base, outstanding color, sgd in pontil with monogram "M" and "L" **200.00**

Flask, 9-1/2" h, elongated neck, pinched bulbous base, gold irid glass, Art Nouveau sterling silver floral overlay, polished pontil, imperfections . . **750.00**

Garniture set, blood red, multicolored variegated oil-spot motif, matched pr of sq 9-3/4" h vases in metal frames, rect matching 4-1/2" h x 9" l x 4" d planter in ornate brass mounted frame, emb pond lily dec **1,950.00**

Inkwell

3-1/4" h, 4" w, highly textured and irid surface, four blown-out corners, deep cobalt blue glass, brass fittings **300.00**

3-1/2" h, amethyst, sq, irid, web design, bronze mouth **125.00**

Jack-in-the-pulpit vase

10" h, Persian flask shape, dimpled bulbous body, spotted irid Papillon surface dec, polished pontil **635.00**

11-1/2" h, gold irid flower and stem, applied raised large leaf on dome foot, blue irid **1,300.00**

14" h, silver blue gold irid surface, floriform blossom, green body, knotty tree bark texture, polished pontil **425.00**

Lamp shade

3-3/4" h, 3-3/4" d, mottled yellow shaded to blue sphere, layered in brick red, etched as leafy branches with berry clusters, sgd "Richard" at side **230.00**

5" h, 2-1/4" fitter, deep butterscotch bronze, band of deep blue irid gold spots, slight roughness on fitter rim **300.00**

Lamp, mantel, 11" h, octopus, brown vasiform layered in white and blue glass, Federzeichnung air-tray design, enameled diaper border around rim, mounted on round turned wooden lamp base with int. single-socket fitting **290.00**

Lamp, table

16-1/2" h, 5-1/2" d opening, domed amber and gold mushroom shade, patinated metal tripod supports **1,555.00**

19-1/2" h, 9-1/2" d, table, globular shade, bulbous base, allover irid oil-spot motif, orig brass oil fittings **3,000.00**

Luminaire, 11" h, yellow opaque, Phanomen Gre dec, orig Art Nouveau hardware, c1915 . . . . **1,840.00**

Pitcher, 8-5/8" h, pinched bulbous body, purple and green irid, applied handle, gilt metal mount with cast foliate motif. **650.00**

Rose bowl, 6-1/2" d, ruffled purple irid raindrop dec **265.00**

Salt, open, 2-3/4" d, 1" h, irid blue ground, blue and gold oil-spot motif **600.00**

Sweetmeat jar, cov, 5" h, irid silver spider web dec, green ground, sgd **450.00**

Town pump and trough, 10" h, 9" w, random threading all over, slight irid colors, applied base with pale pink-peach open flower, green leaves **400.00**

Urn, 9-1/4" h, ovoid, irid, blue oil-spot motif, inscribed "Loetz, Austria" **1,600.00**

Vase

3" h, 5" d, squatty, platinum gold trails meandering over rosy pink body. **450.00**

3-1/8" h, small flared rim, angular green glass body, three applied handles, silver blue Papillon dec, polished pontil with inscribed artist's cipher for Marie Kirschner, c1905, minor nicks **375.00**

3-3/4" h, bulbous stick, lustrous Papillon design, cobalt blue ground, internal rim nicks, possibly trimmed, unmarked....... **180.00**

3-3/4" h, dimpled shoulder, pink combed design, dotted with irid silvery blue rondals over golden oil spots, salmon ground ... **1,800.00**

3-3/4" h, ovoid, green body with serpentine textured surface, light blue irid surface, polished pontil **375.00**

4" h, Acorn, ftd, irid blue-green **400.00**

4" h, green, bluish-gold Papillon design, nicks and polished area on rim **175.00**

4-1/2" h, cameo-etched, Powolny design, two layer floral dec, deep blue over intense orange, three applied handles, sgd "Richard" **1,725.00**

4-3/4" h, green, oilspot dec, crimped edge, large polished pontil, fake LCT signature **230.00**

5" h, bulbous, green irid body, pinched shoulder, ruffled rim, silver Art Nouveau floral overlay **1,600.00**

5" h, colorless oval, tricorn ruffled rim and dimpled sides, overall small gold circles and large red roundels, polished pontil, attributed to Koloman Moser for Loetz **1,725.00**

5" h, pinched, tricorn rim over pinched ovoid pale pink-amber body, pulled silver blue and magenta irid windings, muted gold ground, polished pontil inscribed "Loetz, Austria" **750.00**

5-1/2" h, onyx, shades of mint green, baby blue, and red, gilt dec, c1890 .... **460.00**

6" h, 3-1/2" d, green wave dec from top to bottom, gold ground, broad gold chainwork dec around center **2,100.00**

6-3/4" h, gold ground, irid feathers pulled from base to rim, slight rim chip, gaffer's sliver chip next to polished pontil........... **300.00**

6-3/4" h, reeded, King Tut, gold irid body, applied handles, polished pontil **295.00**

Vase, King Tut, reeded, applied handles, gold irid body, polished pontil, 6-3/4" h, **$295.** *Loetz photos courtesy of David Rago Auctions.*

6-7/8" h, double-gourd shape, colorless, Papillon dec on gold irid ground, Art Nouveau-style poppies silver overlay, minor nicks **1,265.00**

7" h, shaded from salmon to yellow to black base, gold swirl dec, sgd "Loetz/Austria" **7,475.00**

7-1/8" h, flared mouth, broad shouldered green body, draped pale blue irid threads, light irid sheet, polished pontil, c1900 .... **460.00**

7-1/4" h, green, oilspot dec, turned-down rim, large polished pontil................. **150.00**

71/4" h, classic shape, neck dec with enameling surrounded by minute gilt scrolling, marbled glossy surface, pink cased int. ... **650.00**

7-3/8" h, Marmorierte, quatreform rim on raised neck, ovoid body, flared to foot, opaque pink cased to swirled orange, white, and red marble base, enamel dec with intricate border at top portion in pink and white, gilt highlights, polished pontil, minor enamel wear **575.00**

7-1/2" h, metallic silver and blue Phanomen Gre 7966 dec over irid red base glass, c1900, partial paper label............ **5,000.00**

8-1/2" h, two handles, emerald green, Papillion pattern in irid gold-blue, threading applied to neck and handles fastened by buttons to lower body, polished pontil with paper label marked "F. Schultze & Co., Cincinnati, O," heat check in one handle...... **350.00**

9-5/8" h, flared rim, raised neck over ovoid vessel, colorless body with four pulled irid blue-green feathers, gold luster ground, Art Nouveau-style poppies silver overlay.............. **2,550.00**

11" h, irid peach ground, red combed feather dec **750.00**

11-1/4" h, Pampas floral form, scalloped rim, irid blue infused with green entwined trails...... **650.00**

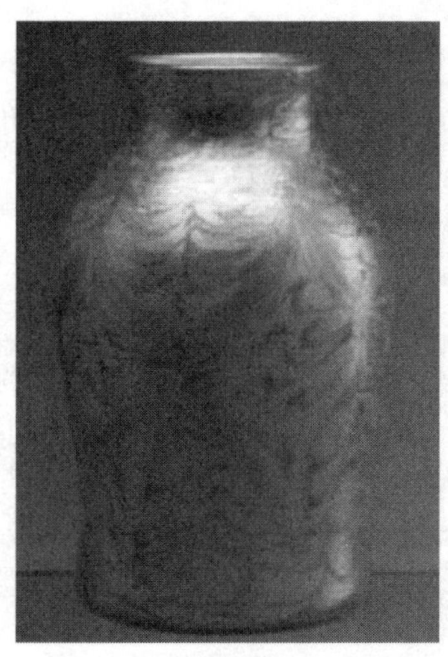

Vase, green wave decoration from top to bottom, gold ground, broad gold chainwork decoration around center, 6" h, 3-1/2" d, **$2,100**

11-1/2" h, neck dec with applied blue glass coil, three applied blue prunts on green body, polished pontil **400.00**

11-3/4" h, trumpet form, irid luster of assorted pulled color designs, metallic magentas, topaz, carmine purple, copper, rich blues, and green, inscribed "Loetz Austria" on polished pontil........ **13,000.00**

12-1/2" h, 6-1/2" d, Titania, silver overlay, polished pontil, internal bruise around top rim ... **2,300.00**

13-1/2" h, flared ruffled rim, bulbed neck, elongated oval form, spotted gold, blue, and irid green glass, polished pontil inscribed "Loetz Austria 5611"............ **700.00**

18-1/2" h, whirling irid golden silver motifs mingling with butterscotch, pearlized ground, acorn form body, pedestal with brackish oceanic wave motifs, ivory incorporated within pulled design, unsigned, design attributed to Franz Hofstatter............ **30,000.00**

McKee Glass

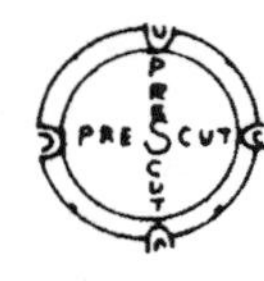

c1852–1950 1904–30s

History: The McKee Glass Co. was established in 1843 in Pittsburgh, Pennsylvania. In 1852, it opened a factory to produce pattern glass. In 1888, the factory was relocated to Jeannette, Pennsylvania, and began to produce many types of glass kitchenwares, including several patterns of Depression glass. The factory continued until 1951 when it was sold to the Thatcher Manufacturing Co.

The McKee Glass Company produced many types of glass, including window panes, tumblers, tablewares, Depression glass, milk glass, and bar and utility objects.

McKee named its colors Chalaine Blue, Custard, Seville Yellow, and Skokie Green. McKee glass may also be found with painted patterns, e.g., dots and ships. A few items were decaled. Many of the canisters and shakers were lettered in black to show the purpose for which they were intended.

There are many so-called "McKee" animal-covered dishes. Caution must be exercised in evaluating pieces because some authentic covers were not signed. Furthermore, many factories have made, and still are making, split-rib bases with McKee-like animal covers or with different animal covers. The prices listed are for authentic McKee pieces with either the cover or base signed.

Another area of McKee glass collecting that must be carefully approached is the Bottoms Up tumblers and coasters. Reproductions of these whimsical pieces have been well documented by experts such as Mark Chervenka in his book, *Antique Trader Guide to Fakes & Reproductions*.

References: Tom and Neila Bredehoft, *Fifty Years of Collectible Glass*, 1920-1970, Volume I, Volume II, Antique Trader Books, 2000; Gene Florence, *Kitchen Glassware of the Depression Years*, 6th ed., Collector Books, 2001; ——, *Very Rare Glassware of the Depression Years*, 6th Series, 1999, Collector Books; Lowell Innes and Jane Shadel Spillman, *M'Kee Victorian Glass*, Dover Publications, 1981; M'Kee and Brothers, *M'Kee Victorian Glass*, Dover Publications, 1971, 1981 reprint.

Animal dish, cov
- Canary, nest base, milk glass **145.00**
- Cat, milk glass **190.00**
- Dove, round base, beaded rim, vaseline, sgd **365.00**
- Hen, milk glass, orig eyes... **140.00**
- Horse, milk glass **195.00**
- Rabbit, milk glass......... **170.00**
- Squirrel, split rib base, milk glass **150.00**
- Turkey, white milk glass, 4-1/2" h 1vM.................. **40.00**

Wren house, gray body, red roof, **$150.**

Banana stand, Britannic pattern, ruby stained **100.00**

Basket, 15-1/2" h, 11" w, cut and pressed, floral and bird with butterfly **50.00**

Berry set, Hobnail with Fan pattern, blue, master berry and eight sauce dishes..................... **170.00**

Bird house, gray body, red roof **165.00**

Bowl
- 5" d, 4-1/2" h, Skokie Green.... **9.75**
- 6-1/2" d, Skokie Green....... **16.00**
- 8" d, Star Rosetted pattern ... **18.00**
- 9" d, Laurel pattern, Skokie Green **15.00**
- 9" d, Seville Yellow, green dots **35.00**
- 9-1/2" d, Skokie Green, flower band pattern.................. **35.00**
- 10" l, oval, Skokie Green, Autumn pattern.................. **50.00**
- 10-1/2" d, Chalaine Blue **145.00**

Bread plate
- Queen pattern, canary yellow . **40.00**
- Star Rosetted pattern, "A Good Mother Makes A Happy Home" **65.00**

Butter dish, cov
- Britannic pattern, ruby stained **125.00**
- Eureka pattern, heavy brilliant flint **75.00**
- Gothic pattern, colorless, pyramid shaped finial **50.00**
- Queen pattern, canary yellow, domed lid **85.00**
- Red ships, white ground **27.50**
- Star Rosetted pattern, colorless **45.00**
- Strigil pattern, colorless...... **45.00**
- Wiltec pattern, Pre-Cut Ware, frosted **70.00**

Cake stand
- Queen pattern, amber **65.00**
- Rock Crystal, green, low **55.00**

Candlesticks, pr
- 9" h, Rock Crystal, amber... **130.00**
- 9" h, Rock Crystal, colorless. **165.00**
- 10" h, crucifix form, Christ figure and "INRI"" plaque, hexagonal base, colorless.............. **125.00**

Candy dish, cov, 7-3/4" h, orange body, gold trim, gold finial, colorless pedestal base **35.00**

Canister, cov
- Cereal, 48 oz, Skokie Green, round **35.00**
- Coffee, 24 oz, Skokie Green, faded **30.00**
- Drippings, 2-3/4" h, 4-1/4" d, Skokie Green................. **30.00**
- Flour, 24 oz, Skokie Green ... **55.00**
- Sugar, 40 oz, Seville Yellow .. **75.00**
- Sugar, 40 oz, Skokie Green .. **65.00**

Carafe, Champion pattern, ruby stained by Beaumont Glass Works **125.00**

Castor set, three bottles, toothpick handle **270.00**

Celery tray, Britannic pattern, ruby stained.................... **80.00**

Celery vase
- Champion pattern, ruby stained by Beaumont Glass Works **95.00**
- Eugenia pattern, heavy brilliant flint **95.00**
- Gothic pattern, colorless, ruby stain, scalloped **90.00**
- Strigil pattern, colorless **25.00**

Champagne
- Eugenia pattern, colorless, heavy brilliant flint............. **90.00**
- Eureka pattern, colorless, heavy brilliant flint............. **90.00**

Cheese and cracker set, Rock Crystal pattern, red **170.00**

Clock, Daisy and Button pattern, tambour shapeAmethyst...... **750.00**
- Vaseline **450.00**

Coach bowl, Daisy and Button pattern
- Amber.................. **75.00**
- Blue, rim flake, chips on wheels **60.00**

Cologne bottle, Britannic pattern, ruby stained.................. **145.00**

Compote
- Brittanic pattern, green...... **60.00**
- Eugenia pattern, heavy brilliant flint, 8" d................... **150.00**
- Queen pattern, apple green.. **85.00**
- Star Rosetted pattern, colorless, 8-1/2" d................. **70.00**

Console bowl, 8-1/2" d, Autumn pattern, Skokie Green **40.00**

Cookie jar, cov, 6" h, Skokie Green, diagonal Art Deco design, ftd . . . **95.00**

Cordial

Eugenia pattern, colorless, heavy brilliant flint . . . **90.00**
Eureka pattern, colorless, heavy brilliant flint . . . **85.00**
Gothic pattern, colorless . . . **45.00**
Rock Crystal pattern, colorless . . . **35.00**

Creamer

Comet pattern, colorless . . . **55.00**
Eugenia pattern, colorless, heavy brilliant flint . . . **190.00**
Eureka pattern, colorless, heavy brilliant flint . . . **155.00**
Gothic pattern, ruby stain . . . **65.00**
Masonic pattern, colorless . . . **45.00**
Queen pattern, canary yellow . **45.00**
Rock Crystal pattern, colorless **35.00**
Star Rosetted pattern, colorless . . . **40.00**
Strigil pattern, colorless . . . **35.00**

Custard cup, Champion pattern, ruby stained by Beaumont Glass Works . . . **30.00**

Decanter set, decanter, six whiskey glasses, pink ground, ring dec. . **125.00**

Dinnerware, Oxford pattern, 26-pc set, c1940 . . . **42.00**

Dish

4" x 5", red ships, white ground . . . **20.00**
6" sq, Sunbeam pattern, turned up corners, green . . . **30.00**

Dripping bowl, cov, 4" x 5", Skokie green . . . **30.00**

Egg beater bowl, spout

Ivory . . . **30.00**
Skokie Green . . . **32.00**

Egg cup, Custard . . . **8.00**

Fish dish, 7" l, oval, Skokie green **14.00**

Flour shaker

Chalaine Blue . . . **125.00**
Red Dots, Seville Yellow ground . . . **115.00**
Red Ship, white ground, red ship . . . **30.00**
Roman Arch, custard . . . **30.00**

Fruit bowl, Colonial pattern

Caramel, 12" d . . . **140.00**
Seville Yellow, 12" d . . . **85.00**
Skokie Green, 12" d . . . **95.00**

Goblet

Britannic pattern, ruby stained **80.00**
Eugenia pattern, heavy brilliant flint . . . **90.00**
Eureka pattern, heavy brilliant flint . . . **75.00**
French Ivory . . . **40.00**
Gothic pattern, ruby stain . . . **65.00**
Puritan pattern, pink stem . . . **35.00**
Queen pattern, amber . . . **45.00**
Rock Crystal pattern, colorless **25.00**
Star Rosetted pattern, colorless . . . **40.00**
Strigil pattern, colorless . . . **35.00**

Grapefruit bowl, Rock Crystal pattern, red . . . **45.00**

Honey dish, Britannic pattern, ruby stained, cov, sq . . . **185.00**

Iced tea tumbler, Rock Crystal pattern, red . . . **35.00**

Jelly compote, Gothic pattern, colorless, scalloped rim . . . **20.00**

Lamp

Dance de Lumierre, green . . **750.00**
Eugenia pattern, heavy brilliant flint, whale oil burner . . . **165.00**
Nude, green . . . **175.00**
Ribbed Tulip pattern, 9-1/2" h, colorless font, milk glass base . . . **125.00**

Measuring cup

Glassbake, four-cup, crystal, red lettering . . . **25.00**
Red ships, white ground . . . **28.00**
Seville Yellow, ftd, four-cup . . **150.00**
Seville Yellow, red dots, two-cup . . . **55.00**
Skokie Green, nested set, four-pc . . . **125.00**

Measuring pitcher, white . . . **25.00**

Mixing bowl, Red Ship, white ground, red or black dec

6" d . . . **15.00**
7" d . . . **20.00**
8" d . . . **20.00**
9" d . . . **24.00**

Mug

Bottoms Down, Seville Yellow **150.00**
Mug, Brittanic pattern, ruby stained . . . **35.00**
Troubadour, opaque blue, 4-5/8" h . . . **40.00**

Mustard bottle, Eugenia pattern, colorless, heavy brilliant flint . . . **35.00**

Pepper bottle, Eugenia pattern, colorless, heavy brilliant flint . . . **30.00**

Pickle dish, oval

Queen pattern, blue . . . **25.00**
Star Rosetted pattern, colorless . . . **20.00**

Pin tray, hand shape, milk glass **20.00**

Pitcher

Aztec pattern, colorless, 5" h . **20.00**
Dark Skokie Green, 16 oz. . . . **75.00**
Eugenia pattern, colorless, heavy brilliant flint . . . **125.00**
Gothic pattern, colorless . . . **75.00**
Queen pattern, blue . . . **85.00**
Skokie Green, 16 oz . . . **37.00**
Star Rosetted pattern, colorless . . . **70.00**
Sunburst pattern, colorless, marked "Prescut" . . . **65.00**
Yutec Eclipse pattern, colorless, marked "Prescut" . . . **45.00**
Wild Rose and Bowknot pattern, frosted, gilt dec, 8" h . . . **65.00**

Plate, Rock Crystal, amber, 9" d, **$24.**

Plate

Holly pattern, 8" d, Skokie Green . . . **12.00**
Laurel pattern, 9" d, Skokie Green . . . **10.00**
Rock Crystal pattern, 12" d, colorless . . . **18.00**
Serenade pattern, 6-3/8" d, opaque white . . . **60.00**

Platter, Glassbake, 17-1/2" l, fish shape, crystal . . . **25.00**

Punch bowl set, bowl, 12 mugs, Tom and Jerry, red scroll dec . . . **65.00**

Razor hone, stropper, milk glass. **20.00**

Reamer, pointed top, Skokie Green . . . **45.00**

Refrigerator dish, cov

Custard, 4" x 5" . . . **22.00**
Red Ship, 5" x 8", white ground, red dec . . . **25.00**
Seville Yellow, 6-1/2" sq . . . **55.00**
Skokie Green, 4" x 5" . . . **12.00**
White, 5" x 8" . . . **18.00**

Relish

Gothic pattern, colorless . . . **20.00**
Hickman pattern, 8" l, green, gold trim . . . **30.00**
Prescut, milk glass . . . **25.00**

Ring box, cov, Seville Yellow . . . **20.00**

Rose jar, Colonial pattern, green, 10" h . . . **85.00**

Salt and pepper shakers, pr
Red Dots, Seville Yellow ground **75.00**
Red Ships, white ground, red dec, black tops........ **35.00**
Roman Arches, black **60.00**
Roman Arches, Seville Yellow ground, black lettering **48.00**
Skokie Green, 2-1/4", sq **14.00**
Sauce
Eugenia pattern, heavy brilliant flint **12.00**
Gothic pattern, ruby stain.... **20.00**
Queen pattern, colorless, ftd . **12.00**
Strigil pattern, colorless **8.00**
Sandwich server, center handle
Brocade pattern, pink, 10-1/2" d **50.00**
Rock Crystal pattern, red ... **140.00**

Sherbet, etched floral swag pattern, colorless, **$8.**

Sherbet
Laurel pattern, Skokie Green . **10.00**
Rock Crystal pattern, colorless **12.00**
Skillet, Range-Tee, crystal **5.00**
Spooner
Eugenia pattern, heavy brilliant flint **45.00**
Queen pattern, amber **35.00**
Stars and Stripes pattern, colorless, minor roughness.......... **22.00**
Strigil pattern, colorless **20.00**
Sugar bowl, cov
Comet pattern, colorless **55.00**
Eugenia pattern, heavy brilliant flint **190.00**
Eureka pattern, heavy brilliant flint **155.00**
Gothic pattern, ruby stain.... **65.00**
Laurel pattern, Skokie Green . **15.00**
Masonic pattern, colorless ... **45.00**
Queen pattern, canary yellow. **45.00**
Rock Crystal pattern, colorless **35.00**
Star Rosetted pattern, colorless **40.00**
Strigil pattern, colorless...... **35.00**
Sugar shaker
Chalaine Blue **125.00**
Red Dots, Seville Yellow ground **115.00**
Tankard pitcher, Britannic pattern, ruby stained, applied handle **175.00**
Toothbrush holder, Skokie Green **20.00**
Toothpick holder
Aztec pattern, colorless...... **25.00**
Figural, hat shape, Vaseline .. **35.00**
Gothic pattern, ruby stain, scalloped rim........ **85.00**
Rock Crystal pattern, colorless **40.00**
Tumbler
Bottoms Up, orig coaster, Seville Yellow **180.00**
Bottoms Up, orig coaster, Skokie Green **170.00**
Eugenia pattern, heavy brilliant flint **45.00**
Flower Band pattern, 3-1/2" h, Skokie Green **1.00**
Gladiator pattern, cobalt blue, gold trim **50.00**
Gothic pattern, colorless **35.00**
Ivory, 4" h, flat **12.00**
Ivory, 4-1/2" h, ftd........... **12.00**
Queen pattern, blue **45.00**
Ribbed Palm pattern, colorless **70.00**
Rock Crystal pattern, colorless **25.00**
Sextec pattern, colorless, 4" h, flat **20.00**
Seville Yellow, 4-1/2" h, ftd.... **14.00**
Vase
Auto, 6-1/4" h, crystal **45.00**
Auto, 6-1/2" h, Colonial pattern, Cut No. 1, crystal............ **45.00**
Brocade pattern, 7-1/2" h, crystal, two handles, gold trim...... **50.00**
Clothed Woman, three-sided, Skokie Green **175.00**
Hickman pattern, 10" h, green, gold trim **65.00**
Nude, 8-1/2" h, Chalaine Blue **175.00**
Rock Crystal pattern, 11" h, amber **85.00**
Sarah pattern, Chalaine Blue, 11-1/2" h **115.00**
Sarah pattern, Skokie Green, 8" h **48.00**
Water bottle, 21" h, Radium Emanator Filter, vaseline, orig box **325.00**
Window box, 5" x 9", lion, Skokie Green **85.00**
Wine, Britannic pattern, ruby stained **60.00**

Mercury Glass

History: Mercury glass is a light-bodied, double-walled glass that was "silvered" by applying a solution of silver nitrate to the inside of the object through a hole in its base.

F. Hale Thomas of London patented the method in 1849. In 1855, the New England Glass Co. filed a patent for the same type of process. Other American glassmakers soon followed. The glass reached the height of its popularity in the early 20th century. However, production was always somewhat limited and few forms exist. Because of the highly toxic nature of the silver nitrate linings, collectors need to handle this type of glassware with care.

Butler's ball, pedestal base, 10-1/2" h, **$450.** *Photo courtesy of Alderfer's Auction.*

Atomizer, colored floral bud-shaped glass stopper **50.00**
Bottle, 7-1/2" h, 4-1/4"d, bulbous, flashed amber panel cut neck, etched grapes and leaves dec, corked metal stopper, c1840 .... **175.00**
Bowl
4-3/4" d, enameled floral dec, gold luster int........ **50.00**
6" d, enameled white floral dec **45.00**
8" d, small plug in bottom, some wear **120.00**
Cake stand, 8" d, pedestal base, emb floral dec **80.00**
Candlesticks, pr
4" d, plain **40.00**
5-1/2" d, enameled white floral dec, domed base........ **70.00**
8" h, baluster........ **150.00**
10-1/2" h **225.00**
11" h, enameled floral dec .. **150.00**

12-3/4" h, baluster, domed circular foot, amber, enameled floral springs **300.00**

Candy dish, cov, 8-1/4" h, 4-1/4" d, pedestal base, colorless glass domed cov **45.00**

Carafe, 12" h, 5-1/2" d, mushroom stopper, dated 1909 . . . . **65.00**

Christmas ornament, 7" d, ball, brass collar and hanger, c190 . . . . **50.00**

Cologne bottle, 4-1/4" x 7-1/2", bulbous, flashed amber panel, cut neck, etched grapes and leaves, corked metal stopper, c1840 . . . **160.00**

Compote, 7" h, 6-1/2" d, enameled white floral dec, gold luster int. . . **65.00**

Creamer

6" h, etched grapevine dec, applied colorless handle **115.00**

6-1/2"h, etched ferns, applied colorless handle, attributed to Sandwich. **140.00**

Cup and saucer, etched floral dec **65.00**

Curtain tieback, 2-5/8" d, pewter fitting, starflower dec. **65.00**

Curtain tiebacks, 3-1/8" d, 4-1/2" l, etched grape design, price for pr **140.00**

Door knob set, 2-1/4" d **80.00**

Garniture, 14" h, baluster, raised circular molded foot, everted rim, enameled foliate motif **215.00**

Goblet

5" d, gold, white lily of the valley dec **40.00**

6-7/8" h, silver, etched Vintage pattern, gold luster int. **65.00**

7-1/2" h, Ivy pattern, engraved grape leaves and grapes **145.00**

Mug, 2-7/8" h, silver, applied colorless handle. **35.00**

Perfume bottle, emerald green ground, cut and enameled dec, orig stopper **225.00**

Pitcher

9-3/4" h, 5-1/2" d, bulbous, panel cut neck, engraved lacy florals and leaves, applied colorless handle, c1840 . . . . **225.00**

12-1/2" h, bulbous, applied colorless handle **185.00**

Reflecting globe, 10" d, silver int., rests on white columnar form satin glass base, 19th C, minor silver loss, base chip, pr **450.00**

Salt, 3" x 3", price for pr **100.00**

Scent bottle, 4" l, cobalt blue over mercury glass ground, cut with shaped oval panels, silver mounted, early 20th C **320.00**

Lightning rod ball, quilt-raised diamond pattern, silver mercury, sheared collared mouths with metal collars marked "Kretzer Brand/Trademark," America, 1870-1920, 5" d, ***$300.*** *Photo courtesy of Norman C. Heckler and Co.*

Spooner, Vintage pattern **75.00**

Sugar bowl, cov, 4-1/4" d, 6-1/4" h, low foot, enameled white foliage dec, knob finial **65.00**

Sweetmeat dish, cov, 4" d, 7-1/2" h, pedestal base, colorless cov . . . **50.00**

Tazza, 5-3/4" d, 2-3/4" h, etched birds and leaves dec **75.00**

Toothpick holder

3-1/2" h, gold, pedestal base . **40.00**

5" h, gold, pedestal base, etched ferns **45.00**

Urn, 13" h, baluster, marked "Harnish & Co. London" **250.00**

Vase

4-3/4" h, silver, sanded foliage dec **45.00**

8" h, cut to show emerald glass ground, marked "Harnish & Co. London Pat.". **115.00**

8-3/4" h, emerald green, hand-painted floral dec, c1890, pr **185.00**

9-3/4 h, cylindrical, raised circular foot, everted rim, bright enameled yellow, orange, and blue floral sprays and insects, pr **225.00**

10-1/4" h, paneled sides, frosted palm trees, flowers, gold luster int., pr **225.00**

10-1/2" h, cylindrical, hand-painted floral and leaf band around center **125.00**

12" h, ribbed, emerald green, enameled floral and bird dec **145.00**

13" h, trumpet shape, enameled panel of orange, yellow, green, and blue floral clusters and butterflies **220.00**

Walking stick, 42-1/2" l, red, blue, yellow, and silver swirls, some wear to silvering **200.00**

Wig stand, 10-1/4" h **150.00**

Wine, engraved Vintage dec, amber int.. . . . . **100.00**

Witch ball, emerald green, attached base **185.00**

MILK GLASS

History: Opaque white glass attained its greatest popularity at the end of the 19th century. American glass manufacturers made opaque white tablewares as a substitute for costly European china and glass. Other opaque colors, e.g., blue and green, also were made. Production of milk glass novelties came in with the Edwardian era.

The surge of popularity in milk glass subsided after World War I. However, milk glass continues to be made in the 20th century. Some modern products are reissues and reproductions of earlier forms. This presents a significant problem for collectors, although it is partially obviated by patent dates or company markings on the originals and by the telltale signs of age.

Collectors favor milk glass from the pre-World War I era, especially animal-covered dishes. The most prolific manufacturers of these animal covers were Atterbury, Challinor-Taylor, Flaccus, and McKee.

References: E. McCamley Belknap, *Milk Glass*, Crown Publishers, 1949, out of print; Frank Chiarienza and James Slater, *The Milk Glass Book*, Schiffer, 1998; Regis F. and Mary F. Ferson, *Today's Prices for Yesterday's Milk Glass*, published by authors, 1985; —, *Yesterday's Milk Glass Today*, published by authors, 1981; Everett Grist, *Covered Animal Dishes*, Collector Books, 1988, 2000 value update; Lorraine Kovar, *Westmoreland Glass*, two vols., Antique Publications, 1991; S. T. Millard, *Opaque Glass*, 4th ed., Wallace Homestead, 1975, out of print; Betty and Bill Newbound, *Collector's Encyclopedia of Milk Glass*, Collector Books, 1995, 2000 value update.

Collectors' Club: National Milk Glass Collectors Society, 500 Union Cemetery Rd, Greensburg, PA 15601, http://www.nmgcs.org.

Museum: Houston Antique Museum, Chattanooga, TN.

Notes: Numbers in listings prefixed with a letter refer to books listed in the references, wherein the letter identifies the first letter of the author's name.

Animal dish, cov

Baboon, fleur de lis base, seated baboon, facing to one side, attributed to Flaccus (F114) **600.00**

Chick emerging from egg, basketweave base **80.00**

Deer, fallen tree base, sgd "E. C. Flaccus Co., Wheeling, WV" (F34) **185.00**

Dog, setter, white base, sgd "Flaccus," repair to lid **150.00**

Duck, Atterbury, white opaque, dated under base, 11" l, 5" h, two chips under tail, replaced eyes **80.00**

Elephant with Rider (F1).... **700.00**

Fish, 8-3/4" l, walking, divided horizontally, five central fins support body, detailed scales, red glass eyes (B167b) **195.00**

Hen, large, almond......... **90.00**

Hen, large, blue head, white body **45.00**

Hen, large, gray, Kemple ... **300.00**

Hen, marbleized, head turned to left, lacy base, white and deep blue, Atterbury (F8)........... **165.00**

Hen on sleigh **90.00**

Lamp, octagonal picket base, blue body, white head, Westmoreland (F87)................. **115.00**

Pintail duck, basketweave base, traces of old paint, numbered **65.00**

Rabbit, patent date on base, Atterbury (F48).......... **175.00**

Robin with Berry (F217) **75.00**

Rooster, wide rib base, blue, marked "I" inside base, Westmoreland Specialty Co., 4-1/4" h **30.00**

Squirrel, acorn base (F15) .. **155.00**

Swan, closed neck, basketweave base (M278)............. **95.00**

Turkey, small, blue, Kemple . **200.00**

Turkey, white, McKee, 4-1/2" h, very minor mold roughness inside base rim **40.00**

Bell, 5-1/4" h, 3-3/8" d base, handle formed by three molded chain links **60.00**

Bonbon, scoop shape, Eagle Glass Co., 1899 (F597) **45.00**

Bottle, figural

Bear, 10-1/4" h, facing forward, sitting, forelegs folded across chest (F132)............ **125.00**

Duck, 11-1/2" h, vertical bill, head, and neck form flanged opening, rimmed oval for label, no closure, Atterbury (F433)......... **350.00**

Bowl

Arch Border pattern, 8" d, alternating wade curved arches and interlocking narrow pointed arches, Challinor, Taylor (B100a) ... **50.00**

Ball and Chain pattern, 8" d, openwork rim (B100b) **50.00**

Cut Star pattern, 7-1/4" d, blue, scalloped edge, 12 rated stars (F289)................. **75.00**

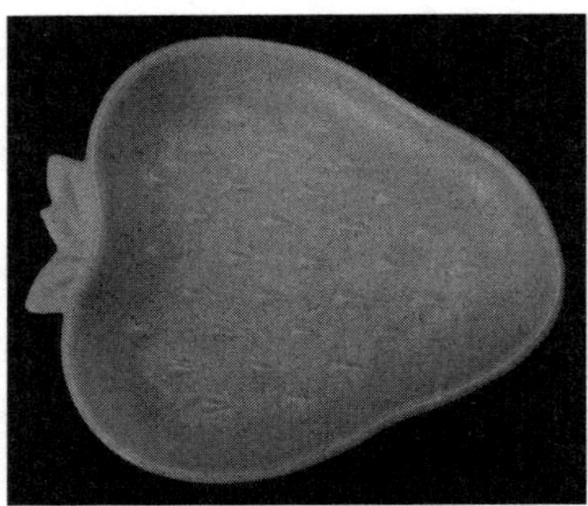

Dish, figural strawberry, detailed stippling, unmarked, **$10.**

Daisy, 8-1/4" d, allover leaves and flower design, open scalloped edge (F165).............. **85.00**

King's Crown, 8" d, basketweave pattern, slanted sides, vertical bar pattern on base, eight triangular points forming crown (B1078b) **75.00**

Bread tray, basketweave border, motto "Give Us Our Daily Bread" inscribed on rim, Atterbury (F345) **75.00**

Butter dish, cov

Challinor's #313, multicolored dec, Challinor, Taylor & Co., 5-1/2" d lid, 6" h **90.00**

Cosmos, yellow, pink, and blue dec, Consolidated Lamp & Glass Co., 8" d, 6" h **160.00**

Crossed Fern pattern, 6"d, animal claw grasping ball feet and finial, scalloped edge, Atterbury (F232) **75.00**

Gooseberry pattern, narrow beaded edges, band of fruit on cov and base, berry finial, Sandwich (F248) **120.00**

Roman Cross pattern, 4-7/8" w, sq, ftd base curves outward toward top, cube shape finial (F240) **75.00**

Calling card receiver, bird, wings extended over fanned tail, head resting on leaf, detailed feather pattern (F669) **150.00**

Candlestick

3-3/8" h, clown, bust rises from wide curved neck ruffle (F129) ... **75.00**

7-3/4" h, swirl, ribbing twists counter-clockwise from base, column, cup, and was guard (F522) **50.00**

Candy container, figural, top hat, tin threaded lid (W12A)........... **45.00**

Celery vase

Blackberry Pattern, 6-5/8" h, scalloped rim, plain band above vertical surface, Hobbs Brockunier (F317)................. **110.00**

Burred Hobnail pattern...... **45.00**

Child's mug, Little Bo Peep (M-92) **85.00**

Compote

Atlas, lacy edge, blue...... **185.00**

Blackberry pattern, 9" h, large figural blackberry finial on cov, Hobbs Brockunier (B121) **160.00**

Chick and Eggs, 11" h, pedestal, chick emerging from heaped eggs, finial cov, mounted on curved tripod, central support, rounded lacy edge base, emb Atterbury patent date, Aug. 6, 1889 inside cov (F362) **185.00**

Lattice Edge pattern, 8-1/2" d, floral dec, Daisy and Button type pattern pedestal base, Challinor, Taylor (M116a) **100.00**

Prism pattern, 8" d, 5-1/2" h, wafer connection between Prism bowl and foot **155.00**

Cracker jar, cov, Challinor's #313, multicolored dec, satin finish, Challinor, Taylor & Co., 4-1/2" d, 7" h...... **90.00**

Creamer

Beaded Circle pattern, applied handle (F322)............ **65.00**

Blackberry pattern **45.00**

Burred Hobnail pattern...... **45.00**

Forget Me Not pattern **40.00**

Melon with Leaf and Net pattern, Atterbury **45.00**

Paneled Wheat pattern, Hobbs Brockunier (F255) **65.00**

Roman Cross pattern (F239) . **50.00**

Trumpet Vine pattern, fire painted dec, sgd "SV"............ **70.00**

Cruet, Tree of Life pattern, blue . **80.00**

Dresser box, cov, horseshoe, horse, floral dec **40.00**

Egg cup, cov, 4-1/4" h, bird, round, fluted, Atterbury (F130)....... **135.00**

Fish set, figural fish platter, four serving dishes, Atterbury, emb patent date **250.00**

Hurricane lamp, 10-1/2" h, Rainbow Art Co., #183, ruby and gold hand painted dec, two-pc, c1947.......... **125.00**

Inkwell, horseshoe, circular inkwell in center, pen rests (F449) **45.00**

Jar, cov, figural

Eagle, "Old Abe," leafy base, "E. Pluribus Unum" on encircled banner, gray (F568) **115.00**

Owl, glass eyes **85.00**

Lamp, 11" h, Goddess of Liberty, bust, three stepped hexagonal bases, clear

and frosted font, brass screw connector, patent date, Atterbury (F329) **300.00**

Match holder

Indian Head (B219) **125.00**

Jolly Jester, patent date on rear (F201) **135.00**

Minstrel Boy **195.00**

Trilby, patent date with reversed "9" **150.00**

Match safe, 4-1/2" h, baby in black hat, corrugated match striker (F534). **350.00**

Mug

Ceres, blue, Atterbury & Co., 3-1/4" h **30.00**

Ivy in Snow pattern, 3" h **40.00**

Liberty Bell, Centennial dates emb between two bells (F674) . . **185.00**

Mustard, cov

Bull's head (F14) **150.00**

Tryolean Bears, 3-1/4" d, 4-1/8" h, traces of green paint, Westmoreland Specialty Co., two annealing lines on lid **25.00**

Perfume bottle, 4-1/2" h, 4" d, orig lid, emb ivy leaves around body, one on lid, orig label "John Davis & Co. Manfg," directions for filling after emptied by orig owner, three flakes on neck. . **25.00**

Pitcher

Birds on Branch pattern, trio of small birds on leafy branch, cold painted dec (F519). **110.00**

Dart and Bar pattern, 8" h, blue, rect handle, ftd (B85a) **100.00**

Fish pattern, 7-1/4" h, finely detailed, Atterbury (F328) **185.00**

Plate

Ancient Castle, 7" d **50.00**

Cats, 6" d, two cats form upper edge, bracketed dog head, open work, swirling leaves, emb "He's all right" (B20d) **125.00**

Colonial Hearth, center black decal, lacy edge, Kemple Glass . . . **15.00**

Plate, color decal of fruit, original Fostoria label, 8-1/4" d, repaired, **$5.**

Plate, Trumpet Vine decoration, lattice border, Challinor, Taylor, 10-5/8" d, **$35.**

Columbus, 9-3/4" d, center bust with dates 1492-1892 across chest, shell and club border **45.00**

Cupid and Psyche, 7" d **45.00**

Dog and Cats (B20d) **50.00**

Donkey, 7" d **45.00**

Easter Horseshoe (W150Ac) . **85.00**

National, flag, eagles, patent date on back, 7" d **50.00**

Roger Williams Memorial, 7-1/4" d, Williams monument emb in center, flags, eagles, and fleur de lis, patent date, Westmoreland (F639) **150.00**

Roses, 12" d, Imperial, c1950. **35.00**

Small Mouth Bass, multicolored center dec, lacy heart border, Kemple Glass, 6-1/2" h. **15.00**

Star, 5-3/8" d, six pointed center star, lacy filigree fills in spaces between points **15.00**

Woof Woof **45.00**

Platter

Blaine Logan Campaign, 13-1/8" l, emb bust of Blaine faces Logan, notched border (F564). . . . **365.00**

Retriever, 13-1/4" l, swimming dog pursuing duck through cattails, lily pad border (B53) **120.00**

Salt shaker

Atterbury Dredge, 3-3/8" h, combination octagonal paneled and pepper shakers shaped as small cov stein (F415) **95.00**

Brownie, 2-3/8" h, Palmer Cox Brownies in different poses on each of four vertical sides (F448) **120.00**

Diamond Point and Leaf pattern, 2-3/4" h, blue (F489). **50.00**

Shaving mug, Atterbury's Robin, 3-5/8" d, 3-3/8" h **30.00**

Spooner

Beaded Circle pattern, 5-5/8" h, scalloped, ftd, flint, attributed to Sandwich (F321). **70.00**

Melon with Leaf and Net, Atterbury **40.00**

Monkey, scalloped top, 5-1/8" h (F275) **125.00**

Paneled Flower, 4-5/8" h, ribbing separates six diamond point panels, stylized floral dec, scalloped edges, Challinor, Taylor (F284) **60.00**

Sugar bowl, cov

Almond Thumbprint, 7-1/2" h, large scalloped edges (F367) . . . **120.00**

Beaded Circle pattern, applied handle (F322) **65.00**

Blackberry pattern. **45.00**

Burred Hobnail pattern **45.00**

Ceres pattern, 7-1/4" h, cameo profiles in beaded circles, leafy sprays, bust finial (B127) . . **115.00**

Forget Me Not pattern **40.00**

Melon with Leaf and Net pattern, Atterbury **45.00**

Nine Panel patter, Ihmsen Glass Co, flared bowl, cov fits inside base edge (F670) **450.00**

Paneled Wheat pattern, Hobbs Brockunier (F255) **65.00**

Roman Cross pattern (F239). . **50.00**

Sunflower pattern (B82b) **65.00**

Trumpet Vine pattern, fire painted dec, sgd "SV" **70.00**

Sugar shaker

Apple Blossom, Northwood Glass Co., 4-1/2" h **160.00**

Netted Oak pattern, 4-1/4" h, oak leaf centered on netted panels, green top band, Northwood (F495). **85.00**

Paneled Sprig, fired-on green dec, gilt accents, Northwood Glass Co., 4-3/4" h, wear to dec **65.00**

Quilted Phlox, white, hand painted blue flowers, Northwood Glass Co./Dugan Glass Co., 4-1/2" h **100.00**

Royal Oak, Northwood Glass Co. **190.00**

Syrup pitcher, orig top

Acorn pattern, 6-1/2" h, blue, Beaumont Glass Co. **190.00**

Acorn pattern, 6-1/2" h, white shading to pink, Beaumont Glass Co.. **210.00**

Alba pattern, 6-1/2" h, enameled floral sprays, Ditheridge (F139) **150.00**

Argus Swirl pattern, 4-1/" h, netted floral transfer dec on shoulder,

Magazine tear sheet, from Crockery and Glass Journal, *March 1961,* **$8.50.**

attributed to Consolidated Lamp & Glass Co. **150.00**
Beehive, 5-5/8" h, emb beehive center, ribbed top and base, strap handle (F372) **185.00**
Bellflower pattern, single vine, dated, Collins & Wright (F155C0) **245.00**
Challinor's #313, 6-1/4" h, blue, Challinor, Taylor & Co. **140.00**
Challinor's #313, 6-3/4" h, white, multicolored dec, Challinor, Taylor & Co., wear to dec **50.00**
Challinor's Forget-Me-Not, semi-opaque pink, 5-1/4" h, Challinor, Taylor & Co. **140.00**
Double Fan Band, 7" h, white, dainty hand painted floral dec, Dithridge & Co. **50.00**
Ribbed melon, 6" h, white, hand painted floral dec, pressed handle **50.00**

Toothpick holder, Tramp Shoe (F194) **65.00**

Tumbler, Royal Oak, orig fired paint, green band. **50.00**

Whimsey, rowboat, Atterbury, patent date **45.00**

Wine, Feather pattern **40.00**

MILLEFIORI

History: Millefiori (thousand flowers) is an ornamental glass composed of bundles of colored glass rods fused together into canes. The canes were pulled to the desired length while still ductile, sliced, arranged in a pattern, and fused together again. The Egyptians developed this technique in the first century B.C. It was revived in the 1880s.

Reproduction Alert: Many modern companies are making Millefiori items, such as paperweights,

Reference: Kenneth Wilson, *American Glass, 1760-1930: The Toledo Museum of Art, Volume I, Volume II*, Hudson Hills Press and The Toledo Museum of Art, 1994.

Basket

3-1/4" h, blue and amber canes, matte finish, orig millefiori handle, Italian **100.00**
3-1/2" h, yellow and blue canes, matte finish, orig millefiori handle, Italian **100.00**
10-1/2" h, 6-1/2" w, random pattern of millefiori canes, white opal ground cased in colorless, butterscotch irid surface, applied pale pink loop handle **200.00**

Bottle

9" h, 4-1/2" d, V.E.M., by Gulio Radi, corseted, flat shoulder, amethyst murrines, silver and gold inclusions, unmarked. . . . **4,025.00**
10-1/2" h, 4" d, V.E.M., by Ansolo Fuga, teardrop shape, four panels of murrines in different colors, gold foil ground, unmarked . . . **4,600.00**

Bowl

2" d, pink, green, and white canes, applied colorless handles . . **48.00**
4" d, blue and white canes, applied colorless handles. **80.00**
8" d, tricorn, scalloped, folded sides, amethyst and silver deposit **125.00**
8" d, 3" h, V.E.M., designed by Gulio Radi, black glass, fold foil and large murrines, unmarked . **150.00**
8" d, 3-3/4" h, Fratelli Toso, multicolored murrines, applied foot rim, 1910s, unmarked . . . **4,315.00**

Box, cov, 3" d, multicolored . . . **125.00**

Creamer

4" h, white ground, scattered millefiori, applied handle . . **250.00**
4-1/2" h, 3" d, white and cobalt blue canes, yellow centers, satin finish **110.00**

Bowl, multicolored murrines, applied foot rim, Fratelli Toso, 1910s, unmarked, 8" d, 3-3/4" h, **$4,325.** *Photo courtesy of David Rago Auctions.*

Cruet, orig stopper

6" h, bulbous, multicolored canes, applied frosted rope handle, c1920 .... **400.00**

7" h, slender, multicolored canes, matte finish, Italian, c1950 .. **75.00**

Cup and saucer, white and cobalt blue canes, yellow center, satin finish . **90.00**

Decanter, 12" h, deep black ground, all over multicolored flux and canes, including peachblow, and opal, enamel dec, Gundersen **1,450.00**

Dish

4-3/8" d, 1-1/2" h, close concentric millefiori, blue, white, and amethyst canes, signature Whitefriars monk cane, dated "1977" **80.00**

5" d, octagonal, blue and white canes.................. **125.00**

Door knob, 2-1/2" d, paperweight, center cane dated 1852, New England Glass Co. **395.00**

Flask, 4-1/2" x 3" x 1", millefiori separated by blue and white filigrana threads **275.00**

Goblet, 7-1/2" h, multicolored canes, colorless stem and base **150.00**

Jack-in-the-pulpit vase, multicolored canes, matte finish, Italian, c1950 **65.00**

Inkwell, 4-1/2" h, sgd "Paul Ysart" **200.00**

Jug, 2-1/4" h, multicolored canes, applied colorless handle **95.00**

Lamp

11-1/2" h, pear-shaped shade with frosted button finial, matching baluster form base, old fittings, European plug........... **450.00**

14-1/2" h, 8-1/2" d dome shade, glass base, electric....... **795.00**

Miniature lamp

8-1/2" h, mushroom cap shade, bulbous base, multicolored canes **375.00**

11" h, mushroom cap shade, matching glass lamp shaft, red, blue, and white, gilt metal "Bryant" electrical fittings **1,200.00**

Perfume bottle, round body, seven portrait canes, orig metal mountings, Venetian, c1930-40........... **450.00**

Pitcher, 6-1/2" h, multicolored canes, applied candy cane handle **195.00**

Rose bowl, 6" h, crimped top, multicolored, cased, white lining **145.00**

Slipper, 5" l, camphor ruffle and heel **140.00**

Sugar, cov, 4" h, 3-1/2" d, white canes, yellow centers, satin finish **125.00**

Toothpick holder, ruffled top, multicolored canes, c1890 .... **200.00**

Tumble-Up, 8-3/4" h, multicolored canes, matte finish, Italian, c1950 **85.00**

Vase

3-1/2" h, waisted, ruffled top, light blue, cobalt blue, medium blue, and white canes, four applied knob handles................. **65.00**

4" d, handkerchief, red ground, gold dust ext. **180.00**

4" d, multicolored canes, applied double handles **100.00**

5-1/2" h, purple bands, white oval lines and bands, red flowers, yellow centers **175.00**

8" h, ruffled rim, multicolored canes, applied colorless handles . **190.00**

14-1/2" h, 7" d, V.E.M., designed by Ansolo Fuga, executed by Luciana Ferro, applied dec of red, green, and yellow murrines, blue, yellow, and red bands, paper label from collection of Lucaino Ferro **6,900.00**

MINIATURE LAMPS

History: Miniature oil and kerosene lamps, often called "night lamps," are diminutive replicas of larger lamps. Simple and utilitarian in design, miniature lamps found a place in the parlor (as "courting" lamps), hallway, children's rooms, and sickrooms.

Miniature lamps are found in many glass types, from amberina to satin glass. Miniature lamps measure 2-1/2 to 12 inches in height, with the principle parts being the base, collar, burner, chimney, and shade. In 1877, both L. J. Atwood and L. H. Olmsted patented burners for miniature lamps. Their burners made the lamps into a popular household accessory.

References: Marjorie Hulsebus, *Miniature Victorian Lamps*, Schiffer Publishing, 1996; Ann Gilbert McDonald, *Evolution of the Night Lamp,* Wallace-Homestead, 1979; Frank R. and Ruth E. Smith, *Miniature Lamps* (1981), Book II (1982) Schiffer Publishing; John F. Solverson, *Those Fascinating Little Lamps: Miniature Lamps and Their Values*, Antique Publications, 1988, includes prices for Smith numbers.

Collectors' Club: Night Light, 38619 Wakefield Ct, Northville, MI 48167.

Reproduction Alert: Study a lamp carefully to make certain all parts are original; married pieces are common.

Note: The numbers given below refer to the figure numbers found in the Smith books.

Figure III-I, Artichoke, pink **225.00**

Figure VII-I, Santa Claus **2,700.00**

Figure VII-II, satin, rainbow, Kosmos Brenner burner, 10-1/2" h.... **2,750.00**

Figure VIII-I, cameo, white maidenhair fern and butterflies, citron ground **5,500.00**

Figure XVIII-II, overshot, frosted, house scene, 5-1/2" h **850.00**

Figure XXIX-II, satin, swirled emb ribbed rose shade, emb scene, SS pedestal base, 13-1/2" h **800.00**

#9-I, opaque white, Fire Fly, orig dated burner.................. **250.00**

#11-1, milk glass, pedestal base and shade, clear pressed font, Sandwich, 6-3/4" h.................. **275.00**

#20-II, blue glass shade, Aladdin type **275.00**

#25-II, cranberry, Berger lamp.. **275.00**

#28-II, milk glass, Glow Lamp, melon ribbed.................. **165.00**

#29-I, nutmeg, white milk glass, brass band and handle **80.00**

#30-I, green glass shade, tin holder, acorn border **120.00**

#36-I, Little Buttercup, blue **75.00**

#40-I, opalescent, cranberry, Spanish Lace pattern, applied handle, hornet border.................. **325.00**

#49-I, cobalt blue, Little Butter Cup, 2" h, pr **275.00**

#49-II, Little Banner **90.00**

#50-I, log cabin, blue, handle **1,100.00**

#59-II, clear, emb "Vienna"..... **125.00**

#68-I, finger lamp, blue with stars, emb "Wide Awake".............. **115.00**

#82-II, Block pattern, milk glass, matching globe, 6-1/2" h **100.00**

#85-II, blue opaque, base only .. **35.00**

#95-II, clear, applied handle **70.00**

#106-I, clear, block font and base, nutmeg burner **90.00**

#109-I, Beaded Heart, clear, emb **115.00**

#110-I, Bull's Eye, clear, stem.... **45.00**

#111-I, Bull's Eye, teal blue, stem, 4-7/8" h.................. **190.00**

#112-I, Bull's Eye, green, burst bubble on one of the points on foot **45.00**

#116-I, Fishscale pattern, amber, nutmeg burner, clear glass chimney **150.00**

#121-I, mercury glass, acorn shape, emb acorn cap base, acorn burner **125.00**

#125-I, Christmas Tree, white milk glass, gold trim.............. **125.00**

#143-I, Lincoln Drape, frosted amber, acorn burner **140.00**
#144-I, Westmoreland pattern . . **325.00**
#153-I, milk glass, pink and gold, emb **115.00**
#156-I, milk glass, emb flower and scrolls, 8" h **125.00**
#165-II, clear, fine ribbing, acorn burner, patent collar **115.00**
#166-I, Greek Key, clear, acorn burner **90.00**
#171-I, Pond Lily, emb, inside painting **140.00**
#177-I, custard glass, rough shade **55.00**
#184-II, Swirl, orig reflector **85.00**
#190-I, Block and Dot pattern, milk glass, 7-3/4" h **140.00**
#192-I, Block pattern, clear, hand painted blue and green flowers, acorn burner, 6-1/2" h **85.00**
#193-I, Apple Blossom, white milk glass, pink bands and flowers, ball shade, several chips on shade . . **80.00**
#194-I, Apple Blossom, white milk glass, green bands, pink flowers, umbrella shade, 7-1/4" h, chip on shade **90.00**
#203-I, Plume pattern, opaque white, gilt dec, nutmeg burner, 8-1/4" h **115.00**
#211-I, Medallion, milk glass, emb **45.00**

Cut glass, 8-1/2" h, **$200.** *Photo courtesy of Joy Luke Fine Art Brokers and Auctioneers.*

Satin, MOP, diamond quilt pattern body, pink, 8-1/2" h, **$1,350.**

#212-I, pink milk glass with shells, base of shade damaged **145.00**
#213-I, milk glass, emb, yellow, pink, and white **135.00**
#214-I, Maltese Cross, milk glass, emb rough top shade **50.00**
#226-I, white milk glass, traces of gilt dec, Fleur-de-Lys with scroll and beading, 6-3/4" h, roughness **60.00**
#230-I, Acanthus, milk glass, emb. yellow and white **125.00**
#231-I, Drape pattern, pink and white milk glass **75.00**
#233-I, blue opaque, emb circle and bead design, period burner, 4" h, flake on base **25.00**
#240-I, Defender, blue opaque, base only **50.00**
#240-I, Defender, green milk glass, 8-1/2" h **250.00**
#241-I, Paneled Cosmos, white milk glass, multicolored floral dec, 8-1/4" h, small chip on top rim of shade . . **370.00**
#286-I, Cosmos, pink cased, Consolidated Lamp & Glass Co., 7" h, flat chip **325.00**
#286-I, Cosmos, white milk glass, multicolored floral dec, pink trim bands, 7-1/2" h **275.00**
#279-I, basket, base only, clear cased yellow, burner and chimney, Consolidated Lamp & Glass Co., 3-1/4" h **35.00**

#311-I, white milk glass, orange, green and brown ground, 8" h, no harm fish scale flake on shade fitter edge **350.00**
#317-I, milk glass, pink and yellow flowers, shaded green ground . **300.00**
#325-I, pink milk glass, angel dec **165.00**
#327-II, swan, milk glass, shade with crack **300.00**
#330-II, elephant, wrong shade **225.00**
#368-I, Beaded Rib, spatter glass, hornet burner **400.00**
#368-II, milk glass, blue bands, pink flowers, green leaves, Dietz Night Light burner **475.00**
#369-I, Beaded Swirl, end of day **300.00**
#370-I, cranberry, Beaded Swirl **200.00**
#389-I, satin, blue, melon ribbed base, pansy ball shade, chip on shade **155.00**
#390-I, melon ribbed, cased, yellow **525.00**
#394-I, satin, blue, puffy diamond quilted pattern base and umbrella shade, nutmeg burner, clear glass chimney, 9" h **475.00**
#400-I, green beaded **125.00**
#403-I, Beaded Drape, cranberry opalescent, nutmeg burner, 9-1/2" h **350.00**
#409-II, cranberry, threaded base **125.00**
#421-II, milk glass, banquet style shape, three tiers, brass pedestal base **550.00**
#422-II, banquet, cranberry Hobbs Optic shade, white metal with brass finish, filigree font holder, solid textured stem and ornate foot, 16-1/2" h, electrified. **130.00**
#432-I, Twinkle, cobalt blue, 7" h, slight flake on shade fitter edge **175.00**
#439-I, cranberry, Hornet burner, 8" h, some roughness at top of shade **200.00**
#457-II, blue opaque, base only . **40.00**
#459-II, satin, red shading to pink, emb scrolled leaves and swirl, 10" h **1,650.00**
#460-I, cranberry, white enamel floral dec, 11-5/8"h **450.00**
#474-I, Spanish Lace filigree . . **750.00**
#482-I, Daisy and Cube, vaseline, nutmeg burner, 8" h. **365.00**
#483-II, satin, light blue, enameled tulips and leaves, gold trim **450.00**
#488-II, amber, applied handle . . **75.00**
#490-I, Skeleton, 5-1/2" h **8,000.00**

#497-I, owl, black, gray, orange eyes **1,100.00**
#499-I, swan, glossy pink slag, 7-3/4" h, three very small flakes on top of shade **2,250.00**
#502-I, opalescent, amber, pink feet **3,000.00**
#508-I, Spanish Lace, opalescent, nutmeg burner **350.00**
#509-I, Reverse Swirl, opalescent, 7-3/8" h, roughness and chips to top edge of shade **125.00**
#521-II, cranberry, globular font, interior honeycomb design, three clear applied glass feet, burner, and chimney, no shade **50.00**
#536-I, cranberry shading to clear on both shade and base, applied colorless feet, 7-1/2" h **450.00**
#538-I, amberina, paneled, amber fee, 9-1/4" h **1,500.00**
#546-I, Swirl, blue, 8-1/2" h..... **600.00**
#555-I, glossy satin glass, pink and butterscotch **1,550.00**
#595-I, satin, MOP, DQ, shading from pink to apricot, burner ring damaged **1,050.00**
#600-I, satin, MOP, Raindrop, four petal feet, 8-3/4" h **600.00**
#610-I, Burmese, Webb, brown and green foliage, red berries.... **4,000.00**
#625-I, Glow Lamp, amber, replaced glass burner, 4-1/2" h **40.00**
#625-I, Glow Lamp, ruby, orig glass burner, 4-1/2" h.............. **100.00**
#625-I, Glow Lamp, white milk glass, floral dec, burner **30.00**
Marriage, Smith #285-I shade, Smith #284-I base, red satin, petal type shade, emb base **110.00**

Unlisted

Banquet, white opaque font, stem, and ball shade, blue transfer and white enameled floral dec, brass connector, sq brass foot, 4-1/2" h shade, 12-1/2" h lamp, burner missing, connector rod replaced **300.00**

Base only, Snowflake, cranberry opalescent, Hobbs, Brockunier & Co., 3-3/4" h, electric adjuster in collar **40.00**

White milk glass, emb scroll and floral design on base and matching shade, flowers dec in maroon, yellow centers, dark green leaves and scrolls, band of light green at bottom of shade and below collar of base, 7-7/8" h **475.00**

MONT JOYE GLASS

History: Mont Joye is a type of glass produced by Saint-Hilaire, Touvier, de Varreaux & Company at its glassworks in Pantin, France. Most pieces were lightly acid etched to give them a frosted appearance and were also decorated with enameled florals.

Bowl

3-3/4" d, frosted ground, enameled floral dec, sgd **275.00**

9" d, 5" h, textured emerald green ground, purple and pink poppies, golden foliage, pulled and tolled rim sponged with gold, narrow open bubble near rim..... **275.00**

Ewer, cov, cameo cutting, crystal, green, and gold, brass spout and handle, removable cover, artist sgd "Cristalle Rie Depantin"....... **550.00**
Inkwell, green, enameled lavender flower..................... **180.00**
Jar, cov, 8" h, cylindrical, crystal ground, etched, enameled iris, gilt leaves, crystal knob, gilt factory mark, c1900..................... **275.00**
Pitcher, 10" h, amethyst, enameled flowers, aqua, blue, pink, and gold, sgd **350.00**
Rose bowl, 3-3/4" h, 4-1/4" d, pinched sides, acid etched, enameled purple violets, gold stems and dec ... **295.00**

Vase

4" h, pink enameled poppy and gold leaves, frosted textured ground, marked................ **275.00**

5-1/8" h, spherical, cylindrical neck and foot, frosted ground, etched and gilt oak leaves and acorns, gilt signature **215.00**

5-1/2" h, swirled shape, green, enameled flowers, c1890, sgd "Mont Joye" **445.00**

5-3/4" h, elongated sq form, light yellow transparent textured glass, etched lily of the valley blossoms and leaves dec on sides, few small rim nicks............... **215.00**

6-1/2" h, green frosted ground, cut poppies, crimson enamel and gilt trim **265.00**

7-1/2" h, dark green satin ground, enameled pink iris dec.... **400.00**

8" h, light turquoise ground, etched iris dec, gold highlights, acid etched frosting, gold band around crimped edge........... **395.00**

8-1/4" h, teal ground, enameled daffodils on gold stalks, raised gold scroll design applied to neck and shoulder, silver rim marked "Sterling" **900.00**

*From left: Cameo trumpet vase, burgundy tousled thistle petals, textured iridescent honey glass ground, decorative rim, 12" h, **$500**; vase with profusion of enameled lavender hydrangea blossoms, gold leaves, silver and gold highlights, acid-etched colorless body with frosted berried vines below scalloped cut rim, 16" h, **$1,300**; cameo vase, life size emerald green irises, two dragonflies, frosted textured ground, raised gold detailing, 15-1/2" h, **$600**; cameo vase, melon ribbed base, slender neck, enameled violets strewn on slight iridescent frosty textured surface, gilt highlights, cameo leaves and stems,* **$750.** *Photo courtesy of Cincinnati Art Galleries.*

8-1/2" h, cameo, icy frosted ground, enameled leaves, deep red poppies, sgd............ **450.00**

9-1/2" h, 6" w, ovoid, acid etched, lilies outlined in gold, body slightly ribbed, indented fluted top with gold accents, sgd, c1900.. **600.00**

10" h, bulbous, narrow neck, clear to opalescent green, naturalistic thistle dec, gold highlights . **375.00**

11" h, tomato red ground, lacy gold dec, enameled iris and foliage dec **250.00**

12" h, trumpet form, cameo-etched burgundy tasseled thistle petals, textured irid honey ground, decorative rim............ **500.00**

13-1/4" h, frosted texture, gold acid cut Art Nouveau border of flowers and leaves dangling above yellow enameled teasel blossoms, raised gold stems **400.00**

13-3/4" h, flattened ovoid shape, cameo, crystal ground, etched, molded and enameled iris, gilt leaves, c1900 .... **350.00**

15-1/2" h, cameo-etched emerald green irises, two dragonflies, frosty textured ground, raised gold detailing **600.00**

16-1/2" h, cameo-etched green foliated vine encircling textured Depression glass pink body, sponged gold highlights... **500.00**

15-1/2" h, cameo-etched leaves and stems, melon ribbed base, elongated stick neck, enameled violets, irid frosty textured surface, gilt highlights **750.00**

16" h, scalloped cut rim, profusion of enameled lavender hydrangea blossoms, golden leaves, enhanced by silver, raised gold highlights, colorless body acid etched with frosty berried vines **1,300.00**

18" h, green, enameled purple flowers, gold leaves, sgd .. **325.00**

19-3/4" h, swollen at top, narrow stem, flared foot, translucent emerald green body, textured acid finish, cameo-etched borders at top and bottom, enameled silvered acorns, gold, and silvered leaves on dark gilt ground, Mont Joye shield in gold enamel on base, minor wear to gilt **3,200.00**

25-3/4" h, flaring waisted bottle form, green metallic flaked ground, overlaid foliate dec, MOP beads, base stamped "Mont Joye," c1910 .... **1,200.00**

Violet vase, 6" h, frosted etched surface, colorless glass, naturalistic enameled purple violet blossoms, gold highlights, base marked "Dimier Geneve".................. **260.00**

Morgantown Glass Works

History: The Morgantown Glass Works, Morgantown, West Virginia, was founded in 1899 and began production in 1901. Reorganized in 1903, it operated as the Economy Tumbler Company for 20 years until, in 1923, the word "Tumbler" was dropped from the corporate title. The firm was then known as The Economy Glass Company until reversion to its original name, Morgantown Glass Works, Inc., in 1929, the name it kept until its first closing in 1937. In 1939, the factory was reopened under the aegis of a guild of glassworkers and operated as the Morgantown Glassware Guild from that time until its final closing. Purchased by Fostoria in 1965, the factory operated as a subsidiary of the Moundsville-based parent company until 1971, when Fostoria opted to terminate production of glass at the Morgantown facility. Today, collectors use the generic term, "Morgantown Glass," to include all periods of production from 1901 to 1971.

Morgantown was a 1920s leader in the manufacture of colorful wares for table and ornamental use in American homes. The company pioneered the processes of iridization on glass, as well as gold and platinum encrustation of patterns. It enhanced Crystal offerings with contrasting handle and foot of India Black, Spanish Red (ruby), and Ritz Blue (cobalt blue), and other intense and pastel colors for which the company is famous. It conceived the use of contrasting shades of fired enamel to add color to its etchings. Morgantown was the only American company to use a chromatic silk-screen printing process on glass, its two most famous and collectible designs being Queen Louise and Manchester Pheasant.

The company is also known for ornamental "open stems" produced during the late 1920s. Open stems separate to form an open design midway between the bowl and foot, e.g., an open square, a "Y," or two diamond-shaped designs. Many of these open stems were purchased and decorated by Dorothy C. Thorpe in her California studio, and her signed open stems command high prices from today's collectors. Morgantown also produced figural stems for commercial clients such as Koscherak Brothers and Marks & Rosenfeld. Chanticleer (rooster) and Mai Tai (Polynesian bis) cocktails are two of the most popular figurals collected today.

Morgantown is best known for the diversity of design in its stemware patterns, as well as for its four patented optics: Festoon, Palm, Peacock, and Pineapple. These optics were used to embellish stems, jugs, bowls, liquor sets, guest sets, salvers, ivy and witch balls, vases, and smoking items.

Two well-known lines of Morgantown Glass are recognized by most glass collectors today: #758 Sunrise Medallion and #7643 Golf Ball Stem Line. When Economy introduced #758 in 1928, it was originally identified as "Nymph." By 1931, the Morgantown front office had renamed it Sunrise Medallion. Recent publications erred in labeling it "dancing girl." Upon careful study of the medallion, you can see the figure is poised on one tiptoe, musically saluting the dawn with her horn. The second well-known line, #7643 Golf Ball, was patented in 1928; production commenced immediately and continued until the company closed in 1971. More Golf Ball than any other Morgantown product is found on the market today.

References: Jerry Gallagher, *Handbook of Old Morgantown Glass*, Vol. I, published by author (420 First Ave. NW, Plainview, MN 55964), 1995; —, Old Morgantown, Catalogue of Glassware, 1931, Morgantown Collectors of America Research Society, n.d.; Ellen Schroy, *Warman's Depression Glass*, 2nd edition, Krause Publications, 1997; Hazel Marie Weatherman, *Colored Glassware of the Depression Era*, Book 2 published by author, 1974, available in reprint; —, *1984 Supplement & Price Trends for Colored Glassware of the Depression Era*, Book 1, published by author, 1984.

Collectors' Clubs: Old Morgantown Glass Collectors' Guild, P.O. Box 894, Morgantown, WV 26507.

Bowl

#1 Berkshire, Crystal w/#90 Starlet cutting, 8" d **58.00**

#12 Stella, Nanking Blue, #2 Cover, 8" d **315.00**

#12-1/2 Woodsfield, Genova Line, 12-1/2" d **545.00**

#12-1/2 Woodsfield, Pomona Line, 12-1/2" d............... **550.00**

#14 Fairlee, Glacier decor, 8" d **525.00**

#17 Calypso, Spanish Red, 7-3/4" d **235.00**

#19 Kelsha, Danube Line, 12" d **425.00**

#19 Kelsha, Genova Line, 12" d **425.00**

#22 Linwood, Topreen Line, Spiral Optic, 10" d **355.00**

#26 Greer, Neubian Line, 10" d **750.00**

#26 Greer, Topreen Line, 10" d **465.00**

#35-1/2 Elena, Old Amethyst, applied Crystal rim, 8" d... **425.00**

#35-1/2 Elena, Old Bristol Line, 9-1/2" d................ **745.00**

#67 Fantasia, Bristol Blue, 5-1/2" d **75.00**

#71 Vienna, Stiegel Green w/Crystal Italian Base, 12" d **1,400.00**

#101 Heritage, Gypsy Fire, matte finish, 8" d............... **70.00**

#101 Heritage, Peacock Blue, 8" d **48.00**

#103 Elyse, Steel Blue, 7" d .. **48.00**

#111 Dodd, Bristol Blue, 5" d. **65.00**

#1102 Crown, Moss Green, 9" d **45.00**

#1102 Crown, Steel Blue, 9" d **50.00**

#4355 Janice, Crystal, #787 Maytime etch, 13" d **195.00**

#4355 Janice, Crystal, Glacier Decor w/Snow Flowers, 13" d.... **565.00**

#4355 Janice, 14K Topaz, Carlton/Madrid, 13" d..... **185.00**

#4355 Janice, Ritz Blue, 13" d **445.00**

#4355 Janice, Spanish Red, 13" d **445.00**

#7643 Celeste, Spanish Red, Crystal trim, covered, 6" d **1,200.00**

#7643 Truman, Spanish Red, Crystal trim, rare, 10" d......... **4,500.00**

#9937 Revere, Pineapple, 4-1/2" d **45.00**

#9937 Revere, Ruby, 6" d.... **75.00**

Bud vase

#26 Catherine 10" h, Anna Rose, #758 Sunrise Medallion etch **745.00**

#26 Catherine 10" h, Azure, #758 Sunrise Medallion etch.... **270.00**

#26 Catherine 10" h, Jade Green, Enamel Floral Decor, crimped **250.00**

#36 Lara, 10" h, Thistle...... **95.00**

Crockery and Glass Journal, published monthly at New York, by Demarest Publications, Inc., 45 East 17th St., New York, N. Y. Subscriptions, $3 per year. Entered as second-class matter September 2, 1920, at the Post Office at New York, under the Act of March 3, 1879.
Vol. 109. No. 9. September, 1931.

Ad showing Golf Ball, #7643, ruby bowls. The Crockery and Glass Journal, *September 1931.*

#53 Serenade 10" h, Opaque Yellow **430.00**
#53 Serenade 10" h, Spanish Red **425.00**
#53 Serenade 10" h, Venetian Green, #756 Tinker Bell etch **595.00**
#124 Bodden, 6" h, Thistle . . . **40.00**
#7621 Ringer, 10" h, Opaque Yellow **475.00**

Candleholders, pair

#37 Emperor, Genova Line, 8" h **625.00**
#37 Emperor, Stiegel Green, 8" h **625.00**
#37 Emperor, 14K Topaz, 8" h **625.00**
#60 Rhoda, Bristol Blue **80.00**
#60 Rhoda, Hurricane Lite, plain rim, Lime, 8" h **110.00**
#64 Monet, Peacock Blue. . . . **90.00**
#80 Modern, Moss Green, 7-1/2" h **70.00**
#81 Bravo, Gypsy Fire, 4-1/2" h **70.00**
#81 Bravo, Peacock Blue, 4-1/2" h **528.00**
#81 Bravo, Thistle, 4-1/2" h. . **135.00**
#82 Cosmopolitan, Moss Green, slant, 7" h **75.00**
#82 Cosmopolitan, Gypsy Fire, slant, 7" h **75.00**
#87 Hamilton, Evergreen, 5" h **75.00**
#87 Hamilton, Steel Blue, 4" h. **50.00**
#88 Classic, Nutmeg, 4-3/4" h **55.00**
#104 Slant, Burgundy **45.00**
#105 Coronet, Cobalt Blue, slant, 8-3/4" h **120.00**
#105 Coronet, Ebony, slant, 8-3/4" h **120.00**
#110 Sonata, Pineapple **90.00**
#135 Ricardo, Moss Green (Golden Moss) **50.00**
#1254 Wickliffe, Moss Green (Golden Moss) **35.00**
#7620 Fontanne, Ebony filament, #781 Fontinelle etch **1,000.00**
#7643 Dupont, Crystal, rare, 4-5/8" h **385.00**
#7643 Golf Ball, Torch Candle, single, Ritz Blue, 6" h **280.00**
#7643 Jacobi, Anna Rose, rare, 4" h **525.00**
#7643 Jacobi, Venetian Green, rare, 4" h **525.00**
#7662 Majesty, Randall Blue, 4" h **750.00**
#7662 Majesty, Spanish Red, 4" h **395.00**
#7690 Monroe, Ritz Blue, 7" h, rare **1,200.00**
#7949 Bertonna, Danube Line, 8-3/4" h **835.00**
#7951 Stafford, Crystal w/#25 gold band, 3-1/8" h **685.00**
#9913 Federal, heavy Spiral Optic, Gypsy Fire **45.00**
#9913 Federal, Lime **28.00**
#9913 Federal, Pineapple **25.00**
#9913 Federal, Spiral Optic, Moss Green **22.50**
#9923 Colonial, Peacock Blue, chimney. **65.00**
#9923 Cosmopolitan, light amethyst, slant, thistle base **30.00**
#9935 Barton, Burgundy, 3-3/4" h **12.00**
#9935 Barton, Ebony, light blue and white sticker **70.00**
#9935 Barton, Peacock Blue, 3-3/4" h **30.00**
#9935 Barton, Pineapple. **50.00**

Candy jar

#14 Edmond, Danube Line, #4 cover, rare, 8-1/2" h. **625.00**
#14 Guilford, Genova Line, #3 cover, 10-3/4" h **500.00**
#15 Lisbon, Crystal w/#734 American Beauty etch, #2 cover, 8-1/2" h **525.00**
#16 Rachel, Crystal, Pandora cutting, 6" h **385.00**
#71 Jupiter, Steel Blue, 6" h. . . **95.00**
#108 Bethann, Topreen Line, 5" h **595.00**
#127 Yorktown, Steel Blue, 7-1/2" h **75.00**
#200, Mansfield, Burgundy matte, 12" h **195.00**
#1114 Jerome, Bristol Blue, 11-1/2" h **135.00**
#1212 Michael, Spanish Red, Crystal finial, 5-1/2" h. **1,000.00**
#2938 Helga, Anna Rose, Meadow Green finial, 5" h **1,500.00**
#7643-1 Alexandra, Randall Blue/Crystal Duo-Tone, 5" h **825.00**
#9949 Christmas Tree, Crystal, four-part stack jar, 11" h . . . **140.00**
#9952 Palace, Ruby, 6-12" h . . **60.00**

Champagne

#7565 Astrid, American Beauty etch, 6 oz **45.00**
#7577 Venus, Ritz Blue, Pillar Optic, 5-1/2 oz **55.00**
#7606-1/2 Athena, Ebony filament, #777 Baden etch, 7 oz **75.00**
#7617 Brilliant, Spanish Red . . **22.00**
#7621 Ringer, Anna Rose, 7 oz **65.00**
#7621 Ringer, Aquamarine, 6 oz **55.00**
#7623 Pygon, D.C. Thorpe satin open stem, 6-1/2 oz **165.00**
#7630 Ballerina, #757 Elizabeth etch, 6 oz **55.00**
#7640 Art Moderne, Ebony open stem, 5 oz. **85.00**
#7634 Golf Ball, 5-1/2 oz, Crystal **22.50**
#7643 Golf Ball, 5-1/2 oz , Ritz Blue **60.00**
#7643 Golf Ball, 5-1/2 oz , Spanish Red. **55.00**
#7643 Golf Ball, 5-1/2 oz , Stiegel Green **55.00**
#7660 Empress, Spanish Red, 6 oz **48.00**
#7664 Queen Anne, Azure, #758 Sunrise Medallion etch, 6-1/2 oz **95.00**
#7668 Galaxy, Crystal, Lace Bouquet etch **35.00**
#7678 Old English, 6-1/2 oz, Ritz Blue **48.00**
#7678 Old English, 6-1/2 oz, Spanish Red. **45.00**
#7678 Old English, 6-1/2 oz, Stiegel Green **40.00**
#7690 Monroe, red and crystal **35.00**
#7705 Hopkins, Toulon gold decor, 5 oz **145.00**
#7860 Lawton, Azure, Festoon Optic, 5 oz **50.00**
#8445 Plantation, Cobalt Blue **75.00**

Cocktail

#7577 Venus, Anna Rose, Palm Optic, 3 oz **38.00**
#7577 Venus, Azure, Palm Optic, 3 oz **38.00**
#7577 Venus, Crystal, Bramble Rose etch **30.00**
#7577 Venus, Nanking Blue . . **35.00**
#7577 Venus, Venetian Green, Palm Optic, 3 oz **35.00**
#7586 Napa, Azure, Festoon Optic, 3-1/2 oz **48.00**
#7617 Brilliant, Spanish Red . **15.00**
#7620 Fontanne, Ebony filament, #781 Fontinelle etch, 3-1/2 oz **135.00**
#7630 Ballerina, #765 Springtime etch, 3 oz **45.00**
#7643 Golf Ball, 3-1/2 oz, Ritz Blue **42.00**
#7643 Golf Ball, 3-1/2 oz, Spanish Red. **42.00**
#7643 Golf Ball, 3-1/2 oz, Stiegel Green **42.00**
#7646 Sophisticate, Picardy etch **28.00**
#7654 Hold in Home, reverse twist stem, Spanish Red. **55.00**
#7654-1/2 Legacy, Spanish Red, 3 oz **45.00**

#7654-1/2 Legacy, Manchester Pheasant Silk Screen, 3-1/2 oz 185.00
#7667 Georgian, Spanish Red and Crystal 30.00
#7668 Galaxy, Crystal, American Beauty etch 30.00
#7668 Galaxy, Crystal, Mayfair etch 25.00
#7700 Salem, Crystal, red filament, Pillar Optic 45.00
#8445 Plantation, Cobalt Blue . 67.50
#8445 Plantation, Spanish Red 40.00
Chanticleer, Pink Champagne bowl, 4 oz 45.00
Chanticleer, Ruby bowl 47.50
Mai Tai, Topaz stem, 4 oz 50.00
Modern American, Seafoam . . 30.00
Old Crown, 6-1/4" h, 5-1/2 oz. . 85.00

Compote

#12 Stella, Moss Green (Golden Moss), 8" 40.00
#12 Stella, Peacock Blue, 4" . . 48.00
#65 Withers, Bristol Blue 38.00
#65 Withers, Lime 55.00
#201 Inverness, Meadow Green, Peacock Optic, 4-1/2" d, 7-1/2" h 155.00
#203 Marietta, Ruby, 9-1/2" . . . 75.00
#206 Colette, Burgundy, 7-1/2" h 65.00
#7556 Helena, low with cover, Crystal, Snowberry cutting, 4-1/2" d 265.00
#7556 Toledo, high with cover, Crystal, Forever cutting, 4-1/2" d 315.00
#7620 Rarey, Spanish Red bowl, 6" d, 6-1/2" h 255.00
#7654 Reverse Twist, Anna Rose, 6-1/2" d, 6-3/4" h 195.00
#7654 Reverse Twist, Aquamarine, 6-1/2" d, 6-3/4" h 195.00
Miramar, Danube Line, Crystal, Nanking Blue stem 125.00
Miramar, Laurel Line, Crystal, Meadow Green stem 125.00
Miramar, Laurel Line, Crystal, Meadow Green stem and cutting 125.00
Palmer, Laurel Line, Crystal, Meadow Green stem and cutting 125.00
Stella, Gypsy Fire 30.00
Valencia, Danube Line, Crystal, Nanking Blue jewel 250.00

Console bowl

#1933 El Mexicana, Ice, 10" d 285.00
#1933 El Mexicana, Seaweed, 10" d 325.00

Cordial

#788-1/2 Roanoke, Spanish Red, 1-1/2 oz 50.00
#7565 Astrid, Anna Rose, #734 American Beauty etch, 3/4 oz 155.00
#7570 Horizon, #735 Richmond etch, 1 oz 55.00
#7577 Venus, Anna Rose, #743 Bramble Rose etch, 1-1/2 oz 165.00
#7587 Hanover, #733 Virginia etch w/#25 Minton Gold band, 1 oz. 55.00
#7616 Wescott, crystal, red filament, 4-1/8" h 65.00
#7617 Brilliant, Spanish Red . 45.00
#7617 Brilliant, Ritz Blue, 1-1/2 oz 135.00
#7617 Brilliant, Spanish Red, 1-1/2 oz 135.00
#7640 Art Moderne, Ebony stem, 1-1/2 oz 135.00
#7643 Golf Ball, 1-1/2 oz, Pastels 55.00
#7643 Golf Ball, 1-1/2 oz, Ritz Blue 58.00
#7643 Golf Ball, 1-1/2 oz, Spanish Red. 55.00
#7643 Golf Ball, 1-1/2 oz, Stiegel Green 52.00
#7654 Lorna, Nantucket etch, 1-1/2 oz 105.00
#7660-1/2 Empress, Spanish Red, 1-1/2 oz 87.50
#7668 Galaxy, Mayfair etch, 1-1/2 oz 87.50
#7668 Galaxy, #810 Sears' Lace Bouquet etch, 1-1/2 oz. 50.00
#7668 Virginia, crystal, 4-1/4" h 35.00
#7673 Lexington, Ritz Blue filament, #790 Fairwin etch, 1-1/2 oz 165.00
#7678 Old English, Spanish Red, 2 oz. 70.00
#7909 Blake, Spanish Red filament, 1 oz. 65.00
#8445 Plantation, Cobalt Blue 145.00

Creamer, #9074 Belton, Crystal with Golden Iris foot 95.00

Finger bowl, #7634, 4-1/4" d, Old Amethyst, crystal foot, set of four 125.00

Flower Lite

#9920 Nova, Peach 125.00
#9941-1/2 Vesta, Gypsy Fire, with candle frog 65.00
Sharon, Burgundy. 45.00
Sharon, Peacock Blue 50.00

Goblet, Adonis Etch, crystal, #7606-1/2, 9 oz, Venetian Green stem and foot, **$145.**

Goblet

#300 Festival, Gloria Blue, 8 oz 35.00
#7565 Astrid, #734 American Beauty etch, punty cut stem, 10 oz. . 65.00
#7568 Horizon, #735 Richmond etch, 10 oz 48.00
#7577 Venus, Anna Rose, Azure foot, Tulip Optic, 9 oz 60.00
#7577 Venus, Anna Rose, Palm Optic, 9 oz. 50.00
#7577 Venus, Anna Rose, #743 Bramble Rose etch, 9 oz. . . . 95.00
#7577 Venus, Azure Blue, Palm Optic, 9 oz. 30.00
#7577 Venus, Crystal, #743 Bramble Rose etch, 9 oz 80.00
#7577 Venus, Nanking Blue . . 50.00
#7586 Napa, Biscayne etch, gold banding on rim 58.00
#7587 Hanover, Virginia etch . 30.00
#7589 Laurette, #735 Richmond etch, 9 oz 42.00
#7590 Kingswood, Priscilla etch, gold band 55.00
#7591 Lismore, Crystal, Nanking foot, bowl and stem iridized . 35.00
#7604 Princeton, Amber, Panel Optic, Homa's Delight etch, 9 oz 65.00
#7604-1/2 Heirloom, Bramble Rose etch. 55.00

#7604-1/2 Heirloom, Crystal, #751 Adonis etch, 9 oz **60.00**
#7604-1/2 Heirloom, 14-K Topaz, #751 Adonis etch, 9 oz . . . **125.00**
#7606-1/2 Athena, Carlton, crystal cased black filament **145.00**
#7614 Hampton, Anna Rose stem, Queen Louise Silk Screen, 9 oz **225.00**
#7614 Hampton, Golden iris, Virginia etch, 9 oz **65.00**
#7617 Brilliant, Ritz Blue, 10 oz **115.00**
#7617 Brilliant, Spanish Red, 10 oz **55.00**
#7623 Pygon, D. C. Thorpe satin open stem, 9 oz **185.00**
#7624 Paragon, Ebony open stem, 10 oz. **200.00**
#7625 Paramount, Meadow Green open stem, #765 Springtime etch, 10 oz. **165.00**
#7630 Ballerina, Aquamarine/Azure, Yukon cutting, 10 oz. **120.00**
#7630 Ballerina, Crystal bowl and stem, Gloria Blue foot, light copper wheel cutting on bowl. **35.00**
#7636 Square, open stem, 9 oz **245.00**
#7637 Courtney, D.C. Thorpe satin open stem, 9 oz **195.00**
#7638 Avalon, Anna Rose, Peacock Optic. **28.00**
#7638 Avalon, Venetian Green, Peacock Optic, 9 oz. **45.00**
#7640 Art Moderne, Ritz Blue, Crystal open stem, 9 oz . . . **155.00**
#7643 Golf Ball, 9 oz, Alabaster **150.00**
#7643 Golf Ball, 9 oz, Crystal . **35.00**
#7643 Golf Ball, 9 oz, Pastels. **55.00**
#7643 Golf Ball, 9 oz, Ritz Blue **58.00**
#7643 Golf Ball, 9 oz, Spanish Red **55.00**
#7643 Golf Ball, 9 oz, Stiegel Green **52.00**
#7644-1/2 Vernon, Venetian Green, Pineapple Optic, 9 oz. **55.00**
#7646 Sophisticate, Picardy etch, 9 oz. **65.00**
#7654 Lorna, Ritz Blue bowl, reverse twist stem **75.00**
#7654 Lorna, Sunrise Medallion crystal, alabaster stem and foot **250.00**
#7659 Cynthia, #746 Sonoma etch, 10 oz. **68.00**
#7664 Queen Anne, #758 Sunrise Medallion etch, 10 oz **95.00**
#7664 Queen Anne, Manchester Pheasant Silk Screen, 10 oz **275.00**
#7668 Galaxy, Azure, 9 oz. . . . **35.00**
#7668 Galaxy, Crystal, American Beauty etch **40.00**
#7668 Galaxy, Crystal, Charlton etch **40.00**
#7668 Galaxy, Crystal, Lace Bouquet etch. **30.00**
#7678 Old English, 10 oz, Ritz Blue **55.00**
#7678 Old English, 10 oz, Spanish Red **55.00**
#7678 Old English, 10 oz, Stiegel Green **65.00**
#7690 Monroe, Golden Iris, Amber, 9 oz **80.00**
#7810 Monaco, Crystal, Adam etch **35.00**
#8445 Plantation, Spanish Red and Crystal. **65.00**

Guest set

#23 Trudy, Alabaster, 6-3/8" h **175.00**
#23 Trudy, Anna Rose, Palm Optic, 6-3/8" h **90.00**
#23 Trudy, Baby Blue, 6-3/8" h **85.00**
#23 Trudy, Baby Blue carafe, India Black tumbler, 6-3/8" h **140.00**
#23 Trudy, Bristol Blue, 6-3/8" h **125.00**
#23 Trudy, Jade Green, 6-3/8" h **90.00**
#23 Trudy, Opaque Yellow carafe, India Black tumbler, 6-3/8" h **195.00**
#23 Trudy, Venetian Green, Palm Optic, 6-3/8" h **95.00**
#24 Margaret, Anna Rose, enamel decor, 5-7/8" h. **170.00**
#24 Margaret, Azure/Aquamarine, enamel decor, 5-7/8" h **575.00**
#24 Margaret, Jade Green, 5-7/8" h **185.00**
#24 Margaret, Golden Iris, pulled spout, handled **425.00**
Festoon Optic, Anna Rose. . . . **90.00**

Iced tea

#1962 Crinkle Line, Topaz, ftd. **15.00**
#1928 Ivy, Stiegel Green, 15 oz **75.00**
#7621 Ringer, Spanish Red, 14 oz **65.00**
#7622 Bracelet, Ritz Blue, 14 oz **85.00**
#7643 Golf Ball, Spanish Red . **55.00**
#7643 Golf Ball, Stiegel Green **40.00**
#7646 Sophisticate, ftd **40.00**
#7668 Galaxy, Crystal, Carlton etch **40.00**
#7668 Galaxy, Crystal, Lace Bouquet etch, ftd. **30.00**
#7678 Old English, Stiegel Green **65.00**
#7703 Sextette, Old Bristol, ftd, 11 oz **185.00**

Ice tub

#1933 El Mexicano Ice, 6" d. **210.00**
#1933 El Mexicano, Seaweed, 6" d. **215.00**

Ivy ball

#7643, Kimball, Ritz Blue, 4" **195.00**
#7643, Kimball, Spanish Red, 4" **110.00**
#7643, Kimball, Stiegel Green, 4" **125.00**

Jug

#6 Kaufmann, Old Bristol line, 54 oz **1,500.00**
#6 Kaufmann, #510 Doric Star Sand Blast, 54 oz **275.00**
#8 Orleans, #90 Starlet cutting, 54 oz **315.00**
#8 Orleans, #131 Brittany cutting, 54 oz **385.00**
#14 Eiffel, #282 needle etch, 65 oz **325.00**
#25 Olympic, Crystal, green handle, Spiral Optic **225.00**
#33 Martina, #518 Lily of the Valley Sand Blast dec, 46 oz, seven-piece set **585.00**
#33 Rawsthorne, Anna Rose, Peacock Optic, 48 oz. **465.00**
#36 Bolero, Pomona Two-Tone Line, 54 oz **985.00**
#37 Barry, Anna Rose handle and foot, Palm Optic, 48 oz. . . . **390.00**
#37 Barry, Zurich Two Tone Line, covered, 48 oz **860.00**
#303 Cyrano, #203 needle etch, 54 oz **385.00**
#545 Pickford Spiral, Amber, 54 oz **135.00**
#1933 LMX Del Rey, Randall Blue non-opaque, rare, 54 oz . . **675.00**
#1933 LMX Ockner, Ice, 64 oz **210.00**
#1933 LMX Ockner, Seaweed, 64 oz **210.00**
#1962 Ockner, Crinkle Line, 64 oz, Amethyst **145.00**
#1962 Ockner, Crinkle Line, 64 oz, Green **95.00**
#1962 Ockner, Crinkle Line, 64 oz, Pink Champagne **115.00**
#1962 Ockner, Crinkle Line, 64 oz, Pink Champagne, frosted . **165.00**
#1962 Ockner, Crinkle Line, 64 oz, Topaz Mist **95.00**
#1962 San Juan, Crinkle Line, Amethyst, Tankard, 64 oz. . **125.00**
#1962 Tijuana, Crinkle Line, Peacock Blue, Juice/Martini, 34 oz **80.00**

#7621 Carona, Anna Rose, 54 oz 350.00
#7622-1/2 Ringling, 54 oz, Golden Iris 650.00
#7622-1/2 Ringling, 54 oz, Randall Blue 535.00
#7622-1/2 Ringling, 54 oz, Spanish Red 695.00
#9844 Swirl, Burgundy, 54 oz 195.00
#20069 Melon, Alabaster, Ritz Blue trim 1,250.00
Karma, Nanking Blue, applied crystal handle 395.00
Pickford, Anna Rose, Palm Optic 265.00

Juice tumbler

#1962 Crinkle Line, India Black, flat, 6 oz 85.00
#7667-1/2 Jacobean, Spanish Red, crystal foot, 5 oz 28.00
#7711 Callahan, Crystal, Floret etch, 5 oz, ftd 22.00

Martini mixer

#78 Sexton, Steel Blue, 16 oz . 40.00
#78 Sexton, Thistle, silver and dark blue triangle sticker, 16 oz .. 55.00
#9906 Normandie, Steel Blue . 40.00

Parfait

#7643 Golf Ball, Cobalt blue . 125.00
#7711 Versailles, Callahan stem 65.00

Patio light

#9915 Federal, Bristol Blue ... 55.00
#9915 Federal, Evergreen 55.00
#9915 Federal, Pineapple 45.00
#9915 Federal, Ruby 55.00

Plate, #1500

#734 American Beauty etch, Anna Rose, dessert, 7" d 55.00
#734 American Beauty etch, Crystal, dessert, 7" d 45.00
#737 Victoria Regina dec, Meadow Green, dessert, 7" d 22.00
#743 Bramble Rose etch, Anna Rose, salad/luncheon, 8-1/2" d 55.00
#751 Adonis etch, 14-K Topaz, dessert, 7"d 58.00
#776 Nasreen etch, Alexandrite, dessert, 7" d 135.00
#776 Nasreen etch, 14-K Topaz, salad, 7-3/4" d 55.00
#810 Sear's Lace Bouquet etch, Crystal, dessert, 7" d....... 25.00
#1933 El Mexicano, ice, 6" d .. 18.00
#1933 El Mexicano, ice, 7" d .. 25.00
#1933 El Mexicano, ice, 9" d .. 45.00

Sherbet

#1962 Crinkle Line, 6 oz, Peacock Blue 18.00
#1962 Crinkle Line, 6 oz, Pineapple 32.50
#1962 Crinkle Line, 6 oz, Pink 24.00
#1962 Crinkle Line, 6 oz, Ruby 27.50
#3011 Montego, Gypsy Fired, 6-1/2" oz 38.00
#3011 Montego, Peacock Blue, 6-1/2 oz 24.00
#7577 Venus, Nanking Blue .. 30.00
#7620 Fontanne, #781 Fontinelle etch, 6 oz 165.00
#7640 Art Moderne, Ritz Blue, 5-1/2 oz 65.00
#7643 Golf Ball, 5-1/2 oz, Pastels 35.00
#7643 Golf Ball, 5-1/2 oz, Ritz Blue 45.00
#7643 Golf Ball, 5-1/2 oz, Spanish Red.................... 38.00
#7643 Golf Ball, 5-1/2 oz, Stiegel Green 35.00
#7646 Sophisticate, Picardy etch, 5-1/2 oz 48.00
#7654 Lorna, Meadow Green stem, #766 Nantucket etch, 5-1/2 oz 55.00
#7654-1/2 Legacy, Manchester Pheasant Silk Screen, 6-1/2 oz 135.00
#7668 Galaxy, Crystal, Carlton etch 40.00
#7690 Monroe, Old Amethyst, 6 oz 85.00
#7690 Monroe, Spanish red, 6 oz 70.00
#7780 The President's House, 6 oz 20.00

Shrimp cocktail

#1962, Crinkle Line, Peacock Blue 22.00
Floret, Crystal, orig liner 45.00

Torte plate, Crystal, Hollywood Platinum/Red band dec, 14" d . 395.00

Tumbler

#1962 Crinkle Line, Amberina, flat water, 10 oz 120.00
#1962 Crinkle Line, Peacock Blue, 12 oz, flat 12.00
#1962 Crinkle Line, Topaz, flat, 10 oz.................... 8.00
#7622 Ringling Red, 3" d, 4-1/2" h 35.00
#7640 Art Moderne, cobalt blue, ftd, 6-1/2" h................ 95.00
#7664 Queen Anne, Aquamarine/ Azure, #758 Elizabeth etch, 11 oz.....................115.00
#7668 Galaxy, Pink Champagne, ftd, 9 oz..................... 22.00
#7668 Galaxy, #778 Carlton etch, 9 oz...................... 22.00

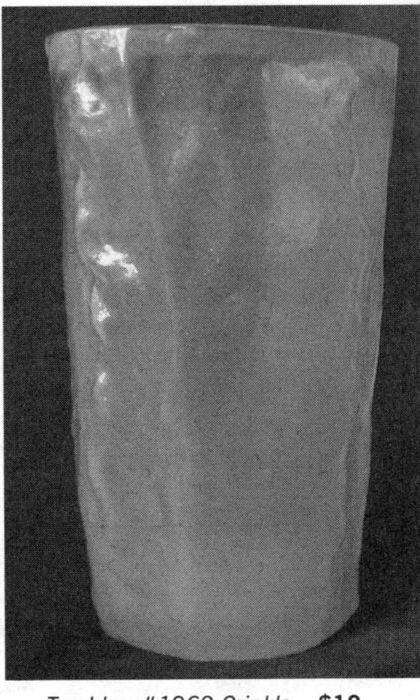

Tumbler, #1962 Crinkle, **$10.**

#7667-1/2 Jacobean, Spanish Red, crystal foot, 9 oz 45.00
#7678 Old English, Ritz Blue, ftd, 6-1/4" h 40.00
#7711 Callahan, Crystal, Floret etch, 10 oz, ftd 24.00
#8701 Garrett, American Beauty etching, short Zombie...... 30.00
#8701 Garrett, American Beauty etching, tall Zombie 38.00
#9051 Zenith, Venetian Green, Peacock Optic, bar, 2 oz.... 45.00
#9069 Spanish red and crystal, 12 oz 20.00
#9074 Belton, Golden Iris, #733 Virginia etch, 12 oz 48.00
#9074 Belton, Primrose, Vaseline, Pillar Optic, 9 oz 125.00
#9079 Economy, Bristol Blue.. 45.00
#9844 Swirl, Burgundy, 12 oz . 12.00
#9844 Swirl, Evergreen, 12 oz. 12.00
#9844 Swirl, Gloria Blue, 9 oz .. 9.50
#9844 Swirl, Gloria Blue, 10 oz 12.00
#9844 Swirl, green, 9 oz 9.50
#9844 Swirl, pink, 9 oz 9.50

Vase

#12 Viola, Rainbow Line, Spiral Optic, 8" h 120.00
#18 Lynda, Burgundy, Spiral Optic, 8" h 45.00
#18 Lynda, Evergreen, 8" h ... 35.00
#18 Lynda, Gypsy Fire, Pillar Optic, 8" h 40.00
#18 Lynda, Peacock Blue, 8" h 30.00
#24 Roseanne, Baby Blue, Allegheny Bird Screen Print, 10" h 350.00

#24 Roseanne, Topreen, (topaz body, Meadow Green foot, ruffled top, 10" h **325.00**
#25 Olympic, #734 American Beauty etch, 12" h **650.00**
#32 Donna, India Black, 6" h . **65.00**
#35-1/2 Electra, Continental Line, Old Amethyst, 10" h **1,000.00**
#36 Lara, Bristol Blue, slant top, 10" h **28.00**
#36 Lara, Burgundy, slant top, 8" h **28.00**
#36 Lara, Burgundy, slant top, 10" h **28.00**
#36 Lara, Ebony, slant top, 10" h **38.00**
#36 Lara, Gypsy Fire, slant top, 8" h **35.00**
#36 Lara, Pineapple, slant top, 8" h **28.00**
#36 Lara, Peacock Blue, slant top, 10" h, orig label **30.00**
#36 Uranus, Nanking Blue ... **95.00**
#43 Encino, Peacock Blue, 10-1/4" h **1,255.00**
#45 Catherine, Crystal with Meadow Green foot, Spiral Optic and iridized, 10" h **125.00**
#45 Catherine, Ebony with gold encrusted Minton band, 10" h **125.00**
#45 Catherine, Laurel Line, Crystal with Meadow Green foot, Spiral Optic, 10" h.............. **95.00**
#45 Catherine, Topreen, Topaz with Meadow Green foot, Spiral Optic, 10" h **275.00**
#46 Petite, Anna Rose, crystal foot, 6" h **50.00**
#46 Petite, Gloria Blue, Crystal foot, Palm Optic, 6" h **55.00**
#53 Serenade, Anna Rose .. **125.00**
#53 Serenade, Jade **145.00**
#53 Serenade, Stiegel Green **125.00**
#54 Media, Golden Iris, Pillar Optic, 10" h **225.00**
#61 Chanson, Bristol Blue ... **48.00**
#61 Chanson, Pineapple **28.00**
#61 Chanson, Spiral Optic, Burgundy **25.00**
#61 Chanson, Peacock Blue . **45.00**
#61 Chanson, Spiral Optic, Moss Green **18.00**
#61 Chanson, Steel Blue **45.00**
#67 Fantasia, Bristol Blue.... **58.00**
#67 Grecian, Ebony, Saracenic Art Line, 6" h..............**1,200.00**
#70 Maxwell, Bristol Blue **48.00**
#70 Maxwell, Peacock Blue, 9-1/2" h **25.00**
#73 Radio, Ritz Blue, 6" h... **895.00**
#78 Elinor, Burgundy........**30.00**
#90 Daisy, Crystal, Green and White Wash, 9-1/2" h...........**450.00**
#91 Lalique, Crystal Satin, 8-1/4" h **650.00**
#108 Wheatley, Peacock Blue, Spiral Optic, 11-1/2" h...........**65.00**
#114 Tuscany, Bristol Blue....**48.00**
#122 Kathleen, Bristol Blue...**28.00**
#122 Kathleen, Gypsy Fire, orig label **30.00**
#122 Kathleen, Moss Green (Golden Moss)..................**25.00**
#122 Kathleen, Spanish Red..**28.00**
#123 Diana, Moss Green (Golden Moss)..................**25.00**
#124 Bodden, Evergreen **30.00**
#206 Colette, Amethyst......**75.00**
#1160 Baronet, Bristol Blue...**35.00**
#1160 Baronet, White Opaque **48.00**
#1161 Finale, Opaque White..**35.00**
#1161 Finale, Pineapple **45.00**
#1933 Gaydos, LMX Seaweed, 6-1/2" h **785.00**
#1933 Santiago, Ice.........**85.00**
#1962 Snowball, Moss Green .**30.00**
#1205 Spindle, White Opaque, candleholder/vase.........**65.00**
#7261 Ringer, Aquamarine/Azure, flip, 8" h **295.00**
#7643 Golf Ball, urn, Spanish Red **125.00**
#9902 Adams, Bristol Blue, slant top, 7" h **28.00**
#9902 Adams, Burgundy, slant top, 7" h **22.50**
#9902 Adams, Evergreen, slant top, 9" h **40.00**
#9902 Adams, Evergreen, slant top, 12" h **55.00**
#9902 Adams, Lime Green, slant top, 7" h................**28.00**
#9902 Adams, Lime Green, slant top, 12" h...............**75.00**
#9902 Adams, Peacock Blue, slant top, 7" h................**22.50**
#9902 Adams, Peacock Blue, slant top, 12" h...............**65.00**
#9902 Adams, Pineapple, slant top, 7" h **22.50**
#9902 Adams, Smoke, slant top, 9" h **18.00**
#9902 Adams, Spanish Red, slant top, 7" h................**28.00**
#9912 Marlborough, Peacock Blue **55.00**
#9956 Carleen, Bristol Blue...**30.00**
#9956 Carleen, Burgundy, Panel Optic **35.00**
#9956 Carleen, Burgundy, Spiral Optic **35.00**
#9956 Carleen, Moss Green (Golden Moss), Panel Optic........ **35.00**
#9956 Carleen, Ruby **35.00**
#9986 Metropolitan, Bristol Blue **65.00**
Flamenco, Gypsy Fire, 12" h . **35.00**
Lido, Amberina............ **45.00**
Lido, Bristol Blue **45.00**
Lido, Jade............... **40.00**
Lido, Ritz Blue **75.00**
Lido, Ruby **75.00**

Wine

#7565 Astrid, Anna Rose, #734 American Beauty etch, 3 oz **125.00**
#7560 Horizon, #735 Richmond etch, 3 oz **55.00**
#7577 Venus, Anna Rose, #743 Bramble Rose etch, 3-1/2 oz **145.00**
#7577 Venus, Genova Artware, 1921 .... **55.00**
#7587 Hanover, #733 Virginia etch w/#25 Minton Gold band, 3 oz **45.00**
#7616 Wescott, crystal, red filament, 4-7/8" h................ **75.00**
#7643 Golf Ball, 3 oz, Alabaster **145.00**
#7643 Golf Ball, 3 oz, Pastels. **60.00**
#7643 Golf Ball, 3 oz, Ritz Blue **65.00**
#7643 Golf Ball, 3 oz, Spanish Red **60.00**
#7643 Golf Ball, 3 oz, Stiegel Green **55.00**
#7617 Brilliant, Ritz Blue, 2-1/2 oz **120.00**
#7640 Art Moderne, ebony stem, 3 oz **145.00**
#7654 Lorna, Nantucket etch, 3 oz **85.00**
#7660-1/2 Empress, Spanish Red, 3 oz **85.00**
#7662 Majesty, Spanish Red, 3-1/2 oz **85.00**
#7668 Galaxy, Azure, 2-1/2 oz **40.00**
#7668 Galaxy, #810 Sears' Lace Bouquet etch, 2-1/2 oz..... **48.00**
#7673 Lexington, Ritz Blue filament lament, #790 Fairwin etch, 3 oz **135.00**
#7678 Old English, Spanish Red **55.00**
#7693 Warwick, Stiegel Green, 2-1/2 oz **55.00**
#7706 Octave, ruby filament . **55.00**
#7720 Palazzo, Violet, 3-1/2 oz **120.00**
#7721 Panama, Sharon decor, 3 oz **225.00**
#8445 Plantation, Cobalt Blue **125.00**

#8445 Plantation, Lotus Green, 3 oz **125.00**
#8446 Summer Cornucopia, Copen Blue bowl, 3 oz **325.00**
#9074 Belton, Peacock Optic, Meadow Green **20.00**

MOSER GLASS

Moser / Moser Karlsbad

History: Ludwig Moser (1833-1916) founded his polishing and engraving workshop in 1857 in Karlsbad (Karlovy Vary), Czechoslovakia. He employed many famous glass designers, e.g., Johann Hoffmann, Josef Urban, and Rudolf Miller. In 1900, Moser and his sons, Rudolf and Gustav, incorporated Ludwig Moser & Söhne.

Moser art glass included clear pieces with inserted blobs of colored glass, cut colored glass with classical scenes, cameo glass, and intaglio cut items. Many inexpensive enameled pieces also were made.

In 1922, Leo and Richard Moser bought Meyr's Neffe, their biggest Bohemian art glass rival. Moser executed many pieces for the Wiener Werkstätte in the 1920s. The Moser glass factory continues to produce new items.

References: Gary Baldwin and Lee Carno, *Moser—Artistry in Glass*, Antique Publications, 1988; Gary Baldwin, *Moser—Artistry in Glass, Second Edition*, Antique Publications, 1997; Mural K. Charon and John Mareska, *Ludvik Moser, King of Glass*, published by author, 1984; Jan Mergl and Lenka Pankova, *Moser 1857-1997*, Austrian Publisher, English version distributed to Eaton's Glass Books, (http://glassbooks.com), 1997.

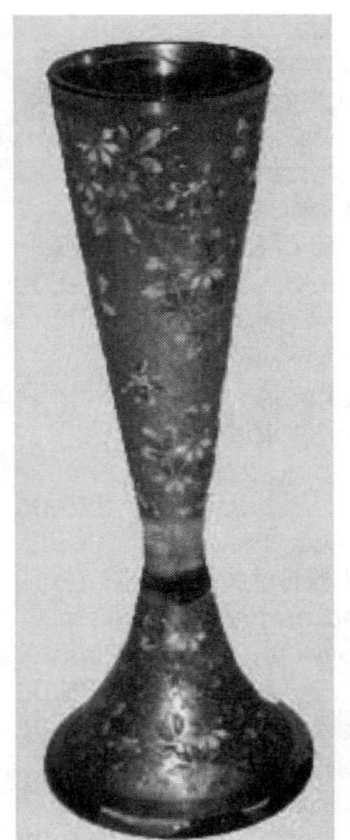

Bud vase, allover floral decoration and gilding, signed, 6-1/4" h, **$325.** *Photo courtesy of Joy Luke Fine Art Brokers and Auctioneers.*

Basket, 5-1/2" h, green malachite ground, molded cherubs dec, pr **800.00**

Bell, 5-1/2" h, cranberry cut to colorless, gold scrolling, orig clapper **110.00**

Bowl
7-1/4" d, 5-5/8" h, opalescent pink shaded ground, multicolored enameled oak leaves and foliage, applied lustered acorns, sgd in gold on base **1,200.00**
8" d, sapphire blue ground, colorless applied feet, enameled and gilt floral dec, script sgd "Moser" **200.00**

Box, cov
3-3/8" h, circular, deep purple ground, gold enameled fauns and maidens, fitted cov, four ball feet, etched "Made in Czechoslovakia Moser Karlsbad" **1,200.00**
4-1/2" l, red ground, enameled blue and white floral motif, gilt highlights **550.00**
6" d, 3-3/4" h, cranberry ground, white enameled woman carrying cornucopia and grapes, gold enameled vine and berries **650.00**

Cabinet vase, 2" h, 2-1/2" w, bulbous, citron green ground, applied brass rim, three black glass acorns, gold and yellow florals and leaves, three flying insects, sgd "Moser Carlsbad" under base. **200.00**

Calling card holder
Cranberry ground, turquoise jewels, gold prunts, four scrolled feet **375.00**
Crystal ground, two multicolored enameled birds of paradise in center, bird on ruffled rim. . **225.00**

Centerpiece
5" x 9", green ground, intaglio cut flowers **425.00**
11" d oval bowl, intaglio, emerald green shading to clear ground, sgd **215.00**

Chalice, cov, 9-1/2" h, amber and colorless ground, faceted, central landscape frieze, gold leaves outlined in white, gold and black dots, white dotted blossoms, neck, base, and orange stopper heavily gold encrusted **425.00**

Cologne bottle
7-1/2" h, 3-1/2" d, amethyst shaded to clear ground, deep intaglio cut flowers and leaves, orig stopper, sgd **695.00**
9-1/2" h, deep cobalt blue ground, enameled floral scene, matching stopper, script engraved "Moser" **225.00**

Compote
4" h, 8-1/4" d, hollow base, pale amber ground, electric blue rigaree and four applied dec, int. deck of 12 painted leaves, brown branches, gold leaves, white cherries, matching branch on base **650.00**
9-1/2" h, quatraform, crystal ground, gilt enameled heavy scrollwork reserves, matching dec on pedestal foot, crystal stem, pr **400.00**

Cordial
1-3/8" h, cranberry bowl, colorless stem, multicolored enameled flowers, bee, and insect dec on base **100.00**
2-1/2" h, Alexandrite, flared cup, dichroic light blue to pink glass, facet cut with 12 panels, c1925 . . . . **115.00**

Cordial set
9" h cordial decanter with broad faceted stopper, inverted cone-shaped vessel of colorless glass, dec with diagonal bands of engraved lines, six 3" h matching cordials, "Moser" acid stamp in polished pontil of decanter . **375.00**
10-1/4" h frosted and polished smoky topaz decanter, four cordials, molded nude women, five-pc set **265.00**

Cruet, 13" h, pigeon blood ground, 11 raised acorns, raised enameled tracery branches and dragonfly, trefoil spout, applied handle, orig paper label **1,850.00**

Cup and saucer, amber ground, gold scrolls, multicolored enameled flowers **295.00**

Decanter
10-1/2" h, ovoid, flattened sides, colorless ground **125.00**
11-1/2" h, 4-1/4" d base, cranberry and white opaque overlay, six opaque petal shapes with gold tree and branch design, gilt dec around each petal, top formed by six cut petals edged in gold, gold vertical lines, tulip-shaped stopper with six opaque white petal shapes with conforming dec, c1880. . **1,375.00**
Underplate, 10" h, white overlaid in pink, cut to crystal, thumbprints

and leafage, script engraved "Moser" 275.00

Demitasse cup and saucer, amber shading to white, enameled gilt flowers 100.00

Ewer

5-3/4" h, 2-3/4" d, crystal shaded to gold ground, multicolored enameled flowers and green leaves, pedestal base, unsgd 285.00

9" h, cov, horn shape, aquamarine ground, all over gold leaves, vines and flowers, pedestal base 925.00

10-3/4" h, cranberry ground, gilt surface, applied acorns and clear jewels 2,000.00

Fernery, 7" d, deep amethyst ground, inverted thumbprint, enameled florals, script sgd "Moser" 450.00

Finger bowl, matching underplate

6" d bowl, 7" d underplate, scalloped, shaded pink to lavender ground, gold, silver, and blue enameled Arabesque dec, white petit-point dec 975.00

6-1/2" d bowl, Alexandrite ground, sgd 250.00

Flask, 7-1/2" l, powder horn shape, deep cranberry ground, multicolored enameled fern dec, brass spigot, fittings and orig chain 775.00

Goblet

4-1/2" h, cranberry ground, enameled, gold overlay, wheel cut design, ftd stem with gold overlay on base, six-pc set....... 500.00

5-1/4" h, 3-1/2" d, colorless ground, gold overlay, relief amethyst sq blocks................ 225.00

8" h, cranberry ground, Rhine-style, enameled oak leaves, applied acorns, four-pc set...... 1,800.00

Ice cream set, master bowl and four serving bowls, clear shading to gold ground, mermaid relief, gilt highlights 395.00

Jar, cov, 10-3/4" h, goblet form, amber ground, polished faceted panels, conforming inset cov......... 315.00

Juice tumbler, colorless ground, enameled florals, lace-type trim, 83 applied glass jewels 235.00

Lamp, 18" h, 7-1/4" w globe, cranberry opaque ground, multicolored enamel floral dec, gilt scroll dec, finely cut pattern on globe and base, acid etched signature on base, c1920 .... 4,800.00

Mug, 4-1/4" h, topaz colored crackle ground, heavy gold handle and base edging, four applied insects with polychrome dec 345.00

Nappy, 5" w, 1-3/4" h, pastel green, yellow, blue, and pink, four enameled foxes, applied loop handle, polished disc base 500.00

Pansy vase, 14" h, colorless ground, multicolored dec........... 1,000.00

Patch box, cov

2" d, 1-1/4" h, light amber, enamel and gilt dec............. 140.00

2-3/8" d, 1-1/2" h, green, ribbed, enamel and gilt dec 160.00

Perfume bottle

4-3/4" h, pink-lavender Alexandrite ground, faceted panels, matching stopper, sgd in oval....... 275.00

5" h, emerald green ground, allover floral dec, orig stopper 275.00

6-1/2" h, 4-1/4" d, Malachite ground, molded bottle and stopper, slab polished sides and top 295.00

Pitcher

5" h, aqua blue crackle ground, 3" l enameled brown, tan, and orange lobster and seaweed, applied colorless handle, polished pontil 850.00

5-1/2" h, chartreuse craquelle ground, two wading storks among cattails and flowers, applied angled handle, enamel chip to stork beak 275.00

5-1/2" h, cranberry crackle ground, applied colorless handle, polished pontil 575.00

6-3/4" h, amberina ground, inverted thumbprint pattern, four yellow, red, blue, and green applied glass beaded bunches of grapes, pinched in sides, three-dimensional bird beneath spout, allover enamel and gold leaves, vines, and tendrils 3,200.00

8" h, light amber crackle ground, multicolored enameled fish and underwater plants, applied colorless handle, polished pontil 750.00

8-1/2" h, amber ground, multicolored enameled florals 275.00

11-3/4" h, bright transparent blue ground, heavy gilding, enameled fern fronds, birds, and insects, applied salamander handle 2,400.00

Plate, 7-3/8" d, amber ground, gold dec 150.00

Pokal, cov, 8" h, cut, faceted, and enameled, amethyst body with cut panels, gold and high relief floral dec, wafer foot with cut stem 700.00

Portrait vase, 8-1/2" h, colorless ground, multicolored portrait of woman, gold leaves, light wear 450.00

Rose bowl, 6" h, 6-1/2" d, colorless ground, outward flared ruffled top, allover gold enamel dec, vines, flowers, and lattice, c1858 .... 475.00

Scent bottle

5" h, emerald green ground, multicolored leaves and berries, ball stopper 195.00

11" h, cranberry ground, leaves, white and gold dec 400.00

Sherry, 4-1/4" h, crystal ground, gold and white beading, knobbed stem, wafer base................ 225.00

Sweetmeat dish, round, cranberry ground, engraved, gold band.. 225.00

Toothpick, cranberry ground, colorless pedestal, cut, sgd.......... 145.00

Tumbler

3-1/2" h, octagonal, ruby cut to clear ground, gold dec 85.00

4" h, green, red, and blue, elaborately dec with floral, scrolled, beading, and gild, some beads missing, nine-pc set...... 460.00

Urn, 15-3/4" h, cranberry ground, two gilt handles, studded with green, blue, clear, and red stones, highly enameled surface, multicolored and gilt Moorish dec 3,500.00

Vase

5-1/4" h, 2-5/8" w, light green ground, coralene beaded dec around top, gilt coralene leaf design, white enameled branches, blue dot enameled highlights, center five-petal flower with two sprays of leaves, white enameled opaque scene of tree and mountains, between spray of leaves on front, c1890 .... 500.00

6" h, vertical ribs crown rim in graceful golden waves, thick enameled pansies and foliage in natural colors, golden grasses, amethyst shading to colorless ground 325.00

6-1/2" h, colorless, Inverted Thumbprint body, MOP luster, two fish enameled on front, entire school on obverse, chip to enamel of one fin 275.00

6-1/2" h, cranberry ground, heavy applied dec of scrolls, abstract flowers, and butterflies, four ftd, #2208................. 950.00

7" h, paneled amber baluster body, wide gold medial band of women warriors, base inscribed "Made in Czechoslovakia-Moser Karlsbad" **550.00**
7-1/4" h, amber, cut and polished, optic cube panels, 12-sided tapered form, later inscribed "Moser, Austria" **200.00**
7-3/4" h, long neck shading from emerald green shading to clear ground, bulbous base, gold and platinum floral dec, diamond point signature **375.00**
8" h, octagonal tapered form, crystal, cut and polished, rows of optic cubes **100.00**
8-1/4" h, diamond form, smoky, cut and polished, nick on base. **100.00**
8-1/4" h, 6-1/2" w, bulbous base, narrow neck, three applied rolled handles, blue ground, enameled dec of green and pink grasshopper, delicate pastel flowers, and leaves, round pink enameled circle with brown and turquoise beetle and spray of pink and blue flowers with green leaves, gilt dec, vertical stripe, enameled pink and white flowers, gilt and turquoise green leaves . . **1,200.00**
9" h, cranberry ground, two gilt handles, medallion with hp roses, sgd **1,050.00**
10" h, flared purple cylinder, broad medial band of etched griffins, urns, and swags, enameled in gold, polished pontil **375.00**
10" h, heavy walled dark amethyst faceted body, etched and gilded medial scene of bear hunt, spear-armed men and dogs pursuing large bear. **345.00**
10" h, trumpet, red Venetian ground, heavy gold filigree surrounding central Greek Goddess Diana wearing clinging dress, one bare breast, standing next to buck, other side with Diana holding bird, standing next to doe **450.00**
10-1/2" h, cylindrical, frosted green, enamel dec butterflies fluttering around meadow grasses. . . **350.00**
10-1/2" h, octagonal, smoky, cut and polished horizontal panes . . **225.00**
11" h, emerald green ground, intricately enameled fish, four applied pickerel, handles . . **900.00**
11-1/4" h, bifurcated rim, conical shaped vessel with honeycomb-cut zigzag band in colorless glass on transparent cobalt blue optic-ribbed flared base, acid etched "Moser" on polished pontil, c1940 . . . . **965.00**
11-1/2" h, alternating blue and yellow bands, ivory enameled florals, script engraved "Moser" . . **385.00**
12" h, triangular baluster, ruby ground, gold enameled children dec **265.00**
12-1/8" h, 3-7/8" w, flaring neck, stepped pedestal base, delicate gold all over fern and floral design on neck and body, 2-3/8" border with gold design, acid cutback dots above and below border, pink, white, purple, orange and magenta floral dec of pansies, bell flowers, mums, daisies and clematis, shaded green foliage all around base, orig paper label with design number, c1880 . . . . **2,800.00**
12-1/4" h, cobalt blue ground, large enameled florals and gold dec, script engraved "Moser" . . **220.00**
12-1/2" h, cranberry ground, stylized gilt florals, script engraved "Moser" **275.00**
12-1/2" h, green ground, six gold cartouche with jewels surrounded by seed pearls, gold filigree around neck and base, minor wear **300.00**
12-1/2" h, 5-1/2" w, aventurine glass, deep emerald green, allover gold flecking, Art Nouveau style gold and painted enamel dec, sgd "Bares Moser Karlsbad". . . **275.00**
14-1/2" h, cranberry shading to colorless, swirled body, enameled florals, script engraved "Moser" **175.00**

Vase, amethyst, signed, 4-1/4" h, **$425.** *Photo courtesy of Joy Luke Fine Art Brokers and Auctioneers.*

15-1/2" h, clear and frosted ground, deeply etched thistles, inscribed "Moser/Karlsbad" **420.00**
23-1/2" h, cranberry ground, enameled leaf surface, applied acorns, three dimensional eagle and bird, sgd "Moser," stand **8,250.00**

Water set, 8" h pitcher, six 4" h tumblers, colorless, ribbed body, dec with peasant seated on bench holding stem, three tumblers with same design, three with peasant women doing chores, gold trim, some scratches **600.00**

Wine
Rainbow glass, funnel shaped cup, Inverted Baby Thumbprint pattern, enameled grapes and leaves dec, applied row of gold knobs around top **365.00**
Turquoise shading to clear ground, allover gold leaf dec, heavy applied prunts. **425.00**

Mount Washington Glass Company

History: In 1837, Deming Jarves, founder of the Boston and Sandwich Glass Company, established for his son, George D. Jarves, the Mount Washington Glass Company in Boston, Massachusetts. In the following years, the leadership and the name of the company changed several times as George Jarves formed different associations.

In the 1860s, the company was owned and operated by Timothy Howe and William L. Libbey. In 1869, Libbey bought a new factory in New Bedford, Massachusetts. The Mount Washington Glass Company began operating there again under its original name. Henry Libbey became associated with the company early in 1871. He resigned in 1874 during the general Depression, and the glassworks was closed. William Libbey had resigned in 1872 when he went to work for the New England Glass Company.

The Mount Washington Glass Company opened again in the fall of 1874 under the presidency of A. H. Seabury and the management of Frederick S. Shirley. In 1894, the glassworks became a part of the Pairpoint Manufacturing Company.

Throughout its history the Mount Washington Glass Company made different types of glass including pressed, blown, art, lava, Napoli, cameo, cut, Albertine, and Verona.

References: George C. Avila, *The Pairpoint Glass Story,* Reynolds-DeWalt Printing, Inc., 1968; Sean and Johanna S. Billings, *Peachblow Glass, Collector's Identification & Price Guide,* Krause Publications, 2000; Kyle Husfloen, contributing editor Louis O. St. Aubin, Jr., *Antique Trader's American & European*

Decorative and Art Glass Price Guide, 2nd ed., Krause Publications, 2000; Edward and Sheila Malakoff, *Pairpoint Lamps*, Schiffer Publishing, 1990; *Pairpoint Manufacturing Company 1894 Catalogue Reprint,* Antique Publications, 1997; Kenneth Wilson, *American Glass 1760-1930: The Toledo Museum of Art, Volume I, Volume II,* Hudson Hills Press and The Toledo Museum of Art, 1994.

Collectors Club: Mount Washington Art Glass Society, P.O. Box 24094, Fort Worth, TX 76124-1094

Museum: The New Bedford Glass Museum, New Bedford, MA.

Additional Listings: Burmese; Crown Milano; Peachblow; Royal Flemish.

Basket, mother of pearl satin

6-3/4" h, 6-1/2" w, deep pink shading to pale pink, Diamond Quilted pattern, applied frosted loop handle **200.00**

9" h, 7" w, deep blue shading to pale white, Herringbone pattern, applied camphor edge, large twisted and frosted thorn handle **300.00**

9-1/2" h, 5" w, shaded apricot pink to off white, Herringbone pattern, applied frosted loop handle **150.00**

9-1/2" h, 7-1/2" w, bright spring daffodil yellow shading to pale yellow, Herringbone pattern, ruffled edge, applied frosted loop handle with thorns **250.00**

11" h, 11" w, deep yellow shaded ext. bright pink shading to deep red int., Diamond Quilted patterned, applied ruffled camphor edge, applied camphor thorn handle **500.00**

Beverage set, mother of pearl satin

Coralene, yellow sea weed dec, glossy finish, 9" h, bulbous water pitcher, three-spout top, applied reeded shell handle, three matching 4" h tumblers, two blisters on pitcher, three-pc set . . . **750.00**

Herringbone, 9" h bulbous water pitcher, 7" w, applied frosted handle, deep rose to deep pink to pink, to off white, enameled and painted white wild roses, green, brown, and gold leaves, stems, branches, and thorns, four 3-3/4" h tumblers, damage to tumbler, five-pc set. **1,750.00**

Biscuit jar, cov, 7" h, 5" w, raised swirl patter, white shading to beige, white enamel beading, pink and white enameled rose, orig silver plated fittings **200.00**

Bottle, 3-1/2" h, raised neck, flattened ovoid, opaque white, enameled pink and cream daisies, gilt rim, wear to enamel **275.00**

Bowl

4-1/2" d, satin, pink floral dec . **95.00**

4-1/2" d, 2-3/4" h, Rose amber, fuchsia, blue swirl bands, bell tone flint. **295.00**

10-1/2" d, blue satin int., chrysanthemums and leaves dec on ext., ruffled **280.00**

Box, cov

4" h, 7" d, colorless frosted ground, molded swirls, Royal Flemish type dec, yellow blossoms on leafy blossoms, central enamel outlined cartouche with single red bead, gilt-metal hinged rim, wear, no lining **2,645.00**

4" h, 7" d, colorless frosted ground, molded swirls, Royal Flemish type dec, Wavecrest style dancing flamingoes, gilt-metal hinged rim, wear, lining soiled **3,450.00**

4-1/2" h, 6-1/2" d, opalware, mint green ground, deep pink roses, small red cornflowers, gold trim, blown-out floral and ribbon design, #3212/20 . . . . **1,750.00**

4-3/4" h, 6-1/2" d, opalware, soft beige ground, portrait of reclining colonial lady, base numbered "3212/90," repairs needed to hinge **1,100.00**

Bride's basket, 10-1/2" d, 10-3/4" h, MOP satin, Diamond Quilted pattern, deep pink shading to pale pink to off-white, Mt. Washington rectangular form bowl, applied frosted edge, orig fancy silver plated Victorian "Manhattan Silver Company," holder has been resilvered **400.00**

Calling card tray, 6-1/4" d, white lusterless, ruffled, flowers and two butterflies dec **65.00**

Candlesticks, pr, 8-7/8" h, 3-1/4" d base, pressed, emerald green, petal socket joined by wafer to fluted standard, sq base with chamfered corners, attributed to Mt Washington Glass Works or American Flint Glass Works, both South Boston, MA, 1840-55, large loss to one base, other with imperfections and flaw, price for pr **2,100.00**

Caster set, satin, multicolored enameled floral dec, SP Pairpoint holder **250.00**

Collars and cuffs box, opalware, shaped as two collars with big bow in front, cov dec with orange and pink Oriental poppies, silver poppy-shaped finial with gold trim, base with poppies, white ground, gold trim, bright blue bow, white polka dots, buckle on back, sgd "Patent applied for April 10, 1894," #2390/128 . . . . **950.00**

Compote

5-1/2" h, 7-3/8" d, Napoli, colorless dish, reverse painted maroon with blue and yellow blossoms and leaves, gold highlights on int., silvered ribbed metal base marked "Pairpoint B4702". **500.00**

11" h, 4-1/2" h, Ambero, thick bowl with reverse painted enameled grapes and leaves, thin layer of lemon flashing on base and wafer foot, rolled over rim, sgd "Ambero C" **950.00**

11" h, 10-1/4" d, Napoli, deep cranberry colored ground, painted and gilded dec of peaches, green leaves, naturalistic colors, Art Nouveau style silver plated Pairpoint base with elaborate poppy design, some orig gold wash on base, sgd "Pairpoint Manufacturing Company, New Bedford, Mass Quadruple Plate #B4704" **650.00**

Cracker jar, 9-1/2" h, 7-1/2" w, opalware, bright yellow ground, pink Oriental poppies, green leaves dec, blown-out floral and leaf design on base, orig metal hardware, base marked "3930/230," cov marked "Pairpoint" **525.00**

Creamer, 3" h, melon ribbed, enameled leaf and floral dec, SP handle and spout **200.00**

Cruet

Acid Cut, enameled blue and white flowers, soft yellow shaded throat, handle, and stopper. **1,950.00**

Acid Cut, white body, leaves and blue berries, yellow throat, handle, and stopper **1,950.00**

Dresser box, cov, 6-1/4" h, 8" w, painted satin finish ground shading from tan to gold and brown, large enameled poppies, buds, and leaves, shades of yellow, tan, brown, red, and white, top with large blown out central flower with gold highlights, hinged, orig emb silver plated trim, worn orig green satin lining, base numbered "4655/820" **1,750.00**

Ewer

7" h, bulbous, gilt orange enameled floral vine, textured overlay flaming body cov in Roman gold, hand and rim with traces of gold, hand numbered 6-1093/15 over P510 . . . . **250.00**

7-3/4" h, conical lusterless white ground, hand painted and enameled thistle blossoms and leaves, elongated pouring lip, applied reeded handle **195.00**

13" h, satin, shaded blue mother of pearl, white lining, applied frosted and twisted rope handle, white pedestal base **775.00**

Flower holder, 5-1/4" d, 3-1/2" h, mushroom shape, white ground, blue dot and oak leaf dec **425.00**

Flower frog, 3" h, 5-1/2" d, mushroom shape, pedestal base, painted Burmese coloration, top dec with white, yellow, and tan daisies and leaves **250.00**

Fruit bowl, 10" d, 7-1/2" h, Napoli, solid dark green ground painted on clear glass, outside dec with pale pink and white pond lilies, green and pink leaves and blossoms, int. dec with gold highlight traceries, silver-plated base with pond lily design, two applied loop handles, four buds form feet, base sgd "Pairpoint Mfg. Co. B4704" . . **2,200.00**

Humidor, 5-1/2" h, 4-1/2" d top, hinged silver-plated metalwork rim and edge, blown-out rococo scroll pattern, brilliant blue Delft windmills, ships, and landscape, Pairpoint **950.00**

Jewel box, 4-1/2" d top, 5-1/4" d base, 3-1/4" h, opalware, Monk drinking glass of red wine on lid, solid shaded green background on cover and base, fancy gold-washed, silver-plated rim and hinge, orig satin lining, artist sgd "Schindler" **550.00**

Jar, covered, apricot, white daisies decoration, silver-plated fittings signed "Pairpoint," 3" h, **$190.**

Jug

6" h, 4" w, satin, Polka Dot, deep peachblow pink, white air traps, Diamond Quilted pattern, unlined, applied frosted loop handle **475.00**

6" h, 5-1/2" w, Verona, yellow, gold, and purple spider mums and buds, green leaves dec **450.00**

Lamp, parlor, four dec glass oval insert panels, orig dec white opalware ball shade with deep red carnations, sgd "Pairpoint" base, c1890. . . . . . **1,750.00**

Lamp shade, 4-1/4" h, 5" d across top, 2" d fitter, rose amber, ruffled, fuschia shading to deep blue, Diamond Quilted pattern **575.00**

Miniature lamp, 17" h, 4-1/2" d shade, banquet style, milk glass, bright blue Delft dec of houses and trees, orig metal fittings, attributed to Frank Guba **795.00**

Mustard pot

3-1/4" h, 1-3/4" w, melon ribbed, satin finish, yellow shaded to white ground, enameled pink apple blossom dec, green leaves, orig silver plated notched cover, brass bail handle **175.00**

4-1/2" h, ribbed, bright yellow and pink background, painted white and magenta wild roses, orig silver-plated hardware **185.00**

Perfume bottle

5-1/4" h, 3" d, opalware, dark green and brown glossy ground, red and yellow nasturtiums, green leaves, sprinkler top **375.00**

6" h, 2-1/4" w, sq, satin, woman in 1890s dress, script on back "Hout's Milk White March 19, 1894-50th Performance Boston Theatre Boston," orig threaded atomizer **175.00**

Pickle castor, deep cranberry satin ground, Optic Diamond and Inverted Thumbprint pattern insert, gold spider mums dec, ftd Simpson Hall frame, ornate engraved cov, orig silvering **700.00**

Pitcher

5" h, 5" w, Verona, gold fish swimming among coral, rust, purple, and green sea plants, blue ground, green plants on handle, gold trim, spout and rim . . **1,000.00**

5-1/2" h, 3-1/4" d, Hobnail pattern, Burmese, deep salmon shading to bright yellow ground, acid finish, applied bright yellow handle **1,600.00**

Salt shaker, Egg and Blossom, 2-1/2" h, **$135.**

6" h, 3" w, satin, Diamond Quilted pattern, mother of pearl, large frosted camphor shell loop handle **325.00**

8" h, Verona, bulbous, maiden hair fern dec, gold highlights, applied colorless reeded handle . . . **265.00**

Plate

7" d, country scene of stone bridge, cottage, and lake, factory dec, orig paper label **125.00**

12" d, twin cupids, leaf and floral border **125.00**

Rose bowl, 4" h, 5" d, satin, bright yellow, enameled red berries, pale orange leaves and branches, eight large ribbed swirls **145.00**

Salt and pepper shakers

Chicks, 2-1/4" h, 2-1/2" l, opal, hand painted floral dec, figural metal chicken head covers, pr . . . **450.00**

Egg shape, Egg in Blossom . **135.00**

Fig shape, 2-3/8" h, light yellow over white opaque, hand painted floral dec, wear to dec **80.00**

Fig shape, 2-1/2" h, mauve, forget-me-not dec, orig top. **225.00**

Fig shape, 2-1/2" h, pastel yellow ground, pine cone motif, orig top **200.00**

Fig shape, 2-1/2" h, white ground, floral dec, orig top. **225.00**

Holly dec, holder, pr **385.00**

Little Apple, blue, satin finish, hand painted floral dec, 1-7/8" h, wear to dec **90.00**

Little Apple, pink, satin finish, hand painted floral dec, 1-7/8" h, wear to dec **90.00**
Little Apple, tan shading to white, glossy finish, hand painted floral dec, 1-7/8" h, wear to dec .. **95.00**
Melon ribbed, shades from pink to white, yellow and white daisy dec, screw on pewter lid, 2" h, 2" w, pr **150.00**
Tomato shape, biscuit color, enameled blue raspberries and white blossoms, screw on top, 1-3/4" h **85.00**
Tomato shape, coral shading to yellow, hand painted floral dec, orig lid, 1-3/4" h **110.00**
Tomato shape, light blue-green shading to white, satin finish, hand painted floral dec, orig lid, 1-3/4" h **90.00**
Tomato shape, opal glass, pink and yellow pansy dec, 2-1/4" h, 2-1/2" w **95.00**
Tomato shape, pale pink, blue and yellow iris and foliage, screw on top, 1-3/4" h **90.00**
Tomato shape, pale yellow, fall leaves, screw on cap, 1-3/4" h **80.00**
Tomato shape, tinted pink, yellow daisies, eroded cap secured by later adhesive, 1-3/4" h..... **50.00**
Tomato shape, white, hand painted floral dec, orig lid, 1-3/4" h . **100.00**
Tomato shape, yellow shading to white, hand painted floral dec, orig lid, 1-3/4" h **110.00**

Scent bottle, lusterless white ground, reserve with couple, basket of flowers on reverse **200.00**

Sugar shaker

2-1/2" h, tomato, yellow shading to white, satin finish, pink floral dec **400.00**
3-3/4" h, ostrich egg shape, opalware, light pink, satin finish, hand painted multicolored floral dec **400.00**
4" h, fig shape, white, satin finish, hand painted leaves, yellow floral dec **1,650.00**
4" h, 3-1/4" d, egg shape, pastel pansies, pronged top..... **590.00**
4-1/4" h, egg shape, opalware, soft pink background, hand painted floral dec, two-piece metal lid **400.00**
4-1/2" h, Albertine, egg shape, orig top **295.00**

Syrup pitcher, Colonial Ware, 15 Dresden floral sprays, white melon ribbed body, fancy gold scrollwork, pewter-like collar and lid, **$950.** *Photo courtesy of Clarence and Betty Maier.*

4-1/2" h, egg, beige, glossy finish, pink floral dec, marked "Pat'd" under base **175.00**
4-1/2" h, egg, light blue shading to cream, satin finish, dainty blue and white floral dec **350.00**
4-1/2" h, egg, white, satin finish, dainty blue and white floral dec **250.00**
4-1/2" h, egg, white, satin finish, pink and green fern and leaf dec **275.00**
5-1/2" h, Inverted Thumbprint pattern, lighthouse shape, Bluerina, orig metal top.... **350.00**

Syrup pitcher, 7-1/2" h, opaque white, violets and leaves dec, silver plated lid, collar, and handle have oxidized, pitcher inscribed "351"...... **1,250.00**

Toothpick holder, satin glass, Brownie Policeman, billy club in hand, holding another Brownie by scruff of neck, sitting Brownie on back **575.00**

Tumbler, 4" h, satin, c1880

Diamond Quilted, heavenly blue **165.00**
Diamond Quilted, shaded yellow to white **165.00**
Herringbone, shaded blue .. **165.00**

Vase

5" h, 4" w, melon ribbed, ruffled tricorn top, mother of pearl satin, Alice Blue, white lining, applied frosted edge, 1880s...... **275.00**
5-1/4" h, Verona, swirled ridges, ruby luster wild rose sprigs, raised gold, enamel detailing on ruffled rim, flat nicks on rim and base **200.00**
5-1/4" h, 4-1/2" w, bulbous, flaring neck, Lava, glossy black ground, numerous green, blue, white, and gray flux, one large burst bubble near surface........... **1,200.00**
5-3/4" h, Lava, dense black vasiform, surface dec with irregular squares of blue, green, pink, and gray, applied reeded handles at shoulders, some bubbles at surface............... **2,100.00**
5-3/4" h, Lava, flared black glass oval, surface dec with irregular patches of red, blue, pink, green, gray, and small opal white speckles, applied reeded handles at shoulders, some bubbles, minor surface scratches **1,840.00**
5-3/4" h, 4-1/4" w, satin, heavenly blue shading to white, white lining, hobnails, four fold, folded in-top **675.00**
6" h, 3-1/4" w, bulbous stick, satin, flaring rim, apricot shading to white, Diamond Quilted pattern **375.00**
6-1/4" h, 5-1/2" w, satin, melon ribbed, mother of pearl, Bridal White, muslin pattern, applied frosted edge, c1880...... **425.00**
6-1/2" h, satin, Alice Blue, pr **275.00**
6-1/2" h, 3" w, satin, Raindrop, Bridal White, mother of pearl, applied frosted edge, pr......... **550.00**
6-1/2" h, 6" w, satin, bulbous, Diamond Quilted pattern, deep rose shading to pink, two applied frosted "M" handles with thorns, cut edge, c1880............ **750.00**
8" h, Ring, black ground, gold storks in flight, gold floral dec, spoke bottom, pr.............. **550.00**
8" h, mother of pearl satin, Raindrop, butterscotch, applied camphor edge.................. **375.00**
8" h, trumpet, Napoli, pedestal, chrysanthemums and daisies dec inside ribbed vase and underside, gilt edges, trim, sgd, numbered **500.00**
8" h, 7" w, bulbous, mother of pearl satin, Alice Blue, Muslin pattern, applied frosted edge, three-petal top **675.00**
8-1/4" h, 5" w, satin, amberina coloration, mother of pearl

Diamond Quilted pattern, deep gold diamonds, white lining, slightly ruffled top **1,250.00**

8-1/2" h, 5" d at base, Napoli, int. dec in turquoise, blue, green, and rust, ext. outlined in gold, frog sitting in bulrushes dec, eight vertical ribs, some paint loss on int. **975.00**

9" h, 3-1/2" w at shoulder, mother of pearl satin glass, deep gold, Raindrop pattern sheet lining, applied tightly crimped camphor edge, c1880 .... **285.00**

9" h, 5-1/2" w, pink opalware, Delft windmill with person in front, gold trim top and base, Pairpoint **725.00**

9-1/4" h, 4-1/4" w, mother of pearl satin, shaded rose, Diamond Quilted pattern, ruffled edges, white lining, c1880, pr..... **875.00**

9-1/2" h, 6" w, mother of pearl satin, shaded yellow to white, Diamond Quilted pattern, painted and enameled landscape design, white and blue floral dec **150.00**

10" h, Neapolitan Ware, yellow, purple, rust, and gold spider mums, green leaves, gold spider webbing on ext., sgd "Napoli," #880 .... **1,450.00**

Vase, decorated with open lily blossom, buds, leaves, 24 optic ribs in colorless body, 7" h, **$285.** *Photo courtesy of Clarence and Betty Maier.*

11-1/4" h, gourd shape, 6" l flaring neck, satin, deep brown shading to gold, white lining, enameled seaweed design all over .. **550.00**

11-1/2" h, Napoli, 1-1/4" mouth, int. painted bouquet of spring flowers, eight exterior swirling ribs delineated on int. with black dots, brilliant gold ext., each petal and leaf outlined, fine gold network, brushed gold highlights to crown-like top, sgd "Napoli 821" **2,950.00**

11-7/8" h, bulbous stick, Colonial ware, glossy white, gold dec, allover vine and berry dec, two wreath and bow dec at top, sgd, #1010 .... **550.00**

12" h, Opal Ware, dec with migrating Guba Ducks, setting sun, peachblow colored sky, hand numbered 1562 over 615.. **500.00**

12-3/4" h, 5-1/2" w, Colonial ware, shaped like Persian water jug, loop handle on top, small spout, bulbous body, pedestal base, glossy white ground, pale pink and purple lilies, green leaves and stems, overlaid gold dec of leaves, stems, and daisies, sgd and #1022 .... **2,200.00**

17-1/2" h, hp floral dec, white satin glass, swirl ribbed tall cylinder body.................. **400.00**

18" h, Napoli, snipped and flared tricorn rim, elongated ribbed colorless oval body, hand painted chrysanthemum blossoms on int., gold tracery on ext., inscribed "Napoli 841" on base, some wear to gold, rim possibly retouched **635.00**

Murano Glass

History: Murano, Italy, is the home of several interesting Italian glassmakers. The Barovier and Toso Studio and the Ermanno Nason Murano Studio are modern makers which produced glassware in the 1950s. The Venini Glassworks was established in 1925 by Paolo Venini and is currently operated by his descendants.

Venini Glassworks revived several old Venetian glass techniques, such as millefiori, and has also developed several new distinctive styles.

Principal designers of Venini Glassworks include Ludovico Diaz De Santillana, and the Finnish designer, Tapio Wirkkala, who served as art director of the firm for many years.

Modern Italian glassware is currently selling quite well in some of the major auction houses. Works by artists such as Ermanno Nason are realizing high prices.

Items made by the Barovier and Toso Studio are often identified by a signature which reads "Murano/Antica Vetreia/F 11: TOSO," and may even include a design or style number. Items made by Venini Glassworks may be engraved or acid stamped. Some are marked "Venini Murano, Made in Italy," or "Venini Murano, Italia."

Bottle

8" h, Fratelli Toso, vetro a spirale technique with red and cobalt blue glass, orig stopper, unsigned **380.00**

8" h, 4" d, Archimede Seguso, gourd shape, blue murletto, unmarked **2,760.00**

8-1/2" h, 5-1/2" d, Venini & Co., by Carlo Scarpa, green and gold sommerso, ovoid, four-line acid stamp, "Venini/Murano/Made in Italy" **4,315.00**

9-1/4" h, 3-3/4" d, Barovier E. Toso, striato, red swirls, matching stopper, unmarked **265.00**

10" h, 9" d, Venini & Co., by Vittorio Zecchin, ribbed, gourd shape, soffiati, sheer blue glass, crinoline detail, acid stamped "Venini/Murano".......... **815.00**

11" h, 6" d, V.E.M., by Aldo Nason, from Yokohama series, red and white murrines on cobalt ground, gold and silver foil, unmarked **4,600.00**

12-1/2" h, 3-1/4" d, Aureliano Toso, gourd-shape, by Dino Martens, robin's egg blue, vertically twisted filigree, unmarked...... **2,070.00**

12" h, 3-1/2" h, Venini & Co., giada stopper, olive green with copper inclusions, three-line acid stamp, "Venini/Murano/Italia" ... **1,850.00**

12" h, 6-1/2" d, Venini & Co., gourd shape, by Ludvica di Santillana, smokey, coral drips, three-line acid stamp, "Venini/Murano/Italia" **2,070.00**

14" h, 7" d, Cenedese, sommerso, tall neck, red and blue casing, unmarked **300.00**

Bowl

10-3/4" d, 4" h, Archimede Seguso, shaded green, silver, and amethyst, silver inclusions, c1953, unmarked **195.00**

16-1/2" l, 6-1/2" w, Salvati, by Luciano Gaspari, fish shape, rose and blue accents, colorless body, incised "Luciano Gaspari" . **115.00**

Brandy snifter, 12" h, fused transparent red, green, blue, and colorless stripes in diagonal design, cobalt blue pedestal stem and foot, design attributed to Fulvio Bianconi for Venini **1,725.00**

Candlesticks, pr, 9-1/2" h, Soffiato, clear glass baluster form, domed circular foot, applied cobalt blue dec, Venini **800.00**

Center bowl, 18" d, broad shallow colorless irid bowl, bright blue rim wrap, molded dished pattern at center, Venetian Revival style **300.00**

Chandelier, by Ettore Sottsass for Venini, spherical fixture, bright brass ring surrounded by suspended hand blown clear rods with two rows of green disks, orig Venini shipping boxes **815.00**

Charger, 22" d, shallow bowl, applied rows of stringing, wide rim, attributed to Zecchin Martinuzzi **550.00**

Chimera vessel, Barovier E. Toso

- 6-1/2" x 5-1/2", from Corniola series, 1959, unmarked **3,450.00**
- 7" x 9-1/4", from Eugenio series, green, unmarked **2,870.00**

Compote, 9" h, 8-1/2" d, Salviati, blue and white zamfirico and latticinio, ruffled rim, unmarked **4,600.00**

Dish, 1-1/4" h, 9" d, Venini, shallow, marbleized vitri latticinio and amethyst, acid-etched two-line signature . **100.00**

Figure

- 3-1/2" h, apple, white ground, gold highlights, gold stem and leaf, 1930s, unmarked **100.00**
- 6" l, fish, opalescent, applied red details, unmarked. **65.00**
- 6" h, penguin, Archimede Seguso, amber shading to clear glass, orig foil labels, price for pr. **145.00**
- 6-1/2" l, fish, Cenedese, colorless, purple and green sommerso, unmarked **85.00**
- 6-3/4" h, 8" l, bird, colorless swallow, latticinio core and gold, bipartite pedestal foot, attributed to Barovier & Toso. **175.00**
- 7" x 7", bird, Venini & Co., by Tyra Lundgren, corroso, c1938, four-line, acid stamp, "Venini/Murano/Made in Italy" **865.00**
- 7-1/2" x 13", yak, Cenedese, by Antonio Da Rose, orange and vaseline sommerso, orange swirled horns, unmarked **690.00**
- 8-1/2" h, rooster, multicolored striated dec, applied gilt glass dec, orig paper label, Fratelli Toso **350.00**
- 11-1/2" h, fish, aventurine, black glass oval body, applied fish-face lips, eyes, and fins, round platform base inscribed "Salviani Murano" **260.00**
- 12-1/2" l, fish, flat sided, opaque white cased with clear glass, internally dec with beige and turquoise stripes, aubergine glass eyes, acid stamped "VENINI MURANO ITALIA," orig paper label, designed by Ken Scott, c1962 . . . . **650.00**
- 13-1/2" x 3-1/2", man, whimsical, Cenedese, by Antonio Da Rose, blue, green, and clear sommerso, unmarked **920.00**

Fountain, attributed to Barovier and Toso, c1940

- 38" h, 26" d, pink ftd bowl with gold inclusions central pink and gold fixture supporting five intricately blown nude female figures with florets, bowl cracked and restored **3,000.00**
- 60" h, 28" h, sectional pedestal base with gold inclusions, supporting broad blue plastic basin with light fittings, central blue and gold fixture supporting five intricately blown nude opalescent female figures holding gold garlands alternating with striated rose flowerheads. **9,500.00**

Lamp, hanging fixture, 14" l, 15" d, Vistosi, cobalt blue ext., single large murrine to one side, white int., unmarked, two chips to int. fixture ring at top **410.00**

Lamp shade, hanging, Venini

- 14" h, cigar shape, orange ground, blue, green and red horizontal striped border **700.00**
- 14" h, cigar shape, yellow ground, blue, green, and red horizontal striped border **700.00**
- 14" h, waisted cylindrical form, thin stripes, cobalt blue, green, and red horizontal striped border. . . **400.00**
- 20" h, cigar shaped, white ground, blue, red, and green horizontal striped border **1,200.00**
- 20" h, onion form, white ground, thin caramel stripes **700.00**

Paperweight

- 2" h, 4" d, Vistosi, sommerso, concentric white, olive, and black glass rings, etched signature **290.00**

Vessel, sommerso, squatty, by Carlo Scarpa, mint-colored swirls, two-line acid stamp "Venini/Murano," 9" x 5-1/2", **$11,150.**

- 7-1/2" l, Neopolitico, stylized fish form, white stone dec, yellow eyes, designed by Ercole Barovier for Barovier and Toso, c1954, pr **400.00**

Pitcher

- 8" h, 5-1/4" w, blue, ribbed, applied flowers and handle. **1,200.00**
- 11" x 6-1/2", Aureliano Toso, mezza-filigrana, by Dino Martens, black, white, and gold, exaggerated spout, unmarked **1,380.00**
- 14" h, 8" d, Barovier E. Toso, from Eugenio series, eggplant and green luster, unmarked . . **2,070.00**

Plate, 11" d, black aubergine with oro antico aventurine, six matching pcs of glass fruit, design by Ercole Barovier for 1934 Biennale **320.00**

Sconce, 12" h, 8" w, Gino Cenedese, scavo, applied figural dec, titled "La Fornace," from "La Lozrazione Del Vetro" series by Napolene Martinuzzi, c1953, unmarked **5,175.00**

Sculpture

- 6-1/4" d, face, Fucina Degli Angeli, freeblown fiery amber, corroso green-black surface, engraved signature and "Alfo3" on reverse, designed by Max Ernest, from 1966 series. **575.00**
- 6-1/2" h, 14" d foot, Desert Bandits, whimsical cactus with etched and colored faces, arms raising holding wide removable sky bowl, among tumbleweeds and rabbit, base inscribed "Bandits in the Desert US of America 1952/Dis. Bruno Saeeti/Seguso Murano" . . . **920.00**
- 7-1/4" x 9" x 2-1/4", aquarium block, attributed to Cenedese, colorless, internal polychrome dec of fish and marine life, unmarked **290.00**

Urn, Fratelli Toso, carnivale, unmarked, 10" h, 10-1/2" h, price for pair, **$2,070.**

12" h, Apparenza, colorless head, applied turban ornament, burgundy colored masquerade mask with eye slits, button mouth, ruffled collard base, lower edge inscribed "Max Ernst" and below Ferro e Lazzarini-Murano," designed by Max Ernst, executed by Ferro-Lazzarini **1,035.00**

13-1/2" h, portrait in red glass, applied blue eye and ear, raised on colorless columnar candlestick body base, etched and painted polka dot skirt, stockings, and black pumps, base engraved "Miro/Messega IVR Murano," design by Jean Miro, execution attributed to Ermanno Nason, chip on back corner of base .. **2,300.00**

13-3/4" h, form of woman, hands on hips, anger in stance, black on white glass, marked "Picasso" at lower edge, base engraved "Picasso IVR Mazzega Murano," design by Pablo Picasso, rigaree chip **2,530.00**

Urn, Fratelli Toso

4-1/2" h, 4" d, Floriale, bulbous, applied handles, white and green inlaid with pink and yellow flowers, unmarked **1,840.00**

10" h, 10-1/2" h, Carnivale, 1920s, unmarked, price for pr .. **2,070.00**

14" h, 4-1/2" d, Carnivale, black handles, 1920s, orig retail label from Naples, Italy **3,450.00**

Vase

4-1/2" h, 5-1/2" d, Venini, by Carlo Scarpa, Art Deco, flared, faceted, green sommerso, unmarked **2,070.00**

7-1/2" h, 6-1/2" d, Venini, by Carlo Scarpa, emerald green corroso, flaring, organic form, partially obscured four-line acid stamp, "Venini/Murano/Made in Italy" **3,775.00**

8" h, 8" d, Archimede Seguso, white murletto double-lobed, flaring, green and amber banded rim, unmarked **9,780.00**

9-3/4" h, 7" w, Venini, by Carlo Scarpa, bulbous, amber, lug handles, slightly fumed surface, three-line acid stamp, "Venini/Murano/Italia" **3,775.00**

10" h, 7-1/2" d, Cenedese, by Antonia Da Rose, sommerso momento, flattened rect form, mid 1950s, orange, blue, and green casing, unmarked **2,700.00**

10-1/4" h, Venini, design attributed to Fulvio Biancoti, Italy, mid-20th C, Venini Fasce Veticale, flared rim, tapered neck, cylindrical body of fused green and blue bands, acid stamped "Venini Murano Italia" in polished pontil **350.00**

10-1/2" h, 2-1/2" d, Venini & Co., cigar-shaped patchwork, smokey, black, clear, and amber, by Fulvio Bianconi, three-line acid stamp, "Venini/Murano/Italia" **8,050.00**

10-1/2" h, 4-1/2" d, Archimede Seguso, plume teardrop shape, amber, amethyst feathers, 1956, unmarked **6,275.00**

11" h, 4" d, Aureliano Toso, by Dino Martens, double-spouted, with hold, blue melted powders on surface, 1952, unmarked. **1,610.00**

11" h, 9" w, Fratelli Toso, flaring pillow shape, aventurine glass, broad orange bands, unmarked. **1,485.00**

11" h, 12-1/2" d, Venini & Co., by Fulvio Bianconi, fazzoletto, pink and white zanfirico, three-line acid stamp, "Venini/Murano/Italia" **1,850.00**

11-1/2" h, 8" d, Barovier E. Toso, by Carlo Barovier, irid colorless body, controlled bubbles, applied leaf and vines, late 1930s, unmarked **2,760.00**

12-1/2" h, 3-3/4" d, Venini, by Tobia Scarpa, four-sided, red ochhi, paper label, three-line acid stamp "Venini/Murano/Italia" .. **10,925.00**

12-1/2" h, 7" d, Cenedese, by Antonia Da Ros, sommerso flattened hemispherical, mid 1950s, amethyst casing, unmarked **865.00**

12-1/2" h, 7" d, Fratelli Toso, nerox terrazzo murrine, ovoid, lavender, blue, red, and white, unmarked **8,050.00**

13-1/2" h, Paolo Venini for Venini, cylindrical mosaico zanfirico, slanted rim, turquoise, white netting, acid-etched "Venini/Murano/Italia" ... **7,475.00**

14" h, 6-1/2" d, Aureliano Toso, designed by Dino Martins, pierced asymmetrical-shaped body, tooled rim, clear glass with enclosed patchwork red, yellow, white, blue, and black, with latticinio, aventurine, and black and white Murrhina star, paper label, c1950, few scratches **8,100.00**

16-1/2" h, 13" d, Barovier E. Toso, by Ercole Barovier, autunno gemmato, applied buttressed shoulders, 1935-36, unmarked..... **5,350.00**

17" h, 8-1/2" d, Barvoier-Seguso-Ferro, designed by Flavio Poli, executed by Alfred Barbini, Laguna, pink, gold snake handles, 1932, unmarked **20,125.00**

19" h, 7-1/2" d, Cenedese, designed by Gino Cenedese, teardrop shape, applied trailing dec on striped clear and cobalt blue scavo background, unmarked . **8,050.00**

Vessel

5-1/4" h, 5-1/2" d, Alfredo Barbini, corroso sommerso, cranberry red, unmarked **600.00**

6" h ewer, 4-3/4" h ewer, 3-1/2" h two-handled vase, Barovier, Eugenio, vermillion, red details, two with paper labels, third pc with remnant of label, price for three-pc set **1,725.00**

7" h, 9" w, Barovier E. Toso, colorless, ribbed, spherical shape, mica inclusions, applied grape clusters at shoulder, orig paper label **1,150.00**

9-1/2" h, 7" w, Salier, by Mirco Casaril, double spouted, acid-etched aboriginal animals, geometric design, Pauly & C. paper label **6,275.00**

Nailsea-Type Glass

History: Nailsea-type glass is characterized by swirls and loopings, usually white, on a clear or colored ground. One of the first areas where this glass was made was Nailsea, England, 1788-1873, hence the name. Several glass houses, including American factories, made this type of glass.

Basket, 5-1/2" h, 5" w, pink loopings, white satin ground, applied frosted feet, applied frosted handle **385.00**

Bell, 11-3/4" h, white, rose loopings **95.00**

Bellows bottle

- 9" h, red, white loop design, applied colorless rim, quilling, fine rigaree, prunts, handle, northeastern US, late 19th C **200.00**
- 10" h, red, white loop design, applied colorless rim, quilling, fine rigaree, prunts, handle, northeastern US, late 19th C **200.00**
- 11-1/2" h, colorless, white marbrie, applied turquoise rim, quilling, leaf, and prunt, colorless rigaree and handles, England or eastern US, 19th C, imperfections..... **125.00**

Bottle

- 6-1/2" h, medium gray-blue ground, white loopings, pewter threading, pontil scar, cap missing, attributed to Germany, mid-18th C . . **1,750.00**
- 7-5/8" h, rect, beveled edges, medium sapphire blue ground, white loopings, pewter threads, pontil scar, attributed to Germany or Northern Europe, c1750 .... **1,250.00**

Bowl, 4-1/4" d, 2-1/4" h, citron ground, narrow white looping, applied rigaree loop dec, rim, ground pontil ... **200.00**

Candlestick, 10" h, colorless, white loopings, folded socket rim, hollow blown socket drawn out to a double knop, bulb-shaped stem, two additional knops, inverted cone shaped base, early 19th C **375.00**

Cologne bottle, 5-3/8" h, opaque white body, blue and cranberry loopings, colorless stopper with white, pink, and blue loopings, pontil scar, New England, 1840-60 .... **485.00**

Decanter

- 11" h, colorless, white marbrie dec, applied rings on neck, England or eastern US, 19th C, imperfections **175.00**

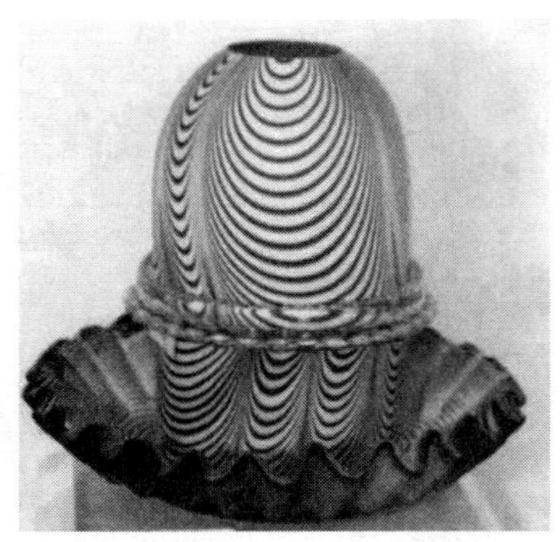

Fairy lamp, ruby ground, profuse white loopings, 7" d bowl-shaped base with 26 evenly spaced pleats, clear glass candle holder signed "S. Clarke Patent Trade Mark Fairy," **$975.** *Photo courtesy of Clarence and Betty Maier.*

- 13-1/4" h, colorless, opalescent marbrie dec, applied colorless rim, neck rings, Prince of Wales feathers, rigaree, prunt, handles, and stepped disk base, England or eastern US, 19th C **195.00**

Fairy lamp

- 5-1/4" h, 6-1/4" d, frosted blue, opaque white loopings, colorless Clarke insert **695.00**
- 6" h, blue shade, matching ruffled trifold rim base, colorless glass candle cup insert **750.00**
- 6-1/2" h, red, sweeping white loops, dome shaped shade, ruffled triangular base, colorless glass candle cup with ruffled edge, orig "Price's Royal Castle Night Light" candle **985.00**

Finger bowl, 4-1/4" d, ftd, colorless ground, swirled streaks of deep blue ad white, foot drawn from body, applied colorless handles imp with cherub's face........................ **90.00**

Flask

- 3-1/4" h, ovoid, opalescent body, pink marbrie loop dec, England or eastern US, 19th C, imperfections **1,225.00**
- 4" h, flattened spherical colorless body, blue and white swirled cane dec, England or eastern US, 19th C, imperfections **1,125.00**
- 4" h, flattened spherical colorless body, red cane, England or eastern US, 19th C, imperfections **1,125.00**
- 4-1/2" h, amber, diagonal white pulled loop designs, half-pint, England or eastern US, 19th C, imperfections **245.00**
- 5-1/2" h, lime green, swirling ribbed body, white undulating design, half-pint, England or eastern US, 19th C, imperfections..... **285.00**
- 6-3/8" h, white, pink and blue loop designs, half pint, England or eastern US, 19th C, imperfections **225.00**
- 7-1/2" h, colorless, light blue and pink loop design, pint, England or eastern US, 19th C, imperfections **260.00**
- 7-5/8" h, white, pink marbrie, pint, England or eastern US, 19th C, imperfections **245.00**
- 7-7/8" h, colorless, spiral ribbed, transparent red, white, and blue striations, pint, England or eastern US, 19th C, imperfections . **275.00**
- 8-1/4" h, white, blue and pink marbrie, pint, England or eastern US, 19th C, imperfections . **250.00**
- 8-1/4" h, colorless, transparent pink and white loop dec, applied white rim, pint, England or eastern US, 19th C, imperfections..... **235.00**
- 9-3/4" h, amber, white loop designs, applied white rim, matching stopper, England or eastern US, 19th C, imperfections..... **200.00**

Gemel bottle

- 8-1/4" h, colorless, pink and white loop design, applied colorless rigaree, England or eastern US, 19th C, imperfections..... **315.00**
- 9" h, colorless, pink and white loop design, applied colorless rigaree, England or eastern US, 19th C, imperfections **325.00**
- 10-7/8" h, red, white loop designs, cased in colorless glass, applied colorless rigaree, England or eastern US, 19th C, imperfections **295.00**

Fancy-back bar bottle, America, 1870-1900, colorless with pink and white Nailsea-type decoration with swirled stripes, sheared mouth with applied rim, ground pontil scar, 10-7/8" h, **$1,500.**

Lamp, 11-1/2" h, colorless ground, pink and white loopings on font and ruffled shade, applied colorless feet, berry prunt **2,500.00**
Mug, 5-1/4" h, 3-5/8" d, colorless ground, white and blue loopings, cylindrical, tapering slightly to rim, applied colorless solid handle, rough pontil **375.00**
Pipe, 18" l, white ground, red loopings, bulbous bowl, knopped stem . . . **275.00**
Pitcher
- 6-1/2" h, 4" d, colorless ground, white loopings, ftd, solid applied base, triple ribbed solid handle with curled end, flaring formed mouth, attributed to South Jersey, c1840-60 . . . . **1,200.00**
- 9-1/2" h, cranberry ground, thick white loopings, applied clear handle with five crimps, applied colorless handle with five crimps, applied colorless foot, pontil scar, attributed to South Jersey, c1840-50 . . . . **4,100.00**

Powder horn
- 11" h, colorless ground, blue and white loopings, tooled lip, pontil scar, ground lip, mid-19th C **125.00**
- 13" l, colorless ground, white loopings and red stripes, stand **250.00**

Rolling pin
- 13-3/4" l, free blown, rose and white loopings, colorless ground, ground mouth, smooth base, 1850-80 . . . . **220.00**
- 16-1/2" l, colorless ground, deep ruby loopings, 1883 English coin trapped inside, attributed to Nailsea district, England, 1880s **400.00**
- 18" l, colorless ground, pink and white loopings **265.00**

Salt, open, 3-1/4" d, 1-1/4" h, colorless ground, white loopings, wide gauffered rolled rim, applied cobalt blue rim band, applied solid foot, polished pontil **450.00**
Tankard, 7" h, aqua ground, white loopings, applied solid aqua handle, pontil scar, crack at upper handle attachment, attributed to South Jersey, mid-19th C **425.00**
Tumbler, white ground, blue loopings **120.00**
Vase
- 6-1/4" h, ruby, hexagonal rim, white loop dec, applied colorless ribbed and scrolled handles, rigaree, disk base, England or eastern US, 19th C, imperfections **175.00**
- 11-3/4" h, transparent light green, opalescent loop designs, England or eastern US, 19th C, minor scratches **115.00**
- 24-1/8" h, colorless, white loop and spiral patterns, England or eastern US, 19th C, imperfections . **195.00**

Witch ball
- 4-3/8" d, white ground, pink and blue loopings **450.00**
- 5-1/4" d, colorless ground, opaque white casing, red loopings, attributed to Pittsburgh. . . . **275.00**
- 16" h, matching ball and vase stand, colorless ground, white loopings, pontil scar, attributed to Pittsburgh or New Jersey, 1840-50 . . **1,250.00**

Nash Glass

History: Nash glass is a type of art glass attributed to Arthur John Nash and his sons, Leslie H. and A. Douglas. Arthur John Nash, originally employed by Webb in Stourbridge, England, came to America and was employed in 1889 by Tiffany Furnaces at its Corona, Long Island, plant.

While managing the plant for Tiffany, Nash designed and produced iridescent glass. In 1928, A. Douglas Nash purchased the facilities of Tiffany Furnaces. The A. Douglas Nash Corporation remained in operation until 1931.

Reference: Kenneth Wilson, *American Glass 1760-1930: The Toledo Museum of Art, Volume I, Volume II,* Hudson Hills Press and The Toledo Museum of Art, 1994.

Bottle, 4-1/2" h, squatty, pinched sides, amber irid, green and amber irid striated feather dec, inscribed "LCT B1," c1890 . . . . **1,250.00**
Bowl
- 4-7/8" d, 1-3/4" h, green pastel opalescent, sgd on side. . . **650.00**
- 5-1/4" d, inverted rim, leaf design, sgd **200.00**
- 7-3/4" d, 2-1/2" h, Jewel pattern, gold phantom luster **285.00**
- 13" d, Diamond Optic pattern, colorless ground, cranberry threads, wide rim **295.00**
- 15-1/2" d, Chintz amber, blue, and green opalescent, turned down rim **325.00**

Candlestick
- 4" h, Chintz ruby and gray, sgd **450.00**
- 4-1/2" h, irid blue, sgd and numbered. **500.00**
- 5" h, Chintz blood red and silver dec **550.00**

Champagne, 5" h, pale irid amber, shallow cup splitting to three stems continuing to domed circular base **750.00**
Cologne bottle
- 5" h, flaring bulbed base, Chintz wide pale green stripes separated by wide pale green stripes with thing blue centers, clear stopper with controlled bubble, sgd "Nash/1008?jj". **600.00**
- 6" h, cylindrical, Chintz paperweight stopper **275.00**

Compote
- 6" d, 2" h, fold over rim, Chintz, green-blue bowl, colorless pedestal foot, sgd. **225.00**
- 7-1/2" d, 4-1/2" h, Chintz transparent aquamarine, wide flat rim of red and gray-green controlled stripe dec, base inscribed "Nash RD89" **865.00**

Console bowl, 11-1/2" d, 3-1/2" h, Chintz, clear ground, pink and green chintz, sgd "501/DD/Nash" **250.00**
Cordial, 5-1/2" h, Chintz, green and blue **95.00**
Creamer, 4-1/4" h, pale orchid and green design, applied colorless handle **325.00**
Dish, cov, 5" d, 2-1/2" h, internally molded leaf design, amber ground, lustrous gold irid, conforming cover, rim chips. **260.00**
Finger bowl, 4-3/4" d, matching underplate, opalescent rays, cranberry rim, sgd **225.00**
Goblet
- 6-1/2" h, Chintz **185.00**
- 6-3/4" h, feathered leaf motif, gilt dec, sgd **295.00**

Console bowl, Chintz, colorless ground, pink and green chintz stripes, signed, 11-1/2" d, 3-1/2" h, **$250.** *Photo courtesy of David Rago Auctions.*

Perfume bottle
- 7-1/2" h, bulbous bottle shape over blown-in-mold apron, irid gold, conforming stopper with 7" l wand, sgd "Nash 523" **975.00**
- 7-7/8" h, blue and lilac rays, pale blue foot, silver-blue irid, orig pointed amber stopper.... **850.00**

Plate
- 4-1/2" d, irid amber, scalloped edge, sgd and numbered....... **325.00**
- 6-1/2" d, Spiral pattern, orchid and clear spirals, sgd **200.00**
- 8" d, Chintz, green and blue. **195.00**

Salt, open, 4" d, 1-1/4" h, irid gold, ruffled rim, sgd and numbered . **350.00**

Sherbet, bluish-gold texture, ftd, sgd, #417..................... **275.00**

Vase
- 4-1/4" h, red, blue-gray dots, swirled vertical ribs, smooth pontil . **775.00**
- 4-3/4" h, blue-gold irid, pedestal base, inscribed "Nash 644" **350.00**
- 5-1/4" h, square mouth, round base, four heavy pillar ribs extending from mouth to base, polished pontil, sgd "541 Nash" **650.00**
- 5-1/2" h, Chintz, brilliant red oval, controlled black, brown, gray striped dec, base inscribed "Nash" **865.00**
- 5-1/2" h, Chintz, deep rose red-red oval, alternating wide and narrow vertical silver luster stripes, base inscribed "Nash RD 66" ... **990.00**
- 5-1/2" h, Chintz, pastel, transparent oval, internally striped with pastel orange alternating with yellow chintz dec.............. **175.00**

Vase, footed, iridescent gold, marked "544 Nash," 4-1/8" h, **$375.**

- 6-1/4" h, 3-1/2" d, trumpet shade, Chintz, sgd and numbered . **375.00**
- 7-1/2" h, beaker, Chintz, blood red, sgd "Nash RD 1025"...... **475.00**
- 7-3/4" h, baluster, brilliant irid pumpkin, lemon-yellow int. **3,500.00**
- 7-3/4" h, cylindrical, spreading foot, Chintz, blue............. **525.00**
- 8-1/2" h, Chintz, green, brown, and gold flecks.............. **325.00**
- 9" h, Chintz, blood red and ray, ball-shaped clear stem **475.00**
- 9" h, Polka Dot, deep opaque red oval, molded with prominent sixteen ribs, dec by spaced white opal dots, base inscribed "Nash GD154" **1,100.00**
- 9-1/2" h, green and gold irid body, colorless irid circular base . **325.00**
- 11" h, trumpet shape, gold luster, blue, green, and pink highlights, lightly textured body, sgd in polished pontil......... **1,250.00**
- 12" h, trumpet shape, orange and yellow vertical stripes, inscribed "Nash 62AA" **450.00**
- 13-1/4" h, 4-1/4" w, hourglass shape, bright orange, cobalt blue vertical stripes, polished pontil **350.00**

Wine, 6" h, Chintz, pink and green **175.00**

New Martinsville Viking

History: The New Martinsville Glass Manufacturing Company, founded in 1901, took its name from its West Virginia location. Early products were opal glass decorative ware and utilitarian items. Later productions were pressed crystal tableware with flashed-on ruby or gold decorations. In the 1920s, innovative color and designs made vanity, liquor, and smoker sets popular. Dinner sets in patterns such as Radiance, Moondrops, and Dancing Girl, as well as new colors, cuttings, and etchings, were produced. The 1940s brought black glass formed into perfume bottles, bowls with swan handles, and flower bowls. In 1944, the company was sold and reorganized as the Viking Glass Company.

The Rainbow Art Glass Company, Huntington, West Virginia, was established in 1942 by Henry Manus, A Dutch immigrant. This company produced small, hand-fashioned animals and decorative ware of opal, spatter, cased, and crackle glass. Rainbow Art Glass also decorated for other companies. In the early 1970s, Viking acquired Rainbow Art Glass Company and continued the production of the small animals.

New Martinsville glass predating 1935 appears in a wide variety of colors. Later glass was made only in crystal, blue, ruby, and pink.

Look for cocktail, beverage, liquor, vanity, smoking, and console sets. Amusing figures of barnyard and sea animals, dogs, and bears were produced. Both Rainbow Art Glass and Viking glass are handmade and have a paper label. Rainbow Art Glass pieces are beautifully colored, and the animal figures are more abstract in design than those of New Martinsville. Viking makes plain, colored, cut, and etched tableware, novelties, and gift items. Viking began making black glass in 1979.

References: Tom and Neila Bredehoft, *Fifty Years of Collectible Glass, 1920-1970, Volume 1, Volume II*, Antique Trader Books, 2000; James Measell, *New Martinsville Glass, 1900-44*, Antique Publications, 1995; Hazel Marie Weatherman, *Colored Glassware of the Depression Era, Book 2*, Glassworks, Inc., 1982.

Animal, crystal
- Angel fish **75.00**
- Bear, baby, sun colored **35.00**
- Bear, mama **225.00**
- Chick, baby **45.00**
- Dog, amber, 8" l **60.00**
- Eagle **80.00**
- Elephant................. **85.00**
- Gazelle.................. **60.00**
- Hen, 5" h, head down....... **45.00**
- Horse, head up............ **95.00**
- Horse, rearing............ **115.00**
- Piglet, standing........... **145.00**
- Polar bear............... **50.00**
- Police dog **80.00**
- Porpoise on wave......... **550.00**
- Rooster, large............ **80.00**
- Sea horse **65.00**
- Seal, baby **70.00**
- Seal, large **75.00**
- Squirrel................. **65.00**
- Swan, Janice, 12".......... **55.00**
- Wolf hound **95.00**

Ashtray
- Fish, 4" d................. **12.00**
- Moondrops, ruby **32.50**
- Skillet, 5" d **15.00**

Basket
- Janice, #4552, light blue, 11" **295.00**
- Radiance, ruby............ **85.00**

Bobeche, Radiance, ruby..... **125.00**

Bonbon
- Janice, crystal **20.00**
- Radiance, amber **15.00**

Bookends, pr, crystal
- Clipper ships **110.00**
- Cornucopia, 5-3/4" h........ **80.00**
- Daddy bear, 4-1/4" h....... **150.00**
- Elephants, 5-1/2" h, #237 ... **200.00**
- Lady's heads **250.00**
- Nautilus shell **70.00**
- Police dog **85.00**
- Rooster................. **80.00**
- Ship **65.00**
- Squirrels **120.00**
- Starfish **170.00**
- Wolfhound **90.00**

Bowl
Florentine, 13" d, flared, crystal **45.00**
Janice, 11" d, three ftd, amber **45.00**
Janice, 11-1/2" d, ruffled, crystal **45.00**
Janice, 12" d, crystal **55.00**
Meadow Wreath, 5-1/2" d **10.00**
Moondrops, ruby, ftd, 8-1/4" d . **45.00**
Muranese, peach blow, ruffled **165.00**
Peachblow, yellow-caramel shading to peach to beige, scalloped rim, 5" h **60.00**
Prelude etching, ftd, 12" d **25.00**
Radiance, amber, 12" d **40.00**
Radiance, ruby, 13" d **70.00**
Swan, sweetheart shape, emerald green, crystal handle, 5" h .. **30.00**
Teardrop, 11" d, light blue, straight sides **65.00**

Butter dish
Moondrops, cobalt blue..... **325.00**
Radiance, crystal, sterling silver overlay **110.00**

Cake plate
Basket etching **20.00**
Hostmaster, amber **25.00**
Prelude etching **57.00**

Candle lamp, owl, ruby, 7" h **45.00**

Candlesticks, pr
Epic, #1196, ruby **45.00**
Hostmaster, 8-1/2" h, cobalt blue, sterling silver trim **40.00**
Janice, 5" h, #4554, ruby..... **60.00**
Janice, 5-1/2" h, crystal **55.00**
Prelude etching, 5" h, 1-lite, #4554 .... **130.00**
Moondrops, one-lite, amber, 2" h **40.00**
Moondrops, one-lite, crystal, wings, #25 etch, single **85.00**
Moondrops, three-lite, crystal, floral cutting on base **100.00**
Radiance, two-lite, #42, light blue, pr **230.00**
Radiance, two-lite, #4536, blue, pr **125.00**
#414 .... **40.00**
#4531, 6" h **40.00**
#5515, three-lite, crystal **55.00**

Candy basket, Prelude, crystal, 6-1/2", two handles **50.00**

Candy box, cov, Moondrops, three-part, amber, etch #26 .... **160.00**

Candy dish, cov, Roberto, #104, crystal **50.00**

Casserole, cov, Moondrops, amber **155.00**

Celery tray
Janice, #4521, 11" l, crystal... **40.00**
Meadow Wreath, 10" l **15.00**
Radiance, #42, ruby, 10" **85.00**

Champagne, Moondrops, ruby . **40.00**

Cheese and cracker set
Prelude etching **85.00**
#26, crystal **45.00**

Cheese comport
Radiance, ruby **47.50**
#26, crystal **15.00**

Cigarette holder, cart shape ... **20.00**

Cocktail shaker, Hostmaster, c1935, ruby **80.00**

Compote
Griffin, crystal, Moondrops, 5-3/4" w, 3-7/8" h **45.00**
Radiance, ruby, cupped, 5" .. **70.00**

Console bowl
Meadow Wreath, #4511/31... **35.00**
Moondrops, ruby, winged... **125.00**
Wild Rose, ruffled **48.00**

Console set
Epic, turquoise **60.00**
Swan, 10-1/2" d swan shaped center bowl, 4-1/2" h pr swan-shaped candlesticks, amber bodies, crystal necks, c1940-60.... **75.00**

Cordial, 1 oz
Mildred, Hostmaster, ruby bowl, chrome stem **25.00**
Moondrops, amber **35.00**
Moondrops, cobalt blue, metal stem and foot **42.00**
Moondrops, dark green **25.00**
Radiance, ruby, silver trim ... **37.50**

Creamer
Janice, crystal **12.50**
Moondrops, individual size, ruby **28.00**
Moondrops, large, dark green **17.60**
Moondrops, large, ruby **20.00**
Radiance, amber **20.00**
Radiance, ruby **32.50**
#26, crystal **15.00**
#34, amber **12.50**

Cream soup
#34, 5" d, amethyst **20.00**
#34, 5" d, red **35.00**

Cup and saucer
Janice, crystal **10.00**
Janice, ruby **30.00**
Moondrops, amber **15.00**
Moondrops, amethyst **20.00**
Moondrops, cobalt blue **24.50**
Moondrops, pink **19.50**
Moondrops, ruby **20.00**
Radiance, amber **22.00**

Decanter
Mildred, Hostmaster, amber, 6-3/4" h **45.00**
Moondrops, amethyst, 10" h.. **65.00**
Roberto, evergreen, fan-shaped crystal stopper **55.00**

Dresser set, Small Diamond, ice blue, puff box, two matching colognes **155.00**

Epergne, Princess, crystal, bowl, one vase **68.00**

Goblet
Hostmaster, cobalt blue...... **24.00**
Mt. Vernon, cobalt blue **20.00**
Prelude etching, crystal...... **28.00**

Honey jar, cov, Radiance, ruby .. **45.00**

Iced tea tumbler, ftd, Prelude etching, crystal **15.00**

Ice tub
Hostmaster, 5-1/2" h, amber, c1935 .... **40.00**
Hostmaster, 5-1/2" h, ruby, c1935 .... **55.00**

Jug, Oscar, sterling silver overlay **145.00**

Juice tumbler, Moondrops, cobalt blue **18.00**

Lamp base, police dog, pink satin **125.00**

Luncheon set, Janice, blue, 12 luncheon plates, cups, and saucers, two serving plates **275.00**

Marmalade, cov, Janice, crystal . **25.00**

Mayonnaise, cov, underplate, Radiance, amber **25.00**

Mug, Georgian, ruby **18.00**

Nut dish, Radiance, amber, two handles **10.00**

Oil and vinegar cruet set, Prelude **125.00**

Paperweight
Owl, amber, 3" **50.00**
Pear, ruby, green stem....... **45.00**

Perfume
Diamond, transparent green, orig dauber **50.00**
Modernistick, light green, orig dauber **275.00**
Pilsner, Mildred, Hostmaster, 7-3/4" h, pink, set of 10 .... **350.00**

Pitcher, Oscar, pink **125.00**

Plate
Canterbury etch, 8-1/2" d, crystal **10.00**
Florentine, 9" d, crystal **15.00**
Janice, 7" d, crystal, handle, cut flowers and leaves **10.00**
Janice, 13" d, ruby, two handles **65.00**
Meadow Wreath, 11" d, crystal **20.00**
Moondrops, 8-1/2" d, amber ... **6.00**
Moondrops, 9-1/2" d, green... **25.00**
Moondrops, 9-1/2" d, pink.... **18.50**
Prelude, dinner, crystal **45.00**
Radiance, 8-1/4" d, amber ... **16.00**
#34, amber, 8" d **5.00**
#34, amethyst, 8" d **12.00**
#34, ruby, 8" d **10.00**

Platter, Radiance, 14", amber . . . **38.00**

Powder jar

Cinderella Coach, crystal **35.00**

Diamond, three toes, frosted, lavender, celluloid lid **25.00**

Small Diamond, amber, flat lid, multisided finial. **30.00**

Punch bowl

Janice, amber, ball shape, 8" h **555.00**

Radiance, black **245.00**

Relish

Florentine, three-part, 12" l, crystal **35.00**

Janice, two-part, 6" l **10.00**

Meadow Wreath, three-part, crystal **28.00**

Moondrops, 8-1/2" l, three toed, amber **12.00**

Prelude, three-part, crystal . . . **45.00**

Prelude, four-part, crystal, 8" d, sterling base. **45.00**

Radiance, ruby, #4427/28, three-part, metal handle, 8" d **85.00**

Salad bowl, 11" d, Wild Rose etching **25.00**

Salt and pepper shakers, pr

Creased Waist, blue opaque, 3-3/8" h **50.00**

Creased Waist, white opaque, 3-3/8" h **40.00**

Radiance, pink **275.00**

Saucer

#34, amber **1.50**

#34, amethyst **3.50**

Server, center handle

Griffin, pink, cupped up edges, 9" d **125.00**

Prelude etching. **55.00**

Princess, crystal **32.00**

Sherbet

Janice, ruby **22.50**

Moondrops, amber **14.00**

Moondrops, crystal, low **15.00**

Moondrops, crystal, tall **15.00**

Moondrops, ruby, low **20.00**

#34, jade green. **12.00**

Sugar bowl, cov, large

Florentine **15.00**

Meadow Wreath **12.00**

Moondrops, amber **14.50**

Moondrops, ruby **20.00**

Radiance, amber **20.00**

#34, amber **12.50**

#34, amethyst **15.00**

Sugar bowl, individual, Moondrops, ruby **18.00**

Torte plate, 15" d, Prelude etching **60.00**

Tray, Meadow Wreath, 10-1/4" handle to handle **38.00**

Shot glass, Gene, medium blue, 2-1/4" h, **$35.** *Photo courtesy of Michael Krumme.*

Tumble-Up, carafe and tumbler

Volstead Pup, crystal. **65.00**

Volstead Pup, pink. **80.00**

Tumbler

Georgian, ruby, 9 oz **25.00**

Janice, light blue, ftd **35.00**

Janice, ruby, ftd. **35.00**

Hostmaster, cobalt blue. **10.00**

Moondrops, amber, 4-3/4" h . . **15.00**

Moondrops, cobalt blue, 5 oz . **24.00**

Moondrops, ruby, 3-5/8" h **17.50**

Moondrops, ruby, 4-3/4" h **20.00**

Oscar, amber, 9 oz **12.00**

Oscar, cobalt blue, flat **25.00**

Prelude, crystal, 5-3/4" h, ftd . . **18.00**

#34, amethyst, ftd **18.50**

#34, cobalt blue, ftd. **27.50**

Vanity set

Jade green cologne with black stopper, jade green power box with black lid, black tray. **215.00**

Judy, three pcs, green and crystal, cologne bottle, stopper, tray . **95.00**

Thousand Eye, puff box and pr colognes **90.00**

#18/2, pink, puff box and two colognes, slight chips **100.00**

Vase

Janice, 8" h, three ftd, flared, amber **65.00**

Janice, 8" h, three ftd, flared, black **125.00**

Modernistic, pink satin, 8-1/2" h **125.00**

Prelude, #7539, 8" **35.00**

Radiance, #4232, 10" h, crimped, etch #268, crystal **135.00**

Water set

Heart in Sand, 8-3/4" h pitcher, four 4-1/8" h tumblers, ruby stained **3,200.00**

Oscar, pitcher, six 4-5/8" h tumblers, ruby **265.00**

Whiskey

Moondrops, amber **11.00**

Moondrops, 2 oz, amethyst . . . **20.00**

Moondrops, 2 oz, cobalt blue . **16.00**

Mount Vernon, ruby **15.00**

Wine

Moondrops, metal stem, 3 oz, cobalt blue **24.00**

Moondrops, metal stem, 3 oz, red **20.00**

Northwood Glass

History: The Northwood Glass Company was incorporated in 1887 in Martins, Ferry, Belmont County, West Virginia by Henry Helling, Henry Floto, William Mann, Thomas Mears, and Harry Northwood. Production started in early January 1888, with blown ware, consisting of lamp shades, tablewares, water sets, and berry sets. Harry Northwood was the designer and general manager and surely used the years of experience he had working with the former Hobbs, Brockunier, and La Belle Glass Works to develop new glass techniques and patterns. The Northwood Company soon became known for its numerous patterns and items, as well as the vivid colors and types of art glass it produced. Harry Northwood was also responsible for obtaining several patents for glass manufacturing devices.

In November of 1888, he obtained a patent for a speckled type of glassware. This technique was often used with colored grounds, such as cranberry, and produced an innovative type of glassware known as spatter. Production reports of many types of colorful wares can be found. By April 1889, however, the directors dissolved the company and attempted to settle affairs. It appears from most written accounts that, although the products were wonderful, the sales force could not carry through. The Northwood Company reorganized as an Ohio corporation. Accomplished glassmakers continued to produce quality products and added fine examples of cased, satin, and agate-type wares. Patterns requiring skilled workmanship, such as Royal Ivy, were developed and widely advertised.

By 1898, the Northwood Glass Company was beginning to feel pressure from the giant United States Glass conglomerate. Natural supplies were becoming more expensive; Harry Northwood even invested in a natural gas company in an effort to keep prices low. Plans to relocate developed and in 1892, incorporation papers were filed in Pennsylvania. Lawsuits related to the business began to shake its foundation, as the company moved to Ellwood City, Pennsylvania. By 1898, the company was failing and closed late in the year.

Harry Northwood went on to the Indiana Glass Company, Indiana, Pennsylvania. His presence became quickly known as new products were developed, including some intricate pressed patterns to rival cut glass.

Northwood & Co. was founded in 1902 by Harry Northwood and Thomas Dugan in Wheeling, West Virginia. The first items produced by the new company were ornate tableware patterns, as well as lemonade sets. Ironically, the company was located in the former Hobbs, Brockunier plant, where the young Englishman, Harry Northwood, held his first glassmaking job.

By 1907, H. Northwood & Co. was established as one of America's finest glassware manufacturers. Novelties and pressed patterns were produced in

opalescent colors, as well as solid green, amethyst, and blue—some of which featured gold decorations. Carnival glass production began in 1908, but continued only until 1915. Despite its popularity, it was discontinued due to hard financial times. H. Northwood & Co. continued to pioneer glass formulas and produced a fine line of custard patterns, as well as an imitation marble-type glass.

Harry Northwood died in 1919, and the company reorganized. Several new patterns and colors were added. Competition from companies such as Westmoreland, Fenton, and Imperial was becoming fierce and the company began to falter. By 1925, Northwood & Co. ceased production and the plant was closed.

References: Marion T. Hartung, Northwood *Pattern Glass In Color, Clear, Colored, Custard, and Carnival*, privately printed, 1969; William Heacock, James Measell, Berry Wiggins, *Harry Northwood: The Early Years, 1881-1900*, Antique Publications, 1990; —, *Harry Northwood: The Wheeling Years, 1901-1925*, Antique Publications, 1992; Kenneth Wilson, *American Glass 1760-1930: The Toledo Museum of Art, Volume I, Volume II*, Hudson Hills Press and The Toledo Museum of Art, 1994.

Museums: The Chrysler Museum, Norfolk, VA; The Corning Museum of Glass, Corning, NY; The Toledo Museum of Art, Toledo, OH.

Additional Listings: See Carnival glass, Custard Glass, Opalescent Glass, and Pattern Glass.

Basket

4" h, white carnival, basketweave, eight sided, open handles, ftd, sgd **125.00**

4-1/2" h, 4-1/2" d, bushel-basket shape, blue opalescent. . . . **140.00**

11-1/2" h, 12" w, deep red with pale orange cream color, bright shocking pink int. lining, applied crystal edges, four applied rosette prunts, four large thorn ribbed feet, double applied crystal rope handle, Victorian **1,250.00**

Berry set, master and six individual sauces

Intaglio, custard, green and gilt dec, 8-3/4" d master, 4-1/2" d sauces **250.00**

Leaf Medallion pattern, cobalt blue, gold trim **315.00**

Memphis pattern, green **200.00**

Biscuit jar, cov, Cherry Thumbprint pattern, colorless, ruby and gold trim **150.00**

Bonbon, Stippled Rays pattern, carnival, blue **60.00**

Bowl

6-1/2" d, cobalt blue, gold highlighted florals and beaded pattern, gold on rim, sgd "Northwood" **50.00**

8" sq, 2-3/4" h, Shasta Daisy, amethyst, gilt dec, turn-up sides, part of Verre D'Or line, sgd "H. Northwood & Co.," wear to gilt **70.00**

9" d, 4-1/2" h, satin, gold and pink stripes on white ground, white int., applied frosted crimped edge **500.00**

Bride's bowl, 10-1/2" d, 4" h, Opaline Brocade, Spanish Lace, vaseline, round, crimped rim **120.00**

Bud vase, six-sided, pulled top, green, marked **35.00**

Butter, cov

Cherry Thumbprint pattern, colorless **110.00**

Leaf Umbrella pattern, cranberry **600.00**

Peach pattern, colorless, gold and red trim. **95.00**

Spanish Lace pattern, vaseline opal **445.00**

Springtime pattern, carnival, purple **215.00**

Venetian pattern, cobalt blue, gold trim, enamel dec **135.00**

Calling card tray, ftd, Opal, blue opalescent. **40.00**

Candlesticks, pr

4-1/2" h, #636, blue irid stretch **55.00**

10" h, Chinese Red pattern . .**115.00**

Candy dish, cov

#636, blue irid stretch, one-pound size. **70.00**

#659, russet stretch, half-pound size **60.00**

Celery vase

Block pattern, blue opalescent **55.00**

Leaf Mold pattern, cranberry **135.00**

Ribbed Pillar pattern, pink and white spatter **95.00**

Cologne bottle, Leaf Umbrella pattern, mauve, cased, orig stopper . . . **275.00**

Compote, Pearl and Scale pattern, green. **80.00**

Condiment tray, Chrysanthemum Sprig pattern, custard, gold and color dec, script mark. **450.00**

Console set, Chinese Red pattern, 9-1/2" d ftd compote, pr matching candlesticks **185.00**

Creamer

Cherry and Plum pattern, colorless, ruby and gold trim **85.00**

Leaf Umbrella pattern, cranberry, breakfast size. **225.00**

Lustre Flute pattern, carnival, green **50.00**

Paneled Sprig pattern, blue opalescent, white spatter, 6" h **95.00**

Peach pattern, colorless, gold and red trim **60.00**

Pods and Posies pattern, green, gold trim **70.00**

Creamer and sugar, No. 12 pattern, colorless, gilt trim, marked. **75.00**

Cruet, orig stopper

Daisy and Fern pattern, blue opalescent, Parian Swirl mold **175.00**

Intaglio pattern, white opalescent **165.00**

Wild Bouquet pattern, custard, enamel dec. **550.00**

Finger bowl, Leaf Umbrella pattern, blue, cased **100.00**

Goblet

Grape and Gothic Arches pattern, custard, nutmeg stain **75.00**

Nearcut, colorless **35.00**

Strawberry and Cable pattern, colorless **40.00**

Jelly compote

Intaglio pattern, white opalescent, c1903 . . . . **45.00**

Poppy pattern, green **35.00**

Lady's spittoon, Inverted Fan and Feather, blue opalescent, c1903 . . . . **275.00**

Marmalade jar, cov, Paneled Sprig pattern, cranberry, SP rim, cov, and bail handle **195.00**

Mug, Dandelion, custard, nutmeg stain **150.00**

Nappy

Lustre Flute pattern, carnival, marigold **35.00**

Memphis pattern, "Compliments L. H. Cahn & Co/Furniture/236-240 W. Federal St" in center, "N" in circle mark, c1900 . . . . **65.00**

Nut bowl, Leaf and Beads pattern, carnival, purple **65.00**

Pickle castor

Paneled Sprig pattern insert, cranberry, enameled floral dec on panels, ornate silver plated frame, lid, orig tongs, 9" h **600.00**

Royal Ivy, frosted rubena, silver plated Webster frame, 9-1/2" h **250.00**

Pitcher

Apple Blossom, white opaque, dec, 8" h, most dec worn off **25.00**

Cherry and Plum pattern, colorless, gold trim **165.00**

Chrysanthemum Sprig, 9" h, lime green, white spatter, satinized handle. **475.00**

Coin Dot pattern, carnival, marigold **170.00**

Daisy and Fern pattern, cranberry, ball shape **175.00**
Leaf Mold pattern, cranberry, white spatter **300.00**
Leaf Umbrella pattern, blue opaque, 72 oz **650.00**
Opaline Brocade, Spanish Lace, blue, 9-1/2" h, residue on int. **200.00**
Paneled Holly pattern, green, gold trim **250.00**
Royal Oak pattern, colorless . **75.00**

Plate

Paneled Cherry pattern, colorless, red cherries, gold leaves, 10-1/2" d **45.00**
Thistle pattern, colorless, 10" d **30.00**
Three Fruits pattern, custard, 7-1/2" d **25.00**

Rose bowl

Pearl and Scale pattern, stem, blue **90.00**
Pull Up, 8" h, 6" w, deep green and red, brilliant pink lining, three applied crystal thorn feet **1,200.00**
Royal Ivy, 4" h, 2-1/4" d rim, frosted rubena, minute roughness inside rim **150.00**

Salt and pepper shakers, pr, orig tops

Bow and Tassel pattern, milk glass **65.00**
Carnelian pattern, custard .. **450.00**
Leaf Umbrella pattern, mauve, cased **165.00**

Sauce

Cherry Thumbprint pattern, colorless, ruby and gold trim **15.00**
Regent pattern, amethyst, gold trim **40.00**
Wild Bouquet pattern, white opal, no dec **20.00**

Server, 11" d, center handle, #698, blue irid stretch **48.00**

Spooner

Aurora pattern, pink satin ground, white patter **85.00**
Cherry and Plum pattern, colorless, ruby and gold trim **75.00**
Chrysanthemum Sprig pattern, opaque blue, gold trim.... **245.00**
Gothic Arches pattern, colorless **35.00**
Klondyke, blue opalescent, 4-1/4" d, 4-1/4" h **70.00**
Memphis pattern, green..... **75.00**
Singing Birds pattern, colorless **70.00**

Sugar bowl, cov

Cherry and Plum pattern, colorless, ruby and gold trim **85.00**
Cherry Thumbprint pattern, colorless, ruby and gold trim **100.00**
Paneled Sprig pattern, milk glass, green and gold dec **125.00**
Peach pattern, colorless, ruby and gold trim **85.00**
Utopia Optic pattern, cranberry **120.00**

Sugar shaker

Jeweled Heart, apple green, 4-1/2" h **300.00**
Jeweled Heart, blue, 4-3/4" h **300.00**
Jeweled Heart, colorless, traces of gilt dec, 4-1/2" h **90.00**
Leaf Mold, cased blue, satin finish, orig top **375.00**
Leaf Mold, light blue, satin finish, 4" h **325.00**
Leaf Umbrella, blue, satin finish, 4-1/2" h **425.00**
Leaf Umbrella, cased yellow, 4-1/2" h **275.00**
Royal Ivy, frosted, 4-1/4" h... **110.00**
Royal Ivy, rainbow craquelle, 4-1/2" h **550.00**

Syrup pitcher

Coin Spot and Swirl, blue, 6" h **220.00**
Coin Spot and Swirl, white, 6" h **100.00**
Jeweled Heart, apple green, 6" h, reproduction lid **550.00**
Jeweled Heart, blue, 5-1/2" h **700.00**
Leaf Umbrella pattern, cranberry, white spatter **250.00**
Nine Panel, blue, 5-3/4" h ... **150.00**
Paneled Sprig, blue speckled, 5-1/2" h **1,800.00**
Ribbed Pillar, pink and white spatter, front of lid marked "Pat. April 26, 81, March 28, 82," 6-1/2" h . **350.00**
Stripe, bulbous, vaseline, front of lid marked "Pat. April 26, 81, March 28, 82," 6-1/4" h.......... **650.00**
Stripe, tall, white, leaf design in upper end of applied handle, inside of lid marked "Pat. July 15, 84," 7-1/4" h.......... **120.00**

Table set, cov butter, creamer, spooner, and cov sugar

Belladonna pattern, green, gold trim **325.00**
Nearcut, colorless, gold trim . **250.00**
Paneled Holly pattern, green, gold trim **475.00**
Peach pattern, green, gold trim, marked "N" **350.00**

Sugar castor, Leaf Umbrella, cased blue, **$225.**

Tankard pitcher, 11-1/2" h, blue, multicolored enamel floral dec, gold rim, ftd band at base, marked...**110.00**

Toothpick holder

Maple Leaf pattern, custard. **550.00**
Memphis pattern, green..... **50.00**
Ribbed Optic pattern, rubena **165.00**
Threaded Swirl pattern, rubena **250.00**

Tumbler

Atlas pattern, opaque pink... **35.00**
Flower and Bud pattern, colorless **50.00**
Leaf Umbrella, blue, opal plated interior, 3-3/4" h **60.00**
Oriental Poppy pattern, colorless, gold trim.......... **25.00**
Paneled Holly pattern, colorless **45.00**
Peach pattern, colorless..... **45.00**
Regent pattern, amethyst, gold trim **75.00**
Strawberry and Cable pattern, colorless.......... **40.00**

Vase

7-1/2" h, 6" w, Jewel, medium blue over white satin body, vertical pattern of 30 ribs, orig white lining **450.00**
Daisy and Drape pattern ... **300.00**
Diamond Point pattern, 7" h . **150.00**

Water set

Daffodils, 9-1/2" h bulbous water pitcher, six 4" h tumblers, opalescent blue, tightly crimped rim, small flakes **900.00**
Peach, 8-1/2" h pitcher, two 4" h tumblers, green, gilt dec, wear to gilt **130.00**

Whiskey tumbler, Threaded Swirl pattern, Rubena **65.00**

Wine set, Cornflower pattern, green, gold trim, decanter, orig stopper, four matching wines.......... **165.00**

Opalescent Glass

History: Opalescent glass, a clear or colored glass with milky white decorations, looks fiery or opalescent when held to light. This effect was achieved by applying bone ash chemicals to designated areas while a piece was still hot and then refiring it at extremely high temperatures.

There are three basic categories of opalescent glass: (1) blown (or mold blown) patterns, e.g., Daisy and Fern and Spanish Lace; (2) novelties, pressed glass patterns made in limited quantity and often in unusual shapes such as corn or a trough; and (3) traditional pattern (pressed) glass forms.

Opalescent glass was produced in England in the 1870s. Northwood began the American production in 1897 at its Indiana, Pennsylvania, plant. Jefferson, National Glass, Hobbs, and Fenton soon followed.

References: Gary Baker et al., *Wheeling Glass 1829-1939*, Oglebay Institute, 1994, distributed by Antique Publications; Bill Banks, *Complete Price Guide for Opalescent Glass*, 2nd ed., published by author, 1996; Bill Edwards, *Standard Encyclopedia of Opalescent Glass*, Collector Books, 1997; William Heacock, *Encyclopedia of Victorian Colored Pattern Glass*, Book II, 2nd ed., Antique Publications, 1977; William Heacock and William Gamble, *Encyclopedia of Victorian Colored Pattern Glass, Book 9, Cranberry Opalescent from A to Z*, Antique Publications, 1987; William Heacock, James Measell, and Berry Wiggins, *Dugan/Diamond*, Antique Publications, 1993; —–, *Harry Northwood* (1990), Book 2 (1991) Antique Publications; —–, *Harry Northwood: The Early Years 1881-1900*, Antique Publications, 1990; —–, *Harry Northwood: The Wheeling Years 1901-1925*, Antique Publications, 1991.

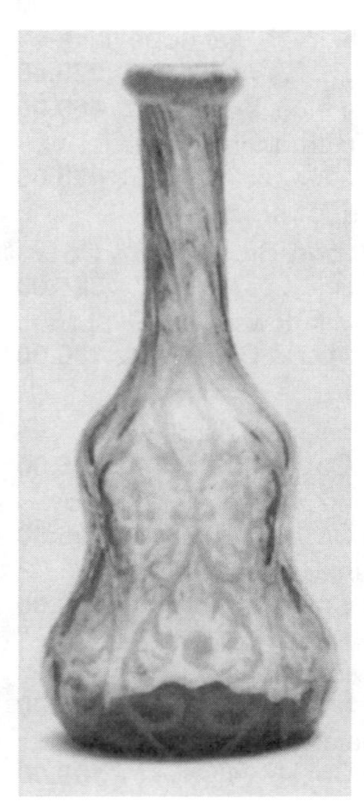

Barber bottle, cylindrical, flattened bulbous body, long neck, cranberry, Coin Spot, tooled mouth, smooth base, 7-1/2" h, **$180.** *Photo courtesy of Norman C. Heckler and Co.*

Blown

Barber bottle
- Raised Swirl, cranberry **295.00**
- Spanish Lace, cranberry ... **700.00**
- Swirl, blue **225.00**

Basket, Daisy and Fern, vaseline, looped handle **190.00**

Berry bowl, master, Chrysanthemum Base Swirl, blue, satin **95.00**

Biscuit jar, cov, Spanish Lace, vaseline **275.00**

Bowl
- Ruffles and Rings, green **40.00**
- Seaweed, white, 9" d **80.00**
- Swirling Maze, cranberry, ruffled **145.00**

Bride's basket, cranberry, SP holder
- Bubble Lattice **200.00**
- Poinsettia, ruffled top **275.00**

Butter dish, cov
- Hobbs Hobnail, vaseline ... **250.00**
- Spanish Lace, blue........ **265.00**

Celery vase
- Consolidated Criss-Cross, rubena, satin finish **250.00**
- Daffodils, blue.............**115.00**
- Reverse Swirl, cranberry ... **175.00**
- Ribbed Lattice, cranberry .. **245.00**
- Seaweed, cranberry....... **250.00**
- Windows, cranberry, ruffled rim **115.00**

Cheese dish, Hobb's Swirl, cranberry **350.00**

Compote, Ribbed Spiral, blue .. **70.00**

Creamer
- Buckeye Lattice, cranberry . **450.00**
- Coin Dot, cranberry **190.00**
- Windows Swirl, cranberry... **500.00**

Cruet, orig stopper
- Chrysanthemum Base Swirl, white, satin **175.00**
- Fern, blue **345.00**
- Hobb's Hobnail, blue **225.00**
- Ribbed Opal Lattice, white.. **135.00**
- Spanish Lace, canary yellow **185.00**
- Stripe, blue, applied blue handle **185.00**
- Windows, Plain, cranberry .. **375.00**
- Windows, Swirled, cranberry **350.00**

Custard cup, Panel Hobnail, white **15.00**

Finger bowl
- Hobb's Hobnail, cranberry ... **65.00**
- Hobb's Optic Diamond, cranberry **70.00**
- Spanish Lace, blue......... **50.00**

Lamp, oil
- Inverted Thumbprint, white, amber fan base **145.00**
- Snowflake, cranberry **800.00**

Lamp shade, Swirl pattern, cranberry ground, 8-1/2" d.............**110.00**

Cruet, white opalescent stripes, sapphire blue applied handle, sapphire blue stopper, 5-1/2" h, **$285.** *Photo courtesy of Clarence and Betty Maier.*

Miniature lamp, Reverse Swirl, vaseline **95.00**

Mustard, cov, Reverse Swirl, vaseline **65.00**

Pickle castor, Daisy and Fern, blue, emb floral jar, DQ, resilvered frame **650.00**

Lamp, Cobweb, cranberry ground, clear Eason base, ground under foot, **$550.** *Photo courtesy of Green Valley Auctions.*

Pitcher

Arabian Nights, white **450.00**
Buttons and Braids, blue ... **220.00**
Christmas Snowflake, cranberry **2,100.00**
Coin Spot, cranberry
Clover leaf crimp **325.00**
Triangular crimp, windows mold, #261................ **400.00**
Daisy and Fern, cranberry .. **500.00**
Fern
Blue **450.00**
Cranberry, applied crystal handle, 9" h, 6" d **600.00**
Hobb's Hobnail, cranberry .. **315.00**
Reverse Swirl, blue, satin, speckled **495.00**
Seaweed, blue **525.00**
Stars and Stripes, cranberry **2,100.00**
Windows, cranberry **695.00**

Rose bowl

Opal Swirl, white........... **40.00**
Piasa Bird, blue........... **100.00**

Salt shaker, Reverse Twist, blue, original top, **$65.**

Salt shaker, orig top

Coin Spot, cranberry **200.00**
Consolidated Criss-Cross, cranberry **85.00**
Reverse Swirl, blue......... **65.00**
Ribbed Opal Lattice, cranberry **95.00**

Spooner

Bubble Lattice, cranberry... **145.00**
Reverse Swirl, cranberry ... **165.00**
Ribbed Spiral, blue........ **110.00**

Sugar bowl, cov

Bubble Lattice, cranberry ... **195.00**
Reverse Swirl, cranberry **350.00**
Spanish Lace, blue **175.00**

Sugar shaker

Bubble Lattice, blue, 4-3/4" h **325.00**
Chrysanthemum Base Swirl
Blue, Buckeye Glass Co., 4-3/4" h.............. **275.00**
Cranberry, Buckeye Glass Co., 4-3/4" h.............. **400.00**
Coin Spot
Bulbous base, blue, Hobbs, Brockunier & Co./Beaumont Glass Co., 4-3/4" h **160.00**
Bulbous base, white, Hobbs, Brockunier & Co./Beaumont Glass Co., 4-3/4" h **80.00**
Nine-panel mold, blue, Northwood Glass Co., 4-1/2" h.............. **200.00**
Nine-panel mold, white, Northwood Glass Co., 4-1/2" h.............. **100.00**
Ring neck, blue-green, Hobbs, Brockunier & Co., 4-3/4" h **130.00**
Ring neck, rubena, Hobbs, Brockunier & Co., 4-1/2" h **220.00**
Tapered, white, Hobbs, Brockunier & Co., 5-1/4" h **100.00**
Wide waisted, cranberry, Northwood Glass Co./Buckeye Glass Co., 4-1/2" h **250.00**
Wide waisted, green, Northwood Glass Co./Buckeye Glass Co., 4-1/2" h.............. **160.00**
Wide waisted, white, Northwood Glass Co./Buckeye Glass Co., 4-3/4" h.............. **100.00**
Daisy and Fern
Northwood mold, blue, Northwood Glass Co., 4-1/4" h **210.00**
Northwood mold, cranberry, Northwood Glass Co., 4-1/4" h **400.00**
Wide waisted mold, blue, Northwood Glass Co., 4-1/4" h **180.00**
Wide waisted mold, cranberry, Northwood Glass Co., 4-1/4" h **325.00**
Wide waisted mold, white, Northwood Glass Co., 4-1/4" h **70.00**
Poinsettia
Blue, H. Northwood & Co., 5" h **475.00**
Colorless, H. Northwood & Co., 5" h **130.00**
Polka Dot, cranberry, Northwood & Co., 4-1/4" h............ **800.00**
Reverse Swirl
Blue, satin, Buckeye Glass Co./Model Flint Glass Co., 4-3/4" h **300.00**
Cranberry, Buckeye Glass Co./Model Flint Glass Co., 4-1/2" h **300.00**
Vaseline, Buckeye Glass Co./Model Flint Glass Co., 4-3/4" h **300.00**
White, Buckeye Glass Co./Model Flint Glass Co., 4-3/4" h. **120.00**
Ribbed Opal Lattice, tall
Blue, 4-1/2" h.......... **170.00**
Cranberry, 4-1/2" h...... **220.00**
White, 4-1/2" h **90.00**
Spanish Lace
Cranberry, Northwood Glass Co., 4-1/2" h **325.00**
Vaseline, Northwood Glass Co., 4-1/2" h **275.00**
White, Northwood Glass Co., 4-1/2" h **110.00**
Stripe, wide, cranberry, 4" h . **600.00**
Swirl
Bulbous base, light blue, Hobbs, Brockunier & Co., 4-3/4" h **350.00**
Bulbous base, vaseline, Hobbs, Brockunier & Co., 4-3/4" h, minor ext. wear **350.00**
Cranberry, 5" h, chips ... **375.00**
Green, 5-1/4" h, flat edge flake **275.00**
Tapered, blue, 5-1/2" h .. **400.00**
Tapered, cranberry, 5-1/4" h **425.00**
Swirled Windows
Blue, Hobbs, Brockunier & Co., 5" h **325.00**
Swirled Windows, white, Hobbs, Brockunier & Co., 5" h.. **130.00**
Twist
Nine panel, blue, Northwood Glass Co., 4-1/2" h **275.00**
Nine panel, green, Northwood Glass Co., 4-1/2" h **295.00**
Nine panel, white Northwood Glass Co., 4-1/2" h **100.00**
Wide waisted, vaseline, Northwood Glass Co., 4-3/4" h **325.00**
Wide waisted, white, Northwood Glass Co., 4-3/4" h **100.00**

Syrup pitcher

Aztec Medallion (Swirl), green, 6" h **2,400.00**
Baby Coin Spot, white, applied handle with pressed leaf crimp, 7-1/2" h **125.00**
Beatty Swirl, blue, Beatty and Sons, 6-3/4" h **800.00**
Coin Dot, blue, squatty, 4-1/2" h **250.00**
Coin Spot, cranberry **175.00**
Coin Spot and Swirl, blue, applied loop handle, orig tin cover . **150.00**
Daisy and Criss-Cross, white. **545.00**
Daisy and Fern, blue, bulbous. **285.00**
Daisy and Fern, white, bulbous, 6" h, wear to lid **100.00**
Double Greek Key, blue, applied blue handle with curl, Nickel Plate Glass Co., Fostoria, OH, 6" h **4,600.00**
Reverse Swirl
- Blue, Buckeye Glass Co./Model Flint Glass Co., 6-3/4" h . **375.00**
- Collard, blue, Buckeye Glass Co./Model Flint Glass Co., 6" h, crack in top of handle. . . **225.00**
- Vaseline, Buckeye Glass Co./Model Flint Glass Co., lid marked "Pat. April 26, 81, March 28, 82," 7-1/4" h **350.00**
- White, Buckeye Glass Co./Model Flint Glass Co., lid marked "Pat. April 26, 81, March 28, 82," 7" h, internal fracture below base of handle. **60.00**

Seaweed
- Blue, Hobbs, Brockunier & Co., 5-3/4" h **850.00**
- Cranberry, Hobbs, Brockunier & Co., 6" h **1,150.00**

Spanish Lace, white, Northwood Glass Co., old reeded handle, 6-1/4" h, reproduction lid . . . **140.00**
Stripe, wide, blue, curl at base of applied handle, front of lid marked "Pat April 26, 81, Mar 28, 82," 6-1/4" h **800.00**
Windows, Swirled, white, front of lid marked "Pat. April 26, 81, Mar 28, 82," Hobbs, Brockunier & Co., 6-3/4" h **300.00**

Tankard pitcher

Chrysanthemum Swirl Variant, cranberry. **2,500.00**
Poinsettia, cranberry **2,500.00**

Toothpick holder

Consolidated Criss-Cross, cranberry **500.00**
Overall Hobnail, blue **65.00**
Ribbed Lattice, blue **165.00**

Tumbler

Acanthus, blue **90.00**
Beatty Honeycomb, blue . . . **275.00**
Bubble Lattice, cranberry. . . **135.00**
Christmas Snowflake, blue, ribbed **125.00**
Maze, swirling, green **95.00**
Reverse Swirl, cranberry **65.00**
Seaweed, cranberry **150.00**
Spanish Lace, green **65.00**
Swirl, blue **95.00**
Windows, cranberry **125.00**

Vase, Dahlia, blue **60.00**
Waste bowl, Hobbs Hobnail, vaseline **75.00**
Water set, Christmas Snowflake, cobalt blue, six pcs **400.00**
Whimsy, bowl, Piasa Bird, blue . **85.00**

Novelties

Back bar bottle, 12-1/4" h, robin's egg blue ground, opalescent stripes swirled to the right **100.00**
Barber bottle, 8" h, sq, diamond pattern molded form, light cranberry, white vertical stripes **275.00**

Basket

4" h, 5" w, cranberry, white opalescent stripes and clear ribbing interspersed with silver mica, ruffled edge, applied clear twisted center loop handle. **150.00**
7-1/2" h, 5" w, rose bowl form, cranberry, deep white opalescent extends half way down, applied clear rigaree top, applied crystal five-footed base, small loop applied crystal handle **200.00**

Bowl

Cashews, blue, crimped. **60.00**
Grape and Cherry, blue **85.00**
Greek Key and Ribs, green . . **75.00**
Jolly Bear, white **85.00**
Leaf and Beads, green, twig feet **60.00**
Many Loops, blue, crimped, fluted **65.00**
Ruffles and Rings, white. **35.00**
Winter Cabbage, white. **45.00**

Bushel basket, blue **75.00**
Chalice, Maple Leaf, vaseline. . . **45.00**

Compote

Dolphin, vaseline **95.00**
Squirrel and Acorn, green, ruffled **175.00**

Cruet, Stars and Stripes, cranberry **575.00**
Hanging vase, 8-1/2" h, green opalescent vase with thorns, clear crystal vine as holder for vase, pressed green daisy-like flower on holder, Victorian **115.00**
Hat, Opal Swirl, white. **35.00**
Jack-in-the-pulpit vase, 8-1/2" h, Squirrel and Acorn pattern, opalescent, white **115.00**
Mug, Singing Birds, blue **145.00**
Plate, Wishbone and Drape, green **35.00**

Rose bowl

Leaf Chalice, green, pedestal . **65.00**
Palm and Scroll, green, three ftd **75.00**

Vase, corn, white **125.00**

Pressed

Banana boat, Jewel and Fan, green **115.00**

Berry bowl, master

Alaska, blue. **195.00**
Everglades, vaseline, gold trim **200.00**
Tokyo, green **75.00**

Berry set

Beatty Swirl, blue, seven pcs **325.00**
Inverted Fan and Feather, white **260.00**
Iris and Meander, blue, six pcs **380.00**
Swag with Brackets, green, seven pcs **275.00**

Bowl

Argonaut Shell, vaseline, shell ftd **100.00**
Beaded Stars, low base, green **45.00**
Beatty Rib, blue, rect. **65.00**
Diamond Spearhead, 9" d, blue **45.00**
Iris with Meander, 8" d, vaseline **135.00**
Jewel and Fan, blue **35.00**
Jeweled Heart, green, crimped **40.00**
Many Loops, crimped, green . **25.00**
Peacocks, Northwood, blue, ruffled, ribbed back. **145.00**
Peacock and Fence, blue . . . **300.00**
Waterlily and Cattail, blue **65.00**

Bride's basket, Lattice, cranberry, sq, ruffled rim, 4" h, 7" d **240.00**

Butter dish, cov

Argonaut Shell, white. **245.00**
Beatty Rib, white **95.00**
Drapery, blue, gold trim. **215.00**
Everglades, vaseline **345.00**
Fluted Scrolls, blue **200.00**
Idyll, green. **350.00**
Jackson, blue **155.00**
Sunburst and Shield, blue. . . **345.00**
Swag with Brackets, green . . **100.00**

Tokyo, blue **300.00**
Water Lily and Cattails
Blue **300.00**
White **230.00**

Calling card receiver
Fluted Scrolls
Vaseline **65.00**
White **40.00**
Inverted Feather, vaseline. . . **225.00**

Celery vase
Alaska, blue, dec **150.00**
Diamond Spearhead, green . **275.00**
Wreath and Shell, vaseline, dec **140.00**

Compote
Diamond Spearhead, vaseline **150.00**
Intaglio, vaseline. **70.00**
Tokyo, blue **60.00**

Cracker jar, cov
Beaded Drape, pale blue ground, mate finish, silver plated hardware, 11" h, 6-1/2" w, wear to silver plate **100.00**
Wreath and Shell, vaseline . . **750.00**

Creamer
Alaska, blue, 3-1/2" h **75.00**
Beaded Shell, green. **165.00**
Fluted Scrolls
Blue **70.00**
Vaseline **85.00**
Gonterman Swirl, blue, frosted **625.00**
Hobnail, rose, clear applied handle, polished pontil, 5" h **110.00**
Inverted Fan and Feather, blue **125.00**
Intaglio, white **85.00**
Paneled Holly, white **70.00**
Scroll with Acanthus, green . . **65.00**
Swag with Brackets, green. . . **90.00**
Tokyo, blue **125.00**
Wild Bouquet, green. **140.00**
Wreath and Shell, vaseline, dec **135.00**

Cruet
Alaska, vaseline, enameled dec **275.00**
Christmas Pearls, white **260.00**
Daisy and Fern, blue, Parian Swirl mold paneled stopper, 6" h **110.00**
Everglades, vaseline. **275.00**
Fancy Fantails, blue **375.00**
Fluted Scrolls, blue, clear stopper **295.00**
Intaglio, white, no stopper, 5-1/2" h **25.00**
Jackson, blue **185.00**
Paneled Sprig/Lattice, white, no stopper, 6-1/2" h **50.00**
Scroll with Acanthus, blue . . . **200.00**
Swirl, green, clear applied handle, orig stopper, 6-1/2" h. **170.00**
Tokyo, green, no stopper, 4-1/2" h, int. residue. **70.00**

Epergne, Jackson, blue. **155.00**

Goblet, Diamond Spearhead, cranberry **85.00**

Jelly compote
Diamond Spearhead, vaseline **85.00**
Everglades, blue, gold trim . . . **85.00**
Intaglio, blue **55.00**
Iris with Meander, vaseline . . . **95.00**
Wild Bouquet, blue **160.00**

Match holder, Beatty Rib, white . **35.00**

Mug
Diamond Spearhead, cobalt blue **85.00**
Stork and Rushes, blue **90.00**

Nappy, Hobbs' Hobnail, blue, polished pontil, sq, 4-1/2" w, 1-3/4" h, set of six **170.00**

Pitcher
Beatty Swirl, canary yellow . . **195.00**
Fern, white, sq top, applied colorless handle **190.00**
Fluted Scrolls, vaseline **300.00**
Gonterman Swirl, amber top . **375.00**
Intaglio, blue **215.00**
Jeweled Heart, blue **250.00**
Swag with Brackets, vaseline **225.00**
Swirl, blue, applied blue handle, ruffled top, 9-1/2" h **200.00**
Wild Bouquet, blue **300.00**

Plate
Palm Beach, blue, 10" d, set of six **895.00**
Tokyo, ftd, green **70.00**
Water Lily and Cattail, amethyst **85.00**

Rose bowl
Beaded Drape, blue **60.00**
Fancy Fantails, cranberry, four clear applied feet **650.00**
Fluted Scrolls, blue **125.00**
Fluted Scrolls, vaseline **115.00**

Salt and pepper shakers, pr
Everglades, vaseline **400.00**
Jewel and Flower, canary yellow, orig tops **250.00**

Salt, open, individual
Beatty Rib, white **42.00**
Wreath and Shell, blue **65.00**

Sauce
Alaska
Blue. **65.00**
White. **20.00**
Argonaut Shell, blue **40.00**
Circled Scrolls, blue **50.00**
Drapery, Northwood, dec, blue **35.00**
Iris with Meander, yellow **25.00**
Jewel and Flower, white **25.00**
Regal, green. **65.00**
Water Lily and Cattails, white . **35.00**
Wild Bouquet, blue. **40.00**

Spooner
Argonaut Shell, French Opal **170.00**
Beatty Rib, white. **45.00**
Flora, blue. **110.00**
Fluted Scrolls, blue, dec. **70.00**
Intaglio, white **45.00**
Iris with Meander, canary yellow **95.00**
Klondyke, blue, 4-1/4" h **70.00**
Palm Beach, vaseline **95.00**
Tokyo, blue **85.00**
Swag with Brackets, blue **50.00**
Wreath and Shell
Vaseline **120.00**
White **285.00**

Sugar bowl, cov
Alaska, vaseline **155.00**
Circled Scroll, green. **85.00**
Diamond Spearhead, vaseline **235.00**
Fluted Scrolls, blue. **130.00**
Gonterman Swirl, amber. . . . **235.00**
Intaglio, blue. **75.00**
Jewel and Flower, vaseline. . . **90.00**
Swag with Brackets, blue **95.00**
Tokyo, blue, gold trim **115.00**

Sugar shaker, Beatty Honeycomb, white, Beatty & Sons, 3-1/2" h . . . **110.00**

Syrup pitcher
Diamond Spearhead, green. **350.00**
Flora, white, gold trim **275.00**

Toothpick holder
Beatty Rib, white. **30.00**
Diamond Spearhead
Green. **75.00**
Vaseline **80.00**
Flora, white, gold trim **150.00**
Gonterman Swirl, amber top **150.00**
Iris with Meander, blue **115.00**
Ribbed Spiral, blue. **90.00**
Wreath and Shell, blue **275.00**

Tumbler
Alaska
Blue **110.00**
Vaseline **85.00**
Beatty Rib, white. **35.00**
Beatty Swirl, white **45.00**
Drapery, blue **90.00**
Everglades, vaseline **50.00**
Fluted Scrolls, vaseline. **75.00**
Intaglio, white **45.00**
Jackson, green. **50.00**
Jeweled Heart, blue **85.00**

Paneled Holly, blue **100.00**
S-Repeat, blue. **45.00**
Wild Bouquet, white. **25.00**
Wreath and Shell
Collared, blue **90.00**
Ftd, blue **375.00**

Vase
Fluted Scrolls and Vine, blue . . **70.00**
Inverted Fan and Feather, blue **85.00**
Northwood Diamond Point, blue **75.00**
Water Lily and Cattail, amethyst **75.00**

Water set
Daffodils, 9-1/2" h bulbous water pitcher, six 4" h tumblers, blue, tightly crimped rim, Northwood, small flakes **900.00**
Diamond Spearhead, tankard pitcher, six tumblers, green. **445.00**
Everglades, pitcher, six tumblers **700.00**
Fluted Scrolls, blue, pitcher and six tumblers **645.00**
Jeweled Heart, blue. **650.00**
Swag with Brackets, vaseline **695.00**
Tokyo, green **675.00**

Opaline Glass

History: Opaline glass was a popular mid to late 19th-century European glass. The glass has a certain amount of translucency and often is found decorated with enamel designs and trimmed in gold.

Basket
5" h, ruffled, applied colorless handle **60.00**
6-1/2" h, 6" d, clambroth color, applied pink snake loop around handle, gold rim **100.00**

Biscuit jar, cov, white ground, hp, florals and birds dec, brass lid and bail handle **165.00**

Bouquet holder, 7" h, blue opaline cornucopia shaped gilt dec flower holders issuing from bronze stag heads, Belgian black marble base, English, Victorian, early 19th C, pr **725.00**

Bowl, 8" d, 2 h, rose opaque body **50.00**

Box, cov
5-3/8" l, rect, domed cov, blue, gilt metal mounts, Continental, early 20th C. **250.00**
7-1/2" l, egg shaped, blue, gilt metal mounts, Continental, early 20th C **295.00**

Bride's bowl, 7-1/2" d, 10-1/2" h, round pink bowl, clear ruffled rim, Meriden frame with cupid medallions on handles **200.00**

Candelabra, Louis XV style
18-1/2" h, gilt bronze and blue opaline, scrolled candle arms and base, two-light, late 19th C **175.00**
26-1/2" h, gilt metal and blue opaline, five-light, late 19th C **400.00**

Candlestick, 7-1/4" h, white opaque clambroth body, rib molded **150.00**

Casket, 6" l, 4" h, hinged, beveled and hand polished inserts, gilded beaded frame, four scrolled feet with emb design, French, few beads missing on lower front. **100.00**

Chalice, white ground, Diamond Point pattern **35.00**

Cheese dish, cov, white opaque body, gold enamel dec **185.00**

Child's mug, 2-1/4" h, paneled scenes of Dutch children, pr **65.00**

Clock, 6" d, white opaque body, hanging type, circular frame, hand painted, Welch Company, Forestville, CT, clockworks, orig brass chain **275.00**

Cologne bottle
6" h, jade green opaque body, orig stopper **95.00**
8-3/4" h, jade green opaque body, gold ring dec, orig stopper . . **90.00**

Creamer, shaded yellow to white opaque body, pink roses and blue forget me nots, SP rim and handle **125.00**

Cup plate, Lee-Rose 258, white opaque body, minute rim roughage **75.00**

Dresser jar, 5-1/2" d, egg shape, blue ground, heavy gold dec. **200.00**

Ewer, 13-1/4" h, white ground, Diamond Point pattern. **135.00**

Fairy lamp, 17" h, French blue, four large faceted purple and dark blue jewels, filigree brass mountings. **285.00**

Jack-in-the-pulpit vase, 5-1/2" h, robin's egg blue opaque body, applied amber feet **95.00**

Jar, cov, 5" h, 6-1/4" d underplate, gilt Greek key banding, short bell-shaped jar, spreading foot, tapered lid, French, 19th C, price for pr. **525.00**

Jardinières, 5-1/4" h, gilt bronze and blue opaline, sq, Empire style, tasseled chains, paw feet, early 20th C, pr **1,610.00**

Mantel lusters, 12-3/4" h, blue, gilt dec, slender faceted prisms, Victorian, c1880, damage, pr. **250.00**

Match holder, 1-3/8" h, blue opaque body, gold flowers and leaves . . . **40.00**

Miniature, bride's bowl, 5" d, 5-1/2" h, Brocade Spanish Lace, cranberry ground, plain frame marked "WBsS, EP 1243," wear on silver frame **250.00**

Oil lamp, 24" h, dolphin-form stepped base, clear glass oil well, frosted glass shade, late 19th C, converted to electric, chips. **460.00**

Casket, hinged, beveled and hand polished inserts, gilded beaded frame, four scrolled feet with embossed design, French, few beads missing on lower front, 6" l, 4" h, **$100.** *Photo courtesy of Cincinnati Art Galleries.*

Oil lamp base, 22" h, blue, baluster turned standard on circular foot, 20th C, converted to electric, pr **635.00**

Perfume bottle

2-3/4" h, blue opaque body, gold flowers and leaves, matching stopper.................. **60.00**

3-1/8" d, 7-3/4" h, tapering cylinder, flat flared base, ring of white opaline around neck and matching teardrop stopper, gold trim. **115.00**

4" h, blue opaque body, gold, white, and yellow dec, matching stopper **75.00**

Pitcher

4-1/4" h, pink opaque body, applied white handle............. **75.00**

12" h, pink, applied ruby paste stones, beaded enamel swag, applied handle, French, 19th C **110.00**

Posy holder, 8" h, blue opaque body, figural hand holding small vase, ruffled rim **85.00**

Salt and pepper shakers, pr, 4" h, pansy dec, damage to both covers, worn dec, pr **45.00**

Salt, open, boat shaped, blue dec, white enamel garland and scrolling **75.00**

Sugar, cov, shaded yellow to white opaque body, pink roses and blue forget me nots, SP cover, rim, and handle **150.00**

Toothpick holder, lavender opaque body, small ball feet........... **85.00**

Tumbler, white opaque body, enameled pink rose **25.00**

Tumble-up, carafe, tumbler, and underplate, pale green opaque body, gold beading, black and white jeweled dec, three pcs.............. **325.00**

Urn, 13" h, blue opaque body, enameled blue flowers, gilt trim, flared rim, pr **350.00**

Vase

5" h, blue, platinum stars dec, Czechoslovakian **55.00**

5" h, 3-3/4" d, pink, applied green tightly ruffled rims, green thorn handles, swirled rib bodies, price for pr.................. **150.00**

5-1/2" h, cased light blue opaline, blue applied ribbon handles, marked "Czecho-slovakia".. **50.00**

8" h, swirled and mottled colors over opaline, applied clear pinched handles, Czechoslovakian .. **35.00**

16-1/4" h, oviform, circular cushioned foot, parcel gilt, enameled, turquoise blue opaque body, gilt rimmed molded border and handles, oval panels with artists' portraits, one with Raphel, other Van Dyke, brown, claret, white, and flesh tones, gilt borders with scrolling foliate edges, French, 19th C, pr **2,500.00**

Violet bowl, 3-1/2" d, 3" h, peachblow pink ground, blue and white enameled flowers, gray leaves and vines, base sgd, Mt Washington **275.00**

Water pitcher, 12-1/4" h, blue, high looped handle, bulbous, early 20th C **230.00**

Whiskey taster, white opaque clam-broth colored body

Lacy, Sandwich, Lee, plate 150-5, minute rim nicks **45.00**

Ten Panel, handle, small chip on bottom.................. **85.00**

OVERSHOT GLASS

History: Overshot glass was developed in the mid-1800s. To produce overshot glass, a gather of molten glass was rolled over the marver upon which had been placed crushed glass. The piece then was blown into the desired shape. The finished product appeared to be frosted or iced.

Early pieces were made mainly in clear glass. As the demand for colored glass increased, color was added to the base piece and occasionally to the crushed glass.

Pieces of overshot generally are attributed to the Boston and Sandwich Glass Co., although many other companies also made it as it grew in popularity.

Museum: Sandwich Glass Museum, Sandwich, MA.

Basket

7" h, 9" w, pink opalescent ruffled body, three rows of hobnails, twisted vaseline handle.... **190.00**

7-1/4" h, 5" d, transparent green shading to colorless, ruffled swirled edge, sq thorn handle, melon-ribbed base with pineapple-like design, entire surface with overshot finish. **285.00**

10" h, 7-1/2" d, rect, shaded cranberry to crystal, applied crystal ruffled edge, applied thorn overshot handle.......... **225.00**

Biscuit jar, cov, 7" h, 5" d, colorless melon ribbed body, applied cranberry overshot, coiled snake handle .. **250.00**

Bowl, 6" d, 3-7/8" h, pale blue opaque, applied amber rigaree around top, applied green leaves, white, pink, and blue applied flowers.......... **235.00**

Bowl, cov, underplate

4-1/4" d, 2-1/4" h bowl, 7" d underplate, colorless, applied red coiled snake on cover, c1880 .... **850.00**

4-1/4" d, 2-1/4" h bowl, 7" d underplate, colorless, applied sterling silver cherries and leaves, c1880................. **850.00**

Bride's bowl, 8-5/8" d, 6-5/8" h, shaded clear to blue ground, lobed, crimped edge, dec brass holder....... **215.00**

Celery vase, 6" h, 3-1/2" d, scalloped top, cranberry ground......... **90.00**

Cheese dish, dome cov, 8" d, 7" h, cranberry ground, enameled crane and cattails, applied colorless faceted finial **425.00**

Compote

6-3/4" h, 8-3/8" d, cranberry shaded to clear bowl, applied clear scalloped and ruffled edge, fancy brass dome ftd pedestal base **125.00**

9" h, 8-7/8" d, colorless ground, applied gold dec, cranberry serpent around stem **125.00**

10-1/4" h, 10" d, cranberry ground, wide rounded bowl, scalloped crown gilt trimmed rim, compressed knop on cylindrical pedestal, wide flaring foot, late 19th C................ **300.00**

12-3/4" h, 8-1/2" d, rubena overshot bowl, white metal bronze finished figural standard **135.00**

14" h, 9" d, rubena overshot bowl, white meal bronze finished figural standard............... **165.00**

Custard cup, pink ground, applied clear ground, Sandwich **60.00**

Decanter, colorless ground, ice bladder, orig stopper......... **750.00**

Epergne, single lily, rubena overshot, fishnet dec................. **300.00**

Ewer, 13-1/2" h, trefoil top, colorless ground, twisted rope handle, Sandwich **275.00**

Fairy lamp, 4-1/4" h, 3" d, opalescent, figural, crown shape, colorless pressed "Clarke" base **195.00**

Finger bowl, pink ground, fluted and swirled....................**115.00**

Goblet, flint, cut cotton twist stem, American................. **300.00**

Ice cream tray, 13" l, colorless, gold trim, Portland............... **40.00**

Lamp shade, 7-7/8" d, 2-7/8" d fitter ring, sapphire blue shaded to clear ground, ruffled............. **125.00**

Lemonade set, 9" h colorless pitcher with swirled body, polished pontil, twisted claw patterned colorless handle, six 3-1/2" h tumblers with swirled body and overshot, c1880 . . . . **650.00**

Marmalade jar, cov, matching underplate, green ground, gold snake entwined on cov, attributed to Boston and Sandwich Glass Co. **315.00**

Mug, 3" h, colorless ground, applied colorless handle **35.00**

Pitcher

- 6" d, cranberry ground, bulbous, applied colorless reeded handle **125.00**
- 7" h, cranberry ground, bulbous, applied colorless reeded handle, attributed to Sandwich **900.00**
- 7" h, cranberry shading to clear, cylindrical, applied colorless handle **750.00**
- 8" d, bulbous, colorless ground, heavy enamel dec of white roses, blue forget me nots and green leaves, applied colorless handle **150.00**
- 8" d, ovoid, cranberry ground, swirled melon ribbed body, cylindrical neck, pinched spout, applied colorless reeded handle **250.00**
- 8-1/4" h, green ground, amber shell handle, Sandwich, c1875, brown age line near lip **225.00**
- 9" h, tankard, cranberry ground, applied colorless reeded handle, hinged metal lid **195.00**
- 10-1/2" h, colorless, applied crystal rigaree around top, rope-twist handle, ice bladder, attributed to Boston and Sandwich Glass Co., c1870-77 . . . . **950.00**
- 11-1/4" h, colorless, twisted rope handle, tricorn rim, gold accents, c1850 . . . . **850.00**
- 11-1/2" h, golden yellow, glass threading at neck, honey-comb spiral shape, glass prunt at base of handle, large colorless disk base, attributed to Boston and Sandwich Glass Co., c1870-77 . . . . . **875.00**
- 13" h, colorless, claw handle, trifold spout, ice bladder opening trimmed with rigaree, c1880 **795.00**
- 13-1/2" h, colorless, twisted rope handle, two large glass strawberry prunts, attributed to Boston and Sandwich Glass Co., c1870-77 . . . . **1,100.00**

Punch cup, pink ground, applied colorless handle, attributed to Boston and Sandwich Glass Co., set of eight **300.00**

Rose bowl, 3-3/4" d, rubena ground, applied flowers and pale green leaves **165.00**

Tazza, 5-3/4" h, 7-3/4" d, colorless ground, flint glass. **195.00**

Vase

- 5-1/2" h, pink ground, applied random amber threading . . **225.00**
- 7-1/2" h, bulbous base, slender neck, colorless ground, gold overshot, silver floral dec . . **125.00**
- 8-1/2" h, opalescent pink ground, fluted, applied colorless handle **135.00**
- 11" h, cranberry ground, two applied pink flowers, green branch and leaves, clear ruffled edge, applied amber feet. **300.00**
- 11-1/4" h, cylindrical, pink shading to vaseline base, crystal overshot, crystal rigaree circling down to base with scalloped rigaree **1,500.00**
- 12" h, 2-1/2" sq base, colorless overshot, pink ground, 2" vaseline overlay flower with two leaves and 7" l stem. **1,000.00**

Paden City Glass

History: Paden City Glass Manufacturing Co. was founded in 1916 in Paden City, West Virginia. David Fisher, formerly of the New Martinsville Glass Manufacturing Co., operated the company until his death in 1933, at which time his son, Samuel, became president. A management decision in 1949 to expand Paden City's production by acquiring American Glass Company, an automated manufacturer of bottles, ashtrays, and novelties, strained the company's finances, forcing it to close permanently in 1951.

Although Paden City glass is often lumped with mass-produced, machine-made wares into the Depression glass category, Paden City's wares were, until 1948, all handmade. Its products are better classified as "elegant glass" of the era, as it ranks in quality with the wares produced by contemporaries such as Fostoria, New Martinsville, and Morgantown.

Paden City kept a low profile, never advertising in consumer magazines of the day. It never marked its glass in any way because a large portion of its business consisted of sales to decorating companies, mounters, and fitters. The firm also supplied bars, restaurants, and soda fountains with glassware, as evidenced by the wide range of tumblers, ice cream dishes, and institutional products available in several Paden City patterns.

Paden City's decorating shop also etched, cut, hand painted, and applied silver overlay and gold encrustation. However, not every decoration found on Paden City shapes necessarily come from the factory. Cupid, Peacock and Rose, and several other etchings depicting birds are among the most sought after decorations. Pieces with these etchings are commanding higher and higher prices, even though they were apparently made in greater quantities than some of the etchings that are less-known, but just as beautiful.

Paden City is noted for its colors: opal (opaque white), ebony, mulberry (amethyst), Cheriglo (delicate pink), yellow, dark green (forest), crystal, amber, primrose (reddish-amber), blue, rose, and great quantities of ruby (red). The firm also produced transparent green in numerous shades ranging from yellowish to a distinctive electric green that always alerts knowledgeable collectors to its Paden City origin.

Rising collector interest in Paden City glass has resulted in a sharp spike in prices on some patterns. Currently, pieces with Orchid etch or Cupid etch are bringing the highest prices. Several truly rare items in these etchings have recently topped the $1,000 mark! Advanced collectors seek out examples with unusual and/or undocumented etchings. Colored pieces which sport an etching that is not usually found on that particular color are especially sought after, and bringing strong prices. In contrast, prices for common items with Peacock and Rose etch remain static, and the prices for dinnerware in ruby Penny Line and pink or green Party Line have inched up only slightly, due to its greater availability.

Contrary to popular belief and previously incorrect printed references, The Paden City Glass Manufacturing Company had absolutely no connection with the Paden City Pottery Company, other than their identical locale.

References: Jerry Barnett, *Paden City, The Color Company,* published by author, 1979, out-of-print; Tom and Neila Bredehoft, *Fifty Years of Collectible Glass, 1920-1970,* Antique Trader Books, 1997; Lee Garmon and Dick Spencer, *Glass Animals of the Depression Era,* Collector Books, 1993; Naomi L. Over, *Ruby Glass of the 20th Century,* The Glass Press, 1990, 1993-94 value update; Paul and Debra Torsiello, Tom and Arlene Stillman, *Paden City Glassware,* Schiffer Publishing, 2001; Hazel Marie Weatherman, *Colored Glassware of the Depression Era 2,* Glassbooks, 1974; *Paden City Catalog Reprints from the 1920s,* The Glass Press, 2000.

Periodical: *Paden City Glass Collectors Guild,* 42 Aldine Rd, Parsippany, NJ 07054.

Animal

Bunny, ears down, cotton dispenser . . . **95.00**
Dragon Swan, crystal . . . **175.00**
Dragon Swan, light blue (Barth Art) . . . **495.00**
Goose, crystal . . . **60.00**
Goose, light blue . . . **125.00**
Horse, rearing (Barth Art) . . . **275.00**
Pheasant, light blue . . . **170.00**
Pony, tall . . . **100.00**
Pony, 12" h, light blue . . . **150.00**
Squirrel (Barth Art) . . . **30.00**

Banana split dish, #191 Party Line, green . . . **20.00**

Bookends, pr

Eagle, crystal . . . **300.00**
Pouter Pigeons, crystal . . . **170.00**

Bowl

#191 Party Line, pink, 4-5/8" d . **9.00**
#300 Archaic, Peacock and Rose etching, pink, 11" d . . . **130.00**
#412 Crow's Foot, round, three ftd, flared, ruby . . . **65.00**
#440 Nerva, 8" d, silver overlay, marked "Sterling" . . . **95.00**
Cupid etch, rolled edge, pink, 10-1/2" d . . . **350.00**
Emerald Glo, Coppertone metal base, 10" d . . . **40.00**
Gadroon, cobalt blue, 8" d . . . **85.00**
Gazebo etching, crystal, 13" d **55.00**

Bowl, serving, two-handled

#210 Regina, Black Forest etch . . . **110.00**
#210 Spire, Eden Rose etch . . **29.00**
#211 Spire, gold trim, four gold encrusted broader bands separated by alternating crystal etches . . . **65.00**
#215 Glades, Spring Orchard etch . . . **50.00**
#221 Maya, light blue . . . **60.00**
#411 Mrs. B, Gothic Garden etch, yellow . . . **135.00**
#411 Mrs. B, Ardith etch, pink . **50.00**
#412 Crow's Foot Square, Orchid etch . . . **68.00**
#412 Crow's Foot Square, silver overlay . . . **60.00**
#440 Nerva, Fuchsia etch . . . **52.00**

Cake salver, footed

#210 Regina, Black Forest etch . . . **90.00**
#215 Glades, cutting . . . **40.00**
#300 Archaic, Gothic Garden etch, topaz . . . **99.00**
#300 Archaic, Peacock and Rose etch, Cheriglo . . . **95.00**
#300 Archaic, Lela Bird etch, green . . . **125.00**
#411 Mrs. B., Ardith etch, yellow . . . **55.00**
#411 Mrs. B., Gothic Garden, green . . . **50.00**
#412 Crow's Foot Square, Orchid etch, yellow . . . **95.00**
#412 Crow's Foot Square, opal **50.00**
#895 Lucy, silver deposit . . . **40.00**

Candleholders, pr

#191 Party Line, dome foot, Gypsy cutting, medium blue . . . **25.00**
#210 Regina, Black Forest etch . . . **140.00**
#211 Spire, Spring Orchard etch . . . **50.00**
#215 Glades, double, ruby . . . **75.00**
#215 Glades, single, Spring Orchard etch . . . **45.00**
#220 Largo, crystal, satin finish, silver deposit . . . **30.00**
#220 Largo, light blue . . . **125.00**
#300 Archaic, Cupid etch, pink . . . **140.00**
#300 Archaic, Lela Bird etch, pink . . . **135.00**
#300 Archaic, Nora Bird etching, amber . . . **100.00**
#412 Crow's Foot Square, keyhole style, Orchid etch . . . **125.00**
#412 Crow's Foot Square, keyhole style, ruby, 6-1/2" h . . . **70.00**
#412 Crow's Foot Square, mushroom, black . . . **90.00**
#412 Crow's Foot Square, red, 5-1/4" h . . . **125.00**
#412 Crow's Foot Square, white, silver Venus and Cupid design . . . **85.00**
#440 Nerva, crystal, pr . . . **65.00**
#444 Vale, three-light, cutting . **40.00**
#701 Triumph, Eden Rose etch, pink . . . **90.00**
#881 Gadroon, double, Frost etch . . . **95.00**
#890 Crow's Foot Round, three-light, ruby . . . **165.00**

#2000 Mystic double candleholders, ruby, pair **92.00**
Luli, double, crystal, Frost etch, single **75.00**

Candy box, cov, flat
#411 Mrs. B., Ardith etch, green **150.00**
#411 Mrs. B., Orchid etch, pink **325.00**
#412 Crow's Foot Square, square shape, ebony w/crystal lid . . **60.00**
#412 Crow's Foot Square, square shape, ruby **125.00**
#412 Crow's Foot Square, Orchid etch, ruby **230.00**
#412-1/2 Crow's Foot Square, cloverleaf shape, cobalt blue **225.00**
#412-1/2 Crow's Foot Square, cloverleaf shape, ruby. **96.00**
#513 Black Forest etch, crystal **65.00**

Candy dish, cov, footed
#191 Party Line, ftd, Black Forest etch **149.00**
#191 Party Line, pink. **50.00**
#412-1/2 Crow's Foot Square, cloverleaf-shaped covered candy, cobalt blue **195.00**
#555, w/beaded edge, ruby . . **67.00**
#890 Crow's Foot Round, amber **95.00**

Candy tray, #300 Gothic Garden, 11" d, center handle, light green **150.00**

Cheese and cracker
#215 Glades, crystal, Spring Orchard etch **35.00**
#440 Nerva, crystal, plate with domed lid style **65.00**
#513 Black Forest, pink, plate with compote style **250.00**

Cigarette box, cov, #220 Largo, ruby, very rare **240.00**

Cocktail shaker
#191 Party Line Green, with spout **95.00**
#902, three-part w/strainer and stopper, cut **50.00**
Speakeasy, green **45.00**

Cocktail, #215 Glades, Spring Orchard etch, 3 oz. ftd **12.50**

Compote
#142 Crow's Foot Square, amethyst **65.00**
#191 Party Line, pink, ftd, 11" . **35.00**
#191 Party Line, with cutting, green **28.00**
#211 Spire, flared, Ardith etch. **85.00**
#211 Spire, Gothic Garden, Trumpet Flower etch, 7" w, 6" h **95.00**
#300 Archaic, Cupid etch, blue **450.00**

Compote, #890 Crow's Foot, ruby, round foot, 7-1/8" w, 3-7/8" h, **$60.** *Photo courtesy of Michael Krumme.*

#300 Archaic, Cupid etch, pink **100.00**
#411 Mrs. B, Ardith etch, yellow **75.00**
#411 Mrs. B, Gothic Garden etch, ebony, rolled edge **90.00**
#411 Mrs. B, Gothic Garden etch, yellow, flared **90.00**
#412 Crow's Foot Square, short stem, pink. **25.00**
#412 Crow's Foot Square, tall stem, silver encrusted edge and floral etch, cobalt blue **200.00**
#412 Crow's Foot Square, 6-1/2", ruby **70.00**
#412 Crow's Foot Square, 6-1/2", Orchid etch, ruby. **120.00**
#412 Crow's Foot Square, 6-1/2", Orchid etch, cobalt blue . . **135.00**
#412 Crow's Foot Square, 6-1/2", opal, silver overlay **180.00**
#412 Crow's Foot Round, 9", ruby **50.00**
#440 Nerva, tall, double Columbine etch **155.00**
#444 w/ball stem, ruby **40.00**
Luli, low, light cutting **48.00**
Mr. B, light blue, 10" d, 5-1/2" h **145.00**

Condiment set, Emerald Glo, cut stars, orig lids and spoons **45.00**

Console bowl
#191 Party Line, rolled edge, light blue **45.00**
#210 Regina 13" d, Black Forest etch, ebony **185.00**
#220 Largo, crimped, 12" d, Spring Orchard etch **125.00**
#220 Largo, flat rim, Ruby Satin **95.00**
#220 Largo, three-footed, cupped up, light blue **70.00**
#220 Largo, three-footed, flat rim, light blue, Garden Magic etch **127.00**
#221 Maya, amber **95.00**
#300 Archaic, 11" d, Cheriglo, Cupid etch **230.00**
#411 Mrs. B, Gothic Garden etch, green. **95.00**
#411 Mrs. B, Gothic Garden etch, yellow **50.00**
#412 Crow's Foot Square, rolled edge, cobalt blue **60.00**
#440 Nerva, 11" d, flat rim, light blue **50.00**
#503, amber, cutting, 7" d, three-footed base **25.00**
#881 Gadroon, Frost etch **65.00**
#881 Gadroon, flat rim, satin Peacock dec **95.00**
#888 12" low scalloped edge bowl, Floral Medallion etch. **59.00**
#890 Crow's Foot Round, flat rim, Leeuwen etch **135.00**

Cordial, #991 Penny Line, ruby, platinum rings. **25.00**

Cordial set, New Martinsville Radiance cordial decanter with Paden City's Trumpet Flower etching, five plain cordials. **250.00**

Cracker plate, Spire, 11-1/2" d, crystal, gold encrusted. **65.00**

Creamer
#90 Chevalier, ruby. **18.00**
#411 Mrs. B, amber. **12.50**
#412 Crow's Foot Square, Orchid etching, ruby. **40.00**
Cupid etch, 5" h, ftd, pink . . . **200.00**

Creamer and sugar
#191 Party Line, Cheriglo **24.00**
#210 Regina, Black Forest etch, crystal **75.00**
#210 Regina, Black Forest etch, green. **115.00**
#220 Largo, ruby. **155.00**
#300 Archaic, Cupid etch, green **295.00**
#411 Mrs. B, Gothic Garden etch, crystal **45.00**
#411 Mrs. B, Gothic Garden etch, topaz. **85.00**
#412 Crow's Foot Square, mulberry **42.00**
#412 Crow's Foot Square, ruby **35.00**
#412 Crow's Foot Square, Orchid etch, ruby **265.00**
#503, no optic, pink. **20.00**
#503, no optic, Cupid etch w/gold-encrusted medallion, pink **495.00**
#555 Gazebo etch. **42.00**
#881 Gadroon, ruby **60.00**
#890 Crow's Foot Round, mulberry **155.00**
#994 Popeye and Olive, ruby . **70.00**

Cream soup bowl
- #412 Crow's Foot Square, amber, ftd **10.00**
- #412 Crow's Foot Square, ruby **25.00**
- #890 Crow's Foot Round, amber, with underplate.......... **35.00**

Cruet, orig stopper, Emerald Glo, cut stars.......... **45.00**

Cup and saucer
- #215 Glade, ruby **15.00**
- #220 Largo, light blue.......... **25.00**
- #220 Largo, ruby **27.50**
- #330 Cavendish, ruby.......... **16.50**
- #411 Mrs. B, amber **7.50**
- #411 Mrs. B, cobalt blue, set of eight **120.00**
- #411 Mrs. B, ruby.......... **10.00**
- #411 Mrs. B, topaz, Ardith etch **15.00**
- #412 Crow's Foot Square, amber **10.00**
- #412 Crow's Foot Square, ruby **20.00**
- #890 Crow's Foot Round, forest green **18.00**
- #890 Crow's Foot Round, ruby **24.00**
- #991 Penny Line, ruby **18.00**
- #994 Popeye and Olive, ruby. **30.00**
- Hotcha, ruby, set of eight ... **110.00**

Decanter
- Georgian, cobalt blue, cobalt blue stopper.......... **195.00**
- Lobed-shape decanter, five Penny Line wines, Spring Orchard etch **80.00**

Epergne, #888, Forest Green, three pcs **175.00**

Finger bowl
- #991 Penny Line, ruby **22.00**
- #994 Popeye and Olive, w/liner, royal blue **127.00**
- #994 Popeye and Olive, ruby. **34.00**

Goblet
- #210 Regina, green, Black Forest etch, tall stem.......... **230.00**
- #991 Penny Line, mulberry, low foot **18.50**
- #991 Penny Line, Stiegel Green **22.00**
- #991 Penny Line, ruby **32.50**
- #994 Popeye and Olive, 6-1/8" h, cobalt blue.......... **35.00**

Guest set
- Amber, pitcher with lid **60.00**
- Peacock blue, pitcher, lid, matching tray.......... **135.00**

Ice bucket
- #902, Black Forest etch, pink **255.00**
- #902, Cupid etch, pink **225.00**

Ice cream soda, ftd
- #191 Party Line, 7" h, amber . **18.50**
- #191 Party Line, 7" h, pink ... **25.00**

Ice tub
- #191 Party Line, green **19.00**
- #895 Lucy, Blue Willow etch . **130.00**
- #991 Penny Line, green.......... **25.00**
- Cupid etch, green, 4-3/4" ... **300.00**

Iced tea tumbler, ftd
- #991 Penny Line, 12 oz, amethyst **22.50**
- #991 Penny Line, 12 oz, ruby . **35.00**

Jug, cov
- #189-60, blown, amber body, wide Panel Optic, Neptune Blue cover and applied handle.......... **295.00**
- #191 Party Line, 74 oz, green . **95.00**

Lemonade pitcher, #210 Black Forest, 10-1/4" h, cov **870.00**

Marmalade
- #191 Party Line, crystal, chrome cov **20.00**
- #207, two-handled cov jam dish, orig ladle.......... **32.00**
- Emerald Glo, coppertone lid .. **40.00**
- Emerald Glo, star cut, coppertone lid **45.00**

Mayonnaise bowl
- #412 Crow's Foot Square, opal **40.00**
- #555 beaded edge, Gazebo etch, wing handles.......... **65.00**

Mayonnaise set, bowl and underplate
- #215 Glades, Spring Orchard etch **33.00**
- #300 Archaic, Cupid, green, with orig ladle **325.00**
- #300 Archaic, Nora Bird etch, Cheriglo.......... **135.00**
- #895 Lucy, Oriental Garden etch **58.00**

Mayonnaise set, bowl, underplate, and ladle, three pcs
- #411 Mrs. B, Ardith etch, yellow **160.00**
- #777 Comet, frosted rim, cut stars **25.00**
- #881 Gadroon, Black Forest etch, w/ladle.......... **125.00**
- Cupid, amber, gold panels .. **225.00**
- Cupid, green **275.00**

Napkin holder, #210 Regina, green **150.00**

Nappy
- #412 Crow's Foot Square, 5", ruby **35.00**
- #412 Crow's Foot Square, 7", Orchid etch, yellow **40.00**

Old fashioned tumbler, Georgian, 3-1/4" h, ruby **15.00**

Parfait, #191 Party Line, ftd, green **20.00**

Perfume bottle
- #191 Party Line, transparent blue, orig dauber **115.00**
- #499, 1 oz, crystal body, three rings at base, black stopper.......... **45.00**

Pitcher, #994 Popeye and Olive, cobalt blue **395.00**

Plate
- #131 Party Line, 6" d, amber .. **3.00**
- #210 Regina, 8" d, Black Forest etch **35.00**
- #330 Cavendish, 10" d, ruby . **30.00**
- #411 Mrs. B, 8-1/2" d, amber .. **6.00**
- #412 Crow's Foot Square, 6" w sq, ruby **5.00**
- #412 Crow's Foot Square, 8-1/2" d, ruby **10.00**
- #412 Crow's Foot Square, 11-1/2" d, ruby, gold-encrusted etch .. **90.00**
- #890 Crow's Foot Round, 6-1/2" d, amber.......... **10.00**
- #890 Crow's Foot Round, 6-1/2" d, blue **6.00**
- #890 Crow's Foot Round, 8-1/2" d, amber.......... **7.00**
- Glades, 6" d, ruby, set of eight **50.00**
- Hotcha, 6" d, ruby, set of eight **50.00**

Platter
- #211 Spire, Gothic Garden, gold etch and trim **55.00**
- #220 Largo, 14" l, three toes, ruby, floral silver overlay **55.00**
- #412 Crow's Foot Square, ruby **35.00**
- #440 Nerva, 11" l, silver overlay **65.00**

Puff box, cov, #499, 1 oz, crystal body, three rings at base, round foot, black lid **28.00**

Punch bowl set, #555, crystal, bowl, seven cups **75.00**

Relish
- #890 Crow's Foot Round, three-part, 11" l oblong, crystal, star cut **35.00**
- Mr. B, three-part, 10" x 7" oval, Pam's Floral etch **38.00**

Saucer
- #411 Mrs. B, amber **2.00**
- #411 Mrs. B, pink **2.00**
- #411 Mrs. B, yellow **2.00**
- #412 Crow's Foot Square, ruby **5.00**
- #890 Crow's Foot Round, ruby. **7.00**

Serving plate, center handle
- #210 Regina, Black Forest etch **78.00**
- #215 Glades, Spring Orchard, crystal.......... **65.00**
- #220 Largo, ruby **95.00**
- #300 Archaic, Cupid etching, pink **160.00**
- #411 Mrs. B, amber **18.00**

#411 Mrs. B, pink 20.00
#411 Mrs. B, yellow, Ardith etch 58.00
#412 Crow's Foot Square, Orchid etch, ruby 165.00
#412 Crow's Foot Square, Delilah Bird etch, amber 95.00
#412 Crow's Foot Square, opal, rare 350.00
#555 Gazebo etch, crystal . . . 65.00
#701 Triumph, aquamarine blue, cutting 18.00
#701 Triumph, Delilah Bird etch 40.00
#881 Gadroon, ruby 75.00
#890 Crow's Foot Round, amber 65.00
#890 Crow's Foot Round, crystal, cupped up, floral etch 50.00
#1504 Chaucer, crystal 35.00
#1504 swan-shaped handle, Gazebo etch 85.00
#1504 swan-shaped handle, silver overlay 95.00
Cupid etch, 10-3/4" d, pink . . 200.00
Gothic Garden etch, yellow . . . 55.00
Mr. B, crystal, Gazebo etch . . . 65.00
Peacock and Rose etch, green, 10-3/4" d 145.00

Sherbet

#69 Line, Georgian, ruby 12.50
#191 Party Line, pink 8.50
#991 Penny Line, mulberry, low foot 12.50
#991 Penny Line, ruby, tall 13.00

Soda tumbler, #191 Party Line, tall, ftd, green 24.00

Soup bowl, #412 Crow's Foot, green, 7" d, tiny base nick 20.00

Sugar bowl

#191 Party Line, green 15.00
#411 Mrs. B, amber 12.50
#411 Mrs. B, Gothic Garden etching, green 45.00
#412 Crow's Foot Square, amber 10.00
#412 Crow's Foot Square, ruby 15.00
#911 Penny Line, ruby 22.00

Sugar pourer

#94 bullet-shape, screw-on nickel base, green 175.00
#153 Rena, Cheriglo, swirl pattern, metal top 125.00
#153 Rena, green, screw-on metal cap 215.00

Syrup pitcher, glass lid

#180, green, floral cutting 70.00
#198, crystal, cutting 35.00

Top hat, Eden Rose etch, small 135.00

Tray, two handled

#210 Regina, Black Forest etch, pink 95.00
#411 Mrs. B., Gothic Garden, ebony 40.00
#412 Crow's Foot Square, Sasha Bird etch 122.00

Tumbler

#69 Georgian, 3-1/2" h, ftd, "V" shape, ruby 10.00
#191 Party Line, 3-1/2" h, ftd, amber 9.50
#191 Party Line, 5" h, cone shape, green 7.75
#191 Party Line, 5-3/4" h, cone shape, green 8.75
#191 Party Line, 5-3/4" h, cone shape, pink 9.75
#210 Regina, 5-1/2" h, Black Forest etch, pink 80.00
#890 Crow's Foot Round, amber 35.00
#991 Penny Line, 3-1/4" h, ruby 8.00
#991 Penny Line, 4-1/8" h, ruby 10.00
#991 Penny Line, 5-1/4" h, ruby 12.00
Blown tumbler, 5" h, Ardith etch, green 22.00
Blown tumbler, 5-3/4" h, Black Forest etch, Cheriglo 75.00

Vase

#11, 9" h, Utopia etch, ebony, box shape 270.00
#182, 8" h, elliptical, Cheriglo, Cupid etch 650.00
#182, 8" h, elliptical, crystal, Trumpet Flower etch 115.00
#182, 8" h, elliptical, ebony, gold encrusted Peacock and Rose etch 335.00
#182, 8" h, elliptical, ebony, Lela Bird etch 125.00
#182, 8" h, elliptical, green, Orchid etch 300.00
#182, 8" h, elliptical, green with gold trim, Sunflower etch 200.00
#182, 8" h, elliptical, pink, Daisy etch 145.00
#182-1/2, 5" h, elliptical vase, Ardith etch, ormolu holder 75.00
#184, 10" h, bulbous, Lady with Grapes etch, Cheriglo 260.00
#184, 10" h, bulbous, Leli Bird etch, ebony 150.00
#184, 10" h, bulbous, Utopia etch, ebony 195.00
#184, 10" h, bulbous, Peacock and Rose etch, Cheriglo 165.00
#184, 10" h, bulbous, Rose Bouquet etch, green 158.00
#184, 10" h, Orchid etch, ruby, 10" 330.00
#184, 10" h, Utopia etch, ruby, 10" 590.00
#184, 12" h, bulbous, Daisy etch, Cheriglo 170.00
#184, 12" h, bulbous, Eden Rose etch, ebony 145.00
#184, 12" h, Cupid silver deposit 230.00
#184, 12" h, Gothic Garden etch, ruby 205.00
#184, 12" h, Orchid etch, ebony 225.00
#184, 12", Utopia etch, ruby . 205.00
#184, 12" h, Leeuwen etch . . 155.00
#191 Party Line, fan, green . . . 40.00
#191 Party Line, fan, green . . . 48.00
#210 Regina, 6-1/2" h, Harvesters etch, ebony 145.00
#210 Regina, 6-1/2" h, Black Forest etch, green 150.00
#412 Crow's Foot Square, 10" h, flared, ruby 96.00
#412 Crow's Foot Square, 10" h, flared, Daisy etch, ruby 225.00
#412 Crow's Foot Square, 10" h, Gothic Garden etch, ruby . . 430.00
#412 Crow's Foot Square, 11-1/2" h, flared, amber 150.00
#412 Crow's Foot Square, 12" h, cupped, Rose Bouquet etch 180.00
#513 Black Forest etch, 6-1/2" h, black, squatty 175.00
#513 Black Forest etch, 6-1/2" h, green 150.00
#513 Black Forest etch, 10" h, black 250.00
#513 Black Forest etch, 10" h, crystal 195.00
Delilah Bird etch, 6-3/4" h, green 125.00
Shoe Box, pink, rect, silver overlay, marked "Sterling" 135.00
Unknown #, small, bulbous, Orchid etch, ruby 465.00
Unknown #, 12" h, cylindrical, Rose Bouquet etch, green 305.00
Utopia etch, 10" h, black 195.00
Utopia etch, 10" h, crystal . . . 135.00
Utopia etch, 10" h, yellow 85.00

Water set, #210 Regina tall jug, four blown tumblers, Black Forest etch, green 1,825.00

Wine, #991 Penny Line, ruby, platinum rings 22.00

PAIRPOINT

History: The Pairpoint Manufacturing Co. was organized in 1880 as a silver-plating firm in New Bedford, Massachusetts. The company merged with Mount Washington Glass Co. in 1894 and became the Pairpoint Corporation. The new company produced specialty glass items often accented with metal frames.

Pairpoint Corp. was sold in 1938 and Robert Gunderson became manager. He operated it as the Gunderson Glass Works until his death in 1952. From 1952 until the plant closed in 1956, operations were maintained under the name Gunderson-Pairpoint. Robert Bryden reopened the glass manufacturing business in 1970, moving it back to the New Bedford area.

Pairpoint was known for its "puffy" featured glassware. This term refers to a mold that included an extra molded section, usually pushed out from the main surface of the object. Lampshades with puffy features often had additional decoration in these sections, giving even a more three-dimensional look.

References: George C. Avila, *The Pairpoint Glass Story,* Reynolds-DeWalt Printing, Inc., 1968; Marion and Sandra Frost, *The Essence of Pairpoint*, Schiffer, 2001; Leonard E. Padgett, *Pairpoint Glass,* Wallace-Homestead, 1979; John A. Shuman III, *Collector's Encyclopedia of American Art Glass*, Collector Books, 1988, 1994 value update; *Pairpoint Lamp Catalog: Shade Shapes Ambero Through Panel*, Schiffer, 2001; —, *Pairpoint Lamp Catalog: Shade Shapes Papillon Through Windsor,* Schiffer, 2001; Kenneth Wilson, *American Glass 1760-1930: The Toledo Museum of Art, Volume I, Volume II,* Hudson Hills Press and The Toledo Museum of Art, 1994.

Collectors' Clubs: Mount Washington Art Glass Society, P.O. Box 24094, Fort Worth, TX 76124-1094; Pairpoint Cup Plate Collectors, P.O. Box 890052, East Weymouth, MA 02189.

Museum: New Bedford Glass Museum, New Bedford, MA; Pairpoint Museum, Sagamore, MA.

Dresser box, molded-in rococo swirls, fancy centered swirled button, gold floral decoration, single petal rose decoration, pastel blue background, Wedgwood blue border, gold floral swags on base, gilt metal fittings, loose gold velvet liner, 7-1/2" d, 3" h, **$785.** *Photo courtesy of Clarence and Betty Maier.*

Decorative objects

Bell, 9-3/4" h, ruby base, crystal swirled handle **200.00**

Biscuit jar, cov

5" h, squatty, shaded pink to yellow ground, floral and leaf dec, enameled flowers, ormolu molded base, sgd "P" in diamond on lid **275.00**

6-1/2" h, 6" d, 16 panels, gold/beige ground, white and deep pink roses, green leaves, cov sgd "Pairpoint-3932," base sgd "3932/222," fancy metal work **595.00**

6-3/4" h, 7-1/2" w, Mt. Washington opalware, pistachio green top and bottom, 3-1/2" w band of deep pink and red roses, green leaves, gold trim, fancy silver-plated cov, handle, and bail, cov sgd "Pairpoint –3912," base sgd "3912-268" **725.00**

7" h, 6" d, molded bulbous base, hand painted, daisy dec, apricot ground, SP rim, cov, and bail handle, sgd and numbered **300.00**

8-1/2" h, Rose Velvet finish, pink and white quilted satin body, cased white int., silver plated rim and lid, marked, bail handle missing **325.00**

Bowl

7-3/4" d, 3-1/4" h, Peppermint Stick, star-cut frosted round form, rosaria rim cut in vertical stripes, medial band of cut diamond motif, fitted into silvered metal Aesthetic design holder **185.00**

8" d, 6-1/2" h, cov, raised gold chrysanthemum blossoms and foliage, eggshell white ground, gold striped handles, fish floral, sgd and numbered **600.00**

8-1/2" d, 3-1/2" h, Ambero, heavy walls, textured ext., int. painted with trailing vines, three pink lotus blossoms, lush green leaves floating on pool of lime green water, sgd "Ambero L" **775.00**

Box, cov, 7-1/4" l, 2-3/4" h, molded quatraform oval, opal ground, gold enameled floral dec, hinged metal rim fittings, sgd on base "PMC 9524" **475.00**

Calling card receiver, 5" d, engraved floral dec, clear controlled bubble ball connector, saucer base **145.00**

Candlesticks, 3" h, glossy Burmese, Robert Bryden, irregular areas on one stem **80.00**

Candlesticks, pr, 9-1/2" h, Mt. Washington opalware glass, silver-plated overlay, deep pink painted ground, white peony dec, fancy Art Nouveau-styled silver overlay base and socket, sgd "Pairpoint Mfg. Co" **1,250.00**

Centerpiece, 12" h, 13" l, swan, ruby glass brown body, applied clear swan's neck and head **450.00**

Champagne, 5-1/8" h, Flambo pattern, crystal **60.00**

Cologne bottle, 8" h, applied vertical cranberry ribbing, elaborate flower form cranberry and clear stopper **115.00**

Compote, cov

8-1/2" d, ruby, bubbled finial and ball stem **145.00**

14-1/4" h, ovoid colorless vessel cut and etched with florals and swags, lid with air bubble spire finial, baluster stem with air bubble sphere, weighted Watson sterling silver trumpet foot, late 19th/early 20th C, price for pr **2,300.00**

Compote, open, 10" h, 5-1/2" d, Fine Arts Line, Aurora, brilliant cut deep amber glass bowl, brass and onyx base with full figured cherub holding up bowl, marked "C1413 Pairpoint" **475.00**

Console set

Three-pc set, 12" d bowl, matching 3" h candlesticks, Tavern glass, bouquet of red, white, and green flowers **575.00**

12" d, bowl, matching mushroom candlesticks, Flambo Ware, tomato red, applied black glass foot, c1915 . . . . **1,950.00**

Decanter, 10" h, Old English pattern, quart, matching stopper **1,250.00**

Hat, 4-1/4" h, deep red ground, white spatter, controlled bubbles, orig paper label **90.00**

Inkwell, 4" h, colorless, allover controlled bubbles, sterling silver cap **200.00**

Jewel box, cov, robin's egg blue opal glass, six scalloped pink, yellow, and coral rose medallions with green leaves, brown traceries, painted gold trim, four ball feet, gold washed silver plated base, sgd and numbered **350.00**

Pickle castor insert, 3" d rim, 4-3/4" h, Pink Plush, two pickle jars, swirled ribs, pink shading from dark to light, satin finish, polished pontil, rim flakes, price for pr **400.00**

Pitcher, 8-1/2" h, amberina, applied ruby handle **190.00**

Plate, 5-1/8" d, enameled floral dec, artist sgd "P. Kiluk," diamond mark with "P" **125.00**

Salt, master, colorless, controlled bubbles **85.00**

Scent bottle, 5" h, 3-1/4" d, patterned millefiori stopper with two rose canes, other pastel canes, yellow translucent ground, clear controlled bubbles in body **70.00**

Smoking stand, three opal bowls, 3-3/4" x 3-1/2" h, 3" x 2" h, and 2-1/4" x 2-1/4" h, Delft dec, windmills, houses, people, trees, and sailing ships, brass rims, maple shield shape, fancy brass trim and feet, brass cigar holder . **565.00**

Tray, 6" d, 1-3/4" h, glossy Burmese, Robert Bryden, "potato chip" type, rough pontil, sliver chips **50.00**

Urn, ruby, swirl connector, applied cactus handles **350.00**

Vase

- 5-1/2" h, 4-1/2" w, Tavern glass, bulbous, enameled floral dec of vase of flowers, base numbered **225.00**
- 6" h, Tavern glass, bulbous, enameled sailing galleon on wavy sea, sgd "D. 1507," c1900-38 . . . . **300.00**
- 9" h, Ambero, int. painted with scene of couple strolling down country lane, textured finish **750.00**
- 10" h, purple, hexagonal sides, sgd **120.00**
- 14-1/2" h, flared colorless crystal trumpet form, bright-cut floral dec, gilt metal foliate molded weighted pedestal base, imp "Pairpoint C1509" **490.00**
- 15" h, winged cherub, flowing pink drape with tray of peonies, reverse with spray of multicolored poppies, gold borders, powder blue rim shading to cobalt blue ground, applied cobalt blue openwork handles **1,400.00**

Lamps

Boudoir

- 11-3/4" h, 5-1/2" d puffy pansy shade with open top, yellow, orange, red, and purple pansies, green ground, sgd "Pat. Applied for" in gold on outside bottom edge, urn-shaped base with antique brass finish sgd "Pairpoint" **3,300.00**
- Boudoir, 14-3/4" h, 9" closed top Papillon shade, pink and red roses, yellow and green butterflies, brass Pairpoint base with green paint **4,750.00**

Candle lamp

- 8" h, blown-out pansy dec reverse painted shade, multicolored, mahogany pedestal with glass candleholder **920.00**
- 8" h, 4-1/2" d puffy blown-out poppy shade, orange, purple, and yellow flowers, orig wooden base, shade glued onto base **1,100.00**
- 16-1/2" h, puffy shades dec with red and yellow roses, Windsor background, marked "Pairpoint #B6131," matched pr **5,750.00**

Floor, 16" d Springfield shade, 57" h, painted soft yellow and peach ground, purple azalea flowers, sgd "Pairpoint Corp." **2,000.00**

Table

- 8" puffy shade, Stratford, yellow and red roses, blue background, black border, sgd base **2,800.00**
- 19" h, 12" d puffy shade, seven clumps of deep purple grapes molded with green, teal, and red leaves, open topped shade, base with stem covered with grapevines and leaves, sq foot, shade sgd "Pat. Applied For," base sgd "Pairpoint Mf'g B 3010" and "P" in diamond shape **14,560.00**
- 19" h, 13" d, puffy shade, tapestry floral motif shade, mint green ground, base sgd "Pairpoint Mfg Co." with "P" in diamond mark **4,335.00**
- 19-1/2" h, 18" w corner to corner, 14" d side diameter, reverse painted ribbed shade, four Venetian water scenes, gondola, three scenes with sailboats, San Mara Square in background, moored boats, flying birds, boys floating on water, blue sea and sky, closed top, tasseled cloth, green, yellow, and black dec, surrounding bright red flower, scalloped four footed base with simple stem, shade sgd "The Pairpoint Mfg Co. B 3040," and "P" within diamond shape. . . . **8,400.00**
- 20" h, 12" d, blown-out, deep green ground, brilliant colored deep rose azaleas, orig brass collared base with fancy floral design, sgd "Pairpoint Mfg Co. 3099," slight flake on int. rim, covered by ring **11,000.00**
- 20-1/2" h, 16" puffy shade, colorful garlands of irises, roses, daisies, and mums, ribbed, scalloped border, white flowers meet on top, base with four ribbed stem, sq foot, two sides have raised flowered design, other two have long leaves, two acorn pulls, shade marked "The Pairpoint Corp," base marked "Pairpoint Mft Co. B3016" and "P" within diamond shape . . . **8,950.00**
- 21" h, 14-3/4" d, Carlisle reverse painted Venetian harbor scene, sailing boats in front of Venetian city, naturalistic colors, shade artist "H. Fisher" sgd and stamped "Pairpoint Corp," in gold, two-light reeded standard over urn form base, two leafy handles, white metal with dark green patina, base imp with Pairpoint diamond mark and number, c1915, few chips to shade, wear to patina . . . **2,045.00**
- 21" h, 18" d reverse painted shade, jungle scene, four multicolored parrots, large fronds from background are painted in sage green, purple, blue-gray, and tan, scattered pink and white flowers, base with concentric layers on egg-shaped stem, octagonal foot, base sgd "Pairpoint D 3038," and "P" in diamond shape . . . **4,760.00**
- 21-1/2" h, 13-1/2" Stratford puffy shade, two red and green hummingbirds flying over border of red, pink, orange, and yellow roses, silvered base with stylized leaf design, marked "Pairpoint C 3006"and "P" within diamond on base **5,320.00**
- 22" h, 12" d shade, Albernal, puffy garland of American Beauty roses being inspected by two colorful butterflies, intricate background of white scrolls, flowers, and spiral strands, teal and green ground, brass base emb with floral motifs, marked "Pairpoint Mfg Co.," and numbered, "P" in diamond logo **7,750.00**
- 22" h, 14" d, Lilac, closed puffy scalloped shade, eight clumps of white and light pink highlighted lilacs, blue and green leaves, two yellow, red, blue, and orange painted butterflies, shade drilled for finial, vasiform base with two handles, flower garlands, painted red, green, and gold, shade sgd "Pairpoint Corp," base sgd "73" with "P" in diamond shape **21,850.00**
- 22" h, 16" d, Hollyhock, colorful flowers, rare mint green ground, shade sgd "Patent July 9, 1907/The Pairpoint Corp," rare tree-trunk

form base, base sgd "Pairpoint Mfg Co.," with "P" in diamond mark **19,555.00**

22" h, 17" d Berkeley shade, wisteria design, trees with pale pink and yellow leaves, rare glass dec base with green finish, flat chip on base **2,700.00**

23" h, 17" d Exeter shade, pink, yellow, and purple chrysanthemums on brown and black border, orig paper label, fancy silver plated sgd Pairpoint base. **4,700.00**

23" h, 17" d flared and domed Four Seasons shade, etched glass sections reversed painted depict Spring, Summer, Autumn, and Winter, three-socket baluster metal base with bronzed finish, sgd and numbered "D3051". **3,750.00**

23-1/2" h, 17-1/2" d Carlisle conical reverse painted shade, exotic tropical trees and plants, four brightly colored cockatoos, silvered tripartite urn form metal base, imp "Pairpoint D3070" **6,625.00**

26" h, 21" d Carlisle reverse painted shade, figures in Italian landscape, naturalistic colors, ink stamp "The Pairpoint Corp'n," two-handled urn form bronzed metal base, imp Pairpoint diamond mark, c1915, few rim chips, replaced socks **1,850.00**

27-1/2" h, 17" d Directorie scenic hexagonal heavy walled shade, reverse painted as six continuing panels, colorful landscaped ground with columned waterfront building, irid background coloring, paneled borders above and below, "The Pairpoint Corp.n" on border, gilt metal, onyx, and cut glass candle lamp form base, imp "Pairpoint Mfg. Co. E30001" **2,645.00**

Paperweights

History: Although paperweights had their origin in ancient Egypt, it was in the mid-19th century that this art form reached its zenith. The finest paperweights were produced between 1834 and 1855 in France by the Clichy, Baccarat, and Saint Louis factories. Other weights made in England, Italy, and Bohemia during this period rarely match the quality of the French weights.

In the early 1850s, the New England Glass Co. in Cambridge, Massachusetts, and the Boston and Sandwich Glass Co. in Sandwich, Massachusetts, became the first American factories to make paperweights.

Popularity peaked during the classic period (1845-1855) and faded toward the end of the 19th century. Paperweight production was rediscovered nearly a century later in the mid-1900s. Baccarat, Saint Louis, Perthshire, and many studio craftsmen in the U.S. and Europe still make contemporary weights.

References: *Annual Bulletin of the Paperweight Collectors Association, Inc.*, available from association (P.O. Box 1263, Beltsville, MD 20704), 1996; Monika Flemming and Peter Pommerencke, *Paperweights of the World*, Schiffer, 1994; Robert G. Hall, *World Paperweights, Millefiori and Lampwork*, Schiffer, 2001; John D. Hawley, *Glass Menagerie*, Paperweight Press, 1995; Sibylle Jargstorf, *Paperweights*, Schiffer, 1991; Paul Jokelson and Dena Tarshis, *Baccarat Paperweights and Related Glass*, Paperweight Press, 1990; George N. Kulles, *Identifying Antique Paperweights-Lampwork*, Paperwork Press, 1987; Edith Mannoni, *Classic French Paperweights*, Paperweight Press, 1984; Bonnie Pruitt, *St. Clair Glass Collectors Guide*, published by author, 1992; Pat Reilly, *Paperweights*, Running Press, Courage Books, 1994; Lawrence H. Selman, *All About Paperweights*, Paperweight Press, 1992; ——, *Art of the Paperweight*, Paperweight Press, 1988; ——, *Art of the Paperweight, Perthshire*, Paperweight Press, 1983; ——, *Art of the Paperweight, Saint Louis*, Paperweight Press, 1981 (all of the Paperweight Press books are distributed by Charles E. Tuttle Co., 1996); Kenneth Wilson, *American Glass 1760-1930*, two vols., Hudson Hills Press and The Toledo Museum of Art, 1994.

Periodicals*:* *Paperweight Collectors Bulletin*, Paperweight Collectors Assoc., Inc., P.O. Box 1263, Beltsville, MD 20704; *Paperweight Gaffer*, 35 Williamstown Circle, York, PA 17404; *Paperweight News*, 761 Chestnut St., Santa Cruz, CA, 95060; *The Gatherer*, Museum of American Glass at Wheaton Village, Glasstown Rd., Millville, NJ 08332.

Collectors' Clubs: Arizona Paperweight Collectors, 21405 N. 142nd Drive, Sun City West, AZ 85375; Caithness Collectors Club, 141 Lanza Ave., Building 12, Garfield, NJ 07026; Cambridge Paperweight Circle, 34 Huxley Rd., Welling, Kent DA16 2EW, U.K.; Delaware Valley Chapter, Paperweight Collectors International, 49 East Lancaster Ave, East Frazer, PA 19355-2120; Evangline Bergstrom Paperweight Collectors, 1008 North 14th St., Manitowoc, WI 54220; Indiana Paperweight Collectors, 123 North 9th St., Zionsville, IN 46077-1217; International Paperweight Society, 761 Chestnut St., Santa Cruz, CA 95060, http://www.paperweight.com; MD-DC-VA Paperweight Collectors, P.O. Box 20083, Baltimore, MD 21284-0083; Mid-Atlantic Paperweight Collectors, P.O. Box 6259, High Point, NC 27262; Montreal Paperweight Collectors, 3275 Shebrooke St., East, #2, Montreal, Quebec H1W IC3 Canada; New England Paperweight Collectors, 168 Oxbow Rd, Wayland, MA 01778; Northern California Paperweight Collectors, 10110 Longview, Atwater, CA 95301; Ohio Paperweight Collectors, 2303 Glendon Rd, University Heights, OH 44118; Ontario Paperweight Collectors, 16 Tanburn Place, Don Mills, Ontario M3A 1X5 Canada; Paperweight Club of Deutchland, Postfach 1733, D-82145 Planegg, Germany; Paperweight Collectors Assoc. Inc., P.O. Box 1264, Beltsville, MD 20704, http://www.collectoronline.com/paperweights/PCA.html; Paperweight Collectors Assoc. of Chicago, 535 Delkir Ct, Naperville, IL 60565; Paperweight Collectors Assoc. of Texas, 19302 Marlstone Ct, Houston, TX 77094-3082; San Diego Paperweight Collectors, P.O. Box 881463, San Diego, CA 92168.

Museums: Bergstrom-Mahler Museum, Neenah, WI; Corning Museum of Glass, Corning, NY; Degenhart Paperweight & Glass Museum, Inc., Cambridge, OH; Museum of American Glass at Wheaton Village, Millville, NJ; Toledo Museum of Art, Toledo, OH.

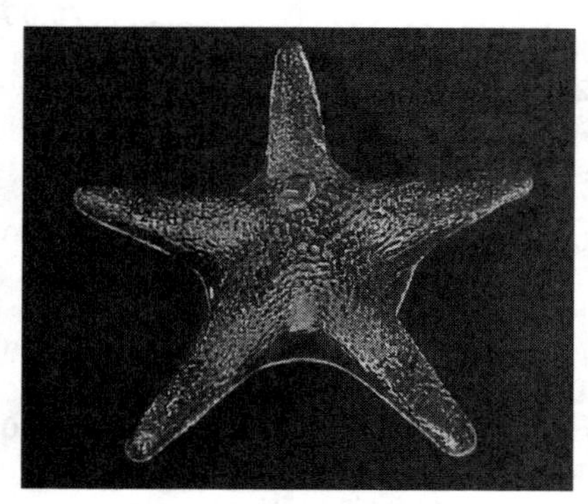

Blenko, starfish shape, introduced 1994, 9", **$18.** *Photo courtesy of Blenko.*

Antique

Baccarat, France

Anemone, red-tipped cupped white petals on single blossom, leafy stem, row of oval facets around base, small star-cut on base, c1845-55, 1-3/4" h, 2-3/4" d **920.00**

Butterfly with garland, millefiori canes set in multicolored wings, surrounded by garland of alternating green and white canes, star-cut base, mid 19th C, 2" h, 3" d, dings, wear **2,415.00**

Clematis, white and red blossoms surrounded by leaves and stem with bud, blue and white millefiori border, star-cut base, c1845, 1-3/4" h, 2-3/4" d, imperfections **2,185.00**

Close millefiori featuring several animal silhouette canes, including pelican, monkey, dog, rooster, squirrel, and kangaroo, c1848, 1-7/8" h, 3" d, some wear to lower edge................. **2,530.00**

Dog, central star honeycomb millefiori cane surrounded by five blue and white petals, five green leaves and stem, star cut base, 2" d, 1-3/8" h, minor surface spalls and surface scratches.... **800.00**

Dog Rose, central millefiori cluster of pink whorl and white star canes, five red and white petals, well centered with six and one faceting, star cut base, 2-1/4" d, 1-5/8" h, several surface scratches, one spall, minor nicks and dings **800.00**

Pansy, yellow, purple, and red pansy and bud, bright green leafy stem, star-cut base, 2-1/4" h, 3" d, imperfections............ **350.00**

Primrose, center cluster of pink whorl and white stars, six red and white petals, star cut base, 2" d, 1-1/2" h **900.00**

Trefoil, double interlaced, arrowhead, six-pointed stars and whorl canes, pedestal base with pink and white torsade, 3" d, 2-6/8" h **2,500.00**

Boston & Sandwich Glass Co., Sandwich, MA, c1870

Cruciform, blue and red cross, red petals, two green leaves, 2-1/8" d, 1-1/2" h, polished pontil, wear on base **400.00**

Cruciform and Heart, pink and green cruciform, red and green heart sits among four branches, two with pink leaves, two with blue leaves, green stems, 2-3/4" d, 1-3/4" h, one pink step separated from stem, surface scratches on top .. **350.00**

Dahlia, red petal flower, white cone center, green leafy stem, white latticinio ground, 2" h, 3-1/8" d, surface scratches **460.00**

Poinsettia, double poinsettia, red flower with double tier of petals, green and white Lutz rose, green stem and leaves, bubbles between petals, 3" d **1,200.00**

Queen Victoria, colorless and frosted, portraits of Queen Victoria and Prince Consort, 1851, 1-1/4" h, 3-1/2" w **220.00**

Clichy, France

Clichy Rose, large pink center rose, surrounded by green and red canes in star pattern, white lace ground, five over five round facets, one at top center, c1845-55, 2-1/4" h, 3" d, minute nicks........... **2,450.00**

Close Packed Millefiori, various complex canes including signature "C" cane, stave basket, 2-3/8" d, 1-5/8" h, annealing crack in stave **700.00**

Concentric Millefiori, central pink rose cane, surrounded by row of pink, white, and green canes, outer concentric row of pink/white and amethyst/white and green canes, multi-faceted surface, 2" d, 1-3/16" h, ring of carbon and bubbles surrounds design . **200.00**

Garland Trefoil, pink and white whorl canes clustered in green cane, central Clichy rose and five other complex canes, 2" d, 1-1/4" h, minor surface scratches, wear to base **900.00**

Millefiori, multicolored complex canes, central pink and green Clichy rose, upset muslin background, 10 side facets, one bruise at side, 2-1/8" d.... **490.00**

Millefiori, white center, red surround, green and purple outer rim **200.00**

Mushroom, close concentric design, large central pink and green rose surrounded by pin, white, cobalt blue, and cadmium green complex millefiori, middle row of canes with 10 green and white roses alternating with pink pastry mold canes, pin and white stems, 2-3/4" d............... **6,600.00**

Nosegay, three floral canes, including a Clichy rose on five green leaves and stem, 2" d, 1-1/4" h................ **600.00**

Open Concentric, florette and millefiori canes, pink, blue, white, and green, on clear background, well centered, 2-1/4" d, 1-1/2" d h **425.00**

Patterned Millefiori, central floret surrounded by pink and green cog canes, garland of six-pointed star canes and bundled rods, 2" d, 1-1/2" h, minor roughage on base, minor surface imperfections **250.00**

Patterned Millefiori, central millefiori cane surrounded by ring of nine white and green Clichy roses, outside ring of ten pink and green Clichy roses, purple millefiori canes, 1-3/4" d, 1-1/4" h, minor wear on base **800.00**

Patterned Millefiori, central pink and green Clichy rose surrounded by clusters of white six-pointed stars and a garland of pink and green canes, 1-3/4" d, 1-1/4" h, minor surface wear **600.00**

Patterned Millefiori, two concentric millefiori white and green rings, central green and white complex cane, outer garland of white, green, blue, and red canes, red background, 2-3/8" d, 1-3/4" h, two surface spalls, one surface pit **800.00**

Quatrefoil Patterned Millefiori, pink and white quatrefoil canes, spaced complex millefiori blue and green canes, sodden snow background, 3" d, 2" h **2,150.00**

Scattered millefiori, clear background, six Clichy roses, florets, and other complex canes, 2-3/4" d, 1-1/2" h......... **850.00**

Scattered millefiori, cobalt blue background, one Clichy rose cane, other complex canes, 3" d, 2-1/4" h **2,650.00**

Scramble, whole and partial canes, one whole and one partial rose cane, 2-3/4" d, 2-1/8" h, minor surface scratches, wear on bottom **700.00**

Star, purple and green canes around pink circlet, central cane centered white star, base scratches, 2" d **215.00**

Swirl, alternating purple and white pinwheels emanating from white, green, and pink pastry mold cane, minor bubbles, 2-5/8" d.. **2,200.00**

Swirl, green and white, central cane cluster of pink whorls and white florets, 2" d, 1-1/2" h, minor surface wear, wear on base....... **900.00**

Trefoil, interlaced, blue and pink canes, upset muslin background, large central millefiori cane, 2-5/8" d, 1-7/8" h **850.00**

Gillinder

Buddha, amber, opalescent, sgd **325.00**

Turtle, orange, moving appendages in hollow center, pale orange background, molded dome, 3-1/16" d **500.00**

Millville, umbrella pedestal, red, white, green, blue, and yellow int., bubble in sphere center, 3-1/8" d, 3-3/8" h. **800.00**

New England Glass Co., Cambridge, MA, c1860

Concentric Millefiori, canes on muslin background, faceted, many internal fractures, 2-3/4" d.. **115.00**

Crown, red, white, blue, and green twists interspersed with white latticinio emanating from a central pink, white, and green complex floret/cog cane, minor bubbles in glass, 2-3/4" d......... **2,400.00**

Double Overlay, red rose, yellow over white cut to clear, six side facets, one top facet, 2-3/4" d **230.00**

Fruit cluster, red, yellow, and green, latticinio basket, c1860, imperfections, 1-7/8" h, 2-3/4" d **550.00**

Fruit cluster with leaves, center of white latticinio basket, 2" h, 2-5/8" d, wear **225.00**

Leaf Spray, three clusters of pink, blue, green, and amethyst leaves, latticino background, 2-1/2" d, one leaf spray has two separated leaves **200.00**

Open Concentric Millefiori, complex canes including three rabbit canes, upset muslin background, 10 side facets, one top facet, 2" d, 1-3/4" h **1,000.00**

Poinsettia, central yellow millefiori cluster, cobalt blue petals, green stem, three green leaves, red jasper background, 2-3/4" d, 1-5/8" h, flower off-center, two of the petals have splits, polished pontil, wear on base...... **100.00**

Sailboat, enameled white ship silhouette, red flag, blue water, three facets, 4" h, 3-3/4" d **3,450.00**

Saint Louis, France

Bouquet, four upright flowers and green leaves, white spiral torsade, star cut base, 3" d, 2-1/2" h, very minor surface scratches and wear on base **2,600.00**

Clematis, 12 pastel blue ribbed petals, green leafy stem, white latticino bed, six outer facets, center "SL 1972" cane, 3" d. **260.00**

Faceted Posey, central floral arrangement of four millefiori canes, green leaves, surrounded by ring of blue and green millefiori canes, six-sided facets, one top facet, 2-1/4" d, 3" h....... **600.00**

Fruit Bouquet, apple, two pears, three cherries, six green leaves, latticino background, polished base, 2-1/2" h, 1-3/4" h.... **800.00**

Millefiori, close concentric millefiori, central silhouette of couple dancing, chartreuse, cadmium green, white, opaque pink, mauve, salmon, peach, powder blue, and ruby florets, cross canes, cogs, and bull's eyes canes, 3-3/16" d **5,750.00**

Nosegay, four millefiori flower canes nestled on five green leaves and stems, blue, white, and yellow cane garland, strawberry cut base, 2-1/2" d, 1-3/4" h......... **600.00**

Pattern Spaced Millefiori, canes of six-pointed stars and cogs in six clusters, red jasper background, 2-1/4" d, 1-1/2" h **125.00**

Pattern Spaced Millefiori, red, white, blue, and yellow canes, upset muslin background, 3" d, 2" h, polished pontil, wear on base **300.00**

Pears and cherries among foliage, white latticinio basket, 2" h, 2-3/4" d **900.00**

Pompon, pink petals, bundle of yellow rod canes in center of flower, one pink blossom, five green leaves with stem, star-cut base, 2-3/4" d, 2" h, one bubble floats about flowers, minor surface scratches, wear on base... **850.00**

Scramble, various pieces of complex canes, polished pontil, 2-3/4" d, 1-3/4" h, wear on base **200.00**

Turnips, six turnips, one red, two white, two yellow, one purple, green tops, double-spiral white lattice ground, c1848, 2" h, 2-1/4" d **650.00**

Union Glass Company, Somerville

Bird, pair of egrets and egg-filled nest, 3-3/4" d............ **300.00**

Central red flower, words "E. E. Rines, Somerville," garland of 12 flowers surrounds design, 4" d, 2-7/8" h, surface scratches, central flower has in-the-making imperfection **175.00**

Fantasy Flower, blue petals with yellow dots, green leaves, sitting on red, white, and blue marbric background, 3-1/4" d, 3" h, one surface spall **500.00**

Poinsettia, red, split petals, 3-1/8" d, scratched **50.00**

Whitefriars, close concentric millefiori, pink, blue, purple, green, white, and yellow cog canes, 1948 date cane, minor bubble in dome, 3-5/8" d . **900.00**

Modern

Ayotte, Rick, Nashua, NH

Black capped chickadee perched on branch, top facet, five semi-circular side facets, inscribed "4/50," inscribed with signature and date on lower side, 1-3/4" h, 2-3/4" d **620.00**

Butterfly, shaded blue and black butterfly above layer of blue leafy branches with yellow blossoms, inscribed "Ayotte 1985," 1-3/4" h, 3-1/4" d **690.00**

Cardinal on branch, green leaves, light blue base inscribed "50/50," inscribed with signature and date on lower side, 2" h, 2-1/4" d **600.00**

Daisies and blueberries magnum, three light blue, white, and pink daisies, clusters of blueberries on a branch, inscribed "Rick Ayotte LE/35 '99," 2-1/4" h, 3-3/4" d **750.00**

Hawaiian Floral Bouquet, two Lady Slipper orchids, six Hawaiian flowers, green and brown leaves, sgd in script "Rick Ayotte ED/50 '95," 3-1/2" d, 2" h........ **600.00**

Hummingbird, two ruby- throated hummingbirds, fuchsia blossoms, colorless ground, inscribed "Rick Ayotte LE/35 '99," 2-1/4" h, 3-1/2" d................ **690.00**

Thrush, spray of purple flowers, green and yellow leaves, yellow ground, inscribed "Ayotte 21/75 '85" at side, 1985, 2" h, 3-3/4" d................ **865.00**

Trio of red roses with foliage, small white blossoms, top circular facet, six oval side facets, inscribed "ED/50," inscribed with signature and date on lower side, 2-1/4" h, 3-1/4" d................ **575.00**

White-crowned sparrow perched on double layer of green leafy branches with yellow pods, inscribed "Ayotte 15/50 '83" at side, 2" h, 2-3/4" d **865.00**

Baccarat, France

Church, closed pack millefiori, zodiac silhouette canes, date cane "1968," acid etch mark underneath, 2-3/4" h, 1-3/4" h................ **400.00**

Concentric Millefiori, concentric rings of reds, whites, and greens, acid-sgd on reverse, 2-3/8" d, 1-3/4" h, some distortion to canes during making **50.00**

Gridel pelican cane surrounded by five concentric rings of yellow, pink, green, and white complex canes, pink canes contain 18 Gridel silhouette canes, lace background, 1973 date cane, signature cane, sgd and dated, limited edition of 350, 3-1/16" d........... **850.00**

Gridel, pheasant, large central Gridel silhouette of pheasant cane, surrounded by ring of 17 smaller Gridel animal silhouettes, outer ring of white millefiori canes,

translucent blue ground, signature and date 1975 cane, acid stamp on base, inscribed 1975, 2-1/4" h, 2-7/8" d **375.00**

Multicolored millefiori carpet ground, acid mark on base, 1968 year cane, 1-7/8" h, 3" d **435.00**

Pink pompon with green leaves and stem encircled by ring of millefiori on clear ground, star-cut base, signature cane, acid-etched mark, inscribed "50/150," and "1992," 2-1/4" h, 3" d **815.00**

Banford, Bob, Hammonton, NJ

Daffodil, two yellow blossoms, two buds, green leaves, cobalt blue background, multifaceted base, sgd with signature red "B" cane, 2-7/8" d, 2-1/2" h **376.00**

Floral bouquet, pink, blue, and white blossoms, entwined leafy stems, signature cane near stem, 2-3/8" h, 2-7/8" d **650.00**

Fruit, quatrefoil arrangement of pears, cherries, and leaves on white lace ground, green, blue, and white twisted tape border, "B" signature cane on base, 2-1/2" h, 2-7/8" d **435.00**

Wheat Flower, yellow blossom and bud, brown dots on petals, green foliage on stem, transparent cobalt blue star-cut base, signature cane near stem, 2-1/2" h, 3" d ... **645.00**

Banford, Ray, Hammonton, NJ

Faceted lily of the valley, white blossoms, leafy stem, transparent cranberry red ground, round facet on top with six semi-circular side facets, signature cane near stem **520.00**

Iris, purple iris blossom, two buds, green leaves, star cut white background, sgd with signature "B" cane, 3" d, 2" h **275.00**

Rose Bouquet, three white roses, green leaves, powder blue pebble background, sgd in underside with black "B," 2-3/8" d, 2-1/8" h . **275.00**

Pink rose, two buds, deep green foliage, white lace ground, surrounded by pink and blue spiral torsade, black and white initial B cane on reverse, 2-1/2" h, 3" d **500.00**

Bireifer, twig and berry weight, sgd "Bireifer 9-76" **90.00**

Buzzini, Chris

Bindwind and Wild Flax, two pink morning glories entwined with wild flax blossoms, buds, and leaves, numbered "33/40," sgd and dated with signature cane, script sgd "Buzzini '94," 3" d, 2-1/4" h. **700.00**

Floral bouquet, four wild rose bouquet, three pink wild roses, one yellow wild rose, five buds, green leaves, brown stems, numbered "37/40," sgd and dated in script "Buzzini '90," sgd and dated with "Buzzini 90" signature cane, 3" d, 2-3/8" h................ **450.00**

Floral bouquet, three red azaleas surrounded by purple bellflowers, three yellow wild flowers, sgd and dated with signature cane, script sgd "Buzzini '87," 3" d, 2" h **500.00**

Two purple asters with bud, one yellow wild rose with two buds, green leaves, brown stems, sgd and dated with signature cane, script sgd "Buzzini '91," numbered "25/40," 3" d, 2-1/4" h..... **500.00**

Lupine, three pink and amethyst blossoms, three white blossoms, yellow stamens, green leaves, brown stems, numbered "69/75," sgd and dated "Buzzini '90" with signature cane and script, 3" d, 2-5/8" h................ **450.00**

Orchid, pink, white, and orange orchid, bud, leaves, and roots, sgd and dated "Buzzini '87" with signature cane and script, 2-7/8" d, 2-1/4" h................ **475.00**

Vetch, amethyst and white blossoms, green leaves and stems, brown roots, sgd and dated with signature cane, script sgd "Buzzini '91," numbered "16/40," 3" d, 2-1/4" h................ **400.00**

Violet, two purple flowers, yellow and orange centers, green stems, two buds, four heart-shaped green leaves, bulbous root system, signature and date cane "Buzzini '89," also sgd in script "Buzzini LSV 8912," 3" d, 2-1/4" h...... **550.00**

Correia, orchid, orange flower, green stem and leaves, black background, frosted ext. front window facet, limited edition of 200, numbered "106," sgd "Correia," dated "1983," 2-58" d, 2-1/4" h **180.00**

Diacons, John, floral latticinio, pink blossom, stardust cane at center, leafy stem, cushion of spiral latticinio, signature cane "JD," 1-7/8" h, 2-1/2" d, imperfections............... **230.00**

DePalma, Tony, rose, pink to white crimped petals, four green leaves, clear pedestal foot, sgd and dated on bottom "A DePalma 1986," 3-1/4" d, 4-1/2" h **150.00**

Crider, swirls, blue and white, signed, **$90.**

Grubb, Randall, floral bouquet, 11 flowers, pastel pink, blue, and amethyst, green leaves and stems, sgd in script "Randall Grubb '92," 3" d, 2-3/8" h.................... **375.00**

Hamon, Bob, crimped blue flower, green leaves, clear pedestal, six side facets, one top facet, sgd on bottom with emb "H," 2" d, 2-1/8" h **75.00**

Hansen, Robert, lily of the valley, three white blossoms, eight buds on green stem with leaves, pink background, six side facets, one top facet, base sgd "Robert Hansen," 2-1/8" d, 1-" h **125.00**

Hansen, Ronald E., single flower, blue five-petaled flower, central millefiori cane, six green leaves, cobalt blue background, six side facets, one top facet, base sgd "Ronald E. Hansen," 1-3/4" d, 1-1/4" h.............. **50.00**

Isle of Wright Glass, England, crackled gold-colored overlay on colorless glass, red center, paper label "Isle of Wright Glass/Hand Made England".................... **90.00**

Kaziun, Charles

Blue aventurine heart surrounded by ring of pink, green, and blue millefiori canes, pink, green, and white twisted garland with initial cane, white opaque ground, gold K on reverse, 1-3/4" h, 2-1/8" d **460.00**

Concentric millefiori, central cane cluster with red heart surrounded by eight millefiori red, white, and green canes, upset muslin background, underside sgd with blue on white "K" signature cane, 1-1/2" d, 1-1/8" h, several minute bubbles exist within muslin. **375.00**

Concentric, millefiori, heart, turtle silhouette, shamrocks, six-pointed stars, and floret canes encircled by purple and white torsade, turquoise background flecked with goldstone, K signature cane, 2-1/16" d **1,200.00**

Concentric millefiori, multicolored canes surrounded by pink, blue, and white twisted garland with initial cane, set on aventurine and opaque turquoise ground, gold K on reverse, 1-3/4" h, 2-1/8" d **550.00**

Four pink roses, green foliage, surrounded by pink and white twisted garland, initial cane, opaque light blue ground, gold bee on one leaf, initial K on reverse, 1-1/2" h, 2" d **425.00**

Morning glory, white and blue striped blossom and bud, green leafy vine on white trellis, amethyst ground, gold bee on leaf, K on reverse, 1-5/8" h, 2-1/4" h . **1,035.00**

Open Concentric Millefiori, central fish silhouette cane surrounded by six silhouette canes of turtles and shamrocks, robin's egg blue with gold aventurine background, pink torsade surrounds design, sgd with black and white signature cane, reverse side sgd with gold "K" **500.00**

Paperweight stopper on Gunderson bottle, stopper with heart and shamrock millefiori canes, aventurine and blue ground, initial cane beneath, set in teardrop-shaped colorless glass bottle, sq base, Gunderson foil label, 11" h **1,265.00**

Silhouette of boy, large oval black on white silhouette flanked by six white, pink, and blue millefiori canes, pink and white twisted garland with initial cane, pale opaque yellow ground, gold K on reverse, 1-5/8" h, 2-1/4" d . . **700.00**

Silhouette of girl wearing bonnet, large oval black on white silhouette flanked by six white, pink, and blue millefiori canes, white twisted garland with initial cane, pink opaque ground, gold K on reverse, 1-3/4" h, 2-1/4" d **700.00**

Snake, green, beige, and yellow spotted snake, black head, coiled by pink rose, gold bee on green leaf, opaque white ground, two gold Ks on reverse, 1-1/2" h, 2" d **700.00**

Lotton, Charles, four pink blossoms with leafy stems, transparent colorless glass, sgd "MultiFlora Charles Lotton 1975" **125.00**

Lundberg, Steven, Lundberg Studios, CA

Clematis, pink blossoms and upright bud, leafy stems, blue ground, signature cane, inscribed "Steven Lundberg, Lundberg Studios 1990 051119," 2-1/2" h, 3-1/8" d . **250.00**

Daffodils, pink on white striped daffodils accompanied by tall leaves, signature cane, inscribed "Steven Lundberg, Lundberg Studios, 1990 082867," 3" h, 3" d **250.00**

Gardenia, flower and leaves on transparent blue ground, fluted ribbed side facets leaving six-petal top facet, inscribed "Lundberg Studios/1991, Daniel Salazar, Carole Trevia 092617," 2-3/8" h, 3-1/2" d **300.00**

Lily, upright orange lily blossom, green leaves, gray and brown stamen, pedestal base, inscribed "Steven Lundberg, Lundberg Studios, 1986, 012308," 3-3/8" h, 3-1/4" d **265.00**

Lily, upright white lily blossom, green leaves, gray and brown stamen, pedestal base, inscribed "Steven Lundberg, Lundberg Studios, 1988 082961," 3" h, 2-3/4" d. **275.00**

Tropical fish, three fish at top, turquoise ground, waves of gold, green, and cream, inscribed "Lundberg Studios, 1976" . . **225.00**

Orient & Flume, CA

Five heart-shaped leaves on green-blue ground, inscribed "Orient & Flume 225 j 1977" **185.00**

Four-leaf clover, radiating design in green, brown, and blue, inscribed "Orient & Flume 501 in 1975" **175.00**

Veiled pale green core, burgundy pulled feathers lining perimeter, topped by colorful butterfly on solitary blossom, script sgd "Orient and Plume-1978" **100.00**

Parabelle

Patterned millefiori, central Clichy rose surrounded by seven green and white millefiori canes in ring of 12 Clichy-type roses, garland of eight circlets, green moss carpet background, sgd and dated on reverse side with cane "PB1992," 2-3/4" d, 2" h **650.00**

Spaced millefiori, various complex canes, red opaque background, signature and date cane "PB1990," orig paper label, 2-3/4" d, 1-5/8" h **145.00**

Perthshire

Christmas, 1983, Christmas holly wreath, green and red bow, upset muslin background, sgd and dated on bottom with signature cane, 2-5/8" d, 2" h **150.00**

Christmas, 1984, poinsettia and white Christmas flower bouquet, sgd with "P" signature cane, strawberry cut base, 2-3/4" d, 2-1/4" h **125.00**

Christmas, 1987, word "Noel," white Christmas flower, two boughs of holly and five white stars, six side facets, one top facet, sgd "P 1987," 3" d, 2" h **150.00**

Crown, central complex cane with projecting red and blue twisted ribbons alternating with latticinio ribbons, 1985 date cane, signature cane, limited edition of 268, 3" d **850.00**

Double overlay, single pink flower resting on latticino background, cut red and white double overlay, sgd with "P" signature cane, orig label, 2-7/8" d, 2-1/4" h **225.00**

Double overlay, single upright flower, pink petals, green leaves, central "P" signature cane, blue and white double overlay, eight side facets, one top facet, strawberry cut bottom, 2-1/4" d, 1-1/2" h . . **200.00**

Double overlay, three flower bouquet, three white lily-of-the-valley flowers, swirl cut green and white double overlay, "P" signature cane, 2-3/8" d, 1-3/4" h **175.00**

Miniature, six-petaled pink flower, central "P" signature cane, two green leaves, stem hovering over pink and white basket, 1-3/4" d, 1-1/2" h **175.00**

Silk Worm, green, black, and red silk worm rests on two green leaves, top and side faceting, sgd underneath leaf with "P" signature cane, 2-3/8" d, 2-1/4" h. . . . **150.00**

Single Flower, five-petaled amethyst and white flower, central "P" signature cane, green leaves and stems, eight side facets, one top facet, strawberry cut base, 2-1/4" d, 1-1/2" h. **100.00**

Rosenfield, Ken

Bouquet of red, purple, and white flowers and buds, green leafy stems, translucent blue ground, initial "R" cane, inscribed "4/25 Ken Rosenfield '93," 2-1/2" h, 3-1/4" d **490.00**

Bouquet of red tulips and bud, purple crocus, white blossom and bud, green stems terminating in cluster of foliage on transparent blue base, inscribed signature, signature cane on side, 1987, 1-7/8" h, 3-1/4" d **425.00**

Floral bouquet, yellow, orange, blue, and purple blossoms, terminating in cluster of foliage on sand ground, inscribed signature, signature cane on side, 1990, 2-1/8" h, 31/4" h **575.00**

Four purple crocus, three yellow blossoms, two yellow buds, green stems, foliage below, transparent blue base, inscribed signature, signature cane at side, 1-7/8" h, 3" d **365.00**

Purple crocus, and yellow blossoms on green stems with foliage, inscribed signature, signature cane at side, 2" h, 3-1/4" d **395.00**

Wheat flowers, three yellow flowers with brown spots, two purple and blue clovers, two red blossoms with blue buds, stems with foliage, angled cut on base for upright display, signature cane, etched "KR 93," 1-3/8" h, 3-7/8" h . . **350.00**

Saint Louis, France

Abundance Fruit Basket, latticino fruit basket filled with lamp worked bananas, applies, pears, cherries, plums, and leaves, limited edition of 150, sgd in script "St. Louis 1993," numbered "114/150," 4-1/4" l, 3-1/4" w. **750.00**

Butterfly, blue, red, white, black, and amethyst millefiori, white star dust carpet background, sgd and dated with signature cane on underside, 2-7/8" d, 1-7/8" h **300.00**

Clematis, six-petaled red flower, central signature and date cane "SL 1982" on cobalt blue background, orig paper label, 2-1/2" d, 2" h **175.00**

Double-overlay dahlia bouquet, salmon and blue blossoms on leafy stems, set on clear base, blue cut to white cut to clear on five round-cut side facets, large round cut on top, signature cane at center of salmon flower, 1975, 2-1/4" h, 3" d **575.00**

Egg Shape, hand cooler type, oval, white latticinio alternating with pink to blue twists, "SL1976" cane, 2-7/8" h. **230.00**

Five Flower Bouquet, three blue clematis, one white double clematis, red and white primrose, green leaves and stems, underside with date and signature cane "SL 1986," 2-3/4" d, 2" h **350.00**

Mushroom, double overlay, close concentric millefiori, central signature cane "SL 1970," encased in pistachio over white double overlay, five side facets, one top facet, 2-7/8" d, 2" h. **425.00**

Pie Douche, close concentric millefiori, complex canes, latticinio pedestal basket, signature and date "1972" cane, 3" d, 3" h **950.00**

Red and white honeycomb carpet background, rings of C-shaped red and white complex canes, central signature and date "1974" cane, sgd "SL 1974," 2-3/4" d, 2-1/4" h **350.00**

Rose, single pink rose and bud, green leaves and stems, pale amethyst background, six side facets, one top facet, sgd and dated on reverse with "SL1978" signature cane, 3-1/8" d, 2" h **275.00**

Rose Spray, red bud and blossoms, thorny branch, six side facets, sgd "SL1976" cane under white cushion, 3" d. **175.00**

Sulphide, double eagle, blue background, encased in red over white double overlay, five side facets, one top facet, acid etched signature on base, 3" d, 2" h **125.00**

Upright Bouquet, three flowered upright bouquet, red, white, and blue, green leaves, latticinio cushion, white flower has a date and signature cane 'SL 1978," six side facets, one top facet, 2-7/8" d, 2" h **275.00**

Simpson, Josh, MA, Inhabited Planet, grays, blues, and brown, inscribed "Simpson 1986 P4.20," 3" h, 3-1/4" d **225.00**

Stankard, Paul

Chokeberry, white blossoms, leafy stem next to red berry cluster on orange leafy stem, signature cane on lower side, numbered, c1976, 2" h, 2-7/8" d. **1,265.00**

Five-petal white blossom with three partially open buds, leafy stems with root and bulb, signature cane at side, inscribed "B869 1989," 1-1/4" h, 3" d **1,610.00**

Pickerel bud, white and yellow blossoms, ant over tangle of roots, spirit and word canes "Fertile, Seeds, Scent," inscribed "Paul Stankard 1998 C 27," 2-1/4" h, 3" d **2,200.00**

Three orange spider orchid blossoms, green leafy stem with white roots, signature cane at side, inscribed "34/75 AO 34 1978," 2-1/8" h, 2-3/4" d **1,000.00**

Three yellow blossoms with six buds, leafy green stems, signature cane at side, inscribed "B109 1978," 2" h, 2-7/8" d **955.00**

Wildflower, white blossom, two buds, two clusters of blackberries, yellow and orange blossoms, "S" signature cane on side, inscribed "1/6" and numbered, 2" h, 3" d **1,850.00**

Wild rose, pink blossom on leafy foliage, set on clear ground, five round facets on side, one on top, signature "PS" and incised number on side, 1-7/8" h, 2-1/2" d **1,265.00**

Taristano, Debbie, Long Island, NY

Bouquet, yellow and blue centered pink blossom, bright blue flowers on green leafy vines, "DT" cane on reverse, 3" d **415.00**

Dahlia, purple flower, yellow stamens, green leaves, centered on star cut base, DT signature cane, 3" d, 2" h **650.00**

Orange and purple bird of paradise flower on stalk, striped green leaves, star cut background, DT signature cane, 2-15/16" d . **550.00**

Lalique, Deux Aigles, deep amber, c1914, wheel cut signature "R. Lalique," 3" h, **$690.** *Photo courtesy of David Rago Auctions.*

Red blossoms with buds, leafy green stem, round top facet, six side facets, indistinct signature cane under leaf, 2" h, 3" d, minor scratch to base **690.00**

Three flower bouquet, three pink five-petaled blossoms, two buds, four smaller pale blue flowers, green leaves, brown stems, star cut base, signature cane present, but unreadable, 3-1/8" d, 2-1/4" h **650.00**

Yellow centered purple-blue, yellow, and pink zinnia blossoms with red and blue buds, leafy stems, "DT" cane on reverse, 3-1/4" d . . **850.00**

White blossom on brown stem, green leaves, small star-cut base, signature cane at end of stem, 2-1/4" h, 3" d, imperfections **575.00**

Taristano, Delmo, Long Island, NY

Coiled green snake, realistic earth and translucent green background, sgd with "DT" signature, 3-3/8" d, 2-1/4" h **750.00**

Earth Life Series, open-mouth snake entwined in pink, lavender, and blue flowers, rocky ledge background, "DT" cane in design, 4-1/4" d **1,750.00**

Gray spider with red-orange back, clusters of vegetation on sandy ground, signature cane near edge, 2-3/8" h, 3-1/4" d **1,380.00**

Two peaches on brown branch, green leaves, round top facet, six side facets, transparent blue ground, 2" h, 2-1/2" d **690.00**

Tarisitano, Victor, red trumpet flower, yellow centers, one single bug on branch, four green leaves, rock background, sgd underneath with "T" signature cane, 3" d, 2-1/4" h . . **400.00**

Trabucco, David and John

Floral Bouquet, two yellow flowers, two blue flowers with yellow centers, six blue buds, seven small yellow flowers, green leaves and stems, sgd in script "Trabucco 1990 DJ," 3" d, 2-1/2" h . . . **150.00**

Raspberry Bouquet, three red raspberries, two pink flowers, yellow center stamens, four pink buds on branch, seven green leaves, signature "T" cane underneath one leaf, sgd in script "Trabucco 1991 DJ," 3" d, 2-3/4" h **225.00**

Wild Rose, 14 petal pink and white flower, white stamens, one bud and five small white flowers, nine green leaves, sgd underneath one leaf with black on green "T," script sgd "Trabucco 1992 DJ," 1-7/8" d, 1-5/8" h **125.00**

Trabucco, Victor, Buffalo, NY

Blue blossoms and buds, small white flowers, yellow berries on leafy stems, etched "Trabucco, D. J., 1990," on side, 2-1/2" h, 3-1/8" d **425.00**

Blue blossoms and two buds, leafy stem, inscribed "Trabucco 1989 D. J.," 2-1/4" h, 2-3/4" d **400.00**

Floral and fruit, white and purple blossoms and buds, trio of lemons connected on leafy branch, inscribed "Trabucco 1989" on base, 3-1/4" h, 4" d **750.00**

Pink blossom on brown twig, three red berries and leaves, inscribed "Trabucco 1990 D. J.," 1-3/4" d, 2" h **375.00**

Raspberry and Roses Magnum, red berries, white blossoms, "VT" leaf cane, side inscribed "Trabucco 1996," 3-3/4" d. **690.00**

Rose Bouquet, single large pink rose, two pink buds, eight white bellflowers, eight green leaves and stems, translucent cobalt blue background, sgd underneath one leaf with a "VT" signature cane, script sgd "Trabucco 1987," 3" d, 2-5/8" h **250.00**

Two red flowers with pale pink blossoms and bud, leafy green stems, signature cane at base, inscribed "Trabucco 1982 16/50" at side **425.00**

Violet**,** three violet blossoms, two buds, five heart-shaped leaves, green stems, sgd underneath one leaf with "VT" signature cane, 1983, 3" d, 2-3/8" h **175.00**

Unknown maker, millefiori, concentric rings of red, white, and blue floral canes, 4" h, 3-1/2" d, price for pr **480.00**

Val St. Lambert, Belgium, 20th C, planet form, swirls of browns, greens, and blues, paper label at top, inscribed "Val St. Lambert SJH" at base, 3-1/4" h, 4-1/2" d **115.00**

Whittemore, Francis

Acorns, two green and brown acorns on branch with three brown and yellow oak leaves, translucent cobalt blue background, circular top facet five oval punties on sides, 2-3/8" d **300.00**

Degenhart, portrait of Elizabeth Degenhart, designed by Jack Choko of Millville, NJ, made by Imperial Glass for Crystal Art Co., introduced 1977, **$175.**

Nosegay, titled four flower nosegay, one contains a "W" signature cane and five green leaves, opaque white background, clear pedestal base, also sgd on reverse with blue and white "W" signature cane, 1-3/8" d, 2-3/4" h. **250.00**

Pompon Bouquet, seven pink pompons, green leaves and stems, snow white background, sgd with signature black on yellow "W" signature cane, 2-3/8" d, 1-3/4" h **325.00**

Rose, pink rose and bud, green leaves and stems, cobalt blue background, sgd with black on yellow "W" signature cane on underneath side of one petal, 2-1/2" d, 1-7/8" h. **225.00**

Rose, yellow crimped rose, three green leaves, clear pedestal foot, signed with signature black on white "W" cane, 1-3/4" d, 2-1/2" h **225.00**

Three flower bouquet, single five-petaled clematis blossom, white and yellow calla lily, yellow and green stylized blossom, green leaves and stems, red translucent background, sgd with signature black on yellow "W" cane, 2-3/8" d, 2" h **200.00**

Violet, two partially opened violets, one bud, green stems and leaves, opaque white background, sgd with signature black on white "W" cane, seven side facets, one top facet, 1-7/8" d, 1-5/8" h. . . . **150.00**

Ysart, Paul, green fish, yellow eye, yellow and white jasper background encircled by pink, green, and white complex cane garland, PY signature cane **550.00**

Pate-de-Verre

History: The term "pate-de-verre" can be translated simply as "glass paste." It is manufactured by grinding lead glass into a powder or crystal form, making it into a paste by adding a 2 percent or 3 percent solution of sodium silicate, molding, firing, and carving. The Egyptians discovered the process as early as 1500 B.C.

A WALTER NANCY

In the late 19th century, the process was rediscovered by a group of French glassmakers. Almaric Walter, Henri Cros, Georges Despret, and the Daum brothers were leading manufacturers.

Contemporary sculptors are creating a second renaissance, led by the technical research of Jacques Daum.

Animal

Dog, translucent blue and purple, tree-form base with gilt border, inscribed "Daum France" on base, 20th C **130.00**

Dragon, translucent purple, tree-form base with gilt border, inscribed "Daum France" on base, 20th C **130.00**

Komodo dragon, translucent green, tree-form base with gilt border, inscribed "Daum France" on base, 20th C **230.00**

Goat, leaping, colorless, tree-form base with gilt border, inscribed "Daum France" on base, 20th C **130.00**

Horse, leaping, translucent blue, tree-form base with gilt border, inscribed "Daum France" on base, 20th C **130.00**

Monkey, translucent amber, tree-form base with gilt border, inscribed "Daum France" on base, 20th C **130.00**

Opossum, translucent amber and aqua, tree-form base with gilt border, inscribed "Daum France" on base, 20th C.......... **130.00**

Snake, translucent green, tree-form base with gilt border, inscribed "Daum France" on base, 20th C **130.00**

Tiger, translucent amber, tree-form base with gilt border, inscribed "Daum France" on base, 20th C **130.00**

Turtle, translucent green, inscribed "Daum France" on base ... **200.00**

Water buffalo, translucent moss green, tree-form base with gilt border, inscribed "Daum France" on base, 20th C.......... **130.00**

Wild boar, translucent green and amber, tree-form base with gilt border, inscribed "Daum France" on base, 20th C **130.00**

Ashtray

3-1/2" sq, mottled turquoise and midnight blue, two rect compartments, molded bumblebee with black and orange body, green wings, deep brown head, molded signature "A Walter/Nancy" and "Berge/SC," c1925....... **900.00**

6-1/4" l, 3-1/2" w, center medallion with Egyptian head, molded in reds and purples, small flower buds around edge, raised lattice work on bottom **1,650.00**

Atomizer, 5-3/4" h, red berries, green leaves, molded signature "H. Berge" **1,200.00**

Bookends, pr, 6-1/2" h, Buddha, yellow amber pressed molded design, seated in lotus position, inscribed "A Walter Nancy".................... **2,450.00**

Bowl

4" d, 8-3/4" h, Almeric Walter, designed by Jules Cayette, molded blue green glass, yellow center, green around border, three brown scarab beetles with long black antennae, inscribed "A. Walter Nancy," and also "J. Cayette," "Made in France" on base **4,600.00**

4-3/4" h, oviform, turquoise blue ground, molded green band of stylized flowers, molded "A. Walter Nancy" **1,600.00**

6-1/2" d, 4" h, mottled violet bowl, molded with animated hunting scene of wild boar, deer, and fowl being speared by arrows, molded "G. Argy-Rousseau"..... **8,250.00**

9-3/4" d, 4" h, octagonal coupe, solid foot, dec by swags of stylized leafy purple and black branches, mottled colorless near transparent background, ext. molded "G. Argy Rousseau" **6,500.00**

Center bowl, 10-3/8" d, 3-3/4" h, blue, purple, and green press molded design, seven exotic long-legged birds, central multi-pearl blossom, repeating design on ext., raised pedestal foot, sgd "G. Argy-Rousseau"..... **6,750.00**

Clock, 4-1/2" sq, stars within pentagon and tapered sheaves motif, orange and black, molded sgd "G. Argy-Rousseau," clock by J. E. Caldwell **2,750.00**

Bowl, pedestal, purple grape motif, signed "Gargy-Rousseau," 4" d, **$950.**

Dagger, 12" l, frosted blade, relief design, green horse head handle, script sgd "Nancy France"... **1,200.00**

Dish, leaf form

2-1/8" h, 8" l, fig leaf with trio of polished figs and small lizard, green, purple, and amber translucent glass, inscribed "Daum France" on base, 20th C... **215.00**

2-1/4" h, 7-1/4" l, maple leaf with two snails, purple and green translucent glass, inscribed "Daum France" on base, 20th C... **200.00**

2-3/8" h, lizard and moth resting on elongated oval shaped leaf, translucent green and purple, inscribed "Daum France," 20th C **150.00**

2-5/8" h, group of shells on rocky foundation, light blue, purple, and amber translucent glass, inscribed "Daum France," 20th C.... **150.00**

2-3/4" h, winged insect on small leaf, green and purple translucent glass, inscribed "Daum France," 20th C **165.00**

3-1/2" h, large moth alighting on leaf, amber, blue, and purple translucent glass, inscribed "Daum France," 20th C.......... **155.00**

4-7/8" h, three overlapping grape leaves, hibiscus blossom, polished snails in full relief, translucent gray purple and amber glass, inscribed "Daum France," 20th C.... **575.00**

Display plaque, 4-4/5" l, 2-5/8" h, rect, golden amber, brown, and colorless, raised molded brown lettering "Les Pates de Verre d'Argy-Rousseau" **2,530.00**

Fig bowl, 7-5/8" h, flared rim, broad shouldered bowl, tapering to base, molded fig leaves, two lizards, polished figs around sides, translucent amber, purple, and green, inscribed "Daum France" on side, 20th C **2,100.00**

Bowl, yellow leaves and purple vines, marked "Argy-Rousseau," 3-3/4" d, 2" h, **$900.**

Fruit

3" h, translucent purple fig, pierced by bronze arrow, inscribed "Daum France" on base, 20th C ... **90.00**

4-3/8" h, translucent amber pear, pierced by bronze arrow, inscribed "Daum France" on base, 20th C **90.00**

4-7/8" h, translucent green apple, pierced by bronze arrow, inscribed "Daum France" on base, 20th C **90.00**

Hand mirror, 12-1/2" l, pate de verre handle depicting woman's head, flowing hair in form of grape leaves and grape clusters, translucent purple and aqua glass, bronze oval leafy vine frame, inscribed "Daum France," 20th C **250.00**

Inkwell, double, 6-1/2" l, 3" h, black and brown beetle, brilliant orange and yellow glass, central beetle motif, orig conforming covers, sgd "Walter" **4,500.00**

Jewelry

Earrings, pr, 2-3/4" l, teardrop for, molded violet and rose shaded tulip blossom, suspended from rose colored swirl molded circle **2,200.00**

Pendant, 1-1/4" d, molded amethyst portrait of Art Nouveau woman, flowing hair, gilt metal mount **400.00**

Pendant, 2-1/8" x 2-1/4", pierced glass, butterfly, blue, green, red-orange wings, colorless and gray ground, inscribed "GAR" in design (G. Argy-Rousseau) **2,415.00**

Pendant, 2-1/2" x 1-3/4", deep amethyst, red and brown spatter, detailed moth, orig silk tassel, necklace, and red bead, G. Argy Rousseau **1,750.00**

Paperweight

2-1/2" h, 3-1/2" w, brown snail, realistic detailing, brilliant green, blue base, sgd "A. Walter" **2,500.00**

2-5/8" h, Papillion de Nuit, cube, internally streaked gray, deep forest green highlights, molded full relief moths, molded "G. Argy-Rousseau," c1923 . **2,400.00**

3-1/2" h, mouse, gray body, eating from brown walnut shell perched on green grassy knoll, marked by designer and "A. Walter Nancy" in mold **7,500.00**

3-3/4" h, 3-1/2" w, lizard, naturalistic dark brown and black, brilliant blue and green sculptured base, sgd "A. Walter" **5,250.00**

Plaque

5" d, blue, black, and brown moth, Art Deco-inspired patterned base, sgd "Walter" **2,400.00**

6-1/2" d, 7-1/4" h, amber ground, two stalking black striped orange tigers emerging from stylized panels ribbed as tall grasses, molded "G. Argy-Rousseau," No. 28.11, designed as lighting plate on electrolier stand........ **5,750.00**

8-1/2" l, 4" w, figural, white ground, salmon pink mythical creature with blue eyes............. **1,500.00**

Sculpture

8" h, Faune, man/goat, gray-green glass, inscribed "66/250" on base, marked "Daum/J. P. Demarchi" on neck and plinth, 1980s **690.00**

9-5/8" l, crab in sea grasses, lemon yellow, chocolate brown, pale mauve, and sea green, sgd "A. Walter/Nancy" and "Berge/SC" **8,500.00**

10-3/4" h, seated cat, gray-green glass, inscribed "53/250" on base, marked in mold, c1980 .... **690.00**

Tray

6" x 8", apple green, figural green and yellow duck with orange beak at one end, sgd "Walter, Nancy" **950.00**

7" l, 5" w, angular mottled orange-yellow oval, full bodied black and brown center scarab, imp "A. Walter/Nancy"... **2,750.00**

Vase

3" h, small oval, yellow glass, dec with border of raised stylized flowers, touches of yellow-orange, rust, and green to border, inscribed designer "M. Corrette" at mid-section and "A. Walter Nancy" near base, c1925 ...... **1,380.00**

4" h, smoky gray mottled with violet, rose, and green, relief molded with clusters of white berried branches, violet leaves, molded "G. Argy-Rousseau France".. **7,250.00**

4-3/4" h, spherical, black spiders spinning intricate webs from yellow, orange, amber, and black bramble bushes, side molded "A. Argy-Rousseau," base molded "France" internal 1/2" fracture at mid center **2,990.00**

5-1/8" h, striated aubergine purple and colorless cone shaped body, integrated disk foot molded with four repeating spiked devices, imp "Decorchemont" in horseshoe stamp, numbered C199 on base **3,600.00**

5-1/4" h, 4-7/8" l, golden amber and brown ground, central conical bud vase in oval plinth base, molded and stylized birds of prey at each side, marked "G. Argy-Rousseau" **4,025.00**

5-3/8" h, raised and flared rim, ovoid pate de verre body, molded dec of trailing vines with fruit, pale aqua, green, gray, and orange-grown, molded "G. Agry Rousseau" signature near base, opaque int., c1915, int. crack to shoulder **575.00**

5-1/2" h, press molded and carved, mottled amethyst and frost ground, three black and green crabs, red eyes, naturalistic seaweed at rim, center imp "G. Argy-Rousseau," base imp "France"...... **5,500.00**

9" h, molded goblet form, yellow amber ground, shaded green to orange at base, highly detailed and realistic green-black lizard wrapped around stem, imp "A. Walter" and "H. Berge SC," orig thin rim area........... **6,325.00**

Veilleuse, night light

6-1/2" h, domed form, deep aqua blue glass, molded trailing vines, yellow flower, mounted on circular wrought-iron stand, removable domed cap molded "A. Walter Nancy" **6,000.00**

7-1/4" h, gray body, molded with amethyst accents on medial band of black and brown leafy branches, wrought iron cap and base with lamp socket, molded "G. Argy-Rousseau" at side.. **4,900.00**

8-1/4" h, oval molded shade, mottled gray-lavender, three repeating

red-centered purple blossoms within black V-shaped devices, molded "G. Argy-Rousseau," four ball feet on wrought iron base, fitted with night light, conforming cap **5,300.00**

8-1/2" h, press molded oval lamp shade, frosted mottled gray glass, elaborate purple arches with three teardrop-shaped windows of yellow, center teal-green stylized blossoms on black swirling stems, imp "G. Arty-Rousseau" at lower edge, wrought iron frame, three ball feet centering internal lamp socket, conforming iron cover **6,900.00**

Vide Pouche, irregular-shaped dish

6-1/4" l, welled crescent shape, mottled tangerine shading to pale lemon, molded along with side with two spotted langoustines, one teal, the other burgundy, molded "A. Walter Nancy" and "Berge S.C." **4,000.00**

6-3/4" l, 3-3/4" h, shallow oval, mottled orange and black, surmounted by green spotted black lizard molded in full relief, molded "A. Walter Nancy Berge" **4,500.00**

7-1/4" l, 2-3/4" h, petal shape, seafoam green, molded in low relief with amber seaweed, full relief molded orange and brown seashell, molded "A. Walter Nancy Berge S.C." **4,000.00**

11" l, elongated rectangular, mottled sky blue, molded at each end with burgundy and black moth, stylized star burst, molded "A. Walter Nancy Berge S.C." **4,000.00**

Wall sconce, 16-1/2" l, 11" h, shell-shaped wall pocket, trio of mermaids in frosted and translucent amethyst glass, polished high relief areas, lit from behind with three-socket fixture, inscribed "Daum France," 20th C..................... **980.00**

Pattern Glass

History: Pattern glass is clear or colored glass pressed into one of hundreds of patterns. Deming Jarves of the Boston and Sandwich Glass Co. invented one of the first successful pressing machines in 1828. By the 1860s, glass-pressing machinery had been improved, and mass production of good-quality matched tableware sets began. The idea of a matched glassware table service (including goblets, tumblers, creamers, sugars, compotes, cruets, etc.) quickly caught on in America. Many pattern glass table services had numerous accessory pieces such as banana stands, molasses cans, and water bottles.

Early pattern glass (flint) was made with a lead formula, giving many items a ringing sound when tapped. Lead became too valuable to be used in glass manufacturing during the Civil War; and in 1864 Hobbs, Brockunier & Co., West Virginia, developed a soda lime (non-flint) formula. Pattern glass also was produced in transparent colors, milk glass, opalescent glass, slag glass, and custard glass.

The hundreds of companies that produced pattern glass experienced periods of development, expansions, personnel problems, material and supply demands, fires, and mergers. In 1899, the National Glass Co. was formed as a combine of 19 glass companies in Pennsylvania, Ohio, Indiana, West Virginia, and Maryland. U.S. Glass, another consortium, was founded in 1891. These combines resulted from attempts to save small companies by pooling talents, resources, and patterns. Because of this pooling, the same pattern often can be attributed to several companies.

Sometimes various companies produced the same patterns at different times and used different names to reflect current fashion trends. U.S. Glass created the States series by using state names for various patterns, several of which were new issues, while others were former patterns renamed.

References: Gary Baker et al., *Wheeling Glass 1829-1939*, Oglebay Institute, 1994, distributed by Antique Publications; E. M. Belknap, *Milk Glass*, Crown, 1949; George and Linda Breeze, *Mysteries of the Moon & Star*, published by authors, 1995; Bill Edwards, *The Standard Encyclopedia of Opalescent Glass*, Collector Books, 1992; Elaine Ezell and George Newhouse, *Cruets, Cruets, Cruets*, Antique Publications, 1992; Regis F. and Mary F. Ferson, *Yesterday's Milk Glass Today*, published by author, 1981; William Heacock, *Encyclopedia of Victorian Colored Pattern Glass (all published by Antique Publications):Book 1: Toothpick Holders from A to Z*, 2nd ed. (1976, 1992 value update); —, *Book 2, Opalescent Glass from A to Z, (1981);* —, *Book 3, Syrups, Sugar Shakers, and Cruets*, (1981); —, *Book 4, Custard Glass from A to Z*, (1980); —, *Book 5: U. S. Glass from A to Z* (1980), —, *Oil Cruets from A to Z, (1981);* —, *Book 7: Ruby Stained Glass from A To Z* (1986), *Book 8: More Rugy Stained Glass* (1987), Antique Publications; —, *Old Pattern Glass*, Antique Publications, 1981; —, *1000 Toothpick Holders*, Antique Publications, 1977; —, *Rare and Unlisted Toothpick Holders*, Antique Publications, 1984; William Heacock, James Measell, and Berry Wiggins, *Dugan/Diamond: The Story of Indiana, Pennsylvania, Glass*, Antique Publications, 1993; —, *Harry Northwood: The Early Years, 1881-1900*, Antique Publications; 1990; —, *Harry Northwood: The Wheeling Years*, Antique Publications; 1991; Ann Hicks, *Just Jenkins*, published by author, 1988; Kyle Husfloen, *Collector's Guide to American Pressed Glass*, Wallace-Homestead, 1992; Bill Jenks and Jerry Luna, *Early American Pattern Glass—1850 to 1910*, Wallace-Homestead, 1990; Bill Jenks, Jerry Luna, and Darryl Reilly, *Identifying Pattern Glass Reproductions*, Wallace-Homestead, 1993; William J. Jenks and Darryl Reilly, *American Price Guide to Unitt's Canadian & American Goblets Volumes I & II*, Author! Author! Books (P.O. Box 1964, Kingston, PA 18704), 1996; —, *U. S. Glass: The States Patterns*, Author! Author! Books, Inc., 1998.

Minnie Watson Kamm, *Pattern Glass Pitchers*, Books 1 through 8, published by author, 1970, 4th printing; Lorraine Kovar, *Westmoreland Glass: 1950-54, Volume I (1991); Volume II (1991)*, Antique Publications; Thelma Ladd and Laurence Ladd, *Portland Glass: Legacy of a Glass House Down East*, Collector Books, 1992; Ruth Webb Lee, *Early American Pressed Glass*, 36th ed., Lee Publications, 1966; —, *Victorian Glass*, 13th ed., Lee Publications, 1944; Bessie M. Lindsey, *American Historical Glass*, Charles E. Tuttle, 1967; Robert Irwin Lucas, *Tarentum Pattern Glass*, privately printed, 1981; Mollie H. McCain, *Collector's Encyclopedia of Pattern Glass*, Collector Books, 1982, 1994 value update; George P. and Helen McKearin, *American Glass*, Crown Publishers, 1941; James Measell, *Greentown Glass*, Grand Rapids Public Museum Association, 1979, 1992-93 value update, distributed by Antique Publications; James Measell and Don E. Smith, *Findlay Glass: The Glass Tableware Manufactures, 1886-1902*, Antique Publications, 1986; Alice Hulett Metz, *Early American Pattern Glass*, published by author, 1958 (reprinted by Collector Books, 2000, with revisions); —, *Much More Early American Pattern Glass*, published by author, 1965 (reprinted by Collector Books, 2000, with revisions); S. T. Millard, *Goblets I* (1938), *Goblets II* (1940), privately printed, reprinted Wallace-Homestead, 1975; John B. Mordock and Walter L. Adams, *Pattern Glass* Mugs, Antique Publications, 1995.; Kirk J. Nelson, *50 Favorites: Early American Pressed Glass Goblets: Sections from the Dorothy and Jacque D. Vallier Collection*, University of Wisconsin, 1993;

Arthur G. Peterson, *Glass Salt Shakers*, Wallace-Homestead, 1970; Ellen T. Schroy, *Warman's Pattern Glass*, 2nd ed., Krause Publications, 2000; Jane Shadel Spillman, *American and European Pressed Glass in the Corning Museum of Glass*, Corning Museum of Glass, 1981; —, *Knopf Collectors Guides to American Antiques, Glass*, Vol. 1 (1982), Vol. 2 (1983), Alfred A. Knopf; Ron Teal, R., *Albany Glass, Model Flint Glass Company of Albany, Indiana*, Antique Publications, 1997; Doris and Peter Unitt, *American and Canadian Goblets*, Clock House, 1970, reprinted by The Love of Glass Publishing (Box 629, Arthur, Ontario, Canada NOG 1AO), 1996; —, *Treasury of Canadian Glass*, 2nd ed., Clock House, 1969; Peter Unitt and Anne Worrall, *Canadian Handbook, Pressed Glass Tableware*, Clock House Productions, 1983; John and Elizabeth Welker, *Pressed Glass in America: Encyclopedia of the First Hundred Years, 1825-1925*, Antique Acres Press, 1985; Kenneth Wilson, *American Glass 1760-1930*, 2 vols., Hudson Hills Press and The Toledo Museum of Art, 1994.

Periodicals: *Glass Shards*, The National American Glass Club, Ltd., P.O. Box 8489, Silver Spring, MD 20907; *News Journal*, Early American Pattern Glass Society, P.O. Box 266, Colesburg, IA 52035;

Collectors' Clubs: Early American Pattern Glass Society, P.O. Box 266, Colesburg, IA 52035, http://www.eapgs.org; Moon and Star Collectors Club, 4207 Fox Creek, Mount Vernon, IL 62864; The

National American Glass Club, Ltd., P.O. Box 8489, Silver Spring, MD 20907.

Museums: Bennington Museum, Bennington, CT; Corning Museum of Glass, Corning, NY; Historical Glass Museum, Redlands, CA: Jones Museum of Glass and Ceramics, Sebago, ME; National Museum of Man, Ottawa, Ontario, Canada; Sandwich Glass Museum, Sandwich, MA; Schminck Memorial Museum, Lakeview, OR; The Chrysler Museum, Norfolk, VA; The Toledo Museum of Art, Toledo, OH; University of Wisconsin-Stevens Point, Stevens Point, WI, Wheaton Historical Village Assoc. Museum of Glass, Millville, NJ.

Reproduction Alert: Pattern glass has been widely reproduced.

Additional Listings: Bread Plates, Children's Toy Dishes, Cruets, Custard Glass, Milk Glass, Sugar Shakers, Toothpicks, and specific companies.

Note: Prices listed are for colorless (clear) pieces, unless otherwise noted.

Ale
- Ashburton, flint, 5" h **90.00**
- Dancing Goat, frosted goat . . **55.00**
- Mephistopheles **95.00**

Apothecary jar, Mascotte, ruby stained, clear ground stopper with thumbprints, pattern at top of jar and stem, 24" h. **2,300.00**

Banana stand
- Amazon, etched **95.00**
- Art, ruby stained, 10" d, high standard **170.00**
- Broken Column **185.00**
- Delaware, green, gold trim . . . **95.00**
- Eyewinker, flat. **85.00**

Bar bottle
- Nine Panel Flute, flint, pint . . . **65.00**
- Waffle, flint, quart **155.00**

Basket
- Broken Column, applied handle, 15" l. **135.00**
- Dakota, etched **250.00**
- Haley, blue semi-translucent, butterfly on top of handle, band of flowers and leaves around rim, four feet, marked "Pat'd July 21st 1874 April 5th 1881," Atterbury & Co., 9" l, 6-1/4" w, 5" h, rim chip, flake on one foot **50.00**
- Paneled Thistle **85.00**
- Portland, gold trim **85.00**
- Snail **85.00**
- Vermont, gold trim **45.00**

Eyewinker pattern, front: small covered jar, chips, ***$50****; rear: compote, covered, pedestal base, 12-1/2" high,* ***$200.*** *Photo courtesy of Joy Luke Fine Art Brokers and Auctioneers.*

Berry bowl, master
- Adonis, canary-yellow **20.00**
- Croesus, green **165.00**
- Daisy and Button, oval, amber **45.00**
- Jacob's Ladder, ornate SP holder, ftd **125.00**
- Nestor, blue, gilt and white enamel dec, 8-3/4" d, 5" h, wear to gilt at rim **50.00**
- O'Hara Diamond **25.00**
- Shell and Tassel **35.00**
- Three Panel, amber **45.00**
- Wreath and Shell, 8-1/2" d **45.00**

Berry set
- Bull's Eye and Daisy, green stain, five pcs **115.00**
- Cord Drapery. **75.00**
- Croesus, amethyst, seven pcs **625.00**
- Delaware, green, gold trim, seven pcs **175.00**
- Feather Duster, gold rim, seven pcs **55.00**
- Jacob's Coat, master berry, 11 flat sauces, emerald green **60.00**
- Manhattan, seven pcs **50.00**
- Sunflower Patch pattern, ruby stained, seven pcs **275.00**
- Thumbnail pattern, ruby stained, five pcs **165.00**

Biscuit jar, cov
- All-Over Diamond **65.00**
- Art, ruby stained. **150.00**
- Big Button, ruby stained. . . . **135.00**
- Broken Column, ruby stained **185.00**
- Minnesota, ruby stained. . . . **165.00**
- Pennsylvania, emerald green **100.00**
- Reverse Torpedo **145.00**
- Three Face, 9-1/2" h **1,700.00**

Bonbon, Georgi **35.00**

Bowl, open
- All-Over Diamond **25.00**
- Art, ruby stained. **60.00**
- Banded Portland, maiden's blush stain, oval, shallow, 10" l, 7-1/2" w, 2" h, several rim flakes **25.00**
- Barred Ovals, ruby stained, 7" sq **45.00**
- Beveled Diamond and Star, ruby stained, 8" d **100.00**
- Block and Fan, ruby stained, 6" d. **40.00**
- Broken Column, ruby stained, 8" d. **145.00**
- Buckle, flint, 10" d. **65.00**
- Button Arches, ruby stained, 8" d. **65.00**
- Crystal Wedding, ruby stained, 6" d, scalloped rim **75.00**
- Dakota, ruby stained **85.00**
- Daisy and Button, blue, triangular **45.00**
- Delaware, boat-shaped bowl, orig SP frame, rose **400.00**
- Fleur-de-lis, 9" d **28.00**
- Heart with Thumbprint, ruby stained, 6" h. **75.00**
- Honeycomb, flint, 8" d, ftd . . . **20.00**
- King's #500, Dewey Blue, gold trim, 7" d. **35.00**
- Locket on Chain, ruby stained, 8" d **145.00**
- New Hampshire, gold trim, flared, 8-1/2" d. **20.00**
- Royal Lady, Belmont's, 11-1/4" l, flat, oval, cov. **145.00**
- Ruby Thumbprint, ruby stained, 7" d **50.00**
- Thousand Eye, blue **85.00**
- Torpedo, ruby stained **75.00**
- Triple Triangle, ruby stained, 10" l, rect. **65.00**
- Truncated Cube, ruby stained, 8" d **50.00**
- Utah **20.00**
- Westmoreland, 4-1/4" x 7" sq, orig SP frame **125.00**

Brandy tray, Willow Oak, amber **125.00**

Roman Rosette, compote, cover, hs, 7-1/4" d, 11-1/2" d, **$60.**

Bread plate

Actress, Miss Neilson **80.00**
Basketweave, canary-yellow .. **35.00**
Beveled Diamond and Star, ruby stained, 7" d **85.00**
Broken Column, ruby stained **140.00**
Cape Cod **45.00**
Cupid's Hunt **90.00**
Deer and Pine Tree, amber .. **110.00**
Lion, motto, blue **135.00**
Roman Rosette, 9" x 11" **55.00**
Train **75.00**
Triple Triangle, ruby stained. . **125.00**

Butter, covered

Alaska, vaseline opal **350.00**
Art, ruby stained **115.00**
Atlas, ruby stained, copper wheel engraving **145.00**
Beaded Loop **75.00**
Bird and Strawberry, color ... **100.00**
Bull's Eye and Daisy, cranberry eyes, gold trim **65.00**
Croesus, amethyst **275.00**
Crystal Wedding, ruby stained **145.00**
Daisy and Button, amber, bell cover, orig clapper, 6-1/4" d, 8" h, flat chips to flange edge **70.00**
Dakota, ruby stained, copper wheel engraved dec **175.00**
Deer, Dog, Hunter **225.00**
Duncan's Thumbprint, ruby stained **225.00**
Empress **125.00**
Eureka, ruby stained **125.00**
Flat Iron, blue, 8-1/2" l, 5" w, 3-3/4" h **60.00**
Frog, blue, Bryce, Higbee & Co., 8-1/2" l, 6-1/2" w, 3" h, chip, two rough points on base flange **200.00**
Garfield Drape **95.00**
Galloway, maiden's blush **85.00**
Holly **150.00**
Horn of Plenty, flint, Washington head finial **995.00**
Illinois **55.00**
Jockey Cap **400.00**
Jumbo **550.00**
Liberty Bell, 1876 .... **85.00**
Locket on Chain, ruby stained **260.00**
Loop and Jewel **95.00**
Maryland, gold trim **75.00**
Nestor, amethyst, dec **125.00**
Nestor, blue, gilt and white enamel dec, 6" h, two minor flakes .. **70.00**
Pennsylvania **50.00**
Prize, ruby stained **185.00**
Red Block, ruby stained, 6" d, 5" h, annealing lines **80.00**
Reverse 44, cranberry, gold trim **125.00**
Rose in Snow, sq **50.00**
Ruby Thumbprint, ruby stained **150.00**
Thousand Eye, vaseline **90.00**
Torpedo, ruby stained **150.00**
Truncated Cube, ruby stained. **100.00**
Wreath and Shell, vaseline .. **250.00**
Zipper **75.00**

Butter pat

Horn of Plenty **20.00**
Shell and Tassel **15.00**

Cake stand

Atlas, ruby stained, 9" d, high standard **120.00**
Bellflower, single vine, flint, matching patterned domed foot, 9-1/4" d, 3-3/4" h, extremely rare .. **4,600.00**
Beveled Diamond and Star, ruby stained, 9" d, high standard **115.00**
Button Arches, ruby stained, high standard **185.00**
Bird and Strawberry **75.00**
Crystal Wedding **95.00**
Daisy and Button with Thumbprint Panel, amber, 10" d, 6-1/2" h **60.00**
Daisy and Button with Thumbprint Panel, blue, 10" d, 6-1/2" h. . **110.00**
Festoon **48.00**
Finecut and Panel, blue **75.00**
Good Luck, 10" d **75.00**
Hand **60.00**
Horn of Plenty, flint, waffle type pattern under foot, 8-1/4" d, 4-1/4" h **1,800.00**
Holly, 10-1/2" d **110.00**
Missouri **35.00**
Pogo Stick **45.00**
Rose in Snow **95.00**
Ruby Thumbprint, ruby stained, 10" d, high standard **175.00**
Shosone, 10-1/2" d **45.00**
Texas **125.00**
Wildflower, vaseline, 9-1/2" d, 6" h, light scratching **100.00**
Willow Oak, amber **55.00**

Calling card receiver

Colorado, blue **45.00**
Heart with Thumbprint, ruby stained **90.00**

Carafe

Barred Ovals, ruby stained ... **95.00**
Block **30.00**
Bull's Eye **45.00**
Excelsior **150.00**
Galloway, rose stained **85.00**
Heart with Thumbprint, ruby stained **165.00**
Honeycomb **100.00**

Castor set

Alabama, four bottles, glass frame **125.00**
Bellflower, single vine, flint, five bottles, Britannia stand **750.00**
Daisy and Button, vaseline, four bottles, glass stand **85.00**
King's Crown **185.00**
Ruby Thumbprint, ruby stained, four bottles, orig stoppers and frame **350.00**

Celery tray

Barred Ovals, ruby stained ... **85.00**
Broken Column **45.00**
Nail, etched **45.00**
Triple Triangle, ruby stained .. **85.00**

Celery vase

Art, ruby stained **60.00**
Ashburton, flint, 9" h **90.00**
Atlas, ruby stained **75.00**
Baby Face, 7-3/4" h, bruise ... **70.00**
Bellflower, single vine, flint, 8-1/4" h **325.00**
Chandelier **25.00**
Diamond Thumbprint, flint ... **150.00**
Eureka, ruby stained **80.00**
Francesware Swirl **75.00**
Good Luck **35.00**
Heart with Thumbprint **145.00**
Hexagon Block, ruby stained **130.00**
Honeycomb, flint **45.00**
Jacob's Ladder, 9" **30.00**

Locket on Chain, ruby stained **175.00**
Moon and Star **35.00**
Plume **35.00**
Prize, ruby stained **160.00**
Ruby Thumbprint, ruby stained, etched **85.00**
Shoshone, ruby stained **120.00**
Torpedo, ruby stained **125.00**
Truncated Cube, ruby stained **115.00**
US Coin, quarters **210.00**
Waffle and Thumbprint, flint .. **95.00**
Wreath and Shell, vaseline .. **245.00**

Champagne

Broken Column, ruby stained **175.00**
Diamond Thumbprint, flint, polished rim **425.00**
Flamingo Habitat **50.00**
Hamilton with Frosted Leaf, flint, 4-7/8" h **275.00**
Inverted Fern, flint, plain base, 5" h **150.00**
Ivy in Snow, ruby stained **85.00**
Mardi Gras **26.00**
Minerva, 5" h, tiny flake under foot **600.00**
Morning Glory, flint, 5" h **210.00**
New England Pineapple, flint, 5-1/4" h **210.00**
New York, flint **65.00**
Ribbed Ivy, flint **275.00**
Ribbed Palm, flint **120.00**
Ruby Thumbprint, ruby stained **50.00**
Sawtooth, flint **65.00**
Three Face, hollow stem, 3-1/2" d, 4" h **5,100.00**
Three Face, saucer type, 3-3/4" d, 4-3/8" h **350.00**
Waffle and Thumbprint, flint . **110.00**

Cheese dish, cov

Actress **225.00**
Esther, ruby stained **150.00**
Flamingo Habitat **150.00**
Horseshoe **215.00**
Lion, rampant lion finial **400.00**
Snail **95.00**
Thumbprint, etched **145.00**
Zipper **65.00**

Claret

Broken Column **85.00**
Diamond Point, flint **90.00**
Lattice and Oval Panels, flint **110.00**
Three Face **115.00**

Cologne bottle

Bull's Eye, flint, orig stopper .. **50.00**
Massachusetts **45.00**
Thousand Eye, apple green . **100.00**

Compote, covered

Barley, 7" d, high standard ... **65.00**
Beaded Band, 8" d **85.00**
Crystal Wedding **75.00**
Daisy and Button with Thumbprint Panel, blue, 6-1/2" d, 10-1/2" h, flake **70.00**
Dakota, 5" d, high standard, etched leaf **30.00**
Dakota, 6" d, high standard... **40.00**
Early Thumbprint, high standard, ball form, double step hollow stem with 12 flutes, circular foot with 24 scallops, single band of 24 thumbprints under foot, wafer construction, 14-3/4" h, 9-3/4" h base, 8" d rim, 5-1/2" d foot, three flakes on base rim, three chips on side, large chip on int. rim of lid, three large chips on outside edge **3,700.00**
Frosted Chicken, 7" d, high standard **200.00**
Frosted Circle, 7" h **125.00**
Frosted Eagle, 8" d, low standard **275.00**
Frosted Lion, 7" d, oval **85.00**
Frosted Lion, 8-1/4" d, oval ... **95.00**
Good Luck, 8" d **175.00**
Heart Stem, 6" **85.00**
Honeycomb, 8" d, high standard, melon finial **90.00**
Jumbo **275.00**
Lion and Cable, high standard, etched leaf and berry, frosted lion finial, 9" d **150.00**
Paneled Forget Me Not, 7" d, high standard **50.00**
Peacock Feather, 8" d **125.00**
Pleat and Panel, 8" d, high standard **145.00**
Ribbon, 10-7/8" h, 7-3/4" d **55.00**
Ribbon Candy, 7" d **85.00**
Sequoia **55.00**
Snail, 7" d, 12" h **145.00**
Texas, 6" d, scalloped lid **195.00**

Compote, open

Almond Thumbprint **45.00**
Amazon **45.00**
Belmont, vaseline, 10-3/4" d, 8-1/2" h **180.00**
Bird and Strawberry, 8" d, ruffled edge **110.00**
Brilliant, Royal's, 6" d **20.00**
Broken Column, 5-1/2" **75.00**
Cable, 8" d, flint **75.00**
Daisy and Button, amber, star type, wafer, 10-1/2" d, 6-1/2" h, minor wear **90.00**
Frosted Foot **45.00**
Good Luck, 9" d **235.00**
Grape Band **35.00**

Jacob's Ladder, compote, oblong dolphin stem, **$300**

Horn of Plenty, flint, oval, matching pattern under foot, 8-1/4" l, 5-3/4" w, 6" h **1,500.00**
Interlocking Crescents **35.00**
Jacob's Ladder, 6" x 8-1/2", flared **30.00**
Locket on Chain, high standard, 8-1/2" d **145.00**
New England Pineapple, 8" d. **70.00**
Paneled Daisy and Button, amber, paneled bowl, inverted funnel foot, scalloped lower edge, 8-1/4" d, 10" h **90.00**
Paneled Forget Me Not **35.00**
Rope and Thumbprint, amber **40.00**
Sawtooth **55.00**
Teardrop and Tassel **55.00**
Two Panel, blue, high standard **140.00**

Cordial

Almond Thumbprint, flint **50.00**
Atlas, ruby stained **45.00**
Basketweave, apple green... **45.00**
Bellflower, single vine, vine ribbed, knob stem, rayed base, barrel shape **115.00**
Early Thumbprint, flint, knob stem, 3-1/4" h **200.00**
Feather **95.00**
King's Crown **45.00**
Star and File **20.00**
Thousand Eye **30.00**

Creamer

Actress **90.00**
Adonis **20.00**
Alaska, vaseline opal **85.00**
Barberry **55.00**
Beaded Band **30.00**
Bellflower, double fine, 6-3/4" h **210.00**
Bellflower, single vine, flint, ribs to end of lip, 6" h **275.00**
Bird and Strawberry **65.00**
Bird in Ring **25.00**

Bleeding Heart 55.00
Block and Fan 25.00
Block and Honeycomb 65.00
Broken Column 40.00
Cabbage Rose 55.00
Cardinal Bird 25.00
Chain and Shield 20.00
Chandelier, leaf and berry etch . 25.00
Classic Medallion 40.00
Cord and Tassel 30.00
Cottage 30.00
Croesus, amethyst, individual size 170.00
Croesus, green 140.00
Dart 30.00
Dewey, cov, amber 75.00
Diamond Point Band 60.00
Drapery 45.00
Early Thistle, applied handle . . 75.00
Egyptian 50.00
Frosted Stork 35.00
Garland of Roses, triple stem . 35.00
Garfield Drape 45.00
Georgia Gem, gold trim 35.00
Good Luck 40.00
Grace 65.00
Grape 20.00
Grape and Festoon 55.00
Grasshopper, no insect 30.00
Heart with Thumbprint, individual size 25.00
Hobnail, ball foot 20.00
Horn of Plenty, flint, small, two chips 250.00
Horseshoe 25.00
Intaglio 35.00
Jumbo 150.00
Louis XV, green 45.00
Mascotte, etched 45.00
Memphis, green 75.00
Minerva 50.00
Nailhead 30.00
Oasis 30.00
One-O-One 21.00
One Hundred One 40.00
Paneled Chain 36.00
Pennsylvania, gold trim 35.00
Popcorn 32.00
Pressed Leaf 45.00
Prize, ruby 110.00
Psyche and Cupid 50.00
Reverse 44, ftd, platinum trim . 40.00
Roman Rosette 60.00
Seedpod, green, gold trim, c1899 . . . . 65.00
Stashed Swirl 20.00
Stippled Chain 25.00
Stippled Grape and Festoon . . 25.00
Sunbeam 45.00
Teardrop and Tassel, opaque white 85.00
Threading 15.00
Three Face 85.00
Torpedo, 6" 36.00
Tremont 20.00
Truncated Cube, individual size, ruby stain 40.00
Two Band 36.00
Wheat and Barley 15.00
Wreath and Shell, blue, decorated 235.00

Cruet

Beaded Grape, green, 5-1/2" h, roughness on shoulder 40.00
Beaded Swirl and Lens, ruby stained, no stopper, 5" h . . . 40.00
Brazillian, green, no stopper, 7" h 30.00
Cone, pink satin, replaced stopper, 5" h 110.00
Croesus, amethyst, small, orig stopper 375.00
Cut Log, orig stopper 40.00
Daisy and Button, amber, bulbous, 6-1/4" h 130.00
Duchess, maiden's blush, no stopper 125.00
Empress, gold trim, orig stopper 195.00
Illinois, sq, orig stopper 50.00
Jeweled Heart, apple green, replaced stopper, 7" h 80.00
King's Crown, orig stopper . . . 45.00
Oneida, orig stopper 20.00
Paneled Thistle, orig stopper . 30.00
Stars and Bars, amber, orig stopper, 7-1/2" h 90.00
Sterling, amber stained, orig stopper 225.00
Sunflower, orig stopper 40.00
Tacoma, orig stopper 20.00
Zenith, blue, replaced stopper, 7" h 50.00
Zipper and Panel, faceted stopper 30.00

Cruet tray

Croesus, amethyst 115.00
Nestor, blue, gold trim 65.00

Cup and saucer

Basketweave, blue 35.00
Cornell, green, gold grim 30.00
Currier and Ives 30.00
Fleur de Lys with Drape 30.00
King's Crown 55.00
Star and Ivy 35.00
Torpedo 50.00
Wisconsin 50.00

Custard cup

Bull's Eye and Fan 12.00
Fine Rib, flint, 3-7/8" h 325.00
New Hampshire, rose stain . . 15.00
Snail 32.00
Wisconsin 25.00

Decanter

Aurora, ruby stained, 11-3/4" h 95.00
Bellflower, single vine, flint, pint, orig stopper, 8-1/2" h, large chip on stopper 750.00
Bigler, bar type, flint 60.00
Corona, ruby stained 110.00
Fine Rib with Cut Ovals, flint, quart, tiny nick 200.00
Honeycomb, flint, quart, no stopper 40.00
Peerless, flint 45.00
Ribbed Ivy, flint, orig hollow flower form stopper, 7" h, flake on stopper 400.00
Sandwich Star, quart, no stopper 25.00
Sawtooth, flint, quart, orig stopper 135.00
Torpedo, ruby stained, 8" h . . 150.00
Truncated Cube, ruby stained, 12" h 150.00
Tulip and Sawtooth, flint, pink, bar lip, orig stopper 150.00
Waffle and Thumbprint, orig stopper, canary, applied lip, polished pontil, 13-1/4" h 6,250.00

Dish

Heart with Thumbprint, heart shaped, handle 32.50
Shell and Tassel, 8" w, octagonal, amber 50.00
Shoshone, 5" l, handle, Dewey Blue 65.00

Doughnut stand

Paneled Thistle 45.00
Prayer Rug 75.00
Ribbon Candy, 3" h 150.00

Egg cup, flint

Ashburton 25.00
Bellflower 45.00
Bull's Eye, cov, 5-1/4" h, small flake on lid 250.00
Bull's Eye with Diamond Point, flint, 4" h 180.00
Cable 55.00
Colonial 35.00
Frosted Lion 50.00
Hamilton 45.00
Hercules Pillar, double 65.00
Horn of Plenty 45.00
Huber 25.00
Lattice and Oval Panels, flint . . 45.00
Magnet and Grape with Frosted Leaf, flint 80.00
New England Pineapple 60.00
Ribbed Palm 45.00
Sawtooth, cov, flint, nicks on foot 70.00
Washington, flint 90.00

Goblet, Garden of Eden, plain stem, **$40**

Fruit bowl, Shell and Tassel, 10" d, Meriden SP holder **100.00**

Goblet

Almond Thumbprint **10.00**
Atlanta, light int. wear **45.00**
Apollo, etched **35.00**
Arched Grape **35.00**
Arched Grape Variant **35.00**
Argus, barrel, flint **40.00**
Art, ruby stained **60.00**
Ashburton, flint, plain stem . . . **28.00**
Ashman **30.00**
Atlas, etched **45.00**
Austrian **35.00**
Baby Face, fern and berry etching **325.00**
Banded Portland, maiden's blush stain, 5-5/8" h **50.00**
Banded Portland, yellow stain, 5-3/4" h **45.00**
Bar and Swirl **25.00**
Barberry **35.00**
Barred Forget Me Not **20.00**
Basketweave, amber **16.00**
Beaded Acorn **25.00**
Beaded Bands **20.00**
Beaded Dart Band, ruby stained **60.00**
Beaded Mirror, flint, etched grape and fern in ovals and around top band, 5-3/4" h **100.00**
Beaded Panels **20.00**
Bessiner Flute, flint **25.00**
Beveled Diamond and Star, ruby stained **75.00**
Bigler, flint **35.00**
Birds at Fountain **40.00**
Blackberry **35.00**
Block, ruby stained **90.00**
Bradford Grape, flint **135.00**
Broken Column, ruby stained . **160.00**
Buckle, flint **35.00**
Bull and Swirl Band with Etched Leaf and Fern **20.00**
Bull's Eye, flint, knob stem, 6-5/8" h **100.00**
Bull's Eye and Broken Column, flint **100.00**
Bull's Eye with Daisy, green stain **42.00**
Bull's Eye with Diamond Point, flint, 6-7/8" h **130.00**
Bull's Eye with Fleur-De-Lys, flint **100.00**
Bull's Eye and Spearhead **50.00**
Button Arches, ruby stained . . **45.00**
Cabbage Rose **25.00**
Cable, flint **210.00**
Canadian **55.00**
Cape Cod **45.00**
Cartridge Belt, flint **25.00**
Chain with Star **25.00**
Colonial with Diamond Band, flint **75.00**
Comet, flint **120.00**
Cord and Tassel **85.00**
Cottage **20.00**
Curled Leaf **27.00**
Currant **25.00**
Curtain Tieback **35.00**
Currier and Ives **30.00**
Dakota, etched **55.00**
Deer and Dog, etched **50.00**
Deer and Pine Tree **50.00**
Dewdrop **20.00**
Diamond Point, flint **45.00**
Diamond Ridge **30.00**
Diamond Thumbprint, flint, 6-3/4" h **700.00**
Divided Diamonds, flint **35.00**
Double Disced Prism, flint, green **80.00**
Drapery **35.00**
Duquesne, flint **25.00**
Early Paneled Grape Band, flint **50.00**
Early Thumbprint, flint, unlisted short knob stem **200.00**
Egg in Sand **25.00**
Egyptian **50.00**
Elongated Honeycomb, flint . . **30.00**
Esther, ruby stained by Beaumont Glass Works **85.00**
Excelsior, barrel, flint **30.00**
Falcon Strawberry **20.00**
Fairfax Strawberry **45.00**
Fan with Diamonds **20.00**
Feather **35.00**
Fedora Loop, flint **50.00**
Finecut and Block **30.00**
Finecut and Panel, vaseline . . **25.00**
Fine Diamond Point, flint **30.00**
Fine Rib with Bellflower Border, flint, 5-1/2" h **2,100.00**
Flamingo **195.00**
Flower Band, frosted **95.00**
Flower Medallion, flint **25.00**
Flying Stork **65.00**
Frosted Lion **70.00**
Frosted Magnolia **100.00**
Frosted Stork **50.00**
Fruit Panels **20.00**
Garfield Drape **20.00**
Giant Baby Thumbprint, flint . . **85.00**
Giant Bull's Eye, flint **50.00**
Giant Prism, flint **50.00**
Girl with Fan **100.00**
Good Luck, knob stem **35.00**
Gooseberry **35.00**
Grand **20.00**
Grape Band **20.00**
Grape Vine Under **35.00**
Grape With Thumbprint **32.00**
Hairpin with Thumbprint, flint . **35.00**
Hamilton with Frosted Leaf, flint **130.00**
Harp, flint, 6-1/8" h, extremely rare **2,750.00**
Harvard Yard, rose **45.00**
Harvest Blackberry **35.00**
Hawaiian Pineapple, flint **90.00**
Heart with Thumbprint **65.00**
Hickman, ruby stained **55.00**
Hidalgo, etched **20.00**
Hinoto, flint **70.00**
Honeycomb **20.00**
Honeycomb, Elongated, flint . **30.00**
Horsemint **20.00**
Huber **20.00**
Hummingbird, blue **145.00**
Icicle with Chain Band, flint . . **45.00**
Inverted Fern, flint **30.00**
Jacob's Ladder **55.00**
Knives and Forks, flint **25.00**
Knobby Bull's Eye, gold trim, amethyst stain **20.00**
Kokomo **35.00**
Lattice and Oval Panels, flint, 6-1/8" h **210.00**
Lincoln Drape, flint **120.00**
Loganberry and Grape, round rim **20.00**
Loop, ruby stained **90.00**
Loop and Dart, Diamond Ornament **20.00**

Loop and Pyramid **16.00**
Lotus and Serpent **325.00**
Magnet and Grape with Frosted Leaf, American shield, flint, 6-1/2" h **300.00**
Maple Leaf, 6" h **170.00**
Maryland **30.00**
Melrose, etched **42.50**
Michigan **40.00**
Minerva **70.00**
Minnesota **36.00**
Morning Glory, flint **1,850.00**
Nail, etched **45.00**
Nailhead **32.00**
Netted Swan, amber **95.00**
New England Centennial **245.00**
New Hampshire, gold trim **20.00**
New Jersey, gold trim **25.00**
Nickel Plate's Richmond **25.00**
Nova Scotia Grape and Vine . . **60.00**
Oak Leaf Band with Loops, flint **80.00**
Odd Fellow **48.00**
Open Rose **25.00**
Oval Mitre, flint **25.00**
Oval Panels, vaseline **35.00**
Owl and Possum **85.00**
Owl in Fan **35.00**
Owl in Horseshoe **110.00**
Paneled Forget Me Not **45.00**
Paneled Ovals, flint **40.00**
Paneled Potted Flower **55.00**
Paneled Diamonds **20.00**
Paneled Fern, frosted, flint . . . **270.00**
Paneled Flattened Sawtooth, flint **170.00**
Pavonia **30.00**
Persian Spear, flint **85.00**
Plain Sunburst **20.00**
Pleat and Panel **35.00**
Plume, engraved **20.00**
Polar Bear **125.00**
Polar Bear, frosted **100.00**
Portland Tree of Life, emb "P.G. Co. Patent," flint **60.00**
Portrait, non-flint, rare **850.00**
Prism and Flute, flint **32.00**
Queen, amber **15.00**
Queen, colorless **38.00**
Rayed Heart **700.00**
Reverse 44, burgundy, gold trim **65.00**
Reverse 44, platinum trim **25.00**
Ribbed Droplet Band, frosted, amber stained, etched **55.00**
Ribbed Grape, flint, plain band **25.00**
Ribbed Ivy, flint, barrel **40.00**
Roman Key, flint **35.00**
Rose in Snow **20.00**
Rose Leaves **20.00**

Rosette Palm **20.00**
Sawtooth, flint **40.00**
Scarab, flint **175.00**
Seneca Loop **30.00**
Shell and Tassel **55.00**
Shrine **85.00**
Star in Box **65.00**
Star in Bull's Eye **32.00**
Stippled Medallion, flint **25.00**
Stippled Peppers **35.00**
Stocky Mirror, flint **45.00**
Stork **85.00**
Straight Huber, flint, etched . . **35.00**
Strawberry **55.00**
Strawberry and Currant **35.00**
Tape Measure, flint **20.00**
Teardrop and Tassel **175.00**
Teardrop and Thumbprint **20.00**
Texas **95.00**
Texas Bull's Eye **20.00**
Texas Centennial **95.00**
Thousand Eye, blue **60.00**
Three Face **110.00**
Three Panel, vaseline **30.00**
Thumbprint, hotel style **21.00**
Tree of Life, Portland, flint, faintly marked "P.G.Co. Patent" under foot **50.00**
Tulip with Sawtooth, flint **45.00**
US Coin, frosted dimes **575.00**
Vermont, green, gold trim **68.00**
Waffle and Thumbprint, flint . . **60.00**
Waffle with Fan Top **20.00**
Washington, flint **120.00**
Ways Current **35.00**
Wedding Ring, flint **70.00**
Wildflower **20.00**
Willow Oak, amber **35.00**
Yoked Lump, flint **25.00**
Yuma Loop, flint **25.00**
Zenith **20.00**
Zig Zag **36.00**

Hat

Daisy and Button, blue, large . **45.00**
Thousand Eye, vaseline **48.00**

Honey dish

Alabama cov **60.00**
Beaded Grape Medallion, open **12.00**
Bellflower, single vine, flint, scallop and point rim, star base, 3" d, normal flaking **100.00**
Broken Column, ruby stained, open, flat **45.00**
Diamond Thumbprint, flint . . . **25.00**
Horn of Plenty, cov, flint, rect, unrecorded orig undertray, 6-1/2" l, 4" w, 3" h dish, 7" l, 4-1/2" w, 1-1/4" tray, extremely rare, sold at auction by Green Valley Auctions, Inc. **14,000.00**

Dakota, pitchers, water, tankard, left: Bird and Fern etching, 4-1/2" d, 12" h, **$125;** *right: Fern and Berry etching, 4-7/8" w, 9" h,* **$95.**

Lily of the Valley **12.00**
Oregon #1 . . . . **12.00**
Ruby Thumbprint, ruby stained, cov, 8" sq, tab handles **245.00**

Horseradish dish, Duncan Block #331, ground stopper **40.00**

Ice cream tray

Block and Fan **75.00**
Sherwood, 8-1/2" x 13-1/2" **1,100.00**

Jelly compote

Croesus, green, gold trim . . . **225.00**
Diamond Spearhead, cobalt blue **200.00**
Florida, green **25.00**
Reverse Torpedo **35.00**

Juice tumbler

Cut Log **35.00**
Daisy and Button, amber **15.00**
Massachusetts **15.00**
Pennsylvania **8.00**

Ketchup bottle, Daisy and Button with Crossbar, amber, orig stopper, 8-1/4" h **50.00**

Lamp, oil

Acanthus Leaf, flint, 11-1/2" h **150.00**
Beaded Bull's Eye and Fleur-de-Lis, green, tall standard **115.00**
Bellflower, single vine, flint, pattern on inside of font, wafer, scalloped base, 9" h, replaced collar . **650.00**
Crystal Wedding **245.00**
Elongated Loop, finger lamp, medium emerald green, applied handle, pewter collar, single tube burner, Boston & Sandwich Glass Co., 1840-60, 3-1/2" h top of burner, missing tip of curl on handle **850.00**
Excelsior, flint, 4-3/4" h, finger type **195.00**
Harp, flint, 4" h, finger type . . **365.00**

Harp, flint, 9" h **290.00**
One-O-One, finger **95.00**
Pleat and Panel. **250.00**
Ringed Framed Ovals, flint, 9" h **140.00**

Lamp shade

Button Arches, gas type **55.00**
Mardi Gras, electric type **45.00**
Teepee, electric type **70.00**

Lemonade pitcher

Bull's Eye and Fan **85.00**
Pavonia. **125.00**

Lemonade tumbler

Bull's Eye and Fan **20.00**
Honeycomb, flint. **40.00**
Plume **30.00**

Marmalade jar, cov

Actress **95.00**
Atlanta. **95.00**
Atlas, ruby stained **115.00**
Bow Tie, pewter lid **75.00**
Butterfly with Spray. **80.00**
Deer and Pine Tree. **90.00**
Esther, ruby stained by Beaumont Glass Works **100.00**
Log Cabin. **275.00**
Ruby Thumbprint, ruby stained **185.00**
Snail **95.00**
Three Face **200.00**
Viking, ground stopper **175.00**
Wisconsin **125.00**

Milk pitcher

Art, ruby stained. **160.00**
Bellflower, double vine, flint, straight sides, one quart **550.00**
Beveled Diamond and Star, ruby stained **145.00**
Button Arches, ruby stained. **130.00**
Cane Horseshoe. **40.00**
Cape Cod **65.00**
Colorado, green, gold trim . . **325.00**
Cupid and Venus **95.00**
Daisy and Button with Crossbars, vaseline **130.00**
Eyewinker **75.00**
Francesware Swirl. **125.00**
Frosted Lion, non-flint, applied handle, 7" h **6,000.00**
Good Luck **225.00**
Paneled Thistle **65.00**
Pleat and Panel. **155.00**
Rosette **50.00**
Ruby Thumbprint, ruby stained **150.00**
Tiny Lion **70.00**
Truncated Cube, ruby stained **1,100.00**
Willow Oak **40.00**

Mug

Arched Fleur-De-Lis, ruby stained **30.00**
Beaded Swirl **15.00**
Bird and Owl **80.00**
Cupid and Venus. **30.00**
Kansas. **45.00**
Lyre with Bird on Nest, 3" h . . . **30.00**
Minnesota **15.00**
Thousand Eye, apple green . . **30.00**
US Coin **185.00**

Mustard, cov

King's Crown **75.00**
Wisconsin **70.00**

Nappy

Amazon, 4". **12.00**
Bird and Strawberry. **70.00**
Colorado, emerald green **35.00**
Galloway, rose stain **50.00**
Heart with Thumbprint, green, handle **85.00**
Lily of the Valley. **25.00**

Olive

Arched Fleur-De-Lis. **17.50**
Beaded Grape. **20.00**
Illinois. **20.00**
Kentucky **25.00**
Maryland, gold trim **15.00**
Thousand Eye, amber **40.00**

Pickle castor

Broken Column **175.00**
Cupid and Venus, silver-plated frame **295.00**
Daisy and Button with V Ornament, vaseline **120.00**
Feather. **150.00**

Pickle dish

Aegis **20.00**
Barberry. **25.00**
Lily of the Valley, scoop shape **20.00**
Jacob's Ladder, handle **10.00**
Maryland **18.00**
Missouri **20.00**
US Coin, frosted, chips **40.00**
Utah **20.00**

Plate

Arched Fleur-De-Lis, 7" sq. . . . **18.00**
Beautiful Lady, 8" d **20.00**
Beaded Grape, 8-1/4" sq **30.00**
Bellflower, single vine, flint, 6" d **60.00**
Broken Column, ruby stained, 5" d **60.00**
Button Arches, ruby stained, 7" d **35.00**
Croesus, 8" d **145.00**
Egyptian, 10" d, tab handle . . . **95.00**
Elaine, swan border. **110.00**
Heart with Thumbprint pattern, ruby stained, 6" d **40.00**
Horn of Plenty, flint, canary, 6-1/4" d, mold roughness, edge flaking **700.00**
Illinois, 7" d **55.00**
Jacob's Ladder, 6" d **27.00**
King's Crown, 7" w, sq **65.00**
Maryland, gold trim, 7" d **25.00**
O'Hara Diamond, 8" d **30.00**
Ribbed Grape, flint, 5-3/4" . . . **45.00**
Stippled Cherry, 6" d **12.00**
Stippled Forget Me Not, 9" d, kitten center. **55.00**
The States, 6" d **12.00**
Willow Oak, 9" d, blue. **45.00**
Wisconsin, 7" d. **45.00**

Platter

Actress Miss Neilson **60.00**
Cape Cod. **45.00**
Frosted Stork, One Hundred One border **85.00**
Knights of Labor, amber, oval, 11-3/4" l, 8-3/4" w, rim flake **100.00**
Knights of Labor, blue, oval, 11-3/4" l, 8-3/4" w **210.00**
Maple Leaf, blue, oval **55.00**
Pleat Panel **25.00**

Puff box, Banded Portland, irid stain, 2-1/2" d, 2-1/4" h **40.00**

Punch bowl set

Aztec, bowl, stand, 20 cups. **100.00**
Manhattan, bowl, 12 cups . . . **80.00**
The States, bowl, eight cups **125.00**

Punch cup

Bird and Strawberry **22.00**
Button Panels **10.00**
Galloway. **8.50**
Hickman **10.00**
Iowa, gold trim **15.00**
Kentucky. **8.00**
King Arthur **8.00**
Louise. **8.00**
Pennsylvania **10.00**
Roman Rosette. **15.00**
US Rib, green, gold band . . . **15.00**

Relish

Amazon, etched. **30.00**
Art, ruby stained. **60.00**
Block and Fan pattern, Richards & Glass Co. oval **45.00**
Broken Column, ruby stained, 11" l, oval. **165.00**
Bull's Eye and Fan, pink stain. **20.00**
Crystal Wedding, ruby stained **45.00**
Currier and Ives **20.00**
Dewey, flower flange, serpentine, amber. **45.00**
Horn of Plenty, flint, 5" x 7" . . . **42.50**

Grouping of salt containers, from left: Pennsylvania, individual salt, **$20;** *Frosted Lion, master salt,* **$150;** *Sawtooth, individual salt,* **$110;** *Sandwich, covered, master salt,* **$65;** *Wooden Pail, individual salt,* **$20**

Jacob's Ladder, 9-1/2" x 5-1/2" **12.00**
King's #500, Dewey Blue, gold trim . . . **30.00**
Magnet and Grape, stippled leaf . . . **18.00**
New Hampshire, rose stain, diamond shape . . . **24.00**
New Jersey, ruby stained, 8" l **110.00**
Oregon #1 . . . **18.00**
Texas, blushed . . . **55.00**
Wisconsin . . . **25.00**
Zipper . . . **18.00**

Rose bowl

Kokomo, small . . . **20.00**
Paneled Thistle . . . **50.00**
Snail, 5" h . . . **45.00**
Wreath and Shell, blue . . . **145.00**
Zippered Swirl with Diamond, emerald green . . . **35.00**

Salt and pepper shakers, pr

Actress . . . **120.00**
Atlas . . . **25.00**
Banded Portland, maiden's blush stain, 1-1/4" d, 3" h . . . **45.00**
Columbia, Belmont's . . . **85.00**
Croesus, green . . . **250.00**
Cut Log, orig tops . . . **130.00**
Delaware, green, gold trim . . . **500.00**
Diamond Ridge . . . **45.00**
Flower Band . . . **100.00**
Westmoreland . . . **60.00**
X-Ray, green, gold trim . . . **225.00**

Salt, individual

Atlanta, frosted . . . **42.00**
Bird, salt cellar on napkin ring, pepper shaker in front, 4" d, 5" h, crack in base . . . **160.00**
Button Arches . . . **15.00**
Illinois . . . **15.00**
Lacy Daisy . . . **5.00**
Moon and Star . . . **18.50**
Morning Glory, flint, 2" d . . . **110.00**
Pressed Diamond, vaseline, 1-3/4" d, 7/8" h, set of four . . . **50.00**
Snail . . . **20.00**
Zipper . . . **8.00**

Salt, master

Amazon . . . **20.00**
Argus . . . **30.00**
Cabbage Rose, ftd . . . **25.00**
Daisy and Button with Thumbprint Panel, vaseline, 2-5/8" sq, 1-1/2" h, flakes . . . **25.00**
Electric . . . **12.00**
Excelsior, flint . . . **30.00**
Jacob's Ladder . . . **22.00**
Lily of the Valley, cov . . . **125.00**
Ribbed Ivy, flint, 4-1/2" h, flake on lid . . . **190.00**
Royal Lady . . . **30.00**
Sawtooth . . . **50.00**
Torpedo . . . **25.00**

Sauce/individual berry bowl

Acorn, 5" d . . . **18.00**
Actress, ftd . . . **27.00**
Adonis, 4" d . . . **12.00**
Alaska, vaseline opal . . . **45.00**
Amazon . . . **10.00**
Bleeding Heart, flat . . . **15.00**
Colorado, ruffled . . . **18.00**
Cupid and Venus, ftd . . . **18.00**
Dakota, ftd, 4" d . . . **6.00**
Derby, Riverside, vaseline . . . **35.00**
Diagonal Band with Fan, set of six . . . **95.00**
Duncan's 2000, amber stained, 4-3/4" d . . . **40.00**
Florida, sq, emerald green . . . **10.00**
Frosted Lion, ftd, 4" . . . **20.00**
Good Luck, 4" d, ftd . . . **15.00**
Grace, Duncan, 4-1/2" d . . . **17.50**
Jacob's Ladder, flat, 4-1/2" d . . **8.00**
Japanese, ftd . . . **15.00**
Leaf Medallion, amethyst . . . **30.00**
Minerva . . . **10.00**
Reverse Torpedo . . . **12.00**
Shell and Tassel, ftd, 4" d . . . **8.00**
Squirrel in Bower . . . **10.00**
Thumbprint, flint . . . **12.00**
Wreath and Shell, vaseline . . . **40.00**
Zipper, ftd . . . **15.00**

Shoe

Boot, blue, marked under base, "Bouquet Holder, Patented Dec 1886," 5-1/2" h . . . **100.00**
Daisy and Button, colorless, sole dated "Pat'd 1888" . . . **95.00**
Shoe on roller skates, blue, 6" l, 3-7/8" h, minor roughness . . **40.00**

Soap dish, Wash Tub, blue, washboard and clothes on int., Bryce, Higbee & Co., 4-3/4" d, 2-1/4" h, flake . . . **100.00**

Spill vase

Buckle with Star . . . **60.00**
Diamond Point, flint . . . **50.00**
Honeycomb, flint . . . **30.00**
Sandwich Star . . . **30.00**

Spittoon, Wreath and Shell, vaseline . . . **150.00**

Spooner

Alaska, vaseline opal . . . **55.00**
Bellflower, double vine, flint, six-scallop rim, short stem, rayed base, 5" h . . . **140.00**
Berry Cluster . . . **28.00**
Cable, flint . . . **55.00**
Cathedral . . . **25.00**
Columbian Coin, frosted coins . . . **100.00**
Croesus, green . . . **100.00**
Elephant . . . **550.00**
Fine Rib, flint . . . **45.00**
Garfield Drape . . . **38.00**
Grace, Duncan . . . **55.00**
Grape and Festoon . . . **35.00**
Hexagon Block . . . **25.00**
Japanese . . . **35.00**
Klondike . . . **75.00**
Lorraine, frosted . . . **45.00**
Louis XV, green . . . **45.00**
Magnet and Grape, Frosted Leaf, flint . . . **95.00**
Mascotte, etched . . . **28.00**
Morning Glory, flint . . . **160.00**
Pleat and Panel . . . **28.00**
Prize, ruby . . . **95.00**
Snail . . . **25.00**
Victor, green . . . **75.00**
Wreath and Shell, vaseline, dec . . . **195.00**
X-Ray, amethyst, gold trim . . **110.00**

Spoon tray

Daisy and Button, blue, orig Tuffs quadruple plate frame, marked #2083, 7" l, 6-1/4" h, small bruise and internal crack . . . **150.00**
Empress, vaseline, gilt dec, 9" l, 6" w, small flake on underside of tab handle . . . **25.00**

Sugar, covered

Alaska, vaseline opal . . . **300.00**
Bellflower, double vine, flint, 8-3/4" h, flaking on lid . . . **230.00**
Bellflower, single vine, flint, octagonal, 5-3/4" d, chip along lid, extremely rare . . . **1,550.00**
Bradford Grape . . . **55.00**
Cathedral, amber . . . **45.00**
Cranesbill . . . **40.00**
Croesus, green . . . **175.00**

Diamond Cut with Leaf **50.00**
Frosted Eagle **200.00**
Heart with Thumbprint, individual size **25.00**
Hinto, flint **75.00**
Horseshoe **85.00**
Inverted Fern, flint, two chips on lid **60.00**
Log Cabin **455.00**
Louis XV, green. **90.00**
Mascotte, etched **450.00**
Nail, etched **48.00**
New England Pineapple **65.00**
New Jersey **50.00**
Plain Band, Heisey #1225, gold band **35.00**
Rose Point Band **65.00**
Snail, breakfast size **85.00**
Way's Beaded Swirl **35.00**

Sugar, open

Actress **50.00**
New England Pineapple **45.00**
Ray, flint **65.00**
Roman Rosette **18.00**

Sweetmeat, cov

Almond Thumbprint, flint. **70.00**
Bellflower, single vine, 6" h, high standard **300.00**
New Jersey, gold trim. **50.00**
Ohio, etched **30.00**

Syrup pitcher

Adonis, Gonterman Swirl, amber top, opalescent base, Aetna Glass & Mfg. Co., 6-3/4" h **600.00**
Alba, white, colored florals . . . **65.00**
Bellflower, double vine, flint, hollow handle, tin top, 7-1/4" h, unrecorded. **1,300.00**
Chrysanthemum Base, blue speckled, Buckeye Glass Co., 6-1/2" h **700.00**
Cord Drapery, chocolate . . . **350.00**
Currier and Ives **95.00**
Dahlia, amber **85.00**
Hercules Pillar, amber, 8-1/2" h **110.00**
Inverted Thumbprint, pinched base, blue, 6-7/8" h **80.00**
Inverted Thumbprint, tapered, apple green, 7" h **100.00**
Jeweled Heart, apple green, 6" h **550.00**
Jeweled Moon and Star, dec, lid missing **185.00**
King's 500, cobalt blue, 5-1/4" h, minor roughness. **300.00**
Knobby Bull's Eye. **85.00**
Louise **75.00**
Medallion Sprig, blue fading to clear, 8" h, crack in top of handle, missing thumb tab **90.00**
Patee Cross **65.00**
Robin's Nest, amber, 7-1/4" h, thumb tab missing **50.00**
Rope and Thumbprint, amber, marked inside lid "Pat. Jan 29, 84" **60.00**
Star and Punty, blown, flint . . **385.00**
Thousand Eye, blue. **225.00**
Waffle Variant, reeded pressed handle, 6" h **60.00**
Waffle Variant, colorless and frosted, bulbous body, ribs on neck, 7" h **85.00**
York Herringbone. **125.00**

Table set

Atlanta, four pcs **450.00**
Baby Face, four pcs **600.00**
Empress, green, gold trim, four pcs **325.00**

Tankard pitcher

Delaware, green, gilt dec, 9-3/8" h, wear to gilt. **70.00**
King's Crown, ruby stained, engraved "Mineola 1893," 8" h **90.00**

Tazza, Paneled Daisy and Button, etching **95.00**

Toothpick holder

Atlas, etched leaf and berry . . **20.00**
Banded Portland **40.00**
Beaded Grape, green, gold trim **70.00**
Box in Box **30.00**
Box in Box, green, gold trim . . **70.00**
Bull's Eye and Fan **40.00**
Colonial, blue, two handles . . . **35.00**
Croesus, green **125.00**
Daisy and Button with "V" Ornament **35.00**
Delaware, rose stained **125.00**
Diamond Spearhead, green . . **50.00**
Empress, gold trim **85.00**
King's Crown **45.00**
Lower Manhattan, amethyst stain **35.00**
Medallion Sunburst **35.00**
Michigan, yellow stained, floral dec **85.00**
Minnesota, green. **165.00**
Paneled Cherry **25.00**
Portland **20.00**
Queen's Necklace **35.00**
Scalloped Skirt, green, enamel dec **55.00**
Reverse 44, platinum trim **95.00**
Rising Sun, pink suns **25.00**
The States **50.00**
Thousand Eye, amber **35.00**
Tree of Life, amber, two small nicks **75.00**
Washington, Knights Templar enameling **60.00**
X-Ray, green, gold trim **25.00**

Tray

Bulky Mule, 10" d **40.00**
Columbian Shield, vaseline . **300.00**
Feather Duster, 11", green . . . **32.00**
Nellie Bly, oval, minor chips . **200.00**
Scroll Cane Band, amber stain **60.00**
Two Panel, blue, oval, handles, 15" l, 10-1/4" w, 1-3/4" h, flake on handle **40.00**

Tumbler

Amazon, etched **42.50**
Beaded Swirl, green, gold trim **40.00**
Bellflower, flint **90.00**
Bird and Strawberry **45.00**
Bleeding Heart, ftd **95.00**
Broken Column, ruby trim. . . . **65.00**
Bull's Eye and Diamond Panels **50.00**
Cherry and Cable, color trim . **20.00**
Cranes and Herons, etched . . **30.00**
Croesus, amethyst **90.00**
Dakota, etched fern and berry dec **35.00**
Delaware, cranberry, gold trim **40.00**
Empress, green, gold trim . . . **55.00**
Esther, green, gold trim **45.00**
Excelsior, bar **75.00**
Festoon. **20.00**
Flower with Cane, colorless, green stain, gold trim **20.00**
Gibson Girl **75.00**
Hand. **75.00**
Heavy Drape **20.00**
Herons, etched fish in mouth . **25.00**
Hobnail **40.00**
Horn of Plenty. **50.00**
Hummingbird **50.00**
Illinois **55.00**
King's 500, cobalt blue, gold trim **50.00**
Memphis, emerald green, faded gold trim. **25.00**
Michigan, narrow gold stripe near rim **35.00**
Peacock Feather **30.00**
Pillow Encircled, ruby. **40.00**
Shell and Jewel **15.00**
Stag, etched, yellow and mauve tints **40.00**
Stippled Leaf **45.00**
Waffle and Thumbprint, flint, ftd, mold roughness **90.00**
Wildflower, apple green **45.00**
Wreath and Shell, blue **80.00**
X-Ray, amethyst, gold trim . . . **65.00**

Block and Fan, water bottle, 4-1/4" d, 8-1/4" h, **$50.**

Vase

Ashburton, scalloped rim, flint, 10-1/2" h, 5-1/2" d foot **170.00**
Colorado, blue, 12" h **90.00**
Daisy and Button, hand holding cornucopia, ruby stained, 6" h, chip under foot **130.00**
Illinois, 6" h, sq **25.00**
Massachusetts, green, 10" h . . **65.00**
Michigan, bud **18.00**
New Hampshire, amethyst stain **30.00**
Paneled Thistle 9-1/4" h **25.00**

Vegetable bowl

Beaded Grape Medallion, cov, ftd **75.00**
Eyewinker, 6-1/2" l **35.00**
Horseshoe **35.00**
Lily of the Valley **35.00**

Violet bowl

Chandelier **40.00**
Colorado, blue **35.00**
Snail **50.00**

Waste bowl

Block and Fan **30.00**
Festoon **38.00**
King's 500, frosted **45.00**
Pavonia **65.00**
Polar Bear **95.00**
Two Panel, amber **35.00**

Water bottle, Banded Portland, maiden's blush stain, 8-1/2" h . . . **110.00**

Water pitcher

Actress, frosted under bowl and stem, 9-1/4" h **350.00**
Aquarium **165.00**
Bellflower, double vine, flint, straight sides, 1-1/2 quarts **450.00**
Classic, log feet **315.00**
Cleat, flint **325.00**
Clematis, frosted, purple and amber staining, 8" h, wear to staining **50.00**
Cut and Block, amber trim . . **125.00**
Daisy and Button with Thumbprint Panel, amber **225.00**
Dewey, Gridley **95.00**
Diamond Thumbprint, flint . **1,350.00**
Feather, green **200.00**
Florida, emerald green **45.00**
Honeycomb, flint, "pat'd 1865" . **90.00**
Horn of Plenty, flint, heat check on handle **875.00**
Huckle, green **65.00**
Hummingbird **125.00**
Inverted Thumbprint, amber, multicolored enamel floral dec, triangular rim, applied clear reeded handle, 8-1/2" h **150.00**
Klondike, amber stained, sq. **900.00**
Nestor, blue, dec **150.00**
Peapods **40.00**
Reverse 44, burgundy, gold trim, jug **65.00**
Squirrel **350.00**
Swan **295.00**
Valentine **325.00**
Wildflower **35.00**
Wreath and Shell, vaseline . . **525.00**
X-Ray, green **140.00**

Water set

Basketweave, pitcher, six goblets, 12" d scenic tray, amber . . **125.00**
Button Arches, 10" h tankard pitcher, four tumblers, ruby stained, finely engraved foliage and "To Bert and Grace," chip on one tumbler **275.00**
Croesus. 11-1/2" h pitcher, four 3-3/4" h tumblers, green, gilt dec, flake on pitcher, wear to gilt **140.00**
Delaware, tankard, six tumblers, green, gold trim **375.00**
Heart in Sand, 8-3/4" h pitcher, four 4-1/8" h tumblers, ruby stained, New Martinsville **3,200.00**
Hexagon Block, tankard, two tumblers, etched, amber stain **225.00**
Inverted Thistle, green, gold trim, seven pcs **280.00**
Peach, 8-1/2" h pitcher, two 4" h tumblers, green, gilt dec, wear to gilt **130.00**
Shell and Jewel, pitcher, eight tumblers **145.00**
Two Panel, blue **345.00**

Banded Portland water set, maiden's blush, pitcher and six tumblers, **$375.** *Photo courtesy of Joy Luke Fine Art Brokers and Auctioneers.*

Water tray

Currier and Ives, bulky mule center **35.00**
Daisy and Button, blue, round, two tab handles, 12" d **90.00**
Daisy and Button with Thumbprint, yellow stain **95.00**
Hummingbird, amber **95.00**
Polar Bear, frosted **300.00**

Whiskey

Argus, applied handle **75.00**
Bellflower, single vine, fine ribbed, 3-1/2" h **260.00**
Bull's Eye **85.00**
Comet, flint, 3" h **180.00**
Diamond Point, flint, applied handle **85.00**
Diamond Thumbprint, flint, 3" h **130.00**
Excelsior **95.00**
Fine Rib, flint, handle, 3" h . . . **300.00**
Horn of Plenty, flint **180.00**
Ribbed Ivy, flint, handle, 2-3/4" h **230.00**

Wine

Ashburton, flint **40.00**
Banded Portland, gold trim . . . **42.00**
Barberry **40.00**
Beaded Band **32.00**
Beaded Tulip **25.00**
Bird and Strawberry **40.00**
Bleeding Heart **225.00**
Canadian **42.00**
Candlewick **12.00**
Cathedral, amber **40.00**
Co-op, Royal **15.00**
Cupid and Venus **70.00**
Currier and Ives, blue **55.00**
Cut Log **20.00**
Daisy and Button with Crossbar, amber, blue, or vaseline **25.00**
Dakota, etched **15.00**
Diamond Quilted, blue **25.00**

Diamond Ridge. **25.00**
Diamond Thumbprint, flint . . **150.00**
Galloway. **45.00**
Halley's Comet **15.00**
Hartley **22.00**
Heart with Thumbprint **42.50**
Horn of Plenty, flint **140.00**
Hourglass **15.00**
Jacob's Ladder. **24.00**
King's Crown, yellow stain . . . **15.00**
Lady Hamilton. **25.00**
Lattice and Oval Panels, flint . **35.00**
Magnet and Grape, Frosted Leaf, flint **195.00**
Mascotte. **25.00**
Massachusetts **35.00**
Melrose. **15.00**
Minnesota. **15.00**
Mirror and Fan **24.00**
Morning Glory, flint **200.00**
Nailhead **15.00**
New England Pineapple, flint . **90.00**
Paisley **20.00**
Paneled Nightshade. **35.00**
Popcorn **35.00**
Portland, gold trim **30.00**
Primrose, green **40.00**
Prize, ruby. **225.00**
Rose Point Band. **20.00**
Spirea Band, blue. **20.00**
S-Repeat, blue **50.00**
Teardrop and Thumbprint, etched **25.00**
The States. **18.00**
Three Face **190.00**
Triple Triangle, ruby stained . . **25.00**
Two Panel, green **35.00**
US Coin. **225.00**
Wisconsin **75.00**
Wyoming. **85.00**

Wine decanter, S-Repeat, blue **120.00**

Wine set, Daisy and Button with Narcissus, decanter, tray, six wines **145.00**

PEACHBLOW

History: Peachblow, an art glass that derives its name from a fine Chinese-glazed porcelain, resembles a peach or crushed strawberries in color. Three American glass manufacturers and two English firms produced peachblow glass in the late 1880s. A fourth American company resumed the process in the 1950s. The glass from each firm has its own identifying characteristics.

Hobbs, Brockunier & Co., Wheeling peachblow: Opalescent glass, plated or cased with a transparent amber glass; shading from yellow at the base to a deep red at top; glossy or satin finish.

Mt. Washington "Peach Blow": A homogeneous glass, shading from a pale gray-blue to a soft rose color; some pieces enhanced with glass appliqués, enameling, and gilding.

New England Glass Works, New England peachblow (advertised as Wild Rose, but called Peach Blow at the plant): Translucent, shading from rose to white; acid or glossy finish; some pieces enameled and gilded.

Thomas Webb & Sons and Stevens and Williams (English firms): Peachblow-style cased art glass, shading from yellow to red; some pieces with cameo-type relief designs. Occasionally found with cameo-type designs in relief.

Gunderson Glass Co.: Produced peachblow-type art glass to order during the 1950s; shades from an opaque faint tint of pink, which is almost white, to a deep rose.

Marks: Pieces made in England are marked "Peach Blow" or "Peach Bloom."

References: Sean and Johanna S. Billings, *Peachblow Glass, Collector's Identification & Price Guide,* Krause Publications, 2000; Kyle Husfloen, *Antique Trader's American & European Decorative and Art Glass Price Guide,* 2nd ed., Krause Publications, 2000.

Museums: Huntington Museum of Art, Huntington, WV; New Bedford Glass Museum, New Bedford, MA; Oglebay Institute Glass Museum; The Corning Museum of Glass, Corning, NY; The Toledo Museum of Art, Toledo, OH.

Gundersen-Pairpoint

Butter dish, cov, 9" d, 5" h, satin finish, scalloped edge, applied finial, c1960 . . . . **415.00**

Candlesticks, pr **275.00**

Compote, 5" h, Pairpoint **250.00**

Creamer and sugar, 3-1/2" h, 5-3/4" d, acid finish, deep pink, vertical stripes, applied reeded handles. **475.00**

Cruet, 8" h, 3-1/2" w, matte finish, ribbed shell handle, matching stopper with good color. **875.00**

Cup and saucer. **275.00**

Decanter, 10" h, 5" w, Pilgrim Canteen form, acid finish, deep raspberry to white, applied peachblow ribbed handle, deep raspberry stopper **950.00**

Goblet, 7-1/4" h, 4" d top, glossy finish, deep color, applied Burmese glass base **285.00**

Hat, 3-1/4" h, satin finish, Diamond Quilted pattern **150.00**

Jug, 4-1/2" h, 4" w, bulbous, applied loop handle, acid finish **450.00**

Mug, satin finish, dec, orig paper label, c1970 . . . . **125.00**

Pitcher

5-1/2" h, Hobnail, matte finish, white with hint of pink on int., orig label **550.00**

6-1/4" h, 3-1/2" w, Camellia, peachblow body, pedestal, applied clear handle, waffle pontil, orig silver label. **950.00**

Plate, 8" d, luncheon, deep raspberry to pale pink, matte finish **375.00**

Punch cup, acid finish **275.00**

Tumbler, 3-3/4" h, matte finish . **275.00**

Urn, 8-1/2" h, 4-1/2" w, two applied "M" handles, sq cut base, matte finish **550.00**

Vase

4-1/4" h, 3" d, acid finish. . . . **225.00**
5" h, 6" w, ruffled top, pinched-in base **525.00**
9" h, 3-1/4" w, Tappan, acid finish **425.00**
10-1/4" h, tapered, tricorner rim **120.00**

Wine glass, 5" h, glossy finish . **175.00**

Mount Washington

Biscuit jar, cov, 7-1/4" h, satin finish, enameled and jeweled dec, sgd **700.00**

Bride's basket, 11" d, pink ext., peachblow int., gold stylized flowers dec, ornate silver plated holder with aquatic motif, marked "Pairpoint Mfg Co" **875.00**

Bride's bowl, 9-7/8" d, 3" h, 3-3/4" base, glossy finish, deep pink shading to pale **250.00**

Condiment set, 3" h salt and pepper shakers, mustard pot, acid finish, ribbed barrel form, enameled flub and white forget-met-nots, delicate green leaves and tracery, orig silver plated tops, replated silver plated stand marked "Pairpoint Mfg Co New Bedford Mass 705" **3,850.00**

Bowl, 3" x 4", shading from deep rose to bluish-white, mother of pearl satin int. **150.00**

Cream pitcher, 3-1/4" h, paper-thin walls, apple blossom pink to blue/gray base, tiny pointed spout, applied blue-gray handle. **3,250.00**

Perfume bottle, 5" h, satin finish, enameled sprays of dainty white flowers, orig matching faceted cut stopper **650.00**

Pitcher, 6-7/8" h, bulbous, sq handle **3,750.00**

Tumbler, satin finish, band of apple blossom pink shades to soft blue-gray **1,500.00**

Vase

7" h, trumpet, fold-over rim, satin finish. **800.00**
8" h, slender neck, bulbous body, satin finish **1,400.00**
8-1/4" h, lily form, satin finish **1,850.00**

New England Glass Works, tumbler, satin finish, deep raspberry red shading to creamy yellow to creamy white, delicate thin walls, 3-3/4" h, **$450.** *Photo courtesy of Clarence and Betty Maier.*

New England

Bowl

- 5-1/2" d, 3" h, 10-ruffled top, deep raspberry shading to creamy white **750.00**
- 6" d, 3" h, acid finish, soft pink shading to off-white base, ruffled rim, polished pontil **325.00**

Celery vase

- 7" h, 4" w, Hobnail, satin finish, pale creamy white to rose pink . . **475.00**
- 7" h, 4" w, square top, deep raspberry with purple highlights shading to white **785.00**

Creamer and sugar, 2-3/4" h creamer, 3-1/4" h open sugar, satin finish, ribbed, applied white handles **500.00**

Cruet, 6-3/4" h, 4" d at base, petticoat form, applied white handle and stopper, three lip top, acid finish **1,950.00**

Darner **175.00**

Finger bowl, 5-1/4" d, 2-1/2" h, ruffled rim. **385.00**

Pear, 4-1/4" h, hollow, free blown, crooked stem, pink to white coloring **300.00**

Pitcher

- 6-1/4" h, satin finish, 10-crimp top, applied white handle. . . . **1,200.00**
- 6-3/4" h, 7-1/2" w, 3-1/4" w at top, bulbous, sq top, applied frosted handle, 10 rows of hobs . . . **550.00**

Punch cup, satin finish, deep rose shading to white, applied white acid finished handle. **450.00**

Rose bowl, 4" d, 4" h, glossy finish, deep color **495.00**

Salt shaker, 3-3/4" h, acid finish, deep color, orig silver plated top. **550.00**

Spooner, 4-1/2" h, scalloped rim, acid finish, Wild Rose. **200.00**

Toothpick holder, 5" h, 2-3/8" h peachblow holder, shiny finish, silver plated Kale Greenaway holder, little girl holding peachblow toothpick holder in outstretched arms, holder sgd "James W. Tufts Warranted Quadruple Plate 3405," incised "XM 89," and "Mother 7 10" **1,075.00**

Tumbler

- 3-3/4" h, shiny finish, deep color upper third, middle fading to creamy white bottom, thin walls **450.00**
- 3-3/4" h, velvety satin finish, deep raspberry red extends 2/3 down, faces to 1/2" pure white band **400.00**

Vase

- 3-1/4" h, 2-1/2" d, bulbous bottom, ring around neck, flaring top, matte finish. **550.00**
- 5-1/2" h, satin finish, bulbous **485.00**
- 6-1/2" h, 3" w at top, lily, glossy finish, deep pink shading to white **650.00**
- 6-5/8" h, 2-7/8" d, lily, tricorner rim, satin finish **395.00**
- 7" h, lily, satin finish, wafer base **945.00**
- 8-3/4" h, 4" w, bulbous stick, deep raspberry to white, matte finish **950.00**
- 9-1/2" h, trumpet, deep rose tricorn rim **375.00**
- 10-1/2" h, 5" w at base, bulbous, tapering neck, cup top, deep color, orig glossy finish **1,250.00**
- 10-1/2" h, 5" w at base, bulbous gourd shape, deep raspberry with fuchsia highlights to white, coloring extends two-thirds way down, four dimpled sides. **1,450.00**
- 15-1/2" h, 6" w at top, lily, deep raspberry pink to white . . **1,450.00**

New Martinsville

Bowl, 5" d, scalloped rim, yellow-caramel shading to peach to beige **65.00**

Bride's bowl, 11" d, wavy ruffled rim, cased int. **125.00**

Dish, 5" d, 2-1/2" h, wavy ruffled rim **100.00**

Webb

Biscuit jar, cov, 6" h, 4-1/2" d, acid finish, heavy gold prunus blossoms, pine needles and butterfly dec, rich creamy white lining, silver plated rim, lid, and handle. **950.00**

Celery vase, 6-1/2" h, acid finish **220.00**

Cologne, 5" h, bulbous, raised gold floral branches, silver hallmarked dome top **900.00**

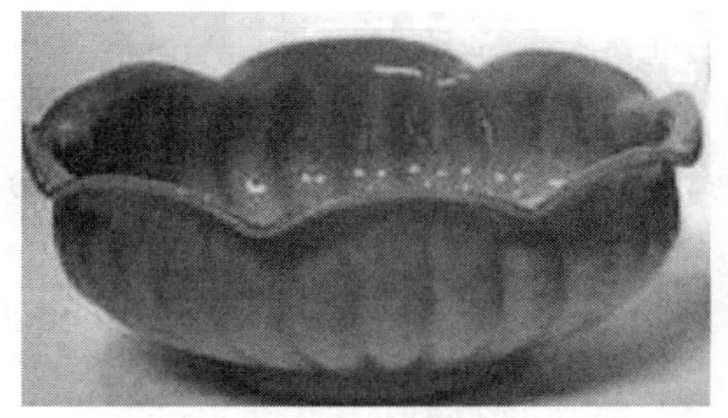

New Martinsville, peachblow exterior, sunglow (iridescent yellow) interior, 28 molded-in ribs, crimped edge, 5" d, 2" h, **$165.** *Photo courtesy of Clarence and Betty Maier.*

Creamer, satin finish, coralene dec, rolled rim, flat base. **650.00**

Finger bowl, 4-1/2" d, cased. . . **195.00**

Mustard jar, 2-1/2" h, satin finish, hand painted prunus dec, gold trim . . **425.00**

Plate, 8-1/4" d, glossy finish, crimped edge, gold enameled butterfly and blossoming prunus branches . . **450.00**

Punch cup, glossy finish, creamy white lining. **150.00**

Scent bottle, 3-7/8" h, 2-3/4" d, satin finish, dainty blue, white, and yellow enameled flowers, green leaves, monarch butterfly, creamy white lining, hallmarked sterling silver top . . . **725.00**

Vase

- 8-3/4" h, slightly flared rim, double bulbed vase, rich red shading to pink-white at base, gilt enamel dec of leafy branches, umbrels, and wasp alighting, base sgd "520/1 L 103," attributed to Thomas Webb & Sons or Stevens & Williams. **230.00**
- 10" h, shaded pink, white opal casing, enameled gold pendant blossoming branches **300.00**
- 11-1/4" h, 6-1/2" d, pine needles, boughs, and trailing prunus blossoms, buds, and branches, two butterflies in flight, deep cherry red shading to pink-peach, creamy white lining, gold trim at top and base, dec by Jules Barbe. . **750.00**
- 12-1/4" h, 4-1/4" d base, coral shades to rose then to light pink, white opaque lining, pink, mauve, and gilt flowers and leaves, gilt around base, polished pontil **785.00**

Wheeling

Bowl, 3-3/4" d, satin finish, ground rim **190.00**

Carafe, glossy finish **725.00**

Cream pitcher, 4" h, glossy finish, sq top, name etched on shoulder . . **700.00**

Cruet

6-1/4" h, ball shaped, mahogany neck and spout, fuchsia shoulders, cream base, Hobbs, Brockunier **1,950.00**

7-3/8" h, Catalog #312 Oil, deep mahogany shading to amber, creamy lining, applied dark amber reeded handle, faceted amber stopper Hobbs, Brockunier **1,600.00**

Decanter, 9-1/8" h, satin finish, applied amber twisted handle, orig stopper **1,250.00**

Ewer, 6-3/4" h, 4" w, glossy finish, duck bill top, applied amber loop handle **3,500.00**

Jardinière, 6-1/8" h, bulbous form, Hobbs, Brochure, top rim ground evenly **600.00**

Lamp, 11" h, base of glossy Morgan vase affixed to P & A Hornet fluid lamp fittings, glass chimney........ **500.00**

Mustard, silver plated cov and handle **475.00**

Pear

4-3/4" w, 3" w base, hollow, blown, matte finish, bright red and yellow, white lining, very tip of stem gone **900.00**

5-1/2" h, 3" w base, hollow, blown, glossy finish, tip of stem gone **800.00**

Punch cup, 2-1/2" h, Hobbs, Brockunier **535.00**

Salt and pepper shakers, pr, 2-3/4" h, squatty round form, extra deep fuchsia color shading to amber, orig pewter caps.................... **690.00**

Sugar shaker, 5-1/2" h, satin finish, orig metal top **700.00**

Toothpick holder, 2-3/4" h, 2-1/2" d, bulbous, deep color, glossy finish, two external cracks on outer layer of glass **70.00**

Tumbler, 3-1/2" h, shiny finish, deep colored upper third shades to creamy base.................... **385.00**

Vase

9-1/2" h, flared and ruffled rim, applied amber edge above oval body, molded drapery design, Hobbs Brockunier **1,200.00**

13" h, acid finish **975.00**

Peking Glass

History: Peking glass is a type of cameo glass of Chinese origin. Its production began in the 1700s and continued well into the 19th century. The background color of Peking glass may be a delicate shade of yellow, green, or white. One style of white background is so transparent that it often is referred to as the "snowflake" ground. The overlay colors include a rich garnet red, deep blue, and emerald green.

Bead necklace, 22-1/2" l, jade green, gold wash and bead flower clasp, knotted between each bead **45.00**

Bottle, 10" h, opaque yellow ground, carved birds in flight and orchid plants **425.00**

Bowl

5-3/4" d, rounded form, ext. with cranes and lotus plants, green overlay, white ground **90.00**

6-1/8" d, floral shaped rim, ext. with birds among lotus, lotus leaf form foot, red overly, white ground **1,150.00**

7" d, raised lotus petals on ext., opaque blue with white int., 19th C **375.00**

7" d, rounded form, shaped rim, ext. with flowering lotus continuing to a lotus leaf-form foot rim, green overlay, white ground **575.00**

Candlestick, cock's foot **230.00**

Cup, 2-1/2" h, deep form, gently flaring rim, ring foot, continual band of overlapping dragons, cloud collar border, lappet border, red overlay, Snowflake................ **2,185.00**

Dish, 11-3/4" l, flattened round form, bright yellow, 19th C.......... **850.00**

Ginger jar, cov, 9-1/4" h, three different scenes, cinnabar red over white **750.00**

Rose jar, cov, 7-1/2" h, 8" d, emerald green over flint white ground, carved bird on hawthorne tree, matching carved cover **325.00**

Snuff bottle

2" h, colorless ground, Imperial yellow exterior, carved in shape of three circles with windows . **150.00**

2" h, colorless ground, red-purple overlay carved as lotus flower, silver stopper with red stones **150.00**

2-1/2" h, colorless ground, red overlay carved as spider and spider web **175.00**

2-1/2" h, opaque white ground, olive green overlay of cows under tree on one side, carved rooster on obverse **150.00**

2-1/2" h, opaque white ground, red overlay carved fish and aquatic plants.................. **175.00**

2-3/4" h, colorless ground, red overlay carved with Tao Tieh design **175.00**

2-3/4" h, yellow, enameled fruit, jade stopper and spoon....... **250.00**

2-3/4" h, 1-1/4" w, amber, stone cap **225.00**

3" h, colorless ground, blue overlay caved as hydra, blue bamboo design carved on sides ... **175.00**

4" h, colorless, carved monkey **300.00**

4-1/2" h, opaque white ground, green overlay, carved ivory cap and attached spoon...... **400.00**

Vase

7" h, high shouldered form, ducks swimming among tall lotus plants, green overlay, white ground, pr **500.00**

7-1/2" h, ovoid, elongated neck, red overlay, Snowflake pattern, body with two dragons and two phoenix, neck with dragon and phoenix, Qianlong period, pr **4,600.00**

8" h, high shoulder form, red overlay, white ground, female figures in garden, 18th C, pr **1,840.00**

8-3/4" h, hand carved, green over white lotus design, small rim chip **900.00**

9" h, opaque white ground, Chinese red cameo, deep cut leaves and berries, baluster, c1900 ... **575.00**

9-1/4" h, ovoid, opaque raised yellow flowers, translucent yellow ground, 19th C................ **525.00**

10" h, baluster, opaque white ground, carved blue overlay, florals and foliate, price for pr.... **700.00**

Vase, opaque white ground, hand-carved red floral pattern, 8" h, **$425.**

10" h, baluster, opaque white ground, carved red overlay, goldfish and water lily dec, pr **700.00**

11-1/2" h, hand carved cobalt blue florals and butterflies, white satin ground, Chinese, 19th C. **1,100.00**

12" h, baluster, opaque white ground, yellow overlay cut with exotic fish, pond, lilies, pads, and aquatic grasses, pr **700.00**

Perfume, Cologne, and Scent Bottles

History: The second half of the 19th century was the golden age for decorative bottles made to hold scents. These bottles were made in a variety of shapes and sizes.

An atomizer is a perfume bottle with a spray mechanism. Cologne bottles usually are larger and have stoppers, which also may be used as applicators. A perfume bottle has a stopper that often is elongated and designed to be an applicator.

Scent bottles are small bottles used to hold a scent or smelling salts. A vinaigrette is an ornamental box or bottle that has a perforated top and is used to hold aromatic vinegar or smelling salts. Fashionable women of the late 18th and 19th centuries carried them in purses or slipped them into gloves in case of a sudden fainting spell.

References: Roselyn Gerson, *The Estée Lauder Solid Perfume Compact Collection, 1967 to 2001,* Collector Books, 2001; Jacquelyne Jones-North, *Commercial Perfume Bottles,* 3rd, Schiffer Publishing, 1996; —, *Perfume, Cologne and Scent Bottles,* 3rd ed., Schiffer Publishing, 1999; Jacquelyne Y. Jones-North, et. al., *Czechoslovakian Perfume Bottles and Boudoir Accessories, Revised Ed.,* Antique Publications, 1999; L-W Book Sales, *Diamond I Perfume Bottles Price Guide and other Drugstore Wares,* L-W Book Sales, 2000; Monsen and Baer, *A Century of Perfume: The Perfumes of François Coty,* published by authors, 2000; —, *Beauty of Perfume,* published by authors (Box 529, Vienna, VA 22183), 1996; —, *Legacies of Perfume,* published by authors, 1997; —, *Memories of Perfume,* published by authors, 1998.

Periodicals and Internet Resources: *Art & Fragrances Perfume Presentation,* FDR Station, P.O. Box 5200, New York, NY 10150-5200; *Montage,* http://www.cicat.com/montage; *Passion for Perfume,* http://passionforperfume.com.

Collectors' Clubs: International Perfume Bottle Assoc., 3314 Shamrock Rd, Tampa, FL 33629, http://www.perfumebottles.org; Miniature Perfume Bottle Collectors, 28227 Paseo El Siena, Laguna Niguel, CA 92677; Parfum Plus Collections, 1590 Louis-Carrier Ste 502, Montreal Quebec H4N 2Z1 Canada.

Lalique, Clairfontaine, clear and frosted glass, c1950-80, 5" h, price for pair, **$525.** *Photo courtesy of David Rago Auctions.*

Atomizer

3" h, opaque black ground, gold Art Deco dec.................. **75.00**

4-1/2" h, Moser, sapphire blue, gold florals, leaves, and swirls, melon ribbed body, orig gold top and bulb... **275.00**

6-1/4" h, Cambridge, stippled gold, opaque jade, orig silk lined box **140.00**

7" h, Carder Steuben, gold aurene tapered body, gilt metal DeVilbiss fittings, orig rubber bulb intact, but hardened.................. **865.00**

7-3/4" h, Galle, cameo, purple bleeding hearts, frosted ground, orig hardware, sgd "Galle" in cameo **925.00**

8" h, Czechoslovakian, cobalt blue, large enameled and faceted crystal stopper, c1930 .... **80.00**

8" h, Galle, cameo, lavender flowers and foliage, shaded yellow and frosted ground.................. **1,250.00**

9-1/2" h, 3" w, green cut to clear overlay, floral and panel cutting, fancy metal holder, emerald and pearl jewel accents, attributed to Czechoslovakia **400.00**

10" h, DeVilbiss, dark amethyst, goldstone spider-web dec, bulb missing **90.00**

10" h, faceted citron green transparent bottle suspended from conforming angular chromed metal holder, Art-Deco style, some int. stains, minor metal scratches............. **700.00**

12" h, deep amethyst cameo cut blackberries and leaves, blue ground, sgd "Richard" **490.00**

Cologne

3-1/8" h, apple green, pressed base, cut stopper **150.00**

3-5/8" h, C & B, irregular six-sided form, bulbous neck, sapphire blue, tooled mouth, pontil scar, attributed to America, 1840-60 .... **140.00**

4" h, satin, heat reactive rose-red shaded to green, cased to opal glass int., threaded silver rim and hammered screw-on cap, imp "Gorham Sterling" **345.00**

4-1/2" h, vaseline, attributed to New England Glass Co., flint, orig stopper **225.00**

4-3/4" h, figural, elephant with rich trappings, colorless, tooled flared mouth, pontil scar, America, 1840-60 .... **500.00**

5" h, diamond form, full figured Indians on two sides, oval label panels on other two sides, aquamarine, inward rolled mouth, pontil scar, America, 1840-60 .... **90.00**

5-1/2" h, flat corseted form, palmette, scrolled acanthus, and cross hatching, brilliant sapphire blue, inward rolled mouth, pontil scar, America, 1840-60 .... **1,800.00**

5-1/2" h, pattern molded, 16 vertical ribs, bright sapphire blue, inward rolled mouth, faint pontil scar, Midwest America, 1820-60............ **240.00**

5-7/8" h, Baccarat, colorless, panel cut, matching stopper............. **75.00**

6" h, 4" d, blown molded, opaque blue, petal-form rim, paneled octagonal neck, round body with white and gold enamel scrolling leaf and vine designs, shaped faceted hexagonal stopper, America, second half 19th C, shedding surface.................... **320.00**

6-1/4" h, front panel with bunch of grapes with leaves, back panel with fancy leaf designs, two sides panels are fluted, aquamarine, tooled flared mouth, pontil scar, America, 1840-60, old label on side panel with medication adv **375.00**

6-1/2" h, domed cylindrical bottle, molded colorless glass, dec with scales over repeating rows of bees, round stopper, marked in mold "Guerlain Bottle, Made in France" **110.00**

7" h, cut glass, cranberry cut to colorless, cane cut, matching stopper **250.00**

7" h, 5" d, paperweight, double overlay, crimson red over white over colorless squatty bottle, five oval facet windows reveal concentric millefiore cane int., matching stopper............ **460.00**

7-1/4" h, Tiffany Favrile, irid gold, double bulbed amber body, eight applied prunts trailing threads to base, matching gold irid stopper, inscribed

"L. C. T. Q4736," some int. stain 2,415.00

7-3/4" h, blown molded, deep blue-green, Elongated Loop Pattern, hexagonal paneled neck and body with loop designs, faceted stopper, attributed to New England, c1840-70, rim chip and crack 460.00

8-1/8" h, clambroth, enameled portrait medallion of young lady, gilt highlights, orig stopper 90.00

9" h, domed cylindrical bottle, molded colorless glass, dec with scales over repeating rows of bees, round stopper, paper label, marked in mold "Guerlain Paris," minor staining to label .. 100.00

11" h, art glass, transparent green bottle, delicate floral design, colorless pedestal foot, faceted teardrop stopper 175.00

11-1/2" h, blue cut to opalescent, swirls on lower section, elongated ovals with panels on upper section, two applied faceted neck rings, fitted in ormolu and brass cathedral-style stand, stopper missing, chip on base 90.00

Perfume

2" h, 1-1/2" d, German, green glass, colored enamel coat of arms, fine enamel trim on body and matching green stopper 60.00

2-3/8" h, Venetian, globular body, Lion of Venice portrait cane on surface of opaque yellow and silver glass, crowned with ornate cap dec with flowers, no stopper 335.00

2-1/2" l, dark cobalt blue, sheared top, cork closure, c1890........... 75.00

3" h, paperweight, Kaziun, stopper with spider lily on cobalt and aventurine ground, colorless glass bottle, base with matching spider lily dec, gold K beneath each lily 750.00

3-9/16" h, cherub sulfide surrounded by ornate faceting on all sides, gilded copper cap, glass stopper 365.00

3-11/16" h, Clichy, ext. dec with alternating blue and white swirled bands, stopper and base dec with 16K gold chased with delicate patterns, base marked "D. J.," fitted leather carrying case............... 990.00

4-1/2" h, Steuben, amber, melon ribbed, teardrop stopper, long dauber . 265.00

4-3/4" h, Steuben, Verre de Soie, jade green 310.00

5" h, paperweight type, spherical bottle, teardrop stopper, each with multi-petaled yellow rose blossom, Francis Whittemore "W" canes . 450.00

Perfume bottle, silver deposit, bulbous, floral and flowing leaf motif, 3-3/8" h, **$175.**

5" h, Quezal, flattened teardrop form, irid multicolored ground, foliate mounts, bulbous stopper, c1915 .... 625.00

5-1/2" h, Rene Lalique, Sirenes, frosted mermaids with traces of gray patina, molded signature on base, no cover 250.00

6-3/8" h, Baccarat, molded and frosted, acid stamped "Baccarat/France," mid-20th C 650.00

6" l, satin, Diamond Quilted MOP, shading yellow to white, lay down horn type...................... 415.00

6-1/2" h, American Brilliant Period Cut Glass, Button and Star pattern, rayed base, faceted stopper 125.00

6-1/2" h, 8" w, display, Tresor Lancome, faceted sq stopper set in black ring neck, broad vessel of colorless glass, tapering steps to black base, enamel trademark, manufacturer's label on base, wear to enamel......... 115.00

7-1/2" h, blue, enamel and gilt dec, orig blue steeple stopper, wear to dec 80.00

7-5/8" h, colorless, encased in heavy gold color metal dec, price for pr 150.00

9-1/4" h, cameo, bleeding hearts and vine, midnight blue overlay, mustard ground, sgd "Richard" in cameo . 800.00

Scent

1-5/8" h, white, red, and blue speckling 95.00

2" h, blue-green, waisted, paneled, pewter screw cap............ 90.00

2-1/4" h, cobalt blue, spiraling ribs 75.00

2-1/4" h, teardrop form, ruby, enameled, gilt metal mounting, Victorian, late 19th C, stopper missing........ 80.00

Scent, cylindrical, flared base, frosted and cut glass, light to dark blue, gold plated cap and chain, orig dauber, 2-3/4" l, **$150.**

2-1/2" h, Early American glass, amethyst, teardrop shape, emb sunburst design 225.00

2-1/2" h, 1-1/4" d, Frances Whittemore, paperweight type, white rose with four green leaves, sgd underneath with black on yellow "W" signature cane, white swirl stopper 115.00

2-3/4" h, teardrop form, blue, enameled, gilt metal mounting, Victorian, late 19th C, stopper missing 80.00

2-7/8" h, Early American glass, teardrop form, 19 vertical ribs, citron, sheared mouth, pontil scar, attributed to America, 1840-60, light overall int. haze 230.00

3" h, Early American glass, teardrop form, pattern molded, ribbed and swirled to the right, 15 ribs, colorless, sheared mouth, pontil scar 300.00

3" h, Early American glass, teardrop form, 25 swirled ribs, emerald green, sheared mouth, pontil scar, c1840-60, some light int. residue........ 100.00

3-1/4" h, double overlay, pink over white, early 20th C, cap and stopper missing 100.00

3-1/2" h, double overlay, cobalt blue over white, early 20th C, cap and stopper missing............. 100.00

3-3/4" h, satin, Peacock Eye, MOP, bridal white, orig glass stopper, push-on silver plated lid with monogram "C" 435.00

4" d, satin, bridal white, 24 white vertical stripes, 12 silk ribbons alternating with 12 muted satin ribbons, sterling silver flip top cap, collar stamped "CS, FS, STd, SILr," engraved name 400.00

4-1/8" h, Early American, blown, colorless, cranberry and white stripes, white and gold metallic twist **95.00**

4-1/4" h, ruby, faceted sides, double silver mounts with repousse molded top, early 20th C............. **175.00**

4-1/2" h, white overlay, ruby glass body, silver mount, early 20th C...... **185.00**

44-3/4" h, cobalt blue, faceted sides, double silver mounts with repousse molded top, early 20th C **175.00**

5-1/2 h, double, cobalt blue, faceted cylindrical sides, silver mounted repousse tops............... **225.00**

5-1/2" h, four triangular scenes encased in trelliswork banding, dec gilt metal foliate mounts, cut glass stoppers, French, early 20th C.......... **115.00**

Vinaigrette

2-1/4" x 1", cranberry, rect, allover cutting, enameled tiny pink roses, green leaves, gold dec, hinged lid, stopper, finger chain................. **185.00**

3-7/8" l, cut glass, cobalt blue, yellow flashing, SS overlay, emb SS cap **125.00**

PHOENIX GLASS

History: Phoenix Glass Company, Beaver, Pennsylvania, was established in 1880. Known primarily for commercial glassware, the firm also produced a molded, sculptured, cameo-type line in 1932, when 45 to 50 molds from the Consolidated Glass Company were moved to Phoenix and used until early 1936.

The earliest art glass production at Phoenix was called the "Reuben Line." These items were made with an oval paper label. One key to identifying Phoenix's Reuben Line is to watch for solid color finishes in light blue, dark blue, green, white, and yellow. Another popular Phoenix line was its Sculptured Art Ware. Most of the designs are credited to Kenneth Haley. These early items in this line were marked with silver paper labels. Later items featured a gold paper label. This line was produced on and off into the 1960s. The company is still in business, but does not have facilities to make hand-molded glass or the Sculptured Art Ware.

References: Tom and Neila Bredehoft, *Fifty Years of Collectible Glass, 1920-1970, Volume 1, Volume II*, Antique Trader Books, 2000; Jack D. Wilson, *Phoenix & Consolidated Art Glass*, Antique Publications, 1989.

Collectors' Club: Phoenix & Consolidated Glass Collectors Club, 41 River View Drive, Essex Junction, VT 05452, http://www.collectoron-line.com/club-PCGCC-wp.html.

Ashtray, Praying Mantis, white ground, relief molded insect, triangular... **65.00**

Basket, 4-1/2" h, pink ground, relief-molded dogwood dec..... **65.00**

Bowl

Bittersweet, relief molded, white ground, 9-1/2" d, 5-1/2" h.. **165.00**

Swallows, purple wash..... **150.00**

Bowl, cov, Lace Dew Drop, #811, 8-1/2" d, blue and white....... **275.00**

Candlesticks, pr, 3-1/4" h, blue ground, bubbles and swirls **65.00**

Canoe, 13-1/2" l, opal ground, sculptured blue lovebirds **325.00**

Centerpiece bowl, 14" d, opaque white ground, sculptured diving nudes, three colors.................... **250.00**

Charger, 18" d, blue ground, relief molded white dancing nudes .. **525.00**

Cigarette box, Phlox, white milk glass, cocoa brown **140.00**

Compote

8-1/2" d, butterscotch ground, relief molded dragonflies and water lilies dec.................... **85.00**

11" w, 6-1/2" h, Lacy Dewdrop, heavy caramel irid **115.00**

Dish, cov, 8-1/2" l, oval, amber ground, sculptured lotus blossoms and dragonflies................. **100.00**

Floor vase, 18" h, Bushberry, light green.................... **450.00**

Ginger jar, cov, frosted ground, bird finial...................... **80.00**

Lamp

Boudoir, Wild Rose, brown highlights, milk glass ground **150.00**

Ceiling, 15" sq, Flying Birds, heavy custard glass, metal mounts **1,500.00**

Table

22-1/2" h, 18" reverse painted dome shade, blue shading to yellow to blue, water landscape of Indian paddling canoe, rib molded round ftd base **2,500.00**

23" h, 16" d reverse painted shade, landscape with windmill, cottage, and barn, pale pink, yellow, and blue ground, green and brown landscape, minor edge flake **650.00**

26" h, 16" d, reverse painted shade, brilliant yellow and pink ground, large trees and rocks by stream, orig fancy metal Art Nouveau-style base, emb floral design **1,250.00**

Thistle, umbrella shape, blue and irid white, 25" h............ **400.00**

Lamp base, Cockatoos, blue, brown, custard **200.00**

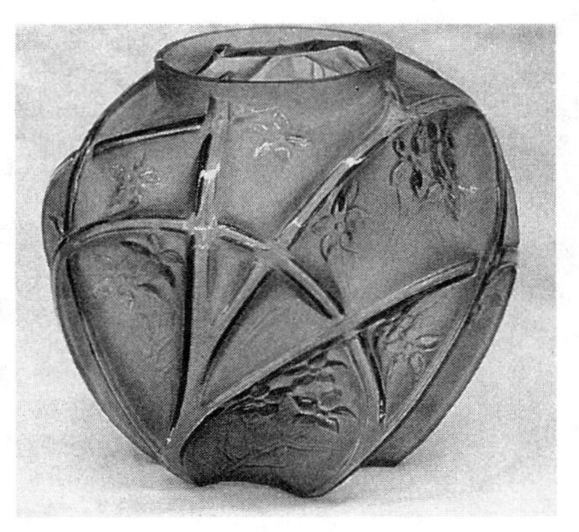

Vase, light blue, globular, Lalique-type pattern, 6-3/4" h, 7" w, **$165.**

Planter, 8-1/2" l, 3-1/4" h, white ground, relief molded green lion **95.00**

Plate, 8-1/2" d, frosted and clear ground, relief molded cherries... **60.00**

Powder box, cov, 7-1/4" d, pale lavender ground, sculptured white violets..................... **115.00**

Rose bowl, rose pink ground, relief molded starflowers and white bands **150.00**

Tumbler, Lace Dew Drop, blue and white, set of four............. **75.00**

Umbrella stand, 18" h, 9" w, Thistle, green wash................ **600.00**

Vase

Bellflower, burgundy pearlized **175.00**

Bittersweet, white stained crystal, Reuben line............. **150.00**

Bluebell, brown, 7" h **125.00**

Cameo, #345, sculptured, blue highlights, 6" h........... **130.00**

Cockatoos, aqua, bulbous, cream ground, beige branches, lavender berries, 9" h, 9" w **325.00**

Cosmos, cocoa brown, white milk glass **125.00**

Daisies, white milk glass, pale blue/gray painted ground, allover daisies, 9-1/2" h, 9" w **500.00**

Dragonfly, purple cased **350.00**

Fern, #261, burgundy, pearlized white ferns, 7-1/4" h....... **250.00**

Flying Geese

Cocoa brown, white milk glass **220.00**

Pillow form, white on brown **260.00**

Foxglove, rose, green, white, 10-1/2" h **125.00**

Freesia, fan, cocoa brown, white milk glass **125.00**

Gold Fish, pale green, peach colored fish, 9-1/4" h, 8" w.. **425.00**

Grasshoppers and reeds dec, clear and frosted, 8-3/4" h...... **125.00**
Jewel, powder blue, pearlized **80.00**
Line 700, blue crystal, 6-1/2" h **350.00**
Madonna, cocoa brown, white milk glass.................. **220.00**
Magnolia, white milk glass, 5" h **55.00**
Peony, yellow, green, custard, 9-1/2" h................ **160.00**
Philodendron, Wedgwood blue, white milk glass **160.00**
Regent, fan shape, white, violets dec, gold border **145.00**
Starflower, cocoa brown, white milk glass.................. **140.00**
Thistle, powder blue pearlized **520.00**
Wild Geese, #357, pearlized white birds, blue ground **225.00**
Wild Rose, blown out, pearlized dec, dark rose ground, orig label, 11" h **275.00**
Zodiac, raised white figures, peach colored ground, 10-1/2" h.. **700.00**

PICKLE CASTORS

History: A pickle castor is a table accessory used to serve pickles. It generally consists of a silver-plated frame fitted with a glass insert, matching silver-plated lid, and matching tongs. Pickle castors were very popular during the Victorian era. Inserts are found in pattern glass and colored art glass.

Amber

Daisy and Button pattern insert, silver-plated frame **370.00**
Inverted Thumbprint pattern insert, silver-plated frame **275.00**
Light, Panel with Diamond Point pattern insert, Central Glass Co., Meriden frame, leaves on legs, 9-1/2" h................ **220.00**
Zipper Variant pattern insert, Pairpoint frame with tongs, 11" h, several rim flakes **160.00**

Amberina, melon ribbed Inverted Thumbprint pattern insert, silver plated lid, ftd frame, lid, tongs, c1875-95 .... **720.00**

Blue

Currier and Ives pattern insert, orig silver-plated frame **195.00**
Daisy and Button pattern insert, silver-plated Wilcox frame, lid, and tongs **250.00**
Daisy and Button with V Ornament pattern insert, Meriden frame, lid, and tongs, 2-1/2" h, two rim flakes **210.00**

Cranberry insert with diamond quilted satin ground, enameled gild spider mums and leaves, ornate gold-toned frame with figural leaves holding jar in place, footed, gold-tone cover, marked "Rogers Smith," **$395.** *Photo courtesy of Joy Luke Fine Art Brokers and Auctioneers.*

Sprig pattern insert, ornate Reed and Barton frame, orig fork and fancy lid................ **200.00**

Colorless

Acid etched insert, floral dec with bird medallion, octagonal 11-3/4" h silver-plated frame, marked "Meriden Co. 182"........ **200.00**
Block-type pressed pattern insert, Rockford frame with tongs, 11-1/2" h **120.00**
Cupid and Venus patterned insert, silver-plated frame......... **295.00**
Engraved insert, dark Brittania frame, leafy gingerbread-type dec, orig tongs, matching finial on lid, c1865 .... **115.00**

Colorless and frosted, six panels with various detailed birds and cherubs on pressed insert, Meriden frame with tongs, classical busts around base of frame, 12" h, two rim flakes **300.00**

Cranberry

Barrel-shaped insert, multicolored enamel flowers, figural frame with acorns and dog's paw feet . **425.00**
Bulbous cranberry insert, Inverted Thumbprint pattern, fancy Tuffs frame with emb floral design, 12-3/4" h, internal crack near rim, frame appears to have been dropped, minor repair **475.00**
Inverted Fern and Daisy pattern insert, enamel multicolor floral dec, Reed and Barton frame, 13" h **250.00**
Inverted Thumbprint pattern insert
  Enameled blue and white florals, green leaves, shelf on frame dec with peacocks and other birds **325.00**
  Jar fitted with filigree sleeve, Middletown frame, lid, and tongs, 11" h.......... **850.00**
  Meriden frame, handles on sides, 7" h **275.00**
  Multicolored floral dec, Derby frame, 13" h.......... **500.00**
  White enamel and gilt floral dec, Middletown frame and tongs, 11" h **325.00**
Paneled Sprig pattern insert, Forbes frame, flat lid, 10" h **220.00**

Double, colorless inserts

Block and star type pattern, Wilcox frame, 10" h **100.00**
Emb fans and flowers, matching cov, fancy tulip finials, Viking head ftd oval handled frame, sgd "Meriden" **275.00**
Engraved band at top, Panel with Diamond Point pattern, Central Glass Co., ornate Rogers, Smith and Co. frame, cherub on handle **350.00**

Double, vaseline, pickle leaves and pieces, resilvered frame **800.00**

Emerald green, paneled insert with enameled florals, ornate silver plated frame..................... **245.00**

Mold blown, Wild Rose, frosted, Meriden frame and tongs, 12-1/2" h **350.00**

Mount Washington, 11" h, 6" d, decorated satin glass insert, blue enamel and painted yellow roses, green leaves, orange and yellow blossoms, silver-plated Rogers stand and tongs **875.00**

Opal insert, 11" h, shaded pale green to white ground, pink flowers, fancy silver-plated frame with tongs.. **500.00**

Opalescent

Coin Spot pattern insert, cranberry ground, polychrome enameled flowers, opalescent spots, silver

Double, pressed Block and Star patterned insert, Viking feet, Meriden, c1884, 10-1/2" h, 6-3/4" w, **$325.**

plated frame with lion and shield finial **225.00**

Daisy & Fern pattern insert, blue, emb DQ floral jar, resilvered frame **650.00**

Vertical white stripes pattern insert, colorless ground, resilvered angel frame, elephant's head and trunk feet **725.00**

Pigeon blood, Torquay pattern insert, silver plated frame and tongs . . . **400.00**

Pink, shiny pink Florette pattern insert, white int., bowed out frame **325.00**

Rubena

Inverted Thumbprint pattern insert, multicolored enameled floral dec, Rockford frame with fork, 10" h, flake on jar rim **325.00**

Rubena, frosted, Royal Ivy pattern insert, Webster frame, 9-1/2" h **250.00**

Satin

Cranberry, Optic Diamond and Inverted Thumbprint pattern insert, gold spider chrysanthemum dec, ftd Simpson Hall frame, ornate engraved cov, orig silvering . **625.00**

Yellow barrel shaped insert, flowers and butterfly dec, cherubs on front and back corners of frame, marked "Rogers" **750.00**

Sapphire blue, Beaded Dart pattern insert, fancy silver-plated Simpson, Hall & Miller stand **350.00**

Vaseline

Blown insert, fancy silver-plated Meriden frame, orig tongs, 12" h **375.00**

Daisy and Button variant insert, pattern band at top and bottom of jar, plain notched center band, Aurora frame, 11" h **200.00**

Pink Slag

History: True pink slag is found only in the molded Inverted Fan and Feather pattern. Quality pieces shade from pink at the top to white at the bottom.

Reproduction Alert: Recently, pieces of pink slag made from molds of the now-defunct Cambridge Glass Company have been found in the Inverted Strawberry and Inverted Thistle patterns. This is not considered true pink slag and brings only a fraction of the price of the Inverted Fan and Feather pieces.

Bowl

9" d, ftd **600.00**

10" d **750.00**

Butter dish, cov, 7-5/8" d, 7" h cov, 2-1/4" h base with four molded feet, fiery opalescent coloring **1,485.00**

Creamer **465.00**

Cruet, 6-1/2" h, orig stopper . . **1,300.00**

Jelly compote, 5" h, 4-1/2" d, scalloped top **375.00**

Marmalade jar, cov **875.00**

Pitcher, water **775.00**

Punch cup, 2-1/2" h, ftd **275.00**

Salt shaker **300.00**

Sauce dish, 4-1/4" d, 2-1/2" h, ball feet **200.00**

Spooner **350.00**

Sugar bowl, cov **550.00**

Toothpick holder **825.00**

Tumbler, 4-1/2" h. **475.00**

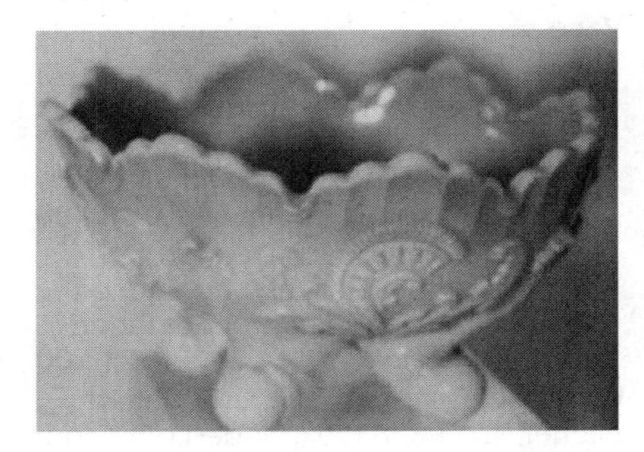

Sauce dish, footed, 4" d, 2-1/2" h, **$200.** *Photo courtesy of Clarence and Betty Maier.*

Pomona Glass

History: Pomona glass, produced only by the New England Glass Works and named for the Roman goddess of fruit and trees, was patented in 1885 by Joseph Locke. It is a delicate lead, blown art glass, which has a pale, soft beige ground and a top one-inch band of honey amber.

There are two distinct types of backgrounds. Making fine cuttings through a wax coating, followed by an acid bath, produced first ground, made only from late 1884 to June 1886. Rolling the piece in acid-resisting particles and acid etching made second ground. Second ground was made in Cambridge until 1888 and until the early 1900s in Toledo, where Libbey moved the firm after purchasing New England Glass works. Both methods produced a soft frosted appearance, but fine curlicue lines are more visible on first-ground pieces. Some pieces have designs that were etched and then stained with a color. The most familiar design is blue cornflowers.

Do not confuse Pomona with Midwestern Pomona, a pressed glass with a frosted body and amber band.

References: Joseph and Jane Locke, *Locke Art Glass*, Dover Publications, 1987; Kenneth Wilson, *American Glass 1760-1930*, 2 vols., Hudson Hills Press and The Toledo Museum of Art, 1994.

Bowl

4-1/2" d, 3" h, first ground, rich deep amber staining **275.00**

5" d, Rivulet pattern, second ground, fluted, blue stain **125.00**

5-1/4" d, Cornflower pattern, second ground, fluted **85.00**

10" d, Cornflower pattern, second ground. **450.00**

Butter dish, cov, 4-1/2" h, 8" d underplate, first ground, gold stained acacia leaf dec, reeded curlicue handle **1,275.00**

Celery vase, 6-1/8" h, 4-1/2" d, first ground, acacia leaf dec **550.00**

Champagne, 5" h, stemmed, second ground, amber staining **245.00**

Creamer

Cornflower pattern, second ground, blue flower, ruffled top, applied crystal crimped base, 3" h, 6" w **225.00**

Daisy and Butterfly pattern, second ground, applied colorless handle, three applied colorless feet **275.00**

Cruet, orig ball stopper

5-1/2" h, Blueberry pattern, first ground, gold leaves, applied colorless handle **300.00**

7-1/4" h, Cornflower pattern, first ground. **365.00**

7-1/4" h, Pansy and Butterfly pattern, second ground, unstained dec and handle, irid amber stopper . **500.00**

Finger bowl

Cornflower pattern, first ground 75.00

Diamond Quilted pattern, second ground, 4-3/4" d, 2" h 50.00

Ruffled rim, second ground, 5-1/2" d, 2-1/2" h 60.00

Goblet

5-1/8" h, 2-3/4" d rim, first ground, Diamond Quilted pattern . . 210.00

6" h, first ground, little amber stain remains. 115.00

Lemonade mug

5-3/4" h, Cornflower pattern, first ground, blue flowers. 295.00

5-3/4" h, Optic Diamond Quilted pattern, first ground, irid, colorless handle and upper border. . 200.00

Mustard, 3-1/8" h, Flower and Pleat pattern, light stain, SP top 95.00

Nappy, 5-1/4" d, Cornflower pattern, first ground, blue flowers, applied handle 150.00

Pitcher

3" h, 6-1/2" d, ruffled rim, bowl form, tooled spout rim, etched first ground, blue floral dec band, gold leaves and border, applied handle 900.00

5-1/2" h, first ground, applied unstained handle, sq mouth. 235.00

6-1/4" h, Cornflower pattern, first ground 400.00

8-3/4" h, 4-1/2" w, acanthus leaf dec, first ground, deep amber stain 465.00

12" h, Diamond Quilted pattern, second ground, slightly tapering cylindrical body, amber stain at top and applied handle, polished pontil 200.00

Mustard, Flower and Pleat, washed color, silver-plated top, 3-1/8" h, **$95.**

Tumbler, first ground, Fern and Daisy, enameled decoration, **$175.**

Punch cup

Cornflower pattern, first ground, blue staining 145.00

Cornflower pattern, second ground 110.00

Inverted Thumbprint pattern, first ground, amber staining. 85.00

Rivulet pattern, second ground, amber stained rim. 185.00

Spooner, 4-3/4" h, 3" d rim, Inverted Thumbprint pattern, ruffled rim, applied scalloped foot, second ground . . 80.00

Tankard pitcher, 6-3/4" h, first ground, optic diamond quilted body, gold stain on clear glass handle and upper border 385.00

Tumbler

Cornflower pattern, second ground, diamond quilted body, excellent staining, 4" h 95.00

Cornflower pattern, second ground, diamond quilted body, honey amber stain top and bottom, rich blue stained flowers, 3-3/4" h, 2-5/8" d 145.00

Oak Leaf Band pattern, second ground. 100.00

Pansy and Butterfly pattern, first ground. 145.00

Vase

3" h, 6" w, fan, Cornflower pattern, first ground, blue stained flower dec and violet spray 250.00

5-3/8" h, 5-1/8" d, Diamond Quilted pattern, sq ruffled rim 60.00

6" h, first ground, rigaree around ruffled top and neck ring, etched waisted body, first ground, faded amber stain 215.00

Water set, 7-1/4" h Blueberry pattern, pitcher, six 3-3/4" h expanded diamond tumblers, etched second ground surface, iridized gold stain above and below, some wear to dec 550.00

Powder Jars

History: Ladies have been powdering their noses ever since the days of Cleopatra. As dressing tables evolved through the years, more elaborate containers to hold loose powder came into style. Today, collectors are enchanted with these colorful boxes. Many of the boxes had enough room to accommodate a soft puffy. One of the most popular types is the figural boxes created by Depression-era glass manufacturers.

Reference: Ellen Bercovici, Bobbie Zucher Bryson, Deborah Gillham, *Collectibles for the Kitchen, Bath & Beyond,* Krause Publications, 2001.

Art glass

3-1/2" d, 2-1/2" h, green, simple enamel and gilt dec 90.00

3-1/2" d, 3-1/2" h, cobalt blue, enameled lily dec 80.00

3-3/4" d, 3-1/4" h, green, white enamel and gilt dec, wear to gilt 70.00

4" d, 1-1/2" h, Lalique, frosted, three dancing nudes 590.00

4" d, 3-1/2" h, blue, white enamel dec on lid, three brass feet, wear to dec 70.00

5" d, 3-1/4" h, blue clambroth, white enamel dec, gilt and black accents on lid. 120.00

5" d, 3-3/4" h, cranberry, white enamel and gilt dec 130.00

5-1/2" d, 3-1/2" h, hinged top, squatty form, frosted colorless glass, enamel dec with polychrome medallions, gilt linear highlights, gilt metal mount, attributed to France, c1930. . . . 175.00

7" d, 3" h, Belleware, hinged top, opal glass, dec with vignette of a child picking roses, naturalistic tones, dark green ground, raised pink and gilt scrollwork and highlights, gilt metal mounts, satin liner in top, enameled "Belle Ware" on base, minor spotting to metal mount. 1,500.00

7-1/2" d, 4" h, C. F. Monroe, hinged top, ornate molded opal glass in sq format, dec with pink roses, olive green ground, gilt highlights, gilt-metal mount, black Nakara stamp on base, c1900, minor wear to gilt. 1,500.00

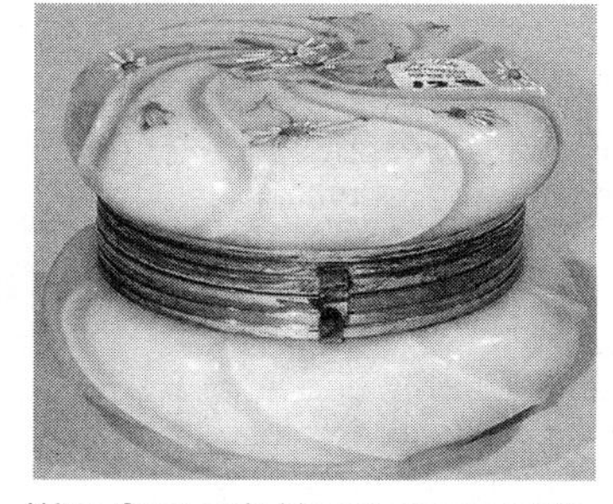

Wave Crest-style hinged, opaque white ground decorated with flowers, 5" d, 3" h, 5" d, **$185.** *Photo courtesy of Joy Luke Fine Art Brokers and Auctioneers.*

Figural, Depression-era

Annette, crystal **75.00**
Babs II, frosted pink. **165.00**
Bambi, crystal, Jeanette. **35.00**
Basset hound, frosted pink. . . . **165.00**
Carrie, black, painted flowers. . **355.00**
Court jester, frosted pink. **160.00**
Crinoline lady
- Crystal. **85.00**
- Crystal, green paint. **150.00**
- Green frosted. **165.00**

Curtsy, frosted pink. **150.00**
Elephant
- Miniature, frosted pink. **200.00**
- Trunk down, frosted green. . . **140.00**
- Trunk down, frosted pink. . . . **125.00**

Horse-drawn coach, frosted green, orig paint. **300.00**
Jackie, frosted pink. **165.00**
Jester, frosted vaseline. **145.00**
Lovebirds, frosted green. **130.00**
Minstrel
- Crystal. **130.00**
- Frosted green. **120.00**
- Frosted pink. **120.00**

Nude sisters, 6-1/2" d, 7-1/4" h, frosted green, wear, few chips. **300.00**
Parakeets, crystal. **155.00**
Parrots, frosted crystal. **40.00**
Penguin, peaked, frosted pink. **245.00**
Roxana, frosted green. **145.00**
Royal coach, frosted pink, white over-spray, gold over-spray highlights, black lid. **225.00**
Scottie dog
- Cobalt blue, 5-3/8" h, chip on inside of lid. **500.00**
- Pink, Jeanette. **70.00**
- White opaque, Akro Agate. . . . **85.00**

Spring nymph, frosted green. . **375.00**
Three birds, frosted pink. **85.00**
Twins, frosted green. **185.00**

Pattern glass

Banded Portland, U.S. Glass Co., irid stain, 2-1/2" d, 2-1/4" h **40.00**

Vanity type

3-1/2" d, 2-1/4" h, Art Deco, pressed glass bottom, peach and green enameled accents on orig chrome top **20.00**

3-7/8" d, 2-1/2" h, Czechoslovakian, green slag glass to imitate malachite, entwined nudes on lid and jar, metal hinged mounts **395.00**

6" d, 5" h, cased opaque pink, melon ribbed body and matching cover. **10.00**

Purple Slag

History: Challinor, Taylor & Co., Tarantum, Pennsylvania, c1870s-1880s, was the largest producer of purple slag in the United States. Since the quality of pieces varies considerably, there is no doubt that other American firms made it as well.

Purple slag also was made in England. English pieces are marked with British Registry marks.

Other slag colors, such as blue, green, and orange, were used, but examples are rare. Another common name for purple slag is "marble glass" and generally the other color combinations are identified by "slag" or "marble glass."

Videotape: National Imperial Glass Collectors Society, "Glass of Yesteryears, The Renaissance of Slag Glass by Imperial," RoCliff Communications, 1994.

> **Reproduction Alert:** Purple slag has been heavily reproduced over the years and still is reproduced at present.

Additional Listings: Greentown Glass (chocolate slag) and Pink Slag.

Note: Prices listed are for purple slag pieces, unless otherwise noted.

Animal covered dish
- Rabbit. **285.00**
- Rooster, small, caramel slag, Kemple. **300.00**

Ashtray, 6" sq, chocolate slag, Imperial IG mark **25.00**
Basket, 5-1/2", caramel slag basket, white milk glass handle, Imperial **50.00**
Bowl
- 6" d, Beaded Rib pattern, cov **85.00**
- 8" d, Dart and Bar pattern . . . **60.00**
- 8" d, Heart and Vine pattern. . **50.00**
- 9" d, Open Rose pattern, caramel slag, Imperial IG mark **50.00**

Bread tray, Notched Daisy pattern, c1890. **120.00**
Butter dish
- Cov, Paneled Grape pattern. . **75.00**
- Plain paneled sides, cow shaped finial **50.00**

Cake stand
- Flute pattern **75.00**
- Plain, pedestal base. **60.00**

Candlesticks, pr, figural dolphin stems **250.00**
Celery vase
- Blackberry pattern, 6-5/8" h, scalloped rim, Hobbs Brockunier **115.00**
- Jeweled Star pattern, 10" h, c1890 . . . . **125.00**
- Plain, pedestal base. **45.00**

Compote
- 4-1/2" d, crimped top, plain bowl **70.00**
- 5" d, Beaded Hearts pattern. . **85.00**
- 8" d, 8" h, Openwork Lattice pattern **95.00**

Creamer
- Crossbar and Flute pattern. . . **85.00**
- Figural, fish shape **95.00**
- Flower and Panel pattern **85.00**
- Flute pattern **90.00**
- Oak Leaf pattern. **75.00**
- Scroll with Acanthus pattern. . **90.00**

Goblet, Flute pattern **40.00**
Jack-in-the-pulpit vase, 6" h . . . **45.00**
Jar, cov, figural
- Bull's head, Westmoreland . . . **50.00**
- Owl, glossy, green slag, Imperial IG mark **60.00**

Match holder, Daisy and Button pattern, green. **30.00**
Monument, obelisk top, English, c1880, two flat base chips **125.00**
Mug
- Bird in nest, smiling cat, purple, Challinor Taylor, c1890 . . . . . **75.00**
- Rabbit **65.00**

Pitcher
- Fan and Basketweave pattern. **250.00**
- Windmill pattern, glossy, Imperial IG mark **45.00**

Plate, 10-1/2"d, closed lattice edge **75.00**
Platter, oval, notched rim, wildflowers dec, nick. **20.00**
Shoe
- 3-1/4" h, cowboy boot, stirrup and spur. **65.00**
- 6" h, lady's, high-button style, beaded diamond-shaped base **75.00**

Spooner
- Crossbar and Flute pattern . . . **85.00**
- Flower Panel pattern **80.00**
- Scroll with Acanthus pattern . . **65.00**

Sugar bowl, cov
- Crossbar and Flute pattern . . . **85.00**
- Flower Panel pattern **80.00**
- Flute pattern **190.00**
- Scroll with Acanthus pattern . **125.00**

Toothpick holder, Scroll with Acanthus pattern **125.00**
Tumbler
- Flute pattern, 3-1/4" h **50.00**
- Ribbed pattern, 4-1/2" h **45.00**
- Scroll with Acanthus pattern . . **65.00**

Vase
- 5" h, fan shaped, rich variegated purple, emb floral base, Victorian **50.00**
- 10" h, wispy purple swirls against frosted and clear body **125.00**

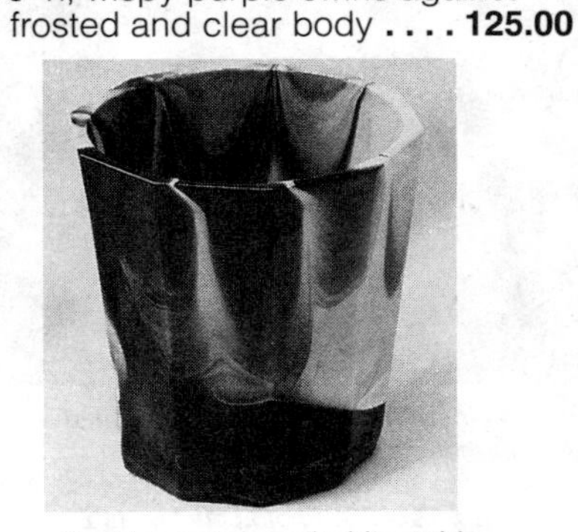

Tumbler, purple and white swirls, paneled body, 3-1/4" h, **$50.**

QUEZAL

Quezal

1901–25

History: The Quezal Art Glass Decorating Company, named for the quetzal—a bird with brilliantly colored feathers—was organized in 1901 in Brooklyn, New York, by Martin Bach and Thomas Johnson, two disgruntled Tiffany workers. They soon hired Percy Britton and William Wiedebine, two more Tiffany employees.

The first products, which are unmarked, were exact Tiffany imitations. Quezal pieces differ from Tiffany pieces in that they are more defined and the decorations are more visible and brighter. Quezal developed no new techniques, but created stunning glassware that was well received at the time.

Johnson left in 1905. T. Conrad Vahlsing, Bach's son-in-law, joined the firm in 1918 but left with Paul Frank in 1920 to form Lustre Art Glass Company, which copied Quezal pieces. Martin Bach died in 1924, and by 1925, Quezal had ceased operations.

The "Quezal" trademark was first used in 1902 and placed on the base of vases and bowls and on the rims of shades. The acid-etched or engraved letters vary in size and may be found in amber, black, or gold. A printed label, which includes an illustration of a quetzal, was used briefly in 1907.

Automobile vase, 10-1/2" h, irid gold amber ground, folded rim, elongated conical form, marked "Quezal" . **165.00**

Bowl

5-1/2" d, irid gold ground, flared rim **275.00**

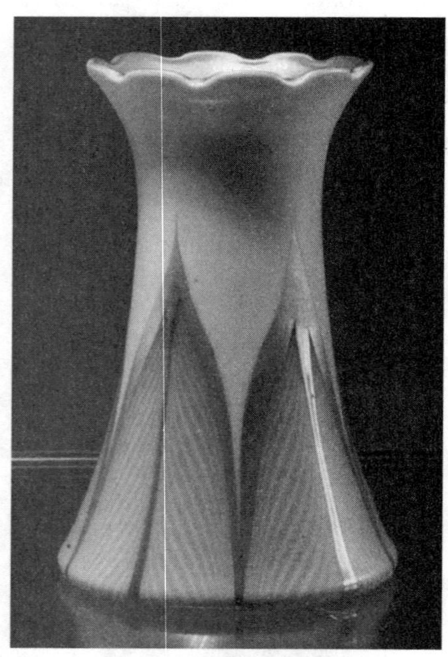

Cabinet vase, green and gold pulled feather decoration, scalloped rim, intense gold iridescent liner, signed, 5" h, **$1,400.** *Photo courtesy of David Rago Auctions.*

6" d, 3-3/4" h, irid blue, flared, raised rim, broad shouldered bowl tapering to base **275.00**

6-3/4" d, 1-1/2" h, shallow, ambergris, lustrous blue irid, silver base mark **230.00**

7-1/2" d, irid butterscotch ground, ftd, sgd **350.00**

9-1/2" d, gold calcite ground, stretch rim, pedestal foot, sgd "Quezal" **800.00**

12" d, peacock blue ground, hammered silver base, marked "Oscar B Bach, NY" **475.00**

Bud vase

5" h, lily, pinched quatraform rim, slender transparent golden bud vase, five subtle green spiked feathers, large partial label covers pontil, "Art Quezal – rooklyn" **1,035.00**

10-1/2" h, bronze mount, polished pontil, inscribed and silvered mark, imperfections to int. base .. **800.00**

12-3/4" h, ruffled rim on trumpet form vase, irid gold, wheat husks on textured bronze base, inscribed "Quezal" **865.00**

18-1/2" h, flared rim on trumpet form vase, irid gold, bronze mount dec with two snakes and foliage in relief, imp "C" **2,070.00**

Candlestick, 7" h, white King Tut dec, blue irid ground, fully sgd ... **1,050.00**

Chandelier

25" drop, six gold irid ribbed floriform shades, hung with orig chains, additional chains swag to each extended length of chain and shade **3,650.00**

30" drop, five 4-1/2" d diameter ribbed floriform gold shades with flared rims, affixed to extended adjustable metal arms... **1,120.00**

35" drop, sgd pulled green feather dec on each of six bell-shaped shades............... **4,200.00**

Cologne bottle, 7-1/2" h, irid gold ground, Art Deco design, sgd "Q" and "Melba"................... **250.00**

Compote

4-5/8" h, pale pastel blue ground, pedestal foot, sgd and numbered **525.00**

5-1/4" d, 4-1/4" h, two-tone, irid marigold, bluish-gold knobbed pedestal, silver signature on foot, factory blemishes **850.00**

Creamer, 2-1/2" h, irid gold ground, applied lip and handle **550.00**

Cruet, white opal ground, green pulled feather design, yellow stopper and applied handle **2,500.00**

Cup and saucer, irid gold int., opal hooked feather pattern, sgd and numbered **1,200.00**

Finger bowl and underplate, 4-1/2" d x 2-5/8" h, 5-3/4" d ribbed, scalloped edge underplate, contoured Flower Pod design on gold ext. with pink and blue highlights, blue irid int., sgd "Quezal" on base **750.00**

Flask, 8-1/2" h, brilliant irid rainbow ground, finely chased silver overlay carnations, inscribed "Quezal," Alvin Corp. mark stamped on silver. **1,200.00**

Jack-in-the-pulpit vase

8-3/4" h, gold, stretched irid on rounded blossom, sgd "Quezal 176" on base with scrolls. **1,150.00**

14-3/4" h, irid deep amber ground, green and pink highlights, silvery blue and amber loopings and trailings, wide flaring turned up rim, cylindrical standard, circular domed foot, c1905-20 ... **2,500.00**

Knife rest, 3-1/2" l, irid gold ground, two sq ends, twisted bar, polished pontil with signature **150.00**

Lamp base, 12" h, golden leaves with coiled tips pulled from base, emerald green ground, opal shoulder with gold pulled design, repeated at rim, mounted on metal base, marked "Lion Electric Mfg. Design Patent" .. **1,600.00**

Lamp

Desk, 14-1/2" h, gold irid shade with green and white pulled feather dec, inscribed "Quezal" at rim, gilt metal adjustable crook-neck lamp **575.00**

Mantel, gold irid 10-rib bell shade, rim marked "Quezal," gilt metal weighted single-socket base, 9" h, pr **575.00**

Opal glass shade with gold outlined green feather dec, inscribed "Quezal" at rim, gilt metal tripod base with twisted shaft, pr. **750.00**

Lamp shade

4-1/4" h, 6-1/2" d, puffy, colonial blue feathers with amber tips, pearl ground, irid gold int., ruffled rim, sgd, minor factory irregularities **700.00**

4-5/8" h, 2-1/8" d aperture, bulbous form, gold pulled feather pattern, white opalescent ground, sgd "Quezal," chip on fitter rim. **145.00**

4-3/4" h, 2-1/4" d aperture, reptilian pattern, irid gold, white accents, factory bubble near fitter . . . **130.00**

4-7/8" h, 10-ribbed bell-form shade, irid gold, inscribed "QUEZAL" on rim, minor chips on fitter ring . . . **185.00**

5" h, 16-ribbed bell-form, irid gold and white pulled dec, gold int., inscribed "QUEZAL" around rim . . . **520.00**

5" h, 2" d, bell form, gold pulled feathers tipped with green, ribbed opal ground, marigold int., sgd . . . **225.00**

5" h, 2-1/4" d, opal tulip form, gold entwined vines and scattered emerald green leaves, inscribed on fitter . . . **225.00**

5-1/4" h, double bulbed shade, flared rim, irid gold, inscribed "QUEZAL" on rim . . . **200.00**

5-1/2" h, 2-1/8" d aperture, trumpet form, green pulled feathers with gold borders, white opalescent ground, stretched ruffled rim, sgd "Quezal," price for pr . . . **575.00**

5-3/4" h, 2" d aperture, morning-glory shape, irid gold combed feathers with bluish-gray tips, yellowish opal ground, set of four, provenance includes documentation of ownership by John A. Ferguson, last president of Quezal . . . **850.00**

6" h, 2" d aperture, irid golden pulled feathers over opal ground, satin irid sheet, bright gold int., inscribed . . . **200.00**

8" h, 3" d aperture, molded opal flame form, two-tone irid gold, inscribed on fitter, flat chip on ext. . . . **650.00**

Lamp, table, 18" h, 10 gold irid fluted lily shades, 10 graceful arms meet at center to form ribbed center stem, large circular foot base, shades all sgd . . . **4,000.00**

Newell post lamp, 29-1/2" h, three-ball shade, zipper dec, brilliant yellow on oyster white, white meal and brass Victorian newel post . . . **500.00**

Nut dish, irid gold ground, triangular rim, gently rounded body, inscribed "Quezal" . . . **150.00**

Perfume bottle, 5" h, irid gold ground, flattened teardrop shape, bulbous stopper, Gorham sterling silver monogrammed foliate mounts . . **600.00**

Plate

5-7/8" d, irid gold ground, scalloped rim, sgd on pontil . . . **200.00**

8" d, irid gold ground, scalloped . . . **250.00**

10-3/4" h, fiery irid stretched orange-gold ground, ambergris dec, sgd "Quezal" across polished pontil, set of six . . . **1,500.00**

Salt, open

1-1/8" h, ruffed rim, ribbed body, lustrous gold, polished pontil inscribed "QUEZAL" . . . **550.00**

1-1/4" h, 1-1/2" d, ruffled rim, strong pink highlights, sgd . . . **450.00**

Toasting goblet, 4" h, white opal ground, fiery irid gold int., gold and green pulled feather dec, gold chain border, sgd "Quezal" inside applied hollow stem pedestal, pr . . . **1,750.00**

Toothpick holder, 2-1/4" h, melon ribbed, pinched sides, irid blue, green, purple and gold, sgd . . . **200.00**

Vase

4-1/4" h, irid gold ground, green and gold threads, slender body, circular foot, folded back surface, sgd "Quezal 167" . . . **1,200.00**

Vase, creamy white exterior, green pulled feathering, gold chain decoration wraps around center, gold interior, 10-1/4" h, **$3,335.** *Photo courtesy of David Rago Auctions.*

4-1/2" h, flared rim, bowl form body, translucent amber, delicate green and gold feathers on thin opal surface, folded gold irid rim, base inscribed "Quezal," surface bubbles in feather area . . . **920.00**

4-5/8" h, double dec opal body, hooked and pulled gold feathers below green hooked elements, medial gold band, gold irid surface above and within flared rim, base inscribed "Quezal 490" . . **2,070.00**

4-3/4" h, candlestick form, opal cylinders, applied disk foot, green and gold pulled feather dec, gold irid int., inscribed "Quezal" on base, accompanied by gold metal candle cup bobeches, pr . . **690.00**

4-3/4" h, cased cylinder, five pointed gold irid feathers on opal white body, flared golden foot inscribed "Quezal" on base . . . **575.00**

4-3/4" h, 3" h, watermelon green body, hooked feather, ric-rack, and pulled feather dec on oyster white, irid finish, purple and blue highlights, sgd . . . **2,750.00**

4-3/4" h, 5-1/2" w, oyster white ground, green pulled feather, gold trim, sgd . . . **900.00**

5" h, green and gold pulled feather dec, intense irid gold lining, scalloped rim, sgd . . . **1,380.00**

5-1/2" h, green pulled feathers outlined in gold, gold int. **1,050.00**

5-1/2" h, irid gold, floral form, tri-petal stretched rim, trumpet form body, magenta hues, inscribed "Quezal" . . . **475.00**

5-1/2" h, laminated, fine polished stone appearance, one side strewn with agate crystals, obverse with large haloed colors, inscribed "Quezal" . . . **2,300.00**

6-3/8" h, flared and slightly ribbed rim, elongated neck over ovoid body of pale amber glass, five opaque white pulled feathers rising from base, strong irid gold ground, polished pontil inscribed and gilded "Quezal 692," minor imperfections . . . **920.00**

7" h, white opal ground, five detailed green pulled feather leaf forms, gold outlines, bright irid gold int., flared trumpet floriform, inscribed "Quezal S 206" . . . **1,200.00**

7-1/4" h, 5" d, white opal ground, gold and green feathered leaves, flower form top, sgd . . . **1,750.00**

7-3-4" h, 9-1/2" d, large flared bulbous ambergris body cased to opal, dec with green pulled and coiled feathers obscured by lavish overall gold irid, inscribed "Quezal C357" on base **5,175.00**

8-1/4" h, baluster, ambergris with blue irid, purple luster above shoulder, inscribed "Quezal" on base **700.00**

8-1/2" h, flared oval amber body, gold irid, pulled and hooked white all over tracery, base inscribed "Quezal" **1,500.00**

8-1/2" h, trumpet, green and gold pulled feather dec, brilliant white ground, gold liner, sgd ... **2,530.00**

9" h, irid ribbon dec, sgd ... **880.00**

9" h, white opal and irid gold ground, gold pulled feather design, gold chain of hearts under rim, bright irid orange-gold int., Martin Bach design, sgd "Quezal 6" .. **1,200.00**

9-1/2" h, platinized gold feathering, emerald green tips pulled down into ivory shoulder, golden int., pale ric-rac design on lower part of body, raised bump inside rim, some slight ext. scuffs..... **650.00**

9-1/2" h, white, opal ground, reverse pulled irid gold feathers above symmetrical spider web criss-cross designs, elongated bottle form, sgd "Quezal C 369" **1,500.00**

10-1/4" h, five combed cucumber green feathers tipped with wide lustrous gold bands, gray-opal ground, circumference embellished with 10 applied irid gold ridged shells that trail to polished pontil, pontil inscribed "Quezal," some cooling lines **5,000.00**

10-1/4" h, gold int., creamy white ext., green pulled feathering from top and from bottom, gold chain dec wraps around center **3,335.00**

11" h, Luster Art, opal feathers pulled from polished pontil, wrapped in fine gold thread, gold ground, unsigned **850.00**

11-1/2" h, white spatter on black ground, base etched in silver "20120-12 K -QUE-O" **400.00**

12-1/4" h, ambergris oval body, cased to white, pulled gold feathers over bright green pulled feather motif, folded gold irid rim, Martin Bach manner, unsigned **3,200.00**

12-5/8" h, flared rim, urn form, bulbed base, irid gold swirl pattern **900.00**

Wall sconce, 14" h, irid floriform shade, white opal ground, gold pulled feather design, gold int., molded brass sconce, foliage and mirror dec, sgd at base of shade **300.00**

Whiskey taster, 2-3/4" h, oval, gold irid, four pinched dimples, sgd "Quezal" on base **200.00**

Rose Bowls

History: A rose bowl is a decorative open bowl with a crimped, scalloped, or petal top which turns in at the top, but does not then turn up or back out again. Rose bowls held fragrant rose petals or potpourri, which served as air fresheners in the late Victorian period. Practically every glass manufacturer made rose bowls in virtually every glass type, pattern, and style.

Rose bowls usually have a small opening which may be crimped, pinched, scalloped, or even petaled like flowers. Most rose bowls are round in shape, although a few examples can be found in an egg shape.

Reference: Johanna S. Billings with Sean Billings, *Collectible Rose Bowls,* Antique Trader Books, 1999.

Reproduction Alert: Rose bowls have been widely reproduced. Be especially careful of Italian copies of Victorian art glass, particularly Burmese and mother-of-pearl, imported in the 1960s and early 1970s.

Amber, 3" h, white spatter tortoiseshell type dec, applied gold dec **150.00**

Amberina, 6" h, 5" d, ribbed, cranberry shaded to olive-amber, enameled white and pink blossoms, tan branches **275.00**

Amethyst, squatty, enameled dec, fluted top **115.00**

Bohemian, 5" h, deep amber, pinched rim, applied feet, enameled florals **75.00**

Cameo, 3-1/2" h, 4" d, shaded deep rose to red, cameo-etched white florals, white lining, Diamond Quilted pattern, ground pontil **1,500.00**

Carnival

- Beaded Cable, Northwood, aqua opalescent, four toes, lightly ruffled top **500.00**
- Concave Flute, Westmoreland, green, ruffled top, collar foot **135.00**
- Fenton Flowers, ftdGreen . . . **125.00**

Marigold **35.00**

Powder blue **125.00**

White **95.00**

- Honeycomb, Northwood, peach opalescent **80.00**
- Horse Medallion, Fenton, marigold, three toes, ruffled top **175.00**
- Imperial Star and File, dark marigold **45.00**
- Leaf and Beads, Northwood, ftd
  - Blue **65.00**
  - Electric blue **85.00**
  - Floral int., green **325.00**
  - Marigold **60.00**
  - Purple **85.00**

Pattern glass, Tacoma pattern, green, 3-1/2" d, **$35.**

Cased, 5" h, 4-1/2" w, pink over white, ribbed, five triangular crimps, two white applied glass flowers **85.00**

Colorless, 7" d, ruffled rim **165.00**

Crackle, 3-1/4" h, 4-1/4" d, cranberry ground, Arboresque pattern, opaque white design, tightly crimped top **150.00**

Cranberry

- 4-1/4" h, 4-3/8" d, six-crimp top **95.00**
- 4-1/2" h, 5" d, Coin Spot pattern, eight-loop top **195.00**
- 5-5/8" h, 5-1/4" d **110.00**

Cut glass, small, Hobstars/Panels, American Brilliant Period **45.00**

Daum Nancy, 3" h, 3-1/4" d, mottled gold ground, acid cut river's edge landscape, enameled highlights, three-petal top **650.00**

Fenton

- 2-1/2" h, 3" w, Burmese miniature "Love Bouquet" with a rose, rosebud, lily of the valley and forget me nots, embossed butterfly in the bottom, sgd "Mary Walrath, 1986," also sgd "Handpainted by Pam Miller" **75.00**
- 5-1/2" h, Hobnail pattern, opalescent cranberry **165.00**

Legras

- 9" h, enameled grapes and vines, acid finish background, ground pontil, marked "LEG" **175.00**
- 9-1/2" d, 9" h, enamel grape and leaves dec, bright orange-red and black, sgd "Legras" **950.00**

Moser, 2-1/2" h, 2-1/2" w, green, intaglio engraved with lily, polished pontil, six delicate crimps **250.00**

Northwood, 301/8" h, 4-1/2" d, satin, light tan ground, mauve pulled feather dec, robin's egg blue lining, tightly crimped top **1,000.00**

Opalescent

- Beaded Drape pattern, green . **50.00**
- Button Panels pattern, colorless, Northwood **45.00**
- Fancy Fantails pattern, cranberry **65.00**
- Inverted Fan and Feather, colorless, ftd, Northwood **90.00**
- Stripe pattern, blue **90.00**
- Stripe pattern, cranberry, enameled forget-me-nots dec **95.00**

Pattern glass

- Champion pattern, McKee & Brothers, dec by Beaumont Glass Works, colorless, amber stain **60.00**
- Eureka pattern, National Glass Co., colorless, ruby stained **85.00**
- Heart with Thumbprint pattern, Tarentum Glass Co., colorless, ruby stained **115.00**
- Scalloped Six Points pattern, George Duncan Sons & Co., colorless **50.00**
- Torpedo pattern, Thompson Glass Co., colorless **90.00**

Peachblow

- 2-3/8" h, 2-1/2" d, Diamond Quilted pattern, mother of pearl, deep red shaded to amber pink, eight crimp top, Webb **375.00**
- 5-1/2" h, 7" d, pale-yellowed stain encircles bottom ext. **100.00**

Peloton, 3-7/8" h, 3-1/2" d, white opaque cased ribbed ground, multicolored filaments, pulled to four points on top **360.00**

Rossler, enameled, large, cranberry **145.00**

Rubena

- 3-5/8" h, 4-1/4" d, overshot type dec, eight crimps **125.00**
- Frosted, 4" h, 2-1/4" d rim, Royal Ivy, Northwood, minute roughness inside rim **150.00**

Satin

- 3-1/2" h, 4" w, yellow shading to white, white lining, ground pontil **40.00**
- 4" h, 4" w, Cabbage Rose pattern, pink blown out petals, white lining, rough pontil **225.00**
- 4-1/2" d, 31/2" h, blue shaded to pale blue ground, mezzotint of cherub wearing bright blue cape, vines and leaves dec, Mt. Washington **200.00**
- 5-1/2" d, pale blue ground, life-like pansy, numbered "617" on bottom, Mt. Washington **575.00**

5-1/2" h, 5" h, lusterless white ground, eight crimp top, orig matte finish, Mt. Washington, c1870 .... 100.00

5-1/2" h, 5-1/2" w, ovoid, opaque white shading to light blue, three orange flowers and foliage, crimped rim, hand blown .. 175.00

Stevens and Williams

4-1/2" h, swirled blue, and yellow, white opalescent edges, ribbed mold, ground pontil 150.00

4-3/4" h, 5-3/8" d, sapphire blue, 12-crimp top, ribbed effect, enameled pink and white flowers 220.00

6-1/4" h, 4-5/8" d, sapphire blue, applied crystal feet, applied crystal drippings from scalloped top edge 155.00

Webb, 3" h, 3-1/8" d, deep red shading to warm pink-amber, acid finish, cream lining, eight-crimp top 250.00

Royal Flemish

1892

History: Royal Flemish was produced by the Mount Washington Glass Co., New Bedford, Massachusetts. Albert Steffin patented the process in 1894. Royal Flemish was only produced for a limited time, as the technique involved was labor intensive and therefore costly.

Royal Flemish is a frosted transparent glass with heavy raised gold enamel lines. These lines form sections—often colored in russet tones—giving the appearance of stained-glass windows with elaborate floral or coin medallions.

Royal Flemish wares were not all singed, although a round paper label is found on some pieces. A red enameled mark was also used.

References: John A. Shuman III, *The Collector's Encyclopedia of American Art Glass*, Collector Books, 1988, 1994 value update; Kenneth Wilson, *American Glass 1760-1930: The Toledo Museum of Art*, Vol. I and Vol. II, Hudson Hills Press and The Toledo Museum of Art, 1994.

Collectors' Club: Mount Washington Art Glass Society, P.O. Box 24094, Fort Worth, TX 76124-1094

Museums: New Bedford Museum, New Bedford, MA; Sandwich Glass Museum, Sandwich, MA; The Corning Museum of Glass, Corning, NY; The Toledo Museum of Art, Toledo, OH.

Biscuit jar, cov

8" h, ovoid, large Roman coins on stained panels, divided by heavy gold lines, ornate SP cov, rim, and bail handle, orig paper label "Mt. W. G. Co. Royal Flemish" . 1,750.00

8-1/2" h, 6" d, Roman coin dec, four large medallions, three with coins, one with griffin, deep maroon, beige, and brown ground, orig fancy metal hardware, minor loss to paint 1,100.00

9" h, 6" w, maroon and rust ground, four Roman coins, replaced SP top 1,150.00

Bowl, 10-1/2" d, 4" h, enameled chrysanthemum dec, gold outlined panels.................. 1,750.00

Box, cov, 5-1/2" d, 3-3/4" h, swirled border, gold outlined swirls, gold tracery blossoms, enameled blossom with jeweled center on lid.... 1,500.00

Cologne bottle, 5-1/2" h, frosted body, enameled butterfly and daisy dec, heavy gold tracery, dark maroon enameled neck and stopper . 4,000.00

Compote, 11" d, 16" h, dec Royal Flemish bowl, held in figural silver plated base with putti holding bowl overhead, base sgd "Pairpoint" 5,320.00

Ewer

9" h, 7" w, Heraldic, brown, rust, and tan dec, gold floral design, 2" band of various coats of armor at neck, rope handle........... 1,380.00

9-1/2" h, Cupid slaying dragon, raised gold, mythological fish in medallions, pastel blue and violet blossoms within side panels, gold tracery on extended neck, applied twisted rope handle..... 4,500.00

Ewer, sepia-colored body, eight vertical panes framed by heavy raised gold, four panels tinted pale mauve, other panels and sweeping around perimeter of body are raised gold tendrils laden with multi-petaled blossoms of encrusted gold and tinted autumn leaves, cerise-colored shoulders, 16 sky-blue circular medallions, cerise spout, frosted colorless glass handle, 5-1/2" d, 12" h, very slight loss to gilt trim, **$7,500.** *Photo courtesy of Clarence and Betty Maier.*

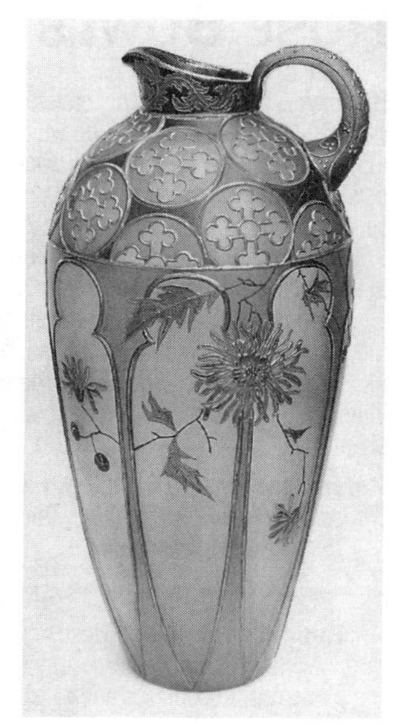

Ewer, alternating pale blue and tan lower panels surmounted by circlets of dark blue with centered light blue crosses, circlets on field of cerise, raised gold separation lines, chrysanthemum blossoms, and foliage, 11-1/2" h, **$4,000.**

10-1/2" h, 9" w, 5" d, circular semi-transparent panel on front with youth thrusting spear into chest of winged creature, reverse panel shows mythical fish created with tail changed into stylized florals, raised gold dec, outlines, and scrolls, rust, purple, and gold curlicues, twisted rope handle with brushed gold encircles neck, hp minute gold florals on neck, burnished gold stripes on rim spout and panels............ 4,950.00

12-1/4" h, flag staff dec on segmented stained glass type ground, fierce rampant lion above company masthead double eagle emblem shield, applied rope handle 3,000.00

Jar, cov, 8" h, classical Roman coin medallion dec, simulated stained-glass panels, SP rim, bail, and cov, paper label "Mt. W. G. Co. Royal Flemish" 1,650.00

Mug, 7" h, tankard form, band of leaves and berries, deep blue band, 18 circles separated by gold line, gold rope handle 3,510.00

Rose bowl, eight-scalloped top, pale brown shading to frosted, white and blue asters, brown and green stems and leaves, pontil with purple number 1,400.00

Rose jar, cov, 9" h, bright panels, Roman coins on obverse, raised gold florals on reverse, finial with old repair 2,100.00

Sugar bowl, cov, 6-1/4" d, 2-1/2" h, pink and yellow apple blossoms, gilt enameled dec, applied reeded handles 450.00

Temple jar, cov, 16" h, 8" d, St. George and the dragon motif, brown, beige, and green shaded background, maroon trim on neck and cover, pinhead flake on top of finial **11,500.00**

Vase

- 4" h, 4-1/2" d, mythical winged gargoyle, tail becoming part of stylized foliage that sweeps around the perimeter, gold embellishments, irregular-sized angular panels of subdued shades of brown, dark tan, lighter tan and frosted clear form background **985.00**
- 6" h, double bulbed, frosted, colorful pansies, allover gold enameling **1,210.00**
- 6" h, 6" w, frosted colorless ground, allover purple violet dec, sgd and numbered "533" **1,210.00**
- 6-1/2" h, 6" d, bold stylized scrolls of pastel violet, realistically tinted sprays of violets randomly strewn around frosted clear glass body, carefully drawn brilliant gold lines define violet nosegays and frame scrolls, daubed gold accents, two tiny handles, sgd with logo and "0583" **2,200.00**
- 7-1/2" h, 7-1/2" d, squatty, smaller squatty form as collar, 14 pastel pansies, clear frosted ground, four rayed suns, painted foliage-like gold tracery **1,400.00**
- 8" h, 6-3/4" d, tan and brown, raised gold winged gargoyle, stylized florals **2,750.00**
- 8" h, 8" w, central cartouche of two owls sitting on bough, sun in background, reverse with single own sitting on bough, gold scrolling, two snail handles, sgd and numbered "599" . . . **17,250.00**
- 9-1/2" h, double bulbed body, allover training enameled roses, shades of pink and green, raised gold enamel outlines, stylized gilt trellis of blue spiral accents, red enamel mark on base, c1894, slight wear to gilt **3,335.00**
- 10" h, floral and butterfly dec, rust colored ground, ruby moiré throat band, gold enamel dec, gilt metal mounts **2,250.00**
- 10" h, 4" d, jeweled, colorless frosted ground, gold and red raspberries with leaves, loss to several glass jewels **2,130.00**
- 10" h, 8" d, bulbous, winged serpent and dragon, large pinwheel type stars, deep maroon and green ground **4,025.00**
- 14" h, Snow Geese, five geese in flight over bright sun, gold stars, blue, green, and beige stained ground, deep maroon collar **10,350.00**
- 14" h, 4" d, winged creature in flight, gold dec, maroon, tan, brown, beige, and green panels, heavy gold raised dec, 1" gold floral dec band on neck and base . . **5,750.00**
- 14" h, 7" d, bulbous, large winged creature, brightly colored lavender, blue, and green ground, heavy gold dec, deep blue sections **6,325.00**

Vase, cov

- 6-1/4" h, squatty bulbous, colorless ground heavily dec with butterflies and colorful stylized blossoms between two maroon tapestry-like reserves, gold enameled embellishments, conforming cov, unsigned **3,750.00**
- 15" h, frosted colorless body, elaborately dec with red and opal beaded gold enameled peacock perched on blossom-laden branches, scrolling designs, conforming ornamental stopper, base marked in rd "RF 594," some int. stain, stopper finial flat on one side. **4,325.00**

Rubena Glass

History: Rubena crystal is a transparent blown glass that shades from clear to red. It also is found as the background for frosted and overshot glass. Several glass companies, including Northwood and Hobbs, and Brockunier & Co. of Wheeling, West Virginia, made it in the late 1800s.

Rubena was used for several patterns of pattern glass including Royal Ivy and Royal Oak.

Biscuit jar, cov

- Aurora, inverted rib, Northwood **325.00**
- Cut fan and strawberry design, fancy sterling silver cov, 7" h, 6" w **1,150.00**
- Diamond-Quilted pattern, 7-1/4" h, 6-1/4" d, squatty bulbous body, ornate SP rim, domed cov, and scrolling bail handle, resilvered **375.00**

Bowl

- 4-1/2" d, Daisy and Scroll pattern **65.00**
- 9" d, Royal Ivy pattern, frosted **135.00**

Pitcher, enameled apple blossom motif, 7-1/2" h, **$475.**

Butter dish, cov, Royal Oak pattern, fluted **250.00**

Castor set, Venecia pattern, salt and pepper shakers with orig tops, cov mustard jar, cruet with orig stopper, glass handled frame **275.00**

Cologne bottle, 6-3/4" h, 2-3/4" d, gold bands, overall stippling, orig cut faceted stopper with gold trim, St. Louis **150.00**

Compote, 14" h, 9" d, rubena overshot bowl, white metal bronze finished figural standard **170.00**

Creamer, Hobbs' Hobnail pattern, sq top, polished pontil, 4" h. **220.00**

Creamer and sugar bowl, cov

- Medallion Spring pattern. . . . **315.00**
- Royal Ivy pattern **250.00**

Decanter, 9" h, bulbous body, narrow neck, applied colorless handle . **170.00**

Finger bowl

- Hobbs' Hobnail pattern, satin finish **90.00**
- Royal Ivy pattern **65.00**

Marmalade jar, cov, enameled dec, sgd "Moser" **325.00**

Perfume bottle, 3-1/4" h, SP top rim, cranberry cut stopper **125.00**

Pickle castor

- Enameled daisy dec, ornate sgd frame with two handles, pickle fork in front **245.00**
- Royal Ivy pattern insert, frosted, Webster frame, 9-1/2" h . . . **250.00**

Punch set, 7-1/2" d, 12" h globe shaped cov bowl, six 3-3/4" h handled mugs, ribbed optic, copper wheel engraved dec, int. rim chips on bowl, mugs with flakes, one missing handle **160.00**

*Royak Oak pattern, all frosted rubena, from left: salt shaker (2), each, **$75**; square lidded dish, **$245**; open square dish, **$195**; covered sugar bowl, **$245**; creamer, **$185**; cruet **$185**; toothpick holder, **$90**. Photo courtesy of Joy Luke Fine Art Brokers and Auctioneers.*

Rose bowl, 4" h, 2-1/4" d rim, Royal Ivy, frosted, Northwood, minute roughness inside rim **150.00**

Salt shaker
- Coquette pattern, orig top . . **150.00**
- Royal Ivy pattern, frosted, no top **75.00**

Sauce dish, Royal Ivy pattern. . . **35.00**

Sugar, cov, Royal Ivy pattern, #79 . . . . **235.00**

Sugar, open, Royal Ivy pattern, #78 . . . . **135.00**

Sugar shaker
- Royal Ivy pattern, Northwood Glass Co., 4-1/4" h **275.00**
- Royal Ivy pattern, frosted, Northwood Glass Co., 4" h. **400.00**
- Royal Oak pattern, frosted . . **300.00**

Syrup pitcher, Royal Oak pattern **265.00**

Table set, creamer, cov sugar, spooner, lid for butter (no base), Royal Oak, frosted **300.00**

Tankard pitcher
- Enameled floral dec, applied reeded handle, 9-1/4" h **200.00**
- Reverse rubena, collar etching **175.00**

Toothpick holder
- Optic pattern. **150.00**
- Royal Ivy pattern. **85.00**

Tumbler
- Hobbs' Hobnail, 3-7/8" h. **60.00**
- Medallion Sprig pattern **100.00**
- Royal Oak pattern. **90.00**

Tumble-up, tumbler and carafe, Baccarat Swirl **175.00**

Vase
- 6" h, 4-1/2" w, acid etched flowers and leaves, frosted, vertical ribbed int., bell-shaped top, Mt. Washington. **295.00**
- 10" h, ruffled rim, hp enameled flowers, gold trim, Hobbs, Brockunier & Co. **175.00**
- 10" h, trumpet, enameled gold dec **150.00**

Water pitcher
- Opal Swirl pattern, Northwood **275.00**
- Royal Ivy pattern, frosted. . . . **295.00**

Water set
- Royal Ivy, frosted, 8" h pitcher, four 3-3/4" tumblers, Northwood, minor rim flakes on tumblers. **280.00**
- Royal Ivy, frosted and clear, 8-1/4" h pitcher, six 3-3/4" h tumblers, Northwood, minor rim flakes on tumblers **110.00**
- Royal Oak pattern, pitcher and four tumblers **565.00**

RUBENA VERDE GLASS

History: Rubena Verde, a transparent glass that shades from red in the upper section to yellow-green in the lower, was made by Hobbs, Brockunier & Co., Wheeling, West Virginia, in the late 1880s. It often is found in the Inverted Thumbprint (IVT) pattern, called "Polka Dot" by Hobbs.

Modern glassblowers have tried to duplicate this technique and some new pieces do exist. But the amount of labor involved to reheat the gather (molten or semimolten state of glass) to create the color variations prohibits mass production.

Basket, 10" h, 5" d, egg-shaped form, pink and white morning glories, cut-away top, applied green base with gold dec, pale green U-shaped handle **250.00**

Bowl
- 7-1/2" w, 3" h, sq, Hobbs' Hobnail pattern, Hobbs, Brockunier & Co., several open bubbles on int. **130.00**
- 9-1/2" d, Inverted Thumbprint pattern, ruffled. **175.00**

Butter dish, cov, Daisy and Button pattern **250.00**

Celery vase, 6-1/4" h, Inverted Thumbprint pattern. **225.00**

Compote, 8" h, 8" d, Honeycomb pattern **145.00**

Creamer and sugar bowl, cov, Hobnail pattern, bulbous, applied handle **550.00**

Cruet, 7" h, Inverted Thumbprint pattern, teepee shape, trefoil spout, vaseline handle and faceted stopper, Hobbs, Brockunier **550.00**

Finger bowl, Inverted Thumbprint pattern, 2-1/2" h **95.00**

Jack-in-the-pulpit vase, 8" h. . . **250.00**

Pickle castor, Hobbs' Hobnail pattern, SP frame, cov, and tongs **500.00**

Salt and pepper shakers, pr, Inverted Thumbprint pattern **210.00**

Sugar shaker, Hobbs' Coloratura pattern, enameled floral dec, metal lid **320.00**

Toothpick holder, 4" h, Hobnail pattern, opalescent hobs **125.00**

Tumbler, Inverted Thumbprint pattern **125.00**

Vase
- 7" h, bulbous, scalloped rim, enameled floral dec **225.00**
- 9-1/4" h, paneled body, enameled daises dec **85.00**
- 10-1/4" h, applied colorless edge, sq mouth, colorless rigaree band spiraling from top to base, applied colorless foot **200.00**
- 10-1/2" h, Neptune, polished rim, Bohemian. **230.00**
- 12-1/8" h, 5-1/4" d, cranberry shading to green, enameled flowers, green leaves, lacy gold foliage, blue bow ribbon accents **225.00**

Water pitcher
- 7-1/2" h, Hobbs' Hobnail pattern **395.00**
- 8" h, Reverse Thumbprint pattern, sq top, applied vaseline handle **295.00**
- 8-1/2" h, Inverted Thumbprint pattern, applied vaseline handle **350.00**

Water set, 8-1/2" h pitcher, four 3-3/4" h tumblers, heavy ribbed optic, yellow enamel and gilt palm tree dec . **550.00**

*Vase, Neptune, polished rim, Bohemian, 10-1/2" h, **$230.** Photo courtesy of David Rago Auctions.*

Sabino Glass

History: Sabino glass, named for its creator Ernest Marius Sabino, originated in France in the 1920s and is an art glass which was produced in a wide range of decorative styles: frosted, clear, opalescent, and colored. Both blown and pressed moldings were used. Hand-sculpted wooden molds that were cast in iron were used and are still in use at the present time.

In 1960, the company introduced fiery opalescent Art Deco-style pieces, including a line of one- to eight-inch high figurines. Gold was added to a batch of glass to obtain the fiery glow. These are the Sabino pieces most commonly found today. Sabino is marked with the name in the mold, as an etched signature, or both.

Animal

Bird

Babies, 3" h, two chubby babies perched close on twig with berries leaves, oval molded base, relief molded "Sabino" **35.00**

Feeding, 1-1/2" x 2" **90.00**

Five birds perched on branch, 7" x 8" **1,250.00**

Hopping, 1-1/2" x 2" **85.00**

Jumping, 3-1/4" x 3-1/2" . . . **85.00**

Mocking, 6" x 4-1/2" h **115.00**

Nesting, 1-1/2" x 2" **90.00**

Pair, 3-1/2" x 4-1/2" **250.00**

Resting **60.00**

Shivering **75.00**

Teasing, 2-1/2" x 3", wings up **85.00**

Trio, 5" x 5" **265.00**

Butterfly, opalescent, relief molded "Sabino" **25.00**

Cat

Napping, 2" h **45.00**

Sitting, 2-1/4" h **50.00**

Figure, dragonfly, 6" h, **$125.**

Chick

Drinking, wings down **50.00**

Standing, 3-3/4" h, wings up **60.00**

Collie, 2" h **50.00**

Dragonfly, 6" h, 5-3/4" l **125.00**

Elephant **45.00**

Fish, large **110.00**

Fox **35.00**

Gazelle **100.00**

German Shepherd, 2" h **45.00**

Hen **35.00**

Heron, 7-1/2" h **125.00**

Lovebirds, pr, 3-3/4" x 5", sgd "Sabino, Paris" **650.00**

Mouse, 3" h **60.00**

Owl, 4-1/2" h **70.00**

Panthers, 5-3/4" x 7-1/4", grouping **225.00**

Pekinese, 1-1/4" h, begged, opalescent, relief molded "Sabino" **35.00**

Pigeon, 6-1/4" h **150.00**

Poodle, 1-3/4" h **35.00**

Rabbit, 1" x 2" **75.00**

Rooster, 7-1/2" h **500.00**

Scottie, 1-1/2" x 3" x 4" **115.00**

Snail, 1" x 3", relief molded "Sabino" **45.00**

Squirrel, 3-1/2" h, eating acorn, oval molded base, relief molded "Sabino" **45.00**

Stork, 7-1/4" h **145.00**

Turkey, 2-1/4" h, 2-1/2" l, molded signature "Sabino, France" . **45.00**

Turtle, small **35.00**

Zebra, 5-1/2" l, 5-1/2" h **165.00**

Ashtray

Shell, 5-1/2" l, 3-1/2" w **35.00**

Violet, 4-1/2" d **40.00**

Blotter, 6" l, rocker type, crossed American and French flags **275.00**

Bowl

Beehive **150.00**

Berry, 5-3/4" d, relief molded . **70.00**

Fish, 5" d **85.00**

Shell **50.00**

Box, cov, Petalia **145.00**

Candlestick, two-lite, relief molded grapes **140.00**

Center bowl, 10-1/4" d, 4-1/4" h, heavy walled, frosted, three high relief oyster shells, tripod feet, star, and pearls between, center marked "Sabino France," int. wear **500.00**

Charger, 11-3/4" d, opalescent, Art Deco molded spiral design, three nude women swimming, central molded mark "Sabino Paris" **550.00**

Clock, 6-1/8" h, opalescent, arched case, overlapping geometric devices, molded festoons centered by circular chapter ring, molded "SABINO," c1925 . . . . **1,725.00**

Hand, left **200.00**

Knife rest

Butterfly, 4" l **50.00**

Duck **25.00**

Lamp, 15-1/4" h, opalescent glass shade, marble base with gilt mounts, sgd "Minuet" **1,500.00**

Luminiere, 9" h, 12" l, deeply opalescent, molded as fish, conforming illuminating gilt-metal base, glass molded "SABINO FRANCE" . . **1,300.00**

Napkin ring, birds, opalescent . . **45.00**

Perfume bottle, opalescent, semi-nudes, 1920s **250.00**

Plate, 8-1/2" d, sailing ships . . . **250.00**

Powder box, small **40.00**

Scent bottle

Nudes, 6" h, inscribed "Sabino France" **125.00**

Petalia **150.00**

Pineapple, 5" h **175.00**

Statue

Cherub, 2" h **45.00**

Draped Nude, 7-1/4" h **425.00**

Kneeling Nude, 6" h **250.00**

Madonna, 5" h **120.00**

Maiden, 7-3/4" h, opalescent, draped in contrapposto with raised right arm, etched "Sabino Paris" **885.00**

Nude, 6-3/4" h, opalescent, long flowing hair, sgd "Sabino Paris" on back **625.00**

Venus de Milo, large **75.00**

Tray

Butterfly, round **90.00**

Shell, figural **50.00**

Thistle, figural **60.00**

Vase

7" h, press molded sphere, raised bumblebees clustered on angular honeycomb and floral latticework, engraved mark on base "Sabino Paris" **460.00**

7-1/2" h, 7" d, amber, sunrise on one side, obverse with sunset, seven swallows **650.00**

7-1/2" h, 9-1/2" d, colorless elliptical body, full-bodied nude women at each side, frosted blossoming flower bends, molded script mark on base "Sabino Paris" . . **1,495.00**

8-1/2" h, blown-out blossoms, eight panels **350.00**

9-7/8" h, opalescent, rounded rect form, Art Deco female nude each side, joining hands around vessel, etched 'Sabino Paris" **1,870.00**

15-1/2" h, tall oval body, molded three swallows in flight, fiery amber, base inscribed "Sabino France" in script **1,035.00**

SALT AND PEPPER SHAKERS

History: Collecting salt and pepper shakers, whether late 19th-century glass forms or the contemporary figural and souvenir types, is becoming more and more popular. The supply and variety is practically unlimited; the price for most sets is within the budget of cost-conscious collectors. In addition, their size offers an opportunity to display a large collection in a relatively small space.

Specialty collections can be by type, form, or maker. Great glass artisans, such as Joseph Locke and Nicholas Kopp, designed salt and pepper shakers in the normal course of their work.

The clear colored and colored opaque sets command the highest prices; clear and white sets the lowest. Although some shakers, e.g., the tomato or fig, have a special patented top and need it to hold value, it does not lower the price to replace the top of a shaker.

Sentiment and whimsy are prime collecting motivations, especially in the areas of figural and souvenir shakers. The large variety of shakers and their current low prices indicate a potential for long-term price growth.

Generally, older shakers are priced by the piece, and prices below are noted how they are priced. All shakers are assumed to have original tops unless noted. Arthur Goodwin Peterson's *Glass Salt Shakers: 1,000 Patterns* provides the reference numbers given below. Peterson made a beginning; there are still hundreds, perhaps thousands of patterns to be catalogued.

References: Larry Carey and Sylvia Tompkins, *1003 Salt & Pepper Shakers*, Schiffer Publishing, 1997; —; *1004 Salt & Pepper Shakers*, Schiffer Publishing, 1998; —; *1006 Salt & Pepper Shakers*, Schiffer Publishing, 2000; Melva Davern, *Collector's Encyclopedia of Figural & Novelty Salt and Pepper Shakers*, Collector Books, First and Second Series, 2000 value updates; Helene Guarnaccia, *Salt & Pepper Shakers*, Vol. I (1985, 1999 value update), Vol. II (1989, 1998 value update), Vol. III (1991, 1998 value update), Vol. IV (1993, 2001 value update), Collector Books; Mildred and Ralph Lechner, *World of Salt Shakers*, 2nd ed., Collector Books, 1992, 1998 value update; Arthur G. Peterson, *Glass Salt Shakers*, Wallace-Homestead, 1970, out of print; Sylvia Tompkins and Irene Thornburg, *America's Salt and Pepper Shakers*, Schiffer, 2000.

Collectors' Clubs: Antique and Art Glass Salt Shaker Collectors Society, 1775 Lakeview Drive, Zeeland, MI 49464, http://www.cbantiques.com/ssc; British Novelty Salt & Pepper Collectors Club, Coleshill, Clayton Rd, Mold, Flintshire CH7 1SX UK; Novelty Salt & Pepper Shakers Club, P.O. Box 677388, Orlando, FL 32867-7388.

Museum: Judith Basin Museum, Stanford, MT.

Art glass (priced individually)

Blue, Inverted Thumbprint, sphere **125.00**

Burmese, satin finish, barrel, ribbed, floral motif, two-piece pewter top with finial, Mt. Washington **225.00**

Cobalt blue, 4" h, deep color, sterling push-on lid with English hallmarks "E.E.," "HH" and a lion facing left, sterling collar marked "E.E.," anchor, and lion facing left **185.00**

Cranberry, Inverted Thumbprint, sphere **175.00**

Fig, enameled pansy dec, satin, orig prong top, Mt. Washington..... **120.00**

Libbey, satin, egg shape, flat side, pewter top, made for Columbian Exposition, 1893 (28-B) **75.00**

Peachblow, Wheeling, bulbous. **460.00**

Scrollware, blue scrolling **170.00**

Wave Crest

Erie Twist body, hp flowers, 2-1/2" h **185.00**

Tulip, white opaque shading to yellow, hand-painted floral dec, 2-1/2" h, dec very worn **40.00**

Depression glass (priced by pair)

Aunt Polly, blue............. **220.00**

Cloverleaf, black............. **75.00**

Colonial, green **140.00**

Madrid, amber............. **125.00**

Raindrops, green **315.00**

Royal Lace, cobalt blue....... **250.00**

Sandwich (Indiana), crystal..... **18.00**

Sharon, pink **55.00**

Swirl, ultramarine............. **45.00**

Tea Room, green............. **30.00**

Figurals (priced by set)

Binoculars, shakers set into matching glass frame, blue shading to amber, Bryce, Higbee & Co., 3-3/4" h, 5-1/4" l, base appears to have been cut down, roughness on edge of both shakers **130.00**

Chick, pedestal, C. F. Monroe, white opal, not dec, 3" h **285.00**

Christmas, barrel shape

Amber **80.00**

Amethyst **145.00**

Ducks, 2-1/2" h, sitting, glass, clear bodies, blue heads, sgd "Czechoslovakia" **45.00**

Egg shape

Opaque white body, holly dec, 23 red raised enameled berries, Mt. Washington **185.00**

Pastel tint, pink enameled blossoms, lid loose **65.00**

Opalescent glass (priced individually)

Argonaut Shell, blue **65.00**

Beatty Honeycomb, blue (22-Q) . **45.00**

Circle Scroll, blue, tin top (156-S) . **85.00**

Fluted Scrolls, vaseline **65.00**

Jewel and Flower, blue, (164-J), replaced top **45.00**

Reverse Swirl, blue, 2-3/8" h, no harm open bubble on side.......... **70.00**

Ribbed Opal Lattice, cranberry, 3-1/4" h, dent in lid **150.00**

Ribbon Vertical, white **40.00**

Seaweed, Hobbs, cranberry.... **60.00**

Windows, Hobbs, blue, pewter top **50.00**

Opaque, butterfly, original pewter top, made by Eagle Glass Co., c1890, P-23B, **$35.**

Opaque glass (priced individually)

Acorn, short

Coral, shaded light to dark, orig brass dome, 2-1/2" h **25.00**

Pink, variegated, orig brass dome lid, 2-1/2" h.............. **25.00**

Acorn, tall

Dark blue, U.S. Glass Co., 3" h **40.00**

Pink, U.S. Glass Co., 3" h.... **35.00**

Apple Blossom, milk white, Consolidated Lamp and Glass Co. **35.00**

Beaded Dahlia
- Cased, clear with pink casing, Consolidated Lamp and Glass Co., 2-1/2" h **30.00**
- Light blue, Consolidated Lamp and Glass Co., 2-1/2" h **30.00**
- Medium blue, Consolidated Lamp and Glass Co., 2-1/2" h **30.00**

Broken Rib, blue, 3" h **30.00**
Brownie, 2-3/8" h, rounded cube, four vertical sides, Palmer Cox Brownies in different poses on each (F-488) . . **90.00**
Bulging Petal, flat
- Cased, clear with pink casing, Consolidated Lamp and Glass Co., 2-1/8" h **20.00**
- Dark blue, Consolidated Lamp and Glass Co., 2-1/8" h **30.00**
- Light blue, Consolidated Lamp and Glass Co., 2-1/8" h **30.00**

Carnelian, custard, Northwood . **225.00**
Chocolate, Cactus, Greentown . . **50.00**
Chrysanthemum Sprig, custard **150.00**
Clover Leaf, pink, cased, Dithridge & Co., 3-1/4" h **20.00**
Cone, pink, Consolidated Lamp and Glass Co., 3" h **45.00**
Cord and Tassel
- Blue, glossy, Consolidated Lamp & Glass Co., 2" h, damage to lid **35.00**
- Pink, satin finish, Consolidated Lamp & Glass Co., 2" h, damage to lid **30.00**
- Satin finish, Consolidated Lamp & Glass Co., 2" h, damage to lid **20.00**

Cosmos, tall, blue, Consolidated Lamp & Glass Co., 3-1/2" h **30.00**
Cotton Bale, pink
- Satin finish, Consolidated Lamp & Glass Co., 2-1/2" h, split in lid . **30.00**
- Semi-transparent, variegated, glossy, Consolidated Lamp & Glass Co., 2-1/2" h, split in lid **30.00**

Creased Neck, opalware, hand painted floral dec **25.00**
Creased Waist
- Blue, New Martinsville Glass Mfg. Co., 3-3/8" h **25.00**
- White, New Martinsville Glass Mfg. Co., 3-3/8" h **20.00**
- Yellow, Couderspot Glass Co. **35.00**

Daisy Sprig **50.00**
Dithridge Princess Swirl, pink, cased, Dithridge & Co., 2-1/4" h **25.00**
Double Fan Band, pink, cased, Dithridge & Co., 3-1/2" h **20.00**
Egg in Blossom **100.00**
Everglades, purple slag, white and gold highlights, pewter (160-K) . . **85.00**
Fantasia, pink, Coudersport Tile & Ornamental Glass Co., 2-1/2" h . . **25.00**
Flaming, clear, pink casing, satin, Consolidated Lamp & Glass Co., 3" h **45.00**
Florette, clear, pink casing, satin, Consolidated Lamp & Glass Co., 2-1/4" h **30.00**
Flower Bouquet, green, Challinor Taylor & Co., 3-1/4" h, two flakes on base **25.00**
Forget-Me-Not
- Blue, Challinor, Taylor & Co., 2-1/2" h **40.00**
- Green Challinor, Taylor & Co., 2-1/2" h **30.00**
- Pink, variegated, Challinor, Taylor & Co., 2-1/2" h **35.00**
- White, Challinor, Taylor & Co., 2-1/2" h **25.00**

Guttate
- Green, Consolidated Lamp & Glass Co., 3" h **48.00**
- Pink, Consolidated Lamp & Glass Co., 3" h, damage to lid **15.00**

Inverted Fan and Feather, pink slag (31-O) **250.00**
Knobby, heavy opaque white, hp pastel flowers, shading to pale yellow, orig pewter top **45.00**
Leaf Double, clear, pink casing, Dithridge & Co, 3-5/8" h **25.00**
Leaf Hanging, blue, 4-1/4" h **25.00**
Little Shrimp
- Blue, Dithridge & Co, 1-1/2" h, lid damage **55.00**
- Light green satin, hand painted floral dec, 1-1/2" h, no lid **35.00**

Narrow Base Scroll, clear, pink casing, Consolidated Lamp & Glass Co., 3-7/8" h, lid split **30.00**
Overlapping Leaf, pink, blue, or green, Consolidated Lamp & Glass Co., 1-7/8" h **40.00**
Palm Leaf, green or blue, Consolidated Lamp & Glass Co., 2-1/2" h **30.00**
Pineapple, blue, Consolidated Lamp & Glass Co., 3-1/8" h, damage to lid **15.00**
Pointed Rib, blue, Dithridge & Co., 2-1/4" h **40.00**
Punty Band, custard **45.00**
Scroll and Net
- Blue or green, Consolidated Lamp & Glass Co., 3" h **25.00**
- Clear, pink casing, Consolidated Lamp & Glass Co., 3" h **25.00**

Scroll in Scroll, blue, Dithridge & Co., 2-1/4" h **45.00**
Square Scroll, blue, Dithridge & Co., 3-1/2" h **15.00**
Sunset, white, 3" h, Dithridge & Co. (40-U) **35.00**
Tall Vertical Panel, blue, 3-3/4" h **15.00**
Tapered Pillar, opalware, band painted with heron, similar to Boston and Sandwich, 3-3/4" h **20.00**
Winged Scroll, custard **80.00**

Pattern glass (priced individually)

Actress, pewter top **45.00**
Banded Portland, maiden's blush **40.00**
Barred Ovals, ruby stained, orig top **40.00**
Beautiful Lady, colorless, 1905 . . **25.00**
Block and Fan, colorless, 1891 . **20.00**
Cane, apple green **30.00**
Croesus, amethyst, gold trim . . . **75.00**
Crown Jewel, c1880, etched . . . **35.00**
Dakota, ruby stained, orig top . . . **85.00**
Diamond Horseshoe, ruby stained **45.00**
Diamond Point and Leaf, blue milk glass (F-489) **40.00**
Double Deck, opaque green **40.00**
Feather (28-N) **25.00**
Flower and Rain, red **425.00**
Four Square, Billows **100.00**

Three miscellaneous melon ribbed satin glass salt shakers, all with white opaque ground, hand-painted flowers, yellow and orange pansies on first two from left, blue-purple violets on right, **$150.** *Photo courtesy of Joy Luke Fine Art Brokers and Auctioneers.*

Francesware, Hobbs, Brockunier Co., c1880, hobnail, frosted, amber stained 45.00
Haines 45.00
Little Apple, ftd 110.00
Lobe, squatty 120.00
Locket on Chain, Heisey, ruby stained, orig top 125.00
Maine (22-M) 25.00
Medallion Sprig, 3-1/4" h, shaded cobalt blue to white, orig base (33-S) 75.00
Mikado, vaseline 30.00
O'Hara Diamond, ruby stained . . 35.00
Paneled Sprig, milk glass, green dec 37.50
Scrolled Panel, opaque green . . 35.00
Stars and Stripes (173-S) 25.00
Thousand Eye, vaseline 30.00
Tulip 100.00
Twelve Panel, scrolled pink . . . 130.00
Wheat and Barley, blue 40.00
Whirligig, colorless, tin top, (177-A) 20.00

SALTS, OPEN

History: When salt was first mined, the supply was limited and expensive. The necessity for a receptacle in which to serve the salt resulted in the first open salt, a crude, hand-carved, wooden trencher.

As time passed, salt receptacles were refined in style and materials. In the 1500s, both master and individual salts existed. By the 1700s, firms such as Meissen, Waterford, and Wedgwood were making glass, china, and porcelain salts. Leading glass manufacturers in the 1800s included Libbey, Mount Washington, New England, Smith Bros., Vallerysthal, Wave Crest, and Webb.

Open salts were the only means of serving salt until the appearance of the shaker in the late 1800s. The ease of procuring salt from a shaker greatly reduced the use of and need for the open salts.

Place setting size or individual sized salts were often sold as sets. They would be included in a place setting, complete with a tiny spoon for each user. Master salts are larger and often covered vessels. They held a larger quantity of salt and were often used on tables or side boards if place setting size salts were not used.

References: William Heacock and Patricia Johnson, *5,000 Open Salts*, Richardson Printing Corporation, 1982, 1986 value update; L. W. and D. B. Neal, *Pressed Glass Dishes of the Lacy Period 1925-1950*, published by author, 1962; Allan B. and Helen B. Smith have authored and published 10 books on open salts beginning with *One Thousand Individual Open Salts Illustrated* (1972) and ending with *1,334 Open Salts Illustrated: The Tenth Book* (1984). Daniel Snyder did the master salt sections in volumes 8 and 9. In 1987, Mimi Rudnick compiled a revised price list for the 10 Smith Books; Kenneth Wilson, *American Glass 1760-1930*, two vols., Hudson Hills Press and The Toledo Museum of Art, 1994.

Periodical: *OSCAR*, Open Salt Collectors of the Atlantic Region, 820 Sunlight Dr., York, PA 17402; *Salty Comments*, 401 Nottingham Rd, Newark, DE 19711; *Salt Talk*, New England Society of Open Salt Collectors, P.O. Box 177, Sudbury, MA 01776.

Collectors' Clubs: New England Society of Open Salt Collectors, P.O. Box 177, Sudbury, MA 01776; Open Salt Collectors of the Atlantic Region, 820 Sunlight Dr., York, PA 17402.

Note: The numbers in parenthesis refer to plate numbers in the Smiths' books.

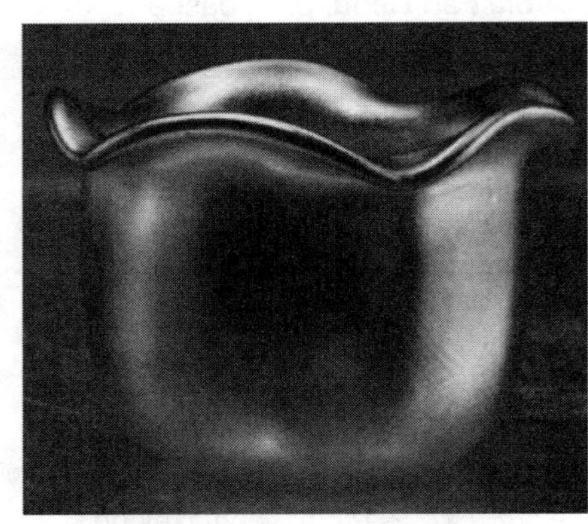

Art glass, Quezal, ruffled edge, strong pink highlights on gold iridescent ground, 1-1/2" d, 1-1/4" h, **$275.** *Photo courtesy of David Rago Auctions.*

Art glass

Baccarat, double salts, clear, pedestal, paneled sides, one salt with frosted panels, sgd (395) 125.00

Cameo glass

Galle, green pedestal, enamel dec, sgd, early, place setting size (205) 295.00
Webb, red ground, white lacy dec around bowl, place setting size, matching spoon (137) 600.00

Steuben, cobalt blue, pedestal, place setting size (485) 250.00
Tiffany, irid bluish-gold, ftd, ribbed body, waisted rim, inscribed "L.C.T." 2-1/4" d, 1-1/2" h 300.00

Colored glass

Aventurine, narrow base, master size (316) 75.00
Cambridge, Decagon pattern, amber, place setting size (468) 40.00
Clambroth, Sawtooth, Sandwich, c1850, master size 65.00
Cobalt blue, wafer base, 2-1/6" h, 2-1/16" d, master size 150.00

Cranberry

Emb ribs, applied crystal ruffed rim, silver-plated holder with emb lions heads, master size, 3" d, 1-3/4" h 160.00
Ruffled salt held by rigaree in wire holder, unmarked, place setting size (373) 190.00

Green, light, dark green ruffled top, open pontil, master size (449) . . . 90.00
Milk glass, turquoise, double, sgd "Vallerystahl, Made in France," place setting size 45.00
Moser, cobalt blue, pedestal, gold bands, applied flowers, sgd, place setting size (380) 70.00
Opalescent, blue, silver rim, English, registry number, master size (384) 115.00
Opaque blue, double, molded rim form, 3-1/2" h 185.00

Purple slag

Emb shell pattern, place setting size, place setting size 50.00
Leaf and Flower, master size (313) 65.00

Raspberry, heavy, sq, Pairpoint, master size (444) 75.00
Sapphire blue, white enameled stylized leaves, blossoms, and scrolls, touches of pink, green, and yellow, gold rim and wafer foot, place setting size 3-1/8" d, 1-1/2" h 290.00
Vaseline, 3" d, 2-1/4" h, applied crystal trim around middle, silver-plated stand, master size 125.00

Cut glass

2" d, 1-1/2" h, cut ruby ovals, allover dainty white enameled scrolls, clear ground, gold trim, scalloped top, place setting size 60.00
2" d, 2" h, green cut to clear, silver-plated holder, master size . 115.00

Early American glass

Cobalt blue

3" h, paneled with diamond foot 125.00
3-1/8" l, Neal CN 1a, two feet replaced, small chips 200.00
3-3/8" h, facet cut, fan rim, sq foot, edges ground 125.00

Colorless

2-5/8" l, colorless, variant, Neal MN3, chips 305.00
3" h, colorless, blown, expanded diamond bowl, applied petal foot 145.00
3" l, colorless, lacy, eagle, Neal EE1, chips 200.00

Opalescent, fiery
3-1/8" l, 3-1/8" l, Neal BS2, chips **275.00**
3-1/4" l, fiery opalescent, eagles, Neal EE3b, chips.......... **500.00**

Sapphire blue, 3-5/8" l, Neal BT 2, very minor flakes **1,075.00**

Vaseline, 2-3/8" h, 2-3/4" d, pressed, emb rib, silver-plated ftd holder .. **55.00**

Figurals

Basket, 3" h, 2-3/4" d, coral colored glass, silver-plated basket frame, salt with cut polished facets **55.00**

Boat, lacy, colorless, New England, Neal BT-9, slight rim roughness . **160.00**

Bucket, 2-1/2" d, 1-5/8" h, Bristol glass, turquoise, white, green, and brown enameled bird, butterfly and trees, silver-plated rim and handle..... **75.00**

Pattern glass, colorless unless noted otherwise

Bakewell Pears, master size.... **30.00**

Barberry, pedestal, master size.. **40.00**

Basketweave, sleigh, master size (397) **100.00**

Crystal Wedding, place setting size **25.00**

Diamond Point, cov, master size **75.00**

Eureka pattern, ruby stained, master size **40.00**

Excelsior, master size **30.00**

Eyewinker, pedestal, master size (346) **90.00**

Fine Rib, flint, place setting size . **35.00**

Gothic Arches variant, pedestal, 2-1/2" h, c1865, master size (3606) **35.00**

Grasshopper, master size...... **35.00**

Hamilton, pedestal, master size (344) **40.00**

Hawaiian Lei, place setting size (477) **35.00**

Hobnail, round, master size (407) **40.00**

Horizontal Framed Ovals, master size **30.00**

Horn of Plenty, master size (329) **85.00**

Liberty Bell, oval, place setting size **25.00**

Palmette, master size (471)..... **65.00**

Paneled Diamond, pedestal, master size (331) **50.00**

Pineapple and Fan, place setting size **25.00**

Red Block, ruby stained, master size **65.00**

Ruby Thumbprint, ruby stained, sq, master size **65.00**

Sawtooth Circle, master size ... **35.00**

Scrolled Heart, green, master size **275.00**

Snail, ruby stained, master size . **75.00**

Square Pillared, master size (341) **35.00**

Sunflower, pedestal, master size (346) **40.00**

Three Face, place setting size .. **40.00**

Thumbprint pattern, double salts, octagonal, place setting size (394) **90.00**

Torpedo, ruby stained, master size **65.00**

Viking, master size **30.00**

Vintage, master size (340) **40.00**

Sandwich Glass

History: In 1818, Deming Jarves was listed in the Boston Directory as a glass maker. That same year, he was appointed general manager of the newly formed New England Glass Company. In 1824, Jarves toured the glassmaking factories in Pittsburgh, left New England Glass Company, and founded a glass factory in Sandwich.

Originally called the Sandwich Manufacturing Company, it was incorporated in April 1826 as the Boston & Sandwich Glass Company. From 1826 to 1858, Jarves served as general manager. The Boston & Sandwich Glass Company produced a wide variety of wares in differing levels of quality. The factory used the free-blown, blown three mold, and pressed glass manufacturing techniques. Both clear and colored glass were used.

Competition in the American glass industry in the mid-1850s resulted in lower-quality products. Jarves left the Boston & Sandwich company in 1858, founded the Cape Cod Glass Company, and tried to duplicate the high quality of the earlier glass. Meanwhile, at the Boston & Sandwich Glass Company, emphasis was placed on mass production. The development of a lime glass (non-flint) led to lower costs for pressed glass. Some free-blown and blown-and-molded pieces, mostly in color, were made. Most of this Victorian-era glass was enameled, painted, or acid etched.

By the 1880s, the Boston & Sandwich Glass Company was operating at a loss. Labor difficulties finally resulted in the closing of the factory on January 1, 1888.

References: Raymond E. Barlow and Joan E. Kaiser, *Glass Industry in Sandwich*, Vol. 1 (1993), Vol. 2 (1989), Vol. 3 (1987), Vol. 4 (1983), and Vol. 5 (1999), distributed by Schiffer Publishing; —, *A Guide to Sandwich Glass: Cut Ware, A General Assortment and Bottles,* Schiffer Publishing, 1999; —, *Price Guide for the Glass Industry in Sandwich Vols. 1-4*, Schiffer Publishing, 1993; Ruth Webb Lee, *Sandwich Glass Handbook*, Charles E. Tuttle, 1966; —, *Sandwich Glass*, Charles E. Tuttle, 1966; George S. and Helen McKearin, *American Glass*, Random House, 1979; W. and D. B. Neal, *Pressed Glass Dishes of the Lacy Period 1925-1950,* published by author, 1962; Catherine M. V. Thuro, *Oil Lamps II*, Collector Books, 1994 value update; Kenneth Wilson, *American Glass 1760-1930,* two vols., Hudson Hills Press and The Toledo Museum of Art, 1994.

Museum: Sandwich Glass Museum, Sandwich, MA, http://www.sandwichglassmuseum.org.

Bank, 12" h, colorless, applied peacock blue rigaree, rooster finial, two silver U.S. dimes dated 1835 within knob stem **8,000.00**

Basket, 5-1/2" h, 5-1/2" w, ruffled box pleated top, White Burmese, candy pink to yellow peachblow-type, applied frosted thorn handle.......... **795.00**

Bowl
6-1/2" d, pressed, Peacock Eye pattern, grape border, lacy, colorless, ftd, shallow flake on foot **500.00**
7-1/2" d, pressed, lacy, Tulip and Acanthus pattern, slight roughness **45.00**
9-1/2" d, pressed, Gothic Arches pattern, lacy, colorless, Lee 129 .... **185.00**

Butter dish, cov
Bluerina, 4-7/8" h, enameled dec **675.00**
Gothic pattern, colorless, flint **200.00**
Horn of Plenty pattern, colorless, flint, bust of George Washington finial, small scallop chips **1,700.00**

Candlesticks, pr, pressed
9-3/4" h, 3-5/8" d base, vaseline, petal socket over dolphin standard, small head, sq double-step base, c1845-70, imperfections. **1,265.00**
10-1/4" h, canary, dolphin, single step, chip and flakes on socket petals **1,100.00**
10-1/4" h, vaseline, petal socket over dolphin standard, large heads, sq single-step base, c1845-70, very minor imperfections and flaws **2,650.00**
10-1/4" h, 3-1/4" d, turquoise, petal socket over dolphin standard with large head, well-defined eye, sq base, c1845-70, imperfections **4,600.00**
10-1/4" h, 3-3/4" d, light blue, petal socket over dolphin standard, large head, well-defined eyes, sq base, c1845-70, minor flaws and imperfections **9,775.00**
10-1/4" h, 3-3/4" d, vaseline, petal socket over dolphin standard, large head, well-defined eyes, sq base, c1845-70, cracked sockets, imperfections **980.00**
11" h, blue hexagonal sockets with scrolling leaf designs joined by

clambroth wafers over acanthus leaf dec baluster-form standard, sq base, c1840-50, one with repaired standard **1,265.00**

Celery vase

7-3/4" h, Excelsior pattern, colorless, flint **90.00**

8-1/2" h, Diamond Thumbprint pattern, colorless, flint **150.00**

9" h, Loop pattern, dark blue, ground base, flakes around base. . **420.00**

11-1/4" h, Arch pattern, cobalt blue, cascade base **500.00**

Salt shaker, Christmas, yellow ground, green leaves, brown decoration, original top, marked "Pat Dec 25, 1877," 2-3/4" h, 1-3/4" d, some wear to design, **$95.**

Christmas salt, orig 5" x 5-1/2" box, amethyst, teal blue, canary, yellow, and sapphire blue salts, marked caps and agitators, ground mouth, smooth base, box marked "Dana K. Alden's World Renowned Table Salt Bottles" . . **500.00**

Claret, 4-1/2" h, Horn of Plenty pattern, flint, set of eight **500.00**

Cologne bottle

5-1/2" h, paneled, 12-sided form, teal blue, fiery blue opalescent neck, tooled flared mouth, smooth base, 1860-80 . . . . **350.00**

5-5/8" h, sq tapered form, thumbprint pattern on side panel, herringbone corners, fiery blue opalescent, opaque blue neck and mouth, tooled mouth, smooth base, c1860-80 . . . . **800.00**

6" h, blown three mold, medium amethyst, flared mouth, pontil scar, c1820, McKearin GI-7, type 4 . . . . **300.00**

6" h, paneled, corseted form, amethyst, tooled mouth, pontil scar, c1840-60 . . . . **700.00**

6-3/8" h, tapered monument building form, cobalt blue, tooled flared mouth, smooth base, c1860-80, mouth roughness and numerous chips **120.00**

6-3/4" h, blown molded, green canary, Elongated Loop pattern, paneled octagonal body with petals at base, stopper with six-petal base, c1840-70, very minor imperfections and flaw **435.00**

7" h, two-pc mold, 12 body panels, deep sapphire blue, flared mouth, smooth base, period stopper, c1860 . . . . **250.00**

7-1/8" h, paneled, 12-sided form, colorless, inward rolled mouth, smooth base, nearly perfect label reads "Daisy/Cologne/Fragrant And Lasting/L. M. Wardner/ Druggist/St. Regis Falls, N.Y.," c1860-80 . . . . **160.00**

7-1/4" h, paneled, 12-sided form, sapphire blue with purple tone, outward rolled mouth, pontil scar, 1840-60 . . . . **250.00**

Compote

6" d, 5-7/8" h, Horn of Plenty pattern bowl, Waffle pattern base, flint, minor chips and roughness **145.00**

9" d, 12" h, Sandwich Star pattern, electric blue. **5,500.00**

10-1/2" d, 4-3/4" h, cranberry overlay, oval cuts, enameled birds and flowers on inner surface, c1890 . . . . **495.00**

Creamer

4-1/2" h, Heart and Scale, flint, normal flaking, mold roughness **40.00**

4-1/2" h, 2-3/4" d, blown three mold, cobalt blue, paneled and reeded body, applied handle, c1825-40, very minor imperfections. **2,875.00**

Cup and saucer, lacy, colorless **200.00**

Cup plate

Blue, lacy, ship **125.00**

Violet Blue, lacy, heart **325.00**

Curtain tiebacks, pr, 3" d, flower, white opalescent, orig hardware **165.00**

Decanter, blown three mold

McKearin GI-29, sapphire blue, flared mouth, smooth base, half pint, 1860-80, top surface of mouth ground, no stopper **70.00**

McKearin GII-18, colorless, flared mouth, pontil scar, pint, period stopper, 1820-40 . . . . **110.00**

McKearin GII-18, colorless, flared mouth, pontil scar, quart, period stopper, 1820-40 . . . . **130.00**

McKearin GIII-5, colorless, flared mouth, pontil scar, quart, period stopper, 1820-40, some int. haze near base. **120.00**

McKearin GIII-6, colorless, flared mouth, pontil scar, pint, no stopper, 1820-40 . . . . **80.00**

Waffle and Thumbprint, orig stopper, canary, pint, applied lip, polished pontil, 13-1/4" h **6,250.00**

Dish, cov, Princess Feather Medallion and Basket of Flowers, lacy, grape border around rim of base, 10-1/2" l, 8-3/4" w, 5" h **6,500.00**

Dish, open, colorless

5-3/4" l, Rayed Peacock Eye pattern, flint **185.00**

6-1/4" l, Tulip and Arches Leaf pattern, lacy **145.00**

8" d, Scotch Plaid pattern, lacy, pontil mark **150.00**

12" l, 9" w, 1-3/4" h, Peacock Eye pattern, flint **800.00**

Egg cup, 3-3/4" h, Horn of Plenty pattern, flint **90.00**

Ewer, 10-7/8" h, clambroth body, green applied handle and band, pewter fittings **65.00**

Flat iron, amethyst, three minor flakes on edges, handle check **650.00**

Flip, 5-5/8" h, blown three mold, colorless, sheared rim, pontil scar, 1820-40, McKearin GII-18. . . . . **130.00**

Girandole, Star and Punty, three-light center girandole with matching single light side sticks, five opaque powder blue with sand finish fonts, each set into spun brass sockets, alternating bright and satin finish bands, center girandole fitted with two brass scrolled arms, figural standard of cavalier and his maiden, rect marble base, side sticks with matching standards and marble bases, all fonts with removable top mounted brass leaf band coronets, hanging Star and Rosette prisms, c1840-60, 19-1/2" h center, 17" h sides, old staple repair to one font, missing 12 prisms **3,500.00**

Goblet

Gothic pattern, colorless, flint 12-pc set **650.00**

Horn of Plenty pattern, colorless, flint, 6" h. **150.00**
Paneled Fern, flint, frosted. . . **270.00**
Paneled Fern, flint, low resonance **80.00**
Sandwich Star, flint, 6-1/2" h **1,500.00**
Sandwich Vine, colorless, flint, gilt highlights on pattern and stem, 6-1/4" h, extremely rare . **10,500.00**
Sandwich Vine, colorless, flint, hexagonal foot, gilt dec rim, 6-3/8" h, wear to gilt. **1,700.00**
Sandwich Vine, colorless, flint, round foot, mint gilt dec rim, 6-1/2" h **2,400.00**

Honey dish, lacy, medium red-amber, two scallops missing **120.00**

Inkwell

2-3/8" h, sq, honey amber, applied brass collar, hinged cap, smooth base **40.00**
2-9/16", cylindrical domed form, colorless, pink and white stripes, sheared mouth, applied pewter collar and cap, smooth base **2,300.00**

Jewel casket, cov, 6-1/2" l, oblong, lacy, colorless, Lee 162 . . . . . **1,200.00**

Lamp, fluid, cut overlay

10-5/8" h, transparent amethyst cut to clear font, quatrefoil, oval, and punty cut designs, flared fluted columnar standard, sq stepped marble base with brass trim, c1860-80, minor wear . . . **2,530.00**
11" h, 4-3/4" d base, pink cut to white cut to clear font, quatrefoil, oval, vesica, and star cut designs, reeded standard, stepped marble base, second half 19th C, minor base imperfections **1,955.00**
11-3/4" h, cobalt blue cut to white cut to clear font, slash, punty, and oval cut designs, flared fluted columnar brass standard, sq stepped marble base with brass trim, c1860-80, minor imperfections, price for pr **4,025.00**
12" h, 4-1/2" d base, cobalt blue cut to white cut to clear font, oval, star, vesica, and quatrefoil cut designs, clear wafer, reeded brass standard, stepped marble base, second half 19th C, minor flaws and imperfections **1,100.00**
12" h, 4-3/4" d base, red cut to white cut to clear font, oval, quatrefoil, star, and vesica cut designs, reeded standard, stepped marble base, second half 19th C . . **865.00**
12" h, 5" d base, cobalt blue cut to white cut to clear font, oval, star, vesica, and quatrefoil cut designs, clear wafer, reeded brass standard, stepped marble base, second half 19th C, very minor flaws and imperfections . . **1,100.00**
12-1/4" h, 5-1/8" d base, pink cut to white cut to clear font, quatrefoil, oval, and star cut designs, reeded brass standard, stepped marble base, second half 19th C, minor flaws and imperfections . . **2,070.00**
12-1/2" h, cranberry cut to white cut to clear font, quatrefoil, star, and oval cut designs, flared fluted columnar brass standard, sq stepped marble base with brass trim, c1860-80, very minor wear **2,070.00**
12-3/4" h, 5" d, base, cobalt blue cut to white cut to clear font, oval, star, vesica, and punty cut designs, clear wafer, brass standard, stepped marble base, second half 19th C, minor imperfections **2,300.00**
12-3/4" h, 5" d base, white cut to ruby font, quatrefoil, oval, vesica, and star-cut designs, clear wafer, reeded base standard, stepped marble base, second half 19th C, imperfections **1,150.00**
12-7/8" h, opaque white cut to ruby font, punty, and oval cut designs, fluted opal baroque base, 1860-80, minor imperfections **1,380.00**
13" h, 5" d, cobalt blue cut to white cut to clear font, oval and punty cut designs, reeded brass standard, stepped marble base, second half 19th C, flaw and minor imperfections **1,610.00**
13" h, 5-3/8" d base, cobalt blue cut to white cut to clear font, oval, quatrefoil, star, and vesica cut designs, clear wafer, reeded standard, stepped marble base, second half 19th C, minor imperfections **3,220.00**
13" h, 5-1/2" d font, 5-3/4" sq base, Bellflower, rose cut to white cut to clear font, eight three-petal blooms alternating upward and downward, double row of punties on lower section, brass connection to white opaque Baroque base with gilt dec, c1860-80 . . . . **1,550.00**
13-1/4" h, 5-1/4" d base, white cut to emerald green font, quatrefoil, star, oval, and vesica cut designs, black pressed glass reeded standard, baroque base with gilt accents, c1860-80, gilt dec worn, possibly re-plastered. **6,325.00**
13-1/2" h, 5" d, opaque medium blue cut to clear font, quatrefoil and punty cut designs, glass standard of medium blue cut to clear with elongated oval and punty cut designs, stepped marble base, second half 19th C **690.00**
13-1/2" h, 5" d base, ruby cut to white cut to clear font, punty, vesica, and oval cut designs, pressed glass standard, baroque base with gilt embellishments, c1860-80, very minor gilt wear **1,380.00**
13-1/2" h, 5-1/8" d base, white cut to medium blue glass font, oval, punty, and slash cut designs, medium blue pressed glass reeded hexagonal standard, sq base with gilt foliate motifs, minor imperfections **1,955.00**
13-1/2" h, 6-1/2" d base, white cut to emerald green font, quatrefoil, star, and oval cut designs, pressed clambroth glass reeded standard, baroque base, gilt dec, c1860-80, minor flaws, imperfections, gilt wear **4,890.00**
13-5/8" h, cobalt blue cut to white cut to clear, oval and punty cut designs, gilt scroll dec, opaque white fluted standard, sq base, 1860-70, imperfections, several heat cracks under base . **1,265.00**
13-3/4" h, 5" d base, white cut to peacock blue font, oval, punty, and slash cut designs, pressed glass reeded standard, baroque base, c1860-80. . . . . **1,610.00**
14" h, opaque white cut to clear, punty and oval cut designs on font, floral gilt band, octagonal fluted opal standard, sq base, 1860-70, worn gilt borders, minor imperfections **525.00**
14-3/8" h, ruby cut to clear font, floral and vine gilt band, punty and oval cut design, octagonal opal fluted standard, sq base with gilt borders, c1860-70, minor gilt wear **1,035.00**
15-1/2" h, 6" d base, white cut to red font, quatrefoil oval, star, and slash cut design, foliate brass rings, punty and oval cut standard, stepped marble base, second half 19th C **2,415.00**
16" h, 5-1/2" d, cobalt blue cut to white cut to clear font, punty cut designs, conforming cut double

overlay standard, stepped marble base, c1860-80, minor imperfections to base... **29,900.00**

16-1/4" h, cobalt blue cut to white cut to clear glass font, oval cut designs, brass connector joins similar overlay and cut design standard, sq stepped marble base with gilt metal trim, c1860-80, minor imperfections **12,650.00**

16-1/4" h, cobalt blue cut to white, cut to clear glass font, slash, punty, and oval cut designs, brass connector joins font to similar standard, sq stepped marble base, gilt-metal trim, c1860-80, minor imperfections **9,775.00**

16-1/4" h, 5-1/2" d base, white cut to clear glass font, punty cut designs, conforming glass standard, stepped marble base, c1860-80, minor imperfections to base **4,025.00**

17" h, cranberry cut to white cut to clear font, oval, punty, and vesica cut designs, double overlay standard with similar designs, sq stepped marble base, c1860-80, crack to font **460.00**

21" h, 6-3/4" d base, white cut to green font, quatrefoil punty and oval cut designs on opaque pale green glass standard, stepped marble base, mid-19th C, restoration............. **4,320.00**

28-1/2" h, 6" d base, baluster-shaped frosted cut-glass shade over foliate ring, baluster standard embellished with foliage and eagle centering image of George Washington, prisms, stepped marble base, 19th C, wear to gilding and minor imperfections **2,415.00**

28-1/2" h, 6" d, frosted cut-glass shade over scrolling foliate ring on overlay white cut to clear standard, prisms, stepped marble base, 19th C, minor wear to gilding and other minor imperfections **1,265.00**

33-1/4" h, 6-1/4" d, frosted and cut colorless glass shade, slash and quatrefoil cut designs in font, punty standard and gilt metal and stepped marble base, 1860-80, minor imperfections **10,350.00**

Lamp, fluid, pressed

9-1/2" h, 3" d base, Bigler pattern, octagonal concave paneled standard, sq base, c1840-60, amethyst, minor imperfections **2,185.00**

9-1/2" h, 3" d base, Bigler pattern, octagonal concave paneled standard, sq base, c1840-60, deep amethyst, imperfections . **2,185.00**

9-3/4" h, 3" d base, Bigler pattern, octagonal concave paneled standard, sq base, c1840-60, price for pr **4,600.00**

10-1/2" h, 3-1/2" d base, Waisted Loop pattern, yellow canary, pressed monument base, c1840-60, minor chips to base **2,990.00**

11-1/2" h, ring punty, ellipse, punty, and diamond point colorless fonts, brass collar, triple-pressed glass dolphin standard, stepped round base, one base opal glass, other translucent medium blue, c1860-80, imperfections, price for pr.................. **4,600.00**

Marble

1-3/4" d, spangled, green, red, white, and blue **150.00**

2-1/8" d, cranberry and white swirl, Lutz-type **150.00**

2-1/8" d, spangled, multicolored, roughness and some nicks. **145.00**

2-5/8" d, spangled, red, white, and blue **525.00**

Milk pan, 7-1/4" d, 3" h, free blown, folded rim, pinched lip, green .. **375.00**

Mustard pot, cov, Peacock Eye pattern, lacy, colorless **395.00**

Pitcher, 10" h,

Amberina Verde, fluted top .. **325.00**

Electric Blue, enameled floral dec, fluted top, threaded handle. **425.00**

Reverse Amberina, fluted top **400.00**

Plate, colorless

6" d, Plaid pattern, few scratches **65.00**

6" d, Shell pattern, lacy **165.00**

7" d, Rayed Peacock Eye pattern **125.00**

8" d, Plaid pattern, few chips.. **85.00**

9-1/2" d, Quatrefoil, lacy ... **1765.00**

Pomade jar, figural, bear

Blue, base imp retailer's name "X. Bazin, Philada," 4-1/2" h, chips **300.00**

Clambroth, imp retailer's name "F. B. Strouse, N.Y.," 3-3/4" h, chips **525.00**

Deep amethyst, chips, wear .. **95.00**

Relish, 8-1/8" l, Pipes of Pan pattern, colorless.................. **250.00**

Salt, open, master, lacy, Chariot, opaque blue, Neal CT-1, **$600.**

Salt, open

1-3/4" h, blown three mold, cobalt blue, sheared rim, pontil scar, c1820-40, McKearin GIII-3. **600.00**

2" h, 3-1/8" d, blue, pressed, floral, Barlow 1460, minor chips, mold imperfections **690.00**

Sauce bottle, 5-7/8" h, Horn of Plenty, colorless, flint, arched panel engraved "Heswan," two small annealing lines at top **120.00**

Sauce dish, colorless

Beaded Scale and Eye pattern, daisy center **75.00**

Horn of Plenty pattern, flint, 4-1/2" d **40.00**

Peacock Eye pattern, flint.... **50.00**

Roman Rosette pattern, fiery opalescent **100.00**

Shell Medallion pattern, octagonal **70.00**

Waffle pattern, flint **50.00**

Scent bottle

Deep emerald green, violin shape, orig pewter screw top, McKearin 241-31 .... **225.00**

Medium purple-blue, McKearin 241-55 .... **150.00**

Spillholder, 5" h, Sandwich Star pattern, electric blue, several small chips on base corners **800.00**

Spooner, colorless, flint, Gothic pattern **85.00**

String holder, 4" h, 3-7/8" d, colorless, cobalt blue rim and ring around string hole **375.00**

Sugar, cov, colorless, flint

Acanthus Leaf pattern **350.00**

Horn of Plenty pattern, 7-1/2" h **250.00**

Sweetmeat, cov, Waffle pattern, colorless, flint, one scallop rim chipped **95.00**

Talcum shaker, clambroth **135.00**

Toddy plate, 5-7/8" d, star and fan border, eight-pointed center star, raised sq hobs **120.00**

Toilette ewer, 10-1/2" h, panel-cut, cut glass, attributed to Boston and Sandwich Glass Co. or New England Glass Co., c1845-55.......... **120.00**

Vase, blown, 8-3/4" h, ribbed amber olive body, 20 textured icicles riding from icy base, rigaree trim, int., scratches **600.00**

Vase, pressed

9-1/2" h, 4-1/4" d, paneled tulip, blue-green, slightly flared scalloped rim and paneled sides, octagonal base, c1845-65, imperfections.......... **4,025.00**

10" h, 3" d base, Loop pattern, amethyst, gauffered rim, octagonal standard, sq base, mid-19th C, minor imperfections..... **2,070.00**

10" h, 4" d base, Loop pattern, emerald green, gauffered rim, six elongated loops, hexagonal standard, circular base, c1840-60, crack in base extends into standard **1,610.00**

10" h, 4" d base, Twisted Loop pattern, amethyst, gauffered rim, hexagonal standard, circular faceted base, c1840-60, minor imperfections.......... **3,220.00**

10" h, 4-1/4" d, tulip, emerald green, flaring scalloped rim, paneled sides, octagonal base, c1845-65, minor imperfections, price for pr **9,200.00**

10" h, 4-3/8" d, tulip, amethyst, flaring scalloped rim, octagonal base, c1845-65, very minor imperfections.......... **4,600.00**

11-1/8" h, 3" d base, amethyst, gauffered rim, faceted, octagonal ringed standard, tiered octagonal base, mid-19th C, minor imperfections.......... **2,185.00**

11-1/4" h, 3" w sq base, Bigler pattern, amethyst, gauffered rim, octagonal concave paneled standard, c1840-60, minor imperfections.......... **2,175.00**

11-1/2" h, 4-1/2" w, vaseline, four-printie, gauffered rim, hexagonal base, c1840-60, minor imperfections, price for pr. **1,035.00**

Vegetable dish

10-1/2" l, lacy, colorless, grape border, cov, Lee 151-1 .. **5,500.00**

10-3/4" l, medium amethyst, thinly blown bell, Three Printie Block pattern, expanded rim, heavy octagonal standard, sq base, c1845-60............. **1,250.00**

Vinegar bottle, 6-3/4" h, blown three mold, deep amethyst, cobalt blue stopper **395.00**

Whiskey taster

Clambroth, lacy, Lee pate 150-5 .... **120.00**

Cobalt blue, nine panels.... **185.00**

Wine, Sandwich Star, flint, 4-1/2" h **325.00**

SATIN GLASS

History: Satin glass, produced in the late 19th century, is an opaque art glass with a velvety matte (satin) finish achieved through treatment with hydrofluoric acid. A large majority of the pieces were cased or had a white lining.

While working at the Phoenix Glass Company, Beaver, Pennsylvania, Joseph Webb perfected mother-of-pearl satin glass in 1885. Similar to plain satin glass in respect to casing, mother-of-pearl satin glass has a distinctive surface finish and an integral or indented design, the most well known being diamond quilted.

The most common colors are yellow, rose, or blue. Rainbow coloring is considered choice.

Additional Listings: Cruets, Fairy Lamps, Miniature Lamps, and Rose Bowls.

Reproduction Alert: Satin glass, in both the plain and mother-of-pearl varieties, has been widely reproduced.

Basket

4-1/2" h, 4" w, pastel pink, herringbone patterned body, cased in white, very tightly ruffled rim, applied clear frosted handle **150.00**

4-3/4" h, 4" w, pink shaded to white, applied twisted and frosted rope handle **95.00**

5" h, 10" w, deep pink shading to white, leaf form shaped bowl, orange enamel dec, applied frosted leaf basket, large applied frosted thorn handle, Victorian **150.00**

5-1/2" h, 4" w, blue, herringbone patterned body, mother-of-pearl, applied frosted camphor feet **95.00**

6" h, 4-1/2" w, shaded rose to pink, herringbone patterned body, mother-of-pearl, applied frosted squared-off handle....... **150.00**

7" h, 5-1/2" w, pink and blue stripes, opaque white ext., ruffled edge, ornate twisted frosted handle **100.00**

8" h, 7" w, brilliant robin's egg blue over white, melon rib shape, heavily crimped and ruffled edge, frosted loop handle....... **100.00**

8-1/2" h, 8-1/2" w, candy stripe, deep pink, red, and white stripes, white int. lining, frosted thorn handle, slight roughage to handle.. **175.00**

8-3/4" h, 5-1/2" w, glossy, herringbone patterned body, deep pink shading to pale pink, applied amber V-shaped handle ... **110.00**

9" h, 5-1/2" w, herringbone-patterned body, mother-of-pearl, rose bowl shape, shaded deep rose to pale pink to off white, applied U-shaped handle................. **225.00**

9-1/2" h, 10" l, deep peach int., pale green ext., fancy ruffled edge, twisted frosted thorn handle, applied leaf feet, Victorian . **200.00**

10-1/2" h, 6" w, moiré patterned body, mother-of-pearl, chartreuse yellow shading to deep cranberry in amberina type coloration, box pleated top on deep basket, four frosted thorn feet, frosted loop handle, minor roughage to one foot **400.00**

11-3/4" h, 8-1/2" w, moiré patterned body, mother-of-pearl, deep red shading to pink, matching lining shading to white, applied frosted "V" shaped handle, four fancy thorn feet............... **600.00**

Biscuit jar, cov, 9" h, 5" d, diamond quilted patterned body, mother-of-pearl, shiny finish, rainbow stripes, flared cylindrical base, silver plated bail handle and cov, marked "Patent" **995.00**

Bowl

4" d, 3" h, diamond quilted, butterscotch, opal plated interior, polished pontil............ **80.00**

4-1/2" d, 2-3/4" h, ribbed body, mother-of-pearl, shaded pink ground, very tightly crimped ribbon edge **350.00**

5-7/8" d, 4-1/2" h, blue diamond quilted patterned body, mother-of-pearl, three applied frosted thorny glass vases forming feet, white lining, ruffled edge **365.00**

6-1/2" w, 4-1/2" h, bright pink and blue, white lining, Coin Spot pattern, scalloped rose bowl like top, three thorn feet, berry prunt **750.00**

7" d, 3-3/4" h, cased, raindrop, crimped ruffled rim, white ext., robin's egg blue int. **60.00**

10-1/2" d, 4-1/2" h, squatty, mother-of-pearl, gold, amber, and red moiré, lusterless white lining, deeply crimped rim **375.00**

Bride's basket, 9" d, 13-1/2" h, cased rose diamond within diamond int., white ext., clear ruffled rim, pinched sides, Middletown frame **425.00**

Bride's bowl

11" d, tri-corner form, cased pink shading to white, int. with purple and yellow enamel floral dec, intricate scalloped rim, Mt. Washington. **400.00**

11-1/2" d, 5-1/2" h, diamond quilted, reddish-orange shading to peach ext., hand enameled flowers and gilt leaves and birds, cased pale pink int. **1,300.00**

12" d, 14-3/4" h, cream ext., mother-of-pearl lining, enamel floral dec, ruffled clear edge with gold trim **450.00**

Bud vase, 7-1/2" h, bulbous, small tapered neck, opaque white, price for pr **90.00**

Celery vase

Herringbone-patterned body, mother-of-pearl, white base shades to raspberry to deep cranberry rim, applied clear frosted ruffled edge, silver plated holder marked "Aurora silver plated MFG" quadruple plate, attributed to Mt. Washington, c1885 . . . . **1,200.00**

8" h, pink shaded to white ext., white cased int., multicolored enamel floral dec with dragonflies around rim, Tufts frame. **450.00**

Cologne bottle, long dauber, green, oval foot, green, Lancaster Glass **95.00**

Cream pitcher, 4-1/2" h, 3-1/8" d, blue, raindrop patterned body, mother-of-pearl, frosted blue reeded handle, white lining, bulbous, round mouth. **195.00**

Cup and saucer, 3" h cup, 5" d saucer, pink to white raindrop patterned body, mother-of-pearl, frosted handle. **395.00**

Dish, 5-1/4" d, raspberry ground, ivory ruffled rim. **65.00**

Ewer

8-3/8" h, Herringbone, blue shading to white, cased int., applied colorless crimped handle. . **150.00**

8-1/2" h, pink, mother-of-pearl, frilly spout, thorn handle **385.00**

9-1/2" h, diamond quilted patterned body, mother-of-pearl, deep apricot shading to light ground, applied colorless thorn handle. **350.00**

10" h, cased red shading to pink, multicolored enamel floral dec, applied colorless crimped handle **150.00**

10-1/4" h, yellow shading to white, applied frosted handle, ftd, chip on lower tip of handle. **80.00**

19-1/2" h, ovoid creamy beige ground, light blue floral sprays, outlined in gold, floral emb metal mount with satyr head on handle, Victorian **900.00**

Finger bowl and underplate, blue diamond quilted patterned body, mother-of-pearl, sgd "Patent". . . **585.00**

Hatpin holder, 3-1/4" h, diamond quilted-patterned body, mother-of-pearl, pink ground, enameled floral dec. **175.00**

Jar, cov, 6-1/4" h, diamond quilted patterned body, mother-of-pearl, salmon ground, applied colorless floral final. **325.00**

Pair satin glass mantel lusters with cut glass prisms—electrified, **$145.** *Photo courtesy of Joy Luke Fine Art Brokers and Auctioneers.*

Marmalade jar, cov, 4-1/2" h, 3-1/2" d, diamond quilted-patterned body, mother-of-pearl, shaded pink ground, black etched dec of bird among berries and leaves, frosted applied shell ruffled top, silver-plated holder **250.00**

Mug

2-3/4" h, 2-1/4" d, barrel shape, deep rose to amber, diamond quilted-patterned body, creamy white lining, frosted loop handle, English. **175.00**

3-1/2" h, pink and gold looping, white ground, applied frosted reeded handle **175.00**

Nappy, 6" l, 2-1/2" h, handle, white, diamond quilted-patterned body, mother-of-pearl, triangular shaped top, applied frosted handle, allover gold dec, deeply crimped edge **425.00**

Paperweight, diamond quilted, turquoise blue, attributed to Fenton **60.00**

Perfume bottle, 4-1/2" h, 4" d, swirl patterned body, mother-of-pearl, shaded pink ground, white and orange flowers dec, atomizer missing. . **150.00**

Pitcher, bulbous

6" h, Herringbone patterned square body, yellow shading to white, opal plated interior, applied colorless handle, polished pontil. . . . **170.00**

6" h, 4-1/2" d, diamond quilted patterned body, mother-of-pearl, shaded blue ground, enameled pink and yellow floral dec, green leaves, oval top, applied handle **350.00**

7" h, light blue, multicolored enamel floral dec, opal plated interior, applied frosted handle, polished pontil **140.00**

7-1/2" h, pink, yellow plated interior, applied frosted handle, polished pontil **160.00**

7-3/4" h, dark blue-green shading to light, opal plated interior, applied frosted handle, polished pontil **190.00**

7-3/4" h, 6" d, melon ribbed body, mother-of-pearl, shaded pale pink to white ground, enameled white and gold coral dec, applied frosted handle **750.00**

8-1/2" h, white, hand-painted dec of thistle and two beetles, polished pontil, wear to dec **70.00**

9" h, red shaded to pink ext., opal plated interior, applied frosted thorn handle and rim, polished pontil **400.00**

Rose bowl

3" d, 2-1/2" h, mottled pink, polished pontil **50.00**

3-3/8" d, 4" h, shaded heavenly blue, herringbone-patterned body, mother-of-pearl, six-crimp top **195.00**

3-1/2" d, 2-3/4" h, blue, ground pontil mark. **385.00**

3-3/4" d, 2-3/8" h, heavenly blue, ribbon pattern, mother-of-pearl, nine-crimp top, white lining **235.00**

Vase, swirl, mother of pearl, shading blue to gold to tan, Stevens & Williams, 10" h, **$650.** *Photo courtesy of David Rago Auctions.*

4" h, shaded blue to white, Mezzotint cherub dec, Victorian **175.00**

4-1/2" d, bright yellow to white, enameled berries, leaves, and stems, Victorian **145.00**

5" d, 4-3/8" h, shaded blue, white lining, six-crimp top, lavender enameled leaves dec **115.00**

5-1/2" d, 5" h, bright green shading to pale green, enamel blue, pale yellow, and gold floral dec . **295.00**

Scent bottle, 4-3/8" l, tapered conical form, blue, silver repousse top, American, early 20th C, stopper missing **300.00**

Sugar bowl, cov, 5" h, 3-3/4" d, dark pink shading to light, enamel dec, silver-plate rim and cov **100.00**

Toothpick holder, 2-1/2" h, diamond quilted patterned body, mother-of-pearl, yellow ground **160.00**

Tumbler

3-1/2" h, rainbow, diamond quilted patterned body, mother-of-pearl, enamel floral dec, three white and pink single-petaled blossoms, four buds, four leaves and grass, gold rim **750.00**

3-3/4" h, 2-3/4" d, diamond quilted-patterned body, amberina, polished pontil **85.00**

3-3/4" h, 2-3/4" d, diamond quilted-patterned body, apricot **80.00**

3-3/4" h, 2-3/4" d, diamond quilted-patterned body, blue **70.00**

3-3/4" h, 2-3/4" d, diamond quilted-patterned body, pink **60.00**

3-3/4" h, 2-3/4" d, diamond quilted-patterned body, yellow **60.00**

3-3/4" h, 2-3/4" d, herringbone-pattern body, blue **65.00**

3-3/4" h, 2-3/4" d, raindrop-pattern body, pink and white **65.00**

4" h, apricot to pink to white, diamond quilted-patterned body, mother-of-pearl, c1880, small blister **60.00**

Vase

4-1/2" h, 5-5/8" d, ribbon-patterned body, mother-of-pearl, light blue, three-way top, pinched in side **375.00**

4-3/4" h, 4" d, diamond quilted-patterned body, mother-of-pearl, shaded heavenly blue, heavy gold floral dec, red enameled spider with mark on base "Whitehouse Glass Works, Stourbridge" **260.00**

5-1/2" h, 2-3/4" d, raindrop-patterned body, mother-of-pearl, blue, frosted amber edge ruffled fan top, white lining **145.00**

5-3/4" h, hobnail, mother-of-pearl, pink shades to pale pink base, four folded-in sides **500.00**

6-1/2" h, brown shaded to white, diamond quilted, blue, white, and orange enameled forget-me-nots dec, mother-of-pearl int. . . . **825.00**

7" h, Morgan, opaque white . . **90.00**

7" h, 3-5/8" d, diamond quilted patterned body, mother-of-pearl, shaded pink ground, blue flowers and morning glory dec, bee in flight **125.00**

7" h, 4-1/2" d, mother-of-pearl, Federzeichnung, bold air-traps randomly sweep down around perimeter, chocolate-colored ground, squiggly lines of burnished gold tracery, quadric-form top with gold embellishments in individual folds, gold enamel signature in pontil "Pat 9159" **2,500.00**

9" h, 3-1/2" w, swirl patterned body, mother-of-pearl, gold to pale pink-white, Mt Washington . **325.00**

Vase, vertical, ribbed, pinched tricorn top, pink, Stevens and Williams, 3" h, **$375.**

9-1/2" h, bulbous, diamond quilted, peach shading to white, opal plated interior, polished pontil, Mt Washington **300.00**

9-1/2" h, 5" w, blue shading to white, Coin Spot, lightly crimped rim pulled down to shoulder at 3 points, Mt Washington. **675.00**

10-1/2" h, 5-1/2" w, diamond quilted patterned body, mother-of-pearl, bulbous, heavenly blue shading to pale blue, creamy white lining, English **265.00**

10-3/4" h, diamond quilted-patterned body, mother-of-pearl, spray of carnations, long green stems, rose pink fading to pale pink at base **175.00**

11-1/2" h, 4" w, diamond quilted-patterned body, mother-of-pearl, bulbous, deep blue shading to white, four petal top, white flowers and orange branches dec, Victorian . . . **185.00**

SCHNEIDER GLASS

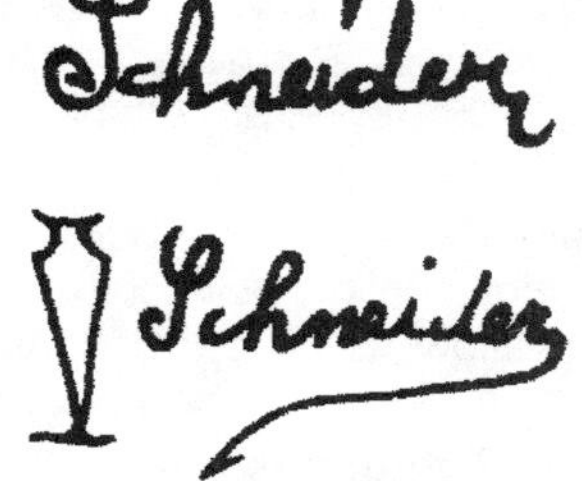

History: Brothers Ernest and Charles Schneider founded a glassworks at Epiney-sur-Seine, France, in 1913. Charles, the artistic designer, previously had worked for Daum and Gallé. Robert, son of Charles, assumed art direction in 1948. Schneider moved to Loris in 1962.

Although Schneider made tablewares, stained glass, and lighting fixtures, its best-known product is art glass, which exhibits simplicity of design and often has bubbles and streaking in larger pieces. Other styles include cameo-cut and hydrofluoric-acid-etched designs.

Schneider glass was signed with a variety of script and block signatures, "Le Verre Francais," or "Charder."

Bowl

5-1/4" d, 4-3/4" h, inverted rim on cylindrical colorless form, two applied geometric handles, green mottled disk foot, body etched with geometric border over stylized bowl of fruit, foot inscribed "Schneider," c1928....... **750.00**

6-3/4" h, inverted rim on cylindrical mottled pale orange overlaid with mottled orange and green, cameo etched stylized leaves and hanging flowers, ftd base, sgd "Charder" at lower side, incised "Le Verre Francais" at side of base, base wear............. **920.00**

13-1/2" d, 4-3/4" h, upright rim on shallow bowl, mottled purple and brown to burgundy, frosted purple base, inscribed "Schneider" at side of base, scratches to int. and base **650.00**

14" d, flared rim, shallow bowl, pink glass dec with frosted ext. design of lines and circles, ftd base, etched "Schneider" at lower side, base wear............ **1,850.00**

Box, cov, 3" h, Art Dec, glossy citron cover, mottled royal blue and citron base, enameled script sgd "Schneider," interior rim nicks **200.00**

Candlesticks, 7" h, 8-1/2" h, 9-1/2" h, colorless crystal, hexagonal shape, ground base, three-pc set..... **125.00**

Center bowl, 12" d, 3-1/4" h, mottled orange border, yellow and white body, edge inscribed "Schneider," base inscribed "France-Ovington New York," inside wear **345.00**

Charger, 15-1/2" d, three pulls on curved rim, shallow bowl of mottled blue to yellow, inscribed "Schneider" at side, scratches **450.00**

Cigarette lighter base, 7-1/2" h, 3" h mottled yellow pear-shaped glass, etched purple and rose-pink Art-Deco elements, inscribed "Le Verre Francais" on gilt metal atomizer top **375.00**

Compote

8" d, 3-1/4" h, flared flattened rim tapering to squatty green vessel, trapped bubbles, black ground, ftd base, inscribed "Schneider" at side of base, scratches to base . **290.00**

10" d, 8-1/2" h, tango red, mottled blue-black rim, shaped bowl, wrought metal pedestal foot, three glass beads, glass stem inscribed 'Schneider France" **690.00**

15" d, 6-1/4" h, folded rim on broad centerbowl, Tango Red streaked with aubergine, applied purple and black stem, foot inscribed "Schneider"............ **525.00**

Dish, 13-1/2" x 5-1/2", mottled orange and dark blue, amethyst with white ribbing, pedestal base........ **275.00**

Ewer, 15-1/2" h, ovoid, pointed spout, thick cushion foot, mottled white frosted ground, mottled orange and green overlay, etched floral bands, applied purple angled handle at shoulder, engraved "Charder Le Verre Francais" **1,250.00**

Lamp, 15-1/2" d, hanging, creamy glass half-round light bowl, speckled yellow and red, edge inscribed "Schneider," suspended by twisted and knotted cord and wire chain, three matching glass beads **1,380.00**

Night light, 5" h, 3-3/4" w, round glass globe, acid finish shading from yellow to blue spatter, pewter-style figural ftd base, three butterflies hold the shade, some bends to silver-plated base **650.00**

Pitcher

6-1/2" h, bulbous tango red body, elongated mottled blue-brown neck and spout, applied purple glass handle, inscribed "Schneider"............ **635.00**

6-1/2" h, mottled Art Deco orange bulbous body, aubergine base, applied angular handle, marked "Schneider" at lower edge . **345.00**

13-3/4" h, oval mottled brown and yellow ground, silver foil inclusions, amethyst-purple angular applied handle, point nicked at end **460.00**

Serving plate, 14" d, 3" h, transparent green-yellow dish, mottled orange pedestaled foot, inscribed "Schneider France".................... **345.00**

Tazza, 15-1/2" d, 3-1/2" h, slightly triangular top with three pulled points, shades of yellow, orange, and dark purple spattering, purple striped short pedestal **850.00**

Vase

4" h, Bijou, tomato red, four applied cabochons, sgd "Schneider, France" in script........ **1,500.00**

6-3/4" h, flared rim, cylindrical, sea foam green, swirled ribs starting at base, dec with raised repeating stylized "V" motif under rim, enclosed bubbles, etched "Schneider" on side...... **990.00**

7" h, oviform, wide everted rim, applied black applications on two sides, carved as overlapping flowerheads, carved "Schneider" **1,700.00**

7-1/4" h, squat waisted form, everted rim, internally dec with air bubbles, three applied handles, engraved "Schneider/France" **1,000.00**

9" h, Jade, violets with yellow centers, soft pink ground. **1,100.00**

9" h, spherical, medial band of applied sunbursts in amber glass, ftd base, etched "Schneider," scratches **650.00**

9" h, 7-1/2" w, bulged rim over high-shouldered vessel, small black angular handles from rim to top of shoulders, orange, rust, and brown veined body **3,100.00**

10" h, 10-1/2" w, flat rim over short neck, body flares out in teepee shape, blue ground, gold veining dec, narrows back to socket base which fits into bronze mount, three orange berries and tendrils attached to ftd base..... **1,680.00**

Vase, Bijou, tomato red, four applied cabochons, signed "Schneider, France" in script, 4" h, **$1,500.** *Photo courtesy of David Rago Auctions.*

11-1/2" h, flared sq rim, bulbous pinched dimpled vessel of colorless glass, mottled burgundy flecks, small enclosed bubbles, base etched "Schneider" . . **520.00**

12" h, Jade Berluze, muted oranges and blues, sgd "Schneider" with urn **460.00**

12" h, quatraform, fiery yellow amber int., bright blue and maroon splotches, dark purple platform foot, inscribed "Schneider" above, "France" on base **1,250.00**

12" h, 4-1/4" d, pink and white spatter shading to maroon and pink base, disk foot, bright yellow sunflower dec **3,900.00**

12-1/2" h, upright rim on shouldered mottled yellow and orange vessel, etched "Schneider" at lower side, "France" at base, base wear **1,150.00**

12-1/2" h, flattened oval, mottled pastel blue body, bright royal blue overlay, two stripes of etched foliated elements, sgd "Charder" on cameo at side, foot inscribed "Le Verre Francais France" **1,150.00**

12-1/2" h, 5-1/2" d, colorless, applied amethyst base, two carved handles in form of Art Deco bouquets, sgd "Schneider France" **4,000.00**

13-1/4" h, raised rim, bulbed cylindrical neck, flared base, heavy walled bubbled colorless glass, internal streaks of grass green and opaque white, acid mark "Schneider" near base, large polished pontil **1,495.00**

14" h, mottled and veiled oval body, rose pink, yellow, and orange above pink-red and brick glass, two applied amethyst handles at top, foot inscribed "Schneider" **1,265.00**

14-1/2" h, Croecus, green jade flower, deep amethyst foot, sgd **2,185.00**

15" h, 7-1/4" d, smoke bubbled ovoid body, disk foot, applied green and white mottled ear type handles **3,920.00**

15-1/2" h, 12" d, oval colorless and mottled white body, internally decorated with broad orange and purple aubergine strokes and splotches, inscribed "Schneider" mark at side. **1,725.00**

19-3/4" h, flared rim, cylindrical neck, rounded squared body, colorless glass with internal bubbles and streaks of blue, green, yellow, and pink, etched "Schneider" at lower side, base wear **1,840.00**

Silver Deposit and Silver Overlay Glass

History: Silver deposit glass was popular at the turn of the century. A simple electrical process was used to deposit a thin coating of silver on glass products. After the glass and a piece of silver were placed in a solution, an electric current was introduced which caused the silver to decompose, pass through the solution, and remain on those parts of the glass on which a pattern had been outlined.

Silver overlay is silver applied directly to a finished glass or porcelain object. The overlay is cut and decorated, usually by engraving, prior to being molded around the object.

Glass usually is of high quality and either crystal or colored. Lenox used silver overlay on some porcelain pieces. Most designs are from the Art Nouveau and Art Deco periods.

Reference: Lillian F. Potter, *Re-Introduction to Silver Overlay on Glass and Ceramics*, published by author, 1992; Kenneth Wilson, *American Glass 1760-1930: The Toledo Museum of Art,* Volume I, Volume II, Hudson Hills Press and The Toledo Museum of Art, 1994.

Basket, 5" h, 7-1/2" w, deep emerald green ground, applied loop handles with berry prunts, six rows of applied glass openwork forming reticulated base, silver overlay **500.00**

Perfume bottle, florals and scroll motif, matching stopper, opaque blue ground, 4-1/2" h, **$110.**

Bottle, 3-1/2" h, sq form bottle with rows of emb X-form domed squares, beaded floral emb motif, threaded cap, London, 1935, imp marks "CS" and "FS". **230.00**

Box, cov, 7" d, 4-1/2" h, dark amethyst, int. divided into three compartments, repeating silver foliate dec. **230.00**

Candlesticks, pr, 7-1/4" h, opal, amber streaked ground, irid threading on base, SS rim, attributed to Loetz **750.00**

Compote, 6" h, 6-1/2" d, black ground, overlaid in Art Deco gazelles and stylized foliate motifs, Rockwell type dec, minor silver loss, pr **225.00**

Decanter

7-1/2" h, squatty colorless base, star-cut base, heavily overlaid in silver scrolling devices, monogrammed "FGS" in reverse, stamped "9/1000 fine" and numbered, conforming stopper **550.00**

8" h, satin body, chased silver cap, chain, and mounts, elongated neck over spherical opal white glass cased to light yellow, air-trap dec in peacock eye pattern, small polished pontil, silver highlights, late 19th C, minor dent to cap **690.00**

10" h, cut glass body, foliage emb and engraved silver mount and lid, marked "Gorham" **575.00**

Ewer, 11-1/2" h, bulbous colorless body, elongated neck, rim and handle encased in silver, body with silver overlay foliate and scroll dec, cartouche on front, spreading circular foot, frosted and cut base, faceted silver overlay ball stopper **1,955.00**

Perfume bottle, orig stopper

3-1/2" h, colorless, Art Nouveau-style silver overlay **125.00**

4" h, squatty, colorless ground, silver cut iris blossoms, stems, and scrolls, orig stopper, marked "999/1000 fine – 3105" **500.00**

5-1/2" h, spherical, teal green, layered at shoulder with silver floral dec, stopper missing, stamped "sterling" **345.00**

Syrup pitcher, 9" h, cut glass body, silver rim and spout **350.00**

Tankard pitcher, 10-3/4" h, 6" w, cranberry, heavy silver overlay, grape and vine dec, large shield, applied clear handle **2,800.00**

Vase

3-1/4" h, gourd form, orange spotted silver irid vase, overlaid with secessionist-style silver overlay, enameled "586 M655" . . **1,600.00**

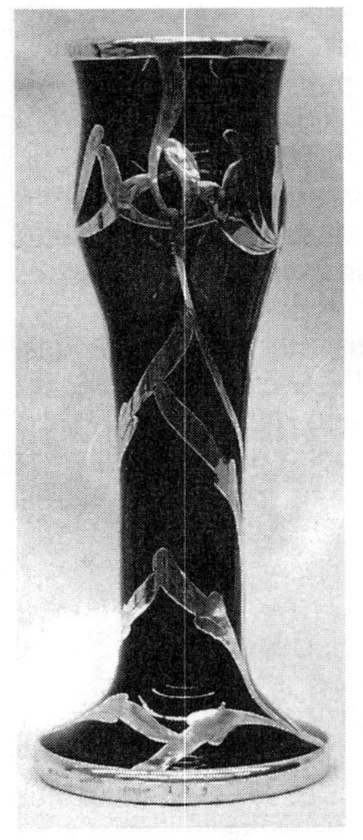
Vase, green ground, overlay marked "Sterling Silver Deposit 196," 6" h, 2-3/8" d, **$225.**

3-1/2" h, bulbous, trefoil rim, blue irid, silver Art Nouveau floral silver, attributed to Loetz **800.00**
3-5/8" h, flat rim, mold blown green glass irid oval, scroll and floral dec, imp "L Sterling," design worn **635.00**
3-3/4" h, irid green oval body, four applied protrusions, silver floral motif stamped "patented 3419-999/1000 fine," hallmarked **635.00**
4-1/2" h, oviform, pinched around neck, silver-blue oil-spot motif, geometric silver overlay, attributed to Loetz............... **2,300.00**
4-1/2" h, ruffled quatraform rim, dimpled oval body, gold irid surface overlaid in scrolling silver foliage dec, polished pontil, Austrian **550.00**
7-1/2" h, green/yellow irid ground, silver plated swan and lily dec, attributed to Loetz **500.00**
8-3/4" h, raised flared rim, broad amber oval irid body overlaid on front with pendant berry and leaf silver dec, leaf imp "L. Sterling," Austrian **1,380.00**
9" h, oval dark amethyst body, three buttress-form feet, foliage border with animal medallions, "sterling" engraved in design, minor silver loss.................. **175.00**
10" h, cased turquoise blue cylinder, layered in sterling dec, full-length floral designs, two butterflies **175.00**
10" h, pinched oval ambergris body internally dec with metallic pulled feathers, external silver overlay intricate rose blossoms with stylized Art Nouveau motif, polished pontil, attributed to Loetz **4,600.00**
10-1/2" h, translucent apple green body, scrolled silver overlay with tropical parrot landing on floral branch, silver rim bands at top and disk foot................. **50.00**
10-1/2" h, 6-1/2" w, deep red shading to green with Loetz type iridescence, elaborate silver overlay of flowers and vines, minor loss to silver............. **325.00**
12" h, bright rose-red tapered body, opal white int., overlaid in elaborate silver floral motif with scrolls and swirling stems, centering medallion crest **1,380.00**
12" h, 5" d, cylindrical, white glass ground, silver floral overlay. **175.00**
14" h, cobalt blue gooseneck body, silver irid papillon dec, elaborate silver overlay in scrolling foliate designs, recessed polished pontil, Austrian, minor damage . **2,415.00**
14-1/4" h, colorless oval, internally flashed in amber, amethyst, pink, and frosted landscape scene, overlaid with tall tree, antlered deer center, base stamped "Rockwell" in shield, some paint loss, wear, stain **690.00**
22" h, baluster, peach ground, elaborate stylized silver floral overlay, attributed to Loetz **4,500.00**

SMITH BROS. GLASS

History: After establishing a decorating department at the Mount Washington Glass Works in 1871, Alfred and Harry Smith struck out on their own in 1875. Their New Bedford, Massachusetts, firm soon became known worldwide for its fine opalescent decorated wares, similar in style to those of Mount Washington.

Smith Bros. glass often is marked on the base with a red shield enclosing a rampant lion and the word "Trademark."

References: Kenneth Wilson, *American Glass 1760-1930*, two vols., Hudson Hills Press and The Toledo Museum of Art, 1994.

Reproduction Alert: Beware of examples marked "Smith Bros."

Atomizer, melon ribbed, creamy white satin ground, hand-painted carnations outlined in gold, red rampant lion mark **625.00**

Biscuit jar, cov
7" h, 5" d, barrel shape, beige ground, seven deep brown, rust, maroon, green, and gold pansies, metal cov marked "S. B. 4412," base also sgd **750.00**
7" h, 7" d, melon rib shape, enameled pansies, c1875 . **795.00**
8-1/2" h, 7-1/2" d, pale pink draped over shoulder with hp lacy border, four cream-colored textured enameled tassels, six-sectioned body, satin finish, metal fittings, lid sgd "S B 4402".......... **675.00**
8-1/2" h, 7-1/2" d, tan, floral dec, melon shaped, matching lid, lion trade mark **275.00**

Bowl
2-3/4" d, 2-3/8" h, buff ground, hand-painted multicolored flowers, yellow rim, white dots......**110.00**
2-3/4" d, 2-1/2" h, buff ground, hand-painted multicolored pansies, blue rim, white dots **110.00**
6" d, 2-3/4" h, melon ribbed, two shades of gold prunus dec, beaded white rim........ **375.00**
8-3/4" d, narrow ribbed body, creamy white satin ground, oak leaves and acorns outlined in gold, metal rim, marked **550.00**
9" d, 4" h, melon ribbed, beige ground, pink Moss Rose dec, blue flowers, green leaves, white beaded rim............ **675.00**

Box, cov, 4" d, melon ribbed, beige satin ground, blue florals, sgd . **375.00**

Bride's bowl, 9-1/2" d, 3" h bowl, 16" h overall, opal glass bowl, painted ground, 2" band dec with cranes, fans, vases, and flowers, white and gray dec, fancy silver-plated holder sgd and numbered 2117............ **1,450.00**

Creamer and sugar
4" d, 3-3/4" h, shaded blue and beige ground, multicolored violet and leaves dec, fancy silver plated metalware............. **750.00**
4" h, ribbed melon-form, white asters, yellow centers, silver-plated

scrolled rims, cov with woman's profile cartouche **450.00**

Fernery

10" d, orig insert, melon ribbed, creamy white shiny finished satin ground, hand-painted violets and leaves, rampant lion mark, sgd "Smith Bros." **450.00**

10" d, 4" h, squatty, 10 ribbed bulbous oval body, wild rose dec, outlined in gold, raised edge, silver-plated rim, red rampant lion mark **600.00**

Ginger jar, cov, 5-1/2" h, ovoid vessel, opal glass, berry prunt finial, dec with blue, yellow, and brown asters, light blue ground, unsigned, wear to int. rim **225.00**

Humidor, cov, 6-1/2" h, 4" d, cream ground, eight blue pansies, melon-ribbed cov **850.00**

Jar, cov, 4-1/2" h, squatty, melon ribbed, creamy white satin ground, hand painted pansy dec, openwork silver top **275.00**

Juice tumbler, blue, stork dec . . . **50.00**

Mayonnaise dish, creamy white satin ground, floral dec, fancy silver-plated top and handle, sgd **275.00**

Mustard jar, cov, 2" h, ribbed, gold prunus dec, white ground **300.00**

Perfume bottle, 5" h, creamy white satin ground, enameled floral dec, floral emb cap, rampant lion mark . . . **450.00**

Plate, 7-3/4" d, Santa Maria, beige, brown, and pale orange ship, commissioned by Libbey for Columbian Exposition of 1902-03 . . . . **595.00**

Potpourri jar, cov, 5-3/4" d, 3-3/4" h, open white lotus blossom, trailing stem, partially opened bud, framed by two naturalistic tinted leaves, shadowy blue ripples of cream-colored pond, another floating stem with leaf and bud on other side, silver-plated lid with lotus blossom finial, lion-in-shield signature . . . **585.00**

Rose bowl

2-1/4" h, 3" d, cream ground, jeweled gold prunus dec, gold beaded top, sgd **285.00**

2-1/4" h, 3-3/4" d, creamy ext., gold gilt, floral leaf and vine dec, beaded rim, sgd **225.00**

4-1/2" d, fat bulbous shape, beige ground, two sprays of daisy-type flowers, beaded top **325.00**

Salt, open, 2" w, 1-1/4" h, white satin melon ribbed body, blue, orange, and green small flowers and leaves, orange beaded top **90.00**

Rose bowl, creamy exterior, gold decoration, floral leaf and vine decoration, beaded rim, signed, 3-3/4" d, 2-1/2" h, **$175.** *Photo courtesy of David Rago Auctions.*

Sugar shaker

5-3/4" h, pillar ribbed, white ground, pink wild rose and pale blue leaves, blue beaded top, orig cov fair **495.00**

6" h, 2-1/2" d, cylindrical, vertical ribs, opaque white body, stylized dec of pink, blue, and gray summer blossoms, wispy stalks, pewter top **575.00**

Sweetmeat, jar, cov, 5-1/4" d, 5-1/4" h, melon ribbed body, creamy white satin ground, enameled daisy spray, emb silver plated collar and bail, sgd **575.00**

Toothpick holder

2" h, ribbed blank, purple and blue violets, beaded top **285.00**

2-1/4" h, barrel shape, opaque white body, swag of single petaled blossoms **265.00**

2-1/4" h, pillar ribbed, white ground, pink wild rose and pale blue leaves, blue beaded top . . **250.00**

2-1/2" h Little Lobe, pale blue body, single petaled rose blossoms, raised blue dots on rim . . . **245.00**

Vase

3-1/2" w, 2-1/4" h, melon ribbed, ivory satin ground, gold prunus blossoms, gold trim, sgd, top rim may be repainted **40.00**

5-1/4" h, 3-1/2" d, pinched-in, apricot ground, white wisteria dec, gold highlights, sgd **375.00**

5-1/4" h, 4" d, triangular shape, pale yellow ground, white daisy-like flowers, sgd **425.00**

5-1/2" h, petticoat shape, flared base, pink ground, multicolored foliage and herons, stamped mark on base, "Smith brothers- New Bedford, MA," pr **850.00**

7" h, soft pink ground, inverted dec of white pond lily, blue-green and black leaves, brown stems, maroon trim, c1870, pr. **375.00**

7-1/4" h, 8" d, double canteen, pink rose sprays centered in three decorative reserves, lime-yellow ground, two restored enameled dots, small int. chip **325.00**

7-1/4" h, 8-1/4" w, 2-1/4" deep, double canteen, one side with naturalistic executed enamel dec of wisteria blossoms clinging to vine which sweeps across front and over shoulder, each blossom outlined in raised gold, olive-green leaves overhang floral cluster, raise gold borders, other canteen depicts Roman columns draped with stylized ivory, obverse with Venetian harbor scene, gondolier in foreground, two sail boats, several abstract sails in distance, smaller canteen shows solitary wisteria cluster clinging to vine from other side, background color simulates Mount Washington's Burmese, Smith Bros. lion-in-shield mark **1,950.00**

8" h, conical shape, pink, white blossoms and hummingbird dec, script sgd, pr. **225.00**

8" h, Verona, quatraform rim, cylindrical colorless body flaring to base, int. ribbing, enamel dec with purple and white iris on green leafy stems, gilt highlights, minor wear to enamel **230.00**

8-1/2" h, 3-3/4" w, Verona, colorless ground, painted and enameled pink and yellow orchids, leaves, stems, and buds, int. vertical ribs **495.00**

Smith Brothers created several different vessels in this same floral motif. This one is slightly smaller and has a smaller opening; at 3-1/4" d, 2-1/4" h, it is valued at **$195.**

8-1/2" h, 6-1/2" w, 1-1/2" neck, canteen shape, pale pink shading to cream ground, purple wisteria dec, raised heavy gold leaves and branches, beaded top, sgd **1,250.00**

10" h, 6" d, pillow, soft ground, purple wisteria, green, and gold leaves, slight roughage on base **925.00**

10" h, 8" w, shaded rust, brown, yellow and gold ground, white apple blossoms, green leaves, and branches, painted beige int. **595.00**

12-1/2" h, Verona, colorless ground, deep purple and white irises, gold trim, green leaves and stems, int. vertical ribs **550.00**

L. E. Smith Glass Company

History: L. E. Smith Glass Company was founded in Mount Pleasant, Pennsylvania, in 1907 by Lewis E. Smith. Although Smith left the company shortly after, it still bears his name. Early products were cooking articles and utilitarian objects such as glass percolator tops, fruit jars, sanitary sugar bowls, and reamers.

In the 1920s, green, amber, canary, amethyst, and blue colors were introduced, along with an extensive line of soda-fountain wares. The company also made milk glass, console, dresser sets, and the always-popular fish-shaped aquariums. During the 1930s, Smith became the largest producer of black glass. Popular dinner set lines were Homestead, Melba, Do-Si-Do, By Cracky, Romanesque, and Mount Pleasant.

L. E. Smith glass is handmade and usually unmarked. Some older pieces bear a "C" in a circle and a tiny "S." Currently, a paper label is used. If you collect older items, carefully study the black and Depression glass pieces. The Moon and Star pattern has been reproduced for many years. Smith glass of recent manufacture is found in house sales, flea markets, and gift and antiques shops.

References: Lee Garmon and Dick Spencer, *Glass Animals of the Depression Era*, Collector Books, 1993; Hazel Marie Weatherman, *Colored Glassware of the Depression Era 2*, Glassbooks, 1982.

Animal
- Cat, black, reclining, c1930, marked **35.00**
- Goose, black, reclining, c1930, marked **25.00**
- Horse, lying down, amberina **125.00**
- Rooster, black, reclining, c1930, marked **25.00**
- Swan, opaque white **30.00**

Aquarium, kingfish
- Crystal **195.00**
- Green **250.00**

Ashtray, elephant, black **35.00**

Bonbon, ftd, handle
- Cobalt blue **15.00**
- Green **10.00**

Bookends, pr, rearing horse
- Amber, 8" h, c1940 .... **45.00**
- Cobalt blue, c1930 .... **65.00**
- Crystal, c1930 .... **45.00**
- Green **45.00**

Bowl
- 10" d, Wig Wam pattern, ftd, oval, cobalt blue **150.00**
- 10" d, Wig Wam pattern, ftd, round, cobalt blue **150.00**
- 10" d, Wig Wam pattern, ftd, round, crystal **95.00**
- 10-1/2" d, Melba pattern. green, ruffled **35.00**
- 10-1/2" d, Romanesque pattern, green **45.00**

Cake plate, Do-Si-Do pattern, handles **17.50**

Candlestick, Moon 'n' Star, Heritage Collection, yellow shading to red, 4-3/4" h, **$8.**

Candlesticks, pr
- By Cracky pattern, green **20.00**
- Mt. Pleasant pattern, black **25.00**
- Romanesque pattern, pink **20.00**
- Veined Onyx pattern, black **40.00**
- Wig Wam patternBlack **100.00**
  - Cobalt blue **80.00**
  - Crystal **50.00**

Casserole, cov, Melba pattern, 9-1/2" l, oval **15.00**

Compote, cov, Moon 'n' Star pattern, amberina **35.00**

Cookie jar, amber, 8" h **75.00**

Creamer
- Do-Si-Do pattern **6.00**
- Homestead pattern, pink **8.00**
- Moon 'n' Star pattern, amberina **12.00**

Cruet, Moon 'n' Star pattern, ruby **35.00**

Cup and saucer, Melba pattern
- Amethyst **10.00**
- Pink **9.00**

Dish, cov, Stagecoach, detailed. **45.00**

Fern bowl, flower frog, Greek Key pattern, 4-1/4" h
- Cobalt blue **75.00**
- Dark amethyst **35.00**
- Vaseline **85.00**

Flower block, By Cracky pattern, 3" h **5.00**

Flower pot, 4" h, black, silver floral dec **15.00**

Goblet
- Do-Si-Do pattern **5.00**
- Homestead pattern, pink **7.00**
- Moon 'n' Star pattern, amberina **17.50**

Jardiniere, Greek Key pattern, three ftd, dark amethyst, silver overlay **25.00**

Macaroon jar, cov, 7-1/4" h, dark amethyst **85.00**

Mayonnaise, Kent pattern **10.00**

Parfait
- Do-Si-Do pattern **7.00**
- Homestead pattern, pink **9.00**
- Soda Shop pattern **10.00**

Plate
- 6" d, Melba pattern, amethyst . **7.50**
- 7" d, Romanesque pattern, octagonal, green **10.00**
- 7-1/8" d, round, aqua **6.00**
- 8" d, Homestead pattern, pink . **8.00**
- 8" sq, Do-Si-Do pattern, amethyst **12.00**
- 8" d, Maple Leaf pattern, cobalt blue **15.00**
- 8" d, Melba pattern, octagonal, pink **8.00**
- 8" d, Mt. Pleasant pattern, pink, scalloped edge **8.00**
- 8" w, Romanesque pattern, octagonal, green **10.00**
- 9" d, Homestead pattern, pink, grill **15.00**
- 9-1/4" d, Lincoln, backward "C" border, milk glass, c1960 ... **50.00**
- 11" w, Romanesque pattern, octagonal, amber **30.00**

Platter, 11-1/2" w, Melba pattern, octagonal, pink **15.00**

Salt and pepper shakers, pr
- Dresden pattern, white **20.00**
- Mt. Pleasant pattern, cobalt blue **30.00**

Sherbet
- Do-Si-Do pattern **9.00**
- Romanesque pattern, vaseline **15.00**

Slipper, Daisy and Button pattern, amber, 2-1/2" h **10.00**

Soda tumbler, crystal

Jumbo pattern, ribbed, pedestal foot **9.00**

Soda Shop pattern. **10.00**

Sugar, cov

Do-Si-Do pattern **9.00**

Homestead pattern, pink. **12.00**

Kent pattern. **10.00**

Melba pattern **12.00**

Moon 'n' Star pattern, amberina **15.00**

Tray, crystal, 15" l, 6" w, oval **12.00**

Urn, two handles, 7" h, dancing girls, cobalt blue **40.00**

Vase

Moon 'n' Star pattern, blue, 7" h **20.00**

Romanesque pattern, green, fan, ftd **45.00**

#433/4-C, dark amethyst, dancing figures, handles, 7" h. **50.00**

#1931, dark amethyst, dancing figures, crimped top, 6-3/4" h **50.00**

Violet bowl, Hobnail pattern, white opaque **10.00**

Window box, F. W. Woolworth . . . **30.00**

Wine

Dancing figures, dark amethyst, 8" x 3-1/2" **65.00**

Moon 'n' Star pattern, amberina **15.00**

Ruby body, crystal stem and foot **7.00**

SPANGLED GLASS

History: Spangled glass is a blown or blown-molded variegated art glass, similar to spatter glass, with the addition of flakes of mica or metallic aventurine. Many pieces are cased with a white or clear layer of glass. Spangled glass was developed in the late 19th century and still is being manufactured.

Originally, spangled glass was attributed only to the Vasa Murrhina Art Glass Company of Hartford, Connecticut, which distributed the glass for Dr. Flower of the Cape Cod Glassworks, Sandwich, Massachusetts. However, research has shown that many companies in Europe, England, and the United States made spangled glass, and attributing a piece to a specific source is very difficult.

Apothecary jar, 6-1/2" h, bulbous, pink and white, silver mica flecks, matching stopper **175.00**

Basket

6-1/2" h, 5-1/2" w, bean pot shape, sq top, deep pink int., shaded deep apricot with spangled gold, applied crystal loop handle. **325.00**

7" h, 6" l, ruffled edge, white int., deep apricot with spangled gold, applied crystal loop handle, slight flake **225.00**

7-1/2" h, 5" w, brown-pink shading to amber, vertical stripes with gold spangles, bright pink int., bulbous bean pot type form, applied crystal loop edge and handle **150.00**

7-1/2" h, 7" w, deep rose shading to pink to white, melon ribbed form, twisted crystal handle **100.00**

8-1/4" h, 6" d, blue, cased white int., spangle in vertical rows, colorless looped thorn handle. **190.00**

8-1/2" h, 10" d, deep heavenly blue shading to white, lighter blue edge, large silver mica flecks, three rows of hobnails, ruffled, applied crystal edge, applied crystal rope handle, slight amount of edge roughness **100.00**

8-1/2" h, 10" x 9" body, cased red to white spangled int., white ext., crimped rim with colorless border, applied colorless twisted handle **190.00**

9" h, 10" l, deep blue shading to pale blue to white int., silver spangles, brilliant white ext., deeply crimped and blown-out edge, applied crystal rope handle, Victorian **175.00**

9-1/2" h, 9" d, opaque white ext., int. of pink, green, amber, brown, and silver mica flecks, applied crystal edge, applied crystal twisted rope handle **100.00**

9-1/2" h, 10" l, 8-1/2" w, pink, yellow, and brown-green spatter, silver flecks, white ext., applied crystal twisted rope handle, c1890 **325.00**

10" h, 9-1/2" w, cased amber ext., shocking pink int., gold mica flecks, tightly ribbed, applied amber leaf ftd base, applied amber twisted handle, slight edge roughness **125.00**

10-1/2" h, 11-3/4" w, bright pink cased with white, heavy silver mica flecks, tightly ruffled and pleated rim, applied colorless braided V-shaped handle **300.00**

11" h, 9-1/2" d, large ruffled pulled down rect basket, deep amethyst shading to white, silver mica over opaque white, applied crystal rope handle **150.00**

13" h, 9" w, amber glass, green, pink, maroon, and yellow spangles, white lining, very ruffled edge with crystal applied rim, applied shell reeded feet, strap-type handle **150.00**

Beverage set, bulbous pitcher, six matching tumblers, rubena, opalescent mottling, silver flecks, attributed to Sandwich, c1850-60 . . . . **250.00**

Bowl

4-3/8" d, 2-1/4" h, rainbow, silver mica flecks, white lining . . . **150.00**

9-1/2" d, chartreuse, reverse swirl ext., white cased lining, piecrust star form rim **90.00**

Bride's bowl, 10-3/8" d, multicolored, ruby, cranberry, and green, ivory-yellow ground, silver flecks **125.00**

Candlesticks, pr, 8-1/8" h, pink and white spatter, green Aventurine flecks, cased white int. **115.00**

Condiment set, cranberry, green flecks, silver plated holder, three pcs **215.00**

Creamer and sugar, cov, blue, gold mica flecks **250.00**

Creamer, Hobbs' Spangled, amber, deep blue plated int., melon ribbed, 3-1/2" h **70.00**

Cruet, Leaf Mold pattern, cranberry, mica flecks, white casing, Northwood **450.00**

Decanter, 12" h, 3-1/2" w, dark lavender, silver flecks through, large matching ball stopper, Italian. **40.00**

Ewer, 11" h, colorless, cased pink, mica flecks, twisted applied handle . . **125.00**

Fairy lamp, 6-3/8" h, multicolored, gold mica flecks, orig Clarke insert . . **225.00**

Juice tumbler, 3-3/8" h, white ground, pink spatter, silver mica flecks, white casing. **95.00**

Miniature, bride's bowl, 5-1/2" d, 1-3/4" h, cased blue shading to white, clear "V" scallop rim **25.00**

Pitcher

6-3/4" h, cobalt blue, gold mica flecks, applied amber handle with flecks. **250.00**

7-1/2" h, bulbous, four-sided top, apricot, gold mica flecks form diamond pattern, white casing, pontil **175.00**

8" h, blood red, pink, and light blue spatter, swirled ribbed body, mica flecks, opal plated interior, polished pontil, applied colorless reeded handle **240.00**

8-3/4" h, bulbous, crimped rim with applied colorless edge, deep rose, burgundy spatter, silver mica flecks, applied colorless reeded handle 325.00

10" h, peach ground, ruby spatter, gold mica flecks, white casing, applied amber thorn handle 250.00

Rose bowl, 3-3/8" d, 3-1/2" h, eight-crimp top, cased deep rose, heavy mica coral like dec, white int. 115.00

Sugar shaker, cranberry, mica flecks, white casing, Northwood...... 115.00

Tumbler, pink, white, orange, red, blue, and yellow, silver spangles, 4" h, **$75.**

Tumbler

3-1/2" h, pale blue and white spatter, silver mica flecks form vertical paneled pattern, white casing 85.00

4" h, pink, white, orange, red, yellow, and silver spangles 75.00

Vase

4-1/4" h, ruffled top, melon ribbed, colorless shading to blue body, silver mica inclusions, burgundy specks, wrapped in tangled green threads, Austrian 100.00

4-3/4" h, 4" d, amethyst ground, collared scalloped top, goldstone flecks around body....... 145.00

5" h, 4" d, squatty bulbous body, mottled pink and white, cased, chips.......... 30.00

8" h, modified baluster, tulip shaped lip, deep cranberry casing, colorless casing with gold foil flecks in wide vertical swath, brown, green, yellow, and red spatter.......... 250.00

8" h, 4-1/8" d, tan, beige, oxblood red and pink spatter, silver mica flecks, white casing....... 165.00

8" h, 4-1/4" d, amber, pinched bulbous body, cylindrical neck, heavy solid applied round foot, flat polished rim, bruised on shoulder 30.00

8-1/8" h, 3-5/8" d, cranberry ground, emb swirls, goldstone..... 140.00

9-1/4" h, pink ground, silver mica flecks, white casing, applied vaseline rigaree shell trim, applied vaseline loop handles 165.00

12" h, oviform, squatty circular base, amber, silver mica flecks, pinched neck.......... 100.00

14-1/2" h, melon ribbed, ruffled, pink, white, and green mica flecks 265.00

Water set, 8" h pitcher, four 3-3/4" h tumblers, butterscotch ground, abstract black and brown striping, mica flakes, opal plated interior, applied colorless handle and polished pontil on pitcher, flaking on tumblers........... 400.00

Witch ball, 8" h, tortoiseshell glass ball, attached to amber glass stem and foot 200.00

SPATTER GLASS

History: Spatter glass is a variegated blown or blown-molded art glass. It originally was called "End-of-Day" glass, based on the assumption that it was made from batches of glass leftover at the end of the day. However, spatter glass was found to be a standard production item for many glass factories.

Spatter glass was developed at the end of the 19th century and is still being produced in the United States and Europe. Companies like Northwood and Hobbs, Brockunier produced splendid examples of spatter glass. The Czechoslovakians used vivid color combinations creating some striking pieces of glassware.

References: William Heacock, James Measell and Berry Wiggins, *Harry Northwood: The Early Years 1881-1900*, Antique Publications, 1990; —, *Harry Northwood: The Wheeling Years 1902-1925*, Antique Publications, 1991.

Reproduction Alert: Many modern examples come from the area previously called Czechoslovakia. Reproductions of Northwood pieces have also flooded the marketplace.

Basket

6" h, 6" w, yellow, maroon, green, and brown spatter, white int., three rows of hobnails, rect form, loop thorn handle 125.00

6"h, 6-1/2" l, 6" w, pink and bright yellow spatter, white int. lining, colorless thorn handle, eight-point star-shaped body........ 250.00

6" h, 8" w, pink and white, air traps, star shaped basket, thorn handle with sag in center........ 250.00

6-1/2" h, 6-1/4" l, 5" w, rect, maroon, brown, yellow, blue, red, green spatter, white int. lining, colorless thorn loop handle, tightly crimped edge with two rows of hobnails 250.00

7" h, crystal ground, five rows of applied blue flattened hobs, white and blue spatter, applied crystal twisted thorn handle, Victorian 300.00

7-1/2" h, 5" w, triangular form, bright pink and yellow spatter, white ground, colorless twisted thorn handle, ruffled edge, c1890 225.00

7-1/2" h, 6" l, brown and jade green spatter, white ground, thorn handle, ruffled star-shaped edge, c1890 .... 275.00

8" h, 13" l, 8" d, tortoiseshell, pale ground with white, red, and brown spatter, heavy gold enameled floral dec, applied gold dec loop handle, minor wear to gold handle. 150.00

Bottle, 11" h, rubena, opalescent spatter.......... 150.00

Bowl

8-1/2" d, 4-1/4" h, Le Gras, Tigre, cranberry int., spattered cream opaque with goldstone, amber glass applied wishbone feet 220.00

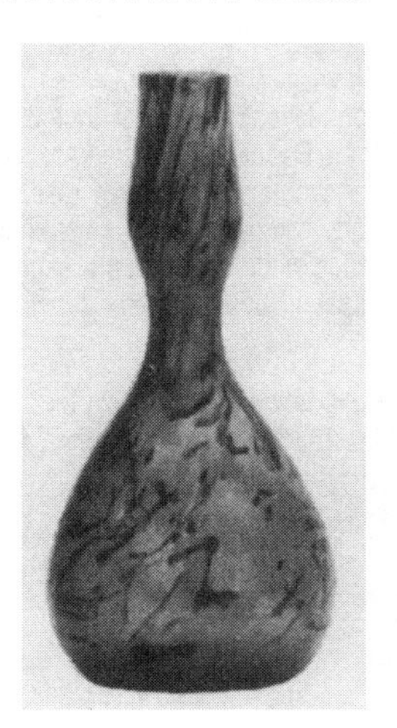

Barber bottle, 7-1/4" h, cylindrical, bulbous body, long bulbous neck, amethyst and light yellow amber mottled design, overall pink iridescent, ground mouth, smooth base, **$325.** *Photo courtesy of Norman C. Heckler and Co.*

9" h, 8" w, triangular shape, white satin ground ext. and int., pink and yellow spatter, large applied twisted thorn handle **100.00**

9-1/2" h, 10" w, pink and white spatter, brilliant opaque yellow ground, three rows of hobnails, ruffled and crimped edge, applied crystal shell feet, twisted thorn handle, flake off one foot... **200.00**

13-1/2" h, 6" h, blown swirl pattern, yellow cased ground, white spatter, two applied amber loop handles, three amber thorn ball feet . **100.00**

Box, 7-1/2" l, 4-1/2" h, egg shaped, hinged, white casing, yellow and blue flowers, gold and white leaves, three applied colorless feet......... **275.00**

Bride's basket, 8" d, 8-3/4" h, vaseline and amethyst round bowl, ruffled rim, multicolored floral and butterfly dec, Strickland pedestal stand, leaf and bird side mounted handles **700.00**

Candlestick, 7-1/2" h, yellow, red, and white streaks, colorless overlay, vertical swirled molding, smooth base, flanged socket...................... **60.00**

Cane, 30-1/2" l, aqua, spiral twist at straight end of handle **150.00**

Cologne bottle

8-1/2" h, etched adv "Rich Secker Sweet Cologne, New York," applied colorless handles **65.00**

Leaf Mold, vaseline spatter, shiny finish **400.00**

Creamer, 4-3/4" h, pink and white, applied colorless handle, Northwood **50.00**

Cruet, orig stopper, applied colorless handle

Amber and white spatter, polished pontil.................... **95.00**

Red and white spatter **125.00**

Darning egg, multicolored, attributed to Sandwich Glass............. **125.00**

Ewer, cranberry spatter, applied colorless handle **65.00**

Fairy lamp, 3-1/4" h, 2-7/8" d, pyramid shape, pink, yellow, and white, white casing, marked "Clarke" base . **100.00**

Finger lamp, 6-1/4" h, 4-1/4" d, peach ground, white and brown spatter, applied colorless handle...... **145.00**

Jack-in-the-pulpit vase, 9-3/8" h, 5-1/2" d, green, white, and peach spatter body, white and peach spatter top, green base............. **125.00**

Perfume bottle, 4-3/4" h, yellow shaded to white ground, gold, blue, yellow, and white spatter **85.00**

Rose bowl, 3-1/2" h, octagonal, crimped top, rose spatter, white casing **115.00**

Salt, 3" l, maroon and pink, white spatter, applied colorless feet and handle.................... **125.00**

Sugar shaker

4-1/2" h, cased cranberry, Leaf Umbrella pattern, Northwood Glass Co. **350.00**

4-1/2" h, rainbow, cased, Royal Ivy, Northwood Glass Co, 4" h . **500.00**

4-1/2" h, rainbow craquelle, Royal Ivy, Northwood Glass Co.. . **550.00**

4-7/8" h, pink and white, SP top **75.00**

Syrup pitcher

6-1/2" h, Ribbed Pillar, pink and white spatter, front of lid marked "Pat. April 26, 81, March 28, 82," Northwood Glass Co. **350.00**

6-3/4" h, ring neck, pink and white spatter, imp curved horizontal lines on upper end of applied handle **150.00**

Toothpick holder, Leaf Mold, cranberry and vaseline spatter.......... **225.00**

Tumbler

3-1/2" h, Inverted Thumbprint pattern, colorless ground, vaseline and white spatter, c1890.... **45.00**

3-3/4"h, emb Swirl pattern, white, maroon, pink, yellow, and green, white int. **65.00**

Tumble-up, bottle and matching tumbler, elongated thumbprint patterned body, green, red, pink, and yellow spatter, white casing, applied colorless feet **300.00**

Vase

7" h, blue opalescent, white spatter, crimped, Dugan **75.00**

7" h, 4-1/2" d, golden yellow and white, enameled bird and flowers, applied colorless handles, colored enamel dec............ **180.00**

7-1/2" h, bulbous, ruffled rim, ruby, white spatter, gold butterflies, flowers, and foliage, pr.... **475.00**

9" h, basketweave, blues, pinks, white, and tortoise, crimpled ruffled rim.................... **75.00**

10" h, pink, yellow, and tan swirls, white casing, cupped goblet type neck, pr................ **300.00**

Water pitcher, cranberry and yellow, cinched neck, crimped top, ground and polished pontil **115.00**

Royal Ivy pattern, creamer, covered sugar, spooner, and toothpick holder, **$475.**
Photo courtesy of Joy Luke Fine Art Brokers and Auctioneers.

Steuben Glass

History: Frederick Carder, an Englishman, and Thomas G. Hawkes of Corning, New York, established the Steuben Glass Works in 1904. In 1918, the Corning Glass Company purchased the Steuben company. Carder remained with the firm and designed many of the pieces bearing the Steuben mark.

1903–32

The most widely recognized wares are Aurene, Verre De Soie, and Rosaline, but many other types were produced. Aurene is the name given to glassware that has an iridized golden sheet and may be found on amber, blue, colorless, or topaz-colored glass.

Examples of Aurene with a red, green, or brown base are rare. Aurene was produced from 1904 through 1933. Verre de Soie is also an iridized type of glass. The silk-like texture is lightly frosted and should have a blue tint. Rosaline is a pink jade type glass with a cloudy appearance. Rosaline pieces are commonly found with alabaster trim, feet, handles, and finials.

The classic shapes and styles can also identify Steuben glassware. Catalog reprints and other types of research materials have led to identification of these distinctive shapes.

The firm is still operating, producing glass of exceptional quality.

References: Thomas P. Dimitroff, Charles R. Hajdamach, Jane Shadel Spillman, and Robert F. Rockwell III, *Frederick Carder and Steuben Glass: American Classic,* Schiffer Publishing, 1998; Paul Gardner, *Glass of Frederick Carder,* Schiffer Publishing, 2001; Kyle Husfloen, *Antique Trader's American & European Decorative and Art Glass Price Guide,* 2nd ed., Krause Publications, 2000; Paul Perrot, Paul Gardner, and James S. Plaut, *Steuben,* Praeger Publishers, 1974; Kenneth Wilson, *American Glass 1760-1930,* two vols., Hudson Hills Press and The Toledo Museum of Art, 1994.

Museums: Corning Museum of Glass, Corning, NY; Rockwell Museum, Corning, NY; The Chrysler Museum, Norfolk, VA; The Rockwell Museum, Corning, NY; The Toledo Museum of Art, Toledo, OH.

Reproduction Alert: Steuben pieces have been reproduced. The coloration can be duplicated, but the silky and iridized finishes originally produced by Steuben are not usually perfected on reproductions.

Acid cut back

Bowl

6-7/8" h, swollen vessel, semi-opaque purple glass cased to rich plum ext., deeply acid etched water lilies over stylized scrolled ground, polished pontil, c1925 . . . . **4,320.00**

8" d, 7-1/4" h, green jade, cut chrysanthemums and leaves dec **650.00**

Candlesticks, pr, 14" h, black cut to colorless, Poussin pattern, flowers and leaves **2,400.00**

Centerpiece bowl, 17-1/2" w, 2-3/4" h, black, four baskets filled with flowers, other floral and ribbon designs, applied flint white rim, sgd **800.00**

Jar, cov, 5-1/2", white ground, apple green leaves and flowers **800.00**

Lamp base

25" h, 5-1/2" d shaft, jade green over alabaster, cut floral and leaves design, fancy orig silver-plated mountings and orig finial. . . **550.00**

26" h, 14" h glass shaft, Catalog No.8006, elongated flared neck over bulbous base, acid etch grape motif, spiraled leaves and vines around neck, mounted to unsigned gilt-metal base and two-socket shaft **920.00**

Vase

7" h, Catalog No. 6078, semi-spherical, Green Jade cut to alabaster in lotus design, polished pontil, minor light scratches **3,450.00**

9-1/4" h, Catalog No. 6142, Green Jade over alabaster, repeating design of two crested birds frolicking on flowering branch, two small int. rim chips **900.00**

9-1/2" h, baluster, green jade cut back to alabaster, Bird pattern, exotic bids, leafy flowering tree branches. **1,200.00**

10-1/4" h, 3-3/4" d, heavy walled, cobalt blue Aurene ground, silver-blue irid, cut to dark cobalt, broad vintage frieze of grapes, leaves, and vines below shoulder dec of stylized leaves and berries, sgd 'Steuben Aurene 2683" on base **4,200.00**

12" h, baluster, raised flared rim, triple layers, peach Cintra cased to alabaster, dark amethyst overlay, acid cut back Pagoda pattern, three repeats in shaped medallion windows with Canton landscapes, floral and fretwork borders. **2,400.00**

Amethyst

Bowl

6-1/4" d, 4" h, flared rim, colorless glass stem with trapped air bubble, amethyst disk base, polished pontil **95.00**

11-3/8" d, 6-1/2" h, Catalog No. 7535, Grotesque, amethyst fading to colorless glass body, polished pontil, inscribed "Steuben 560/766," minor light scratches **225.00**

Center bowl, 12-1/4" d, 4-1/2" h, flared rim, ribbed ftd vessel, polished pontil **135.00**

Cologne bottle, 5-5/8" h, rect vessel with optic-ribbed dec, polished pontil, acid fleur-de-lis mark, machine threaded dec on stoppers, price for pr **575.00**

Figure and flower frog, 9" h, Kuan Yin, Catalog No. 7133; double-tiered flower frog, Catalog No. 7064, c1926-31, minor scratches. **520.00**

Goblet, 6" h, Catalog No. 3140, amethyst body, applied colorless stem, amethyst disk base, polished pontil **100.00**

Perfume bottle, 6-1/2" h, melon ribbed, teardrop stopper **420.00**

Urn, cov, 11-5/8" h, domed cov, flared rim, ftd, polished pontil **290.00**

Vase

9" h, Catalog No. 7090, Grotesque, amethyst shading to colorless, ftd, polished pontil, wear, minor light scratches **275.00**

14" h, flared ruffled amethyst rim tapering to bulbed amethyst stem, colorless disk base, polished pontil, scratches to base . . **260.00**

Animal

Beaver, 6-1/4" h, Catalog No. 8307, colorless, upright, transparent pink eyes, inscribed "Steuben". **875.00**

Cicada, 2-1/2" l, colorless, detailed cuts, frosted accents on wings . **150.00**

Dolphin

6-1/2" l, Catalog No. SP577, colorless, inscribed "Steuben" **400.00**

7-3/4" l, Catalog No. 7880, colorless, bookends, leaping, semi-circular bases **700.00**

Donkey, 10" h, Catalog No. 8137, colorless, standing **400.00**

Duckling, 8" h, Catalog No. 8129, colorless, inscribed "Steuben" . **495.00**

Elephant

5-1/4" h, Catalog No. 8106, colorless, large ears, inscribed "Steuben". **850.00**

6-3/8" h, Catalog No. 7896, colorless, tucked trunk, inscribed "Steuben". **885.00**

7-1/2" h, Catalog No. 8128, colorless, trumpeting, inscribed "Steuben". **950.00**

Giraffe, 15" h, Catalog No. 8119, colorless, supported by dome base, inscribed "Steuben" **1,850.00**

Penguin, 6-3/8" h, colorless, standing, inscribed "Steuben," scratches on base **490.00**

Pheasant, 15-1/4" h, Catalog No. 8243, colorless, extended wings, angular base, inscribed "Steuben" on base **550.00**

Phoenix, 12-3/4" h, Catalog No. 8136, colorless, elongated, perched on colorless stand, inscribed "Steuben" **1,100.00**

Rabbit, rosaline body, alabaster ears, feet, and tail, 4-1/4" l **365.00**

Seal, 8-1/2" l, Catalog No. 5012, colorless, resting on flippers, inscribed "Steuben" **400.00**

Sea sprit, 8-5/8" h, Catalog No. 8047, colorless, on base, inscribed "Steuben" **300.00**

Swan, 8" h, Catalog No. 8149, colorless, arched wings, inscribed "Steuben" **465.00**

Tropical fish, 8-1/8" h, Catalog No. 8236, colorless, large fins, inscribed "Steuben" **1,495.00**

Trout, 8" h, Catalog No. 1002, colorless, leaping with bubbles at scales, gold fly at mouth, designed by James Houston, inscribed "Steuben" **1,160.00**

Walrus, 7-1/4" h, Catalog No. 8335, colorless, silver tucks, inscribed "Steuben" **1,380.00**

Water bird, 9-7/8" h, Catalog No. 8095, colorless, raised wing, cresting wave **600.00**

Aurene

Atomizer, Catalog No. 6407, gilt-metal mount

- Blue bottle with etched floral and lattice band, polished pontil, gilt stamp "DeVilbiss" in pontil, c1924, nick and few scratches, bulb missing **575.00**
- Gilt-metal mount, gold slender vessel with flared base, polished pontil, inscribed "Aurene L12," few scratches, damage to bulb . **435.00**

Basket

- 6-3/4" h, 6-1/4" w, irid gold, brilliant gold, purple, and blue highlights, applied loop handle, applied berry prunts, sgd "Aurene 453" **1,750.00**
- 8" h, 2-3/4" h, rolled in rim, three applied glass feet, highly irid blue surface with purple highlights, sgd "Aurene, #2586," minor interior scratches. **600.00**
- 8-3/4" h, 9-1/2" w, flaring, deep gold, purple and blue irid highlights, sgd "Aurene, #723," minor surface scratching **800.00**
- 9-1/2" h, 8" w, brilliant gold, applied blue-gold handle, raspberry prunt, inscribed "Aurene, #453" **1,800.00**
- 9-1/2" h, 8" w, brilliant gold int., calcite ext., blue-green applied handle **1,300.00**
- 10" d, 2" h, deep irid blue aurene with purple highlights, sgd "Aurene #2586" **500.00**
- 10-1/4" w, 2-1/2" h, gold aurene on calcite, purple highlights, flaring, minor interior scratches . . . **300.00**
- 13" h, 8" w, gold irid, orig metal mounted floral design handle, sgd "F. Carder" **2,000.00**
- 15-3/4" h, 10" w, brilliant blue, green, and purple int., oyster white calcite ext., applied loop handle . **3,500.00**

Bonbon, 4-1/2" d, 1-1/4" h, Catalog No.138, blue, scalloped design, silvery blue luster, base inscribed "Aurene 138" **550.00**

Bowl

- 5" d, 2" h, gold, ruffled edge, sgd "Aurene" in silver **230.00**
- 8" d, 3-3/8" d, gold, stretched flared rim, bowl raised on domed round base, polished pontil **1,150.00**
- 9" d, 3-3/4" h, Catalog No. 2852, blue, round, applied foot, rough pontil, inscribed "Aurene 2852" **920.00**

Bulb bowl, 9-3/4" d, 1-3/4" h, Catalog No.2586, shallow, gold, silvery transparent luster, base scratches **260.00**

Candlestick

- 8-1/4" h, Catalog No.686, blue, rope twist shaft, shiny foot **635.00**
- 10" h, Catalog No.686, blue, rope twist shaft, inscribed "Aurene 686," one with partial label, pr. . **1,840.00**
- 12" h, Catalog No.6405, blue, rope twist shafts, price for mated pr **575.00**

Center bowl

- 8" d, 4" h, gold, deeply pinched scalloped rim manipulated into eight apertures **550.00**
- 10" d, 3" h, Catalog No.158, blue, eight-pointed scalloped rim, amber glass, blue irid, strong luster, inscribed on base "Aurene 158" **1,035.00**
- 12" d, 4-3/4" h, Catalog No.7423, blue, flared form, eight spaced crimps, irid shades from deep purple to golden and silvery cobalt blue **2,300.00**
- 12-1/4" d, 3-1/2" h, gold, inscribed "Aurene, 2879" around waffle pontil **250.00**
- 14" d, irid gold aurene on calcite, minor interior scratching . . **825.00**
- 14" d, 2" h, angular, shallow round bowl, gold aurene on calcite, orange irid luster **420.00**
- 14-1/2" d, 2" h, Catalog No.3579, shallow, gold aurene on calcite, broad decumbent flowers cut on rim, etched white calcite blossoms, one bubble near edge **690.00**

Champagne, 5-3/4" h, Catalog No.2642, gold, lustrous irid, base inscribed **460.00**

Cigarette holder, 4-1/4" l, blue, ribbed **350.00**

Cologne bottle

- 5" h, Catalog No.1455, gold, eight-lobed body, conforming stopper, base inscribed "Aurene 1455" **815.00**
- 6-1/2" h, Catalog No.1455, gold, eight-lobed body, tapered conforming stopper, very minor chips at stopper rim, inscribed "Aurene 1455" **815.00**

Compote

- 6" w, 5" h, deep irid blue, purple highlights, sgd, numbered "2760" **1,100.00**
- 7-1/2" d, 10" d, design #367, deep color, crimped edge, rope twist shaft, base inscribed "Steuben Aurene 367" **1,265.00**
- 8-1/2" d, 7" h, flared deep gold bowl, spiral ribbed calcite shat and round foot **920.00**
- 10" d, 2-3/4" h, gold aurene on calcite, flared bowl, low cupped pedestal foot **460.00**

Finger bowl and underplate, Catalog No.171, 5" d bowl, 6-1/4" d plate, gold, pointed scalloped rim, both marked "Aurene" **690.00**

Goblet, 6" h, Catalog No.2361, gold, flared bell form, applied twist, disk foot, inscribed "Aurene 2361," set of eight **1,840.00**

Jardiniere, 6-1/2" h, gold, pedestal base, three applied handles, base engraved "Steuben Aurene 627" **1,210.00**

Lamp shade

- 4-1/8" h, 2-1/8" d aperture, Catalog No. 2242, bulbous, gold, fleur-de-lis paint stamp, small nick at aperture. **100.00**
- 4-1/2" h, 2-1/4" d aperture, gold, bell shaped **150.00**
- 4-3/4" h, 2-1/4" d aperture, Catalog No. 2286, King Tut ornament in green and gold on cream-colored ground, partial fleur-de-lis stamp mark **700.00**
- 5-1/8" h, 2-1/8" d aperture, Catalog No. 2283, King Tut ornament over gold pulled feathers, chips on both fitted rims, price for pr. . . **1,495.00**

Lamp, table, 11-1/4" h, Catalog No. 6407 Variant, slender gold shaft with flared based, mounted on bronze base with etched textured surface, imp Roycroft orb on base, few light scratches.................. 550.00

Perfume bottle

5-3/4" h, Catalog No. 3422, flame stopper, melon ribbed gold bottle, polished pontil, inscribed "Aurene," c1915-18, chips on one dauber end, price for pr........ 1,955.00

7" h, Catalog No. 3425, Coral Jade floral stopper, Mirror Black glass inserted into raised neck, tapered oval body, disk foot, cobalt blue glass with strong blue irid, base inscribed "Steuben Aurene 3425," gold foil triangular label over polished pontil, stopper reduced 2,415.00

7-1/2" h, Catalog No. 1414, flamed shaped top, raised neck over tapered cobalt blue body, overall blue irid, orig stopper, inscribed "Aurene 1414" around polished pontil, minor nicks to stopper 815.00

Plate, 8-1/2" d, Catalog No.3059, gold, shallow bowl-form, fine irid lustrous surface, inscribed "Aurene 3059," price for pr 345.00

Salt, 1-1/2" h, 2-1/2" w, gold aurene on calcite, pedestal foot......... 375.00

Sherbet and underplate

4" d, 6-1/4" d, Catalog No.2680, blue, 12-rib molded dish and underplate, strong blue-purple luster, each inscribed "Aurene 2680" 520.00

6" d, 3-3/4" h, Catalog No.2960, gold-stemmed bowl with calcite stem, sgd "F. Carder Aurene" on base 290.00

6" d, 4-1/4" h, gold aurene on calcite, irid 225.00

Vase

3" h, irid gold, ruffled top, inscribed "Aurene-162" 350.00

4" h, flared rim, bulbous body, blue, painted "Haviland" mark, paper retailer's label, c1910-15 .. 865.00

5" h, Catalog No.2631, flared bulbous form, 10 prominent ribs, even blue irid, base inscribed "Steuben"............. 1,100.00

6" h, 4" w, platinum, green heart and vine dec, white millefiori flowers, sgd "Aurene #599"...... 2,200.00

6-1/4" h, gold heart and vine dec, white calcite body, sgd ... 575.00

7" h, slightly flared rim, waisted dimpled vessel, gold, polished pontil, few scratches...... 375.00

7-1/4" h, design #136, platinum gold irid, raised quatraform rim on dimpled bulb above elongated stem, integral foot, marked "Aurene 136".................. 920.00

7-7/8" h, Catalog No. 137, quatrefoil rim over bulbed neck, oval body, four pinched recessed, colorless glass with gold irid, inscribed "Aurene 137" around polished pontil, breakdown to irid ... 490.00

8-1/4" h, Catalog No.2683, irid gold body, inscribed "Steuben" 1,300.00

9" h, Catalog No. 723, gold, scalloped rim, flared vessel of colorless glass, strong gold irid, stretched irid at rim, inscribed "Aurene 723" around polished pontil, wear 750.00

9" h, stump, blue, sgd "Aurene" and numbered 865.00

9-1/4" h, Catalog No. 753, wide ruffled stretched glass rim tapering to bulbous base, gold, polished pontil, few minor scratches 1,035.00

9-1/2" h, Catalog No. 6993, flared rim on ovoid vessel, gold, polished pontil, inscribed "Steuben Aurene 6993," scratches......... 980.00

10" h, Catalog No.506, style D, gold aurene on irid green body cased to white int., blossom, heart, and vine dec, base inscribed "Aurene 506" 5,175.00

10-1/4" h, Catalog No. 355 Variant, stretched ruffled rim on cylindrical form, gold, polished pontil, inscribed "Aurene 355".... 690.00

12" h, urn form, blue aurene over calcite, base drilled for table lamp, price for pr............ 1,150.00

10-1/2" h, 5" w, brilliant green ground, irid gold flowers, sgd "Aurene, 244" 4,000.00

12" h, Catalog No.6034, trumpet, molded cone, irid gold, cupped pedestal foot inscribed "Steuben Aurene," numbered and labeled 1,265.00

12" h, elongated slender baluster, organic green leaf-forms pulled into alabaster white dec by gold aurene peacock feathers centering four gold hearts with green peacock eyes, inscribed on base "Aurene/535," 1/2" shallow scratch at side 3,950.00

12-1/4" h, Catalog No.6034, gold, swirled trumpet, cupped pedestal foot, inscribed "Steuben Aurene 6034" 1,380.00

Bristol Yellow

Basket, 14-3/4" h, Catalog No. 1590, applied handle on folded rim, optic-ribbed body, large polished pontil, acid "STEUBEN" mark .. 750.00

Cake set, 10-1/2" d plate, eight 7" d serving plates, two with "Steuben" in block letters, some edge chips, blemishes, nine-pc set 350.00

Candlestick

5" h, Catalog No. 6637, rough pontil 125.00

8" h, Catalog No. 6637, ruffed rim, applied Mirror Black reeding extending down to candle cup, rough pontil, acid "STEUBEN" mark 375.00

Center bowl, 16" d, 4-1/2" d, low ruffled rim, mirror black threads on ext., Steuben fleur-de-lis mark on base 420.00

Compote, 5" h, Mirror Black reeding on bowl, rough pontil, acid "STEUBEN" mark 325.00

Decanter, 9" h, quatraform buttressed form, swirled rib-mold, solid matching stopper 575.00

Dresser jar, 5-1/4" h, square, swirl molded, matching stopper 225.00

Plate, 8-1/8" d, block letter mark. 90.00

Vase

7-1/4" h, Catalog No. 6980, diamond quilted barrel form, white reeding, polished pontil, fleur-de-lis mark, 2nd quarter 20th C....... 350.00

8" h, Catalog No. 6123 variant, trapped bubbles, border of black threading 125.00

8-1/7" h, Catalog No. 6297, optic-ribbed fan, disk base, polished pontil, light wear to base 290.00

10" h, Catalog No.6030, flared oval optic ribbed design, strong twist to the right, fleur-de-lis mark on bulbed foot, small sand grain bubble at side 200.00

12" h, Catalog No.6034, trumpet form, ribbed flared body, applied cupped pedestal foot, fleur-de-lis mark on base........... 490.00

Wine glass, 4-7/8" h, optic-ribbed, acid fleur-de-lis mark............ 125.00

Calcite

Ashtray, 3-3/4" d, 1" h, round dish with applied twisted ring handle, blue Aurene over calcite, c1924-29, minor scratches **575.00**

Bowl

8-3/8" d, inverted rim, shallow round bowl with gold Aurene int., polished pontil, wear **320.00**

10" d, inverted rim, shallow round bowl, gold Aurene int., int. scratches **375.00**

10-1/4" d, Catalog No. 5194, gold, bun foot, short surface scratches **350.00**

Center bowl, 10" d, 2-7/8" h, stretched glass rim, blue Aurene bowl over calcite, polished pontil **920.00**

Finger bowl and underplate, 4-3/4" d bowl, 6" d plate, Catalog No. 5110, flared 12-ribbed calcite bowl with gold int. bowl **250.00**

Lamp shade, 5" l, flared rim, bell-form shade, light irid ivory color, acid-etched pillar and foliate dec, c1915, light scratches **165.00**

Celeste Blue

Box, cov, 5-1/2" d, 4-1/2" h, Catalog No.7540, round swirled blown box, conforming cov, threaded Celeste finial, flat rim chip inside cover **175.00**

Candlestick, 6-1/2" h, green candle cup, triangular looped stem dec with applied Celeste blue loops, domed base, rough pontil. **300.00**

Center bowl, 12" d, 5-1/4" h, ribbed Celeste blue bulbed bowl, cupped transparent topaz amber pedestal foot **300.00**

Compote, cov

6" h, Catalog No. 5128 Variant, Celeste blue ball finial on amber cov bowl, hollow twist Celeste blue stem, amber disk base, polished pontil **230.00**

6-1/2" h, 8" d, Celeste blue bowl, with rosa mica fleck stem, swirl design to bowl and foot, acid fleur-de-lis mark **815.00**

9" h, pear finial on cov, flared rim optic-ribbed bowl, ball-stemmed ftd vessel, rough pontil, wear **750.00**

Compote, open

7" h, Catalog No. 2604 Variant, optic-ribbed flared bowl, twisted stem with swirl prunts, disk base, rough pontil, minor light scratches **525.00**

9-3/4" d, 1-7/8" h, low dish, domed disk base, polished pontil, minor scratches **300.00**

Creamer and sugar, applied amethyst handles **400.00**

Dresser jar, 5-1/4" h, square, swirl molded, matching stopper **225.00**

Finger bowl and underplate, 5" d bowl, 6-1/4" d underplate, Catalog No.204. **200.00**

Goblet, 6" h, ribbed design, crystal stem, fleur-de-lis mark, set of six **300.00**

Perfume bottle, 6-1/2" h, teardrop stopper, fleur-de-lis mark. **350.00**

Urn, cov, 19" h, Catalog No.3114 variant, 16-rib oval vasiform brilliant transparent blue body, conforming raised cover with figural red and yellow glass pear finial with applied green stem, ribbed leaf, some glass bubbles **1,650.00**

Vase

6" h, Catalog No.6287, fan, optic ribbed version, triple wafer stem, pedestal base stamped with fleur-de-lis mark **320.00**

8-3/4" h, broad oval, round applied disk foot, fleur-de-lis mark . **290.00**

Cintra

Bowl, 8" d, 7" h, Catalog No.6856, scalloped rim, mottled and crackled pink, blue, and frosted colorless ground, applied blossoms, three applied twig feet, int. water stain, annealing cracks where two twigs attach to body **1,500.00**

Cologne bottle, 5-1/2" h, oval #3048 bottle, opalescent ground with applied pink-blue-purple Cintra handles, and rim wrap, amethyst turret stopper and dauber. **1,500.00**

Lamp, 32" h, 14" h glass shaft, heavy walled green Cintra oval body overlaid in translucent alabaster, acid etched naturalized wheat stalks and angular grasses, matching wheel molded gilt metal platform base, Art Deco gazelle finial above three-socket fittings **1,725.00**

Plate, 8-1/2" d, opalescent body, blue and red Cintra edge **185.00**

Vase, 12" h, Catalog No.3279, speckled pastel green in colorless and white surround, overlaid with Rosa glass, acid-etched twice to shade stylized blossoms and vertical geometric devices, four chips on blossom petals **3,450.00**

Cluthra

Bowl, 4-3/4" h, Catalog No.6805, green shading to white, fleur-de-lis acid stamp mark **450.00**

Center bowl, 15" d, 7-1/2" h, Catalog No. 6169, conical form, white Cluthra glass, polished pontil, c1928, few chips on base **750.00**

Puff box, cov, 5-1/4" h, Catalog No. 6681, crystal finial on green Cluthra cover, white Cluthra bowl, polished pontil, c1928. . . . . **1,150.00**

Vase

5-1/2" h, flared rim, angled vessel of rose and white Cluthra, polished pontil, acid "STEUBEN" mark, c1928 . . . . **575.00**

6-3/8" h, Catalog No. 2683, black, raised and rolled rim, broad shouldered form, large polished pontil **1,100.00**

10" h, Catalog No. 2683, rose, polished pontil, acid "Steuben" signature, c1928 . . . . **3,150.00**

10" h, Catalog No. 8508, raised and rolled rim, ovoid off-white body, two translucent opal applied "M" handles, polished pontil with script acid stamp, nick, cullet inclusion to rim **1,265.00**

10-3/8" h, Catalog No. 2683, apple green Cluthra body, polished pontil acid stamp fleur-de-lis mark, c1928 . . . . **1,150.00**

12" h, Catalog No. 6875, prong, shading black to white on oval colorless vase, rough center with polished pontil, c1928, wear to base **1,495.00**

Crystal

Audubon plate set, great blue heron, white pelican, flamingo, barred owl, horned grebe, swallow-tail kit, four engraved "Steuben," other two "S," 10" d, unused condition, set of six . . . **2,990.00**

Bowl

7-3/4" d, 3-1/2" h, engraved, orig box, pr. **175.00**

9" d, 7" h, Catalog No.8084, square prunts on pedestal base, design by Donald Pollard, 1957 . . . . . **345.00**

Candleholders, pr, Catalog No.8017, two-arm candelabra, scroll motif, engraved 'Steuben" on base, design by Lloyd Atkins **490.00**

Center bowl

10-3/4" d, 7" h, broad conical form, deep well applied in four swirled leaf forms, "Steuben" engraved on base **320.00**

16" d, Catalog No.3579, rib-molded colorless body, pale Rosa pink folded rim, engraved floral, webbed, and scrolled dec, fleur-de-lis mark on base, some wear scratches **345.00**

Exhibition bowl

9-1/2" h, X1924A designed by George Thompson, engraving by Donald Wier, wood sprite playing stringed instrument among blossoms and bees, below "Sounds and Sweet Airs That Give Delight," inscribed "Steuben" on base **1,495.00**

11-3/4" h, American Ballard Series, "The Arts," design by George Thompson, engraving designed by Sidney Waugh, from patriotic wartime series, conforming cover with finial, matching pedestal knob, inscribed "Steuben" on base **1,840.00**

Figure, Guardian Angel, Catalog No.1027, solid crystal angel, wings outspread, head wreathed in 18K gold vermeil halo, base inscribed "Steuben" **1,955.00**

Goblet

7" h, Catalog No.7737, elegant fluted bowl, broad bubbled stem, engraved "Steuben," designed by Sidney Waugh, six-pc set.. **550.00**

7-1/2" h, Catalog No.8212, first in Seven Sins series, engraved woman watching man from behind tree, inscribed "Steuben" on base, designed by Sidney Waugh **1,380.00**

Luminiere, 13" h, molded glass gazelle set into illuminating rect black plastic base issuing six curved arms each suspending a glass drop, glass inscribed "Steuben," pr...... **2,000.00**

Martini glass, 4-3/4" h, hourglass shape, teardrop bubble in solid base, inscribed "Steuben," eight-pc set **425.00**

Paperweight

3-1/4" h, faceted hand-polished solid crystal rock base embedded with removable 8-1/2" l sterling silver sword, 18 carat gold scabbard, red velvet and leather case, inscribed "Steuben" **1,300.00**

3-1/2" h, spiraled, central teardrop, inscribed "Steuben" **345.00**

Plate

4-1/4" h, tree in snow, inscribed "Steuben" **300.00**

8" d, central monogram "J" above "EF," eight-pc set......... **300.00**

Prismatic ornament

3-1/2" h, Catalog No.4107, Empire Ellipse, engraved Shakespeare Twelfth Night inscription, inscribed "Steuben," design by George Thompson **200.00**

5-3/4" d, Catalog No.8609, Plant Saturn, designed by James Noll **650.00**

Sculpture, 7" h, cut and polished glass rock supporting golden thistle, design by James Houston, inscribed "Steuben" on base, velvet lined red leather case **2,185.00**

Urn, 12-3/4" h, 7" h, Catalog No.7548, Strawberry Mansion, flared bulbed form, sq plinth base, two applied "M" handles, designed by Frederick Carder **750.00**

Vase

6" h, Catalog No.2683, Mansard, frosted colorless crystal cut in repeating stylized Art Deco blossoms, etched fleur-de-list "Steuben" mark at lower edge **1,500.00**

6" h, Sidney Waugh design, wheel-cut parallel lines compacted as squares in quintessential curvilinear expression, marked "Steuben" on base **230.00**

7-1/4" h, Sidney Waugh design, Angus Dei, winged sacred figure, marked "Steuben" on base. **350.00**

7-1/4" h, Sidney Waugh design, stylized Art Deco gazelle figure, marked "Steuben" on base. **400.00**

15" h, six-prong, Catalog No.1-7129, triangular flower holders attached to central disk base, lightly crizzled **920.00**

Wine, 5-1/4" h, trumpet shape, wide angular teardrop stems, designed by Sidney Waugh, 12-pc set...... **750.00**

Flemish Blue

Bowl

5" h, Catalog No. 7091, Flemish blue fading to colorless, acid etched "Steuben" **215.00**

8" l, 4-1/2" l, Catalog No.6380, rect body, optic ridges swirled to right, four applied feet, fleur-de-lis mark on base **490.00**

Compote, 4" h, flattened rim on bowl, bulbed stem, disk base, polished pontil **195.00**

Goblet, 6-1/2" h, blue overlay, coin cut design, faceted colorless stem, star-cut base **95.00**

Perfume jar, 3-3/4" h, Catalog No.6887 variant, swirled optic ribbing and threading, conforming stoppers, fleur-de-lis mark on back, price for pr **460.00**

Vase, Catalog No. 5441 ...... **225.00**

French Blue

Compote

4-3/4" h, ruffled rim, ext. reeding, small trapped bubbles, stem with trapped bubble, round base, polished pontil **200.00**

6-3/4" h, flared rim, shallow bowl, turned stem, domed base, polished pontil, light scratches **250.00**

Creamer and sugar, 4-1/2" h creamer, 3-3/4" h sugar, rims dec with reeding on trapped bubble glass, two handles and disk base on sugar, polished pontils, sugar acid stamped "Steuben," damage to reeding **200.00**

Vase

5" h, quatrefoil rim on cylindrical form, polished pontil, acid fleur-de-lis stamp **215.00**

6" h, reeding around flared rim, ovoid vessel, disk base, polished pontil **175.00**

Gray-Green

Bowl

10" d, Catalog No. 7023, Sea Green flared rim, optic-ribbed ftd gray-green bowl, wear.... **175.00**

11-5/8" d, downward turned rim, spiral ribbed ftd vessel, polished pontil, acid fleur-de-lis mark **220.00**

Vase, 7-3/4" h, flared rim, ribbed body, applied dome base, polished pontil, acid stamp "Steuben," etched "8286" **240.00**

Grotesque

Bowl

5" d, red pillar molded **375.00**

11" d, 6" h, open flower form, Grotesque, deep green shading to colorless, sgd........... **550.00**

12" l, 7-1/4" h, Catalog No.7535, Grotesque, topaz, four-pillar ruffled oval body, light topaz color, "Steuben" inscribed on base foot **400.00**

12-1/2" l, 4-1/4" h, Catalog No.7535, pillar molded, colorless, green upper body, script sgd "Steuben"

on base, small chip on foot edge 175.00

Compote, Catalog #7171, 7-1/4" d, 6-1/4" h, green, two-line pillar molded design, grotesque suggestion in scalloped rim, hollow flared colorless base, fleur-de-lis mark, price for pr 490.00

Vase

5-1/2" h, 10" d, pillar ribbed abstract form, ivory, minor surface stain 345.00

6-1/4" h, Catalog No.7311, jade green, modified four-pillar grotesque design, vertical shading 400.00

9-1/4" h, flared quatraform, amethyst, pillar molded.... 575.00

Vase, Ivorine, flared flattened oval body, 10- rib design, iridescent white Aurene, partial paper label on base, 9-1/2" h, 10-1/2" w, **$550.** *Photo courtesy of Skinner, Inc.*

Ivory, Ivrene, Ivorine

Bowl

6" x 4", Catalog No.7233, unsigned 95.00

8-1/8" d, 6" h, Catalog No. 7303, Grotesque, ivory eight-ribbed bowl, black ftd base, rough pontil **575.00**

12" d, 8-3/4" h, Catalog No. 7307, Grotesque, fan-shaped eight-ribbed ivory ftd vessel, c1930 .... 865.00

Candleholder

3" h, Catalog No.7564, irid opaque white glass, ruffled and folded bobeche about integrated disk foot 435.00

10-1/2" h, Catalog No.7317, florifom, ribbed stems support two candle cups, applied leaf form accents, cupped disk foot 550.00

Center bowl, 10" d, 4-1/4" h, Catalog No.7023, classic flared bowl, integrated disk foot, applied rim wrap of lustrous blue Aurene, satin irid, some minor int. wear...................... 900.00

Goblet, 4-3/4" h, Catalog No. 7040, oval ivory bowl, black domed base, rough pontil, acid fleur-de-lis mark, c1935 .... 235.00

Lamp, 15" h, 11" d shade, Catalog No.2384, matching 12-rib base and shade, irid opaque calcite white, engraved floral motif interspersed through wheel-cut geometric medial design, minimal chipping at top under shade cap 2,070.00

Urn, 12" h, Catalog No.7468, translucent irid white, flared, stepped sq pedestal foot, applied "M" handles, pr...................... 2,100.00

Vase

5" h, 5" d, Catalog No.2533, flared body, 10 prominent optic ridges 460.00

8-1/4" h, Catalog No. 2683 design, oval, raised floral rim 520.00

8-1/2" h, Catalog No. 6875, triangular form tapering to applied star motif on round base, polished pontil, paper label from 1933 Chicago World's Fair............ 435.00

9" h, 6" d, Catalog 7331, ribbed 200.00

10-1/4" h, Catalog Variant No. 8598, rolled and flared rim, ovoid vessel with cushion foot, polished pontil 690.00

10-1/4" h, flared ribbed rim, urn-shaped ftd vessel, semi-polished pontil, inscribed "Steuben," c1936........ 920.00

12" h, Catalog No. 7566, trumpet with two lilies 1,955.00

Jade

Bowl

6" d, Catalog No. 2687, inverted rim on wide shouldered light blue body, c1925 .... 865.00

9" d, 3" h, Catalog No. 2582, light blue wide shallow bowl, applied flint white foot, polished pontil, paper fleur-de-lis label on base, c1925, nick to base, light scratches 750.00

Center bowl, 16" d, 5-1/2" h, Catalog No.3200 variant, broad, flared, opaque yellow, bulbed integrated foot, two small sand grain spots on int... 230.00

Compote

7" d, 3" h, Catalog No.3234, translucent light blue jade above applied opal white alabaster stem and disk foot 575.00

11-5/8" d, 3-3/4" h, wide rim on bowl, circular alabaster foot..... 115.00

Cornucopia, 8-1/4" h, 4-1/2" w at top, green, doomed alabaster foot, sgd, pr 1,150.00

Goblet, 8" h, experimental shape, Oriental Jade green striped bowl, rough pontil.................... 1,100.00

Lamp base

6" h, Catalog No.6199, etched yellow jade, sculptured floral pattern, rectangular glass body, silvered metal platform base and harp lamp fittings 520.00

7" h, green jade glass stick vase shaft mounted with etched silvered metal base, rim, and electrical socket fittings, Roycroft orb mark on base.............. 1,840.00

9-1/2" h, Catalog No.8002, flared vasiform green jade glass shaft, applied mirror black looped rigaree handles, gilt metal lamp fittings attributed to Crest Lamp Co. 460.00

Perfume bottle, 5-3/4" h, green, internally ribbed and tooled, white glass stopper, sgd "F. Carder-Steuben" 675.00

Vase

5-1/2" h, thin ribbed vase, polished pontil, acid stamped "Steuben" 350.00

8-1/8" h, conical form, five horizontal lower ribs, Art Deco style, polished pontil, light minor scratches **300.00**

8-1/2" h, Catalog No. 6287, optic-ribbed Green Jade fan form vase, applied alabaster ftd stem, rough pontil.................. 490.00

8-1/2" h, Catalog No. 7436, dark blue, vertically pillared shape 2,530.00

9" h, Catalog No. 938, ftd, Green Jade cut to alabaster, bird design, polished pontil, light rim scratches 2,100.00

9-1/2" h, Catalog No. 5000, raised rim, ovoid form, Green Jade cut to alabaster, bird design, polished pontil, minor light scratches 2,100.00

10" h, Catalog No. 6873, three prong, Green Jade, alabaster pod vase, acid stamped "Steuben" in block letters, gaffer's sliver chip at pontil **950.00**

11-1/2" h, Green Jade, rect, two applied alabaster lion masks, mounted in leafy metal base **700.00**

Matsu Noke

Candlestick, 10-1/2" h, colorless crystal, applied rim wraps, handles, and Matsu Noke dec in light Pomona Green glass **520.00**

Glass, Catalog No.2239, green handle **290.00**

Vase, Catalog No.3359, rose dec **340.00**

Mirror Black

Bath salts bottle, 5-1/4" h

Catalog No. 6887, threaded gold Aurene mushroom stopper, acid fleur-de-lis mark, few nicks. **200.00**

Catalog No. 7347, threaded gold Aurene mushroom stopper, acid fleur-de-lis mark, few nicks. **300.00**

Bowl, 8" d

3-1/4" h, Catalog No.5023, opaque flared form, fleur-de-lis mark on foot, minor scratches **435.00**

Bowl, 8" d, 4-3/4" h, glossy, wide ribbed pattern ending as four scallops at top **450.00**

Candlestick, 10" h, Catalog No. 5114, applied colorless rope dec, rough pontil **865.00**

Center bowl, 10-1/8" d, 4-7/8" h, Mirror Black bowl, hollow, twisted colorless stem, disk base, polished pontil, light scratches **575.00**

Compote, 7" d, 3-3/8" h, Mirror Black bowl, hollow, twisted colorless stem, disk base, polished pontil, light scratches **400.00**

Jar, cov

4-3/4" h, sq, gold aurene threaded stopper **200.00**

5" h, Celeste blue ground, mirror black reeding, angular black stopper **250.00**

Sherbet, 3-3/4" h, Catalog No. 2680, polished pontil **175.00**

Vase

6-1/4" h, 8" l, Catalog No. 7564, modified four-pillar grotesque form, ivory bowl raised on capped black foot **460.00**

6-1/2" h, Catalog No. 7307, modified grotesque manner, waffle pontil **175.00**

9-7/8" h, Catalog No. 5103, two applied handles, polished pontil **1,380.00**

10-1/2" h, Catalog No. 6873, prong-type, three triangular holders applied to conforming oval pad foot, one with fleur-de-lis stamp mark, price for pr. **920.00**

12" h, Catalog No. 6391, polished raised rim, broad glossy oval, five repeated foliate panels and scrolling devices **1,500.00**

12" h, Catalog No. 6391, polished raised rim, broad glossy oval, Matzu, three full-length stylized Ming trees over cloud formations, fleur-de-lis mark on base. **1,265.00**

Miscellaneous

Bowl

7-3/4" d, 3-1/4" h, crystal, Floret, shape no. 8059, inscribed "Steuben" **225.00**

9" d, 3-1/2" h, Calyx, designed by Donald Pollard, floriform, solid foot of colorless glass, inscribed "Steuben," c1962 . . . . **100.00**

9" d, 7-1/4" h, designed by John Dreves, deep colorless bowl, raised on six scrolled feet, inscribed "Steuben" on base, orig box, c1942 . . . . **350.00**

10" d, 4-1/4" h, crystal, Trillium, shape no. 8089, triangulated rim, inscribed "Steuben" on base **200.00**

Center bowl, 12-1/2" d, Catalog No. 6784, Florentia, flared ruffled rim, gold fumed flower blossom ornament, mica-flecked colorless glass, matte acid-etched finish. **4,715.00**

Champagne, 5-1/2" h, Catalog No. 7160, conical opal body, amethyst cintra-twist stem, polished pontil, c1928 . . . . **175.00**

Compote, 3-1/4" h, 8" d, Catalog No. 3234, shallow bowl supported on short stem, disk foot, topaz with blue rim wrap, polished pontil, c1920, price for pr **350.00**

Decanter, 10-1/2" h, inverted teardrop shape trapped bubble in stopper, colorless bulbous vessel, etched mark on base, scratches on base. . . . **150.00**

Flower frog, 14-1/2" h, Catalog No. 6483, nude female diver, frosted colorless glass, flower frog base designed as polished colorless glass rock form, minor nicks **1,100.00**

Pitcher, 10-1/2" h, elongated flared rim, egg-shaped body, colorless, design by George Thompson, inscribed "Steuben" on base **230.00**

Portrait plaque, 8-1/2" w, 10-1/2" h, rect colorless glass plaque, cast leaded glass portrait of Thomas Edison, acid stamp fleur-de-lis mark, also marked "C1929 C.G.W.," metal luminor base inscribed "Edison Association Illuminating Co.," made as a favor for banquet to celebrate 15th anniversary of Edison's invention of the electric light, and grand opening of Henry Ford Museum, scratches. **1,725.00**

Seafood cocktail, 4-1/4" d flared bowl, round 2-3/4" h ftd base, colorless, designed by George Thompson, inscribed "Steuben" within pontil, price for 12-pc set **900.00**

Sherbet and undertray, 4" h, 6" d undertray, Catalog No. 2961, Rose Dubarry, flared rim, alabaster stem and base, polished pontils, inscribed "Collection Eric E. Ericson/Rose du Barry" **1,150.00**

Shrimp compote, 4-3/4" h, Catalog No. 6252, flared deep orchid glass bowl, alabaster standard and disk foot, c1925 . . . . **225.00**

Vase

6-1/4" h, Catalog No. 429, alabaster, irid gold entwined vines and leaves, soft irid sheen **550.00**

8-1/4" h, 7" w, Catalog No. 6287, slightly ribbed fan of amber glass, green bulbed standard and disk foot, block letter acid stamp in polished pontil, c1925 . . . . . **115.00**

Moss Agate

Lamp, 30" h overall, Catalog No.8026, 11" h angular shouldered oval glass shaft of purple and lavender with mica flecks, swirls of green aventurine, amber, red, and blue, mounted to gilt metal single-socket lamp fittings **1,610.00**

Torchere, 15" h, flared glass shade, eight scalloped rim, mottled amber, green, yellow, rust, red swirled with cluthra bubbles and crackling, black painted cast iron lamp base . . **1,200.00**

Vase, 6" h, flared rim, oval body, mottled green, internally dec with multicolored red, blue, white, brown, black, and metallic clusters swirling powders, recessed polished pontil, attributed to Frederick Carder. . **635.00**

Oriental Poppy

Box, cov, 5-1/2" d, 3-1/4" h, Catalog No.7540, mold blown round dish, opal striped poppy pink transparent crystal,

matching five petal blossom on conforming cov. 1,035.00
Champagne, green stem. 375.00
Cordial, green stem and foot, sgd 325.00
Goblet, 8-1/4" h, flared rib-molded, pink opal, applied Pomona green straight stem 490.00
Lamp, Catalog No.6501. . . . . 1,500.00
Lamp base, 10-3/4" h, Catalog No.8490, rib-molded satin pink opal, elaborate gilt-metal fittings 575.00
Perfume bottle, 10-1/2" h, opal, rose, c1925 . . . . 1,200.00
Sherbet, 4-1/2" h, green stem . . 275.00
Vase

6" h, Catalog No.650, satin smooth flared oval body, pink ground, 16 integrated opal stripes, two potstone blemishes at side 1,380.00

10-1/4" h, Catalog No.8422, flared oval body, vertical opal rib-stripes, rosy-pink surround, applied Pomona Green pedestal foot 1,495.00

Pomona Green, vase, Catalog No. 7331, ribbed, unsigned, 9" h, 5-3/4" d, **$215.** *Photo courtesy of David Rago Auctions.*

Pomona Green

Basket, 4-1/2" h, Catalog No. 644, applied handles with raspberry prunts, looped lattice design, large polished pontil. 290.00
Bowl, 10-1/2" d, 6" h, Catalog No.6241, angular rib-molded green bowl, topaz pedestal foot. 230.00
Candlesticks, 4" h, Catalog No.6384 . . . . 90.00
Center bowl, 10" d, 5-1/4" h, Catalog No.3080, air trap bubbled variation, four hollow stems around central opening 345.00
Compote, 8-1/2" d, 8-1/4" h, Catalog No.6044, rib-molded amber topaz bowl, solid green stem, double cupped base 435.00
Finger bowl and underplate, 5" d bowl, 6-1/4" d underplate, Catalog No.204. . . . . 200.00
Pitcher, 8-1/2" h, Catalog No.6232, ribbed oval green body, applied amber handle 230.00
Vase

6-3/4" h, Catalog No.6031 variant, ribbed sphere. 200.00

8" h, Catalog No.6441, trefoil pinched rim, rib-molded cone form 240.00

9" h, 5-3/4" d, Catalog No. 7221, ribbed, unsigned 215.00

11" h, Catalog No.6287, green round, ridged topaz engraved in floral swag dec, fleur-de-lis mark on base, annealing flaw at pontil 175.00

11" h, Catalog No. 6875, fan. 275.00

Rosaline

Bowl

6-7/8" d, Catalog No. 2687, inverted rim, shouldered vessel, no pontil 550.00

8-1/4" d, 3" h, flared rim, alabaster foot, no pontil, scratches . . 150.00

12-1/2" l, Catalog No. 6081 variant, oval, Rosaline cut to alabaster, grapes pattern, raised applied handles at each end, heat crack on one at rim 2,30.00

Bud vase, 8" h, Catalog No. 7671, Rosaline vase, alabaster foot, acid stamp mark 225.00
Candlesticks, pr, 1-1/2" h, Rosaline cups, alabaster disk base. 250.00
Compote

3-1/2" h, Catalog No. 3234, shallow Rosaline bowl, alabaster stem, disk foot, polished pontil, c1920 200.00

12" d, 2-3/4" h, Catalog No. 506, elegant pink bowl, applied alabaster glass foot, int. bubble 375.00

Cup and saucer, 2-1/4" h cup, 4-1/2" d saucer, alabaster loop handles, disk foot, polished pontil, acid stamp 150.00
Plate, acid stamp mark. 95.00
Powder box, cov, 4" x 3", Catalog No. 2910, unsigned 210.00
Vase

4-3/4" h, Catalog No. 1500 variant, diminutive oval ginger jar form, double etched Chinese pattern surface, alabaster ground 1,265.00

7" h, Catalog No. 6078, semi-spherical shape, Rosaline cut to alabaster, floral design, polished pontil, minor light scratches 1,725.00

Selenium Red

Bowl, 4-1/2" d, 2-3/4" h, oval, fleur-de-lis mark on base, six-pc set 325.00
Center bowl, 14" d, 6" h, Catalog No.3196, sgd "F. Carder/Steuben" 425.00
Goblet, engraved grape vine motif, base marked "Steuben" and fleur-de-lis mark 250.00
Vase

6" h, 4" w at top, red dome foot, rolled edge, deep color . . . 300.00

12" h, Catalog No.6034, ridged trumpet form, brilliant red, grape and vine dec, fleur-de-lis mark on base, four int. bubbles at top rim 920.00

Silverina

Candlesticks, pr

5" h, Catalog No.6637, amethyst, mica-flecked body, controlled bubble pattern 865.00

12" h, Catalog No.3328 variant, colorless crystal internally dec by diamond patterned air-trap mica flecks, mirror black cupped bases stamped "Steuben". 900.00

Center bowl, 11-1/8" d, flared rim on diamond air-trap amethyst bowl with mica flecks, rough pontil, acid fleur-de-lis stamp, wear 1,150.00
Vase, 12" h, topaz bulbous bud vase, decorative mica flecks throughout, applied Pomona Green disk foot 400.00

Spanish Green

Bud vase, 13-1/4" h, Catalog No. 5228 variant, elongated optic-ribbed neck, ftd double gourd bulbous form, polished pontil 115.00
Candlestick, 12" h, Catalog No.2596, optic ribbed baluster form, double ball below candle cup, fleur-de-lis mark on base 250.00
Centerpiece bowl, 14" d, bubbles and reeded dec. 200.00

Champagne goblet, 6-1/4" h, floriform, five applied ribbed leaves under bubbled bowl, raised on nubby stem, folded rim pedestal foot, stamped mark on base, price for 10-pc set . . **1,380.00**

Compote, 7" h, bubbled and reeded design, pr **325.00**

Goblet, 8-1/2" h, Catalog No. 8316, inverted bell form, bubbled glass, five applied leaves above rustic-style stem, disk foot, block letter acid stamp, c1925, price for nine-pc set . . . **980.00**

Shot glass, threading, bubbles, sgd **60.00**

Stemware, nine 7-1/2" h, eight 6-1/4" h, two 3-1/4" h, Catalog No. 6359, flared cups, bulbed stems with decorative prunts, disk feet, bubbled glass threads, some with block letter or fleur-de-lis stamp marks, c1925, price for 19-pc set **1,150.00**

Table service, 12 8" d plates, 12 bouillon cups, 14 serving bowls, 36-pc set **575.00**

Vase

- 8" h, trumpet form, bubbled and reeded design, pr. **400.00**
- 8-1/4" h, optic-ribbed fan, Spanish Green reeding, trapped bubbles on disk base. **195.00**
- 10" h, Catalog No. 6873, three triangular prong forms attached to round base **320.00**

Threaded

Cocktail pitcher, 9-1/4" h, Catalog No.7056, crystal body, applied strap handle, rose reeding, conforming cov, some loss to threading **225.00**

Compote, Catalog No. 2018, crystal, green machine threading, engraved **285.00**

Dresser jar, Catalog No.1169, colorless puff jars, one with ruby random threads, one with black threads, price for pr **325.00**

Goblet, 5-3/4" h, colorless, diamond molded, Pomona blue reeding, applied Bristol yellow disk foot, stamped "Steuben," three-pc set. **225.00**

Plate, 10-7/8" d, colorless, bright blue concentric threads on back rim, inscribed "F. Carder/Steuben". . **220.00**

Salt, 2" h, 2-1/4" d, colorless, Rosa threading applied under flared rim, pedestal. **175.00**

Topaz

Compote, 8-3/8" d, 8" h, curved rim on shallow optic-ribbed topaz colored bowl, applied Green No. 5 stem, domed topaz base. **300.00**

Goblet, 6-1/4" h, Catalog No. 6220, topaz optic-ribbed conical bowl, applied Green No. 5 stem and domed base **175.00**

Vase, 8-5/8" h, Catalog No. 6297, topaz optic-ribbed fan, applied Green No. 5 bulbed stem and disk base, polished pontil. **200.00**

Verre de Soi, perfume bottle, melon ribbed, long celeste blue dauber, 4-1/2" h, **$290.** *Photo courtesy of David Rago Auctions.*

Verre de Soie

Basket

- 10-3/4" h, Catalog No.5069, irid silky body, berry prunt at applied handles **920.00**
- 13" h, 8" w, ruffled rim **600.00**
- 14" h, 10" l, irid, engraving of flowers, leaves, and swags, applied loop handle, sgd "Hawkes Steuben" **900.00**

Bowl

- 8" d, Catalog No. 2687, inverted rim on shouldered vessel, polished pontil **200.00**
- 9-7/8" d, Catalog No. 2851, flared rim, ftd, large polished pontil **225.00**
- 10" d, Catalog No. 2586, inverted rim, shallow body, three applied feet, polished pontil. **240.00**

Bud vase, Catalog No. 451, ruffled rim, polished pontil, c1915 . . . . **190.00**

Candlesticks, pr, 10" h, Catalog No. 5194, half twist stems, unmarked **425.00**

Center bowl, Catalog No.2775, eight pinched apertures around rim . **290.00**

Chandelier, 16" w, four verre de soie ruffled glass #892 shades, mounted to gilt metal ceiling lamp with acorn and oak cluster motif, adjustable drop **1,840.00**

Compote, 6-1/2" h, flared bow, "C" monogram on baluster stem, disk foot **175.00**

Console set, 12" d flared #2764 bowl, pr 3" h mushroom candleholders, ruby reeding on outer rims, stamped fleur-de-lis mark, some threads damage **520.00**

Finger bowl and underplate, 2-3/4" h, Catalog No. 1984 variant, polished pontil **195.00**

Goblet, 3-7/8" h, Catalog No. 2680, polished pontil. **85.00**

Oil and vinegar cruet, 7-3/8" h, Catalog No. 3061, engraved flower and bud on leafy stem, oil and vinegar measurements, polished pontil. **220.00**

Perfume bottle, 4-1/2" h, melon-ribbed, celeste blue trim, long dauber . **290.00**

Tableware, four plates, two goblets, three sherbets, six wines, stamped "Hawkes" at center pontil **750.00**

Sherbet set, 4" h, 3-3/4" d sherbet, 6" d undertray, tinted aquamarine/green **220.00**

Tumbler, 4" h, 3-1/4" w at top, flaring rim, sgd "F. Carder Steuben" . . **450.00**

Tumble-up, 7" h, carafe with mold-blown tumbler, polished pontil **285.00**

Vase

- 5-3/4" h, stretched ruffled fan rim on tapering ftd base, polished pontil **365.00**
- 7" h, Catalog No. 2137 variant, engraved flowers and buds on leafy stems, polished pontil **225.00**
- 7-3/4" h, Catalog No. 2142, engraved floral, foliate, and bow knotted swag motif, polished pontil **245.00**
- 10" h, trefoil rim on optic-ribbed cylindrical base, polished pontil **395.00**

Wisteria, vase, 9-1/8" h, Catalog No. 7388, cylindrical spiral optic, ribbed vase with ball stem, domed base, polished pontil, minor scratches **635.00**

Stevens and Williams

19th C

History: In 1824, Joseph Silvers and Joseph Stevens leased the Moor Lane Glass House at Briar Lea Hill (Brierley Hill), England, from the Honey-Borne family. In 1847, William Stevens and Samuel Cox Williams took over, giving the firm its present name. In 1870, the company moved to its Stourbridge plant. In the 1880s, the firm employed such renowned glass artisans as Frederick C. Carder, John Northwood, other Northwood family members, James Hill, and Joshua Hodgetts.

Stevens and Williams made cameo glass. Hodgetts developed a more commercial version using thinner-walled blanks, acid etching, and the engraving wheel. Hodgetts, an amateur botanist, was noted for his brilliant floral designs.

Other glass products and designs manufactured by Stevens and Williams include intaglio ware, Peach Bloom (a form of peachblow), moss agate, threaded ware, "jewell" ware, tapestry ware, and Silveria. Stevens and Williams made glass pieces covering the full range of late Victorian fashion.

After World War I, the firm concentrated on refining the production of lead crystal and achieving new glass colors. In 1932, Keith Murray came to Stevens and Williams as a designer. His work stressed the pure nature of the glass form. Murray stayed with Stevens and Williams until World War II, and later had a career in architecture.

Basket

7-1/2" h, 6" sq, transparent amber glass, applied green leaves, large amber apples, amber feet, amber thorn loop handle **550.00**

10" h, 6-1/2" d, deep pink int., creamy white ext., three applied amber loop feet which extend up to form three green with cranberry highlights leaf designs which attach and swirl around body, applied amber rope handle with applied cranberry rigaree, top knot finial on center of handle . . . **400.00**

10" h, 9" w, brilliant green over pale yellow, blue lining int., applied blue flowers, four applied vaseline feet, green thorn loop handle, button pontil **400.00**

11" h, 6" w, pale yellow custard body, large applied amber glass flower, applied emerald green leaves, feet and twisted thorn handle. . . **425.00**

13" h, 10-1/2" d, white ribbed ext., blown-out hobnails cased in bright pink shading to pale pink, ornate amber trim, twisted amber handle, applied amber thorn feet, two feet may have been polished in the making **175.00**

13-3/4" h, 8-3/4" d, arabesque, colorless body, white arabesque designs, seven applied bands of cranberry and yellow dec, applied ribbed foot, large crystal loop handle **165.00**

14" h, 7" w, cranberry egg-shaped body, pale cream outer casing, three green applied leaf-like feet which form loops on base, thorn cut edge, large applied amber thorn crossed handle **200.00**

Biscuit jar, 5-1/2" d, 7-3/4" h, creamy opaque ground, applied amber and green leaves, deep pink lining, SP rim, cov, and handle. **295.00**

Bowl

5" d, 2-3/4" h, Jewell Glass, pale dusty-rose, zipper-like air-trap ribs, incised in pontil "Rd 55693" **215.00**

6" d, 3" h, Matsu No Ke, creamy yellow satin bowl, branch of twisted, knurled, and thorny frosted crystal glass winds around perimeter, 36 florets, three feet, one slight chip on one flower . **1,250.00**

8" d, Peachblow, double tier of applied shell rigaree at rim, polished pontil **250.00**

Bride's basket, 10-1/2" h, 10" l, 5" w, off-white ext., Rose Du Barry pink int., two clear red cherries on one side, two amber anjou pears on other, rambling leafed amber branches, golden-amber pie crust ribbon edge and four knurled feet, golden-amber looping handle **1,750.00**

Calling card tray, 10" l, applied amber handle, rolled edge, translucent opalescent ground, three applied berries, blossoms, and green leaves, three applied amber feet. **750.00**

Cologne bottle, 8-1/2" h, cut and engraved crystal, square panel-ribbed crystal with bright-cut floral dec, repeated on conforming cover, stopper chipped at base **375.00**

Compote

3-1/4" h, rosaline bowl, bulbed alabaster stem, disk foot, acid "S & W England" stamp, polished pontil **200.00**

5" w, 4" h, blue bowl, alabaster foot, sgd **100.00**

Creamer and sugar, open, blue opalescent, snail feet, applied raspberry prunts **175.00**

Vase, Grotesque, colorless, applied green lobes, polished pontil, 9-1/4" h, 4-1/2" d, **$200.** *Photo courtesy of David Rago Auctions.*

Ewer, 5-1/4" h, Silveria, silver foil sandwiched between layers of glass, crimson, ruby-red, and gold on upper half, large areas of vivid purple accented by splotches of gold on lower portion, clear green glass entwining vertical trailing overlaid, applied handle, sgd "S&W" in pontil mark **3,450.00**

Lemonade pitcher, 9" h, amber, thumbprint molding, applied blue handle **325.00**

Mug, blue, applied plums **300.00**

Parfait, 4-1/4" h, light blue jade, alabaster foot, wafer connection . **90.00**

Perfume bottle, 6-1/2" h, 3-3/4" w, Pompeiian Swirl, deep gold, brown to red, turquoise blue lining, orig cut frosted stopper. **895.00**

Pitcher

6" h, 5" d, yellow opalescent, vertical stripes, shell reeded handle **225.00**

7" h, 4-1/2" d, overlay, mint green ext., robin's egg blue int., three white and pink tinted blossoms, amber leaves attached to twisting, curling amber tendril continues to form handle, end of tendril ground smooth **385.00**

Powder box, jade, alabaster foot and knob **200.00**

Rose bowl, 5-1/4" d, 5" h, Pompeiian Swirl, shaded brown to gold, robin's egg blue lining, box pleated top, six ruffles **850.00**

Salt, irid gold ground, sterling silver basket, hanging spoon, English hallmarks **165.00**

Toothpick holder, green ground cut to clear, hallmarked sterling silver rim **275.00**

Toupee stand, mushroom shape, rose alabaster **295.00**

Tumbler, 5" h, cut and engraved crystal, oval, foliate dec including foxglove blossoms and birds in flight **125.00**

Vase, blue body, applied amber rim, rigaree, and feet, signed, 7-1/2" w, 7-1/2" h, **$325.**

Vase

- 5-1/4" h, 6-1/2" d, ivory, appliquéd, textured fern frond applied to shoulder, stem forming loop handle, pie crust ruffled rim with amber trim **100.00**
- 5-3/4" h, egg shape, opal and cranberry vertical stripes, gold an black floral dec, applied colorless rigaree extends to three feet, pr **250.00**
- 6" h, 6" w, 4-3/4" w at top, applied dec, Matso Nuke style, ftd, pink-peach peachblow ground, bright cream-yellow lining, colorless applied band of shell-like rigaree at top, three rosettes, three large 5-1/4" l leaf feet, applied raspberry prunt over pontil. **750.00**
- 6-1/2" h, 4" w, Sylvaria, silvery white shading to raspberry, random green threading **1,200.00**
- 6-1/2" h, 5-1/2" d, amber ruffled top edge, amber loop feet, rose lined cream opaque body, three appliqué amber, green, and cranberry ruffled leaves . . . **260.00**
- 7" h, swirled satin, amber shaded to blue cased to opal and yellow, spiraled air trap swirls **575.00**
- 7-1/4" h, Pompeiian Swirl, MOP, powder blue body, pink air-traps, shiny pink ribbons swirl down neck to body, two small ext. flakes **545.00**
- 7-1/4" h, satin, Swirl, shading blue to pink, spiral trapped bubble pattern **750.00**
- 7-1/2" h, swirled satin, tooled crimped rim, green shaded to rose body, cased to opal and yellow with spiraled air trap swirls . **815.00**
- 7-1/2" h, 5" w, striped Swirl, frosted deep pink, rose, and yellow stripes, frosted ground, 36 vertical ribs **425.00**
- 7-3/4" h, 3-3/4" w, double gourd, Pompeiian Swirl, light brown shading to gold **475.00**
- 8" h, 4-1/2" w, bulbous, Pompeiian Swirl, deep rose, white int. . **575.00**
- 9-1/4" h, 4-1/2" d, Grotesque, clear, applied green lobes, polished pontil **200.00**
- 10" h, intaglio cut, pale rose pink cased to transparent green, wheel cut foliate panels below horizontal stepped flared rim. **1,265.00**
- 10" h, slender refined shape, six medallions of applied colorless glass, trailing stems swirling to base, engraved ornate stylized petals and foliage, sgd in pontil "Frederick Carder," Stevens and Williams logo **900.00**
- 10-1/8" h, cameo, rim cut to floral blossom's outline, swollen at top, flared at base, overlaid in white, wheel-carved to deep purple shading to yellow, blossoms, elongated leaves and stems, cipher at base **10,350.00**
- 10-1/2" h, flared trumpet form, colorless, four panels of intaglio blossoms and swirling prunts separated by horizontal notched ribs **300.00**
- 10-3/4" h, 5-3/4" w, bulbous, pedestal base, Pompeiian Swirl, MOP, pale lime green, white lining **850.00**
- 11" h, 6-1/2" base, stick with bulbous base, Pompeiian Swirl, deep amber to bright red **950.00**
- 11-1/2" h, 4" w, rose shading to pink, white and colorless applied flowers and leaves, ruffled top, flaring ribbed neck **225.00**
- 12-1/2" h, 7" d, lily, Verre de Soie, twisted stem, scratches . . . **150.00**

Stiegel-Type Glass

History: Baron Henry Stiegel founded America's first flint-glass factory at Manheim, Pennsylvania, in the 1760s. Although clear glass was the most common color made, amethyst, blue (cobalt), and fiery opalescent pieces also are found. Products included bottles, creamers, flasks, flips, perfumes, salts, tumblers, and whiskeys. Prosperity was short-lived; Stiegel's extravagant lifestyle forced the factory to close.

It is very difficult to identify a Stiegel-made item. As a result, the term "Stiegel-type" is used to identify glass made during the time period of Stiegel's firm and in the same shapes and colors as used by that company.

Enamel-decorated ware also is attributed to Stiegel. True Stiegel pieces are rare; an overwhelming majority is of European origin.

References: Frederick W. Hunter, *Stiegel Glass*, 1950, available in Dover reprint; George and Helen McKearin, American Glass, Crown, 1975; ——, *Two Hundred Years of American Blown Glass*, Doubleday and Company, 1950; Kenneth Wilson, *American Glass 1760-1930*, two vols., Hudson Hills Press and The Toledo Museum of Art, 1994.

Reproduction Alert: Beware of modern reproductions, especially in enamel wares.

Beaker, 5" h, blown peacock blue glass, six panels, enameled birds, dog, tiger, stag, fruit, and florals, loop design around base, polished pontil, c1840, slight lower crizzling **425.00**

Bottle, blown, colorless, enamel dec, Continental, 19th C

- 4-1/4" h, paneled sides, gentleman raising his glass, inscription on reverse, pewter color, imperfection **325.00**
- 5-1/2" h, paneled sides, flowers, heart, birds, and inscription on reverse **265.00**
- 5-7/8" h, paneled sides, floral dec **225.00**
- 5-7/8" h, paneled sides, floral dec, pewter color, imperfection . **200.00**

5-7/8" h, paneled sides, flowers and birds in oval verse, pewter color, imperfection **215.00**

6" h, paneled sides, flowers and bird dec, pewter color, imperfection **220.00**

8-3/4" h, flattened side, dec with cross and various symbols, depicting Crucifixion of Christ, inscription on reverse, pewter screw-cap **295.00**

8-7/8" h, flattened round glass stopper, flowers and leave dec, pewter color, imperfection. . **265.00**

Bottle, half post, colorless, pewter lip, minor enamel flaking

5-1/8" h, polychrome enameled flowers and birds, stain.... **110.00**

5-3/8" h, polychrome enameled flowers and birds......... **360.00**

5-3/8" h, polychrome enameled flowers, man with wine glass **165.00**

5-1/2" h, polychrome enameled flowers, bird in medallion, some residue, threads incomplete **250.00**

5-3/4" h, polychrome enameled flowers, man with bell, threads on lip incomplete, broken blister on man's arm **55.00**

5-7/8" h, polychrome enameled flowers, inscription, fox with birds in basket **300.00**

6-3/4" h, polychrome enameled flowers, man with yoke, and buckets **175.00**

Bride's bottle, 4-7/8" h, blown, opalescent, enameled floral, scroll, and bird dec, Continental, 18th C, minor scratches **525.00**

Christmas light, 4" h, yellow-green, expanded diamond pattern, metal fixture **150.00**

Creamer

3-1/8" h, pattern molded, 15-diamond pattern, emerald green, ovoid, applied handle, tooled rim, pour spout, pontil scar **2,000.00**

3-7/8" h, deep cobalt blue, 20-diamond mold, applied foot and handle, flake on bottom of handle, pinpoint rim flake......... **500.00**

4-1/8" h, cobalt blue, 20 expanded diamonds **350.00**

Firing glass, blown, colorless, European, late 19th C

4" h, Masonic engraving, traces of gilding, pontil scar........ **200.00**

4-1/4" h, copper wheel engraving around rim, hollow stem, pontil scar **175.00**

Flask

4-3/4" h, amethyst diamond and daisy.................. **495.00**

5" h, amethyst, globular, 20 molded ribs, minute rim chip..... **1,380.00**

5" h, blown, flattened oval, enameled Masonic dec, florals and inscription, sheared lip, pontil, scar, German, mid-18th C **295.00**

5-1/4" h, two hearts and dove in round floral bordered reserve, inscription on reverse, half pint **245.00**

5-1/2" h, flowers, scissors, and inscription on reverse, half pint **275.00**

6" h, blown, colorless, chestnut, checkered-diamond pattern, wear, sickness, pinpoint rim flake **725.00**

Flip glass, colorless, sheared rim, pontil scar

3-1/2" h, handle, engraved repeating swag motif around rim, lower body emb with graduated panels, form similar to McKearin plate 22, #2 .... **210.00**

3-7/8" h, band of floral dec, Continental, 18th C....... **215.00**

5-1/4" h, engraved top border frieze of ovals, leaves, and berries beneath loop ribbon design **150.00**

6-1/4" h, engraved floral motif and sunflower, form similar to McKearin plate 22, #2 .... **300.00**

7" h, engraved basket and floral motif, form similar to McKearin plate 22, #2 .... **350.00**

7" h, engraved bird in heart dec within sunburst motif, form similar to McKearin plate 22, #2 .. **400.00**

7-3/4" h, 6" d, engraved Phoenix bird between two tulips **175.00**

7-7/8" h, engraved pair of birds perched on heart within sunburst motif, form similar to McKearin plate 22, #2 .... **475.00**

8" h, engraved large flower and floral motif, form similar to McKearin plate 22, #2 .... **325.00**

8-1/4" h, engraved tulip and floral design, pontil scar, European, late 18th C................. **245.00**

Flip, cov, blown, colorless, sunburst medallion, bird, and floral dec, conical knop, etched spotted border on lid, Continental 18th or 19th C, minor imperfections............. **2,100.00**

Humpen, 9-1/4" h, blown colorless glass, enameled men smoking pipe, florals, and inscriptions, pontil scar, etched "FH 304/1" on base, European, late 19th C **275.00**

Jar, cov, 10-1/2" h, colorless, engraved sunflower and floral motifs, repeating dot and vine dec on cov, applied finial, sheared rim, pontil scar, form similar to McKearin plate 35, #2 and #3 . . **750.00**

Miniature, flip glass, 3" h, colorless, engraved bird within sunburst motif, seared mouth, pontil scar **325.00**

Mug, enameled, center shield with carpenter and blacksmith tools, floral decoration on sides, "Das ihre bare Huff and Wassen Schmidt Hand Werck," dated 1790, **$350.**

Mug, blown, colorless

3-3/8" h, enameled polychrome dec of birds, hearts, and flowers, applied strap handle, European, 18th C **395.00**

5-1/4" h, engraved floral design, pontil scar, applied strap handle with medial crease, Bohemia, mid-18th C **275.00**

6" h, cov, engraved floral motif, strap handle................. **425.00**

6-1/8" h, elaborate frosted engraving, large applied strap handle................. **265.00**

Perfume bottle, Daisy in Hexagon pattern, flake on neck....... **4,000.00**

Pitcher, 9-3/4" h, blown, aqua, twelve bands of threading around neck, enameled polychrome floral design, c1820-40 .... **2,000.00**

Salt, blown
- 2-5/8" h, blue, checkered diamond pattern **750.00**
- 2-3/4" h, colorless, ogee bowl, 18 vertical ribs, applied petaled foot **225.00**
- 2-7/8" h, 2-1/4" d, pattern molded, cobalt blue, checkered diamond pattern, double ogee bowl with short stem from same gather, plain applied circular foot, sheared rim, pontil scar, attributed to Amelung Glass Works, Frederick, MD, 1785-1797 . . . . **1,200.00**
- 3" h, deep violet-blue, 11-diamond mold, applied foot, minor pinpoint rim flakes **365.00**

Stein, 6" h, opalescent, applied strap handle, flowers and portrait of gentleman in round floral bordered reserve, Continental, 18th C, minor scratches. **550.00**

Sugar, cov, deep sapphire blue, 11 expanded diamond pattern. . . **2,650.00**

Tankard, handle, cylindrical, applied solid reeded handle, flared foot, sheared rim, pontil scar, form similar to McKearin plate 22, #4
- 5-1/2" h, milk glass, red, yellow, blue, and green enameled dec of house on mountain with floral motif, old meandering fissure around body of vessel **150.00**
- 5-3/4" h, colorless, engraved with bird in elaborate sunburst motif **500.00**
- 6-1/4" h, colorless, engraved elaborate bird and tulip dec **475.00**

Tumbler, blown, colorless
- 2-7/8" h, paneled, polychrome enameled flowers. **220.00**
- 3-1/8" h, enameled polychrome dec of bird, heart, and foliage, minor enamel wear. **265.00**
- 3-5/8" h, enameled polychrome floral dec and phrase "We two will be true," minor enamel wear . . **650.00**
- 4-3/8" h, 3-1/2" d, 22 vertical flutes, engraved dec, cross-hatched ovals. **50.00**

Whiskey tumbler, blown
- Cobalt blue, pattern mold, 12 ogival diamonds over 12 flutes design **500.00**
- Colorless, enameled man on prancing horse. **275.00**

Stretch Glass

History: Stretch glass was produced by many glass manufacturers in the United States between 1915 through 1935. The most prominent makers were Cambridge, Fenton (which probably manufactured more stretch glass than any of the others), Imperial, Northwood, and Steuben. Stretch glass is pressed or blown-molded glass, with little or no pattern, that is sprayed with a metallic salt mix while hot, creating a iridescent, onionskin-like effect, that may be velvety or shiny in luster. Look for mold marks. Imported pieces are blown and show a pontil mark.

References: Kitty and Russel Umbraco, *Iridescent Stretch Glass*, published by authors (6019 Arlington Blvd, Richmond, CA 94805) 1972; Berry Wiggins, *Stretch Glass*, Antique Publications, 1972, 1987 value update.

Collectors' Club: Stretch Glass Society, P.O. Box 573, Hampshire, IL 60140.

Ashtray, sapphire blue **18.00**

Basket
- 5" d, Tiffany, pink shading to white stretch glass basket, gold-plated metal basket frame **2,395.00**
- 6" h, blue, applied colorless reeded handle **65.00**
- 10-1/2" d, white ground, applied colorless handle **140.00**

Bobeches, pr, vaseline, scalloped **45.00**

Bowl
- 7-1/2" d, 3" h, green, ftd. **35.00**
- 7-1/2" w, sq, orange, Imperial . **65.00**
- 8" w, sq, ruffled, dark marigold, stretch irid, Imperial **65.00**
- 9" d, low, blue irid **45.00**
- 9" d, 4" h, orange, flared, Imperial cross mark. **65.00**
- 10" d, green, rolled rim **25.00**
- 10" d, irid green, straight sided, flared, Dugan **28.00**
- 10" d, 4-1/2" h, yellow irid, Imperial **85.00**
- 12" d, white, Fenton. **45.00**
- 13" d, blue, wide rim, collared base **115.00**

Compote, Tiffany Favrile, iridescent blue, 8" d, 4-1/2" h, **$1,350.**

Bud vase, 11-3/4" h, pink **50.00**

Cake server, green, center handle **35.00**

Candlesticks, pr
- 6" h, celeste blue, Fenton, #249 . . . . **165.00**
- 8-1/2" h, Colonial Panels, olive-green **85.00**
- 9-1/2" h, light green **60.00**
- 10" h, emerald green **70.00**
- 10-1/2" h, vaseline **60.00**

Candy dish, cov, topaz, Fenton . **60.00**

Cheese dish, 4-1/2" d, 2-1/2" h, yellow ground, black edge, pedestal base, Northwood. **50.00**

Compote
- 6-1/2" d, 5-1/2" h, bright green, zipper notched pedestal base **50.00**
- 7-5/8" d, 4-1/2" h, irid green, clear stem, amber base **75.00**
- 9-1/2" d, 5-1/2" h, vaseline, tree bark patterned stem, sgd "Northwood" **175.00**

Console bowl
- 11-1/2" d, orange, rolled rim. . **40.00**
- 14" d, red **175.00**

Creamer and sugar, tangerine, Rings pattern. **75.00**

Hat, 4" h, purple, Imperial **55.00**

Lemonade pitcher, celeste blue, applied cobalt blue handle **215.00**

Mayonnaise, ftd, orig liner, Twisted Optic, Iris Ice, Imperial **68.00**

Mayonnaise ladle, Celeste **25.00**

Nappy, 7" w, vaseline, Fenton . . . **40.00**

Nut cup, yellow, Northwood **50.00**

Plate
- 6" d, red, paneled, Imperial . . **50.00**
- 7-1/2" d, amber glass with stretched irid to rim, gold luster surface, small polished pontil, attributed to Imperial Glass Co., early 20th C **115.00**
- 8-1/4" d, Aurene, gold **75.00**
- 8-1/2" d, blue **35.00**
- 9" d, amethyst ice, paneled, Imperial **48.00**
- 9" d, green, laurel leaf dec . . . **25.00**
- 10" d, brown and orange **35.00**
- 11-1/2" d, Panels, russet. **65.00**

Powder jar, cov, ice blue **50.00**

Ring tree, 5" d, yellow, enameled floral dec **45.00**

Salad set, 14" d bowl, six 8-1/2" plates, mayonnaise bowl with underplate, vaseline, c1920 . . . . **125.00**

Sandwich server, sq, green, center handle **30.00**

Sherbet

4" h, red, melon ribbed **60.00**

5-1/2" h, green, fluted **40.00**

Tumbler, Colonial Panels pattern, red **95.00**

Vase

5-1/2" h, baluster, pink, Imperial **75.00**

5-1/2" h, 6" w at top, 3-1/2" d base, Smooth Panels, white **60.00**

5-1/2" h, 7-1/2" w at top, 3-1/2" d base, Smooth Panels, white . **60.00**

6" h, cylindrical, rolled rim, clear ribbed int., hand painted florals and leaves. **45.00**

6" h, fan, green, ribbed **45.00**

7" h, vaseline, fan shape **40.00**

10" h, blue, vertical cut **60.00**

Studio Art

History: Studio art of the 1990s may be the collectibles of the 21st century. Collectors are becoming aware of some of the distinctive examples of studio glassware being currently produced. Many of the fine art glass examples we treasure today began as studio art in the preceding decades.

Collectors may decide to center their collections on specific types of glassware or a particular craftsman. Collectors should buy studio glass to be enjoyed, as well as treasured. Careful documentation of additions to collections will be valuable as the collector's interests grow. Well-made, tastefully decorated glassware will surely increase in collectibility. Collectors of studio art often include paperweights in this collecting category, as they are individual works of art. This is one of the most interesting and unexplored glass collecting categories in the antiques and collectibles field.

Reference: Leslie Piña, *Fifties Glass*, Schiffer, 1994.

Periodicals: *Glass Art Society Journal*, 1305 4th Ave. #711, Seattle, WA 98101-2401; *Glass Magazine*, New York Experimental Glass Workshop, Inc., 142 Mulberry St., New York, NY 10013; *Neu Glaz* (New Glass), Rudolf - Diesel - Str. 5-7, Frechen 50226 Germany; *Vetri, Italian Glass News*, P.O. Box 191, Fort Lee, NJ 07024-0191.

Museums: The Chrysler Museum, Norfolk, VA; The Corning Museum of Glass, Corning, NY.

Additional Listings: Murano Glass and Paperweights.

Ashtray, 5-1/2" d, 2-1/2" h, by Floris Meydam for Leerdam Glass Works (Holland), thick, colorless, orange and green stripes, etched "Meydam Leerdam" **450.00**

Basket

7" h, 8-1/4" w, by Per Lutken, for Holmegaard, sommerso, dark green casing, etched "Holmegaard/PL/1957" **700.00**

14" h, 9" w, large free flowing basket, shelf attached overhead handle, bright red, control bubbles, mica flecks, cased in clear, Barbini type **70.00**

Bottle

4-1/4" h, irid ovoid vessel, swirling elements below moon and earth representations, base inscribed "Lewis '74, (John Conrad Lewis Studio)". **345.00**

15" h, by Floris Meydam for Leerdam Glass Works (Holland), opalescent, etched "M Leerdam" **1,100.00**

Bowl

3-1/2" h, deep blue int., white ext., blue and purple flowers, Robert Levin. **350.00**

5-3/4" d, 2-3/4" h, trio of pinched handles, coral Verdi color, coral blush on base, inscribed "Labino-5, 1981" **275.00**

8" d, 6-3/4" h, sea-form, seedy colorless body shaded to smoky topaz, dark red doted repeating rim border, base inscribed "For Tommy/Chihuly 1980," Dale Chihuly, minor int. water stain **1,035.00**

8-1/4" d, 2-1/2" h, Michael Higgins, speckled, green and aqua, three white and yellow circular designs, gold highlights **100.00**

15-3/4" l, 2-1/2" h, by Floris Meydam for Leerdam Glass Works (Holland), organically shaped, broad flat rim, colorless, cobalt blue and amethyst stripes, etched "Leerdam 7 M" **600.00**

Charger, 17" d, Michael Higgins, amethyst, chartreuse and blue geometric inclusions, sgd in gold **125.00**

Decanter

8-1/2" h, colorless oval bottle cased to opal white internally dec with lavender-pink pulled striations, conforming ball stopper, base fully signed "Joel Phillip Myers," dated 1973 . . . . **230.00**

18" h, figural, colorless, applied colored glass hair, eyes, nose-mouth, nipples and navel, stamped and labeled "Rosenthal," designed by Jean Hans Arp **990.00**

Disk, 21" d, broad freeblown form, bluish-tined transparent glass, dec by hot manipulated squares and bits of color, attributed to Rhode Island School of Design. **175.00**

Fantasia cup, 5" h, purple, black, and red, Robert Levin **650.00**

Figure, 7" h, pear, Cenedese, pink scavo glass, design attributed to A. Barbini, unmarked **300.00**

Goblet

7-3/8" h, whimsical, glass banana supporting curved striped stem, cased yellow and green goblet glass, frosted base, inscribed "Levin 1977," titled "Cup with A-Peel," Robert Levin Studio **1,150.00**

9-1/4" h, colorless goblet with minute filligrana webbing, blue and white latticino figural teapot as stem, applied black base, white checked murrine on foot, base inscribed "Marquis © 1991," design by Richard Marquis **1,500.00**

Jack-in-the-pulpit vase

13" h, heavily cased clear over purple-amethyst body, irid flared top with continuous winding green stem from calla lily top to base, overshot dec, etched by artist "C. Funk 87" for Chris Funk, CA **225.00**

Black body, irid face, contemporary flared body, by Stuart Abelman, CA, c1982 . . . . **300.00**

Sculpture

3" h, 3-1/2" w, solid colorless body, central oval bubble and three int. spiraled green, blue, and red veils, polished facets, stepped ridges on ext. surface, base inscribed "K. Karbler 787120 Michael David" **175.00**

7-3/4" h, 14" l, abstract vessel, nippled protrusions, colorless body cased with striated opal, beige, yellow, and turquoise inclusions, base sgd "Marvin Lipovsky" dated '74 . . . . **365.00**

9" h, 13" l, transparent teal glass abstraction, flowing protuberances rising from single ringed base opening, inscribed at lower edge "Samuel J. Herman," England, c1970 . . . . **635.00**

10" h, 9" l, freeform vessel with nippled inclusions of colorless glass, internally dec with amber circles on opal white core, sgd "Marvin Lipovsky," dated '74 . . . . **420.00**

17" h, figurative glass blossom titled "Midnight Iris," purple, blue, green, and brown coloration crest to roots, sgd "Yaffa Sikorsky-Todd," dated 1988 . . . . **460.00**

Eye To Eye, Göran Wärff, 1996, Kosta Boda, Sweden. Photo courtesy of Kosta Boda.

28" w, Persian Series, each component comprised of brilliant red-orange and golden amber stripes, bright cobalt blue rim wraps, includes slumped centerpiece with colorless ribbed superstructure, folded bowl, wide rim vasiform, two conical vessels, elongated Persian water sprinkler, inscribed "Chihuly 1988" (Dale Chihuly) **16,100.00**

Scent bottle, Charles Lotton, Lansing, IL, multi-floral, gold and ruby. . . **700.00**

Stemware set, crystal, colorless Art Deco style, square gray-topaz base, five water goblets, four wines, six cordials, eight sherbets, each stamped "Rosenthal" with trademark, 29 pcs **435.00**

Tray, 17" d, orange, red, and amber ornamentals, curvilinear geometric devices, edge marked in gold "higgins," (Michael Higgins) . . . **100.00**

Vase

3-3/4" h, crystal, cobalt blue and yellow inclusions, sgd "Labino-6, 1972" **250.00**

4-3/4" h, contorted ovoid transparent body, shaded red and maroon swirls, base inscribed "Labino 1966" (Dominick Labino) . . **345.00**

5" h, stick, deep rose, interior pulls, Paul Manners, sgd **250.00**

5" h, 5-1/4" h, irid, Cypriot type finish **125.00**

5-1/2" h, 5" w, irid, green waves **125.00**

5-1/2" h, 10-1/2" l, Merletto, pinched circular form, fine network of white threads interspersed with aubergine spots, Seguso **3,000.00**

5-1/2" h, very pale apricot, inverted-egg shape, bulbous foot, sgd and dated "Labino-1965" **125.00**

5-3/8" h, ovoid, crystal, wrapped with inclusions of festoons, combined shades of cadmium orange, lemon yellow, and olive, sgd and dated "Labino-11-1975" **750.00**

5-3/4" h, 3-3/4" d, by Per Lutken, for Holmegaard, sommerso, tear shape, amethyst, etched "19H/56" **500.00**

6-1/2" h, Kralik, burgundy swirl, polished rim. **150.00**

7" h, 6-3/4" d, by Floris Meydam for Leerdam Glass Works (Holland), pillow shape, dark green and cobalt stripes, etched "Leerdam/M" **980.00**

7-1/2" h, designed by Bengt Orup for Hadeland Glassworks (Sweden), flaring sommerso, black drips, bubbles, sgd **675.00**

7-1/2" h, brilliant transparent emerald green, occasional opalescent inclusions pulled and tooled into dec protuberances, base inscribed "Labino 5-1083" **425.00**

7-1/2" h, 4" w, irid, loop dec . . . **50.00**

7-3/4" h, 5-1/2" w, brown glass, blue feather dec, c1979 . . . . **145.00**

8-1/4" h, basketweave, irid gold, magenta highlights molded with diamond forms, ruby int. and rim, sgd and dated "Lundberg 2-22-97 AA32" **300.00**

8-1/2" h, designed by Aimo Okkolin for Riihimaen Lasi (Finland), elongated sommerso, purple casing, controlled bubbles at base, etched "Riihimaen Lasi/O.Y./Aimo Okkolin" **165.00**

8-1/2" h, frosted gray glass bucket form, applied stripes of color etched and polished in linear design, base inscribed "T. Noe 1983 ©," Rhode Island School of Design. **175.00**

8-1/2" h, mold blown raised rim, bulbous oval of amber cased to colorless, central opal white core stabilizing honey-amber swirls, bubbles, and convolutions, inscribed "Kent F. Ipsen/Richmond VA 1975" **230.00**

9" h, 3-1/2" d, by Per Lutken, for Holmegaard, sommerso, flame shape, dark green casing, etched "Holmegaard 53" **520.00**

9-1/2" h, 6-3/4" h, 2-3/4" h, Vistosi, designed by Fulvio Bianconi, four-sided smoky glass vases, floating blue and green murrines, 1963, unmarked, price for three-pc set **1,050.00**

10" h, opaque red striated oval, engraved with fire-breathing dragon motif, gold filled incising, sgd "Chris Heilman," dated April 10, 1979, series #4 of 5 . . . **230.00**

10" h, 6-1/2" d, by Floris Meydam for Leerdam Glass Works (Holland), pillow shape, orange and white stripes, etched "Leerdam/22/M," paper label "Crystal Leerdam/ Made in Holland" **3,775.00**

10" h, 8" d, by Seguso Vetri D'Arte, green bullicante, included gold patches, controlled bubbles, pulled surfaces, 1938-40, unmarked. **115.00**

10-1/2" h, heavy walled colorless body, trapped tiny bubbles in symmetrical design, base engraved "G. Nyman/Nuttajarvi—57," designed by Gunnel Nyman, Finnish **425.00**

10-7/8" h, 11-1/4" d, Soffiato, bulbous, cobalt blue, two handles, acid etched "MADE IN ITALY," Seguso. **1,000.00**

11-1/4" h, by Ernest Gordon for Afors (Sweden), elongated sommerso, purple casing, tiny bubbles, etched "Afors/3004". **150.00**

11-3/4" h, 5-1/8" w, upper portion of smoky topaz, triangular crystal control bubble base, sgd "Erickson". **50.00**

12-1/2" h, 3-3/4" d, designed by Tapio Wirkala for Iitalia, bulbous, etched fine white lines, etched "Tapio Wirkkala/Iitalia/55". . **625.00**

13" h, 8" w at base, brilliant yellow, white snail like dec, highly irid, Palmer Konig **500.00**

14-3/4" h, Yokohama, double neck, blue ground, internally dec with gold flecks, green/blue/white murrhines, engraved "Nason Aldo," c1960 . . . . **4,750.00**

19-1/2" h, pink bulbous base, long cylindrical blue neck, hand-etched

"J. P. Holmes BG89 Organic Vase Series," American, c1989 .. **250.00**
20" h, 8" d, Cenedese, designed by Antonio Da Ros, by Giancarlo Begotti, teardrop shape, exhibition piece, acid cut-back hieroglyphics, enameled in purples, greens, blues, and grays inscribed "G. Begotti, A. Da Ros, Cenedese" **11,150.00**

SUGAR SHAKERS

History: Sugar shakers, sugar castors, or muffineers all served the same purpose: to "sugar" muffins, scones, or toast. They are larger than salt and pepper shakers, were produced in a variety of materials, and were in vogue in the late Victorian era.

Reference: William Heacock, *Encyclopedia of Victorian Colored Pattern Glass*, Book III, Antique Publications, 1976, 1991-92 value update.

Amber
Horseshoe, 5" h, no lid........ **25.00**
Paneled Daisy, Bryce Bros./U.S. Glass Co., 4-1/4" h **275.00**
Rope and Thumbprint, Central Glass Co., 5-1/4" h.............. **140.00**
Amethyst, nine panel, attributed to Northwood Glass Co., 4-1/2" h .. **180.00**
Apple green, Inverted Thumbprint, tapered, 5-3/4" h.............. **160.00**
Blue
Inverted Fern, 5" h **325.00**
Blue, nine panel, attributed to Northwood Glass Co., 4-1/2" h **220.00**
Bristol, 6-1/4" h, tall tapering cylinder, pink, blue flowers and green leaves dec **75.00**
Cobalt blue, Ridge Swirl, 4-3/4" h **375.00**
Crackle, cranberry, two part brass lid, 4-1/4" h **60.00**
Cranberry
Argus Swirl, attributed to Consolidated Lamp & Glass Co., 3" h, minor wear........... **350.00**
Baby Inverted Thumbprint, Fenton Art Glass Co., 4-3/4" h...... **210.00**
Bulbous base optic, Hobbs, Brockunier & Co., 5" h...... **210.00**
Bulbous top, tapered base, paneled int., lid stamped "E.R.N.S.," 6-1/2" h **110.00**
Inverted Thumbprint, nine-panel mold, 4-3/4" h **250.00**
Ring neck, optic, 4-3/4" h ... **180.00**
Twelve exterior cut panels, lid stamped "E.R.N.S.," 6-1/2" h. **90.00**

Crown Milano, melon shape, ribbed, dec, Mt. Washington two-pc top **395.00**
Custard, Paneled Teardrop, Tarentum Glass Co., 4-3/4" h............ **110.00**
Cut glass
Heavy cut diamond and fan pattern, 4-1/4" h, flake, as-is lid **90.00**
Plain, engraved stars, 4-1/4" h **95.00**
Russian pattern alternating with clear panels, orig SS top .. **375.00**

Paneled Diamond Block, George Duncan, original top, **$70.**

Emerald green
Aster and Leaf, Beaumont Glass Co., 5" h **450.00**
Hobnail, U.S. Glass Co., 4-1/4" h **170.00**
Melligo, Consolidated Lamp & Glass Co., 4-3/4" h **200.00**
Green, four blown molded panels, diamond and cross design, rib between each panel, lid marked "E. P.," 5-3/4" h, open bubble on surface **100.00**
Light blue, Paneled Daisy, Bryce Bros./U.S. Glass Co., 4-1/4" h .. **375.00**
Milk glass
Apple Blossom, Northwood Glass Co., 4-1/2" h **160.00**
Paneled Sprig, fired-on green dec, gilt accents, Northwood Glass Co., 4-3/4" h, wear to dec **65.00**
Quilted Phlox, white, hand painted blue flowers, Northwood Glass Co./Dugan Glass Co., 4-1/2" h **100.00**
Opalescent
Beatty Honeycomb, white, Beatty & Sons, 3-1/2" h............ **110.00**

Blown twist, nine panel
Blue, Northwood Glass Co., 4-1/2" h **275.00**
Green, Northwood Glass Co., 4-1/2" h **295.00**
White Northwood Glass Co., 4-1/2" h **100.00**
Blown twist, wide waisted
Vaseline, Northwood Glass Co., 4-3/4" h **325.00**
White, Northwood Glass Co., 4-3/4" h **100.00**
Bubble Lattice, blue, 4-3/4" h **325.00**
Chrysanthemum Base Swirl
Blue, Buckeye Glass Co., 4-3/4" h **275.00**
Cranberry, Buckeye Glass Co., 4-3/4" h **400.00**
Coin Spot, bulbous base
Blue, Hobbs, Brockunier & Co./Beaumont Glass Co., 4-3/4" h **160.00**
Coin Spot, bulbous base, white, Hobbs, Brockunier & Co./Beaumont Glass Co., 4-3/4" h **80.00**
Coin Spot, nine-panel mold
Blue, Northwood Glass Co., 4-1/2" h **200.00**
Coin Spot, nine-panel mold, white, Northwood Glass Co., 4-1/2" h **100.00**
Coin Spot, ring neck
Blue-green, Hobbs, Brockunier & Co., 4-3/4" h **130.00**
Rubena, Hobbs, Brockunier & Co., 4-1/2" h **220.00**
Coin Spot, tapered, white, Hobbs, Brockunier & Co., 5-1/4" h.. **100.00**
Coin Spot, wide waisted
Cranberry, Northwood Glass Co./Buckeye Glass Co., 4-1/2" h **250.00**
Green, Northwood Glass Co./Buckeye Glass Co., 4-1/2" h **160.00**
White, Northwood Glass Co./Buckeye Glass Co., 4-3/4" h **100.00**
Daisy & Fern, Northwood mold
Blue, Northwood Glass Co., 4-1/4" h **210.00**
Cranberry, Northwood Glass Co., 4-1/4" h **400.00**
Daisy & Fern, wide waisted mold
Blue, Northwood Glass Co., 4-1/4" h **180.00**
Cranberry, Northwood Glass Co., 4-1/4" h **325.00**
White, Northwood Glass Co., 4-1/4" h **70.00**

Poinsettia
- Blue, H. Northwood & Co., 5" h **475.00**
- Colorless, H. Northwood & Co., 5" h................. **130.00**

Polka Dot, cranberry, Northwood & Co., 4-1/4" h **800.00**

Reverse Swirl
- Blue, satin, Buckeye Glass Co./Model Flint Glass Co., 4-3/4" h **300.00**
- Cranberry, Buckeye Glass Co./Model Flint Glass Co., 4-1/2" h **300.00**
- Vaseline, Buckeye Glass Co./Model Flint Glass Co., 4-3/4" h **300.00**
- White, Buckeye Glass Co./Model Flint Glass Co., 4-3/4" h. **120.00**

Ribbed Opal Lattice, tall
- Blue, 4-1/2" h **170.00**
- Cranberry, 4-1/2" h...... **220.00**
- White, 4-1/2" h **90.00**

Spanish Lace
- Cranberry, Northwood Glass Co., 4-1/2" h **325.00**
- Vaseline, Northwood Glass Co., 4-1/2" h **275.00**
- White, Northwood Glass Co., 4-1/2" h **110.00**

Stripe, wide, cranberry, 4" h . **600.00**

Swirl, bulbous baseLight blue,
- Hobbs, Brockunier & Co., 4-3/4" h **350.00**
- Vaseline, Hobbs, Brockunier & Co., 4-3/4" h, minor ext. wear **350.00**

Swirl
- Cranberry, 5" h, chips ... **375.00**
- Swirl, green, 5-1/4" h, flat edge flake................ **275.00**

Swirl, tapered
- Blue, 5-1/2" h **400.00**
- Cranberry, 5-1/4" h...... **425.00**

Swirled Windows
- Blue, Hobbs, Brockunier & Co., 5" h................. **325.00**
- White, Hobbs, Brockunier & Co., 5" h................. **130.00**

Opalware

Blue shaded to cream, hand-painted dainty floral dec, 5" h, wear spot on back **100.00**

Draped Column, skirt with shaded background, hand painted floral dec, Wave Crest, 5" h, some wear to dec, replaced lid **60.00**

Egg base, soft pink background, hand painted floral dec, two-piece metal lid, Mt. Washington Glass Co., 4-1/4" h **400.00**

Egg shape, light blue, hand-painted lily dec, two-part metal lid, 4" h, wear to leaves........... **80.00**

Erie Twist, hand-painted pansy dec, Wave Crest, 2-1/2" h, lid missing **110.00**

Gillinder Melon, light blue shading to white, satin finish, hand-painted multicolored floral dec, Gillinder & Sons, 4-1/2" h **180.00**

Ostrich egg, overall light pink, satin finish, hand painted multicolored floral dec, Mt. Washington Glass Co., 3-3/4" h, manufacturing bubble on surface........ **400.00**

Tall, tapered, waisted base, light green, hand painted large floral dec, 6" h **70.00**

Tapered
- Blue, hand painted thistle dec, 6" h **80.00**
- Pink, hand painted blue lily of the valley dec, 5-1/2" h, modern lid **30.00**
- Salmon, hand painted blue lily of the valley dec, 6" h...... **50.00**

Opaque

Acorn
- Blue, Beaumont Glass Co., 5" h **230.00**
- White shading to pink, hand painted gilt floral dec, Beaumont Glass Co., 5" h, wear to gilt............... **190.00**

Alba
- Pink, Dithridge & Co., 4-1/2" h **190.00**
- White, Dithridge & Co., 4-1/2" h **90.00**

Argus Swirl, white, netted floral transfer dec on shoulder, attributed to Consolidated Lamp & Glass Co., 3" h **100.00**

Challinor's Forget-Me-Not
- Blue, Challinor, Taylor & Co., 3-3/4" h.............. **150.00**
- Pink, Challinor, Taylor & Co., 3-3/4" h.............. **190.00**
- White, Challinor, Taylor & Co., 3-3/4" h............... **90.00**

Cone
- Blue, Consolidated Lamp & Glass Co., 5-1/4" h **140.00**
- Green, Consolidated Lamp & Glass Co., 5-1/4" h **120.00**
- Pink, Consolidated Lamp & Glass Co., 5-1/4" h **160.00**

Cone, squatty
- Lemon satin, Consolidated Lamp & Glass Co., 3" h....... **270.00**

Opaque, Cone pattern, cased pink, Consolidated Lamp & Glass Co., **$160.**

- Light blue satin, cased, Consolidated Lamp & Glass Co., 3" h............. **190.00**

Little Shrimp
- Ivory, Dithridge & Co., 3" h **100.00**
- Turquoise blue, Dithridge & Co., 3" h **210.00**
- White, Dithridge & Co., 3" h **80.00**
- White, satin finish, hand painted floral dec, Dithridge & Co., 2-3/4" h **100.00**

Owl, full figure, white, plain flat oval on chest, 5" h **50.00**

Parian Swirl, green, hand-painted floral dec, Northwood Glass Co., 4-1/2" h................ **175.00**

Quilted Phlox
- Light green, cased, Northwood Glass Co./Dugan Glass Co., 4-1/2" h **210.00**
- Light blue, cased, Northwood Glass Co./Dugan Glass Co., 4-1/2" h **160.00**
- Mottled pink, Northwood Glass Co./Dugan Glass Co., 4-3/4" h **250.00**

Rings & Ribs, white, hand-painted floral dec, 4-1/2" h **50.00**

Utopia Optic, green, hand-painted floral dec, Buckeye Glass Co./Northwood Glass Co., 4-1/2" h **300.00**

White
- Emb floral dec on front, dec, Eagle Glass & Manufacturing Co., 5" h.............. **60.00**
- Hand-colored transfer floral dec, Eagle Glass & Manufacturing Co., 4-3/4" h........... **50.00**

Square, panels with three emb flowers, traces of dec, 4-1/8" h **50.00**

Ruby stained, Duncan Late Block, orig top **295.00**

Satin, Leaf Mold

Light blue, Northwood Glass Co., 4" h **325.00**

Lime green, Northwood Glass Co., 4" h **550.00**

Satin, Leaf Umbrella, blue, Northwood Glass Co., 4-1/2" h **425.00**

Slag

Bulbous base, purple, Hobbs, Brockunier & Co., 5" h **475.00**

Creased Teardrop, brown shading to green, 4-3/4" h **275.00**

Spatter

Leaf Umbrella, cased cranberry, Northwood Glass Co., 4-1/2" h **350.00**

Reverse Swirl, colorless, frosted, Buckeye Glass Co., 4-3/4" h, internal fracture following one rib **70.00**

Ribbed Pillar, pink and white, Northwood Glass Co., 4-3/4" h **160.00**

Ring neck, cranberry and white, 4-3/4" h **140.00**

Ring neck, white, hint of cranberry, Inverted Thumbprint, 4-3/4" h **60.00**

Royal Ivy, rainbow, cased, Northwood Glass Co., 4" h, splits in lid **500.00**

SWANKYSWIGS

History: Swankyswigs are decorated glass containers that were filled with Kraft Cheese Spreads. The first Swankyswigs date from the early 1930s. Production was discontinued during the last days of World War II because the paint was needed for the war effort. After the war, production resumed and several new patterns were introduced, including Posy or Cornflower No. 2 (1947), Forget-Me-Not (1948), and Tulip No. 3 (1950). The last colored pattern was Bicentennial Tulip (1975).

In the mid-1970s, several copycat patterns emerged. These include Wildlife Series (1975) and Sportsman Series (1976)—most likely Canadian varieties—Rooster's Head, Cherry, Diamond Over Triangle, and Circus. Kraft Cheese Spread is still available, but is sold in crystal-type glass.

Swankyswigs were very popular with economy-minded ladies of the Depression era. After the original contents had been consumed, the containers, which could be used as tumblers or to store juice, served as perfect companions to Depression glass table services. Their cheerful designs helped to chase away the Depression blues.

The first designs were hand applied. When the popularity of Swankyswigs increased, more intricate machine-made patterns were introduced. Designs were test marketed and those that did not achieve the desired results are hard to identify and find.

The lack of adequate records about Swankyswigs makes it very difficult to completely identify all patterns. Since 1979, quite a few look-alikes have appeared. Although these glasses were similar to the originals, only Kraft glasses are considered Swankyswigs.

Ideally, select glasses with patterns clear and brightly colored. Patterns that are more rare include Carnival, Checkerboard, and Texas Centennial. Look-alike patterns from other manufacturers include the Rooster's Head, Cherry, Diamond Over Triangle, and Circus. The look-alike patterns date from the 1930s to the 1960s.

Notes: Lids are valued at $5 each when found in good condition. Certain advertisements can bring a higher price. Glasses with original labels will bring approximately 50 percent more.

Antelope and Star, black and red, 3-1/2" h **4.00**

Antiques

Churn and cradle, orange, 3-3/4" h **5.00**

Coffee grinder and plate, green, 3-3/4" h **5.00**

Spinning wheel and bellows, red, 3-3/4" h **5.00**

Teapot and lamp, blue, 3-3/4" h **5.00**

Band #1, blue and white, 3-3/8" . . **3.75**

Band #2, red and black **2.50**

Band #3, 3-3/8" h **3.00**

Bear and Pig, light blue, 3-3/4" h . **5.00**

Bustlin' Betsy

Blue, 3-3/4" h **4.75**

Brown, 3-3/4" h **6.00**

Orange, 3-3/4" h **4.75**

Red, 3-3/4" h **2.75**

Set, red, blue, brown, yellow, and green **25.00**

Yellow, 3-3/4" h **4.75**

Carnival

Blue, 3-1/2" h **4.25**

Green, 3-1/2" h **4.50**

Red, 3-1/2" h **3.00**

Cars and Wagon, black and white, 3-3/4" h **4.00**

Checkerboard, 3-1/2" d, red and white **16.00**

Circle and Dot

Black, 3-1/2" h **5.50**

Blue, 3-1/2" h **5.00**

Red, 3-1/2" h **5.00**

Cornflower, #1, light blue

3-1/2" h **9.00**

3-3/4" h **15.00**

4-1/2" h **18.00**

Cornflower, #2

Dark blue, 3-1/4" h **12.75**

Dark blue, 3-1/2" h **3.00**

Light blue, 3-1/4" h **12.50**

Light blue, 3-1/2" h **2.75**

Red, 3-1/2" h **2.75**

Yellow, 3-1/4" h **12.50**

Yellow, 3-1/2" h **3.00**

Daisy

Red and white, 3-1/4" h **35.00**

Red, white, and green, 3-1/4" h . **15.00**

Red, white, and green, 4-1/2" h **19.50**

Davy Crockett, 3-1/2" h **8.50**

Dog, black **5.00**

Dog and Rooster, orange, 3-3/4" h . **5.00**

Dots, red, 3-1/2" h **3.00**

Duck and Horse, black, 3-3/4" h . . **5.00**

Elephant and Bird, red **4.75**

Flying Geese, red, yellow, and blue, 3-1/2" h **4.00**

Forget Me Not

Dark blue, 3-1/4" h **15.00**

Dark blue, 3-1/2" h **2.75**

Light blue, 3-1/4" h **12.75**

Light blue, 3-1/2" h **2.75**

Red, 3-1/4" h **15.00**

Red, 3-1/2" h **4.50**

Yellow, 3-1/4" h **14.00**

Yellow, 3-1/2" h **5.00**

Horizontal Lines, black and red, 3-1/4" h **3.00**

Kiddie cup, 3-1/4" h

Black **14.50**

Brown **13.75**

Green **13.75**

Orange **13.75**

Kiddie cup, 3-3/4" h

Black **4.50**

Brown **3.75**

Green **3.75**

Orange **3.75**

Kiddie cup, Squirrel and Deer, brown, 4-1/2" h, **$18.**

Posy, Violet, purple flowers, green leaves, 3-1/2" h, **$5.00.**

Kiddie cup, 4-1/2" h
- Black, ... **22.00**
- Brown **18.00**
- Green **18.00**
- Orange **18.00**

Posy, Jonquil, yellow
- 3-1/4" h. **18.00**
- 3-1/2" h. **6.00**
- 4-1/2" h. **20.00**

Posy, Tulip
- Red, 3-1/4" h **15.00**
- 3-1/2" h. **4.00**
- 4-1/2" h. **12.00**

Posy, Violet, purple
- 3-1/4" h. **18.00**
- 3-1/2" h. **5.00**
- 4-1/2" h. **20.00**

Scotty, red dog, blue fence, 3-1/2" h **6.00**
Squirrel and Deer, brown, 3-3/4" h **5.00**
Spaceships, blue, 3-1/2" d **6.00**
Stars
- Black, 3-1/2" h **2.00**
- Blue, 3-1/2" h **3.75**
- Green, 3-1/2" h. **3.00**
- Red, 3-1/2" h **4.00**

Stripe, red and black........... **4.00**
Tulip, #1, green, 3-1/4" h **15.00**
Tulip, #1, 3-1/2" h
- Black. **3.00**
- Dark blue **3.75**
- Green **2.75**
- Red. **3.50**

Tulip, #1, 4-1/2" h
- Blue **16.00**
- Green **15.00**
- Red. **15.00**

Tulip, #2, dark blue
- 3-1/4" h **15.00**
- 3-3/4" h **4.00**
- 4-1/2" h **18.00**

Tulip, #3, 3-1/4" h
- Light blue **15.00**
- Yellow **14.00**

Tulip, #3, 3-3/4" h
- Dark blue **2.75**
- Light blue **2.75**
- Red. **2.75**
- Yellow **3.00**

Tulip, #3, red, 4-1/2" h. **18.50**

Threaded Glass

History: Threaded glass is glass decorated with applied threads of glass. Before the English invention of a glass-threading machine in 1876, threads were applied by hand. After this invention, threaded glass was produced in quantity by practically every major glass factory.

The art glass manufacturers such as Durand and Steuben revived threaded glass, and it is still made today.

Pitcher, pink and yellow swirl, 6" h, **$175.**

Basket

- 8" h, 7" w, cranberry shading to amber, white opalescent stripes, threaded surface, pale pink twisted thorn handle, Victorian **125.00**
- 11" h, 12" d, pink opalescent and amber basket, threaded and raised hobnail design, twisted thorn handle, Victorian **125.00**

Bowl

- 7" d, 3" h, light pink, green threaded swirl design **45.00**
- 9-1/2" d, 4-1/2" h, deep amethyst ground, silver-blue threading, highly irid surface, shades of green and purple, inscribed "Loetz, Austria" **100.00**

Candlestick, 9-7/8" h, colorless, cut, flared base, bell nozzle with frosted floral and beaded dec, amethyst rim and threading on stem **175.00**

Celery vase, 6-7/8" h, colorless, floral enamel dec.................. **30.00**

Center bowl, 12-1/8" d, 4-7/8" h, flared round Verre de Soie bowl, blue threaded dec, polished pontil, attributed to Carder Steuben ... **350.00**

Champagne tumbler, 4" h, colorless, floral enamel dec............. **30.00**

Cheese dish, cov, 7-1/2" h, colorless, light blue opalescent threading on upper half of bell-shaped dome, faceted knob **140.00**

Claret jug, 11-1/2" h, 3-1/2" d, chartreuse green, emb scrolled French pewter hinged top, handle, and pedestal foot **245.00**

Compote, 4-5/8" h, ruffled rim, gold colored threading on shallow colorless glass bowl, with trapped bubbles, stem with air-trapped bubble, polished pontil **200.00**

Creamer, 4-3/4" h, colorless with slight blue tint, threaded neck and lip, applied ribbed handle, Pittsburgh **170.00**

Epergne, four purple lilies, white threading.................. **375.00**

Finger bowl and underplate

- 4-3/4" d, 2-3/4" h bowl, cranberry, light blue opalescent, ruffled rim, 6-3/4" d underplate........**110.00**
- 5-1/4" d, 2-3/4" h diamond quilted bowl, gold with light cranberry highlights, ruffled rim, 7-3/4" d matching plate, both with polished pontils................ **100.00**

Goblet, 5-3/4" h, colorless, diamond molded bowl, Pomona blue reeding, applied Bristol yellow disk foot, stamped "Steuben," set of three **225.00**

Honey pot, cov, 5-3/4" h, 6-1/2" w, satin finished crystal ground, pulled and twisted pattern of blue and white threads, twig finial on cov, twig-like metal frame **450.00**

Lemonade mug, 5-3/8" h, colorless ground, cranberry threading, Sandwich **125.00**

Luncheon plate

- 8-1/4" d, green threading on flattened rim, colorless ground with trapped bubbles **65.00**
- 8-1/2" d, colorless crystal ground, Pomona Green concentric threads applied to ext. rim, Steuben, set of six.................... **230.00**

Mantel lamp, 13" h, threaded art glass shade with gold, green, and white pulled feather dec, elaborate sculptured metal sphinx base marked "759E W. B. Mfg. Co. Copyright" **1,150.00**

Mayonnaise, underplate, cranberry ground, ground pontil scar **90.00**

Mug, 4-3/4" h, colorless, second gather of glass with swirled ribs, applied handle, copper wheel engraved initials and wreath, threaded neck, attributed to New England Glass Co.... **1,550.00**

Perfume bottle, 5-1/2" h, colorless ground, pink threading........ **175.00**

Pitcher

- 3-7/8" h, colorless, applied threading at neck, applied handle ... **145.00**
- 7" h, Lily Pad, aqua, threaded neck and lip, applied hollow handle **550.00**

Powder jar, 2-1/2" d, 3" h, Palme Koenig, cranberry ground, random irid threading, dec brass lid....... **175.00**

Rose bowl, 6" h, 5" d, colorless ground, pink threading **60.00**

Salt, 2-3/4" d, cranberry ground, opaque white threads, applied colorless petal feet............ **75.00**

Sherbet, 4-3/4" d, 2-3/4" h, colorless bowl, band of ruby threading around rim, ruby machine threading from shoulder to colorless disk base, acid stamp "Steuben" on base, price for pr **200.00**

Tumbler, 3-1/8" h, opalescent ribbed ground, blue threads, Lutz type.. **30.00**

Vase, Palme Koenig, random green threading over iridescent white base, polished rim, 8-1/2" h, **$150.** *Photo courtesy of David Rago Auctions.*

Vase

- 4" h, Palme Koenig, green random threading, polished rim, strong irid **150.00**
- 4-1/4" h, ruffled rim with green threading, Verre de Soie body, polished pontil........... **125.00**
- 6" h, pink threaded flared rim, diamond quilted colorless glass body, polished pontil, Carder Steuben, Catalog No. 6817, minor threading loss **195.00**

7-7/8" h, flared rim, green threading, colorless ftd vessel, rough pontil **95.00**

8" h, petal top, cranberry ground, white threading, sgd "Stevens and Williams" **150.00**

8-1/2" h, Palme Koenig, random green threading, irid base color, polished rim **150.00**

10-1/4" h, Kralik, green threading, strong blue and fuchsia threads, polished rim **195.00**

11-3/4" h, diamond quilted colorless glass, green threading, polished pontil, acid etched Carder Steuben fleur-de-lis mark, Catalog No. 6812 variant, base wear **825.00**

12" h, 4" w, red ground, green random threadings at top, flat flared rim, Loetz type **250.00**

14" h, Palme Koenig, random threading, amber body, gold irid **270.00**

16" h, 6" d, bulbous, amber body, applied green threads, by Archimede Seguso, unmarked **115.00**

TIFFANY

History: Louis Comfort Tiffany (1849-1934) established a glass house in 1878 primarily to make stained-glass windows.

In 1890, in order to utilize surplus materials at the plant, Tiffany began to design and produce "small glass," such as iridescent glass lamp shades, vases, stemware, and tableware in the Art Nouveau manner. Commercial production began in 1896.

Tiffany developed a unique type of colored iridescent glass called Favrile, which differs from other art glass in that it was a composition of colored glass worked together while hot. The essential characteristic is that the ornamentation is found within the glass; Favrile was never further decorated. Different effects were achieved by varying the amount and position of colors.

Most Tiffany wares are signed with the name "L. C. Tiffany" or the initials "L.C.T." Some pieces also are marked "Favrile," along with a number. A variety of other marks can be found, e.g., "Tiffany Studios" and "Louis C. Tiffany Furnaces."

Louis Tiffany and the artists in his studio also are well known for their fine work in other areas—bronzes, pottery, jewelry, silver, and enamels.

References: Victor Arwas, *Glass, Art Nouveau and Art Deco*, Rizzoli International Publications, 1977; Alastair Duncan, *Louis Comfort Tiffany*, Harry N. Abrams, 1992; Alastair Duncan and William J. Fieldstein, *Lamps of Tiffany Studios*, Harry N. Abrams, 1983, reprint 1992; Robert Koch, *Louis C. Tiffany*, Schiffer Publishing, 2001; John A. Shuman III, *Collector's Encyclopedia of American Art Glass*, Collector Books, 1988, 1994 value update; Moise S. Steeg, *Tiffany Favrile Art Glass*, Schiffer, 1997; Kenneth Wilson, *American Glass 1760-1930: The Toledo Museum of Art*, Volume I, Volume II, Hudson Hills Press and The Toledo Museum of Art, 1994.

Museums: Bergstrom-Mahler Museum, Neenah, WI; Corning Glass Museum, Corning, NY; Historical Glass Museum, Redlands, CA; Chrysler Museum, Norfolk, VA; The Toledo Museum of Art, Toledo, OH; University of Connecticut, The William Benton Museum of Art, Storrs, CT.

Decorative objects

Basket, 7" h, 8" w, Favrile, pastel green, deep opalescent white, Diamond Quilted pattern, applied vaseline-yellow colored base, bronze edge handle, enameled dec, bronze mountings inscribed "Louis C. Tiffany Furnaces," numbered................ **1,000.00**

Bottle, 6-1/2" h, sq, orange translucent Favrile, metallic blue, purple and green swirled and pulled opaque bottom, sgd "L. C. T. T5224," small bubble burst hole on base................ **700.00**

Bowl

2-1/4" h, flared rim with onion skin, gold irid ext. sides dec with repeating leaf pattern in relief, polished pontil inscribed "L. C. Tiffany, Favrile/1925" **690.00**

6" d, gold favrile, scalloped edge, sgd "1286 L.C.T. Favrile"... **520.00**

6-1/2" d, gold favrile, stretch irid around edges, sgd "1263 L. C.T. Favrile" **435.00**

7" d, 3" h, irid bluish-gold, waisted rim, ribbed body, inscribed "L.C.T.," small paper label, uneven color to int.. .... **450.00**

7" d, 3" h, irid gold, blue highlights, ribbed, scalloped edge, inscribed "L.C.T. Favrile"........... **400.00**

7-1/4" d, 3" h, ruffled rim, ribbed bowl tapering to base, gold lustrous irid overall, base inscribed "L. C. Tiffany-Inc., Favrile X 128" . **490.00**

8-1/2" d, 2-1/2" h, broad rim, stretched cobalt blue on feather-ribbed bowl of opalescent glass, base inscribed "5-L.C. Tiffany Inc. Favrile 1578," staining **400.00**

9-3/4" d, 2-1/4" h, pastel aqua, broad flat rim, stretched aqua irid at rim shading to opalescent glass, optic ribs, light irid luster overall, polished pontil, paper label, inscribed "1898 L. C. Tiffany Favrile" **1,035.00**

10-1/8" d, 3-3/4" h, flared rim, diamond quilted bowl of pale green and colorless, stretched green irid at rim, inscribed "L. C. Tiffany Favrile X 104" around polished pontil **525.00**

Flower frog, 10" d, favrile, intaglio carved leaves and vine, bowl sgd "578N Louis C Tiffany Furnaces, Inc., Favrile," frog sgd "L. C. Tiffany Favrile" **1,610.00**

Box, cov, 4-1/4" d, 1-1/2" h, Grapevine, gold dore, amber slag glass panels, sgd "Tiffany Studios New York 800" **490.00**

Bud vase

10" h, cobalt blue with strong blue irid luster, elongated flared vase, disk foot, base inscribed "L.C. Tiffany Favrile 9667 K" ... **1,265.00**

Bronze mount

13-5/8" h, trumpet style, gold irid Favrile glass, green irid pulled leaves, bronze base with eight ball feet, glass base inscribed "L. C. T.," bronze base imp "Tiffany Studios/New York/717" **920.00**

16" h, cylindrical, colorless glass, green pulled leaves, bronze artichoke-pattern base, inscribed "L. C. T.," imp "Tiffany New York 1043"...... **1,380.00**

16" h, flared rim on elongated vessel, irid gold, green pulled leaves, bronze artichoke-pattern base, imp "Tiffany Studios 1043" **920.00**

Cabinet vase

2" h, gold favrile, bronze hook design, sgd "L.C.T. Y4419" **1,050.00**

2-1/2" h, swirled irid gold body, opalescent tinge to rim and shoulder, irid blue foot inscribed "L.C.T., 4599," interior straw mark **425.00**

2-1/2" h, 3-1/2" d, raised rim, squatty oval form, cobalt blue ground, variegated green-gray heart-shaped leaves on trailing vines, irid blue ground, base inscribed "2083 J. L. C. Tiffany-Favrile" around polished pontil **3,150.00**

3" h, Cypriote Agate, Cypriote 3/4 way down body, changing to agate at base, brilliant blue int., two

handles, special order mark **3,150.00**

3-1/4" h, slightly flared rim, swollen vessel, amber glass, dec with six pulled prunts on border of horizontal threading, overall strong irid gold luster, polished pontil, base inscribed "L.C.T.," minor loss to threading **375.00**

3-1/2" h, ribbed body, tooled design, irid silvery gold, blue highlights, inscribed and numbered "L.C.T. M6456," small "T.G.D. Co." paper label, glazed over factory nick on rim **200.00**

3-1/2" h, 3" d, elongated neck, angular body of pale amber glass, green heart leaves on trailing brown vines, irid gold ground, base inscribed "L. C. T. Y8387" around button pontil **2,100.00**

Calling card holder

6" l, polished onyx oval dish fitted each end by ribbed gold Favrile handles, inscribed "Schlumberger/Made in France/Tiffany" **865.00**

7-3/4" d, 14 rib circular form, ambergris with pastel opal coloration, stretched luster, polished pontil, early label "TG&D Co" on reverse. **260.00**

Candelabrum, 19" h, two 10-rib gold irid bell glass shades fitted to bronze holder with blown out green candle cups above lappet cushion base, 16 matching glass jewels, base imp TG & D Co. logo, and "Tiffany Studios New York 22323" **2,875.00**

Candleholder/vase, 5" h, gold Favrile, flared integral bobeche rim crowns 11-ribbed swirled body, button pontil inscribed "L. C. T." **425.00**

Candle lamp shade, 7" d, gold favrile, stretch around scalloped edge, sgd "L.C.T." **520.00**

Candlestick

11" h, broad rim, bulbed candle cup over ribbed and tapered standard, ribbed dome base, cobalt blue glass, overall blue irid, base inscribed "1826 L.C.T. Favrile" in small polished pontil **1,380.00**

11-1/4" h, pastel, opalescent aqua holder, wide flanged rim, stretched scalloped edge attached to slender ribbed opal and crystal stem, raised ribbed foot with opal petals, inscribed "L.C.T. Favrile-182G" around polished pontil, small green and gold paper label emb "Tiffany Favrile Glass, Registered Trademark," L.C.T. monogram **1,100.00**

16" h, flared amber ground, gold irid surface, median border of trailing prunts, inserted into bulbed bronze standard, circular foot, internal beaded bronze cup, dore finish, base with imp maker's mark, numbered, loss of trailing threads **1,380.00**

Candlesticks, pr

4" h, gold favrile, inscribed "L.C.T" **1,150.00**

17-3/4" h, beaded bobeche inserted into reticulated bronze cup with blown green glass dec, slender standard over circular base relief dec with Queen Anne blossom, bronze finish, maker's mark **4,600.00**

Centerpiece bowl

9" d, 5-1/4" h, double bulbed rim, jardinière form honey amber bowl, 10 emerald green lily pads at shoulder, orange-gold smooth irid surface, button pontil inscribed "L. C. Tiffany Inc., Favrile 1521-9735 M," 1" shallow scratch at side **1,610.00**

12" d, 2-1/8" h, irid gold, wreath of tangled vines, emerald green leaves, stretched edge finished with tight fold-in rim, central core with flat nick, slight polished top edge concealed by brass holder with scalloped trimming, inscribed "L.C. Tiffany Favrile, 1514M" **600.00**

12-1/4" d, irid gold, green leaf dec, matching frog, each sgd "2039L L.C. Tiffany-Favrile" **1,300.00**

14" d, 9" h, broad shallow brilliant blue irid bowl, strong stretched silver-gold luster, inserted into gold artichoke pattern stem and platform base, imp "Tiffany Studios New York, 1043," bowl inscribed "LC Tiffany-Favrile". **1,380.00**

Champagne, Favrile

3-1/2" h, 4" w, gold, grape and leaf cutting, highly irid surface, blue highlights, sgd **350.00**

5" h, 4" d top, pale yellow with deep green yellow opalescent finish, highly irid, sgd "L. C. T. Favrile #1806" **350.00**

Cologne bottle, 7-1/2" h, gold King Tut pattern, ivory ground, purple and blue irid highlights, gold stopper, sgd **950.00**

Lamp, green Damascene shade on Zodiac bronze base, shade signed "Tiffany Studios," base signed "Tiffany Studios, New York," and numbered, 13" h, 7" d shade, **$6,275.** *Photo courtesy of David Rago Auctions.*

Compote

3-1/2" h, gold favrile, intaglio carved grapes and vine on int., ftd, sgd "L. C. Tiffany Favrile" **575.00**

4-1/4" d, 1-7/8" h, ruffled rim on shallow blue bowl, ftd base of light greenish-blue irid, inscribed "L. C. T.," and "U1070" on base, minor scratches to base **460.00**

5" d, 4-3/4" h, floriform, oval lustrous gold dish with wide five-ruffled rim, solid stem and blue luster disk foot, inscribed "L. C. Tiffany-Favrile 4780C" **1,035.00**

5-1/4" d, 3-1/4" h, deep pink highly irid ground, opalescent leaf design, sgd "LCT Favrile, #1700," retains part of orig label **750.00**

5-1/4" d, 4-1/4" h, ruffled floriform amber bowl, gold irid, cupped pedestal foot, inscribed "L. C. Tiffany Favrile 3472D" **575.00**

5-3/4" h, 6-1/4" d, gold, shallow optic ribbed bowl, slender amber standard, amber disk foot, stretched irid to rim, gold luster on bowl and foot, polished pontil inscribed "L.C.T. Favrile". **1,035.00**

6" d, 2" h, irid gold, blue and purple highlights, mirror base, sgd "L. C. T. Favrile". **550.00**

6-1/4" d, 6" h, green opalescent, feathering pulled around bowl, ftd, sgd "L.C.T. Favrile 1884" . . **990.00**

7-3/4" d, 4" h, gold favrile, scalloped edge, sgd "L.C.T." **860.00**

8-1/2 d, 4" h, gold irid, ribbed base, inscribed "L. C. Tiffany #1847" **950.00**

10" d, 4-1/2" h, 10-rib scalloped cobalt blue dish, conforming blue baluster stem and disk foot, int. with engraved leaf and vine dec, base inscribed "L. C. T. Favrile 1279" **2,760.00**

10" d, 5-3/4" h, floriform, wide flat flared blossom rim, conical dish fitted into petals rising from broad disk foot, stretched blue irid, inscribed "L. C. Tiffany Favrile 1976" **2,530.00**

10-1/4" d, 5" h, deep emerald green shading to white, diamond quilted pattern, orig metal base marked "Tiffany Furnaces Favrile 499" **800.00**

11-3/4" d, 3-1/8" h, extended rim on shallow ftd round blue bowl, base inscribed "L. C. Tiffany Favrile, P" on base, rough pontil **810.00**

Cordial

3-1/2" h, Favrile, waisted flared form, inscribed "L.C.T.," six-pc set **1,400.00**

3-3/4" h, irid gold, amber cut stem, cut floret beneath bowl, inscribed "L.C.T." monogram....... **250.00**

4-1/4" h, greenish-gold, gold irid three layer glass molded with tulip petals rising from florette base, inscribed "L.C.T." on base, tiny flat nick on base............ **120.00**

Cordial set, 9-1/2" h double bulb gourd-shaped gold irid decanter with 12 applied trailing prunts, orig knobbed stopper, inscribed "LCT 29," six matching 2-1/4" h glasses marked "LCT".................... **2,185.00**

Cup, 3-1/2" d, 2-1/2" h, gold favrile, white and gold zig zag design around middle, strong fuchsia int., applied scroll handle, sgd "V698 L. C. Tiffany Favrile," open bubble on int.... **460.00**

Decanter

7-1/4" h, irid gold, ftd, dimpled sides, inscribed "L.C.T. 41," base pinprick, scratches....... **650.00**

10-1/2" h, favrile, twisted, prunt dec, pastel gold, sgd "LCT U6318" **2,100.00**

Dish

4" d, 1-3/4" h, ruffled rim, shallow bowl, irid blue, shaded blue violet disk base, inscribed "U 8899" **290.00**

4-1/4" d, scalloped rim, small shallow gold bowl, inscribed "L.C.T." **290.00**

4-3/4" d, ruffled rim, shallow bowl, amber, center with molded dec of eagle, Liberty Bell, and 1918 Victory banner in relief, overall gold irid, base inscribed "Louis C. Tiffany Favrile," minor mold imperfections **500.00**

Finger bowl and undertray

2-1/2" h, 5-3/4" d, gold favrile, twisted, prunt, bowl sgd "LCT T6462," underplate sgd "LCT" **460.00**

4-1/2" d, 2-3/8" h bowl, 6-1/4" d undertray, gold, ruffled rim, eight-ribbed bowl, similar shallow eight-ribbed tray, bases inscribed "L. C. T.," straw marks, nick on bowl.................... **920.00**

Flower bowl

10" d, cobalt blue ground, golden green lily pads, lustrous stretched irid, integrated two-tier blue glass frog flower arranger, engraved "Louis C. Tiffany Inc. Favrile 1730N," small hidden inside rim chip **1,610.00**

10-1/2" d, stretched gold irid luster on folded rim, five green lily pads centering integrated two-tier glass frog flower arranger, both inscribed "LC Tiffany Favrile" and numbered **1,850.00**

Goblet

8" h, floriform, pastel aqua green, opal ribbed accents, conforming cupped pedestal foot, inscribed "L. C. T. Favrile," one with label, 10-pc set **3,335.00**

8-1/2" h, trumpet bowl, slender stem, domed circular foot, pale irid lavender, opaque white stripes, sgd "L. C. Tiffany Favrile" . . **850.00**

Jar, cov, 4" h, gold amber Favrile cylinder, five pulled green feathers, silver rim, hinged cov and lift handle, monogrammed, marked "Tiffany & Co. Sterling Silver 925-1000," glass base inscribed "L. C. Tiffany Favrile" . **865.00**

Jewelry box

6-3/4" l, 9" w, 3" h, Pine Needle pattern, green and white slag glass, beaded borders, green patina to metal mounts, inscribed near base "Sarita, April 21st 1905," green velvet interior, imp "Tiffany Studios New York 46," minor spotting **3,115.00**

4" l, 6" w, 3" h, Pine Needle pattern, green and white slag glass, beaded borders, warm brown patina to metal mounts, green velvet interior, imp "Tiffany Studios New York 36," c1905, one hinge broken **1,350.00**

Lamp shade

4-1/2" h, lily shape, eight-rib scalloped rim, irid gold . . **1,150.00**

8" h, 2-1/4" d outside rim, opal gold and Favrile, faint diamond optic pattern, teardrop form, numbered "M925" **520.00**

Loving cup, 8" d, ambergris vasiform, three applied reeded handles, three green leaf forms among trailing vines, gold irid luster, inscribed "L. C. Tiffany Favrile 2024D," top rim out of round, light blemish inside rim **2,530.00**

Matchsafe, 4" h, 5" d, Grapevine, gold doré, amber slag glass panels, sgd "Tiffany Studios New York 958". **630.00**

Nut bowl, 3" d, 1-1/4" h, bluish-gold irid ribbed body, irregular ruffled rim, sgd "L.C.T." **275.00**

Perfume bottle, 4-1/4" h, globular, short cylindrical neck, everted lip, ball-shaped stopper, irid green trailing vine and ivy leaves dec, irid amber ground, shaded with pink, numbered, inscribed "L. C. Tiffany, Favrile," c1916 .... **1,000.00**

Pitcher, 5-1/4" h, flared cylindrical form, applied handle, irid gold ground, green leaf and vine dec, polished button pontil base inscribed "L. C. Tiffany-Favrile"............. **1,850.00**

Plate

6-1/2" d, gold favrile, scalloped edge, stretch effect around edges, sgd "LCT R4403"........ **255.00**

8-3/4" d, bright pink rim, opal at reverse, 10 dec wedge-shaped sections, inscribed "L. C. T. Favrile" **550.00**

10-1/2" d, Favrile, pastel irid green, stretched edge, sgd "L. C. Tiffany" **600.00**

Posy vase, 3-1/8" h, Favrile, flared oval, opal, green, and gold, pulled leaf-feather dec, gold irid int., base inscribed "L. C. T. 7973" **865.00**

Prisms, 5-3/4" l, lozenge form, irid honey amber, opalescence to ridged area, set of eight, few flat nicks. **200.00**

Rose bowl, 3-1/2" d, bright cobalt blue body, green centered black heart-shaped leaves and trailing vines, irid luster, base inscribed "LCT Tiffany Favrile 9806E"............. **2,876.00**

Rose water sprinkler, 15-1/2" h, bulbous base, slender gooseneck, peaked rim, lemon yellow, inscribed "3016," paper label marked "L3016" **1,500.00**

Salt, open

1-3/4" d, 1" h, gold favrile, twisted, prunt, sgd "L.C.T.," orig paper label **365.00**

2" d, 1-1/4" h, gold favrile, twisted, prunt, sgd "L.C.T.," orig paper label **365.00**

2-1/2" d, ruffled rim, ribbed body of pale amber glass, irid gold luster, inscribed "L.C.T.," polished pontil **230.00**

2-1/2" d, ruffled rim, shallow bowl, amber glass, irid gold, polished pontil, initialed "L.C.T." on base **250.00**

3" d, ruffled rim, shallow bowl, amber glass, lustrous gold overall, inscribed "L.C.T." on base . **200.00**

Smoke bell, 4-1/2" h, 2-3/4" w, gold irid body, slightly ribbed, clear applied hanger **250.00**

Tazza, 6-1/2" d, 3-1/4" h, irid gold, ruffled stretch rim with radiant rainbow hues, inscribed "L.C.T.," partial paper label, pinpoint nicks on base . . . **550.00**

Tile, 3" sq, opalescent, flower in relief, top border relief "PAT. FEB 8th 1881," lower border "L.C.T. & Co.," loss at corners **150.00**

Toothpick holder

1-3/4" h, flared rim, pinched cylindrical vessel, irid gold, polished pontil, inscribed "L.C.T. 105" on base, imperfections **150.00**

2-1/4" h, eight applied trailing prunts around swollen cylindrical form, inscribed "L. C. T." and "T8044," paper Tiffany Glass and Decorating Co. label **635.00**

3-1/8" h, amber with gold irid luster, cushion base, polished pontil, inscribed "L.C.T. Favrile" . . . **550.00**

Tray, 6-1/2" d, raised scalloped rim, colorless plate dec with Nash-style green panels and amethyst rib-stripes, inscribed "L. C. T. 361" **290.00**

Tumbler, 3" h, oval, gold irid, eight pulled swirl dec, inscribed "LCT" and numbered, three-pc set **1,150.00**

Vase

4" h, bulbed neck, oval-shaped vessel, irid gold, polished pontil inscribed "L. C. Tiffany Favrile" and "5616 H" **575.00**

4" h, flared rim, swollen form, gold irid, green heart-shaped leaves, brown trailing vines, polished button pontil, inscribed "L. C. Tiffany-Favrile 1161C," few tiny rim nicks **1,035.00**

4" h, ruffled rim, bulbed body, four pulled feet, amber glass with gold irid, base inscribed "Y 8359," polished pontil **470.00**

5-1/4" h, finger, irid gold, applied button pontil, inscribed "L. C. Tiffany Favrile," numbered X71-2841, prefix number superimposed over 1086 below pontil **700.00**

5-1/2" h, bulbous amber body, star millefiori, trailings, and finely wheel-carved green leaves, inscribed "L. C. Tiffany-Favrile/ Y5909," sample, hole at base **5,750.00**

5-3/4" h, floriform, irid stretched ruffled rim, bulbous bowl tapering to disk base, gold, unpolished pontil, inscribed "L. C. Tiffany Favrile 1654J," minor nick to base **2,100.00**

5-3/4" h, raised and slightly flared rim, broad shouldered urn form, cobalt blue with strong irid blue luster, inscribed "L. C. Tiffany Inc. Favrile 1147-4236M" around button pontil **2,300.00**

6-1/4" h, floriform, ruffled rim, trumpet form, irid gold, cupped pedestal foot marked "L.C.T. WHH13" **635.00**

Vase, conical white opaque body, white streaks, flat circular pedestal, white opaque base with blue rim, flat top with yellow stretched effect, marked "1546 L. C. Tiffany, Favrile," original paper label, 5-1/2" h, 6" top d, **$1,125.**

6-5/8" h, inverted rim, eight-ribbed conical form, dimpled shoulder, applied round dome foot, gold, inscribed "L.C.T. W3027" . . **900.00**

6-3/4" h, flared, amber with gold irid luster, disk foot, polished pontil, inscribed "L.C.T. Favrile" . . . **650.00**

6-3/4" h, oval, amber irid body, dec with trailings and intaglio wheel-carved heart-shaped green leafage, inscribed "Louis C. Tiffany Furnaces, Inc., Favrile," and "1732n," rim cut down, light wear **1,495.00**

7" h, Special Order, opaque caramel body, irid blue pulled designs on lower area, garnished with two applied bands astride five riveted buttons, translucent honey applied cupped foot, paper label over polished pontil "TGDCO, Tiffany Favrile Glass, Registered Trade Mark," special order #04625 etched on base, cooling contraction line in foot to which stabilizing fixture has been applied **1,100.00**

7" h, 5-1/2" w, peacock eye dec, brilliant purple-green and blue irid ground, sgd "LCT," numbered L645 . . . . **2,400.00**

7-1/4" h, 3-1/2" d, ribbed bottle form, Favrile, highly irid gold ground, purple and blue highlights, sgd "L. C. T. #W7609" **725.00**

7-1/4" h, 4" d, Favrile, paperweight technique, glossy surface, deep brown pulled and hooked dec, irid int. **1,250.00**

7-1/4" h, 5-1/4" d, gold favrile, sgd "L. C. Tiffany Favrile 9770A" **2,100.00**

8" h, handled, slender, flattened oval, eight ribbed body, integrated tooled handles, gold luster, inscribed "L. C. T. Favrile" . . **920.00**

8" h, paperweight, bulbed oval amber body, int. gold luster, internally dec by vertical stripes, gold-amber dots in zipper pattern, inscribed "L. C. T. Favrile" **1,495.00**

8" h, raised folded rim, dark blue bulbous body, pulled and hooked irid swirls, inscribed 'L. C. T. K1073" around prominent pontil button **4,900.00**

8" d, tapered oval transparent green-amber early favrile body, dec at shoulder with double horizontal borders of brick red pulled ribbon design, base inscribed "7380" and "Tiffany Glass & Decorating Co." label . . **1,150.00**

8-3/4" h, Corona, silver combed feather dec, green ground, sq rim, gold throat, dimpled at shoulder **1,625.00**

9-3/4" h, trumpet, gold, sgd "L. C. Tiffany Favrile 1832," orig paper label **1,610.00**

9-7/8" h, raised rim, elongated ovoid vessel, ambergris glass internally dec with rust-red peacock feathers, irid green-blue ground, button pontil, base inscribed "L.C. Tiffany Inc. Favrile 8763" **26,450.00**

10-1/2" h, flared rim, double bulbed lustrous violet green body, 10 applied trailing irid gold-green prunts, disk base, paper label, inscribed "08736," repairs to base **420.00**

10-3/4" h, floriform, inverted rim, elongated stem, dome foot, light amber glass body, dec with five mahogany and opaque white pulled feathers trailing down stem, base with band of pulled white dec, base sgd in script "L.C.T. o7661" **16,675.00**

11" h, cylindrical, irregular stretched ruffled rim, vertical pulled designs in irid gold color, pearly windows, pale opal green leaves strewn about body, monogram TCG acid etched on applied button pontil **1,300.00**

11" h, floriform, tulip shape, lightly scalloped rim, sgd "L.C.T. W6222," orig paper label **2,875.00**

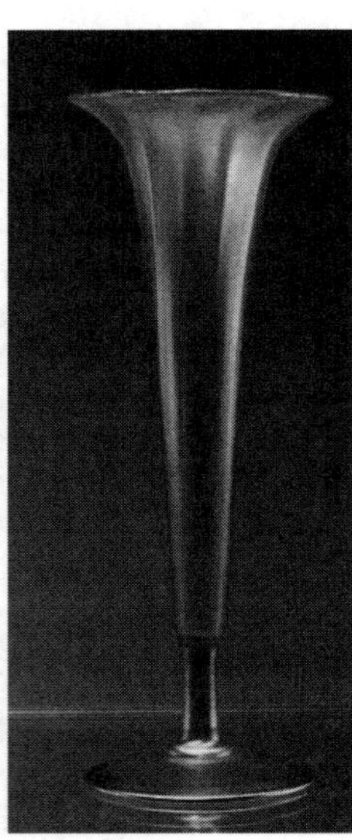

Vase, conical white opaque body, white streaks, flat circular pedestal, white opaque base with blue rim, flat top with yellow stretched effect, marked "1546 L. C. Tiffany, Favrile," original paper label, 5-1/2" h, 6" d top, **$1,125.**

11" h, ruffled rim, stretched opalescent glass, pulled green leaves, amber body, transparent swollen green stem applied to gold cupped base with similar leaf design, inscribed "L. C. T. M8894" on base edge, inclusion . **8,100.00**

11-1/2" h, irid gold, chartreuse and irid gold leaves dangling from vertical golden stems, rough pontil, unsigned, carbon particles, oxidized pitting on surface, irregular coloring on lower body **1,500.00**

11-5/8" h, cylindrical, bulbous base, dichoric yellow ground, gold irid pulled feathers, polished pontil button, base inscribed "LCT" and "F66" **1,495.00**

12" h, wide mouth, bulbed neck and shoulder tapering to flared base, gold irid, inscribed "L. C. Tiffany-Favrile/1974" **2,185.00**

12-1/2" d, flared trumpet, opal white, five green and gold pulled feathers, lustrous gold irid int., base inscribed "LCT Favrile," inserted into artichoke-form etched bronze pedestal base, stamped "Tiffany Studios New York 1043," worn bronze patina **2,530.00**

12-1/2" d, floriform, rib-molded spherical blossom, opal white and rosy irid gold, five green petal forms rising from transparent striated gold stem, conforming ribbed and cupped god an opal pedestal foot, base inscribed "LCT 1622B". **8,625.00**

12-1/2" h, irid gold feathering, white ground, gold foot, sgd . . **1,725.00**

12-3/4" h, floriform, gold favrile, blue highlights, sgd, numbered **1,9855.00**

14" h, trumpet form, irid opal, silvery gold feathers pulled from applied disc panel, cov with soft rainbow essence, boldly script sgd and numbered "L.C. Tiffany-Favrile, 1118-8440 L". **1,200.00**

15" h, paperweight, elongated amber-aquamarine baluster body, internally dec with three repeating clusters of ethereal blossoms centering long slender leaves, warm sienna orange-red irid int., base inscribed "LC Tiffany Favrile 8972D" **6,900.00**

15" h, pinched cylinder, circular bun foot, erected rim, irid gold, inscribed "L.C.T. 509A" . . **2,250.00**

16" h, flared elongated ovoid, colorless glass internally dec with 10 paper-white narcissus blossoms, red and yellow millefiori cane centers, perched on naturalized brown stems, green spike leaves extending from swelled base, inscribed "L. C. Tiffany Favrile 2731G" . . **17,250.00**

Window, 31" w, 47" h, Three Wise Men, presenting their gifts, high profile richly colored garments, shades of golden yellow, green, rose-purple, and ivory white, background of royal blue opalescent glass, entire scene framed by alternating rows of green and shaded amber, heavily plated, additional glass panels on rear, naturally oxidized patina **28,000.00**

Whiskey taster, 1-3/4" h, 1-1/2" w, brilliant irid gold, purple highlights, sgd **200.00**

Wine

3-3/8" h, amber cup raised on pedestal base, engraved with border of grapes on vine, irid int., inscribed "L. C. T." on base, straw mark, price for pr **400.00**

3-3/4" h, 3-3/4" w, Favrile, highly irid gold surface, cut and notched base, stem, and bowl, sgd, four-pc set **1,150.00**

4" h, ambergris, opalescent green rim, int. enhancements, transparent amber stem, disk foot, inscribed "LCT Favrile," set of four . . **980.00**

Lamps

Boudoir, 13" h, bronze harp suspending bulbed glass shade with five pulled green and gold feathers, pale gold luster ground, dome base with incised linear dec, pebbled surface with dark gold finish, shade inscribed "L.C.T.," base imp "Tiffany Studios New York 419" **5,750.00**

Candle

13-1/2" h, gold irid ruffled shade engraved "L. C. T.," splint bamboo bronze base with rich brown patina, base stamped "Tiffany Studios" **1,800.00**

14-1/2" h, Favrile, gold irid base, green and white dec glass column, highly irid gold honeycomb design shade **1,600.00**

16-1/2" h, three-part Electrolier, swirled rib gold irid holder fitted with gilt metal and favrile glass candle supporting gold irid ruffled shade with green pulled and coiled

dec, inscribed "L. C. T" twice, base marked 1,610.00

Ceiling

7-1/4" h, 14-1/2" d, domed shaded leaded with brilliant green glass segments, foliate motif centering around turtleback at apex, hinged to elaborate double beaded bronze ceiling mouth, wide border of 18 matching green rect turtleback tiles, orig dark patina.... **9,775.00**

11" h, six 4-1/2" h shades, 10 green, orange, and yellow turtleback panels, bronzed fixture with brown-green patina, all shades sgd "L.C.T. Favrile"........ **22,400.00**

16" h, 14" d, scalloped beaded rim, fiery golden green translucent leaded Favrile glass shade, curving segments in intricate arrangement ending in hinged trap door framing opalescent glass turtleback, orig hooks on rim attached to bronze beaded chain, single socket ceiling mouth **6,100.00**

Desk

13-1/2" h, 7" d Damescene shade, swirled dec cased irid gold ribbed dome shade, marked "LCT" on rim, swivel socket, etched gold harp desk-type frame, ribbed cushion platform, ball feet, imp "Tiffany Studios New York 419," one ball missing **4,025.00**

13-1/2" h, Nautilus, leaded segments of opal white shading to deep green, formed as nautilus shell, bronze standard, cushion base with striped petal dec, red-brown patina, base imp "Tiffany Studios, New York, 28628" **10,925.00**

14-1/2" h, domed favrile glass shade of cobalt blue cased to opal white int., enhanced by irid gold damascene wavy dec, rim inscribed "5-L.C.T. Favrile," swivel shade mount, gilt bronze swollen shaft tapering to round, domed floriform base, imp "Tiffany Furnaces, Inc., Favrile 16 A" **8,100.00**

14-1/2" h, gold, green, and opal conical 6" d shade, rim inscribed "LCT," four-arm spider support, dark bronze platform base fitted with 16 green glass jewels, base imp "Tiffany Studios New York 255" **3,750.00**

15" h, Zodiac, pair of freeform opal ambergris jewel turtleback inserts fastened on each side of helmeted shade form, swivels on heavy duty wishbone base with patina, marked "Tiffany Studios New York, 541," applied metal ring securing one panel slightly off-center .. **6,000.00**

18" h, domed irid shade, three arm bamboo base, brown/green patina, orig finial, shade inscribed "L. C. T. Favrile," base stamped "Tiffany Studios New York" **3,750.00**

18" h, 7" d irid gold fluted shade, held high on molded tree trunk base, large snake coiled around stem, large green Verde marble ball on foot, shade sgd "L.C.T." **1,980.00**

Floor

20" d leaded shade, blue-green Greek key design with background of butterscotch mottled glass, base with four high ornate feet with scrollwork, onyx stem varies from cream to dark brown veining, two wide metal bands with ornate leaves and vines, third smaller band with beading, vase-like shape with two handles and two more bands at top of stem, shade sgd "Tiffany Studios New York 1907" **31,360.00**

54" h, 10" d Favrile shade, bridge, light green shade with darker green ribbon design, plain stem narrows at top, bulbous section gradually becomes harp design, three curved legs stand on flat leaf pads, base sgd "Tiffany Studios New York 423" **8,400.00**

55-1/2" h, 10" d Favrile shade, counter balance, double curved arm and ball supporting dome shade of opal glass cased to amber, pulled gold dec, inscribed "L. C. T. Favrile," slender standard over five-leg base with flattened spade feet, warm brown patina, base imp "Tiffany Studios New York 568" **8,625.00**

55-1/2" h, 10" d Favrile shade, counter balance, double curved arm and ball supporting dome shade of opal glass cased to cobalt blue with pulled irid and cream colored spiral trailings, inscribed "L. C. T. Favrile," slender bulbed standard over scalloped circular foot, textured surface with dark brown patina, base imp "Tiffany Studios New York 681," damage and repair to shade **7,890.00**

71-1/2" h, 22-1/2" d stepped domed leaded glass shade, blossoming apple branches, pink and white blossoms, dark green leafy branches, pale green shaded to apple green ground, two board bands of yellow and light green, rim tag imp "Tiffany Studios New York 1512-7," three-light Spanish Moss fixture, raised on bronze tripod base, coiled wiretwist and beaded dec, scalloped feet on tripart platform base, brown-green patina, base marked "Tiffany Studios, New York," cracked segments, loss to one segment, province includes 40 years in the offices of Heinz Corp, Pittsburgh, PA **63,000.00**

Floor/ceiling, 24" d leaded wisteria shade, blue blossoms of mottled glass, green and brown leaves, irregular border, green patina on top, sold with orig Tiffany floor base, but also hanging hardware **324,800.00**

Hanging, 18" h, 16" d shade, row of metal beads, nine rows of consistent green-colored glass, centerpiece of round piece of green glass, three chains hold shade, secured to ball on center stem, orig ceiling cap **12,230.00**

Lantern, 10" h, 7" w, hanging globe flares to eight-sided base rim, marigold irid stretch glass shade with random irregular blue and purple threading at top, remaining marigold irid with white calcite lining, sgd "LCT Favrile," hanger and wire replaced **2,000.00**

Night, 8" h, Favrile shade, creamy base, green pulled feathers with gold outlines, orig wood base, shade sgd "L. C. T. Favrile".............. **2,520.00**

Piano, 11-1/2" h, 9-1/2" d irid gold Damascene shade, 10 prominent ribs in amber Favrile glass shade, offset fixed curving shaft, lappet cushion base imp "Tiffany Studios New York 25165" and imp "TG & D Co." mark **4,600.00**

Student

21" h, 7" d opal cased green Damascene irid Favrile glass shade, inscribed "LCTif-," telescoping single burner lamp, spiral beading and smoked diamond design on urn-form font, fine patina, imp "22327," orig vented chimney........ **9,200.00**

23" h, 30" l, double student, mottled green geometric leaded glass shades flanking reticulated Moorish globe resting within arch supported by chain of openwork design, circular base with gallery, shade stamped "Tiffany Studios New York 1658" **20,000.00**

29" h, 10" d, double, dark patina on wire twist dec central font between double post bronze frame, adjustable arm mechanism, beaded spiral on twin burners mounted with translucent green leaded dome Favrile shades **10,925.00**

Table

16" d, Acorn, shade with emerald green glass shading to white, green and mottled green acorns, bronze Greek urn form base, three supporting arms, brown patina, converted to electric, several tight shade cracks **10,925.00**

16" h, 10" abalone linen-fold shade, 12-sided, pleated pale green Favrile Fabrique, bands of horizontally ribbed glass, 12 small round pieces of abalone set into top and finial, stem, and base, shade sgd "Tiffany Studios New York 1928," base sgd "Tiffany Studios New York 604".. **10,640.00**

17-1/2" h, 16" d domed leaded glass shade, radiating caramel glass segments with border of striated green square segments near bottom rim, metal rim tag reads "Tiffany Studios New York," three-light fixture set in pottery base, two buttressed handle on flared bulbous body, dark green drip over mottled glossy maroon glaze, unmarked........ **7,475.00**

21" h, 16" d bronze and leaded glass domed shade, tulip blossoms and leaves, shades of amber, white, blue, and green, metal rim tag imp "Tiffany Studios 1906," three arm bronze base, scrolled wiretwist dec, greenish brown patina, base plate missing **21,850.00**

21" h, 16" d shade, three rows of green mottled glass, wide band of 19 turtleback tiles, five rows of dark green mottled glass to top, simple stick base with four feet, brown-red patina, shade sgd "Tiffany Studios New York"............ **14,000.00**

22" h, 16" d domed leaded glass shade, red stipple glass forms poppies, intense purple centers, each covered with pierced bronzework, border of thin band of turquoise segments between gold segments, mottled background, orig cap and sockets, tendrils curl up stem and meet at overlapping leaves, bumpy type base, four feet, base sgd "Tiffany Studios New York 28617" with Tiffany monogram **72,800.00**

Lamp, table, domed Peony shade, large mauve, fuchsia, purple, and white flowers, green leaves, emerald green ground, imp "Tiffany Studios, New York 1475" on rim, molded bronze base imp "Tiffany Studios, New York 9514," 26" h, 18" d shade, **$34,100.** *Photo courtesy of James D. Julia, Inc.*

22" h, 16" d domed leaded glass shade, three repeating patterns of daffodils in mottled orange-yellow segments, blossoms supported on long stems of light green with yellow striations, segmented leaves on dark green, metal tag imp "Tiffany Studios New York," shade raised on three-socket bronze base with three-arm spider cylindrical shaft, ribbed cushion base with four ball feet, applied scrolled dec, brown and verdigris patina, base imp "Tiffany Studios New York," Tiffany Glass and Decorating Co. mark, "22326" and "20879," c1899-1922, imperfections **27,600.00**

22-1/2" h, 16-1/4" d domed shade, radiating mottled green segments, central floral border composed of clusters of multicolored pansy blossoms in mottled red, blue, orange, purple, white, and yellow, mottled and striated green foliage, sgd with metal tag imp "Tiffany Studios New York, 1448," shade supported on three-socket baluster form standard, upheld by three-prong shaft over domed sq base, base marked with disk imp "Tiffany Studios New York 444," some cracked segments, minor corrosion **29,900.00**

24-1/2" h, 14" d domed shade, Acorn, geometric leaded glass segments of striated green and white glass, border of acorns in yellow, white, and green, metal tag imp "Tiffany Studios New York," three-light base, three-arm spider on adjustable standard over openwork base of stylized branches with berries, green-brown patina, base unmarked............ **24,150.00**

25" h, 20" d pyramid leaded shade, Poppy pattern, red, fuchsia, and purple poppies, centers overlaid with pierced bronze-work, heavily striated background of orange and yellow, deep green leaves, metal worked form within shade to give illusion of veins in leaves, two rows at bottom done in mottled apple green glass, additional orange-yellow row, simple ftd base, sgd "Tiffany 8805," base sgd "Tiffany Studios New York" **89,500.00**

25-1/2" h, 17-3/4" hemispherical leaded shade, radiating mottled green geometric tile segments above a wide band of poinsettia blossoms and foliage of striated pink, green, yellow, blue, and purple segments, two border bands of green and amber rect tile segments, metal tags imp "Tiffany Studios New York 1558," three-socket fixture, geometric paneled bronze standard and disk base, imp marks and number, few cracked segments..... **37,950.00**

28-3/4" h, 2-1/4" d shade aperture, four entwined tendril arms supporting three down-turned and one central upright shade of diamond quilted glass, five pulled feathers, irid blue Favrile ground, inscribed "L.C.T.," bulbed circular lamp base with panels of curvilinear dec, imp "Tiffany Studios New York 25862" **14,950.00**

Wall sconce

14" h, 10" w, white opalescent Favrile glass tiles set in sq bronze links forming chain-mail curtain, suspended by demilune bronze frame with wire scrollwork, two-arm wall mounted fixture, pr. **17,000.00**

15-1/4" h, 16" w, classical bronze mounts with two arms terminating in a shield, each shield comprised of three parts with mottled amber and green glass, 1899-1920, price for pr **17,250.00**

TIFFIN GLASS

c1960

History: A. J. Beatty & Sons built a glass manufacturing plant in Tiffin, Ohio, in 1888. On January 1, 1892, the firm joined the U. S. Glass Co. and was known as factory "R." Quality and production at this factory were very high and resulted in fine Depression-era glass.

Beginning in 1916, wares were marked with a paper label. From 1923 to 1936, Tiffin produced a line of black glassware called Black Satin. The company discontinued operation in 1980.

References: Fred Bickenheuser, *Tiffin Glassmasters*, Book I (1979); *Tiffin Glassmasters, Book II*, Glassmasters Publications, 1981; Fred W. Bickenheuser, *Tiffin Glassmasters, Book III*, Glassmasters Publications, 1985; Jerry Gallagher and Leslie Piña, *Tiffin Glass*, Schiffer, 1996; Ruth Hemminger, Ed Goshe, and Leslia Pina, *Tiffin Glass, 1940-80*, Schiffer, 2001; Kelly O'Kane, *Tiffin Glassmasters, The Modern Years*, published by author, 1998 (P.O. Box 16303, St. Paul, MN 55116-0303, tiffin@pobox.com); Bob Page and Dale Fredericksen, *Tiffin is Forever. A Stemware Identification Guide*, Page-Fredericksen, 1994.

Collectors' Club: Tiffin Glass Collectors Club, P.O. Box 554, Tiffin, OH 44883.

Almond, Flanders, pink, ftd **150.00**

Animal dish, cov, duck, brown . . **65.00**

Animal, goose, crystal. **175.00**

Ashtray

Canterbury, #115, 3-1/2" x 4-1/2", Desert Red **22.00**

Dog, German Shepard

Green **75.00**

Pink **75.00**

Cloverleaf

3", #9123-96, Twilite **25.00**

5", #9123-97, Twilite **45.00**

Rectangular, Desert Red, gold sticker **28.00**

Basket

Black Satin, #9574, 10". **65.00**

Copen Blue, #6533, blue and crystal, 13" **165.00**

Emerald Green, #15151, satin, 7" **55.00**

Light Blue, #310, 3-1/2" d, plain handle **20.00**

Satin, #9574, sky blue, 6" **45.00**

Twilite, 9" h, 5-1/2" w **295.00**

Yellow Satin, 3-1/4" **45.00**

Bell

Cerise, crystal. **75.00**

Cherokee Rose, crystal **65.00**

June Night, #9743

Bead handle, crystal **48.00**

Cut dec, crystal **45.00**

Bonbon

Fuchsia, 6-1/2" d, three ftd . . . **60.00**

Modern

#6224, Wisteria **65.00**

#6281, Killarney Green . . . **65.00**

Bookends, pr, Ships, #9362, amber stain. **325.00**

Bowl

Cadena, 6" d, handle, yellow . **22.00**

Canterbury, Twilite, 9" d, crimped **95.00**

Empress

#5466, Sapphire Blue and crystal **125.00**

#5466, Twilite and Smoke **195.00**

#6561, Smoke and crystal. **65.00**

#9153-108, 10-1/2" d, Twilite **225.00**

First Love, crystal, 5" d **65.00**

Flanders, pink. **50.00**

Fuchsia, #5902, 3-part, 6-3/4" d **28.00**

Killarney Green, 9-1/4" d, ftd, #17430 . . . . **75.00**

Modern

#31, heart shape, controlled bubbles, Twilite **225.00**

#5477, crystal **45.00**

#5550, ram's head style, apple green, c1970 . . . . **45.00**

11" w, Twilite, spike base design **225.00**

Murano, milk glass **45.00**

Swedish Modern

#5948, 15" l, oval, crystal. . **45.00**

#6372, flared, crystal, controlled bubble connector stem . . **80.00**

Whirling Crystal **45.00**

Swedish Optic

#510, Copen Blue, large sand carved flower. **145.00**

#525, 4-1/2" d, three ftd, crystal **45.00**

#17430, 3-1/4" h, 6-1/2" d, Da Vinci foot, wisteria. . . . **75.00**

#17430, 5" h, 8" l, Da Vinci foot, Twilite **165.00**

Bud vase

Bright

#004, green and crystal, Luciana etch **75.00**

#15082, 11" h, crystal, gold band at top and on foot, orig sticker **28.00**

Cerise, #14185, 10" h

Crystal. **28.00**

Crystal, gold encrusted . . . **45.00**

Cherokee Rose, #14185

8" h, crystal. **45.00**

10" h, crystal. **48.00**

Classic, #14185, crystal **95.00**

Fuchsia, five bead, crystal . . **145.00**

Isabella, 10" h, crystal **195.00**

June Night

6-1/4" h, crystal. **45.00**

8" h, crystal. **48.00**

10-1/2" h, crystal. **60.00**

Modern, #14185, 10" h, Killarney Green **35.00**

Swedish Modern, #85, 5" h, Twilite **145.00**

Café parfait

Classic, #185, crystal **70.00**

Persian Pheasant, rose pink . . **95.00**

Cake plate

Fuchsia, 10-1/2" d, crystal. . . . **50.00**

Jack Frost, canary yellow, handle, 9-1/2" d **65.00**

Satin, #179, emerald, center handle, gold tracery and enamel dec **80.00**

Candelabrum, #5831, crystal, pr **38.00**

Candlesticks, pr

Black Satin

#66 . . . . **75.00**

#81 . . . . **65.00**

#319, 10". **95.00**

#15328, 8" h **50.00**

Black Shiny, Art-Deco style, 3-1/2" h, c1970 . . . . **75.00**

Blue Satin

#10 . . . . **28.00**

#315, 9-1/2" h **125.00**

Bright Blue, 5-1/4" d **35.00**

Cerise, two-lite, crystal **75.00**

Cherokee Rose, #5902, two-lite, crystal **165.00**

Classic, crystal **250.00**

Flower Garden with Butterflies, pink **150.00**

Fuchsia, #5902, two-lite, crystal **125.00**

Green Satin, #66, enameled and painted dec. **75.00**

June Night, #5902, crystal . . **100.00**
Juno, #348, green **35.00**
Killarney Green, #17394, 4-1/8" h **65.00**
Medford, squatty, crystal **30.00**
Twilight, block, 2" h **95.00**
White Satin, #10, 3" h **28.00**
Williamsburg, #5902, two-lite, crystal **75.00**

Candy dish, cov
Canterbury, #115, 9-1/4", Desert Red **60.00**
Flanders, pink **590.00**
Oneida, crystal **50.00**
Satin, #330, crystal, cone, enameled flowers on lid **48.00**

Candy jar, cov
Emerald Green, satin, 10" h . . **65.00**
Jack Frost, cone shape, green **55.00**

Celery tray
Cherokee Rose, 10-1/2" l, crystal **35.00**
Fuchsia, crystal **48.00**
June Night, #5902, 10-1/2" l, crystal **58.00**

Centerpiece
Deerwood, #8177, pink, gold trim **245.00**
Flanders, #5813, 13" d, rolled edge, Mandarin Yellow **200.00**
Fontaine, #15033, green, slight use **85.00**
June Night, 13" d, cone **125.00**
La Fleure, #8153, 13" d, yellow **125.00**
Modern, #17430, 12" d, Killarney Green **125.00**
Rambling Rose, #5902, etched, 12" d, crystal **55.00**
Sand Carving, #319, sq, magnolia carving, crystal **75.00**
Swedish Optic, #17430, Twilite, 11" d **225.00**

Champagne
Athens Diana, crystal **25.00**
Barber, #14196, blue **28.00**
Byzantine, crystal **18.00**
Cadena, yellow **30.00**
Capri etch, #15071 . . . . **14.00**
Cerise, #17392, crystal **20.00**
Cherokee Rose, #17403, crystal **28.00**
Classic, crystal **25.00**
Consul, #17679, crystal **18.00**
Enchanto Gold **35.00**
Flanders
Crystal **14.75**
Pink, 6-1/4" h **40.00**
Fontaine, #15033
Pink **35.00**
Twilite, crystal stem **45.00**
Fordham, #17594, crystal **28.00**
Fuchsia, #15803, crystal **14.00**
Interlude, #17726, crystal **30.00**
Jubilation, #17707, pink **25.00**
June Beau, crystal **14.00**
June Night, #17403, crystal . . . **32.50**
Killarney Green, #17394 . . . . . **17.50**
King's Crown, blue **10.00**
Kingsley cutting, #17392, crystal **25.00**
Linda, #17576, crystal **30.00**
Lisette, #17684, crystal **28.00**
Lovelace, #17358, crystal **18.00**
Majesty, #17507, Twilite **32.50**
Mariposa, #17507, crystal **28.00**
Mercedes, #17657, crystal . . . **30.00**
Midnight Mist, crystal **25.00**
Mim, #17501, crystal **30.00**
Moondust, plum **30.00**
Morning Star, #17625, crystal . **28.00**
Optic, Twilite **48.00**
Palasis Versailles, #17594, crystal **75.00**
Persian Pheasant, #17358, crystal **30.00**
Pink Rain, #17477, crystal **50.00**
Princess, #13643, etched, crystal **10.00**
Priscilla, #17361, crystal **25.00**
Queen Astrid, #17358, crystal . **30.00**
Revelation, pink **25.00**
Romance, crystal **25.00**
Silver Pine, #17596, crystal . . . **30.00**
Tea Rose, #17453, crystal **22.50**
Theme, #17644, crystal, orig sticker **16.00**
Thistle, #14197, crystal, 4-7/8" h **22.00**
Tiffin Rose, #17680 . . . . **30.00**
Touraine, #17328, crystal, 6" h **24.00**
Trina, #17565, crystal **22.00**
Wisteria, #17477, crystal, 4-1/2" h, 5 oz **30.00**
Woodstock, #17301, crystal . . **20.00**

Cheese and cracker
Canary Satin **65.00**
Deerwood, etched dome and plate, Rose Pink **235.00**
Flanders, yellow **75.00**
Flower Garden with Butterflies, amber, gold trim **235.00**

Cigarette holder
#15074, Killarney Green, 3-1/2" h **55.00**
#17394, crystal **55.00**

Claret
Cherokee Rose, #17399, crystal, 6" h, 4 oz **40.00**
Fuchsia, #15083, crystal **20.00**
June Night, #17403, crystal . . . **35.00**
Panel Optic, 2-1/2 oz, Twilite . . . **2.00**
Persian Pheasant, #17358, crystal, 4-1/2 oz **40.00**
Roses, crystal, c1931 . . . . **20.00**
Wisteria, #17477, crystal **25.00**

Cocktail
Athens Diana, crystal **18.00**
Byzantine, crystal **14.00**
Cerice, #15071, crystal **18.50**
Cherokee Rose
#17399, crystal **36.00**
#17403, crystal **20.00**
Classic, #14185, crystal, 4-7/8" h, 3 oz **32.00**
King's Crown, cranberry stained **17.50**
Palais Versailles, crystal **95.00**
Strawberry Diamond, Hawkes cut **35.00**

Finger bowl and underplate
Flanders, crystal **75.00**
Minton, crystal, gold border, 4-3/4" d bowl, 6-3/4" d underplate . . **175.00**

Flower arranger
Canterbury, 8-1/2" d, Desert Red **45.00**
Empress
#6552, 7-1/2" d, plum . . . **185.00**
#6553, Ruby and crystal, partial orig label **175.00**
#6553, Smoke and crystal **125.00**
#6569, Sapphire Blue and crystal, both ends turned under **175.00**
#6569, 9" d, Twilite and Smoke **225.00**
Modern, persimmon **45.00**

Flower basket, #6553, Copen Blue and crystal, 13" **165.00**

Flower bowl
Canterbury, #9153-106, 8" d, Citron Green **18.00**
Modern, #9153-108, 10-1/2" d, Twilite **225.00**
Swedish Modern, #4968, crystal **48.00**

Flute
Enchanto Gold **40.00**
Interlude, #17726, crystal **30.00**

Fruit bowl, Open Work, line #310, sky blue, 12" d **75.00**

Garden set, Candlelight, #9153-110, crystal and black, late green shield crest label **110.00**

Goblet, water
Byzantine
Black **45.00**
Crystal **35.00**
Yellow **38.00**
Cadena
Pink **35.00**
Yellow **35.00**
Cerise, crystal **22.00**
Chalet, crystal **50.00**

Cherokee Rose
- #17399, crystal **35.00**
- #17403, crystal **35.00**

Draped Nude, satin stem ... **150.00**
English Hobnail, white milk glass, 6" h **10.00**
Festival, #17640, crystal **24.00**
Flanders, pink, 8-1/4" h **55.00**
Fontaine
- #033, Twilite **65.00**
- #15033, rose pink **95.00**

Fordham, #17594, crystal.... **30.00**
Fuchsia, #15083, crystal
- 6-1/4" h................ **35.00**
- 7-1/2" h................ **35.00**

Interlude, #17726, crystal.... **30.00**
Jubilation, #17707, pink **28.00**
June Night, #17403, crystal, 9 oz.................... **32.00**
Killarney Green
- #17394................ **25.00**
- #17467................ **35.00**

Ad, Tiffinware, showing Flanders and Priscilla patterns. Good Housekeeping, *December 1927.*

Kingsley cutting, #17392, crystal **35.00**
King's Crown
- Cranberry stained......... **8.00**
- Ruby stained............ **15.00**

Lady Carol, #17524, crystal .. **35.00**
Linda, #17576, crystal....... **30.00**
Line
- #011, crystal, green stem, wheel cut **38.00**
- 15003, crystal, amber disk and foot.................. **28.00**
- 15015, Twilite **18.00**
- 17524, Twilite **45.00**

Linear, #17565, crystal **24.00**
Lisette, #17684, crystal...... **30.00**
Lyric, #17601, crystal **25.00**
Majesty, #17507, Twilite...... **45.00**
Mariposa, #17507, crystal.... **30.00**
Mercedes, #17657, crystal ... **30.00**
Midnight Mist............. **25.00**
Moondust, plum............ **30.00**
Morning Star, #17624, crystal . **30.00**
Old Master, #17477, crystal .. **35.00**
Palais Versailles, #17594, 6-7/8" h, 11 oz.................. **115.00**
Panel Optic, #15066, Mandarin yellow, 7" h **20.00**
Persian Pheasant, #17358, crystal, ribbed stem.............. **30.00**
Petite, crystal............. **28.00**
Pink Rain, #17477, crystal.... **55.00**
Princess, #13643, crystal, etched **20.00**
Priscilla, #17361, crystal **35.00**
Psyche, #15106, crystal, green stem **45.00**
Rambling Rose, #17392, crystal **30.00**
Renaissance Platinum....... **35.00**
Resplendent, #17603 .... **35.00**
Revelation, pink........... **25.00**
Romance, crystal........... **25.00**
Royal Splendor, crystal **45.00**
Shamrock, dark green....... **22.00**
Silver Pine, #17596, crystal... **35.00**
Starlight, crystal........... **32.00**
Tea Rose, #17453, crystal, 7-3/8" h **28.50**
Thistle, #14197, crystal, 6-1/4" h **20.00**
Tiffin Rose, #17680, crystal... **30.00**
Touraine, #17328, crystal, 8" h **25.00**
Trina, #17565, crystal **25.00**
Twilite, #17492, crystal **35.00**
Wisteria, #17477, crystal..... **40.00**
Woodstock, #17301, crystal .. **20.00**

Grapefruit

Flanders, yellow, crystal insert **250.00**
Nymph, crystal, Nile Green foot and stem **135.00**

Hat, Black Satin, 4" **245.00**
Hi ball tumbler, Palais Versailles, crystal **75.00**
Iced tea tumbler, 12 oz, ftd
- Cadena, #17065, yellow **44.00**
- Chardonay, crystal **40.00**
- Cherokee Rose, #17403, crystal **35.00**
- Classic, crystal **40.00**
- Enchanto Gold **38.00**
- Flanders, pink **75.00**
- Flying Nun, green, crystal **60.00**
- Fontaine, #15033
  - Green, crystal **33.00**
  - Twilite **95.00**
- Fordham, #17594, crystal **30.00**
- Fuchsia, #15083, crystal **35.00**
- Interlude, #17726, crystal **30.00**
- June Night, crystal **35.00**
- Killarney Green
  - #15077 . . . . **35.00**
  - #17467 . . . . **35.00**
- King's Crown
  - Cranberry stained **16.00**
  - Ruby stained, 5-3/8" h **22.00**
- Linda, #17576, crystal **30.00**
- Linear, #17565, crystal **25.00**
- Lisette, #17684, crystal **30.00**
- Lyric, #17601, crystal **25.00**
- Majesty, #17507, Twilite **45.00**
- Mariposa, #17507, crystal . . . **30.00**
- Mercedes, #17657, crystal . . . **30.00**
- Mona, #17551, crystal **25.00**
- Moondust, plum **30.00**
- Morning Star, #17624, crystal . **30.00**
- Old Master, #17477, crystal . . **35.00**
- Petite, crystal **28.00**
- Pink Rain, #17477, crystal . . . **55.00**
- Priscilla, #17361, crystal **32.00**
- Renaissance Platinum **35.00**
- Resplendent, #17603, crystal . **35.00**
- Royal Splendor, crystal **45.00**
- Silver Pine, #17596, crystal . . **35.00**
- Spiral Optic, crystal bowl, green foot, four-pc set **95.00**
- Starlight, crystal **32.00**
- Tea Rose, #17453, crystal . . . **28.50**
- Trina, #17565, crystal **25.00**
- Westchester Gold **68.00**
- Willow, crystal **28.00**
- Wisteria, #17477, crystal **35.00**
- Woodstock, #17301, crystal . . **20.00**

Ivy ball
- Modern
  - Short stem, large bowl, cobalt blue **275.00**
  - Short stem, small bowl, wisteria **125.00**
  - Tall stem, large bowl, plum **150.00**

Jug
- Athens Diana, #128, crystal . **260.00**
- Classic, cov, crystal **425.00**
- Havana Optic, crystal, Nile Green foot and handle, Hawkes cutting, Hawkes falcon trademark on foot **295.00**
- Spiral Optic, crystal, amber foot, handle, and finial on crystal cover **350.00**
- Swedish Optic, #5935, crystal . **75.00**

Juice tumbler, ftd
- Byzantine, crystal **16.00**
- Cerise, #071, crystal **20.00**
- Cherokee Rose, crystal, 5 oz, ftd **20.00**
- Classic, crystal, 3-1/2" h **35.00**
- Flanders, Mandarin and crystal, 3-3/4" h, 5 oz **25.00**
- June Night, crystal **25.00**
- King's Crown, ruby stained, 4 oz **10.00**
- Wisteria, #17477, 5-1/2" h, 5 oz . **45.00**

Lamp
- Empress, #6565, hurricane, 17" h, ruby and crystal **275.00**
- Killarney Green, gold criss-cross dec, marble base **150.00**
- Mushroom, Blue Satin, 10" h, chips on top of base **165.00**
- Owl **500.00**

Lamp shade, Jack Frost, amber, few chips on connector rim **175.00**
Lemonade set, Swedish Optic, #5959 jug, eight hi-balls, crystal **200.00**
Lily bowl, June Night, #5902, crystal, 13-1/2" d **125.00**
Lily plate, Cherokee Rose, crystal, 13-1/4" d **70.00**
Martini jug
- Modern Optic, late smoke, 4-1/2" d, 12-1/2" h, polished pontil **75.00**
- Twilite, 11-1/2" **450.00**

Mayonnaise set, three pcs
- Cadena, yellow **30.00**
- Cerise, crystal **35.00**
- Cherokee Rose, crystal **45.00**
- Flanders, yellow **60.00**
- Old Gold Bright, #310 . . . . **45.00**

Mint, Flanders, pink, 2-1/2" w, 1-3/4" h, blown stem **195.00**
Nappy, June Night, #5902, 7" . . . **45.00**
Night light, candle holder with finger hold, green satin, #319 . . . . **55.00**
Nut bowl
- Cherokee Rose, 6" d **47.50**
- June Night, crystal, 6" d **45.00**

Olive dish
- Modern, #6647, Killarney Green, 5-1/2" **45.00**
- Teardrop, crystal **20.00**

Oyster cocktail
- Athens Diana, crystal **18.00**
- Cerise, crystal **18.00**
- First Love, crystal **30.00**
- Flanders, crystal **15.00**
- Persian Pheasant, crystal, etched **20.00**

Paperweight, figural
- Apple, controlled bubbles . . **135.00**
- Elephant, 6" h, 4" w, controlled bubbles, standing, trumpeting trunk, Twilite **425.00**
- Pumpkin, yellow, controlled bubbles **125.00**
- Strawberry, small, desert rose, controlled bubbles **95.00**

Parfait
- Byzantine, yellow **32.00**
- Flanders, yellow **60.00**
- Fuchsia, #15083, crystal **60.00**

Pickle dish
- Fuchsia, crystal, 7-3/8" l **45.00**
- La Fleure, yellow, 7-1/2" l **60.00**

Pilsner
- Line 17418, crystal, set of 6 . **150.00**
- Rambler Rose, platinum band, 8-1/2" h, set of 8 . . . . **150.00**

Pipe, souvenir type, crystal **25.00**
Pitcher
- Cherokee Rose, crystal, ftd . **700.00**
- Double Columbine, ftd **225.00**
- First Love, blown **250.00**
- Flanders
  - Crystal, cov **500.00**
  - Pink **475.00**
- Flying Nun, cov, crystal, green base **450.00**
- Threaded Optic, cornflower blue, 4-3/4" h, 32-oz pitcher crystal handle, four 2-5/8" 4 oz tumblers **95.00**

Plate
- Blue Satin, luncheon **15.00**
- Byzantine, crystal, 8-1/2" d **7.50**
- Cadena, yellow, dinner **45.00**
- Cerise, crystal, 8" d **15.00**
- Cherokee Rose, #5902, 8" d . . **30.00**
- Classic, crystal, 10-1/2" d . . . **125.00**
- First Love, crystal
  - 6" d, round **16.00**
  - 7-1/2" sq **45.00**
  - 8" d round **25.00**
- Flanders
  - Crystal, 7" d **9.00**
  - Crystal, 9-1/2" d **195.00**
  - Mandarin yellow, 8" d **24.00**
  - Mandarin yellow, 9-1/2" d . **60.00**
  - Pink, 6" d **22.50**
  - Pink, 8" d **35.00**
- Fontaine, #8833, Twilite, 8" d . **30.00**
- Fordham, #17594, crystal, 8" d **20.00**
- Fuchsia, #8833, crystal, 8" d . **15.00**

June Night, crystal
6" d 16.50
8" d, beaded 25.00
Juno, yellow, 9-1/2" d. 40.00
La Fleure, yellow, 7-1/2" d 15.00
Lyric, #17601, 8" d, crystal . . . 15.00
Mefford, #8836, satin finish, gold trim, 10" d 55.00
Minton, crystal, gold border, 8-1/4" d 12.50
Persian Pheasant
Green, 8" d 14.00
Pink, 8" d. 22.00
Psyche, green, 8" d 20.00
Rain, pink. 45.00
Twilite, luncheon 25.00
Wisteria, #17477, 8" d 25.00

Puff bowl, English Hobnail, white milk glass. 16.00

Puff box, cov
Chipperfield, green 50.00
Dancing Girl, Sky Blue Satin, 6" d 285.00

Punch bowl set, Cascade, crystal, punch bowl and 8 cups 200.00

Punch cup, Caribbean, crystal, cobalt blue handle. 20.00

Relish
Cherokee Rose, crystal
6-1/2" d, round, three parts. 47.50
12" d 80.00
June Night, crystal, 12", three parts 80.00
Rambler Rose, crystal, three parts, 11" l 45.00

Rose bowl
Canterbury, #115
Desert Red 55.00
Greenbriar. 45.00
Twilight, 5". 75.00
Modern, #6120
Short, large bowl, Golden Banana, Diamond Optic. . 75.00
Tall, small bowl, Golden Banana, Diamond Optic 125.00
Tall, small bowl, Plum, Diamond Optic. 125.00
Wisteria 225.00
Oneida, blue encrusted, 7-1/2" d, ftd 65.00
Swedish Optic, #17430, 5" h, 8" d, gold crest label 235.00

Salad bowl
Fuchsia, crystal, 10-1/2" d . . . 120.00
King's Crown, ruby stained . . . 65.00

Salt and pepper shakers, pr
First Love, crystal. 55.00
Fuchsia, crystal 95.00
June Night, crystal. 165.00

Sandwich plate, June Night, #5902, 14" d 125.00

Sandwich tray, Brilliancy, amber 20.00

Seafood cocktail, Palais Versailles, crystal 125.00

Seltzer tumbler, La Fleure, yellow, ftd 20.00

Server, center handle
Canterbury, #115, Greenbriar, 13" w 28.00
Deerwood, pink 75.00
Flanders, pink. 245.00
Green Satin. 25.00
Juno, pink. 85.00

Sherbet
Cadena, low, topaz. 15.00
Cerise, crystal. 10.00
Cherokee Rose, #17399, crystal, tall 20.00
Diamond Optic, #028, vaseline, amber foot, set of eight . . . 225.00
Flanders, crystal, high 28.00
Fontaine, #15033, rose pink . . 33.00
Forever Yours, #17507, crystal . 8.00
Fuchsia, #15083, crystal
4-1/8" h. 18.00
5-3/8" h. 30.00
June Night, #17403, crystal, tall, reed stem 20.00
Killarney Green, #17394. . . . . . 9.50
King's Crown
Cranberry stained 10.00
Ruby stained 12.00
La Fleure, yellow, low 20.00
Maderia, Twilite. 10.00
Wire Optic, #15018, pink, high . 36.00
Wisteria, #17477. . . . . 18.00

Sherry
June Night, crystal, 2 oz. 45.00
Palais Versailles, #17594, crystal, 6-3/8" h, 5-1/2 oz 115.00

Snack set, 10-1/2" d plate and cup
King's Crown
Cranberry stained 35.00
Ruby stained 40.00

Sugar, cov
Cadena, yellow. 37.50
Cerise, crystal. 25.00
Flanders, crystal, 3-1/2" h, ftd . 35.00
June Night, crystal 20.00
Juno, yellow 37.50

Sundae
Cerise, crystal. 20.00
Fontaine, #15033, green. 25.00
La Fleure, Mandarin and crystal, 4-1/2" h. 18.00
Minton, crystal, gold border, four-pc set. 55.00

Sweet pea vase, Swedish Modern, #17350
Copen Blue and crystal, 7" h . 58.00
Killarney Green, 6" h 125.00
Ruby stained 65.00

Tray, Roses, blue opalescent, 11-1/4" l, 9" w. 125.00

Tumbler
Aster, crystal, 8 oz, bell, etched 12.00
Cerise, crystal, 4-7/8" h, ftd . . . 25.00
Cherokee Rose, #17399, crystal, 10-1/2 oz 36.00
Classic, crystal
Flat, 8 oz 45.00
Ftd, 7" h, 7 oz 35.00
Flanders
Mandarin and crystal, 5-5/8" h, 9 oz. 20.00
Pink, 3-3/4" h, 5 oz 60.00
Pink, 4-3/4" h, 9 oz 50.00
Pink, ftd, 5-7/8" h, 12 oz . . . 60.00
Yellow, 4" h, ftd 30.00
Fontaine, crystal, ftd, 10 oz . . . 85.00
Fuchsia, crystal, ftd, 6-5-16" h, 12 oz 32.00
June Night, #17358, crystal, 10 oz 20.00
Killarney Green, #17394, ftd, 6-1/2" h 15.00
La Fleure, Mandarin and crystal, ftd, 5-5/8" h 24.00
Paulina, #14196, yellow, ftd, 4-3/4" h 15.00
Spiral Optic, crystal, green foot, 4" h 75.00
Strawberry Diamond, Hawkes cut 30.00
Wide Optic, #017, rose pink, ftd, 4-3/4", 9-1/2 oz 18.00

Urn
Bright, #9727, Opal, gold band trim 75.00
Cobalt Blue, 10" h, handles . . 195.00
Killarney Green, #17430 . . . . 145.00

Vase
Black Satin
7-3/4" h, gold dec 75.00
8-1/2" h, #16261, open work 85.00
9-1/2" h, #16265, nude torchiere 250.00
10" h, U. S. Glass sticker . . 45.00
Carrara, 11-3/4" h, #329, lily, Pine Green 65.00
Cerise, #14185, crystal, 10" h, gold encrusted 55.00
Crystal, #83, lily, four openings 65.00
Emerald Satin, #16261 8-1/2" h 85.00
Empress
#6550, ruby and crystal, 10 ribs, 16" h 295.00

#6551, ruby and crystal.. **150.00**
#6555, ruby and crystal.. **175.00**
#6570, ruby and crystal, 12-1/2" and 13" h spikes **150.00**
Flanders, pink, 8" h, ftd, flared top **800.00**
Fontaine, pink, 9-1/4" h, blown **595.00**
Killarney Green, #17430, crystal base **35.00**
Modern
Yellow, ball shaped, Saturn optic **50.00**
Whirling Crystal, Twilite .. **265.00**
Oneida, crystal, 10-1/2" h, handle **150.00**
Poppy, Blue Satin, 5" h **40.00**
Sand Carving, #17350, teardrop, roses carving, crystal...... **95.00**
Satin, 8" h, cupped dahlia, two-tone parrot dec............. **150.00**
Swedish Modern
Copen Blue, 9-1/4" h **70.00**
Manzoni, #6448, crystal, ftd, oblong, 9" l........... **125.00**
Small globe, crystal applied stripes **125.00**
Swedish Optic
#5858, Copen Blue, 10" h, flip, sand-carved bellflowers **185.00**
#13750, Copen Blue, 9-1/4", tub type **70.00**
Twilight, 8-1/4" h, ruffled **75.00**
Velva, Crystal, 10" h **85.00**

Water lamp
Crystal, 8" h.............. **125.00**
Emerald Green, tall, ribbed . **225.00**
#111, Rose, faint water mark **145.00**

Whiskey
Classic, #185, crystal, ftd, 2 oz **75.00**
Delores, crystal............ **38.00**
Flanders, pink, 2-3/4" h..... **175.00**
Teardrop, crystal, ftd........ **25.00**

Wine
Byzantine, crystal **22.50**
Cadena, topaz **35.00**
Cerise, crystal............. **30.00**
Chalet, crystal............. **55.00**
Cherokee Rose, #17399..... **38.00**
Elinor, green, 4-7/8" h **35.00**
Empire, #018, pink **125.00**
First Love, crystal **45.00**
Flanders
Crystal **90.00**
Mandarin and crystal, 6" h, 3-1/2" oz.............. **40.00**
Pink **95.00**
Fontaine, #15033
Green and crystal, 1-1/2 oz. **38.00**
#15033, rose pink, 1-1/2 oz . **38.00**
Fuchsia, #1503, crystal, 5-1/16" h **35.00**
Interlude, #17726, crystal **30.00**
Jefferson **35.00**
June Night, #17403, crystal, 3-1/2 oz **35.00**
Kingsley cutting, #17392, crystal **35.00**
La Fleure, Mandarin and crystal, 6" h, 3-1/2 oz **30.00**
Maderia, Twilite **12.00**
Maribelle, #17361, crystal **35.00**
Mimi, #17501, crystal **35.00**
Palais Versailles, #17594, crystal **95.00**
Persian Pheasant, #17358, crystal, etched................. **24.00**
Priscilla, #17361, crystal **35.00**
Rambling Rose, #17441 ..... **30.00**
Thistle, crystal **17.00**
Tiffin Rose, #17680, crystal, 6-3/8" h **30.00**
Twilite, #17507............. **38.00**
Westchester Gold **75.00**
Willow, crystal **35.00**

Toothpick Holders

History: Toothpick holders, indispensable table accessories of the Victorian era, are small containers made specifically to hold toothpicks.

They were made in a wide range of materials: china (bisque and porcelain), glass (art, blown, cut, opalescent, pattern, etc.), and metals, especially silver plate. Makers include both American and European firms.

By applying a decal or transfer, a toothpick holder became a souvenir item; by changing the decal or transfer, the same blank could become a memento for any number of locations.

References: Neila and Tom Bredehoft and Jo and Bob Sanford, *Glass Toothpick Holders,* Collector Books, 1999; William Heacock, *Encyclopedia of Victorian Colored Pattern Glass,* Book I, 2nd ed., Antique Publications, 1976, 1992 value update; —, *1,000 Toothpick Holders*, Antique Publications, 1977; —, *Rare & Unlisted Toothpick Holders*, Antique Publications, 1984; National Toothpick Holders Collectors Society, *Toothpick Holders*, Antique Publications, 1992.

Reproduction Alert: Reproduction toothpick holders abound. Carefully examining details on these small glass objects can be a challenge, but it is often the best way to spot a reproduction.

Collectors' Club: National Toothpick Holder Collectors, P.O. Box 852, Archer City, TX 76351, http://www.collectoronline.com/clubNTHCS.html.

Art and colored glass

Alexandrite, Honeycomb pattern, shot glass shape, straight rim, 2-1/8" h **500.00**

Amberina
Daisy and Button pattern, intense fuchsia coloration........ **385.00**
Diamond Quilted pattern, sq top **350.00**
Inverted Thumbprint pattern, pedestal base, 1000 TPs #15 .... **195.00**
Venetian Diamond pattern, square top, round base **275.00**

Burmese
Gundersen **135.00**
Mt. Washington, hat shape, sq top, hand painted leaf dec, 2-3/4" h **250.00**
Webb, sq top, bulbous body, 2-1/2" h............... **285.00**

Cameo, Daum Nancy, winter scene, sgd **750.00**

Carnival, Kitten pattern, Fenton, amethyst **160.00**

Cranberry
Bulbous base **100.00**
Coin Spot pattern, pedestal base **175.00**
Coralene beaded flowers... **285.00**
Optic Thumbprint pattern... **100.00**

Cut glass
Chain of hobstars, pedestal. **145.00**
Diamonds, fans, and cross-hatching, rayed base............ **125.00**

Latticinio, green, gold, and white **60.00**

Pairpoint, Buffalo, 1000 TPs #21 .... **200.00**

Peachblow, round, plain rim, polished pontil, 2-5/8" h **300.00**

Pigeon blood, Bulging Loops pattern **195.00**

Pomona, first patent, tricorner, New England Glass Co., 2-1/4" h, rim flake **50.00**

Rubena, Royal Ivy, Northwood Glass Co., 2-1/4" h, rim flakes **110.00**

Smith Bros., Columned Ribs pattern, 1000 TPs #31 .... **125.00**

Spatter
Leaf Mold, canary, red spatter, Northwood Glass Co., 1-7/8" h, large chip.............. **20.00**
Royal Ivy pattern, cranberry, crackle **250.00**

Steuben, Grecian Urn, pedestal, applied "M"-shape handles, 2-1/2" h **195.00**

Wave Crest

Cat dec, 1000 TPs #408 .... **165.00**
Kitten dec, 1,000 TP's #32.... **95.00**

Figural

Baby's booties, amber, c1890-95 .... **50.00**
Bird, yellow ground, opaque body **35.00**
Book.......... **25.00**

Art glass, Tiffany, Favrile, iridescent, dimpled sides, etched "LCT" on base, **$175.** *Photo courtesy of Joy Luke Fine Art Brokers and Auctioneers.*

Cat on pillow, Daisy and Button, blue, 3-3/8" h **60.00**
Coal bucket.......... **35.00**
Dog and stump, blue **60.00**
Dog with hat, amber, 3-1/2" h ... **30.00**
Domino **50.00**
Elephant, amber, c1890 .... **75.00**
Kitten on pillow.......... **95.00**
Petticoat hat, vaseline, gold trim **135.00**
Pig, pink.......... **75.00**
Pot belly stove, amber **45.00**
Purse shape, Fine Cut, blue **60.00**
Saddle, blue.......... **45.00**
Squirrel on stump.......... **50.00**
Top hat, fine cut.......... **50.00**
Tramp shoe, milk glass **60.00**
Two roosters, frosted **60.00**
Utility boot.......... **40.00**

Opaque glass

Clambroth, Zipper, fiery opalescent highlights **30.00**
Custard

Fan, Dugan, 2-1/2" h **875.00**
Georgia Gem, jade, gilt highlights, gilt floral dec on two panels, Tarentum Glass Co., 2-3/4" h, gilt wear **50.00**
Harvard, Tarentum Glass Co., 2-1/4" h.......... **45.00**
Ribbed Drape, Jefferson ... **350.00**
Washington.......... **120.00**

Milk glass

Alligator, c1885.......... **70.00**
Florette, turquoise..........**110.00**
Parrot and top hat, c1895.... **45.00**
Scroll, claw ftd, light pink and blue dec, c1900.......... **555.00**

Mount Washington, Ribbed pattern, satin finish, white ground, hand painted blue flowers.......... **175.00**
Satin, Florette, blue opaque **110.00**
Sunset, pink, cased, Dithridge & Co., 2-1/4" h, rim chip.......... **50.00**

Opalescent glass

Beatty Honeycomb pattern, blue ground.......... **165.00**
Beatty Rib, blue, 1-7/8" h **90.00**
Chrysanthemum pattern, cranberry ground.......... **170.00**
Criss-Cross pattern, cranberry ground **600.00**
Daisy pattern, vaseline ground, brass rim **110.00**
Diamond Spearhead pattern, green ground.......... **75.00**
Gonterman Swirl pattern, blue ground **300.00**
Inverted Strawberry pattern, aqua ground, marked "Near Cut"..... **45.00**
Iris Meander pattern, vaseline ground **110.00**
Reverse Swirl pattern, blue ground **85.00**
Ribbed Swirl pattern, blue ground **125.00**
Ringneck Stripe pattern, white ground **125.00**
Shell Wreath pattern, white ground **30.00**
Six Panels pattern, blue ground. **45.00**
Windows Swirl pattern, blue ground **125.00**

Pattern glass, colorless, unless otherwise noted

Adonis/Gonterman Swirl, amber and frosted, Aetna Glass & Mfg. Co., 2-1/2" h **140.00**
Arched Ovals pattern.......... **12.00**
Banded Portland pattern, cranberry **42.00**

Burmese, glossy finish, 2-5/8" h, **$150.**

Box in Box pattern, green, gold trim **42.00**
Continental pattern, Heisey ... **125.00**
Croecus pattern, green, gold highlights, 2-3/4" h **70.00**
Dahlia pattern, double, dec..... **85.00**
Daisy and Button pattern

Blue, round patterned plate type base, with un-patterned cup, 2" h **20.00**
Vaseline, square, 2" h, flake .. **25.00**

Delaware pattern, green, gilt trim, 2-1/2" h, wear to gilt **30.00**
Double Ring Panel pattern **30.00**
Florida pattern, ruby-amber ... **265.00**
Francesware pattern, frosted hobnail **65.00**
Frazier pattern, maiden's blush, enamel floral dec, U.S. Glass Co., 2-3/8" h, nick on rim **80.00**
Hobnail pattern, Apple Green, 1000 TPs #205 .... **55.00**
Holly pattern, Greentown....... **65.00**
Intaglio Sunflower pattern **20.00**
Kansas pattern **45.00**
Michigan pattern, clear, yellow stain **175.00**
New Jersey pattern, gold trim... **55.00**
Peerless pattern, Heisey....... **40.00**
Pineapple and Fan pattern, green, Heisey **185.00**
Spearpoint Band pattern, ruby stained **195.00**
Stars and Stripes pattern...... **15.00**
Sunbeam pattern, emerald **60.00**
Swag with Brackets, amethyst.. **50.00**
Texas pattern, gold trim........ **50.00**

Three Face pattern **40.00**
Truncated Cube pattern, ruby stained **75.00**
Twisted Hobnail pattern. **50.00**
Vermont pattern **40.00**
Vigilant pattern, Fostoria **25.00**
Wisconsin pattern **45.00**

UNION GLASS

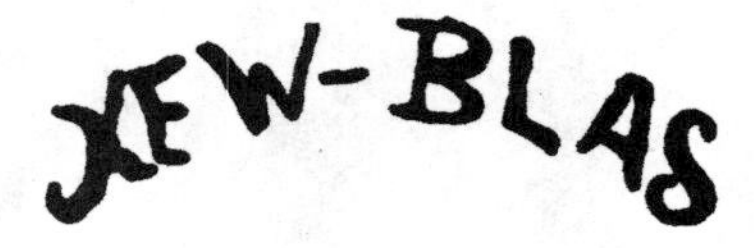

History: Amory and Francis Houghton established the Union Glass Company, Somerville, Massachusetts, in 1851. The company went bankrupt in 1860, but was reorganized. Between 1870 and 1885, the Union Glass Company made pressed glass and blanks for cut glass.

Art-glass production began in 1893 under the direction of William S. Blake and Julian de Cordova. Two styles were introduced: a Venetian style, which consisted of graceful shapes in colored glass, often flecked with gold; and an iridescent glass, called Kew Blas, made in plain and decorated forms. The pieces are similar in design and form to Quezal products but lack the subtlety of Tiffany items.

The company ceased production in 1924.

Museum: Sandwich Glass Museum, Sandwich, MA.

References: John A. Shuman III, The Collector's Encyclopedia of American Art Glass, Collector Books, 1988, 1994 value update; Kenneth Wilson, *American Glass 1760-1930: The Toledo Museum of Art, Volume I, Volume II,* Hudson Hills Press and The Toledo Museum of Art, 1994.

Bowl
- 5" d, irid gold ground, flared, ribbed **225.00**
- 5-1/2" d, irid gold ground, shaped rim, shallow round bowl, sgd "Kew Blas" on base **250.00**
- 14" d, pulled feather, red ground, sgd **1,400.00**

Candlesticks, pr, 8-1/2" h, irid gold, twisted stems. **750.00**

Compote
- 4-1/2" h, 3-1/2" d, gold irid, flared rim, applied pedestal foot with folded edge, inscribed "Kew Blas" on base **460.00**
- 7" h, irid gold ground, pink highlights, ribbed bowl, twisted stem. **550.00**

Console set, 10" d compote
- 5-1/4" h pr candlesticks, transparent green bowl, control bubbled ball stems **590.00**
- 6-3/4" h pr candlesticks, Alexandrite, heat reactive red shaded to blue, chocolate shading, central air trap bubble stem **1,265.00**

Cuspidor, 5-3/4" d, 2-1/2" h, amber ground, irid gold dec, squatty, flattened flared rim, sgd "Kew Blas" **285.00**

Decanter
- 14" h, green-gold irid ground, spherical long stemmed stopper, sgd **375.00**
- 14-1/2" h, 4-3/4" d base, gold irid, ribbed and painted stopper, purple-pink highlights, sgd on base **1,450.00**

Finger bowl and underplate
- 5" d bowl, 6" d plate, ribbed, scalloped border, metallic luster, gold and platinum highlights **475.00**
- 5" d, 7" d plate, 12-ribbed body, scalloped edge, gold irid, inscribed and numbered. . . **425.00**

Goblet
- 4-3/4" h, irid gold ground, curved stem. **250.00**
- 6" h, irid gold ground, knob stem **350.00**

Pitcher
- 4-1/2" h, green pulled feather pattern, deep gold irid int., applied swirl handle, sgd "Kew-Blas" **900.00**
- 5" h, King Tut, white ground, green and gold irid dec, irid blue lining, blue handle, sgd **2,000.00**

Rose bowl, 4" d, scalloped rim, cased glass sphere, green vertical zipper stripes, orange irid int., inscribed "Kew Blas" on base **690.00**

Salt, irid gold. **220.00**

Tumbler
- 3-1/2" h, 3" d, brilliant irid gold exterior, purple irid interior, sgd **275.00**
- 4" h, pinched sides, irid gold, sgd **225.00**

Vase
- 4-1/4" h, 5-1/4" d, deep emerald green, honeycomb pattern, highly irid purple int., sgd. **800.00**
- 4-1/4" h, 5-1/4" d, flared amber ribbed trumpet form, pulled emerald green int. dec, base engraved "Kew-Blas". **815.00**
- 6-1/4" h, cylinder, rolled rim, gold and green swags, pale orange ground, early 20th C, sgd, orig paper label. **950.00**
- 6-1/2" h, 7" w, bulbous, oyster white ground, deep green hooked and pulled feathering, gold irid feathers, gold irid rim on neck, sgd **1,450.00**
- 7" h, cased ambergris oval body, gold irid feathers on opal body, folded irid rim, base inscribed "Kew-Blas" **980.00**
- 7" h, quatrefoil rim, elongated ovoid body of colorless glass, dec with four pulled green and white feathers rising from base, irid gold ground, polished pontil with post production signature, early 20th C **750.00**
- 12-1/2" h, irid gold ground, blue and pink irid highlights, baluster, waisted. **950.00**

Wine glass, 4-3/4" h, curving stem, irid gold **250.00**

Vallerysthal Glass

History: Vallerysthal (Lorraine), France, has been a glass-producing center for centuries. In 1872, two major factories, Vallerysthal glassworks and Portieux glassworks, merged and produced art glass until 1898. Later, pressed glass animal-covered dishes were introduced. The factory continues to operate today.

Animal dish, cov
- Cow, 7" h, clear, pasture scene on cov. 115.00
- Dog on Rug, amber 135.00
- Fish, white milk glass 95.00
- Hen on nest, opaque aqua, sgd 75.00
- Rabbit, white, frosted 65.00
- Snail, figural strawberry base, white milk glass, sgd 115.00
- Squirrel, opaque blue 85.00
- Swan, blue opaque glass . . . 100.00

Box, cov
- 4" h, 3-1/2" d, blue milk glass . 90.00
- 5" x 3", cameo, dark green, applied and cut dec, sgd. 950.00

Breakfast set, hen cov dish, six egg cups, basket form master salt, tray, white milk glass, nine-pc set . . . 500.00

Butter dish, cov, figural
- Lemon, opaque white, sgd . . . 70.00
- Radish, white milk glass 115.00
- Turtle, opaque white, snail finial 100.00

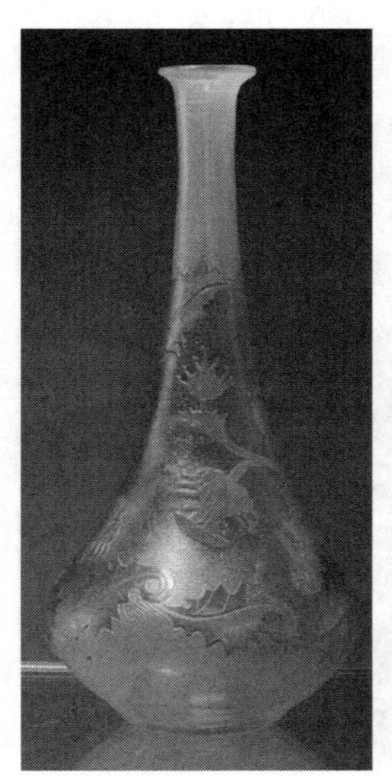

Vase, cameo-etched pink leaves and thistles, accented by light brown tint, colorless ground completely etched with geometric florals, signed on base, 11-1/2" h, **$1,850.** *Photo courtesy of David Rago Auctions.*

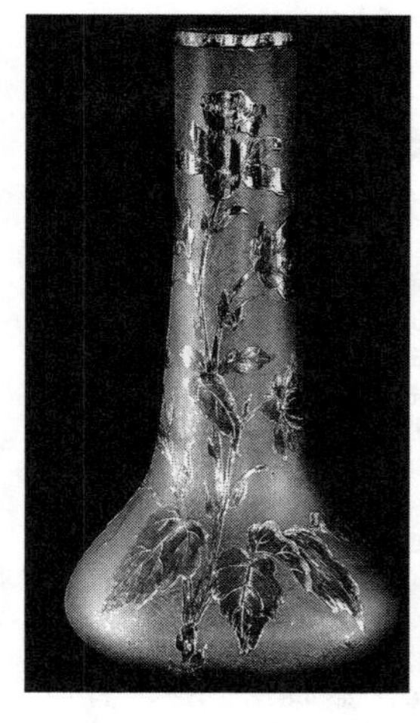

Vase, amberina ground, gold daffodils, 12" h, **$3,500.**

Candlesticks, pr
- Baroque pattern, amber 75.00
- Grecian Girl, frosted 95.00

Candy dish, 4-1/8" d, white milk glass, basketweave base, rope handles and finial 95.00

Compote, 6-1/4" sq, blue opaque glass 75.00

Goblet, blue milk glass, ftd 75.00

Mustard, cov, swirled ribs, scalloped blue opaque, matching cover with slot for spoon 45.00

Pitcher, Grape and Leaf pattern, vaseline, frosted 50.00

Plate
- 6" d, Thistle pattern, green . . . 65.00
- 7-1/2" d, floral dec, blue milk glass 50.00
- 8" d, Thistle pattern, green . . . 75.00

Salt, cov, hen on nest, white opal 65.00

Sugar, cov, 5" h, Strawberry pattern, opaque white, gold trim, salamander finial 85.00

Tumbler, 4" h, blue 40.00

Vase
- 8" h, flared folded burgundy red rim, oval pale green body, matching red enamel berry bush on front, inscribed "Vallerysthal" on base 490.00
- 11-1/2" h, cameo, pink leaves and thistles accented with small amounts of light brown tint, clear ground completely etched with geometric florals, sgd "Vallerystahl" on base 1,850.00

Val St.-Lambert

History: Val St.-Lambert, a 12th-century Cistercian abbey, was located during different historical periods in France, Netherlands, and Belgium (1930 to present). In 1822, Francois Kemlin and Auguste Lelievre, along with a group of financiers, bought the abbey and opened a glassworks. In 1846, Val St.-Lambert merged with the Socété Anonyme des Manufactures de Glaces, Verres à Vitre, Cristaux et Gobeletaries. The company bought many other glassworks.

Val St.-Lambert developed a reputation for technological progress in the glass industry. In 1879 Val St.-Lambert became an independent company, employing 4,000 workers. The firm concentrated on the export market, making table glass, cut, engraved, etched, and molded pieces, and chandeliers. Some pieces were finished in other countries, e.g., silver mounts were added in the United States.

1889

Val St.-Lambert executed many special commissions for the artists of the Art Nouveau and Art Deco periods. The tradition continues. The company also made cameo-etched vases, covered boxes, and bowls. The firm celebrated its 150th anniversary in 1975.

Ashtray, shell, gold label 10.00

Bottle, 6-7/8" h, cameo-etched, green vines and flowers dec, acid finished ground, green cut to clear overlay edge, sgd "Val/St Lambert" 120.00

Bowl, cov, 6-1/2" d, cameo-etched, deep cut purple florals, frosted ground, sgd "Val St Lambert" 750.00

Bowl, open
- 8" d, floral swag dec, sgd 90.00
- 10" d, 4" h, red flashed overlay, sgd 350.00

Bud vase, 11" h, small flared mouth, elongated neck over bulbous body, opal white glass with brick red powder-pulled dec, mottled blue ground, interlocking VSL monogram within base 575.00

Cologne bottle, 6-1/2" h, cameo-etched, textured colorless ground, cranberry florals, cut fern, partial paper label, replaced cut stopper 220.00

Compote, 3-1/2" d, amberina, ruby rim, mottled glass bowl, applied amber foot and handles 175.00

Dresser box, cov, colored 100.00

Finger bowl, 4-1/2" d, crystal, half pentagon, cut edge, sgd 45.00

Goblet, 5-3/8" h, colorless, blown mold, applied foot and stem 50.00

Pitcher, colorless, paneled, cut diamond design, sgd 95.00

Sculpture, Madonna, solid 125.00

Tumbler, 3" h, cameo-etched, blue florals, rim ground 40.00

Tumble-up, decanter and matching tumbler, amber-crystal, marked. . **95.00**

Vase

- 5-1/4" h, 6-3/4" l, lime green transparent elliptical body, acid stamped on base "Val St. Lambert" **345.00**
- 6-1/2" h, flared mouth tapering to neck, ovoid body, opal white glass layered in rosy red, cameo-etched flowering branches, sgd "VSL" in cameo near base, c1910 . . **575.00**
- 7-1/2" h, cameo-etched, colorless frosted ground, emerald green floral cutting, base marked "Made in Belgium, Val St. Lambert" **660.00**
- 8-1/2" h, cameo-etched, colorless frosted ground, emerald green bows and swags cutting . . **385.00**
- 8-1/2" h, heavy colorless oval, engraved rose in center, base inscribed "VSG C. Graffart/Piece Unique 1949," attributed to Charles Graffart **375.00**
- 10" h, cameo-etched, attributed to Desire and Henri Muller, Belgium, c1906, elongated triangular form, opaque white cased to colorless and chartreuse, fluogravure dec of dragonfly over poppies, rust, ochre, and beige colors, script "VSL" signature near base **3,115.00**
- 10" h, cameo-etched, cranberry cut to clear, wide band dec with Greek figures and nymphs above vertical cut ribs **440.00**
- 11-3/4" h, cameo-etched, frosty textured ground, life size enameled teasel and leaves, long woody stems, natural colors, gold highlights **500.00**

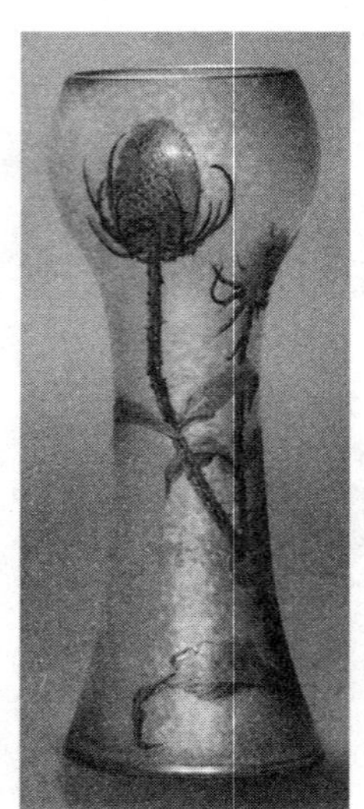

Vase, cameo-etched, frosty textured ground, life size enameled teasel and leaves, long woody stems, natural colors, gold highlights, 11-3/4" h, **$500.** *Photo courtesy of Cincinnati Art Galleries.*

VERLYS GLASS

Verlys   A Verlys France

History: Originally made by Verlys France (1931-1960), this Lalique-influenced art glass was produced in America by The Holophane Co. from 1935 to 1951, and select pieces by the A. H. Heisey Co. from 1955 to 1957. Holophane acquired molds and glass formulas from Verlys France and began making the art glass in 1935 at its Newark, Ohio, facility. It later leased molds to the Heisey Co., and in 1966 finally sold all molds and rights to the Fenton Art Glass Co.

The art glass was made in crystal, topaz, amber, rose, opalescent, and Directorie Blue. Heisey added turquoise. Most pieces have etched (frosted) relief designs.

The French-produced glass can be distinguished from the American products by the signature. Verlys France marked the glass with mold impressed "Verlys France" and "A Verlys France." Holophane (also known as Verlys of America) marked pieces with the mold-impressed "Verlys" and a scratched-script "Verlys" signature. The A. H. Heisey Co. used only a paper label, which reads "Verlys by Heisey."

Reference: Carole and Wayne McPeek, *Verlys of America Decorative Glass*, revised ed., published by authors, 1992.

Ashtray

- 3-1/2" d, floral dec, frosted, script sgd **45.00**
- 4-1/2" d, doves, floral border, frosted, script mark **55.00**
- 6" d, oval, duck perched on side, wave molded base, frosted. . **60.00**

Bowl

- 6" d, Cupids and Hearts pattern, colorless **50.00**
- 6" d, Pine Cone pattern, French blue **110.00**
- 8-1/2" d, 2-3/4" h, Thistle pattern, colorless, frosted and polished, three thistles form small feet, molded signature on int. . . . **250.00**
- 10" d, Chrysanthemum pattern, frosted **130.00**
- 13-1/2" d, Poppies, scratched signature **250.00**
- 13-3/4" d, Kingfisher, sgd **70.00**

Box, cov

- 6-1/2" d, butterflies, frosted, script mark **115.00**
- 6-3/4" d, relief molded bouquet of coreopsis, frosted, molded "Verlys/France" on lid and base **200.00**

Candy dish, cov

- 6" h, Pine Cone pattern, frosted **50.00**
- 6-1/2" h, Lovebirds, frosted, sgd **60.00**
- 7" h, sculptured florals, opalescent **375.00**

Candlesticks, pr, 5-1/2" d, leaftip-molded nozzle, spreading circular foot with molded nasturtiums, etched signature on base **120.00**

Center bowl, 13-1/2" d, molded and frosted colorless bowl, relief dec with water lily blossom on top, three leaves on underside form feet, inscribed "Verlys" on base **100.00**

Charger

- Flying Geese **75.00**
- Tassels, 13" d, script signature **75.00**

Lamp shade, 3-5/8" d, 5-3/4" h, raised birds and fish dec **285.00**

Plate

- 4-7/8" d, Shells pattern, opal **150.00**
- 5" d, fish, frosted. **65.00**
- 6-1/4" h, Pine Cone pattern, mold sgd. **75.00**

Powder box, cov, frosted, lovebirds **85.00**

Vase

- 4" h, Gems pattern, opal, ground base. **90.00**
- 6-1/2" h, 6-3/4" w, frosted and clear, script signature **65.00**
- 8" d, Thistles pattern, dusty rose **275.00**
- 9" h, ovoid, flared flattened rim, topaz, frosted large blossom and leaves, script sgd "Verlys" on base **600.00**
- 9-1/4" h, Mandarin, frosted and clear, script signature **250.00**

Salad bowl, Poppy pattern, Heisey, Newark, script signed, 13-1/2" d, **$135.**

WATERFORD

History: Waterford crystal is high-quality flint glass commonly decorated with cuttings. The original factory was established at Waterford, Ireland, in 1729. Glass made before 1830 is darker than the brilliantly clear glass of later production. The factory closed in 1852. One hundred years later it reopened and continues in production today.

Manufacturer/Distributor: Waterford Wedgwood USA Inc., P.O. Box 1454, Wall, NJ 07719.

Reproduction Alert: Several importers have been exposed as having falsely claimed that their products were genuine Waterford.

Magazine tear sheet, showing Sheila pattern, Crockery & Glass Journal, *March 1961,* **$5.**

Animal
- Bird **65.00**
- Fish **65.00**
- Seahorse **200.00**

Apprentice bowl, 7-3/4" d, 3-1/2" h, center cut with star framed in rays, connected shuttle designs on sides, centralized stars, vertical cut border, scalloped rim, stamped, 1/8" chip on scallop **175.00**

Ashtray, 5" d **95.00**

Biscuit barrel, 6-1/2" h, vertical relief plain diamond bands alternating with cut furrows, spear cut rim, star in base, disc lid with central cut star, faceted knob, stamp mark **110.00**

Bowl
- 6" d, allover diamond cutting **70.00**
- 8" d, DQ, thumbprint stem **125.00**
- 8-1/2" d **155.00**
- 9" d, leaf cut border over trellis-work sides **100.00**
- 10" d, ftd, Benjamin Franklin Liberty Bowl, American Heritage collection **275.00**

Bud vase **60.00**

Cake plate, 10" d, 5-1/4" h, sunburst center, geometric design **85.00**

Cake server, cut glass handle, orig box **80.00**

Candlesticks, pr, 7" h, pear shape, hollow center, horizontal oval cuts on wafers between fluted to and rayed base, looped cross cuttings in two sizes, downward spray of star cut **175.00**

Champagne flute, 6" h, Coleen pattern, 12-pc set **450.00**

Claret jug, 12" h, lapidary stopper, bulbous body, with relief plain diamond cutting, neck with honeycomb pattern, notched handle, double knob stem, rayed base, stamped "Waterford," cloudy int. ring **150.00**

Compote, 5-1/2" h, allover diamond cutting above double wafer stem, pr **400.00**

Creamer and sugar, 4" h creamer, 3-3/4" d sugar, Tralee pattern **85.00**

Cruet, 5" h, waisted body, short fluted neck, fluted rim, strawberry leaves and fan cutting, faceted stopper **120.00**

Decanter, orig stopper
- 10" h, ship's, colorless diamond cutting **200.00**
- 10-1/2" h, large lapidary stopper, corset form body, relief cut vesicas above cut ridges, stamped "Waterford," interior cloudiness **90.00**

12-3/4" h, colorless allover diamond cutting, monogram, pr **300.00**
13-1/4" h, colorless diamond cutting **100.00**

Goblet
Cameragh pattern **40.00**
Glengarett pattern **45.00**

Honey jar, cov............... **70.00**

Jar, cov, 6" h, diamond cut body, triple spring chain bordering thumb cut rim and star cut lid, faceted knob finial **100.00**

Lamp
13-1/2" h, parlor type, relief plain diamond cutting, open plain diamond designs applied to shade and base, stamp marks, minor chip, polished area on base **350.00**
14" h, Victorian style **350.00**
23" h, 13" d umbrella shade, blunt diamond cutting, Pattern L-1122 .... **450.00**

Letter opener **45.00**

Napkin ring, eight-pc set **165.00**

Old fashioned tumbler, 3-1/2" h, Comeragh pattern, pr **70.00**

Pitcher
6-3/4" h, Lismore pattern, shaped spout, applied strap handle **125.00**
10" h, diamond cuttings, applied handle **200.00**

Plate, 8" d, diamond cut center **100.00**

Ring dish, 5" d, colorless, cut glass, price for three-pc set......... **110.00**

Pitcher, ribbed, applied handle, 10-1/2" h, **$215.**

Rose bowl, 5-1/2" d, laurel border, spike diamond band **50.00**

Salt, 3-7/8" d, oval, diamond cut . **75.00**

Scent bottle, 4-1/2" l, diamond cut **75.00**

Sweetmeat, cov, pr, double dome cov, Fan pattern, scalloped rim, sq pedestal base, pr **700.00**

Tumbler, allover cutting **80.00**

Vase, 7" h, bulbous, top to bottom vertical cuts separated by horizontal slash cuts, sgd **140.00**

Wine
5-1/2" h, Patrick, eight-pc set **220.00**
7-3/8" h, Coleen, 12-pc set .. **725.00**

Wine cooler, 6-1/2" x 6-1/2" **195.00**

WAVE CREST

WAVE CREST WARE

c1892

History: The C. F. Monroe Company of Meriden, Connecticut, produced the opal glassware known as Wave Crest from 1898 until World War I. The company bought the opaque, blown-molded glass blanks from the Pairpoint Manufacturing Co. of New Bedford, Massachusetts, and other glassmakers, including European factories. The Monroe Company then decorated the blanks, usually with floral patterns. Trade names used were "Wave Crest Ware," "Kelva," and "Nakara."

References: Wilfred R. Cohen, *Wave Crest*, Collector Books, out-of-print; Elsa H. Grimmer, *Wave Crest Ware*, Wallace-Homestead, out-of-print; Kyle Husfloen, *Antique Trader's American & European Decorative and Art Glass Price Guide*, 2nd ed., Krause Publications, 2000; Carrol Lyle and Whitney Newland, *The C. F. Monroe Co. Catalogue No. 11, 1906-1907*, L & N Associates; Kenneth Wilson, *American Glass 1760-1930: The Toledo Museum of Art, Volume I, Volume II*, Hudson Hills Press and The Toledo Museum of Art, 1994.

Collectors' Club: Wave Crest Collectors Club, P.O. Box 2013, Santa Barbara, CA 93120.

Ashtray and match holder, 6" w, 3" h, white ground, pink enamel flowers, white centers, green leaves, marked "Wavecrest," small flat flake on inner rim of match holder, Cohen, page 79, top left........................ **600.00**

Biscuit jar, cov
5" w, 6" h, rococo, square, fancy blown-out mold, white shaded to pale blue ground, all around pink rose dec, green leaves, fancy silver plated emb metal trim, marked "Wavecrest"............. **300.00**
5-1/2" d, 5-1/2" h, pink and white background, melon ribbed, hp flowers, unmarked........ **250.00**
5-1/2" d, 5-3/4" h, tan and white shaded ground, white and magenta transfer lily flowers, no lid, unmarked............... **45.00**
7-1/2" d, 5-1/2" h, squatty, white shaded to ivory ground, raised rococo leaf design, blue, green, yellow, and brown transfer floral dec, small repair to bail handle, unmarked.............. **235.00**
8" h, blue and white ground, swirled, cherry blossoms dec, lid with handle, unmarked **150.00**
8" h, white ground, fern dec, unmarked.............. **200.00**
9" h, 6-1/4" w, white shading to yellow ground, raised rococo swirls on front and back, transfer dec of apple blossoms and leaves, pink, tan, green, and orange, silver plated bail and lid, hardware may be a replacement, unmarked **200.00**

Bonbon, 7" h, 6" w, Venetian scene, multicolored landscape, dec rim, satin lining missing **1,200.00**

Box, cov
3" d, double Shell, white, peach shells, blue, gray, and peach flowers **235.00**
3" d, hexagon, orig lining, sgd "Nakara," Cohen 126..... **485.00**
3" d, 2-1/2" h, swirl, white ground, small pink floral enamel, orig clasp, no lining, unmarked **165.00**
3" d, 3-1/4" h, Rococo, soft blue ground, pink apple blossoms with green leaves on lid, no lining, repaired hinge, marked "Wavecrest" **150.00**
3-1/2" d, 3-1/4" h, hexagonal, pale mauve, applied white flowers and yellow centers, orig clasp and lining, minor wear to some applied petals **650.00**
3" d, 4-1/2" h, Elephant's Foot mold, white shading to tan ground, transfer and enameled tiny pink roses, green leaves, four tiny nicks on cover, one small flake, orig lining worn, unmarked **400.00**
3-3/4" d, 3" h, blown-out asters, round base, ivory and pink top, shaded green and pink base, small burst bubble on lid, good metal trim, orig base lining, marked "Nakara".............. **500.00**
4" d, blown-out pansy dec, cream ground blue and lavender flowers **650.00**

4" d, blown-out shell, pin round, hp forget-me-not, lining replaced, marked **400.00**
4" d, Helmschmeid Swirl, paper label **275.00**
4" d, Shell, blue, ftd **325.00**
4" d, 3" h, hexagonal, mottled bright pink ground, six pale blue enameled flowers on lid, orig trim and clasp, no lining, marked "Kelva".................. **550.00**
4-1/4" d, bright blue ground, pink and white flowers, emb shell pattern, hinged **425.00**
4-1/4" d, 3" h, Belle Ware, round, smooth finish, pale blue and pink ground, pink roses and buds, orig metal fittings and clasp, marked "Belle Ware" **200.00**
4-1/4" d, 3-1/2" h, Bishop's Hat shape, brown-orange ground, pink flowers on lid, no lining, stamped "Nakara" **340.00**
4-1/4" d, 4" h, Bishop's Hat shape, solid blue ground shading to ivory, enameled bead work and pink and white apple blossoms with green leaves on cov, metal mountings, no lining, clasp possibly restored, marked "Nakara"......... **400.00**
4-1/2" d, 2-3/4" h, round, mottled blue ground, three large pink flowers, green leaves on lid, plated metal trim, worn clasp, orig worn lining, marked "Kelva"..... **350.00**
4-1/2" d, 2-3/4" h, round swirl base and lid, pink shading to white, blue and white forget me nots, green and gray leaves, some wear to lid dec, unmarked **115.00**
4-1/2" d, 3" h, round, blue and white ground, swirled, wild flowers on lid, unmarked **225.00**
4-3/4" d, 2-3/4" h, blown-out aster lid, pink floral dec, floral garland encircles base, remnants of orig lining **985.00**
5" d, 3" h, decorated crystal, holly leaves and berries dec, irid interior, sgd "C. F. Monroe" **300.00**
5" d, 3-1/4" h, shaded yellow and butterscotch ground, white beaded dec and scene of three Kate Greenaway figures having tea, excellent metal trim, no lining, marked "Nakara"......... **600.00**
5" d, 4" h, peach shaded to butterscotch ground, enameled cross on lid, white dot dec, four pale blue flowers, ftd, metal mounts, minor bead wear, replaced lining, marked "Nakara" ... **450.00**
5" d, 5-3/4" h, egg crate, white ground interspersed with irregular panels surrounded by lavender enamel, heavily dec with whit and tan daisies and forget-me-nots, tan stems and leaves, ornate metal fittings and clasp, orig lining, unmarked............. **1,000.00**
5-1/8" l, 3" h, oval, pale yellow ground shading to white, blue, gray, and white daisies and buds on lid, orig clasp, partial orig lining, marked "Wavecrest"...... **325.00**
5-1/4" l, oval, hp lilies, red Kelva mark **650.00**
5-1/4" d, 3-3/4" h, Bishop's Hat, butterscotch and yellow shaded to white solid ground, 13 blue, gray, white, and magenta azalea flowers and buds, good metal fittings and clasp, no lining, marked "Nakara"............... **450.00**
5-1/2" d, Baroque Shell, pink daisies in medallion, enamel beading, lined, marked **675.00**
5-1/2" d, 3-1/4" h, crystal, Helmschmeid Swirl, pale translucent green, enameled leaves, ribbons, large raised flower on cov................. **225.00**
5-1/2" d, 3-1/2" h, Bishop's Hat shape, gray-blue ground, pink and purple floral dec, orig lining, stamped "C.F.M. Co. Nakara" **425.00**
6" d, courting couple, sgd "Nakara" **1,050.00**
6" d, 3-1/2" h, round, mottled blue ground, six pink, yellow, and pale green Shasta daisies, worn orig lining in lid only clasp missing, marked "Kelva" **350.00**
6" d, 3-1/2" h, round, mottled green ground, seven large pink and white flowers, green and yellow centers, good metal trim and clasp, plating slightly worn, no lining, marked "Kelva" **400.00**
6" d, 3-1/2" h, round, scenic, peach colored ground, lavender panels, courting couple scene on lid, blue floral dec on base, orig clasp, replaced lining, marked "Nakara" **1,000.00**
6" d, 4-1/2" h, swirl, white satin ground, beige lily of the valleys enamel dec, green leaves, brown highlights, orig clasp, orig lining, three small burst bubbles, unmarked............. **225.00**
6-1/4" d, Swirl, pink ground, hp forget-me-nots, orig lining, marked **675.00**
6-1/2" d, 4-1/4" h, Swirl pattern, crystal, holly leaves and berries dec, irid int., marked "C. F. Monroe" **700.00**
6-1/2" d, 4-1/2" h, Bishop's Hat, shaded green to pale pink round, large central pink and white rose with bud on top, surrounded by pale green frame, white beading, pale green and white beading on base, some wear to beading, tiny chip on top edge, no lining, no clasp, marked "Nakara" ... **650.00**
6-1/2" d, 4-1/2" h, octagonal, soft mint green ground, darker green overlaid shadow flowers, white beading, pink and white azalea flowers on lid, orig clasp, partial orig lining, marked "Wavecrest" **700.00**
6-3/4" d, 4-1/8" h, relief molded pinwheel cov, enameled egrets in flight with sunset in background, gilt enameled scrolled border dec, hinged brass mounting on gilt and enameled floral dec box, acid finished opalescent glass, pink, green, and peach shading, marked "Nakara," late 19th/early 20th C, small area of gilt loss ... **1,265.00**
6-3/4" d, 5-1/4" h, egg crate, glossy chocolate brown shaded to beige and rust ground, heavily enameled white and green lupine flowers, fancy ormolu trim with clasp and feet, unmarked **1,100.00**
7" d, 3-3/4" h, Baroque Shell, glossy forest green ground, heavy overall gold spatter dec, top cartouche of Gibson-type girl portrait, fancy Victorian dress, beaded hat outlined in lavender enamel, good metal, trim, and clasp, no lining, marked "Wavecrest" **1,000.00**
7" d, 4" h, round, irid crystal, holly dec, Cohen, page 51 ..... **750.00**
7" d, 4" h, shaded green, peach, light burgundy, yellow shaded ground, small enameled white flowers outlined in lavender with gold raised scroll work, pale blue top cartouche with nine storks in flight, shades of white, gray, and black, red beaks and feet, orig work lining, small burst bottom near bottom rim............ **3,700.00**
7" d, 4" h, swirl, glossy dark green ground, pink and white roses with

green leaves, which dotting, outlined in lavender enamel, no lining, unmarked......... **700.00**

7-1/4" d, 3-3/4" h, Baroque Shell, raised pink-gold rococo shells, fancy Arabic pale turquoise dec, opaque white ground, lace-like network of hundreds of precisely placed raised white enamel beads, shiny metal work, satin lining missing............... **1,450.00**

8" d, 3-3/4" h, strong mottled green ground, large enameled pink, white, and yellow poppies on bas and lid, orig trim and clasp, no lining, marked "Kelva" **600.00**

8" d, 4" h, Burmese colored ground shading from pink to yellow, large enameled pale blue and white flowers, minor bead wear, good metal trim and clasp, partial orig lining, marked "Nakara" . . **1,000.00**

8" l, 4-1/2" w, 3-1/2" h, oval, shaded tan to white ground, small blue and white asters, orig lining, marked "Wavecrest" **850.00**

Cake box, cov, 3-1/2" h, 7-1/2" d, glossy dark green ground, pink enameled florals on base, six large blown-out flowers on lid in soft pink and white, yellow centers, lavender enamel trim, orig trim and clasp, marked "Wavecrest"............... **2,150.00**

Cigar band box, 3-3/4" d, 2-1/2" h, crystal ground, cigar bands with various dec, missing glass liner over orig paper liner, replaced royal blue cloth lining **1,250.00**

Cigar holder, 3-3/4" h, 4" d, white ground, blue forget-me-nots, yellow leaves, beaded centers, metal handled rim, metal base ftd base, unmarked **250.00**

Cologne bottle, 5-3/4" h, 2-1/8" w, glossy white ground, transfer dec of pink flowers, green and brown leaves, unmarked **650.00**

Comb and brush holder, 4-1/2" h, 9" at widest point, white ground shading to pink, blue and purple enameled aster type flowers, marked "Wavecrest," minor wear to floral dec on top panel **2,100.00**

Collars and cuff box

7" d, 7-1/2" h, white shading to tan ground, ornate raised scroll work, "Collars & Cuffs" in pink and gold enamel, lid dec of dark and light pink chrysanthemum flowers, small pink daisies and leaves, sgd "Wavecrest" **1,100.00**

Dresser jar, flowers decoration, silk lining, 4-1/4" d, 3-1/2" h, **$250.** *Photos courtesy of Joy Luke Fine Art Brokers and Auctioneers.*

8" d, pink and white florals, sgd "Nakara," clasp missing, Cohen 145 .... **1,200.00**

8" d, 3-3/4" h, pale green shading to gray and pink, cover cartouche with full length portrait of Queen Louise in red and white robe surrounded by white dotting and apple blossoms, flowers to continue to base, metal trim and clasp, replaced lining, unmarked Nakara............... **2,100.00**

8" d, 6-1/4" h, Swirl pattern base and lid, shaded white to soft pink, enameled gray and green leaves, pink and white forget me not flowers, metal bottom, metal feet, trim, and clasp, no lining. . . **700.00**

8" d, 6-3/4" h, Spindrift, soft pink ground shading to white, ornate lavender and pink pansy dec, green shaded leaves, metal fittings with orig clasp, orig peach satin lining **2,500.00**

Clock, 14" h, 7" w, ornate metal case, bottom glass panel of two cherubs wrapped in blue and red cloth, identical clock face plate and save Wavecrest finial with blue and gray floral dec, non-working Waterbury Clock, orig key **1,950.00**

Cracker jar, cov

7-1/4" h, 5" w, swirl shape, satin finish blank, shades from white to powder blue, white beading in panels, enameled white and gray pond lilies with tiny pink blossoms, green leaves, fancy silver plated metal trim, ornate twisted handle, unmarked **400.00**

7-3/4" h, 5-1/2" w, white satin ground shading to yellow and peach, overall quarter moon dec, yellow, pink, and gray accented with brown and peach enameling, white dotting, one small rubbed int. spot, unmarked.............. **200.00**

8" h, glossy, center panel flanked by three smaller panels, transfer floral dec, silver plated mount and lid, minor wear to transfer, poor re-plating starting to peel. . **100.00**

8" h, satin, light blue and white, square body with scroll panels, transfer daisy dec, silver plated mouth, lid, and bail handle, wear to blue, very worn silver..... **160.00**

8-1/2" h, 4-1/2" d, hand painted multicolored floral dec, silver plated collar, bail handle, and cover **375.00**

10-1/2" h, 6" d, barrel shape, green-blue ground, yellow emb crests, hp yellow and brown wild roses, leaves, and stems, silver-plated cover and handle **675.00**

11-1/4" h, 5" w, square, four sides with blown-out dec, pink roses and buds, leaves, medium blue ground, emb metal hardware, sgd "Wave Crest" in pink banner..... **675.00**

Creamer

2-1/2" h, pink shaded to white, floral transfer dec, nickel plated mount and spiral handle, wear to nickel **30.00**

3-1/2" h, Erie Twist, rose transfer dec, silver plated mount........ **90.00**

Creamer and sugar, cov

3" h, light blue shading to white, cupid transfer dec, twisted handles, transfer on sugar lighter in color..................**110.00**

3-1/4" h x 3-1/4" w creamer, 3" h x 4" sugar, Swirl, white ground, blue and white enameled forget me nots on stems, leaves, silver plated trim on both, unmarked....... **350.00**

3-3/8" h creamer, 5-1/2" h cov sugar, Helmschmeid Swirls, line of white enamel dots separates which upper portion of eight swirls from pastel-tan lower section, rose garland, single-petaled pink blossoms, shiny silver plated rims, handle, and cov......... **750.00**

Dresser jar

4" d, 2-7/8" h, blown-out shell on lid, pale green and white, hand panted floral dec, sgd banner bark **280.00**

4" d, 3" h, blown-out shell on lid, light blue and white, hand painted floral dec, sgd banner mark **230.00**

4" l, 4-3/4" w, sq, clear frosted box, shell type pattern, lavender enameled flowers, green leaves, brass fittings and clasp, marked 175.00

4-1/8" l, 2-3/4" h, oblong, molded cartouche design, sage green, hand-painted waterscape with two boats and cattails, transfer cupid design, waterscape repeated on base, sgd with two line mark, light wear................... 260.00

4-1/4" d, 3-7/8" h, ftd, blown-out shell on lid, light blue and white, dainty hand-painted floral dec, sgd banner mark, corrosion on foot 240.00

4-1/2" d, 2-7/8" h, Helmschmied Swirl, white, hand-painted floral dec 260.00

5-1/2" d, 3-1/4" h, Baroque Shell, sage green, hand-painted daisy dec, orig satin lining, minor wear 325.00

7" d, Helmschmied Swirl, pink forget-me-nots on cov and front of base, hint of pale blue to swirls, replaced make-shift hinge pin 200.00

7" d, 4" h, Helmschmied Swirl, buff, dainty hand-painted blue and white floral dec, light wear 525.00

Dresser jar, flowers decoration, metal frame, four brass feet, silk lining, 5-1/2" d, 4" h, **$395.**

Ewer

14-1/2" h, fishing scene, unmarked 110.00

16" h, blue ground, melon ribbed, courting scene, unmarked, pr 250.00

Fernery

6-1/4" d, 3-1/2" h, light blue with white panels, hand-painted floral dec, sgd banner mark, liner missing 230.00

7" d, 2-1/2" h, pale blue, swirled, yellow flowers, unmarked .. 150.00

Flask, 6" h, 3" w at shoulder, white ground, hand-painted blue flowers and green leaves, brown stems, minor wear to dec, unmarked 150.00

Frame, 6-1/2" h

Embossed, soft yellow ground, hp pink roses, ormolu rim, marked 500.00

Puffy, cream ground, pink wild roses, marked................ 475.00

Glove box, cov, 9-1/2" l, 5-3/4" w, 5-1/2" h, white shaded to yellow ground, central dec of two large enameled pink, ivory, and white roses, green and pink leaf trim, ormolu feet, orig worn lining, orig locking device 1,550.00

Humidor

3-3/4" h, 2-7/8" w, powder blue ground, small pink and white enameled florals, "Cigarettes" written in lavender enamel, rare transfer scene of Niagara Falls and floral enamel on top, orig clasp, marked "Wavecrest"...... 900.00

4-3/4" h, 3-3/4" w, white satin ground, orange swags, tiny pink roses, "Tobacco" enameled in black, brass trim, unmarked..... 400.00

5" h, 3-1/2" w, pale green ground, enamel dec on front, back, and lid, small blue forget me nots with white beading, green leaves, "Tobacco" enameled in purple on front, good trim, orig clasp, marked "Wavecrest" 450.00

5" h, 3-1/2" w, round, mottled green ground, 11 orange poppies and buds, "Cigars" enameled in purple on front, clasp missing, marked "Kelva" 500.00

5" h, 4-1/2" w, "The Old Sport," glossy white, russet and brown ground, transfer dec of bulldog and mug, monogrammed silver plated lid with two figural pipes, unmarked.............. 450.00

5" h, 6-1/2" w, egg crate, glossy white ground, allover profuse floral and leaf dec, white enamel with russet, lavender, green, and gray, pink enameled "Cigars" on lid, removable pate and clasp missing, unmarked.............. 650.00

5-1/2" h, soft green and pink florals, marked "Nakara" 975.00

5-1/2" h, 6" w, inverted bear shaped body shading dark to light green, whimsical owl perched on tree branch, orig brass lid, marked "Nakara"............. 1,300.00

5-1/2" h, 6-1/4" w, transfer portrait of Indian chief in head dress, white enameled bead work, shaded green to tan ground, orig brass lid, some wear to beading, marked "Nakara" 1,500.00

5-3/4" h, 6-1/4" w, green ground shades to pin, seven enameled pink, white, and pale green flowers, word "Tobacco" enameled in lavender and gold, marked "Nakara" 900.00

5-3/4" h, 6-1/2" w, solid blue shading to ivory ground, seven pink and white chrysanthemum flowers, int. shelf for sponge, clasp missing, marked "Nakara"....... 1,300.00

6" h, 4-1/4" w, blown-out shell lid, pink shaded to white ground, all over blue and lavender daisies with white enamel and green and gray leaves, "Cigars" on front, marked "Wavecrest"............ 850.00

6" h, 5" w, blown-out mold, brilliant glossy cobalt blue ground, blown out floral lid, allover dec of pink chrysanthemums, green leaves, lavender enamel highlights and word "Cigars," minor wear to purple enamel scroll work, no key, marked "Wavecrest" 1,650.00

6-1/4" h, 4-1/4" w, barrel-shaped opaque body, shading yellow to russet ground, portrait of monk smoking cigar, pipe on reverse, dec both transfer printed and hand painted, some wear to dec, loose fitting cover, unmarked Nakara 350.00

8-3/4" h, blue body, single-petaled pink rose, pink "Cigar" signature, pewter collar, bail, and lid, flame-shaped finial, sgd "Kelva" 685.00

Jar, cov, 5" h, 6" w, melon ribbed, swirl and "Souvenir" on lid, off-white ground, blue and rust daisy-type flowers, white lettering on lid, unmarked 325.00

Jewel stand, 4" d, 3" h, green and white ground, scroll design, pink floral dec, unmarked.................. 90.00

Jewel tray, 3-1/2" d, egg crate . 145.00

Lamp

Banquet, 13-1/2" h to top of collar, buff to light brown ground, paneled font with emb cartouche chain below, design repeated on stem, hand painted multicolored floral dec, sgd in reverse with Wave Crest two line mark under font, brass connectors, open work foot, wear to dec............. 160.00

Boudoir, 7" h, 3-1/4" h x 2-1/2" w glass stem, blue shaded to white glass stem with pink and gray enamel forget-me-not dec, wear to brass plating and cord, unmarked, pr **500.00**

Table, 31" h, 9" h x 9" w shade with glossy white shaded to beige ground, large pink and blue chrysanthemum dec, green leaves surrounded by lavender enamel scrolls and dots, white beaded top rim, heavily emb brass font and base, ornate reticulated scroll work and lions heads and human faces on foot, font and base connected by green onyx stem, has been electrified, but not drilled . . **950.00**

Letter holder, 5-1/2" l, 4" h, puffy, metal top rim, white ground with pink, lavender, and blue flowers, white enameled centers, minor wear to white beading, int. burst bubble, unmarked **200.00**

Memo file, 7" h, 3-1/8" w, eight-sided white body, small blue forget-me-not enamel dec, orig brass finish figures, unmarked **450.00**

Mustard jar, cov

Burmese shaded ground, yellow to pink with gray, yellow, white, and green daisies, green leaves, hinged cover with slot for spoon, marked "Nakara" **350.00**

Green ground, floral dec, matching spoon, unmarked **140.00**

White ground shaded to yellow, three colored fern dec, unmarked **100.00**

Paperweight, 3-1/4" d, 1-1/4" h, white octagonal weight, metal fittings, small blue forget me nots and leaves, unmarked, brass fittings show wear **600.00**

Perfume bottle

4-1/2" h, 3-1/2" w, white ground, pink transfer roses, small yellow flower, cloth bulb cover worn, unmarked **275.00**

4-3/4" h, white satin ground, blue, and pink enameled flowers, green leaves, metal fitting, no bulb, marked "Wavecrest". **225.00**

Pickle castor, 5-1/2" h, white ground, floral dec, fork holder on both sides of SP holder, unmarked. **150.00**

Pin cushion, 1-1/2" h, 4" w, white shading to green ground, rococo mold, small pink and purple daisies, orig metal trim, brown velvet cushion, marked "Wavecrest" **200.00**

Pin dish, open

3-1/2" d, 1-1/2" h, pink and white, swirled, floral dec, unmarked **35.00**

3-3/4" d, Sunbonnet Baby, marked **250.00**

4-1/4" d, 2" h, pink and white, eggcrate mold, blue violets dec, marked **80.00**

5" d, 1-1/2" h, white, scrolls, pink floral dec, marked **80.00**

Pin tray

3" d, 1" h, Egg Crate, dainty hand painted floral dec, openwork tab handles **50.00**

4-1/2" d, 1-5/8" h, Helmschmied Swirl, buff, hand-painted floral dec **80.00**

5" l, 4-1/2" w, molded opal glass, pale pink and green flowers, ftd, brass ormolu base with handle and leaves, sgd "Wavecrest" . . . **600.00**

Plaque, hanging

8" w, 10" h, satin ground, shaded pale pink to white, pink and russet nasturtium flowers, green, blue, and russet leaves, numerous small buds, 16" h x 9" orig frame, orig back and chips **3,000.00**

8" x 10-1/2", landscape with trees, rocks, and mountains in background, green border, orig fancy metal frame, marked "C. F. Monroe" **5,000.00**

Plate, 7" d, reticulated border, pond lily dec, shaded pale blue ground. . **750.00**

Playing card holder, 4" w, 1-1/4" d, 2-1/2" h, satin finish background shades from white to pale blue, pink roses dec, small edge chip covered by metal rim, marked "Wavecrest," Cohen, pg 74 middle **300.00**

Ring box, cov, 2-1/2" d, 2-1/4" h

Shaded green ground, portrait on cover of Victorian lady, worn orig lining, marked "Nakara" . **1,000.00**

White ground, pink flowers with green leaves on lid, dec worn, marked "Wavecrest" **175.00**

Salt and pepper shakers, pr

Cylinder, glossy white and beige ground, pink, brown, and green aster type dec, orig screw-on pewter caps with agitators, 4" h, 1-1/2" w, unmarked **80.00**

Shape No. 6, blue and white ground, fox and hound dec **75.00**

Square, glossy white and pink ground, blue aster dec, 2-3/4" h, 1-1/4" w, damage to one metal cov, unmarked **200.00**

Square, swirling panels of yellow, tan, and blue, blue and lavender forget-me-nots, orig pewter lids, 2-1/4" h, 1-3/4" h, unmarked **150.00**

Swirl and Bulge, yellow shading to white, floral transfer dec, 2-3/4" h **200.00**

Swirled, light yellow ground, floral dec, unmarked. **75.00**

Thumbprint, opalware, worn floral dec, 2-1/8" h. **45.00**

Tulip, brown and white ground, birds and floral dec. **60.00**

Tulip, white opaque shading to yellow, hand-painted floral dec, 2-1/2" h, dec very worn **40.00**

Salt, open, 1-1/8" h, 3" w, pale green ground, small pink and white enameled flowers, white beaded rim, sgd "Nakara" **325.00**

Spooner, 4-1/4" h, Erie Twist, rose transfer dec. **225.00**

Sugar bowl, cov

Erie Twist, rose transfer dec, silver plated mounts and lid, 4-1/4" h, wear to silver **125.00**

Glossy, cupid transfer dec, nickel plated lid, spiral bail handle, wear to transfer. **50.00**

Glossy shaded tan to white ground, transfer dec of blue bird sitting on fence entwined with blue flowers, silver-plated bail and lid, 2" h, 4" w, unmarked. **100.00**

Swirl, hp white and blue florals, marked. **375.00**

Sugar shaker

2-1/2" h, Erie Twist, hand-painted pansy dec **110.00**

3" h, Helmschmeid Swirls, cream ground, blue and lavender violets, marked. **425.00**

3" h, 3-1/4" d, 8 Helmschmied Swirls, creamy pink ground, hp Johnny Jump-Up sprigs, SP metal cov with emb blossoms and leaves. **585.00**

3" h, 3-1/4" d, Helmschmeid Swirls, pale lime-yellow ground, pastel pink rococo swags, raised gold borders, tendrils of gray blossoms rising from base of each of eight swirls, metal lid with emb florals and rococo swags **585.00**

5" h, Draped Column, opalware, skirt dec with shaded background, hand-painted floral dec, replaced lid, wear to dec **60.00**

5" h, 2-3/4" w, teepee shape, glossy white ground, blue daisies, green, and gray leaves, brass plated lid **125.00**

Sweetmeat jar, open

1-3/4" h, 4" w, handled, six-sided base, painted Burmese shading from yellow to pink, blue enamel flowers, white enameled scroll work, fancy brass plated rim and bail handle, minute wear to enamel dots, marked "Nakara" **200.00**

3-3/4" h, 7" w, Belle Ware, textured crystalline finish, white and pale pink ground, pink roses and buds, wear to silver plated trim, marked "Belle Ware" **350.00**

Syrup pitcher

Draped Column, opalware, skirt with shaded background, hand-painted floral dec, metal lid, 6" h ... **260.00**

Helmschmied Swirl, ivory colored body, blue and white floral dec, smoky-gray leafy branches, SP lid and collar **485.00**

Toothpick holder, 2" d, 2-1/8" h, straight sided, solid white, pink apple blossoms, green leaves, gold trim around top, white beaded edge, unmarked **300.00**

Tray

4" w, 4-1/2" h, pale blue and white ground, pink and yellow blossoms, white enamel dottings, orig beveled mirror, replaced lining, marked "Wavecrest" **500.00**

5" w, 1-7/8" h, mottled orange ground, purple violet dec, gold finished fancy metal trim, replaced lining, marked "Kelva"..... **250.00**

6" w, 2-1/4" h, round, shaded green ground, pink, white, and yellow chrysanthemums, small burst bubble on int. rim, minor int. scratching, marked "Nakara" **150.00**

Trinket dish, 1-1/2" x 5", blue and red flowers **175.00**

Urn, 15-1/2" h, 4-1/2" w, baluster shape, center shades from ivory to pale blue, heavily dec in brown, tan, green, pink, and white phlox-type flowers and tiny brown ferns, ornate emb brass finish base with gargoyle heads, ornate spouts and handles with emb heads and phoenix-type bird, unmarked, pr **600.00**

Vase

4" h, 4" w, bulbous, mottled pale blue and white ground, front panel of three pink flowers with white beading outlined in purple, white beaded rim, marked "Belle Ware" **450.00**

4-3/4" h, 3-1/4" w, two handles, shaded white to pale green body, orange daisies on front and back, gold finish metal mounts, marked "Wavecrest" **300.00**

5" h, 1-3/4" w, pale blue ground, white oval panels, small pink flowers and green leaves, ormolu foot and rim, unmarked ... **300.00**

6-1/8" h, 2-1/2" w, white ground, small enamel pink and blue flowers outlined in purple, bright metal trim, unmarked.............. **200.00**

6-1/8" h, 3-1/4" w, pale white ground, front and back panels of blue forget-me-nots framed by lavender enamels, metal mountings, unmarked.............. **300.00**

8" h, 3" w, mottled pink ground, nine blue, white, and gray flowers with white enameled centers, pink beaded top rim, plain glass base, marked "Kelva," price for matched pr **800.00**

8" h, 3-1/2" w, dark green mottled ground, seven pink and yellow lilies, buff trim at base, plain brass rim, marked "Kelva" **350.00**

8-1/2" h, baluster form, opal, mottled blue ground, pink blossoms, gold scrolls, silver plated foot, red "Kelva Trade/Mark" on base **490.00**

9-3/4" h, 3" w at shoulder, fancy emb mold, front and back with soft pink and blue pansies, white dotting, top beaded rim, small enclosed bubble on base, unmarked **250.00**

Vase, flowers decoration, molded shell at base, four metal feet, 6-1/2" h, **$485.**

10" h, pale pink accents on white, pink and orange chrysanthemums, enameled foliage, beaded white top.................... **600.00**

12" h, deep green ground, pink and purple poppy dec, marked "C. F. Monroe Kelva," presently mounted as lamp **225.00**

12" h, white daisies on shaded maroon ground, white dec and light pink shell motif, ornate gilt mounted handles and base...... **2,240.00**

12" h, 7-1/2" w, dark green mottled ground, five central roses surrounded by smaller flowers and buds, metal mounts, unmarked Kelva................ **2,500.00**

12-1/2" h, 4-1/4" w, yellow shaded to russet ground, three large lavender and white iris blossoms, round top, flaring to six-sided base resting on four metal feet, unmarked Nakara **900.00**

Watch box, cov, 3-3/4" w, 2-1/2" h, round, soft blue ground, cov dec with two cupids framed by panels with white beading, clasp missing, partial orig lining, marked "Nakara" **400.00**

Whisk broom holder, shaded white to ivory ground, enameled pink, lavender, blue, and butterscotch pansies with white enamel beading, outlined in lavender enamel, ormolu trim, orig satin lining.................. **2,100.00**

Webb, Thomas & Sons

History: Thomas Webb & Sons was established in 1837 in Stourbridge, England. The company probably is best known for its very beautiful English cameo glass. However, many other types of colored art glass were produced, including enameled, iridescent, heavily ornamented, and cased.

References: Victor Arwas, *Glass Art Nouveau to Art Deco*, Rizzoli International Publications, Inc., 1977; Sean and Johanna S. Billings, *Peachblow Glass, Collector's Identification & Price Guide*, Krause Publications, 2000; Ray and Lee Grover, *English Cameo Glass*, Crown Publishers, Inc., 1980; Charles R. Hajdamach, *British Glass, 1800–1914*, Antique Collectors' Club, 1991; Albert C. Revi, *Nineteenth Century Glass*, reprint, Schiffer Publishing, 1981.

Basket

6" d, 5-1/2" h, Mat So No-Ke, crimped-in rose bowl form, four applied crystal handles, eight trailing crystal leaves and flowers, three applied ball crystal feet, applied crystal raspberry, English registration number RD15353 .... **400.00**

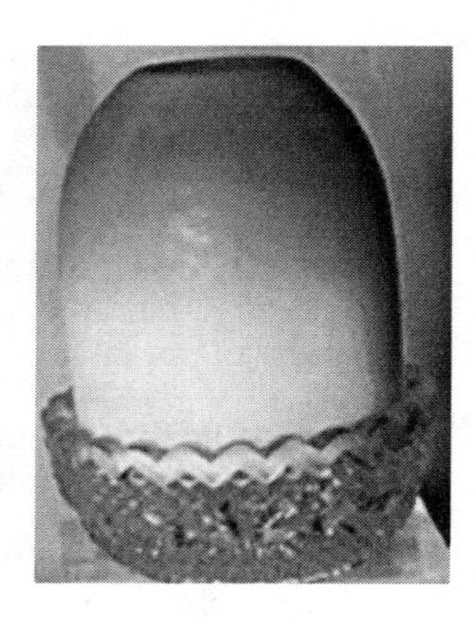
Fairy Lamp, Burmese shade, clear glass base, candle insert signed "S. Clarke's Pyramid Fairy," 3-3/4" h, **$335.** *Photo courtesy of Clarence and Betty Maier.*

8" l, 6-1/2" h, diamond quilted patterned body, vaseline opalescent shading to pink, petal edge, twisted pink handle, c1890 . . . . **265.00**

Beverage set, 11-3/4" h x 6" w pitcher, four 3-3/4" tumblers, pale cream ext., brilliant cranberry cased int., large cranberry loop handle, white, yellow, and magenta roses and leaves dec **875.00**

Bottle, 5-1/4" h, cameo, round cylindrical vial, yellow ground, white overlay, cameo cut and carved leafy spray of blossoms, two flying insects, double linear borders, hallmarked silver cov. **800.00**

Bowl

3" w, 2-1/2" h, tricorn, shaded brown satin, gold prunus blossoms and butterfly dec, creamy int., gold trim **345.00**

5-1/2" w, 5" h, tricorn, Rainbow mother-of-pearl satin, deep pink, yellow, blue, and white, applied thorn feet, raspberry prunt, sgd "Patent" **1,500.00**

5-3/4" d, 4-1/2" h, avocado green, sapphire blue stripes, mica flakes, crystal applied fancy drippings on sides, applied crystal rigaree around top edge, applied clear feet, clear berry pontil **235.00**

10" d, 3-3/4" h, deep rose shading to pink to white ground, diamond quilted patterned body, mother-of-pearl satin, box pleated top, applied solid frosted base **775.00**

Bride's basket, 10" d, diamond quilted patterned body, mother-of-pearl satin, pink ground, ruffled edge, metal base, sgd **400.00**

Cologne bottle, 6" h, cameo, spherical, clear frosted body, overlaid white and red, carved blossoms, buds, leafy stems, and butterfly, linear pattern, hallmarked silver dec, molded and chased blossoms dec **3,200.00**

Compote, 6-1/2" d, 2" h, Alexandrite, ruffled rim, honeycomb molded bowl, shaded brilliant blue-purple to pink to amber, applied amber pedestal and foot **2,000.00**

Cream pitcher

3-1/4" h, sepia to pale tan ground, heavy gold burnished prunus blossoms, butterfly on back, gold rim and base, clear glass handle with brushed gold **385.00**

3-3/4" h, 2-1/2" d, bulbous, round mouth, brown satin, cream lining, applied frosted handle **210.00**

Cup and saucer, 3-1/2" d cup, 4-7/8" d saucer, Alexandrite, moiré ridged, molded handless cup, shading from blue to pink to yellow **1,200.00**

Ewer, 9" h, 4" d, satin, deep green shading to off-white, gold enameled leaves and branches, 3 naturalistic applies, applied ivory handle, long spout, numbered base **425.00**

Flower holder, 12-1/2" l, 8-3/4" w, gold irid glass foot, brass leaves and branches, four irid gold ribbed flower shaped vases **550.00**

Jar, cov, 5" d, blue, diamond quilted patterned body, mother-of-pearl satin, berries dec, silver plated hallmarked collar, lid, and bail handle **475.00**

Perfume bottle, 4-1/4" h, undulating body, yellow overlaid in white, cut and carved as swimming dolphin, inscribed registry mark, "Rd. 18100," rim and cap missing **4,950.00**

Pitcher, 8-3/4" h, 8-1/2" w, deep rose to pale pink peachblow type satin glass body, creamy white int., white and yellow enamel floral dec, green leaves, gold stems, applied frosted loop handle **200.00**

Rose bowl

2-3/4" h, 3-1/2" d, deep rose, ground pontil, shiny signature "Patent" **385.00**

3-3/4" d, blue swirled mother-of-pearl satin, green satin glass leaf-shaped base **250.00**

6-1/4" d, 5-1/4" h, brown shading to yellow to cream satin, creamy white int., box pleated top, sic crimps **350.00**

Salt, master, frosted, Adam and Eve, butterfly signature. **80.00**

Scent bottle, 1-1/4" h, 4-1/4" l, lay down, gold prunus blossoms, green shaded to yellow satin ground, hallmarked sterling silver domed monogrammed cap. **425.00**

Toothpick holder, Alexandrite, ruffled edge **1,100.00**

Tray, 12" l, clamshell, shaded pink over white, enameled butterfly and floral, acid script sgd "Webb" **300.00**

Vase

3-1/2" h, 5-1/2" w, pocket type, Flower and Acorn pattern, bridal white, mother-of-pearl satin, gold flowers and leaves **650.00**

4-1/4" h, Alexandrite, white body, optic honeycomb dec, gentle flare from shoulder to short neck, pie crusted sapphire blue crimped rim **1,250.00**

4-3/4" h, White Burmese, creamy-white body, allover rosy glow int., sepia-colored Oriental motif drawings, floral branch sweeps across, two small panels in center, one with cottage scene, other with bird in flight, line drawing of two happy birds on reverse, sepia line accents at rim and base **485.00**

5" h, 6" w, 18" circumference, shaded blue, sky blue to pale white cream, applied crystal edge, enameled gold and yellow dec of flowers, leaves, and buds, full butterfly, entire surface acid-cut in basketweave design **425.00**

5-1/4" h, 3-1/2" d, opaque ivory, cut leaves and berries, brown staining, circular cameo mark on base "Simulated Ivory English Cameo Glass," hallmarked silver rim and frosted ball feet **625.00**

Vase, orange cased satin glass, 4" h, **$400.** *Photo courtesy of Joy Luke Fine Art Brokers and Auctioneers.*

5-1/2" h, transparent yellow, wheel cut and frosted pond lilies and leaves, acid stamped "Webb-Made in England" **130.00**
6-1/2" h, heat reactive amber to rose, cream lining, white overlay, cameo cut wild geraniums and grasses, top rim possibly ground, unsigned **1,200.00**
6-7/8" h, peachblow, acid finish, deep cream lining, shaded rose to cream, heavy gold daisies and leaves, large gold dragonfly on back **675.00**
7" h, cased, deep ruby over white, gold Art Deco thistle, propeller trademark **385.00**
7" h, gourd-shaped body, butterscotch yellow shaded to turquoise blue, cased to opal white, outer layer etched and carved as five-petaled rose on front, ornamental grasses on back, linear borders above and below **1,955.00**
7" h, 4" d, satin, robin's egg blue, leaves, berries, and vines dec, flowing gold and scroll design, white lining **450.00**
7" h, 5" w, basketweave patterned body, mother-of-pearl satin, bulbous base shading from deep blue to pale blue, creamy lining **750.00**
7-1/4" h, 4" w at shoulder, Rainbow mother-of-pearl satin, pink, yellow, blue, and white, diamond quilted patterned body, flaring top, broad shoulder, tapered body, glossy white int., sgd "Patent" .. **1,250.00**
7-1/4" h, Japonesque, pale oval heat reactive body, white Burmese to pink at top, overall delicate oriental sepia scenes............ **345.00**

Vase, cameo, narrow neck, bulbous base, cameo cut white chrysanthemum blossoms and foliage, peach ground, signed with dragonfly, 7-1/4" h, ***$900.*** *Photo courtesy of Freeman/Fine Arts of Philadelphia, Inc.*

7-1/2" h, 5-5/8" d, shaded orange overlay, off-white lining, gold flowers and fern-like leaves, gold butterfly on back, applied bronze-colored glass handles **255.00**
8" h, 4" w, satin, pink and white stripes, fancy frilly top, bulbous base, unlined **425.00**
8-1/2" h, cased, pink shading to white, enameled floral swags and gold scrolling, three ball feet, acid script sgd "Webb" **175.00**
8-1/2" h, 4" w, cased, deep peach pink ext., creamy white lining, dec with spring flowers, blue, pink and white daisies, enameled gold, leaf and branch, pulled down tops with blue and gold enameled dec, pr **200.00**
9" h, white opaque over yellow wash, enameled florals and scrolls, acid black letter sgd "Webb"... **250.00**
9-3/4" h, cameo, tricolor, broad citron yellow oval body, overlaid in bright Webb red and opal white, cameo etched and carved blossoms on leafy stems, wild grasses at sides, stepped and angular borders, base circular mark "Thos. Webb & Sons Cameo".......... **4,600.00**
10" h, Old Ivory, six floral designed cartouches set among bamboo leaves and stalks, applied scale covered handles at each side, intricate borders above and below, semicircular mark "Thomas Webb & Sons," design attributed to George Woodall........ **3,000.00**
10" h, 4" w, satin, pulled down edges, deep rose shading to pink, creamy lining, ruffled top, dome foot, pr **550.00**
10-1/2" h, gourd shape, satin, bright yellow shading to pale yellow, creamy white lining, bleed-through in pontil................ **285.00**
10-1/2" h, 4" w, bulbous, gold floral prunus blossoms, leaves, branches, pine needles, and insect, satin ground shaded brown to gold, creamy white lining, Jules Barbe dec **450.00**
10-5/8" h, cameo, designed by Ludwig Kny, closed-in rim, tapered body, flared base, colorless glass layered in blue, green, and brown transparent glass, carved Japanese flower blossoms on shoulder, repeating flowers and buds on stem, leaf blades below, polished surface, base inscribed "Murrhina," "TCW," and "Lu Kny," minor scratches **5,100.00**
12-1/4"h, colorless oval body, allover etched surface, raised enameled iris flowers, frosted mallard duck poised for flight, base inscribed "Thomas Webb & Corbett Ltd/Stourbridge England" .. **750.00**

Wine, 5-1/4" h, cranberry cut to clear, fine overlay, faceted teardrop stems, elaborate star bases, three stamped "Webb," set of six............ **650.00**

Westmoreland Glass Company

History: The Westmoreland Glass Company was founded in October 1899 at Grapeville, Pennsylvania. From the beginning, Westmoreland made handcrafted high-quality glassware. During the early years, the company processed mustard, baking powder, and condiments to fill its containers. During World War I, candy-filled glass novelties were popular.

Although Westmoreland is famous for its milk glass, other types of glass products were also produced. During the 1920s, Westmoreland made reproductions and decorated wares. Color and tableware appeared in the 1930s; but, as with other companies, 1935 saw production return primarily to crystal. From the 1940s to the 1960s, black, ruby, and amber objects were made.

In May 1982, the factory closed. Reorganization brought a reopening in July 1982, but the Grapeville plant closed again in 1984.

Collectors should become familiar with the many lines of tableware produced. English Hobnail, made from the 1920s to the 1960s, is popular. Colonial designs were used frequently, and accessories with dolphin pedestals are distinctive.

The trademark, an intertwined "W" and "G," was imprinted on glass beginning in 1949. After January 1983, the full name, "Westmoreland," was marked on all glass products. Early molds were reintroduced. Numbered, signed, dated "Limited Editions" were offered.

References: Tom and Neila Bredehoft, *Fifty Years of Collectible Glass, 1920-1970, Volume 1, Volume II*, Antique Trader Books, 2000; Lorraine Kovar, *Westmoreland Glass*, vols. I and II, The Glass Press, 1991; Hazel Marie Weatherman, *Colored Glassware of the Depression Era, Book 2*, Glassbooks, Inc., 1982; Chas West Wilson, *Westmoreland Glass*, Collector Books, 1996, 1998 value update.

Collectors' Clubs: National Westmoreland Glass Collectors Club, P.O. Box 372, Westmoreland City, PA 15692; Westmoreland Glass Collectors Club, 2712 Glenwood, Independence, 64052; Westmoreland Glass Society, 4809 420th St. SE, Iowa City, IA 52240.

Museum: Westmoreland Glass Museum, Port Vue, PA.

Miscellaneous

Animal, covered dish type

Camel, kneeling, white milk glass 75.00
Cat, blue eyes, white milk glass 75.00
Chick on eggs, iridized 85.00
Fox, brown eyes, lacy base, white milk glass 75.00
Lovebirds, white milk glass, 6-1/2" 40.00
Rooster, standing, white milk glass 50.00
Rooster, wide rib base, blue opaque, marked "I" inside base, 4-1/4" h 30.00
Swan, raised wing, white milk glass 115.00

Animal, covered dish, turkey, gold goofus-type ground, 6-1/4" l, 5-1/4" w, 7" h. 125.00
Ashtray, turtle, crystal. 15.00
Banana split, Colonial, crystal, keystone mark, 7-1/2" 22.00

Basket

Amber, 6" h 95.00
Belgium Blue, 6" h 155.00
Ice Blue, 6" h. 155.00
Pansy, white milk glass 20.00

Bell

Beaded Bouquet, coral, sgd "L. Kemmerer, 1978," 6" h . . 35.00
Mary Gregory, blue mist 45.00

Branch for wrens, white milk glass 25.00
Butter dish, cov, Flute, red 35.00
Candlesticks, pr, Ring & Petal . . 22.00

Candy dish, cov

Argonaut Shell, ruby, orig label. 40.00
Ashburton, white milk glass . . 18.00
Beaded Bouquet, blue milk glass 35.00
Wakefield, crystal, low 45.00

Child's mug, chick, #603, dec, orig label. 30.00

Children's dishes

Creamer, File & Fan, ruby carnival 20.00
Pitcher, Flute, cobalt blue, white floral dec 40.00
Sugar, cov, File & Fan, ruby carnival 30.00
Table set, File & Fan, cov butter, creamer, cov sugar, white milk glass. 45.00
Tumbler, Flute, green, white floral dec 15.00

Cigarette box, turtle, crystal 45.00

Compote

Colonial, dark blue mist, tall, handle 30.00
Lotus, blue frosted, open stem, 6" 18.50
Sawtooth, Golden Sunset, 9" h, 12" w, orig label. 75.00

Creamer and sugar, cov, Swan, white milk glass 70.00
Cruet, Colonial, 2 oz, blue 75.00
Goblet, Colonial, Bermuda Blue . 18.50
Knife, Thumbguard, crystal, dec. 52.00
Pansy basket, white milk glass . . 25.00
Picnic basket, cov, white milk glass 30.00
Pitcher, Colonial, Bermuda Blue . 95.00

Plate

7-1/2" d, Fleur de Lis, white milk glass, hp blue and green parakeets 25.00
9" d, #30, black, wicket border 18.50
10-1/4" d, dinner, #1800 Daisy Decal, dark blue mist, scalloped edge 45.00

Punch cup, Three Fruits, white milk glass. 10.00
Punch set, Fruits, white milk glass, 12 pc set 150.00
Server, two tiers, Forget-Me-Not border, white milk glass 50.00
Slipper, figural, almond milk glass . 20.00
Toothpick holder, Swan, white milk glass. 24.00
Vase, 7" h, horn-shape, Lotus, #9 . 35.00
Water set, 1776 Colonial, amber, flat water pitcher, six goblets, price for seven-pc set. 70.00

Wedding bowl, cov, 10" d

Ruby stained 40.00
White milk glass. 35.00

Patterns

American Hobnail, Pattern #77, white milk glass

Ashtray, 4-1/2" d, round 6.50
Bonbon, cov 25.00
Candleholders, pr, 5" h 30.00
Compote, 6" h, ftd 20.00
Creamer and sugar 22.00
Cup and saucer. 10.00
Goblet 12.50
Mayonnaise, bell rim, ftd 20.00
Puff box, cov 25.00
Rose bowl, cupped, ftd 20.00

Beaded Edge, Pattern #22, white milk glass

Berry bowl, hand-painted fruit center 8.00
Bowl, cov, 9", sq, ftd 50.00

Magazine cover, China, Glass & Tablewares, *November 1964, showing milk glass Sawtooth Bowl,* **$7.50.**

Coupe plate

Center dec with apples . . . 15.00
Center dec with cardinal . . 22.50
Center dec with cherries . . 15.00
Center dec with florals, multicolored. 20.00
Center dec with florals, pink. 15.00
Center dec with grapes . . . 15.00
Center dec with strawberries 15.00

Cup, red apple 15.00
Nappy, 5" d, hand-painted fruit dec 12.00

Plate

6" d. 5.00
7" d, red edge 10.00
10-1/2" d, dinner 20.00

Beaded Grape, Pattern #1884, white milk glass, Golden Sunset

Ashtray

4" d, white milk glass 15.00
5" d, white milk glass 20.00

Bowl, cov

4" d, sq, white milk glass . . 25.00
5" d, flared, white milk glass 55.00
7" d, ftd, white milk glass . . 35.00
9" d, sq, white milk glass . . 55.00

Bowl, open

7" d, Golden Sunset. 30.00
9" w, sq, ftd, white milk glass 55.00

Candlesticks, pr, white milk glass 22.50
Candy dish, cov, 9" d, ftd, white milk glass. 40.00

Compote, open, ftd
7" sq, white milk glass..... **18.00**
9" sq, white milk glass..... **30.00**
Goblet, 8 oz, white milk glass . **30.00**
Honey, cov, 5" d
White milk glass **25.00**
White milk glass, gold fruit dec **35.00**
White milk glass, roses and garland dec **45.00**
Puff box, cov, sq, white milk glass **40.00**
Sugar bowl, cov
Individual size, white milk glass **10.00**
Table size, white milk glass. **15.00**

Bramble/Maple Leaf, Pattern #1928, white milk glass
Bowl, 4-1/2" d, round, ftd..... **25.00**
Compote, crimped, ftd **25.00**
Creamer.................. **15.00**
Rose bowl, 4-1/2" d, ftd...... **25.00**
Sugar.................... **15.00**

Della Robia, candlestick, 2-lite, **$40.**

Della Robbia, Pattern #1058. Made in crystal and crystal with hand applied stained dec
Cake stand, 14-1/4" d
No color **85.00**
Staining on fruit, wear to stain **85.00**
Candlesticks, pr, light luster .. **32.00**
Compote
3-1/4" d, stained dark luster colors **35.00**
6" d, stained **25.00**
Creamer and sugar
Blue.................... **55.00**
Stained **25.00**
Cup and saucer, crystal...... **15.00**
Dish, heart shape, handle, stained **70.00**
Goblet, 8 oz
Dark stain **30.00**
White milk glass **15.00**
Nappy, heart shaped, handle, 8", stained **35.00**
Plate, 14" d, blue and gold... **65.00**
Punch set, cupped punch bowl, 19" d liner, ladle, 10 cups, stained dark luster colors **675.00**
Salad plate, dark stain **22.00**
Salt and pepper shakers, pr, stained **70.00**
Sherbet, 10-3/4" h, light stain . **26.00**
Torte plate, 14" d, light stain . **125.00**
Tumbler
Flat, dark stain, 8 oz...... **28.00**
Footed, blue and gold, 8 oz **27.50**
White milk glass, 6" h..... **22.50**
Wine, 4-5/8" h, white milk glass **17.50**

Dolphin
Bowl, 8-1/2" d, oval, ftd, white milk glass.................. **25.00**
Candlesticks, pr
4" h, cobalt blue.......... **95.00**
4" h, white milk glass **25.00**
9" h, white milk glass **45.00**
Compote, open, ftd
8" d, white milk glass **45.00**
8" d, 7" h, amber **70.00**
Console set, pr 9" h candlesticks, 11" d console bowl, amber. **180.00**
Lamp, #1049/1, amber..... **145.00**

English Hobnail
Basket
5", handle, crystal **20.00**
9" h, ruby, crystal handle .. **60.00**
Bonbon, 6-1/2" l, handle, crystal **19.50**
Bowl
4-3/4" d, crystal **6.00**
6-1/2" d, crystal **18.50**
7-3/4" l, oval, crystal...... **35.00**
9-1/2 d, crimped, white milk glass **25.00**
Butter dish, cov, square, 6", crystal **25.00**
Candy, cov
Amber, cone shape **45.00**
Green, silver worn on finial **25.00**
Ruby stained, crystal lid, cone shape................ **30.00**
White milk glass, cone shape **20.00**
Champagne, round foot, crystal **12.50**
Cheese dish, lid, 6" d, crystal. **40.00**
Cocktail
Round base, crystal, 4-1/2" . **7.50**
Square base, crystal **7.50**
Condiment set, individual size, salt dip, pepper shaper, cruet, tray, white milk glass........... **50.00**
Cordial
Round base, 1 oz, crystal.. **27.50**
Square base, crystal....... **7.50**
Creamer
Flat, crystal.............. **7.50**
Footed, amber **24.00**
Footed, crystal **12.50**
Cruet, orig stopper
Individual size, white milk glass **25.00**
Large size, white milk glass **20.00**
Cup, crystal................ **8.50**
Finger bowl, crystal, 4-3/8" d... **7.00**
Goblet
Round base, crystal, 6-1/8" h **15.00**
Square base, crystal, 6-1/8" h **12.00**
Hat, high, white milk glass.... **10.00**
Ivy ball, #555/2, white milk glass, crimped top, ftd, 6-1/2" h ... **45.00**
Loving cup, two handles, hexagonal foot, 8" h, white milk glass... **35.00**
Marmalade, chrome lid, crystal. **25.00**
Mayonnaise, 6" d, crystal **14.50**
Mustard, cov, spoon, square base, white milk glass........... **25.00**
Nappy, 4" d, white milk glass... **5.00**
Nut dish, Golden Sunset..... **15.00**
Old-fashioned tumbler, 5 oz, crystal **12.50**
Plate
5-1/2" d, round, crystal..... **7.50**
7-1/2" w, square, crystal... **10.00**
8" w, square, crystal **10.00**
8-1/2" w, pink **15.00**
Platter
9-1/2" l, oval, crystal **40.00**
12" l, oval, crystal **42.00**
Salt and pepper shakers, pr
Barrel shape, white milk glass **25.00**
Round base, white milk glass **22.00**
Square base, crystal...... **40.00**
Salt, open, ftd
Golden Sunset **17.50**
Pink.................... **18.00**
Salts bottle, orig stopper, green **50.00**
Sherbet, round foot
Amber.................. **12.50**
Crystal................... **6.00**
Sherbet, square foot, crystal... **8.00**
Sugar
Hexagonal foot, crystal.... **12.50**
Square foot, crystal........ **8.00**

Tumbler
3-3/4" h, square foot, crystal . **6.50**
4-5/8" h, square foot, crystal. **10.00**
5-3/8" h, flat, crystal **15.00**
Whiskey, 2-1/2" h, crystal **15.00**
Wine, square base, 4-1/2" h, crystal **15.00**

Lotus, plate, 8-3/4" d, green **18.50**

Old Quilt, Pattern #500, white milk glass
Bowl
5" d, ftd, flared **30.00**
6" d, ftd, bell shape **32.00**
7-1/2" d, ftd **35.00**
Box, cov, sq **25.00**
Butter dish, cov, 1/4 lb, milk glass **30.00**
Candlesticks, pr, 4" h, milk glass **24.00**
Candy dish, cov, 4-1/2" d, ftd . **25.00**
Celery, ftd **20.00**
Cheese, cov **50.00**
Compote
Cov, antique blue milk glass **35.00**
Open, cupped, 6" d, octagonal foot................. **30.00**
Open, ftd, 7" d, bell shape bowl **26.00**
Creamer
Individual, 3-1/2" **15.00**
Large **38.00**
Cruet, stopper............. **30.00**
Cup and saucer **32.50**
Dinner plate, 10-1/2" d **65.00**
Fruit bowl, 9" d, ftd, crimped, #43 .... **45.00**
Goblet, 8 oz **18.00**
Honey, cov, 5" d **28.00**
Iced tea tumbler, flat, 11 oz .. **20.00**
Juice pitcher, pint, 7-1/2" h ... **35.00**
Juice tumbler **6.00**
Nappy, 5-1/2" d, bell shape .. **25.00**
Pitcher, 8-1/2" h, three pint ... **35.00**
Salt and pepper shakers, pr .. **25.00**
Spooner, 6-1/2" h **28.00**
Sweetmeat, cov, 6" h, ftd **30.00**
Sugar bowl, cov
Large **28.00**
Small **10.00**
Vase, 7" h, ftd, fan.......... **20.00**
Wine **25.00**

Paneled Grape, Pattern #1881, white milk glass, limited production in other colors.
Appetizer canapé set, white milk glass, three pcs, orig labels. **75.00**
Ashtray, sq, 5", white milk glass **45.00**
Basket, 6-1/2" l, oval, white milk glass **30.00**
Bowl, open
4-1/2" d, white milk glass .. **22.00**
5" d, handle, white milk glass **30.00**
6-1/2" l, oval, white milk glass **30.00**
9" d, lipped, ftd, white milk glass **95.00**
9" d, 6" h, ftd, white milk glass **45.00**
9-1/2" d, lip, white milk glass **100.00**
9-1/2" d, scalloped, white milk glass................ **125.00**
10-1/2" d, ftd, white milk glass **100.00**
11" l, oval, lipped, skirted pedestal base, white milk glass **95.00**
Bud vase
9-1/2" h, white milk glass .. **30.00**
10" h, white milk glass, orig label **30.00**
18" h, white milk glass..... **50.00**
Butter dish, cov, 1/4 lb, white milk glass **35.00**
Cake salver, skirted, white milk glass **85.00**
Candelabra, three-lite, white milk glass **245.00**
Candlesticks, pr
Three-lite, white milk glass **285.00**
4" h, white milk glass...... **30.00**
4" h, white milk glass...... **27.50**
5" h, handle, white milk glass **80.00**
Candy dish
Cov, crimped, 8" d, three legs, white milk glass **40.00**
#26, white milk glass...... **30.00**
Celery vase, 6" h, white milk glass **40.00**
Champagne, white milk glass . **35.00**
Cheese dish, cov, white milk glass **60.00**
Chip and dip set, white milk glass **25.00**
Chocolate box, cov, round, white milk glass **50.00**
Cocktail, crystal............ **15.00**
Compote, cov, 7" d Golden Sunset **40.00**
Compote, open, ftd,
6" d, crimped, white milk glass **40.00**
7" d, orig label, white milk glass **20.00**
6" d, 9" d, white milk glass, clear foot **75.00**
Cordial, 3-1/4" h
Crystal **20.00**
White milk glass......... **24.50**
Creamer, 6-1/2 oz, orig label, white milk glass **16.00**
Creamer and sugar on tray, individual size, white milk glass **27.00**
Creamer and sugar, ice blue . **65.00**
Cruet, stopper, white milk glass **40.00**
Cup and saucer, white milk glass **25.00**
Decanter, stopper
Amber **125.00**
White milk glass........ **200.00**
Epergne
10-1/2" d lipped bowl, one vase, cone-shaped foot, white milk glass **295.00**
12" d lipped bowl, 8-1/2" h vase, white milk glass....... **185.00**
Flower pot, white milk glass .. **50.00**
Fruit cocktail, white milk glass **20.00**
Fruit cocktail underplate, white milk glass.................. **9.00**
Goblet, 5-3/4" h, 8 oz, white milk glass.................. **25.00**
Gravy boat and underplate, white milk glass **70.00**
Iced tea tumbler, 12 oz, white milk glass.................. **25.00**
Ivy ball, 7", white milk glass .. **65.00**
Jardinière
5", ftd, white milk glass ... **28.00**
6-1/2" h, ftd, white milk glass **42.00**
Jelly, cov, white milk glass ... **30.00**
Juice pitcher, pint, white milk glass **40.00**
Mayonnaise, three pcs, white milk glass.................. **28.00**
Parfait, crystal............. **25.00**
Pickle dish, white milk glass.. **20.00**
Pitcher
7-3/4" h, white milk glass .. **45.00**
8-1/2" h, white milk glass .. **35.00**
Planter
4-3/4" x 8-3/4", white milk glass **45.00**
5" x 9", white milk glass ... **48.00**
Plate
6" d, white milk glass **17.50**
6-1/2" d, salad, white milk glass **25.00**
8-1/2" d, luncheon, white milk glass **27.50**
10" d, dinner, white milk glass **65.00**
Puff box, cov, white milk glass. **30.00**

Punch bowl base, white milk glass 115.00
Punch cup, white milk glass ..15.00
Punch ladle, #1800, ice lip, white milk glass 98.00
Punch set, white milk glass, red hooks and ladle, 13" d, 15-pc set 595.00
Rose bowl, 4" d, ftd, white milk glass 30.00
Salt and pepper shakers, pr, ftd, white milk glass...........25.00
Sauce boat and underplate, white milk glass 70.00
Saucer, white milk glass 8.50
Sherbet, ftd
- Amethyst...............20.00
- White milk glass 16.00

Spoon holder, cov, white milk glass 40.00
Sugar bowl, cov, lace edge, white milk glass 35.00
Sugar bowl, open
- Individual size, white milk glass 8.00
- Table size, white milk glass. 15.00

Toilet bottle, orig stopper, 5 oz, white milk glass 45.00
Toothpick holder, white milk glass 35.00
Tray
- 9" l, oval, white milk glass . . 75.00
- 13-1/2" l, oval, white milk glass 75.00

Tumbler
- Flat, white milk glass......12.50
- 12 oz, white milk glass 20.00
- 3-3/4" h, crystal..........18.50
- 4-7/8" h, 10 oz, crystal 18.50
- 5-7/8" h, crystal, gold encrusted dec 32.00

Vase
- 6" h, ftd, bell-shape, white milk glass.................15.00
- 9" h, ftd, bell-shape, white milk glass.................40.00
- 15" h, swung-type, white milk glass.................20.00

Wedding bowl, cov, 8", white milk glass, roses and bows dec . . 60.00
Wine, 2 oz, white milk glass. . . 24.50

Princess Feather

Bowl, 5-1/4" d, rolled edge, crystal 15.00
Cocktail, crystal............10.00
Cup and saucer, crystal......12.50
Goblet, six-pc set 150.00
Plate
- 7-1/4" d, crystal...........9.00
- 8" d, crystal.............15.00

Wine, 2 oz, crystal 12.00

Roses and Bows

Compote, cov, 7" d, green ... 65.00
Honey, cov, Beaded Grape .. 45.00
Vase, 9" h, bud 30.00
Vegetable bowl, cov........ 75.00
Wedding bowl, large, "Best Wishes" dec.................... 75.00

Thousand Eye

Bowl
- 11-1/4" d, crystal, flashed color 48.00
- 12" l, oblong, crimped, crystal, purple, and marigold.... 35.00

Candlesticks, pr, crystal..... 55.00
Cocktail, marigold.......... 15.00
Decanter, stopper, purple, wear to color on bottle 65.00
Plate, 18" d, crystal, flashed color 85.00
Saucer, crystal 2.50
Sherbet, 4-1/4" h
- Crystal 12.00
- Crystal and purple....... 15.00

Vase, 5-1/2" h, crystal, flashed color 65.00
Wine, 5" h, crystal, flashed color 18.50

Waterford

Bonbon, cov, crystal........ 45.00
Cake salver, ruby stained.... 75.00
Candy dish, cov, ruby stained, 9" d................... 35.00
Comport, 7" d, ruby stained .. 45.00
Goblet, ruby stained........ 15.00
Tumbler, ftd, 4-3/4" h, crystal . 15.00
Urn, cov, ruby stained 95.00

WHIMSIES

History: During lunch or after completing their regular work schedule, glassworkers occasionally spent time creating unusual glass objects known as whimsies, e.g. candy-striped canes, darners, hats, paperweights, pipes, and witch balls. Whimsies were taken home and given as gifts to family and friends.

Because of their uniqueness and infinite variety, whimsies can rarely be attributed to a specific glass house or glassworker. Whimsies were created wherever glass was made, from New Jersey to Ohio and westward. Some have suggested that style and color can be used to pinpoint region or factory, but no one has yet developed an identification key that is adequate.

Glass canes are among the most collectible types of whimsies. These range in length from very short (under one foot) to 10 feet or more. They come in both hollow and solid form. Hollow canes can have a bulb-type handle or the rarer C- or L-shaped handle. Canes are found in many fascinating colors, with the candy striped being a regular favorite with collectors. Many canes are also filled with various colored powders, gold and white being the most common and silver being harder to find. Sometimes they were even used as candy containers.

References: Gary Baker et al., *Wheeling Glass 1829-1939*, Oglebay Institute, 1994, distributed by Antique Publications; Joyce E. Blake, *Glasshouse Whimsies*, published by author, 1984; Joyce E. Blake and Dale Murschell, *Glasshouse Whimsies: An Enhanced Reference*, published by authors, 1989; Kenneth Wilson, *American Glass 1760-1930: The Toledo Museum of Art, Volume I, Volume II*, Hudson Hills Press and The Toledo Museum of Art, 1994.

Collectors' Club: Whimsey Club, 20 William St., Dansville, KY 14437.

Bird drinking font, 4-1/2" h, blown molded, applied cobalt blue ball top and rim...................200.00
Bird feeder, 5-1/4" h, bottle green, emb bird and "Don't Forget To Feed Me" 150.00
Bellows bottle, blown
- 5-1/4" h, colorless, applied rim, quilling at neck, prunts, rigaree handles, England or eastern U.S., late 19th C, imperfections. . 165.00
- 7" h, colorless, white marbrie loop dec, applied rim, quilling at neck, prunts, rigaree handles, England or eastern U.S., late 19th C, imperfections 195.00
- 8" h, light aqua with applied rims, rigaree, prunts, handles, feather dec, England or eastern U.S., late 19th C, imperfections 175.00
- 8-3/8" h, colorless, applied prunt, rigaree, and handles, England or eastern U.S., 19th C, imperfections 145.00
- 8-3/4" h, colorless, applied rim, neck rings, rigaree, prunts, Prince of Wales feathers, handles, England or eastern U.S., late 19th C, imperfections 75.00
- 9-3/4" h, pale aqua, applied prunt, rigaree, and handles, England or eastern U.S., 19th C, imperfections 185.00
- 9-3/4" h, transparent ruby with white marbrie, applied ruby quilling at neck, colorless rigaree, prunt handles, circular base, England or eastern U.S., late 19th C, imperfections 260.00
- 10-3/8" h, yellow-green, ribbed neck and body, applied prunt, rigaree and handles, England or eastern U.S., 19th C, imperfections. 125.00
- 11-1/4" h, cobalt blue with white marbrie, applied colorless rigaree, prunt, leaf, handles, and circular base, England or eastern U.S., late 19th C, imperfections 345.00

11-3/4" h, white with red and blue loop design, applied colorless rim, quilling at neck, prunt, rigaree, handle, and circular base, England or eastern U.S., late 19th C, imperfections **460.00**

12" h, colorless, white marbrie, applied colorless rim, quilling, rigaree, prunt, and handles, England or eastern U.S., 19th C, imperfections **215.00**

12-1/4" h, colorless, translucent red and opaque white loop designs, applied colorless rigaree, prunt, handle, and circular base, England or eastern U.S., late 19th C, imperfections, one handle missing **290.00**

13-1/4" h, colorless, opalescent loop design, applied colorless rim, neck rings, rigaree, Prince of Wales feathers, prunt, handles, disk base, England or eastern U.S., late 19th C. **145.00**

14-3/8" h, colorless, applied quilling, neck ring, rigaree, raspberry prunts, leaf, handles, disk base, England or eastern U.S., late 19th C. **115.00**

14-1/2" h, colorless, chartreuse, white, and pink loop designs, applied colorless quilling at neck, raspberry prunts, rigaree, handles, leaf, and tall bulbed shaft, circular base, England or eastern U.S., late 19th C, imperfections. **260.00**

14-1/2" h, 5" w, 2" d, attributed to MA, c1885, Marbrie, applied lip over alternating red and white loops within colorless glass bellows form body, applied clear rigaree and bellows handles, applied clear round foot, stopper missing **375.00**

16" h, transparent pink, white marbrie applied rigaree, Prince of Wales feathers, prunts, handles, and circular foot, England or eastern U.S., late 19th C, imperfections **500.00**

Bracelet

2" to 3" d, Lutz type, clear, multicolored twists and spirals, gold **85.00**

3" d, solid glass, varied colored stripes. **65.00**

Buttonhook

5" to 10" l, plain, bottle green . **35.00**

5 to 10" l, plain, colorless **25.00**

7" h, bottle green, elaborately twisted body, amber ends **75.00**

Cane, blown

25-1/4" l, colorless, entwined spiraling red, white, and blue canes, America, late 19th/early 20th C, imperfections **175.00**

27-1/2" l, pale aqua, spiraling ribs, bulbous top, America, late 19th/early 20th C, imperfections **115.00**

38" l, amber, corkscrew spiral shaft, America, late 19th/early 20th C, imperfections **120.00**

38" l, light aqua twisted glass, attributed to Mid-western U.S., late 19th/early 20th C, imperfections **195.00**

38-1/4" l, colorless, spiraling ribs, transparent gold canes, America, late 19th/early 20th C, imperfections **125.00**

38-1/2" l, colorless with entwined cobalt blue spirals, America, late 19th/early 20th C, imperfections **195.00**

38-1/2" l, pale aqua with spiraling incised line, red, white, and blue canes, America, late 19th/early 20th C, imperfections **145.00**

38-3/4" l, colorless, bulbous top, tapering to corked end, America, late 19th/early 20th C, imperfections **85.00**

41-1/2" l, white, spiraling pink canes, America, late 19th/early 20th C, imperfections **200.00**

42" l, amber, spiral shaft, America, late 19th/early 20th C, imperfections **200.00**

42" l, colorless, red, white, and blue spiraling canes, America, late 19th/early 20th C, imperfections **120.00**

44" l, white, red vertical canes, America, late 19th/early 20th C, imperfections **220.00**

45-3/4" l, colorless, red, white, and blue spiraling canes, America, late 19th/early 20th C, imperfections **120.00**

47-1/2" l, white, spiraling canes, bulbous top, cased in colorless glass, America, late 19th/early 20th C, imperfections **230.00**

52" l, white canes in spiral pattern in colorless glass, light aqua twisted glass, attributed to Mid-western U.S., late 19th/early 20th C, imperfections **245.00**

53" l, colorless, red, white, and blue spiraling canes, America, late 19th/early 20th C, imperfections **120.00**

53-1/2" l, red, yellow, and blue canes in spiral pattern in colorless glass, light aqua twisted glass, attributed to Mid-western U.S., late 19th/early 20th C, imperfections. **225.00**

61" h, colorless, bulbous top, tapering undulating shaft, spiraling red and blue canes, applied white cane, America, late 19th/early 20th C, imperfections. **195.00**

Darners, from left: red and green spatter on white ground, ***$90;*** *blue iridescent,* ***$115;*** *red and blue stripes, colorless ground,* ***$125;*** *red, green, and tan spatter on white ground,* **$95.**

Egg, hollow, milk glass, various colored splotches

2" h **65.00**

4-1/2" h **85.00**

Fly catcher, 7" h, removable dome top, colorless, 19th C **250.00**

Gemel bottle, blown

10-1/2" h, pale green, applied rigaree and leaf design, England or eastern U.S., 19th C, imperfections **195.00**

12" h, colorless, transparent blue loop designs, and rim, applied colorless rigaree, England or eastern U.S., 19th C, imperfections **165.00**

Hat, free blown

1-1/2" h, milk glass, c1910 . . . **50.00**

1-1/2" h, 4" d, amber, attributed to Keene, c1860. . . . . **165.00**

1-3/4" h, 3-3/8" d, light citron, inward rolled rim, pontil scar, attributed to New York state glass house, 1830-50 . . . . **375.00**

2-1/4" h, blown three mold, over pattern mold vertical ribbing, colorless, 24 ribs, folded rim, pontil scar, attributed to Boston and Sandwich Glass Works, Sandwich, MA, 1820-40, 3/4" manufacturer's fissure in pontil scar **150.00**

Horn

8-1/2" l, French-horn type, candy stripes **300.00**

20" l, trumpet type, red, white, yellow, purple, and green candy stripes **175.00**

Pen, root beer-colored swirled body, colorless flame swirled pointed nib, **$35.**

Ladle, 10" l, hollow, gold powder filled, colored splotches, curved handles **65.00**

Mallet-style hammer, 8" l, colorless, red, and blue splotches on head, c1920 . . . . **85.00**

Pen

- Elaborate, green, finely twisted applied bird finial. **85.00**
- Simple design, amber, colorless nib, 7" l **35.00**

Pen holder, 3" h, 3-1/2" d paperweight base, blown spatter glass, cobalt blue, red, and white solid round sphere, pulled into six coils to hold pen . **175.00**

Pipe, blown, England or eastern U.S., 19th C, imperfections

- 7-1/2" l, colorless, twisted stem **95.00**
- 11" l, colorless, white threads **115.00**
- 17" l, cobalt blue, double looped stem, gauffered bowl rim. . . **225.00**
- 18-1/2" l, opaque wavy pink and white, applied bowl rim **185.00**

Potichomanie ball, 12" d, blown, aqua, paper cut-outs of flowers, etc., matching 24" h stand, attributed to Lancaster, NY **600.00**

Powder horn

- 6-1/2" h, 28 vertical ribs, olive amber, applied ring and lip, pontil scar, New England, 1790-1830 **1,500.00**
- 10" l, colorless, white marbrie, applied rings at neck, England or America, 19th C, imperfections **115.00**
- 11" h, Nailsea type, ftd, colorless ground, blue and white loopings, tooled ground lip, pontil scar, mid-19th C. **500.00**
- 12" l, colorless, white Nailsea loopings, raspberry colored drape type striping, early Pittsburgh, 1930-50 . . . . **350.00**

Rolling pin

- 14" l, black or deep olive green, white dec, early Keene or Stoddard **150.00**
- 15" l, Nailsea type, cobalt blue ground, white loopings. . . . **165.00**

Shoe, 5-1/2" l, Button and Daisy pattern, toboggan form, emb snow shoes, ice blue crystal **45.00**

Sock darner, England or America, 19th C

- 5" l, amber head, applied colorless handle **200.00**
- 6-1/2" l, white, multicolored pastel speckles and striations, cased in colorless glass **95.00**
- 7" l, white ground, blue Nailsea loopings **195.00**
- 7-1/4" l, white, multicolored speckles and striations, cased in colorless glass. **95.00**
- 7-1/2" l, spatter glass, pink, green, blue, and yellow splotches, c1920 . . . . **175.00**
- 7-1/2" l, white, red Nailsea looping **250.00**

Sword, colorless, colored spirals in handle, attributed to Sandwich Glass Works, late 19th C, pr **400.00**

Vase, blown, Marbrie, red and opalescent white, flared scalloped rim, applied base with knop and round foot, attributed to New England or New Jersey, c1860-80, minor wear . **1,955.00**

Wine thief, 18-1/2" l, colorless, etched, England or America, 19th C . . . **100.00**

Witch ball, blown, England or eastern US

- 2-1/8" d, multicolored, loop closure **195.00**
- 4" d, white, blue, and pink marbrie **225.00**
- 5-1/8" d, colorless, white swirl design, fabric American flag **7500.00**
- 6" d, colorless, white marbrie **300.00**
- 6-3/4" d, white, pink, blue and yellow flecks. **315.00**

Witch ball on stand, attributed to Boston & Sandwich Glass Co., Sandwich, MA, c1850-70, free-blown

- 15" h, 7" d, Marbrie, clear ball with four white loops, conforming columnar stand with swelled base **1,050.00**
- 15-1/4" h, 8" d, Marbie, clear ball with four white loops, baluster and ball-form standard, one stand with loss at base, price for pr. **1,150.00**
- 16" h, 8" d, Marbrie, clear ball with four white loops, conforming columnar stand with swelled base **1,050.00**

Witch ball, vase-type holder with wafer foot, colorless, white Nailsea loopings, **$695.**

INDEX

E

F

G

H

I

J

K

L

M

N

O

P